APPLIED
DEMOGRAPHY

APPLIED DEMOGRAPHY

Applications to Business, Government, Law, and Public Policy

Jacob S. Siegel

J. Stuart Siegel Demographic Services
North Bethesda, Maryland

ACADEMIC PRESS

An Imprint of Elsevier

San Diego   San Francisco   New York   Boston   London   Sydney   Tokyo

Academic Press
An Imprint of Elsevier
525 B Street, Suite 1900, San Diego, CA 92101-4495, USA
http://www.academicpress.com

Academic Press
Harcourt Place, 32 Jamestown Road, London, NW1 7BY, UK
http://www.academicpress.com

Library of Congress Catalog Number: 2001090929

International Standard Book Number: 0-12-641840-3

PRINTED IN THE UNITED STATES OF AMERICA
06 QW 9 8 7 6 5 4 3 2

In memory
David W. Siegel, 1919–1998

■ CONTENTS

4 Limitations of Census and Survey Data

5 Geodemography: Geographic Area Concepts and Information Systems for Demographic Applications

6 Demographic Applications in Business Planning

7 Demographic Applications to Government and Private Nonprofit Organizations

8 The Demography of the Labor Force and of the Workforce of Organizations

9 Population Estimates: Basic Demographic Characteristics

10 Population Projections: Basic Demographic Characteristics

11 Estimates and Projections of Socioeconomic and Health Characteristics

12 Some Political Applications of Demographic Data and Methods

13 Demographic Aspects of Selected Public Policy Issues

14 The Demography of Organizational Populations

Epilogue

■PREFACE

This volume differs from a typical general text in demography, which is concerned mainly with demographic principles, trends, problems, and theories. Rather, *Applied Demography* explores the practical issues with which demographers working for government agencies, private nonprofit organizations, and businesses deal. Government and business are increasingly recognizing the desirability, even need, for demographers' input to analyze effectively and solve planning and management problems. Whether the task is marketing a new product, planning a new school, or delineating legislative districts, demographic knowledge, skills, and perspectives can be helpful in resolving the problem or increasing the chances for success of the operation or activity. Demographers now work directly, or indirectly as consultants, for a variety of state and local government agencies and business organizations as well as national and international agencies. Readers generally are familiar with the affiliation of demographers with academic institutions as teachers and researchers, but they may be unaware that many of these demographers, particularly those in state universities, have a joint affiliation with institutes, bureaus, or centers that apply demography in the service of their states or communities.

Many demographers direct their principal efforts toward the preparation of population estimates and projections and the analysis of population changes for small areas, such as metropolitan areas, counties, cities, and minor civil divisions. Apart from the value of these estimates and projections as news material, they are required for program planning and implementation, both by local governments and by local businesses and other local organizations. Anticipating the supply of and demand for many goods and services in communities requires a close look at local population shifts. Applied demographers may be called on to advise in planning the operations of local governments and businesses to the degree that demographic skills, knowledge, and perspectives are viewed as useful for such planning.

The baby boom of 1946 through 1964 triggered considerable popular interest in population phenomena as a significant factor in influencing and shaping the course of public affairs. In recent years, heated public debate about such issues as teenage pregnancy, abortion, illegal immigration, welfare-to-work programs, the costs of health care, and the solvency of the Social Security system has maintained this interest. The public's interest is also reflected in the fact that the term *demographics* has entered the common vocabulary, even if the more established term *demography* has not. Scholars in the federal government and universities have long understood the considerable influence of population on our public life. Federal agencies spend hundred of millions of dollars annually on demographic projects, particularly the decennial census, national household surveys, and compilation of vital statistics. In addition, several billion dollars flow from the federal government to state and local agencies each year through programs and funding formulas that incorporate demographic data.

A newer development has been the recognition by states, local governments, and private organizations, especially businesses, of the importance of population phenomena in the evolution of events and in the management of their affairs. Now every state has a state demographer or other analyst dedicated to the pursuit of population studies, and many major private profit and nonprofit organizations employ at least one demographic analyst.

The emphasis of applied demography on applications underlies the treatment in this book of issues in a variety of related disciplines (e.g., economics, gerontology, public policy, sociology, public administration, and business management). The orientation of these disciplines is taken into account, but limited use is also made of the methods and materials of statistics, actuarial science, geography, history, law, and computer science. One aim of this book is to inform the reader of the wide range of applications of demography, including not only the areas narrowly defined as demographic but also a broad range of nondemographic ones, such as insurance programs, manufacturing processes, and the dynamics of organizations as population units. The topics covered in this book generally reflect the areas in which applied demographers in the United States work today, as suggested by the newsletter of the Southern Demographic Association and by the programs of the biennial Conferences on Applied Demography held at Bowling Green State University during the late 1980s and the 1990s.

Practical limits had to be set in the book on the scope of the applications considered, both geographically and substantively, however. Certain topics that might appear appropriate for inclusion are specifically excluded. Among them are, for example, family planning, the relation of population to resources and food supply, and environmental degradation. These are public issues of great importance, especially in less developed countries. Space limitations did not permit the detailed exposition of many other relevant topics, although some of them are treated briefly (e.g., comparative international practice and experience, development of geographic information systems, computer programs and applications, sample survey design, and problems in legislative and school redistricting). Sources of material on some of these topics are cited in the text, endnotes, and suggested readings.

Chapter 1 is devoted to describing, in general terms, the scope of applied demography and its basic measurement techniques. Chapter 2 presents a summary of recent population trends in the United States and then discusses some of their implications for and linkages with selected social programs. Chapter 3 covers the major sources of demographic data used by the applied demographer and the ways of accessing them. In this chapter, the decennial census, the various registration systems, and the major national surveys are considered, as well as the main sources of economic information useful in demographic analysis. Chapter 4 examines the quality of demographic data, including the various sources of error, ways of measuring it, the findings, and some problems of using and interpreting census and survey data. Since applied demography focuses so heavily on local area issues, Chapter 5 describes the geographic structure of the U.S. population as embedded in the decennial population census and national population surveys and as generally observed by applied demographers.

The next three chapters take us to the heart of the matter, namely, the application of demographic data and methods to the conduct of business (Chapter 6), the management of nonprofit private and public organizations (Chapter 7), and the national labor force and the workforces of individual companies (Chapter 8). In the course of these discussions, we consider some of the principal concepts that the census data represent (e.g., race, labor force, income, poverty, and families and households). The explication of these concepts appears in the chapter where it is deemed most appropriate.

Chapters 9, 10, and 11 focus on the methods of making population estimates and projections, particularly for subnational areas. Chapters 9 and 10 deal only with the basic demographic characteristics—that is, total population and age, sex, and race distribution—and Chapter 11 deals with socioeconomic characteristics. Chapters 12 and 13 focus on applications of demographic data and methods to political issues and other selected issues of public policy. Chapter 12 deals with their use in political representation and the allocation of public funds. Chapter 13 presents brief demographic analyses of a few selected public policy issues, such as the future state of the Social Security system and the role of population changes in the rising costs of health care. Finally, Chapter 14 focuses on sets of large-scale organizations considered as populations, to illustrate how demographic logic may be extended to nonhuman populations.

This book has been designed to serve more than one purpose. Its primary purpose is as a text in a one-semester course in applied demography for advanced undergraduates and graduate students. The book can stand alone for this purpose, but it will be used most advantageously if such a course is taken following or concurrently with a basic course in population, particularly a course in techniques of population analysis, and a course in survey research. Although this book reviews the basic methods of demography and recent U.S.

population trends (Chapters 1 and 2), this review is highly condensed and it would be helpful, therefore, for the reader to be familiar with these areas in advance of pursuing the study of applied demography. Other relevant but optional areas of preparation in the social sciences are introductory economics, political science, and business administration.

Prospective users of a book of this kind often ask about their mathematical and statistical readiness to take advantage of what it offers. Success in understanding and applying the material in this book can be achieved only with some mathematical and statistical training. For the most part, a term of college mathematics and a basic course in statistics will take the reader through the material. Those who are more firmly grounded in these fields will profit more from study of this book. Hence, my advice is to take appropriate training concurrently if it is not already part of the student's intellectual preparation. Such additional training would include first-year college mathematics and a year of social statistics.

The second purpose of this book is as a reference handbook for practitioners—that is, demographers and nondemographers who are engaged in practicing applied demography or who could effectively incorporate it in their work. A course based on this book can introduce the student to the subject matter, but experience at applying the material and the opportunity to revisit the book under working conditions will prove even more useful.

Much of applied demography has relevance to a particular country. It is closely tied to the record systems, the geographic concepts, the governmental structure, and the legal system of the country. This book is mainly intended to explore the data, methods, and practice of applied demography in the United States. If no other geographic reference is given, the reader should assume that the area referred to is the United States. Nevertheless, readers from other countries, particularly the more developed countries, will find much in it of value for them.

Considerable attention is given to the U.S. population census and the work of the U.S. Census Bureau. This may be taken to reflect my longtime association with that agency, but the more relevant consideration is the primary importance of the Census Bureau in producing the data on which applied demographers in the United States depend so heavily. The U.S. Census Bureau provides in the decennial census and in its current estimates program uniform small-area demographic data in easy-to-access media. The Census Bureau has also defined the basic concepts underlying much of the data applied demographers use. Moreover, it is responsible for the conduct of several of the most important national sample surveys and has set the standard for the conduct of such surveys.

Many publications of the U.S. government are cited in this book. They are consistently listed under the name of the U.S. agency that sponsored the publication; the name of the specific author, if known, is then added as part of the citation. Since the place of publication and the publisher of U.S. government publications are known to readers (i.e., Washington, DC, U.S. Government Printing Office), in the interest of economy this information is uniformly omitted when a U.S. agency is the source.

Some methodological examples are presented here for which the exposition is too limited to serve as a paradigm for applying the method. For further information, the reader is advised to refer to one of the several texts on demographic techniques, particularly Henry S. Shryock, Jacob S. Siegel, and Edward F. Stockwell, *The Methods and Materials of Demography: Condensed Edition* (Academic Press, 1976), or the *Revised Condensed Edition* of the latter work (Academic Press, 2002), edited by David A. Swanson and Jacob S. Siegel.

In the course of preparing this work, the author has had occasion to consult a number of colleagues on their areas of expertise and special interest. I am particularly grateful to Murray Gendell, Professor of Demography (retired), my former colleague in the Department of Demography, Georgetown University, who took time out from a busy "retirement" schedule to prepare background material for my use in writing Chapter 2. I have called on numerous federal analysts and researchers for information and advice. It would be impractical to name all of them and, with apologies to those whom I may have overlooked, I acknowledge with pleasure a number of them, in no particular order: Howard Fullerton, Peter Haro, Thomas Raby, and Anne E. Polivka of the Bureau of Labor Statistics; Shirley Smith of the Bureau of International Labor Affairs; Alfred Nucci, J. Gregory Robinson, Frederick Hollmann, Jennifer Day, Martin O'Connell, Kevin Deardorff, Elizabeth Martin, Howard Hogan, Wendy Bruno, Diane Schmidley, Prithwis Das Gupta, Valerie Strang, Denise Smith, Janice Valdisera, Eric Neuberger, Sam Davis, Joseph Dalaker, Gerald Feuer, David Waddington, and Patrick Caldwell of the Bureau of the Census; George Downey and Clifford Woodruff of the Bureau of Economic Analysis; David Huckabee of the Congressional Reference Service; Harry Rosenberg, Kenneth Kochanek, Stephanie Ventura, Robert Bilgrad, Deborah Blackwell, Julia Kowaleski, Robert Anderson, and Linda Peterson of the National Center for Health Statistics; Anne Martin of the Health Care Financing Administration; Bruce Phillips of the Small Business Administration; Robert Warren of the Immigration and Naturalization Service; and Debra Gerald of the National Center for Education Statistics.

Among those with whom I consulted outside the federal government are Paula Hollerbach of the Academy for Educational Development, Jeffrey Passel of the Urban Institute, Susan de la Cruze of TIAA-CREF, and Kenneth Hodges of Claritas Corporation. Ken Hodges was especially helpful in providing material on the history of private data-vending companies. Paul Voss of the University of Wisconsin and Louis Pol of the University of Nebraska, as well as several anonymous reviewers, gave me numerous valuable comments. Next, I express my thanks to Marilyn Jeffery, computer consultant, for aiding me in the solution of various technical problems and in the preparation of some of the tables and charts.

Finally, I express my appreciation to the Academic Press staff. J. Scott Bentley, Senior Editor, lent his support and encouragement throughout the period this work was in gestation. Jocelyn Lofstrom, Production Manager, gently coordinated my later efforts so that this work could emerge as a finished product on schedule. Finally, Mara Conner, Promotions Manager, has been diligent in ensuring that prospective users learned about the book and would be interested in taking advantage of it.

Although I consulted many persons, I wrote the entire work. Therefore, I have to take full responsibility for all of it, including any deficiencies it may have. My hope is that it serves as a useful tool in advancing the training of demographers and expanding serious interest in the field of applied demography.

1

SCOPE AND METHODS OF APPLIED DEMOGRAPHY

THE FIELD AND SCOPE OF APPLIED DEMOGRAPHY

Definition of Applied Demography

Applied demography is a subfield of demography. To understand the domain of applied demography, then, it may be useful to begin with the definition of demography. Demography is the scientific study of human population or, more specifically, the study of the size, geographic distribution, age-sex structure, and socioeconomic composition of populations and the factors that effect changes in these dimensions of population, namely, fertility, mortality, and migration. The socioeconomic characteristics referred to include mainly marital status and living arrangements, race and ethnic composition, education, economic status, and, in an extended definition, health status. We may view

1

these socioeconomic fields as representing a band around the core area of formal demography, which is concerned with the size and age-sex structure of populations and their dynamics.

Simply defined, applied demography is the subfield of demography focusing on practical applications of demographic materials and methods. Some of this work is done at the local level so that applied demography is often viewed as state and local demography. Some of it is done for use by management in business and nonprofit organizations so that applied demography is also viewed as business demography. Applied demography has a special orientation with respect to time and place. Typically, as an applied field, it is concerned with particular geographic areas and with the present and future, not the past. Accordingly, many applied demographers are engaged in analyzing current population trends and making population forecasts for specific areas. Applied demography is not concerned with broad demographic theories or basic demographic research, such as the behavioral determinants of population changes. It may, however, pursue research into the design of general solutions proposed for demographic problems or conduct evaluation studies to test the effectiveness of specific solutions implemented.

A more ample definition of **applied demography**, then, is that it is the subfield of demography concerned with the application of the materials and methods of demography to the analysis and solution of the problems of business, private nonprofit organizations, and government, at the local, national, and international levels, with a primary orientation toward particular areas and the present and future. Accordingly, we can characterize applied demography as a decision-oriented science concerned with aiding managers, administrators, and government officials in making practical decisions congruent with the policy or goals of the organization or institution for which they work.[1]

Applied demography may be defined in other ways than in terms of its goals. It may be defined in terms of the principal academic disciplines with which it interfaces, the principal roles of those who pursue this work, and the principal topics it has embraced. These topics have linked applied demography with many other disciplines, including business management, regional planning, government administration, law, public policy, sociology, economics, and gerontology, but the common theme is that this field of demography seeks to apply its insights and tools to the solution of practical problems in these areas of study. Applied demography is engaged with other disciplines as well, such as geography, statistics, actuarial science, computer science, and history, to develop and expand the tools with which it works.

Most applied demographers are associated with government agencies, business organizations, or nonprofit organizations—that is, organizations outside academia. There are many applied demographers in government agencies at all levels. Those in the federal government are often engaged in developing basic demographic data of various types. Some applied demographers work independently and serve as private consultants or as expert witnesses in litigation. Some universities have well-developed training and research programs in applied demography, and applied demographers are found there also. Much of the material covered in courses in demographic techniques is directly applicable to applied demography and the instructors often have a strong interest in applied demography.

Work of Applied Demographers

I have described the work of applied demographers in the most general terms. To give a more specific indication of their work, I enumerate the principal subjects that concern them in a systematic form. This list virtually provides an outline of the topics covered in this book:

1. Collection and compilation of demographic and quasi-demographic data.
   a. Development of forms, questions, and tabulation plans of population censuses and sample surveys.
   b. Participation in editing of census and survey returns (i.e., developing editing rules and reviewing preliminary tabulations to judge the adequacy of the application of editing rules).
   c. Implementation, conduct, and evaluation of population censuses and sample surveys.
   d. Development of data sources for demographic uses, including particularly administrative records, at the national, state, and local level.
   e. Application of geographic information systems to the compilation of demographic and related data for particular areas.
2. Analysis of data compiled in population censuses and surveys.
   a. Analysis of demographic changes in particular local areas, including trends in population size and population characteristics.
   b. The measurement and interpretation of internal migration and the characteristics of internal migrants.
   c. Application of graphic methods to the analysis of demographic data.
3. Preparation of population estimates and projections.
   a. Preparation of national, state, and local estimates and projections of total population.
   b. Preparation of estimates and projections of demographic (age, sex, race) and socioeconomic (households, education, labor force, income, health) characteristics at the national, state, and local levels.
4. Application of the methods and materials of demography to the problems of business administration.
   a. Site location (e.g., new plants, malls, retail stores, service outlets).
   b. Marketing (e.g., tracking current and potential demand for products and services).
   c. Human resources planning, including personnel planning related to the demographic characteristics of the workforce and retirees.
   d. Study of the internal population dynamics of the workforce of a particular company.
5. Study of the population dynamics of the national labor force, regional labor forces, and the labor forces of industries.
6. Application of the methods and materials of demography to the problems of state and local government administration.

      a. Site location (e.g., libraries, schools, police and fire stations, trash dumps, airports).

      b. Measurement of the need for public services and facilities (e.g., public housing, parks, community mental health clinics, "senior" centers).

      c. Estimation of budget changes required by population changes.

7. Analysis of various legal and political issues involving population data, such as use of adjusted census data for fund allocation, legislative redistricting, and redrawing school districts.

8. Demographic analysis of public policy issues such as the solvency of the Social Security system, effectiveness of welfare-to-work programs, and the role of population and other factors in the rise in health care costs.

9. Application of demographic methods to nonhuman populations.[2]

      a. Application of demographic methods to manufactured products and the built environment (e.g., life tables for housing units or automobiles).

      b. Demographic analysis of sets of organizations, such as businesses and colleges.

I can provide an even more realistic sense of the types of work applied demographers do by giving examples drawn from observation of their activities as employees, researchers, managers, and private practitioners. Demographers carry out analyses of the dynamics of the workforce of large companies and of the effect of different retirement policies on retirement trends in the company. Business demographers track changes in the age structure of the general population, with a focus on the effect of these changes on advertising plans of the company and on the volume of sales. Large corporations, implementing recruitment plans that call for persons with specific skills, racial affiliation, and women may employ demographers to aid in the location of such recruits.

Demographers in utility companies make projections of households for local service areas and track changes in the types of households in these areas. This work recognizes that different types of telephone services may be required for different types of households, or that the demand for energy is affected by shifts in the size of households since large households the use more energy than single-person households or childless families. State demographers make population estimates for their states and substate areas as a basis for a great number of planning uses and participate, in effect, in the solicitation of federal funds allocated on the basis of population. Local government demographers project demands for health care, education, welfare, and public-safety services, making forecasts, for example, of juvenile arrests, public assistance caseloads, and high school enrollments. To aid further in the planning process, they may extend these in the form of forecasts for public facilities such as hospitals, schools, libraries, detention centers, and fire stations and in the form of budget estimates of the costs of these services and facilities.

Applied demographers also deal with broader questions of public policy. For example, they advise government officials on the role of demographic factors in the prospective demands on the Social Security system in order to aid in resolving the problem of the system's future financial solvency. They prepare studies of the trends in work participation of women in relation to the shifts in the ages of marriage and childbearing in order to support efforts to create jobs for women and provide child-care services. They develop and interpret data on trends in teenage pregnancy and analyze its effects on the subsequent socioeconomic conditions of the mothers. They try to measure the extent of illegal immigration and to estimate the impact of illegal immigration on state and local budgets. They evaluate the impact of national and state population trends on national and state budgets and on the distribution of legislative power in the Congress, state legislatures, and city councils. Apart from dealing with specific problems of the types mentioned, many applied demographers are engaged in compiling the basic data—through censuses, vital statistics, immigration data, and sample population surveys—that are needed for other applied demographers or researchers to carry on their work.

Definition of Demographics

The term **demographics** has entered the popular vocabulary with several meanings, namely, (1) a synonym of *demography* or *applied demography*, (2) the production of current demographic data and the data themselves, (3) the demographic characteristics of a population, and (4) the demographic background of a problem. The public also tends to think of demographics mainly as a business producing masses of demographic data, not as a science. I think, therefore, that the first meaning listed is especially unfortunate since I prefer to think of demography and applied demography as sciences or at least science-cum-art. It is better for scholars to avoid use of the term to mean (1) demography or applied demography, (2) the basic demographic characteristics of a population, or (3) the demographic background of a problem. I suggest limiting the use of the term *demographics* to the second meaning given here and propose the following definition: (1) the relatively mechanical production of demographic data on a current basis that are used to serve the marketing needs of business and industry and (2) the resulting data. The types of basic data usually included in the packages called demographics are the total population, age of the population, number of households, and household income, for such small substate political and statistical areas as counties, minor civil divisions, places, and census tracts, and such economic areas as metropolitan areas and zip code areas. While demographics is not considered a scientific discipline or a major subdiscipline of demography, some may choose to view it as a subdivision of applied demography serving the narrow purpose just defined.[3]

CENSUS AND DEMOGRAPHIC CONCEPTS

This book is replete with demographic concepts representing types of data collected and compiled in population censuses, population surveys, and vital registration systems because they are deemed useful to meet policy and programmatic needs. The U.S. decennial census employs such population concepts as age, race, Hispanic origin, household, marital status, and migration, and their variants and subcategories. It also employs such socioeconomic concepts as housing unit, labor force, educational level, and income, and their variants and subtypes. The vital statistics system deals in such concepts as birth, death, life expectation, marriage, and divorce, and their varants and subtypes, as well as some of the demographic concepts already noted. These concepts serve as operationally serviceable tools—albeit only proxies for real-world phenomena—for collecting and compiling the data that may provide the information needed to deal with practical problems of management and public policy. Such concepts are, then, the link between raw data, on the one hand, and information that may serve some use, on the other.

The concepts must be given formal definition if respondents and interviewers are to know how to interpret the census or survey questions and users are to know exactly what the data represent. The formal definition for many of these demographic concepts is given in other chapters, where the definition is relevant to the subject matter of the chapter. For a more complete explanation of particular concepts, the reader may refer to the official sources cited in this book or to *The Methods and Materials of Demography, Revised Condensed Edition.*

SELECTED GENERAL DEMOGRAPHIC RELATIONS AND PROCESSES

The basic concepts of applied demography are the same, for the most part, as those of general demography. I summarize many of these and follow that discusssion with a summary discussion of a number of methods employed in the practice of applied demography. The list of methods discussed is not comprehensive, but it includes many of those commonly used. Most of these techniques are distinguished from general statistical techniques in employing demographic data and dealing mainly with demographic issues. They may be thought of, however, as a subset of general statistical techniques. Many general methods of statistical analysis, such as regression analysis, time series analysis, and measurement of sampling errors, are often applied to demographic data or materials, but the full exposition of these topics is more appropriate for a general statistical text. Methods of this sort are considered in this book only briefly in special applications.

Population Estimating Equation and Its Variants

Demographic methodology is grounded in a simple linear relationship that links populations at different dates with the basic factors accounting for change in the intervening period, namely births, deaths, in-migrants, and out-migrants:

$$P_1 = P_0 + B - D + I - O \tag{1}$$
$$P_1 - P_0 = B - D + I - O \tag{2}$$

Equation (1) is called the **population estimating equation**. This equation expresses the fact that the population at one date (P_1) depends on the population at some earlier date (P_0) and the births (B), deaths (D), in-migrations (I), and out-migrations (O) that occur between the two dates. The second equation expresses the fact that the difference in the populations at two dates is theoretically equivalent to the excess of births over deaths plus the excess of in-migrations over out-migrations. With actual data this equivalence is not achieved and there is an error term. There are, then, only two ways for a general population to grow—births and in-migrations—and only two ways for a general population to decline—deaths and out-migrations. The components are often regrouped to combine births and deaths as natural increase (NI) and in-migrations and out-migrations as net migration (NM):

$$P_1 = P_0 + NI + NM \tag{3}$$

Demographers are concerned with changes in population size and the degree to which fertility (i.e., births), mortality (i.e., deaths), and migration (i.e., movement into and out of an area) contribute to these changes.

These equations and variants of them serve as the basis for a variety of demographic calculations—postcensal and intercensal population estimates, evaluation of population census totals, evaluation of the components of change, and estimates of net migration—as suggested by the following equations:

$$\text{Evaluation:} \quad E = (P_1 - P_0) - (B - D) - (I - O) \tag{4}$$

$$\text{Net migration:} \quad I - O = (P_1 - P_0) - (B - D) \tag{5}$$

E, called the error of closure, denotes the discrepancy between the change in population and the algebraic sum of the components of change. $I - O$, net migration, is measured as the difference between total change and natural increase. If this equation is limited to special populations, it may be used to measure their net migration (e.g., the foreign-born population and the military population):

$$\text{Foreign-born population } (FB): \quad (I - O)^{FB} = (P_1^{FB} - P_0^{FB}) + D^{FB} \tag{6}$$

$$\text{Military population } (M): \quad (I - O)^{M} = (P_1^{M} - P_0^{M}) + D^{M} \tag{7}$$

Note that in both equations the birth component does not appear since it is not relevant. In equation (7), the P's represent overseas military population and D represents overseas deaths. $(I - O)^{M}$ represents net in-movement into the overseas military population and, disregarding net entries into the military abroad, net out-movement of the military from the United States.

If the elements in the population estimating equation are appropriately modified, it may serve to represent the basic dynamics of such populations as the national labor force, the workforce of a company, public assistance caseloads, the housing inventory, or even automobile batteries in use. Like the general population, these populations change in numbers between two dates as a result of entries and exits, but here the entries and exits may include non-demographic and special demographic processes as well as the usual demographic ones.

We do not need to know the components of change during a period to measure net population growth during the period. We need to know only the population totals at the beginning and end of the period, as is indicated in equation (2). These figures may be available from two censuses, a census and a population estimate, or two population estimates. Moreover, we can calculate the average annual rate of growth during the period merely on the basis of the two population figures, using one or another growth formula, as will be explained.

As suggested earlier, in practice, use of equation (1) and its variants proves problematic because the elements in it are subject to measurement error even if the equations specify the relations exactly. Population at the two dates and the components must have a consistent definition (e.g., geographic coverage, type of population) even though they may be derived from different collection systems. Data on the populations and the components of change are subject to errors of completeness of coverage, reporting, or sampling. Reported data may be lacking for some component or parts of some component (e.g., U.S. emigration data, net immigration of U.S. citizens) and must be estimated. The change in population is very likely to disagree with the change represented by the sum of natural increase and net immigration.

A simple extension of equation (1) representing particular ages permits the demographer to carry out many additional computations that are central to demographic practice. They include postcensal population estimation, population projection, and evaluation of census coverage, for age groups. Such a variation of the equation makes possible special types of estimates for age groups—that is, intercensal estimates of net internal migration, intercensal estimates of the net immigration of the foreign born, evaluation of the components of change, and reconstruction of the very old population:

Population estimation: $\quad P_{1c} = P_{0c} - D_c + I_c - O_c$ $\hfill (8)$

Net migration: $\quad (I - O)_c = (P_1 - P_0)_c + D_c$ $\hfill (9)$

Population evaluation: $\quad E_c = (P_1 - P_0)_c + D_c - (I_c - O_c)$ $\hfill (10)$

Reconstruction of oldest population: $\quad P^y_{85+} = {}_y\Sigma^\infty D_c$ $\hfill (11)$

where subscript y represents a particular year and c represents data for a "cohort," here an age group that becomes 1 year older in each successive calendar year (see below). Equation (11) states that the population 85 years and over may be estimated by cumulating deaths for the cohort from year y to some very high age in later years; the component of births is not relevant and immigration may be disregarded.

The equations for the new birth cohorts, the groups of births occurring since the start of the estimation process, are not given, but they are analogous. In making estimates and projections for age groups by calculations in terms of cohorts, we may consider the method as having introduced a new component of change, **aging** (i.e., the process by which groups attain higher ages with the passage of time).

Survival rates from life tables, measures of the chance of dying between one age and another, may be substituted in these equations to allow for deaths in the calculation of population estimates, net migration, and estimates of the error of closure. It is standard practice to use survival rates in calculating population projections. The use of survival rates changes the structure of the component equation since the rates have to be applied to the population and to any entrants (e.g., immigrants, in-migrants, other entrants) and exits (e.g., emigrants, out-migrants, other exits) during the period.

Cohort Data and Cohort Analysis

Perhaps the most important variable demographers deal with is age. While persons get older and assume new ages with the passage of time, they have a fixed year of birth. Persons with ages x years apart in calendar years x years apart have the same year of birth. A group of people who have a common initial demographic characteristic, such as year of birth, and who are followed up in later years with respect to some other demographic characteristic, such as survival, marriage, or childbearing, is called a **cohort**.[4] Thus, a group of children born in the same year and analyzed with respect to its survival history in later years is a birth cohort subject to survival/longevity analysis.

There are many other types of cohorts in addition to birth cohorts. We can also have marriage cohorts, year-of-immigration cohorts, interstate migration cohorts, and even death cohorts (who would be tracked backward in time). The concept is easily extended to encompass types of socioeconomic cohorts. Some examples are a labor force cohort, a group entering the labor force in the same year or a group hired at the same time in a work organization; a consumer cohort, a group adopting a product or service, or ceasing to purchase a product or service, in the same year; and an education cohort, a group entering the first grade, or a group graduating high school, at the same time. The cohort name's indicates its initial common characteristic but cohort "status" also requires being subjected to life-history analysis of some kind. Such analysis is called **cohort analysis**. Cohort analysis links the role of year of birth, year of marriage, year of immigration, year of labor-force entry, and other temporally defined demographic characteristics to outcomes with respect to such other demographic characteristics as educational attainment, work history, marriage, fertility, and socioeconomic status. These outcomes cannot be fully understood, however, without relating the shared experiences of the members of the cohort, called **cohort effects**, to so-called **period effects** (i.e., the effect of differences in the calendar year) and so-called **age-cycle effects** (i.e., the effect of differences in age). Interpreting the change in the status of a group with respect to some demographic characteristic must take into account the role of these three factors.

Understanding the relative contribution of cohort effects, age-cycle effects, and period effects to changes in demographic, economic, and social phenomena over time at a particular age, or in the same year across ages, is a central issue in demographic analysis. An illustrative question for analysis might be, why did the percentage of men in the labor force decline at ages 55–64 between 1985 and 1995? Or, why was the percent of high school graduates lower at ages 55–64 than at ages 35–44 in 1995? A cohort is subject to changes resulting from the fact that both the ages of the members are changing as it grows older and the calendar year is advancing. These are the so-called age-cycle effects and period effects, respectively. Changes over time at the same ages are subject to period and cohort effects, and differences between ages in the same year are subject to age-cycle and cohort effects. To return to the example of the decline in the percentage of men participating in the labor force at ages 55–64 between 1985 and 1995, the interpretation should encompass cohort effects and period effects since the birth cohorts and the calendar years are different but the ages are the same. In the second example, the lower level of education at ages 55–64 than at ages 35–44 in 1995 is to be explained in terms of cohort effects and age-cycle effects; the calendar year is the same.[5] The triad of factors cannot be separated fully except under very restrictive assumptions. Demographers have developed a variety of tools, both statistical and graphic, to analyze cohorts.[6]

Effect of Birth Fluctuations on Age Changes

The *number* of persons in a segment of an age distribution is determined by the size of the original cohort of births, the survival rates pertaining to the cohort, and the net migration occurring to the cohort as it ages. When the numbers of births fluctuate greatly, the sizes of the same age groups in different years tend to differ greatly from one another, as do the sizes of the different age groups in the same year. Since the mid-1930s, fluctuations in the numbers of births have become the norm. The moderate increase from the late Depression years up to the end of World War II was followed by the "baby boom" from 1946 to 1964, which was followed by the "baby bust" from 1965 to 1984, and more recently, by a number of "boomlets" and "bustlets" around near-subreplacement fertility (i.e., just below the level of fertility needed to replace the population). Business and government forecasters often take account of variations in the size of age groups by building their specialized projections on general population projections that have been developed as extensions of current estimates for age groups.

At present in the United States, mortality does not exact a heavy toll on new birth cohorts until the older ages since infant and early childhood mortality have been reduced to low levels. This development and a spectacular reduction since the late 1960s in death rates at the older ages have contributed to a rapid rise in the numbers of elderly survivors. Net immigration has also become an important factor in growth, particularly at the young-adult ages.

The broad contours of the age distribution and shifts in these contours require a somewhat different explanation than do the changes in the numbers in each age group. The level of the birth rate in the previous century, but especially in the previous several decades, mainly determines the general shape of the age distribution, with a secondary contribution from the death rate. Short-term changes in the age distibution, for example, an increase in the proportion of elderly persons, are determined jointly by changes in the birthrate, changes in the level and age pattern of death rates, and changes in the numbers of persons reaching old age. The graphic form called a **population pyramid** is commonly employed to depict the age-sex structure of a population. In a population pyramid, horizontal bars representing the size of each sex-age group are stacked from the youngest ages at the bottom to the oldest ages at the top. Males are placed on the left and females on the right of a central vertical axis, from which the size measurements are made. The chart takes the form of a pyramid, which, in stylized form, varies in shape from an equilateral triangle to a beehive.

The shift in the shape of the age pyramid of the population from its roughly triangular shape in the middle of the 19th century to its anticipated near-beehive shape in the middle of the 21st century reflects mainly the long-term decline in the birthrate. These changes are intensified by the long-term reductions in death rates over all ages, with relatively greater increases in survival rates at the older ages than at younger ages in recent decades, and the advent of the baby-boom cohorts at the older ages. Immigration has not had a major effect on the age distribution because immigrants are less concentrated by age and are less numerous than births and deaths.

SELECTED GENERAL MEASURES

Ratios, Proportions, and Rates

To conduct both descriptive and analytic studies in applied demography, demographers calculate many different types of **ratios**, an expression that one number is divided by another. These are usually, but not always, either **proportions**, which show the share that one population group makes up of a larger population

$$P_a \div (P_a + P_b) \tag{12}$$

or **rates**, which show the ratio of a given demographic or socioeconomic event to the population group at risk of experiencing the event. Two measures of the relative frequency of unemployment illustrate the difference. We can calculate the proportion of an age group that is unemployed at some date (e.g., unemployment ratio on April 1, 1999) or the chance that the members of the age group will become unemployed during a given year (e.g., unemployment rate between April 1, 1999, and April 1, 2000). The first deals with the number in a given status at some specific time, the second with events over a period of time.

A probability is a special type of rate that expresses precisely the chances that a given population will experience a given event over a designated subsequent period. The contrast is illustrated by the difference between an age-specific central death rate and a mortality rate, the probability of a group losing members through death between one exact age and another:

$$m_x = \frac{D_x}{P_x} \times 1000 \tag{13}$$

$$q_x = \frac{d_x}{p_x} \times 1000 \tag{14}$$

where D_x represents deaths during a year at age x and P_x is the midyear population at this age, while d_x represents the deaths occurring between exact age x and exact age $x + 1$ to the cohort of exact age x at the beginning of a year, and p_x is the population at exact age x at the beginning of the year.

A list of some common demographic ratios that are *not* proportions or rates is presented in Figure 1.1, a list of some common demographic proportions is presented in Figure 1.2, and a list of some common demographic rates, including probabilities, is given in Figure 1.3.[7] The formulas are largely self-explanatory.

FIGURE 1.1   Illustration of Ratios Used in Demographic Analysis That Are Not Proportions or Rates

Measure	Description
Population density	Population per square mile or per square kilometer
Residential density	Housing units per acre
Age dependency ratio	(Persons under age 18 and 65 and over ÷ persons 18–64) $\star$ 100
Child dependency ratio	(Children under age 18 ÷ persons 18–64) $\star$ 100
Aged dependency ratio	(Persons aged 65 and over ÷ persons 18–64) $\star$ 100
Sex ratio	(Ratio of males to females) $\star$ 100
Race ratio of death rates	(Ratio of death rate of blacks to death rate of whites) $\star$ 100

Average Measures

Demographic analysis frequently involves calculation of some type of "average," or measure of central tendency, to summarize the distribution of a demographic variable. Several such measures are available—arithmetic mean, median, mode, geometric mean, quadratic mean, harmonic mean—and the demographer must choose among them in analyzing the distributions of specific demographic variables. In making this choice, consideration should be given to several factors, namely, the logic of applying the measure to the variable, the ease or difficulty of calculating the measure, the ease or difficulty of statistically manipulating it, and its statistical appropriateness, taking account of the variable's distribution. Most demographic variables are *not* normally (i.e., symmetrically) distributed but are skewed to the right. Consider, for example, the distributions of the age of the population, the size of households, household income, educational level, the number of children ever born, the number of births to married women, and the percentage error in population

FIGURE 1.2   Illustrations of Proportions Used in Demographic Analysis

Measure	Formula[a]
Proportion net undercount in a census	P_U/P_{U+C}
Proportion elderly in the total population	P_{65+}/P_T
Proportion of children in the total population	$P_{<18}/P_T$
General labor force participation ratio	$_{16+}P_{LF}/_{16+}P_T$
Labor force participation ratio, age-specific	$_aP_{LF}/_aP_T$
General unemployment ratio	$_{16+}P_U/_{16+}P_T$
Unemployment ratio, age-specific	$_aP_U/_aP_T$
General proportion of high school graduates	$_{25+}P_{HSG}/_{25+}P_T$
General proportion married	$_{15+}P_M/_{15+}P_T$
Proportion married, age-specific	$_aP_M/_aP_T$
General proportion of citizens of voting age in the total voting-age population	$_{18+}P_C/_{18+}P_T$
Proportion of single-person households	H_S/H_T
Proportion of housing units with incomplete plumbing	HU_{IP}/HU_T

[a] Usually expressed as percentage: Proportion $\star$ 100. The numbers represent age ranges.

FIGURE 1.3   Illustrations of Rates Used in Demographic Analysis

Measure	Comment
Birthrate (crude)	Central rate
Death rate (crude)	Central rate
Death rate, age-specific	Central rate
Mortality rate, age-specific	Cohort rate (probability)
Out-migration rate, age-specific	Cohort rate (probability)
Unemployment rate, age-specific[a]	Cohort rate (probability)
Labor force withdrawal rate, age-specific[b]	Cohort rate (probability)
Marriage rate, age-specific	Central rate
Marriage rate, age-specific[b]	Cohort rate (probability)
Divorce rate, age-specific	Central rate
Divorce rate, age-specific[b]	Cohort rate (probability)
High school graduation rate[c]	Cohort rate

[a] Numbers becoming unemployed at a particular age a in a year divided by the labor force in the exact age a at the beginning of the year. Differs from the conventional "unemployment rate," which is a proportion.

[b] Analogous in form to the unemployment rate. See footnote a.

[c] This measure can take various forms. One form is as follows: Students graduating high school at the end of a school year divided by the number of high school students enrolled in grade 9, 3 years earlier.

Note: Crude rates are based on the total population not disaggregated by age. Central rates are based on the midyear population. Cohort rates (probabilities) are based on the population in the cohort at the beginning of the year in which the events occur. For some of these measures the conventional multiplier is 100; for others it is 1000. The denominators of these rates, especially the probabilities, are tailored to fit the event in the numerator. For example, the probability of first marriage at age 25 during year y may be computed approximately as the number of marriages of single persons at age 25 in year y divided by the single population at age 25 at midyear plus one half the deaths of single persons at age 25 during the year plus one-half the marriages of single persons at age 25 during the year.

estimates for small areas. Illustrations of measures of central tendency used for demographic variables are given in Figure 1.4.

Medians

The median is that value of a distribution that divides the distribution arrayed by size into two equal parts according to the number of cases.[8] The details of calculation of a median differ for continuous and discontinuous (i.e., discrete) quantitative variables. Examples of the first are age and income, and examples of the second are number of children ever born and size of household. In computing the median for continuous variables, the lower limit of the median class corresponds to the exact lower limit of the class. For example, 20.0 is the lower limit for the age class 20–24 years. The formula for the median is

$$Md = L_{Md} + \left[(.5T - \Sigma fx) \div x \right](i) \qquad (15)$$

where L_{Md} is the lower limit of the median class, T is the total number of cases, $.5T$ identifies the median case and the median class, Σfx is the sum of the cases up to the median class, x is the number of cases in the median class, and i is the width of the class interval.

FIGURE 1.4   Illustrations of Measures of Central Tendency for Demographic Variables

Measure	Comment[a]
Mean age of the population	
Median age of the population	
Median size of household	
"Average" size of household	Arithmetic mean. Size of households if population were distributed evenly among households.
Children ever born per 1000 women of reproductive age	Arithmetic mean. Size of family if children were distributed evenly among women of reproductive age.
Median (individual) income	
Per capita income	Arithmetic mean. Amount of income per person if all income were distributed equally. Tends to be much higher than median income.
Median years of school completed	
Average annual rate of growth	Essentially a geometric mean, the type of average used in time series. If applied continuously, would yield the recorded growth over the whole period under study.

[a] The underlying distributions for all of these variables, except the annual rate of growth, are skewed to the right. Therefore, the means are higher than the corresponding medians.

For discrete variables, the reported integral values are designated as the midpoints of the assumed intervals. For example, 3.0 is the midpoint of the interval for size class three persons per household. The intervals are then assumed to range from 0.5 below to 0.5 above the midpoint of the interval, as, for example, 0.5–1.5, 1.5–2.5, 2.5–3.5, 3.5–4.5, for midpoints 1.0, 2.0, 3.0, and 4.0. Then, if all households had three persons, the median value would be 3.0, as is logical.[9]

For variables that can be considered either continuous or discrete, there is no obvious solution and either method can be applied, although consistency within a presentation is necessary. An example of such a variable is educational attainment. My preference is to treat it as a continuous variable even though credit for completing a given level of school is not given until the end of the school year.

Arithmetic Means

The arithmetic mean is the average of the distribution of a variable that corresponds to the value each member of the population would have if the aggregate value of the variable over the entire population were distributed equally among them. For example, the mean size of household is obtained by dividing the total aggregate population in households by the number of households. The formula for grouped data is

$$M = {}_1\Sigma^{\omega} f_x m_x \div {}_1\Sigma^{\omega} f_x \tag{16}$$

where f_x are the frequencies (e.g., number of households) in each (e.g., household size) class, m_x is the midpoint of each (household size) class, and the size classes are numbered from 1 to the largest size reported (ω). Arithmetic means are used to summarize a variety of demographic distributions in addition to household size, among them distributions of age, income, number of children ever born to women, and absolute percentage error in population estimates. The arithmetic means obtained are, in addition to persons per household, respectively, mean age, per capita income, average number of children ever born to a woman, and mean absolute percentage error (MAPE).

Since the arithmetic mean can be pulled sharply in the direction of the longer tail of an asymmetric distribution and the median is drawn in the direction of the skew only moderately—generally a desirable feature—the median is frequently used as a measure of central tendency for demographic distributions. The median does not take account of all the information in the distribution and is not as statistically manipulable as the arithmetic mean, however. Sometimes both the arithmetic mean and the median are calculated for the same distribution if their alternative interpretations are plausible for the variable. Thus, in Census Bureau tables, we may encounter both median income and per capita income and both median size of household and persons per household. Both measures may be calculated also because there may be interest in the effect of the skewness of the distribution per se on the average, and the difference between the median and mean reflects this effect.

Interpolation within Intervals

With grouped data, the shortcut method of calculating an arithmetic mean calls for assigning a midpoint value to represent each interval (e.g., each income class). The midpoints are normally taken as the center of the interval on the assumption of **rectangularity**, or evenness, of the distribution of the variable in the interval. Rectangular interpolation assumes a constant density of the population having a characteristic within an interval and corresponds to an assumption of **linearity** in the cumulative values of the variable. An assumption of rectangularity is conventionally employed in interpolating in the median class when computing the median of a distribution.

An assumption of rectangularity is problematic if the interval is wide. In this case, **Pareto interpolation** may be used. Pareto interpolation assumes a decreasing density of population within an interval. This assumption may be employed, for example, for selected classes of the distribution in computing per capita income, particularly the open-end interval at the end of the distribution, or for the median class in computing the median income of the population if the width of the interval exceeds some designated amount, say $2,500.

Geometric Mean/Average Annual Rates of Growth

The use of the geometric mean is normally limited to time series, since in such series growth is compounded over time. The average annual rate of growth of a population over some period can be measured by the geometric mean (M_G) of the distribution of annual growth rates (r_i) of the population:

$$M_G = \sqrt[t]{{_1\Pi^t}(1 + r_i)} - 1 = \sqrt[t]{P_t \div P_0} - 1 \qquad (17)$$

where Π is the operator for continuous multiplication and i varies from 1 to t.

Alternatively, the geometric formula assumes annual compounding of population growth at a constant rate. To derive M_G, it is not necessary to know the annual growth rates, however, only the population at the initial and terminal dates.

The average annual rate of growth of a population is now commonly calculated by the **exponential** formula, which assumes continuous compounding of population growth at a constant rate. If the frequency of compounding is increased without limit, the population grows by r rather than by M_G. The exponential growth formula for r is

$$P_t = P_0 e^{rt} \tag{18}$$

$$r = \ln(P_t \div P_0) \div t \tag{19}$$

where ln refers to the system of natural logarithms, e is the base of the system of natural logarithms, and t is the number of years between P_0 and P_t. The exponential formula is more realistic than the geometric formula for measuring and analyzing population growth, although the two formulas give nearly the same results for r over short periods. The exponential formula is also easier to compute.

Average annual rates for the components of change—births, deaths, and net migration—consistent mathematically with the average annual growth rate for the total population just described—can also be calculated by the exponential formula. Assuming that the numbers of births, deaths, and net migrations sum to the difference between the two population figures, we seek three rates that sum to the average annual rate of growth for the total population. For this purpose, we divide the total number of births, deaths, and net migrants in the overall period by the number of **person–years lived** during the period.[10] The denominators of each rate are the same, therefore. For a 10-year intercensal period, the formula for the average annual birthrate (b_r) is

$$b_r = \left(\sum_{y=1}^{y=10} b_y \right) \div \left(\int_{t=0}^{t=10} P_t dt \right) \tag{20}$$

where b_y is the number of births in each year of the decade. Reducing this formula to computational form by solving the integral, we obtain

$$b_r = \left(r \sum_{y=1}^{y=10} b_y \right) \div (P_{10} - P_0) \tag{21}$$

For example, if the initial population of an area in the decade is 10,000, the terminal population in the decade is 12,214, and the total number of births in the decade is 1500, we can derive the annual average growth rate (r) by the formula for continuous compounding as follows:

$$r = \ln e^{10r} \div 10 = \ln(12,214 \div 10,000) \div 10 = \ln 1.2214 \div 10 = .02 \tag{22}$$

and then evaluate the formula for the annual average birthrate (b_r) as follows:

$$b_r = r\Sigma(b) \div (P_{10} - P_0) = .02(1500) \div (12{,}214 - 10{,}000)$$
$$= 30 \div 2{,}214 = .0136 \tag{23}$$

If the population is declining, the numerator and denominator will both be negative. For example, if $r = -.01$, the initial population is 10,000, the terminal population is 9048, and births in the decade number 1500, we have,

$$-.01(1500) \div (9048 - 10{,}000) = -15 \div -952 = .0158 \tag{24}$$

An analogous formula is used for deaths and net migrants. The three formulas for the birthrate (b_r), the death rate (d_r), and the net migrant rate (m_r) sum to the formula for r, the average annual growth rate based on continuous compounding. That is, if

$$P_{10} - P_0 = \sum_{y=1}^{y=10} b - \sum_{y=1}^{y=10} d + \sum_{y=1}^{y=10} m \tag{25}$$

then

$$r = b_r - d_r + m_r \tag{26}$$

Other Averages

The mode is the value with the maximum frequency and is not affected by the skewness of the distribution, but it has several disadvantages as judged by our criteria. The quadratic mean is not often used to measure the average of the distribution of a demographic variable, but is frequently used to measure the average deviation from the mean of a distribution, as in variance calculations, designated *RMSE*. **RMSE** is an abbreviation for root-mean-square-error, a name that suggests the structure of the calculation:

$$RMSE = \sqrt{\frac{\Sigma(X - \overline{X})^2}{N}} \tag{27}$$

where X is each value in the distribution, $\overline{X}$ is the mean of these values, and N is the number of observations.

Observed versus Adjusted Measures

The measures cited here are observed measures in the sense that they directly reflect or describe the experience of the population to which they refer. For example, a crude death rate for a given year and the corresponding age-specific death rates are observed rates. A crude death rate of 8 per 1000 population says, in effect, that 0.8% of the population died in the year. It is possible that more than one measure may describe essentially the same experience, with more or less verisimilitude. For example, the average annual rate of growth computed by continuous compounding and the average annual rate computed by periodic compounding are observed measures that describe the rate of growth in nearly the same way. Similarly, the mean and median of a distribution are both observed measures that characterize a distribution in terms of central tendency, though their levels are somewhat different. Demographers also deal with many observed measures that are highly disaggregated and are designed to reflect some very limited aspect of the population's condition. Consider, for example, an age-sex-marital status-marital duration-specific death probability, illustrated by the probability that a 26-year-old woman married between 2 and 3 years at the beginning of a year will die during the year.

Age Adjustment

Many demographic measures are not observed measures, however, but **adjusted measures**—that is, hypothetical representations of some demographic aspect of the real population, designed usually for analytic purposes. They are typically aggregated measures that combine schedules (usually for a range of age groups) of proportions or rates by arbitrary weighting patterns rather than the actual weighting patterns by which they are implicitly combined in the real population. For example, a standardized or age-adjusted death rate is derived by weighting a set of observed age-specific death rates with a standard or arbitrary age distribution, to create a hypothetical death rate for use in comparisons with other similarly derived death rates. The primary purpose of standardization or age-adjustment is to eliminate the effect of differences in age distribution between the all-ages rates or proportions being compared.

A part of the difference between the crude rates or general proportions of two populations, or of the total change in the crude rates or general proportions of a population over time, can be explained by the differences or shifts in the age-specific rates or proportions and a part can be explained by the differences or shifts in the age composition of the population (the population "weights"). Crude death rates for two areas may differ simply because the age structures of the population of the two areas differ, without any essential difference between their schedules of age-specific death rates. Standardization may be used as a tool for partitioning the total difference between the observed rates or proportions into the contribution of the two factors, the difference in age composition $(p_a/\Sigma p_a)$ and the difference in the age-specific schedules of the rates or proportions (m_a). Standardization achieves the purposes mentioned by substituting a standard weighting pattern for the observed weighting patterns:

$$Observed\ death\ rate,\ \text{population } p_1 = \frac{d^1}{p^1} = \frac{\Sigma m_a^1 p_a^1}{\Sigma p_a^1};$$

$$\text{population } p_2 = \frac{\Sigma m_a^2 p_a^2}{\Sigma p_a^2} \tag{28}$$

$$Standardized\ death\ rate,\ \text{population } p_1 = \frac{\Sigma m_a^1 P_a}{\Sigma P_a};$$

$$\text{population } p_2 = \frac{\Sigma m_a^2 P_a}{\Sigma P_a} \tag{29}$$

where p_a is the actual population in an age group, P_a is an arbitrary replacement for p_a to be used in all death rates to be compared, and 1 and 2 identify the two populations being compared.[11]

An important historical development is the plan of the U.S. National Center for Health Statistics to introduce a new standard age distribution for computing its age-adjusted death rates beginning with data for the year 1999. The new standard, the projected U.S. population for the year 2000 published by the U.S. Bureau of the Census, will replace the existing 1940 standard age distribution. The rates adjusted by the new standard will be much higher than the 1940 ones, because the population is much older than in 1940, but the trends and differences between the adjusted rates will not vary greatly for most categories because of the change of standard.[12]

Implications of Variations in Age-Specific Rates or Proportions

Age-specific rates and proportions in the same schedule are so variable that the change in the crude rate or overall proportion during a period cannot be used to represent the change in a proportion or rate at some age during the period. Age-specific changes may be very different from one another and are essentially independent of one another. The relative size of the shift in the age-specific proportions or rates over time may be illustrated by the change in the murder rate between 1990 and 1994. The overall murder rate in the United States declined by 4% in this period. However, the rate of murders committed by adults 25 years and over declined by 18%, that for youths 18–24 years of age rose by 2%, and the rate for teenagers 14 to 17 years of age rose by 22%.[13] The murder rate varies widely by age and tends to change at each age, for the most part, independently of the changes at other ages. Politicians can deliberately, and journalists can inadvertently, misrepresent the trend of the murder rate by overlooking these important differences in explaining the nature and causes of violent crime.

This generalization applies to population numbers as well. Percent changes in population for age groups may differ greatly from one age group to another. (See Table 2.1 for percentage changes in age groups for the United States between 1985 and 1995.) Hence, it is a serious fallacy to infer the percentage change in the overall population from the percentage change in some age group. Specifically, beware of inferring the change in the size of an area's population from the change in school enrollment, which merely reflects the change in the school-aged population.

SELECTED SPECIALIZED MEASURES

The Life Table

The life table represents a much used and versatile methodological and analytic tool of demographers. It has as its most common uses the tracking of the survival history of a birth cohort of persons from birth to extinction of the cohort, the calculation of survival rates, and the measurement of a group's life expectancy. The life table and its extensions have also been used in the analysis of lifetime changes in a wide range of social and economic characteristics, such as school enrollment, labor force participation, internal migration, and marital status. Life tables have been used in the study of health, disability, and institutionalization. They have been used for the analysis of the survival or "reliability" history of cohorts of nonhuman living things such as mammals, manufactured products such as household furnishings, and organizations such as private businesses. The reader is probably familiar with the use of life tables in the insurance and annuity industries to determine the prices (premiums) of their products and services and to calculate the expenses to the company (benefits) paid to those who purchase these products and services. The life table incorporates the application of several general demographic techniques, especially the use of probabilities of failure, cohort analysis, and age-adjustment or standardization.

The structure of the life table may vary from a simple conventional life table to a complex multistate life table. The conventional life table involves the reduction over the age scale of the original cohort of births solely by mortality. Multiple-decrement life tables incorporate other factors or events that reduce the size of the original cohort over the age scale, such as first marriage in a first-marriage formation table or various causes of death in a cause-of-death life table. Multistate life tables incorporate the transitions between states of one or more variables and death at each age. For example, a multistate table of marriage formation and dissolution incorporates appropriate transitions between the never-married state, the married state, the widowed state, and the divorced state, in addition to transitions to death from each marital state. In this chapter the conventional life table is briefly described and the sources of the official life tables are noted. Other forms of life tables are considered in later chapters.

A conventional **life table** for a given year displays the survival record by age of a newborn cohort from birth to the extinction of the cohort, employing the schedule of observed age-specific central death rates ($_nm_x$) in the reference year. The abridged life table for the United States in 1995 is shown in Table 1.1. The conventional abridged life table presents the following functions (i.e., columns of interdependent data): (1) survivors to every fifth age out of an initial cohort of 100,000 births (l_x); (2) age-specific probabilities of dying from one exact age to another over each 5-year age period ($_nq_x$); (3) deaths in each 5-year age group ($_nd_x$); (4) the person-years of life lived by the cohort in each age interval, designated the stationary population ($_nL_x$); (5) the person-years of life lived in that age and all remaining ages (T_x); and (6) the expectation of life at 5-year intervals (e_x). Usually, as in the illustrative table, ages under 1, 1 to 4, and 85 and over are treated separately in abridged tables.

In the construction of the life table, observed $_nm_x$'s are converted to $_nq_x$'s by one of several formulas. Then the survivors (l_x) are obtained as the iterative product of l_x and $_nq_x$. $_nL_x$, the stationary population, is derived by formula from l_x, and T_x is obtained by reverse cumulation of $_nL_x$. Life expectation (e_x) is derived by dividing the cumulated stationary population at age x (T_x) by the survivors to age x (l_x).

The age structure of the stationary population of the life table ($_nL_x$) is consistent with a constant annual number of births (l_0) and the current schedule of age-specific death rates ($_nm_x$) or probabilities of dying ($_nq_x$). The age structure of the stationary population is generated entirely from these observed death rates and may differ greatly from the observed age distribution, which has

▬ TABLE 1.1 Abridged Life Table for the Total Population: 1995

Age interval	Proportion dying	Of 100,000 born alive		Stationary population		Average remaining lifetime
Period of life between two exact ages stated in years	Proportion of persons alive at beginning of age interval dying during interval	Number living at beginning of age interval	Number dying during age interval	In the age interval	In this and all subsequent age intervals	Average number of years of life remaining at beginning of age interval
(1)	(2)	(3)	(4)	(5)	(6)	(7)
x to $x+n$	$_nq_x$	l_x	$_nd_x$	$_nL_x$	T_x	e_x
0–1	0.00757	100,000	757	99,363	7,578,845	75.8
1–5	0.00160	99,243	159	396,599	7,479,482	75.4
5–10	0.00099	99,084	98	495,153	7,082,883	71.5
10–15	0.00126	98,986	125	494,687	6,587,730	66.6
15–20	0.00415	98,861	410	493,375	6,093,043	61.6
20–25	0.00535	98,451	527	490,964	5,599,668	56.9
25–30	0.00595	97,924	583	488,161	5,108,704	52.2
30–35	0.00800	97,341	779	484,803	4,620,543	47.5
35–40	0.01049	96,562	1,013	480,421	4,135,740	42.8
40–45	0.01376	95.549	1,315	474,692	3,655,319	38.3
45–50	0.01862	94,234	1,755	467,104	3,180,627	33.8
50–55	0.02796	92,479	2,586	456,336	2,713,523	29.3
55–60	0.04276	89,893	3,844	440,407	2,257,187	25.1
60–65	0.06706	86,049	5,770	416,802	1,816,780	21.1
65–70	0.09826	80,279	7,888	382,527	1,400,178	17.4
70–75	0.14606	72,391	10,573	336,442	1,017,651	14.1
75–80	0.21256	61,618	13,140	277,041	681,209	11.0
80–85	0.31884	48,678	15,520	204,800	404,168	8.3
85 and over	1.00000	33,158	33,158	199,368	199,368	6.0

Source: U.S. National Center for Health Statistics, *Monthly Vital Statistics Report* 45(11): Supplement 2, June 12, 1997, "Report of final mortality statistics: 1995," Table 3.

been generated by a historically unique set of birthrates, death rates, and net immigration rates.[14]

A principal application of the life table is to calculate survival rates for use in making allowances for deaths in preparing population estimates and projections. Generally the $_nL_x$ function is employed for this purpose, although at times the l_x function must be used. Some illustrations are as follows:

5-year age group/5-year time period	$L_{60-64}/L_{55-59} = 416{,}602/440{,}407 = .94595$
Terminal age group/5-year time period	$T_{85}/T_{80} = 199{,}368/204{,}800 = .97348$
Survival from birth to age under 1	$L_0/l_0 = 99{,}363/100{,}000 = .99363$
Survival of 5 birth cohorts to under 5	$L_{0-4}/5l_0 = 495{,}962/500{,}000 = .99192$

The official life tables for the United States and the states are published by the U.S. National Center for Health Statistics. Abridged life tables for the

United States are available for each year from 1945 to 1998,[15] and unabridged life tables are available for decennial years from 1900–1902 to 1989–1991. Life tables for states are available for decennial years from 1929–1931 to 1989–1991.

Life tables are discussed further in other chapters, where applications to specific subject areas are considered. Refer to *The Methods and Materials of Demography: Revised Condensed Edition*, for a more detailed discussion of life tables and paradigms for their construction.[16]

Residual Estimation of Demographic Changes

Estimates for some demographic variables that are components of change in various estimating equations but for which direct data are lacking can be obtained as residuals from these equations. Examples of components that can be estimated by the **residual method** are net migration, net labor force accessions or withdrawals (e.g., retirements), and net marital formations or dissolutions (e.g., net widowings at older ages). The residual method provides an algorithm for estimating residuals of survival calculations between two census or survey figures for the same birth cohort at different dates. Forward and reverse formulas for estimating net migration for birth cohorts by the residual method are

$$M_1 = (P_2 - P_1 s) \div \sqrt{s} \tag{30}$$

$$M_2 = \left[(P_2 \div s) - P_1 \right] \sqrt{s} \tag{31}$$

where P_1 and P_2 are the population figures at the beginning and end of the period, respectively, for the cohort, s is the survival rate for the cohort for the period, and $\sqrt{s}$ is a survival rate representing an adjustment for deaths of migrants during the period. It can be shown that the forward and reverse formulas yield the same result (i.e., $M_1 = M_2$) and that, therefore, a single formula can replace the forward and reverse formulas:

$$(P_2 - P_1 s) \div \sqrt{s} = \left(\frac{P_2}{s} - P_1 \frac{s}{s} \right) \div \frac{\sqrt{s}}{s} = \left(\frac{P_2}{s} - P_1 \right) \sqrt{s} \tag{32}$$

It is expedient simply to apply the forward formula.[17] The assumption has to be made with these equations that the survival rates for the main elements in the equation (i.e., population and migrants) are the same for any particular birth cohort and that the population figures are comparable with respect to definition and coverage.

The residual formula for net labor force accessions and withdrawals parallels that for net migration. We replace the population at the beginning and end of the period by the corresponding labor force figures. Assuming that the labor force figures are comparable with respect to definition and coverage, that survival rates of the labor force and the population are the same, and that net immigration for the cohort during the period can be disregarded, the formula is

$$w_1 = (L_2 - L_1 s) \div \sqrt{s} = \left[(L_2 \div s) - L_1 \right] \sqrt{s} = w_2 \tag{33}$$

where w_1 and w_2 represent net withdrawals from the labor force, L_1 and L_2 represent the labor force for the birth cohort at the beginning and end of the period, respectively, s represents the survival rate for the labor force and the population during the period, and $\sqrt{s}$ represents the survival rate of net withdrawals or net accessions during the period at the same "hazard" rate as for labor force and population.[18]

Model Construction

Demographic models abound in demography in general and in applied demography in particular. **Demographic models** are generalized representations of demographic relationships that are frameworks or instruments for analysis, estimation, or projection. For example, the population estimating equation discussed previously is a model. The form of it for estimating residuals is a more specialized model. The life table is a complex model, with submodels embedded in it, such as the model of a stationary population associated with a particular level of life expectancy. To broaden the reader's view of the role of models in applied demography, three other models used in the field among the many that could be discussed are described. One is a strictly demographic model, the second an economic model, and third a statistical model. More specifically, they are the cohort-component method, econometric and employment-type models, and multiple regression.

Demographic Model: Cohort-Component Method

The name, cohort-component method, points to the fact that the method involves birth or other cohorts that are modified by mortality, migration, and other appropriate components. The cohort-component model is applied in many ways, most commonly to estimate postcensal population and to project population.

Consider the application of the method to the preparation of national population projections. The base population, distributed by single ages, sex, race, and Hispanic origin, is carried forward each year by projected life-table survival rates for these groups and the addition of a fixed amount and age-sex distribution of net immigrants for each year:

$$_{y+1}P_{a+1} = {_y}P_a \, _a s_{a+1} + {_a}M_{a+1} \tag{34}$$

$$_y B_{y+1} = ({_y}f_a + {_{y+1}}f_a) * \left({_y}P_a^f + {_{y+1}}P_a^f\right) \div 4 \tag{35}$$

where y refers to year, a to age, $_a s_{a+1}$ to the survival rate from age a to age $a+1$, f to birthrate, P^f to female population, M to net migration, and B to births. A new birth cohort is added to the population each year. The number of births is obtained by applying age-specific fertility rates to the female population of the particular race/Hispanic origin group. The projections of fertility, mortality, and immigration are guided by general assumptions expressed in terms of the total fertility rate for a terminal year such as 2050, life expectation at birth in the terminal year, and the annual total amount and age-sex distribution of net immigration, respectively. (See Chapter 10 for further discussion.)

Cohort methods do not necessarily involve either components or birth cohorts. Projections of school enrollment by grade can be prepared by carrying forward enrolled students by grade on a grade-cohort basis by use of grade-cohort ratios. A simplified version of the projection model is

$$_{g+1}E_{y+2} = {}_gE_{y+1}({}_{g+1}E_{y+1} \div {}_gE_y) \tag{36}$$

where y refers to year, g to grade, and E to numbers enrolled. Alternatively, the components of mortality, promotion, nonpromotion, and net migration can be incorporated in the model. (See Chapter 11 for further discussion.)

Economic Model: Econometric/Employment Analysis

Various economic models have been developed by economists as tools for preparing population projections, particularly subnational population projections. Two general types of economic models, an econometric model and an employment analysis model, may be distinguished. Their essential common feature is their use of economic variables in a system seeking to produce demographic data, in contrast to the demographic model, in which demographic variables are assumed to operate in a self-contained system. In the economic models, demographic variables are treated as both endogenous (i.e., dependent) and exogenous (i.e., independent) variables. A principal variable in economic models is employment, which may be disaggregated by major industry. Consider the preparation of state population projections by the method of employment analysis. The state ratio of population aged 18–64 to employment may be projected as a function of the change in the corresponding U.S. ratio, as is done in the latest projections of state population prepared by the U.S. Bureau of Economic Analysis. Alternatively, an econometric model links economic variables and demographic variables in a multiple regression equation. In this model, projections of population, personal income, employment, and other variables may be included in the equation as independent variables to reestimate one or other of them. Such a model allows for the reciprocal relation between demographic and economic variables. (See the section that follows and Chapter 10 for further discussion.)

Statistical Models: Multiple Regression

Demographers often have occasion to study the relationship between variables. Multivariate linear regression is a widely used statistical technique for describing the relationship between a dependent variable and several independent variables, for studying the causal relationship between them, or for assessing the strength of their relationship. There are many different regression formulas to express relationships among two or more variables, but formulas expressing linear relationships are most common. Many actual relationships are of the linear form or can be approximated closely by linear equations. Multivariate linear regression is a statistical model of the form.

$$Y_c = \beta_0 + \beta_1 x_1 + \beta_2 x_2 + \cdots + \beta_k x_k \tag{37}$$

where Y_c is a random variable whose value we want to "predict" in terms of given values of the independent variables $x_1, x_2, \ldots, x_k$; $\beta_1, \beta_2, \ldots, \beta_k$ are regression coefficients, numerical constants that must be determined from actual data; and β_0 the intercept of the equation, or the value of Y_c when the regression coefficients are zero.

The regression coefficients, β_i's, are usually estimated by the method of least squares. The least squares estimates of the β_i's are the values for which the sum of the squared differences between the actual values of Y and the values of Y estimated from the equation are a minimum:

$$_1\Sigma^n(Y_i - {_c}Y_i)^2 \min \tag{38}$$

To determine the values of the β_i's, we need $k + 1$ normal equations. We can solve the normal equations by computer using statistical packages or by hand, preferably using matrix algebra.[19]

When the dependent variable is a dichotomous variable (e.g., poor, not poor; disabled, not disabled), a variant of the multiple linear regression equation, the logistic regression model, is usually employed. In logistic regression the dependent variable is expressed in the form of logits, or the "logs" of odds ratios, a continuous variable that can take on any value in the range $(-\infty, +\infty)$. The logit of P is

$$\text{Logit } P_i = \ln[P_i \div (1 - P_i)] \tag{39}$$

where P_i is the probability that the ith person is in the category of interest (e.g., poor) and $(1 - P_i)$ is the probability that he or she is in the other category (e.g., not poor). The logistic regression model for the log odds is

$$\text{Ln}[P_i \div (1 - P_i)] = \beta_0 + \beta_i x_{i1} + \beta_2 x_{i2} + \cdots + \beta_k x_{ik} \tag{40}$$

given a particular vector, or array, of data on k predictor variables.[20] The β_i's here also can be derived by the least squares principle.

Some Measures of Inequality and Geographic Concentration

In analyzing distributions of variables, demographers often wish to measure the degree to which a variable is unequally distributed within a population or the degree to which the inequality of the distribution of a variable differs between two populations. For example, the population of an area may not be distributed equally with respect to type of household, income, assets, or other demographic, social, and economic variables, or the degree of inequality of household type, income, assets, or other variable may differ from one population to another. Furthermore, populations differ from one another with respect to the geographic distributions of these characteristics. Several measures of the inequality of the distribution of a characteristic in relation to a geographic area or the number of persons, and of the relative inequality of the distributions of a characteristic over two or more populations, have been developed. For this introductory discussion, only three of these—quintile analysis, the index of dissimilarity, and the Gini index—are considered. An application of the index of dissimilarity, along with other measures of spacial separation/integration, are described in Chapter 6 in connection with the issue of residential segregation.

Quintile Analysis

In quintile analysis, the question posed is, what percent of the aggregate of the variable is associated with each fifth of the population? For example, in 1995 the lowest quintile of the U.S. population received 4% of aggregate household income, the second quintile received 9%, the middle quintile received 15%, the next-to-the-highest quintile received 23%, and the highest quintile received 49%.[21] In other words, 40% of the population received only 13% of aggregate household income. Several alternative definitions of household income yield similarly uneven distributions of income in the population.

Index of Dissimilarity

The **index of dissimilarity** (*ID*) is calculated from the equation

$$ID = 1/2\Sigma[(X_i \div X) - (Y_i \div Y)] \tag{41}$$

where X_i is the number in group a (e.g., blacks) in category i (e.g., census tract), X is the total in group a over all categories (e.g., blacks in all tracts in a city), Y_i is the number in group b (e.g., nonblacks) in category i (e.g., census tract), and Y is the total in group b over all categories (e.g., nonblacks in all tracts in a city).[22] The formula requires calculating the proportions in the groups for each category (e.g., blacks in census tract i; nonblacks in census tract i) out of the totals for the groups (e.g., blacks in all census tracts; nonblacks in all census tracts [$(X_i \div X)$ and $(Y_i \div Y)$]), taking the differences between the proportions for each group in each category, summing the differences in the proportions over all categories, and dividing the sum in half. The index of dissimilarity varies between zero and one, zero representing perfect equality between the distributions and one representing complete inequality between the distributions.[23] The value of the *ID* indicates the amount by which the proportions in the distribution of the first population (e.g., blacks in census tracts) would have to be shifted up for negative differences and down for positive differences to make the distribution of that population agree exactly with the distribution of the second population (e.g., nonblacks in census tracts).

Since the index of dissimilarity is affected by the number of units (e.g., census tracts) in the distribution, *ID*'s based on different numbers of units (e.g., for different cities) are not fully comparable. It is desirable, therefore, to make some type of adjustment for the number of units, One can combine the units (e.g., census tracts) in order to achieve equality in the number of units beween areas.[24] Alternatively, a rough mathematical adjustment of the number of units could be employed to reduce the lack of comparability. The *ID* for each area could be divided by the cube root of the number of areas or, more conservatively, by the fourth root of the number of areas:

$$\frac{ID}{\sqrt[3]{N}} \qquad \frac{ID}{\sqrt[4]{N}} \tag{42}$$

These adjusted measures tend to be compressed toward zero and hence do not vary from zero to one.

The index of dissimilarity has some other shortcomings as a measure of the concentration of a characteristic. When the index of dissimilarity is used for continuous quantitative variables (e.g., educational level), the choice of categories is arbitrary (e.g., education <8, 8+; or <12, 12+) and influences the value of the index. Another disadvantage is that the use of the measure is limited to a comparison of two groups (e.g., poor and nonpoor). If a characteristic of interest has more than two groups, the groups can be compared only in pairs. The Theil coefficient, or entropy index, H, can take account of the distribution of variables with multiple groups, even those that are nominal.[25]

Gini Ratio

The **Gini ratio** (Gini index of concentration or Gini coefficient) is a summary measure of the inequality of distributions similar to the index of dissimilarity and related to it.[26] It has had considerable use in comparing the inequality of the income distributions in two or more populations or in a single population over time. The Gini ratio ranges from zero to one. An index of 1 indicates perfect inequality; for example, with respect to income, one household or unrelated person has all the income and the others have none. A ratio of 0 indicates perfect equality—that is, each household or unrelated person has the same share of aggregate income as any other household or unrelated person.

The calculation of the Gini ratio may best be described geometrically.[27] First, calculate the cumulative shares of aggregate income corresponding to specified cumulative shares of household units. Next, plot the results on a rectangular grid, with household units from 0 to 100 (percent) on the x-axis and with aggregate income from 0 to 100 (percent) on the y-axis. (See Figure 1.5.) This line is designated the line of inequality, or Lorenz curve. Third, plot a

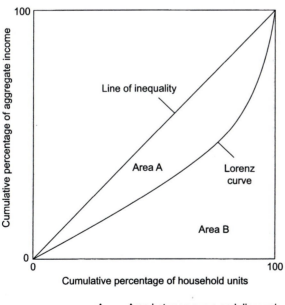

$$\text{Gini ratio} = \frac{A}{A+B} = \frac{\text{Area between curve and diagonal}}{\text{Area under diagonal}}$$

FIGURE 1.5 Schematic diagram of Lorenz curve and Gini ratio.

straight (diagonal) line from (0, 0) to (100, 100), representing a perfectly equal distribution of income and household units (theoretical line of equality). The Gini ratio represents the proportion of the total (triangular) area under the diagonal line that lies in the area between the diagonal line and the Lorenz curve. In the figure, B represents the area under the Lorenz curve and A represents the area between the diagonal line and the Lorenz curve. The Gini ratio is calculated as the share that area A constitutes of area (A + B).[28] The widening inequality of household income is indicated by the Gini ratios for 1970, 1980, 1990, and 1995. The figures are 0.394, 0.403, 0.428, and 0.450.[29]

NOTES

1. See the discussion of this question in David A. Swanson, Thomas K. Burch, and Lucky M. Tedrow, "What is applied demography?" *Population Research and Policy Review* **15**(5/6): 403–418, 1996; and Hallie J. Kintner and Louis G. Pol, "Demography and decision-making," *Population Research and Policy Review* **15**(5/6): 579–584, 1996.

2. I exclude the application of demographic methods to animal and plant populations, which calls for specialized knowledge of particular fields of biology. One could, however, reasonably extend the domain of applied demography to encompass demographic studies of household pets.

3. The use of the term *demographics* as referring to the demographic characteristics of a population is consistent with its etymology ("description of people"). The term is not listed in Roland Pressat's *Dictionary of Demography*, Christopher Wilson, ed., Basil Blackwell, Oxford, 1985, so that it is not recognized abroad as part of the terminology of demography. The term also does not appear in International Union for the Scientific Study of Population, *Multilingual Demographic Dictionary*, 2nd ed., adapted by Etienne van de Walle, from the French Section, edited by Louis Henry, Liège: Ordina Editions, 1982.

4. The concept is variously interpreted to allow new entrants, such as immigrants into a birth cohort, or to exclude them. We may call one type of cohort an open cohort and the other type a closed cohort. Except in special applications, it is not necessary to make this distinction.

5. The relations are more complex than set forth here. There is an interaction between the factors. For example, the *different* cohorts experience the same ages but in *different* calendar years, so that, in addition to the direct contribution of the factors to the total change or difference, there is the contribution of an interaction term.

6. Palmore (1978) and Halli and Rao (1992), following Hobcraft *et al.* (1982), present solutions with different degrees of refinement. Halli and Rao employ logistic regression to determine the proportion of variation in rates that can be explained by various age, period, and cohort models. Erdman Palmore, "When can age, period, and cohort be separated?" *Social Forces* **57**(5): 282–295, 1978; S. S. Halli and K. V. Rao, *Advanced Techniques of Population Analysis*, New York: Plenum, 1992, esp. Chapter 3; J. Hobcraft, J. Menken, and S. Preston, "Age, period, and cohort effects in demography: A review," *Population Index* **48** (Spring): 4–43, 1982. For a general treatment of cohort analysis, see Norvel D. Glenn, *Cohort Analysis*, Beverly Hills, CA: Sage, 1977.

7. The formulas for rates vary greatly depending on the specificity of the event and the precision of the measure. The conventional multiplier ("k" factor) varies for these measures. Some, such as the birthrate and death rate, are conventionally expressed per 1000 population. Others, such as survival rates, are usually expressed per unit. Proportions, such as high school graduation ratios and labor force participation ratios, are usually expressed per 100 population (i.e., as percentages).

8. The median should be calculated only for quantitative variables, such as age, size of household, and income. It makes no sense to speak of the average person in relation to attributes, or nonquantitative variables, such as urban-rural residence, marital status, citizenship, or race, as is so often done in journalistic contexts. We read, for example, that "the average person is a woman living in a metropolitan area," meaning, I suppose, that more than half of the population is female and more than half of the population, male and female, lives in a metropolitan area.

9. If all 1000 households in a community had exactly three persons, then the median is calculated as follows:

Class	Frequency	Notes: Median household $= 1/2(1000) = 500$;
0	—	median class $= 2.5$–3.5; median class share $= 500/1000$
1	—	$= .5$; $Md = 2.5 + .5(1) = 3.0$.
2	—	
3	1000	
4	—	
5	—	
Total	1000	

10. Person-years lived or person-years of exposure represents the product of the number of persons alive during the period and the number of years each lived during the period.

11. Kitagawa (1964) showed how to decompose the difference between two rates into two factors (i.e., age-specific rates and age distribution). The solution determines a unique set of population weights and eliminates the interaction term. The interaction term(s) is a measure of the effect of the difference in the population weighting pattern on the contribution of the difference in age-specific rates to the total difference between crude rates. It recognizes the fact that the contribution of the difference in age-specific rates to the total difference between crude rates varies on the basis of the weighting pattern used to combine the rates. See Evelyn M. Kitagawa, "Standardized comparisons in population research," *Demography* 1: 296–315, 1964.

Research on standardization and decomposition of rates, proportions, and indices in the past several decades has refined and extended the methods of standardization and decomposition from the solution for the comparison of two rates for two populations for two factors. Das Gupta (1993) has set forth formulas for decomposing the difference between two rates into multiple factors and for decomposing the differences between multiple rates into two or more factors, eliminating interaction terms. See U.S. Bureau of the Census, "Standardization and decomposition of rates: A user's manual," by Prithwis Das Gupta, *Current Population Reports*, P23-186, 1993.

12. U.S. National Center for Health Statistics, "Age standardization of death rates: Implementation of the year 2000 standard," by Robert N. Anderson and Harry M. Rosenberg, *National Vital Statistics Reports* 47(3), 1998.

13. James Alan Fox, "The calm before the juvenile crime storm," *Population Today* 24(9): 4–5. Washington, DC: Population Reference Bureau, September 1996.

14. The life table has a death rate ($LTDR = l_0 \div T_0$), which is the same as its birthrate ($LTBR = l_0 \div T_0$). It can be expressed as the cumulative product over all ages of the age-specific life table death rates ($_nm_x = {_nd_x} \div {_nL_x}$) and the stationary population at each age ($_nL_x$):

$$LTDR = (\Sigma_n m_x * {_nL_x}) \div \Sigma_n L_x = \Sigma_n d_x \div T_0 = l_0 \div T_0$$

This is a form of standardization of the observed crude death rate in which the stationary population of the life table is the weighting pattern for the age-specific life table death rates (which, as noted, agree with or approximate the observed age-specific death rates). By extension, life expectancy at birth, the reciprocal of the life table death rate, is a standardized measure, the population weights being the same as for the life table death rate (i.e., the life table stationary population). Note that, since the weighting pattern differs from life table to life table, these measures do not fully eliminate the effect of differences in age distributions.

15. In recent life tables, many of the functions have been interpolated to single ages.

16. For a more advanced discussion of the conventional life table and its extensions, see Krishnan Namboodiri, *Demographic Analysis: A Stochastic Approach*, San Diego: Academic Press, 1991, and for a discussion of the multistate life table in particular, see Robert Schoen, *Modeling Multigroup Populations*, New York: Plenum, 1987, Chapter 4.

17. This formula can replace the forward/reverse/average survival calculations sometimes proposed for estimating net migration. The new formula does not suffer from the bias characteristic of the earlier forward and reverse formulas.

18. There is a consistent formula employing labor force participation ratios, but it also requires a figure for the labor force at the beginning of the period. See Murray Gendell and Jacob S. Siegel, "Trends in retirement age by sex, 1950–2005," *Monthly Labor Review* 115(7), July 1992.

19. See John E. Freund and Roland E. Walpole, *Mathematical Statistics*, 4th ed., Englewood Cliffs, NJ: Prentice Hall, 1987.

20. Shiva S. Halli and K. Vaninadha Rao, *Advanced Techniques of Population Analysis*, New York: Plenum, 1992.

21. U.S. Bureau of the Census, "Money income in the United States: 1995," *Current Population Reports*, P60-193, 1996, Table E, p. xv.

22. An illustration of the calculation is given in *The Methods and Materials of Demography: Revised Condensed Edition*.

23. The index of dissimilarity is also expressed as a percentage and then the range is from 0 to 100.

24. Comparability is affected directly by how the units are combined when the number of units is equated between two areas. In particular, the pattern by which plus and minus differences in the distribution are combined in achieving an equal number of units will influence the result.

25. For the formulas and illustrative results, see Michael J. White, *American Neighborhoods and Residential Differentiation*, A Census Monograph Series, The Population of the United States in the 1980s, New York: Russell Sage Foundation, 1987, Chapter 4.

26. The Gini coefficient is the most popular measure, among sociologists and economists, of inequality of income and wealth among a class of related measures. These coefficients perform differently under different conditions. The Gini coefficient does well in measuring changes in the middle range of income or wealth, but not in the top income or wealth groups. Because of such characteristics, Gini coefficients and other measures should be used in comparisons only with the same measures.

27. See U.S. Bureau of the Census, "Money income of families and persons in the United States: 1978," *Current Population Reports*, Series P-60, No. 123, June 1980. See *The Methods and Materials of Demography: Condensed Edition*, for an illustration of the calculation of a Gini ratio.

28. The index of dissimilarity may also be represented in Figure 1.5 as the maximum vertical distance between the line of equality and the Lorenz curve.

29. U.S. Bureau of the Census, "Money income in the United States: 1995," *Current Population Reports*, P60-193, 1996, Table B-3, p. B-6.

SUGGESTED READINGS

Overview and General Studies

Debartolo, G. (1996). *Elementi di Analisi Demografica e Demografia Applicata*. Universita degli Studi della Calabria, Rende, Italia.

Kintner, Hallie J., and Pol, Louis G. (1996). "Demography and decision-making." *Population Research and Policy Review* 15(5/6): 579–584.

Kintner, Hallie J., Merrick, Thomas W., Morrison, Peter A., and Voss, Paul R. (eds.) (1994). *Demographics: A Case Book for Business and Government*. Boulder, CO: Westview Press.

Merrick, Thomas W., and Tordella, Stephan J. (1988, February). "Demographics: People and markets." *Population Bulletin* 43(1). Washington, DC: Population Reference Bureau.

Morrison, Peter A. (1988, September). "Applied demography: Its current scope and future direction in the United States," Rand Corporation, paper presented at the Conference on Local Area Demography in Business and Government, Nottingham, England.

Murdock, Steve H., and Ellis, David R. (1991). *Applied Demography: An Introduction to Basic Concepts, Methods, and Data*. Boulder, CO: Westview Press.

Pol, Louis G., and Thomas, R. K. (1997). *Demography for Business Decision Making*. Westport, CT: Greenwood Press.

Rao, K. Vaninadha, and Wicks, Jerry W. (eds.) (1994). *Studies in Applied Demography: International Conference on Applied Demography*. Population and Society Research Center. Bowling Green, OH: Bowling Green State University.

Swanson, David A., and Wicks, Jerry W. (eds.) (1987). *Issues in Applied Demography, Proceedings of the 1986 National Conference*. Population and Society Research Center. Bowling Green, OH: Bowling Green State University.

Swanson, David A., Burch, Thomas K., and Tedrow, Lucky M. (1996). "What is applied demography?" *Population Research and Policy Review* 15(5/6): 403–418.

U.S. Bureau of the Census. (1980). *Census '80: Continuing the Fact-Finder Tradition*, Charles P. Kaplan and Thomas L. VanValey (eds.).

U.S. Bureau of the Census. (1981). *Census '80 Projects for Students*.

Weeks, John R. (1996). *Population: An Introduction to Concepts and Issues*, 6th ed. Belmont, CA: Wadsworth, Chapter 16.

Methods

Halli, S. S., and Rao, K. V. (1992). *Advanced Techniques of Population Analysis*. New York: Plenum.

Hobcraft, J., Menken, J., and Preston, S. (1982). "Age, period, and cohort effects in demography: A review." *Population Index* **48**: 4–43.

Namboodiri, Krishnan. (1991). *Demographic Analysis: A Stochastic Approach*. New York: Academic Press.

Pol, Louis G. (1997). "Demographic methods in applied demography: An American perspective." *Genus* **53(1–2)**: 159–176.

Shryock, Henry S., Siegel, Jacob S., and Associates. (1976). *The Methods and Materials of Demography: Condensed Edition* by Edward F. Stockwell. New York: Academic Press. See also Revised Condensed Edition, David A. Swanson and Jacob S. Siegel (eds.), San Diego: Academic Press, 2002.

2
RECENT POPULATION TRENDS AND PROSPECTS AND INTERRELATIONS WITH SELECTED SOCIAL AND ECONOMIC PROGRAMS

The purpose of this chapter is to describe the main demographic and socioeconomic trends since World War II and to link these trends illustratively to actual social and economic programs. The first section of this chapter

Murray Gendell, Professor of Demography (retired), Georgetown University, collaborated with the author in preparing this chapter by providing background material, particularly on linkages with various social and economic programs.

presents a general overview of the principal demographic trends in the post–World War II period, focusing particularly on the changes since 1970, and the principal prospective changes in the first part of the 21st century. This summary provides important information for interpreting and analyzing many of the issues that applied demographers are concerned with and that we will consider in later chapters. The second section of this chapter presents several illustrations of links between population trends and various public and private programs. For this purpose, education, housing, local transit management, and revenue administration are the topics considered.

The discussion of population trends in this chapter is quite limited both in terms of the selection of the topics and the depth of their treatment. The reader should view this chapter as background material for the exploration of applications of demographic data and methods presented later. Most of the discussion in this chapter relates to the nation as a whole. Many applied demographers deal with national data and issues, but most of them are primarily concerned with subnational matters. For the most part, the uses of subnational data are discussed in other chapters. However, to broaden the coverage of state and local materials and to illustrate the variation subnationally with regard to various subject items, several tables and a figure that present selected data for states and other subnational areas are included as an appendix to this chapter. The state tables and figure show data on population size, growth, net migration, life expectancy, fertility, racial/Hispanic composition, and household income.

RECENT POPULATION TRENDS AND PROSPECTS

Population Size and Age–Sex Structure

The U.S. population has undergone vast changes in the decades since World War II and, as the population projections of the U.S. Census Bureau suggest, is expected to undergo marked changes in the next several decades as well. The population changes have been associated with vast changes in U.S. social and economic life and have profound implications for the way the country manages its institutions in the years to come.

Changes in Total Population, Age Groups, and Baby-Boom Cohorts

The population of the United States has been growing more slowly in recent decades than in most of the decades of the 20th century. At present the growth rate is about 0.9% per year, in the 1960s it averaged 1.3%, and in 1900–1910 it averaged 1.9%. Currently net immigration contributes over one-third of the net population gain and natural increase (i.e., the excess of births over deaths) contributes somewhat less than two-thirds. The relative contribution of net migration has been rising and that of natural increase has been falling. According to the middle series of projections of the Census Bureau, in the next few decades (i.e., by 2025) the annual average growth rate will fall to 0.7%, as a result of a rise in the crude death rate and a fall in the net immigration *rate*.[1]

A comparison of the changes in age groups for 1985–1995 and as projected for 1995–2005 and 2015–2025 reveals that in these decades the age changes have been, and are expected to continue to be, very variable (Table 2.1). There is great variation both from age group to age group during the same decennial period but also from one decennial period to the next for the same age group. This variation can be illustrated by comparing the changes in some selected age groups with the relatively stable change in the total population of 8 to 10% during these 10-year periods. The number of youths 18–24 years old dropped 14% in the 1985–1995 decade, but is expected to increase 13% in the 1995–2005 decade. The population aged 55–64 years is expected to show a massive increase, 40%, between 1995 and 2005 after falling slightly in the preceding decade. The age group 85 years and over shows increases of over one-third in the first two periods, 1985–1995 and 1995–2005, after which its growth rate is expected to fall off.

The changes involving the "baby-boom" cohorts are of particular interest. The baby boom is the name popularly given to the huge number of babies born from 1946 through 1964. The baby-boom cohorts are far larger than the preceding cohorts:

Age group	Numbers (in thousands)			Percentage change	
	1975	1995	2015	1975–1995	1995–2015
10–29	78,369[a]	74,022	84,314	−5.6	+13.9
30–49	48,669	81,895[a]	77,440	+68.3	−5.4
50–69	45,570	44,711	76,664[a]	−1.9	+71.5

[a]Baby-boom cohorts, measured with approximate ages.
Source: U.S. Bureau of the Census, *Current Population Reports*, P25-1130, 1996.

Some 77 million persons are anticipated in the 50 to 69-year group in 2015 (i.e., about 72% more than in the same age group in 1995). Note also, however, that the succeeding cohorts are expected to be very large as well.

Aging of the Population

The population of the United States has generally been aging throughout its history. The steady rise in the proportion of the elderly population recorded between 1970 and 1990 continued into the 1990s, albeit very slowly. The process actually came to a halt in the second half of the decade, but is expected to resume its rise without much delay. The percentage of persons 65 and older was 10 in 1970 and 13 in 1997, and is expected to rise to 20 in 2030 (Table 2.2). Similarly, the median age in 1997, 35 years, was well above the figure for 1970, 28 years, and the figure in 2025 is expected to be even higher, 38 years.

The rise in the ratio of persons 85 years and over to persons 65 years and over until 2010, shown in Table 2.2, informs us that the extreme aged population, those 85 years and over, has been growing faster than the elderly population under age 85 and that the elderly population has itself been *aging*. The aging of the elderly population will continue until the baby-boom cohorts begin to reach age 65. For the following two decades the elderly population becomes *younger* as the baby-boom cohorts move into the ages 65 to 84. After 2030 the process reverses again as these cohorts reach age 85. Table 2.2 also records another important demographic by-product of the baby boom—the expected sharp rise in the ratio of elderly persons to persons of working age

TABLE 2.1 Percentage Change in Resident Population According to Age: 1985 to 2025 (Estimates for 1985 and 1995; Middle Series of Projections for 2005 and Beyond)

Age group	Population (in thousands)			Percentage change			
	1985	1995	2005	1985–1995	1995–2005	2005–2015	2015–2025
All ages	237,924	262,755	285,981	+10.4	+8.8	+8.4	+8.0
Under 5	17,842	19,591	19,127	+9.8	−2.4	+0.7	+6.3
5–17	44,781	49,149	52,837	+9.8	+7.5	+1.0	+9.3
18–24	28,902	24,932	28,268	−13.7	+13.4	+8.0	−0.5
25–34	41,696	40,873	36,306	−2.0	−11.2	+13.2	+5.0
35–44	31,691	42,468	42,165	+34.0	−0.7	−10.8	+12.7
45–54	22,460	31,079	41,506	+38.4	+33.5	−0.7	−10.5
55–64	22,135	21,139	29,605	−4.5	+40.0	+33.9	−0.3
65–74	16,858	18,759	18,369	+11.3	−2.1	+42.9	+35.0
75–84	8,890	11,145	12,898	+25.4	+15.7	+1.8	+48.4
85 and over	2,667	3,628	4,899	+36.0	+35.0	+26.4	+13.8
65 and over	28,415	33,532	36,166	+18.0	+7.9	+24.5	+36.0
75 and over	11,557	14,773	17,797	+27.8	+20.5	+8.6	+37.3

Note: A revised set of population projections was issued by the U.S. Census Bureau in January 2000.
Source: U.S. Bureau of the Census, *Current Population Reports*, Series P25-1130, 1996; P-25, No. 1095; PPL-41.

after 2010. These changes have important implications for the management of the Social Security system and the requirements for long-term care.

The aging of the American population has also been geographically pervasive, as the population of nearly every state showed a higher percentage

TABLE 2.2 Resident Population and Population Ratios for Broad Functional Age Groups: 1980 to 2050 (Estimates for 1997; Middle Series of Projections for 2010 and Beyond)

Ages (years)	1980	1990	1997	2010	2030	2050
Number (thousands) Total population	226,546	248,765	267,636	297,716	346,899	393,931
Under 18	73,754	63,942	69,528	72,511	83,442	96,118
18–64	137,241	153,742	164,032	187,797	193,779	218,954
65 and over	25,550	31,081	34,076	39,408	69,378	78,859
85 and over	2,240	3,022	3,871	5,671	8,455	18,223
Ratio per 100 population						
Under 18/total	28.1	25.7	26.0	24.4	24.1	24.4
18–64/total	60.6	61.8	61.3	63.1	55.9	55.6
65+/total	11.3	12.5	12.7	13.2	20.0	20.0
65+/18–64	18.6	20.2	20.8	21.0	35.8	36.0
85+/total	1.0	1.2	1.4	1.9	2.4	4.6
85+/65+	8.8	9.7	11.4	14.4	12.2	23.1

Source: U.S. Bureau of the Census, *Current Population Reports*, P25-1130, 1996, Table F. See also *Statistical Abstract of the United States, 1998*, Tables 14 and 17, 1998.

of elderly persons in 1995 than in 1970. Florida is by far the "oldest" state, with about 19% of the population 65 years and over in 1997, as compared to the national average of 13%. Many states in the Northeast and Midwest show proportions above the national average either because of historically low fertility or because of out-migration of youth. Aging of the population does not preclude increases in the child population. Of the 10 states with the fastest growing elderly population, 5 had the fastest growing child population as well.[2]

Sex Composition and Deficit of Men

In recent decades, the balance of the sexes in the total population and over the age cycle has shown a predictable regularity. The overall deficit of males in relation to the number of females was about 4% in 1997. There is an excess of boys and young men, but at ages 85 years and over there is a massive excess of women. The number of males per 100 females declined rather steadily over the age scale, from 105 at ages under 15 to about 40 at ages 85 and over (Table 2.3). The implications of a largely female older population are wide-ranging. For example, these older women are mostly widowed, often poor, and at relatively high risk of institutionalization. They often live alone and, partly as a result of their isolation, often suffer from mental health problems. Any substantial change in this pattern depends primarily on future changes in the relative mortality of males and females.

Fertility, Mortality, and Immigration

Fluctuating Low Fertility, Increased Nonmarital Fertility, and Rise in Median Age of Childbearing

Fertility reached a postwar peak in 1957 in the midst of the baby boom. A "baby bust" followed in the two decades after the baby boom but the decline in fertility was gradual. Hitching on to this decline, the birthrate went on a moderate roller-coaster ride in the last three decades of the 20th century. For

TABLE 2.3   Males per 100 Females in the Resident Population, for Age Groups: 1980 to 2025 (Estimates for 1997 and Middle Series of Projections for 2025)

Age (years)	1980 (April 1)	1990 (April 1)	1997 (July 1)	2025 (July 1)
All ages	94.5	95.1	95.9	96.0
Under 15	104.6	104.9	104.9	105.1
15 to 24	101.7	104.5	105.8	104.1
25 to 44	97.4	98.9	99.5	97.7
45 to 64	90.7	92.5	93.9	93.5
65 to 84	70.3	71.0	74.5	87.8
85 and over	43.7	38.6	40.3	52.4
65 years and over	67.6	67.2	69.8	82.9

Source: U.S. Bureau of the Census, *Current Population Reports,* P25-1130, 1996; P-25, No. 1095; and PPL-91.

example, it was 18.4 births per 1000 population in 1970, 14.6 in 1975, 16.7 in 1990, and 14.6 in 1998. The total fertility rate, the average number of children born to a women in her lifetime, has fluctuated in somewhat the same way since 1970. It was 2.48 in 1970, 1.77 in 1975, 2.08 in 1990, and 2.06 in 1998, slightly below the replacement level of 2.09 for that year. Total fertility rates vary substantially around the replacement level among the states, but none are very high (Table 2.A.1, see Appendix A). Most are quite low in comparison with the national average. Utah, with a rate of 2.63, has the highest rate and Vermont, with a rate of 1.57, has the lowest rate.

The principal measures of nonmarital fertility have shown a spectacular rise in the past few decades. The rate of births to unmarried women 15 to 44 years of age increased by over half since 1980 and the percentage of births to unmarried women nearly doubled (from 18 in 1980 to 33 in 1999). Over two-thirds of births to black women are nonmarital.

Teenage pregnancy, mostly outside marriage, remains high, although the rates in 1999 are below those of 1991, the previous high year. An estimated 10% of teenagers 15 to 19 years of age became pregnant in 1999, although only 5% became mothers. Some 7% of girls 15 to 17 years of age and 14% of girls 18 to 19 became pregnant in that year. (See Table 2.A.1 for national and state data on teenage motherhood for 1997.)

The median age of childbearing has been rising in recent decades. The figure was 27.4 years in 1997, as compared with 25.1 years in 1980. This change is associated with a rise in the median age at marriage and also with postponement of motherhood within marriage, especially by parents jointly pursuing work careers.

Declines in Death Rates, with Continuing Sex and Race Disparities

The crude death rate, 8.6 per 1000 population in 1997, changed little in the previous two decades, being restrained by the continued aging of the population. There were low points in 1979 and 1982 at 8.5 deaths per 1000 population. Death rates at every age have continued to decline, however. Life expectancy at birth in 1997, at 76.1 years for both sexes combined, was at a historically all-time high (Table 2.4), while the infant mortality rate, at 7.2 per 1000 live births, was at a historically all-time low. The corresponding figures in 1975 were 72.7 and 20.0, respectively, reflecting a rise of 3.4 years in life expectancy and a decline of 12.8 infant deaths per 1000 live births in this period. A substantial part of the increase in life expectancy during this period occurred as a result of declines in death rates at the ages over 65. In fact, there have been such marked declines in death rates at the older ages that the increase in life expectancy at age 65 has accelerated. Life expectancy at age 65 in 1975 was 14.9 years; the corresponding figure in 1997 was 17.7 years.

Life expectancy at birth and life expectancy at age 65 are still considerably lower for males than females in spite of the fact that the increases between 1975 and 1997 were greater for males. At birth there was a gap of 7.8 years in 1975 and a gap of 5.8 years in 1997. At age 65 the corresponding figures were 3.8 years in 1975 and 3.3 years in 1997. The gap between the mortality of whites and blacks remains wide, although it has narrowed a little since 1975.

■ **TABLE 2.4** **Expectation of Life at Birth in Years, by Race/Hispanic Origin and Sex: 1975 to 2025**

Year	All races Male	All races Female	White Male	White Female	Black Male	Black Female	Hispanic[a] Male	Hispanic[a] Female
1975	68.8	76.6	69.5	77.3	62.4	71.3	(NA)	(NA)
1985	71.2	78.2	71.8	78.7	65.3	73.5	(NA)	(NA)
1995	72.5	78.9	73.4	79.6	65.2	73.9	74.9	82.2
1997	73.6	79.4	74.3	79.9	67.2	74.7	75.0	82.5
2015[b]	74.8	81.1	76.3	82.1	65.8	76.0	77.4	84.7
2025[b]	76.2	82.0	77.9	83.2	67.2	77.0	79.3	86.0

NA: Not available.

[a] Hispanics may be of any race.

[b] Middle series of projections. Based on data through 1994.

Source: U.S. National Center for Health Statistics, *Vital Statistics of the United States,* "Life Tables," various issues; *National Vital Statistics Reports* **47**(28), "United States life tables, 1997," 1999; and U.S. Bureau of the Census, *Current Population Reports,* P25-1130, 1996.

(State figures on life expectancy at birth for whites and blacks, by sex, for 1989–1991 are shown in Table 2.A.2.)

Massive Immigration, Increasing Racial Heterogeneity, and Growth in Foreign Born

Immigration has played a large and increasing role in recent U.S. population growth, although it has been a minor factor in the shifts in age composition. Net immigration is approaching 1 million persons per year. Recent immigrants have come increasingly from Asia, Africa, and Latin America, especially Mexico and the Caribbean area, instead of their former origins in Europe (Table 2.5). The massive flow of immigrants has contributed to a sharp rise in the proportion of foreign-born persons and a major change in the racial/ethnic complexion of the population. The changes in the character of our immigration have resulted from large admissions of refugees, a sizable influx of illegal immigrants, mainly from Mexico and Central America, and, most of all, the passage of new immigration legislation, especially in 1965 and 1990. This legislation liberalized the ceilings on immigration numbers, equalized quotas from the countries in the southern continents with those from Europe, and modified the categories receiving preference for entry.

Legal alien immigration averaged 863,000 persons per year between 1992 and 1996, and an estimated 300,000 illegal immigrants were added to the population in each year of this period.[3] Net immigration in 1997 was 868,000. This figure allows for legal alien immigration, illegal immigration, alien emigration, movement to and from Puerto Rico, and net movement of the U.S. armed forces, civilian federal employees, and their dependents. The migration of most of these categories has to be estimated since there are no direct data on them. Legal alien immigration (including the "flexible cap," refugees, and asylees) is now set at about 800,000 per year by law.

In combination with the differences in the fertility levels of the racial/Hispanic groups, immigration is contributing to the racial/ethnic heterogeneity of the American population. Two of every three people added to the population through net immigration in the mid-1990s were Hispanic or Asian, less than one in ten was black, and only one in five was non-Hispanic white (Table 2.5 and U.S. Bureau of the Census, 1996, *op.cit.*). The huge immigration of Caribbean blacks, Asians, and Hispanics since the 1960s and the higher fertility of blacks and Hispanics than of non-Hispanic whites are reflected in rapid increases in these racial/Hispanic groups in the population (Table 2.6). Groups other than non-Hispanic whites, that is, so-called racial-Hispanic minorities, constitute over one-quarter of the population at the turn of the century. Eleven percent of the population is Hispanic, 12% is non-Hispanic black, and 4% is Asian and other, leaving only 73% non-Hispanic white. In 1980 non-Hispanic whites made up about 80% of the total population. As a result of the new immigration, the share of foreign-born persons in the total population has risen from its low point of 5% around 1970 to about 10% by 1997.

The racial/ethnic metamorphosis of the population is expected to continue. Before 2010, Hispanics will become the largest racial/ethnic minority, outpacing blacks, as their share of the total population reaches 14%. The racial/Hispanic minorities are expected to constitute an increasing share of the total population. This share is projected at one-third in 2010 and nearly two-fifths in 2025. In numerous communities of the nation, particularly in the West region, the racial/Hispanic "minorities" have already become the

TABLE 2.5 Immigrants According to World Region and Country of Birth: 1980–1990 and 1995–1996 (Periods Extend from July 1 to June 30)

Region and country of birth	Numbers (in thousands) 1980–1990[a]	Numbers (in thousands) 1995–1996	Percentage 1980–1990	Percentage 1995–1996
All countries	733.8	915.9	100.0	100.0
Europe	70.6	147.6	9.6	16.1
Soviet Union, former	8.4	62.8	1.1	6.9
Asia	281.7	307.8	38.4	33.6
China[b]	38.9	41.7	5.3	4.6
India	26.2	44.9	3.6	4.9
Korea	33.9	18.2	6.6	2.0
Philippines	49.5	55.9	6.7	6.1
Vietnam	40.1	42.1	5.5	4.6
North America	312.5	340.5	42.6	37.2
Mexico	165.3	163.6	22.5	17.9
Caribbean	89.3	116.8	12.2	12.8
Central America	45.9	44.3	6.3	4.8
South America	45.6	61.8	6.2	6.7
Africa	19.2	52.9	2.6	5.8
Other countries[c]	4.2	5.3	0.6	0.6

[a] Annual average.
[b] Includes Taiwan.
[c] Includes Australia, New Zealand, and unknown countries.
Source: Based on U.S. Immigration and Naturalization Service, *1997 Statistical Yearbook of the U.S. Immigration and Naturalization Service*, 1999, Table 3.

■ **TABLE 2.6 Percentage Distribution of the Resident Population by Race/Hispanic Origin: 1970 to 2025**

Year	Total (in thous.)	White	Black	American Indian[a]	Asian and Pacific Islander	Hispanic[b]
1970	203,235	87.6	11.1	1.3	1.3	(NA)
1980	226,546	85.9	11.8	0.6	1.6	6.4
1990	248,765	83.9	12.3	0.8	3.0	9.0
1997	267,636	82.7	12.7	0.9	3.7	11.0
2005[c]	285,981	81.3	13.2	0.9	4.6	12.6
2015[c]	310,134	79.7	13.7	0.9	5.6	15.1
2025[c]	335,050	78.3	14.2	1.0	6.6	17.6

NA: Not available.

[a] Including Eskimo and Aleut.

[b] Persons of Hispanic origin may be of any race.

[c] Medium series of population projections.

Source: U.S. Bureau of the Census, *Current Population Reports*, Series P25-1130, 1996, and Series P-25, No. 1095; and *Population Paper Listings* PPL-91.

racial/Hispanic majorities. This emerging pattern is already suggested by state data on the distribution of the population by racial/Hispanic groups for 1997 (Table 2.A.3). The percentages of racial/Hispanic minorities in seven selected states as estimated for 1997 and projected for 2010 are as follows:

State	Percentage 1997	2010
Arizona	32	36
California	49	59
Florida	31	36
New Jersey	30	38
New Mexico	51	54
New York	34	40
Texas	44	48

Source: U.S. Bureau of the Census, *Population Paper Listings*, PPL-47; *Statistical Abstract of the United States, 1998*, Table 34.

An associated change is the recent rapid increase in the foreign-born population in the several states where the immigrants have been settling in the largest numbers. The states that had more than 10% foreign-born persons in 1990[4] and the percentage of all foreign-born persons in these states that immigrated in the 1980–1990 decade are as follows:

State	Percentage foreign born	Percentage entered 1980–1990
United States	8	44
California	22	50
New York	16	42
Hawaii	15	41
Florida	13	40
New Jersey	12	40

Source: U.S. Bureau of the Census, 1990 Census of Population, *Social and Economic Characteristics, U.S. Summary*, 1993, Table 132.

The new immigrants settled mainly in the several large states in which immigrants had settled before. A substantial share of the foreign-born population in every state in 1990 were recent immigrants, having arrived in the United States in the 1980–1990 decade.

The pattern of heavy concentration of recent immigrants among the foreign born has continued into the 1990s since the immigrant flow has continued unabated. Of the foreign-born population in 1997, over two-fifths (44%) were Hispanic, one-quarter (24%) Asian or Pacific Islander, one-twelfth (8%) black, and one-quarter (24%) were non-Hispanic white. These percentages contrast sharply with the racial/Hispanic distribution of the native population, which is three-quarters non-Hispanic white, one-eighth black, one-twelfth Hispanic, and a few percent Asian and Pacific Islander.

It is apparent that the massive immigration that the U.S. population is experiencing has direct implications for the country's future population size, racial/ethnic composition, and regional distribution. It is less obvious that it has many indirect implications with respect to educational administration, public welfare administration, tax administration, law enforcement, the language situation, the Social Security program, the environment, and public health. Some of these implications are considered further in later parts of this book.

Marriage and Households

Rise in Age at First Marriage; Increase in Divorce, Remarriage, and Nonmarriage

Men and women are marrying later in life than they did a quarter century ago, about 4 years later on the average for each sex. In 1997 median age at first marriage was 25.0 years for women and 26.8 years for men; in 1970 the corresponding figures were 20.6 and 22.5. In this 27-year period, marriage also became less common. While the rate of divorce has declined slightly from about five to four divorces per 1000 population, the relative impact of divorce has not waned. The divorce rate was only one-third the marriage rate in 1970, but it was half the marriage rate in 1995. The percentage of women 18 years old and over who were divorced rose from 4 to 11 between 1970 and 1997.

The percentage of women who have never married also has been rising. This increase in nonmarriage can be measured indirectly from the percentage of women 45 to 54 years old reporting "never married" in 1970 and 1997 in the Current Population Survey. These figures are 5% and 7%, respectively. Another view of the trend toward nonmarriage is given by the rapid increase in cohabitation. The share of unmarried couples grew from 3% in 1980 to 7% in 1997. Yet marriage is not unpopular. Most divorced persons remarry. Nearly half the marriages occurring in the late 1980s involved a remarrying partner, as compared with only one-third in 1970.

Declines in Household Size and in Family Households

On average, the size of households has been getting smaller. The number of households grew faster than the population in the several decades between

1950 and 1990 and, as a result, average household size declined steadily during this period (Table 2.7). It was 3.37 in 1950 and 2.63 in 1990. During the 1990s it remained nearly steady and it is expected to change little in the early years of the new century. The most rapid decline in average household size, 0.38, occurred during the 1970s. In this decade the population grew more slowly than at any time since the 1930s (11%), and the number of households grew more rapidly than in any decade since the beginning of the century (27%). Most of the areas that were losing population were in fact gaining households.[5]

Associated with the drop in average household size during these decades has been a shift in the distribution of households by size. The share of one- and two-person households increased, and the share of five-person and larger households decreased (Table 2.8). For example, during the 1970–1997 period, the share of one-person households increased from 17% to 25%.

From the data on age of householder in Table 2.8, we can infer that the impact of the baby boom on the growth of households was relatively strong during the 1970s and relatively weak during the 1980s. The percentage of householders who were members of the baby-boom cohorts rose from 8% in 1970 to about 32% in 1980 and 44% in 1990.[6] The reason for the weakening of the impact of the baby-boom cohorts on the housing market during the 1980s was that housing became much less affordable during that decade, especially for young adults. This group constitutes the main market segment for first-time homeowners and renters.

A number of related demographic changes account for the drop in average household size. One is that nonfamily households increased more rapidly than

TABLE 2.7 Change in Resident Population, Households, and Average Household Size: 1950–1960 to 1998–2010

Period	Resident population[a]	Households[a]	Persons per household[b]	
			Number[c]	Change[d]
1950–1960	18.5	21.1	3.33	−.04
1960–1970	13.3	20.1	3.14	−.19
1970–1980	11.4	27.4	2.76	−.38
1980–1990	9.8	15.5	2.63	−.13
1990–1997	7.3	8.2	2.64	+.01
1998–2010	10.3	13.6	2.53[e]	−.07[e]

[a] Percent change during period.

[b] Based on the noninstitutional population, including members of the armed forces living on post but excluding all other members of the armed forces.

[c] Average size of household at end of period.

[d] Absolute change in persons per household. The average number of persons per household was 3.37 in 1950.

[e] As projected in series 1.

Source: Based on U.S. Bureau of the Census, *Statistical Abstract of the United States, 1988*, Table 56, and *1998*, Tables 2, 69, and 70; and *Current Population Reports*, P23-49, 1974, Table 3.13, and P25-1129, 1996, Table 1.

TABLE 2.8 Percentage Distribution of Households by Age of Householder and Size of Household: 1970 to 1997 (as of March; Based on Current Population Survey)

Age and size	1970	1980	1990	1997 Family households Total	Married couple	Female householder	Nonfamily households
Total	100	100	100	100	100	100	100
Age of householder (years)							
15–24	7	8	5	5	2	10	7
25–29	10	12	10	9	7	10	10
30–34	9	12	12	11	11	12	8
35–44	19	17	22	24	27	29	16
45–54	19	16	16	19	21	17	14
55–64	17	15	13	12	14	9	11
65–74	12	12	13	12	11	7	15
75 and over	8	8	9	10	6	6	19
Size of household							
One person	17	23	25	25	(X)	(X)	83
Two persons	29	31	32	32	40	43	14
Three persons	17	17	17	17	21	30	2
Four persons	16	16	16	15	23	16	1
Five persons	10	8	7	7	10	7	(Z)
Six persons or more	11	5	3	3	5	4	(Z)

X: Not applicable. Z: Less than 0.5%.
Source: U.S. Bureau of the Census, *Current Population Reports*, P20-509, earlier reports, and unpublished data. See also U.S. Bureau of the Census, *Statistical Abstract of the United States, 1998*, Tables 72 and 73. *Statistical Abstract of the United States, 1988*, Table 59.

family households (Table 2.9).[7] The percentage of all households which were family households dropped between 1970 and 1997 from 81% to 70%, while the share of nonfamily households rose commensurately. The decline in the share of family households occurred because of a large drop in the share of households with a married couple. The latter decline took place because of the large increase in divorce, the rise in the percentage of persons who had never married, the increase in cohabitation, the trend toward delayed marriage, and the increased popularity of living alone.

The share of female-headed households, including those with children under 18, has been growing. In 1997 the share with children was 7.8% while in 1980 it was 6.7%. During the second part of this period, 1990 to 1997, there was an increase of 550,000 (2.2%) in the number of married-couple households with children, after a decrease in this group between 1980 and 1990—suggesting a possible resurgence of the conventional household structure. During the same period, however, households headed by women with minor children increased by nearly one-fifth. Women are the sole earners in these female-headed households and their earnings tend to be lower than those of males. As a result, these households are more likely to be poor as compared

TABLE 2.9 Percentage Distribution of Households by Type: 1970 to 2010 (Estimates for 1970 to 1997 Based on the Current Population Survey; Series 1 Projections for 2010)

Type of household	1970	1980	1990	1997	2010
Households (thousands)	63,401	80,776	93,347	101,018	114,825
Percentage	100.0	100.0	100.0	100.0	100.0
Family households	81.2	73.8	70.8	69.5	67.8
Married couples	70.5	60.8	56.1	53.1	51.7
Male householder[a]	1.9	2.1	3.1	3.8	4.1
Female householder[a]	8.7	10.8	11.7	12.7	12.1
Nonfamily households	18.8	26.2	29.3	30.5	32.2
Male householder	6.4	10.9	12.4	13.6	15.0
Female householder	12.4	15.3	16.8	16.9	17.2
One person[b]	17.1	22.7	24.6	25.1	26.8

[a] No spouse present. Other relatives, usually children, are present.
[b] Included in figures for nonfamily households.
Source: U.S. Bureau of the Census, *Current Population Reports*, P20-509, P25-1129, 1996, and unpublished data. See also U.S. Bureau of the Census, *Statistical Abstract of the United States, 1998*, Tables 69 and 70.

with both married-couple households, particularly those in which both parents are working, and male-headed households.

A larger proportion of elderly persons, even of the older aged, are now living alone (i.e., in their own households) than did so a quarter of a century ago. The share of persons 65 years and over living alone was less than one-quarter (23%) in 1970 and nearly one-third (31%) in 1997. The percentage living alone increases sharply with advancing age. In 1997 the share for those aged 65 to 74 was 24%; for those 75 and over it was 40%. Since most elderly persons (59% in 1997) are women, it is not surprising that a large majority (over three-quarters in 1997) of elderly persons living alone are women.

Socioeconomic Characteristics and Population Redistribution

Educational Attainment, Labor Force Participation,[8] and Income

Educational attainment is closely associated with several other social and economic variables so that progress in this area is of immense importance. Its effect on labor force participation, income, longevity, fertility levels, migration tendencies, household structure, and other variables can be documented. Gains in the educational attainment of the population in the past several decades have been rather impressive. The share of persons who have completed high school and the share who have completed college have risen sharply since 1970. Moreover, the gaps between the sexes and the races have narrowed for some categories of educational attainment. The percentage of persons 25 years old or more completing high school increased from 52 in 1970 to 82 in 1997, and the percentage of persons completing college increased from 11 to 24 (Table 2.10). During this period the gap between white and black high-school-completion ratios narrowed by nearly two-thirds. While Hispanics and

■ **TABLE 2.10   Percentage High School and College Graduates of the Population 25 Years Old and Over, According to Sex and Race/Hispanic Origin: 1970 to 1997 (as of April 1 for 1970, 1980, and 1990; Sample Data from the Census; as of March for 1998; Sample Data from Current Population Survey)**

Year	All races[a] Male	Female	White Male	Female	Black Male	Female	Asian and PI[b] Male	Female	Hispanic[c] Male	Female
Completed 4 years of high school or more										
1970	51.9	52.8	54.0	55.0	30.1	32.5	(NA)	(NA)	37.9	34.2
1980	67.3	65.8	69.6	68.1	50.8	51.5	(NA)	(NA)	44.7[d]	43.2[d]
1990	77.7	77.5	79.1	79.0	65.8	66.5	84.0	77.2	50.3	51.3
1997[e]	82.0	82.2	82.9	83.2	73.5	76.0	(NA)	(NA)	54.9	54.6
Completed 4 years of college or more										
1970	13.5	8.1	14.4	8.4	4.2	4.6	(NA)	(NA)	7.8	4.3
1980	20.1	12.8	21.3	13.3	8.4	8.3	(NA)	(NA)	9.4	6.0
1990	24.4	18.4	25.3	19.0	11.9	10.8	44.9	35.4	9.8	8.7
1997[e]	26.2	21.7	27.0	22.3	12.5	13.9	(NA)	(NA)	10.6	10.1

NA: Not available.

[a] Includes other races, not shown separately.

[b] PI represents Pacific Islanders.

[c] Persons of Hispanic origin may be of any race.

[d] Approximated.

[e] High school graduates and those with a BA degree or higher.

Source: U.S. Bureau of the Census, *U.S. Census of Population, 1970* and *1980*, Vol. 1; *Current Population Reports* P20-505; and unpublished data. See also U.S. Bureau of the Census, *Statistical Abstract of the United States, 1998*, Table 261.

blacks are still lagging greatly behind whites in both high school and college completion, Asians stand in front of the all other racial groups and Hispanics in their educational attainment.

Since 1970 the labor force has been shifting sharply toward a greater balance of the sexes, as the labor force participation of men declined, that of women increased, and the share of two-earner households, including married-couple households with children, increased. As Figure 2.1 shows, labor force participation for every age group among males declined between 1970 and 1997, especially for ages 45 and over, and labor force participation for every age group among females increased except for ages 65 years and over. The female increases under age 65 were considerable. While the labor force participation ratios for males are generally still well above those for females in 1997, much of the difference in labor force participation of the sexes recorded for 1970 has been erased. Of special note is the fact that the labor force participation of wives in married couples with children has increased sharply in the past several decades. Between 1970 and 1997, the labor force participation ratio of wives increased from 41% to 62%, and among those with children under 6 years of age the increase was even greater, from 30% to 64%.[9] The percentage of working couples will probably continue to rise.

Working married women and working women with minor children are facing the challenge of juggling the needs of their families and the requirements of their jobs. Moreover, with the growth of the aged population, families are

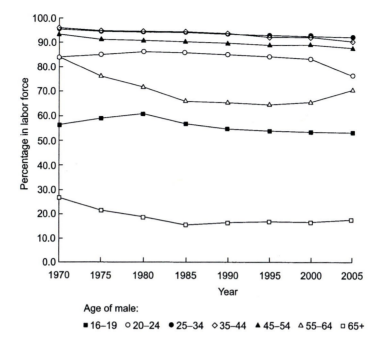

Age of male:

■ 16–19 ○ 20–24 ● 25–34 ◇ 35–44 ▲ 45–54 △ 55–64 □ 65+

Age of female:

■ 16–19 ○ 20–24 ● 25–34 ◇ 35–44 ▲ 45–54 △ 55–64 □ 65+

Figure 2.1 Trend of labor force participation of males and females, according to age: 1970 to 2006. Labor force participation is represented by the proportion of each specified group in the civilian labor force. Ratios are based on annual averages of monthly labor force figures and the annual average civilian noninstitutional population in each specified group. Based on the Current Population Survey. Data for 1990, 1995, and 1998 are not strictly comparable with data for earlier years. *Source*: U.S. Bureau of Labor Statistics, *Employment and Earnings*, monthly, January issues; *Monthly Labor Review*, November 1997; and unpublished data.

increasingly confronted with the need to provide care to their aged parents as well as their children, even as they devote major portions of their time to earning a living. With low fertility and increasing longevity, larger proportions of middle-aged parents have to care for aging and disabled parents without the benefit of siblings, while also trying to earn a living.

These changes in labor force participation have been associated with a decline in the median age of retirement of both men and women. It amounted to about 5 years between the early 1950s and the early 1990s, as the young elderly retired at a greater rate than the old elderly. The fall in retirement age slowed during the 1970s and may have come to a halt by the end of the 1990s. The decline in retirement age and the increase in life expectation since 1950 have contributed to an increase of over 5 years for men and over 6 years for women in the time spent in retirement since 1950.

Since 1970 the baby-boom cohorts have been moving through the working ages and, now at the turn of the century, at ages 35 to 53, are partly in the peak ages of labor force participation (i.e., ages 25 to 44) and partly beyond them. They are now also in the peak ages of earnings and expenditures.

Median household income in real terms (that is, adjusted for changes in the Consumer Price Index) has increased only modestly since 1970 (data not shown). Real gains were somewhat greater for blacks than for whites, but the figures for Hispanics hardly changed. Accordingly, the black-white income gap has narrowed a little in real dollars since 1970. The Current Population Survey showed a median household income for blacks of $25,050 and a median household income for whites of $38,972 in 1997, reflecting a relative deficit of 36% for black households (Table 2.11). In 1970 the black-white relative deficit was 39%. On the other hand, the Hispanic-white income gap has widened since 1970, from 28% to 32%. We see that median household incomes of whites, on the one hand, and blacks and Hispanics, on the other, remain far apart.

There are many demographic categories that show income disparity in addition to the racial categories. Table 2.11 presents data on variations in median household income in 1997, and the estimated change since 1989, for types of households, age of the householder, age of household members, and nativity of the householder. We observe, for example, that family households, particularly married-couple households with children under 18, have far higher incomes than nonfamily households. Further, we note that their median income improved during the 1990s, while that of nonfamily households retrogressed.

Income disparity among the nation's families has been steadily increasing since 1970. In 1996, the one-fifth of the families with the lowest income received only 4% of aggregate income, while the top fifth of the families received 47% of aggregate income.[10] In comparison, in 1970 the lowest and highest income quintiles were appreciably closer; the figures were 5% for the lowest group and 41% for the highest group. In interpreting these estimates, note that they do not take into account nonmoney income or variations in the size of family and that they are based on pretax income.[11]

Median household income varies greatly among the states. Figure 2.A.1

TABLE 2.11   Median Household Income for Selected
Characteristics of Households: 1997 (Households as of March 1998)

Characteristic of householder or household	Median household income	Percent change, 1989 to 1997[a]
All households	$37,005	−0.8
Race/Hispanic origin		
White	38,972	−0.7
Not Hispanic	40,577	+1.0
Black	25,050	*+6.2
Asian or Pacific Islander	45,249	−2.9
Hispanic origin[b]	26,628	−5.5
Type of household		
Family households	45,347	*+1.6
Married-couple households	51,681	*+3.5
With related children under 18	54,518	(NA)
Female householder[c]	23,040	+3.3
Male householder[c]	36,634	−6.3
Nonfamily households	21,705	*−2.3
Male householder	27,592	*−5.0
Female householder	17,613	−1.4
With related children under 18	19,752	(NA)
Age of household members		
With members 65 years and over	22,369	(NA)
With related children under 18	44,791	(NA)
Age of householder (years)		
15 to 24	22,583	*−6.0
25 to 34	38,174	−0.7
35 to 44	46,359	−4.5
45 to 54	51,875	*−3.5
55 to 64	41,356	*+3.5
65 to 74	25,292	(NA)
75 and over	17,079	(NA)
65 and over	20,761	+1.8
Nativity of householder		
Native	37,643	(NA)
Foreign-born	31,318	(NA)
Not a citizen	26,959	(NA)

NA: Not available.

* Statistically significant at the 90-percent confidence level.

[a] Percentage change in real (i.e., adjusted for change in consumer price index) household income.

[b] Persons of Hispanic origin may be of any race.

[c] No spouse present.

Source: U.S. Census Bureau, *Current Population Reports*, P60-200, Tables A and F. Current Population Survey, March 1998.

(see Appendix A) ranks the states according to their median household incomes in 1995–1997. In interpreting these estimates, note that they do not take into account cost-of-living differences among the states.

Interstate Migration; Metropolitan and Nonmetropolitan Growth

Internal migration is often a more important determinant of population change in state and local areas than natural increase. The two main types of internal migration in the United States have been the movements among the regions and states and those along the metropolitan-nonmetropolitan and urban-rural axes.

The strong westward movement of the population, which has been occurring since Europeans first settled in North America, has continued to the present. California, in particular, has been the destination of millions of migrants from all other parts of the country for much of U.S. history, although the direction of this internal movement has reversed itself in recent years. Prior to World War II there was also a movement out of the economically depressed South to the industrial centers of the Midwest and the Northeast regions. Since that war, and especially since the late 1960s, however, the direction of net migration has shifted from movement into the Northeast and Midwest states from the South to movement out of them to the South and West. This movement has been complemented by a generous flow of immigrants from abroad to all the regions. Data for 1996–1997 suggests the most recent pattern (Table 2.12). As a result of immigration, the South and West regions recorded large gains through net migration. In all regions except the South, potential losses through internal migration were offset by immigration. The South gained heavily through both types of movement.

TABLE 2.12   Migration between Regions: 1996–1997 (in Thousands, as of March, Based on the Current Population Survey)

Region	Northeast	Midwest	South	West
1996–1997				
Total in-migrants	481	661	1338	688
From Northeast	(X)	107	392	101
From Midwest	94	(X)	492	228
From South	256	333	(X)	358
From West	131	221	454	(X)
Total out-migrants	600	814	947	806
To Northeast	(X)	94	256	131
To Midwest	107	(X)	333	221
To South	392	492	(X)	454
To West	101	228	358	(X)
Net internal migration	−119	−154	391	−118
Movers from abroad	239	169	445	450
Net total migration				
1996–1997	+120	+15	+836	+332
1990–1991	−376	+193	+784	+784
1980–1981	−35	−226	+899	+675

X: Not applicable.

Source: U.S. Bureau of the Census, *Current Population Reports*, P20-510, 1998. See also U.S. Bureau of the Census, *Statistical Abstract of the United States, 1998*, Table 31.

An array of state data on estimated population changes between 1990 and 1997 indicates that all but two states and the District of Columbia registered population increases in this period, even though over one-third of them experienced an estimated net out-migration (Table 2.A.4). The considerable net out-migration from some states was more than offset by a large net immigration from abroad and natural increase. California, Illinois, Massachusetts, New Jersey, and New York had this experience.

Another prominent historical movement has been the trend toward urbanization and metropolitanization, and the decline in the nonmetropolitan and rural populations, including particularly the rural-farm population. The rapid metropolitanization of the population was the result of the migration of population out of many large central cities into the suburbs and the nearby nonmetropolitan areas. It was accompanied by population losses in many central cities and, in recent decades, by a modest resurgence of the nonmetropolitan population.

The reversal of the historical trend of nonmetroplitan population loss began in the 1970s. During that decade the population of nonmetropolitan areas increased at a greater rate than the population of metropolitan areas. Over 80% of the counties then defined as nonmetropolitan added 8.4 million people to their numbers, with a resulting gain of 16% (Johnson, 1999, p. 3).[12] This growth took place mainly because more people moved into these areas from metropolitan areas and fewer left them for metropolitan areas; the contribution of natural increase was smaller than net in-migration. Many of the nonmetropolitan areas that gained are far from the small towns and sparsely settled open spaces that the term "rural" often brings to mind. However, remote areas also grew.

During the 1980s, the rural rebound slowed; only 45% of rural counties gained population in this decade (Johnson, pp. 4–6). About 1.3 million persons were added to the rural population, representing a gain of merely 2.7%. There was a net out-migration from these areas, but natural increase more than made up the loss. During the 1990s, the rural rebound resumed. The population of more than 70% of the rural counties increased; 3.6 million persons were added, representing 7.1% of the rural population. Again, the gain resulted mainly from net migration rather than natural increase. Fewer rural residents moved to metropolitan areas, while more metropolitan residents moved to rural counties. This rebound took place in nearly every part of the country and was not limited to a particular region. The rural population gains since 1990 have been most common in retirement and recreational areas and least common in farming and mining areas (Johnson, p. 11). The rural rebound of the 1990s and the turnaround of the 1970s bear a great resemblance.

A growing phenomenon, one characterizing some rural counties for many decades and now occurring in numerous rural counties, is **natural decrease**, an excess of deaths over births. It is a result of the out-migration of persons in the prime childbearing ages and the increase in the share of elderly persons, who tend to "age in place." Between 1990 and 1998, nearly 650 rural counties experienced an excess of deaths over births (Johnson, p. 6). These counties are concentrated in the West North Central Division and the West South Central Division. (See Figure 5.1 for the definition of the divisions.)

Our central cities and metropolitan areas are now being reshaped by important trends. The share of population in the giant cities—those over 500,000—out of the total population in incorporated places is declining while the share of population in midsize cities—those 50,000 to 500,000—is increasing (Table 2.13). The small cities and towns under 10,000 are losing population share. In 1970, 20.0% of the population in incorporated places lived in places of this size, but by 1996 the share had fallen to 17.5%. The populations of many large central cities continue to decline even as the metropolitan areas in which they fall continue to grow (Tables 2.A.5 and 2.A.6). The population of almost all large central cities in the Northeast, Midwest, and upper South Atlantic declined between 1970 and 1990, and the declines have continued into the 1990s. St. Louis topped the list, with a loss of over two-fifths of its population in the 1970–1996 period. The percentage losses recorded for a dozen major cities between 1970 and 1996 were, in rank order, as follows:

City	Percentage	City	Percentage
St. Louis	43	Cincinnati	24
Detroit	34	Philadelphia	24
Cleveland	34	Chicago	19
Pittsburgh	33	Milwaukee	18
Washington	28	St. Paul	16
Baltimore	25	Boston	13

New York lost only 7% of its population in this period.

Central city residents have been departing for the suburbs in large numbers since the 1950s. For the most part, the suburbs have less expensive housing,

TABLE 2.13   Population and Number of Incorporated Places According to Population Size: 1970 to 1996

Population size	1996				Population Percentage of total		
	Places		Population				
	Number	Percentage of total	Number (mil.)	Percentage of total	1990	1980	1970
Total	19,335	100.0	162.6	100.0	100.0	100.0	100.0
1,000,000 or more	10	0.1	22.3	13.7	13.0	12.5	14.2
500,000 to 999,999	14	0.1	8.8	5.4	6.6	7.8	9.8
250,000 to 499,999	42	0.2	15.3	9.4	9.3	8.4	7.9
100,000 to 249,999	153	0.8	22.2	13.7	12.5	11.8	10.5
50,000 to 99,999	347	1.8	23.4	14.4	13.9	12.3	12.2
25,000 to 49,999	597	3.1	20.7	12.7	13.0	13.1	11.9
10,000 to 24,999	1366	7.1	21.4	13.2	13.3	14.1	13.3
Under 10,000	16,806	86.9	28.5	17.5	18.4	20.0	20.0

Source: U.S. Bureau of the Census, *Census of Population: 1970* and *1980*, Vol. 1; *1990 Census of Population and Housing, Population and Housing Unit Counts* (CPH-2-1); computer diskette PE-59; and unpublished data. See also *Statistical Abstract of the United States, 1998*, Table 47.

better schools, increased job opportunities, less crime, and more efficient public services. Suburban-to-suburban economic exchanges are increasing as city-to-suburban economic exchanges decline. Large central cities at first lost whites to the suburbs in the 1950s but, by the 1970s, and especially in the 1980s, middle-class blacks were joining the flow. Middle-class blacks continue to depart for the suburbs as the black middle class grows rapidly.

In line with the general trend, some small and moderate size cities, such as Henderson, Nevada, Palmdale, California, Chandler, Arizona, Las Vegas, Nevada, Pembroke Pines, Florida, and Plano, Texas, have been growing with extreme rapidity. In fact, these six cities showed the highest growth rates between 1990 and 1996 among cities with 100,000 inhabitants or more in 1996, according to Census Bureau Estimates.

Central-city-bound immigration is made up largely of persons of African, Asian, and Latin origin, and the percentage of foreign-born persons in these cities is growing. In some large cities, the share of foreign born is extremely high, for example, one-third of New York and one-fifth of Boston residents are foreign born. Racial/ethnic groups that figure heavily among the new immigrants in central cities include Mexicans, Salvadoreans, Chinese, Jamaicans, Dominicans, Colombians, Koreans, and Vietnamese. Most of these new immigrants work in low-skilled occupations, such as service workers in restaurants and hotels, taxi drivers, and garment workers. Many of them entered illegally, or entered legally and stayed on illegally. They are relatively uneducated, have few work skills, tend to be poor, and are likely to be suffering from various health conditions. As a result, they require more government services than the earlier immigrants and native population in cities or the suburban population.

This immigration has been occurring at a time when the economic base for providing the additional services required, particularly from the manufacturing industry and the presence of more affluent households, is eroding. As the vast numbers of new immigrants moved into large central cities, the immigrants who arrived in previous decades and the natives have been leaving for the suburbs in droves. These new suburban residents show a greater tendency than in the past to work in the suburbs rather than in the city. Because the central cities cannot extend their boundaries, they face a difficult and deteriorating situation, characterized by continued population loss, increased concentration of poor racial/ethnic minorities, and a widening income gap in comparison with the suburbs.

Numerous, large middle-class communities in the suburbs are now predominantly black. In some communities, blacks have the same or higher average incomes than whites. In the borough of Queens in New York City, for example, the median incomes of black and white households were essentially the same in 1990. On the other hand, the income disparity within cities, reflecting often black /Hispanic versus non-Hispanic-white differences, can be extreme. For example, the top quintile in the borough of Manhattan in New York City received 32 times as much income as the lowest quintile in 1990.[13] The considerable disparity in income between the most and least affluent segments of the cities has been widening.

INTERRELATIONS WITH VARIOUS SOCIAL AND ECONOMIC PROGRAMS

General Note

Population trends exert pressures on society and the economy to change in many ways, even though the influences go in both directions. That is, population is not purely an **exogenous** (i.e., independent) variable and may be an **endogenous** (i.e., dependent) one. Population changes influence the provision of health, education, recreational, welfare, and protective services, and hence, programs of public finance and the content of government budgets. They affect housing demand and supply. They influence the work of financial institutions, the communications industry, travel and recreation agencies, the transportation industry, and the investment business. They affect the programs of religious, charitable, and fraternal organizations. In sum, demographic influences are pervasive in every facet of social, economic, and political life. These varied demographic/programmatic connections are illustrated in this and several later chapters. This chapter briefly examines the role of population in education, housing, local transit, recreation, and tax administration.

Education

For the first area, education, the focus is mainly on the relation between the trend of the birthrate and the changing volume and character of immigration, on the one hand, and school enrollments and the requirements for teachers and school facilities, on the other.

The 5-year average annual birthrate (births per 1000 population) rose from a low point in the mid-1930s to 19.1 in the late 1930s and then to 19.9 during the early 1940s. The average annual number rose from 2.5 million in 1935–1939 to 2.7 million in 1940–1944. With the end of World War II and the return home of the armed forces, the number of births jumped precipitously, by 33% to 3.8 million in the 2 years from 1945 to 1947. This gain was regarded widely by demographers as a short-term event, resulting from the war-time absence of millions of men and the postwar union and reunion of millions of couples. However, the baby boom persisted; the annual number of births rose above 4 million by 1955 and remained there until 1964. The baby boom was now popularly defined as the 76 million babies born from 1946 through 1964. The subsequent decline was gradual compared to the rise. A low of 3.1 million births was reached in 1973–1976 as the total fertility rate (i.e., average number of children born to a woman in her lifetime) fell to replacement level (2.11). In spite of the low fertility rate, the number of births increased again as women born during the baby-boom period reached childbearing age. It rose gradually to 4 million again in 1989. The fluctuations in the birthrate described were reflected in the record for all parts of the country and all major demographic groups.

School systems across the country felt the impact of the postwar baby boom by the early part of the 1950s. It began with kindergarten about 1952 and moved predictably to elementary school about 1953, middle school about

1959, high school about 1962, and college about 1965. For over a decade, each high-school graduating class was "replaced" by a much larger group of first-grade pupils, beginning with the graduating class of 1954 (i.e., the survivors of the diminutive birth cohort of 1936). This super-replacement of each older birth cohort by the younger one continued until the 1947 birth cohort graduated from high school in 1965. Enrollment in grades K through 8 continued to grow until 1970, however, when the last of the baby-boom cohorts entered kindergarten. High-school enrollment reached a peak a few years later in 1975.

As the baby-boom cohorts arrived at school, local school systems had to absorb a giant wave of students at each successive grade, recruit new teachers, and find additional classroom space. They were not prepared for this onslaught since they, too, held the view that the rapid rise in births in the late 1940s was a temporary phenomenon. There was insufficient time to build new schools and to recruit new teachers, and there was concern about the disposition of the additional schools and teachers once the "short-term" need for them had passed. Compounding the problem for the local school systems was the difficulty of assessing the magnitude and character of local variations in migration, which could rapidly and unexpectedly change.

The result was enormous overcrowding, which new construction could not fully alleviate. The number of elementary schools reached an early peak in 1955 and then gradually declined through the next several decades. Many teachers had more than 40 students in a classroom, not simply because there were not enough classrooms but also because there were not enough teachers. The numbers of teachers fell because the cohorts born in the 1930s, which would provide the new teachers in the 1950s, were very small. Teachers' colleges could not produce enough new teachers to meet the postwar need. Moreover, many potential teachers preferred to accept other positions because the remuneration was better and the work conditions were superior. The national shortage rose to 72,000 by the early 1950s, according to Jones (1980, p. 58).[14] Underqualified teachers, makeshift classrooms in churches and vacant stores, and the sharing of books and desks were some of the desperate measures to which school systems resorted.

As the baby-boom avalanche rolled to a halt in the late 1960s and the 1970s, local school systems increasingly had to deal with the opposite situation. Elementary school enrollment plummeted over the decade of the 1970s. Community leaders were now debating which schools to close and which districts to consolidate. Thousands of schools, many of which were constructed when the first of the baby-boom cohorts came along, were closed and converted into day-care centers, "senior-citizen" centers, and other community facilities.

As mentioned, high-school enrollments responded after 1960 to the fluctuations in births associated with the baby boom. High-school enrollments expanded until the late 1970s. Between the late 1970s and 1990, enrollments fell by about 20%. Since then, high-school enrollments have risen and are expected to continue rising for some years into the new century.

College Enrollment

Many of the returning World War II veterans were college-age youth who immediately sought to enroll in a college of their choice. The community-college system was created to accommodate the hordes of returning veterans seeking a college education. These college-age youth often did not return to the rural and small-town areas from which they originally came, but rather moved to metropolitan areas or university towns.

College enrollments exploded after the war for a number of reasons. There was, first, the usual crop of college-bound students and the pent-up demand of college-age youth who had postponed their college education. Numbers were vastly augmented, however, by the addition of large numbers of veterans supported through college by the GI Bill. This is reflected in rising enrollment ratios both among those 18 to 21 years of age, the main college ages, and also among those 22 to 34 years old and older. After 1964, the baby-boom children were also arriving. College enrollments grew from about 3 million in 1960 to 9 million in 1970 and 12 million in 1980. Further gains came more slowly during the 1980s but enrollments rose to somewhat more than 14 million during the early 1990s.

Some Consequences for Educational Planning

We have seen that the fluctuations in the number of births since the 1940s have played out in waves of students, of larger or smaller amplitude, at each grade level. Larger waves of births and students were followed by smaller waves, which were then followed by the "echo" of the larger waves, and so forth. These waves of school enrollments combine with one another in the various grade groups. The fluctuations present continuing difficulties for public educational systems in planning the expansion and contraction of facilities and personnel. The efficacy of long-term planning of local educational systems depends on the planner's ability to predict fertility or to predict it within a reasonable range of uncertainty. National enrollments in most grades have considerable short-term predictability, but the situation grows increasingly problematic as the projection period extends beyond 5 years and as the geographic area of administrative concern grows smaller. Since educational planning must be done at the local level, there is the need to develop fertility projections for local areas with as limited a range of uncertainty as possible.

The fluctuations in enrollments at the local level resulting from the earlier fluctuations in the number of births are intensified or damped by the movement of families into and out of the area. Projections of school enrollment must take account of such local movements also. Much is known regarding patterns of migration and the factors influencing it to guide the analysis. For example, families with elementary-school-age children have relatively low migration rates, but rates are higher for families with preschool-age children and high-school-age children, and "skyrocket" for college-age youth.

Changes in the age structure and the socioeconomic composition of the population of an area tends to create a demand for additional or alternate services and improvements in infrastructure, including renovation of old schools and construction of new schools. The cost of these services and improvements in facilities could be difficult to meet under changing demographic conditions.

Funding education, in particular, is especially difficult in areas where the number of young residents is declining and the number of old residents is increasing. One of the reasons for the difficulty is that long-time residents tend to regard additions and improvements to the educational program and the associated facilities as unnecessary tax burdens, since they have no children in school. Retirees, an important new component of the metropolitan-to-rural migratory stream, may well resist efforts to increase appropriations for educational uses for the same reason.

The difficulty of funding the costs for new schools and educational programs, as well as other services and facilities, is not confined to nonmetropolitan areas. Rapidly growing suburban counties within metropolitan areas have to cope with the same problem. Efforts to do so have included raising fees paid by home builders to offset the extra costs of adding new housing units or a new housing development or, more drastically, legislating limits to growth. Not surprisingly, both measures are controversial. Similarly, old central cities, experiencing the continuing loss of their more affluent residents—typically middle-class families with children seeking better schools—suffer from an erosion of their tax base and find it more difficult to support and improve their schools. In turn, a shrinking tax base resulting from out-migration makes it difficult to provide the services needed to hold the middle class in the city.

The massive influx of immigrants since the 1960s has been posing a special challenge to the public schools. Immigration has always posed a great challenge to the U.S. educational system because most of the immigrants come with a different culture and language. The relation of the new immigration to our schools is much more problematical. The difference is due to the shift in their countries of origin and their culture, their relation with their native countries, the density of their settlement here, their age distribution, their knowledge of English, and the programs designed for their linguistic assimilation.

As noted earlier, the origins of the new immigration have shifted largely from countries in Europe to countries in Latin America, Asia, and Africa. Unlike the great waves of immigration around the turn of the 20th century, many of the new immigrants maintain a continuing "personal" relation with their native countries (e.g., Mexico, El Salvador) and seek to perpetuate their native language as their primary language not only at home but in their public life. The 1990 census found that nearly 14% of persons aged 5 years or more spoke a language other than English at home. Spanish was by far the most common other language. Unlike the *old* immigration, many of the new immigrants are school-age children who speak their native language at home. The large size of their settlement areas has created mini-countries-of-origin. These facts have made it more difficult to educate the children in the regular classes. For this and other reasons, bilingual education programs supported by the federal government have been introduced. They tend to complicate the whole educational enterprise and greatly increase the costs of public education. In some areas, bilingual education is offered in several languages and bilingual teachers knowledgeable in these languages have to be retained.

The problem of educating immigrants is most severe in the states bordering Mexico and in certain East-coast states, where the new immigrants are concentrated. The states with the heaviest concentrations (i.e., over 20%) of persons speaking a language other than English at home are Arizona, California, New Mexico, Texas, and New York. In California particularly, there are many immigrants of high-school age who cannot be integrated directly into existing classes and who are particular candidates for bilingual education programs.[15]

Postwar trends in family structure, the labor force, and income distribution have greatly complicated the tasks confronted by the educational system. These changes encompass many of the major demographic and socioeconomic changes characterizing the post–World War II years. They include the increase in the proportions of female-headed family households, teenage parents, non-marital births, two-earner households, and young children who will have spent several years in a single-parent household. They include the high and increasing share of children living in poverty and the widening income disparity between the poorest and richest segments of our population. Female-headed family households—products often of divorce, teenage parenthood, and nonmarital parenthood—are commonly poorer than other family households. By all these measures, blacks and Hispanics fare less favorably than non-Hispanic whites.

When there is a single parent, or both parents have to work, or the parents are very young, there is less time for parenting and educational stimulation of the children, and more children enter school lacking fundamental childhood knowledge and skills and desirable personality traits. Teenage mothers are often forced to curtail their education, while being poorly prepared to rear their children, who then enter school under severely disadvantaged conditions. The children of such households usually require more individual attention from teachers, particularly in the early school years, and schools are forced to add new special faculty and perform some of the functions of the family. Schools have become more heavily engaged in maintaining discipline and psychological counselling while being pressed to maintain academic standards. With these added burdens in the classroom, the favorable labor market, and the opportunity for higher remuneration in other fields, many capable teachers are choosing to leave the profession and fewer students are choosing to prepare for careers in public education. As a consequence, there is dearth of qualified teachers, which further exacerbates the problem of providing a good public education.

Housing

The demand for new housing responds in the short term to immediate economic conditions such as inflation, unemployment ratios, per capita income, and mortgage interest rates, but in the longer term it responds also to underlying demographic forces and trends. Clearly a large increase in population, like an increase in real per capita income, tends to support an increase in the demand for and supply of housing. Substantial in-migration to a local area resulting in large local population growth becomes a strong impetus for an increase in the demand for and supply of housing units in the area. The supply of housing units in an area moves more or less in step with the growth in the number of households in the area, being sensitive to the changes in the number of residents and potential residents. Not only must housing units be built to accommodate the growing demand of households for living space, but the households and housing units must be matched in terms of a variety of characteristics of the household, such as type of household, number of members, and household income, on one side, and characteristics of the housing unit, such as type of stucture, cost, and amenities, on the other. Moreover, needs for housing space are specific with respect to geographic location. In sum, the housing industry must try to meet current and prospective requirements of households for housing units of many specific types in the areas needed if the supply of and demand for living space are to be in reasonable balance.[16]

The changes in household size and type and in living arrangements that were identified in the first section of this chapter should be of considerable interest to the housing industry in planning the types of housing units and structures that should be in demand. The increase in the share of persons living alone and of female-headed family households and the decreasing size of households suggest the need for modest-size apartments, condominiums, and small townhouses. At the same time, the many affluent two-earner families, with children (including those planned), in the prosperous economic environment of the late 1990s, will be looking for more spacious and expensive units (i.e., large detached houses with many rooms). Since most aged persons live in conventional housing units but their homes are not designed to fill their special physical needs, homebuilders need to plan for the redesign of homes to give the aged more housing options and to allow them to function better at home. The sharp increase in aged persons, many of whom have serious functional limitations but wish to live independently, supports such an innovation in homebuilders' designs.

As the reader may recall, the rate of household formation was high in the postwar period until the 1980s, when it fell markedly. Among the reasons for the slowdown were poor economic opportunities for many young adults, the continuing postponement of marriage, and economic conditions and policies that adversely affected the construction and purchase of housing.[17] The decline in homeownership ratios during the 1980s and early 1990s occurred mainly among households with householders under age 45 (Table 2.14). Homeownership ratios turned up again by the mid-1990s, as mortgage interest rates began to fall from prohibitive levels.[18] By the late 1990s, there was a huge spurt in homebuying. Increases in homeownership occurred at every age and homeownership ratios reached all-time highs.

An important demographic factor affecting the housing market and contributing to the huge wave of homebuying experienced in the late 1990s is the concentration of the population in the narrow segment of ages representing the baby-boom cohorts. At the beginning of the year 2000, these cohorts were 35 to 53 years of age—ages of high and increasing homeownership. The general economic prosperity of the mid- and late-1990s and the large proportion of two-earner families generating large family incomes also contributed to the surge in homebuying. In particular, the increasing share of wives and mothers who have joined the labor force has added greatly to the purchasing power of families. This is especially true of younger households, since each new cohort coming along has higher labor force participation ratios and higher propor-

TABLE 2.14 Homeownership Ratios According to Age of Householder: 1985 to 1998 (in Percentages; Figures Represent the Ratios of Owner Households to the Total Number of Households in Each Age Group of Householder)

Age of householder (years)	1985	1990	1995	1998
All ages	63.9	63.9	64.7	66.3
Less than 25	17.2	15.7	15.9	18.2
25–29	37.7	35.2	34.4	36.2
30–34	54.0	51.8	53.1	53.6
35–44	68.1	66.3	65.2	66.9
45–54	75.9	75.2	75.2	75.7
55–64	79.5	79.3	79.5	80.9
65–69	79.5	80.0	81.0	81.9
70–74	76.8	78.4	80.9	82.2
75 and over	69.8	72.3	74.6	76.2

Source: U.S. Bureau of the Census, Current Population Survey/Housing Vacancy Survey. See U.S. Bureau of the Census, *Statistical Abstract of the United States, 1999*, Table 1215.

tions of dual earners. As a result, they are in a position to afford homeownership and to purchase homes that suit their needs now or as anticipated.

Whether or not a residence is owned or rented has considerable economic and social implications. For many people, home equity is their largest financial asset. They are motivated to protect this asset not only by maintaining or improving the condition of their property but also by supporting community institutions. They are likely to build stronger social ties with their community and to move less often. The mobility rate is much lower for persons living in owner-occupied housing units than for persons living in renter-occuped units.

As expected, there is a positive association between homeownership and the age of the householder. Among householders 25 to 29 years old in 1998, only 36% owned their primary residence (Table 2.14). Of those 35 to 44 years old, 67% were owners. The percentage rose with increasing age up to a peak of 82% at ages 70 to 74 years. There is a fall-off to 76% at ages 75 years and over. While the decline at these older ages would tend to diminish the strength of the association with age, it may reflect a cohort effect—that is, the movement into these ages of new cohorts arriving with lower homeownership ratios. Since the drop occurs in the data for each calendar year, however, most likely it reflects movement into relatives' homes or group quarters on the occasion of late-life disability, a factor that applies particularly at the very oldest ages.[19]

There is also, as expected, a strong positive association between homeownership and household income, a stronger one than that between homeownership and age. In this case, the percentage of homeownership increases steadily with increasing household income. For example, in 1996 only 40% of households whose income was less than $10,000 owned their primary residence while 87% of households whose income was $75,000 or more owned their primary residence.[20] Given the positive association between the age of the householder and household income, the two associations just described reflect each other to some extent.

Similarly, there is an association between homeownership and race/ethnicity. It reflects to a degree the two associations involving the age of the householder and household income, especially the latter. In 1995, 69% of white householders owned their homes, while only 44% of black householders and 42% of Hispanic householders did so.[21] Given the higher median age of the adult (20 years and over) white population than of the black and Hispanic populations, white householders tend to be older, on average, than black or Hispanic householders. In 1995, the median age of the adult white population was 44 years, that of blacks 40 years, and that of Hispanics 37 years.[22] Differences between the median household incomes of the race groups were noted earlier. It is likely that, if the effects of age of householder and household income on homeownership were eliminated, the association between homeownership and ethnicity would be greatly reduced.

There is a considerable variation in home ownership ratios among the 50 states and it is a challenging question to determine the basis for this variation. The national figure was 66% in 1997. The highest figures were about 9 percentage points greater, and the lowest figures ranged from 7 to 16 percentage points lower (table not shown).[23] The four states with the highest ratios had figures of about 75% (Kentucky, Maine, Minnesota, and West Virginia), and the four states with the lowest ratios had figures ranging from 50 to 59% (Hawaii, New York, California, and Rhode Island). The state variation in the age distribution, median household income, or the cost of housing do not appear to have an association with the state variation in homeownership.[24] Perhaps the cost of housing in relation to household income may be a useful explanatory variable for interpreting it. For interpreting variation in homeownership among cities, race/ethnic composition is likely to be a relevant factor.

Local Transit and Commuting

Local governments and urban planners, especially in large cities and metropolitan areas, have to deal continuously with problems associated with local transit and commuting. They need to monitor traffic patterns and review their system of traffic control on a ongoing basis so as to effect a free flow of traffic and minimize congestion. This analysis may affect the placement of stop signs, stop lights, and traffic officers, the timing of stop lights, the widening of roads, and the building of overpasses. Proposals for managing local traffic can involve several components, which may be called vehicle control, workforce practices, space control, workplace location, and residence location. The first of these deals with the forms of transit, the second with the conditions of work, the third with the supply and use of road space, and the fourth and fifth with the location of workplaces and residences, respectively. The discussion here is limited mainly to the first and second of these, namely, the forms of transit and conditions of work.

The movement of the population outward from central cities has meant a large expansion of the land area of metropolitan centers, often increasing the distance between home, on the one hand, and place of work, stores, places of entertainment, and the residences of friends and relatives, on the other. Since public transportation is much less available or convenient in the suburbs than in the cities, there has been a relative decline in the use of public transit for the journey to work and other places of interest and an increase in the use of private vehicles for these purposes. These private vehicles are overwhelmingly automobiles.

Much of this shift away from public transportation took place in the 1970s and there has been some easing up since then:

| | Vehicle used for commuting | | | |
	1969	1977	1983	1990
All households	100.0	100.0	100.0	100.0
Automobile	82.7	80.5	77.6	91.4
Truck	8.1	12.5	14.8	(NA)[a]
Public transit	8.4	4.7	5.8	5.5
Other	0.8	2.3	1.8	3.1

[a] Not available. It appears that all, or almost all, "truck" responses were reclassified in the 1990 data to the automobile category.

Source: U.S. Federal Highway Administration, *National Personal Transportation Survey, Survey of Travel Trends, 1969, 1977, 1983,* and *1990.* See also U.S. Bureau of the Census, *Statistical Abstract of the United States, 1998,* Table 1039.

Viewed alternatively, the percentage of automobiles and trucks used for commuting remained fairly steady within a narrow range of 91 to 93% of all journey-to-work trip-modes during the 1969–1990 period. The use of trucks (including sport utility vehicles but excluding pickups and other light trucks) rose greatly and the use of automobiles fell by about the same amount during the period. Since the number of households increased sharply during this period, from 62.5 million to 93.3 million (or by 49%), it is apparent that the number of household vehicles used in commuting rose sharply as well.

The total number of vehicles owned by households, including those used in commuting, climbed steeply between 1969 and 1990.[25] The number rose from 72.5 million to 165 million, reflecting a 128% increase. Since there was a much smaller increase in the number of households during this period, the average number of vehicles per household jumped sharply—from 1.2 to 1.8. There was a large drop (33%) during the same period in the number of households with no vehicle. In 1990, only 9% of the 93.3 million households had no vehicle, as compared with 21% in 1969. The number with one vehicle remained virtually unchanged at about 30 1/2 million, despite a 109% increase in the number of one-person households. Thus, a large rise in the number and percentage of households with two or more vehicles accounts for the increase in the average number of vehicles per household. The number with two vehicles rose 117% while the number with three or more climbed a steep 535%. As a result, the number of vehicle trips made by households and the number of vehicle miles traveled by households nearly doubled in the 1969–1990 period.

Most workers drive to work alone, and average vehicle occupancy for the trip to work has been declining in spite of strong official efforts to encourage carpooling. According to the 1980 census, 64% of workers drove to work alone and 20% went to work in carpools (Robey, 1985, p. 92).[26] The 1990 census showed that the share of commuters driving alone had increased to 73% and the share of commuters carpooling had dropped to little more than 13%. Between 1977 and 1990, average vehicle occupancy for home-to-work trips declined by 15%, from 1.3 persons per vehicle to a mere 1.1 persons per vehicle.[27]

Of particular interest in local transit analysis is the origin-destination patterns of commuters. Do suburban commuters mainly travel to the city or stay in the suburbs? Do central-city commuters mainly stay in the central city? Jobs as well as people have increasingly relocated to the suburbs. As a result, the typical commuter now both lives and works in the suburbs and commuting between suburbs is increasingly displacing travel between suburb and city.[28]

Kasarda answered the origin-destination question by examining 1990 census data on suburb-to-city and suburb-to-suburb one-way trips from home to work in 10 large metropolitan areas.[29] In each of these areas, the number of intrasuburban trips was considerably greater than the number going from the suburbs to the city. The suburb-to-suburb commuters typically outnumbered the suburb-to-central city commuters by a margin of at least 3-to-1. Moreover, the time was much shorter for the intrasuburban commuters. Suburb-to-suburb work trips were nearly 50% shorter on average than suburb-to-central city work trips. For example, the mean one-way commuting time of suburban residents who work in New York City was 51 minutes in 1990 compared with 19 minutes for suburban residents who commute to jobs in the New York City suburbs. In the Chicago area, the comparable times were 41 minutes and 22 minutes. Suburbanization helps explain why there was little change in the U.S. average travel time from 1980 to 1990 (21.7 minutes versus 22.4 minutes). The shorter distance of suburban commuting offset the increasing congestion of city commuting.

Geographically, commuting time and distance varied inversely with the size of the area. The longest travel time occurred in the states of the Northeast and the shortest in the states of the West and the West North Central Divison (data not shown). According to the 1990 Census of Population and Housing, the range extended from 28.6 minutes for New York to 13.0 minutes for North Dakota.[30] These data also indicate that the more densely settled parts of the country experienced larger commuting distances than the less densely settled areas.

Commuting time and time lost in commuting have been growing greater because of traffic congestion. The annual numbers of hours of delay per eligible driver in the United States has increased from 16 in 1982 to 34 in 1990 and 45 in 1997. The comparable figures for particular congested areas are much greater. For example, for Washington, D.C., which has the second worst congestion in the country after Los Angeles, they are 30 hours (1982), 58 hours (1990), and 76 hours (1997).[31]

Since congestion is already severe in many areas and these trends are likely to continue, finding better ways to cope with the problem has been receiving considerable attention.[32] The main alternatives proposed are building more roads and expanding mass transit. The proponents of mass transit argue that more roads simply induce more traffic whereas expanded and more flexible mass transit would reduce the share of commuters using their own vehicles. Those who disagree contend that it is infeasible to expand mass transit enough, especially in the growing suburbs, to justify the large capital and operating costs of the expansion. Moreover, they doubt that the convenience and flexibility provided by private vehicles can be matched by mass transit. The prospects for settling this long-running debate in the near future seem dim.

Some amelioration of the situation has been achieved through the adoption of flexible work schedules and through advances in information technology and telecommuncations. Flexible work schedules have lengthened the morning and evening rush hours, and presumably the staggered traffic is not as congested as it would have been without flexible work schedules. To what extent "flextime" has been implemented is not clear; many employers do not offer this option to their employees.

Telecommuting, involving work at home through computer use and home-office setups, is another development that may be contributing to traffic "decongestion." It has grown rapidly in recent years. The International Telework Association and Council said that 4 million people "telecommuted" in the United States in 1990 and that nearly 20 million were telecommuting in 1999. In the Washington, D.C., metropolitan area, 7% of the area's workforce of about 2 million people telecommuted either part time or full time in 1996.[33] Only 2 years later the figure was 12%. A survey conducted by researchers at Rutgers University and the University of Connecticut in January 2000 found that, nationally, only 16% of employers offer this option and only 9% of the workers are actually working this way.[34] Considering the recency of this practice, these are impressive numbers. Telecommuting has the potential to mitigate road congestion substantially.

The reader may be wondering about the relationship between commuting and applied demography. As set forth in the next chapter, the 2000 population census, like the 1990 population census, includes several questions relating to commuting: method of travel to work, carpooling, time of departure for work, and travel time required for commuting. The demographic analyst may be called on to compile and interpret the data on commuting in the census and in other sources in addition to those on population and households. The study of alternative patterns of labor force participation, including flexible work schedules and telecommuting, as well as trends and issues in conventional commuting, are interests of economic and geographic demographers. Many of the measures used in the analysis of commuting parallel measures employed in conventional demography. Finally, to manage the metropolitan traffic problem, current population estimates and projections for commuting regions and small geographic segments within them are required The preparation of such figures is a central concern of applied demographers.

Federal Tax Collection

The wide-ranging population changes in the second half of the 20th century have been responsible for a great increase in the burden on tax collection agencies, from the town tax office and the state office of tax administration to the

Internal Revenue Service.[35] Every change in a jurisdiction's population, including its size, demographic characteristics, and socioeconomic composition, has an impact on the work of the tax collection agency of the jurisdiction. This impact goes far beyond the increase in work resulting from the growth in the number of families and individuals filing tax returns. The changes in age structure, type of family, living arrangements, migration history, disability status, income level, sources of income, and labor force participation also have an impact on the work of tax collection agencies.

The work of the Internal Revenue Service (IRS) is affected by such a wide range of demographic conditions that it is an especially informative example of how demographic conditions can influence the administration of a public program. The movement of the baby-boom cohorts through the life cycle; the changing earnings, spending, and savings patterns associated with it; the increase in the share of elderly persons in various stages of retirement; the tremendous increase in the number and proportion of women in the labor force; the changes in the styles and patterns of work; and the rise in incomes and the diversification of their sources—all these changes have added to the variety and complexity of the tax returns and the job of processing them.

The proliferation of more varied and complex forms of the family has been particularly important in this regard. Recall that families are smaller than in earlier decades, that there is more divorce and remarriage, and that there is a greater proportion of childless couples, one-parent families, blended families, individuals living alone, and couples cohabiting. The emergence of the two-earner family as the norm; the great increase in families and individuals receiving income from alternative sources, reporting home businesses, or contributing wages to retirement accounts; and the increase in "retired" persons who continue to work part-time, often as self-employed independent contractors, and who also receive retirement income—all these changes have led to a great increase in the number of tax filers who report multiple sources of income, itemize deductions, or file supplementary forms.

With the new family structures, many filers are paying or receiving alimony while claiming exemptions for children by former marriages. The increase in the divorce rate, remarriages, and blended families has complicated the matter of identifying the taxpayer who has a proper claim on a particular child as an exemption on a tax return. This situation is leading some to claim certain children as exemptions incorrectly, even falsely.

Rising family income has increased the number of filers at the lower end of the income distribution and the number of filers with very high incomes. High-income filers add to the work and costs of the IRS because their sources of income are more varied and complex, they itemize their deductions, file more supporting forms, and hence, tend to make more errors. Both the low-income filers and the high-income filers are more likely to receive "unearned" income, not covered by employers' tax-withholding forms, and hence to underreport their incomes. Now that more than half of the American population has invested money in the stock market, leading to the receipt of income from capital gains, the numbers of filers required to complete the complicated supplementary form for reporting this income has become sizable.

The large immigration in the past several decades of many illiterate and other English-incompetent workers who may be required to file tax returns also adds to the burden and complexity of the work of the IRS and other tax agencies. Forms are more likely to be illegible and improperly completed. The IRS and state tax departments have had to take on staff members competent in various foreign languages to assist these immigrants in completing their returns.

The continuing redistribution of the resident population imposes on the IRS the task of establishing new offices in various parts of the country as it follows the population to the South and West. At the state level, the internal migration of workers creates an additional burden for tax auditors—and filers. There are special rules for reporting income earned as nonresidents in another state and this income usually has to be reported on a special form.

Because of the changes in the labor force and in the economy, and a limited budget, the IRS also has continuing problems in recruiting a sufficient number of competent accountants and programmers. Changes such as the aging of the baby-boom workers, early retirements of senior personnel, reduced cohorts entering the labor force, and the tight labor market are occurring even as the IRS has to deal with an increasing and more complex workload.

All these demographically induced changes in tax reporting practices have immensely complicated the government review of tax returns. Recognizing these demographic complexities, the IRS may be induced to hire some demographers as well as more accountants and computer programmers! More important, because of the demographic changes that have affected the individual household and the tendency of the tax code to try to fit "every" variation in the demographic and socioeconomic characteristics of respondents, the effort to prepare an accurate federal tax return has become extremely burdensome, if not impossible, for a substantial share of American households. This experience explains the support for the many proposals for a flat tax rate, with possibly three levels to make the tax burden progressive.

Demography of Almost Anything

The preceding illustrations of the links between demographic trends and prospects, on the one hand, and social programs and institutions, on the other, suggest the possible application of the demographic approach to understanding the nature of any defined population group or activity in our society. From this broad viewpoint one can reasonably study the demography of "almost anything." The "anything" can be a demographic group, characteristic, or event, or it can be a nondemographic group or event whose demographic characteristics are of interest. This general guideline leads to the possibility of a demography of our major institutions—political, juridical, economic, educational, familial, religious, health, and recreational. Some illustrative areas of application of demographic analysis within these categories are as follows:

- *Political and juridical demography.* Voting, representation and redistricting, jury selection, criminal justice, prison population

- *Economic demography.* Labor force, retirement, gender and race inequality in the workplace; income inequality, occupational groups, housing characteristics
- *Demography of education.* Educational attainment, enrollment studies, school redistricting
- *Demography of the family.* Family trends, family cycle, living arrangements, nursing-home population
- *Demography of religion.* Variations by socioeconomic status, membership analysis, processes of growth, intermarriage
- *Health demography.* Health providers, categories of patients, socioeconomic variations in health, disabled population
- *Demography of recreation.* Use of discretionary time, participation in leisure activities and the arts, gambling, pet ownership

Such a list suggests a myriad of possibililities of groups for demographic study. Here are some, in no particular order: people who buy used luxury cars, people who smoke, sex workers, persons who converted to Judaism, Olympic medal winners, ballet-season subscribers, ex-white-collar convicts, gambling addicts, people who had open-heart surgery, last-year's new home buyers, overseas tourists of the previous year, people who eat most meals outside their home, sports-team owners, operating-room nurses, adults with Type 1 diabetes, and so on. The commercial magazine *American Demographics* has exploited this idea intensively and frequently carries articles about the demography of such specialized groups. Such information is of great interest to various business and nonprofit organizations that have one or another of these groups as their actual or potential clients.

Recreation

To illustrate this avenue of exploration, consider the subject of recreation. Recreation relates to activities pursued during leisure time (i.e., free or discretionary time). Demographers have neglected the study of recreation and the use of time, particularly discretionary time, although it has been a subject of interest to other disciplines. Demographers could, for example, participate in the development of surveys relating to recreation and the use of discretionary and nondiscretionary time. Demographic study of discretionary time could encompass the extent of participation in various leisure activities, the demographic and socioeconomic characteristics of the participants, and the analysis of the participation process. Many organizations, both public and private, are greatly interested in this type of information. Demographic techniques would be useful in projecting the needs for recreational personnel, facilities, and programs.

For the present discussion, recreation specifically relates to the participation of adults in various leisure activities and their participation in and attendance at various arts activities. The former includes such activities as attendance at movies, sports events, and amusement parks, and participation in sports, an exercise program, charity work, gardening, and computer hobbies. The latter includes such activities as attendance at art museums and historic parks, reading literature, photography, creative writing, and pottery work. Pet ownership and travel for pleasure are additional types of recreation not included in the two main categories described.

A survey conducted by the U.S. Endowment for the Arts in 1997 asked adults (18 years and over) about attendance at or participation in specified leisure-time activities at least once during the previous 12-month period.[36] The most popular leisure activities reported were participation in exercise programs (76%), attendance at the movies (66%), and engaging in home improvement/repair (66%). (See Table 2.15.) Among arts activities, the most popular by a wide margin was reading literature (63%).

The findings show that, as expected, a much larger percentage of men than women attended a sports event, played sports, engaged in home improvement/repairs, and had computer hobbies, and a much larger percentage of women than men engaged in charity work. There were virtually no gender differences relating to movies, exercise programs, and amusement parks. The percentage of adults engaging in recreational activities was inversely related to age. Only a small proportion of the elderly played sports or attended sports events (less than one-fifth), but their participation in exercise programs was high (three-fifths). A much larger percentage of whites than blacks played sports (48 versus 34%), engaged in home improvement/repair (70 versus 51%), and had computer hobbies (43 versus 37%). Although race differences were

TABLE 2.15 Percentage of Adults Participating in Various Leisure and Arts Activities: 1997 (Percentage of Persons 18 Years Old and Over, Covers Activities Engaged in at least Once in the Prior 12 Months)

Activity	Sex			Race		Age		Education	
	Total	Male	Female	White	Black	25–34	65–74	Grade school	Graduate school
Participation in various leisure activities	Percentage								
Movies	66	66	65	68	60	79	38	14	81
Sports attendance	41	49	34	44	35	51	21	13	55
Amusement park	57	58	57	56	55	70	29	34	53
Exercise program	76	75	77	78	74	82	56	46	88
Playing sports	45	56	35	48	34	63	23	13	57
Charity work	43	40	46	45	44	41	40	20	67
Home improvement/repair	66	71	61	70	51	63	55	40	73
Computer hobbies	40	44	37	43	37	51	11	1	59
Participation in various arts activities									
Jazz performance	12	13	11	12	16	13	8	2	28
Classical musical program	16	14	17	18	10	11	18	2	45
Art museums	35	34	36	36	31	37	28	6	70
Historic park	47	48	46	51	37	49	37	13	73
Reading literature	63	65	71	65	60	61	59	29	86
Modern dancing	13	13	12	12	11	13	14	4	15
Pottery work	15	16	14	16	11	17	10	7	13
Photography	17	16	16	17	18	18	10	8	22
Creative writing	12	10	14	12	14	13	5	2	19

Source: U.S. National Endownment for the Arts, *1997 Survey of Public Participation in the Arts*, Research Division Note #70, July 1998. See also U.S. Bureau of the Census, *Statistical Abstract of the United States, 1998*, Tables 444, 446, and 447.

considerably smaller in the case of the other leisure activities, the percentage of whites always exceeded that of blacks.

The percentage of adults participating in various leisure activities increased as educational level rose. The range of variation was greatest for movie attendance (from 14 to 82%). The range reported for adults attending the movies, for different educational levels, is similar to that for age (from 88 to 28%) but, unlike age, education is positively related to movie attendance and other leisure activities. To explain this anomaly is an intriguing problem. It may be surmised that the variation by education is associated with the variation by income, which is also positively associated with various leisure activities (data not shown in Table 2.15). Since many of these activities are not expensive, the greater income of the better educated respondents is not likely to account for much of the association between education and participation in the leisure activity. More likely, the data for the higher educational levels are heavily weighted by younger persons, whose movie attendance and other leisure activities are relatively high. Detailed analysis of cross-tabulations of the data could resolve the question.

The percentages attending artistic events or participating in artistic activities were generally much lower than those reported for the leisure activities just described (Table 2.15). Gender and race differences were also generally smaller for the arts than the leisure activities. The most pronounced differences were the female/male difference in reading literature (71 versus 55%), the white/black difference in attendance at historic parks (51 versus 37%), and the black/white difference in attending jazz performances (16 versus 11%).

Age variations in attending artistic events or participating in artistic activities were usually negligible, and modest at best, but variations by education and income were pronounced.[37] As expected, the percentages increased with the rise in education and income. Strikingly large variations by education were shown for attendance at art museums, attendance at historic parks, and reading literature. It is notable that one in every four adults with only a grade-school education read literature even though the figures for other educational groups were higher. It is even more impressive that 45% of all adults with an income under $10,000 read literature, although many of these may be college students and the quality of the literature read may be questioned. These socioeconomic variations should be of special interest to booksellers and magazine vendors.

Let us examine next some demographic data on another form of recreation, pet ownership. First, it is a very common form of recreation. National survey data compiled by the American Veterinary Medical Association for 1996 show that about one-third (32%) of all households own dogs and about one-quarter (27%) own cats as pets. The demographic characteristics of these households, whether the age of the householder, the size of the household, the type of household, and the household's income, are of considerable interest to companies purveying pet products and services and should be of interest to professionals concerned with family relations. For example, according to the data for 1996, households owning pets tend to be larger than households that do not own pets:

Household size	Households owning		All households
	Dogs	Cats	
Total	100.0	100.0	100.0
One person	13.2	16.8	25.0
Two persons	31.0	32.6	32.6
Three persons	21.4	20.6	16.8
Four or more	34.5	29.9	25.6

Source: American Veterinary Medical Association, Schaumberg, IL, U.S. *Pet Ownership and Demographics Sourcebook, 1997.* See also U.S. Bureau of the Census, *Statistical Abstract of the United States, 1998,* Tables 72 and 431.

These larger families with the disproportionate share of pets would tend to have more children. Fortunately for the pet business, the decline in the size of household seems to have reached a lower asymptote. Households with larger incomes tend to own a disproportionate share of the pet population.

To conclude these introductory comments on recreational demography, we may note that the U.S. National Telecommunications and Information Administration has compiled data on the demographic characteristics of households with a computer and with online service. We can learn, for example, the percentage of U.S. households in 1997 owning a computer, according to the race, Hispanic origin, age, educational attainment, and income of the householder, the region of residence, and the household type.

LIMITATIONS OF DEMOGRAPHIC DETERMINISM

Admittedly in identifying the forces influencing the work, character, success, or failure of our social and economic institutions, my primary emphasis in this chapter and elsewhere in this book has been on demographic factors. The reader should avoid adopting a stance of demographic determinism, however. Demographic factors alone cannot account for the changes observed. For example, demographic facts alone cannot serve as the basis for decisions to expand programs of publicly funded arts programs. The problems of local commuting and of providing the housing needed by a community cannot be analyzed entirely in demographic terms. Demographic facts alone cannot serve as the basis for decisions to expand health services or deploy health resources. One cannot employ demographic factors as the sole guidelines for managing investments. They cannot predict the success of the pharmaceutical industry and certainly not of a particular pharmaceutical firm. Commonly, demographic forces act in concert with many other factors. These other factors may partly or competely offset the effects of demographic influences or intensify their effects. On the other hand, however many nondemographic factors are considered and evaluated for their role in institutional changes and in public and private planning, it would be a serious error to neglect the role of demographic factors in the analysis.

To reiterate, the demographic variable is not a purely exogenous variable in many social and economic interrelations. It may be both exogenous and endogenous at once in an interactive relation. For example, while the death rate and birthrate influence the role of the pharmaceutical industry in particular, and the health industry in general, the effectiveness of the pharmaceutical industry and the health industry also influences the death rate and the birthrate.

APPENDIX A: DATA FOR STATES, METROPOLITAN AREAS, AND CITIES

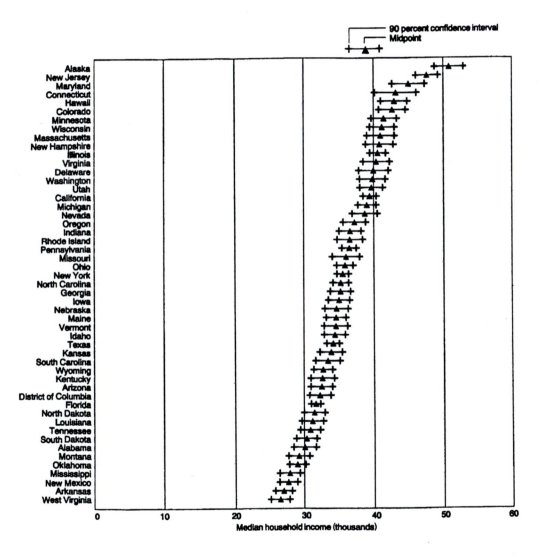

Figure 2.A.1   Median household income for states: 1995–1997 3-year average. *Note:* Income in 1997 dollars. *Source:* U.S. Bureau of the Census, Current Population Survey, March 1996, 1997, and 1998. *Current Population Reports*, Series P60-200, 1998.

TABLE 2.A.1   Total Fertility Rates and Birth Rates for Teenagers 15–19 Years, by Age of Mother, for States: 1997[a]

State	Total fertility rate	Teenage birthrate 15–19 years		
		Total	15–17 years	18–19 years
United States	2,032.5	52.3	32.1	83.6
Alabama	1,917.0	66.6	43.4	100.2
Alaska	2,390.5	44.6	25.1	73.6
Arizona	2,433.0	69.7	44.0	111.2
Arkansas	2,076.0	72.9	42.9	119.2
California	2,230.5	57.3	36.2	90.5
Colorado	2,064.5	48.2	29.9	77.2
Connecticut	1,852.5	36.1	22.5	58.1
Delaware	1,865.0	55.8	36.8	83.3
District of Columbia	1,972.0	91.0	65.9	122.4
Florida	2,064.0	57.7	35.1	94.2
Georgia	2,062.5	67.2	44.0	102.8
Hawaii	2,208.0	43.8	25.3	69.6
Idaho	2,231.0	43.3	23.3	72.5
Illinois	2,129.5	54.7	34.4	87.6
Indiana	1,969.0	54.2	32.1	87.6
Iowa	1,914.5	35.7	20.1	60.4
Kansas	2,084.5	48.5	27.5	81.7
Kentucky	1,868.5	59.6	35.4	95.0
Louisiana	2,022.0	66.3	42.1	101.4
Maine	1,596.5	32.0	15.4	58.3
Maryland	1,836.5	43.9	28.2	68.8
Massachusetts	1,705.5	31.7	19.1	50.8
Michigan	1,883.5	43.9	25.4	72.2
Minnesota	1,945.0	32.0	17.8	55.1
Mississippi	1,991.0	73.7	50.2	108.8
Missouri	1,972.5	51.5	29.6	86.3
Montana	1,957.0	37.6	20.1	65.2
Nebraska	2,053.0	37.2	21.3	61.6
Nevada	2,422.0	67.7	42.2	109.1
New Hampshire	1,647.5	28.6	14.0	53.0
New Jersey	1,980.0	35.0	21.3	56.7
New Mexico	2,246.5	68.4	44.4	106.3
Nee York	1,949.0	38.8	23.4	62.3
North Carolina	2,008.0	61.3	37.7	97.3
North Dakota	1,921.5	30.1	14.3	55.0
Ohio	1,909.5	49.8	28.6	82.6
Oklahoma	2,121.0	64.3	37.3	107.4
Oregon	2,026.0	46.9	27.0	78.2
Pennsylvania	1,758.0	37.3	21.9	61.3
Rhode Island	1,732.5	42.7	27.6	65.6
South Carolina	1,862.0	61.4	40.0	93.0
South Dakota	2,028.0	39.7	21.8	66.3
Tennessee	1,927.5	64.5	38.5	103.8
Texas	2,343.0	71.7	47.1	110.1
Utah	2,632.0	42.6	23.7	68.3

(*continues*)

TABLE 2.A.1 *(continued)*

State	Total fertility rate	Teenage birthrate 15–19 years		
		Total	15–17 years	18–19 years
Vermont	1,573.5	26.9	12.1	51.2
Virginia	1,784.0	44.2	26.1	70.8
Washington	1,978.5	42.5	24.5	70.7
West Virginia	1,649.0	49.1	27.5	80.3
Wisconsin	1,835.0	35.9	21.4	58.8
Wyoming	2,014.5	43.3	23.3	75.8

a By place of residence. Total fertility rates represent the total number of children a thousand women would have in their lifetime according to the age-specific birthrates of 1997. They are calculated by summing birthrates for 5-year age groups and multiplying by five. Birthrates for age groups are live births per 1000 women resident in specified areas in specified age groups.

Source: U.S. National Center for Health Statistics. "Births: Final data for 1997," *National Vital Statistics Reports* 47(18), 1999, Table 10.

TABLE 2.A.2 **Life Expectancy at Birth in Years by Race and Sex for States: 1989–1991**

State	White Male	Female	Black Male	Female
United States	72.72	79.45	64.47	73.73
Alabama	71.12	78.85	64.37	73.76
Alaska	72.82	79.40	*	*
Arizona	73.04	79.84	67.20	74.90
Arkansas	71.54	78.89	64.06	73.58
California	72.61	79.26	65.43	74.07
Colorado	73.88	80.13	68.96	75.89
Connecticut	74.25	80.37	66.04	75.44
Delaware	72.75	78.62	65.51	72.91
District of Columbia	71.36	81.06	57.53	71.61
Florida	73.19	80.46	64.26	73.28
Georgia	71.46	78.94	63.98	73.34
Hawaii	75.12	81.09	*	*
Idaho	73.90	79.93	*	*
Illinois	72.83	79.33	62.41	72.39
Indiana	72.44	79.03	65.87	73.56
Iowa	73.98	80.62	*	*
Kansas	73.72	80.25	67.48	75.04
Kentucky	71.01	78.24	66.06	74.13
Louisiana	71.15	78.54	63.84	73.16
Maine	72.98	79.61	*	*
Maryland	73.20	79.23	64.99	74.31
Massachusetts	73.54	79.95	68.17	76.50
Michigan	73.06	79.14	63.68	73.18
Minnesota	74.78	81.02	*	*
Mississippi	70.74	78.82	64.66	73.82
Missouri	72.43	79.48	63.87	73.52

(continues)

TABLE 2.A.2 *(continued)*

State	White Male	Female	Black Male	Female
Montana	73.59	79.92	*	*
Nebraska	73.87	80.44	*	*
Nevada	71.26	77.99	*	*
New Hampshire	73.48	79.74	*	*
New Jersey	73.37	79.34	63.87	72.88
New Mexico	72.66	79.53	*	*
New York	72.01	79.03	63.86	74.35
North Carolina	72.21	79.44	64.38	74.24
North Dakota	74.74	81.32	*	*
Ohio	72.70	78.95	65.80	74.29
Oklahoma	71.76	78.59	67.10	74.48
Oregon	73.28	79.73	*	*
Pennsylvania	72.81	79.28	63.93	73.02
Rhode Island	73.31	79.97	*	*
South Carolina	71.62	78.97	64.07	73.35
South Dakota	74.30	81.59	*	*
Tennessee	71.38	79.10	64.41	73.24
Texas	72.08	79.42	65.36	74.23
Utah	75.00	80.44	*	*
Vermont	73.25	79.65	*	*
Virginia	73.04	79.48	65.75	74.37
Washington	73.97	79.81	67.91	75.58
West Virginia	70.66	78.02	65.00	74.36
Wisconsin	73.99	80.27	66.42	75.27
Wyoming	73.27	79.46	*	*

* Figure does not meet standards of reliability or precision (based on fewer than 20 events).
Source: U.S. National Center for Health Statistics, *U.S. Decennial Life Tables for 1989–1991*, Vol. 1, No 3, *Trends and Comparisons*, 1998, Table F.

TABLE 2.A.3 **Percent Distribution of the Resident Population of States by Race/Hispanic Origin: 1997**

State	Total	White	Black	American Indian[a]	Asian and PI[b]	Hispanic[c]
United States	100.0	82.7	12.7	0.9	3.7	11.0
Alabama	100.0	73.1	25.9	0.3	0.6	0.9
Alaska	100.0	75.9	3.9	15.9	4.4	21.9
Arizona	100.0	88.8	3.5	5.5	2.0	21.9
Arkansas	100.0	82.7	16.1	0.5	0.7	1.8
California	100.0	79.9	7.4	1.0	11.7	30.8
Colorado	100.0	92.4	4.3	0.9	2.3	14.3
Connecticut	100.0	88.3	9.2	0.2	2.3	7.9
Delaware	100.0	78.6	19.1	0.3	1.9	5.2
Dist. of Columbia	100.0	33.8	62.9	0.4	3.0	7.2

(continues)

TABLE 2.A.3 (*continued*)

State	Total	White	Black	American Indian[a]	Asian and PI[b]	Hispanic[c]
Florida	100.0	82.5	15.4	0.4	1.7	14.4
Georgia	100.0	69.5	28.4	0.2	1.8	2.8
Hawaii	100.0	33.4	2.9	0.6	63.1	8.0
Idaho	100.0	97.0	0.6	1.3	1.1	7.1
Illinois	100.0	81.3	15.3	0.2	3.2	9.9
Indiana	100.0	90.6	8.3	0.2	0.9	2.3
Iowa	100.0	96.5	2.0	0.3	1.3	1.9
Kansas	100.0	91.5	5.9	0.9	1.7	5.1
Kentucky	100.0	91.9	7.2	0.2	0.7	0.8
Louisiana	100.0	66.2	32.1	0.4	1.2	2.6
Maine	100.0	98.4	0.5	0.5	0.7	0.7
Maryland	100.0	68.5	27.4	0.3	3.8	3.5
Massachusetts	100.0	90.1	6.3	0.2	3.4	5.9
Michigan	100.0	83.6	14.2	0.6	1.5	2.6
Minnesota	100.0	93.4	2.8	1.2	2.5	1.7
Mississippi	100.0	62.6	36.4	0.4	0.7	8.0
Missouri	100.0	87.3	11.2	0.4	1.1	1.5
Montana	100.0	92.8	0.3	6.3	0.6	1.7
Nebraska	100.0	93.8	4.0	0.9	1.2	4.1
Nevada	100.0	86.3	7.5	1.8	4.4	15.1
New Hampshire	100.0	98.0	0.7	0.2	1.1	1.4
New Jersey	100.0	79.9	14.5	0.3	5.3	11.9
New Mexico	100.0	86.9	2.5	9.1	1.4	40.1
New York	100.0	76.6	17.7	0.4	5.3	8.2
North Carolina	100.0	75.4	22.1	1.3	1.2	2.0
North Dakota	100.0	93.9	0.6	4.7	0.8	1.1
Ohio	100.0	87.3	11.4	0.2	1.1	1.5
Oklahoma	100.0	83.1	7.7	7.8	1.3	3.7
Oregon	100.0	93.7	1.8	1.4	3.1	5.9
Pennsylvania	100.0	88.6	9.7	0.1	1.7	2.5
Rhode Island	100.0	92.5	4.8	0.5	2.2	6.9
South Carolina	100.0	68.8	30.1	0.2	0.9	1.2
South Dakota	100.0	90.8	0.7	7.9	0.7	1.1
Tennessee	100.0	82.4	16.5	0.2	0.9	1.1
Texas	100.0	84.6	12.2	0.5	2.7	29.4
Utah	100.0	95.3	0.9	1.4	2.5	6.5
Vermont	100.0	98.3	0.5	0.3	0.8	0.8
Virginia	100.0	76.3	20.0	0.3	3.4	3.5
Washington	100.0	89.2	3.5	1.8	5.5	6.1
West Virginia	100.0	96.2	3.2	0.1	0.5	0.6
Wisconsin	100.0	92.1	5.5	0.9	1.5	2.5
Wyoming	100.0	96.0	0.8	2.3	0.8	5.8

[a] Includes Eskimo and Aleut.
[b] Includes Pacific Islanders.
[c] Persons of Hispanic origin may be of any race.
Source: U.S. Bureau of the Census, "Estimates of the population of states by race and Hispanic origin, July 1, 1997," 1998. See also U.S. Bureau of the Census, *Statistical Abstract of the United States, 1998*, Table 34.

TABLE 2.A.4 Resident Population of States, 1980, 1990, and 1997, and Components of Population Change: 1990–1997 (in Thousands, except Percentages; Covers Periods April 1, 1990, to July 1, 1997, and April 1, 1980, to April 1, 1990)

| State | Population | | | 1980–1990, percentage | Net change, 1990–1997[a] | | Births | Deaths | Net movement from abroad | | Net domestic migration |
	1980	1990	1997		Number	Percentage			International migration	Net federal movement	
United States	226,546	248,765	267,836	9.8	18,871	7.8	29,016	16,297	5,627	525	—
Alabama	3,894	4,040	4,319	3.8	279	6.9	446	300	10	7	101
Alaska	402	550	609	36.9	59	10.8	79	17	6	8	-17
Arizona	2,718	3,665	4,555	34.9	890	24.3	515	241	87	8	452
Arkansas	2,286	2,351	2,523	2.8	172	7.3	257	189	7	2	98
California	23,668	29,786	32,268	25.8	2,482	8.3	4,193	1,592	1,789	86	-1,962
Colorado	2,690	3,294	3,893	14.0	596	18.2	396	173	47	14	320
Connecticut	3,108	3,287	3,270	5.8	-17	-0.5	338	210	51	4	-192
Delaware	594	666	732	12.1	65	9.8	77	45	7	2	26
District of Columbia	638	607	529	-4.9	-78	-12.8	72	49	24	3	-128
Florida	9,746	12,938	14,654	32.7	1,716	13.3	1,392	1,040	415	33	925
Georgia	5,463	6,478	7,486	18.6	1,008	15.6	810	407	74	25	514
Hawaii	965	1,108	1,187	14.9	78	7.1	140	52	39	19	-65
Idaho	944	1,007	1,210	6.6	203	20.2	128	60	14	2	120
Illinois	11,427	11,431	11,896	(Z)	465	4.1	1,374	768	272	10	-436
Indiana	5,490	5,544	5,864	1.0	320	5.8	610	377	19	1	74
Iowa	2,914	2,777	2,852	-4.7	78	2.7	275	201	15	(Z)	-10
Kansas	2,364	2,478	2,595	4.8	117	4.7	272	168	21	8	-24
Kentucky	3,661	3,687	3,908	0.7	221	6.0	386	265	11	10	79
Louisiana	4,206	4,222	4,352	0.4	130	3.1	497	282	20	9	-106
Maine	1,125	1,228	1,242	9.1	14	1.2	110	84	2	2	-15
Maryland	4,217	4,781	5,094	13.4	314	6.6	546	293	93	15	-39
Massachusetts	5,737	6,016	6,118	4.9	101	1.7	617	396	112	3	-221
Michigan	9,262	9,295	9,774	0.4	479	5.1	1,021	595	69	2	-162
Minnesota	4,076	4,376	4,686	7.4	310	7.1	473	264	38	1	66
Mississippi	2,521	2,575	2,731	2.2	155	6.0	305	191	5	6	35

(continues)

TABLE 2.A.4 (continued)

State	Population 1980	Population 1990	Population 1997	1980–1990, percentage	Net change, 1990–1997[a] Number	Net change, 1990–1997[a] Percentage	Births	Deaths	Net movement from abroad International migration	Net movement from abroad Net federal movement	Net domestic migration
Missouri	4,917	5,117	5,402	4.1	285	5.6	547	383	27	5	86
Montana	787	799	879	1.6	80	10.0	82	54	2	2	49
Nebraska	1,570	1,578	1,657	0.5	78	5.0	171	109	11	4	5
Nevada	800	1,202	1,677	50.1	475	39.5	170	82	34	3	349
New Hampshire	921	1,109	1,173	20.5	63	5.7	113	65	4	(Z)	13
New Jersey	7,365	7,748	8,053	5.2	305	3.9	853	526	289	5	−305
New Mexico	1,303	1,515	1,730	16.2	215	14.2	200	86	35	6	62
New York	17,558	17,991	18,137	2.5	146	0.8	2,045	1,217	841	11	−1,513
North Carolina	5,882	6,632	7,425	12.8	793	12.0	746	453	42	37	430
North Dakota	663	639	641	−2.1	2	0.3	83	43	3	3	−25
Ohio	10,798	10,847	11,186	0.5	339	3.1	1,153	747	39	4	−107
Oklahoma	3,025	3,146	3,317	4.0	172	5.5	339	231	21	10	38
Oregon	2,633	2,842	3,243	7.9	401	14.1	309	197	49	1	244
Pennsylvania	11,864	11,883	12,020	0.2	137	1.2	1,151	912	84	3	−170
Rhode Island	947	1,003	987	5.9	−18	−1.6	96	60	12	2	−86
South Carolina	3,122	3,486	3,760	11.7	274	7.9	391	233	12	17	91
South Dakota	691	696	738	0.8	42	6.0	78	49	3	2	9
Tennessee	4,591	4,877	5,368	6.2	491	10.1	535	357	21	6	301
Texas	14,229	16,986	19,439	19.4	2,453	14.4	2,344	969	598	43	461
Utah	1,461	1,723	2,059	17.9	336	19.5	280	75	21	2	87
Vermont	511	563	589	10.0	26	4.7	54	35	3	(Z)	5
Virginia	5,347	6,189	6,734	15.8	545	8.8	687	371	106	60	70
Washington	4,132	4,867	5,610	17.8	744	15.3	570	289	96	20	352
West Virginia	1,950	1,793	1,816	−8.2	22	1.2	158	146	3	(Z)	11
Wisconsin	4,706	4,892	5,170	4.0	278	5.7	505	322	19	(Z)	85
Wyoming	470	454	480	−3.4	26	5.8	47	25	2	1	1

—represents zero. Z represents less than 500.

[a] Includes residual change, not shown separately. The residual is the effect of national "controls" on subnational estimates. It is the difference between the results of the national estimates model and the county/state estimates model and is distributed among the states.

Source: U.S. Bureau of the Census, "ST-97-3 Estimates of the population of states: Annual time series, July 1, 1990, to July 1, 1997, and demographic components of population change, annual time series, July 1, 1990, to July 1, 1997," January 1998; PPL-110 and P-25, No. 1095.

■ **TABLE 2.A.5 Population of the 75 Largest Metropolitan Areas and Distribution by Race/Hispanic Origin: 1997**

Metropolitan area[a]	Total population (1,000)	Percentage of total metropolitan population			
		Black	American Indian, Eskimo, Aleut	Asian and Pacific Islander	Hispanic origin[b]
New York-Northern New Jersey-Long Island, NY-NJ-CT-PA CMSA/NECMA[c]	19,876	19.4	0.3	6.4	17.1
Los Angeles-Riverside-Orange County, CA CMSA	15,609	8.3	0.7	11.1	38.5
Chicago-Gary-Kenosha, IL-IN-WI CMSA	8,642	19.2	0.2	4.0	13.5
Washington-Baltimore, DC-MD-VA-WV CMSA	7,207	25.8	0.3	4.9	5.1
San Francisco-Oakland-San Jose, CA CMSA	6,701	8.8	0.7	18.2	19.1
Philadelphia-Wilmington-Atlantic City, PA-NJ-DE-MD CMSA	5,972	19.4	0.2	2.8	4.8
Boston-Worcester-Lawrence-Lowell-Brockton, MA-NH NECMA	5,828	5.8	0.2	3.5	5.3
Detroit-Ann Arbor-Flint, MI CMSA	5,439	20.8	0.4	1.9	2.4
Dallas-Fort Worth, TX CMSA	4,683	14.2	0.6	3.5	15.5
Houston-Galveston-Brazoria, TX CMSA	4,320	18.3	0.4	5.0	24.3
Atlanta, GA MSA	3,627	25.8	0.2	2.8	3.2
Miami-Fort Lauderdale, FL CMSA	3,515	19.7	0.3	1.8	37.2
Seattle-Tacoma-Bremerton, WA CMSA	3,388	5.1	1.3	7.8	4.2
Cleveland-Akron, OH CMSA	2,908	18.6	0.2	1.3	2.3
Phoenix-Mesa, AZ MSA	2,840	4.1	2.4	2.2	20.2
Minneapolis-St. Paul, MN-WI MSA	2,792	4.5	1.0	3.6	2.1
San Diego, CA MSA	2,723	6.4	0.9	10.3	25.8
St. Louis, MO-IL MSA	2,558	17.6	0.2	1.2	1.4
Pittsburgh, PA MSA	2,361	8.4	0.1	1.0	0.8
Denver-Boulder-Gresley, CO CMSA	2,318	5.3	0.8	2.8	14.3
Tampa-St. Petersburg-Clearwater, FL MSA	2,227	10.5	0.3	1.8	9.1
Portland-Salem, OR-WA CMSA	2,113	2.7	1.0	4.1	5.9
Cincinnati-Hamilton, OH-KY-IN CMSA	1,934	11.6	0.1	1.0	0.7
Kansas City, MO-KS MSA	1,709	13.3	0.5	1.5	3.7
Sacramento-Yolo, CA CMSA	1,656	7.0	1.3	9.9	14.8
Milwaukee-Racine, WI CMSA	1,637	14.9	0.6	1.6	4.8
Norfolk-Virginia Beach-Newport News, VA-NC MSA	1,545	30.1	0.4	3.3	3.0
San Antonio, TX MSA	1,511	6.5	0.4	1.7	53.2
Indianapolis, IN MSA	1,503	13.6	0.2	1.0	1.2
Orlando, FL MSA	1,467	14.1	0.4	2.5	11.1
Columbus, OH MSA	1,460	13.2	0.2	2.0	1.0
Charlotte-Gastonia-Rock Hill, NC-SC MSA	1,350	20.5	0.4	1.5	1.7
New Orleans, LA MSA	1,308	34.9	0.3	2.1	4.9
Las Vegas, NV-AZ MSA	1,262	9.1	1.2	4.3	15.1
Salt Lake City-Ogden, UT MSA	1,248	1.3	0.8	3.1	7.7
Buffalo-Niagara Falls, NY MSA	1,165	11.6	0.7	1.3	2.6
Greensboro-Winston-Salem-High Point, NC MSA	1,153	19.6	0.4	1.0	1.4
Nashville, TN MSA	1,135	15.7	0.2	1.4	1.2
Hartford, CT NECMA	1,105	9.4	0.2	2.3	8.3

(*continues*)

TABLE 2.A.5 *(continued)*

Metropolitan area[a]	Total population (1,000)	Black	American Indian, Eskimo, Aleut	Asian and Pacific Islander	Hispanic origin[b]
		Percentage of total metropolitan population			
Rochester, NY MSA	1,086	10.1	0.4	1.9	3.8
Memphis, TN-AR-MS MSA	1,083	42.1	0.2	1.1	1.2
Austin-San Marcos, TX MSA	1,071	10.0	0.5	3.0	25.1
Raleigh-Durham-Chapel Hill, NC MSA	1,050	24.1	0.3	2.5	2.3
Jacksonville, FL MSA	1,035	22.6	0.4	2.5	3.5
Oklahoma City, OK MSA	1,031	10.8	4.7	2.2	4.8
Grand Rapids-Muskegon-Holland, MI MSA	1,026	7.3	0.6	1.3	3.8
West Palm Beach-Boca Raton, FL MSA	1,019	14.7	0.2	1.5	10.3
Louisville, KY-IN MSA	993	13.0	0.2	0.8	0.8
Dayton-Springfield, OH MSA	945	14.5	0.2	1.3	0.9
Richmond-Petersburg, VA MSA	943	29.9	0.3	1.8	1.5
Providence-Warwick-Pawtucket, RI NECMA	905	4.9	0.5	2.3	6.6
Greenville-Spartanburg-Anderson, SC MSA	905	17.9	0.2	0.8	1.1
Birmingham, AL MSA	900	29.0	0.2	0.5	0.7
Albany-Schenectady-Troy, NY MSA	876	5.1	0.2	1.8	2.2
Honolulu, HI MSA	870	3.8	0.5	64.3	7.4
Fresno, CA MSA	869	4.9	1.3	9.3	42.0
Tucson, AZ MSA	780	3.8	3.5	2.4	28.7
Tulsa, OK MSA	764	8.6	6.6	1.1	2.8
Syracuse, NY MSA	741	6.3	0.6	1.5	1.7
El Paso, TX MSA	702	3.5	0.5	1.5	74.4
Omaha, NE-IA MSA	687	8.6	0.6	1.6	4.6
Albuquerque, NM MSA	675	3.4	5.7	2.0	38.9
Knoxville, TN MSA	654	6.4	0.3	1.1	0.9
Bakersfield, CA MSA	629	6.4	1.7	4.4	34.5
Scranton-Wilkes-Barre-Hazleton, PA MSA	622	1.0	0.1	0.7	0.8
Harrisburg-Lebanon-Cartisle, PA MSA	615	7.7	0.1	1.5	2.3
Allentown-Bethlehem-Easton, PA MSA	614	2.5	0.1	1.5	6.0
Toledo, OH MSA	612	12.3	0.3	1.3	4.0
Youngstown-Warren, OH MSA	595	10.3	0.2	0.5	1.6
Springfield, MA NECMA	591	7.8	0.2	2.0	10.0
Baton Rouge, LA MSA	570	31.2	0.2	1.3	1.7
Little Rock-North Little Rock, AR MSA	552	20.9	0.3	0.8	1.7
Stockton-Lodl, CA MSA	543	5.7	1.1	15.3	28.4
Sarasota-Bradenton, FL MSA	539	7.0	0.3	0.8	4.4
Wichita, KS MSA	531	8.1	1.1	2.4	5.6

Note: as of July 1. Areas as defined by U.S. Office of Management and Budget, June 30, 1996. Covers 273 metropolitan areas: 17 consolidated metropolitan statistical areas (CMSAs), 245 metropolitan statistical areas (MSAs) located outside of New England, and 11 county metropolitan areas (NECMAs) in New England.

[a] Metropolitan areas are shown in rank order of total population.

[b] Persons af Hispanic origin may be of any race.

[c] Includes data for New Haven-Bridgeport-Stamford-Waterbury-Danbury, CT NECMA.

Source: U.S. Bureau of the Census, *Statistcal Abstract of the United States, 1999*, Table 44. See also U.S. Bureau of the Census. *State and Metropolitan Area Data Book, 1997–1998*, 1999.

TABLE 2.A.6   Population of Cities with 500,000 or More Inhabitants, 1990 and 1998, Percentage Distribution by Race/Hispanic Origin, 1990, and Percentage Change: 1990–1998

State	Population, 1990 Total[a]	Percentage of total Black	Asian[b]	Hispanic[c]	Population, 1998	Percentage change, 1990–1998
Austin, TX	472	12.4	3.0	23.0	552	17.0
Baltimore, MD	736	59.2	1.1	1.0	646	−12.3
Boston, MA	574	25.6	5.3	10.8	555	−3.3
Charlotte, NC	420	31.8	1.8	1.4	505	20.3
Chicago, IL	2,784	39.1	3.7	19.6	2,802	0.7
Columbus, OH	633	22.6	2.4	1.1	670	5.9
Dallas, TX	1,008	29.5	2.2	20.9	1,076	6.8
Detroit, MI	1,028	75.7	0.8	2.8	970	−5.6
El Paso, TX	515	3.4	1.2	69.0	615	19.3
Houston, TX	1,638	8.1	4.1	27.6	1,787	9.1
Indianapolis, IN	731	22.6	0.9	1.1	741	1.4
Jacksonville, FL	635	25.2	1.9	2.6	694	9.2
Los Angeles, CA	3,486	14.0	9.8	39.9	3,598	3.2
Memphis, TN	619	54.8	0.8	0.7	604	−2.4
Milwaukee, WI	628	30.5	1.9	6.3	578	−7.9
Nashville-Davidson, TN[d]	488	24.3	1.4	0.9	510	4.5
New York, NY	7,323	28.7	7.0	24.4	7,420	1.3
Philadelphia, PA	1,586	39.9	2.7	5.6	1,436	−9.4
Phoenix, AZ	984	5.2	1.7	20.0	1,198	21.7
Portland, OR	464	7.7	5.3	3.2	504	8.7
San Antonio, TX	959	7.0	1.1	55.6	1,114	16.1
San Diego, CA	1,111	9.4	11.8	20.7	1,221	9.9
San Francisco, CA	724	10.9	29.1	13.9	746	3.0
San Jose, CA	782	4.7	19.5	26.6	861	10.1
Seattle, WA	516	10.1	11.8	3.6	537	4.0
Washington, DC	607	65.8	1.8	5.4	523	−13.8

Note: Lists cities with 500,000 or more inhabitants as estimated for July 1, 1998. Population as of April 1 for 1990; numbers in thousands. Data refer to boundaries in effect in December 1994. Minus sign (−) denotes decrease.

[a] Includes other races not shown.

[b] Includes Pacific Islanders.

[c] Hispanic persons may be of any race.

[d] Represents the portion of a consolidated city that is not within one or more separately incorporated places.

Source: U.S. Bureau of the Census, *1990 Census of Population and Housing, Population and Housing Unit Counts* (CPH-2) and *General Population Characteristics* (CP-1); and "Population estimates for places: Annual time series, July 1, 1990, to July 1, 1998," June 1999.

APPENDIX B: NOTE ON FOREIGN POPULATION TRENDS

For the most part, the demographic forces at work in the other industrialized countries resemble those in the United States. A major difference between the United States, on the one hand, and most countries of Europe and Japan, on the other, is the difference in their fertility rates and the role of immigration in national growth. In the United States, the total fertility rate is at just about the level (2.06 in 1998) at which the population would replace itself (2.09), while in the countries of Europe and Japan the rate is well below replacement (1.4). This difference has serious implications for the long-term growth of the United States and the other countries. Unless the latter countries can raise their fertility rates or accept a larger influx of immigrants than they have done in the past, their populations will begin to decline, as is now projected for them. With the current level of immigration to the United States, even though fertility has been below replacement level in all the years since 1972, there is no prospect of population decline.

Moreover, the populations of these countries will age more rapidly than the United States population and the ratio of elders to workers will be greater. According to the World Bank's 1994 population projections, the ratio of persons aged 65 years and over to persons 15 to 64 years of age, for the United States, Japan, and three of Europe's largest countries, is expected to change as follows:

| | Ratio per 100 | | |
	1990	2010	2030
France	20.8	24.6	39.1
Germany	21.4	30.1	47.1
Japan	17.3	34.1	43.5
United Kingdom	29.2	25.5	38.3
United States	18.7	19.1	31.9

The pervasive and powerful impact of these changes on pensions, health care, and social benefits, as well as the economy and the national budget, is well recognized in these countries. These and many other similarly situated countries have been grappling with the difficult task of preparing for the social and economic consequences of the prospective shifts in age distribution.

The population of the world is increasing by more than 80 million persons per year and virtually all (i.e., 98%) of this growth is occurring in the less developed countries. In the medium series of the United Nations population projections, which assumes that women have two children in their lifetime on average, the world's population will grow to 9.4 billion in 2050 from 6.0 billion in 1999 and reach a stationary level of 11 billion in the following century.

Some of the demographic forces now at work in the less developed countries were foreshadowed and triggered by earlier developments in the United States and other industrialized countries. Generally speaking, the demographic changes that occurred in the United States in the earlier decades of the 20th century are now occurring in the less developed countries. The major demographic movements in these countries are as follows: high, albeit diminishing, rates of population growth; high, but declining, birthrates; very high, but falling, proportions of children and youth, and continued numerical dominance of these groups; relatively low crude death rates but high infant mortality rates; relatively low, but rising, life expectancy; very low percentages of elderly persons but rapid growth in the numbers of elderly persons; low but increasing participation of women in the paid labor force; a high percentage of rural residents but rapid urbanization; high and rising population density; low but rising educational attainment; and extremely low per capita income (Table 2.B.1).[38] These indicators vary widely among the less developed regions of

■ **TABLE 2.B.1** Demographic Indicators for Countries with More Than 30 Million Inhabitants: 1999

Country	Population (millions) 1999	2010	Natural increase (percentage)[a]	Total fertility rate[b]	Life expectancy at birth	Infant mortality rate	Percentage aged Under 15	65 and over	Percentage urban	GNP per capita, 1997 (U.S. $)
Africa										
Algeria	30.8	38.3	2.4	4.1	68	44	39	4	49	1,500
Congo, Dem. Rep. of	50.5	70.3	3.2	6.6	49	106	49	3	29	110
Egypt	66.9	80.3	2.0	3.3	65	52	39	4	44	1,200
Ethiopia	59.7	74.8	2.5	7.0	42	128	46	3	20	340
Nigeria	113.8	150.3	3.0	6.2	54	74	46	3	20	110
South Africa	42.6	46.6	1.6	3.3	58	52	34	5	45	3,210
Tanzania	31.3	39.4	2.5	5.7	47	100	45	3	21	210
Asia										
Bangladesh	125.7	150.3	1.8	3.3	59	82	43	3	20	360
China	1,254.1	1,394.3	1.0	1.8	71	31	26	7	30	860
India	986.6	1,167.3	1.9	3.4	60	72	36	4	28	370
Indonesia	211.8	247.5	1.6	2.8	63	46	33	4	38	1,110
Iran	66.2	78.9	1.8	3.0	69	26	40	4	61	1,780
Japan	126.7	127.6	0.2	1.4	81	3.7	15	16	79	38,160
Korea, South	46.9	50.6	1.0	1.6	74	11	22	7	79	10,550
Myanmar	48.1	56.6	2.0	3.8	61	83	33	5	26	(NA)
Pakistan	146.5	181.1	0.3	5.6	58	91	41	4	32	500
Philippines	74.7	91.9	2.3	3.7	67	35	38	4	26	(NA)
Thailand	61.8	67.3	1.1	2.0	72	25	27	5	31	2,740
Turkey	65.9	76.3	1.5	2.6	68	43	31	5	64	3,130
Vietnam	79.5	94.2	1.5	2.7	66	35	35	5	20	310
Europe										
Germany	82.0	81.7	−0.1	1.3	77	4.9	16	16	86	28,280
Italy	57.7	57.5	Z	1.2	78	5.5	15	17	90	20,170
France	59.1	61.7	0.3	1.7	78	5.0	19	16	74	26,300
Poland	38.7	40.2	0.1	1.5	73	10	21	12	62	3,590
Russia	146.5	144.7	−0.5	1.2	67	17	20	13	73	2,680
Spain	39.4	39.8	Z	1.2	78	5.5	15	16	64	14,490
Ukraine	49.9	47.4	−0.6	1.3	68	14	19	14	68	1,040
United Kingdom	59.4	60.8	0.2	1.7	77	5.9	19	16	89	20,870
North America										
Canada	30.6	35.1	0.4	1.5	79	5.6	20	12	77	19,640
United States	272.5	297.7	0.6	2.0	77	7.0	21	13	75	29,080
Latin America										
Argentina	36.6	41.5	1.2	2.6	73	22	29	9	89	8,950
Brazil	168.0	190.9	1.5	2.3	67	41	32	5	78	4,790
Colombia	38.6	47.3	2.0	3.0	69	28	33	4	71	2,180
Mexico	99.7	118.2	2.2	3.0	72	32	35	5	74	3,700

NA: Not available.

Z: Less than 0.05.

[a] Annual percentage change.

[b] Rate per woman.

Source: Population Reference Bureau, *1999 World Population Data Sheet*, Washington, DC: Population Reference Bureau, 1999.

the world. The least favorable values are found in sub-Saharan Africa and the most favorable ones are found in East Asia (excluding Japan).

The growing desire for smaller families and greater access to family planning services are helping couples in the less developed countries achieve the family size desired, with resulting declines in birthrates and proportions of children and youth. At the same time, the very high prevalence of AIDS in these countries, particularly the countries of sub-Saharan Africa, has emerged as a major factor in raising death rates, reducing per capita income, and limiting economic growth.

NOTES

1. Since this work was prepared, the U.S. Census Bureau has published a revised set of population projections (2000). The most recent population outlook is for slightly greater net growth than previously projected. The revised total population is 404 million in 2050, as compared with 394 million in the series described here.

2. Population Reference Bureau, *Population Today*, Washington, DC: Population Reference Bureau, March 1996.

3. Population Reference Bureau, *Population Today*, Washington, DC: Population Reference Bureau, March 1996.

4. State data on the foreign-born population are not available for postcensal years.

5. Bryant Robey, *The American People*, New York: Truman Talley Books, E. B. Dutton, 1985, p. 49.

6. See also U.S. Bureau of the Census, *Statistical Abstract of the United States, 1998*, Table 73.

7. A family household is one in which the members are related to the householder, or head of the household. A nonfamily household is one in which the members are not related to the householder.

8. Note that a full chapter, Chapter 8, is devoted to the demography of the labor force.

9. U.S. Bureau of the Census, *Statistical Abstract of the United States, 1998*, Tables 653 and 654.

10. See U.S. Bureau of the Census, *Statistical Abstract of the United States, 1998*, Table 747.

11. Allowance for these factors would probably bring the figures closer together but, without testing, we cannot be sure about the effect.

12. Kenneth M. Johnson, "The rural rebound," *Reports on America* 1(3): Washington, DC: Population Reference Bureau, September 1999. The present discussion of nonmetropolitan and rural trends is based largely on this study.

13. Andrew Beveridge, *Footnotes*, Washington, DC: American Sociological Association, January 1996, p. 8. Based on analysis of 1990 census data.

14. Landon Y. Jones, *Great Expectations: America and the Baby Boom Generation*, New York: Coward, McCann, and Geoghegan, 1980.

15. The children of the old immigrants were typically natives of this country since the immigrants themselves were commonly unmarried youths. The children were strongly imbued by their parents with the desirability of immediate assimilation and total immersion, often at the expense of forsaking their native language and at a loss to the nation of considerable linguistic resources. Bilingual education in the public schools was unknown, although the native languages of some immigrant groups (e.g., German, Spanish, Italian) were offered as foreign languages in the regular curriculum in some cities.

16. Since a household is defined as the person or group of persons who occupy a housing unit, the counts for these two concepts are identical although the concepts are different. It should be evident, therefore, that there is a strong interactive relation between changes in households and changes in housing units, a relation that achieves a perfect equilibrium in the number of households and the number of occupied housing units. The point where the equilibrium is achieved determines whether there is a shortage of acceptable housing units or a surplus of units, representing the extent

of vacancies. Potential households seek housing units, but if an actual physical structure of the type sought by the potential household is not available, neither a household nor an occupied housing unit comes into being.

17. These conditions and policies included a recession in 1982, high inflation, and high mortgage interest rates, especially during the first half of the decade. Sales of existing single-family houses dropped precipitously from the late 1970s to the early 1980s—from 4 million in 1978 to 3 million in 1980 and 2 million in 1982. Purchases of new houses and sales of existing houses may or not affect homeownership ratios, depending on whether the purchaser was previously a homeowner. Purchasers of new houses are usually new homeowners. Trading up to more expensive houses affects the number of sales of existing houses, but does not affect the extent of homeownership. See U.S. Bureau of the Census, *Statistical Abstract of the United States, 1998,* Tables 1204 and 1215.

18. Interest rates dropped somewhat in the latter part of the 1980 decade. Compared to interest rates of 13 to 16% from 1980 to 1985, rates around 10% from 1985 to 1990 looked attractive. In addition, they allowed many more people to qualify for mortgage loans. Hence, given the pent-up demand, sales of existing single-family houses rebounded to more than 3 million by 1985 and reached nearly 4 million again by 1994. See U.S. Bureau of the Census, *Statistical Abstract of the United States, 1998,* Tables 1204 and 1215.

19. Jacob S. Siegel, *A Generation of Change: A Profile of America's Older Population,* New York: Russell Sage Foundation, 1993, p. 351.

20. U.S. Bureau of the Census, *Current Population Reports,* P60–197. See also U.S. Bureau of the Census, *Statistical Abstract of the United States, 1998,* Table 740.

21. U.S. Bureau of the Census, *Current Housing Reports,* Series H150/95, *American Housing Survey in the United States.* See also U.S. Bureau of the Census, *Statistical Abstract of the United States, 1998,* Table 1214.

22. U.S. Bureau of the Census, Population Paper Listing 91. See also U.S. Bureau of the Census, *Statistical Abstract of the United States, 1998,* Table 22.

23. U.S. Bureau of the Census, *Statistical Abstract of the United States, 1998,* Table 1216.

24. U.S. Bureau of the Census, *Statistical Abstract of the United States, 1998,* Tables 1204 and 1205.

25. U.S. Federal Highway Administration, *National Personal Transportation Survey, Summary of Travel Trends, 1969, 1977, 1983,* and *1990.* See also U.S. Bureau of the Census, *Statistical Abstract of the United States, 1998,* Table 1039.

26. Bryant Robey, *The American People,* New York: Truman Talley Books, E.P. Dutton, 1985.

27. U.S. Federal Highway Administration, *National Personal Transportation Survey, Summary of Travel Trends, 1969, 1977, 1983,* and *1990.*

28. William H. Frey, "The new geography of population shifts," in Reynolds Farley (ed.), *State of the Nation: America in the 1990s,* Vol. 2: *Social Trends,* New York: Russell Sage Foundation, 1995, p. 275.

29. John D. Kasarda, "Industrial restructuring and the changing location of jobs," in Reynolds Farley (ed.), *State of the Nation, America in the 1990s,* Vol. I: *Economic Trends,* New York: Russell Sage Foundation, 1995, pp. 237–238.

30. U.S. Bureau of the Census, *Statistical Abstract of the United States, 1998,* Table 1038.

31. *Washington Post,* February 4, 2000, p. A20.

32. Traffic congestion is not confined to the Monday-to-Friday workweek. Traffic on the weekends has grown considerably and in some areas the traffic on Saturday is more congested than during the week. With more dual-earner households, more single-parent households, and more persons living alone, the weekend has increasingly become the preferred time for shopping. In the suburbs, the use of a car is virtually required for trips to the supermarket and the shopping mall. Between 1969 and 1990, the average annual number of vehicle trips for shopping per household rose from 213 to 345 (i.e., by 62%) and the average annual number of vehicle miles traveled for shopping per household swelled from 929 to 1,743 (i.e., by 88%). U.S. Federal Highway Administration, *National Personal Transportation Survey, Summary of Travel Trends, 1969* and *1990.* See also U.S. Bureau of the Census, *Statistical Abstract of the United States, 1998,* Table 1039.

33. *Washington Post,* January 31, 2000, p. E13.

34. *Washington Post*, February 11, 2000, p. E10.

35. See, for example, Peter A. Morrison and Paola Scommegna, "Demographic trends tax the IRS," *Population Trends and Public Policy* Series 11, Washington, DC: Population Reference Bureau, 1986.

36. U.S. National Endowment for the Arts, *1997 Survey of Public Participation in the Arts*, Research Division Note #70, July 1998. See also U.S. Bureau of the Census, *Statistical Abstract of the United States, 1998*, Tables 444 and 446.

37. U.S. National Endowment for the Arts, *1997 Survey of Public Participation in the Arts*, Research Division Note #70, July 1998. See also U.S. Bureau of the Census, *Statistical Abstract of the United States, 1998*, Tables 446 and 447.

38. See also U.S. Bureau of the Census and U.S. Agency for International Development, Bureau of Global Programs, Field Support, and Research, *World Population Profile: 1998*, by Thomas M. McDevitt, 1999; Population Reference Bureau, *World Population Data Sheet, 1999*, Washington, DC: Population Reference Bureau, 1999.

SUGGESTED READINGS

Recent Population Trends

Ahlburg, Dennis A., and DeVita, Carol J. (1992). "New realities of the American Family," *Population Bulletin* 47(2). Washington, DC: Population Reference Bureau.

Annie E. Casey Foundation. (1998). *1998 Kids Count Data Sheet*. Baltimore, MD: Annie E. Casey Foundation.

DeVita, Carol J. (1996). "The United States at mid-decade," *Population Bulletin* 50(4). Washington, DC: Population Reference Bureau.

Farley, Reynolds. (1996). *The New American Reality: Who We Are, How We Got Here, Where We Are Going*. 1990 Census Research Series. Vol. III. New York: Russell Sage Foundation.

Farley, Reynolds (ed.) (1995). *State of the Union: America in the 1990s*. 1990 Census Research Series. Vol. I. *Economic Trends*. Vol. II. *Social Trends*. New York: Russell Sage Foundation.

Frey, William H. (1990). "Metropolitan America: Beyond the transition," *Population Bulletin* 45(2). Washington, DC: Population Reference Bureau.

Frey, William H. (1995). "The new geography of population shifts." In Reynolds Farley (ed.), *State of the Nation: America in the 1990s*. Vol. II. *Social Trends*. New York: Russell Sage Foundation.

Hernandez, Donald J. (1995). *America's Children: Resources from Family, Government, and the Economy*. New York: Russell Sage Foundation.

Johnson, Kenneth M. (1999). "The rural rebound." *Reports on America* 1(3), September. Washington, DC: Population Reference Bureau.

Levy, Frank. (1998). *The New Dollars and Dreams: American Incomes and Economic Change*. New York: Russell Sage Foundation.

Lieberson, Stanley, and Waters, Mary C. (1988). *Ethnic and Racial Groups in Contemporary America*. New York: Russell Sage Foundation.

Martin, Philip, and Midgley, Elizabeth. (1994). "Immigration to the United States: Journey to an uncertain destination," *Population Bulletin* 49(2). Washington, DC: Population Reference Bureau.

Myers, Dowell. (1997). *Analysis with Local Census Data: Portraits of Change*. Boston: Academic Press.

Population Reference Bureau. (1999a). *1999 United States Population Data Sheet*. Washington, DC: Population Reference Bureau.

Population Reference Bureau. (1999b). *1999 World Population Data Sheet*. Washington, DC: Population Reference Bureau.

Roberts, Sam. (1993). *Who We Are: A Portrait of America Based on the Latest U.S. Census*. New York: Times Books/Random House.

Robey, Bryant. (1985). *The American People*. New York: Truman Talley Books, E. B. Dutton.

Schneider, Mark, and Phelan, Thomas. (1993, May). "Black suburbanization in the 1980s." *Demography* 30(2): 269–280.

Siegel, Jacob S. (1993). *A Generation of Change: A Profile of America's Older Population.* New York: Russell Sage Foundation.

Spain, Daphne. (1999, May). "America's diversity: On the edge of two centuries." *Reports on America* 1(2). Washington, DC: Population Reference Bureau.

Spain, Daphne, and Bianchi, Susan M. (1996). *Balancing Act: Motherhood, Marriage, and Employment among American Women.* New York: Russell Sage Foundation.

U.S. Bureau of the Census and U.S. Agency for International Development, Bureau of Global Programs, Field Support, and Research. (1999). *World Population Profile: 1998,* by Thomas M. McDevitt.

U.S. Bureau of the Census. (1998). "Population Profile of the United States: 1997." *Current Population Reports,* Series P-23, No. 194.

U.S. National Center for Health Statistics. (1999). "Some trends and comparisons of United States life table data: 1900–1991," by Robert N. Anderson. *U.S. Decennial Life Tables for 1989–91.* Vol. 1, No. 3.

Links to Selected Social and Economic Programs

De Vita, Carol. (1989). *America in the 21st Century.* A series of reports including "Human Resource Development," "Social and Economic Support Systems," "Governance and Politics," and others. Washington, DC: Population Reference Bureau.

Godbey, Geoffrey, and Robinson, John. (1999). *Time for Life: The Surprising Ways Americans Use Their Time.* University Park, PA: Penn State University Press.

Morrison, Peter A. (1988, June). "Demographic factors shaping the U.S. market for new housing," Rand Corporation paper presented at the Institutional Investor's Japanese Real Estate Seminar, Tokyo, Japan.

Morrison, Peter A., and Scommegna, Paola. (1986, April). "Demographic trends tax the IRS," *Population Trends and Public Policy,* Series 11. Washington, DC: Population Reference Bureau.

Myers, Dowell, and Welch, Jennifer R. (1995). "The polarization of housing status." In Reynolds Farley (ed.), *State of the Union: America in the 1990s.* Vol. I. *Economic Trends.* New York: Russell Sage Foundation.

O'Hare, William P. (1987, September). "America's welfare population: Who get's what?" *Population Trends and Policy,* Series 13. Washington, DC: Population Reference Bureau.

Pisarski, Alan. (1996). *Commuting in America II: Second National Report on Commuting Patterns and Trends.* Lansdowne, VA: Eno Foundation for Transportation.

3

BASIC SOURCES OF DEMOGRAPHIC AND SOCIOECONOMIC DATA AND WAYS OF ACCESSING THEM

INTRODUCTION

The sources of data useful for applied demography may be classified in several ways, including the methods of collecting and compiling the data, the agencies that collect and compile the data, the ways of accessing the data, and the publications that present them. This discussion is organized mainly around the agencies that collect the data, but considers the other bases of classification in a subsidiary fashion.

The basic methods of collecting demographic data may be listed as enumeration, registration, and maintenance of administrative records. In **enumeration**, the collecting authority, usually the government, initiates contact with the members of a population in order to collect and compile data about the *status* of the population at a specified *date* (e.g., sample survey, census). In the **registration** method, the members of the population report an *event* to the collecting authority, usually the goverment, *as it occurs* (e.g., birth and death registration). The collection of immigration data is a hybrid of methods, but it essentially employs the registration method. In this case, an event is recorded as the government and the immigrant meet at the nation's ports. A **population register** is a registration system that serves as a continuous and comprehensive system of population accounting, covering international migration and internal geographic mobility as well as vital events. Individuals report these events to local record offices as they occur. The **administrative records method** first calls for a general registration/enumeration to initiate a file of individuals eligible or obligated to register, and then for a continuing registration by individuals as they become eligible for registration. Administrative records are usually established as an administrative file to collect nondemographic data. In spite of its having features in common with the other methods, this method is distinctive enough to be listed separately (e.g., Social Security records, drivers license registrations, Medicare records).

A distinction may be made between **primary sources** and **secondary sources** according to whether the agency named collects and compiles the data itself or republishes data collected by others and merely reshapes them into a new form. Alternatively viewed, the primary sources are the publications reporting original data, and the secondary sources are those that reproduce previously published data. Federal and other government agencies are typically primary sources, but they may be secondary sources for either government or private data. For example, the decennial census reports of the U.S.Census Bureau are the primary source of population census data, but the *Statistical Abstract of the United States,* published annually by the Census Bureau, is a secondary source for most of the data contained in it. The following discussion of sources of demographic data, essentially organized in terms of agencies, distinguishes federal sources, state and local government sources, and private sources in that order.

FEDERAL SOURCES

Federal Statistical Agencies

There are more than 70 agencies in the federal government that produce statistical data, and much of this material has some utility for the applied demographer. Among the several statistical agencies in the federal government concerned with the collection and compilation of data about the population, the major ones are the Bureau of the Census (Department of Commerce), the

National Center for Health Statistics (Department of Health and Human Services), and the Bureau of Labor Statistics (Department of Labor). Among the other statistical agencies producing data of value to the applied demographer are the National Agricultural Statistics Service (Department of Agriculture), the Economic Research Service (Department of Agriculture), the National Center for Education Statistics (Department of Education), the Bureau of Economic Analysis (Department of Commerce), the Bureau of Justice Statistics (Department of Justice), and the Bureau of Transportation Statistics (Department of Transportation). In addition to the nine statistical agencies named, some administrative agencies have important statistical units, such as the Office of Research and Statistics of the Social Security Administration, the Statistics of Income Division of the Internal Revenue Service (Department of the Treasury) and the Statistics Branch of the Immigration and Naturalization Service (Department of Justice). Most federal agencies engage in some statistical activities or support statistical activities in other agencies. For example, the Administration on Aging has a statistical unit and the National Institutes of Health support statistical work in other federal agencies as well as in private organizations.

Bureau of the Census: Population and Housing Censuses

As the single largest producer of primary demographic data, the U.S. Bureau of the Census is given major attention in this book. The other agencies, though they may also be important producers of primary data, have a far more narrow subject focus and hence are covered in much less detail. The Census Bureau ranks first in the demographic importance of its data, their volume, their historical continuity, and the scope of the subject matter. In fiscal year, 1995–1996, the activities of the Census Bureau represented more than a quarter of the total estimated federal expenditures for statistical programs. In that year, the Census Bureau received $294 million in direct funding from the Congress out of a total of $1106 million appropriated to the principal federal statistical agencies.[1]

The Bureau of the Census takes the Censuses of Population and Housing every 10 years. The census serves many purposes. First and foremost, it provides the population counts needed to apportion seats among the states in the U.S. House of Representatives. This is a Constitutional requirement. The Bureau of the Census provides the national and subnational data used to serve many critical needs during the decade following the census and later. Federal uses include allocating funds appropriated under federal grant programs, identifying areas requiring child assistance programs, enforcing fair lending practices, determining compliance with the Voting Rights Act and its amendments, and assessing the need for Equal Employment Opportunity programs. State and local governments require census data to delineate federal congressional districts, state legislative districts, and local legislative bodies, develop social service programs, analyze commuting patterns and plan transportation systems, plan school district boundaries and school construction programs, and for many related purposes. Academic researchers use the data for the analysis of population growth and social and economic trends. Business organizations need the census to assess the adequacy of labor pools, select sites for new plants, and select areas and populations for marketing goods and services. Similarly, other private organizations need the census data to develop programs and policies, implement them, and evaluate the results of their programs.

The decennial Census of Population has a strong legal basis. The Constitution of the United States and Title 13 of the U.S. Code constitute the principal legal instruments governing the operation of the Census Bureau.[2] The framers of the Constitution wrote a requirement for a census into the document as a basis for apportioning the Congress of the United States among the states. Article I, Section 2, of the Constitution states:

> The actual enumeration shall be made within three years after the first meeting of the Congress of the United States, and within every subsequent term of ten years in such manner as they shall by law direct.

Since the first census was taken in 1790, as mandated, the legal obligations of the federal government, particularly the Census Bureau, to collect and compile data have expanded immensely. Now, at the beginning of the 21st century, the Census Bureau conducts censuses and surveys authorized by law on a wide variety of subjects. Title 13 of the U.S. Code spells out the specific authority not only for the decennial census of population, but also for censuses of housing, governments, and agriculture, and several economic censuses. Title 13 also states that the Secretary of Commerce may "make surveys deemed necessary to furnish annual and other interim current data on the subjects covered by the censuses."

A significant portion of the work performed by the Census Bureau is done for other agencies of the federal government and is carried out under the authority of Title 31, Section 686, of the U.S. Code. This law permits federal departments and agencies to exchange services with one another and to pay the corresponding costs.

Some Issues in Taking the Population and Housing Censuses in 2000

The congressional committee overseeing the programs of the Census Bureau criticized the 1990 census on the grounds that it cost too much and its quality was unacceptably low. The cost of the decennial census has exploded over the past several decades. It grew from $250 thousand in 1970 to $1 billion in 1980 to $2.6 billion in 1990. Only a small part of the massive increase between 1980 and 1990 can be explained by population increase and price inflation. The prolongation of the field operations, needed in order to complete the census, appears to have been a major contributor to the runaway cost. The 1990 census was also faulted for having a large undercount—larger than in 1980—and, especially, for showing larger differences in undercount levels between the races than in 1980. In 1990 the estimated overall net undercount was 1.8%, and the estimated black and nonblack net undercounts were 5.7% and 1.3%, respectively.[3] Chapter 4 discusses census errors in greater detail.

The high cost of the 1990 census and the perception of its poor quality instigated a congressional demand that the Census Bureau find ways of conducting a more economical and more accurate census in 2000. Given the Constititutional requirement that an enumeration be taken once every 10 years to apportion the Congress among the states, the simplest alternative to the present census procedure is a mere head count without the accompanying battery of questions on the characteristics of the population and their housing. The general structure of the census calls for asking merely a handful of questions of everyone in the population but a large array of questions of only one in six households. There is a widespread but unsupported belief that simplifying the census in the way suggested would contribute to a much more economical and a much more complete count. To comply with Public Law 94-171, however, most of the present group of six to eight 100% (or nonsample) questions would have to be included in the census. This federal law requires the U.S. Census Bureau to make available census data on the total and voting-age population (i.e., 18 years and over) for race/Hispanic groups for areas as small as blocks to state governments at their request. It supports Supreme Court decisions mandating certain guidelines regarding the delineation of legislative districts, including congressional districts.

A census of the population conducted merely to obtain the counts needed for apportionment of the Congress would expend much of the money and effort needed to conduct an expanded census, such as was taken in 1990. The basic census operations, such as the development of complete and verified address lists, comprehensive geographic files, hiring and deployment of a large army of temporary employees, and processing of the questionnaires, would still have to be carried out. Research conducted by the Census Bureau shows that the incremental cost of asking the additional questions is substantial, but far below the cost of the basic census. Moreover, all the questions in the 2000 census fill a legislative mandate for data on the subject.

Inevitably an abbreviated census would still be incomplete. In the past, this fact has given rise to a demand that the census be adjusted to include the estimated population that was missed. Efforts to compel the Census Bureau to make such an adjustment by court action have consistently failed. For the 2000 census, the Census Bureau favored such an adjustment. Its plan was to develop a single integrated count, representing a combination of the count based directly on the field enumeration and estimates of persons not counted, to be derived by matching of special post-enumeration samples with the census records.

To improve the method of taking the 2000 census, the Census Bureau carried out various tests of alternative procedures. Specifically, in the 1995 procedural test, three long forms (i.e., the forms containing sample questions) of different lengths were tested, sample follow-up of nonresponses and of incomplete responses was undertaken at an early stage, and a special post-enumeration survey was employed for matching with the census lists in the attempt to estimate the number and characteristics of persons omitted or counted erroneously. A **post-enumeration survey** is a survey of a representative sample of the population following the census for purposes of evaluation or adjustment of the census count. The plan of the Census Bureau for 2000 was to count *at least* 90% of the households in each census tract (i.e., small areas within counties) and then conduct a special post-enumeration survey, designated the Integrated Coverage Measurement Survey, to develop an estimate of the remainder of the population. The program was called the **Integrated Cov-**

erage Measurement Program. The program would involve a limited follow-up of nonrespondents in the census in order to achieve the 90% initial coverage for census tracts. Then, the basic field count would be supplemented by use of the special post-enumeration survey. The survey would consist of a representative sample of blocks. Persons listed in the Integrated Coverage Measurement Survey would be matched to persons listed in the original count, and persons listed in the survey but not matched would become the basis of estimates of persons to be added to the count in every block and census tract. Another sample, this one taken from the original census, would probe for duplications in the original count.

Throughout the years that this census design was being tested, there was strong political opposition in the U.S. Congress to this use of sampling to obtain the final census count. The Republican-dominated Congress passed a bill prohibiting the use of sampling until the Supreme Court ruled on its constitutionality. Following an appeal to the Supreme Court by the U.S. Department of Commerce, the Court ruled against the use of sampling as a means of supplementing the census count for apportionment purposes (*Department of Commerce v. House of Representatives*, 1999). Other legal and technical aspects of this dispute are described in Chapter 12.

Choices and Final Plans for the Year 2000 Census

The possible choices considered up to 1998 as available to the Census Bureau for conducting the year 2000 population census ranged from repeating the past practice (i.e., conducting a conventional census) to carrying out the Integrated Coverage Measurement Program, and from employing the long form, perhaps with fewer questions, to eliminating the long form and resorting to **continuous measurement**, a program of continuing sample surveys.[4] Various legislative proposals have been made with regard to the treatment of the census long form, for example, to decouple the long form and the short form, to eliminate the long form and resort to continuous measurement, and to retain the procedure of 1990.

As of early 2000, the Census Bureau plans to repeat the procedure of 1990 in carrying out the year 2000 census since it could not secure support from the Congress for the Integrated Coverage Measurement Program and the Supreme Court has ruled against the adjustment of the data for apportionment of the Congress. To replace the Integrated Coverage Measurement Survey, it will conduct the **Accuracy and Coverage Evaluation Survey**. This survey will serve both as a basis for evaluating the coverage of the census and as a basis for preparing adjusted figures, which will be made available to states for redistricting, allocation of funds, and other uses at their discretion. The Congress has already expressed its opposition to the use of adjusted figures in redistricting, and some states have already ruled against it. The form of the year 2000 census emerged out of a long tug-of-war between the White House (then Democrat controlled), the Congress (Republican controlled), and the courts, particularly the Supreme Court. The technical merits of the census plans and the independent judgment of the specialists at the Census Bureau have had little influence. This is the first census where other branches of government have been intimately involved in the decision of how the census should be taken.

Subjects in the 1990 and 2000 Population and Housing Censuses

In 1990 a short (or 100%) form, containing seven population items and five housing items, was used to collect information for about 83% of the population (i.e., five out of six housing units). A long (or sample) form, containing the short-form items and a large number of other demographic, social, economic, and housing items, was used to collect information for the remaining 17% of the population (i.e., one out of six housing units). The long form contained 26 population items and 19 housing items. The short-form population items were as follows:

Name	Race
Relationship to the reference person	Hispanic origin
Sex	Marital status
Date of birth/age	

The long-form items included the following:

State or country of birth	Military service
Citizenship	Labor force participation
Year of immigration	Hours worked
School attendance	Unemployment
Years of school completed	Occupation and industry
Ancestry or ethnic origin	Class of worker
Residence 5 years ago	Place of work
Language spoken at home	Commuting experience
Knowledge of English	Year last worked
Children ever born	Work status last year
Disability	Income

In connection with the planning of the 2000 census, a review of the needs for census data, both with respect to subjects and geographic areas, by users of all kinds was conducted. As a result, the 2000 census questionnaire emerged with essentially the same content and design as in 1990. Only a few changes were made in the items on population; there were more extensive changes in the housing items. Overall, the following changes in questionnaire content were made. Five subjects were removed from the short form and shifted to the long form: one population item (i.e., marital status) and four housing items (i.e., units in structure, number of rooms, value of home, and monthly rent). Children ever born, source of water, sewage disposal, and condominium status—all long-form items in 1990—were dropped from the census and year last worked was abbreviated. As a result of these and related changes, the short form in the 2000 census contains six population items and one housing item (tenure). One item has been added on the long form, called for by recent welfare reform legislation, namely, responsibility of grandparents for care of grandchildren in their home. In total, the census contains 54 subjects including the housing items and counting only the main questions (i.e., not the parts of questions), 7 on the short form and 47 on the long form. The population items number 6 and 26 on these forms, respectively. An abbreviated copy of the short-form and long-form questionnaires employed for the 2000 Population and Housing Censuses are shown as Figures 3.1a and 3.1b.

The items in these censuses can be divided into three groups on the basis of federal legislative and programmatic needs (Figure 3.2).[5]

United States
Census 2000

U.S. Department of Commerce • Bureau of the Census

This is the official form for all the people at this address. It is quick and easy, and your answers are protected by law. Complete the Census and help your community get what it needs — today and in the future!

Start Here
Please use a black or blue pen.

1. How many people were living or staying in this house, apartment, or mobile home on April 1, 2000?

[ ] Number of people

INCLUDE in this number:
- foster children, roomers, or housemates
- people staying here on April 1, 2000 who have no other permanent place to stay
- people living here most of the time while working, even if they have another place to live

DO NOT INCLUDE in this number:
- college students living away while attending college
- people in a correctional facility, nursing home, or mental hospital on April 1, 2000
- Armed Forces personnel living somewhere else
- people who live or stay at another place most of the time

2. Is this house, apartment, or mobile home — *Mark ☐ ONE box.*
- ☐ Owned by you or someone in this household with a mortgage or loan?
- ☐ Owned by you or someone in this household free and clear (without a mortgage or loan)?
- ☐ Rented for cash rent?
- ☐ Occupied without payment of cash rent?

3. Please answer the following questions for each person living in this house, apartment, or mobile home. Start with the name of one of the people living here who owns, is buying, or rents this house, apartment, or mobile home. If there is no such person, start with any adult living or staying here. We will refer to this person as Person 1.

What is this person's name? *Print name below.*

Last Name

First Name   MI

OMB No. 0607-0856: Approval Expires 12/31/2000

Form **D-61A**

4. What is Person 1's telephone number? *We may call this person if we don't understand an answer.*

Area Code + Number

5. What is Person 1's sex? *Mark ☐ ONE box.*
- ☐ Male   ☐ Female

6. What is Person 1's age and what is Person 1's date of birth?

Age on April 1, 2000

Print numbers in boxes
Month   Day   Year of birth

NOTE: Please answer BOTH Questions 7 and 8.

7. Is Person 1 Spanish/Hispanic/Latino? *Mark ☐ the "No" box if not Spanish/Hispanic/Latino.*
- ☐ **No,** not Spanish/Hispanic/Latino   ☐ Yes, Puerto Rican
- ☐ Yes, Mexican, Mexican Am., Chicano   ☐ Yes, Cuban
- ☐ Yes, other Spanish/Hispanic/Latino — *Print group.*

8. What is Person 1's race? *Mark ☐ one or more races to indicate what this person considers himself/herself to be.*
- ☐ White
- ☐ Black, African Am., or Negro
- ☐ American Indian or Alaska Native — *Print name of enrolled or principal tribe.*

- ☐ Asian Indian   ☐ Japanese   ☐ Native Hawaiian
- ☐ Chinese   ☐ Korean   ☐ Guamanian or Chamorro
- ☐ Filipino   ☐ Vietnamese   ☐ Samoan
- ☐ Other Asian — *Print race.*   ☐ Other Pacific Islander — *Print race.*

- ☐ Some other race — *Print race.*

If more people live here, continue with Person 2.

FIGURE 3.1a Short form for U.S. Censuses of Population and Housing, 2000.

Person 2

Your answers are important! Every person in the Census counts.

1. What is Person 2's name? *Print name below.*
Last Name

First Name   MI

2. How is this person related to Person 1? *Mark* ☐ *ONE box.*
- ☐ Husband/wife
- ☐ Natural-born son/daughter
- ☐ Adopted son/daughter
- ☐ Stepson/stepdaughter
- ☐ Brother/sister
- ☐ Father/mother
- ☐ Grandchild
- ☐ Parent-in-law
- ☐ Son-in-law/daughter-in-law
- ☐ Other relative — *Print exact relationship.*

If NOT RELATED to Person 1:
- ☐ Roomer, boarder
- ☐ Housemate, roommate
- ☐ Unmarried partner
- ☐ Foster child
- ☐ Other nonrelative

3. What is this person's sex? *Mark* ☐ *ONE box.*
- ☐ Male   ☐ Female

4. What is this person's age and what is this person's date of birth? *Print numbers in boxes.*
Age on April 1, 2000   Month   Day   Year of birth

NOTE: Please answer BOTH Questions 5 and 6.

5. Is this person Spanish/Hispanic/Latino? *Mark* ☐ *the "No" box if* **not** *Spanish/Hispanic/Latino.*
- ☐ **No,** not Spanish/Hispanic/Latino
- ☐ Yes, Mexican, Mexican Am., Chicano
- ☐ Yes, other Spanish/Hispanic/Latino — *Print group.*
- ☐ Yes, Puerto Rican
- ☐ Yes, Cuban

6. What is this person's race? *Mark* ☐ *one or more races* to indicate what this person considers himself/herself to be.
- ☐ White
- ☐ Black, African Am., or Negro
- ☐ American Indian or Alaska Native — *Print name of enrolled or principal tribe.*

- ☐ Asian Indian
- ☐ Chinese
- ☐ Filipino
- ☐ Other Asian — *Print race.*
- ☐ Japanese
- ☐ Korean
- ☐ Vietnamese
- ☐ Native Hawaiian
- ☐ Guamanian or Chamorro
- ☐ Samoan
- ☐ Other Pacific Islander — *Print race.*

- ☐ Some other race — *Print race.*

If more people live here, continue with Person 3.

Person 3

Census information helps your community get financial assistance for roads, hospitals, schools, and more.

1. What is Person 3's name? *Print name below.*
Last Name

First Name   MI

2. How is this person related to Person 1? *Mark* ☐ *ONE box.*
- ☐ Husband/wife
- ☐ Natural-born son/daughter
- ☐ Adopted son/daughter
- ☐ Stepson/stepdaughter
- ☐ Brother/sister
- ☐ Father/mother
- ☐ Grandchild
- ☐ Parent-in-law
- ☐ Son-in-law/daughter-in-law
- ☐ Other relative — *Print exact relationship.*

If NOT RELATED to Person 1:
- ☐ Roomer, boarder
- ☐ Housemate, roommate
- ☐ Unmarried partner
- ☐ Foster child
- ☐ Other nonrelative

3. What is this person's sex? *Mark* ☐ *ONE box.*
- ☐ Male   ☐ Female

4. What is this person's age and what is this person's date of birth? *Print numbers in boxes.*
Age on April 1, 2000   Month   Day   Year of birth

NOTE: Please answer BOTH Questions 5 and 6.

5. Is this person Spanish/Hispanic/Latino? *Mark* ☐ *the "No" box if* **not** *Spanish/Hispanic/Latino.*
- ☐ **No,** not Spanish/Hispanic/Latino
- ☐ Yes, Mexican, Mexican Am., Chicano
- ☐ Yes, other Spanish/Hispanic/Latino — *Print group.*
- ☐ Yes, Puerto Rican
- ☐ Yes, Cuban

6. What is this person's race? *Mark* ☐ *one or more races* to indicate what this person considers himself/herself to be.
- ☐ White
- ☐ Black, African Am., or Negro
- ☐ American Indian or Alaska Native — *Print name of enrolled or principal tribe.*

- ☐ Asian Indian
- ☐ Chinese
- ☐ Filipino
- ☐ Other Asian — *Print race.*
- ☐ Japanese
- ☐ Korean
- ☐ Vietnamese
- ☐ Native Hawaiian
- ☐ Guamanian or Chamorro
- ☐ Samoan
- ☐ Other Pacific Islander — *Print race.*

- ☐ Some other race — *Print race.*

If more people live here, continue with Person 4.

FIGURE 3.1a (*Continued*)

Persons 7 – 12

If you didn't have room to list everyone who lives in this house or apartment, please list the others below. *You may be contacted by the Census Bureau for the same information about these people.*

Person 7 — Last Name

First Name   MI

Person 8 — Last Name

First Name   MI

Person 9 — Last Name

First Name   MI

Person 10 — Last Name

First Name   MI

Person 11 — Last Name

First Name   MI

Person 12 — Last Name

First Name   MI

The Census Bureau estimates that, for the average household, this form will take about 10 minutes to complete, including the time for reviewing the instructions and answers. Comments about the estimate should be directed to the Associate Director for Finance and Administration, Attn: Paperwork Reduction Project 0607-0856, Room 3104, Federal Building 3, Bureau of the Census, Washington, DC 20233.

Respondents are not required to respond to any information collection unless it displays a valid approval number from the Office of Management and Budget.

Thank you for completing your official U.S. Census 2000 form.

The "Informational Copy" shows the content of the United States Census 2000 "short" form questionnaire. Each household will receive either a short form (100-percent questions) or a long form (100-percent and sample questions). The short form questionnaire contains 6 population questions and 1 housing question. On average, about 5 in every 6 households will receive the short form. The content of the forms resulted from reviewing the 1990 census data, consulting with federal and non-federal data users, and conducting tests.

For additional information about Census 2000, visit our website at **www.census.gov** or write to the Director, Bureau of the Census, Washington, DC 20233.

FOR OFFICE USE ONLY

| **A.** JIC1 | **B.** JIC2 | **C.** JIC3 | **D.** JIC4 |

FIGURE 3.1a (*Continued*)

United States
Census 2000

U.S. Department of Commerce
Bureau of the Census

This is the official form for all the people at this address. It is quick and easy, and your answers are protected by law. Complete the Census and help your community get what it needs — today and in the future!

The "Informational Copy" shows the content of the United States Census 2000 "long" form questionnaire. Each household will receive either a short form (100-percent questions) or a long form (100-percent and sample questions). The long form questionnaire includes the same 6 population questions and 1 housing question that are on the Census 2000 short form, plus 26 additional population questions, and 20 additional housing questions. On average, about 1 in every 6 households will receive the long form. The content of the forms resulted from reviewing the 1990 census data, consulting with federal and non-federal data users, and conducting tests.

For additional information about Census 2000, visit our website at **www.census.gov** or write to the Director, Bureau of the Census, Washington, DC 20233.

Start Here
Please use a black or blue pen.

1 How many people were living or staying in this house, apartment, or mobile home on April 1, 2000?

Number of people

INCLUDE in this number:
- foster children, roomers, or housemates
- people staying here on April 1, 2000 who have no other permanent place to stay
- people living here most of the time while working, even if they have another place to live

DO NOT INCLUDE in this number:
- college students living away while attending college
- people in a correctional facility, nursing home, or mental hospital on April 1, 2000
- Armed Forces personnel living somewhere else
- people who live or stay at another place most of the time

Please turn the page and print the names of all the people living or staying here on April 1, 2000.

If you need help completing this form, call 1–800–XXX–XXXX between 8:00 a.m. and 9:00 p.m., 7 days a week. The telephone call is free.

TDD – Telephone display device for the hearing impaired. Call 1–800–XXX–XXXX between 8:00 a.m. and 9:00 p.m., 7 days a week. The telephone call is free.

¿NECESITA AYUDA? Si usted necesita ayuda para completar este cuestionario llame al 1–800–XXX–XXXX entre las 8:00 a.m. y las 9:00 p.m., 7 días a la semana. La llamada telefónica es gratis.

The Census Bureau estimates that, for the average household, this form will take about 38 minutes to complete, including the time for reviewing the instructions and answers. Comments about the estimate should be directed to the Associate Director for Finance and Administration, Attn: Paperwork Reduction Project 0607-0856, Room 3104, Federal Building 3, Bureau of the Census, Washington, DC 20233.

Respondents are not required to respond to any information collection unless it displays a valid approval number from the Office of Management and Budget.

OMB No. 0607-0856: Approval Expires 12/31/2000

Form **D-61B**

FIGURE 3.1b Long form for U.S. Censuses of Population and Housing, 2000.

List of Persons

Please be sure you answered question 1 on the front page before continuing.

2 Please print the names of all the people who you indicated in question 1 were living or staying here on April 1, 2000.

Example — Last Name

J O H N S O N

First Name   MI

R O B I N   J

Start with the person, or one of the people living here who owns, is buying, or rents this house, apartment, or mobile home. If there is no such person, start with any adult living or staying here.

Person 1 — Last Name

First Name   MI

Person 2 — Last Name

First Name   MI

Person 3 — Last Name

First Name   MI

Person 4 — Last Name

First Name   MI

Person 5 — Last Name

First Name   MI

Person 6 — Last Name

First Name   MI

Person 7 — Last Name

First Name   MI

Person 8 — Last Name

First Name   MI

Person 9 — Last Name

First Name   MI

Person 10 — Last Name

First Name   MI

Person 11 — Last Name

First Name   MI

Person 12 — Last Name

First Name   MI

● Next, answer questions about Person 1.

FOR OFFICE USE ONLY			
A. JIC1	**B. JIC2**	**C. JIC3**	**D. JIC4**

Form D-61B

2

FIGURE 3.1b *(Continued)*

Person 1

Your answers are important! Every person in the Census counts.

1 What is this person's name? *Print the name of Person 1 from page 2.*

Last Name

First Name   MI

2 What is this person's telephone number? *We may contact this person if we don't understand an answer.*

Area Code + Number

3 What is this person's sex? *Mark* ☐ *ONE box.*
☐ Male
☐ Female

4 What is this person's age and what is this person's date of birth?

Age on April 1, 2000

Print numbers in boxes.
Month   Day   Year of birth

NOTE: Please answer BOTH Questions 5 and 6.

5 Is this person Spanish/Hispanic/Latino? *Mark* ☐ *the "No" box if not Spanish/Hispanic/Latino.*
☐ **No**, not Spanish/Hispanic/Latino
☐ Yes, Mexican, Mexican Am., Chicano
☐ Yes, Puerto Rican
☐ Yes, Cuban
☐ Yes, other Spanish/Hispanic/Latino — *Print group.* ➚

6 What is this person's race? *Mark* ☐ *one or more races to indicate what this person considers himself/herself to be.*
☐ White
☐ Black, African Am., or Negro
☐ American Indian or Alaska Native — *Print name of enrolled or principal tribe.* ➚

☐ Asian Indian   ☐ Native Hawaiian
☐ Chinese   ☐ Guamanian or Chamorro
☐ Filipino
☐ Japanese   ☐ Samoan
☐ Korean   ☐ Other Pacific Islander — *Print race.* ➚
☐ Vietnamese
☐ Other Asian — *Print race.* ➚

☐ Some other race — *Print race.* ➚

7 What is this person's marital status?
☐ Now married
☐ Widowed
☐ Divorced
☐ Separated
☐ Never married

8 a. At any time since February 1, 2000, has this person attended regular school or college? *Include only nursery school or preschool, kindergarten, elementary school, and schooling which leads to a high school diploma or a college degree.*
☐ No, has not attended since February 1   *Skip to 9*
☐ Yes, public school, public college
☐ Yes, private school, private college

☞ Question is asked of all persons on the short (100-percent) and long (sample) forms.

FIGURE 3.1b *(Continued)*

Person 1 (continued)

8 b. What grade or level was this person attending?
Mark ☐ ONE box.

☐ Nursery school, preschool
☐ Kindergarten
☐ Grade 1 to grade 4
☐ Grade 5 to grade 8
☐ Grade 9 to grade 12
☐ College undergraduate years (freshman to senior)
☐ Graduate or professional school *(for example: medical, dental, or law school)*

9 What is the highest degree or level of school this person has COMPLETED? *Mark ☐ ONE box. If currently enrolled, mark the previous grade or highest degree received.*

☐ No schooling completed
☐ Nursery school to 4th grade
☐ 5th grade or 6th grade
☐ 7th grade or 8th grade
☐ 9th grade
☐ 10th grade
☐ 11th grade
☐ 12th grade, **NO DIPLOMA**
☐ **HIGH SCHOOL GRADUATE** — high school DIPLOMA or the equivalent *(for example: GED)*
☐ Some college credit, but less than 1 year
☐ 1 or more years of college, no degree
☐ Associate degree *(for example: AA, AS)*
☐ Bachelor's degree *(for example: BA, AB, BS)*
☐ Master's degree *(for example: MA, MS, MEng, MEd, MSW, MBA)*
☐ Professional degree *(for example: MD, DDS, DVM, LLB, JD)*
☐ Doctorate degree *(for example: PhD, EdD)*

10 What is this person's ancestry or ethnic origin?

(For example: Italian, Jamaican, African Am., Cambodian, Cape Verdean, Norwegian, Dominican, French Canadian, Haitian, Korean, Lebanese, Polish, Nigerian, Mexican, Taiwanese, Ukrainian, and so on.)

11 a. Does this person speak a language other than English at home?

☐ Yes
☐ No　*Skip to 12*

b. What is this language?

(For example: Korean, Italian, Spanish, Vietnamese)

c. How well does this person speak English?

☐ Very well
☐ Well
☐ Not well
☐ Not at all

12 Where was this person born?

☐ In the United States — *Print name of state.*

☐ Outside the United States — *Print name of foreign country, or Puerto Rico, Guam, etc.*

13 Is this person a CITIZEN of the United States?

☐ Yes, born in the United States　*Skip to 15a*
☐ Yes, born in Puerto Rico, Guam, the U.S. Virgin Islands, or Northern Marianas
☐ Yes, born abroad of American parent or parents
☐ Yes, a U.S. citizen by naturalization
☐ No, not a citizen of the United States

14 When did this person come to live in the United States? *Print numbers in boxes.*

Year

15 a. Did this person live in this house or apartment 5 years ago (on April 1, 1995)?

☐ Person is under 5 years old　*Skip to 33*
☐ Yes, this house　*Skip to 16*
☐ No, outside the United States — *Print name of foreign country, or Puerto Rico, Guam, etc., below; then skip to 16.*

☐ No, different house in the United States

Form D-61B

4

FIGURE 3.1b *(Continued)*

Person 1 (continued)

15 b. Where did this person live 5 years ago?

Name of city, town, or post office

[ ]

Did this person live inside the limits of the city or town?

☐ Yes
☐ No, outside the city/town limits

Name of county

[ ]

Name of state

[ ]

ZIP Code

[ ]

16 Does this person have any of the following long-lasting conditions:

	Yes	No
a. Blindness, deafness, or a severe vision or hearing impairment?	☐	☐
b. A condition that substantially limits one or more basic physical activities such as walking, climbing stairs, reaching, lifting, or carrying?	☐	☐

17 Because of a physical, mental, or emotional condition lasting 6 months or more, does this person have any difficulty in doing any of the following activities:

	Yes	No
a. Learning, remembering, or concentrating?	☐	☐
b. Dressing, bathing, or getting around inside the home?	☐	☐
c. (Answer if this person is 16 YEARS OLD OR OVER.) Going outside the home alone to shop or visit a doctor's office?	☐	☐
d. (Answer if this person is 16 YEARS OLD OR OVER.) Working at a job or business?	☐	☐

18 Was this person under 15 years of age on April 1, 2000?

☐ Yes   *Skip to 33*
☐ No

19 a. Does this person have any of his/her own grandchildren under the age of 18 living in this house or apartment?

☐ Yes
☐ No   *Skip to 20a*

b. Is this grandparent currently responsible for most of the basic needs of any grandchild(ren) under the age of 18 who live(s) in this house or apartment?

☐ Yes
☐ No   *Skip to 20a*

c. **How long has this grandparent been responsible for the(se) grandchild(ren)?** *If the grandparent is financially responsible for more than one grandchild, answer the question for the grandchild for whom the grandparent has been responsible for the longest period of time.*

☐ Less than 6 months
☐ 6 to 11 months
☐ 1 or 2 years
☐ 3 or 4 years
☐ 5 years or more

20 a. Has this person ever served on active duty in the U.S. Armed Forces, military Reserves, or National Guard? *Active duty does not include training for the Reserves or National Guard, but DOES include activation, for example, for the Persian Gulf War.*

☐ Yes, now on active duty
☐ Yes, on active duty in past, but not now
☐ No, training for Reserves or National Guard only   *Skip to 21*
☐ No, never served in the military   *Skip to 21*

b. **When did this person serve on active duty in the U.S. Armed Forces?** *Mark ☐ a box for EACH period in which this person served.*

☐ April 1995 or later
☐ August 1990 to March 1995 (including Persian Gulf War)
☐ September 1980 to July 1990
☐ May 1975 to August 1980
☐ Vietnam era (August 1964—April 1975)
☐ February 1955 to July 1964
☐ Korean conflict (June 1950—January 1955)
☐ World War II (September 1940—July 1947)
☐ Some other time

c. **In total, how many years of active-duty military service has this person had?**

☐ Less than 2 years
☐ 2 years or more

2045

Form D-61B

5

FIGURE 3.1b   *(Continued)*

Person 1 (continued)

21 LAST WEEK, did this person do ANY work for
either pay or profit? *Mark ☐ the "Yes" box even if the
person worked only 1 hour, or helped without pay in a
family business or farm for 15 hours or more, or was on
active duty in the Armed Forces.*

☐ Yes
☐ No   *Skip to 25a*

22 At what location did this person work LAST
WEEK? *If this person worked at more than one location,
print where he or she worked most last week.*

a. Address (Number and street name)

*(If the exact address is not known, give a description
of the location such as the building name or the nearest
street or intersection.)*

b. Name of city, town, or post office

**c. Is the work location inside the limits of that
city or town?**

☐ Yes
☐ No, outside the city/town limits

d. Name of county

e. Name of U.S. state or foreign country

f. ZIP Code

23 **a. How did this person usually get to work LAST
WEEK?** *If this person usually used more than one method
of transportation during the trip, mark ☐ the box of the
one used for most of the distance.*

☐ Car, truck, or van
☐ Bus or trolley bus
☐ Streetcar or trolley car
☐ Subway or elevated
☐ Railroad
☐ Ferryboat
☐ Taxicab
☐ Motorcycle
☐ Bicycle
☐ Walked
☐ Worked at home   *Skip to 27*
☐ Other method

● If "Car, truck, or van" is marked in 23a, go to 23b.
Otherwise, skip to 24a.

23 **b. How many people, including this person,
usually rode to work in the car, truck, or van
LAST WEEK?**

☐ Drove alone
☐ 2 people
☐ 3 people
☐ 4 people
☐ 5 or 6 people
☐ 7 or more people

24 **a. What time did this person usually leave home
to go to work LAST WEEK?**

[   ] ☐ a.m.   ☐ p.m.

**b. How many minutes did it usually take this
person to get from home to work LAST WEEK?**

Minutes

● Answer questions 25–26 for persons who did not
work for pay or profit last week. Others skip to 27.

25 **a. LAST WEEK, was this person on layoff from
a job?**

☐ Yes   *Skip to 25c*
☐ No

**b. LAST WEEK, was this person TEMPORARILY
absent from a job or business?**

☐ Yes, on vacation, temporary illness, labor
  dispute, etc.   *Skip to 26*
☐ No   *Skip to 25d*

**c. Has this person been informed that he or she
will be recalled to work within the next 6 months
OR been given a date to return to work?**

☐ Yes   *Skip to 25e*
☐ No

**d. Has this person been looking for work during
the last 4 weeks?**

☐ Yes
☐ No   *Skip to 26*

**e. LAST WEEK, could this person have started a
job if offered one, or returned to work if recalled?**

☐ Yes, could have gone to work
☐ No, because of own temporary illness
☐ No, because of all other reasons *(in school, etc.)*

26 When did this person last work, even for a
few days?

☐ 1995 to 2000
☐ 1994 or earlier, or never worked   *Skip to 31*

FIGURE 3.1b *(Continued)*

Person 1 (continued)

27 Industry or Employer — *Describe clearly this person's chief job activity or business last week. If this person had more than one job, describe the one at which this person worked the most hours. If this person had no job or business last week, give the information for his/her last job or business since 1995.*

a. For whom did this person work? *If now on active duty in the Armed Forces, mark ☐ this box and print the branch of the Armed Forces.* ☐

Name of company, business, or other employer

b. What kind of business or industry was this? *Describe the activity at location where employed. (For example: hospital, newspaper publishing, mail order house, auto repair shop, bank)*

c. Is this mainly — *Mark ☐ ONE box.*
☐ Manufacturing?
☐ Wholesale trade?
☐ Retail trade?
☐ Other (agriculture, construction, service, government, etc.)?

28 Occupation

a. What kind of work was this person doing? *(For example: registered nurse, personnel manager, supervisor of order department, auto mechanic, accountant)*

b. What were this person's most important activities or duties? *(For example: patient care, directing hiring policies, supervising order clerks, repairing automobiles, reconciling financial records)*

29 Was this person — *Mark ☐ ONE box.*
☐ Employee of a PRIVATE-FOR-PROFIT company or business or of an individual, for wages, salary, or commissions
☐ Employee of a PRIVATE NOT-FOR-PROFIT, tax-exempt, or charitable organization
☐ Local GOVERNMENT employee (city, county, etc.)
☐ State GOVERNMENT employee
☐ Federal GOVERNMENT employee
☐ SELF-EMPLOYED in own NOT INCORPORATED business, professional practice, or farm
☐ SELF-EMPLOYED in own INCORPORATED business, professional practice, or farm
☐ Working WITHOUT PAY in family business or farm

30 a. LAST YEAR, 1999, did this person work at a job or business at any time?
☐ Yes
☐ No   *Skip to 31*

b. How many weeks did this person work in 1999? *Count paid vacation, paid sick leave, and military service.*
Weeks

c. During the weeks WORKED in 1999, how many hours did this person usually work each WEEK?
Usual hours worked each WEEK

31 INCOME IN 1999 — *Mark ☐ the "Yes" box for each income source received during 1999 and enter the total amount received during 1999 to a maximum of $999,999. Mark ☐ the "No" box if the income source was not received. If net income was a loss, enter the amount and mark ☐ the "Loss" box next to the dollar amount.*

For income received jointly, report, if possible, the appropriate share for each person; otherwise, report the whole amount for only one person and mark ☐ the "No" box for the other person. If exact amount is not known, please give best estimate.

a. Wages, salary, commissions, bonuses, or tips from all jobs — *Report amount before deductions for taxes, bonds, dues, or other items.*
☐ Yes   Annual amount — Dollars
$ | | | .00
☐ No

b. Self-employment income from own nonfarm businesses or farm businesses, including proprietorships and partnerships — *Report NET income after business expenses.*
☐ Yes   Annual amount — Dollars
$ | | | .00   ☐ Loss
☐ No

Form D-61B

FIGURE 3.1b *(Continued)*

Person 1 (continued)

31 **c. Interest, dividends, net rental income, royalty income, or income from estates and trusts** — *Report even small amounts credited to an account.*

☐ Yes   Annual amount — *Dollars*

$ _____ .00   ☐ Loss

☐ No

d. Social Security or Railroad Retirement

☐ Yes   Annual amount — *Dollars*

$ _____ .00

☐ No

e. Supplemental Security Income (SSI)

☐ Yes   Annual amount — *Dollars*

$ _____ .00

☐ No

f. Any public assistance or welfare payments from the state or local welfare office

☐ Yes   Annual amount — *Dollars*

$ _____ .00

☐ No

g. Retirement, survivor, or disability pensions — *Do NOT include Social Security.*

☐ Yes   Annual amount — *Dollars*

$ _____ .00

☐ No

h. Any other sources of income received regularly such as Veterans' (VA) payments, unemployment compensation, child support, or alimony — *Do NOT include lump-sum payments such as money from an inheritance or sale of a home.*

☐ Yes   Annual amount — *Dollars*

$ _____ .00

☐ No

32 **What was this person's total income in 1999?** *Add entries in questions 31a—31h; subtract any losses. If net income was a loss, enter the amount and mark* ☐ *the "Loss" box next to the dollar amount.*

Annual amount — *Dollars*

☐ None   OR $ _____ .00   ☐ Loss

☞ Question is asked of all households on the short (100-percent) and long (sample) forms.

HOUSING QUESTIONS

● Now, please answer questions 33—53 about your household.

☞ **33** **Is this house, apartment, or mobile home —**

☐ Owned by you or someone in this household with a mortgage or loan?
☐ Owned by you or someone in this household free and clear (without a mortgage or loan)?
☐ Rented for cash rent?
☐ Occupied without payment of cash rent?

34 **Which best describes this building?** *Include all apartments, flats, etc., even if vacant.*

☐ A mobile home
☐ A one-family house detached from any other house
☐ A one-family house attached to one or more houses
☐ A building with 2 apartments
☐ A building with 3 or 4 apartments
☐ A building with 5 to 9 apartments
☐ A building with 10 to 19 apartments
☐ A building with 20 to 49 apartments
☐ A building with 50 or more apartments
☐ Boat, RV, van, etc.

35 **About when was this building first built?**

☐ 1999 or 2000
☐ 1995 to 1998
☐ 1990 to 1994
☐ 1980 to 1989
☐ 1970 to 1979
☐ 1960 to 1969
☐ 1950 to 1959
☐ 1940 to 1949
☐ 1939 or earlier

36 **When did this person move into this house, apartment, or mobile home?**

☐ 1999 or 2000
☐ 1995 to 1998
☐ 1990 to 1994
☐ 1980 to 1989
☐ 1970 to 1979
☐ 1969 or earlier

37 **How many rooms do you have in this house, apartment, or mobile home?** *Do NOT count bathrooms, porches, balconies, foyers, halls, or half-rooms.*

☐ 1 room   ☐ 6 rooms
☐ 2 rooms   ☐ 7 rooms
☐ 3 rooms   ☐ 8 rooms
☐ 4 rooms   ☐ 9 or more rooms
☐ 5 rooms

Form D-618

8

FIGURE 3.1b   (*Continued*)

Person 1 (continued)

38 How many bedrooms do you have; that is, how many bedrooms would you list if this house, apartment, or mobile home were on the market for sale or rent?

- ☐ No bedroom
- ☐ 1 bedroom
- ☐ 2 bedrooms
- ☐ 3 bedrooms
- ☐ 4 bedrooms
- ☐ 5 or more bedrooms

39 Do you have COMPLETE plumbing facilities in this house, apartment, or mobile home; that is, 1) hot and cold piped water, 2) a flush toilet, and 3) a bathtub or shower?

- ☐ Yes, have all three facilities
- ☐ No

40 Do you have COMPLETE kitchen facilities in this house, apartment, or mobile home; that is, 1) a sink with piped water, 2) a range or stove, and 3) a refrigerator?

- ☐ Yes, have all three facilities
- ☐ No

41 Is there telephone service available in this house, apartment, or mobile home from which you can both make and receive calls?

- ☐ Yes
- ☐ No

42 Which FUEL is used MOST for heating this house, apartment, or mobile home?

- ☐ Gas: from underground pipes serving the neighborhood
- ☐ Gas: bottled, tank, or LP
- ☐ Electricity
- ☐ Fuel oil, kerosene, etc.
- ☐ Coal or coke
- ☐ Wood
- ☐ Solar energy
- ☐ Other fuel
- ☐ No fuel used

43 How many automobiles, vans, and trucks of one-ton capacity or less are kept at home for use by members of your household?

- ☐ None
- ☐ 1
- ☐ 2
- ☐ 3
- ☐ 4
- ☐ 5
- ☐ 6 or more

44 Answer ONLY if this is a ONE-FAMILY HOUSE OR MOBILE HOME — All others skip to 45.

a. Is there a business (such as a store or barber shop) or a medical office on this property?

- ☐ Yes
- ☐ No

b. How many acres is this house or mobile home on?

- ☐ Less than 1 acre   *Skip to 45*
- ☐ 1 to 9.9 acres
- ☐ 10 or more acres

c. In 1999, what were the actual sales of all agricultural products from this property?

- ☐ None
- ☐ $1 to $999
- ☐ $1,000 to $2,499
- ☐ $2,500 to $4,999
- ☐ $5,000 to $9,999
- ☐ $10,000 or more

45 What are the annual costs of utilities and fuels for this house, apartment, or mobile home? *If you have lived here less than 1 year, estimate the annual cost.*

a. Electricity

Annual cost — *Dollars*

$ ⌶ ⌶ .00

OR

- ☐ Included in rent or in condominium fee
- ☐ No charge or electricity not used

b. Gas

Annual cost — *Dollars*

$ ⌶ ⌶ .00

OR

- ☐ Included in rent or in condominium fee
- ☐ No charge or gas not used

c. Water and sewer

Annual cost — *Dollars*

$ ⌶ ⌶ .00

OR

- ☐ Included in rent or in condominium fee
- ☐ No charge

d. Oil, coal, kerosene, wood, etc.

Annual cost — *Dollars*

$ ⌶ ⌶ .00

OR

- ☐ Included in rent or in condominium fee
- ☐ No charge or these fuels not used

FIGURE 3.1b   (*Continued*)

Person 1 (continued)

46 Answer ONLY if you PAY RENT for this house, apartment, or mobile home — All others skip to 47.

a. What is the monthly rent?

Monthly amount — *Dollars*

$ [ ] . [ ].00

b. Does the monthly rent include any meals?

☐ Yes
☐ No

47 Answer questions 47a—53 if you or someone in this household owns or is buying this house, apartment, or mobile home; otherwise, skip to questions for Person 2.

a. Do you have a mortgage, deed of trust, contract to purchase, or similar debt on THIS property?

☐ Yes, mortgage, deed of trust, or similar debt
☐ Yes, contract to purchase
☐ No   *Skip to 48a*

b. How much is your regular monthly mortgage payment on THIS property? *Include payment only on first mortgage or contract to purchase.*

Monthly amount — *Dollars*

$ [ ] . [ ].00

OR

☐ No regular payment required   *Skip to 48a*

c. Does your regular monthly mortgage payment include payments for real estate taxes on THIS property?

☐ Yes, taxes included in mortgage payment
☐ No, taxes paid separately or taxes not required

d. Does your regular monthly mortgage payment include payments for fire, hazard, or flood insurance on THIS property?

☐ Yes, insurance included in mortgage payment
☐ No, insurance paid separately or no insurance

48 **a. Do you have a second mortgage or a home equity loan on THIS property?** *Mark ☐ all boxes that apply.*

☐ Yes, a second mortgage
☐ Yes, a home equity loan
☐ No   *Skip to 49*

b. How much is your regular monthly payment on all second or junior mortgages and all home equity loans on THIS property?

Monthly amount — *Dollars*

$ [ ] . [ ].00

OR

☐ No regular payment required

49 **What were the real estate taxes on THIS property last year?**

Yearly amount — *Dollars*

$ [ ] . [ ].00

OR

☐ None

50 **What was the annual payment for fire, hazard, and flood insurance on THIS property?**

Annual amount — *Dollars*

$ [ ] . [ ].00

OR

☐ None

51 **What is the value of this property; that is, how much do you think this house and lot, apartment, or mobile home and lot would sell for if it were for sale?**

☐ Less than $10,000
☐ $10,000 to $14,999
☐ $15,000 to $19,999
☐ $20,000 to $24,999
☐ $25,000 to $29,999
☐ $30,000 to $34,999
☐ $35,000 to $39,999
☐ $40,000 to $49,999
☐ $50,000 to $59,999
☐ $60,000 to $69,999
☐ $70,000 to $79,999
☐ $80,000 to $89,999
☐ $90,000 to $99,999
☐ $100,000 to $124,999
☐ $125,000 to $149,999
☐ $150,000 to $174,999
☐ $175,000 to $199,999
☐ $200,000 to $249,999
☐ $250,000 to $299,999
☐ $300,000 to $399,999
☐ $400,000 to $499,999
☐ $500,000 to $749,999
☐ $750,000 to $999,999
☐ $1,000,000 or more

52 Answer ONLY if this is a CONDOMINIUM —

What is the monthly condominium fee?

Monthly amount — *Dollars*

$ [ ] . [ ].00

53 Answer ONLY if this is a MOBILE HOME —

a. Do you have an installment loan or contract on THIS mobile home?

☐ Yes
☐ No

b. What was the total cost for installment loan payments, personal property taxes, site rent, registration fees, and license fees on THIS mobile home and its site last year? *Exclude real estate taxes.*

Yearly amount — *Dollars*

$ [ ] . [ ].00

● **Are there more people living here? If yes, continue with Person 2.**

FIGURE 3.1b *(Continued)*

Person 2

Census information helps your community get financial assistance for roads, hospitals, schools and more.

① **What is this person's name?** *Print the name of Person 2 from page 2.*

Last Name

First Name   MI

☞ **②** **How is this person related to Person 1?**
Mark ☐ ONE box.

☐ Husband/wife
☐ Natural-born son/daughter
☐ Adopted son/daughter
☐ Stepson/stepdaughter
☐ Brother/sister
☐ Father/mother
☐ Grandchild
☐ Parent-in-law
☐ Son-in-law/daughter-in-law
☐ Other relative — *Print exact relationship.*

If NOT RELATED to Person 1:

☐ Roomer, boarder
☐ Housemate, roommate
☐ Unmarried partner
☐ Foster child
☐ Other nonrelative

☞ Question is asked of Persons 2–6 on the short (100-percent) and long (sample) forms.

For Person 2, repeat questions 3-32 of Person 1.

INFORMATIONAL COPY

2051

FIGURE 3.1b *(Continued)*

FIGURE 3.2   Comparison of 1990 and 2000 Census Subjects Classified by Federal Legislative Needs: (a) Population and (b) Housing

Mandatory subjects (M): Decennial census data about these subjects are specifically cited in legislation.

Required subjects (R): Data about these subjects are required (1) by law (although not specifically decennial census data), and decennial census data are the only source, or the source historically used or (2) to fill case law requirements imposed by the federal court system.

Programmatic subjects (P): Data about these subjects are used for program planning, implementation, and evaluation, or to provide legal evidence.

| | **(a) Population subjects** | | | | |
| | | 100% | | Sample | |
	Status in 1990	1990	2000	1990	2000
Mandatory in 2000					
Age	M	x	x	x	x
Sex	M	x	x	x	x
Relationship	M	x	x	x	x
Race	M	x	x	x	x
Hispanic origin	M	x	x	x	x
Marital status	M	x	([a])	x	x
Place of birth	M			x	x
Citizenship	M			x	x
Year of immigration	M			x	x
Education	M			x	x
Language spoken at home	M			x	x
Veteran status	M			x	x
Journey to work	M			x	x
Place of work	M			x	x
Income	M			x	x
Grandparents as caregivers	([b])			([b])	x
Required in 2000					
Ancestry	P			x	x
Disability	R			x	x
Residence 5 years ago	P			x	x
Labor force status	R			x	x
Industry	R			x	x
Occupation	R			x	x
Class of worker	R			x	x
Work status last year	P			x	x
Programmatic in 2000					
Children ever born	P			x	([c])
Year last worked[d]	P			x	([c])
	(b) Housing subjects				
Mandatory in 2000					
Rooms	M	x	([a])	x	
Tenure (owner or renter)	M	x	x	x	x
Farm residence	M			x	x
Vehicles available	M			x	x
Year structure built	M			x	x

(continues)

FIGURE 3.2 (*continued*)

	Status in 1990	100% 1990	2000	Sample 1990	2000
Required in 2000					
Units in structure	R	x	(^{a})	x	x
Value	P	x	(^{a})	x	x
Monthly rent	R	x	(^{a})	x	x
Bedrooms	R			x	x
Plumbing facilities	R			x	x
Kitchen facilities	R			x	x
Telephone	P			x	x
House heating fuel	R			x	x
Year moved into unit	R			x	x
Shelter costs (incl. utilities)	R			x	x
Programmatic in 2000					
Source af water	P			x	(^{c})
Sewage disposal	P			x	(^{c})
Condominium status	P			x	(^{c})

[a] Moved to sample in 2000.

[b] New in 2000.

[c] These subjects were not recommended for census 2000 because they do not have an explicit legislative requirement.

[d] An abbreviated screener question about work history was included with questions about industry, occupation, and class of worker in census 2000. This will aid in defining the "experienced labor force."

Source: Adapted from U.S. Bureau of the Census, Public Documents.

1. Mandatory items, for which decennial census data are specifically cited in legislation, such as age, marital status, income, tenure (i.e., owner or renter).[6]
2. Required items, for which data are required by law (although not specifically decennial census data) and for which decennial census data are the only source or the source historically used, such as disability, labor force status, and value (programmatic in 1990) or rent of housing unit.
3. Programmatic items, for which data are needed for program planning, implementation, or evaluation, or to provide legal evidence. All programmatic items of 1990 were required in 2000 (such as residence 5 years ago, ancestry, and work status last year) or eliminated (such as children ever born).

A few actual examples of the applications of census data may be given. The Special Supplemental Food Program for Women, Infants, and Children requires data on income (and several other census items) at the state and county levels. The Low-Income Energy Assistance Program requires data on house heating fuel and income for counties. The Older Americans Act uses data on migration (residence 5 years ago) at the zip code level to implement various programs. All of these programs are authorized in Title 42 of the U.S. Code. The question on grandparents as caregivers is based on the requirements of Public Law 104-193 and is designed to identify grandparents who have primary responsibility for the care of grandchildren in their home.

Race/Hispanic Origin Classification

Because of their pervasive impact on data tabulations and the uses of census data, the items on race and Hispanic origin on the census questionnaire have been selected for more detailed discussion here. As indicated earlier, race and Hispanic origin are both mandatory census items and have been carried on the census questionnaire as 100% (short-form) items. They are needed to fill the requirements of the Voting Rights Act, the Civil Rights Act, and other federal legislation. The data are widely used for programmatic purposes at all levels of government and in court contests relating to civil rights (e.g., workplace discrimination, access to banking services, voting rights), jury selection, and legislative redistricting. The data are used to measure allocations of funds for education, housing, and health research. Perhaps because of the use of the race/Hispanic origin data in so many adversarial contexts, much controversy has arisen with respect to the classification used in the official statistics on race and Hispanic origin.

The classification used was governed by the Office of Management and Budget (OMB) Directive 15 until 1997. This directive provided specific guidelines on terminology and classification of the races and Hispanic origin. Data on race and Hispanic origin in the 1990 census were tabulated in two forms, both consistent with OMB guidelines. The first tabulation classifies the races as white, black, American Indian (plus Eskimo and Aleut), and Asian and Pacific Islander.[7] As indicated by the 1990 census questionnaire, Asian and Pacific Islander includes various national-origin groups (e.g., Japanese, Chinese, Korean, Asian Indian, Filipino, and Hawaiian). The category, "some other race," was listed on the questionnaire but such responses were reassigned in part to one of the other racial groups where a national origin was named (except a Hispanic national origin). Persons of Hispanic origin include persons of Mexican, Puerto Rican, Cuban, or other Spanish origin, regardless of race. The second tabulation separates Hispanics and non-Hispanics and, by excluding Hispanics from each of the race categories (e.g., non-Hispanic whites, non-Hispanic blacks, etc.), represents a set of mutually exclusive race/Hispanic origin categories. Much data are presented in the census for the principal race/Hispanic-origin groups, but rather limited data are presented for the specific national-origin/race groups, the specific national-origin/Hispanic groups, and the Hispanic population in association with non-Hispanic segments of specific race groups.

In the decennial census and the surveys conducted by the Census Bureau currently, race is self-reported (i.e., the individual determines his or her own race). This is consistent with self-enumeration as the method of census taking. Under such circumstances, persons with some "black blood" and persons with some "American Indian blood" have tended to report themselves as black and American Indian, respectively. In censuses before self-enumeration was used, race was determined by observation made by a census enumerator. Nevertheless, for blacks these practices appear to have produced comparable results between censuses and between surveys. For American Indians, however, the data are not comparable from one census to the next because there has been a progressive tendency for respondents to prefer this category.[8] Massive misinterpetation of the race question by Hispanics led to a serious unstatement of whites and blacks in 1990 and 1980. A large share (about 40%) of Hispanics did not report one of the conventional races; rather, they reported "other race." To achieve greater consistency with data on race in prior censuses and in other collection systems (e.g., vital statistics registration), the Census Bureau has prepared and released adjusted race data for 1990 and 1980 for the nation and the states.[9]

Various criticisms have been made of the race/Hispanic-origin classification and the census-questionnaire design supporting it. It is argued that (1) the concepts of race and Hispanic origin cannot be logically and reliably separated, (2) people of mixed race have no way of indicating this fact on the questionnaire, (3) some national-origin groups should be listed separately or differently, and (4) the order of the questions prejudices the count of Hispanics. Accordingly, consideration has been given to various alternative designs for obtaining data on race and Hispanic origin. They include, among other more limited changes, combining the Hispanic-origin question and the race question into a single ethnic-origin question, adding to the race question a category "mixed race," allowing the respondent to check more than one race, and reversing the order of the two questions.

Many members of racial minorities and most Hispanics are, in fact, of mixed race as a result of racial intermarriage and interbreeding over a long period. Currently about one-third of Hispanics, largely Mexican-Americans, marry non-Hispanics; and a substantial share, between one-quarter and one-half, of Asian-Americans and American Indians marry persons of another racial group.[10]

The Office of Statistical Policy in the Office of Management and Budget (OMB) reviewed these issues with the intent of promulgating a new directive. Under its aegis, the Census Bureau and the Bureau of Labor Statistics tested various alternatives in the field during 1995 and 1996. These tests showed that relatively few persons reported themselves as of mixed race, whether by checking a separate mixed-race category or by checking more than one race category. They also showed that combining the questions on race and Hispanic origin did not provide the detailed data needed on race groups and Hispanic origin.

Following the tests, the OMB issued a Revised Directive 15 on the collection and classification of racial statistics that governs all statistical programs of the federal government and statistical reporting to the federal government by other public and private entities. Most important, the new standards are being used in the year 2000 census and must be adopted by all federal agencies by the end of the year 2002. Revised Directive 15 calls mainly for (1) retention of separate questions on race and Hispanic origin, as in the 1990 census; (2) placing the Hispanic-origin question before the race question in the 2000 census, in contrast to the practice in 1990; (3) allowing multiple responses to the race question, a rule also unlike that of 1990; and (4) separating the category Asian or Pacific Islander into two categories, Asian, and Native Hawaiian or Other Pacific Islander. A mixed race category would not be added, as many had proposed.

In sum, the new racial categories with the new name changes are as follows:

White
Black, African-American, or Negro
Asian
Native Hawaiian or other Pacific Islander
American Indian or Alaska Native
Some other race

For Hispanic ethnicity, the categories are Spanish/Hispanic/Latino, and Not Spanish/Hispanic/ Latino. As in 1990, the year 2000 census form lists a number of national-origin groups for Asian, Native Hawaiian or other Pacific Islander, and Hispanics. (See the extract of the Census 2000 form in Figure 3.1.) The Hispanic groups to be listed are Puerto Rican, Mexican/Mexican American/Chicano, Cuban, and other Spanish/Hispanic/Latino.

With regard to tabulations of the 2000 census data, the OMB has ruled that the total number reporting more than one race must be made available, whether by reporting all or a collapsed set of multiple-race combinations or by reporting the total for each race both alone and in combination with other races. The Census Bureau plans to display the figures for 63 race categories, representing those reporting single races (six basic race categories) and those reporting combinations of two or more races (57 categories).[11]

Accessing the 1990 and 2000 Population Censuses

The data from the 1990 population census were made available in seven forms: (1) printed reports, (2) computer tapes with tabulated data, (3) microfiche, (4) computer tapes with microdata samples, (5) compact disks, (6) flexible diskettes, and (7) online computer data transmission. Selected data were made available in each of these forms, and some data were made available in more than one form.

The printed data from the 1990 censuses were presented in three categories of reports: (1) reports presenting population data only (CP), (2) reports presenting housing data only (CH), and (3) reports presenting both population and housing data (CPH). The various reports within each category may be distinguished in large part by whether they present 100% data only (that is, data only on subjects asked of all persons), sample data only, or a combination of 100% data and sample data. CP-1, CH-1, CPH-1, and CPH-2 present 100% data only; CP-2, CH-2, and CPH-5 present data on sample subjects only; and CPH-3 and CPH-4 present data on both 100% subjects and sample subjects:

	Printed reports
CP	Population data only
	CP-1 100% data only
	CP-2 Sample data
CH	Housing data only
	CH-1 100% data only
	CH-2 Sample data
CPH	Population and housing data
	CPH-1 and CPH-2 100% data only
	CPH-3 and CPH-4 100% and sample data
	CPH-5 Sample data

Computer tapes with tabulated data include summary tape files (STFs), Public Law 94-171 counts (i.e., Redistricting Data File), the Equal Employment Opportunity Special File, and the TIGER/Line files (geographic files). Other 1990 census machine-readable products include microfiche,[12] public-use microdata samples (PUMS) on computer tapes; compact disks (CD-ROM— compact disks-read only memory),[13] and CENSTATS, the Census Bureau's online system of computer data transmission.

Summary tape files (STF) 1A, 1B, and 1C contain detailed population and housing data based on the (100%) census short form, while STF 3A, 3B, and 3C are derived from data collected on the (sample) census long form:

Summary tape files: Population and housing data

100% data	Sample data
1A	3A
1B	3B
1C	3C

The various lettered segments differ in the geographic detail provided.[14]

CD-ROMs permit access to large databases on personal computers. The 1990 Census of Population and Housing has been released on several series of CD-ROMs with data at all geographic levels from the nation down to individual blocks. To use CD-ROMs, in addition to a personal computer, a CD-ROM reader (D-drive on the computer) and some applications software, which may be included on the disk, are needed.

With a PUMS tape, the researcher can design his or her own tabulations, subject to geographic restrictions and sampling error. PUMS provide original census data for individuals, after the identifying personal information has been deleted. The geographic identification in each tape is limited to a class of areas. PUMS tapes are available for 1% of the population (metropolitan areas) and 5% of the population (county groups).[15] Such tapes have been prepared for many prior censuses, making possible comparable historical tabulations on subjects of the user's interest.

The Census Bureau has also "gone on line" with many of its products; that is, they can be accessed by computer via the internet. CENSTATS is a quick alternative for accessing selected data from the STF tapes for the 50 states and the District of Columbia, all counties and places, and county subdivisions in selected states. The online data can be downloaded to create a file or they can be printed out.

The 2000 census data will also be released in several forms, including printed tables, summary files, public-use microdata sample (PUMS) files, CD-ROMs, and online transmission. All the data except the public-use microdata sample will be made available on the Internet. The principal reports, to be made available both in printed form and on the Internet, are as follows:

Title	Planned release date	Lowest geographic level
Summary: Population and Housing Characteristics	January–November 2002	Places
Population and Housing Unit Counts	2003	Places
Summary: Social, Economic, and Housing Characteristics	2003	Places

Source: U.S. Bureau of the Census, information sheet dated 9/00.

A variety of summary files, including a redistricting data summary file and Summary Files 1 to 4, provide 100% data and sample data:

> Summary File 1 (SF1): 100% data down to blocks
> Summary File 2 (SF2): 100% data down to census tracts
> Summary File 3 (SF3): Sample data down to block groups
> Summary File 4 (SF4): Sample data down to census tracts

All summary files will be made available both on the Internet and on CD-ROM.

There will be an electronic query system. American Factfinder will allow users to create and receive tabulations from the full microdata file via the Internet. It will enable the user to access the 1990 and the upcoming 2000 Censuses of Population and Housing (as well as the American Community Survey and the 1997 Economic Censuses). American Factfinder will enable the user to obtain population and housing data for any particular city, county, state, or congressional district as well as reference maps showing boundaries for a geographic area and thematic maps displaying statistical data. The URL is *www.factfinder.census.gov.*

All printed reports issued by the Census Bureau since January 1996 are available on the Census Bureau Web site (*www.census.gov*).[16] FERRET is another Internet tool, developed and supported by the U.S. Bureau of the Census in collaboration with the U.S. Bureau of Labor Statistics to provide users with specially tailored data based on microdata files (*www.bls.census.gov*). Appendix A presents a list of Internet sites for many leading sources of demographic data.

American Community Survey

In anticipation of eliminating the long form from future censuses, the Census Bureau has initiated the **American Community Survey** (ACS), a large sample survey covering both the short-form and the long-form questions. After it is fully operative in 2003, it will provide data for large and small areas over the entire country on a continuing basis The present plan is to conduct a large sample survey at the census date and then take **rolling sample surveys** throughout the decade. The large size of these sample surveys and the cumulation of data from several surveys would provide the desired data on a variety of subjects for the nation and areas within it. More specifically, for **continuous measurement** of the characteristics of the population, a survey of about 250,000 households would be taken monthly and the results would be averaged over several years in order to derive accurate results for small areas such as census tracts (small statistical subdivisions of counties).

After being tested at a series of experimental sites, the ACS would be extended to every county by 2003. From 2003 on, 3 million households would be selected for interview annually. When the full sample is included, the survey would provide annual data for all states and all other entities of 65,000 population or more. For smaller areas, 3-year averages would be taken. For areas under 20,000 population, such as census tracts, sample data would be cumulated for 5 years. As planned, the first census-tract statistics would be based on data collected in 2003–2007 and published in 2008. Under the plan, the long form employed in the past several decennial censuses would be eliminated in the 2010 census.

The implementation of the ACS will have a profound effect not only on federal and state statistical programs but on the programs for allocating funds to the states and local areas. Federal agencies will have a more efficient means of allocating funds authorized by Congress, and state agencies will be able to meet the needs of local areas for funds more efficiently. Cities will have more timely and accurate data on which to make determinations for road, school, and hospital construction, and private business will have more timely and accurate data for business planning. Additional types of data could be developed for local areas by the combination of data collected by various federal agencies and the data provided by the ACS. One obvious but not a serious shortcoming of the program is the indefinite reference date and time lag for much of the data.

National Center for Health Statistics

The National Center for Health Statistics (NCHS) is the principal source of comparable national, state, and county data on births, deaths, and fetal deaths. It is also the principal source of national data on the marriage, divorce, and health of the American population. Since the registration of vital events is a state function, the vital statistics (excluding health statistics) are obtained through state-administered registration systems. The NCHS secures copies of vital records from the registration offices of the states, the District of Columbia, and New York City (a separate registration area). Standard forms for the collection of the data and model procedures for the uniform registration of the events are developed and recommended for state use through cooperative activities of the states and the NCHS. Provisional data on births, deaths, marriages, and divorces are published monthly for the nation with a lag of about 9 months, and final data on births and deaths, including detailed tabulations, are published for a given year with a lag of about a year and half following the close of the reference year (*National Vital Statistics Reports*, formerly *Monthly Vital Statistics Report*). The NCHS also compiles national and state data on fetal deaths and induced terminations of pregnancy (abortions).

Comprehensive data on births, deaths, infant deaths, and fetal deaths for the nation, states, and counties, and national life tables, have been published for each year in sets of bound volumes (one on natality and two on mortality) since the establishment of the birth and death registration areas early in the 20th century (*Vital Statistics of the United States*). In recent years the volumes have been appearing with a considerable lag. The volumes for 1993 appeared in 1999. Because of budgetary restrictions, these will be the last in this series. Hereafter, the detailed tabulations can be obtained on the Internet or by special request from the NCHS. Public use tapes based on these data are available for sale from the NCHS. Bound volumes on marriages and divorces were published until 1988, but this series has been discontinued. The last annual marriage and divorce reports in the National Vital Statistics Reports series presenting comprehensive data appeared in 1990. National abridged life tables have been published annually since 1945, and national unabridged life tables for the death registration area were published decennially from 1900–1902 to 1989–1991. They are curently published annually (since 1998). Unabridged state life tables were published decennially from 1929–1931 to 1989–1991.

Certificates of birth, death, fetal death, and induced terminations of pregnancy contain a considerable amount of demographic and socioeconomic information. For example, information on age, race, Hispanic origin, educational level, and marital status of mother, and birth order and sex of child, as well as several characteristics of the father, is available on the birth certificate. It is furnished mainly by the mother. Information on pregnany history and the health condition of the newborn, shown on the birth certificate, comes from hospital records. Information on the age, sex, race, Hispanic origin, educational level, marital status, place of birth, military service, and usual occupation of the decedent is recorded on the death certificate by the funeral director in collaboration with the next of kin. Medical certification of cause of death is furnished by a physician or medical examiner. The report of fetal death contains similar information. Copies of the U.S. Standard Certificate of Live Birth, the Standard Certificate of Death, and the Report of Fetal Death, as revised in 1989, are shown as Figures 3.3a, 3.3b, and 3.3c. The standard certificates are revised decennially. The review and revision process is now under way and the new certificates will probably go into effect in 2003 or 2004.

The NCHS maintains a National Death Index, a continuing and cumulative computer database containing the records of all deaths reported in the United States since 1979. This file is available for research purposes only. The NCHS has also developed a Linked Birth/Infant Death File. As of the end of 1999, linked birth/infant death data sets for the birth cohorts of 1983 to 1991 and 1995 to 1998 are available. Finally, the NCHS sponsors several national sample surveys that mainly relate to the health of the population, enumerated here.

An important online source of data on mortality is the Web site of the Centers for Disease Control and Prevention. It makes available a number of data sets, including the Compressed Mortality File (CMF). This file has data for 1979 to 1997 on deaths and population for counties, with age, sex, race, and cause-of-death detail. The database permits the calculation of national, state, and county death rates for race/sex/age/cause-of-death groups of interest. The Web site for accessing these data is *www.wonder.cdc.gov.*

Immigration and Naturalization Service

The Immigration and Naturalization Service (INS) is the federal administrative agency that compiles and publishes data on immigation into the United States and on naturalizations. The basic data are presented in its *Statistical Yearbook of the Immigration and Naturalization Service* (formerly *Annual Report*). The INS also offers a public use tape from which special tabulations can be developed. The yearbook provides data on international admissions by type—that is, immigrants, nonimmigrants (i.e., temporary admissions), refugees, asylees, and parolees, and on naturalizations, apprehensions, and deportations. No direct data are currently available on emigrants (i.e., immigrants departing)

TYPE/PRINT IN PERMANENT BLACK INK FOR INSTRUCTIONS SEE HANDBOOK

CHILD

U.S. STANDARD
CERTIFICATE OF LIVE BIRTH

LOCAL FILE NUMBER   BIRTH NUMBER

1. CHILD'S NAME (First, Middle, Last)	2. DATE OF BIRTH (Month, Day, Year)	3. TIME OF BIRTH M

4. SEX	5. CITY, TOWN, OR LOCATION OF BIRTH	6. COUNTY OF BIRTH

7. PLACE OF BIRTH ☐ Hospital ☐ Freestanding Birthing Center
☐ Clinic/Doctor's Office ☐ Residence
☐ Other (Specify)___

8. FACILITY NAME (If not institution, give street and number)

CERTIFIER/ATTENDANT

DEATH UNDER ONE YEAR OF AGE Enter State File Number of death certificate for this child

9. I certify that this child was born alive at the place and time and on the date stated.
Signature ▶

10. DATE SIGNED (Month, Day, Year)

11. ATTENDANT'S NAME AND TITLE (If other than certifier) (Type/Print)
Name ___
☐ M D ☐ D O ☐ C N M ☐ Other Midwife
☐ Other (Specify)

12. CERTIFIER'S NAME AND TITLE (Type/Print)
Name ___
☐ M D ☐ D O ☐ Hospital Admin. ☐ C N M ☐ Other Midwife
☐ Other (Specify)

13. ATTENDANT'S MAILING ADDRESS (Street and Number or Rural Route Number, City or Town, State, Zip Code)

14. REGISTRAR'S SIGNATURE ▶

15. DATE FILED BY REGISTRAR (Month, Day, Year)

MOTHER

16a. MOTHER'S NAME (First, Middle, Last)	16b. MAIDEN SURNAME	17. DATE OF BIRTH (Month, Day, Year)

18. BIRTHPLACE (State or Foreign Country)	19a. RESIDENCE—STATE	19b. COUNTY	19c. CITY, TOWN, OR LOCATION

19d. STREET AND NUMBER	19e. INSIDE CITY LIMITS? (Yes or no)	20. MOTHER'S MAILING ADDRESS (If same as residence, enter Zip Code only)

FATHER

21. FATHER'S NAME (First, Middle, Last)	22. DATE OF BIRTH (Month, Day, Year)	23. BIRTHPLACE (State or Foreign Country)

INFORMANT

24. I certify that the personal information provided on this certificate is correct to the best of my knowledge and belief.
Signature of Parent or Other Informant ▶

INFORMATION FOR MEDICAL AND HEALTH USE ONLY

MOTHER
FATHER

25. OF HISPANIC ORIGIN? (Specify No or Yes—If yes, specify Cuban, Mexican, Puerto Rican, etc.)	26. RACE—American Indian, Black, White, etc. (Specify below)	27. EDUCATION (Specify only highest grade completed) Elementary/Secondary (0-12) College (1-4 or 5+)
25a. ☐ No ☐ Yes Specify:	26a.	27a.
25b. ☐ No ☐ Yes Specify:	26b.	27b.

MULTIPLE BIRTHS Enter State File Number for Mate(s) LIVE BIRTH(S)

FETAL DEATH(S)

28. PREGNANCY HISTORY (Complete each section)			29. MOTHER MARRIED? (At birth, conception, or any time between) (Yes or no)	30. DATE LAST NORMAL MENSES BEGAN (Month, Day, Year)
LIVE BIRTHS (Do not include this child)		OTHER TERMINATIONS (Spontaneous and induced at any time after conception)		
28a. Now Living	28b. Now Dead	28d.	31. MONTH OF PREGNANCY PRENATAL CARE BEGAN—First, Second, Third, etc. (Specify)	32. PRENATAL VISITS—Total Number (If none, so state)
Number ___ ☐ None	Number ___ ☐ None	Number ___ ☐ None	33. BIRTH WEIGHT (Specify unit)	34. CLINICAL ESTIMATE OF GESTATION (Weeks)
28c. DATE OF LAST LIVE BIRTH (Month, Year)		28e. DATE OF LAST OTHER TERMINATION (Month, Year)	35a. PLURALITY—Single, Twin, Triplet, etc. (Specify)	35b. IF NOT SINGLE BIRTH—Born First, Second, Third, etc. (Specify)

36. APGAR SCORE		37a. MOTHER TRANSFERRED PRIOR TO DELIVERY? ☐ No ☐ Yes If Yes, enter name of facility transferred from:
36a. 1 Minute	36b. 5 Minutes	37b. INFANT TRANSFERRED? ☐ No ☐ Yes If Yes, enter name of facility transferred to:

38a. MEDICAL RISK FACTORS FOR THIS PREGNANCY (Check all that apply)

Anemia (Hct. <30/Hgb. <10)	01 ☐
Cardiac disease	02 ☐
Acute or chronic lung disease	03 ☐
Diabetes	04 ☐
Genital herpes	05 ☐
Hydramnios/Oligohydramnios	06 ☐
Hemoglobinopathy	07 ☐
Hypertension, chronic	08 ☐
Hypertension, pregnancy-associated	09 ☐
Eclampsia	10 ☐
Incompetent cervix	11 ☐
Previous infant 4000+ grams	12 ☐
Previous preterm or small for gestational-age infant	13 ☐
Renal disease	14 ☐
Rh sensitization	15 ☐
Uterine bleeding	16 ☐
None	00 ☐
Other	17 ☐
(Specify)	

38b. OTHER RISK FACTORS FOR THIS PREGNANCY (Complete all items)

Tobacco use during pregnancy ... Yes ☐ No ☐
Average number cigarettes per day ___
Alcohol use during pregnancy ... Yes ☐ No ☐
Average number drinks per week ___
Weight gained during pregnancy ___ lbs.

38c. OBSTETRIC PROCEDURES (Check all that apply)

Amniocentesis	01 ☐
Electronic fetal monitoring	02 ☐
Induction of labor	03 ☐
Stimulation of labor	04 ☐
Tocolysis	05 ☐
Ultrasound	06 ☐
None	00 ☐
Other	07 ☐
(Specify)	

40. COMPLICATIONS OF LABOR AND/OR DELIVERY (Check all that apply)

Febrile (>100°F. or 38°C.)	01 ☐
Meconium, moderate/heavy	02 ☐
Premature rupture of membrane (>12 hours)	03 ☐
Abruptio placenta	04 ☐
Placenta previa	05 ☐
Other excessive bleeding	06 ☐
Seizures during labor	07 ☐
Precipitous labor (<3 hours)	08 ☐
Prolonged labor (>20 hours)	09 ☐
Dysfunctional labor	10 ☐
Breech/Malpresentation	11 ☐
Cephalopelvic disproportion	12 ☐
Cord prolapse	13 ☐
Anesthetic complications	14 ☐
Fetal distress	15 ☐
None	00 ☐
Other	16 ☐
(Specify)	

41. METHOD OF DELIVERY (Check all that apply)

Vaginal	01 ☐
Vaginal birth after previous C-section	02 ☐
Primary C-section	03 ☐
Repeat C-section	04 ☐
Forceps	05 ☐
Vacuum	06 ☐

42. ABNORMAL CONDITIONS OF THE NEWBORN (Check all that apply)

Anemia (Hct. <39/Hgb. <13)	01 ☐
Birth injury	02 ☐
Fetal alcohol syndrome	03 ☐
Hyaline membrane disease/RDS	04 ☐
Meconium aspiration syndrome	05 ☐
Assisted ventilation <30 min	06 ☐
Assisted ventilation ≥30 min	07 ☐
Seizures	08 ☐
None	00 ☐
Other	09 ☐
(Specify)	

43. CONGENITAL ANOMALIES OF CHILD (Check all that apply)

Anencephalus	01 ☐
Spina bifida/Meningocele	02 ☐
Hydrocephalus	03 ☐
Microcephalus	04 ☐
Other central nervous system anomalies (Specify)	05 ☐
Heart malformations	06 ☐
Other circulatory/respiratory anomalies (Specify) ___	07 ☐
Rectal atresia/stenosis	08 ☐
Tracheo esophageal fistula/Esophageal atresia	09 ☐
Omphalocele/Gastroschisis	10 ☐
Other gastrointestinal anomalies (Specify) ___	11 ☐
Malformed genitalia	17 ☐
Renal agenesis	13 ☐
Other urogenital anomalies (Specify) ___	14 ☐
Cleft lip/palate	15 ☐
Polydactyly/Syndactyly/Adactyly	16 ☐
Club foot	17 ☐
Diaphragmatic hernia	18 ☐
Other musculoskeletal/integumental anomalies (Specify) ___	19 ☐
Down's syndrome	20 ☐
Other chromosomal anomalies (Specify) ___	21 ☐
None	00 ☐
Other ___ (Specify)	22 ☐

CDC 64.91
REV. 1/89

FIGURE 3.3a U.S. Standard Certificate of Live Birth: Revision of 1989.

TYPE/PRINT IN PERMANENT BLACK INK FOR INSTRUCTIONS SEE OTHER SIDE AND HANDBOOK

U.S. STANDARD
CERTIFICATE OF DEATH

LOCAL FILE NUMBER

STATE FILE NUMBER

DECEDENT

1. DECEDENT'S NAME (First, Middle, Last)　　2. SEX　　3. DATE OF DEATH (Month, Day, Year)

4. SOCIAL SECURITY NUMBER　5a. AGE—Last Birthday (Years)　5b. UNDER 1 YEAR (Months / Days)　5c. UNDER 1 DAY (Hours / Minutes)　6. DATE OF BIRTH (Month, Day, Year)　7. BIRTHPLACE (City and State or Foreign Country)

8. WAS DECEDENT EVER IN U.S. ARMED FORCES? (Yes or no)　9a. PLACE OF DEATH (Check only one; see instructions on other side)　HOSPITAL: ☐ Inpatient ☐ ER/Outpatient ☐ DOA　OTHER: ☐ Nursing Home ☐ Residence ☐ Other (Specify)

9b. FACILITY NAME (If not institution, give street and number)　9c. CITY, TOWN, OR LOCATION OF DEATH　9d. COUNTY OF DEATH

10. MARITAL STATUS—Married, Never Married, Widowed, Divorced (Specify)　11. SURVIVING SPOUSE (If wife, give maiden name)　12a. DECEDENT'S USUAL OCCUPATION (Give kind of work done during most of working life. Do not use retired.)　12b. KIND OF BUSINESS/INDUSTRY

13a. RESIDENCE - STATE　13b. COUNTY　13c. CITY, TOWN, OR LOCATION　13d. STREET AND NUMBER

13e. INSIDE CITY LIMITS? (Yes or no)　13f. ZIP CODE　14. WAS DECEDENT OF HISPANIC ORIGIN? (Specify No or Yes—If yes, specify Cuban, Mexican, Puerto Rican, etc.) ☐ No ☐ Yes Specify:　15. RACE—American Indian, Black, White, etc. (Specify)　16. DECEDENT'S EDUCATION (Specify only highest grade completed) Elementary/Secondary (0-12) College (1-4 or 5+)

PARENTS

17. FATHER'S NAME (First, Middle, Last)　18. MOTHER'S NAME (First, Middle, Maiden Surname)

INFORMANT

19a. INFORMANT'S NAME (Type/Print)　19b. MAILING ADDRESS (Street and Number or Rural Route Number, City or Town, State, Zip Code)

DISPOSITION

20a. METHOD OF DISPOSITION ☐ Burial ☐ Cremation ☐ Removal from State ☐ Donation ☐ Other (Specify)　20b. PLACE OF DISPOSITION (Name of cemetery, crematory, or other place)　20c. LOCATION—City or Town, State

21a. SIGNATURE OF FUNERAL SERVICE LICENSEE OR PERSON ACTING AS SUCH　21b. LICENSE NUMBER (of Licensee)　22. NAME AND ADDRESS OF FACILITY

PRONOUNCING PHYSICIAN ONLY

Complete items 23a-c only when certifying physician is not available at time of death to certify cause of death.　23a. To the best of my knowledge, death occurred at the time, date, and place stated. Signature and Title ▶　23b. LICENSE NUMBER　23c. DATE SIGNED (Month, Day, Year)

ITEMS 24-26 MUST BE COMPLETED BY PERSON WHO PRONOUNCES DEATH

24. TIME OF DEATH ___ M　25. DATE PRONOUNCED DEAD (Month, Day, Year)　26. WAS CASE REFERRED TO MEDICAL EXAMINER/CORONER? (Yes or no)

CAUSE OF DEATH

27. PART I. Enter the diseases, injuries, or complications that caused the death. Do not enter the mode of dying, such as cardiac or respiratory arrest, shock, or heart failure. List only one cause on each line.　Approximate Interval Between Onset and Death

IMMEDIATE CAUSE (Final disease or condition resulting in death) → a. ___ DUE TO (OR AS A CONSEQUENCE OF):

Sequentially list conditions, if any, leading to immediate cause. Enter UNDERLYING CAUSE (Disease or injury that initiated events resulting in death) LAST　b. ___ DUE TO (OR AS A CONSEQUENCE OF):

c. ___ DUE TO (OR AS A CONSEQUENCE OF):

d.

PART II. Other significant conditions contributing to death but not resulting in the underlying cause given in Part I.　28a. WAS AN AUTOPSY PERFORMED? (Yes or no)　28b. WERE AUTOPSY FINDINGS AVAILABLE PRIOR TO COMPLETION OF CAUSE OF DEATH? (Yes or no)

29. MANNER OF DEATH ☐ Natural ☐ Accident ☐ Suicide ☐ Homicide ☐ Pending Investigation ☐ Could not be Determined　30a. DATE OF INJURY (Month, Day, Year)　30b. TIME OF INJURY ___ M　30c. INJURY AT WORK? (Yes or no)　30d. DESCRIBE HOW INJURY OCCURRED

30e. PLACE OF INJURY—At home, farm, street, factory, office building, etc. (Specify)　30f. LOCATION (Street and Number or Rural Route Number, City or Town, State)

CERTIFIER

31a. CERTIFIER (Check only one)
☐ CERTIFYING PHYSICIAN (Physician certifying cause of death when another physician has pronounced death and completed Item 23) To the best of my knowledge, death occurred due to the cause(s) and manner as stated.
☐ PRONOUNCING AND CERTIFYING PHYSICIAN (Physician both pronouncing death and certifying to cause of death) To the best of my knowledge, death occurred at the time, date, and place, and due to the cause(s) and manner as stated.
☐ MEDICAL EXAMINER/CORONER On the basis of examination and/or investigation, in my opinion, death occurred at the time, date, and place, and due to the cause(s) and manner as stated.

31b. SIGNATURE AND TITLE OF CERTIFIER　31c. LICENSE NUMBER　31d. DATE SIGNED (Month, Day, Year)

32. NAME AND ADDRESS OF PERSON WHO COMPLETED CAUSE OF DEATH (ITEM 27) (Type/Print)

REGISTRAR

33. REGISTRAR'S SIGNATURE　34. DATE FILED (Month, Day, Year)

NAME OF DECEDENT: For use by physician or institution

DEPARTMENT OF HEALTH AND HUMAN SERVICES – PUBLIC HEALTH SERVICE – NATIONAL CENTER FOR HEALTH STATISTICS – 1989 REVISION

PHS-T-003
REV. 1/89

FIGURE 3.3b　U.S. Standard Certificate of Death: Revision of 1989.

TYPE/PRINT IN PERMANENT BLACK INK FOR INSTRUCTIONS SEE HANDBOOK

U.S. STANDARD
REPORT OF FETAL DEATH

STATE FILE NUMBER

1. FACILITY NAME (If not institution, give street and number)

2. CITY, TOWN, OR LOCATION OF DELIVERY

3. COUNTY OF DELIVERY

4. DATE OF DELIVERY (Month, Day, Year)

5. SEX OF FETUS

PARENTS

6a. MOTHER'S NAME (First, Middle, Last)

6b. MAIDEN SURNAME

7. DATE OF BIRTH (Month, Day, Year)

8a. RESIDENCE-STATE

8b. COUNTY

8c. CITY, TOWN, OR LOCATION

8d. STREET AND NUMBER

8e. INSIDE CITY LIMITS? (Yes or no)

8f. ZIP CODE

9. FATHER'S NAME (First, Middle, Last)

10. DATE OF BIRTH (Month, Day, Year)

MOTHER

11. OF HISPANIC ORIGIN? (Specify No or Yes—If yes, specify Cuban, Mexican, Puerto Rican, etc.)

12. RACE—American Indian, Black, White, etc. (Specify below)

13. EDUCATION (Specify only highest grade completed)
- Elementary/Secondary (0-12)
- College (1-4 or 5+)

14. OCCUPATION AND BUSINESS/INDUSTRY (Worked during last year)
- Occupation
- Business/Industry

11a. ☐ No ☐ Yes Specify:

12a.

13a.

14a.

14b.

FATHER

11b. ☐ No ☐ Yes Specify:

12b.

13b.

14c.

14d.

MULTIPLE BIRTHS
Enter State File Number for Mate(s)
LIVE BIRTH(S)

FETAL DEATH(S)

15. PREGNANCY HISTORY (Complete each section)

LIVE BIRTHS

OTHER TERMINATIONS (Spontaneous and induced at any time after conception)

16. MOTHER MARRIED? (At delivery, conception, or any time between) (Yes or no)

17. DATE LAST NORMAL MENSES BEGAN (Month, Day, Year)

15a. Now Living Number ___ ☐ None

15b. Now Dead Number ___ ☐ None

15d. (Do not include this fetus) Number ___ ☐ None

18. MONTH OF PREGNANCY PRENATAL CARE BEGAN—First, Second, Third, etc. (Specify)

19. PRENATAL VISITS—Total Number (If none, so state)

20. WEIGHT OF FETUS (Specify Unit)

21. CLINICAL ESTIMATE OF GESTATION (Weeks)

15c. DATE OF LAST LIVE BIRTH (Month, Year)

15e. DATE OF LAST OTHER TERMINATION (Month, Year)

22a. PLURALITY—Single, Twin, Triplet, etc. (Specify)

22b. IF NOT SINGLE BIRTH—Born First, Second, Third, etc. (Specify)

MEDICAL AND HEALTH INFORMATION

DEPARTMENT OF HEALTH AND HUMAN SERVICES – PUBLIC HEALTH SERVICE – NATIONAL CENTER FOR HEALTH STATISTICS – 1989 REVISION

23a. MEDICAL RISK FACTORS FOR THIS PREGNANCY (Check all that apply)

Anemia (Hct. < 30/Hgb. < 10) .... 01 ☐
Cardiac disease .... 02 ☐
Acute or chronic lung disease .... 03 ☐
Diabetes .... 04 ☐
Genital herpes .... 05 ☐
Hydramnios/Oligohydramnios .... 06 ☐
Hemoglobinopathy .... 07 ☐
Hypertension, chronic .... 08 ☐
Hypertension, pregnancy-associated ..... 09 ☐
Eclampsia .... 10 ☐
Incompetent cervix .... 11 ☐
Previous infant 4000 + grams .... 12 ☐
Previous preterm or small-for-gestational age infant .... 13 ☐
Renal disease .... 14 ☐
Rh sensitization .... 15 ☐
Uterine bleeding .... 16 ☐
None .... 00 ☐
Other .... 17 ☐
(Specify)

23b. OTHER RISK FACTORS FOR THIS PREGNANCY (Complete all items)

Tobacco use during pregnancy .... Yes ☐ No ☐
Average number cigarettes per day ____
Alcohol use during pregnancy .... Yes ☐ No ☐
Average number drinks per week ____
Weight gained during pregnancy ____ lbs.

24. OBSTETRIC PROCEDURES (Check all that apply)

Amniocentesis .... 01 ☐
Electronic fetal monitoring .... 02 ☐
Induction of labor .... 03 ☐
Stimulation of labor .... 04 ☐
Tocolysis .... 05 ☐
Ultrasound .... 06 ☐
None .... 00 ☐
Other .... 07 ☐
(Specify)

25. COMPLICATIONS OF LABOR AND/OR DELIVERY (Check all that apply)

Febrile (>100°F. or 38°C.) .... 01 ☐
Meconium, moderate/heavy .... 02 ☐
Premature rupture of membrane (>12 hours) .. 03 ☐
Abruptio placenta .... 04 ☐
Placenta previa .... 05 ☐
Other excessive bleeding .... 06 ☐
Seizures during labor .... 07 ☐
Precipitous labor (< 3 hours) .... 08 ☐
Prolonged labor (> 20 hours) .... 09 ☐
Dysfunctional labor .... 10 ☐
Breech/Malpresentation .... 11 ☐
Cephalopelvic disproportion .... 12 ☐
Cord prolapse .... 13 ☐
Anesthetic complications .... 14 ☐
Fetal distress .... 15 ☐
None .... 00 ☐
Other .... 16 ☐
(Specify)

26. METHOD OF DELIVERY (Check all that apply)

Vaginal .... 01 ☐
Vaginal birth after previous C-section ..... 02 ☐
Primary C-section .... 03 ☐
Repeat C-section .... 04 ☐
Forceps .... 05 ☐
Vacuum .... 06 ☐
Hysterotomy/Hysterectomy .... 07 ☐

27. CONGENITAL ANOMALIES OF FETUS (Check all that apply)

Anencephalus .... 01 ☐
Spina bifida/Meningocele .... 02 ☐
Hydrocephalus .... 03 ☐
Microcephalus .... 04 ☐
Other central nervous system anomalies (Specify) _____ 05 ☐
Heart malformations .... 06 ☐
Other circulatory/respiratory anomalies (Specify) _____ 07 ☐
Rectal atresia/stenosis .... 08 ☐
Tracheo esophageal fistula/Esophageal atresia .. 09 ☐
Omphalocele/Gastroschisis .... 10 ☐
Other gastrointestinal anomalies (Specify) _____ 11 ☐
Malformed genitalia .... 12 ☐
Renal agenesis .... 13 ☐
Other urogenital anomalies (Specify) _____ 14 ☐
Cleft lip/palate .... 15 ☐
Polydactyly/Syndactyly/Adactyly .... 16 ☐
Club foot .... 17 ☐
Diaphragmatic hernia .... 18 ☐
Other musculoskeletal/ integumental anomalies (Specify) _____ 19 ☐
Down's syndrome .... 20 ☐
Other chromosomal anomalies (Specify) _____ 21 ☐
None .... 00 ☐
Other .... 22 ☐
(Specify)

CAUSE OF FETAL DEATH

28.
PART I. Fetal or maternal condition directly causing fetal death.

Enter only one cause per line for a, b, and c.

IMMEDIATE CAUSE
a. _____ Specify Fetal or Maternal

Fetal and/or maternal conditions, if any, giving rise to the immediate cause(s), stating the underlying cause last.

DUE TO (OR AS A CONSEQUENCE OF):
b. _____ Specify Fetal or Maternal

DUE TO (OR AS A CONSEQUENCE OF):
c. _____ Specify Fetal or Maternal

PART II. Other significant conditions of fetus or mother contributing to fetal death but not resulting in the underlying cause given in Part I.

29. FETUS DIED BEFORE LABOR, DURING LABOR OR DELIVERY, UNKNOWN (Specify)

30. ATTENDANT'S NAME AND TITLE (Type/Print)

Name _____

☐ M.D. ☐ D.O. ☐ C.N.M. ☐ Other Midwife
☐ Other (Specify) _____

31. NAME AND TITLE OF PERSON COMPLETING REPORT (Type/Print)

Name _____

Title _____

PHS-T-007
REV. 1/89

FIGURE 3.3c U.S. Standard Report of Fetal Death: Revision of 1989.

and nonemigrants (i.e., temporary admissions departing), although data were once tabulated on these movements.

The data on immigrants are published in limited cross-classification for such variables as major category of admission, country of last residence, country of birth, state of intended residence, age, sex, marital status, and major occupation group. Somewhat fewer but similar data are shown for naturalizations. The yearbook presents little demographic data on nonimmigrants and refugees, asylees, and parolees, and on apprehensions and deportations. Data relevant to the movements of Puerto Ricans, members of the armed forces, and other U.S. citizens must be derived from other sources and the movements must be estimated.

Other Federal Agencies

Many other federal agencies produce demographic data, or **administrative data** (i.e., information on individuals created for administrative purposes) useful in carrying out demographic studies. Some of these agencies are statistical or research agencies and others are administrative agencies with statistical duties. The statistical agencies include, in addition to the Bureau of the Census and the National Center for Health Statistics, the Bureau of Labor Statistics, the National Center for Education Statistics, and the Bureau of Economic Analysis. The administrative agencies include, in addition to the Immigration and Naturalization Service, the Social Security Administration, the Internal Revenue Service, and the Health Care Financing Agency. Other statistical and administrative agencies produce administrative data of lesser demographic importance. As a group, these agencies furnish historical data, estimates, and projections, or data useful for making estimates and projections, on employment, school enrollment, farm ownership and residence, family income, tax exemptions, and similar subjects. For example, the Bureau of Labor Statistics provides sample household data, via the Current Population Survey, on the labor force and employment, and the Social Security Administration provides data on retirement (i.e., beneficiaries) and data on employment (i.e., covered workers).

Major National Sample Surveys

The following section is intended to introduce the reader to some of the major national sample surveys. Most of these are either conducted by federal agencies, sponsored by them, or heavily financed by them. The list is selective and does not include many of the specialized surveys now under way.

Role of the Census Bureau

The U.S. Census Bureau plays a major role in the conduct of national sample surveys. In addition to the direct funds the Census Bureau receives, it also receives funds from other federal agencies for reimbursable work. Generally this work consists of conducting household sample surveys and processing the data collected. Much of this work is carried out at the request of the Departments of Labor, Justice, Housing and Urban Development, and Health and

Human Services and deals with the areas of labor force, criminal justice, housing, health, and income and assets. The Census Bureau has no administrative or policy-making functions, and in this way the production of data is separated from program administration and policy development. Sometimes the sponsoring agency does not have administrative functions either, but the Census Bureau is selected because of its première position in survey taking. Funds are commonly appropriated to the sponsoring agency and are then transferred to the Census Bureau, which collects and compiles the required data. Analysis of the data is the task of the sponsoring agency.

Although response to the decennial censuses of population and housing is mandatory, this is not the case for the many surveys conducted by the Census Bureau. Over the years, the Census Bureau has been successful in obtaining the cooperation of the general public in responding to the surveys, in spite of the fact that response to the surveys is voluntary and the Census Bureau may have been serving only as the data-collection agent for another federal agency. The Bureau of the Census and the sponsoring agency can use the data collected only for statistical purposes and for purposes revealed to the individual respondent. In this connection, statements of informed consent for voluntary surveys, and of the purpose of the survey for mandatory surveys, must be provided to the respondent.

The Bureau of the Census collects extensive current information on the demographic, social, and economic characteristics of the U.S. population through five national sample surveys, namely, the Current Population Survey, the Survey of Income and Program Participation, the American Housing Survey, the Consumer Expenditure Survey, and the National Health Survey. All of these surveys except the Survey of Income and Program Participation are sponsored in whole or part by other federal agencies. The Census Bureau also processes the data collected, editing and weighting the data as required with the appropriate sampling weights, and adjusting the inflated data to independent estimates of age, sex, race/Hispanic groups in the population, the so-called **survey controls** (discussed later and in Chapter 4). The survey controls now include an adjustment for net undercounts in the 1990 census, even though the official census data themselves do not include such an adjustment.

Current Population Survey

The oldest of the surveys conducted by the Census Bureau is the Current Population Survey (CPS), which was initiated in the mid-1930s. The CPS is a monthly survey of about 50,000 occupied households (as of 1997), conducted for the Bureau of Labor Statistics. The CPS covers the civilian noninstitutional population of the United States for labor force data, plus members of the armed forces living off post or with their families on post in the United States for other subjects. The present CPS sample consists of 754 sampling areas selected from 2007 counties or groups of contiguous counties (minor civil divisions in New England and Hawaii) into which the country is divided. There is coverage in every state and the District of Columbia. The sample was selected from the 1990 decennial census files but is continually updated to account for new residential construction. The CPS collects data through direct interviews for each person 15 years old and over in each sample household.

The CPS is primarily designed to collect data on the labor force and employment and is the source of the official monthly estimates of unemployment. From time to time, supplements relating to the labor force are added to the survey questionnaire. Each March and October, other supplements are added, which inquire about a host of demographic, social, and economic items. Subjects of special reports based on the supplements are marital status and living arrangements, families and households, school enrollment, educational attainment, fertility, race, Hispanic origin, nativity, geographical mobility, income, and poverty.

In the CPS estimation procedure, the sample results are adjusted for noninterviews, inflated for the sampling ratio (i.e., the probability of selection, or the proportion of the population included in the sample), and then adjusted to independent estimates of the civilian noninstitutional population of the United States disaggregated by state and by age, sex, race, and Hispanic origin. The independent estimates, the survey controls, are based on statistics from the 1990 census of population; an adjustment for undercoverage in the 1990 census; statistics of births, deaths, and net immigration since the census date; statistics on the size of the armed forces; and estimates of the institutional population. Accordingly, the CPS in effect provides data only on the *proportional* distribution of the population in each control class (i.e., age, sex, race, and Hispanic origin) for some social or economic characteristic (e.g., marital status). This relation can be represented approximately by the following algebraic expression for the estimate (P') of the widowed population in one control group:

$$_T P'_{a,s,r,h,w} = {_T}P_{a,s,r,h} \star \frac{_E P_{a,s,r,h,w}}{_E P_{a,s,r,h}} \tag{1}$$

where P refers to population, a, s, r, h refers to an age/sex/race/Hispanic control category (e.g., non-Hispanic black women 30–34 years old), T to the independent estimate for this control group, E to the survey estimate, and w to the widowed population.[17]

The CPS publishes data mainly for the United States, with only limited data for regions, the larger states, and the larger metropolitan areas, because of the large sampling errors for the smaller areas. For demographic data for smaller geographic units one must turn to the decennial census and, within a few years, to the American Community Survey. The labor force estimates from the CPS are published monthly by the Bureau of Labor Statistics in *Employment and Earnings*. Income and poverty estimates for households, families, and persons are published annually by the Bureau of the Census in *Current Population Reports*, Series P-60. The data on demographic and social topics, such as families, households, and marital status, provided by the March supplement, are published annually or less frequently in *Current Population Reports*, Series P-20 or P-23. A public-use tape is available for sale to private users to develop special tabulations.

Because of periodic changes in the design of the CPS (involving questionnaire redesign, other design changes, and changes in collection and processing), intended to improve the quality and reliability of the data, to reduce costs, and to satisfy changing data needs, current data are not strictly comparable with data for earlier years. The most recent redesign occurred in 1994–1995.[18]

Survey of Income and Program Participation

The Survey of Income and Program Participation (SIPP) is a national longitudinal survey sponsored and conducted by the U.S. Census Bureau. It is designed to provide data on the dynamics of income and assets and on eligibility for and participation in income programs. In addition to money income, the survey collects information on the receipt of noncash benefits from both public and private sources, taxes paid, and assets and liabilities. Unlike the CPS, the SIPP design makes it readily possible to gauge movement along the income distribution and into and out of poverty for the same person in 2 consecutive years.[19] The SIPP includes both a core questionnaire covering basic items and topical modules covering items of current or specialized interest. Data files are made available for the full panel for a year, or for various waves of a panel.

The SIPP became fully operational in 1982–1983. Approximately 61,200 persons were initially eligible to be interviewed; however, 45,400 were classified as interviewed for the life of the panel. Hence, there was a nonresponse rate of 25%. The 1995 panel of the SIPP sample is located in 230 primary sampling units, each consisting of a county or group of counties. The sample is based on lists of addresses from the 1990 census and is continually updated to account for new housing construction. A sample person is visited in the first 4 months and in each of the eight successive 4-month periods thereafter (waves). The reference period is the 4 months preceding the interview month. The period covered by the panel consists of 32 interview months (eight interviews). Several stages of weight adjustments are used in processing the longitudinal data collected in the SIPP, as for the Current Population Survey: the base weights, which are equal to the inverse of the probability of selection, two noninterview adjustments, and an adjustment to independent estimates of the population classified in age, sex, race, and Hispanic groups. Data obtained from the SIPP are not entirely comparable with data obtained from other sources, such as the CPS.[20] They are published in *Current Population Reports*, Series P-70.

American Housing Survey

The American Housing Survey (AHS), called the Annual Housing Survey before 1984, is a national sample survey sponsored by the Department of Housing and Urban Development, with data collection and compilation by the Bureau of the Census. The survey provides much data on housing characteristics, conditions, size, costs, values, equipment, and fuels, and some data on the demographic, social, and, economic characteristics of the occupants and neighborhood conditions. It provides information on changes in the quality of the nation's housing, the extent of overcrowding, the relationship between costs and family income, and the extent of failures in housing systems.

The AHS includes a national component, conducted in odd-numbered years for national, regional, and metropolitan/nonmetropolitan data, and a metropolitan component, consisting of surveys in 46 metropolitan statistical areas that are conducted in 4-year cycles of 12 metropolitan areas each year. All housing units in the United States are represented by the sample for the

AHS, numbering on average 55,000 housing units. Each metropolitan area sample consists of 4800 or more housing units. The AHS sample consists of addresses and data that are gathered from the same housing units each other year by computer-assisted interviewing technology.[21]

Consumer Expenditure Survey

The Consumer Expenditure Survey (CES) is a national sample survey conducted by the Bureau of the Census on behalf of the Bureau of Labor Statistics and provides data on the buying habits of American consumers according to a variety of socioeconomic characteristics. The program consists of two surveys, the quarterly Interview Survey and the Diary Survey, each with its own questionnaire and sample. The Interview Survey, provides data on relatively large nonrecurring expenditures, such as purchases of property or vehicles; the Diary Survey provides detailed data on expenditures for small, frequently purchased items, such as food or housekeeping supplies. In the Interview Survey, respondents report data to an interviewer five times over an 18-month period. In the Diary Survey, respondents complete a diary of expenses for two consecutive one-week periods. The CES uses a rotating panel design and respondent reports are obtained on a continuing basis. Prior to 1984, the CES was conducted roughly every 10 years.[22]

Consumer Price Index

An important application of the expenditure data in the Consumer Expenditure Survey is their use in the construction of the Consumer Price Index (CPI). The CPI was designed by the Bureau of Labor Statistics to measure the changes in the price of goods and services on the basis of a fixed market basket of goods and services. It is an important tool in the interpretation and use of the income data provided by the Current Population Survey and the Survey of Income and Program Participation. It is used in computing the cost-of-living adjustments for Social Security benefits, retirement pensions of federal workers and veterans, and several means-tested programs, such as Food Stamps and Supplemental Security Income (SSI). It is used to adjust income tax brackets for inflation in federal income tax returns, as well as to compute cost-of-living adjustments for wages and salaries in many union contracts. Clearly, the level and changes in the index can have a substantial effect on the disposable income of many segments of the population. It is for this reason that the CPI is of interest to demographers.

The Consumer Price Index is shown in Table 3.1 for each year since 1980 and at quinquennial intervals between 1960 and 1980. The figures reflect the considerable inflation during this period. The base period for the current indexes is 1982–1984; so that the average of the indexes for these years is 1.00. The index has typically been revised every 10 years to reflect the changes in the buying patterns of consumers over the 10-year period. As of 1998, however, 1982–1984 has been retained as the base period of the index.[23]

National Health Interview Survey

The National Health Interview Survey (NHIS) is sponsored by the National Center for Health Statistics, with data collection and processing by the Bu-

TABLE 3.1   Annual Consumer Price Index (CPI-U): 1960 to 1997 (1982–1984 = 100; Represents Annual Averages of Monthly Figures for All Urban Consumers)

Year	CPI-U	Year	CPI-U
1960	29.6	1987	113.6
1965	31.5	1988	118.3
1970	38.8	1989	124.0
1975	53.8	1990	130.7
1980	82.4	1991	136.2
1981	90.9	1992	140.3
1982	96.5	1993	144.5
1983	99.6	1994	148.2
1984	103.9	1995	152.4
1985	107.6	1996	156.9
1986	109.6	1997	160.5

Note: The percentage change in prices between any earlier year and 1997 is computed by dividing the Consumer Price Index (CPI-U) for 1997 by the Consumer Price Index for the earlier year.

Source: U.S. Bureau of Labor Statistics, *Monthly Labor Review* and *Handbook of Labor Statistics*, periodic. See also U.S. Bureau of the Census, *Statistical Abstract of the United States, 1998*, Table 772.

reau of the Census. NHIS is a national survey of health conditions (including illnesses, injuries, impairments, and activity limitations), access to health care, health services utilization, prevalence of risk behaviors, health promotion activities, and health insurance coverage. In addition to securing health information of the types mentioned, the survey obtains information on the demographic and social characteristics of the respondents. The NHIS is a continuing national sample survey of the civilian noninstitutional population. Information is obtained by personal household interviews for about 100,000 persons during a year. Cross-sectional survey data are cumulated over various periods to secure reliable data for major tabulation categories.[24] The National Center for Health Statistics also sponsors the National Health and Nutrition Examination Survey, the National Health Care Survey, the National Survey of Family Growth, the National Mortality Followback Survey, and the National Maternal and Infant Health Survey.

Other National Sample Surveys

There are other national sample surveys of greater or lesser interest to applied demographers. This interest stems partly from their use in specialized demographic studies and partly from their use in providing national "controls" for synthetic estimates of the demographic and socioeconomic characteristics of subnational areas (see Chapter 11). Among these surveys are the National Assessment of Educational Progress, the National Household Education Survey, the National Health and Retirement Survey/AHEAD, the Panel Study of Income Dynamics, Monitoring the Future, the National Crime Victimization Survey, the National Longitudinal Study on Aging (a supplement of the National Health Interview Survey), the National Long-Term Care Survey, and the National Longitudinal Surveys of the Bureau of Labor Statistics. All of these surveys are supported by federal funds but not all of them are sponsored and directed by federal agencies. The titles of these surveys indicate their principal emphasis, with the possible exceptions of AHEAD and Monitoring the Future. AHEAD is concerned with the health and economic dynamics of the older aged population, and Monitoring the Future consists of annual surveys of 8th-, 10th-, and 12th-grade students, designed to explore the values, lifestyles, and behaviors of American youth.

Economic Censuses, Economic Surveys, and Administrative Records

Some economic censuses and surveys and some administrative record systems provide economic data useful in demographic applications. In the federal government, economic censuses and economic sample surveys are conducted by the Bureau of the Census, administrative data on economic subjects are compiled by the Social Security Administration and the Internal Revenue Service, and other economic data are developed by the Bureau of Economic Analysis, the Small Business Administration, and the Council of Economic Advisors.

The economic censuses of the U.S. Census Bureau include seven censuses: manufactures, retail trade, wholesale trade, transportation, services, mineral industries, and construction industries. The economic censuses are taken every 5 years. The last set of economic censuses was taken in 1997 and, as of early 2000, the processing of these censuses was completed and most of the results have been released.[25] The data are classified according to the new North American Industry Classification System (NAICS), which replaces the earlier Standard Industrial Classification (see Chapter 6); some data are also tabulated according to the earlier system. Of interest to the demographer, for example, are the data relating to the size of establishments in the form of payrolls, employment, dollar sales, and taxes, provided by the Census of Retail Trade, and data from the Survey of Minority-Owned Business.

The data from the economic censuses and surveys are referred to as **establishment data** while those from the population and housing censuses and CPS and SIPP are referred to as **household data**. They are so described because in the former case the response unit is the business establishment while in the latter case the response unit is the household. Because of the differences in collection systems, question wording, and processing, data from one source are not considered comparable with the corresponding data from the other source.

The Social Security Administration (SSA) maintains files on covered workers, or workers required to pay payroll taxes to SSA ("Continuous Work History File"), beneficiaries ("Master Beneficiary File"), and applicants for Social Security numbers (Social Security Number File, or "Numident File"). From the covered workers file, for example, sample data on employment in each state are tabulated. The SSA publishes the *Social Security Bulletin* each month and an *Annual Statistical Supplement*. The Internal Revenue Service maintains an individual master file of federal individual tax filers and publishes the *Statistics of Income Bulletin*. Other economic data of interest to demographers are compiled by the Bureau of Economic Analysis, the Small Business Administration, and the Council of Economic Advisors. Additional discussion of sources of economic data appears in later chapters, particularly Chapters 6 and 14.

NONFEDERAL SOURCES

State and Local Sources

Some agencies in state and local governments play an important role in compiling, repackaging, and disseminating decennial census and other population-related data. They are a major source of population data for their state and the local governments within it. State governments have developed a considerable capability in the management and manipulation of large data files over the past few decades. On the other hand, with the exception of some of the larger cities and counties, local governments have acquired little or no capability in this regard. Access to and mastery of census data have become dependent on the technical capability of the staff and on the availability of funds for purchasing and managing large census data files.

State and local area needs for computer skills and money to buy the appropriate census products are a result, in large part, of changes in the way the Census Bureau disseminates census data. It has moved from mainly printed reports to mainly computer tapes, compact disks, and tabulation software. The Census Bureau no longer publishes much of the data it compiles. Its new policy of disseminating census data was motivated by the desire to provide more information to users and more flexibility to them in securing the tabulations they want, to reduce its costs by getting users to pay their own way, and to make the data available more promptly. At the same time, the policy has adversely affected many local governments and private nonprofit organizations as well as individual users, who do not have the necessary technical capability and funds. The private business sector, which can afford to hire the appropriate technical staff and buy data and statistical services, has not suffered from this change of policy.

State data centers (discussed later) have contributed greatly toward providing data services for state and local governments, nonprofit organizations, and individuals, while private data-vending companies are servicing mainly the business community. In California the Regional Councils of Government have also played the role of providing data and technical assistance to public and private users of census data.

State, regional, and local governments also compile many series of public administrative data for their areas useful in demographic analysis.[26] Among the data series are automobile registrations, building permits issued, voter registrations, and driver licenses issued. Some quasi-administrative series are developed as management records by private organizations, particularly utility companies,which can be adapted for other uses by public agencies. These series include electric, gas, water, and telephone customer records. State and local government agencies also prepare population estimates and projections for many different areas. In fact, an important use of the administrative data series made by the planning or analysis offices of these governments is the preparation of population estimates and projections.[27] Another is the review and evaluation of census data. Population estimates and projections of many types are also prepared by businesses, but these are proprietary and hence are not publicly available.

State Data Centers

State data centers (SDC) represent an important public resource for securing census data, especially when the Census Bureau's printed reports do not fill a specific need for local data. SDCs can provide data that go well beyond those published by the Census Bureau and hence they may be able to fill the local need. The SDCs specialize in providing data for small geographic areas within their states, such as city blocks, census tracts, zip code areas, and specially designated areas. Their products may cover data that the Census Bureau has not published or does not plan to publish.

Every state has at least one data center and some have more than one.[28] A lead data center may head up a network of affiliated centers. For example, California has six SDCs and the Department of Finance in Sacramento is the lead data center. The Southern California Association of Governments (SCAG), a sponsor of one of the SDC's of California, offers access to the computer tape files for all the 1990 census data. The SCAG SDC also prepares made-to-order demographic tabulations and reports on an at-cost basis. Many SDCs also "bank" data from other federal and state agencies, which can be integrated or merged with decennial census data.

The Census Bureau has designated the SDCs to perform this service for local government agencies, businesses, nonprofit community organizations, and individuals. The purchasers of the service primarily use the data to identify, measure, and describe target populations in which they are interested. Data may be provided on a wide variety of census subjects, including demographic, social, economic, and housing characteristics. The centers' products may be geographic profiles, standardized tabulations, custom-made tabulations, or charts. The data may be furnished in a variety of formats, including hard-copy printouts, magnetic tapes, diskettes, and CD-ROMs.

Commercial Data-Vending Companies

Specially tailored tabulations from the last census and special current estimates and projections may be purchased from many private companies as well as from state data centers. The private companies specialize in marketing standard and special compilations of data for small areas. The emphasis in the work of these companies is on subnational data, particularly substate data. However specialized, the products of private vendors rely on the statistical and geographic foundation provided by the federal statistical system. Most of the demographic data sold by private vendors is based on data developed by the Census Bureau.

There are numerous companies in the population data-vending business. Three of the leading ones are CACI, Claritas, and Polk. The kinds of printed products these companies market can be illustrated with a summary description of some leading products of CACI and Claritas. CACI sourcebooks present a variety of demographic information for counties, census tracts, places, and zip-code areas. For example, the *Sourcebook of Zip Code Demographics* presents data on population, households, age distribution, race, income in a variety of forms (per capita income, median household income, household income distribution, average disposable income), and other items, for 1995 (population data for 1980, 1990, and 2000 also), for all 29,523 residential zip-code areas and more than 12,730 nonresidential zip-code areas. Similarly, the *Sourcebook of County Demographics* presents such information for 3141 counties. The format includes software for quickly accessing the data, sorting them, and "exporting" them to a database or "spreadsheet." The software also permits users to locate zip-code areas or counties that they wish to analyze, or to locate zip-code areas or counties with specified demographic characteristics.

Claritas offers similar products, designated Market Trend, REZIDE, Trendline-GIS, and Building Blocks. With Market Trend, customers may identify any market area with its geographic boundaries down to small neighborhoods and obtain 1990 census data, current estimates, and 5-year projections, for a wide range of subjects including population, households and families, race and Hispanic origin, age by sex, age by income, and household wealth. Data are updated annually. REZIDE profiles every zip code in the United States with a broad array of demographic statistics and 5-year household projections. Trendline-GIS is a demographic database designed for geographic information systems (GIS) and desktop mapping users. It simplifies mapping of the demographic data in several databases, each of which provides data from censuses, current estimates, and 5-year projections on a variety of demographic, socioeconomic, and housing subjects. Building Blocks are large databases, available for demographic analyses on mainframe computers and consisting of 1980 and 1990 census data, current estimates, and 5-year projections. These products can be delivered in hard copy, diskette, CD-ROM, or magnetic tape.

Many smaller companies are players in this field. Geolytics of East Brunswick, New Jersey, for example, provides 1990 STF-3 data and estimates and short-term projections for numerous variables, including population, socioeconomic characteristics, and consumer spending, for five geographic levels (block group, census tract, zip code, county, and state).

The data-vending business is expected to continue to expand. A next step, already under way, is the dissemination of products through the Internet. For example, Claritas is now providing access to its new product, Connect, through the Internet.

ADMINISTRATIVE RECORDS AS SOURCES OF DEMOGRAPHIC DATA

General Considerations

As mentioned, numerous administrative files are compiled and maintained by agencies in the federal, state, and local governments. Large private companies also maintain administrative files on employees for payroll management and human resources planning, and on customers for advertising, sales, and billing.

Many public administrative data series have been adopted for demographic uses by demographers and others. Among such data series at the federal level are several files maintained by the Department of Housing and Urban Development (e.g., public housing data); the Social Security Administration (SSA) covered-worker, beneficiary, and Numident files; Medicare enrollments of the Health Care Financing Administration; and the Internal Revenue Service Individual Master File. SSA's Numident files are cumulative files of all initial applications for Social Security numbers and contain several demographic items.

The compilations of birth, death, fetal deaths, marriage, and divorce data made by the states are public administrative data that demographers tend to view as demographic data. In addition to vital statistics, many series of data compiled at the state and local levels for purely administrative uses have been appropriated for demographic uses by demographers. These include drivers license registrations, auto registrations, tax returns, building permits, voting registrations, public school enrollments, public assistance lists (PRWO),[29] Head Start participants, and recipients of food stamps. From the criminal justice system, there are lists of probationers, parolees, and prisoners. Various commercial lists, such as telephone subscribers, utility customers, and city directories, can also serve many of the same demographic functions as the administrative lists already enumerated.

Administrative data may be available in the form of aggregate data or in the form of individual records (i.e., microdata files). State administrative data are normally provided outside the state government only in aggregate form, but microdata can be obtained where state law permits it and under prescribed curcumstances. Administrative data compiled by private companies about their employees and retirees are proprietary data available only within the company and are typically restricted to specified areas of company operation. Analysts within these organizations may have access to the records for research purposes under restricted conditions.

The Census Bureau plans to use administrative records in connection with the year 2000 census only in a limited way—that is, only as tools in the coverage improvement and evaluation programs. As an evaluative tool, administrative records data can be compared in aggregate form with census data, or selected administrative records can be matched to the sample blocks identified for matching in the Accuracy and Coverage Evaluation Program.[30] An **administrative records match** is a procedure in which a sample of the population is matched to the records in an administrative record file, a sample from the administrative record file is matched to the population, or a sample from one administrative record file is matched to the records in a second administrative record file. Administrative records from several sources can be integrated into a single composite, unduplicated file, and the names and addresses of persons in this file can be compared to the census address files, the census persons listed, or the lists of persons for the sample blocks of the Accuracy and Coverage Evaluation Survey. Persons omitted from the census can be then added to the count of persons omitted by the census or to the census count itself.

As sources of demographic data, administrative records offer a number of potential benefits, among them, increasing the currency and frequency of demographic and economic information, expanding its detail, lowering the costs of data collection, and reducing respondent burden in censuses and surveys. Use of administrative data can also reduce the nonresponse workload, provide responses to items not answered for respondent households, and supplement information used in the coverage evaluation program of the census. For these reasons, the Census Bureau is engaging in considerable research to assess the feasibility of a greater use of administrative records in census taking and its other population programs. Specifically, research now under way is designed to determine the feasibility of employing administrative records as part of continuous measurement during the postcensal years, as a principal basis for postcensal population estimates, and as a major element in the year 2010 census. The research relates to the selection of administrative records to be used for each program, the procedures for obtaining an unduplicated list when combining administrative records, the procedures for matching administrative records to other records, and the effectiveness of the use of such records in terms of quality and cost.

Limitations and Issues

The user of administrative data, particularly microdata, has to confront a number of issues. One set of issues relates to access to the data, involving use restrictions mandated by law, fair exchange of data between collection agencies, and confidentiality, and the other relates to the quality of the data for demographic uses.

Title 13, Section 6, requires that the Census Bureau use administrative records to the maximum extent possible in lieu of asking respondents for the information again. However, the administrative agency may operate under legislation that restricts its ability to provide the data. Then the two agencies must negotiate the terms of the exchange to find a common ground free of legal barriers.

There are several types of legal barriers in accessing public administrative records: (1) federal laws that specify who can access the data and for what purpose; (2) federal laws that permit access to the data of various agencies for program uses; (3) the Federal Privacy Act, which permits access to data only for statistical purposes under a routine-use exemption; and (4) state laws that govern access to specific state data. State laws vary widely so that access may be easy to secure in one state and difficult in another. The Internal Revenue Service (IRS) and the Social Security Administration (SSA) limit access to their data to research uses. An agreement between agencies to exchange data may facilitate the receipt of the desired data. For example, the Census Bureau and the SSA have a long-standing agreement allowing exchange of statistical data. When data are transferred between these agencies, the receiving agency agrees to use the transferred records for statistical purposes only. When IRS and SSA agree to transfer data to the Census Bureau, as they have done, they may allow access only to sample files. Confidentiality of the transferred data is an important issue, and its protection is discussed further in the next chapter.

All administrative records, whether in aggregate form or in the form of individual records, require adjustment before they can be employed as demographic data in a specific situation. First, like all records, they are error prone and, to the extent possible, should be **cleaned** (i.e., corrected for missing, unreasonable, and inconsistent entries) before they are used. Next, coverage of a particular population group that the records are intended to represent may be incomplete, as is true of Medicare enrollments used to represent the number of persons aged 65 years and over or IRS tax records used to represent the entire population under 65 years of age. The IRS file excludes families and individuals who are not required to file tax returns because of insufficient income. A file may include some persons who have died, as when Social Security beneficiary files continue to carry some decedents because of the family's failure to report the death or processing errors. A file may contain two records for the same person if that person has two Social Security numbers as a result of processing or other errors. Files may have serious geocoding problems (i.e., problems in assigning persons to a particular geographic place). This is true for Medicare and IRS tax records. When IRS tax records are used in making population estimates for local areas, a modification of the residence inquiry on the form is required so that the Census Bureau can accurately assign filers and their dependents to the appropriate area of residence.

Record Linkage

A researcher may wish to link two or more record sets in some demographic application. **Record linkage** involves matching individuals, households, or businesses in two or more records, usually with the goal of producing a new file or files based on the matched individuals, households, or businesses. Record linkage may be viewed as another source of demographic data in that the new file has different properties and uses than the original files.

Linkage of files has a number of advantages over taking another census or survey or adding data to existing records through additional inquiries. The matching operation is usually less costly, can provide the desired data on a more current basis, may provide some data not otherwise available, and can be used to improve the quality of the data. Linking records can be used in a great variety of ways: to measure the coverage of a census or survey, to measure the completeness of birth and death registration, to trace individuals through life course experiences, to secure more accurate estimates of a demographic or socioeconomic characteristic, to set up a sampling frame for surveys, and to secure information supplementary to the census or survey. There are many illustrations of the application of record linkage in the health area, particularly in longitudinal studies where various life cycle changes are involved. Record linkage may be used to generate disease registries (e.g., by combining hospital admissions, clinical records, death registrations) and to create patient-oriented rather than event-oriented records (e.g., for cancer registries).[31] The analysis of the life cycle of an individual with respect to health involves linking various data sources over time, such as health surveys and birth and death registration records. Matching is employed in demographic applications for reasons other than the creation of a new file, however, as when a file of records is matched to a list of surnames in order to identify or count persons of a specified ethnic group (see Chapter 12).

An illustration of the linkage of large files is the Exact Match File of Social Security records, income tax records, and the Current Population Survey in 1973. A principal purpose of this linkage was to evaluate income information in the Current Population Survey, but a secondary purpose was to evaluate the coverage of the Current Population Survey. In another major match study, the 1990 census records were matched with a post-enumeration survey to evaluate the completeness of coverage of the census. In Canada, the National Population Health Survey, a longitudinal survey, is being linked to the respondents' provincial health records. The U.S. National Center for Health Statistics has been linking infant deaths with births in order to provide data on infant mortality classified by the expanded list of characteristics available on either the birth or death certificate.

The National Death Index (NDI) is being used to retrieve information given on death certificates that matches information on deaths provided by researchers and other users to the National Center of Health Statistics. Figure 3.4a lists the criteria for determining whether the particular NDI record qualifies as a positive record match with a particular user-provided record. To qualify as a positive match, both records must satisfy at least one of the 12 conditions or matching criteria listed. The information provided by researchers and other users is often incomplete and inexact. Whenever a user-provided record matches one or more NDI records, an NDI retrieval report is generated. Figure 3.4b is a hypothetical example of a retrieval report. It shows one user record that matches four NDI records. All items provided on the user record match the items on the NDI record exactly in only one of the four cases.

Errors occur in the matching operation. The identifiers used in the matching operation, such as names and addresses, are not unique and may appear in different forms. The matching algorithm makes a great difference in the **match ratio**—that is, the proportion of records in one file that are matched

---

FIGURE 3.4a   National Death Index: Matching Criteria

---

1. Social Security number, first name
2. Social Security number, last name
3. Social Security number, father's surname
4. If the subject is female: Social Security number, last name (user's record),
    and father's surname (NDI record)
5. Month and exact year of birth, first and last name
6. Month and exact year of birth, first name, father's surname
7. If the subject is female: month and exact year of birth, first name, last name (user's record)
    and father's surname (NDI record)
8. Month and exact year of birth, first and middle initials, last name
9. Month and + or − 1 year of birth, first and middle initials, last name
10. Month and + or − 1 year of birth, first and last name
11. Month and day of birth, first and last name
12. Month and day of birth, first and middle initials, last name

---

Note: All matches on last name and father's surname are performed on the basis of either exact spelling or NYSIIS Phonetic Codes (New York State Identification and Intelligence System). To qualify as a possible match, both records must satisfy at least 1 of the 12 conditions or matching criteria listed. The specified data items must agree on both records.

Source: U.S. National Center for Health Statistics, Division of Vital Statistics.

Retrieval Report

Whenever a user record matches with one or more NDI records, an NDI Retrieval Report is generated. Presented below is a *hypothetical* example of a Retrieval Report which shows one user record matching with four NDI records.

USER REQUEST RECORD   (POSSIBLE MATCHES =   4)

				NDI APPL NO 842899				CONTROL NO 4507		

POSSIBLE DECEDENT NAME	FATHERS SURNAME	SOC SEC NO	BIRTH DATE MO DY YR	AGE	SEX	RACE	MS	SOR	SOB	USER DATA
REGINA HANES	-	114576493	12 10 18	-	F	-	M	PA	LA	011560

POSSIBLE NDI RECORD MATCHES   (IN RANKED ORDER)

STATE OF DEATH	CERT NUMBER	DATE OF DEATH	NAME F M L	FATHERS SURNAME	LN/FS	SOC SEC NO	BIRTH DATE MO DY YR	AGE	SEX	RACE	MS	SOR	SOB
* PENNSYLVANIA	861098	02-01-81	X B X	-		XXXXXXXX	X X X		X	X	X	X	X
LOUISIANA	421304	07-07-80	X X :	-		--XXXX-X	X X +01		X	-	X	X	X
LOUISIANA	A 421304	07-07-80	I B X	-		--XXXX-X	X X +01		X	-	-		
INDIANA	698637	03-21-79	X N	-	N	---X--X--	X X -05		X	-	?		

Column heading abbreviations:

LN/FS = Last name on user record compared to father's surname on NDI record.

MS = Marital status

SOR = State of residence

SOB = State of birth

Symbols used within the table:

* = All items provided on user record matched exactly with items on NDI record.

X = User data item and NDI data item matched exactly.

Blank = User data item and NDI data item did not match.

- = Data item not provided by user. For SSN: specific digits did not match. For LN/FS: comparison was not attempted.

? = Insufficient information on NDI record.

A = Alias name on NDI record.

I = Only first initial of first name matched.

N = Names matched only on NYSIIS phonetic codes.

B = Middle initials not provided on either record. This occurrence is treated as a match on middle initial.

+01 = Birth year on the NDI record is one year more than the year on the user record.

-05 = Birth year on the NDI record is five years less than the year on the user record.

FIGURE 3.4b National Death Index: Hypothetical example of a retrieval report. *Source:* U.S. National Center for Health Statistics, Division of Vital Statistics.

with records in the other file. Given the errors in records, if the records in the two files must agree on too many items, the match ratio may be unrealistically low, and if they must agree on too few items, the match ratio may be unrealistically high. Associated with the match ratio are various types of match error ratios. In general, the **match error ratio** is the proportion of records in one file erroneously matched with records in the other file or erroneously not matched.[32]

The match ratio is in part dependent on the resources available to carry out the record-matching operation. Experience suggests that the greater the effort and resources applied in the operation, the higher the percentage of matches achieved. The match error ratio tends to be higher if the files being matched differ greatly in size. The explanation for the higher ratios of false positive matches or false negative matches under these circumstances is not evident, but the small match ratio for the larger file resulting from the difference in the number of records in the two files may contribute to this outcome.

Considerable research is under way to reduce and control error ratios in record linkage. Two approaches to this problem are cited here, but a full explanation of the proposed methods is best reserved for more specialized texts. The first approach, the Scheuren–Winkler approach, is based on recent developments in edit/imputation (i.e., cleaning files) of microdata employing computer software. Edit/imputation procedures are combined with regression analysis in a recursive (i.e., iterative) process to improve the record-linkage results.[33]

In the second approach, the Fair–Kestenbaum approach, a probabilistic method is used to determine whether or not two records are true matches. The method uses identifiers (e.g., name, birth date) in addition to Social Security number in order to improve the accuracy of the record-linkage operation. Decisions have to be made about the identifiers to be employed in the match, the algorithm for determining the probability of a match, and the bounds for establishing a certain match and a certain nonmatch. To apply the probabilistic method, a score is computed, which represents the odds that a linkage between a record from file A and a record from file B, being compared with respect to a set of identifiers selected for linkage purposes, is a true match.[34]

APPENDIX A: SELECTED INTERNET WEB SITES FOR DEMOGRAPHIC DATA

The principal offices and agencies producing demographic data have Internet Web sites through which they release data, including some data that they have released or will release in printed form. Much of their data may be made available in no other form. The following list of Internet Web sites includes both general addresses and a few specific addresses. In most cases, if users employ the general address, they will have to continue with extensions of the address in order to locate the data they seek. Consider the two addresses for the Immigration and Naturalization Service. The first is the general address for the agency and the second will take users directly to displays of statistical data.

Federal Interagency Council on Statistical Policy	www.fedstats.gov
Federal Interagency Forum on Child and Family Statistics	www.childstats.gov

Federal Interagency Forum on Aging Related Statistics	www.dhhs/cdc/nchs/oaehp/dhua
U.S. Bureau of the Census	www.census.gov
American Factfinder	www.factfinder.census.gov
Population data	www.census.gov/population
Housing and household economics	www.census.gov/hhes
Population estimates	www.census.gov/population/www/estimates/popest.html
Population projections	www.census.gov/population/www/projection/popproj.html
Publications	www.census.gov/prod/www/titles
Publications from 1997 economic censuses	www.census.gov/epcd/www/econ97.html
International data base	www.census.gov/ipc/www/idbnew.html
TIGER	www.census.gov/geo/www/tiger
U.S. Bureau of Economic Analysis	www.bea.doc.gov
U.S. Centers for Disease Control and Prevention	www.cdc.gov
Wonder	www.wonder. cdc.gov
U.S. National Center for Health Statistics	www.cdc.gov/nchs
Natality data	www.cdc.gov/nchs/births
Mortality data	www.cdc.gov/nchs/about/major/dvs/mortdata.html
Healthy People 2010	www.health.gov/healthypeople
U.S. National Center for Education Statlstics	www.nces.ed.gov
U.S. Bureau of Labor Statistics	www.bls.gov
U.S. Bureau of Labor Statistics/Census Bureau FERRET site	www.bls.census.gov
U.S. Social Security Administration	www.ssa.gov
Office of the Actuary	www.ssa.gov/oact/pubs.html
U.S. Internal Revenue Service	www.irs.gov
U.S. Immigration and Naturalization Service	www.ins.usdoj.gov
Statistical data	www.ins.usdoj/graphics/aboutins/statistics/index.html
U.S. Economic Research Service (Dept. of Agric.)	www.econ.ag.gov
U.S. National Library of Medicine, Medline	www.igm.nlm.nih.gov
Annie E. Casey Foundation	www.aecf.org
Council of Professional Associations or Federal Statistics	www.copafs.aol.com
Environmental Systems Research Institute, Inc.	www.esri.com
Minnesota Population Research Institute	www.ipums.umn.edu
National Academy of Sciences	www.nas.edu
Population Reference Bureau	www.prb.org
Population Today	www.poptoday.prb.org
International and U.S. population data	www.worldpop.org/prbdata.htm
U.S. demographic trends	www. Ameristat.org
Population Council	www.popcouncil.org
Population Index	www.popindex.princeton.edu
Public Data Queries, Inc. (PDQ-Explore)	www.pdq.com
Public Health Foundation	www.phf.org
Rand Corporation	www.rand.org
Social Science Data Network (SSDAN)	ssdan.net/ssdan-class.html ssdan.net/chip
Statistics Canada	www.statcan.ca
Survey Research Center, Institute of Social Research, University of Michigan	www.icpsr.umich.edu
United Nations	www.un.org
Urban Institute	www.urban.org

APPENDIX B: CENSUS 2000 DATA PRODUCTS

Planned release date*	100% data products	Lowest geographic level
Mar.–Apr. 1, 2001	**Census 2000 Redistricting Data Summary File** • State population counts for legislative redistricting *Media: Internet, CD-ROM*	Blocks
Jun.–Sep. 2001	**Demographic Profile** • Population totals and selected population and housing characteristics in a single table *Media: Internet, CD-ROM, paper*	Places Census tracts (*Internet only*)
Jun.–Sep. 2001	**Congressional District Demographic Profile** • Population totals and selected population and housing characteristics in a single table fr congressional districts only *Media: Internet, CD-ROM, paper*	Congressional districts of the 106th Congress
Jul. 2001	**Race and Hispanic or Latino Summary File on CD-ROM** *Medium: CD-ROM*	Places
States: Jun.–Sep. 2001 *Advance national:* Nov–Dec. 2001 *Final national:* May–Jun. 2002	**Summary File 1 (SF 1):** • Population counts for 63 race categories and Hispanic or Latino • Population counts for many detailed race and Hispanic or Latino categories, and American Indian and Alaska Native tribes • Selected population and housing characteristics (Urban/rural data are on the final national file—this is the only difference from the advance national file) *Media: Internet, CD-ROM*	Blocks Census tracts Blocks/Census tracts
States: Sep.–Dec. 2001 *Advance national:* Mar.–Apr. 2002 *Final national:* Jun.–Jul. 2002	**Summary File 2 (SF 2):** • Population and housing characteristics iterated for many detailed race and Hispanic or Latino categories, and American Indian and Alaska Native tribes (Urban/rural data are on the final national file—this is the only difference from the advance national file) *Media: Internet, CD-ROM*	Census tracts
States: Apr.–Dec. 2001 *National:* Nov. 2001–Apr. 2002	**Quick Tables** • Table shells with population and housing characteristics where the user can specify a geographic area and a population group *Medium: Internet*	Census tracts
States: Apr. 2001–Jan. 2002 *National:* Dec. 2001–Aug. 2002	**Geographic Comparison Tables** • Population and housing characteristics for a list of geographic areas (e.g., all counties in a state) *Medium: Internet*	Places
Sep.–Dec. 2001 (Release subject to policy decisions on access and confidentiality)	**Advanced Query Function** • User specifies contents of tabulations from full microdata file • Includes safeguards against disclosure of identifying information about individuals and housing units *Medium: Internet*	User defined down to block groups

(continues)

Appendix B: Census 2000 Data Products (*continued*)

Planned release date*	100% data products	Lowest geographic level
Jan.–Nov. 2002	**Census 2000: Summary Population and Housing Characteristics** *Media: Internet, paper (printed report)*	Places
2003	**Census 2000: Population and Housing Unit Totals** *Media: Internet, paper (printed report with selected historical counts)*	Places
Dec. 2001–Mar. 2002	**Demographic Profile** • Demographic, social, economic, and housing characteristics presented in three separate tables *Media: Internet, CD-ROM, paper*	Places Census tracts (*Internet only*)
Dec. 2001–Mar. 2002	**Congressional District Demographic Profile** • Demographic, social, economic, and housing characteristics presented in three separate tables for congressional districts only *Media: Internet, CD-ROM, paper*	Congressional districts of the 106th Congress
Jun.–Sep. 2002	**Summary File 3 (SF 3):** • Population counts for ancestry groups • Selected population and housing characteristics *Media: Internet, CD-ROM*	Census tracts Block groups/ Census tracts

Oct. 2002–Feb. 2003	**Summary File 4 (SF 4):**
	 • Population and housing characteristics iterated for many detailed
	    race and Hispanic or Latino categories, American Indian and
	    Alaska Native tribes, and ancestry groups
	 Media: Internet, CD-ROM
		Census tracts

Jun. 2002–Feb. 2003	**Quick Tables** • Table shells with population and housing characteristics where the user can specify a geographic area and a population group *Medium: Internet*	Census tracts
Jul. 2002–Jan. 2003	**Geographic Comparison Tables** • Population and housing characteristics for a list of geographic areas (e.g., all counties in a state) *Medium: Internet*	Places
For 1% sample: 2002 *For 5% sample*:	**Public Use Microdata Sample (PUMS) Files** • 1% sample (information for the nation and states, as well as substate areas where appropriate) • 5% sample (information for state and substate areas)	Super Public Use Microdata Areas (Super-PUMAs) of 400,000+
2003	*Medium: CD-ROM*	PUMAs of 100,000+
Dec. 2002–Mar. 2003 (Release subject to policy decisions on access and confidentiality)	**Advanced Query Function** • User specifies contents of tabulations from full microdata file • Includes safeguards against disclosure of identifying information about individuals and housing units *Medium: Internet*	User defined down to census tracts
2003	**Census 2000: Summary Social, Economic, and Housing Characteristics** *Media: Internet, paper (printed report)*	Places

(*continues*)

Appendix B: Census 2000 Data Products (*continued*)

Planned release date*	100% data products	Lowest geographic level
2003	**Congressional District Data Summary File** • 100% and sample data for the redistricted 108th Congress *Media: Internet, CD-ROM*	Census tracts within congressional districts

General—Census 2000 data products are designed to meet a variety of data needs for different segments of the data user community. The data products described here provide a summary of the general tabulation and publication program for the 50 states, the District of Columbia, and Puerto Rico (which is treated as a state equivalent for each data product). Constraints with staffing and budget, federal guidelines regarding the tabulation of data by race and ethnicity, data processing, or other considerations may result in changes to the types of data products prepared or the timing of their release.

* The dates in this column refer to the first medium of release.

Source: U.S. Bureau of the Census, public document.

NOTES

1. In subsequent years, funds appropriated to the Census Bureau for periodic programs (e.g., 2000 census planning) increased sharply. In fiscal year 1998–1999, the Census Bureau received 61% of funds appropriated to the principal federal statistical agencies. See U.S. Office of Management and Budget, *Analytical Perspectives, Budget of the United States Government*, Fiscal Year 2001.

2. The U.S. Code is a codified listing of U.S. federal laws. The principal divisions of the U.S. Code are called Titles and Title 13 of the U.S. Code groups together the federal legislation governing the operations of the U.S. Census Bureau.

3. J. Gregory Robinson, Bashir Ahmed, Prithwis Das Gupta, and Karen A. Woodrow, "Estimation of population coverage in the 1990 United States census based on demographic analysis," *Journal of the American Statistical Association* 88(423): 1061–1074, September 1993.

4. The reader will note the omission, from the list of proposals seriously considered by the Census Bureau for 2000, of some radical approaches that were proposed in pursuance of the effort to reinvent the year 2000 census. These approaches include substituting for the conventional census a population register, administrative records, or a continuous sample census, or handing over the conduct of the census to the U.S. Postal Service or to a private company.

The conventional census has been under fire in several countries of northern Europe, which have also been concerned about excessive costs. Denmark, Finland, Germany, and the Netherlands have all turned away from conventional census-taking and rely more heavily on population registers, administrative records, and special surveys.

5. The assignment of some items shifted from one category to another between 1990 and 2000.

6. Decennial census data on all the short-form items are specifically cited in legislation but this is also true of many items relegated to the long form. The short-form items in the 1990 and 2000 censuses were selected out of the total list of census questions on the basis of legal, political, programmatic, and demographic considerations.

7. Anthropologists generally recognize three major racial groups, with a few smaller groups not specifically classified: Caucasoid ("white"), Negroid ("black"), Mongoloid (mainly American Indian and most Asian and Pacific Islanders). Hawaiian is one of the unclassified groups. The races are distinguished by a congeries of physical traits, of which skin color is secondary. For example, most Middle Easterners and most Asian Indians are caucasoid.

8. Jeffrey S. Passel, "The Growing American Indian Population, 1960–1990: Beyond demography," pp. 79–102, in Gary D. Sandefur, Ronald R. Rindfuss, and Barney Cohen (eds.), *Changing Numbers, Changing Needs: American Indian Demography and Public Health*, Washington, DC:

National Academy Press, 1996.

9. U.S. Bureau of the Census, "Age, sex, race, and Hispanic origin information from the 1990 census: A comparison of census results with results where age and race have been modified," 1990 CPH-L-74, August 1991. U.S. Bureau of the Census, "U.S. population estimates, by age, sex, race, and Hispanic origin: 1980 to 1991," *Current Population Reports* P25–1095, by Frederick W. Hollmann, February 1993, Table E and Table 1 (pp. 6 and 28).

10. See U.S. Bureau of the Census, *Statistical Abstract of the United States, 1998*, Table 67; *Current Population Reports*, Series P-20, No. 509; and decennial census reports on marital characteristics.

11. The 63 race categories are distributed as follows: a single race (6), two races (15), three races (20), four races (15), five races (6), and six races (1). A minimum tabulation would have seven categories: six single race categories and one for two or more races. If Hispanic origin is taken into account, 126 categories would result (63 times 2).

Since only 2 to 3% of the population reported more than one race in the 1998 Dress Rehearsal for the 2000 census, it is not likely that the change in the form of the race question will affect the final tabulations for the single-race categories very much.

12. Microfiche are flat sheets of film with statistical data. One square inch of microfiche contains a page of census data. They are available for most printed reports.

13. Read-only memory means that the user cannot change or update the information found on the disk. The computer can read the data on the disk but cannot write on it or change it. The data are on the disk as long as the disk lasts.

14. Maps are essential to relate the geographic area names and codes on the STFs to actual geographic areas. For example, to learn the boundaries of block group 4 in census tract 1001 and the boundaries of census tract 1001, the user must refer to a plotter-generated map prepared by the Census Bureau. The Census Bureau has developed a map series that is useful in working specifically with STF data.

15. Computer tapes with census data can be purchased from the Census Bureau. To use these tapes, researchers need appropriate software programs. They can purchase the software from a commercial vendor, or they can secure the services of a State Data Center or a private data-vending company (see text). Information service specialists in the Census Bureau's regional offices and the national office are also available to offer technical assistance relating to the Census Bureau's products.

16. These documents are in Adobe Acrobat Portable Document Format (PDF). To view these publications, the user needs an Acrobat Reader, available from the Adobe Web site. There is a link to this site from the Census Bureau Web site. The direct URL is *www.census.gov/prod/www/titles /html*.

17. See U.S. Bureau of the Census, "Current Population Survey—Design and methodology," *Technical Paper* 63, 2000, for a discussion of the application of population controls in the processing of the Current Population Survey. See also the methodological appendixes of *Current Population Reports*, Series P-60 and P-20, published since 1994.

18. The change of design is described in U.S. Bureau of Labor Statistics, *Monthly Labor Review* 116(9), September 1993, and in U.S. Bureau of the Census, "Current Population Survey—Design and methodology," *Technical Paper* 63, 2000.

19. This is because SIPP is a panel survey designed to track the same respondents over time while CPS is essentially a cross-sectional survey. Although CPS does keep some rotation groups in the survey for more than one interview, a match over time can be made only if the household does not move. In a panel survey the household is tracked to the new address if it moves during the period that it is retained in the sample and if it continues to reside in the primary sampling areas.

20. The lack of comparability results from use of different concepts and procedures and differences in nonsampling errors, even though the same population "controls" are used. A description of the survey and and a summary of its history are presented in Dawn Nelson, David McMillan, and Daniel Kasprzyk, "An overview of the Survey of Income and Program Participation," *Working Paper Series* No. 8401, U.S. Bureau of the Census, June 1984.

21. For a description of the sample design, see U.S. Bureau of the Census, "The American Housing Survey for the United States in 1989,"*Current Housing Reports*, Series H150-89.

22. For a description of the Consumer Expenditure Survey and recent results, see U.S. Bureau of Labor Statistics, *Consumer Expenditure Survey, 1994–1995*, Bulletin 2492, 1997.

23. Many economists believe that the CPI as currently constructed overstates actual price changes for consumer goods and services (i.e., it overstates inflation). According to the Advisory Commission to Study the Consumer Price Index, it suffers from three major upward biases. In total, these biases cause the CPI to overstate inflation by about 1.1%. Because of price inflation, consumers change their buying patterns and shift to less expensive alternatives. In this way they maintain their level of living on a lower budget. This factor causes the CPI to overstate inflation by a fraction (0.4) of a percent. With price inflation, consumers also shift to lower price discount outlets for their purchases (0.1%). A part of the total bias results from failure to allow adequately for the improved quality of existing products (0.6%). Other limitations of the current CPI are the failure to introduce new products into the market basket at sufficiently frequent intervals for the index to reflect the actual buying practices of consumers and the failure of the index to represent the variations in the cost of living for age groups or geographic regions. For example, the elderly have higher expenses than the general population for health goods and services, including prescription drugs, because of their much greater need for these products. A more realistic cost-of-living index would measure the cost of obtaining a fixed level of economic well-being for major segments of the population, but it may not be possible to design such a series of measures.

In the wake of the considerable criticism of the CPI as designed, the Bureau of Labor Statistics (BLS) has made some changes in it, modifying the selection of goods and services included, the weights for combining them, and the statistical method of combining the weighted components. The BLS has also been considering carefully the factors identified by the Advisory Commission as biasing the current CPI and concluded that the index has not been overstating the cost of living, as claimed by the Advisory Commission. Given this disagreement among experts, further evaluation of the CPI is in progress.

See U.S. Bureau of Labor Statistics, "Planned change in the Consumer Price Index formula April 16, 1998," *Consumer Price Indexes*, 1999.

24. A description of the survey and some recent results are given in National Center for Health Statistics, "Current estimates from the Health Interview Survey," by V. Benson and M. Marano, *Vital and Health Statistics* 10(199), 1998.

25. Data from the 1997 economic censuses are available in a variety of forms, like those from the 1990 Population and Housing Censuses. The entire 1997 economic censuses will be available on a series of CD-ROMs.

26. A "Guide to State Statistical Abstracts," a list of the latest Statistical Abstracts for the states, is given in Appendix I of the U.S. Bureau of the Census, *Statistical Abstract of the United States, 1999*.

27. These noncensus or nonsurvey products are mentioned here because of the common sponsorship and common product-packaging of census data, postcensal population estimates, and projections by state data centers and private data-vending companies. See Chapters 9 and 10 for further discussion of population estimates and projections.

28. A list of state data centers and their addresses may be secured at the Census Bureau Web site (www.census.gov) under "Federal Stats, Related Sites, State Data Centers."

29. The PRWO program replaces AFDC (Aid to Families with Dependent Children), the federal-state program of public assistance to needy families. Under the PRWO program, federal block grants are made available to states to finance the new welfare-to-work program authorized by the 1996 Personal Responsibility and Work Opportunity Reconciliation Act.

30. As explained more fully in Chapter 4, use of administrative records for matching in evaluation studies does not always require that the administrative record file be complete, only that it be statistically independent of the census.

31. See Martha E. Fair, "Record linkage in an information society," pp. 903–919, in U.S. Bureau of the Census, *1996 Annual Research Conference*, Washington, DC: U.S. Bureau of the Census, 1996.

32. The match error ratio may be calculated in several ways. One useful distinction is that between the net match error ratio and the gross match error ratio. Erroneous matches (false positive matches) are offset by erroneous nonmatches (false negative matches) in the net error ratio. False positive matches and the false negative matches are combined in the gross error ratio.

33. William Winkler and Fritz Scheuren, "Linking data to create information," in Statistics Canada, *Proceedings of Statistics Canada Symposium 95—From Data to Information—Methods and Systems*, November 1995, Ottawa: Statistics Canada; Fritz Scheuren and William Winkler,

"Recursive analysis of linked data files," pp. 920–935, in US. Bureau of the Census, *1996 Annual Research Conference,* Washington, DC, 1996.

34. Bert Kestenbaum, "Probability linkage using Social Security Administration files," pp. 893–902, in U.S. Bureau of the Census, *1996 Annual Research Conference,* Washington, DC, 1996; Martha E. Fair, "An overview of record linkage in Canada," pp. 139–150, in U.S. Internal Revenue Service, *Turning Administrative Systems into Information Systems,* Bettye Jamerson and Wendy Alvey (eds.), Selected Papers Given in 1995 at the Annual Meetings of the American Statistical Association, 1995.

SUGGESTED READINGS

Federal Statistical Programs

U.S. General Accounting Office. (1996, July 1). *Federal Statistics: Principal Statistical Agencies' Missions and Funding.* GAO/GGD-96-107.

U.S. Office of Management and Budget. (1997, October 30). "Revisions to the standards for the classification of federal data on race and ethnicity." *Federal Register:* 62 (210).

U.S. Office of Management and Budget. (2000, March 9). "Guidance on aggregation and allocation of data on race for use in civil rights monitoring and enforcement." *OMB Bulletin,* No. 00-02.

Censuses of Population and Housing

Anderson, Margo. (1988). *The American Census: A Social History.* New Haven: Yale University Press.

Anderson, Margo, and Fienberg, Stephen E. (1999). *Who Counts? The Politics of Census-Taking in Contemporary America.* Vol. V, in the 1990 Census Research Series. New York: Russell Sage Foundation.

Dodd, David J. (2000). "Tabulating diversity: Race and ethnicity categories in census 2000." *Applied Demography* 13(2). Newsletter of the Applied Demography Interest Group, Population Association of America.

Edmonston, Barry. (1999), "The 2000 census challenge." *Reports on America* 1(1), Washington, DC: The Population Reference Bureau.

Edmonston, Barry, and Schultze, Charles (eds.). (1994). *Modernizing the U.S. Census.* Washington, DC: National Academy Press.

National Research Council, Panel on Alternative Census Methodologies. (1999). *Measuring a Changing Nation: Modern Methods for the 2000 Census.* Washington, DC: National Academy Press.

Petersen, William. (1987). "Politics and the measurement of ethnicity." In William Alonzo and Paul Starr (eds.), *The Politics of Numbers,* pp. 187–233. New York: Russell Sage Foundation.

Robey, Bryant. (1989, April). "Two hundred years and counting: The 1990 census," *Population Bulletin* 44(1). Washington, DC: Population Reference Bureau.

Stefey, D.L., and Bradburn, N. M. (eds.). (1994). *Counting People in the Information Age.* Washington, DC: National Academy Press.

U.S. Bureau of the Census. (1990a). *Census '90: Basics.*

U.S. Bureau of the Census. (1990b). "Federal legislative uses of decennial census data." *1990 Census of Population and Housing: Content Determination Reports,* 1990 CDR-14.

U.S. Bureau of the Census. (1990c). *Tabulation and Publication Program.*

U.S. Bureau of the Census. (1999). "Updated summary: Census 2000 operational plan." *U.S. Census 2000.*

Registration Systems

U.S. Immigration and Naturalization Service. *Statistical Yearbook of Immigration and Naturalization Service.* Annual report.

U.S. National Center for Health Statistics. "Births: Final data for (year)." *National Vital Statistics Reports*. Annual report.

U.S. National Center for Health Statistics. "Deaths: Final data for (year)." *National Vital Statistics Reports*. Annual report.

U.S. National Center for Health Statistics, *Vital Statistics of the United States*. Vols. I and II, Annual report.

National Socioeconomic and Other Sample Surveys

Juster, F. T., and Suzman, R. M. (1995). "An overview of the Health and Retirement Survey." *Journal of Human Resources* 30 (Supplement): S7–S56.

U.S. Bureau of Labor Statistics. (1997a). *BLS Handbook of Methods*. Chapters on the Consumer Price Index and the Consumer Expenditure Survey.

U.S. Bureau of Labor Statistics. (1997b). *Consumer Expenditure Survey, 1994–95*, Bulletin 2492.

U.S. Bureau of Labor Statistics. (1993, September). Special Section: "Overhauling the Current Population Survey." *Monthly Labor Review* 116(9).

U.S. Bureau of the Census. (2000). *Current Population Survey: Design and Methology*. Technical Paper 63.

U.S. Bureau of the Census. (1998). *SIPP Quality Profile*, 1998. See especially Chapters 1–4.

U.S. National Center for Health Statistics. (1989a). "Data systems of the National Center for Health Statistics," by M. G. Kovar. *Vital and Health Statistics* 1(23).

U.S. National Center for Health Statistics. (1989b). "Design and estimation for the National Health Interview Survey, 1985–94," by J. T. Massey, T. F. Moore, V. L. Parsons, and W. Tadros. *Vital and Health Statistics* 2(110).

U.S. National Center for Vital Statistics. (1998). "Current estimates from the National Health Interview Survey, 1995," by V. Benson and V. Marano. *Vital and Health Statistics* 10(199).

U.S. Office of Management and Budget, Statistical Policy Office. (1986). "Federal longitudinal surveys." Prepared by the Federal Committee on Statistical Methodology. *Statistical Policy Working Paper* 13. See especially Appendix, Case Studies 1 and 2.

U.S. Office of Management and Budget, Statistical Policy Office. (1990). "Survey coverage." Prepared by the Federal Committee on Statistical Methodology. *Statistical Policy Working Paper* 17. See Appendix A-7, "Current Population Survey."

National Economic Censuses and Surveys

U.S. Bureau of the Census. (1990). *Guide to the 1987 Economic Censuses and Related Statistics*, EC87-R2, 1990.

U.S. Bureau of the Census. (1993). *Introduction to the 1992 Economic Census*. EC92-PR-2.

U.S. Bureau of the Census. (2000). *History of the 1997 Economic Census*. POL/00HEC.

Administrative Records and Record Linkage

Fair, Martha E. (1995). "An overview of record linkage in Canada." U.S. Internal Revenue Service, *Turning Administrative Systems into Information Systems,* Bettye Jamerson and Wendy Alvey (eds.), pp. 139–150. Selected papers given at the 1995 Annual Meeting of the American Statistical Association.

Fair, Martha E. (1996). "Record linkage in an information society." U.S. Bureau of the Census, *1996 Annual Research Conference*, pp. 903–919.

Jaro, Matthew A. (1995). "Probabilistic linkage of large public health data files." *Statistics in Medicine* 14: 491–448.

Kestenbaum, Bert. (1996). "Probability linkage using Social Security Administration files." U.S. Bureau of the Census, *1996 Annual Research Conference*, pp. 893–902.

Newcombe, Howard B. (1988). *Handbook of Record Linkage: Methods for Health and Social Studies. Administration and Business*. Oxford, UK: Oxford University Press.

Newcombe, Howard, Fair, Martha, and Lalonde, P. (1992). "The use of names for linking personal records," *Journal of the American Statistical Association* 87: 1193–1209.

Scheuren, Fritz, and Winkler, William. (1996). "Recursive analysis of linked data files." U.S. Bureau of the Census, *1996 Annual Research Conference*, pp. 920–935.

U.S. Department of Commerce, Office of Federal Statistical Policy and Standards. (1980a). "Report on exact and statistical matching techniques." Prepared by the Federal Committee on Statistical Methodology. *Statistical Policy Working Paper 5*.

U.S. Department of Commerce, Office of Federal Statistical Policy and Standards. (1980b). "Report on statistical uses of administrative records." Prepared by the Federal Committee on Statistical Methodology. *Statistical Policy Working Paper 6*.

U.S. Internal Revenue Service. (1985, May 9–10). *Record Linkage Techniques: Proceedings of the Workshop on Exact Matching Methodologies*, Beth Kilss and Wendy Alvey (eds.). Arlington, VA. Publication 1299 (2–86). See also a special issue of *Survey Methodology* 19(1), 1993.

Winkler, William E. (1995). "Matching and record linkage." B. G. Cox, Binder, D. A. and Chinappa, A. (eds.), *Business Survey Methods*, pp. 355–384. New York: John Wiley.

Winkler, William, and Scheuren, Fritz. (1995). "Linking data to create information." In Statistics Canada, *Proceedings of Statistics Canada Symposium 95—From Data to Information—Methods and Systems*. November 1995. Ottawa: Statistics Canada.

4

■LIMITATIONS OF CENSUS AND SURVEY DATA

INTRODUCTION

All data derived from censuses and surveys are subject to error and, in fact, census and survey data suffer from substantial error—large and small errors of many types. For example, the precise numbers of residents of the states and their demographic characteristics on any date are indeterminate. An instrument called a census is periodically employed for measuring such phenomena, but this instrument has serious limitations, cannot be made perfect, and yields only approximations to the true numbers. Even the census "count" of the total U.S. population is a refined estimate at best, plagued by omissions and duplications and shored up by "substitutions" and a variety of "coverage improvement procedures." Some of these procedures involve estimation by sampling and other nonenumerative devices.

The reference to errors in censuses and surveys implies the existence of true values, but the question has been posed, not unreasonably, whether there are true, ascertainable values for what censuses or surveys purport to measure. To measure the population of an area at a given moment is like shooting at a moving target since the object—population size—is ephemeral and even fuzzily defined under the special combination of conditions prevailing at any moment. This suggests that a census count is in reality unique, that it cannot be replicated even under the same census conditions, that it is one of a vast number of possible counts, and that the task imposed on the census administrators is in part a metaphysical one.[1] On the other hand, we have statistical tools that can approximate unknown and unknowable numbers, and in spite of measurement difficulties, for some subjects we can reasonably posit that there are true values that lie behind the individual measurements (e.g., age and family income).

This chapter examines the major types of census and survey errors, the ways the errors are measured, their magnitude in decennial population censuses and some federal surveys, and their treatment in tabulations. The discussion is mainly concerned with errors in **cross-sectional data**, data obtained for a single reference date or for independent populations at a series of dates. Such data do not track the *same* persons or households over the life of the survey, as do **panel surveys**. The error profiles of panel surveys are different from those of censuses or cross-sectional surveys, even those that are conducted periodically and thereby produce aggregate data for cohorts.[2] Moreover, the causes of error and the ways of handling them in panel surveys are different. Panel surveys are affected by progressive omission or loss of the households in the sample, called **sample attrition** or sample loss. Errors that present minor problems in the analysis of cross-sectional data may present major problems in the analysis of panel data.

The types of survey errors may be outlined as follows:

> Nonsampling or response errors
> > Coverage errors
> > > Gross coverage errors
> > > > Erroneous inclusions
> > > > Gross omissions
> > > Net coverage error
> > Content or reporting errors
> > > Gross reporting errors
> > > Net reporting error
> > Nonreporting
> Error due to sampling
> > Sampling or probabilistic error
> > Other errors due to sampling

Census and survey errors may be either response errors (also designated nonsampling errors) or errors due to sampling. Errors due to sampling include sampling error, or probabilistic error, and other errors due to sampling. **Sampling error** arises from the fact that the data are based on a sample and hence they differ from the results that would have been obtained if a 100% count were taken. While sampling errors represent possible limitations of the data, they are not errors in the usual sense of the word (i.e., mistakes). However, errors are made as a result of the use of sampling in surveys, including errors in the sample design and errors in the application of the sample design. **Response errors** or **nonsampling errors** encompass all types of errors affecting a census or survey other than those described as errors due to sampling. They include those that result from errors in questionnaire design, interviewer failure, respondent failure, and processing failure.

NONSAMPLING/RESPONSE ERRORS

Most of the space on survey errors is devoted to response or nonsampling errors. This is appropriate for two reasons. First, these sources of error have been the greater focus of attention of applied demographers, whose skills lie more directly in this area and who have been using demographic techniques to measure such errors. Second, for many of the large samples with which applied demographers work (including the census samples and the national survey samples), nonsampling errors tend to be greater in size and to be the more important source of possible misinterpretation of the data.

Nonsampling errors may be classified as coverage errors and content errors (or errors of reporting or classification). Coverage errors may be either **erroneous exclusions** or **erroneous inclusions**—that is, individuals are omitted from the survey or census at their proper address who should have been included and individuals are included in the survey at a particular address who should have been omitted. The difference between these two types of errors is designated **net coverage error**. Erroneous exclusions consist mainly of omissions—that is, persons completely omitted from the census and persons erroneously enumerated at another address. Erroneous inclusions consist of cases of households or persons for whom more than one questionnaire was obtained (**duplications**), for whom fictitious entries for nonexistent housing units were recorded (**curbstoning**), who were reported at the wrong address (**geocoding errors**), and who should be omitted according to the designated scope of the census or survey, such as temporary visitors and tourists from abroad and persons who died before or were born after the designated census or survey date (**out-of-scope cases**). Geocoding errors or geographic misassignments give rise at once to errors of both inclusion and omission since the household is enumerated erroneously at one address and omitted erroneously at another address. Inasmuch as these errors occur at different addresses, they may affect the counts for two different tabulation areas. At the national level and for broad geographic areas, they have little or no net effect on the counts of the population, but they do affect the counts of small areas.

The term **net errors** was previously defined as the difference between erroneous omissions and erroneous inclusions. The term **gross errors** is defined as the sum of these two types of errors. Net errors tend to be smaller than gross errors because in the calculation of the net error the two types of errors offset one another to some degree. If we designate the true number for an area as T, the reported number as N, the erroneous inclusions as i, and the erroneous exclusions as e, the net error for the area is $e - i$:

$$T = N + (e - i) \tag{1}$$

Omissions are much more likely to occur in censuses and surveys than erroneous inclusions, and as a result the net coverage error is also designated the **net undercount**. The corresponding gross error is represented as $e + i$. Attention is given to gross error because it provides a more complete record of the sources of error and of the effectiveness of the survey- or census-taking procedures than the net error.

Coverage Error

The following general statement on the causes of coverage error is succeeded by a description of the procedures that the Census Bureau has employed as part of the census operations to reduce omissions and a description of the methods that are used to measure coverage error. The review of methods of measuring coverage error offers us another view of the causes of census and survey omissions.

Causes of Coverage Error

The causes of omissions from censuses and surveys are numerous and may be classified in a variety of ways. It has proven difficult to quantify these causes as they play out in an actual census, although local ethnographic studies have cast some light on them. The causes of omission may be classified under four headings, not claimed to be mutually exclusive or comprehensive: errors of the professional staff, the actions or inactions of the respondent, problems of the physical environment, and miscellaneous other sources, including mainly machine failure and accidents. Omissions can result from errors in the planning, design, and conduct of census and survey operations on the part of the professional staff. This first source of error is illustrated by an incomplete address register, ambivalent questionnaire instructions, and failure to follow up nonresponses. The second is illustrated by deliberate avoidance, carelessness, or apathy on the part of the respondent. It is well documented that a substantial segment of the population harbors attitudes of alienation toward governmental authority. The third is illustrated by irregular housing and living arrangements, such as unconventional and illegal housing conditions, and the location of housing units in isolated and hazardous areas. A fourth category attributes a portion of the errors to processing problems and accidents. A factor such as the transiency of the population presents a problem, falling under more than one of the four headings listed.

Omissions may be either omissions of an individual from a household that was enumerated or omission of an entire household, including persons living alone. In the decennial censuses and the national sample surveys, omission of persons from enumerated households appears to be a more important reason for census undercount than omission of persons in missed households, at least among groups where the undercount level is relatively high (e.g., blacks). The underlying causes of these two types of omissions are different. Omissions of persons in enumerated households result from neglect, lack of information, or a deliberate effort to omit a household member on the part of respondents. Omissions of entire households result from incompleteness of the address register, unconventional housing conditions, difficult physical conditions for enumeration, and individuals living alone who wish to avoid enumeration. Some omissions of entire households result from processing problems, such as mechanical failure (e.g., failure of microfilm equipment) and accidents during processing (e.g., loss of records as a result of fire or flood). Accordingly, it is useful to distinguish omissions due to **processing losses** and omissions due to **noninterview**, as well as within-household and entire-household omissions.

We can also consider the causes of coverage error from a "compositional" point of view. This approach asks the question, what are the relative coverage rates of age, sex, and race/ethnic groups, types of households, housing-tenure groups (i.e., owners or renters), type-of-housing groups, and other groups in the population? The answer can identify valuable indicators of the undercount problem and suggest ways of designing the census, evaluation, and adjustment programs. Estimates for some of these categories are given in a later section.

Given this array of causes, one can blame the survey takers, the survey respondents, or both, in various degrees, for undercoverage in censuses and surveys. Maybe we should also allow for natural causes and "acts of God." The members of Congress in the political party opposing the Administration routinely tend to place the bulk of the blame for the undercount of the decennial census on the Census Bureau. However, the decennial censuses have been carefully designed by highly competent technicians, considerable publicity has been given to the censuses, and response to the census is mandatory. Through the use of a carefully validated address register, the Census Bureau has a firm basis for obtaining a complete count of households, particularly the residents in conventional housing units, and considerable effort is expended to design and apply many so-called coverage improvement procedures. It is reasonable to conclude that most of the coverage error is due to respondents and reflects a combination of deliberate avoidance of the census, public apathy, and carelessness.

Reduction of Coverage Error

A substantial proportion of the households (i.e., occupied housing units) did not return the census mail-out/mail-back forms in the 1970, 1980, and 1990 censuses. Only 65% of all housing units returned the forms in 1990 compared with 75% in 1980. Note that some housing units are not expected to return the forms; they are vacant or seasonal units. Nevertheless, this experience suggests that willingness to cooperate with the federal government had been diminishing. Anticipating a continuation in 2000 of reduced cooperation of the public, the Census Bureau's budgeted target for this census was 61%. In fact, 66% of the households returned the forms. Note, however, that return of the forms is no guarantee that all persons in these households were properly listed.

Failure to respond in the first phase of a census conducted by mail or of a survey conducted by personal or telephone interviews is followed up by telephone calls and personal visits. More than one visit or additional telephone call may be made. After a specified number of follow-up contacts have been attempted in accordance with the rules of a given census or survey, and an interview has not been obtained, it is necessary to close out the record by handling it as an estimation problem, using the available field information obtained by observation or inquiry of neighbors. Each census or survey has rules specifying the information required to add a person to the count. In the decennial census, a few items, such as sex, race, and relationship to the householder, are considered sufficient to infer the existence of a person. In these cases, a previously processed person or unit is drawn from the file under specified criteria and a full set of characteristics is duplicated for the unenumerated person and unit—a process called **substitution**. The same course is taken if a completed questionnaire is unavailable or unusable (e.g., lost or damaged). Hence, the necessity for such a substitution can arise from either a noninterview or a processing failure.

The measured coverage error of the census does not include these substitutions, since the substitutions are made part of the official count. Their number is important, however, because they are the "nearly missed," and hence they add to an understanding of the true degree of error in the count of the population and of the extent of bias in the reporting of population characteristics. They also suggest possible sources of coverage error. The 1990 census count of the total population included about 1.5 million substitutions, which represents about 0.6% of the population. The use of substitutions figured much more prominently in the 1980 census. The 1980 census count of the population included 3.4 million substitutions, or about 1.5% of the population. Table 4.1 presents some data on the extent of substitutions occurring in the editing operations of the 1990 and 1980 censuses.

In addition to substitutions, the initial field counts of censuses may be augmented by a variety of procedures designated **coverage improvement programs**. Such programs may include some extraordinary procedures to augment the census count. The 1990 census coverage improvement programs included a Shelter and Street Night Enumeration, Transient Night Enumeration, a Vacant/Delete/Movers Check, the recanvass of special areas, a postcensus local review, a special telephone assistance program, and other programs (Table 4.2). One set of programs yielding many additions to the count, called "search/match," included the parolee/probationer program, individual census reports, military census reports, and "Were You Counted?" forms. It added 0.6 million persons to the count. Persons who believed that they were omitted from the census could send in "Where You Counted?" forms. Such a procedure carries a great risk of adding duplicate responses unless the forms are carefully matched against the census records. The greatest yield, 1.5 million

TABLE 4.1   Percentage of Persons Added by Substitution in the 1990 and 1980 Censuses, by Age, by Sex, by Race, and by Region

Subject	1990	1980	Subject	1990	1980
Total	0.6	1.5	Male	0.6	1.5
			Female	0.6	1.5
Age	0.6	1.5			
Under 15	0.5	1.5	Race	0.6	1.5
15 to 19	0.5	1.4	White	0.5	1.3
20 to 24	0.7	1.6	Black	1.2	2.6
25 to 34	0.7	1.6	Hispanic origin	0.6	1.5
35 to 44	0.6	1.5	Northeast	0.8	1.2
45 to 54	0.6	1.5	Midwest	0.5	1.2
55 to 64	0.7	1.5	South	0.7	2.0
65 and over	0.7	1.6	West	0.7	1.5
Household relationship	0.7	1.5	Marital status/15+	0.7	1.5

Source: U.S. Bureau of the Census, *1990 Census of Population*, "General Population Characteristics, United States," 1990 CP90-1-1, 1992, Table 282; *1980 Census of Population*, PC80-1-B1, Tables B-1 and B-4.

███ **TABLE 4.2   Effectiveness of 1990 Census Coverage Improvement Programs**

Coverage improvement method	Housing units added Number (thousands)	Percent	Persons added Number (thousands)	Percent
Programs to Improve the Address List Prior to Enumeration				
Advance Post Office Check I	1353.3	1.3	—	—
Advance Post Office Check II/III and Advance Post Office Check Reconciliation[e]	1171.7[a]	1.1	—	—
Precanvass	5963.0[a]	5.8	—	—
Yellow Card Coding	394.3	0.4	—	—
Precensus Local Review	367.3	0.4	—	—
Casing Check	931.1	0.9	—	—
Questionnaire Delivery and Enumeration				
Rural Update/Leave	399.4	0.4	—	—
Urban Update/Leave	NA	NA	—	—
Urban Update/ Enumerate	NA	NA	NA	NA
Shelter and Street Night Enumeration	—	—	240.1[c]	0.1
Post-Census Day Coverage Improvement				
Telephone Assistance Adds	158.0[b]	0.2	407.0[d]	0.2
Census Closeout Address Check	—	—	0.9[b]	0.0
Vacant/Delete/Movers Check	344.8	0.3	1505.4	0.6
Recanvass	138.6	0.1	178.2[d]	0.1
Postcensus Local Review	80.9	0.1	124.9[d]	0.1
POP One Reenumeration	—	—	56.3	0.0
Primary Selection Algorithm Review	—	—	350.4	0.1
Search/Match Coverage Improvement				
Parolee/Probationer Coverage Improvement Program and Followup	25.0	0.0	447.8	0.2
Other Search/Match Forms[f]	24.9	0.0	603.6	0.2

NA: Not available.

General notes:

Total 1990 housing unit and population counts, used as base of percentages, were 102,264,000 and 248,710,000, respectively. Many coverage improvement programs were conducted only in some areas of the country.

[a] Housing unit adds include all addresses added during the operation, including those addresses that were deleted in later operations. (Housing unit adds for all other operations include only those addresses with a final census status of occupied or vacant.) During precanvass processing, some geographic transfers were not recognized as such and are included in the count of precanvass adds.

[b] Estimated number of adds are based on a sample.

[c] This is a count of the persons enumerated at emergency shelters, shelters for abused women, shelters for runaway and neglected children, and street locations. S-Night was not designed to (and was never intended to be) a complete count of the homeless population.

[d] Estimated number of person adds are based on an average household size of 2.63 persons per household in occupied housing units.

[e] Housing units identified by the USPS as adds during APOC II and III were not added until verified during APOC Reconciliation. Therefore, the number of housing unit adds cannot be separated by APOC and APOC Reconciliation.

[f] Other search/match forms include individual census reports, military census reports, shipboard census reports, usual home elsewhere forms, and were you counted? forms.

Source: U.S. Bureau of the Census, "Programs to improve coverage in the 1990 census," *Evaluation and Research Reports*, 1990 *Census of Population and Housing*, 1990 CPH-E-3, 1993.

persons and 0.3 million housing units, came from the Vacant/Delete/Movers Check. This program reexamined a sample of vacant and deleted units and added persons to them, as needed; many of the units were then reclassified as occupied and vacant. The coverage improvement programs of 1990 added about 3.9 million persons in total to the raw census count. Such programs have been employed for several censuses, and substantial, though smaller, numbers of persons were added from this source in earlier censuses.

Since substitutions and the coverage improvement programs involve estimation as a method for completing the census, it is difficult to distinguish analytically between (1) persons added by these methods and (2) persons estimated by some evaluation method, such as demographic analysis or a post-enumeration survey, to have been omitted from, or erroneously included in, the census. Two bases of distinction may be made. The first is that the former additions to the count have some basis, albeit a limited one, in the actual field work of the census and the second is that it is possible to include them at all geographic levels of the census in time for the apportionment of the Congress. Once the census apportionment figures are tabulated and transmitted to the Congress, any omissions in the counts are viewed as deficiencies in the coverage of the census.

We may designate the use of estimation to increase the initial (raw) census or survey counts as **coverage improvement** and the measurement of the extent of coverage error in the "final" counts as **coverage evaluation.** Survey designs differ as to the place where this line is drawn. As we saw in Chapter 3, in comparison with the procedures used in the 1990 census, a part of the original plan for the year 2000 census, called Integrated Coverage Measurement, shifted the line between coverage improvement and coverage evaluation to the point where adjustment of the count through coverage improvement would have taken care of all undercoverage. Evaluation of undercoverage would then have been reduced to a theoretical zero. In 1994, the Current Population Survey and other national surveys conducted by the Census Bureau underwent a major shift in the use of coverage improvement by adjusting the surveys to "controls" that included the part of coverage error resulting from the 1990 census undercount, as will be explained further.

Measurement of Coverage Error

We may classify the principal techniques of measuring coverage in censuses as demographic analysis, dual systems analysis, and ethnographic analysis. In the context of data evaluation, **demographic analysis** refers to the use of demographic data and methods to develop independent estimates of the expected (i.e., true or correct) population for comparison with the census counts or survey estimates. The kinds of data used in demographic analysis include birth, death, and immigration data, data from prior and current censuses, and administrative record data (e.g., Medicare files, Selective Service data). The methods of demographic analysis include a variety of demographic techniques, among them survival analysis, age-ratio analysis, and sex-ratio analysis. Note that the method of demographic analysis is defined to include comparison of census counts with aggregated administrative records as well as demographic analysis per se.

Figure 4.1 is a **Lexis diagram** that graphically displays the design of the calculations of net census undercount by the method of demographic analysis for 1990, and Table 4.3 enumerates the final steps in deriving estimates of the net undercount in the 1990 census by the method of demographic analysis. The table shows that, before actually comparing the expected numbers with the census counts, it is necessary to make some special adjustments in each set of data to improve comparability (i.e., to add estimates of illegal residents to the expected numbers and to correct the racial distribution in the census counts for the misclassification of race) (see Chapter 3).

For the most part, the estimates of census coverage in the 1990 census

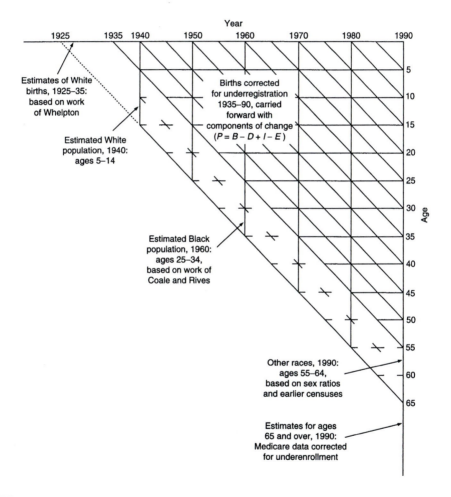

FIGURE 4.1   Lexis diagram showing construction of estimates of coverage in the 1990 census by demographic analysis. *Source:* J. Gregory Robinson et al. "Estimation of population coverage in the 1990 United States census based on demographic analysis." *Journal of the American Statistical Association* **88(423)**: 1061–1074, September, 1993, Figure 1. Reproduced with permission from the *Journal of the American Statistical Association.* Copyright 1993 by the American Statistical Association. All rights reserved.

TABLE 4.3 Final Steps in the Derivation by Demographic Analysis of Estimates of Percentages of Net Undercount in the 1990 Census, by Sex and Race (Numbers in Thousands)

Estimates	Total Both sexes (1)	Male (2)	Female (3)	Black Both sexes (4)	Male (5)	Female (6)	Non Black Both sexes (7)	Male (8)	Female (9)
1. Revised legally resident population, 4-1-1990	250,061	122,928	127,133	32,039	15,625	16,414	218,022	107,303	110,719
2. Illegaly resident aliens, 4-1-1990	3,333	1,792	1,541	281	134	147	3,052	1,658	1,394
3. Total resident population, 4-1-1990 (3 = 1 + 2)	253,394	124,720	128,674	32,320	15,759	10,561	221,074	108,961	112,113
4. Census count, 4-1-1990	248,710	121,239	127,470	29,986	14,170	15,816	218,724	107,069	111,656
5. Race modification	0	0	0	497	250	247	–497	–250	–247
6. Modified census count 4-1-1990 (6 = 4 + 5)	248,710	121,239	127,471	30,483	14,420	16,063	218,227	106,819	111,406
7. Net undercount, 4-1-1990 (7 = 3 – 6)	4,684	3,480	1,204	1,836	1,338	498	2,848	2,142	706
8. Percent net undercount, 4-1-1990 (8 = 7/3 × 100)	1.85	2.79	0.94	5.68	8.49	3.01	1.29	1.97	0.63

Source: J. Gregory Robinson *et al.*, "Estimation of population coverage in the 1990 United States census based on demographic analysis," *Journal of the American Statistical Association* 88(423): 1061–1074, September, 1993, Table 2. Reproduced with permission from the *Journal of the American Statistical Association.* Copyright 1993 by the American Statistical Association. All rights reserved.

were derived by applying the basic demographic accounting equation to each birth cohort:

$$P = B - D + I - E \tag{2}$$

That is, in general, for each birth cohort, births (B), deaths (D), immigration (I), and emigration (E) were combined to obtain the 1990 population expected figures. For example, the estimate of the population 50 years of age on April 1, 1990, was based on births from April 1939 to March 1940, adjusted for underregistration, reduced by deaths to the cohort in each year between 1939 and 1990, augmented by estimates of immigration into the cohort, and diminished by emigration from the cohort over the 51-year period. Prior to 1935 (in particular, 1925 to 1935 for the 1990 calculations), the birth registration figures were inadequate and required special supplementation because not all states were included in the birth registration area until 1933 and underregistration in many states was quite substantial. All ages under 65 in 1990 were essentially estimated on the basis of such cohort analysis. The diagonal lines in Figure 4.1 depict the paths of the birth cohorts. The cohorts born before 1925 (i.e., aged 65 years and over in 1990) could be directly estimated by use of Medicare data corrected for underenrollment.

Demographic analysis demonstrates that the coverage of the population censuses improved steadily from 1940 to 1980 but retrogressed in 1990 (Table 4.4). Estimated overall net census undercount dropped from 5.4% in 1940 to 1.2% in 1980 and then rose to 1.8% in 1990. Moreover, the black/nonblack gap, which had narrowed between 1970 and 1980, widened again in 1990. Throughout the period 1940 to 1980 the gap was 4.3 points (1970) or less, and in 1990 it was 4.4 points.

TABLE 4.4 Historical Estimates of Percentages of Net Undercount Derived by Demographic Analysis, by Sex and Race: 1940 to 1990

Race and sex	1990	1980	1970	1960	1950	1940
Total	1.8	1.2	2.7	3.1	4.1	5.4
Male	2.8	2.2	3.4	3.5	4.4	5.8
Female	0.9	0.3	2.0	2.7	3.8	5.0
Nonblack	1.3	0.8	2.2	2.7	3.8	5.0
Male	2.0	1.5	2.7	2.9	3.8	5.2
Female	0.6	0.1	1.7	2.4	3.7	4.9
Black	5.7	4.5	6.5	6.6	7.5	8.4
Male	8.5	7.5	9.1	8.8	9.7	10.9
Female	3.0	1.7	4.0	4.4	5.4	6.0
Difference						
Male/female	1.8	1.9	1.5	0.8	0.6	0.8
Black/nonblack	4.4	3.7	4.3	3.9	3.6	3.4

Source: J. Gregory Robinson *et al.*, "Estimation of population coverage in the 1990 United States census based on demographic analysis," *Journal of the American Statistical Association* 88(423): 1061–1074, September, 1993, Table 2. Reproduced with permission from the *Journal of the American Statistical Association*. Copyright 1993 by the American Statistical Association. All rights reserved.

Dual systems analysis can be defined as case-by-case matching of records from two (or more) collection systems for the purpose of evaluating one of the sets of records by the other. One of the sets of records is presumed to be the standard for evaluating the other. In the present context, dual systems analysis involves the matching of census individual records to post-enumeration surveys (PES), continuing sample surveys, or administrative records. The fundamental paradigm for making estimates by this method is as follows:

Census enumeration

PES	In	Out	Total
In	$N_{1.1}$	$N_{1.2}$	N_{1+}
Out	$N_{2.1}$	$N_{2.2}$	N_{2+}
Total	N_{+1}	N_{+2}	N_{++}

The dual-systems model classifies each person as being included or not included in the census enumeration and as being included or not included in the PES. The matching operation permits filling all cells except for $N_{2.2}$ and the three row or column totals that are based on $N_{2.2}$, namely N_{+2}, N_{2+}, and N_{++}. Commonly, in the use of this model, independence between inclusion in the census and inclusion in the PES is assumed. That is to say, one's chances of being omitted from the census is not affected by, or correlated with, one's chances of being omitted from the PES. This assumption statistically implies that the estimate of the total population, N_{++}, is equal to

$$N_{++} = (N_{+1})(N_{1+}) \div N_{1.1} \qquad (3)$$

This formula is called the dual-system estimator.[3]

The two basic methods of coverage evaluation have different data requirements, assumptions, and products. The method of demographic analysis depends heavily on the accuracy of the independent estimates of the corrected population and produces mainly estimates of net coverage errors for the national population specific by sex, age, race, and Hispanic origin. The method of dual-systems analysis does not require the collection systems to be complete, not even the system considered as standard, and can measure gross errors (i.e., omissions and erroneous inclusions separately, and coverage and misreporting separately). However, the results are subject to sampling error and various potentially serious biases, especially correlation bias and matching bias. The results may also be biased because of the assumption of homogeneous probabilities within each of the substrata for which the paradigm is applied. The latter assumption can be easily violated by the considerable variation in the characteristics of persons in the cells of the paradigm.

Correlation bias is the bias arising from the failure of the responses in one collection system (e.g., census) and the responses in the other collection system (e.g., PES) to be statistically independent. Logically we would expect a positive correlation bias (i.e., omission from one system is associated with omission from the other), and as a result, the undercount would be understated. It is possible, however, for the correlation bias to be negative, particularly for small areas, and the undercount would be overstated. With either bias, adjustment of the census data could reduce the population count rather than increase it. Because of correlation bias, the PES tends to underestimate coverage in particular for those groups that have high levels of undercoverage. This is evident in the comparative results of the PES and demographic analysis in the 1990 census. Estimates of coverage error in the decennial census of population as measured by a PES or equivalent have consistently, over several censuses, been lower than the estimates of coverage error as measured by demographic analysis for the total population, males, and blacks. To reduce the degree of correlation bias, the PES or its equivalent may be conducted with a lag of several months following the census, but because of changes of address since the census this step increases the chances for matching bias.

Matching bias refers to the bias arising from the tendency for observations in one collection system not to be matched with observations in the other system even though they are the same, or the tendency for observations to be matched even though they are different. Experience shows that matching bias is usually positive—that is, it results in an overstatement of the extent of nonmatches and hence of the percentage of net census undercount. Increased searching effort tends to raise the proportion of matches, but not enough to eliminate all erronenous nonmatches. In practice, then, matching bias tends to offset correlation bias, but probably only in part.

Demographic analysis is a highly effective method for measuring coverage error at the national level and can produce analytically useful estimates at the state level and even the substate level.[4] At present, however, it cannot produce sufficiently accurate results at the state and substate levels for use in correcting the undercounted data. Dual systems analysis is potentially effective at the national and subnational levels, but generally the quality of the estimates decreases with the size of the area.[5] Tables 4.5 and 4.6 summarize the results of the coverage studies of the 1990 census for the United States as shown by demographic analysis and the post-enumeration survey. Table 4.5 compares the results obtained by the two methods for the two sexes and two race categories, and Table 4.6 gives data for selected age groups. These figures do not reflect the additions to the census through substitutions and the coverage improvement programs. The latter additions have been incorporated into the official census counts and are considered part of them.

Ethnographic analysis involves participant observation, by specially trained observers, of small population groups clustered geographically in order to ascertain the true population of the designated area. In this approach, the observers, usually urban ethnographers, take up residence in a neighborhood where racial/ethnic minories reside, become familiar with the membership of each of the households on the block, and try to reconcile these observations with the census reports for these households.[6] Its primary utility is in identifying the possible sources of undercoverage in the census by probing the complexities of family relationships, housing, and residential patterns of the members of the households at the test sites. Thereby, the method offers some qualitative indications of the role of certain factors in the undercoverage of groups that have traditionally been undercounted.

The ethnographic approach has its limitations. Most important, the results are case studies and they cannot be generalized quantitatively to any larger population, especially the national population. The participant observers may be seen as intruders who are spying for the federal government into the pri-

TABLE 4.5   Estimates of Percentages of Net Undercount for Race and Sex Groups in the 1990 Census: Comparison of Demographic Analysis and the Post-Enumeration Survey (Amounts in Thousands)

Race and sex	Demographic analysis		Post-Enumeration Survey		Difference[a]	
	Amount	Percentage	Amount	Percentage	Amount	Percentage
Total	4,684	1.8	4,003	1.6	681	0.3
Male	3,480	2.8	2,384	1.9	1,096	0.9
Female	1,204	0.9	1,619	1.2	−416	−0.3
Nonblack	2,848	1.3	2,612	1.2	236	0.1
Male	2,142	2.0	1,653	1.5	489	0.4
Female	706	0.6	959	0.8	−253	−0.2
Black	1,836	5.7	1,391	4.4	445	1.2
Male	1,338	8.5	731	4.9	608	3.6
Female	498	3.0	660	4.0	−162	−1.0

[a] A positive difference means that the estimate from demographic analysis is higher than the Post-Enumeration Survey estimate; a negative estimate means that the estimate from demographic analysis is lower. Positive signs are omitted.

Source: Unpublished document provided by J. Gregory Robinson, U.S. Bureau of the Census. See also J. Gregory Robinson *et al.*, "Estimation of population coverage in the 1990 United States census based on demographic analysis," *Journal of the American Statistical Association* 88(423): 1061–1074, September 1993, Table 2. Reproduced with permission from the *Journal of the American Statistical Association*. Copyright 1993 by the American Statistical Association. All rights reserved.

vate lives of defenseless minorities and may be fed incorrect information. The essential difficulties of recording the list of residents remain, since the observers must deal with the same ambiguous situations in the living arrangements and residence patterns of the members of these households as regular census takers.

Ethnographic research sponsored by the Census Bureau suggests several causes—many of them related—of the disproportionate undercount of some racial minorities and Hispanics, particularly black and Hispanic men. These include alienation from mainstream society, particularly from the government, deliberate concealment of members to protect sources of household income, irregular and complex household arrangements, including fluid household structures and residence patterns, and the effort of black women to maintain their control of the household. As an example of fluid household arrangements, some children and men "bunk" in more than one household and have no primary attachment to any of them. These factors are associated with residential mobility, lack of knowledge of English and illiteracy, cultural differences in the definition of a household, presence of unrelated individuals, and households formed for purposes of sharing the rent (de la Puente, 1993, *op. cit.*; Martin *et al.*, 1990, *op. cit.*). These factors are usually direct or indirect consequences of poverty and economic marginality and are also reasons mainly for within-household omission. In the test sites, irregular housing is the main reason that entire households are omitted from the census. Irregular housing includes housing units hidden from public view, illegally built units, unconventional units, and units lacking clear numerical designations. Such units may appear in old delapidated buildings, remote rural areas, and sections of large cities where violence is endemic.

TABLE 4.6 Estimates of Percentages of Net Undercount, for Specified Age, Sex, and Race Groups in the 1990 Census: Comparison of Demographic Analysis and the Post-Enumeration Survey (Base of Percentages Is the Estimated "True" Population; a Minus Sign Denotes a Net Overcount)

Age	Nonblack Male	Female	Black Male	Female
Demographic analysis				
All ages	2.0	0.6	8.5	3.0
0–4	2.7	2.8	8.6	8.2
5–9	2.7	2.8	7.7	7.5
10–14	0.5	0.7	4.1	4.0
15–19	−2.3	−1.7	−0.2	0.4
20–24	−0.8	−0.6	5.7	2.5
25–29	4.5	2.1	12.7	4.9
30–34	3.8	0.7	14.0	3.5
35–39	2.6	0.2	11.9	2.2
40–44	1.4	−0.7	10.6	1.5
45–49	2.7	0.6	11.9	2.4
50–54	2.8	0.4	12.0	1.6
55–59	3.0	0.4	12.1	—
60–64	2.6	0.1	10.3	−2.9
65–69	2.2	−0.9	2.1	−7.7
70–74	1.9	−0.1	4.1	−3.8
75+	0.2	1.5	3.2	4.4
All ages	2.0	0.6	8.5	3.0
Under 18	1.5	1.8	5.9	5.9
18–29	1.3	0.2	7.7	2.9
30–49	2.7	0.2	12.3	2.5
50 and over	2.2	0.4	8.3	−0.8
Post-Enumeration Survey				
All ages	1.5	0.8	4.9	4.0
Under 18	2.5	2.5	7.0	7.1
18–29	3.1	2.4	3.6	5.5
30–49	1.3	0.6	6.3	3.2
50 and over	−0.6	−1.2	−0.4	−1.2

Source: Unpublished document provided by J. Gregory Robinson, U.S. Bureau of the Census. J. Gregory Robinson *et al.*, "Estimation of population coverage in the 1990 United States census based on demographic analysis," *Journal of the American Statistical Association* 88(423): 1061–1074, September 1993, Table 3. Reproduced with permission from the *Journal of the American Statistical Association*. Copyright 1993 by the American Statistical Association. All rights reserved.

Coverage of the 1990 Census

According to the method of demographic analysis, the estimated net undercount in the 1990 census was 4.7 million persons or 1.8% of the population (Table 4.5). The corresponding figure for blacks was 1.8 million or 5.7% of the population, while the figure for nonblacks was 2.8 million or 1.3% of the population. Dual systems analysis, linking the 1990 census and the post-enumeration survey (PES), gave slightly lower results than demographic analysis for the overall net undercount (4.0 million persons or 1.6%), but the figure for blacks, particularly males, was much lower (1.4 million or 4.4%) than those shown by demographic analysis. The nonblack percentage was 1.2 and the Hispanic percentage was 5.0 (Hogan, 1993, *op. cit.*). Clearly, the coverage of the nonblack population was much better than for the black population, as shown by both demographic analysis and the PES. The evaluation studies of the 1990 census established the persistence of the considerable black/nonblack gap in coverage. The PES established the fact that Hispanics were missed at a much higher rate than nonblacks in general and at about the same rate as blacks. Demographic analysis demonstrated that the levels of undercount were very high among black males 25 to 64 years of age (Table 4.6). Other PES measurements showed that home ownership or tenure is as important as race in explaining the undercount.

Coverage errors in the census were estimated separately in the two phases of the post-enumeration survey (PES), designated the P sample and the E sample. The proportion of the P sample included in the census is an estimate of the proportion of the true total population included in the census. The E sample consisted of a sample of persons enumerated in the census and was used to estimate the proportion of census enumerations that were erroneous. These enumerations were checked against the census records to determine the extent of duplications, fictitious enumerations, out-of-scope enumerations, and enumerations at the wrong location. The PES showed some 14.1 million erroneous enumerations in the 1990 census, consisting of duplications and fictitious enumerations (4.35 million), geocoding errors (0.7 million), other counting errors (5.5 million), unmatchable cases (2.9 million), and imputed cases (0.7 million). (See Hogan, 1993, *op. cit.*, Table 7.) The 4.35 million duplications and fictitious enumerations have to be subtracted from the census counts before adding in the dual systems estimation from the P sample. If we disregard the 9.76 million geocoding and other errors which represent equal numbers of additions and subtractions, the PES operation accounted for some 8.34 million omissions and some 4.35 million erroneous inclusions in the 1990 census, implying a net undercount of 4.0 million persons in that census. The corresponding percentages are 3.3, 1.7, and 1.6.[7]

Nonresponse rates, the proportions of households that failed to return their mailed questionnaires, have proven to be a sound indicator of the categories of persons who were disproportionately omitted from the 1990 census. Four such categories stand out: racial minorities/Hispanics (i.e., other than non-Hispanic whites), renters, other than husband-wife households, and other than single-family homes. Where *all* these conditions existed, the nonresponse rate was 60%; where *none* of these conditions existed, the nonresponse rate was only 12%.[8] The variation in response rates from 12% to 60% on the basis of these factors applied without reference to geographic location. Such research findings can serve as a basis for developing net undercount rates for small areas as synthetic estimates—that is, as weighted averages of the undercount estimates for these specific categories as observed for larger areas, based on a PES or demographic analysis.

Since the magnitude and distribution of the errors differ from census to census, censuses are never exactly comparable and may sometimes be grossly lacking in comparability, as were the censuses of 1970 and 1980. The plans for taking the 1980 census were so oriented toward making the census "the most complete census ever taken" that the census field operations were stretched out inordinately and, as a result, several million persons were caught in the census net twice. This type of effort was repeated in 1990, with expected results— that is, many duplications but less discontinuity with the 1980 counts. If the year 2000 census succeeds in achieving zero net undercount, as is the goal of the Census Bureau, the 1990 and 2000 censuses will again have a serious comparability problem.

Coverage of National Sample Surveys

The coverage of the Current Population Survey (CPS), as well as other major national surveys conducted by the Census Bureau, can be measured by the extent of the final (second-stage) adjustment of the survey figures after all the preliminary adjustments. The preliminary adjustments include basic weighting, noninterview adjustments, and a (first-stage) ratio adjustment for the black-nonblack population of each state using census data. In the several decades prior to January 1994, the CPS data were then inflated to independent postcensal estimates of the national population consistent with the level of the census counts. An **inflation–deflation procedure** assured that the postcensal population estimates preserved the undercount levels of the previous census at *each age*. In January 1994, the scope of the final or second-stage adjustment was changed. The extent of the final adjustment for coverage deficiency in the CPS was enlarged to encompass not merely the gap between the CPS "provisional" figures and the postcensal estimates consistent with the census level, but also the gap between the census estimates and the adjusted census figures. Thus, no further space was left for undercoverage, coverage evaluation, and adjustment.

In this final adjustment, the CPS data, stratified into several hundred mutually exclusive groups called **control groups**, are reweighted to allow for net omissions in these control groups. The net omissions in the CPS are represented by the gap between (1) the provisional estimates from the survey and (2) independent postcensal population estimates derived by demographic analysis and adjusted for the net undercounts in the 1990 census as measured by the PES. For the reweighting, the independent population estimates are also stratified into the same several hundred control groups. Currently these groups are the groups defined by the cross-classification of age (single years), sex, and race (white, black, other), the cross-classification of Hispanic origin, sex, and age, and the totals 16 years and over for states. The controls are applied sequentially in the reverse order listed; thus, priority is given to the first set of controls listed. The CPS employs "raking," or **iterative proportional adjustment**, in order to close the gap between the provisional survey figures and the independent estimates. (See *The Methods and Materials of Demography: Condensed Edition* for further elaboration of this method.)

Table 4.7 shows the percentage of total net undercoverage in the March 1994 CPS, based on the gap between the March 1994 CPS provisional figures and independent population estimates adjusted for undercoverage in the 1990 census. (This measure of undercoverage excludes all adjustments before the

TABLE 4.7 Estimated Percentages of Total Net Undercount, for Specified Age, Sex, and Race Groups: March 1994 Current Population Survey

Age (years)	All persons Both sexes	Male	Female	Nonblack Male	Female	Black Male	Female
All ages	8.3	10.2	6.4	8.9	5.4	19.8	12.9
Under 15	6.3	6.8	5.7	5.8	4.9	12.0	9.6
15–19	12.4	13.3	11.6	13.6	9.0	11.5	24.9
20–24	16.6	19.2	14.1	17.7	12.3	19.3	24.3
25–29	12.3	15.0	9.7	13.7	9.1	24.5	19.0
30–34	10.5	14.5	6.6	12.0	5.0	32.9	16.7
35–44	9.7	12.5	7.0	10.1	6.0	31.6	13.7
45–54	5.8	7.7	4.0	6.2	3.9	22.2	4.7
55–64	6.2	7.7	4.9	6.8	4.7	16.6	7.1
65–74	4.4	6.8	2.5	6.8	2.3	6.1	4.2
75 and over	−0.7	−1.1	−0.4	−1.9	−0.8	9.0	3.9

Note: Figures represent the difference between the independent population estimates adjusted for undercoverage in the 1990 census on the basis of the PES and the estimated CPS population before ratio adjustment, divided by the independent estimates. A minus sign denotes a net overcount.

Source: U.S. Bureau of the Census, "Money Income in the United States: 1997," *Current Population Reports* P60-200, 1998, Table C-2.

second-stage ratio adjustment, which may be considered coverage improvement procedures.) Net undercoverage of the Current Population Survey in March 1994 in relation to the independent postcensal population estimates was about 8%. The survey undercounts varied greatly by age, sex, and race. The net undercount was larger for males (10%) than for females (6%) and larger for blacks (16%) than for nonblacks (7%). For some age groups, the net undercount of black males in the CPS was considerable. For example, the net undercount of black males 30 to 34 years of age was 33%, far higher than the overall figure for black males (20%).

The total net undercounts of the Current Population Survey of 1994 may roughly be viewed as having two components: (1) the deficit between the provisional CPS figures (i.e., before second-stage weighting) and the independent postcensal estimates consistent with the 1990 census counts and (2) the deficit between the 1990 official census counts and the corrected 1990 census counts. For example, black males in the 35-to-44 age group had a total net undercount of 32%, composed of a 13% net undercount in the 1990 census (ages 30 to 39, Table 4.6) and a 21% gap between the CPS provisional figure and the unadjusted independent postcensal estimate.[9]

SIPP, another major national survey conducted by the U.S. Bureau of the Census, shows similar patterns of coverage errors but somewhat lower levels. Some illustrative percentages of undercount obtained by dividing (1) the difference between the independent population controls adjusted for estimated net undercounts in the 1990 census and the survey estimated population figures (before second-stage weighting) for January 1996 by (2) the independent estimates are as follows:

	Ages 15 and over	Ages 35 to 44
Black males	19.2	24.0
Black females	10.4	7.1
Nonblack males	10.9	8.8
Nonblack females	7.1	4.2

Source: U.S. Bureau of the Census, *SIPP Quality Profile*, 3rd ed., 1998b, Table 11.2.

As a longitudinal survey, SIPP is subject to loss of respondent households over time. Sample loss, or sample attrition, for the 1993 panel rose from about 8.9% at Wave 1 to 26.9% at Wave 9 (U.S. Bureau of the Census, 1998b, *op. cit.*, Table 5.1).

Reporting Error

Censuses and surveys are usually designed to collect data on the characteristics of the persons enumerated as well as to count them. These data are subject to a variety of errors called reporting errors.

Types of Reporting Errors

Several typologies of reporting errors are possible, some identifying the causes of the errors, but others identifying the consequences. Most reporting errors are made by respondents in filling out the questionnaire or in replying to questions by telephone or personal interview. Some are made by enumerators in connection with personal interviews and others occur in connection with processing operations, as a result, for example, of machine misreading of records or accidental destruction of parts of records. All such errors, including blank entries, whether they occur in the collection or in the processing of the data, are described as reporting errors. Considered in terms of consequences rather than causes, errors may be distinguished as net errors (called response bias) and gross errors (called response variability).

Another typology based on the sources of the errors is suggested by the following. The data on the characteristics of persons omitted from the census or survey are omitted from it as well as the persons themselves, and the data on the characteristics of persons erroneously included in the census or survey are erroneously included in it as well as the persons themselves. Hence, the reported data tend to be biased in the direction and to the degree that the number and characteristics of these two groups differ. Next, the characteristics of many persons included in the census or survey have to be assigned because the characteristics were not originally reported or because the data reported are unacceptable for various reasons (e.g., implausibility or inconsistency). Another group, substituted persons, requires the assignment of a whole package of characteristics. Assigned characteristics, especially for substituted persons, have a higher-than-average likelihood of being inaccurate. However, the bulk of reporting errors are imbedded in tabulated data that have passed the tests of plausibility and consistency during the census operations.

In sum, we can classify reporting errors as the misreports that exist in the raw tabulations and appear acceptable; imputation errors, those that occur in the characteristics imputed to substituted or enumerated individuals for whom the information was initially missing or unacceptable; nonreports, representing the omission of information about individuals in the final tabulations because imputation was not used for that subject area; the nonreports resulting from omission of persons; and the misreports resulting from erroneous inclusions. The distinction between the various types of reporting errors may be fuzzy, but it offers a basis for analyzing the causes of reporting errors and methods of reducing them.

Nonreporting and Unacceptable Entries

Some or all the data for persons included in censuses or surveys may be missing or unacceptable prior to editing and tabulation. This is a common occurrence. Missing data or unacceptable entries affect the quality of inferences based on census or survey data because these inferences are based on fewer actual or acceptable reports, certain methods of analysis may not be applicable to the data with missing or unacceptable entries, and inferences based on data with missing or unacceptable entries may be biased.

It is now considered desirable to **impute** or **allocate** values for the missing or unacceptable entries in the hope of enlarging the database, reducing any potential bias, and extending the applicable methods of analysis. Nonimputation was common in earlier censuses and surveys and for some subject items imputation was not done until very recently. The computer has made it a practical possibility to impute values even for multicategoried subject items, such as occupation and state of birth.

When values for the nonreports for some subject item are not imputed but are presented with the reported data on the subject, the user faces the problem of evaluating the effect of the nonreports on the reported data. Here are some rough subjective guidelines. If nonreports number less than 5%, one can safely prorate them (i.e., assume that the nonreports have the same percentage distribution as the reported cases), or assign them in another reasonable way, without seriously biasing the data. A distribution with 5 to 10% of nonreports is generally acceptable. If the percentage exceeds 10% and there is no empirical basis for distributing the nonreports, the interpretation of the data becomes problematic. Distributions of subject items with 20% or more of nonreports may be considered to be inaccurate and unreliable. This may easily occur for some census items for very small areas. Sampling error would diminish the quality of the data further. If values for the nonreports are imputed at such high levels of relative frequency, the quality of the data may be only slightly improved.

Missing information about enumerated individuals is now assigned by computer for most items covered in the census, the CPS, and other national surveys. As suggested earlier, assignments of acceptable codes, made when an entry for a given item is lacking or when the information reported on that item is unreasonable or is inconsistent with other information reported for the person or housing unit, are called **allocations** or **imputations**. Presumably data with the nonreports allocated are more accurate than data that exclude the nonreports or merely show their relative frequency. **Editing rules** designed to modify unreasonable or inconsistent entries are based on the principle that many more erroneous reports than correct ones are eliminated by applying the editing rules and inserting acceptable entries. This would apply to the rule of the Census Bureau that persons under age 15 are excluded from the married population, the rule of the Bureau of Labor Statistics that persons under age 16 are excluded from the labor force, and the rule of the National Center for Health Statistics that females under age 10 and 55 and over (from 1997; 50 and over before 1997) are excluded from the count of mothers. In these cases, age is considered "not stated" and an age is assigned. Inconsistent or unreasonable responses may involve characteristics other than age, as, for example, a "native" who reports a year of immigration on the census form or a report of death of a female from prostate cancer on the death certificate.

A variety of editing procedures are used to adjust the individual records for reporting errors before tabulation. Nearly all surveys taken by federal agencies use editing procedures to detect missing and inconsistent data within a record before tabulation. Applied demographers are often actively involved in developing **editing specifications** for particular demographic subject fields from which edit computer programs are prepared, reviewing results of **edit runs** (i.e., trial tabulations applying new editing specifications), and resolving problems found in them. In this connection, they may also make comparisons of the edit runs with other series, both historical and contemporaneous, to evaluate the need for further editing. As compared with the process of examining individual records for inconsistencies—called **microediting**—the process of **macroediting** involves the examination of aggregated data to detect inconsistencies or irregularities. The examination employs such procedures as range limits, ratio tests, comparison with historical data, comparison with other surveys, and comparison with values estimated in various ways (e.g., regression analysis). Like microediting procedures, macroediting procedures are also used for correcting data as well as evaluating them.

Commonly used imputation or allocation methods include assigning the mean value of the reported data, assigning a randomly selected value from the reported data, applying a "hot-deck" procedure (discussed later), applying various forms of interpolation and extrapolation, and regression. The use of a regression model encompasses deterministic imputation methods (i.e., those that assign predicted values from the regression model for the missing values) and stochastic imputation methods (i.e., those that assign predicted values from the regression model plus randomly chosen residuals).[10]

Allocation for missing and unacceptable entries is currently effected in the census, the CPS, and other national surveys conducted by the Census Bureau by a hot-deck procedure. In the **hot-deck procedure** a characteristic that is missing is derived by computer from the information given about the person or household and information about the last person or household stored in the computer with similar characteristics for whom the missing characteristic is reported. Thus, a person reported as the 20-year-old son of the householder, but lacking an entry for marital status, would be assigned the same marital status as the last son processed in the same age group. Such a procedure introduces some error and even biases, but the resulting data are believed to be more useful and accurate than blanks or inconsistent or implausible entries.

The Census Bureau has used allocation for missing entries for more and more questionnaire items with each successive census. This development has been made possible by extending computer applications in recent censuses. Age, for example, has been assigned since 1940, at first by hand on the basis of random tables of associated characteristics and later by computer. By the 1990 census, missing or unacceptable reports for all characteristics were filled or replaced, including those on the sample (long) form as well as those on the 100% (short) form. Some characteristics (e.g., place of birth and occupation) were not assigned until 1990.

Recent census reports show the percentage of allocations for each subject item. For subject items that were not allocated, the census tables show the percentage of nonreports. Table 4.8 shows the extent of allocations in the 1990 census for most census characteristics. The percentage of allocations was relatively low for the characteristics that are listed on the 100% form (2.5% or less) except for Hispanic origin (10%). In contrast, the percentage of allocations for sample characteristics was often sizable, particularly for the income

TABLE 4.8 **Percentage of Persons with Allocations of Selected Characteristics in the 1990 Census**

Based on 100% data

Total	16.2[a]	Male	1.1	
		Female	1.3	
Age	2.4			
Under 15	2.0	Race	2.0	
15 to 19	1.9	White	1.7	
20 to 24	3.2	Black	2.9	
25 to 34	0.5	Hispanic origin	10.0	
35 to 44	2.3	Northeast	18.0[a]	
45 to 54	2.3	Midwest	15.2[a]	
55 to 64	2.8	South	17.0[a]	
65 and over	3.1	West	14.5[a]	
Household relationship	2.6	Marital status	2.0	

Based on sample data

Sex	0.8	Residence in 1985/5+	6.4	Workers, 16+[b]		
Age	0.9	Year of entry of foreign born	8.0	Labor force status	3.9	
Hh. relationship[c]	1.9	English-speaking ability in households	2.3	Occupation	7.1	
Nativity and citizenship	5.4	Educ. attainment/25+	4.6	Industry	5.9	
		Work disability/16–64	7.8	Place of work	8.0	
Place of birth and nativity	5.4	Household income	18.9	Means of transport.	4.7	
		Type of income	15.2	Travel time to work	7.0	
Poverty, families	25.9	Poverty, unrelat. individuals	19.1			

[a] Percentage with one or more allocations.
[b] All persons 16 years and over for labor force status; employed persons 16 and over for occupation and industry.
[c] Household relationship.

Source: U.S. Bureau of the Census, *1990 Census of Population*, "Social and Economic Characteristics, United States," 1990 CP-2-1, 1993, Table 177; "General Population Characteristics, United States," 1990 CP90-1-1, 1992, Table 284.

questions and their derivatives. Specifically, allocations for the poverty of families amounted to 26% and allocations for poverty of unrelated individuals amounted to 19%. Several of the characteristics had allocation percentages that ranged from 5 to 8% (e.g., year of entry of foreign born, work disability, occupation, place of work, residence in 1985).

The extent of the allocations or nonreports has important implications for the quality of the data. A large percentage of allocations signals poor quality of data, just as a large percentage of nonreports does. Given the high percentages of allocations for household income (19%) and for families and unrelated individuals in poverty in the 1990 census, for example, a question is properly raised about the acceptability of the quality of the data on income and poverty. Often the percentage distribution of a variable is hardly changed when the allocations are included. If it is changed, it is likely that the quality of the data is improved by the process, but we cannot be sure and, in any case, the data may still be defective.

As mentioned earlier, errors in panel data present a different problem from cross-sectional data. The attrition in panel surveys is likely to be selective with respect to various characteristics of the respondents. Hence, the resulting data tend to be biased. In such surveys, missing or unacceptable entries may be bounded—that is, there may be at least one acceptable value before and one acceptable value after the missing or unacceptable value. On the other hand, the missing or unacceptable values may be unbounded—that is, an acceptable value may be lacking either before or after the missing or unacceptable one. Under these circumstances, the analyst can select and apply forms of interpolation or extrapolation, from carrying the last value forward and simple linear interpolation or extrapolation to complex forms of curve fitting or regression.

Misreporting/Content Errors

Even after editing to fill missing entries and replace implausible ones, the data are subject to numerous errors. These errors are called misreporting errors, or content or classification errors. They may affect the data on any subject from age to income and, as with the extent of allocations, may vary from trivial to major, depending on the subject. Interestingly, the quality of many subject items in population censuses and surveys has emerged as an important issue in various applied settings, particularly judicial proceedings.

A variety of measures have been devised to evaluate the accuracy of tabulated data on demographic and socioeconomic characteristics in censuses and surveys. Such information is useful in aiding users of the data to interpret the results and in guiding census and survey planners in their efforts to improve the data. Demographic analysis and dual systems analysis have both contributed to developing measures and estimates of reporting error.[11]

As we have seen, net census error, combining both net coverage error and net reporting error, for age, sex, and race categories, at the national level, can be measured by demographic analysis, and demographic analysis has been used to develop rough estimates of net census error for states for broad age groups.[12] Demographic analysis has also been used to evaluate a variety of socioeconomic subject items in censuses, surveys, and registration systems (e.g., marital status, marriage, nativity and citizenship, racial/ethnic groups, internal migration, and educational attainment).[13] For this purpose, independent estimates of the subject item are typically developed using other data (e.g., prior census data) and compared with the census, survey, or registration data.

Dual systems analysis or case-by-case matching has the advantage of being able to decompose net census errors into coverage error and misreporting/content error. It is also able to decompose content errors so that they can be described both in terms of net misreporting error (i.e., **response bias**) and gross misreporting error (i.e., **response variability**). Dual-systems analysis based on a content reinterview survey was used to measure the reporting errors for most of the population characteristics in the 1990 and 1980 censuses.[14] A similar survey was conducted after each decennial census from 1950 to 1970.

The census results are evaluated against the results of the reinterview survey on the assumption that the survey can be regarded as a standard for judging the census. Probing questions in the reinterview survey support its use as a standard. A content reinterview survey involves selecting a sample of households that were originally enumerated in the census, conducting a second interview with these same households, and then comparing the characteristics of each person in the household in the survey with those obtained in the census. Like the PES, the results are subject to sampling error, but unlike the PES, they are not subject to correlation bias, matching bias, or out-of-scope bias. There are problems in matching characteristics, however, as a result of noninterviews in the reinterview survey and nonreports of characteristics in either the census or the reinterview survey. Hence, the evaluation results may be biased if the patterns of the content errors in the noninterviewed cases and the interviewed cases are different.

Each category for each subject item has a net reporting error and a gross reporting error. The **net reporting error** represents the difference between the number of persons with the characteristic erroneously omitted from the category and the number of persons without the characteristic erroneously included in the category. The **gross reporting error** represents the sum of those numbers. The two components of net and gross errors are called **directional errors**. Directional errors include cases of **reporting out** of a correct category (e.g., from ages 35 to 39 into younger and older ages; from widowed to other marital categories) and **reporting into** an incorrect category (e.g., into ages 35 to 39 from other ages; into widowed from other marital categories). The balance of the errors of reporting erroneously out of a group and the errors of reporting erroneously into the group represents the net reporting error for the group or its **response bias**. The sum of the errors of reporting erroneously into a group and the errors of reporting erroneously out of the group represents the gross reporting error for the group, or its **response variability**. An illustration of the layout of the cross-tabulated data for computing measures of response error from the 1990 Content Reinterview Study is shown for marital status in Table 4.9. The matched reports for widowed persons number 1466, the erroneous omissions number 118 ($= 1584 - 1466$), and the erroneous inclusions number 259 ($= 1725 - 1466$). The net error is $+141$ ($= 259 - 118$) and the gross error is 377 ($= 118 + 259$).

The U.S. Census Bureau has used several measures of net reporting error and gross reporting error based on dual-systems analysis for evaluating cen-

TABLE 4.9 Display of Cross-Tabulated Data on Marital Status for the Computation of Response Error Measures from the Content Interview Survey of 1990 (Unedited Data, Entries in Boldface Represent Counts of Similar Responses in the Census and Reinterview)

Reinterview classification	Total matched persons	Census classification Not reported[a]	Reported	Now married	Widowed	Divorced	Separated	Never married
Total matched persons	29,647	440	29,207	13,811	1,725	1,935	507	11,229
Not reported[b]	4,704	97	4,607	1,588	188	374	128	2,329
Reported	24,943	343	24,600	12,223	1,537	1,561	379	8,900
Now married	12,367	61	12,306	**12,011**	22	77	40	156
Widowed	1,602	18	1,584	51	**1,466**	41	12	14
Divorced	1,582	21	1,561	31	27	**1,368**	94	41
Separated	334	7	327	60	5	34	**212**	16
Never married	9,058	236	8,822	70	17	41	21	**8,673**

[a] Not reported includes individual item nonresponse.

[b] Not reported includes individual item nonresponse, person refusals, movers, and other noninterviews (that is, persons with language barriers, persons who were ill, hospitalized, or temporarily absent, deceased, and so forth).

Source: U.S. Bureau of the Census, "Content Reinterview Survey: Accuracy of data for selected population and housing characteristics as measured by reinterview," *1990 Census of Population and Housing: Evaluation and Research Reports,* 1990 CPH-E-1, 1993, p. 89.

sus and survey results. Unfortunately, they have names that do not tell us much about what they measure or how they are computed. The net difference rate and the index of net shift relative to standard are measures of response bias, and the gross difference rate, the proportion of the standard differently reported, and the index of inconsistency are measures of response variability.[15] The measures of response bias indicate the bias introduced into the estimate of the population characteristic by the reporting errors, and the measures of response variability indicate the variability in the classification of the characteristic over repeated trials caused by the reporting errors.

Treatment of Reporting Error in National Surveys

Earlier we explored the assignment of characteristics by substitution to persons in the census for whom no characteristics were available, and the allocation of characteristics to enumerated persons for whom one or more characteristics was missing or implausible. Similarly persons omitted from the national sample surveys, as indicated by independent population estimates, must have characteristics assigned to them. The Census Bureau uses the method of iterative proportional adjustment, or "raking," for the purpose of adjusting its national sample survey data to the "control" totals in the second-stage adjustment. Omitted persons are assigned socioeconomic characteristics, in addition to basic demographic characteristics, in the process of adjusting the sample data to the figures for the several hundred control groups defined by age, sex, race, Hispanic origin, and state. As we saw, for some of these categories the adjustment of the data is sizable.

While raking to control groups greatly increases the accuracy of the data, the resulting adjusted figures may be biased because the characteristics attributed to the persons who are added by raking are assumed to replicate those of enumerated persons in the control categories. Thus, the raking procedure employed in the CPS assigns socioeconomic characteristics to the omitted persons on the basis of their age/sex/race/Hispanic origin and the socioeconomic characteristics of persons in these groups who were enumerated in the survey. Missed persons may be expected to have different socioeconomic characteristics from enumerated persons, even within the control groups, however. For example, there is evidence that employed persons are more completely enumerated than unemployed persons within the control groups of the CPS. While the differential coverage of the two groups may have only a trivial effect on the overall labor force participation ratio and the overall unemployment ratio, the age-specific ratios may be distorted. Furthermore, any errors are compounded in cross-classifications. For example, persons assigned an erroneous marital status may be further assigned other erroneous characteristics on the basis of the incorrect marital status.

Lack of a Perfect Standard

None of the several evaluation methods can tell us the magnitude of the errors in a census or survey *definitively*. We cannot know all the sources of error and the ways in which they interrelate and combine with one another. Quantifying the components of the total error is very difficult. Incorporated in the total error are systematic errors and random errors. An example of a systematic error is the tendency of some middle-aged persons to represent themselves as younger and an example of a random error is the error contributed by optical reading smudges. Sometimes we have independent observations that permit relatively definitive confirmation of survey reports: for example, matching hospital or doctors' records against respondent reports of illness, or comparing aggregate figures on voting in an election reported in surveys with counts of actual voters. Still, even these calibration sources have coverage and reporting problems, and hence an error stucture of their own. In short, there are no perfect standards for measuring error, only more accurate ones.

ERRORS DUE TO SAMPLING

Errors due to sampling encompass sampling error (i.e., the probabilistic error associated with estimates based on samples of the population) and other errors associated with the taking of samples, such as errors in sample design or errors in sample implementation.

Sampling Error

Sampling error arises from the fact that there are chance variations in the results obtained from samples and these results would differ from those obtained by a complete count using identical procedures. **Confidence intervals** with a stated probability, reflecting these chance variations, can be associated with each sample estimate. For example, an estimate of 100,000, the so-called **point estimate**, may have a confidence interval of 2.25% (i.e., 97,750 to 102,250) with a 95% probability. A 95% probability corresponds to about two **standard errors** on each side of the estimate, and a 95% confidence interval for the sample estimate means that there is a 95% probability that 97,750 and 102,250 contain the true value. Confidence intervals vary for each estimate in a survey for a given probability level. Surveys are normally designed to provide confidence intervals for the leading results of the survey that are small, in terms of a percentages of the survey estimate (e.g., the point estimate plus or minus a few percentages of the point estimate), with a specified probability (e.g., 90%, 95%, 99%).

Control of Sampling Error

A general goal of the survey statistician in designing a survey is to obtain the lowest sampling error (i.e., variance) at an acceptable cost. Some factors save money but tend to cause a rise in sampling error, such as a reduction in sample size. Other elements in the sample design being equal, the larger the sample, the smaller in relative terms the chance variations are. Larger under-coverage errors tend to cause a rise in sampling error by reducing the effective sample size. Among the devices used to reduce sampling error are adjustment of census sample data to marginal totals from the 100% tabulations of the census, ratio adjustment of edited and weighted sample-survey data to independent estimates of population (as in CPS processing), and adjustment of sample survey data to aggregate data from administrative records (e.g., income data from the Internal Revenue Service in various categories of income). Another commonly used device for reducing sampling error of small populations is to oversample these particular groups (while reducing their sampling weights). This device is often used in sample surveys to increase the accuracy of data for racial minorities. In addition to reducing sampling error, these devices may also reduce bias—that is, systematic error.

Presentation and Measurement of Sampling Error

To avoid suggesting that the data are more precise than they really are and to provide an indication of the precision of the data, presentations of sample data should carry some information relating to their sampling errors. What form should this information take? A minimal step is to discuss the issue of sampling error in general terms in the accompanying text. A further step is to present the formulas for computing sampling errors, with illustrations, or generalized tables of standard errors. In this way, readers can calculate sampling errors for whatever survey results they wish. A different approach is to present either one standard error or the sampling error at a specified level of probability for every estimate shown in a table. The usual levels of probability selected are 90% (1.64 standard errors), 95% (1.96 standard errors), and 99% (2.57 standard errors). Many published tables of the U.S. Census Bureau now accompany each sample estimate with its standard error. Another approach is to place an asterisk after every difference between sample figures shown in a table that is statistically significant (i.e., that the difference would not result

TABLE 4.10   Illustration of Presentation of Sampling Errors in Statistical Tables: Median Income of Households by Selected Characteristics of Householder: 1996 and 1997 (Households as of March of the Following Year)

Characteristic	1997 Median income Number (1000)	Value (dollars)	Standard error (dollars)	1996 Median income Number (1000)	Value (dollars)	Standard error (dollars)	Percentage change in real median income 1996–1997[a]
All households	102,528	37,006	171	101,018	36,492	179	*1.9
Type of Residence							
Inside metropolitan areas	82,122	39,381	268	80,950	37,640	245	*2.3
1 million or more	54,687	41,502	254	53,780	39,615	327	*1.9
Inside central cities	20,310	31,789	356	19,934	30,150	385	*3.1
Outside central cities	34,357	47,981	476	33,825	45,526	365	*3.0
Under 1 million	27,455	35,409	335	27,190	34,430	402	.5
Inside central cities	11,597	31,188	425	11,413	30,659	405	−.6
Outside central cities	15,858	38,581	518	15,778	37,399	456	.8
Outside metropolitan areas	20,406	30,057	413	20,088	28,089	396	*4.6
Region							
Northeast	19,810	38,929	525	19,724	37,406	458	1.7
Midwest	24,236	38,316	447	23,972	36,579	365	*2.4
South	36,578	34,346	347	35,693	32,422	288	*3.6
West	21,905	39,162	545	21,829	37,125	387	*3.1
Size of Household							
One person	26,327	18,762	209	25,402	17,897	225	*2.5
Two people	32,965	39,343	352	32,736	37,283	303	*3.2
Three people	17,331	47,115	455	17,065	44,814	422	*2.8
Four people	15,358	53,165	585	15,396	51,405	392	1.1
Five people	7048	50,407	701	6774	47,841	841	3.0
Six people	2232	46,465	1326	2311	42,438	1277	*7.0
Seven people or more	1267	42,343	1688	1334	40,337	1458	2.6
Number of Earners							
No earners	21,280	14,142	152	21,226	13,320	143	*3.8
One earner	35,150	29,780	259	4,026	27,895	237	*4.4
Two earners or more	46,096	57,525	310	45,764	55,547	262	*1.2
Two earners	36,188	54,192	340	35,753	52,416	278	1.1
Three earners	7429	67,182	734	7455	62,426	655	*5.2
Four earners or more	2480	84,816	1324	2556	78,504	1349	*5.6
Work Experience of Householder							
Total	102,528	37,005	171	101,018	35,492	179	*1.9
Worked	73,415	45,877	218	72,377	43,975	237	*2.0
Worked full-time, year-round	53,665	51,336	212	52,899	49,530	307	*1.3
Did not work	29,113	18,143	194	28,641	16,730	171	*6.0
Tenure							
Owner occupied	87,873	45,821	249	66,356	43,793	266	*2.3
Renter occupied	32,954	24,514	256	32,968	23,436	228	*2.3
Occupier paid no cash rent	1701	20,376	1009	1693	21,479	790	−7.3

* Statistically significant change at the 90% confidence level.

[a] Percentage change in real (i.e., adjusted for change in the Consumer Price Index) median household income. A minus (−) sign denotes a decrease.

Source: U.S. Bureau of the Census, "Money income in the United States: 1997," *Current Population Reports*, P60-200, Table 1. Current Population Survey, March 1998.

from chance alone) at a specified level of probability. Table 4.10 illustrates the use of some of these devices in a Census Bureau table relating to median income of households in 1996 and 1997.

A rather different procedure is to present the sampling errors graphically by bands on time series charts or by short lines spanning the range of the point estimate plus and minus about one and two-thirds standard errors or about two standard errors. The latter procedure is illustrated in Figure 2.A.1, with data on median household income in 1995–1997 for states.

The summary measures of distributions most frequently used in the presentation of basic demographic data, such as those published by the U.S. Bureau of the Census, are percentages, medians, means, and differences between them. The basic formula for the standard error of a proportion (i.e., given a random sample) is

$$\text{S.E.}_p = \sqrt{p(1-p) \div n} \tag{4}$$

where p represents the sample estimate of the proportion and n the number of sample cases on which the proportion is based. The formulas for standard errors vary depending on the design of the sample. The standard errors for samples with complex designs tend to be higher than for random samples. National sample surveys, like the CPS, have complex designs and are typically not random samples.

To take account of the sample design of the CPS, a stratified cluster design, the basic formula is modified to include the denominator of the proportion (x) and a special parameter associated with the characteristic in the numerator of the proportion (b):

$$\text{S.E.}_p = \sqrt{\frac{p(1-p) * b}{x}} \tag{5}$$

The calculation of the standard error and confidence interval of a percentage is illustrated by applying this formula to obtain the standard error for the proportion of family households maintained by female householders (with no husband present, but other relatives present) in 1995 shown by the CPS. The sample percentage of family households maintained by female householders in 1995 was 18.0 and the sample estimate of the number of family households was 69,594,000. The b parameter for housholds is 2068, given in a table of the Census Bureau report.[16] Evaluating the formula with these figures, we have

$$\text{S.E.}_p = \sqrt{\frac{18.0(100-18.0) * 2,068}{69,594,000}} = \sqrt{\frac{18.0(82.0) * 2,068}{69,594,000}} = 0.2 \tag{6}$$

The 90% confidence interval is bounded, therefore, by $18.0 - (1.645 * 0.2)$, or 17.7, and $18.0 + (1.645 * 0.2)$, or 18.3.

The basic formula for the standard error of the mean of a distribution of a characteristic (i.e., given a random sample), σ_x, is $\sigma \div \sqrt{n}$, where σ is the standard deviation of the sample distribution of the characteristic and n is the number of cases in the sample. This formula shows that the standard error of the mean of a distribution decreases when n, the sample size, is increased and that when n is increased we can expect values of x to be closer to the true mean.

The standard errors for CPS estimates primarily indicate the magnitude of the sampling error, but they also partially measure the effect of some non-sampling errors in responses and enumeration. On the other hand, they do not measure systematic biases in the data. In the context of sampling, **systematic bias** may be defined as the average over all possible samples of the differences between the sample estimates and the true value:

$$\text{Bias} = \bar{x} - \mathbf{x} \tag{7}$$

where $\mathbf{x}$ denotes the true value and $\bar{x}$ denotes the mean of the sample distribution of estimates. Another component of error is **variance**, which is a measure of the variation of the estimates around their mean, or

$$\text{Var} = \frac{1 \Sigma^n (x_i - \bar{x})^2}{n} \tag{8}$$

The sum of the variance and the square of the bias, called the **mean square error** (MSE), is often used as a summary measure of total error in sample estimates:

$$\text{MSE} = \text{Var} + \text{Bias squared}$$

$$\text{MSE} = \frac{1 \Sigma^n (x_i - \mathbf{x})^2}{n} = \frac{1 \Sigma^n (x_i - \bar{x})^2}{n} + (\bar{x} - \mathbf{x})^2 \tag{9}$$

We see that a biased estimate may show a smaller mean square error than an unbiased one if it has a smaller variance. The measure is sometimes expressed in square-root form as the root-mean-square error.

Some statisticians hold the theoretical position that 100% census counts are also subject to statistical variability or sampling error. This interpretation is based on the statistical reasoning that a particular count is only one of an infinite number of possible results that might be obtained in the same census, given the same instructions, questionaires, enumerators, and plan of administration, but considering variations in weather, the shifting geographic distribution of the population, the chance assignments given to interviewers, and other such factors.

Other Errors Due to Sampling

Other types of errors are linked to sampling in addition to sampling error—types of errors that represent *real* errors. Errors occur in the design of the sample and in its implementation in the field. These general types of errors can be illustrated by the following general cases. The sample may not be representative of the population because of a design error (e.g., faulty demarcation of sample units, defects in the selection of sample units), the questionnaires may not have been distributed correctly according to the planned sampling ratio, sample households may have been deliberately or inadvertently replaced by nonsample households, or the weighting scheme may have been applied incorrectly. One form that the incorrect selection of sample units takes is the exclusion of some cases nonrandomly, resulting in sample-selection bias.

CONFIDENTIALITY ISSUES AND SOLUTIONS

Confidentiality Issues

A fundamental policy issue is the privacy of the data for an individual. Federal statistical agencies work hard to protect it. U.S. Code, Title 13, the body of rules governing Census Bureau activities, makes confidentiality of individual records maintained by the Census Bureau mandatory, and a similar requirement governs the statistical activities of other federal agencies. This policy goal must be balanced against the objective of satisfying the considerable demand for publicly collected data. Federal agencies collecting data employ special methods to prevent disclosure of information about individuals, households, or business establishments. The confidentiality rules require, in effect, that methods be used to minimize the risk of disclosure of the identity of census and survey respondents and information about them. Disclosure can occur on the basis of the data released by an agency or their combination with other publicly available information.

The issue of confidentiality of data about individuals arises in connection with all forms of release of demographic data—published tables, summary tape files (STF), public-use microdata samples (PUMS), and computer-accessed data—as well as all forms of coverage of the population—100% tabular data, sample tabular data, and microdata. Since even aggregate data may reveal the unique records of individuals in certain cells, the issue arises with such data as well as with microdata. The problem is generally more complicated with microdata than aggregate data, however. At the same time, the problem can be especially difficult in connection with aggregate data that are available on online computer access systems, such as CENDATA and American Factfinder planned for the 2000 census.

The need of data collection agencies to protect the confidentiality of their records while providing the maximum amount of data possible to users is complicated by developments in technology (e.g., online computer access to data), the proliferation of data sets, the increased demand for highly disaggregated data, the availability of microdata files, and the linkage of various data sets. The situation is governed in part by federal and state legislation, in part by administrative decisions of government agencies, and in part, where data are to be transferred between agencies, by negotiations between them. The Census Bureau regularly faces the privacy issue not only because of its vast program of censuses and surveys but also because it acquires several types of administrative records from other agencies. Presumably the originating agency has already applied appropriate techniques to both the aggregate and individual data it transfers, to limit disclosure of information about individuals.

Agencies collecting and compiling data have introduced many devices for protecting the privacy of respondents, but these devices are not foolproof. Researchers using microdata, especially when the data are accessed by electronic means, have special responsibilities to maintain the confidentiality of the data. More and more, as researchers link respondents to smaller geographic areas or to administrative records, they are required by government agencies to establish secure research sites protected from Internet access. The responsibility of researchers may include not attempting to subvert the efforts of the agencies to preserve respondent privacy and informing the agencies when they recognize that the latters' efforts have not been wholly successful in this regard.

Confidentiality Solutions

To understand the various approaches to the management of the privacy issue, it is useful to distinguish the terms disclosure limitation, data or cell suppression, and cell modification. Data or cell supression and cell modification are types of **disclosure limitation**. With **cell supression**, certain information is removed from the internal record and is not made available in the release of the data. With **cell modification**, new information is substituted for the information that has to be concealed. Cell suppression has been a common way in the past of limiting disclosure of census and survey data. Since, with cell suppression, the value of the cell can be determined exactly by subtraction of other cells from the marginal total, certain other cells must also be suppressed. The process is called **complementary suppression**. The method of disclosure limitation may vary from one data product to another, and there are many variations of the methods of limiting the disclosure of data through cell supression and cell modification. The need for disclosure limitation tends to be greater if a geographic unit is extremely small, the characteristic applies to very few cases, or the presentation of data for a succession of years is revealing.

The Centers for Disease Control and Prevention employs cell suppression in providing access to its Compressed Mortality File *(wonder.cdc.gov),* a data set based on the national vital statistics system. Data in this file are disaggregated by county, 5-year age groups, race, sex, and specific cause of death. At this level of disaggregation, some table cells will contain very few deaths. The Compressed Mortality File avoids displaying the number of deaths for counties with populations of less than 100,000 if the number in any cell is equal to or less than five.

Since individual records are available to the user of public use microdata samples, information that identifies the respondent has to be suppressed. In addition, the records are subject to cell modification. Names, street addresses, and Social Security number are always deleted. Other information to be suppressed depends on the size and type of geographic area and the level of geographic detail. The geographic detail is always limited; often the identity of the lowest geographic unit is deleted. The number of variables on the file may have to be limited. Additional methods that apply both to microdata and aggregate data, mentioned later, may be used to disguise variables that have high visibility.

Cell suppression has serious disadvantages. It is a complicated and time-consuming procedure and must be performed separately for each data product. It is usually applied on a table-by-table basis. It results in reducing the volume of data published and in modifying the original totals for areas and their basic demographic characteristics.

Procedure Used in the 1990 Census

In the search for an alternative to cell supression that would avoid its disadvantages in limiting disclosure of information about an individual respondent, the Census Bureau employed a method of cell modification in the 1990 census called confidentiality edit. The Census Bureau's confidentiality edit in 1990 was applied in different forms for the 100% data and the sample data.[17] For the 100% data, the Census Bureau used a strategy of cell modification called swapping or switching. A small sample of census households from the microdata was selected, and the data for these households were **swapped** or **switched** with data from other households residing in different geographic locations that had identical characteristics on a certain set of key variables. The key variables were the number of persons in the household, race, Hispanic origin, race of head of household, age group (under 18, 18 and over), number of units in the structure, rent/value, and tenure. Thus, the census counts for these characteristics over a particular geographic area were not affected by the swap. A higher percentage of records were swapped in small blocks because such blocks have a higher risk of disclosing individual data.

For the sample data in 1990, protection of records was achieved by the fact that it was a sample that had to be weighted. Sampling provided sufficient confidentiality protection, except in small block groups. In small block groups some values from the record of one housing unit in the internal file were **blanked out** and new values were imputed using the 1990 census imputation methodology.[18] The public-use microdata were subjected to the same blanking and imputation procedure as the census sample data in addition to the suppression of data on name, address, and specific geographic location, limitation to areas of at least 100,000 persons, and the collapse of detailed categories into broader ones.

The confidentiality edit has the advantages that multidimensional tables can be prepared easily and the disclosure protection applied will always be consistent. In addition, it maintains the totals for most census categories and does not suppress cell counts. On the other hand, it diminishes the underlying quality of the data. The latter effect is often referred to as adding **noise** to the data.

Plan for the 2000 Census

The main change planned for the year 2000 census, as compared with the 1990 census, is to target the most risky records and to use the swapping method for both the 100% data and the sample data.[19] Records would be swapped only if they were unique on the basis of the set of key variables listed earlier. The swapping rate would differ among blocks and have an inverse relationship with block size. The disclosure-limitation procedure will take account of the fact that a higher imputation rate is expected in the 2000 census and that this lowers the disclosure risk of the data. If a designated percentage of the household records in a block are imputed, no swapping will be carried out for the block.

The introduction of American Factfinder, the system that allows users to submit a request and secure the 2000 census data product electronically, complicates the disclosure problem for tabular data. Users can create their own nonstandard geographic areas and, by geographically subtracting the data in two tables that were requested, obtain a table for a small geographic area with one individual in many cells. Hence, some new disclosure-limitation procedures may have to be devised for the tabular data. American Factfinder would be protected in part by filling requests for tables through the system only if the number of households in the designated geographic area exceeded the number of cells in the table by a preset percentage.

Review of Methods

Conducting a sample survey is one method of protecting the confidentiality of data. If the sampling weights used in preparing the estimates are not released, the respondents' data are less identifiable from published totals. In addition, sample estimates, typically small numbers, may be withheld if they do not meet certain specified levels of accuracy. In 100% or sample data, imposing a threshold rule is another way to reduce the risk of disclosure. The rule may be that cells have to contain at least five respondents. If they contain fewer cases, many different devices can be applied.

These devices include the combination of categories, cell suppression, random rounding, controlled rounding, adding random noise, swapping, blanking and imputing, and blurring. Combination of categories includes top-coding, bottom-coding, and recoding (i.e., broadening the highest interval, the lowest interval, and intermediate intervals in published data, respectively). In random rounding, the cell values are rounded up or down (e.g., to a multiple of 5) on a random basis. In controlled rounding, the published entries in each row and column are, in addition, constrained to equal the appropriate marginal totals. Adding noise more narrowly defined involves adding or multiplying by random numbers. We have already referred to swapping, and blanking and imputing, in connection with the confidentiality edit. Finally, blurring may be used (i.e., aggregating across small groups of respondents and replacing one individual value with the average).

Measurement of Effect of Methods

All the methods of statistical disclosure limitation diminish the quality of the data produced by suppressing actual data or modifying them. The question must be asked, then, how the utility of the data is affected by the addition of noise. The two issues—avoidance of disclosure of individual information and the effect on the quality of published data—are intertwined.[20] To evaluate the effect of the disclosure-limitation techniques, the principle measure used is the index of dissimilarity (see Chapter 1). It shows how the distributions of any variable differ from one another before and after the disclosure-limitation operation and what proportion of the cases have to be shifted to restore the original distribution. Enough noise must be introduced in the data to protect them but not so much as to distort them greatly.

NOTES

1. This situation is suggestive of the philosophical difference between phenomena (items experienced by the senses) and noumena (items only intellectually conceived). See William Kruskal, "Introduction," in Paul P. Biemer *et al.*, *Measurement Errors in Surveys*, New York: John Wiley & Sons, Inc., 1991.

2. A panel survey is a longitudinal survey that follows the same individual or household over time for the life of the survey or a particular panel or wave in the survey, even to new residences as necessary. The resulting data are usually referred to as longitudinal data. Aggregate data for

cohorts (e.g., birth cohorts), tracked over time from a series of cross-sectional tabulations, are another type of longitudinal data.

3. See Kirk M. Wolter, "Some coverage error models for census data," *Journal of the American Statistical Association* 81: 338–346, 1986. The method is also called the Chandra Sekar/ Deming formula, named after the two statisticians who refined and tested it. It appears to have been first used at the Bureau of the Census in measuring the underregistration of births and the underenumeration of infants in the 1940 census. See C. Chandra Sekar and W. Edwards Deming, "On a method of estimating birth and death rates and the extent of registration," *Journal of the American Statistical Association* 44(245): 101–115, March 1949. The formula is applied to specified geographic, demographic, social, and economic categories in the census or survey, taking account of factors associated with omission from censuses and surveys, sampling error, and other factors.

4. J. Gregory Robinson *et al.*, "Estimation of population coverage in the 1990 United States census based on demographic analysis," *Journal of the American Statistical Association* 88(423): 1061–1074, September 1993; Christine Himes and Clifford C. Clogg, "An overview of demographic analysis as a method for evaluating census coverage in the United States," *Population Index* 58(4): 587–607, 1992; Samuel H. Preston *et al.*, "Reconstructing the size of the African American population, by age and sex, 1930–1990, *Demography* 35(1): 1–21, 1998; Jeffrey S. Passel, *Demographic Analysis: A Report on its Utility for Adjusting the 1990 Census,* Report prepared for the Special Advisory Panel to the U.S. Department of Commerce. Washington, DC: Urban Institute, 1998; and U.S. Bureau of the Census, "Coverage of Population in the 1980 census," by Robert E. Fay *et al.*, *1980 Census of Population and Housing: Evaluation and Research Reports*, PHC80-E4, 1988. U.S. Bureau of the Census, "Developmental estimates of the coverage of the population of states in the 1970 census: Demographic analysis," by J. S. Siegel *et al.*, *Current Population Reports*, Series P-23, No. 65, 1977.

5. Howard Hogan, "The 1990 Post-Enumeration Survey: Operations and Results," *Journal of the American Statistical Association* 88(423): 1047–1060, September 1993; Howard Hogan and Kirk Wolter, "Measuring accuracy in a post-enumration survey," *Survey Methodology* 14: 99–116, 1988; and U.S. Bureau of the Census/Fay *et al.*, 1988, *op. cit.* (see note 4).

6. Elizabeth Martin, Leslie A. Brownrigg, and Robert E. Fay, "Results of the 1988 ethnographic studies of census coverage and plans for 1990," paper presented to the Bureau of the Census Advisory Committees of the American Statistical Association and the Population Association of America, October 18–19, 1990, Alexandria, VA, U.S. Bureau of the Census, Statistical Research Division; Manuel de la Puente, "Why are people missed or erroneously included by the census: A summary of findings from ethnographic coverage reports," *Proceedings of the Research Conference on Undercounted Ethnic Populations*, Richmond, VA, May 5–7, 1993, U.S. Bureau of the Census, Statistical Research Division, 1993.

7. Based on Howard Hogan and J. Gregory Robinson, "What the Census Bureau's Coverage Evaluation Programs tell us about differential undercount," in *Proceedings of the Research Conference on Undercounted Ethnic Populations*, Richmond, VA, May 5–7, 1993, U.S. Bureau of the Census, Statistical Research Division, 1993.

8. U.S. Bureau of the Census, "Who responds and who doesn't: Analyzing variation in mail response rates during the 1990 census," by David L. Word, *Population Division Working Paper*, No. 19, 1997.

9. Estimates of the part of the total net undercounts of CPS due to undercount in relation to unadjusted independent postcensal estimates can be derived by converting the estimates of net undercount ratios for the age cohorts in the 1990 census into coverage ratios (i.e., taking their complements), dividing the total coverage ratios in CPS by the coverage ratios of the 1990 census, and then converting the resulting partial coverage ratios of the CPS into partial net undercount ratios (i.e., taking their complements). To spell out the example given in the text for black males 35 to 44 years of age, we have the following:

(1) Coverage ratio, 1990 census (for ages 30 to 39) .870
(2) = [1 − (1)] Undercount ratio .130
(3) Total coverage ratio, CPS .684
(4) = [1 − (3)] Total undercount ratio .316
(5) = [(3) ÷ (1)] Coverage ratio, CPS in relation to 1990 census level .786
(6) = [1 − (5)] Undercount ratio .214

10. Stochastic imputation schemes can effectively be applied under conditions that employ multiple imputation techniques. In multiple imputation each missing value is replaced by multiple imputed values and so multiple data sets are created.

11. I exclude a discussion of reporting errors in single ages. This is an important subject on which much has been written. A PES is essentially ineffective in measuring such errors, but demographic analysis by itself or in combination with mathematical analysis has developed a variety of effective measures. See *The Methods and Materials of Demography: Condensed Edition*, for a discussion of this topic.

12. Robinson *et al.* (1993), *op. cit.*; U.S. Bureau of the Census/Siegel *et al.* (1977), *op. cit.*

13. Some illustrative studies are Jeffrey S. Passel and Rebecca L. Clark, "How many naturalized citizens are there? An assessment of data quality in the decennial census and the Current Population Survey," paper presented at the 1997 Annual Meeting of the Population Association of America, Washington, DC, March 27, 1997; U.S. Bureau of the Census, "How well does the Current Population Survey measure the foreign-born population in the United States?" by A. Dianne Schmidley and J. Gregory Robinson, *Working Paper Series*, No. 22, Population Division, 1998; Ellen L. Jamison and Donald S. Akers, "Analysis of the differences between marriage statistics from registration and those from censuses and surveys," *Demography* 5(4): 460–474; and Jeffrey S. Passel, "The growing American Indian population, 1960–1990: Beyond demography," in Gary D. Sandefur, Ronald R. Rindfuss, and Barney Cohen (eds.), *Changing Numbers, Changing Needs: American Indian Demography and Public Health*, Washington, DC: National Academy Press, 1996. A general review of the quality of the data on race and ethnicity in U.S. censuses is given in William Petersen, "Politics and the measurement of ethnicity," pp. 187–233 in William Alonzo and Paul Starr (eds.), *The Politics of Numbers*, Russell Sage Foundation, New York, 1983.

14. U.S. Bureau of the Census, "Content reinterview survey: Accuracy of data for selected population and housing characteristics as measured by reinterview," *1990 Census of Population and Housing, Evaluation and Research Reports*, 1990 CPE-E-1, 1993; U.S. Bureau of the Census, "Content Reinterview Study: Accuracy of data for selected population and housing characteristics as measured by reinterview," *1980 Census of Population and Housing: Evaluation and Research Reports*, PHC80-E2, 1986.

15. For the definition and interpretation of these measures and their formulas, refer to *The Methods and Materials of Demography: Condensed Edition;* and U.S. Bureau of the Census, 1993, *op. cit.* (see note 14).

16. Table D-3 of U.S. Bureau of the Census, *Current Population Reports*, Series P60-193, 1996. For further details refer to Appendix D, "Source and accuracy of estimates," of this report or to more recent P60 reports, e.g., P60-200.

17. R. A. Griffin, F. Navarro, and L. Flores-Baez, "Disclosure avoidance for the 1990 census," pp. 516–521, in *Proceedings, Section on Survey Research Methods*, Alexandria, VA: American Statistical Association, 1989.

18. An illustration is given in U.S. Office of Management and Budget, "Report on statistical disclosure limitation methodology," prepared by the Federal Committee on Statistical Methodology, *Statistical Policy Working Paper* 22, pp. 17–18, 1994.

19. Philip Steel and Laura Zayatz, "Disclosure limitation for the 2000 Census of Housing and Population," unpublished paper, Statistical Research Division, U.S. Bureau of the Census, 1998.

20. U.S. Bureau of the Census, "Preliminary recommendations for disclosure limitation for the 2000 census: Improving the 1990 confidentiality edit procedure," by R. A. Moore, *Statistical Research Division Report*, Series RR 96-06.

SUGGESTED READINGS

General

Biemer, Paul P., Groves, Robert, Lyberg, Lars, Mathiowetz, Nancy A., and Sudman, Seymour (eds.). (1991). *Measurement Errors in Surveys*. New York: John Wiley & Sons.

Ferber, Robert, Sheatsley, Paul, Turner, Anthony, and Waksberg, Joseph. (1980). *What Is a Survey?* Washington, DC: American Statistical Association.

Mosteller, Frederick. (1978). "Nonsampling errors." William H. Kruskal and Judith M. Tanur (eds.), *International Encyclopedia of Statistics*, pp. 208–229. New York: The Free Press/Macmillan.

U.S. Department of Commerce, Office of Federal Statistical Policy and Standards. (1978). "Glossary of nonsampling error terms: An illustration of a semantic problem in statistics," *Statistical Policy Working Paper* 4.

U.S. Office of Management and Budget, Statistical Policy Office. (1991). "Seminar on quality of federal data," prepared by the Federal Committee on Statistical Methodology. *Statistical Policy Working Paper* 20.

Errors in Censuses and Surveys

Bailar, Barbara. (1976). "Some sources of error and their effect on census statistics." *Demography* 13(2): 273–286.

de la Puente, Manuel. (1993). "Why are people missed or erroneously included by the census: A summary of findings from ethnographic coverage reports." *Proceedings of the Research Conference on Undercounted Ethnic Populations*. Richmond, VA, May 5–7, 1993. U.S. Bureau of the Census, Statistical Research Division.

Ellis, Yukiko T. (1995). "Examination of census omission and erroneous enumeration based on 1990 ethnographic studies of census coverage." *Proceedings, Section on Survey Research Methods*. Alexandria, VA: American Statistical Association.

Himes, Christine, and Clogg, Clifford C. (1992). "An overview of demographic analysis as a method for evaluating census coverage in the United States." *Population Index* 58(4): 587–607.

Hogan, Howard. (1993, September). "The 1990 Post-Enumeration Survey: Operations and results." *Journal of the American Statistical Association* 88(423): 1047–1060.

Hogan, Howard, and Wolter, Kirk. (1988). "Measuring accuracy in a post-enumration survey." *Survey Methodology* 14: 99–116.

Iversen, Roberta Rehner, Furstenberg, Jr., Frank F., and Belzer, Alisa A. (1999, February). "How much do we count? Interpretation and error-making in the decennial census." *Demography* 36(1): 121–134.

Martin, Elizabeth, Brownrigg, Leslie A., and Fay, Robert E. (1990). "Results of the 1988 ethnographic studies of census coverage and plans for 1990." Paper presented to the Bureau of the Census Advisory Committees of the American Statistical Association and the Population Association of America, October 18–19, 1990, Alexandria, VA. U.S. Bureau of the Census, Statistical Research Division.

McKay, Ruth B. (1993, September). "Undercoverge of Hispanics in household surveys." *Monthly Labor Review* 116(9): 38–42.

Passel, Jeffrey S. (1990). *Demographic Analysis: A Report on Its Utility for Adjusting the 1990 Census*. Report prepared for the Special Advisory Panel to the U.S. Department of Commerce. Washington, DC: Urban Institute.

Preston, Samuel H., Elo, Irma T., Foster, Andrew, and Fu, Haishan. (1998). "Reconstructing the size of the African American population, by age and sex, 1930–1990." *Demography* 35(1): 1–21.

Robinson, J. Gregory, Ahmed, Bashir, Das Gupta, Prithwis, and Woodrow, Karen A. (1993, September). "Estimation of population coverage in the 1990 United States census based on demographic analysis." *Journal of the American Statistical Association* 88(423): 1061–1074.

Sande, Innis G. (1982). "Imputation in surveys: Coping with reality," *American Statistician* 36(3), Part I: 145–152.

U.S. Bureau of the Census. (1998). *SIPP Quality Profile, 1998*. 3rd ed.

U.S. Bureau of the Census. (1993a). "Content Reinterview Survey: Accuracy of data for selected population and housing characteristics as measured by reinterview." *1990 Census of Population and Housing: Evaluation and Research Reports*. 1990 CPH-E-1.

U.S. Bureau of the Census. (1993b). "Programs to improve coverage in the 1990 Census." *1990 Census of Population and Housing: Evaluation and Research Reports*. 1990 CPH-E-3.

U.S. Bureau of the Census. (1993c). *Proceedings of the Research Conference on Undercounted Ethnic Populations*. Richmond, VA, May 5–7, 1993. U.S. Bureau of the Census, Statistical Research Division.

U.S. Bureau of the Census. (1988). "Coverage of Population in the 1980 census," by Robert E. Fay, Jeffrey S. Passel, and J. Gregory Robinson. *1980 Census of Population and Housing: Evaluation and Research Reports*, PHC80-E4.

U.S. Bureau of the Census. (1986). "Content Reinterview Study: Accuracy of data for selected population and housing characteristics as measured by reinterview." *1980 Census of Population and Housing: Evaluation and Research Reports*, PHC80-E2.

U.S. Bureau of the Census. (1980). *Conference on Census Undercount: Proceedings of the 1980 Conference.* See esp. Conrad Taeuber, "Major conference findings," pp. 3–5.

U.S. Bureau of the Census. (1977). "Developmental estimates of the coverage of the population of states in the 1970 census: Demographic analysis," by J. S. Siegel, J. S. Passel, N. W. Rives, and J. G. Robinson. *Current Population Reports*, Series P-23, No. 65.

U.S. Office of Management and Budget, Statistical Policy Office. (1990a). "Survey coverage," prepared by the Federal Committee on Statistical Methodology. *Statistical Policy Working Paper* 17.

U.S. Office of Management and Budget, Statistical Policy Office, (1990b). "Data editing in federal statistical agencies," by Federal Committee on Statistical Methology. *Statistical Policy Working Paper* 18.

Wolter, Kirk M. (1986). "Some coverage error models for census data." *Journal of the American Statistical Association* 81: 338–346.

Errors in Other Demographic Data

U.S. Immigration and Naturalization Service. (1999). *1997 Statistical Yearbook of the Immigration and Naturalization Service.* Sections of each chapter on "Limitations of data."

U.S. National Center for Health Statistics. (1999a). "Quality of death rates by race and Hispanic origin: A summary of current research, 1999," by Harry M. Rosenberg *et al., Vital and Health Statistics: Data Evaluation and Methods Research* 2(**128**).

U.S. National Center for Health Statistics. (1999b). "Technical appendix." Section 4 in *Vital Statistics of the United States, 1993.* Vol. I. *Natality.*

Confidentiality Issues

Cecil, J. S. (1993). "Confidentiality legislation and the U.S. federal statistical system." *Journal of Official Statistics* 9(2): 519–535.

Griffin, R. A., Navarro, F., and Flores-Baez, L. (1989). "Disclosure avoidance for the 1990 census." *Proceedings, Section on Survey Research Methods*, pp. 516–521. Alexandria, VA: American Statistical Association.

Jabine, T. J. (1993). "Statistical disclosure limitation practices of United States statistical agencies." *Journal of Official Statistics* 9(2): 427–454.

Mugge, R. H. (1983). "Issues in protecting confidentiality in national health statistics." *Proceedings, Section on Survey Research Methods*, pp. 592–594. Alexandria, VA: American Statistical Association.

Steel, Philip, and Zayatz, Laura. (1998). "Disclosure limitation for the 2000 Census of Housing and Population." Unpublished paper. Statistical Research Division, U.S. Bureau of the Census.

U.S. Office of Management and Budget. (1994). "Report on statistical disclosure limitation methodology," prepared by the Federal Committee on Statistical Methodology. *Statistical Policy Working Paper* 22, esp. Chapter II.

5

GEODEMOGRAPHY: GEOGRAPHIC AREA CONCEPTS AND INFORMATION SYSTEMS FOR DEMOGRAPHIC APPLICATIONS

GEOGRAPHIC AREA CLASSIFICATION SYSTEMS

Much of applied demography focuses on subnational demographic issues and geographic variations. To make effective use of geographic or distributional data, a system of geographic area concepts and ways of retrieving, compiling, and analyzing the data are necessary. Moreover, because of the sheer mass of the data, summary methods of comprehending and visualizing the data, such as the use of charts and maps, are virtually required. Geographic classification systems and maps give context to spatial data for particular areas, displaying them in relation to data for other areas.

Census Geographic Categories

Since the most comprehensive and regular source of local area data on population is the decennial census of population, the common system of core geographic area concepts employed in subnational studies is that developed by the U.S. Census Bureau. (As explained in this chapter, the metropolitan area concepts are developed in collaboration with the Office of Management and Budget.) The Census Bureau's system of geographic concepts not only determines the geographic categories for which census data are tabulated and published in a variety of print and nonprint forms, but also the geographic categories for which population and population-related data from many other sources are compiled and by which they can be compared or combined with census data.

Two different classification systems have been applied to geographic areas. They are largely but not wholly independent. The first distinguishes political areas, other administrative areas, and statistical areas. An appropriate combination of political and statistical areas defines a set of hierarchical relationships that covers the entire country. The second classification distinguishes categories reflecting the type of residence of the population. The first classification simply uses "boundary" definitions; the second depends on the distribution of the population by such categories as urban-rural residence, metropolitan residence, and similar socioeconomic categories of residence. Table 5.1 presents a complete list of the geographic entities of the 1990 and 1980 censuses, with the number of each type.[1]

TABLE 5.1   Census Geographic Tabulation Areas, by Number of Entities, in the 1990 and 1980 Population Censuses

	Decennial censuses	
	1980	1990
United States	1	1
States and statistically equivalent entities	57[a]	57[b]
State	50	50
District of Columbia	1	1
Outlying areas	6[a]	6[b]
Counties and statistically equivalent entities	3,231	3,248
Minor civil divisions (MCDs)	30,450	30,386
Sub-MCDs	265	145
Incorporated places	19,176	19,365
Consolidated cities	X	6
American Indian reservations	277	310
American Indian entities with trust lands	37	52
Alaska native villages (ANVs)	209	(See ANVSA)
Alaska Native Regional Corporations (ANRCs)	12	12
Congressional districts	435	435
Voting districts (VTDs)	36,351	148,872[c]
School districts	16,075	16,000[d]
Neighborhoods	28,381	X
Zip code areas	37,000	39,850[d]

(continues)

TABLE 5.1 (*continued*)

	Decennial censuses	
	1980	1990
Statistical entities		
Region	4	4
Divisions	9	9
Metropolitan areas		
Standard metropolitan statistical areas (SMSAs)	323	X
Standard consolidated statistical areas (SCSAs)	17	X
Metropolitan statistical areas (MSAs)	X	268
Consolidated metropolitan statistical areas (CMSAs)	X	21
Primary metropolitan statistical areas (PMSAs)	X	73
Urbanized areas (UAs)	373	405
Alaska native village statistical areas (ANVSAs)	(See ANV)	217
Tribal jurisdiction statistical areas (TJSAs)	X	17
Tribal designated statistical areas (TDSAs)	X	19
County subdivisions	5,827	5,903
Census county divisions (CCDs)	5,512	5,581
Unorganized territories (UTs)	274	282
Other statistically equivalent entities	41	40
Census designated places (CDPs)	3,733	4,423
Census tracts	43,691	50,690
Block numbering areas (BNAs)	3,423	11,586
Block groups (BGs)	156,163	229,192
Tabulated parts	197,957	363,047
Enumeration districts (EDs)	102,235	(See BG)
Blocks	2,473,679	7,017,427
Tabulated parts	2,545,416	X
Traffic analysis zones (TAZs)	160,000[d]	200,000[d]

X: Not applicable.

[a] Includes American Samoa, Guam, Northern Mariana Islands, Puerto Rico, Trust Territory of the Pacific Islands, U.S. Virgin Islands.

[b] Includes American Samoa, Guam, Norhtern Mariana Islands, Palau, Puerto Rico, U.S. Virgin Islands.

[c] Includes only eligible areas participating under Public Law 94-171.

[d] Estimated.

Source: U.S. Bureau of the Census, *Maps and More: Your Guide to Census Bureau Geography*, 1992, p. 1.

Political Areas

Political areas are areas that have boundaries that are recognized by law and that perform political functions. Under this heading come principally states, counties (or county equivalents), minor civil divisions, and incorporated places. There are also some areas that are not part of the basic hierarchy of areas enumerated here. They are American Indian reservations and Alaska Native regional corporations (ANRC); and voting districts and congressional districts. The latter are political areas that serve as voting areas or areas represented by legislators.

In U.S. census tabulations and reports, the "population of the United States" refers ordinarily to the resident population of the 50 **states** and the District of Columbia. Alaska and Hawaii, the two most recent additions to this group, became states in 1959. The 1990 Census treated the District of Columbia, Puerto Rico, and each of the outlying areas (the Virgin Islands of the United States, Guam, American Samoa, the Northern Mariana Islands, and Palau) as statistically equivalent areas for data presentation.[2]

Counties are the first-order divisions of each of the states. Treated as county-equivalents are the District of Columbia and Guam; the parishes of Louisiana; the boroughs and census areas of Alaska; the independent cities in Maryland, Missouri, Nevada, and Virginia; the part of Yellowstone National Park in Montana; the *municipios* of Puerto Rico; and a variety of entities in the other outlying areas. County-equivalents are needed since these areas are not called counties and the entire territory of each state or statistical equivalent of a state must be accounted for. Counties and county-equivalents number about 3200.

The general term for the second-order division of states is **minor civil division** (MCD). (See Appendix A for a list of the acronyms for census geographic areas.) These are legally defined subcounty areas, such as towns or townships. For the 1990 census, these are found in 28 states, Puerto Rico (*barrios*), and several of the outlying areas. There are about 30,400 of them. (See Table 5.2 for an illustration of the geopolitical composition of county populations.)

Within counties some areas are incorporated as a **city**, **town** (excluding the New England States, New York, and Wisconsin), **borough** (excluding Alaska

TABLE 5.2   Geopolitical Components of Boone County, Missouri: 1990 Census

Geographic component	Population
Boone County	112,379
Bourbon township	2,140
Sturgeon city	838
Cedar township	9,233
Ashland city	1,252
Columbia city (pt.)	215
Hartsburg town	131
Centralia township	4,143
Centralia city (pt.)	3,414
Columbia township	38,240
Columbia city (pt.)	29,871
Missouri township	49,428
Columbia city (pt.)	39,015
Rocheport city	255
Perche township	3,475
Harrisburg town	169
Rocky Fork township	5,720
Columbia city (pt.)	—
Hallsville city	917

Note: Parts of Columbia City fall in four townships of Boone County.

Source: U.S. Bureau of the Census, *1990 Censuses of Population and Housing, Population and Housing Characteristics*, 1990 CPH-1-27, 1992.

and New York), or **village**. These **incorporated places** have definite boundaries recognized by the state and have their own local governments. There are about 19,400 of them.

A **voting district** is any of a variety of areas (e.g., election districts, precincts, legislative districts, wards) defined by state and local governments for purposes of conducting elections. In the records of the Census Bureau they may be actual voting districts or areas adjusted to conform with census block boundaries. The term "voting district" in the 1990 census replaces the 1980 census term "election precinct." **Congressional districts** are the 435 areas delineated by state legislatures or, in their default, state commissions or state courts, as the voting areas and the areas represented by members of Congress. Some issues in the delineation of voting districts and congressional districts are discussed in Chapter 12.

Other Administrative Areas

School districts and zip code areas represent two types of nonpolitical administrative areas. **School districts** are areas established by state departments of education for which the Census Bureau prepares special tabulations for the U.S. Department of Education. The various types of districts delineated may overlap, and some territory may not be covered by any district or by a specific type of district. School districts may have no relation to other census geographic areas, sometimes splitting blocks. They numbered about 16,000 in 1990. They function also as political areas in the sense that members of the boards of education of these communities are often elected from these districts. **Zip code areas** are administrative entities of the U.S. Postal Service designed for mail collection and delivery. Data for zip code areas are widely used by business organizations in marketing their products or services. Zip codes areas do not generally coincide with the Census Bureau's political or statistical areas and change according to the needs of the Postal Service. Most zip code areas do not have specific boundaries and their implied boundaries do not necessarily follow clearly identifiable physical features. At the time of the 1990 census, there were an estimated 40,000 such areas, but the Census Bureau tabulated data for only 29,500 residential zip code areas. Population census data for these areas were compiled by private organizations on the basis of data files made available by the Census Bureau. This practice is again being followed in 2000.

Statistical Areas

The Census Bureau has defined a variety of areas that do not conform to political or administrative boundaries, for use in collecting, compiling, and presenting data. These types of areas are called statistical areas. Among them are combinations of political areas (e.g., regions, divisions, metropolitan areas), other specially defined areas (e.g., census county divisions, census-designated places, census tracts), and type-of-residence areas (e.g., urbanized areas, rural areas). In addition, there are various types of statistical areas covering Alaskan native villages and American Indian tribes designed for the purpose of presenting 1990 census data. In the following discussion of these areas, political and statistical areas are considered in their hierarchical relationship first, leaving type-of-residence concepts such as metropolitan areas, urbanized areas, and urban areas for later treatment.

Geographic Hierarchy from Blocks to Regions

There are four geographic **regions**, designated Northeast, Midwest (formerly North Central), South, and West. Each region is a combination of two or three **geographic divisions**, and each division is a combination of several states. The states in each division and the divisions in each region are displayed in Figure 5.1. This grouping of states and divisions has been used since the census of 1960, when a determination was made as to the placement of the two new states, Alaska and Hawaii. The general criteria for grouping states into divisions include geographic contiguity, similarity in economic and physical characteristics, and a common historical development, but other criteria may be invoked. Alaska and Hawaii were both placed in the Pacific Division in 1960, immediately after statehood and in time for the 1960 census, mainly for convenience even though they fit the criteria enumerated for being grouped with the other states in this division only loosely.

The Census Bureau has delineated two types of subcounty areas in cooperation with state and local officials in states where minor civil divisions (MCDs)

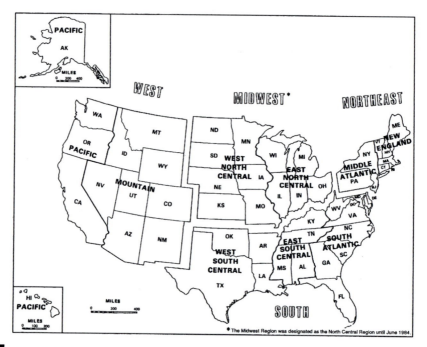

FIGURE 5.1   Outline map of the United States showing census regions, divisions, and states. *Source:* U.S. Bureau of the Census, *State and Metropolitan Area Data Book, 1997–1998*, 1998.

do not exist or are not adequate for reporting subcounty statistics. **Census county divisions** (CCDs) have been delineated in 21 states where MCDs are not legally established, do not have administrative functions, change boundaries frequently, or are not otherwise suitable for reporting subcounty statistics. **Unorganized territories** are subcounty areas delineated by the Census Bureau for those portions of the nine states that are partially covered by MCDs but that lack MCDs in the remainder of the state, or have MCDs in this remainder that are not adequate for reporting subcounty statistics. These two types of areas—census county divisions and unorganized territories—help complete the coverage of all states with a network of subcounty divisions.

The list of incorporated places has been supplemented with a large number (5300) of **census-designated places**, densely settled population centers without legally defined corporate limits or corporate powers. These are defined in cooperation with state officials and local data users. The purpose of delineating such areas is to be able to provide census data for them. Commonly recognized population concentrations that lack politically recognized boundaries may be quite large and populous (e.g., Silver Spring, Maryland, and Levittown, New York).

Selected counties have been divided into **census tracts**, which are small locally delineated statistical areas with stable boundaries and relatively homogeneous demographic and economic characteristics. (See Figures 5.2, 5.3, and 5.4.) They have a population size averaging about 4000 persons, although their populations may range from fewer than 2500 to more than 8000. When the population grows sufficiently, the tract may be subdivided. In 1990, data were compiled for some 50,400 census tracts. For grouping and numbering blocks in 1990 where census tracts had not been established, the Census Bureau delineated 11,500 **block numbering areas** (BNAs) in cooperation with the states.

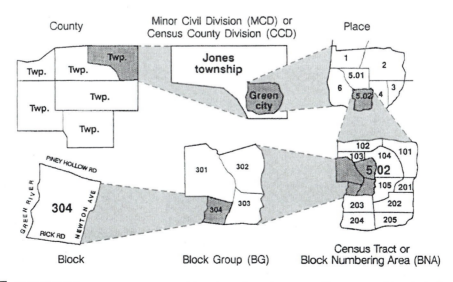

FIGURE 5.2 Stylized illustration of the relationships of census small-area geographic units in the 1990 census. *Source*: U.S. Bureau of the Census, "Census geography—Concepts and products," CFF No. 8 (Rev.), *Factfinder for the Nation*, 1991.

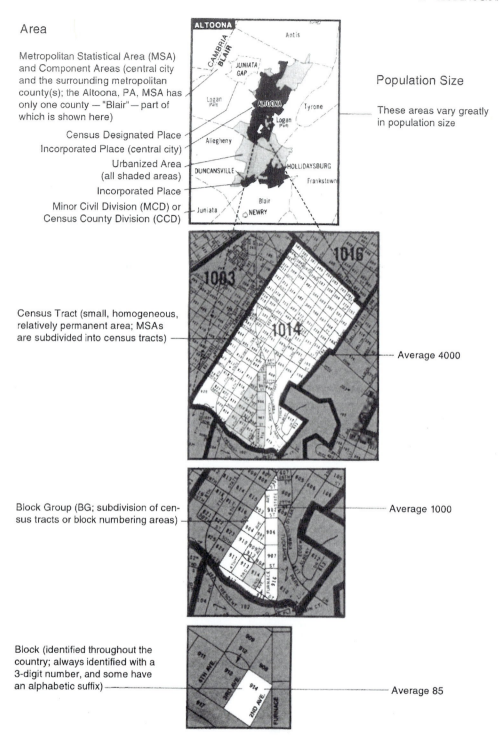

Area

Metropolitan Statistical Area (MSA)
and Component Areas (central city
and the surrounding metropolitan
county(s); the Altoona, PA, MSA has
only one county — "Blair" — part of
which is shown here)

Census Designated Place
Incorporated Place (central city)

Urbanized Area
(all shaded areas)

Incorporated Place

Minor Civil Division (MCD) or
Census County Division (CCD)

Population Size

These areas vary greatly
in population size

Census Tract (small, homogeneous,
relatively permanent area; MSAs
are subdivided into census tracts)

Average 4000

Block Group (BG; subdivision of census tracts or block numbering areas)

Average 1000

Block (identified throughout the
country; always identified with a
3-digit number, and some have
an alphabetic suffix)

Average 85

FIGURE 5.3   Map segments illustrating the geographic subdivisions in a metropolitan county in the
1990 census: Blair County, Pennsylvania (Altoona, Pennsylvania, MSA). *Source*: U.S. Bureau of the Census,
"Census '90 Basics," *Census '90*, 1990.

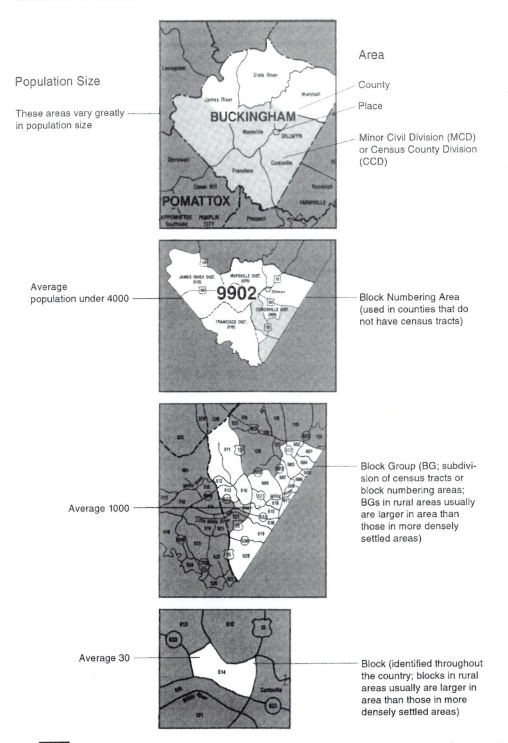

FIGURE 5.4 Map segments illustrating the geographic subdivisions in a nonmetropolitan county in the 1990 census: Buckingham County, Virginia. *Source:* U.S. Bureau of the Census, "Census '90 Basics," *Census '90,* 1990.

Like census tracts, block numbering areas do not cross county boundaries. Block numbering areas were not used for the 2000 census because all areas were tracted in 2000, even rural areas.

Census tracts and block numbering areas are composed of **block groups**, and the latter are composed of **blocks**. Block groups, numbering 230,000 in 1990, are combinations of census blocks sharing the same first digit in their identifying numbers within a census tract or BNA. Blocks are small, usually compact areas, bounded by streets or other prominent physical features as well as certain legal boundaries. They do not cross BNA, census tract, or county boundaries. Blocks are assigned three-digit numbers, with a possible single letter suffix. The 7 million census blocks covered the entire United States in 1990. (See Figures 5.2, 5.3, and 5.4.)

We may summarize the relation of these political and statistical areas in the following hierarchical structure:

> United States
> Region
>   Division
>   State
>   County
>   County subdivision (minor civil division, census county division,
>   unorganized territory)
>   Place (incorporated place, census designated place, or part)
>   Census tract/block numbering area (or part)
>   Block group (or part)
>   Block

Metropolitan Areas and Urbanized Areas

All the counties in the United States, except those in New England (where the operative political units are towns and cities), are classified as metropolitan or nonmetropolitan, depending on whether they are part of a metropolitan area or not. **Metropolitan area** (MA) is a general term encompassing three types of areas. They are **metropolitan statistical areas** (MSAs), **consolidated metropolitan statistical areas** (CMSAs), and **primary metropolitan statistical areas** (PMSAs). These areas are identified and delineated by the Federal Office of Management and Budget (OMB), following a set of standards developed by the OMB in cooperation with other federal agencies and nonfederal users. As currently defined, MAs are based on applying 1990 standards to 1990 decennial census data and to subsequent Census Bureau population estimates and special censuses.[3] (See Figure 5.5 for the location of the MAs in 1999.) MAs are defined in terms of entire counties, except in the six New England states, where cities and towns are used. The general concept of an MA is that of a large population consisting of a population nucleus and the adjacent communities that have a high degree of integration with the nucleus. This general concept has remained essentially the same since MAs were first defined before the 1950 census. The classification provides a nationally consistent set of definitions for collecting, tabulating, and publishing federal statistics for geographic areas consisting of counties or combinations of "related" counties.

An MSA must contain a city with at least 50,000 inhabitants or an urbanized area as delineated by the Census Bureau (discussed later). In the latter case, the MSA must consist of one or more counties containing a population of at least 100,000 (75,000 in cities and towns in New England). Generally, MSAs consist of one or more entire counties that meet specified standards pertaining to population density, commuting patterns, and metropolitan character. Contiguous counties (cities and towns in New England) are included if they have close social and economic links with the area's population nucleus.[4]

An MSA with a population of 1 million or more may be divided into component areas called primary metropolitan statistical areas (PMSA). A PMSA consists of one or more counties (cities and towns in New England) that demonstrate, on the basis of specific standards, strong internal economic and social links, separate from their ties to other portions of the MSA. An MSA is redesignated as a consolidated metropolitan statistical area (CMSA) if PMSAs have been established within the MSA. Every MSA and CMSA—but not every PMSA—has at least one core place, called a **central city**. For example, the Washington-Baltimore, DC-MD-VA-WV CMSA includes three PMSAs (i.e., Baltimore, Maryland, PMSA, Hagerstown, Maryland, PMSA, and Washington, DC-Maryland-Virginia-West Virginia PMSA), three central cities, and 33 counties or independent cities in four states.

We may summarize the metropolitan structure of the population roughly, as we have described it, as follows:

> Metropolitan areas (counties, except New England)
> Metropolitan statistical areas
>   Central city (50,000+) or urbanized area (100,000+)
> Consolidated metropolitan statistical areas (1,000,000+)
>   Central city (50,000+) or urbanized area (100,000+)
>   Primary metropolitan statistical areas
> Nonmetropolitan areas (counties, except New England)

With the June 1998 OMB review, there were 18 CMSAs, comprising 73 PMSAs, and 256 separate MSAs.[5] As of mid-year 1996, 80% of the population lived in MAs, which covered 20% of the land area of the United States. For the list of counties that comprise each MSA, CMSA, and PMSA, refer to the Census Bureau's *Geographic Areas Reference Manual*.[6] This guide was developed to aid data users in applying the geographic concepts and methods used for data presentation in the population, economic, and agriculture censuses.

Prospective Change in Standards for Metropolitan Areas

In line with the practice of periodically reviewing the metropolitan area standards for usefulness and relevance, the Office of Management and Budget (OMB) has been reviewing the recommendations of the Metropolitan Area Standards Review Committee (MASRC) for changes in the OMB's standards for defining metropolitan areas. The committee found that users had concerns about the operational complexity of the standards and about their limited description of the settlement and activity patterns in the country. On the basis of the committee's report, the OMB plans to put into effect a new set of standards for defining metropolitan areas following the year 2000 census.[7]

The MASRC has recommended that MAs be replaced by **core-based statistical areas** (CBSA). The **cores**, densely settled concentrations of population,

Metropolitan Areas of the United States: 1999

FIGURE 5.5 Location of metropolitan areas of the United States: 1999. *Note*: Metropolitan area boundaries and names are those defined by the U.S. Office of Management and Budget on June 30, 1999. All other boundaries and names are as of June 30, 1999. *Source*: U.S. Bureau of the Census, Internet, 1999: www.census.gov/geo/www/mapgallery.

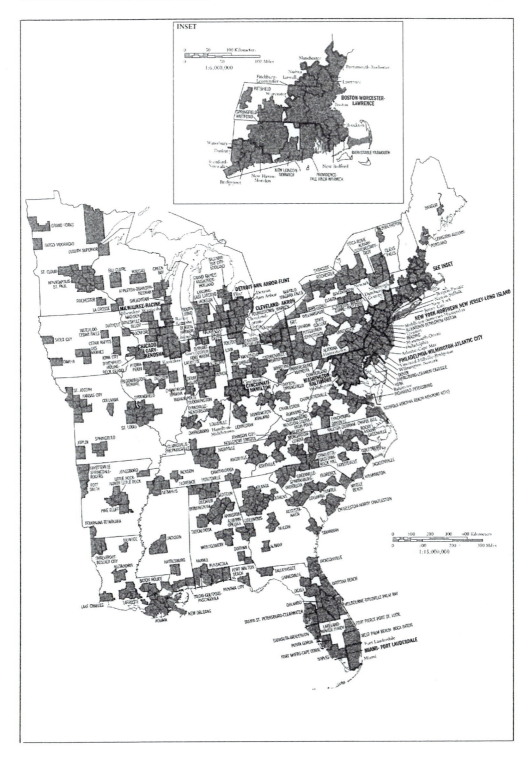

FIGURE 5.5 (*Continued*)

would be **settlement clusters** (SC) or Census Bureau urbanized areas (discussed later), around which the CBSAs would be defined. The settlement clusters are areas that will be newly defined on the basis of the 2000 census. The CBSA classification includes three types of areas based on the total population of the core areas of the CBSAs: (1) megapolitan areas, with cores of at least 1 million population; (2) macropolitan areas, with cores of 50,000 to 999,999 population; and (3) micropolitan population, with cores of 10,000 to 49,999 population. The counties containing the core population would become the central counties of the CBSAs. A single threshold of 25% based on commuting data would be used to establish linkages between the counties containing the CBSA cores and the outlying counties. Counties and equivalent areas are the essential components of the CBSAs. Counties were again selected for this purpose, in preference to subcounty areas such as census tracts, because of the greater availability of data, stability of boundaries, and user familiarity with the geographic components. Territory not included in the CBSAs would be designated as outside core-based statistical areas. The actual areas, based on the 2000 census population and commuting data, will probably be determined in 2003.

Distribution by Type of Residence

The discussion on metropolitan areas is a bridge between areas defined by "boundary" rules and areas defined by type of residence since metropolitan areas may be placed in both classification systems. To describe the residence distribution of the population, we focus on a set of area concepts defined essentially in terms of population density or size. These include the urban population, urbanized areas (UAs), cities/incorporated places, and census-designated places. An **urbanized area** (UA) consists of one or more places (**central place**) and the surrounding densely settled territory (**urban fringe**) having a combined population of 50,000 or more inhabitants. A UA may exclude low density territory in one or more **extended cities**. These are incorporated places that contain substantial territory with a population density of fewer than 100 persons per square mile. The urban fringe, the densely settled area contiguous to the central place of a UA, generally consists of territory having a population density of at least 1000 persons per square mile. One or more central places function as the primary centers of each UA. Each place that is a **central city** of an MSA and lies within the UA is also a central place of the UA. If the UA does not contain a central city, its central place is determined by population size. In 1990 there were 405 urbanized areas.

The **urban population** consists of the population in urbanized areas and the population in places of 2500 or more inhabitants outside urbanized areas. The urban population includes both incorporated places of 2500 or more inhabitants and census-designated places of 2500 or more inhabitants as part of the urban population outside urbanized areas. The **rural population** is the population that is not defined as urban.

We may summarize the relation between these residence concepts as follows:

Urban areas
   Urbanized areas (50,000+)
      Central place (central city in MSA)
      Urban fringe
   Other places of 2500 or more
      Incorporated places
      Census-designated places
Rural areas

In 1990 75% of the population was classified as urban; a current percentage cannot be determined before the year 2000 census results are tabulated.

Special Areas

The Population and Housing Censuses of 1990 included one special area, in addition to voting districts, school districts, and zip code areas already mentioned, namely **traffic analysis zones**. Data for the special areas are compiled on the basis of area definitions submitted by other agencies, mainly state and local government agencies. No other special areas were introduced in the Population and Housing Censuses of 2000. In addition to the standard tabulation areas, congressional districts and zip code areas were employed in the tabulations of the economic censuses of 1997 and 1992. Limited statistics were summarized for individual zip codes in the Censuses of Retail Trade, Service Industries, and Manufactures. Zip code reporting in 1992 took the place of reporting other types of special small areas in the economic censuses before 1992.[8] Trading areas, television marketing areas, and labor market areas are more loosely defined geographic concepts employed in marketing or manpower research (see Chapters 6 and 8).

Comparability of Data from Census to Census

With geographic-area data as with any other type of data, the problem of choosing between currency and comparability of the categories for which the data are tabulated has to be confronted but it is intrinsic to geographic-area data. Area components are added and removed and conceptual frameworks are changed. The definition of a given type of geographic area may be modified. As a result, the boundaries of a whole group of geographic areas or at least the boundaries of some individual areas within the group may change from one census to the next. When changes are instituted and the data have been brought up to date, currrency is achieved but the data for the designated area are no longer comparable.

Some illustrations may be given. The definitions of metropolitan areas have been modified several times since the introduction of the program in the 1950 census and a whole new concept of metropolitan areas is being introduced with the 2000 census. In 1983, about one-third of all MSAs changed boundaries because of changes in commuting patterns identified by the 1980 population census. Consider the evolution of the Washington-Baltimore CMSA, which, as noted, now includes the Washington, D.C., PMSA, the Baltimore, Maryland, PMSA, and the Hagerstown, Maryland, PMSA. In 1985, there were two separate MSAs, Washington, D.C., MSA and Baltimore, Maryland, MSA, and Hagerstown, Maryland, was part of the nonmetropolitan population. With the passage of time and the growth of the surrounding population, many counties were added, the Hagerstown, Maryland, MSA came into existence, and the three MSAs were joined in one CMSA. In comparing metropolitan area data from one census to the next, the analyst may be interested in (1) measuring the change in the population size and characteristics of a given named area, whatever its boundaries, (2) comparing data for common subareas for a series of dates, or (3) reconstituting the present area for past years. These three types of comparisons answer different questions and have different answers.

The second illustration relates to census tracts. These are presumably stable areas but, because of local changes in population numbers and characteristics and boundary changes of various kinds, it often becomes desirable, if not necessary, to revise the census-tract structure in a county. Comparability is maintained by splitting existing tracts into additive geographic parts. For example, the census-tract changes for Wicomico County, Maryland, between 1980 and 1990 included the following splits:

1980	1990
Tract 101 (part) →	Tract 101.10 (part)
Tract 101 (part) →	Tract 101.20 (part)
Tract 105 (part) →	Tract 101.20 (part)
Tract 105 (part) →	Tract 105

For Garrett County, Maryland, and Kent County, Maryland, census tracts and block numbering areas, respectively, were delineated for the first time in 1990; hence comparability with 1980 is not possible. It should be apparent that, even for such "stable" areas as census tracts, comparablility over time can be a difficult and complex problem.

GEOMETRIC DATA RETRIEVAL METHODS, GEOGRAPHIC INFORMATION SYSTEMS, AND TIGER

Geometric Data Retrieval Methods

To be meaningful, demographic data must be assigned to specific locations or geographic areas. A basic step in accomplishing this requirement has been the development of maps covering every street and address in the country. The U.S. Census Bureau must have such maps in order to conduct the decennial census and tabulate the results. The maps of the U.S. census operations are based on a network of coordinate points established by the U.S. Geological Survey. The Census Bureau uses several methods to assign demographic data to locations and geographic areas. These methods are designated area assignment, point assignment, and line assignment.

Area assignment is used by the Census Bureau and private vendors in compiling most data that they disseminate. Aggregate census data are available from the Census Bureau in the form of Summary Tape Files (STF). Census data are retrieved by the Census Bureau by aggregating data for blocks, block groups, or other small geographic units into some required whole, such as a county. STF files are also available from private vendors, who buy STFs from the Census Bureau and sell their clients access to time-sharing equipment and software that the clients can use to manipulate the information on tape. It may be advantageous to secure the STFs from a private vendor on the grounds of price, usability, flexibility, and customization.

Data summaries can be generated for a variety of special areas, such as school districts, telephone exchange areas, radial areas, and polygonal areas. In the delineation of a radial area, the coordinates of a point are read into the computer for the purpose of generating data for a specified area surrounding the point. The area defined, a circle of a specified radius, may be useful for site location of a store or establishing the trading area of a business (see Chapter 6). In the delineation of a polygonal area, the coordinates of several fixed points (e.g., five) form a net and define the boundaries of an area of interest, such as a hospital emergency service zone, a fire station service zone, or a telephone exchange area. Data assigned to locations falling within the net can be aggregated to produce information about the whole area. Note that special software is needed to create circular or polygonal areas when the user works with STFs.

With **point assignment**, a representative sample of records for individual households for a particular geographic area is selected from the complete file and inscribed on computer tape or CD-ROM. If the entire country is covered in this way and the data tape or CD-ROM is made available to the public, the households selected constitute a national Public Use Microdata Sample (PUMS). In the 1990 and earlier censuses, an area had to have a specified minimum population and names, street addresses, and other identifying information were deleted from the housing-unit record to preserve confidentiality. The PUMS records contained geographic codes identifying only large areas called **PUMAs** (public use microdata areas) that had a population of at least 100,000, such as metropolitan areas, large cities, groups of counties, or large groups of census tracts. Because of changes in avoidance-disclosure techniques in the 2000 census, requirements for minimum population are no longer necessary and data can be obtained for the smallest population groups.

Finally, with **line assignment**, street addresses in a geographic area are **geocoded** (i.e., assigned codes corresponding to the longitude and latitude of the address) in order to create a **geobased file** (GBF).[9] (See Figure 5.6.) This file was formerly used in combination with so-called dual independent map encoding (DIME) to assign addresses to particular geographic units, such as census tracts. The analyst can also match data from local administrative records (e.g., local cases of tuberculosis) with the geobased file. The **flagging** of each record with a cartographic code (i.e., attaching an identifying code to the record) allows the analyst to locate residents in a geocoded area. In this way a public health analyst can develop data on cases of tuberculosis in each census tract cross-tabulated by the decennial census characteristics of the tract, or a business can identify customers residing in census tracts that have specified characteristics.

Profiling Specified Areas

The instantaneous generation of a demographic profile for an area of any specified size and shape by the method of area assignment or other method is called **geometric demographic data retrieval**. Commonly geometric retrieval methods are applied to a basic set of data, such as census tracts in tracted

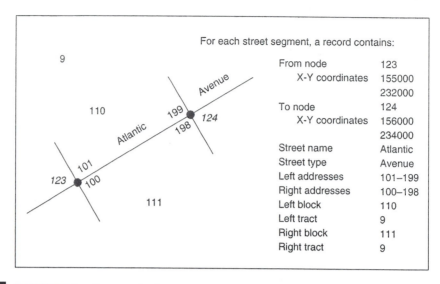

For each street segment, a record contains:

From node   123
    X-Y coordinates   155000
                             232000
To node   124
    X-Y coordinates   156000
                             234000
Street name   Atlantic
Street type   Avenue
Left addresses   101–199
Right addresses   100–198
Left block   110
Left tract   9
Right block   111
Right tract   9

FIGURE 5.6   Contents of a GBF/DIME-File record. *Source:* U.S. Bureau of the Census, *Census '80: Continuing the Factfinder Tradition,* by Charles P. Kaplan, Thomas L. Van Valey, and Associates, 1980, Figure 4–5.

areas, and block numbering areas (BNAs) and minor civil divisions/census county divisions (MCDs/CCDs) in untracted areas. From these units as building blocks, geometrically defined areas can be constructed.[10] Let us assume, for example, that a user or client desires a profile of the population in a circular target area with a specified radius around a designated street-corner address. The data vendor locates the street intersection of the address on maps and establishes the intersection's latitude and longitude. The latitude and longitude are combined in the computer with computer software, which defines the target area, allocates tracts/BNAs or MCDs/CCDs, or portions of them, to the target area, and combines the component pieces of the target area as measured. The area required may be a circle, concentric circles (i.e., a circular band around the designated point), a rectangle, other polygon, or any area which can be drawn exactly on a map.

Schemes vary for determining the portion of the building-block area that will be allocated to the target area when the building-block area straddles the boundary of the target area. Most data-vending companies base their allocation methods on whether the **centroid** (i.e., the geographic center expressed in latitude and longitude) of the principal subdivisions of the census tracts/BNAs (or MCDs/CCDs), that is, block groups (BGs), fall within the target area. Part of the population of the census tract/BNA (or MCD/CCD) is allocated to the target area when the centroids of the BGs split by the boundaries of the target area fall in the target area. The population can be allocated proportionally to the target area on the basis of the relative sizes (in terms of area or, more appropriately, population) of the BGs and the parent census tract. There are many other ways of determining the allocation of the population of subdivisions that straddle the boundary of the target area (see Chapter 6).

Geometric retrieval methods are an established way of securing data on an area's characteristics. Profiles of many alternative areas can be retrieved easily and quickly and compared with one another in preparation for further analysis or decision making. On the other hand, the estimates vary in quality depending on (1) the number and size of geographic units requiring allocation at the boundaries and (2) the internal distribution of the population of these units. The estimates tend to be more accurate, the greater the number and the smaller the size of the units composing the parent area, and the more evenly distributed the population within the units straddling the perimeter of the target area are.[11]

Geographic Information Systems

The linkage of geographic coordinate information and population data is the basis of a geographic information system. A **geographic information system** (GIS) is a computer-automated system of compiling and mapping data identified by geographic coordinates for specified sets of geographic areas identified by geographic coordinates. To accomplish this, the cartographic coordinate points must be **digitized** (i.e., coded in a binary language that a computer can process). The resulting product is a geobased file system for manipulating data. To be operative, a geographic information system requires an automated geographic database to support it. The U.S. Census Bureau developed such a database, identified by the acronym **TIGER** (topologically integrated geographic encoding and referencing), for use in taking the 1990 census.

TIGER

For the 1980 and previous censuses, the Census Bureau depended mostly on local sources to provide the base maps used by census enumerators and census managers to control the census operations. These maps came in a wide variety of shapes and sizes and showed geographic features in different ways. The Census Bureau decided that it needed a better way to produce maps for its censuses and surveys and began to build the TIGER system. For this purpose it joined with the U.S. Geological Survey (USGS) in 1983 to develop a single integrated geographic database for the entire country. The system was largely completed between 1984 and 1987.

For this project, the Census Bureau extended and updated the features in its computerized Geographic Base File/Dual Independent Map Encoding File (GBF/DIME). The TIGER/Line files, an extract from the TIGER system, replace the 1980 census GBF/DIME files. The GBF/DIME files usually covered no more than the urbanized portions of SMSAs, or only about 60% of the population. The TIGER/Line files cover the entire area of the United States. To develop the TIGER/Line files, the GBF/DIME files were joined with digital data from USGS's files.

The TIGER system was designed originally to produce the various geographic products required to support the Census Bureau's censuses and surveys, but its applications have broadened. The TIGER files are a digital cartographic database that contains all the information normally found on a Census Bureau map in a form a computer can manipulate. They are used to assign geographic location codes to addresses for collecting data, either as an address reference file or indirectly in the form of paper maps produced from the file. They provide the geographic structure—that is, the relationship of one geographic area to other geographic areas—that permits assigning an address to the correct census block, census tract, place, or other geographic unit.

Among TIGER's many products are digitized maps and coordinate-based digital map information. The TIGER system makes it possible for users to generate maps by computer at different scales for any geographic area in the country. As compared with the previous method of map preparation, TIGER accelerates map production and makes it easier to update the database that contains the map-drawing information. Using the TIGER database, the Census Bureau generated a wide array of paper maps from the 1990 census. Among them were the series of county block maps, county subdivision maps, and census tract/BNA outline maps. In general, these maps show the boundaries of the featured areas. To apply the TIGER files, user applications software is required. This applications software is available only commercially. Note that the TIGER files do *not* contain statistical data from the Census Bureau's censuses or surveys.

Structure of TIGER

In TIGER, information is related to points, lines, and areas. Each point and each line segment are tagged with their own geographic attribute codes. A 10-digit number identifies each **line segment**. The record contains appropriate

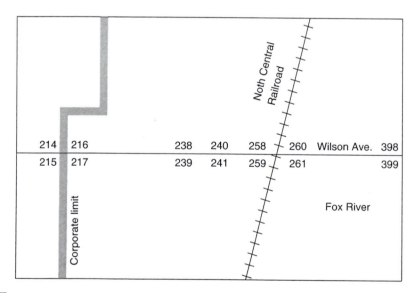

FIGURE 5.7   Illustration of various features of a TIGER/Line file. *Note:* The features depicted were drawn for purposes of illustration only and should not be construed as representative of the content of the TIGER database. *Source:* U.S. Bureau of the Census, *TIGER: The Coast-to-Coast Digital Map Data Base,* 1990.

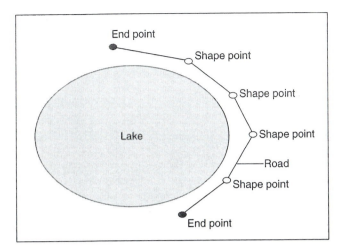

FIGURE 5.8   Illustration of the shape-point coordinates of a TIGER/Line file. End-point coordinates are found in record type 1, shape-point coordinates are found in record type 2. *Source*: U.S. Bureau of the Census, *TIGER: The Coast-to-Coast Digital Map Data Base*, 1990.

codes for latitude and longitude coordinates, the name of the **feature segment** (e.g., road, railroad, river), and alternate names, if any. For areas formerly covered by the GBF/DIME files, the record contains the address ranges and zip codes associated with these ranges for the right and left sides of each line segment. (See Figures 5.6 and 5.7.) Every **end point** of a feature segment is considered a point and is stored as a latitude/longitude coordinate. Considered as a whole, the TIGER database contains a latitude and a longitude coordinate value for each of the more than 28 million feature intersections and end points that define its nearly 40 million feature segments. These, in turn, enclose 12 million polygons in a giant "connect the dots" map of the United States. The end points of the line segments that define the perimeters of these polygons are designated **shape points** (Figure 5.8). The shape points are identified by coordinate values that describe the shape of those feature segments that are not straight.

TIGER/Line files contain selected geographic and cartographic data for the segments of each boundary or feature and the associated areas, including latitude/longitude coordinates of segment end points, the name and type of the feature, the census code identifying the feature segment, adjacent census geographic area codes, and the 1980 and 1990 census geographic area codes. TIGER/Line files also furnish address ranges and associated zip codes for each side-of-street segment for areas approximating the urbanized areas. That is, address-range and zip code information can be found only in those portions of the TIGER/Line files covered originally by the GBF/DIME files. During the course of the 1990 census, the Census Bureau updated and extended address-range and zip code coverage in 20 GBF/DIME file areas.

Availability of TIGER Files and Products

The 1990 Census TIGER/Line files and updates of these files are organized by county and are available from the Census Bureau on computer tape or CD-

ROM. The county files in TIGER/Line contain all the geographic information, including coordinates, codes, names, and relationships (e.g, state in which a county is located) that form the backbone of the TIGER database.

Other TIGER-related geographic products include TIGER/Boundary files. These files contain coordinate data for various 1990 census tabulation-area boundary sets (for example, a file containing state and county boundaries, and a file containing census tract, block-numbering, and block-group boundaries).

The TIGER/Census Tract Comparability File provides geographic comparability information for 1990 and 1980 census tracts in counties that had census tracts in 1990. The TIGER/GICS File provides the names, geographic area codes, and relationships for every geographic area for which the Census Bureau provides data, as well as the latitude and longitude of an internal point (i.e., usually the geographic center) for each geographic area and the area measurement, both land and water. This file enables users of the TIGER/Line files to link a name to a geographic area code without resorting to printed publications. Other files include the Geographic Reference File-Names (PUB-GRF-N), which contains the names associated with 1990 census geographic area codes, and TIGER/Data Base, which facilitates the input of TIGER into GISs.

As noted earlier, user-applications software needed to apply the TIGER/ Line files must be obtained commercially. Although many of the data-vending companies sell other demographic mapping products, in addition to the applications software for TIGER, the production of the applications software is a specialized activity. These products permit the client to create thematic data maps in color for very small geographic areas. The maps can be customized in terms of themes, colors, ranges, and scales. Among the many companies providing geographic products are Business Information Technologies, Caliper Corporation, Environmental Systems Research Institute, Inc. (ESRI), Map-Info Corporation, and Geolytics. ESRI, a large international company, markets ArcView GIS, one of the most widely used desktop GIS and mapping software products.

Applications of GIS and TIGER

Supported by the appropriate software, TIGER/Line files enable the user to combine geographic and cartographic data with data from censuses, vital registrations, and administrative records in order to present the statistical data graphically and analyze them spatially. GIS/TIGER is useful whenever demographic and socioeconomic phenomena present, or are expected to present, distinct patterns that vary according to the different geographic or administrative units in a country or its subdivisions. It provides a basis for analyzing information when variables such as location, distance, area, and geographic shape are involved.

There are numerous possible applications of GIS/TIGER by business, government, and nonprofit organizations. As a general application, the statistical data in the summary tape files from the 1990 census can be linked with the TIGER/Line files, which contain the 1990 census geographic area codes to these data. More specific examples of the uses of GIS/TIGER include geocoding of spatially referenced data for market research (e.g., analysis of market potential for a new product, selection of a store site, sales and inventory control, planning the advertising budget), address-to-area matching (e.g., merging files on health conditions and social characteristics), drawing new political and administrative boundaries (e.g., legislative redistricting, drawing school district boundaries), and planning of community services (e.g., siting public facilities such as recreation centers, schools, libraries, and "senior" centers). Demographic profiles of a target population like the elderly and the poor can be generated for designated geographic reference areas such as counties, cities, and census tracts. GIS/TIGER can be employed in drawing the boundaries for a new school according to defined guidelines, such as avoidance of overcrowding, underuse, excessive travel time, and neighborhood splitting. A county administration can use the TIGER/Line files to keep track of new residential development in a community by exploiting school records, particularly the data in them on student's home address.[12]

Government agencies can use GIS with TIGER to measure and describe the population affected by noise patterns near airports or vulnerable to floods and other natural disasters and plan public action in response to the problem. In the former case, the goal is to map different air traffic patterns, determine the population affected, and redesign flight patterns so as to disturb the smallest population. The same general issue arises in connection with the location and public use of hazardous-waste drop-off sites. The research may seek to determine the optimum location of a new site, involving the measurement of the distribution of residents within specified minutes or miles of the proposed drop-off site, or the rescheduling of drop-off hours at an existing site. GIS/TIGER can be used to reconstruct the record of conditions in an area devastated by flood or hurricane. For example, TIGER/Line files were combined with data from the 1990 census and the appropriate software to locate areas where rescue efforts were most needed and to assess damage from floods in the Midwest and from Hurricane Andrew in Florida and Louisiana in 1992. TIGER/Line files can be the basis of a transportation information system. Public transportation planners can plan and revise public transit routes, emergency-vehicle routing, and car-pool, snow-clearing, and garbage-collection routes, partly on the basis of residence patterns and data on household and housing characteristics.[13]

GIS, supported by TIGER/Line files, can be an important tool to support decision making in community social services planning. In an effort to improve its handling of the problem of spousal abuse, the Baltimore County Police Department geographically coded the spousal abuse cases reported in 1987, using TIGER/Line files. The abuse cases were found to be geographically clustered, and this result made possible a better targetting of police resources. Next, the cases of spousal abuse were linked geographically with variables such as income, employment, and arrests for drunk driving. The maps prepared showing the geographic distribution by census tract of spousal abuse cases and each of these variables afforded the police a better basis for enforcing laws on spousal abuse in the county and county social workers a better understanding of the basis of the problem.[14]

The combination of demographic and health data, and GIS software, can be an important analytic tool to support decision making in public health. GIS allows the analyst to display health phenomena such as the incidence of disease and the location of treatment facilities geographically. The geographic display of the combination of health data with associated demographic and socioeconomic data aids in the analysis of the problem and in planning preventive and treatment programs. Addresses of patients with specific diseases can be combined with population census data to determine the disease incidence rates for specific geographic zones in a city. Hospital, patient, and physician data can be linked, and maps can be prepared for analyzing geographic patterns and correlates of various health conditions.

Gobalet and Thomas (1996) describe several cases in which GIS was used to display and analyze the spatial distribution of public health data.[15] One involved sexually transmitted diseases (STDs) among adolescents in the secondary school districts of Santa Clara County, California. A map depicted the number of cases by proportionally sized circles, and the rates of sexually transmitted diseases by various patterns of shading, for each secondary school district in the county in 1993–1994 (Figure 5.9). Patient-address data collected from physicians and health facilities by the public health department of the county were geocoded and aggregated for secondary school districts. The GIS software made it possible to geocode the STD cases and aggregate them efficiently by school district.

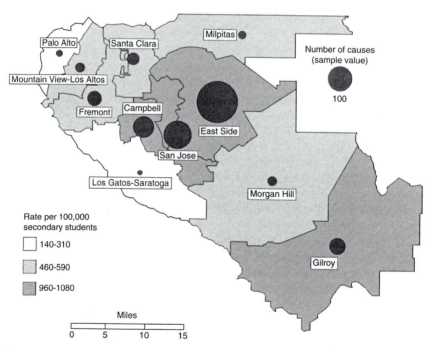

FIGURE 5.9 Map showing number and rates of sexually transmitted diseases among adolescents in the secondary school districts of Santa Clara County, California: 1993–1994. *Source:* Jeanne G. Gobalet and Richard K. Thomas, "Demographic data and geographic information systems for decision making: The case of public health," *Population Research and Policy Review* **15(5/6)**: 537–548, December 1996, Figure 1. © 1996. Reprinted with kind permission of Kluwer Academic Publishers.

SPATIAL DEMOGRAPHIC ANALYSIS

Many methods of statistical analysis of demographic data that show spatial variations have been developed.[16] For most of these, there are complementary versions in the form of graphs, maps, or other pictorial designs. A few notes on some of these measures and mapping devices and a few references for further study are given in the following sections.

Illustrative Techniques

It is commonplace in demographic studies to compute measures of central tendency, and this is no less true in spatial demographic studies. Among the spatial measures of central tendency are the (mean) center of population or the mean point, the median center of population or the median point, and the geographic center. The terms **centroid** and **internal point** have been used to refer to each of these three measures, but centroid usually refers to the mean point and internal point usually refers to the geographic center.

The **geographic center** of an area is the point where the distances to the north and south of the point, and east and west of the point, are equal, without reference to population. Calculation of geographic centers is usually limited to small areas, such as census tracts or block groups. Geographic centers of square degrees of area are employed in the calculation of the center of population of the United States, as explained further next.

The mean point or **center of population** of an area is that point at which a flat and weightless map of the area would balance if (equally valued) weights were placed on it so that each weight represented the location of one person. The estimating algorithm for the U.S. center of population includes the following steps: (1) a mean point for the entire country is assumed; (2) north-south and east-west distances from this assumed mean, representing the distances of persons from the assumed mean, are determined for small geographic areas; (3) the distances for these groups of persons are weighted by the number of persons at the measured distances; (4) the weighted sums east and west of the assumed center, and north and south of the assumed center, are calculated; and (5) the balance of these four weighted sums are used to adjust the location of the assumed center. In practice, the population is grouped in square degrees of area and the geographical center of each of these small areas is used to measure the distance from the assumed mean. The principal measure of dispersion of the population around the center of population of an area is the **standard distance,** a spatial measure analogous to the standard deviation. In 1990 the center of population of the United States was 10 miles southeast of Steelville, Missouri, in Crawford County.

The **median point** of an area is the point of intersection of two median lines, a north-south line, dividing the population of the area in half from east to west, and an east-west line, dividing the population in half from north to south. In 1990 the median point of the population of the United States was located in southwest Indiana (Lawrence County).

Other measures focus on other aspects of the spatial distribution of data. The **point of minimum aggregate travel** is the point from which the total radial

deviations of a population over an area are at a minimum. Another measure
is the number of persons within distance zones from a designated point (i.e.,
within 100 miles, 200 miles, and so on). So-called gravity measures, or measures of **population potential**, adjust for the influence of distance from the
point. They represent the "level of influence" on the population of a point on
a map. The total potential of population at a point is the sum of the reciprocals
of the distances of all persons in the population from the point.

Some measures specifically deal with the inequality of the distribution of
the population in an area. Among the applications of the index of dissimilarity, the Theil coefficient, and the Gini index of concentration (see Chapter
1) are their use as measures of inequality in the distribution of the population among the localities or territorial units of an area. The Lorenz curve is a
graphic device for depicting inequality in population distribution over an area
(see Chapter 1). It is the graphic complement of the Gini index of concentration in measuring inequality. Measures of geographic compactness, population compactness, and population contiguity have also been developed (see
Chapter 12). There are many measures of geographical mobility, varying in
complexity from age-specific migration rates to multiregional life tables. These
are discussed in connection with the estimation and projection of subnational
populations in Chapters 9 and 10.

Maps

As noted earlier, maps are used extensively in the presentation and analysis of
demographic and related data.[17] Maps presenting subject material are called
thematic maps. There are several types of thematic maps. Among these are
choropleth maps, in which the geographic subunits are differentiated by colors,
shades, or patterns to show interarea variations with respect to some variable.
Other types of maps employed in presenting and analyzing demographic data
include dot density maps, proportional symbol maps, and contour maps. A
single map may combine more than one of these mapping techniques. In general, in the design of thematic maps increasing levels of a continuous variable
are represented by increasingly darker (or lighter) shades, increasingly larger
circles or spheres, or increasing density of dots.

Choropleth maps typically display the variation in some variable(s) by
applying one of several (three to six) shading schemes to the coordinate geographic units in the map. (See Figures 5.9 and 5.10.) Figure 5.9 previously
referred to shows that the highest rates of sexually transmitted diseases (among
three class intervals) occur in the Campbell, San Jose, East Side, and Gilroy
school districts and that these four school districts also recorded the greatest number of cases. Figure 5.10 shows the tremendous concentration of the
Hispanic population in the Southwestern part of the United States (six class
intervals).

Two cross-classified variables can be combined on the same map. The variables can be displayed in two ways. Two different schemes of portraying the
variables may be employed. A shading scheme for one variable may be combined with a set of symbols (e.g., circles) for the second variable, as in Figure
5.9. Alternatively, color coding of the cross-classified data may be employed.

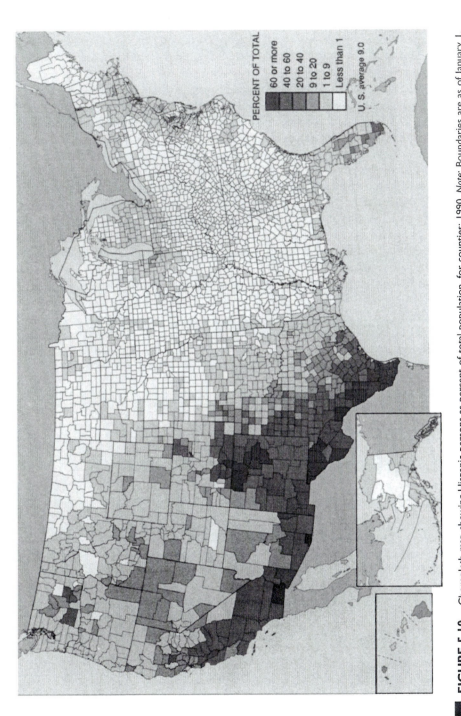

FIGURE 5.10 Choropleth map showing Hispanic persons as percent of total population, for counties: 1990. Note: Boundaries are as of January 1, 1990. *Source*: U.S. Bureau of the Census, *United States Maps*, GE-90. No. 6, 1993.

For example, a map (not illustrated) may show the death rate from cardio-vascular diseases in relation to educational attainment of the population for counties in 1990. The map may have four intervals for the death rate, each represented by a shade of red from light to dark, and four intervals for educational attainment, each represented by a shade of blue from light to dark. Each county would be assigned a color, a mixture of a shade of red and a shade of blue (totaling 16 colors), varying according to the level of the death rate and the level of schooling of the population of the county.

Dot density maps display a dot for a designated fixed number of persons. Figure 5.11, which has one dot for each 7500 persons, shows the tremendous concentration of population in the Northeast and Midwest and the coastal areas of the South and West. Proportional symbol maps use a symbol in each geographic subunit to show the magnitude of the variable. (See Figures 5.9 and 5.12.) Usually a circle is employed; the radius of the circle is proportional to the square root of the population. Sometimes a sphere is employed; the radius is proportional to the cube root of the population. In the case of circles, if the population doubles, the radius increases by 41% ($\sqrt{2}$); in the case of spheres, if the population doubles, the radius increases by 26% ($\sqrt[3]{2}$).

Contour maps of various kinds are independent of conventional political and statistical boundaries and connect lines of common intensity of the variable. One type of contour map incorporates distance and direction simultaneously in measuring the geographic distribution of characteristics from a designated point. Figure 5.13 illustrates this type of map with data on the distribution of household income from the city center in the metropolitan area of

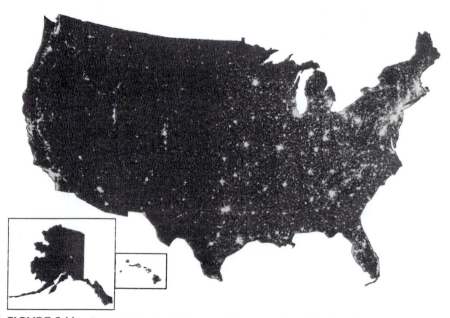

FIGURE 5.11   Dot map showing distribution of the population of the United States: 1990. *Note:* One dot = 7500 persons. *Source:* U.S. Bureau of the Census, *United States Maps*, GE-90, No. 5.

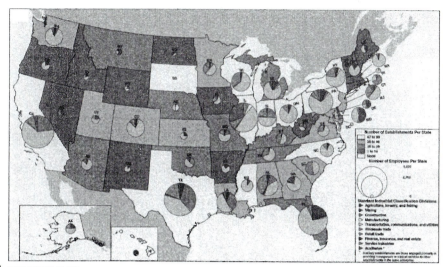

FIGURE 5.12   Map showing distribution of establishments (choropleth) and employment by major industry group (proportional symbols), for states: 1992. *Source*: U.S. Bureau of the Census, Geography Division, 1992 Economic Census, special print.

Indianapolis, Indiana, in terms of standard deviations from the metropolitan area mean. In this case, the contours appear as roughly concentric circles since household income is a radially distributed characteristic.

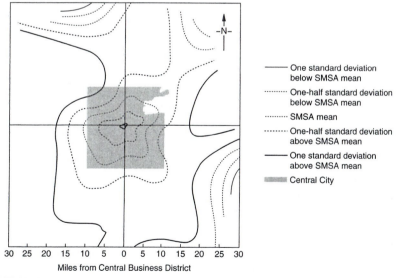

FIGURE 5.13   Map of household income in Indianapolis, IN, metropolitan area, showing contour lines around center city for standard deviations from metropolitan area mean: 1980. *Source*: Michael J. White, *American Neighborhoods and Residential Differentiation*, 1980 Census Monograph Series, New York: Russell Sage Foundation, 1987, p. 144. © Russell Sage Foundation. Reproduced with permission.

The tools for creating maps that depict census and other types of geographic areas, provided by the Census Bureau on its Web site (*www.census.gov/geo/www/tiger*), can be used to create thematic maps. However, the thematic maps produced by GIS/TIGER so far are relatively simple and are limited to single variables. Environmental Research Systems Institute, Inc. (ESRI), has a Web site (*www.esri.com*) that allows ArcView users to download census and other data that can be mapped with GIS software. Their mapmaking tools make possible a wide variety of complex geographic displays of demographic, socioeconomic, housing, and health phenomena.

APPENDIX A: LIST OF ABBREVIATIONS FOR CENSUS GEOGRAPHIC AREAS AND RELATED CONCEPTS

Abbreviation	Geographic area or related concept
ANRC	Alaska Native Regional Corporation
ANV	Alaska native village
ANVSA	Alaska native village statistical area
BG	Block group
BNA	Block numbering area
CBD	Central business district
CBSA	Core-Based Statistical Area
CCD	Census county division
CD	Congressional District
CDP	Census designated place
CMSA	Consolidated metropolitan statistical area
ED	Enumeration district
MA	Metropolitan area
MCD	Minor civil division
MRC	Major retail center
MSA	Metropolitan statistical area
PMSA	Primary metropolitan statistical area
PUMA	Public use microdata area
SC	Settlement cluster
SCSA	Standard consolidated statistical area
SMSA	Standard metropolitan statistical area
SEUA	Special urban economic area
TAZ	Traffic analysis zone
UA	Urbanized area
UT	Unorganized territory
VTD	Voting district
CD-ROM	Compact disk—read only memory
DIME	Dual independent map encoding
GBF	Geographic base file
GIS	Geographic information system
PUMS	Public use microdata sample
STF	Summary tape file
TIGER	Topographically integrated geographic encoding and referencing

APPENDIX B: NOTE ON INTERNATIONAL VARIATIONS IN ADMINISTRATIVE DIVISIONS

Other countries also recognize a set of areas for statistical tabulations built on the hierarchical administrative areas of the country. While these areas may differ in size and political autonomy, they fit into a pattern as primary political subdivisions, secondary political subdivisions, and so forth. On the other hand, administrative units differ from country to country and over time in the same country. The same term or a cognate term may not refer to the same type of geographic unit in different countries. Countries are more likely to differ in the concepts and definitions of the geographic areas used as statistical areas and type-of-residence areas than in those for political areas. Like the United States, many countries have official definitions of metropolitan areas (or urban agglomerations), but the specific definitions may vary widely. The classification of populations as urban/rural, in particular, may differ greatly from country to country because the definition may be based on a different concept. The general concept may be morphological as, for example, population size or population density, or functional as, for example, administrative status or proportion of the population dependent on agriculture.

The hierarchical structure of the administrative systems of various countries is illustrated here by the systems used in three countries: Canada, France, and Mexico. The political/administrative divisions of the Spanish-speaking and Portuguese-speaking countries and the French-speaking countries of Africa are listed in the multilingual demographic dictionaries published by the International Population Union.[18] In all cases, the administrative system gets adapted or converted into the system for statistical classification.

In Canada, the main administrative division is the province (*province*). Canada has 10 provinces and three territories, the Northwest Territories, Yukon Territory, and Nunavut Territory. The administrative organization within the province varies from province to province. The majority of provinces are divided into counties (e.g., Prince Edward, New Brunswick, Nova Scotia). Some are organized into urban municipalities (e.g., Quebec). The principal administrative subdivisions of a few provinces are designated divisions (e.g., Newfoundland) or districts (e.g., British Columbia).

Statistics Canada defines a census agglomeration (CA) as an urban area with at least 10,000 population (known as the urban core), together with the adjacent urban and rural areas (known as urban and rural fringes) that have a high degree of social and economic integration with the urban core. CAs that have urban core populations of at least 50,000 population are subdivided into census tracts. A CA whose urban core population exceeds 100,000 population becomes a census metropolitan area (CMA). A CMA may be consolidated with adjacent CAs if they are socially and economically integrated. This new area is called a consolidated CMA and the component CMAs are called primary census metropolitan areas.

Metropolitan or continental France, including the island of Corsica, is divided into 96 primary political divisions called *départements*.[19] (See Figure 5.B.1.) *Départements* were combined into 22 *régions* for analysis of the 1990 census. For local administrative purposes, *départements* are divided into *communes*, which number about 38,000. The *communes* vary greatly in area and

FIGURE 5.B.1 Census Geographic
Tabulation Areas in the 1990 Census of France

    France
Metropolitan (Métropole)
    Regions
    Political units
        Departments (départements)
            Communes
            Paris
                Arrondissements
                Quartiers
Overseas (Outre-mer)

    France
Rural communes
    Deep rural (rural profond)
    Periurban
Urban units (urbaines unités)
    Under 50,000 inhabitants
    50,000 or more inhabitants
        Principal communes
        Other communes
    Paris metropolitan area (agglomération de Paris)
        Paris
        Suburbs (banlieue)

    Agglomérations
        Center cities (villes centres)
        Suburbs (banlieues)

Source: INED, "La France au recensement de
1990," *Population* 48(6), November/December 1993.

population and often correspond to *municipalités*. While *départements* and *communes* are the two fundamental administrative units, two administrative units are sandwiched between them: *arrondissements* and *cantons*. The large cities are divided into *arrondissements*. Paris has 20 *arrondissements*, each of which is further divided into four *quartiers*. A small share (about 3%) of the French population lives in Overseas France and more than three-quarters of this population live in four overseas departments, namely, Réunion, Guadeloupe, Martinique, and Guiana.

Mexico has 32 primary administrative divisions, including 31 *estados* (states) and a *Distrito Federal* (federal district), a federal entity covering the highly urbanized core of Mexico City. The *estados* are divided into *municipios* (municipalities), which number 2323. Several urban agglomerations are recognized; these represent combinations of central cities and suburban areas. The large urban agglomerations are Mexico City, Guadalajara, Monterrey, Tampico, and Torreon. The metropolitan area of Mexico City, referred to as the Central Metropolitan Zone, or CMZ, has 43 *municipios* and 16 *delegaciones*. The *delegaciones* are all located in the *Distrito Federal*.

The United Nations has been actively involved in standardizing census concepts among the member countries so as to achieve maximum statistical comparability. The standardization of the concepts for geographic and residence categories, particularly urban/rural, however, is a difficult, if not impossible, task, given the differences in political and administrative structures and settlement patterns from country to country.

NOTES

1. For a more comprehensive description of Census Bureau geographic concepts than presented in this book, see U.S. Bureau of the Census, *Maps and More: Your Guide to Census Bureau Geography*, July 1992, and U.S. Bureau of the Census and Association of Public Data Users, *A Guide to State and Local Census Geography*, 1990 CPH-I-18, June 1993.

2. These seven areas of 1990 will be reduced to six in 2000 since Palau became independent in 1994. In 2000 Puerto Rico will be listed in the summary tables for the United States as a whole and for the individual states, but it will be separated from the other data and it will not be included in the population total for the United States. With the exception of American Samoa, people in these areas are U.S. citizens although the areas are not part of the United States.

3. Special censuses are censuses for local jurisdictions carried out by the local government or the Census Bureau on contract, according to Census Bureau standards. During the course of an intercensal decade, several hundred of these may be conducted.

4. See also U.S. Bureau of the Census, "Metropolitan areas as defined by the Office of Management and Budget, June 30, 1993," *1990 Census of Population and Housing, Supplementary Report* 1990 CPH-S-1-1.

5. Based on the 1990 census, 21 CMSAs, comprising 73 PMSAs, and 268 separate MSAs were established.

6. A list of metropolitan areas and their component counties as of June 30, 1998, with population estimates for 1997, is given in U.S. Bureau of the Census, *Statistical Abstract of the United States, 1998*, Tables A and B.

7. U.S. Office of Management and Budget, "Recommendations from the Metropolitan Area Standards Review Committee to the Office of Management and Budget concerning changes to the standards for defining metropolitan areas; Notice," Part IV, *Federal Register* 64(202): 56628–56644, October 20, 1999.

8. The 1987 economic censuses identified a type of statistical entity representing subdivisions of counties called special economic urban areas (SEUAs). There were 433 such areas in 1987. Prior to 1992 the Census of Retail Trade reported data for central business districts (CBDs) and major retail centers (MRCs), both of which contained large concentrations of retail stores within MSAs. Reporting for CBDs and MRCs was discontinued after 1987 because of the high cost of delineating and tabulating data for these areas.

9. In its broader and original sense, geocoding refers to the assignment of geographic codes to data. Hence, it encompasses the assignment of numerical codes to particular states, counties, and other areas and the data for these areas. In a narrower sense, geocoding refers to the assignment of cartographic codes to individual addresses so that they can be placed as points on a map. Even more narrowly defined, geocoding involves the matching of addresses with street segments in GBF/DIME files or TIGER files (an automated geographic database, as discussed herein). Note that matching to individual addresses with STFs or PUMS files cannot be done.

10. Stephen J. Tordella, "Geometric data retrieval methods in commercial sector demography," in David A. Swanson and Jerry W. Wicks (eds.), *Issues in Applied Demography*, Bowling Green, OH: Bowling Green State University, 1987.

11. The use of satellite scanning and aerial photography has been investigated as a means of assigning population data to geographic areas. This procedure has limited capabilities as a source of demographic data, however, because various natural conditions can transform and obscure the images, aerial photography is very expensive, and only a count of structures, not data about occupancy or type of structure, can be obtained.

12. For an excellent presentation of numerous examples of the use of GIS in a wide variety of planning situations employing demographic data, see Andy Mitchell, *Zeroing In: Geographic Information Systems at Work in the Community*, Redlands, CA: Environmental Systems Research Institute, 1997–1998. See Chapter 6 for an illustration relating to school boundaries.

13. See Robert A. Lamacchia, U.S. Bureau of the Census, "Census data available for tranportation planners," paper presented at the Third Annual Conference on Minicomputers in Transportation, sponsored by the American Society of Civil Engineers, San Francisco, CA, June 22, 1989.

14. Reported in U.S. Bureau of the Census, *TIGER: The Coast-to-Coast Digital Map Data Base*, Nov. 1990.

15. Jeanne G. Gobalet and Richard K. Thomas, "Demographic data and geographic information systems for decision making: The case of public health." *Population Research and Policy Review* 15(5–6): 537–548, 1996.

16. For further information, see *The Methods and Materials of Demography*, revised condensed edition. For early classic studies of measures of spatial analysis, see Otis Dudley Duncan, Ray P. Cuzzort, and Beverly Duncan, *Statistical Geography: Problems in Analyzing Areal Data*, The Free Press of Glencoe, Illinois, 1961; and Brian J. L. Berry and Duane F. Marble (eds.), *Spatial Analysis: A Reader in Statistical Geography*, Englewood Cliffs, NJ: Prentice-Hall, 1968.

17. For more extensive treatment of the use of maps for analytic purposes, see G. D. Garson and R. S. Biggs, *Analytic Mapping and Geographic Data Bases*, New York: Sage, 1992; D. A. Plane and P. A. Rogerson, *The Geographical Analysis of Population*, New York: John Wiley, 1994; Borden D. Dent, *Cartography: Thematic Map Design*, 3rd ed., Dubuque, IA: Wm. C. Brown, 1992, especially Chapters 4, 6, 7, 8, and 11; Arthur H. Robinson *et al.*, *Elements of Cartography*, 6th ed., John Wiley and Sons, 1992, Part VI; and Michael J. White, *American Neighborhoods and Residential Differentiation*, New York: Russell Sage Foundation, 1987, Chapter 5.

18. International Union for the Scientific Study of Population, *Dictionnare Démographique Multilingue*, by Louis Henry, Volume Français, 2nd ed., 1981, and *Diccionario Demográfico Plurilingüe*, by Guillermo A. Macció, Versión en Español, 2nd ed., 1985, Liège: Ordina Editions.

19. See the papers in Guy Desplanques (ed.), *La France au recensement de 1990*, special issue of *Population* (Paris) 48(6), November/December 1993, esp. papers by Brigitte Baccaïni, Daniel Courgeau, and Guy Desplanques, and by Patrick Festy.

SUGGESTED READINGS

Geographic Area Definitions

U.S. Bureau of the Census. (1991). "Census Geography—Concepts and Products." CFF No. 8 (Rev.). *Factfinder for the Nation.*

U.S. Bureau of the Census. (1992). *Maps and More: Your Guide to Census Bureau Geography.*

U.S. Bureau of the Census and Association of Public Data Users. (1993). *A Guide to State and Local Census Geography.*

Geometric Data Retrieval and Geographic Information Systems

Agresta, Anthony, and Haub, Carl. (1984, July/August). "Custom-tailoring census data." *Population Today* 12(7/8): 6–7.

Hodges, Ken. (1995). "An evaluation of geometric data retrieval methods." Paper presented at the annual meeting of the Population Association of America, San Francisco, CA, April 6–8.

Mejía Tapia, Miguel Angel. (1992). "Los sistemas de información con referencia geográfica." *Demos: Carta Demográfica Sobre Mexico*, pp. 38–39.

Tordella, Stephen J. (1987). "Geometric data retrieval methods in commercial sector demography." *In* David A. Swanson and Jerry W. Wicks (eds.), *Issues in Applied Demography*. Bowling Green, OH: Bowling Green State University.

U.S. Census Bureau. (1998). "Introducing LandView® III," *Product Profile* PRODPR98-1.

U.S. National Center for Health Statistics. (1979). *Proceedings of the 1976 Workshop on Automated Cartography and Epidemiology, March 18–19, 1976, Arlington, VA.*

TIGER

Marx, Robert W. (1990). "Pixels and censels: Putting people in the picture." Paper presented at the meeting of Commission VII of the International Society of Photogrammetry and Remote Sensing, September 1990, U.S. Bureau of the Census.

Marx, Robert W. (1986). "The TIGER system: Automating the geographic structure of the United States census." *Government Publications Review* 13: 181–201.

U.S. Bureau of the Census. (1990). *TIGER: The Coast-to-Coast Digital Map Data Base.*

Applications

Environmental Systems Research Institute, Inc. (2000). *Map Book: Applications of Geographical Informations Systems*, Vol. 15. Redlands, CA: ESRI Press.

Gobalet, Jeanne G., and Thomas, Richard K. (1996, December). "Demographic data and geographic information systems for decision making: The case of public health." *Population Research and Policy Review* 15(5–6): 537–548.

Lamacchia, Robert, U.S. Bureau of the Census. (1989). "The TIGER file and redistricting." Paper presented at the Conference on Reapportionment and the 1990 Census, sponsored by the National Conference of State Legislatures, Orlando, FL, December 8–9, 1989.

Lang, Laura. (2000). *GIS for Health Organizations*. Redlands, CA: ESRI Press.

Mitchell, Andy. (1997–1998). *Zeroing In: Geographic Systems at Work in the Community*. Redlands, CA: Environmental Systems Research Institute.

Ng, Edward, and Wilkins, Russell, Statistics Canada. (1993). "How far is it to the nearest hospital facility in Canada? Calculating distances using information derived from addresses and postal codes." Paper presented at the XXII General Population Conference of the International Union for the Scientific Study of Population, Montreal, Que., August 24 to September 1, 1993.

Tayman, Jeff, Parrott, Bob, and Carnivale, Sue. (1994). "Locating fire station sites: The response time component." In Hallie J. Kintner, Thomas W. Merrick, Peter A. Morrison, and Paul R. Voss (eds.), *Demographics: A Casebook for Business and Government*, pp. 203–217. Boulder, CO: Westview Press.

Spatial Demographic Analysis

Bachi, Roberto. (1999). New Methods of Geostatistical Analysis and Graphical Presentation: Distributions of Populations over Territories. New York: Kluwer Academic Publishers.

Dent, Borden D. (1992). *Cartography: Thematic Map Design*, 3rd ed. Dubuque, IA: William C. Brown.

Fotheringham, S., and Rogerson, P. (eds.). (1994). *Spatial Analysis and GIS*. Bristol, PA: Taylor and Francis.

Garson, G. D., and Biggs, R. S. (1992). *Analytic Mapping and Geographic Databases*. New York: Sage.

Plane, D. A., and Rogerson, P. A. (1994). *The Geographical Analysis of Population*. New York: John Wiley.

White, Michael J. (1987). *American Neighborhoods and Residential Differentiation*, 1980 Census Monograph Series. New York: Russell Sage Foundation. See Chapter 5.

6
██ DEMOGRAPHIC APPLICATIONS IN BUSINESS PLANNING

INTERFACE OF MARKETING AND DEMOGRAPHY

With this chapter we turn to specific applications of demographic data, methods, and perspectives to various areas of business and government planning and administration. We shall find that there is ample opportunity for demographic applications in connection with decisions regarding business expansion and contraction, and with decisions regarding human resources management. The former aspects of business administration encompass managing the sales force and setting sales goals, setting advertizing goals and allocating the advertising budget, locating branches or outlets, and forecasting demand for consumer products and services. The latter aspects of business administration encompass the recruitment, selection, transfer, and promotion of employees, compliance with the legal requirements relating to these personnel actions, and planning the future size and structure of the workforce of a business. The first of these two areas of business planning and administration is treated in Chapter 6 and the second is treated in Chapter 8.

Both the demographer and the business analyst develop information that business executives can use in decision making, but the demographer's approach to business planning is rather different from that of the business analyst. Demographers are oriented mainly toward use of demographic and socioeconomic data in the framing and analysis of problems, while business analysts tend to focus more on financial and related nondemographic data. Demographic data can be useful in the solution of business problems even if they only supplement nondemographic data in this task. Next, the demographer is likely to employ traditional demographic methods, while the business analyst tends to employ marketing tools, practices, and principles. These tend to be more subjective and informal in character than the more empirical and objective approach of the demographer. He or she generally analyzes the problem by bringing to bear the standard body of techniques in the demographer's toolbox known as demographic methods. Moreover, demographic techniques tailored to fit the business situation can fruitfully supplement standard statistical techniques in the solution of business problems. Finally, the demographer brings a unique perspective to problem solving—let us call it the demographic perspective—and it is perhaps best exemplified by the cohort approach. We can see it in action in various contexts in this and other chapters. In sum, while the purposes for demographic and business analysis overlap, business planning, especially in the area of market research, can be greatly informed by the demographic approach.

Some Concepts of Marketing

In considering the interrelations of business and demography, it is useful at the outset to review some basic concepts of marketing. A **market** is an arena in which transfers of ownership of products, such as commodities, stocks, and precious metals, between buyers and sellers, and performance of services by sellers for buyers, are effected on the basis of mutually agreed-on prices. Any market is the sum of numerous individuals acting on their perceptions of the value of a commodity or service. Two types of markets—industrial markets and consumer markets—may be distinguished. We are mainly concerned with consumer markets, although the industrial markets are also responsive to population changes. The expected total sales of a commodity or service in a consumer market during a given period is called **market potential**. The share of the market expected by an individual company is called its **sales potential**. The **sales quota** is the sales goal assigned to a marketing unit or a sales person for use in the management of sales effort in a specific period, expressed in terms of volume of sales (i.e., dollars spent or units sold). The physical area in which the seller may reasonably expect to sell a profitable volume of goods and services and where other related marketing activities take place is called the **sales territory** or **trading area**.

The task of business planning is somewhat different for businesses that produce or distribute a product nationally and those that produce or distribute a product locally. The distinction may be made, for example, between General Motors and your local auto dealer, or Ben and Jerry's Ice Cream and your local supermarket. The focus on the market is much broader geographically for the first than the second, although national businesses also must pay attention to demographic factors and trends that are local, as in locating a new manufacturing facility or distribution center. So far as analysis of the consumer population is concerned, the national company is more interested in the demographic characteristics of their potential clientele in the nation than in a particular local area.

Demographic and Related Elements Characterizing Potential Buyers

Three elements identify potential buyers in a market. These are as follows:

1. Their number and other basic demographic characteristics
2. Measures of their purchasing power
3. Their buying preferences

These elements can be encapsulated in the concepts of **potential demand** and **effective demand**. The potential demand for a product or service is expressed quantitatively in terms of the number of persons (or households) who want or need a given type of product or service or who can be persuaded to want or need it. Effective demand is limited to those who also have the buying power to express their wants or who can be persuaded to believe that they have such buying power. Potential demand may be defined, therefore, in terms of the first, or perhaps the first and third, elements listed, but effective demand requires all three elements listed. **Actual demand** represents those who are actually buying a given type of product or, from a particular company's point of view, buying their product. Actual demand can be measured in terms of the volume of sales (in terms of dollars spent or units sold) of the product or the service to individuals or families. Measurement of the **target population** then becomes a task of identifying the persons who represent potential, effective, and actual demand. To maintain or expand a business, the owners or managers of the business need to know the demographic, social, economic, and housing characteristics of the actual and potential customers of their products or services. The demographer can provide data on the current and prospective size, distribution, structure, and composition of the target population. The results may be used in budget development, field planning, establishment of additional outlets, and expansion of services in an existing outlet.

The population component listed earlier (item 1) represents potential customers in terms of persons, households, families, age groups, males or females, and race/ethnic groups. Potential consumers may also be distinguished by their marital status, educational level, stage of the family life cycle, family size, occupation, and housing characteristics such as tenure (homeowner or renter), owners of old homes/owners of new homes, or owners of homes heated by gas/owners of homes heated by electricity/other means. The population component is also represented by persons experiencing certain demographic events—that is, birth or parenthood, death, in-migration, out-migration, marriage, widowing, and divorce.

Next in the list of elements identifying potential customers (item 2) are those characteristics that describe a consumer's ability to purchase the product or service offered. Purchasing power is represented by various types of income data, such as individual income, family income, and household income, and by various indicators of income status, such as employment status, home ownership, automobile ownership, and ownership of a personal computer system. Other related indicators are assets, debt burden, savings rate, and patterns of spending. The information may be available in aggregate or summary form, for example, median family income, per capita individual income, median household disposable income, household income in relation to monthly owner costs, percentage of homeowners with incomes in various categories, and percentage of owned homes with values in various categories.

The third item in the list of elements identifying potential customers is a nondemographic attribute of the group, the desire of members of the group to own the product or use the service. Buying preferences are expressed in attitudes about various products or actual buying behavior. These desires and preferences are molded by need; advice of family members, friends, and coworkers; advertising; personal values and beliefs such as pursuit of conspicuous consumption; and other factors.[1] The necessities of the situation may be determinative, as illustrated by the need for a home furnace and heating maintenance service in a New England home or for roofing materials and roofing service in a home where the old roof has expired. Advertising plays a major role in influencing consumer choices, especially in brand selection. Wants are rather elastic, however, and can be expanded to include a product or service if a person's or household's economic condition permits and the product or service is particularly attractive to, or appropriate for, the person or household.

The target population has been identified in terms of demographic (including socioeconomic and housing) characteristics, buying power, and personal needs and desires. To be of practical use in most cases, the characteristics represented by these items, or at least items 1 and 2, need to be cross-classified. For example, we want to know the median income, or the median household income, of persons of a given age/sex group, marital status, household type, level of educational attainment, or occupational group. A fourth element in the characterization of a market is the performance component, as measured by the number of persons or households purchasing the product or service, sales per employee, purchases per 1000 population, and retail outlets per 1000 population. Aggregate or relative estimates of product consumption are available or can be computed, usually on the basis of data in company records. If we need to make forecasts of product consumption, we must make use of the best current and historical information on items 1, 2, 3, and 4 in combination.

Illustrative Tasks of Demographers in Business Planning

The most common general types of problems on which demographers may be called on to assist a business organization are to determine the best prospective location in a metropolitan area of a branch store or service outlet, to forecast the demand for a new product, to interpret a business' compliance with various regulations relating to the conduct of the business, such as antitrust regulations or affirmative action legislation, and to analyze the dynamics of the workforce of a company. The specific types of problems of the first two kinds that demographers may be called on to deal with on behalf of a business are illustrated by the following: choosing the location of a new branch for a bank, assessing a bank's need for a reverse mortgage program, estimating the need for home health care and support services in a community, selecting merchandise lines for a store appropriate for potential customers, selecting the area in which to locate a new supermarket, demonstrating to a bank loan officer that a particular area would be a promising site in which to locate a car wash, determining the best shopping area to be purchased and redeveloped in a metropolitan area, and evaluating the possibilities of increasing the circulation of a newspaper in an area and planning strategies for this purpose. With respect to compliance with legislation controlling the conduct of business, the problem to be resolved may concern housing discrimination and residential patterns of racial minorities, location of environmentally hazardous installations, and discrimination in hiring and promotion. In general, whatever the problem, the role of the demographer is to bring a degree of formal structure to conceptualizing and resolving it. He or she does this by operationalizing the demographic and socioeconomic concepts that define the problem, employing the appropriate demographic and related data sources, and applying the appropriate methods of demographic analysis and the demographic perspective.

Although the tasks enumerated here may differ among one another, they all make use of many of the same types of census data, namely, race/Hispanic origin, household composition, age, income, and housing tenure (i.e., ownership). In addition, they require some special types of census data for use in solving one or another of the tasks presented: data on education for the task of selecting the location of a bank branch and the task of increasing newspaper circulation; data on marital status, disability, and various housing characteristics for estimating the need for home health care and support services; data on marital status, value of home, and shelter costs for assessing the need for a reverse mortgage program; and data on automobile ownership for locating a branch of a bank or a supermarket and securing a loan for opening a car wash.

Classification Systems and Selected Concepts

Among the important tools used in market analysis are standard occupation and industry classifications and standard definitions of various concepts relating to households and income that facilitate the compilation, analysis, and comparison of data of this kind obtained from business establishments or households. The demographer dealing with problems in business planning should become familiar with these classification systems and definitions.

Economic Classification Systems

There are three economic classification systems of interest: the Standard Occupation Classification (SOC), the Standard Industrial Classification (SIC), and the North American Industry Classification System (NAICS). These classifications were developed under the direction of the Office of Management and Budget or, formerly, the Office of Federal Statistical Policy and Standards in the Department of Commerce.

The Standard Occupation Classification (SOC) system provides a comprehensive, mutually exclusive set of categories for presenting data on occupations in the population census, the Current Population Survey (CPS), and other data collection systems of the federal government. The present version of SOC was first used in the 1980 census and the CPS of 1983.[2] **Occupation** is defined as the kind of work a person did during a specified past period (e.g., last week, last year), such as registered nurse, personnel manager, or bricklayer. One very broad set of occupation categories tabulated from the 1997 CPS is as follows: managerial and professional specialty; technical, sales, and administrative support; service occupations; precision production, craft, and repair; operators, fabricators, and laborers; and farming, forestry, and fishing.

The Standard Industrial Classification (SIC) had been used for 50 years until the 1997 economic census to provide a comprehensive, mutually exclusive set of categories for presenting data on industries. **Industry** refers to the kind of business or company a person works for, such as a hospital, newspaper publishing, or construction company. In the SIC, a two- to four-digit coding system is used to classify establishments by type of economic activity (11 industrial sectors), typically on the basis of the product (rather than the process). The broadest industrial categories in the classification are agriculture, forestry, and fishing; mining; construction; manufacturing; transportation, communication, and other public utilities; wholesale trade; retail trade; finance, insurance, and real estate; service industries; public administration; and auxiliaries (i.e., establishments that provide support services to other establishments in the same enterprise). The SIC has been used not only in the economic censuses but also in the population censuses and various national economic and population surveys. For example, the SIC of 1987 is the basis of the classification and tabulation of industry data in the 1990 census of population, the 1992 economic censuses, and the Current Population Surveys from 1992 and later.

For the 1997 economic census, as the group of former economic censuses was called in 1997, SIC has been replaced by the North American Industry Classification System (NAICS). The NAICS increases the level of detail to a five-digit coding system, increases the number of industrial sectors from 11 to 21, and adds or revises several hundred industries. In the NAICS, establishments are classified into industries on the basis of their principal process instead of their principal product. The NAICS substitutes currency (i.e., recency) and international comparability (with Canada and Mexico) for the historical continuity of the SIC.[3]

Definition of Concepts: Families, Households, Housing Units, and Income

Since much of the demographic and socioeconomic data required for business planning are produced by official agencies, many of the concepts commonly used have official standard definitions. The more important ones for business and government planning are described in this and other chapters. This chapter covers the official definitions of the concepts of occupation, industry, household, family, housing unit, and income—concepts that are particularly relevant in business research.[4]

According to the U.S. Census Bureau definition, a **household** consists of all persons who occupy a housing unit. A **housing unit** may be a house, an apartment or other group of rooms, or a single room, which is occupied or intended for occupancy as separate living quarters. That is, the occupants do not live and eat with any other persons in the structure and there is direct access to the unit from the outside or through a common hall. The household includes the related family members and all the unrelated persons, if any, such as lodgers and foster children. A person living alone in a housing unit, a group of unrelated persons sharing a housing unit as partners, and a family are all counted as households. The Current Population Survey definition of a household differs in including related members living away from home at college. The special living arrangements of persons residing in institutions and other units with 10 or more unrelated persons (e.g., military barracks, nursing homes, jails and prisons, and college dormitories) are not counted as housing units and the persons living in them are not part of the household population. These units are designated group quarters and the residents are part of the group quarters population.[5]

A **family** is a household or part of a household consisting of two or more persons related by blood, marriage, or adoption. Note that this definition of the family, whereby all members reside in the same housing unit, does not agree with the popular concept of family as encompassing related persons who may reside in more than one housing unit. Family groups may form part of three different types of households, married-couple households, female-headed family households, and male-headed family households, depending on whether the family includes a married couple or whether the householder is male or female with "no spouse present." The **householder** is the person in whose name the housing unit is owned or rented.[6]

In 1997, of the 101,018,000 households in the United States, 70% were family households and 30% were nonfamily households.[7] Married-couple families made up 53% of all households, family households with female householders 13%, and family households with male householders 4%. One-quarter of the households were persons living alone and over one-fifth of all householders were 65 or older.

According to the definition employed in the decennial census and the Current Population Survey, **income** refers to total money income received in the prior calendar year, excluding noncash benefits and before any deductions such as taxes or union dues. In more operational terms, it is the amount of money received by each person 15 years and over in the preceding calendar year from a specified list of sources. The major sources of income are earnings (of employees and self-employed persons), Social Security and other retirement benefits, survivor and disability benefits, Supplemental Security Income and public assistance, unemployment and workers' compensation, veterans' payments, interests and dividends, rents and royalties, and alimony and child support. The official census measure of income includes money received before payments of personal income taxes and deductions for Social Security, union dues, Medicare, and similar charges, and excludes capital gains and lump-sum or one-time payments. It does not include noncash benefits such as food stamps, health benefits, and subsidized housing; rent-free housing received by some farm families and goods produced and consumed on the farm by them; and free transportation, education, and medical expenses received by some nonfarm workers from their employers.[8]

Median household income is a common measure employing the income concept. There is moderate to considerable variation in median household income according to the type of household, race/Hispanic origin of the householder, age of the householder, and region and metropolitan residence of the household (Table 2.11 and Table 4.10).[9] In 1997 the median income of all households was $37,005, but the median income of family households headed by females was only $23,040. The peak median income was in the age band 45 to 54 years at $51,875, with substantially lower median incomes at the two ends of the adult age distribution. Median household income in metropolitan areas outside central cities ($44,668) greatly exceeded median household income inside central cities ($31,548) and in nonmetropolitan areas ($30,057). The figures differ far less among regions. The lowest figure for the residence categories named falls one-third below the highest, but the median income for the South region, the lowest, falls only 12% below the highest, the West.

There is a tendency for respondents in censuses and household surveys to underreport their income. By comparing independent data on income from administrative records, it has been observed that income other than earnings in the form of wages and salaries is much less completely reported than other types of income. For many categories of income, such as interest, dividends, and private pensions and annuities, there are deficits of over 25%, even after adjustment of the survey data to independent population "controls." In addition to the understatement of income by enumerated persons, the income of the persons missed in the census or survey is omitted along with the persons themselves. The effect of the first type of omission on per capita income or median income of households is uncertain, but it is likely that the second type of omission artificially raises these summary measures as reported because the persons omitted from the survey tend to be poorer than the persons included.

METHODS OF MEASURING THE CHARACTERISTICS OF CUSTOMERS

To identify the target population or potential customers for different products or services, we want information about their demographic and socioeconomic characteristics, such as their age, household size, living arrangements, income, and education. A variety of methods of securing the information needed, from actual and potential customers, have been employed. These methods include the analysis of sales records of customers of existing outlets, exit interviews and surveys in existing outlets, mail surveys of customers, solicitation and analyses of responses to questionnaires accompanying purchased products, and measurement of audiences of the mass communication media and the Internet by various means. Marketing analysis also employs observational research and in-depth interviews focused on how customers go about making their purchasing decisions. The latter methods are typically applied by psychologists and anthropologists.

Analysis of Sales Records and Exit Surveys

The analysis of sales records of customers of existing outlets is employed in business research generally but it is particularly applicable to a small business with only a few outlets seeking to bring in additional customers or to expand the number of its outlets. Sales records are obtained at the point of sale for many products. The records usually contain information on the name of the customer (including his or her address and telephone number) and the specific product or service purchased, the quantity purchased, and the value of the sale (dollars). Such information can reveal the sex of the customer and, depending on the product, a rough measure of his or her age. The sale of life insurance products provides information on the sex, age, general health condition, and sometimes the occupation and income of the customer. An analysis of store or shop records provides data on the distribution of the residences of customers by block, and hence the distances traveled from home to store or shop and the size of the trading area of the business; the time of shopping (month, day); types of products purchased or services received; and the volume of business (number of sales and dollar value). Matching of sales records on the basis of name, address, and telephone number and maintenance of a customer file by computer can provide data on whether shoppers return to the business outlet in question and the relative frequency of return trips made by them. The goal is to develop a **customer information system** that can be accessed and updated as needed by computer.

A sample of customers leaving the store or shop may be selected to provide responses to brief questionnaires asking for demographic/social/economic information, place of residence, distance traveled to the store or shop, products or services purchased, and other items. Although such a survey tends to be biased, this tendency can be reduced by collecting the data on various days of the week and various parts of the day and from a selected sample designed to represent customers "demographically" to the extent possible. This canvas obviously has severe limitations and the information can usually be obtained more easily from sales records.

Mail Surveys and Questionnaires Accompanying Products

Companies may conduct mail surveys of their customers, particularly when the customers first purchase a product or service or when they discontinue purchasing it. For example, financial institutions or magazine publishers may distribute a questionnaire by mail to their customers on such occasions. This method of soliciting information about the purchaser is closely related to the practice of enclosing questionnaires with manufactured products, a practice considered further in the following paragraphs.

Questionnaires enclosed with manufactured products or distributed by mail by service providers are often linked with the registration of the product. This device for collecting data is usually employed in connection with the sale of products or services that have a national distribution or clientele. The practice is quite common. Customers tend to complete the questionnaires because they mistakenly believe that they must do so in order to register the product for warranty purposes. They may also be induced to reply in the hope of winning a prize or gift, receiving discount certificates for various products, or securing information helpful to them (e.g., financial advice). Although such a "survey" is very likely to be biased, such questionnaires tend to be rather comprehensive sources of information about these groups of customers. This device is illustrated by a description of questionnaires enclosed with unassembled furniture, a clock-radio, a free gift of a food item, and a newsletter of an investment company. A wide range of demographic and related information is commonly sought, including age, sex, marital status, number of persons in the household, family income, education, occupation, and home ownership.

Sauder Woodworking of Archbold, Ohio, manufactures ready-to-assemble furniture. In addition to questions regarding the address of the purchaser, the product purchased, and the reason for the purchaser's preference for Sauder furniture, the questionnaire asks for the following information: age (single years) and sex of the household members; marital status of the purchaser (4 classes) and the educational level (7 classes) and occupation (10 classes) of the purchaser and spouse; family income (12 classes); and homeownership and type of housing unit (4 classes). There are three questions on lifestyle interests (61 classes). Figure 6.1 shows the Sauder Woodworking questionnaire in its entirety.

Soundesign Corporation of Jersey City, New Jersey, which manufactures electronic products, and Kraft General Foods of White Plains, New York, ask a similar body of demographic questions, generally with additional detail. Given the virtual identity of these and the Sauder company questionnaires with respect to the demographic data, it is likely that the three companies and possibly many others employ the same promotional services company. Finally, Twentieth Century Mutual Funds of Kansas City, Missouri, a financial services organization, distributes a questionnaire that contains, in addition to some questions on investment issues, several questions about the background of investors. These relate to sex, age, marital status, number of children under age 21, number of grandchildren under age 21, work outside the home, retirement status, self-employment status, homeownership, household income, and

SAUDER woodworking

1. 1. ☐ Mr. 2. ☐ Mrs. 3. ☐ Ms. 4. ☐ Miss
First Name | Initial Last Name

Street | Apt. No.

City | State | ZIP Code

Could you tell us about your new product? *Could you tell us about yourself?*

2. Date of Purchase: Month Day Year

3. Model Number:

4. Name of store where purchased:

5. What brands of ready-to-assemble (prefinished unassembled) furniture have you purchased in the past?
1. ☐ This is my first purchase
2. ☐ Affordable/Ameriwood
3. ☐ Armstrong
4. ☐ Bush
5. ☐ Charleswood
6. ☐ Fournier
7. ☐ IKEA
8. ☐ O'Sullivan
9. ☐ Royal Creations
10. ☐ Sauder Woodworking
11. ☐ Do not remember
12. ☐ Other

6. Where will this furniture primarily be used? (check only 1)
1. ☐ Dining Room 6. ☐ Bedroom
2. ☐ Kitchen 7. ☐ Home Office
3. ☐ Family room/Den 8. ☐ Commercial Office
4. ☐ Living Room 9. ☐ Student Dorm/Apartment
5. ☐ Children's room 10. ☐ Other

7. What two factors most influenced your purchase? (check only 2)
1. ☐ Magazine Ad
2. ☐ Newspaper/Flyer Ad
3. ☐ Catalog
4. ☐ Friend's recommendation
5. ☐ Store display
6. ☐ Sales personnel's recommendation
7. ☐ Brand name
8. ☐ Value for the price
9. ☐ Other

8. Based on your experience with Sauder furniture, would you consider buying another Sauder product in the future?
1. ☐ Yes
2. ☐ No

9. How would you rate the overall quality of the assembly instructions?
1. ☐ Excellent
2. ☐ Good
3. ☐ Fair
4. ☐ Poor

10. Please estimate the amount of time it took to assemble this unit. (check only 1)
1. ☐ Under 30 mins.
2. ☐ 30 mins. - 1 hr.
3. ☐ 2 hrs.
4. ☐ 3 hrs.
5. ☐ 4 hrs.
6. ☐ 5 - 6 hrs.
7. ☐ 6 hrs. or more

11. Who was the primary influence in purchasing this item? (check only 1)

	Male	Female
Under 12 years old	1. ☐	6. ☐
Age 13-17	2. ☐	7. ☐
Age 18-25	3. ☐	8. ☐
Age 26-49	4. ☐	9. ☐
Age 50+	5. ☐	10. ☐

12. Date of birth of person whose name appears above: | 1 9 | Month Year

13. Excluding yourself, what is the SEX and AGE (in years) of children and other adults living in your household?
1. ☐ No one else in household
Male Female Age | Male Female Age
1. ☐ 2. ☐ ____ yrs. 1. ☐ 2. ☐ ____ yrs.
1. ☐ 2. ☐ ____ yrs. 1. ☐ 2. ☐ ____ yrs.

14. Marital Status:
1. ☐ Married 3. ☐ Widowed
2. ☐ Divorced/Separated 4. ☐ Never Married (Single)

15. Occupation:

	You		Spouse
Homemaker	☐	1.	☐
Professional/Technical	☐	2.	☐
Upper Management/Executive	☐	3.	☐
Middle Management	☐	4.	☐
Sales/Marketing	☐	5.	☐
Clerical or Service Worker	☐	6.	☐
Tradesman/Machine Operator/Laborer	☐	7.	☐
Retired	☐	8.	☐
Student	☐	9.	☐
Self Employed/Business Owner	☐	10.	☐

16. Which amount describes your annual family income?
1. ☐ Under $15,000 7. ☐ $40,000-$44,999
2. ☐ $15,000-$19,999 8. ☐ $45,000-$49,999
3. ☐ $20,000-$24,999 9. ☐ $50,000-$59,999
4. ☐ $25,000-$29,999 10. ☐ $60,000-$74,999
5. ☐ $30,000-$34,999 11. ☐ $75,000-$99,999
6. ☐ $35,000-$39,999 12. ☐ $100,000 & over

17. Education: (please check those which apply)

	You		Spouse
Some High School or Less	☐	1.	☐
Completed High School	☐	2.	☐
Vocational/Technical School	☐	3.	☐
Some College	☐	4.	☐
Completed College	☐	5.	☐
Some Graduate School	☐	6.	☐
Completed Graduate School	☐	7.	☐

18. Which credit cards do you use regularly?
1. ☐ American Express, Diners Club
2. ☐ MasterCard, Visa, Discover
3. ☐ Department Store, Oil Company, etc.
4. ☐ Do not use credit cards

19. For your primary residence, do you:
1. ☐ Own a House?
2. ☐ Own a Townhouse or Condominium?
3. ☐ Rent a House?
4. ☐ Rent an Apartment, Townhouse or Condominium?

FIGURE 6.1 Questionnaire accompanying furniture manufactured by Sauder Woodworking to be completed by purchaser. *Source:* Sauder Woodworking, Archbold, Ohio. Information Compiled by Equifax Direct Marketing Solutions, Inc.

(continues)

20. To help us understand our customers' lifestyles, please indicate the interests and activities in which you or your spouse enjoy participating on a regular basis:

1. ☐ Flower Gardening	17. ☐ Camping/Hiking	34. ☐ Crafts	
2. ☐ Grandchildren	18. ☐ Fishing Frequently	35. ☐ Electronics	
3. ☐ Home Furnishing/ Decorating	19. ☐ Hunting/Shooting	36. ☐ Stereo,Records/Tapes/CDs	
	20. ☐ Recreational Vehicles	37. ☐ Needlework/Knitting	
4. ☐ Home Workshop/ Do It Yourself	21. ☐ Sailing	38. ☐ Power Boating	
5. ☐ House Plants	22. ☐ Entering Sweepstakes	39. ☐ Science Fiction	
6. ☐ Vegetable Gardening	23. ☐ Casino Gambling	40. ☐ Photography	
7. ☐ Bicycling Frequently	24. ☐ Real Estate Investments	41. ☐ Science/New Technology	
	25. ☐ Stock/Bond Investments	42. ☐ Self Improvement	
8. ☐ Dieting/Weight Control	26. ☐ Wildlife/Environmental Issues	43. ☐ Sewing	
9. ☐ Golf		44. ☐ Attending Cultural/ Arts Events	
10. ☐ Health/Natural Foods	27. ☐ Our Nation's Heritage		
11. ☐ Physical Fitness/ Exercise	28. ☐ Automotive Work	45. ☐ Fashion Clothing	
12. ☐ Running/Jogging	29. ☐ Avid Book Reading	46. ☐ Fine Art/Antiques	
13. ☐ Snow Skiing Frequently	30. ☐ Bible/Devotional Reading	47. ☐ Foreign Travel	
14. ☐ Tennis Frequently	31. ☐ Buy Pre-Recorded Videos	48. ☐ Gourmet Cooking	
15. ☐ Walking for Health	32. ☐ Coin/Stamp Collecting	49. ☐ Travel in the USA	
16. ☐ Watching Sports on TV	33. ☐ Collectibles/Collections	50. ☐ Wines	

21. Using the numbers in the above list, please indicate the 3 most important activities for:

You ☐☐☐☐☐☐☐   Spouse ☐☐☐☐☐☐☐

22. Please check all that apply to your household:

1. ☐ Regularly Purchase Items Through the Mail	6. ☐ Have a Microwave Oven
2. ☐ Military Veteran in Household	7. ☐ Have a CD Player
3. ☐ Member of Frequent Flyer Program	8. ☐ Have a VCR
4. ☐ Support Health Charities	9. ☐ Use a Personal Computer
5. ☐ Subscribe to Cable TV	10. ☐ Have a Dog
	11. ☐ Have a Cat

Thanks for taking the time to fill out this questionnaire. Your answers will be used for market research studies and reports — and will help us better serve you in the future. They will also allow you to receive important mailings and special offers from a number of fine companies whose products and services relate directly to the specific interests, hobbies, and other information indicated above. Through this selective program, you will be able to obtain more information about activities in which you are involved and less about those in which you are not. Please check here if, for some reason, you would prefer *not* to participate in this opportunity. ☐

FIGURE 6.1 (*Continued*)

type of assets. It is apparent that these questionnaires can serve as the basis of a wealth of demographic and related information regarding specific segments of the population.

Companies like Sauder Woodworking, Soundesign Corporation, Kraft General Foods, and their promotion agencies, secure much information about their customers' interests in particular products, activities, and services in addition to their demographic and socioeconomic characteristics. These data are of value in numerous business operations and can be purchased by other companies for their use in their market research programs. For example, the questionnaires contain entries about interest in specific sports, and companies marketing products for tennis players, skiers, golfers, cyclists, and other participants in sports can secure information about the demographic characteristics of a segment of each of these markets from the responses to the product questionnaires.

Audience Measurement by Diary, Meter, or Internet Contacts

In addition to the methods discussed, some companies secure information about their potential customers on the basis of formal measurement devices. Records of actual listening or viewing activity may be obtained from viewers or listeners themselves. They may be set down in diaries, automatically recorded by meters attached to televison sets, or tabulated as contacts on the Internet.

Marketing by telephone, radio, television, and mail-order catalogs is well established. These media, especially television, may virtually arrange for completing the entire sales operation in that the prospective customer can order and purchase the product being advertised without leaving home. In the process, the media are busy measuring the demographic and socioeconomic characteristics of their readers or viewers.

The Internet eliminates the factors of time, distance, and even most of the effort from shopping. Electronic shopping by computer perfects the sales process in that the customer can complete the entire transaction just by the use of a personal computer at home. Thereby, all the steps of a personal transaction are replicated, even to the point of testing a product by simulation.[10] Access to the Internet—including a personal computer, a modem, communications software, and a telephone line—is all that is required. The marketing of some products is extremely well suited to online sale. An example is office products, especially supplies frequently replenished by small businesses, such as the product lines of Staples or Office Depot. Sales on the Internet still make up a negligible share of all sales, but this form of marketing is growing at sonic speed.

Contact between buyer and seller on the Internet may be made through Usenet newsgroups, Internet relay chat groups, e-mail, or the World Wide Web. There are more than 10,000 newsgroups groups defined by specialized interests, such as tennis or immigration. Once the seller has identified appropriate newsgroups, he or she can be assured of a generally responsive audience. They bring together buyer and seller in an interactive relation without the seller ever having to identify the exact characteristics of potential purchasers in order to locate them. Persons who sell and buy through newsgroups communicate with one another usually with only a little time lag. Some of the them feature big-ticket items, such as home-buying services, and many participants of newsgroups are ready to place orders, even for such major purchases. Chat groups also bring together groups of similar interests but the interchange is in real time.

With e-mail also, the seller and buyer have the opportunity to sell and buy with only a short time lag, but sellers first have to secure address lists of potential buyers on the basis of their characteristics, and potential customers have to be induced to seek out the sellers and contact them. E-mail users have to be asked to provide certain identifying information if the characteristics of such users are to be known. On the other hand, if the seller establishes a home page on the World Wide Web, the buyers may come to him or her. Then the seller will have the task of compiling information about customers who have chosen to visit the seller's home page. Some servers have established electronic malls where several sellers advertise at once. With the increasingly popular electronic auctions, many buyers compete face to face in real-time markets.

Electronic commerce analysts have not yet developed a satisfactory method of determining the characteristics of Internet buyers or potential buyers.[11] They want the best metric for the Internet audience so as to structure their advertising on the Internet most effectively. Interest in data describing the demographic characteristics of Internet users and the online results generated by competing advertisers is now considerable. The relation between Internet access and such demographic variables as age, sex, race, education, and income is generally known. However, "hits," the number of individual requests for information from an Internet site, are not considered very informative in themselves, nor are a variety of other measures of audience activity used to date. One method of determining who the Internet customers are is to examine data about their Internet shopping behavior and infer their characteristics from these data. Measurement of customer behavior can be based on a variety of behavioral markers, such as how the customer reached a site and what the customer ordered. By employing a predictive algorithm that compares customers' behavior to that of past users, customers can be segmented (i.e., assigned to potential-customer categories), even after a brief visit on the Internet and before making any purchases.

FACTORS AFFECTING BUSINESS SITING AND SALES FORECASTING

In selecting a site for the expansion of a firm into a new area, the input of the demographer complements that of the business analyst. As stated earlier, demographic data, methods, and perspectives can play a major role in decisions regarding business expansion, contraction, siting, and forecasting in the local market. The demographic focus is on the demographic, social, economic, and housing characteristics of the prospective customers and their geographic distribution, not on the physical, financial, and accounting matters that primarily concern the business analyst.

Market Segmentation

From surveys of potential customers and other sources, a market analyst will classify potential customers into groups that differ in their preferences for various products or services and their ability to purchase them. **Segmentation marketing** focuses resources on the groups most likely to purchase the product or service in the expectation that this approach produces lower costs per sale or the maximum "hit" rate. Many marketing specialists believe that segmentation marketing is the best way to secure a competitive advantage in one's business.[12] Prospective buyers may be segmented on the basis of demographic, geographic, psychographic (lifestyle and personality features), and other characteristics. Geographic segmentation usually refers to the division of prospective buyers in terms of their region of residence in the country, but it may also refer to their classification in terms of the population density, climate, and size of their city of residence. Segmentation may also be made on the basis of usage of a product or service (e.g., demand for a particular utility such as gas or electric, preference for the particular feature of a product, and other criteria).

However, the most common basis of segmentation is the demographic, socio-economic, and housing characteristics with which demographers are familiar.

Demographic Factors

The demographic and socioeconomic variables that define the target population of national businesses and local businesses are mostly the same. Among the generally applicable demographic and socioeconomic variables are age, sex, race/Hispanic origin, marital status, household status and living arrangements, income, occupation, and educational level. At the local level, residence-to-work commuting patterns and residence-to-store travel patterns (direction, distance, time traveled, and means of transportation), as well as local housing and neighborhood characteristics, are also important in identifying the potential customer. Most of these variables influence a consumer's choice of sales or service outlet and some of them influence the amount and share of income spent on consumer items of various kinds.

Many products are consumed entirely or largely by members of particular population groups. Some products are purchased wholly or mainly by one sex. For example, mostly women purchase women's clothes and accessories, cosmetics, certain kitchen appliances, romance novels, and *Bazaar, Cosmopolitan, New Woman,* and *Glamour* magazines, while mostly men purchase men's clothes and accessories, football and basketball equipment, home repair and maintenance tools, and *Esquire* and *Playboy* magazines. Certain products and services are purchased entirely or largely by persons in particular educational and income categories; for example, *Time* and *Worth* magazines and *The Wall Street Journal* (college graduates), *The Enquirer* and *People* magazines and lottery tickets (persons who have not attended college); Mercedes Benz automobiles, yachts, and riding mowers (more affluent persons), and check-cashing services and kerosene (poor persons). Some newspapers, magazines, radio stations, and TV channels are directed primarily at audiences belonging to a particular race or ethnic group (e.g., *The Chicago Defender* newspaper and *Ebony* magazine for blacks; Univision Communications broadcasting for Hispanics). There are lines of cosmetics, health, and hair products that are specially marketed for black consumers (e.g., Carsons Products, Inc.) and lines of food products that are especially marketed for Latinos (e.g., Goya).

Products used wholly or largely by particular age groups, include, for example, baby foods, children's books and toys, school furniture, *Seventeen* magazine, wheelchairs, dentures, many pharmaceuticals, and long-term care insurance. Attendance at movies and sports events is highly age-selective, attracting mainly younger audiences. The age changes expected in the early part of the 21st century will offer an especially strong opportunity to cater to the needs of the elderly population. Possible services are older assistance, home remodeling, job retraining, and "senior" learning. For example, Gentle Transitions is a relatively new company that helps elderly people move into new dwellings. Most elderly people, however, tend to upgrade their homes rather than move to new homes. Elderly people also spend much time at home—more time than other age segments of the population. With the technology revolution, there has also been a work-style revolution leading to rapid growth of home offices and home-based work. Hence, there are special opportunities for home-renovation contractors, interior designers, and architects. Home remodeling sales have grown sharply in the past few decades, reaching $115 billion in 1996.[13] The prospective changes in age structure will contribute to the growth of the managed care industry, which, in turn, will greatly benefit the pharmaceutical industry. Elderly people consume several times as many prescription drugs as younger persons and the managed care industry prefers dispensing drugs as a treatment protocol rather than providing other more therapeutic and costly treatments.

While the prime consumers of many products are members of particular age groups, the numbers and other characteristics of the persons in these age groups tend to fluctuate with the passage of time. The age changes described in Chapter 2 have important implications for current and prospective changes in consumer demand for many different types of products. For example, consumers between the ages 25 and 34 are important in the purchase of first homes, household furnishings and other durable goods, entertainment, transportation, apparel, and membership in fitness centers, while consumers aged 65 and over are important in the purchase of health and travel services, home repairs and utilities, and food for home consumption (Figure 6.2). The projected 11% decrease in the population 25 to 34 years of age between 1995 and 2005 (see Table 2.1) will tend to depress the sale of products and services directed to this particular age group and to restrain inflation and the demand for credit. To the extent that there is decreased consumer demand for certain products, companies producing these products will tend to have excess capacity and will be disinclined to expand their facilities and increase investments. On the other hand, as a result of the increases in population numbers in other age groups, the sale of products and services to them and related investment prospects may be expected to expand.

The demands for specific types of products and services by *age groups* tend to change slowly compared to the demands by *birth cohorts,* which tend

FIGURE 6.2   Illustrative List of Consumer Products or Services Purchased Disproportionately by Particular Age Groups

Age group	Product or service
Under 25	Transportation, apparel, entertainment, personal care, food away from home, education
25 to 34	Home ownership, household appliances, do-it-yourself products, housing costs, entertainment, apparel, transportation
35 to 49	Apparel, housing costs, home ownership, entertainment, transportation
50 to 64	Travel, recreational products and services, personal insurance, household furnishings
65 to 79	Health, travel, home services, housing repairs, food at home, public transportation
80 and over	Health, home services, housing repairs, food at home

Source: U.S. Bureau of Labor Statistics, *Consumer Expenditures in 1995,* 1997; based on Consumer Expenditure Survey and unpublished data. See also Jacob S. Siegel, *A Generation of Change: A Profile of America's Older Population,* New York: Russell Sage Foundation, 1993, Table 8.24.

to change rapidly. As birth cohorts move up the age scale, they acquire different tastes, needs, and interests, which engender demand for different products and services. In 1960–1980, when many members of the baby-boom cohorts were in their teens, there was a boom in fast foods, musical recordings, and attendance at motion picture shows. By 1998, these cohorts had moved on to the young- and middle-adult ages and had created business booms for a new group of products and services, such as automotive products, household appliances, and computer products. Another shift in the huge demands of these cohorts will occur after 2010 or so, when they begin to reach the older ages and have more need for health products and services, housing repair materials and services, public transportation, and travel products and services.

Many products and services are designed to serve persons experiencing a demographic event. These events represent the major transitions in the life course (i.e., birth, death, migration, marriage, divorce, or widowing). Many illustrations are at hand: moving and storage services for migrants and movers; formal wear and major home furnishings for persons marrying; legal, judicial, and social services for persons divorcing; funeral services and caskets for widowings and other deaths; and obstetrical services, infant foods, and cribs for births and recent parenthood.

Demographic–Economic Interconnections

Prospective changes in the numbers at each age are perhaps the leading demographic factor in defining changing needs and interests in certain products and services but, as indicated earlier, many other demographic factors affect buying patterns and the content of consumer demand. Interconnections between basic demographic characteristics and socioeconomic characteristics are important in defining effective demand for products and services in a local market as illustrated with a few interconnections relating mainly to age, race, household type, family income, and housing characteristics.[14]

Family incomes typically rise and decline over the life course. The middle years are the peak earning years. However, the share of income spent is rather similar for all age groups.[15] Hence, family expenditures typically increase as families move into the ages where they earn more and then decline in later life. Middle-aged adults (45 to 54 years) spend more money than younger and older adults and money spent per consumer unit in these ages is greatest for most consumer items.

Married-couple households tend to be concentrated in the middle-adult ages, to have relatively high incomes, and to own their own homes. These characteristics are associated with relatively high buying power and neighborhood stability. Male-headed and female-headed households, whether family or nonfamily households, tend to have much lower incomes. Persons living alone, in particular, have relatively low incomes and few assets and hence tend to spend less than persons in other living arrangements. Yet they eat out more frequently and move more frequently. Two-earner families have higher incomes and different buying habits than single-earner families. Two-earner families with children have higher incomes and different buying habits than two-earner families without children. For example, a two-earner family without children is prone to eat dinner out; a two-earner family with children is prone to eat dinner in.

A neighborhood has a demographic/socioeconomic profile at any particular time and a life cycle reflecting changes in its profile. Neighborhoods like individuals may be considered new, young, middle-aged, or old according to the stage of their life cycle. Neighborhoods vary according to such factors as the type, age, density of occupancy, tenure (i.e., extent of homeownership), value, and condition of the housing units located in them as well as the characteristics of the households and persons who reside in them. They tend to vary with respect to the age of the householder, the type of household, household income, race and ethnic composition, percentage foreign born, knowledge and use of English in the household, and other characteristics. Taking account of the **life cycle of a neighborhood** is a valuable element in evaluating consumer demand as well as in conducting a siting analysis.

A new neighborhood of single homes with many first-time home buyers aged 25 to 44 years has different purchasing patterns than a neighborhood of apartment dwellers of the same ages or a neighborhood with older second-time buyers. The residents of a new neighborhood of single family homes tend to buy much household equipment and furniture. Nevertheless, neighborhoods with a large share of householders in the middle ages may be expected to spend more than neighborhoods with a large share of younger or older householder. A settled neighborhood with many householders in their late middle years (i.e., 55 to 64 years old) would be in the stage of declining expenditures. An old neighborhood is likely to have a disproportionate share of elderly persons and hence tends to spend less and to spend a disproportionate share of its income on health services and housing maintenance.

Neighborhoods of cities may differ sharply from one another in their race/ethnic composition, but only moderately in the age composition of their residents.[16] Race/ethnic groups tend to cluster greatly within cities (see Chapter 2 and the further discussion in this chapter). Given differences in income and tastes among the races, the buying power and buying practices of neighborhoods may differ greatly. For example, race/ethnic groups differ in their tendency to eat out or eat at home, to pursue recreational activities at home or commercially, and to use certain products or avoid them. Young people of all races are more likely to patronize fast-food restaurants than older persons, but young blacks are especially frequent patrons. Race/ethnic groups differ among one another in the types of cuisine they prefer when they eat out, the types of magazines they read, the radio stations they listen to, and the TV channels they watch.

If certain racial/ethnic groups are concentrated in the low-income classes, as is true for blacks and Hispanics, then an area with a large concentration of such racial groups is likely to have a greatly reduced dollar sales potential, and expenditures for many consumer products may be depressed. Differences in household income and age within a racial group, on the other hand, can reduce, if not eliminate, the differences between different neighborhoods with respect to the amount spent for specific types of products or services. For example, while poorer blacks are likely to eat out often in fast-food restaurants, middle-class blacks are more likely to eat at home, like Hispanics and whites. The more educated, upper middle-class neighborhoods more easily support a bookstore, a health food restaurant, and a computer store than less educated, lower-class neighborhoods, regardless of race.

Nondemographic Factors

The nondemographic variables to be considered in determining the feasibility of establishing a local business or service facility are, for the most part, physical, legal, financial, and administrative. Data for them must generally be secured from sources other than the decennial census of population and similar demographic sources. Among the specific nondemographic variables to be considered are potential competition, the pattern of roadways and physical impediments to commuting, local zoning ordinances, and the master plan describing the current and planned transportation system and use of land. Other related factors are the distances between residences of different types and the proposed business location, indicators of economic growth and prospects for economic growth in the trading area, the quality of management planned for the new facility, and estimates of pedestrian and automobile traffic in front of the prospective retail or service outlet.

The market analyst must consider the specific characteristics of the new business as well as its general features. Even if the general type of store has been predecided, the range of merchandise has to be considered. The store may offer a single product (e.g., shoes, groceries) or a combination of products (e.g., shoes and other types of footware; groceries, prepared food, and a cafe). On the financial side, the analyst must consider such factors as the size of the investment to be made and the expected profitability period. Then, too, attention must be given to the physical situation that is required to support the specific type and size of local business operation to be established.

Illustrations of Use of Demographic and Nondemographic Factors

Our first example relates to a company's basis for expanding its operations and its attention to demographic factors in this regard. The Federal Realty Investment Trust is a successful real estate investment trust specializing in the ownership, management, development, and redevelopment of retail properties, mainly on the East Coast. The *1995 Annual Report* states that the trust makes purchases in areas where it sees "solid demographics, strong retail demand, limited competition, and additional investment opportunities." The trust "focuses on major metropolitan markets, with high household densities and above average median incomes." Areas with "solid demographics" and "strong retail demand" are presumably areas with high population densities around a retail center, with households having high median incomes. Among the nondemographic elements sought by this enterprise are a high quality of the physical state of the properties, a high occupancy rate, accessibility and visibility from main traffic corridors, and the presence of a retailer or retailers with outstanding consumer appeal, which would attract other retailers of this kind.

In the late 1990s, the trust acquired Finley Square in Downers Grove, Illinois, an affluent suburb of Chicago, where more than 270,000 people live within a 5-mile radius of the center of Downers Grove and the median household income exceeds $68,000. Nondemographic factors given as important for this center are its accessibility and visibility from the center's main retail corridor (I-355). Another nondemographic factor viewed as important is the presence of a strong retailer (or retailers) as "anchor(s)" for a retail center. For example, it notes the synergy created by having three dynamic retailers (Fresh Fields, Borders Books, and Bed, Bath & Beyond) as anchors for its redeveloped center at Gaithersburg Square in Gaithersburg, Maryland, in place of the original "undersized" grocery store. In general, a food supermarket is one such anchor since it provides a steady, daily consumer traffic. The principle seems to be that successful retailers breed more successful retailing.

To implement plans for the future location of service and sales outlets, and future production facilities, business planners need, in addition to current estimates of various demographic and nondemographic series, forecasts of them as well, possibly for the nation, the region, and the immediate trading area. Ideally, forecasts should be secured for all the demographic and socioeconomic variables identified as determining demand for a company's products or services. Methods of preparing estimates and projections of a variety of demographic variables are discussed in Chapters 9, 10, and 11. Here we mainly want to call attention to and illustrate the role of forecasts of population and other variables for siting businesses.

In projecting future demand for telephone service in a local area, the projected numbers of persons and households essentially represent actual demand since purchasing power and desire for the product are not major issues. The Bell Atlantic Corporation (reborn as Verizon) needs current estimates and annual population projections for certain constituent areas of the Bell Atlantic region, called LATAs, 20 or so years ahead for age-sex groups. LATAs are composed of specially defined parts of counties, counties, or combinations of counties. They were set up to distinguish local calling areas from long-distance calling areas. None of the types of areas for which data are compiled in the decennial censuses conforms to the market areas of the Bell Atlantic Corporation. However, the boundaries of LATAs can be "digitized," using maps for the LATAs. In this way, the data for the LATAs can be retrieved from the most recent decennial census files by aggregating small area census geographic units to match the LATA's boundaries and, where necessary, applying an estimating rule. Comparable current estimates for them can be developed from available population estimates. Then a methodology for the projections can be designed and applied.

In the example next described, the analyst seeks to identify the variables relevant to the preparation of forecasts of the sales of a particular product, having current estimates of sales on hand, and then employs a regression equation to make the actual forecasts. As reported by Parker and Segura (1970), in order to forecast sales of cans of beer, the American Can Company employed three variables as the independent variables: age distribution of the population, income levels, and number of drinking establishments per 1000 population.[17] In another illustration, forecasting sales in the home furnishings industry, Parker and Segura suggested as independent variables new marriages, housing starts, and disposable personal income for the regression analysis. Once a tentative set of independent variables is selected for a regression analysis, the next steps are to determine the coefficients of the regression equation by solving the corresponding "normal" equations using historical or spatial data as available, determining various future values for the independent variables, inserting them and the coefficients into the regression equation, and solving the equation for the dependent variable (i.e., population or households). Projecting the independent variables is a difficult task—that is, one fraught with great uncertainty—as are most efforts to develop the assumptions required for forecasting. Whatever variation of regression forecasting is used, however, this step must be taken. A further discussion of the procedure for applying regression analysis is given next.

MEASURING THE CONTRIBUTION OF RELEVANT FACTORS

In developing a plan for the siting of a new business, first, relevant demographic and nondemographic variables (i.e., **independent variables**) affecting the profitability of the business must be selected and, then, weights must be assigned to the independent variables to reflect their contribution to some measure of gain, growth, or profitability (i.e., **dependent variable**). The initial selection of the most predictive variables is the analyst's job, but they should ultimately be decided on in collaboration with management. The weights can be developed empirically, in part on the basis of the actual experience of the particular company or, if such data are not available, the actual experience of businesses of similar types and sizes in similar localities. An established company that wishes to expand its operations may have much of the data on hand or can assemble them from the record of its several stores or service outlets, official statistical compendia, and local agencies. Thus, a quantitative relationship between the independent variables and the dependent variable can be established. This makes it possible to "predict" the expected value of the dependent variable in terms of the value(s) of the independent variables.

The **general linear model** is commonly used for this purpose. It can take into account the impact of several variables simultaneously, provide specific predictions in terms of total sales or revenues for each proposed new area, give measures of the contribution of each variable to total sales or revenues, include or exclude variables depending on their predictive value, and provide measures of the quality of the predictions. The model's effectiveness can be measured by a comparison of predictions of performance at existing sites against actual performance, by an analysis of the predictions themselves, and by the usual regression diagnostics, such as in terms of the coefficient of determination (R^2) between the variables. For example, the general linear model can be used to predict sales of a product or revenues from sales in terms of such variables as population, median family income, and unit price, to predict per capita consumption of certain foods in terms of dollars spent to advertise them on television, or to predict family expenditures on entertainment in terms of family income and age of the householder. These are all **interval variables** (i.e., continuous quantitative variables), but noninterval variables (i.e., **ordinal** and **nominal variables**) can also be incorporated into the general linear model as **dummy** variables.

Use of Multiple Linear Regression Analysis

To apply the general linear model, a multiple linear regression equation is used to represent the relation between the dependent variable measuring business performance (e.g., revenues of the company) and a series of independent variables assumed or known to affect the profitability of the business. The weights or coefficients for the independent variables in the equation should be determined by use of actual data for the variables. Given values for the variables in a series of observations recorded for the various local business outlets of the company, we can solve for the weights by an appropriate mathematical criterion. Then, given the weight for each independent variable and observed, assumed, estimated, or projected values of the independent variables, we can evaluate the equation for the value of the dependent variable under the new conditions.[18]

The multiple linear regression equation has the following general form:

$$Y = b_0 + b_1 x_1 + b_2 x_2 + b_3 x_3 + \cdots + b_n x_n + e \qquad (1)$$

where Y is the dependent variable (e.g., total revenues), the x_i the explanatory or independent variables, the b_i the weights, b_0 being the expected value of Y when the x_i are zero, and e is an error term. There are as many x's as there are independent variables; here there are n independent variables. Assuming that we have more than n local business outlets—that is, that there are more units of observation or equations than unknown coefficients (b's)—the system of equations is indeterminate. To solve the system for the b values, then, we need a statistical criterion such as least squares or maximum likelihood. Once the b's are determined, they can be inserted into the general equation along with new values for the x_i's to solve for the Y values. Many computer packages are available for carrying out these regression calculations.

A study by Johnson (1994) illustrates the application of multiple linear regression analysis to a problem in business expansion.[19] A national motel chain, the Welcome Company, owns a large number of motels and wishes to expand its operations by adding several more motels in the country. It wants to apply its experience from its existing motels to determine the possibilities for success in a variety of proposed new locations, using total revenues per motel as a dependent variable. Since it plans to expand in middle-size markets, the experience of its motels in areas of this size will be used in the prediction model. Initially 61 independent variables were considered but the number was reduced to 8. In selecting the variables, the analyst must avoid choosing those that are highly intercorrelated. This situation, called **multicollinearity**, can result in an unreliable indication of the relation between the independent variables and the dependent variable.

The eight variables used in the study to measure the revenues produced by each of the Welcome Company's motels, and their sources for the Eau Claire, Wisconsin, MSA are as follows:

Variable	Source
x_1 Population, 1987	Official state estimates
x_2 Firms, 100+ workers[a]	*County Business Patterns*[b]
x_3 Hotel sales	*1987 Census of Service Industries*[b]
x_4 Daily nonstop commercial flights	*Official Airline Guide*
x_5 Vehicles entering area	State Department of Transportation
x_6 Major events annually	Chamber of Commerce
x_7 Major competitors	Tourist industry sources
x_8 Quality of management	Company operations staff
Constant	Derived from the statistical model

[a] Number of local firms with 100 or more workers.
[b] U.S. Bureau of the Census.
Source: Johnson (1994).

The final regression equation for estimating total revenues per motel in dollars (Y_c), showing the values of the weights (b_i) and the constant (b_0), is

$$Y_c = 101543 + 4.1x_1 + 5147x_2 + 30.8x_3 + 140300x_4 + 2.7x_5 \\ + 11457x_6 - 97843x_7 + 43354x_8 \tag{2}$$

This regression equation can be used to estimate the revenues expected from a proposed motel. A change of one unit in an independent variable x_i, with the other independent variables being held constant, will result in a change of b_i in the dependent variable. For example, if two Welcome locations in two cities were the same in all the variables shown except that one city has one more major event during the year (x_6) than the other, then the additional major event would be expected to bring in \$11,457 in additional revenue annually for the city with the added event.[20]

It is important to test the effectiveness of the regression equation against some actual cases where the value of the dependent variable is known. This test could add credibility to the demographer's analysis (or diminish it). An index could be calculated reflecting the prospective relative success of the proposed facility, as follows:

Market or sales potential index (SPI)

$$= \frac{\text{Weekly sales volume projected for proposed motel}}{\text{Average weekly sales volume of all motels owned}} * 100 \tag{3}$$

A figure of 150, for example, indicates a volume of sales 50% over the average for the company's facilities.

The coefficient of determination (R^2) is one measure of the success of the estimation process. It represents the share of the total variation, which is explained by the fitted line (the multiple regression equation). The formulas for R^2 and the components of error in Y are as follows:

$$R^2 = \Sigma(Y_c - \overline{Y})^2 \div \Sigma(Y_i - \overline{Y})^2 \tag{4}$$

$$\Sigma(Y_i - \overline{Y})^2 = \Sigma(Y_i - Y_c)^2 + \Sigma(Y_c - \overline{Y})^2 \tag{5}$$

R^2 varies from zero to one, and an R^2 of .86, such as was obtained in the Welcome case, suggests a high level of accuracy for the predictions of revenue for the existing locations. For further evaluation of the estimating equation, Johnson categorized every motel either as having inadequate revenue, moderate revenue, or high revenue, set up a two-way classification of the known percentage of motels in each revenue category and the percentage predicted from the regression equation for each revenue category, and then carried out an **odds ratio analysis** of the data. He found, for example, that the odds were 4 to 1 that a unit in a market predicted to generate high revenue would actually do so, whereas the chances were only 1 in 32 that a unit placed in such a market would fail. In general, he found that the regression equation was very effective in predicting motels with inadequate revenue and high revenue but much less able to predict those with moderate revenue.[21] Such evaluations illustrate the strengths and weaknesses of the multiple linear regression model and provide the basis for a rational decision by management for its store-siting plan.

A related problem is illustrated by the case of a grocery chain that is seeking to locate a new supermarket in a metropolitan area and wants to decide in which county among several counties in the area to locate the new supermarket. It wants to identify the county with the potential for the greatest economic growth. The following growth indicators are being considered: population, families, income (median family income), housing units, percentage owner-occupied housing units, car ownership, and grocery store sales. Comparative economic data for supermarkets for the counties of interest may be obtained from the Census of Retail Trade on (1) the number of business outlets, (2) aggregate sales during the year in dollars, (3) aggregate payroll during the year in dollars, and (4) paid employees in the week before the census. (See illustrative data in Appendix A.) The data for the population, socioeconomic, and housing variables, and for car ownership may be obtained from the Population and Housing Censuses, the Census Bureau current estimates programs, state data centers, or private data-vending companies.

To select the county with the greatest growth potential, data for the indicators for an earlier date or two are needed. We could judge the potential for economic growth by the past percentage increase in grocery store sales alone, but systematically taking the group of variables into account provides a stronger basis for the store-siting decision. If they do not point to the same county, we may choose to employ and solve a multiple regression equation for the counties, linking the changes in the group of independent variables and the change in the dependent variable (i.e., some measure of the profitability of grocery supermarkets or the growth of businesses in general). We would implement the equation by inserting projected values of the independent variables for each county and the weights for them determined for the prior period from the company's own or similar experience. The county showing the greatest index of profitability for grocery supermarkets is the choice for locating the new supermarket.

Delimiting the Trading Area

As noted earlier, the **trading area** of a business is the geographic area from which it draws a substantial share of its customers. A trading area has no standard statistical or geographic definition, and different criteria will produce different trading areas, varying in size and shape. One way to determine the size and shape of a particular trading area is to ask shoppers the criteria they used in selecting a particular store. In general, prospective customers for a given product or service will patronize a store only if it is within a specified distance from their residence. An empirical way of determining the boundaries of trading areas is to map the addresses of the current customers and demarcate the continuous area within which about 90% of the customers live. You will still need some quantitative criterion for the border areas, selecting, for example, census tracts from which 5% or more of the customers originate. Alternatively, the trading area can be measured by the "geographic" performance of the business in terms of households represented by customers or sales in dollars, level of customer-individual density, or level of customer-household density.

Different types of businesses have trading areas of different sizes and shapes. A trading area may vary in size from several blocks for a small corner store to an area with a radius of several miles for a large store located in a major shopping area. A supermarket may get the bulk of its customers from residences located within a mile or two of the store, and a combination store, or ultralarge supermarket, may get the bulk of its customers from within a radius of 3 miles. A specialty shop may get its customers over a broader radius.

The trading area of a store in the central business district of a city is normally delineated differently from the trading area of a store in a major suburban shopping area. Place of residence is not usually a determinant of a decision to shop in a downtown store. Typically, the factors defining the trading area of a downtown store are place of work, place of other activities, and the availability of good mass transit facilities or roadways. For the downtown store, the limits of the city can loosely be taken as the bounds of the store's trading area. More precisely, the bounds can be determined by the distribution of the residences of the people who work downtown.

The trading area of a suburban or neighborhood store may be delineated arbitrarily in terms of a circle with a specified radius around the store or other geometrical figure with specified dimensions (e.g., an ellipse of a given length and width), considering the roadway system and the distribution of residences, parks, and offices around the store.[22] Alternatively, the trading area may be delineated in terms of the time needed to travel to the store from a residence. It is likely that a travel time of 20 minutes represents the limit of time for most types of retail shopping. Census data on travel time for shopping are not available, but travel time to work averaged 22 minutes in 1990, being greater in the more densely populated areas. Time allowed for shopping may be expected to be shorter.

Trading areas defined by particular radii for different retail centers tend to overlap. Other things being equal, customers patronize the business that is nearest. The least-distance criterion gives us a way of dealing with stores whose trading areas potentially overlap. Two or three competing retail stores in the same general geographic area may have a variety of retail trading relationships with one another. For example, two such stores may have equal drawing power over a common area or they may have entirely separate trading areas, of the same or different sizes, with an area nearby or in-between that is served insufficiently or not at all by either store. The third store may pick up the potential customers between the two others and even some of their customers.

The fall-off in business with increasing distance from the epicenter (that is, the location of the store, shop, or service station) may be represented by a negative (decay) exponential function or a reverse exponential function. These two models can give very different results. The **negative exponential function** is formulated as follows:

$$R_1 = e^{-rd} \tag{6}$$

where e is the base of the natural logarithm system, d represents the distance in miles from the epicenter, r is the rate of "decay" or fall-off in the volume of business, measured in customers or sales dollars, and R_1 represents the ratio by which the volume of business at d miles from the epicenter is reduced from its theoretical ceiling of 1.0. In this model the rate of fall-off is fixed but the amount of the decline decreases as one moves away from the store. These calculations assume that the population is equally distributed in the 6-mile radius around the store.

The following data illustrate the size of R_1 assuming rates (r) of decay of 0.15, 0.2, and 0.3 for each mile. Each rate may be appropriate for a different type of retail facility:

	R_1 for $r =$		
d	0.15	0.2	0.3
0	1.000	1.000	1.000
1	.861	.819	.741
2	.741	.670	.549
3	.638	.549	.407
4	.549	.449	.301
5	.472	.368	.223
6	.407	.301	.165

For example, with $d = 3$ (miles) and $r = 0.2$,

$$R_1 = e^{-.2(3)} = e^{-.6} = .549 \tag{7}$$

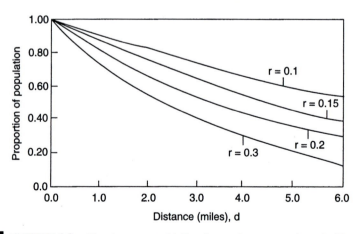

FIGURE 6.3   Negative exponential (decay) curve for various values of r. [$R_1 = e^{-rd}$].

That is to say, with a fall-off rate in customers of 20% per mile ($r = 0.2$), at 3 miles from the facility, the volume of customers would be 55% of its theoretical ceiling. With a uniform fall-off rate of 30% per mile ($r = .3$), the volume of customers at 3 miles would be 41% of its theoretical ceiling. (These results are graphically shown in Figure 6.3.)

If, however, we make the more reasonable assumption that the amount of decline is least in the closest areas and increases with distance from the facility, then a **reverse exponential** is more appropriate. It may be formulated as

$$R_2 = 1 - (e^{rd} - 1) \tag{8}$$

Assuming r values of 0.1, 0.15, and 0.2, the R_2 values are

	R_2 for $r =$		
d	0.1	0.15	0.2
0	1.000	1.000	1.000
1	0.895	0.838	0.779
2	0.779	0.650	0.508
3	0.650	0.432	0.178
4	0.508	0.178	−0.226
5	0.351	−0.117	
6	0.178		

R_2 has the same interpretation as R_1. Note that the graph of the reverse exponential has a convex form, while the graph of the negative exponential has a concave form (Figure 6.4). The rate of decay can be applied either to populaton or households. Alternatively, the R's may be assigned as weights to the different factors influencing the volume of business as the distance from the proposed site increases.

To determine the cumulative share of the customers according to radial miles around the store location, it is necessary to integrate the reverse exponential curve with respect to d. The computational algorithm is[23]

$$2(n + 1) - (e^{r(n+1)}/r) - (2n - e^{rn}/r) \tag{9}$$

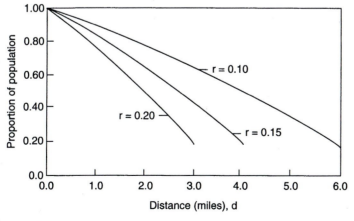

FIGURE 6.4   Reverse exponential (decay) curve for various values of r. $[R_2 = 1 - (e^{rd} - 1)]$.

Applying this result for each mile (n to $n + 1$) for $r = .15$, we obtain, for the proportion of the population in each mile who are likely customers (column 1):

Areas by distance	Proportion of population	Cumulative proportion of customers over 5-mile area
Under 1 mile	0.921	0.361
1.0 to 2.0 miles	0.747	0.653
2.0 to 3.0 miles	0.544	0.866
3.0 to 4.0 miles	0.308	0.987
4.0 to 5.0 miles	0.034	1.000

The second column, the cumulative proportion of customers from the site to the various distances, is obtained by cumulating the proportions in column 1 and calculating the share of the cumulated proportions of the total cumulation. The calculation assumes that the population is distributed equally throughout the area. This exercise tells us, for example, that, with a decay rate of 15% per mile, at 1 to 2 miles from the site, 75% of the population are likely customers and 65% of all the customers reside within 2 miles.[24] (See Figure 6.5.)

Retrieval of Data for Trading Areas

Given a geographic delineation of the trading area, how can the numbers of residents and households and the demographic characteristics of the population of the area be determined? This is a question posed in Chapter 5, but a few more notes are offered here. If the trading area is defined as a circular area of a specified radius around the site of a business facility, the boundaries are likely to cut through all established census areas. Assuming that this is true, one approach is to delineate a group of primary census tracts (i.e., a group of tracts wholly included in the trading area) and a group of secondary tracts (i.e., a group of tracts partly included in the trading area). A determination then has to be made as to which secondary tracts, or the parts of which secondary tracts, should be included in the data for the trading area. In general, the problem is best treated by detailed analysis of the population distribution

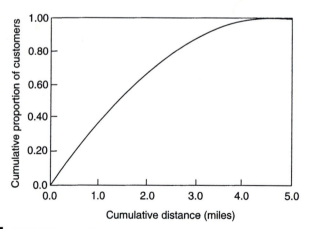

FIGURE 6.5 Cumulative proportion of customers of a retail business according to radial miles around its location, assuming $r = .15$. *Source:* Based on integral of reverse exponential curve.

in the relevant census tracts if the appropriate data are available. In practice, however, depending on the type of data sought and their availability for various geographic units, certain assumptions have to be made to approximate the data for the required area, as suggested next.

If the desired data are available for blocks, the trading area can be approximated rather easily. If the smallest geographic unit for which the required data are available is the census tract, the analyst has several options. He or she can use the data for the entire tracts through which the boundary runs, none of the data for these tracts, or a share of the data for these tracts based on the distribution of the area, population, or housing units within the tracts, as measured in the previous census. A particular tract may be included in entirety if its centroid falls inside the trading area and excluded if its centroid falls outside of it. All of the tract could be included in the trading area if more than 50% of the tract's area is included in it. Alternatively, one could estimate the population in this part of the trading area by geographic or areal interpolation, using an assumption of population **rectangularity** (i.e., evennness of distribution) in space. This assumption is that the share of the tract's *population* in the trading area is the same as the share of the tract's *area* in the trading area. In general, this is a questionable assumption because population is not usually distributed evenly over geographic space, but it applies roughly in most cases. On the other hand, if the geographic units for which data are available are small areas such as block groups, then a rectangular assumption is quite adequate.

I have laid out the issues of delimiting a trading area and retrieving the data because it is important for the analyst to understand the process if he or she is to make a logical choice of the computer software available for this purpose. Commercial data-vending companies employ so-called **geometric retrieval methods**, such as those described earlier, to generate data for specific areas that do not conform to the boundaries of census geographic units. The process of estimating the proportions of population and households, tabulated in the primary source for standard geographic areas, for some arbitrarily defined target area such as a trading area, is called **geographic** or **areal interpolation**. The tools of geographic information systems (GIS), including TIGER, described in Chapter 5, make it possible for an applied demographer to carry out data retrieval involving geographic interpolation from STFs and other special files. These tools automate the processes described previously for delimiting trading areas and effecting data retrieval, and hence they can be very useful to applied demographers engaged in studies of this type.[25]

COMPLIANCE WITH REGULATIONS RELATING TO THE CONDUCT OF BUSINESSES

Businesses have to comply with numerous regulations in the pursuit of their business activities. The design, evaluation, and defense of many of their compliance programs require the use of demographic data and demographic analysis. To illustrate, three areas of activity involving compliance on the part of some class of businesses are considered. They are the sale and rental of housing, businesses' role in environmental protection and equity, and compliance with regulations on expansion and competition.

Housing Discrimination

Demographers and others have carried out many studies that measure the extent of geographic separation, or **residential differentiation,** of race groups and Hispanics, the factors accounting for the racial/ethnic differences in geographic separation, and the share of racial residential differentiation that can be accounted for by **residential segregation** (i.e., involuntary residential separation of the races). Residential differentiation by race can result from such influences as financial inability to rent or buy a housing unit in a particular area, voluntary selection of a particular area on the basis of its ethnic or racial composition, population size and racial composition of an area (e.g., ceiling effect; discussed later), inertia, and racial discrimination. In this conception of the issue, racial discrimination is the factor that results in residential segregation of the races.

The index of dissimilarity is the most commonly used measure of racial residential separation.[26] As explained in Chapter 1, where the formula is given, it ranges from 0 to 100. An index of 100 represents complete separation of the races and an index of 0 represents full integration of the races, with an index above 60 or so being considered high. On the basis of an analysis of 1990 census data for 254 metropolitan areas, Harrison and Weinberg (1992) reported an index of dissimilarity of 69 for blacks, 50 for Hispanics, and 41 for Asians and Pacific Islanders.[27] The results show that the concentration of blacks exceeds that of Hispanics and Asians by a wide margin.[28] A small decline in residential clustering was recorded for blacks between 1980 and 1990, from 74 in 1980 to 69 in 1990. According to Harris (1995), in 1990 the index was over 60 for most large cities. It was over 80 for such cities as Detroit, Chicago, Cleveland, Newark, and New York; it was between 70 and 80 for such cities as Philadelphia, St. Louis, Cincinnati, Los Angeles, and Kansas City; and it was between 60 and 70 for such cities as Boston, Miami, Atlanta, Houston, and Dallas.[29] Blacks and Hispanics of all economic classes have tended to live in distinct neighborhoods, and now the multiethnic neighborhood, in which blacks, Hispanics, and Asian Americans live together, but apart from whites, has emerged.[30]

In measuring and evaluating a community's record on the residential separation of racial/ethnic groups, it is particularly important to consider, among the factors affecting the extent of separation, the racial/ethnic composition of the total population of the area. It is difficult to measure the extent of racial/ethnic discrimination meaningfully in an area, or even prove or disprove its existence, where the "minority" racial/ethnic group constitutes a very high percentage of the population of the area. Under these circumstances, it is also difficult to remedy the problem by public action, such as enforced busing to other sections of the area. As the proportion of a "minority" racial/ethnic group rises above 70% or so, the index of dissimilarity becomes less and less useful as an index of segregation. At this level the ceiling effect leaves little room for racial minorities to live in predominantly white areas. On the other hand, in some metropolitan areas, where the proportion of blacks is small, substantial decreases in racial concentration can occur that are not necessarily the result of declines in discrimination against blacks. In these cases, even if the entire area is integrated, contact between the races will be minimal.[31]

In the interpretation of the index of dissimilarity, researchers in the past have given little weight to the financial inability of most blacks and Hispanics to move into many white neighborhoods. Cutler *et al.* (1999) present evidence, however, indicating that the higher cost of housing in white neighborhoods now plays a significant role in the persistence of the residential concentration of the races.[32] They maintain that in recent years "whites segregate themselves by paying more to live with members of their own race." Some researchers have given more weight to the voluntary preferences of the races than to the cost factor—that is, the preference of blacks for areas that have a large concentration of blacks, and of whites for areas that are mainly white. While blacks are willing to reside in an area with a substantial share of whites (i.e., up to half), whites prefer to reside in an area that is overwhelmingly white (Krivo and Kauffman, 1999, *op. cit.*). There is ample evidence of discrimination in the housing market, so that there is no question about the important role of discrimination in racial residential separation. Many consider racial discrimination the single most important factor accounting for racial residential separation, as has certainly been the case in the past, but the new evidence suggests that the financial factor, joined with voluntary preferences and other "nondiscriminatory" factors, may now be at least of equal importance.

The forms that discrimination takes in the housing industry are (1) implicit or explicit discrimination in advertising the availability of housing, (2) discrimination in (a) handling housing applications, (b) showing housing units to applicants, (c) selecting prospective tenants or owners from lists of applicants, and (d) offering information about housing alternatives, and (3) discrimination in awarding mortgages. The responsible party may be a federal, state, or local government agency, a private management company, or an individual. The government agency may be the Department of Housing and Urban Development (HUD) or a local housing authority.

Reduction of the extent of racial/ethnic residential separation would have several favorable effects. For example, it would make possible greater geographic mobility of inner-city racial groups, increased homeownership by racial minorities, and reduced isolation of racial minorities. It might also improve the accessibility of racial minorities to better neighborhood services and facilities, such as schools, stores, and trash collection. There is evidence that the status of one's neighbors, at least for blacks, has a strong influence on one's economic and social future (Cutler *et al.*, 1999, *op. cit.*; Massey and Denton, 1989, *op. cit.*).

Until the 1960s, housing practices of private entities or individuals were openly discriminatory and such discriminatory practices were legal. After the passage of the Fair Housing Act in 1968 (i.e., Title VIII of the Civil Rights Act of 1968), discrimination in private housing became illegal, as was already the case for discrimination in public housing and discrimination by public agencies.[33] Under the Fair Housing Act of 1968 and the ruling of the Supreme Court in *Jones v. Albert H. Mayer Co.* (1968), it is illegal to discriminate against any person, on the basis of race, color, national origin, and religion, in the sale or rental of housing, the advertising of the sale or rental of housing, the financing of housing, or the provision of real estate brokerage services. Sex, disability, and familial status (i.e., having children under age 18), and protection of the right of older persons to separate housing were added later under a separate act or amendment (1988).

Public housing authorities, like private real estate companies, are subject to various regulations prohibiting restrictions on the clientele to whom they provide public housing. In general, neighborhood covenants cannot be enforced, and discrimination on the grounds of sex, race, age, or family composition and size is prohibited. Just as for private housing, these characteristics may not be used to exclude an applicant from public/subsidized housing.

The extent to which the demographic characteristics of prospective renters and owners can be identified in the law and become the subject of litigation is illustrated by the terms of the Human Rights Act of 1977 of the District of Columbia. Discrimination on the basis of age, sex, race, ethnicity, national origin, religion, sexual orientation, number of children, marital status, enrollment in school, personal appearance, political affiliation, and source of income is prohibited under the law.[34]

A discriminatory act can involve either **disparate treatment** of some group such as a minority racial group (that is, treating the racial groups differently) or **disparate impact** (that is, employing a practice that, indirectly, affects the racial groups differently). For example, the prohibition against a restriction on the number of children is intended to deter discrimination directly against large families and indirectly, by the legal doctrine of **adverse impact**, against blacks and Hispanics, whose families tend to be relatively large. The plaintiff will rely on one approach or another depending on the evidence in the case.

The law applies to all racial/ethnic groups in the population, but certain minority racial/ethnic groups are recognized in the civil rights legislation as **protected** groups. These groups are Hispanics, blacks, Asian and Pacific Islanders, and American Indians. In other words, the principal unprotected group is non-Hispanic whites, who are used for comparison in arguments of disparate impact cases. These groups are more fully described in Chapters 3 and 8.

Several types of evidence have been assembled to prove discrimination in the housing market, but the most carefully designed and convincing are those that use the method of **matched applicants** or matched testers. In the principal version of the method, the matched applicants apply in person for available housing units. The studies pair white and black applicants or testers who otherwise have equal qualifications as renters or owners of housing units and track their separate experiences in seeking to apply for the same housing units. The Housing Discrimination Study, a national fair housing audit study sponsored by HUD, used the method of matched testers in measuring the extent of housing discrimination in 25 metropolitan areas in 1989.[35] It provides evidence of widespread discrimination in housing. The study showed that the probability of unfavorable treatment at some stage in the housing transaction was 46% for black renters, 43% for Hispanic renters, 50% for black homebuyers, and 45% for Hispanic homebuyers.

A pilot study conducted by Massey and Lundy (1999) tested the hypothesis that much racial discrimination occurs without any personal contact between landlords and applicants.[36] It is based on the assumption that the race of the speaker can be inferred from linguistic clues alone, providing landlords and rental agents the opportunity to discriminate over the telephone from the speech patterns of applicants. In this study, native speakers of middle-class white English, black-accented English, and black English vernacular applied by telephone for available housing units in the Philadelphia metropolitan area and their treatment was compared. The researchers found strong and persistent racial discrimination, especially of lower-class black women. Compared with other groups, lower-class black women experience greater hurdles in moving through the process and are more likely to be denied access to rental housing.

Discrimination in mortgage lending on the basis of sex or race was also made illegal by the 1968 act. It has been alleged that there is racial discrimination in awards of mortgages even by public agencies. HUD has been the defendant in many housing discrimination cases, including an east Texas lawsuit involving 36 counties and 70 housing projects (*Washington Post*, November 5, 1993). Reports covering experience under the 1992 Home Mortgage Disclosure Act indicate that disparities in the treatment of the races in the award of mortgages persist. Data from more than 9000 lenders showed that 36% of blacks and 36% of Hispanics were denied home purchase loans in 1992, while the figure for whites was only 16%. The denial rate for blacks in the highest income bracket, 21%, was identical to the rate for whites in the lowest income bracket.

Environmental Equity

Questions of environmental equity have arisen with respect to the location of undesirable facilities, stores, and billboard advertisements in areas where particular demographically defined groups live. It is sometimes claimed that such structures are disproportionately located in "black" neighborhoods and that, thereby, society is supporting the practice of "environmental racism." Specifically, questions have been raised with respect to the adverse effects on the health of racial minorities resulting from the allegedly frequent location of power lines, nuclear waste disposal sites, and other such facilities in rural areas where poor blacks live. Questions of environmental equity have also arisen with respect to the alleged targeting of undesirable commercial products to blacks, such as locating billboards with cigarette advertisements and liquor stores in predominantly black neighborhoods.

Environmental equity would require that, in determining the location of undesirable facilities, no particular population group bear a disproportionate burden in terms of the number and types of undesirable land uses or adverse health effects. Several studies have concluded that racial discrimination plays an important role in the siting of waste dump sites, nuclear power plants, and other locally unwanted land uses.[37] However, a national study of the location of hazardous waste treatment, storage, and disposal facilities (TSDFs), using census-tract-level data, conducted by Anderton *et al.* (1994), concluded that race was not a significant factor in their location.[38] According to this study, when tracts containing TSDFs are compared with tracts that do not contain TSDFs, no significant difference in the percentage of the population that is black was found. The one variable that was found to be significant with respect to TSDF location, after the effect of other independent variables was removed, was the percentage of the population in manufacturing occupations. Other demographic categories than race and ethnicity may be affected by decisions regarding use of the environment. For example, the location of undesirable facilities may place an unequal burden on poor, less educated, and less skilled persons, whether black, Hispanic, or white, and on the rural poor, in particular.

Businesses providing services or making products that affect the natural environment are subject to many regulations relating to their use of the environment. These regulations may limit the proximity of their operations to residential populations and their use of natural products. The regulations may affect the businesses' ability to expand their workforce and to modify the occupational makeup of an area as needed to augment the scope of their operations. In considering the location of a nuclear power plant or a waste disposal dump, for example, the present and prospective number and geographic proximity of the local population, its socioeconomic characteristics, the possible impact of the facility on the health of the local population, and the possible effect on the local labor force—all need to be evaluated. Carefully crafted and comprehensive population projections in radial zones around the proposed location of the plant need to be prepared as part of this evaluation. Demographers may be called on to collaborate in the preparation of environmental impact statements detailing the demographic, social, and economic effects of a proposed, existing, or expanded facility.

Change in the use of an area's environment may affect the proportion of the area's population in the labor force, its unemployment ratio, and the occupational distribution of the labor force. A lumber company may be legally prohibited from expanding or even continuing its operations in an area because of their effect on an endangered species, with the concomitant effect of limiting the employment opportunities in the area. The general issue is usually described as one of jobs versus environmental degradation. The community may depend on a particular industry to provide jobs, either because unemployment is high or because it would be high if the local plant reduced or terminated its operations. Often the very people whose environment is adversely affected support the expansion of industrial operations in an area because of the economic opportunity it provides. The community may have met national pollution standards and the government may have been providing incentives to industry for economic development and job expansion in the particular area. Some associated questions arise: Will the operation be a health hazard? Will local people get the new jobs in view of the possibility that they may lack the necessary skills? Will some racial minority be adversely affected to a disproportionate degree, balancing unfavorable land uses against favorable land uses, in comparison with the experience of other communities in the area? St. James parish in Louisiana has been facing these issues as a Shintec plastic complex is planning to establish a petrochemical plant in the parish at a location closer to the black neighborhoods than the white neighborhoods. The black community is divided on the matter for the reasons mentioned here.

Antitrust and Other Regulatory Areas

The growth of various industries is regulated by the federal government, the states, and local jurisdictions on the basis of current estimates and projections of the need for their products and services by consumers. The regulation may aim to restrict competition or protect it. The federal government can disallow the merger of certain companies in particular industries and withhold the issuance of licenses. In administering federal antitrust legislation, for example, the Federal Trade Commission can either disallow or approve the merger of Office Depot and Staples, two giant office-product chains. The Federal Communications Commission controls the issuance of licenses to operate radio and television stations, and the Federal Reserve Board controls the establishment of new banks. State laws restrict the entry of new firms into certain industries or prohibit the expansion of old firms in these industries. Many types of businesses are subject to special regulations in one state or another, including automobile dealerships, banks, cable television companies, electric utilities, hospitals, and nursing homes. Taxi companies, liquor stores, restaurants, and other types of businesses are subject to local regulation.

In these industries firms cannot freely establish a new outlet in a new area or expand as they choose. They must first obtain approval from the appropriate regulatory agencies. The state regulatory agencies typically grant approval or deny it on the basis of estimates and projections of community need. In estimating and projecting the level of need, the actual and prospective output of current providers is compared with the actual and prospective consumption of the product or service. On the basis of this comparison, the regulatory agency can determine the need, if any, for an additional outlet to meet current or future demand through expansion of an existing firm or entry of a new firm into certain businesses.

In the determination of the need for services and products, estimates and projections of population size and characteristics for some designated area are almost always required. This requirement applies especially to services and products calling for large and expensive facilities, such as hospitals, nursing homes, automobile dealerships, and gambling casinos. For each type of business, some unit of measurement of supply and demand is needed. For health facilities, the unit of measurement of supply and demand is the number of beds per 1000 population. Similar measures can be applied to other businesses.

An example of the application of population estimates and projections in the regulation of a business by a state is given by Smith (1994) relating to automobile dealerships in Florida.[39] Automobile dealers are separate businesses but they operate under agreements with the manufacturers as to certain conditions of sale. In most states, the establishment of a new dealership is restricted by state law for the purpose of protecting existing dealers from competition in the same market area. Such a law exists in Florida. The market area is defined geographically in terms of political units such as counties or in terms of radial distances, and demographically in terms of the population of the trading area. The example given by Smith describes the judicial review of a demand by an automobile dealership, for a given line of automobiles in Northern Dade County, to oppose the establishment in the area of a new dealership by the manufacturer selling the same line of automobiles. The Florida

Department of Highway Safety and Motor Vehicles conducts an administrative hearing in which each of the interested parties, namely, the manufacturer, the proposed dealer, and the opposing dealer, presents its case.[40]

The plaintiff must show at the outset that he or she has **standing**. In general, this means that he or she is an appropriate plaintiff in the case, as shown by the distance between the location of his or her dealership and the location of the proposed dealership, and the size of the population in the market area. In a more legalistic statement of this case, the plaintiff must demonstrate prospective injury to his or her business and the role of the new dealership in causing that prospective injury. In Florida the burden of proving that a new dealership is needed is placed on the defendant—the manufacturer in this case. Estimates and projections of population size for the trading area are indispensable for making the case regarding the need for the new dealership. Information on the social and economic characteristics of the population in the trading area may also be important. The main task of the plaintiff, through his or her demographic expert, is to describe the trading area of the new dealership in terms of geographic boundaries, current and prospective population, sales, distance from competitors, and related variables, setting the ground for a demonstration that the new dealership will pose a severe competitive disadvantage to the plaintiff. The expert for the defendant must provide similar data for the other side.

Note that the demographic experts are retained as advocates for opposing sides in an adversarial proceeding. The issue of the conflict between advocacy and professionalism is apparent. The possibility of bias is heightened by the fact that each expert is beholden to one of the adversaries and not to the court.

APPLICATIONS OF DEMOGRAPHIC TECHNIQUES TO CONSUMER BEHAVIOR, SERVICES, AND PRODUCTS

Many standard demographic techniques are applicable to the analysis of consumer behavior, business services, and manufactured products. I illustrate these applications first with the use of two well-known demographic techniques, cohort analysis and standardization, in the study of consumer behavior. Neither of these has been widely employed in business analysis. Then I present some applications to manufactured products, including the use of life tables.

Cohort Analysis and Standardization

Cohort analysis can be an important tool in understanding changes in consumer behavior as a cohort gets older. A general problem is to analyze shifts over time in the consumption of a product for the purpose of planning the advertising budget and program and projecting demand for the product. Consider, for example, the following question: Will the proportion of a given cohort of new college graduates who subscribe to *Time* magazine persist as the cohort ages? The question is important since the answer would have a bearing on the relative share of advertising to be directed to new college graduates and college graduates at various other ages. To answer the question, it is useful to try to determine the relative contributions of cohort, age-cycle, and period effects on changes in subscriptions (see Chapter 1). Specifically, we want to ascertain the relative role of age-cycle and period influences on the differences in the proportions for recent cohorts of college graduates suscribing to *Time* magazine and the relative role of cohort and period influences on changes in the proportions of subscribers at the same ages over recent decades.

Reynolds and Rentz (1981) conducted an analysis of the consumption of various products by various age groups over the period 1930 to 1980, disaggregating the changes and differences into age, period, and cohort effects on the basis of Palmore's (1978) method.[41] Rentz, Reynolds, and Stout (1983) employed a different method, namely multiple regression, to separate cohort, age, and period effects in a study of soft-drink consumption from 1910 to 1970.[42] If soft-drink consumption declines with age in a given year, it may not mean that age is a major determinant of soft-drink consumption but only that the newer cohorts are consuming more and more soft drinks. If cohort effects are stronger than period and age effects, one conclusion is that the aggregate sales of soft drinks will not necessarily fall because of the aging of the population. On the other hand, if age is an important determinant, the increasing share of elderly could offset, in its effect on the annual sales, any tendency for the newer cohorts to buy more soft drinks.

Standardization is another demographic technique useful in business analysis, particularly as an analytic and interpretive tool in the comparison of markets (see Chapter 1). It may be used, for example, to disaggregate the diffference in the overall consumption rates (e.g., units sold per 100,000 population 21 years and over) for a product in two areas into two factors, namely age composition and age-specific consumption rates. In this way we can determine the extent to which the difference in age composition of the two areas may have contributed to the difference in the overall consumption rates of the two areas. The consumption of many products varies greatly with age. If a market analyst wants to understand why the proportion of the population consuming a particular product is greater in one county than another, he or she could begin by asking whether the age-specific patterns of consumption and the age composition of the two counties differ. Pol and Tymkiw (1991) provided an example in which they compared two markets with regard to beer consumption.[43] Beer is a product whose consumption varies greatly with age. The two markets varied by age composition as well as by age-specific rates of beer consumption. Accordingly, calculation of age-adjusted rates of beer consumption for the two areas—a measure that eliminates the effect of the difference between the two areas in age composition-is useful in measuring the separate contribution of each factor. The results of the calculation of such age-adjusted measures for two or more areas may change the relative market standing of the areas and suggest a change in marketing strategy. Incorporation of sex composition and other variables into the calculations would contribute to the analysis, but standardization for several variables becomes relatively complicated (see Chapter 1).

Disaggregation of rates and proportions can also be a valuable tool in making projections of consumer behavior. Such disaggregation in projections is appropriate when consumption patterns and age composition are expected to change in the future and it is feasible to develop separate assumptions regarding their future changes.

Applications to Manufactured Products

The characteristics of humans that make demographic measures applicable to them are shared by most manufactured items. A large number of units of a product, such as automobiles, railway ties, and electric lamps, are manufactured in a given year, put into service, continued in use until broken or destroyed through wear or obsolescence, and then discarded. Accordingly, we can speak of a "population" of each of these manufactured items and of its "birth" rate, "death" rate, and "morbidity" rate. We can follow it as a real or synthetic cohort over part or all of its life course and construct a life table for it, charting its survival history and calculating its average length of life, as we do for humans (see Chapter 1). In the following illustrations, we apply some common techniques of fertility, mortality, and morbidity measurement to analyze auto repairs and to develop life tables for automobiles, auto batteries, and household furnishings. We can make the logical transformation from products to persons by considering the manufacture or sale of new automobiles as analogous to births, auto accidents and auto repairs as analogous to injuries and sickness (or morbidity), loss of use (or removal) of vehicles by theft, obsolescence, destruction by fire, flood, or accident, and charitable contribution as analogous to deaths, and trade-ins as analogous to a death and a birth or, alternatively, a change in socioeconomic status. Auto repair rates and removal rates are analogous to morbidity rates and death rates, respectively.

Repair Rates for Products on Warranty[44]

In the following example, we assume that the warranty on new cars produced by one manufacturer extends for 12 months or 12,000 miles, whichever comes first. Accordingly, we have "full" records on repairs of these automobiles during the first year after sale or up to the mileage limit. With some effort, we can obtain date of production, date sold, date of repair, type of repair, and order of repair (first, second, etc.) for all the records or for a sample of the records.

The first-year repair rate is analogous in form to an **infant morbidity rate**:

First-year repair rate in model year y

$$= \frac{\text{Warranty repairs in model year } y}{\text{Automobiles built in model year } y} \times 100 \quad (10)$$

This measure has several limitations in informing us about the risk of repairs to autos built in model year y within the first year after sale. During the warranty period, loss of use occurs but, since mileages are still quite low, it is a negligible factor. We have not allowed for it, therefore. Formula 10 does not represent a true cohort rate or probability although it approximates one. Not all repairs are covered by warranty. There are other limitations to the measure. There are several types of "nonreports." Some cars under warranty are not brought to the dealer for repair; the problem is neglected or repaired elsewhere. Some defects in autos under warranty are repaired at the dealer after the warranty period has expired (i.e., the mileage or time limit has been reached) and repair is no longer covered by the warranty. Some defects under warranty appear after the first year. In effect, the repair data may be **censored** by time or mileage, or both.

Next, cars built in model year y may not be sold immediately or even within the model year, and so are not all subject to the risk of repair in the model year. Hence, as in the case of the conventional infant mortality rate, the denominator is not exactly the population exposed to the risk represented in the numerator. In this case, the denominator, the number of automobiles built in year y, is not the number of automobiles exposed to the risk of repair in year y within the 12-month warranty period. Some automobiles under warranty in model year y were sold in the previous model year ($y - 1$) and some automobiles sold in the current model year y will still be under warranty in the following model year ($y + 1$). Since a large share of the repairs required in model year y will be made soon after the purchase of the automobile, most automobiles needing repairs in year y were sold in year y. However, since there is another bunching of repairs at the tail end of the warranty year, many warranty repairs would be made on cars sold in the previous model year. One way to deal with this situation is to employ **separation factors**, which divide the warranty repairs in model year y between the cars sold in year y and the cars sold in year $y - 1$. The rate could then be structured as follows:

Adjusted first-year repair rate in year y $\qquad\qquad\qquad\qquad$ (11)

$$= \frac{\text{Warranty repairs in model year } y \times 100}{[(f) \times \text{new cars sold in year } y + (1 - f) \times \text{new cars sold in year } y - 1]}$$

where f and $1 - f$ are the proportions of new cars repaired in model year y that were sold in year y and year $y - 1$, respectively. Note that this formula mixes repairs to cars *built* in, possibly, three model years (i.e., y, $y - 1$, and $y - 2$).

Rates for "Birth" Cohorts

The adjusted first-year repair rate shown is an approximation to the probability of new car warranty repairs. Another alternative is at hand. We can relate all warranty repairs to cars *built* in model year y, whether the repairs occurred in year y, year $y + 1$, or year $y + 2$, to model year y cars *sold* in year y and year $y + 1$:

Probability of first-year repairs $\qquad\qquad\qquad\qquad\qquad\qquad$ (12)

$$= \frac{\text{Warranty repairs of model year } y \text{ cars in years } y, y + 1, \text{ and } y + 2}{\text{Model year } y \text{ cars sold in years } y \text{ and } y + 1}$$

These relations are depicted in Figure 6.7 in the form of a Lexis diagram. The formula is

$$P_r = \frac{R'_y + R''_{y+1} + R'_{y+1} + R''_{y+2}}{S_y + S_{y+1}} \qquad (13)$$

The elements in this equation are restricted to cars built in year y. The symbols are defined as part of Figure 6.6.

Data on the number of new automobiles built and sold each month by model year and on the number of repairs by model year made under warranty

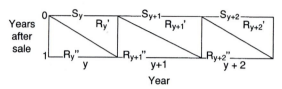

where R_y' = Repairs in year y to cars sold in year y
R_{y+1}'' = Repairs in year y+1 to cars sold in year y
R_{y+1}' = Repairs in year y+1 to cars sold in year y+1
R_{y+2}'' = Repairs in year y+2 to cars sold in year y+1
S_y = Cars sold in year y
S_{y+1} = Cars sold in year y+1
and where *all* four cells defined here and *all* six definitions refer to cars built in year y.
The S's are represented by the horizontal line segments and the R's are represented by tri-
angular areas. The figure does not depict magnitudes but only the relationship of time and age.

FIGURE 6.6   Lexis diagram of relationship among automobiles built in year y, sold in year y or $y + 1$, and repaired in year y, $y + 1$, or $y + 2$.

each month, tabulated by month of manufacture and sale of the vehicle, provide the basis for calculating the rate of repair of new vehicles by number of
months since the sale (i.e., repair rates for monthly birth cohorts). The repair
rates may be designed to show for each month of manufacture and sale of
the cars the rate of repairs over 3-month, 6-month, and 12-month periods. An
analysis of such data would indicate how the repair rate for a given crop of
new cars varies as the period of use of the vehicles increases. This information is extremely important to the automobile company in identifying design
problems so that they can be corrected early in the model year. According
to her analysis of the data on the repair history of monthly cohorts of new
models, Frohardt-Lane (1987, *op. cit.*) found that new models tend to require
many repairs in the early months of use, fewer and fewer repairs as the model
is improved in later months, and, then, as the one-year warranty comes to
an end, an increased number of repairs once again (see Figure 6.7). The rise
toward the end of the warranty period may be due in whole or part to the
accumulation of repairs, which car owners hurry to claim before the year runs
out. The availability of month-of-sale data for new cars and of month-of-repair
data according to date of sale means that we can compile data for true cohorts,
and separation factors are not needed to compute the cohort warranty repair rate.

Some automobiles are returned more than once for the same repair or for
different repairs. To deal with the issue of multiple repairs for the same or
different problem in a given vehicle, the repairs can be tabulated by type of
repair and order of repair—first, second, and third and higher. The cases of
different repairs with the same vehicle (i.e., cases of **comorbidity**) should be
tabulated and analyzed separately. Questions can then be answered, such as
which defects occur alone and which occur in combination, what is their relative frequency, which defects require repeat visits, and how are the individual
defects and combinations of defects related to the age (in months) of the vehicle? Cohort warranty repair rates can be calculated by type of repair, order
of repair, and type and order jointly, for birth cohorts cumulated for months
of age.

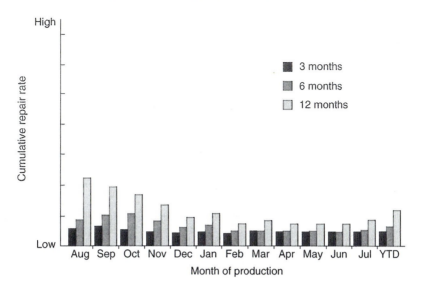

YTD: Year-to-date average.
Note: 1985 models. Data limited to cars that have been sold.

FIGURE 6.7 Cumulative 3-month, 6-month, and 12-month repair rates, for birth cohorts of automobiles by month of production, for each month from August 1984 to July 1985. *Source:* Katharine A. Frohardt-Lane. "On the application of demographic techniques to the analysis of vehicle warranty data," in David A. Swanson and Jerry W. Wicks (eds.), *Issues in Applied Demography: Proceedings of the 1986 National Conference,* Bowling Green, OH: Bowling Green State University, 1987. © Population and Society Research Center, Bowling Green State University. Reprinted with permission.

Total Repair Rate

Let us consider next the possibility of calculating a **total repair rate** (*TRR*), representing the average number of repairs per automobile during the lifetime of a cohort of automobiles. This measure is analogous in form to the total fertility rate—that is, the (age-adjusted) average number of births to a group of women during their lifetime. The total repair rate should be based on annual repair rates according to the age of the automobile, but data are not available to calculate such a measure. If, however, we restrict ourselves to the one-year warranty period and use rates for one-month periods of age, we can derive an age-adjusted measure of the average number of repairs under warranty per automobile (i.e., during the first year).

For this purpose, first calculate the age-specific repair rates for each month of the year, using (1) the data on repairs of cars by month of age since the sale date and (2) the number of automobiles in use by months since the sale date. An age-specific (i.e., 1st-month, 2nd-month, 3rd-month, etc.) repair rate (r_a) is analogous in form to an age-specific annual birth or death rate:

Age-specific repair rate (r_a)

$$= \frac{\text{Repairs } a \text{ months since the sale}}{\text{New cars in use } a \text{ months since the sale}} \times 100 \qquad (14)$$

Next, add these rates up from the lowest ages to the highest ages, to derive the cumulative rate of repairs up to the 12th month. This sum represents the first-year average number of repairs per automobile (TRR):

$$TRR = \sum_{0}^{11} r_a \qquad (15)$$

If the rates for successive months of age (under 1 month, 2 month, etc.) and successive calendar months are combined, we have the total repair rate for a *real cohort*. If the monthly rates for the same (calendar) month and successively older ages (in months) are combined, we have a first-year total repair rate for a *synthetic cohort*. It would be more accurate to make an allowance for the mortality of the automobiles between the date of sale and the current date in the denominators of the age-specific rates, though the effect would be small.

The total lifetime repair rate can be calculated if the manufacturer or other party conducts a longitudinal sample survey of automobile owners or automobiles over the lifetime of the automobiles. Less feasible would be the collection of repair data from a sample of dealers and the countless repair shops. Such a survey would present major problems of sample loss and censored data resulting from change of ownership and mobility of owners. A cross-sectional household survey, gathering data on major automobile repairs in the preceding year and the age of the vehicle, would be a more feasible study.

Life Tables

Given data on a manufactured product's "removals" according to age and date of removal, and the distribution of the product according to age, we can prepare a set of age-specific death rates for the product. From the set of death rates, we can calculate a life table for the product. Calculation of life tables for manufactured products has a long history. Dublin, Lotka, and Spiegelman (1949) described the application of life tables to physical property in their classic book on the life table, *Length of Life*.[45] They cite several studies of this type, which go back to the early part of the 20th century. In a series of studies, published about 1930, Kurtz and Winfrey presented survival curves for such property items as telephone switchboards, telephone poles, electric lamps, locomotives, railway ties made from different woods, automobiles, submarine cables, and agricultural machines.[46]

According to Dublin *et al.*, life table analysis of manufactured products has several uses. First, it gives us a generalized description of the life history of a manufactured product and a measure of its expected life. Next, it charts the distribution of time for the replacements necessary as the original stock wears out and permits a more informed basis for maintenance of the property and projection of the need for replacement. Finally, it makes possible the equitable amortization of the cost of property over the period of useful service, indicates the extent of depreciation of the item for tax or sale purposes, and suggests the desirable period for bond issues.

Automobiles and Auto Parts

Life tables for automobiles and auto parts (e.g., batteries) can be prepared if we can generate the required age- or duration-specific "death" rates. If the rates are compiled for a particular year, a life table charting the survival history of a synthetic cohort of automobiles or an auto part can be constructed. To derive the required death rates for automobiles, for example, we need data on the number of automobiles in use at midyear and the number of automobiles removed from use during the year, each distributed by age (i.e., years since they were first sold as new or put into use). The number removed from use includes autos permanently retired because of theft, charitable donation associated with "old age" or "disability"of the auto, destruction by accident or natual disaster, and unserviceability.

The data in state files on the number of registered automobiles can be used to represent the number of automobiles in use ("population"). In practice, the analyst would take a sample of the records for a sample of states. The registration records show the year of manufacture and year of sale of the automobiles, and hence permit their classification by "age." The total number removed from use during a year can be estimated as a residual by first taking the difference between the number of automobiles registered in 2 successive years (A_1 and A_2), subtracting the number of new automobiles sold in the year (S), and allowing for those shipped overseas after being purchased and registered here (E) and those imported into the country and registered here (I):

$$(-)W = [A_2 - A_1] - S - [I - E] \tag{16}$$

where W, the automobiles removed from use, will normally be negative. The reader should recognize this equation in its standard form (see Chapter 1, equation 1).

$$(-)D = [P_2 - P_1] - B - [I - E] \tag{17}$$

Alternatively, the records can be combed for information on automobiles for which license plates have been returned or owners' registration has not been renewed.

With the appropriate information, age-specific removal rates can be calculated and employed as basic data for constructing the life table. From the age-specific removal rates, probabilities of being removed can be derived. Then, the number of automobiles surviving to each age and the number of remaining years of automobile life at birth and at each later age, for a cohort of 100,000 automobiles, can be computed. The estimated life table median age (i.e., the age corresponding to $1/2T_0$) of automobiles, an age-adjusted measure, may then be compared with the observed median age of automobiles. By comparing life tables for different dates, we can answer questions such as these: Are the automobiles on the streets older on the average than they were a decade ago? Is a greater share of automobiles on the streets more than 10 years old? Is the median age of removal changing?

A similar type of calculation can be used to derive the average life of a battery or other auto part. The number of registered automobiles would provide a measure of auto batteries in use. The number of batteries retired during a year (W) can be approximated by taking the difference between the number of automobiles registered (i.e., batteries in use) at the beginning (A_1) and end of the year (A_2), subtracting the number of new batteries (N) and the number of new automobiles sold (S) during the year, subtracting the number of new batteries and new automobiles imported and sold here (I), and adding the number of new batteries and new automobiles bought here and exported (E), during the year:

$$(-)W = [A_2 - A_1] - [S + N] - [I - E] \tag{18}$$

For life table construction, these data must be disaggregated by years of age.

Manufacturers are interested in forecasting the level of repairs, planning the cost of repairs, and planning the production of replacement parts. For forecasting the future rate of automobile repairs after the warranty period or for forecasting product reliability in general, various studies have shown that the "lives" of mechanical components often follow a Weibull distribution.[47] On this basis, repair data can be projected from warranty data over the lifetime of the mechanical part (e.g., 100,000 miles for automobiles). The demographic techniques described are all useful for the purposes mentioned, especially life table analysis. However, year-to-year changes in model design can be an important factor to be considered in applying current repair rates and current life tables for forecasting.

Household Goods

Economists concerned with family budgets and manufacturers and distributors concerned with how often consumers enter and return to the market are quite interested in data on the service-life expectancy of household goods under one owner. In the 1950s, Pennick and Jaeger (1957) applied actuarial methods to data obtained from household surveys to derive measures of the service-life expectancy of a variety of household goods.[48] Such calculations were carried out for living-room curtains and draperies, living-room sofas and couches, tables in living rooms, living-room rugs and carpets, refrigerators, cookstoves, and radios.

Table 6.1 shows a truncated life table for curtains and draperies in the living room of a sole owner. The basic data for this table were obtained from household sample surveys in which current or prior ownership of the item, year of purchase, and age of the item removed or replaced were ascertained. Age-specific removal rates were applied to a hypothetical cohort of living-room curtains and draperies, assumed to start service simultaneously, reducing it from its starting size at the beginning of its service life to zero at the end, when all items in the starting cohort have been retired or replaced. The age-specific removal rates (q_x) necessary for constructing the life table were derived from data on the inventory and discards of the curtains and draperies by age as reported in the survey.

To simplify the construction of the table, all items were assumed to have been acquired on January 1 of the year of acquisition. In effect, this assumption eliminated the need for converting central removal rates (m_x's) to probabilities of removal (q_x's). The units exposed to risk of removal were obtained by combining the units in the inventory and the units removed. The removal rate then became the ratio of the units removed to the units exposed to risk.

Except for the removal rates, the table is constructed like a conventional life table. The other functions of the table were derived sequentially from the removal rates: The number of units surviving to each age (l_x), the years of service in each age (L_x), the aggregate number of years of service (T_x), and

■ **TABLE 6.1**   Truncated Life Table for Living-Room Curtains and Draperies under One Owner

Age (in years) (1)	Units in inventory[a] (2)	Units removed in year (3)	Units exposed to risk of removal (2)+(3)= (4)	Removal rate (q_x) (3)/(4) = (5)	Survival rate (p_x) (1)−(5)= (6)	Number surviving to age x (l_x) (7)	In age x (L_x) (8)	In age x and later ages (T_x) (9)	Service-life expectancy (e_x) (10)
								Years of service	
0	205	0	205	0	1.0000	1000	1000.0	6830.0	6.83
1	154	24	178	.1348	.8652	1000	932.5	5830.0	5.83
2	102	16	118	.1356	.8644	865	806.5	4897.5	5.66
3	105	20	125	.1600	.8400	748	688.0	4091.0	5.47
4	65	10	75	.1333	.8667	628	586.0	3403.0	5.42
5	21	2	23	.0870	.9130	544	520.5	2817.0	5.18
6	49	10	59	.1695	.8305	497	455.0	2296.5	4.62
7	22	12	34	.3529	.6471	413	340.5	1841.5	4.46
8	12	0	12	0	1.0000	267	267.0	1501.5	5.62
9	10	0	10	0	1.0000	267	267.0	1234.5	4.62
24	4	0	4	0	1.0000	27	27.0	41.5	1.53
25	0	4	4	1.0000	0	27	14.5	14.5	0.54
26	0	0	0	0	0	0	0	0	0

Note: 197 households in the Wilmington urbanized area within Delaware, 1954. Sample data have not been smoothed. Units represent number of curtain and drapery panels.

[a] All items assumed to have been acquired on January 1 of year of acquisition. Excludes units removed during the year.

Source: Based on Jean L. Pennick and Carol M. Jaeger, "Estimating the service life of household goods by actuarial methods," *Journal of the American Statistical Association* 52(278): 175–185, June 1957.

the average number of years remaining for the members of the cohort (e_x). In this experience, the time the article remains in use from age zero, or the mean service-life expectancy, is 6.8 years, the quotient of 6830 and 1000. At age 2, mean service-life expectancy is 5.7 years, the quotient of 4898 (T_2) and 865 (l_2).

Compilation of the data for calculating a life table for household goods presents numerous problems, such as the reporting of out-of-scope removals (i.e., removals that took place outside the period for which such data were sought), failure to report a removal that took place within the period for which removal data were sought, failure to report the age of the items in the inventory and of the items removed, and inexact reporting of age for both items in the inventory and removals. According to Pennick and Jaeger, there is clear evidence of a tendency to understate removals. Many families cannot remember the former appearance of the room and so cannot report what has been removed. There is a basis for suspicion when the age distributions of various household furnishings are very similar but their service-life expectancies are very different.

Finally, two general principals are worth bearing in mind. Since, under the usual conditions of household use, furnishings and equipment are discarded before they reach a state of absolute unserviceability, service-life expectancy rates for periods of economic prosperity, when replacement is easy, will be lower than those for periods of economic recession or depression. Second, it should be recognized that the life table model assumes similarity of products by year of introduction and this assumption is difficult to realize when constructing a conventional life table based on cross-sectional data for many cohorts.

APPENDIX A: SOURCES OF ECONOMIC DATA

Much of the data used in business planning come from the Censuses of Population and Housing and the Economic Censuses. For current national data, several sample surveys—namely, the Current Population Survey, the Survey of Income and Program Participation, the American Housing Survey, and the Survey of Retail and Wholesale Trade—are important primary sources. The *Survey of Current Business* and the *Statistical Abstract of the United States* are important secondary sources, mainly for national data. For current subnational data, the *County and City Data Book,* the *State and Metropolitan Area Data Book,* and *County Business Patterns,* all published by the U.S. Census Bureau, are important secondary sources. They are systematic compilations of series of subnational data on a wide range of subjects of interest to business analysts. For example, the *State and Metropolitan Area Data Book,* which has been published intermittently since 1979, presents data for states, metropolitan areas, and metropolitan counties on a great variety of subjects, including civilian labor force and unemployment (compiled by the Bureau of Labor Statistics from its "Local Area Unemployment Statistics—Time Series" and other sources), and data on personal income (compiled by the Bureau of Economic Analysis from its "Regional Economic Information System").

Currently the Censuses of Population and Housing (1990) and the economic censuses (1997 and 1992) tabulate data for only one type of area that may be considered distinctively economic: zip code areas. The 1990 census sample data were summarized by five-digit zip codes on computer tape and compact disk (CD-ROM). Zip code data from the economic censuses of 1992 and 1997 are also available on CD-ROM.[49]

Private companies may delineate their own marketing areas on the basis of census-defined geographic areas. The Arbitron Company, which rates various television companies and television programs on the basis of their audience listenership, defines areas of dominant influence (ADIs). These are television marketing areas composed of several neighboring counties centered around a major metropolitan area. The A. C. Nielsen Company, another television rating company, defines designated marketing areas (DMAs) in a similar fashion.

Data on numerous demographic and socioeconomic variables that influence the profitability of local stores and services are available from the decennial censuses of population and housing. The analyst needs data for small areas such as counties, census tracts, block groups, and blocks to deal with the problem. Little or nothing is currently available for such areas from the large federal or private national sample surveys, which at most provide usable data for the United States, large states, and large metropolitan areas. As explained in Chapter 3, a new and important source of detailed population and socioeconomic data for small areas will become available in the latter part of the first decade of the 21st century, when the American Community Survey becomes fully operational.[50] A limited range of data for subnational areas are made available through the current estimates programs of the Census Bureau, the Bureau of Economic Analysis, and the Bureau of Labor Statistics, and through commercial data-vending companies, which make forecasts for such areas as well as current estimates.

Some measures that are useful for determining consumer demand for a variety of products and that can be obtained for census tracts from the 1990 and 2000 censuses are listed in Figure 6.A.1. Since both 100% data and sample data were tabulated for census tracts, the sources in terms of summary tape files (STFs) differ for the various measures. The list of subjects and measures is relatively short for blocks, for which only 100% data were tabulated, and relatively long for counties, for which both sample data and 100% data are available from the STFs. The range of subjects for census tracts is intermediate. In general, if we think of census tracts as a proxy for neighborhoods, the demographer has access to a wide range of data for neighborhoods from the census, including numbers of persons, families and households by type and size, housing by value and tenure, employment by occupation and industry, racial and ethnic composition, income distribution, and educational level.

The economic censuses of 1997, 1992, and earlier provide information for retail and wholesale businesses on four indicators of business activity (namely, volume of sales in dollars, number of establishments, number of employees, and payroll), by type of business, for various subnational areas. For example, each state report from the Census of Retail Trade shows data for the state, metropolitan areas, counties and county-equivalents, and incorporated places of 2500 or more. Table 6.A.1 shows illustrative data for Billings, Montana, and Billings, Montana, MSA, for the four indicators of business activity, for a selection of categories of businesses, in 1997. These data are taken from the 1997 Census of Retail Trade and are based on information collected from

---

FIGURE 6.A.1   **Some Measures Available for Census Tracts in 1990 and 2000 Censuses of Population and Housing**[a]

Percentage poor households (S)
Percentage female-headed households (C)
Percentage high school graduates (S)
Percentage Hispanic or race other than white (C)
Median family income (S)
Percentage homeowners (C)
Percentage homes with incomplete plumbing facilities (S)
Median value of owner-occupied homes (C in 1990; S in 2000)
Median gross contract rent for rental units (C in 1990; S in 2000)

Source: U.S. Bureau of the Census, 1990 Censuses of Population and Housing, and public documents relating to the plans for the 2000 census.

[a] C and S identify 100% (C) or sample (S) data.

TABLE 6.A.1 Census-of-Retail-Trade Data on Establishments, Paid Employment, Sales, and Payroll, by Kind of Business, for Billings, MT, and Billings, MT, MSA, 1997: Illustrative Segments (Includes Only Establishments with Payroll; an Establishment Is a Company Operation at a Single Location)

NAICS code	Kind of business	Establishments (number)	Sales ($1000)	Annual payroll ($1000)	Paid employees for pay period including March 12 (number)	Percentage of sales— From administrative records[a]	Estimated[b]
	Billings, MT [segment]						
44–45	Retail trade—Con.						
443	Electronics & appliance stores	30	30,536	4,995	249	4.3	3.1
4431	Electronics & appliance stores	30	30,536	4,995	249	4.3	3.1
44311	Appliance, television, & other electronics stores	22	21,958	3,731	175	5.0	4.1
443111	Household appliance stores	7	12,604	2,040	90	6.0	4.9
443112	Radio, television, & other electronics stores	15	9,352	1,691	85	3.6	2.9
44312	Computer & software stores	7	D	D	[d]	D	D
443120	Computer & software stores	7	D	D	[d]	D	D
444	Building material & garden equipment & supplies dealers	59	144,439	14,461	666	6.7	.5
4441	Building material & supplies dealers	51	D	D	[e]	D	D
44411	Home centers	4	40,959	4,180	230	—	.6
444110	Home centers	4	40,959	4,160	230	—	.6
44412	Paint & wallpaper stores	5	4,090	556	20	—	3.7
444120	Paint & wallpaper stores	5	4,090	556	20	—	3.7
44413	Hardware stores	5	D	D	[d]	D	D
444130	Hardware stores	5	D	D	[d]	D	D
44419	Other building material dealers	37	73,722	7,191	253	11.6	.5
444190	Other building material dealers	37	73,722	7,191	253	11.6	.5

(continues)

TABLE 6.A.1 (continued)

NAICS code	Kind of business	Establishments (number)	Sales ($1000)	Annual payroll ($1000)	Paid employees for pay period including March 12 (number)	Percentage of sales— From administrative records[a]	Percentage of sales— Estimated[b]
4442	Lawn & garden equipment & supplies stores	8	D	D	d	D	D
44422	Nursery & garden centers	8	D	D	d	D	D
444220	Nursery & garden centers	8	D	D	d	D	D
445	Food & beverage stores	35	D	D	e	D	D
4451	Grocery stores	27	D	D	e	D	D
44511	Supermarkets & other grocery (except convenience) stores	25	158,796	15,634	936	5.9	.7
445110	Supermarkets & other grocery (except convenience) stores	25	158,796	15,634	936	5.9	.7
4452	Specialty food stores	5	D	D	c	D	D
4453	Beer, wine, & liquor stores	3	D	D	c	D	D
44531	Beer, wine, & liquor stores	3	D	D	c	D	D
445310	Beer, wine, & liquor stores	3	D	D	c	D	D
446	Health & personal care stores	44	37,935	5,030	272	5.1	.6
4461	Health & personal care stores	44	37,935	5,030	272	5.1	.6
44611	Pharmacies & drug stores	14	21,811	2,185	126	.3	.9
446110	Pharmacies & drug stores	14	21,811	2,185	126	.3	.9
4461101	Pharmacies & drug stores	11	21,387	2,085	117	—	.9
4461102	Proprietary stores	3	424	100	9	13.2	—
44612	Cosmetics, beauty supplies, & perfume stores	5	2,395	291	21	—	—
446120	Cosmetics, beauty supplies, & perfume stores	5	2,395	291	21	—	—

(continues)

TABLE 6.A.1 (*continued*)

NAICS code	Kind of business	Establishments (number)	Sales ($1000)	Annual payroll ($1000)	Paid employees for pay period including March 12 (number)	Percentage of sales— From administrative records[a]	Estimated[b]
44613	Optical goods stores	13	4,137	986	48	24.5	.4
446130	Optical goods stores	13	4,137	986	48	24.5	.4
44619	Other health & personal care stores	12	9,592	1,568	77	8.9	—
446191	Food (health) supplement stores	5	D	D	d	D	D
446199	All other health & personal care stores	7	D	D	d	D	D
447	Gasoline stations	61	85,589	5,292	445	6.7	8.3
4471	Gasoline stations	61	85,589	5,292	445	6.7	8.3
44711	Gasoline stations with convenience stores	45	65,711	3,867	349	3.2	7.2
447110	Gasoline stations with convenience stores	45	65,711	3,867	349	3.2	7.2
44719	Other gasoline stations	16	19,878	1,425	96	18.2	12.0
447190	Other gasoline stations	16	19,878	1,425	96	18.2	12.0
448	Clothing & clothing accessories stores	99	58,209	6,618	647	5.3	8.7
4481	Clothing stores	61	37,041	4,038	439	6.1	6.2
44812	Women's clothing stores	26	9,823	1,177	152	13.9	15.6
448120	Women's clothing stores	26	9,823	1,177	152	13.9	15.6
44813	Children's & infants' clothing stores	3	1,699	401	40	—	—
448130	Children's & infants' clothing stores	3	1,699	401	40	—	—

(*continues*)

TABLE 6.A.1 (*continued*)

NAICS code	Kind of business	Establishments (number)	Sales ($1000)	Annual payroll ($1000)	Paid employees for pay period including March 12 (number)	Percentage of sales— From administrative records[a]	Percentage of sales— Estimated[b]
44814	Family clothing stores	18	20,091	1,852	174	4.0	3.8
448140	Family clothing stores	18	20,091	1,852	174	4.0	3.8
44815	Clothing accessories stores	3	741	111	11	—	—
448150	Clothing accessories stores	3	741	111	11	—	—
44819	Other clothing stores	7	2,537	188	28	3.0	—
448190	Other clothing stores	7	2,537	188	28	3.0	—
4482	Shoe stores	22	11,079	1,364	101	.8	—
44821	Shoe stores	22	11,079	1,364	101	.8	—
448210	Shoe stores	22	11,079	1,364	101	.8	—
4482101	Men's shoe stores	4	D	D	e	D	D
4482104	Family shoe stores	12	5,733	804	56	1.5	—
4482105	Athletic footwear stores	5	3,280	308	30	—	—
4483	Jewelry, luggage, & leather goods stores	16	10,089	1,216	107	7.5	27.7
44831	Jewelry stores	16	10,089	1,216	107	7.5	27.7
448310	Jewelry stores	16	10,089	1,216	107	7.5	27.7
	Billings, MT, MSA [segment]						
443	Electronics & appliance stores	30	30,536	4,995	249	4.3	3.1
4431	Electronics & appliance stores	30	30,536	4,995	249	4.3	3.1
44311	Appliance, television, & other electronics stores	22	21,958	3,731	175	5.0	4.1
443111	Household appliance stores	7	12,604	2,040	90	6.0	4.9

(*continues*)

TABLE 6.A.1 (continued)

NAICS code	Kind of business	Establishments (number)	Sales ($1000)	Annual payroll ($1000)	Paid employees for pay period including March 12 (number)	Percentage of sales— From administrative records[a]	Estimated[b]
44312	Computer & software stores	7	D	D	D [d]	D	D
443120	Computer & software stores	7	D	D	[d]	D	D
444	Building material & garden equipment & supplies dealers	69	169,022	16,294	770	6.0	.6
4441	Building material & supplies dealers	58	137,627	14,503	664	7.3	.7
44419	Other building material dealers	42	82,818	8,439	303	10.3	.7
444190	Other building material dealers	42	82,818	8,439	303	10.3	.7
4442	Lawn & garden equipment & supplies stores	11	31,395	1,791	106	.1	—
44422	Nursery & garden centers	11	31,395	1,791	106	.1	—
444220	Nursery & garden centers	11	31,395	1,791	106	.1	—
445	Food & beverage stores	43	185,878	17,806	1,110	6.6	.6
4451	Grocery stores	34	D	D [f]	D	D	
446	Health & personal care stores	50	41,910	5,431	299	6.1	1.5
4461	Health & personal care stores	50	41,910	5,431	299	6.1	1.5
44612	Cosmetics, beauty supplies, & perfume stores	5	2,395	291	21	—	—
446120	Cosmetics, beauty supplies, & perfume stores	5	2,395	291	21	—	—
44619	Other health & personal care stores	15	10,318	1,663	84	9.2	4.1
447	Gasoline stations	78	125,568	7,149	574	5.0	18.3
4471	Gasoline stations	78	125,568	7,149	574	5.0	18.3
44711	Gasoline stations with convenience stores	57	78,765	4,574	405	3.4	13.1
447110	Gasoline stations with convenience stores	57	78,765	4,574	405	3.4	13.1

(continues)

TABLE 6.A.1 *(continued)*

NAICS code	Kind of business	Establishments (number)	Sales ($1000)	Annual payroll ($1000)	Paid employees for pay period including March 12 (number)	Percentage of sales—From administrative records[a]	Estimated[b]
448	Clothing & clothing accessories stores	99	58,209	6,618	647	5.3	8.7
4481	Clothing stores	61	37,041	4,038	439	6.1	6.2
44819	Other clothing stores	7	2,537	188	28	3.0	—
448190	Other clothing stores	7	2,537	188	28	3.0	—
4483	Jewelry, luggage, & leather goods stores	16	10,089	1,216	107	7.5	27.7

D: Withheld to avoid disclosing data of individual companies; data are included in higher level totals.

[a] Includes sales information obtained from administrative records of other federal agencies.

[b] Includes sales information which was imputed; based on historic company ratios or administrative records, or on industry averages.

[c] 0 to 19 employees.

[d] 20 to 99 employees.

[e] 500 to 999 employees.

[f] 1000 to 2499 employees.

Source: U.S. Bureau of the Census, *1997 Economic Census, Retail Trade,* "Geographic Area Series: Montana," June 1999, Tables 2 and 4.

TABLE 6.A.2 Administrative-Records Data on Establishments, Employment, and Payroll, by Kind of Business, for Baltimore City, MD, Baltimore County, MD, and Baltimore, MD PMSA in 1997: Illustrative Segments

SIC code[a] Major group	Number of employees for week including March 12	Payroll ($1000), Annual	Total number of establishments	Number of establishments by employment-size class[b]								
				1 to 4	5 to 9	10 to 19	20 to 49	50 to 99	100 to 249	250 to 499	500 to 999	1000 or more
Baltimore, MD PMSA—Segment												
Retail trade	206,397	3,181,889	13,818	5,647	3,273	2,349	1,659	585	264	37	4	—
52 Building materials and garden supplies	7,421	142,073	431	174	110	72	44	13	15	3	—	—
53 General merchandise stores	(J)	(D)	273	60	45	42	18	21	67	19	1	—
54 Food stores	30,830	499,470	1,478	541	337	265	148	104	82	1	—	—
55 Automotive dealers and service stations	19,444	495,353	1,334	467	383	277	123	59	22	3	—	—
56 Apparel and accessory stores	(J)	(D)	1,192	424	420	253	81	10	2	1	—	—
57 Furniture and homefurnishings stores	7,764	160,800	966	508	286	107	40	18	7	—	—	—
58 Eating and drinking places	71,769	698,076	4,200	1,537	757	688	873	289	50	6	—	—
59 Miscellaneous retail	30,825	505,458	3,749	1,887	895	609	297	53	7	1	—	—
— Administrative and auxiliary	7,128	291,408	195	49	40	36	35	18	12	3	2	—
Finance, insurance, and real estate	77,293	3,238,655	6,041	3,448	1,270	721	354	137	72	25	9	5
60 Depository institutions	18,593	642,297	1,111	327	396	269	76	20	10	10	1	2
61 Nondepository institutions	(I)	(D)	584	288	149	70	44	16	15	1	1	—
62 Security and commodity brokers	5,685	573,910	344	211	67	23	26	10	3	1	3	—
63 Insurance carriers	(J)	(D)	464	250	55	46	55	32	17	6	—	3
64 Insurance agents, brokers, and service	7,831	292,210	1,128	848	145	71	40	14	7	2	1	—
65 Real estate	17,413	459,812	2,169	1,371	431	215	97	38	16	2	1	—
67 Holding and other investment offices	3,246	152,215	217	144	23	23	14	8	2	—	2	—
— Administrative and auxiliary	(G)	(D)	24	9	3	4	2	1	2	3	—	—
Services	395,065	11,396,336	24,221	13,867	4,623	2,830	1,734	584	396	114	40	33

(continues)

TABLE 6.A.2 (*continued*)

SIC code[a] / Major group	Number of employees for week including March 12	Payroll ($1000), Annual	Total number of establishments	\<10pt\>								
				Number of establishments by employment-size class[b]								
				1 to 4	5 to 9	10 to 19	20 to 49	50 to 99	100 to 249	250 to 499	500 to 999	1000 or more
70 Hotels and other lodging places	8,141	143,834	212	77	20	40	40	13	13	8	1	—
72 Personal services	13,929	195,170	1,937	1,085	458	261	112	13	6	2		—
73 Business services	78,318	2,159,654	4,283	2,574	636	423	331	165	108	28	15	3
75 Auto repair, services, and parking	12,348	279,217	1,708	940	454	221	75	10	4	4		—
76 Miscellaneous repair services	4,833	141,295	664	434	114	66	36	11	2	1		—
78 Motion pictures	(H)	(D)	354	183	56	82	25	8	—			—
79 Amusement and recreation services	11,810	310,615	776	411	93	105	117	38	9	2	1	—
80 Health services	126,654	3,888,533	4,990	2,664	1,223	568	265	93	105	31	16	25
81 Legal services	(I)	(D)	1,686	1,244	235	125	62	12	6	2		—
82 Educational services	31,943	886,122	480	188	71	67	74	40	31	3	3	3
83 Social services	25,976	441,892	1,545	659	319	276	188	49	42	12		—
84 Museums, botanical, zoological gardens	1,417	27,353	47	18	12	7	3	2	4	1		—
86 Membership organizations	19,209	305,825	1,989	1,061	439	286	140	46	13	4		—
87 Engineering and management services	43,312	1,908,371	3,286	2,175	454	277	241	75	43	16	3	2
89 Services, n.e.c.	1,212	52,849	166	125	17	9	10	3	2			—
— Administrative and auxiliary	3,232	164,195	98	29	22	17	15	6	8		1	—
— Unclassified establishments	283	9,500	425	411	9	4	1		—			—
Baltimore County—Segment Retail trade	70,786	1,101,841	4,349	1,617	1,087	801	519	208	101	14	2	—

(continues)

273

TABLE 6.A.2 (continued)

SIC code[a]	Major group	Number of employees for week including March 12	Payroll ($1000), Annual	Total number of establishments	Number of establishments by employment-size class[b]								
					1 to 4	5 to 9	10 to 19	20 to 49	50 to 99	100 to 249	250 to 499	500 to 999	1000 or more
52	Building materials and garden supplies	2,581	51,200	133	48	37	26	10	6	4	2	—	—
521	Lumber and other building materials	1,840	37,975	61	18	14	15	4	5	3	2	—	—
525	Hardware stores	231	3,604	25	11	9	4	—	1	—	—	—	—
526	Retail nurseries and garden stores	407	7,401	30	12	6	6	5	—	1	—	—	—
53	General merchandise stores	8,205	104,155	98	18	13	16	7	8	28	7	1	—
531	Department stores	7,032	86,940	44	3	—	2	—	8	23	7	1	—
533	Variety stores	265	3,255	30	7	9	11	3	—	—	—	—	—
539	Misc. general merchandise stores	908	13,960	24	8	4	3	4	—	5	—	—	—
54	Food stores	10,285	182,635	445	127	122	90	43	33	30	—	—	—
541	Grocery stores	9,120	170,504	289	57	84	54	32	32	30	—	—	—
542	Meat and fish markets	175	2,103	25	11	8	3	3	—	—	—	—	—
546	Retail bakeries	593	5,709	58	20	13	19	5	1	—	—	—	—
549	Miscellaneous food stores	177	2,320	31	16	10	3	2	—	—	—	—	—
55	Automotive dealers and service stations	7,107	186,657	395	131	115	88	25	24	9	3	—	—
551	New and used car dealers	4,515	138,863	58	6	2	2	12	24	9	3	—	—
552	Used car dealers	133	3,250	29	21	4	3	1	—	—	—	—	—
553	Auto and home supply stores	795	17,303	83	21	33	21	8	—	—	—	—	—
554	Gasoline service stations	1,458	22,160	202	73	73	53	3	—	—	—	—	—
555	Boat dealers	125	2,824	14	6	2	5	1	—	—	—	—	—
	Baltimore (IC)—Segment												
	Retail trade	40,027	575,330	3,562	1,791	767	492	368	106	34	4	—	—
52	Building materials and garden supplies	869	18,711	71	35	18	7	7	3	1	—	—	—
521	Lumber and other building materials	626	14,675	33	12	11	2	4	3	1	—	—	—
523	Paint, glass, and wallpaper stores	117	2,413	12	6	2	2	2	—	—	—	—	—

(continues)

274

TABLE 6.A.2 (*continued*)

SIC code[a]	Major group	Number of employees for week including March 12	Payroll ($1000), Annual	Total number of establishments	Number of establishments by employment-size class[b]								
					1 to 4	5 to 9	10 to 19	20 to 49	50 to 99	100 to 249	250 to 499	500 to 999	1000 or more
53	General merchandise stores	1,017	11,326	56	20	16	11	3	2	4	—	—	—
531	Department stores	593	6,286	5	—	—	—	—	1	4	—	—	—
533	Variety stores	305	3,325	33	10	10	10	2	1	—	—	—	—
539	Misc. general merchandise stores	119	1,715	18	10	6	1	1	—	—	—	—	—
54	Food stores	6,764	91,248	436	229	65	56	52	24	9	1	—	—
541	Grocery stores	5,809	80,500	308	161	33	43	37	24	9	1	—	—
542	Meat and fish markets	275	3,437	40	19	15	2	4	—	—	—	—	—
546	Retail bakeries	442	4,648	47	20	13	7	7	—	—	—	—	—
55	Automotive dealers and service stations	2,885	70,740	239	98	77	38	12	11	3	—	—	—
551	New and used car dealers	1,389	47,131	19	2	—	2	3	9	3	—	—	—
552	Used car dealers	114	2,744	31	19	10	2	—	—	—	—	—	—
553	Auto and home supply stores	282	6,234	46	21	17	6	2	—	—	—	—	—
554	Gasoline service stations	1,050	13,222	135	51	50	25	7	2	—	—	—	—
56	Apparel and accessory stores	2,521	30,256	343	145	103	76	16	3	—	—	—	—
561	Men's and boys' clothing stores	330	4,419	48	26	9	10	3	—	—	—	—	—
562	Women's clothing stores	793	7,512	97	29	31	29	8	—	—	—	—	—
564	Children's and infants' wear stores	140	1,569	14	7	—	6	1	—	—	—	—	—
565	Family clothing stores	456	5,086	46	13	16	13	2	2	—	—	—	—
566	Shoe stores	559	8,395	95	43	39	11	2	—	—	—	—	—
569	Misc. apparel and accessory stores	148	1,980	22	13	5	3	—	1	—	—	—	—
57	Furniture and homefurnishings stores	835	17,049	148	85	43	15	4	1	—	—	—	—
571	Furniture and homefurnishings stores	487	10,946	76	42	20	11	2	1	—	—	—	—
5712	Furniture stores	291	7,442	37	19	10	6	1	1	—	—	—	—
5719	Misc. homefurnishings stores	121	1,593	23	13	6	3	1	—	—	—	—	—
573	Radio, television, and computer stores	325	5,867	65	38	21	4	2	—	—	—	—	—
5731	Radio, TV, and electronic stores	117	2,652	30	21	8	1	—	—	—	—	—	—
5735	Record and prerecorded tape stores	164	1,929	25	12	9	2	2	—	—	—	—	—

(*continues*)

275

TABLE 6.A.2 (continued)

SIC code[a]	Major group	Number of employees for week including March 12	Payroll ($1000), Annual	Total number of establishments	Number of establishments by employment-size class[b]								
					1 to 4	5 to 9	10 to 19	20 to 49	50 to 99	100 to 249	250 to 499	500 to 999	1000 or more
58	Eating and drinking places	16,839	179,166	1,292	627	241	171	194	44	12	3	—	—
5812	Eating places	15,533	166,855	1,020	432	195	151	184	43	12	3	—	—
5813	Drinking places	1,306	12,292	270	193	46	20	10	1	—	—	—	—
59	Miscellaneous retail	7,167	125,066	954	547	203	114	75	13	2	—	—	—
591	Drug stores and proprietary stores	2,730	52,324	169	31	37	48	45	8	—	—	—	—
592	Liquor stores	328	11,308	241	191	35	12	3	—	—	—	—	—
593	Used merchandise stores	510	10,094	66	34	20	4	7	—	1	—	—	—
594	Miscellaneous shopping goods stores	1,291	17,621	223	136	51	25	10	1	—	—	—	—
5942	Book stores	236	2,449	34	21	5	6	2	—	—	—	—	—
5944	Jewelry stores	270	5,138	60	40	14	6	—	—	—	—	—	—
5947	Gift, novelty, and souvenir shops	517	5,997	78	44	20	8	5	1	—	—	—	—
596	Nonstore retailers	514	11766	66	37	14	10	3	2	—	—	—	—
5962	Merchandising machine operators	115	3,229	22	15	2	5	—	—	—	—	—	—
5963	Direct selling establishments	329	6,747	29	13	9	2	3	2	—	—	—	—
598	Fuel dealers	284	6,166	14	4	4	1	3	1	—	—	—	—
599	Retail stores, n.e.c.	860	15,787	175	114	42	14	4	1	1	—	—	—
5992	Florists	257	3,400	42	27	5	8	2	—	—	—	—	—
5995	Optical goods stores	117	2,090	33	23	10	—	—	—	—	—	—	—
5999	Miscellaneous retail stores, n.e.c.	409	9,306	81	52	21	5	2	1	—	—	—	—
—	Administrative and auxiliary	1,130	31,768	23	5	1	4	5	5	3	—	—	—

Note: Covers establishments with payroll. An establishment is a company operation at a single location. These industry tabulations exclude most government employees, railroad employees, and self-employed persons. Size class 1 to 4 includes establishments having payroll but no employees during mid-March pay period. D denotes figures withheld to avoid disclosing data for individual companies; the data are included in broader industry totals.

Note: Employment-size classes are indicated as follows: A—0 to 19; B—20 to 99; C—100 to 249; E—250 to 499; F—500 to 999; G—1000 to 2499; H—2500 to 4999; I—5000 to 9999; J—10,000 to 24,999; K—25,000 to 49,999; L—50,000 to 99,999; M—100,000 or more.

[a] Based on 1987 Standard Industrial Classification.

[b] Employees are for the week including March 12.

Source: U.S. Bureau of the Census, *County Business Patterns, 1997,* "Maryland," 1999.

establishments by the Census Bureau. As mentioned, additional economic data for subnational areas are available in the *County and City Data Book,* the *State and Metropolitan Area Data Book,* and *County Business Patterns.* Table 6.A.2 shows illustrative data from *County Business Patterns* for Baltimore City (county-equivalent), Baltimore County, and Baltimore PMSA, Maryland in 1996. Data for three indicators of business activity (namely, establishments, employment, and payroll), for a selection of kinds of businesses are presented. These data are based on administrative records provided by the Internal Revenue Service and the Social Security Administration to the Census Bureau. The latter records in turn are based on records submitted by individual companies to these agencies. More detailed and more current data are shown in *USA County, 1998,* an electronic product of the Census Bureau available on the Internet. The data in Tables 6.A.1 and 6.A.2 are not comparable because of the difference in the collection systems used and the difference in the industry classification systems (NAICS versus SIC).

The statistical compendia of the Census Bureau named earlier contain a wealth of data on nondemographic items for metropolitan areas, counties, and cities. These data are otherwise scattered in numerous sources, both public and private. Finally, reference should be made to the *Statistical Abstract* of an individual state for detailed series of data pertaining to that state and its geographic subunits. All states publish such abstracts or their equivalents.

APPENDIX B: SOME DEMOGRAPHIC ASPECTS OF DOMESTIC AND FOREIGN INVESTMENT

Domestic Investment

Tracking demographic changes should be a leading concern af investment planners. Investment planners have two populations to observe, namely, the actual/potential investors in the investment products they offer and the actual/potential consumers of products and services marketed by the companies in which they have invested funds or may advise clients to invest funds. Investment planners need to ascertain the demographic and socioeconomic characteristics of persons who make investments in the stock, bond, or mutual fund markets, as an aid in identifying likely investors in these types of investment products.[51] The buyers and sellers who participate in the stock and bond markets have demographic characteristics that affect their willingness and ability to buy and sell shares of a particular company's stocks and bonds.

Investment planners and investors also need to identify customers of various types of businesses in terms of their demographic and socioeconomic characteristics in order to evaluate the prospects for growth of these businesses. In addition, demographic changes have a marked influence on the prospects for growth of many businesses and hence on the value of a wide range of stocks. Accordingly, investors and investment management firms should invest funds in companies that can capitalize on current or prospective demographic trends. Perhaps investment companies should have demographic consultants on their staffs or at least have access to them.

Since U.S. society is aging, it seems wise to target companies now that support the emerging needs of an aging saciety. One should look for firms engaged in developing and marketing products and services useful for elderly persons. An illustration of an investment firm that has such a demographic orientation is Phoenix Funds (now Phoenix Investment Partners). As described in its 1997 *Annual Report,* Phoenix Funds sees "aging in America" as a strategic theme, which it defines as a broad trend affecting the investment environment and expected to last 5 years or more. It sees "21st century medicine" as a tactical theme under the umbrella of this strategic theme. Phoenix Funds believes that health care for the elderly population is and will continue to be a growth industry. Within the tactical theme of "21st century medicine," there are various microthemes, such as assisted living, which involves investment in living facilities that provide health care for the elderly population. Supporting this view are the many developments under way in the health care industry, such as production of biotechnology products, research on noninvasive surgical procedures, cost management of health care, and information-automation services.[52]

Many social trends go through a sort of life cycle. The social trends that can be identified as themes of demographic growth are likely to transcend economic cycles and are not likely to be subject to the volatility that stocks experience. The individual investor can take advantage of social or demographic change by investing in groups of stocks or mutual funds (i.e., groups of stocks managed as a single fund) defined by one or more emerging demographic themes, such as health care services, products, and financing.

Foreign Investment

The success of foreign businesses and hence investment prospects abroad are affected by demographic conditions and changes abroad, as are the prospects of U.S. companies doing business abroad. As stated in Chapter 2, in many less developed countries (LDCs), current population changes resemble those in the more developed countries (MDCs) with a lag of several decades. Prospective investors should examine the demographic situation in each region or country separately since it varies from region to region and country to country, but the general trends noted apply to a large number of countries. They foreshadow rapid growth in demand for many products and services, such as telephone services, mass transportation, household appliances, casual clothes, pharmaceuticals, and entertainment. Demand for telephone services and household appliances, for example, is closely associated with increases in the number of households, per capita income, educational level, urbanization, and industrialization.

Many of the products and services that the United States adopted only a few decades ago, such as fast food restaurant services, television sets, automobiles, and telephone equipment, are now being widely adopted in the LDCs. The rapid growth in the teenage population, the number of Western tourists, and the proportion of working women, in particular, is expected to create a boom in demand for fast-food restaurants in the LDCs. The business person can take advantage of this situation by setting up franchises in such countries, buying a franchise for operating such businesses, or providing supplies to existing franchises. The telephone companies could profit from the tremendous potential for growth of telephone services in some areas. For example, the per capita use of telephone service in economically expanding Mexico is far below that of the United States; hence, there is the opportunity for rapid growth of telephone use in Mexico in the coming years, as has occurred in South Korea. The investor can take advantage of the growth situation offered in these countries by investing in local manufacturers, importers, distributors, and providers of the products and services showing demographically driven growth.

The overseas expansion of major U.S. corporations is based on many of the same considerations as those involved in overseas investment in foreign companies by U.S. professional and individual investors. A substantial portion of sales of many U.S. companies (e.g., 3M, Eastman Kodak, Bristol-Myers Squibb, Ford, Exxon, Philip Morris, Microsoft, and IBM) are made in foreign countries, and the list is expected to grow in the future. While economic, political, legal, cultural, and demographic factors all play a part in the decision as to the time, place, and extent of the overseas business expansion, data on the demographic characteristics and the purchasing power of the overseas population are fundamental in selecting markets.

Table 2.A.7 presented several measures of the demographic situation in countries with a population exceeding 30 million inhabitants in 1999 on a country-by-country basis. As the reader may recall, the LDCs are growing much more rapidly than the MDC. Some European countries are losing population and some LDCs have annual growth rates in excess of 2.5%. The LDCs have a great potential for market growth because of their tremendous population size, their huge population growth, and their unfilled need for many products. On the other hand, their per capita income is low and they cannot purchase many goods and services that they need. Part of the basis for the low per capita income in the LDCs is the large proportion of the population which is under age 15, a far higher proportion than in the MDCs.

Even in the LDCs, particular market segments for certain products and services may still support increased demand in the future. Some products and services are sought by fast-growing age segments in the LDC population. Cell phones, for example, are typically purchased by younger, more affluent urban residents, whose numbers are increasing rapidly in some LDCs. Only a few Chinese can afford private cars currently, but car ownership is increasing very rapidly in China.

The movement into the overseas market of the Bristol-Myers Squibb Company, a firm engaged in pharmaceuticals, hair care, over-the-counter medicines, nutritional products, and medical devices, illustrates a business response taking overseas demographic changes into account. In view of the rapid growth of the population in the LDCs, the rising level of living in many of them, and the outlook for a considerable increase in the per capita consumption of health and beauty products in most overseas regions, the company has continued in recent years to "globalize [its] businesses by investing in emerging markets" in Central and Eastern Europe, China, and Latin America.[53] UPSA Medica, part of Bristol-Myers Squibb Consumer Medicines Group, has been actively mining a number of global markets inside and outside those in Central and Eastern Europe, including Russia. In Russia, a successful advertising campaign has been based on the fact that 80% of the households have television sets.

Caution against Demographic Determinism

In spite of the emphasis here on the role of demographic factors in business expansion, consumer markets, and investment, the reader is cautioned against taking a doctrinaire position of demographic determinism in interpreting industrial growth and market changes here and abroad. Demographic trends represent only one of several factors that affect the economies of foreign countries and the investment situation in them. As with domestic markets, the gross size of a market is important, but so are the purchasing power of the population, their wants, needs, and tastes, and a host of other nondemographic factors. Investment plans in an LDC should take into account the country's stage of economic development, its political maturity, and its political stability, as well as its demographic trends and prospects.

Population size favors populous countries such as China and India as overseas markets, but such economic factors as the rate of economic growth, interest rates, relative stock valuations, and relative currency values limit the role of population size and other demographic factors. A lack of diversification in the foreign economy and a decline in the prices of traditional exports may completely offset the effect of demographic influences. These factors may prevent an expected economic boom for a product or service from occurring. Some possibly positive demographic trends, such as extremely rapid growth of the population, may inhibit positive economic growth in already poor countries. Negative demographic trends, such as the rise in death rates in many countries of sub-Saharan Africa, can be a cause of political instability. These demographic, political, and economic factors may keep per capita income from rising or cause it to fall.

Profits may also be restrained by other factors. Foreign investors may not profit even from economies that are growing rapidly. Government regulations may limit foreign investment in various industries or the currency of the country may decline to the same degree as, or to a greater degree than, stock prices rise. In the latter case, the domestic investor can profit from his or her investment while the foreign investor does not.

Prospective long-term demographic changes combine with short-term-demographic changes to determine the role of demographic factors in consumer markers and investment prospects. Even if the influence of demographic trends on consumer and investment markets is taken into account, current demographic information has limited utility since some demographic trends may require a long period to unfold. When the demographic factors are consistently favorable, they generally augur a favorable long-term future outcome for investments. Nondemographic factors are likely to have a much greater influence on consumer markets and investments in the short run than will demographic factors.

NOTES

1. For further discussion of consumer behavior, see Houston G. Elam and Norton Paley, *Marketing for Nonmarketers: Principles and Tactics That Everyone in Business Must Know*, New York: American Management Association, 1993, Chapter 5.

2. The classification system used in the 1970 census and the CPS prior to 1983 were sharply different from the 1980 classification system, and the data compiled from the two classifications are not comparable.

3. The NAICS was implemented in consultation with Canada and Mexico in order to develop common standards for industrial classification in their import and export statistics. The data gathered in the 1997 economic census are being compiled so as to permit tabulations according to both the SIC system and NAICS.

4. The concepts of race and Hispanic origin are treated in Chapter 3, geographic areas in Chapter 5, poverty and education in Chapter 7, and labor force and employment in Chapter 8.

5. Data on group quarters are provided by the decennial census but are excluded from the national sample household surveys such as the Current Population Survey.

6. The Census Bureau discourages use of the phrases female head and male head for householders with no spouse present and refers to them as female householder and male householder. The phrases are used interchangeably here.

7. U.S. Bureau of the Census, "Household and family characteristics: March 1997," *Current Population Reports*, P20–509, 1998.

8. The definition of income employed in SIPP is approximately the same as in CPS. However, the definition of personal income employed by the Bureau of Economic Analysis (BEA) is different. For example, personal income includes various types of nonmoney income, is estimated largely on the basis of existing government records, and has a broader population coverage. The BEA income series is of interest to demographers because it is produced for areas as small as counties on a current basis, unlike income from CPS or SIPP.

9. U.S. Bureau of the Census, "Money income in the United States: 1997," *Current Population Reports*, Series P60-200, 1998, Table A.

10. An excellent discussion on buying and selling on the Internet is given in Lawrence A. Canter and Martha S. Siegel, *How to Make a Fortune on the Information Highway*, New York: HarperCollins, 1994.

11. Steven V. Haar, "Web metrics: Go figure," *Business 2.0*, June 1999, pp. 46–47; James Ryan, "Your online shadow knows," *Business 2.0*, June 1999, pp. 49–55.

12. John Berrigan and Carl Finkbeiner, *Segmentation Marketing: New Methods for Capturing Business Markets*, New York: HarperCollins, 1992.

13. U.S. Bureau of the Census, *Current Construction Reports*, Series C50, *Expenditures for Residential Improvements and Repairs, Fourth Quarter Report, 1997*.

14. Numerous illustrations of such demographic-economic interconnections can be found in the proprietary magazine *American Demographics*, published monthly by Intertec Publishing Company, Stamford, CT.

15. U.S. Bureau of Labor Statistics, *Consumer Expenditures in 1995*, 1997; Jacob S. Siegel, *A Generation of Change: A Profile of America's Older Population*, New York: Russell Sage Foundation, 1993, Tables 8.23 and 8.24.

16. This can be demonstrated by comparing indexes of dissimilarity calculated on the basis of data for census tracts of a city for age (e.g., under 65 and 65 and over) and for race (white non-Hispanic and other).

17. George G. C. Parker and Edilberto L. Segura, "How to get a better forecast," *Harvard Business Review* 49: 99–109, March/April 1971.

18. A short introductory reference for regression analysis is Michael S. Lewis-Beck, *Applied Regression: An Introduction*, Sage University Paper No. 22, Beverly Hills: Sage, 1980. A more recent and comprehensive reference is Alexander von Eye and Christof Schuster, *Regression Analysis in the Social Sciences*, New York: Academic Press, 1998. The multiple linear regression equation is now often formulated and manipulated in terms of matrix algebra. See John E. Freund, Irwin Miller, and Mary Lees Miller, *Mathematical Statistics*, 6th ed., Upper Saddle River, NJ: Prentice-Hall, 1999.

19. Kenneth M. Johnson, "Selecting markets for corporate expansion: A case study in applied demography," pp. 129–143, in Hallie J. Kintner et al. (eds.), *Demographics: A Casebook for Business and Government*, Boulder, CO: Westview Press, 1994.

20. To measure the *relative* importance of the variables, however (i.e., to be able to say that variable x_1 has z times the effect of x_2), the input data must be standardized (i.e., expressed in standard deviation units):

$$Y_o^* = (Y_o - \overline{Y}_o)/\sigma_{Y_o}$$

$$x_i^* = (x_i - \bar{x}_i)/\sigma_i$$

where the difference between the value for each variable (x_i) and its mean (x_i) is divided by the standard deviation of the x_i distribution and the Y_o values over all observation units is similarly modified. The resulting weights, called β (beta) coefficients, are in standardized form, as will be the predicted Y_c values.

21. Another measure of success is the average over all markets of the absolute percentage difference between the actual and predicted revenue for each market. Its value in the Welcome case was 20%.

22. It may reasonably be hypothesized that the number of customers at a retail business center is roughly proportional to the size of the center, as measured by the number of business outlets, aggregate sales in dollars, aggregate payroll in dollars, or number of paid employees. In other words, stores in larger centers attract more business. Stores in larger centers may also be expected to have larger trading areas. We may, for example, geographically represent the trading area of a proposed store in a major retail center as proportional in size to the volume of sales of the major retail centers in the area. If we assume a uniform distribution of sales levels for the trading area of one retail center (A) with a 2-mile radius, then the retail center with sales twice as great (B) would be assumed to have a trading area twice as great and a radius of 2.83 miles. More specifically, if circular trading area A has a radius $r_A = 2$ miles and circular trading area $B (= 2A)$ has a radius r_B, then $A = \pi r_A^2 = 4\pi$ and $B = 2A = 2 * 4\pi = 8\pi = \pi r_B^2$ and $r_B = 2.83$. Similarly, if the radius for trading area A is assumed to equal three miles, the radius for trading area B would equal 4.24 miles under the assumption of proportionality of trading areas.

23. $\int_n^{n+1}[1 - (e^{rd} - 1)]dx = 2d - e^{rd}/r]_n^{n+1} = 2(n + 1) - (e^{r(n+1)}/r) - (2n - e^{rn}/r)$

24. For $R_1 = e^{-rd}$, the comparable integral is $(e^{-r(n+1)} - e^{-rn})/ - r$, and the proportion of the population to be considered customers falls off very slowly. For an r of .15, the proportions are .93 within the first mile and .51 within the fifth mile.

Morrison and Abrahamse propose a different exponential decay function to determine the fraction of residents patronizing a combination store (i.e., an ultralarge supermarket) from the surrounding area. This fraction is proportional to $Ne^{-x/\lambda}$, where N is the number of people in the area and λ is a parameter to be fit to the data, like r above. They derive the fraction of all customers drawn from within a circle of radius x around the store as $1 - (1 + x)/\lambda)e^{-x\lambda}$ and then set λ so that this expression equals 0.77 for $x = 2$ miles and 0.96 for $x = 4$ miles. They determined empirically that 77% of such customers reside within two miles of the store and 96% reside within 4 miles. (Note that my cumulative figures for customers within 2 and 4 miles of the site, given in the text minitable, are 65% and 99%, respectively, for $r = .15$. I determined that $\lambda = .71$ if the expression $1 - (1 + x)/\lambda)e^{-x\lambda}$ equals .77 at 2 miles.) The formula can then be used to interpolate to other radial distances and applied to other similar siting situations. Morrison and Abrahamse based their estimate of the number of sales dollars that would accrue to a hypothetical combination store on the number of households within the trading area, their distribution by household size, and their distribution by income. With the distance-decay function, they weighted these characteristics in relation to their proximity to the proposed store location. See Peter A. Morrison and Allan F. Abrahamse, "Applying demographic analysis to store site selection," *Population Research and Policy Review* 15(5–6): 479–489, December 1996.

25. See, for example, Jeffrey Tayman and Louis Pol, "Retail site selection and geographic information systems," *Journal of Applied Business Research* 11: 46–54, 1995.

26. Residential separation or residential differentiation of the races (commonly called "racial segregation") has been measured over a long period almost solely by the index of dissimilarity. Researchers exploring the facets of residential separation of the races have developed many measures of spatial separation. Massey and Denton (1989, 1988) described five dimensions of

spatial separation and provide formulas for measuring them. (See Douglas Massey and Nancy Denton, "Hypersegregation in U.S. metropolitan areas: Black and white segregation along five dimensions," *Demography* **26**: 373–391, August 1989; Douglas Massey and Nancy A. Denton, "The dimensions of residential segregation," *Social Forces* **67**: 281–315, 1988.) They called these dimensions evenness, exposure, clustering, centralization, and concentration. In this construct of the concept, the index of dissimilarity measures evenness. "Evenness is the degree to which the percentage of minority members within residential areas equals the citywide minority percentage." "Exposure is the degree of potential contact between majority and minority members." Their isolation index of exposure is computed as the weighted average of the shares of a minority in a residential area (e.g., census tracts), the weights being the share of the total population in the residential area which is minority:

$$_xP_x^* = \sum_{i=1}^{n} \left|\frac{x_i}{X}\right| \left|\frac{x_i}{t_i}\right|$$

where x_i is the number of the minority in tract i, X is the number of the minority in the city, and t_i is the total population of the tract. Massey and Denton show that blacks are highly "segregated" on each of the five dimensions and that they are more segregated across all five dimensions than other groups (e.g., Hispanics). They call this hypersegregation.

27. Roderick Harrison and Daniel Weinberg, "How important were changes in racial and ethnic segregation between 1980 and 1990?" pp. 61–67, in *Proceedings of the Social Statistics Section*, Alexandria, VA: American Statistical Association, 1992.

28. Terms such as concentration and clustering are used here in their everyday senses, not in the specialized senses employed by some researchers as described in Note 26.

29. Laura E. Harris (Urban Institute), "Understanding racial residential segregation: Considering racial composition in housing industries," unpublished paper presented at the annual meeting of the Southern Demographic Association, Richmond, VA, 1995.

30. William A. V. Clark, "Residential preferences and residential choices in a multi-ethnic context," *Demography* **29**(3): 451–466, August 1992.

31. Lauren J. Krivo and Robert L. Kaufman, "How low can it go? Declining black-white segregation in a multiethnic context," *Demography* **36**(1): 93–109, February 1999.

32. David M. Cutler, Edward L. Glaeser, and Jacob L. Vigdor, "The rise and decline of the American ghetto," *Journal of Political Economy* **107**(3): 455–506.

33. Jacob S. Siegel, "The role of demographers in public and private suits of racial discrimination in housing," pp. 237–252, in K.V. Rao and Jerry W. Wicks, *Studies in Applied Demography: Proceedings of the International Conference on Applied Demography*, Bowling Green State University, Bowling Green, OH, 1994.

34. Government of the District of Columbia, *Human Rights Act of 1977*, Title 1, Washington, DC, 1991, Chapter 25.

35. Margery A. Turner, Raymon J. Struyck, and John Yinger, *Housing Discrimination Study: A Synthesis*, Urban Institute and Syracuse University, August 1991, prepared for the U.S. Department of Housing and Urban Development, Washington, DC.

36. Douglas S. Massey and Garvey Lundy, "Use of black English and racial discrimination in urban housing markets: New methods and findings," *Urban Affairs Review* **36**(4): 452–469, March 2001.

37. U.S. General Accounting Office, "Siting of hazardous waste landfills and their correlation with racial and economic status of surrounding communities," RCED-93-168, 1983; United Church of Christ Commission for Racial Justice, *Toxic Wastes and Race in the United States: A National Report on the Racial and Socioeconomic Characteristics of Communities with Hazardous Waste Sites*, New York: United Church of Christ, 1987; P. Mohai and B. Bryant, "Environmental racism: Reviewing the evidence," pp. 163–176, in B. Bryant and P. Mohai (eds.), *Race and Environmental Hazards: A Time for Discourse*, Boulder, CO: Westview, 1992; and Michael Greenwood and Michal Cidon, "Broadening the definition of environmental equity: A framework for states and local governments," *Population Research and Policy Review* **16**(4): 397–413, August 1997.

38. D. A. Anderton, A. B. Anderson, J. M. Oakes, and M. R. Fraser, "Environmental equity: The Demographics of Dumping," *Demography* **31**(2): 229–248, May 1994.

39. Stanley K. Smith, "Population estimates, projections, and expert testimony in adversarial legal proceedings: A case study of automobile dealerships," pp. 180–202, in Hallie J. Kintner *et al.*, *Demographics: A Casebook for Business and Government*, Boulder, CO: Westview Press, 1994.

40. An administrative hearing is one that takes place before a hearing officer, an administrative law judge, or an administrative commission or panel appointed under the executive branch of government, whereas a judicial hearing is one that takes place before a judge in a federal or state court.

41. F. D. Reynolds and J. O. Rentz, "Cohort analysis: An aid to strategic planning," *Journal of Marketing* 45(2): 62–70, 1981; and E. Palmore, "When can age, period, and cohort be separated?" *Social Forces* 57(5): 282–295, 1978.

42. J. O. Rentz, F. D. Reynolds, and R. G. Stout, "Analyzing changing consumption patterns with cohort analysis," *Journal of Marketing Research* 20(1): 1–12, 1983.

43. Louis Pol and D. Tymkiw, "A technique to compare demographically different markets," *Marketing Research* 3(1): 29–34, 1991.

44. This discussion of the analysis of repair rates for automobiles draws heavily on Katherine A. Frohardt-Lane, "On the application of demographic techniques to the analysis of warranty data," in David A. Swanson and Jerry W. Wicks (eds.), *Issues in Applied Demography: Proceedings of the 1986 National Conference*, Bowling Green, OH: Bowling Green State University, 1987.

45. Louis I. Dublin, Alfred J. Lotka, and Mortimer Spiegelman, *Length of Life: A Study of the Life Table*, New York: Ronald Press Company, 1949. A more recent volume dealing with life tables for manufactured goods is Wayne Nelson, *Applied Life Data Analysis*, New York: John Wiley and Sons, 1982.

46. For example, E. B. Kurtz, *Life Expectancy of Physical Property*, New York: Ronald Press Company, 1930; and E. B. Kurtz and R. Winfrey, "Life Characteristics of Physical Property," Bulletin 103, Iowa Engineering Experiment Station, Iowa State College, Ames, Iowa, 1931.

47. This note gives a brief technical explanation of the form of the Weibull distribution and a reference for further information. The probability density function of a random variable t corresponding to a Weibull distribution is

$$f(t) = \alpha\beta t^{\beta-1} e^{-\alpha t^{\beta}}$$

If the random variable t is the time to failure of a commercial product and $f(t)$ and $F(t)$ are, respectively, the values of its probability density function and its distribution function at time t, the failure rate at time t is defined as

$$\alpha(t) = \frac{f(t)}{1 - F(t)} = \alpha\beta t^{\beta-1}$$

Thus the failure rate at time t is the probability density of failure at time t, given that failure has not occurred prior to time t. With the Weibull distribution, the failure rate is given by $\alpha\beta t^{\beta-1}$, where α and β are parameters to be determined, α being a scale parameter and β being a shape parameter. The exponential model is a special case of the Weibull model where $\beta = 1$; the failure rate is α and is constant.

For further information, see Shiva S. Halli and K. Vaninadha Rao, *Advanced Techniques of Population Analysis*, New York: Plenum Press, 1992, Chapter 8.

48. Jean L. Pennick and Carol M. Jaeger, "Estimating the service life of household goods by actuarial methods," *Journal of the American Statistical Association* 52(278): 175–185, June 1957.

49. In prior years, data were available from the Census of Retail Trade for two geographic areas especially defined for the census, major retail centers and central business districts, but they were discontinued after 1982. A **major retail center** was defined as a concentration of at least 25 retail stores located inside an SMSA but outside the central business district, including a general merchandise center with floor space greater than 100,000 square feet. The **central business district** was defined as the downtown retail area of the central city of an SMSA or other city of 50,000 persons or more; boundaries were set to correspond to census tract boundaries. The International Council of Shopping Centers employs roughly the same concept in defining "shopping centers" (see the *State and Metropolitan Area Data Book, 1997–1998*, Table A-38).

50. The viability of the American Community Survey depends on congressional support for the full-scale operation on an ongoing basis.

51. Comparable consideration could be given to such related investment products as annuities, life insurance, and real estate unit trusts.

52. For a discussion of developments in biotechnology and their relation to investing in the stock market, see Todd G. Buchholz, "Bionic investing," *Worth*, July/August 1999, pp. 68–70.

53. Bristol-Myers Squibb Company, *1996 Annual Report*, pp. 3, 25, and 31.

SUGGESTED READINGS

General

Beresford, John C. (1987). "Use of the Center for International Research's Demographic and Economic Data Base in Applied Business Demography." In David A. Swanson and Jerry W. Wicks, *Issues in Applied Demography: Proceedings of the 1986 National Conference* (pp. 56–67). Bowling Green, OH: PSRC, Bowling Green State University.

Daniels, John, and Radebaugh, Lee. (1986). *International Business*. Reading, MA: Addison-Wesley.

Day, Adrian. (1982, December). "Demographic factors in foreign investment analysis," *International Demographics* 1(9): 3, 10.

Kintner, Hallie J., Merrick, Thomas W., Morrison, Peter A., and Voss, Peter A. (eds.). (1994). *Demographics: A Case Book for Business and Government*, Boulder, CO: Westview Press.

Lazer, William. (1987). *Handbook of Demographics for Marketing and Advertising: Sources and Trends on the U.S. Consumer*, Lexington, MA: Lexington Books, D.C. Heath and Company.

Mercurio, Joseph W. (1987). "Sociology in marketing research." In Joyce M. Iutcovich and Mark Iutcovich, *The Sociologist as Consultant*, Chapter 5, pp. 75–86. New York, Praeger.

Merrick, Thomas W., and Tordella, Stephen J. (1988, February). "Demographics: People and markets," *Population Bulletin* 43(1), Washington, D.C.: Population Reference Bureau.

Murdock, Steven H., and Hamm, Rita R. (1982). *A Guide to Data Sources and Uses for Business and Government*, A Texas State Data Center Publication, No. 2.

Peterson, Robin T. (1997). *Principles of Marketing*. HBJ College Outline Series. New York: Harcourt Brace.

Pol, Louis G., and Thomas, R. K. (1997). *Demography for Business Decision-Making*. Westport, CT: Greenwood Press.

Root, Franklin R. (1987). *Entry Strategies for International Markets*. Lexington, MA: D.C. Health and Company.

Russell, Cheryl. (1983, June). "The Business of Demographics," *Population Bulletin* 38(3), Washington, D.C.: Population Reference Bureau.

U.S. Bureau of the Census. (1980). "Use of census data in business," by Joseph G. Van Matre, Chapter 12 in *Census '80: Factfinder for the Nation*.

U.S. Bureau of the Census. (1989). *Census ABC's: Applications in Business and Community*.

U.S. Bureau of the Census. (1991). *Case Studies in Using Data for Better Business Decisions*, by Kathy V. Friedman and Frank A. Szumilo (eds.).

U.S. Bureau of the Census. (1993). *Taking Care of Business: A Guide to Census Bureau Data for Small Businesses*, by Barbara Hatchl.

Specific Applications

Ambrose, David M., and Pol, Louis G. (1994). "Motel 48: Evaluating the profitability of a proposed business." In Hallie J. Kintner *et al.* (eds.), *Demographics: A Casebook for Business and Government*, pp. 144–154. Boulder, CO: Westview Press.

Anderton, Douglas L., Anderson, A. B., Oakes, J. M., and Fraser, M. R. (1994, May). "Environmental equity: The demographics of dumping." *Demography* 31(2): 229–248.

Anderton, D.L., Anderson, A. B., Rossi, P. H., Oakes, J. M., Fraser, M. R., Weber, E. W., and Calabrese, E. J. (1994). "Hazardous waste facilities: 'Environmental equity' issues in metropolitan areas." *Evaluation Review* 18(2): 123–140.

Billings, George H., and Pol, Louis G. (1994). "Improving cellular market area valuation with demographic data." In Hallie J. Kintner *et al.* (eds.), *Demographics: A Casebook for Business and Government*, pp. 93–108. Boulder, CO: Westview Press.

Clark, W. A. V. (1992, August). "Residential preferences and residential choices in a multi-ethnic context." *Demography* 29(3): 451–466.

Cutler, David M., Glaeser, Edward L., and Vigdor, Jacob L. (1999). "The rise and decline of the American ghetto." *Journal of Political Economy* 107(3): 455–506.

Frohardt-Lane, Katherine A. (1987). "On the application of demographic techniques to the analysis of vehicle warranty data." In David A. Swanson and Jerry Wicks (eds.), *Issues in Applied Demography: Proceedings of the 1986 National Conference*, pp. 94–99. Bowling Green, OH: PSRC Press, Bowling Green State University.

Greenberg, Michael, and Cidon, Michal. (1997, August). "Broadening the definition of environmental equity: A framework for states and local governments." *Population Research and Policy Review* 16(4): 397–413.

Harrison, Roderick J., and Weinberg, Daniel H. (1992). "How important were changes in racial and ethnic segregation between 1980 and 1990?" In *Proceedings of the Social Statistics Section*, pp. 61–67. Alexandria, VA: American Statistical Association.

Johnson, Kenneth M. (1994). "Selecting markets for corporate expansion: A case study in applied demography." In Hallie J. Kintner et al. (eds.), *Demographics: A Casebook for Business and Government*, pp. 129–143. Boulder, CO: Westview Press.

Krivo, Lauren J., and Kaufman, Robert L. (1999, February). "How low can it go? Declining black-white segregation in a multiethnic context." *Demography* 36(1): 93–109.

Logan, J. R., and Alba, R. D. (1993, May). "Locational returns to human capital: Minority access to suburban community resources." *Demography* 30(2): 243–268.

Massey, Douglas, and Denton, Nancy A. (1988). "The dimensions of residential segregation." *Social Forces* 67: 281–315.

Massey, Douglas, and Denton, Nancy. (1989, August). "Hypersegregation in U.S. metropolitan areas: Black and white segregation along five dimensions." *Demography* 26: 373–391.

Mohai, P., and Bryant, B. (1992). "Environmental racism: Reviewing the evidence." In B. Bryant and P. Mohai (eds.), *Race and the Incidence of Environmental Hazards: A Time for Discourse*, pp. 163–176. Boulder, CO: Westview Press.

Murdock, Steven H., and Hamm, Rita R. (1994). "A demographic analysis of the market for a long-term care facility: A case study in applied demography." In Hallie J. Kintner *et al.* (eds.), *Demographics: A Casebook for Business and Government*, pp. 218–246. Boulder, CO: Westview Press.

O'Hare, William P., and Usdansky, Margaret L. (1992). "What the 1990 census tells us about segregation in 25 large metros." *Population Today* 20(9): 6–7.

Rentz, J. O., and Reynolds, F. D. (1991). "Forecasting the effects of an aging population on product consumption: An age-period-cohort framework." *Journal of Marketing Research* 28(3): 355–360.

Schwemm, Robert G. (1991). *Housing Discrimination: Law and Litigation*. New York: Clark Boardman Callaghan. See especially Chapters 1 and 2.

Siegel, Jacob S. (1994). "The role of demographers in public and private suits of housing discrimination." In K. V. Rao and Jerry W. Wicks (eds.), *Studies in Applied Demography: Proceedings of the International Conference on Applied Demography*, pp. 236–251. Bowling Green, OH: PSRC Press, Bowling Green State University.

Smith, Stanley K. (1994). "Population estimates, projections, and expert testimony in adversarial legal proceedings: A case study of automobile dealerships." In Hallie J. Kintner *et al.* (eds.), *Demographics: A Casebook for Business and Government*, pp. 180–202. Boulder, CO: Westview Press.

Thomas, Richard K. (1944). "Using demographic analysis in health services planning: A case study in obstetrical services." In Hallie J. Kintner *et al.* (eds.), *Demographics: A Casebook for Business and Government*, pp. 159–179. Boulder, CO: Westview Press.

Turner, Margery A., Struyck, Raymond J., and Yinger, John. (1991). *Housing Discrimination Study: A Synthesis*. Urban Institute and Syracuse University, prepared for the Office of Policy Development and Research, U.S. Department of Housing and Urban Development.

United Church of Christ Commission for Racial Justice. (1987). *Toxic Wastes and Race in the United States: A National Report on the Racial and Socioeconomic Characteristics of Communities with Hazardous Waste Sites*. New York: United Church of Christ.

U.S. Environmental Protection Agency. (1992). *Environmental Equity: Reducing Risk for All Communities*.

U.S. General Accounting Office. (1983). "Siting of hazardous waste landfills and their correlation with racial and economic status of surrounding communities."

Voss, Paul R. (1994). "Targeting wealthy ex-Wisconsonites in Florida: A case study in applied demography." In Hallie J. Kintner *et al.* (eds.), *Demographics: A Casebook for Business and Government*, pp. 109–128. Boulder, CO: Westview Press.

7
DEMOGRAPHIC APPLICATIONS TO GOVERNMENT AND PRIVATE NONPROFIT ORGANIZATIONS

TYPES OF ORGANIZATIONAL POPULATIONS

Introduction

In this chapter the discussion moves from business applications to the use of demographic data, methods, and perspectives in dealing with the problems of nonprofit organizations and government agencies. Private nonprofit organizations include colleges and universities, religious organizations, public interest

289

groups, professional and trade associations, charitable organizations, and phil-anthropic foundations. Governments and governmental agencies are, in effect, public nonprofit organizations. From a demographic point of view, the separa-tion made between businesses and nonprofit organizations, especially private nonprofit organizations, is rather arbitrary. The demographic perspective relat-ing to businesses and nonprofit organizations is similar, even though they may deal with different areas of our social life and their goals are different.

In general, three types of populations can be associated with each large-scale organization: the external client population, the internal client popula-tion, and the workforce. Each of these populations merits separate demo-graphic analysis. To simplify our treatment of the subject in Chapter 6, we focused on the **external clients** of businesses, the population to which they offer a product or service, only briefly alluded to their **internal clients**, the population of owners and other "sponsors" (e.g., partners, board of directors, stockholders, bondholders), and did not consider their **workforce** at all. The lines between these populations are sometimes fuzzy, but the distinction has heuristic value in identifying the different types of populations that demog-raphers may be called on to measure, analyze, and forecast. Although often overlapping in their membership, each of these populations can be recognized as theoretically distinct and possibly as having distinctive demographic char-acteristics and dynamics.

The External Client Population

Like businesses, private nonprofit organizations have customers or clients to whom they usually "sell" a product and who must usually "pay" for the prod-uct if the organization is to survive financially. Some nonprofit organizations, such as charitable organizations, offer their products and services free because the clients are indigent and need the product or service to survive. Most gov-ernment products are "free" to the public. The clientele of governments or government agencies may be considered the general public it serves or a des-ignated segment of it. Governments and government agencies are increasingly becoming "privatized," however, offering products for sale directly to the pub-lic, disseminating sales material to elicit public support and to expand their clientele, or marketing their products through private vendors.

Colleges have students as clients who "buy" training and an academic record for entry into, or advancement in, various occupations. Religious orga-nizations have members, followers, or parishioners who "buy," or receive without cost, spiritual services, religious fellowship, or a record of religious affiliation to assure favorable divine intervention when needed. Religious orga-nizations also have another type of external client, segments of the public who are disadvantaged (i.e., are indigent or otherwise in need), to whom supportive services are extended, usually without cost.

Public interest organizations (e.g., Common Cause, League of Women Vot-ers), private-interest groups (e.g., American Association of Retired Persons, Disabled American Veterans), and professional and trade associations (e.g., Population Association of America, AFL-CIO, American Medical Association) are supported by members who contribute dues to these organizations and, hence, function as their external clients (as well as their internal clients, or owners). The organizations work to advance their causes or help them advance their occupational careers and professional status. Charitable organizations and philanthropic foundations solicit contributions from one group of external clients, who are offered in return the opportunity to be charitable and do good works following the tenets of their religious faiths, to support causes in which they believe, to be remembered by posterity, or to receive a generous tax reduction. These organizations also have another group of external clients: the recipients of their beneficence, philanthropic gifts, and grants.

Government agencies market use of public facilities such as parks, sell statistical data such as decennial census reports, provide free health services (Medicaid), and administer a health insurance program (Medicare). The external clients of the government, mainly the members of the general public, benefit from many free government services, but particular segments of the public choose to purchase certain products marketed by the government that are of special value to them.

The Internal Client Population

Nonprofit organizations as well as businesses have to serve groups of clients or members who are essentially internal to the organization. Such internal clients include those who own it, are its creditors, or are its dues-paying members. Some large-scale organizations, especially professional and trade associations, have internal clients who may not be distinct from "customers." A professional association is owned by its dues-paying members, who are also the external clients being served. Dues-paying members of associations may, therefore, be dubbed internal-external clients because they belong both to the owner group and the group being serviced. The distinction between internal and external clients is clearer for businesses. They are owned by their shareholders, a group of partners, or a sole entrepreneur, and these bodies are usually very distinct from the customers of the businesses. Private colleges are "owned" by their financial supporters, such as the alumni who contribute to the college fund, or the foundation or religious organization that sponsors the college. Public colleges are owned by the taxpayers of the relevant jurisdiction. Religious organizations are "owned" by the parent church, or the members who contribute to the building fund and who support the organization financially. A condominium association has similar features. A type of diverse ownership characterizes public organizations such as Public Radio International, which, in effect, is owned by the U.S. National Endowment for the Arts, major private contributors, and listener-contributors.

The Workforce

The third population characterizing organizations is their workforce. All organizations have workforces, the paid workers and the volunteers that do the work of the organization. Once again, we note an overlap. The workforce of many businesses includes their owners (i.e., their internal client populations). For example, the workforce of United Airlines comprises its owners.

The demography of the workforce of organizations is given separate and extended attention in Chapter 8.

USE OF DEMOGRAPHIC DATA AND METHODS BY NONPROFIT ORGANIZATIONS IN COMMUNITY ACTION

The External Client Population

Nonprofit organizations have an interest in knowing about the number and characteristics of their external clients so as to maximize the sale and dissemination of their products, the scope of their influence, or the extent of their power, services, and good works. They may want or need to expand their facilities to meet a growing demand on the part of their external clients. They may want or need to modify their products or methods to satisfy a change in the characteristics or interests of their clients. Colleges, churches, and professional and trade associations all face the same two tasks, maintaining or extending their "membership" and redesigning their programs to accommodate to a changing membership. These tasks are similar to those faced by businesses in expanding their body of customers and accommodating to their changing characteristics and demands.

Four brief illustrations show nonprofit organizations pursuing tasks with demographic components involving external clients: (1) the modification of a college's facilities or programs to meet changing demand, (2) the planning of a job training program by a private service organization aiding "welfare mothers," (3) the setting of fund-raising goals by a charitable organization for house-to-house canvassers, and (4) the improvement of church outreach and community services in a particular metropolitan area.

1. To meet an increase in the number of students, a college may need to expand its campus or department offerings, or add a new campus in a different location. To this end, the college may wish to exploit the available records on its student body and, if necessary, supplement them with a survey, eliciting information about age-sex composition, marital status, income, labor force participation, educational level, living arrangements, and occupational goals. Information of this kind would provide the basis for making a decision on the introduction of new academic departments and the elimination or contraction of others.

2. Planning a private job training program for a local population would make use of census data on age, education, unemployment, language, work experience, and marital status for the area.

3. The charitable organization setting fund-raising goals for a local area could use census data, for the area and its geographic subdivisions, on household composition, income, age, education, value/rent of housing unit, tenure, and year-moved into present residence.

4. To meet its goal of expanding its outreach program, the church management must learn more about the makeup of the communities served by its churches. Accordingly, it could refer to census data for the metropolitan

area and its constituent census tracts. First, it is useful to construct socioeconomic profiles of the local communities on the basis of these data. Using the profiles, the church could learn about the age composition, family structure, income level, ethnic background, occupation, and housing value or rent of the residents in the various neighborhoods. This information tells much about the needs of the communities, and the church is able to plan programs more in line with these needs. These programs might include sponsoring a tutoring program for high-school-age youth, organizing volunteers to assist ailing elderly with shopping or other tasks, and disseminating information about housing assistance programs to people in low-income areas with serious housing problems such as overcrowding and inadequate plumbing. An illustration of data analysis in pursuance of this type of activity by the Evangelical Lutheran Church is described by Ogunwalle (1994).[1]

In all these cases, the choice of areas for which data will be needed depends on the geographic definition of the task. While some data are available at every geographic level from blocks to the entire United States, the detail of the data available tends to diminish as the area gets smaller, with a major divide in data detail between blocks and block groups.

The Internal Client Population

An organization may also have an intense interest in the demographic and socioeconomic characteristics of its internal clients. A college may be interested in the characteristics of its alumni in planning a college development campaign. A corporation may be interested in the characteristics of its stockholders before developing and implementing a reorganization plan that the stockholders must vote on. In planning their campaigns, candidates for high office in a particular religious denomination may wish to secure data on the characteristics of its regular members (i.e., those who have voting rights).

USE OF DEMOGRAPHIC DATA AND METHODS IN LOCAL GOVERNMENT PLANNING AND COMMUNITY ACTION

Demographic data are used by state, regional, and city planners to describe the currrent demographic and socioeconomic situation in local areas, to make estimates of local needs for public services and facilities, to evaluate the effectiveness of programs in operation, to make projections of the demographic and socioeconomic situation in the area, and to devise programs providing for future services. Census data, taken alone or linked with local administrative data, are commonly used in developing the comprehensive plans for local areas and in planning the location of libraries, police stations, playgrounds, public hospitals, and public housing, as well as transportation routes, public safety programs, and community action programs. Geographic analysis and mapping methods can be used to provide the spatial representation for socioeconomic variations in the local area and for analyzing local and regional trends. Census data and local administrative records data can be combined by record linkage systems and geographic information systems (GISs) to derive new series depicting the socioeconomic situation and service needs of an area. It should be apparent that many tasks confronting local and regional governments as well as private nonprivate organizations call for the use of demographic knowledge and skills.

Often, however, these organizations do not have a clear sense of the demographic nature of the questions they have and of the service an applied demographer can provide. As a consequence, the initial discussions between the representatives of such organizations and the demographer must achieve a common and respectful understanding as to the demographic dimensions of the problem and as to the role the demographer can play in dealing with them.

Indicators of the Local Demographic Situation and Local Needs

Local governments need data on a great variety of demographic, social, and economic indicators in order to fill their responsibilities both for the provision of basic services and for the provision of special services to disadvantaged groups. Local governments receive federal and state funds in part according to the numbers in the general population and in special population groups. In addition to such basic characteristics as the total population, its age-sex distribution, and the number of households, the areas of interest in planning local special needs relate to such groups in the population as illiterate adults, children in poor families, female-headed family households, the unemployed, the elderly poor, high school dropouts, pregnant teenagers, and the number of elderly living alone. The demography of social welfare is also concerned with homelessness, institutionalization, drug abuse and crime, and child care, all requiring special attention at the local level.

List of Illustrative Indicators

To identify the nature and measure the extent of local governmental needs, we must devise and calculate appropriate statistical indicators of the community demographic and socioeconomic situation. The indicators can function at once as measures of local needs and measures of the outcomes of social programs. The following list has three parts: measures of the demographic situation, measures of community disorganization or group disadvantage, and measures of health needs and outcomes.[2] Since some indicators serve as measures of local community problems as well as measures of the general demographic and socioeconomic situation, it is difficult to assign the various indicators and measures among the various groups. Health was separated out because of its intrinsic importance to well-being. Inadequate education, low income, unemployment, and inadequate housing are featured among the measures of community disorganization. National data for calculating most of these measures can be obtained from the decennial Censuses of Population and Housing, the Current Population Survey, and the annual reports on vital statistics of the National Center for Health Statistics.

Measures of the Demographic Situation

1. Total population and rate of population growth

2. Age and sex distribution and median age
3. Race and ethnicity distribution
4. Average size of household
5. Median years of school completed (25 years and over)
6. Percentage high-school graduates (25 years and over)
7. Median and mean family or household income
8. Per capita income
9. Net and gross migration rates (5 years and over)
10. Distribution of households by type
11. Percentage living alone (50 years and over)

Measures of Community Disorganization or Group Disadvantage

1. Poverty ratio (persons of all ages)
2. Percentage of children in families with incomes under 125% of the poverty level
3. Percentage of full-time year-round workers with incomes below the poverty level
4. Unemployment ratio (18 years and over in the labor force)
5. Percentage of female-headed family households (family householders under age 50)
6. Proportion of children (under age 18) not living with their parents.
7. Proportion of males 25 to 34 not in the labor force
8. High-school dropout rate
9. Adult illiteracy ratio (18 years and over)
10. Percentage of grade-school children below the modal grade for their age
11. Juvenile crime rate for males and females (under age 18)
12. Adult crime rate for males and females (18 years and over)
13. Proportion of the adult population lacking knowledge of English
14. Proportion illegal immigrants among foreign born
15. Proportion of housing units with 1.01 or more persons per room
16. Proportion of housing units with selected internal deficiences
17. Mean value of owner-occupied housing units in lowest quintile
18. Mean rent of renter-occupied housing units in lowest quintile
19. Median family income in lowest quintile
20. Unemployment ratio in highest quintile

Measures of Health Needs and Outcomes

1. Pregnancy rate for females aged 10 to 14 and 15 to 19
2. Birth rate for unmarried females aged 10 to 14 and 15 to 19
3. Repeat (second-order or higher) birthrate for females aged 10 to 14 and 15 to 19
4. Incidence or prevalence of sexually transmitted diseases
5. Incidence or prevalence of specified infectious diseases (e.g., tuberculosis)
6. Incidence or prevalence of specified chronic diseases (e.g., hypertension)

7. Proportion of disabled persons
8. Infant mortality rate
9. Teenage death rate from accidents, homicide, and suicide (15 to 19 years)

Several measures are used to identify the disadvantaged or needy segment of the community. These measures identify persons who are economically disadvantaged, persons who have limited education, persons who are outside the labor force in the principal working ages or who are unemployed, persons who live under crowded or poor housing conditions, persons whose living arrangements are stressful for them, and persons who have serious health problems or needs. Combinations of criteria help to identify areas having the greatest need. Areas within a city or county ranking lowest (e.g., bottom quintile on median family income) or highest (e.g., top quintile on unemployment ratio) on two or more distinct criteria may be appropriate candidates for public intervention and special assistance. Some of these indicators are considered in greater detail next and their use in selected public programs is illustrated.

Measures of Poverty and Their Limitations

The proportion of persons in poverty or with low income is among the principal criteria used in allocating public funds to economically disadvantaged local areas. The **poverty ratio,** one of the measures of low income, is the proportion of persons living below the official poverty level. In variants of the measure, the criterion of low income specified may be some multiple of the official poverty level, such as 125% or 150% of the poverty level. Low income for a population may also be measured by low per capita (individual) income, low mean family or household income, or low median family or household income.[3] The distribution of families by income may be used to identify the lowest income quintile in the population of an area.

The current official definition of poverty for statistical use was established by the Bureau of the Budget in 1969 and reaffirmed by the Office of Management and Budget in Statistical Policy Directive No. 14. At the core of the definition is the economy food plan, designed by the U. S. Department of Agriculture. After the Department of Agriculture determined, on the basis of the economy food plan, that families of three or four persons spent approximately one-third of their after-tax money income on food, the poverty threshold for families of this size was set at three times the cost of the economy food plan. Other procedures were used to calculate poverty thresholds for two-person households and persons living alone, to compensate for the relatively larger fixed expenses of these smaller units.

The present poverty thresholds vary according to size of family unit (up to nine or more) and number of related children under 18 years old (up to eight or more), with a further distinction according to the age (below age 65 and 65 years and over) of the householder in one- and two-person units. The poverty thresholds for 1997 are shown in Table 7.1. In that year the poverty thresholds ranged from $7698 for a person 65 years or older living alone to $35,719 for a family of nine persons or more with one related child under 18 years. Poverty thresholds are updated each year to reflect changes in the Consumer

■ **TABLE 7.1** Poverty Thresholds in 1997 According to Size of Family and Number of Related Children under 18 Years

| Size of family unit | Weighted average threshold | Related children under 18 years | | | | | | | | |
		None	One	Two	Three	Four	Five	Six	Seven	Eight or more
One person	8,183									
Under 65	8,350	8,350								
65+	7,698	7,698								
Two persons	10,473									
Hh under 65[a]	10,805	10,748	11,063							
Hh 65 or more[b]	9,712	9,701	11,021							
Three persons	12,802	12,554	12,919	12,931						
Four persons	16,400	16,555	16,825	16,276	16,333					
Five persons	19,380	19,964	20,255	19,634	19,154	18,861				
Six persons	21,886	22,962	23,053	22,578	22,123	21,446	21,045			
Seven persons	24,802	26,421	26,586	26,017	25,621	24,882	24,021	23,076		
Eight persons	27,593	29,550	29,811	29,274	28,804	28,137	27,290	26,409	26,185	
Nine persons or more	32,566	35,546	35,719	35,244	34,845	34,190	33,289	32,474	32,272	31,029

[a] Householder under 65 years of age.

[b] Householder 65 years of age or older.

Source: U.S. Bureau of the Census, "Poverty in the United States: 1997," *Current Population Reports*, P60-201, 1998.

Price Index. The 1997 levels are over twice as great as the 1975 levels because of the adjustments for inflation. The updated figures are published annually in the U.S. Bureau of the Census P-60 Series of *Current Population Reports*.

In figuring the current poverty status of a family, the combined before-tax money income of families is compared with the thresholds. Every one in the family unit is assigned the same poverty status. For some administrative and analytic purposes, as suggested earlier, use is made of various multipliers of these thresholds, such as 1.25 (i.e., 125% of the thresholds), or 1.50 (i.e., 150% of the thresholds). These variants of the poverty level correspond to alternative measures of the **ratio of income to the poverty level**. Ratios below 1.00 indicate income below the poverty level or its variant, while ratios above 1.00 indicate income above the poverty level or its variant. Distinctive ratios of income to the poverty level are used in the administration of the Food Stamp program, the Supplemental Security Income program, and other public programs. The 1990 census and the Current Population Survey (CPS) provide data on the distribution of families according to the ratio of family income to the poverty level.

According to the CPS, in 1996 13.7% of the population lived below the poverty level and 18.5% lived below 1.25 times the poverty level. Among blacks, 28.4% lived below the poverty level as compared with 11.2% for whites. About half of blacks in families with female heads and related children under 18 years were poor. Over time, the proportions of the population in poverty have been relatively stable but at the same time there has been considerable movement of individual families into and out of poverty. One-fifth of those in poverty in 1990 were not poor in 1991, while 3% of those not poor in 1990 were poor in 1991. In recent years, stays in poverty lasted an average (median) period of 4 months.[4]

In the 1980 and 1990 censuses, census tracts (in metropolitan areas) and block numbering areas (in nonmetropolitan areas) were defined as **poverty areas** if 20% or more of the population in the tract was determined to be below the poverty level according to the censuses. Poverty areas are not defined or tabulated for larger or smaller geographic units than census tracts. However, the proportion of poor census tracts in a city or county, or the proportion of population in poor census tracts, may be used to describe the city's or county's poverty status relative to that of other cities or counties. In 1990 the overall poverty ratio for such areas was 34%, or about $2^1/2$ times the national average (13.5%). Table 7.2 presents illustrative data on census tracts defined as poverty areas, for the counties of Maryland in 1990. Such poverty areas accounted for 8.7% of the population of Maryland in 1990, while the 1990 census reported a poverty ratio of 8.3% for the state.

The official measure of poverty is subject to several limitations, particularly in connection with its use in formulating policy. The criticisms encompass both the categories entering into the poverty matrix and the thresholds assigned to the categories. First, critics note that the underlying income data omit the income of persons not enumerated in the survey or census and understate the income of persons enumerated. The deficiencies have a differential effect by age, since more people are missed at some ages than others and some types of income are more underreported than others. In particular, transfer payments and other "unearned" income tend to be more underreported than wage and salary income. Omission of the income of persons not enumerated tends to be concentrated among males, particularly black males aged 25 to 54, who receive wages and salaries and public assistance more than other types of income and are more likely to receive low incomes and to be poor.

According to Ruggles (1992), the present measure no longer reflects minimum cost-of-living requirements because of the obsolescence of the consumption data used in constructing the original measure.[5] She maintains that a complete reexamination of the consumption pattern, including each major budget item, and of the variation introduced in the consumption pattern by type and size of family needs to be undertaken.

Money income, as used in the official poverty formula, is not an adequate measure of economic well-being. Money income excludes noncash benefits and represents income before tax or other deductions. Noncash benefits, such as food stamps, free school lunches, subsidized housing, and welfare payments,[6] may contribute substantially to the effective income of the family unit. Medicare and Medicaid are important public noncash benefits and employer-provided health insurance is an important private noncash benefit, but it is difficult to quantify them for use in determining a poverty theshold or a family's effective income level. Another issue is the use of income rather than net worth or assets to serve as the basis for determining poverty status. Ownership of assets clearly promotes economic well-being. The failure to consider assets leads to the anomaly of "poor" college students who are mem-

TABLE 7.2 Number and Population of Census Tracts Designated as Poverty Areas in Maryland, by County: 1990

County	Census tracts or BNAs[a]		Poverty areas		Percentage, population in poverty areas
	Number	Population	Number	Population	
Maryland	1,151	4,780,753	129	414,655	8.7[b]
Allegany	25	74,946	7	20,827	27.8
Anne Arundel	82	427,239	3	2,353	0.6
Baltimore	198	692,134	7	10,352	1.5
Calvert	12	51,372	—	—	—
Caroline[a]	7	27,035	—	—	—
Carroll	25	123,372	—	—	—
Cecil	15	71,347	—	—	—
Charles	21	101,154	—	—	—
Dorchester[a]	9	30,236	1	4,334	14.4
Frederick	33	150,208	2	3,722	2.5
Garrett[c]	7	28,138	—	—	—
Harford	39	182,132	—	—	—
Howard	30	187,328	—	—	—
Kent[a]	5	17,842	—	—	—
Montgomery	160	762,207	—	—	—
Prince George's	172	723,373	5	23,905	3.3
Queen Anne's	11	33,953	—	—	—
St. Mary's[a]	13	75,974	—	—	—
Somerset[a]	7	23,440	1	2,904	12.4
Talbot[a]	9	30,549	—	—	—
Washington	29	121,393	3	8,692	7.2
Wicomico[c]	16	74,339	2	6,799	9.1
Worcester[a]	23	35,028	1	200	0.6
Baltimore city[d]	203	736,014	97	330,557	44.9

Note: A poverty area is a census tract or block numbering area in which 20% or more of the population is below the poverty level.

[a] BNA Block numbering areas, established outside metropolitan area counties.

[b] The 1990 census figure for persons in poverty is 8.3%.

[c] Tracted nonmetropolitan county.

[d] Independent city.

Source: U.S. Bureau of the Census, 1990 Censuses of Population and Housing, 1990 CPH-3, *Population and Housing Characteristics for Census Tracts and Block Numbering Areas*. CPH-3 reports for Maryland, the Washington, DC-MD-VA MSA, Baltimore, MD MSA, Hagerstown, MD MSA, Wilmington, DE-NJ-MD PMSA, and Cumberland, MD-WV MSA.

bers of affluent families, and of "poor" elderly who have substantial assets, including homes and rental property. Admittedly, these assets are often illiquid (i.e., not readily convertible to cash). The thresholds fail to take account of regional and farm-nonfarm differences in income needed to achieve a similar level of living. The problem of measuring the variations in the poverty thresholds geographically is a difficult one. The areas have to be identified, appropriate poverty thresholds ascertained, and cost-of-living indexes developed to allow for annual adjustments for inflation.

Because of these limitations of the official measure of poverty, many proposals have been made to modify it. The Census Bureau has been developing alternative estimates of poverty based on alternative definitions of income.[7] The National Academy of Sciences has proposed a new measure designed to reflect the income actually available to families for purchasing basic goods and services.[8]

Measures of Educational Progress

The list of social indicators of local need for community action includes several measures of educational progress. One's educational progress greatly affects one life's chances and poor educational progress is associated with behavioral difficulties in later years. Numerous measures of educational progress have been devised and applied, six of which are listed here: median years of school completed, percentage of high-school graduates, percentage of grade-school children below the modal grade for their age, high school dropout rate, adult illiteracy ratio, and proportion of the adult population lacking knowledge of English. These measures have their variants when we come to expressing them in an actual computational algorithm.

The **median years of school completed** is a general measure of educational progress for the adult population. It is based on a question or questions seeking the highest grade achieved in regular schools—that is, graded schools that may advance a person toward a certificate, diploma, or degree. When the median is low, say below 10 years, it is a reasonably sensitive and informative indicator of the educational progress of the population. As it approaches 12 years—that is, completion of high school—it becomes increasingly insensitive as a measure, especially for comparing different population groups, and an alternative measure, namely the **percentage of high school graduates** in the population, is generally substituted. The U.S. Census Bureau has been increasingly presenting the latter measure to indicate variations in educational progress in deference to the median years of school completed.

We can measure acceleration or deceleration in movement through the grades by the percentage of grade-school children above and below the **modal grade** (i.e., the commonest grade) for their age. To select the modal grade for each age, we compile an age-grade table of enrollments and for each age identify the modal grade of the students. All students at a given age enrolled in a lower grade than the modal grade are considered to be below the normal grade for their age. A more conservative measure would consider as behind in school only those attending a grade 2 years or more below the modal grade. The measure of educational progress is the percentage that this number is of the total number enrolled at a particular age.

The **high school dropout rate** is an important indicator of the effectiveness of the school system and the educational progress of teenagers. It can be defined operationally in several ways. We can calculate the percentage of teenagers 16 to 19 who are not enrolled in school and are not high school graduates. This is a measure of the proportion of teenagers who are high school dropouts. Longitudinal data are needed to develop a good measure of educational progress in the form of a dropout rate, however. We can calculate the percentage of the cohort of students enrolled in grade 9 who do not graduate high school "4" years later (preferably adjusted for unclassified secondary students, internal migration, deaths, accelerated and delayed students, and students who graduated with GED certificates). A rough estimate can be made on the basis of CPS data by comparing the gross number of fourth-year high school students in a given year and the number of first-year high school students 3 years earlier. At the national level this estimate is affected mainly by international immigration and comparability of CPS data. Another variant for defining the high school dropout rate is the percentage of teenagers enrolled in high school in a given year who dropped out of school in the following year and who did not graduate during the year. Using SIPP data, matched from year to year, one can follow a cohort of 15-year-olds for a few years to determine whether the same individuals are still in school or have graduated. This measure has the advantage of excluding the effect of the population changes that normally occur to a group of teenagers between ages 15 and 18 and that would obscure the estimate of dropouts. The last two measures of educational progress, those relating to illiteracy and knowledge of English, are considered later in connection with the description of a program to reduce adult illiteracy.

The data needed for computing these measures can be obtained from state and local educational agencies and the National Center for Education Statistics as well as the decennial census and national sample surveys, such as CPS and SIPP.[9] The decennial census has the advantage of providing the data for computing measures for small areas, but it has the disadvantage that longitudinal measures cannot be calculated on the basis of a single census.

Measures of Housing Value and Condition

Several indicators in my list relate to housing costs, crowding, and quality or condition. The first, the proportion of housing units with 1.01 or more persons per room, is a measure of crowding. The second, the proportion of housing units with selected internal deficiencies, is a measure of housing quality. These conditions may be the lack of complete plumbing facilities for exclusive use, the lack of a complete kitchen, exposed wiring, and similar substandard housing conditions. The other two measures are indirect measures of housing condition or quality: The housing units in the lowest quintile with respect to monthly value or rent are assumed to be in poor condition.

Table 7.3 compares housing conditions for black, Hispanic, and low-income households with those for all households, on the basis of data on several indicators of internal deficiencies in the housing stock for 1995. The housing conditions for these particular groups are much more deficient than those for the remaining households. These data are illustrative of the current data furnished by the American Housing Survey.

Illustrations of Program Applications

There are numerous special public programs that require the use of demographic data, indicators, or methods. The county Department of Social Services may want to restructure county child care services or to improve its services for teenage pregnant women. The city Department of Parks may want to locate a new playground in an area convenient to children now underserved. The state

TABLE 7.3   Occupied Housing Units with Selected Internal Deficiences, by Type of Deficiency, for Blacks, Hispanics, and Low-Income Households: 1995

Deficiency	Total occupied units	Black	Hispanic	Low-income household
Total units (000s)	97,693	11,774	7,757	14,695
Percentage of total:				
Signs of rats in last three months	2.8	6.7	8.5	5.9
Holes in floors or open cracks or holes	5.7	11.8	10.2	11.0
Exposed wiring	1.8	2.8	3.3	2.8
Water leakage[a]	11.7	15.6	13.1	14.0

[a] During the 12 months prior to the survey.

Source: U.S. Bureau of the Census, *Current Housing Reports,* Series H150/95, "Annual Housing Survey in the United States, 1995," 1998.

Department of Labor may want to plan a job training program for disabled adults. The state Department of Education may want to plan a program to reduce adult illiteracy and to provide instruction in English as a second language. We consider the demographic aspects of some of these programs next.

Improving Services for Teenage Pregnant Women: Measuring the Teenage Pregnancy Rate for Substate Areas

The first task in trying to improve services for teenage pregnant women is to develop estimates of the number of teenagers who are pregnant and the teenage pregnancy rate in the geographic area of interest. The calculation of an estimate of the teenage pregnancy rate is illustrated for a hypothetical county. The method used is called **combination of outcome components.** The number of pregnant women at a given date (t) can be estimated as the sum of the number of live births during the following 9-month period, (induced) abortions during the first 6 months of the period, and (other) fetal losses of 20 weeks or more of gestation during the first 20 weeks of the period:

$$t|\longleftarrow \text{births} \longrightarrow |t + 9 \text{ months}$$
$$t|\longleftarrow \text{abortions} \longrightarrow |t + 6 \text{ months}$$
$$t|\longleftarrow \text{fetal losses} \longrightarrow |t + 20 \text{ weeks}$$

In this special use of the term, fetal losses exclude all abortions (i.e., induced terminations of pregnancy) and other fetal losses of less than 20 weeks of gestation, which are usually not reported. Late-term abortions (6 or more months) are rare and few are reported.

For the most part, only available data are used in the calculation. The explanation of the more specialized techniques of population estimation that may be required are left to Chapter 9. Generally, data on births disaggregated by age of women and population data disaggregated by age and sex, for the county, can be secured from public sources, such as the state government and the U.S. Census Bureau, or can be estimated by procedures to be described in Chapter 9. The number of abortions for counties can be secured from local records or from the Alan Guttmacher Institute.[10] Fetal loss data can be secured for the United States as a whole from the National Survey of Family Growth

(NSFG) for 1995 and earlier years and from the Centers for Disease Control and Prevention. All data on fetal losses suffer from incomplete reporting for a number of reasons: forgetfulness; deliberate failure to report, in order to avoid embarrassment, emotional trauma, or participation in the survey; and lack of knowledge as to the event or the correct gestational period. The NSFG data are also subject to sampling error. These influences contribute to a lack of comparability of the data from area to area and year to year.

Worksheets 7.1 and 7.2 set forth the basic data on population, births, and abortions, and the steps in the calculation of the **pregnancy rate**, for our hypothetical county in the year 1995. For this purpose, the national **fetal loss rates** for teenagers from the NSFG have been adopted for the county. Since births and abortions appear to make up most of the pregnancy outcomes, we can make this assumption without seriously prejudicing the accuracy of our estimates of the pregnancy rate. We initially obtain an estimate of 114.4 pregnancies per 1000 women 15 to 19 years old for county C by adding the county birthrate (67.1), the county abortion rate (31.4), and the national fetal loss rate (15.9).

We can improve the estimate of fetal losses for ages 15 to 19 for the county by taking advantage of the available national data from the NSFG for age groups 15 to 17 and 18 to 19 and for Hispanics and other blacks and whites (see Worksheet 7.2). By applying the national rates for these age-race-Hispanic origin groups to the corresponding county population estimates, we derive a **synthetic estimate** of the fetal loss rate for the county, which can be expected to be a more accurate estimate for the county than the national rate. In this way, if the local population is mainly black, the rate for blacks will be given major weight, as it should be. Worksheet 7.2 illustrates the calculation of this type of synthetic estimate of the fetal loss rate. It is shown in Worksheet 7.1

WORKSHEET 7.1 Calculation of the Teenage Pregnancy Rate for County C by Combining Outcome Components: 1995

Data element	15–17 years	18–19 years	Total, 15–19 years
(1) Female population aged	9,423	7,602	17,025
(2) Births to women aged	438	704	1,142
(3) Abortions to women aged	202	332	534
(4) = (2) ÷ (1) × 1000 Birthrate	46.5	92.6	67.1
(5) = (3) ÷ (1) × 1000 Abortion rate	21.4	43.7	31.4
(6a) = Estimated fetal loss rate, prelim.	15.9	16.0	15.9
(6b) = Estimated fetal loss rate, rev.	16.2	20.3	18.0
(7a) = (4) + (5) + (6a) Estimated pregnancy rate, prelim.	83.8	152.3	114.4
(7b) = (4) + (5) + (6b) Estimated pregnancy rate, rev.	84.1	156.6	116.5

Source: (1) U.S. Bureau of the Census or State Data Center.
(2) U.S. National Center for Health Statistics or State Offices of Vital Statistics.
(3) Centers for Disease Control and Prevention and the Allan Guttmacher Institute.
(6a) Worksheet 7.2.
(6b) Worksheet 7.2.

WORKSHEET 7.2   Calculation of the Teenage Fetal Loss Rate for
County C by the Synthetic Method: 1995

Race/Hispanic	15–17 years	18–19 years	Total, 15–19 years
Female population, county C			
White, non-Hispanic	735	593	1,328
Black, non-Hispanic	5,647	4,634	10,281
Hispanic	3,041	2,375	5,416
Total	9,423	7,602	17,025
Fetal loss rate, United States[a]			
White, non-Hispanic	11.5	12.9	12.0
Black, non-Hispanic	19.1	18.3	18.8
Hispanic	12.0	26.0	17.5
Total	15.9	16.0	15.9
County C, total	16.2[b]	20.3[b]	18.0[c]

[a] Spontaneous fetal losses from recognized pregnancies of all gestational periods as reported by women in the 1995 National Survey of Family Growth.

[b] Derived by weighting the U.S. fetal loss rates shown in this table by the corresponding county populations shown above. Example: $[(.0115 \times 735) + (.0191 \times 5,647) + (.0120 \times 3,041)] \div 9,423 = .0162$.

[c] Derived by weighting the total rates for ages 15 to 17 and 18 to 19 shown for County C by the county populations shown: $[(.0162 \times 9,423) + (.0203 \times 7,602)] \div 17,075 = .0180$.

Source: Incorporates data from U.S. National Center for Health Statistics, S. J. Ventura *et al.*, "Trends in pregnancies and pregnancy rates by outcomes: Estimates for the United States, 1976–1996," *Vital and Health Statistics* 21(56), 2000.

as a revised estimate of the fetal loss rate (18.0). The revised estimate of the pregnancy rate for the county is 116.5.

We may want to measure the teenage pregnancy rate also for subcounty areas, such as census tracts. Then, we need estimates of the female population, birthrates, abortion rates, and fetal loss rates for the teenagers for census tracts. If we lack the abortion rate and the fetal loss rate for these areas, we can proceed as before, weighting the county estimates of the abortion rate and the national estimates of the fetal loss rate with population estimates for census tracts, for age and race groups. The estimates of abortion rates and fetal loss rates for census tracts so derived can then be combined with local birthrates.

Suppose we do not have abortion data for areas within states but only for the state as a whole. For this purpose we may compute the **abortion ratio** for the state (i.e., the number of abortions during a year per 1000 births during the year) and use it to calculate the number of abortions for a particular county. For women 15 to 19 years of age, we can estimate abortions in county C as follows:

Abortions, county C = (births, county C) ⋆ (abortion ratio, state)

With an estimate of abortions in the county, we can calculate an abortion rate (based on population) for the county, derive an estimate of the fetal-loss rate for the county as before, and combine them with the birthrate for the county, to estimate the pregnancy rate for the county. A similar procedure can be used to calculate estimates of abortions and the abortion rates for census tracts, from which pregnancy rates for census tracts may be derived.

Locating Local Government Installations: Locating a Playground in a City

In this example, the parks director in a city wishes to locate a new playground where it will be most effective (i.e., in an area where poor children lack sufficient recreational facilities). This is interpreted by the parks director to mean a census tract that lacks a playground, has available space for a playground, and has a large number of children aged 5 to 14 years living in poverty. She or he could select from any of several measures of low income but decides to choose the official poverty criterion. Pertinent census data for census tracts include the number of children distributed by detailed age and the number of "related" children in low-income families in lesser age detail (i.e., 5 to 17 years). **Related children** are children related to the householder. These data appear in the 1990 census report CPH-3, *Population and Housing Characteristics for Census Tracts and Block Numbering Areas*, and on the CD-ROM files for STF-3A. Other data needed are the locations of existing parks and the locations of available land that is suitable for park use. The Department of Parks already has the former information and the City Planning Office can provide the latter information.

A paradigm for the computation of the number of related children 5 to 14 years old in families with incomes below the poverty level for the census tracts in a hypothetical city, Middletown, USA, in the Middletown, MSA, is shown in Worksheet 7.3. Because of the more limited age detail on poor children for census tracts, it is necessary to estimate the number of children 5 to 14 years of age. For this purpose, we assume that the percentage of children 5 to 14 years old in poverty in each census tract is the same as the percentage of children 5 to 17 years old in poverty in the census tract, using the formula:

$$\text{Related children 5 to 14 in poverty} = \text{Related children 5 to 17 in poverty} \star \frac{\text{Children 5 to 14}}{\text{Children 5 to 17}}$$

The limited nature of the assumption assures us that the estimates are rather robust. On the basis of the estimates, the director of parks in Middletown can select the census tract in which to locate the new playground—a tract lacking a playground, having space for the new facility, and recording the greatest number of children in low-income families.[11]

Planning a State and Local Program to Reduce Adult Illiteracy

Adult literacy and language instruction programs are intended to help people improve their reading and writing skills so that they can qualify for new jobs or for more skilled jobs. In the present case, the task of the demographer is to estimate the number of people in need of literacy and/or English-language instruction in the various parts of a state, identifying the particular pockets of need. There are no direct data on literacy in the 1990 census, other recent censuses, or recent national surveys. A question on literacy was not asked in these censuses and only national information on illiteracy was secured in the

WORKSHEET 7.3 Paradigm for Estimating the Number of Related Children 5 to 14 Years Old in Low-Income Families, for Selected Census Tracts in Middletown, MSA: 1990

Census tract no.	Children 5–17 in low-income families[a] (1)	Total children			Estimated children 5–14 in low-income families (5) = (4) ⋆ (1)
		5–14 years (2)	5–17 years (3)	Proportion (4) = (2)/(3)	
Middletown, MSA	21,158	131,707	177,596	.7416	15,691
Middletown City	10,806	29,282	39,006	.7507	8,112
0001	19	57	78	.7308	14
0002	97	131	174	.7529	73
0003	116	266	343	.7755	90
0004	208	640	828	.7729	161
0005	401	554	706	.7847	315
0006	470	781	1,091	.7159	336
0007	122	375	521	.7198	88
0008	615	956	1,294	.7388	454
0009	194	300	424	.7075	137
0010	159	115	168	.6845	109
0011	98	130	182	.7143	70
0012	144	215	302	.7119	103

[a] Related children (i.e., children related to householder).

Source: Suggesteed by U.S. Bureau of the Census, Data Users Services Division, "Case study: The location of a playground," ca. 1975. For source of data, see U.S. Bureau of the Census, 1990 Censuses of Population and Housing, 1990 CPH-3, *Population and Housing Characteristics for Census Tracts and Block Numbering Areas*, Tables 1 and 19.

1992 national adult literacy survey. This survey was sponsored by the National Center for Education Statistics (NCES). A question on literacy seeks information on the ability of a person to read and write. An **illiteracy ratio** for adults may be defined as the proportion of the population 18 years and over who are unable to read and write.

In the absence of reported data, the extent of illiteracy for states and substate areas must be estimated, either by use of proxy data or a synthetic method. The managers of the programs being planned decided to use census data on elementary-school dropouts and persons lacking knowledge of English, in combination with data on persons unemployed and adults living in poverty, for census tracts, to determine the potential need for reading, writing, and English-language instruction in each community. Data on adults who were living in poverty and data on unemployed persons were viewed as useful guides to accompany the data on adults who had little education and adults who did not speak English well.

Census tract data found in 1990 CPH-3, *Population and Housing Characteristics for Census Tracts and Block Numbering Areas*, and on CD-ROM for STF-3A, show the approximate number of persons 25 years old and over who have less than an 8th grade education, persons 18 and over who do not speak English or do not speak it well, unemployed persons (16 years and over), and persons 18 to 59 who are living in poverty. These data are not generally cross-tabulated, so that most indices have to be examined separately or cross-tabulations have to be estimated. The combined, albeit overlapping, numbers of persons for each census tract falling in these categories can be obtained, and the results may then be ranked. The results will guide the program managers in selecting the best areas in which to concentrate advertising for the program, locate classroom facilities, and estimate the potential pool of students in each of the two types of classes to be conducted. A second method of deriving illiteracy figures, employed by NCES, is a synthetic method, in which the national results of the illiteracy survey are applied to local census data or population estimates to derive local estimates of illiteracy. (See examples earlier in this chapter and in Chapter 11.)

Measuring the Utilization of Institutions

Adequate measures of the utilization of institutions, particularly prisons and nursing homes, are needed to develop public policies regarding punitive and rehabitative programs for lawbreakers and living accommodations for dependent elderly persons, and to plan for institutional personnel and facilities. A number of different measures of the use of institutions can be employed. These vary from simple "status" or "stock" measures, such as the proportion of the population confined in institutions at any particular date, to "flow" measures, such as annual rates of admission or discharge, the lifetime probability of ever being admitted to an institution, and the average years lived before and after entering an institution. Some measures do not fit neatly under either rubric, such as the number of person-days of confinement or care during a year, the average number of inmates or residents per day over a year, and the number of person-days of confinement or care in relation to the number of beds available for use. Regardless of its classification, each measure serves a different purpose.

Different data and methods are required to develop the various measures. Censuses, sample surveys, and administrative records provide the data used to develop both the stock measures and the flow measures. Cross-sectional data, such as those given in censuses, can be manipulated to develop annual rates in cohort form (e.g., age-specific net admission or net discharge rates) and synthetic lifetime measures (e.g., lifetime chances of being confined).

Of the various measures, we focus on three here: the chance of ever entering an institution, the average years at a given age remaining before entering an institution, and the average years of institutional life remaining at a given age. We often want to know the chances of an event ever occurring during the lifetime of an individual from some age forward, whether at birth or some older age. Illustrative events are imprisonment, entering a nursing home, victimization through serious crime, and experiencing a heart attack. The chances of the event ever occurring are not affected by second or additional occurrences of the event, so that we really want to know the proportion of individuals out of an initial cohort who experience a first confinement in a prison, a first entry into a nursing home, a first victimization, or a first heart attack.

Life-Table Methods of Measuring Prison Confinement

The same general demographic tool can be used to deal with any of these events—a life table. The specific life-table method for solving the general questions we have posed may vary for each event or situation because of differences in the form, detail, and quality of the available data. Our first illustration relates to imprisonment. The analysis is restricted to state and federal prisons (i.e., excluding local jails and juvenile detention centers) because of the more limited availability and poorer quality of data for jails and detention centers, the immense number of detainees in the latter facilities, the tremendous turnover of inmates of jails and detention centers, and the temporary status of many inmates who are awaiting trial or sentencing or are serving time for misdemeanors.

The life table to be constructed must go beyond the conventional life table and include some special functions that relate to confinements. Given the appropriate data, we can construct a multiple-decrement table, with deaths and first admissions as the decrements (i.e., factors that reduce the size of the cohort). Such a multiple-decrement table, adapted from work of Bonczar and Beck of the U.S. Bureau of Justice Statistics (1997),[12] is shown as Table 7.4. The table is constructed from two sets of probabilities—probabilities of dying at each age (column 2) and probabilities of first admissions at each age (column 3). Prison records show the prisoners who were confined for the first time according to age during the year. Data of this kind may also be secured from interviews of inmates, so that one source can be used to supplement or validate the other. Central rates of first-time imprisonment at each age were computed from first-time admissions between July 1, 1990, and July 1, 1991, by dividing the new admissions by the population at each age. These central rates of first-time imprisonment were then converted into probabilities of first-time imprisonment by conventional methods described in various texts on demographic analysis. (See, for example, *The Methods and Materials of Demography: Revised Condensed Edition.*) Now we are ready to complete the construction of the life table.

An initial cohort of 100,000 births is subjected to mortality rates (q_x, column 2) and first-time admission rates (r_{nx}, column 3) at each successive age in order to derive the survivors at each age who have not previously been imprisoned (l_{nx}, column 1). The decrements are deaths (d_{nx}, column 4) and first-time prison admissions (i_{nx}, column 5). The accumulation of the first-time admissions (I_{nx}, column 6) gives all first-time admissions from a given age forward to the end of life. Dividing the cumulation of first-time admissions at a given age (I_x, column 6) by the never-imprisoned survivors at the same age (l_{nx}, column 1) gives the chance of being confined in a prison for the first time (or ever being confined) from a given age forward ($\%I_{nx}$, column 7). The life table of the Bureau of Justice Statistics assumes that the first-admission rates of 1991 remain constant through the lifetime of the (synthetic) cohort and that the death rates of the general population apply both to the never-incarcerated population and to the ever-incarcerated population.

From the life table presented here for 1991 and others not shown, the Bureau of Justice Statistics could describe the chances of various groups in the population ever serving time in a federal or state prison. About 5% of the U.S.

population would be confined to a state or federal prison during their lifetime. The probabilities are different for men and women and for blacks, whites, and Hispanics. The lifetime chances that a man will go to prison are much higher (9.0%) than for a woman (1.1%). The lifetime chances that a black person

TABLE 7.4   Double-Decrement Table for First Incarceration in a State or Federal Prison: 1990–1991

Age	l_{nx} (1)	q_x (2)	r_{nx} (3)	d_{nx} (4)	i_{nx} (5)	l_{nx} (6)	$\%l_{nx}$ (7)
0–13	100,000	—	—	1,217	—	5,147	5.15
14	98,783	48	2	48	2	5,147	5.21
15	98,733	67	15	66	15	5,145	5.21
16	98,652	84	62	82	62	5,130	5.20
17	98,508	97	124	96	122	5,068	5.15
18	98,290	104	228	103	224	4,946	5.03
19	97,963	107	302	104	296	4,722	4.82
20	97,563	109	352	106	343	4,426	4.54
21	97,114	111	266	109	257	4,083	4.20
22	96,748	113	299	109	290	3,825	3.95
23	96,349	114	254	109	245	3,536	3.67
24	95,995	114	297	110	285	3,291	3.43
25	95,600	113	228	108	218	3,006	3.14
26	95,274	113	233	108	221	2,788	2.93
27	94,945	114	217	108	206	2,567	2.70
28	94,631	118	219	112	207	2,361	2.49
29	94,312	122	188	115	178	2,153	2.28
30	94,019	128	155	120	146	1,976	2.10
31	93,753	134	188	125	176	1,830	1.95
32	93,452	141	143	133	133	1,654	1.77
33	93,186	151	110	141	102	1,520	1.63
34	92,943	163	113	151	105	1,418	1.53
35	92,687	175	134	162	124	1,314	1.42
36	92,401	189	123	175	113	1,190	1.29
37	92,113	201	117	185	108	1,076	1.17
38	91,820	211	98	193	90	969	1.06
39	91,537	220	90	202	82	879	0.96
40	91,253	230	85	209	78	797	0.87
41	90,966	242	71	221	64	719	0.79
42	90,681	255	67	231	61	655	0.72
43	90,389	270	47	244	42	594	0.66
44	90,103	286	51	258	46	552	0.61
45	89,799	305	44	274	39	506	0.56
46	89,486	326	42	292	37	467	0.52
47	89,157	352	45	313	40	429	0.48
48	88,804	383	45	341	40	390	0.44
49	88,423	418	45	369	40	350	0.40
50	88,014	458	38	403	33	309	0.35
51	87,578	502	20	439	18	277	0.32
52	87,121	552	23	481	20	259	0.30
53	86,620	608	30	528	25	239	0.28
54	86,067	670	28	575	25	214	0.25
55	85,467	737	32	631	26	189	0.22

(*continues*)

TABLE 7.4　　(*continued*)

Age	l_{nx} (1)	q_x (2)	r_{nx} (3)	d_{nx} (4)	i_{nx} (5)	I_{nx} (6)	$\%I_{nx}$ (7)
56–60	84,810	4,834	106	4,100	90	163	0.10
61–70	80,620	17,437	65	14,058	52	73	0.04
71 or older	66,510	99,968[a]	32	66,489	21	21	—

[a] The probability of dying at the terminal age is normally set at 1.0.

— Number rounds to zero or percent rounds to zero.

Notes: Calculations for ages under 14 and ages 56 or older are made for each single year of age and the results are then grouped for presentation in the table. The table appears to make the minor allowance for the joint risk of dying and being imprisoned within a given age. Explanations of columns:

　(1) Hypothetical cohort of 100,000 births reduced by mortality and first incarceration.

　(2) Rates represent the number of persons alive at the beginning of the age interval and dying during the interval per 100,000 persons.

　(3) Calculated by dividing the total number of first admissions during the 12-month period by the number of persons at risk of first incarceration, and then multiplying by 100,000.

　(4) Calculated by multiplying the age-specific mortality rates (column 2) by the number of persons surviving and not previously incarcerated (column 1).

　(5) Calculated by multiplying age-specific first-admission rates (column 3) by the number of persons surviving and not previously incarcerated (column 1).

　(6) Number expected to go to prison at each age and each remaining age. Derived by cumulating the number previously incarcerated (column 5) from the oldest ages to the youngest.

　(7) Calculated by dividing the number expected to go to prison at this or later age (column 6) by the number surviving and at risk of first incarceration (column 1), and multiplying by 100.

Source: U.S. Bureau of Justice Statistics, "Lifetime likelihood of going to state or federal prison," by Thomas P. Bonczar and Allen J. Beck, NCJ-160092, March 1997.

(16.2%) or a Hispanic person (9.4%) will go to prison are much higher than for a white person (2.5%). According to these life-table calculations for 1991, over one-quarter of black men, nearly one-sixth of Hispanic men, and only one out of 23 white men would be imprisoned during their lifetimes.

Estimates of the chances of ever being confined in prison at other ages can be obtained by reading the other values of the $\%I_{nx}$ function of the table. The chances drop steadily with advancing age. For example, only about 2% of persons 30 years of age who have never been imprisoned can be expected to go to prison at some later age. At age 34 the chances for future imprisonment are 1.5%. By age 46 the chances are only about 0.5%.

Other Types of Life-Table Analyses

The portion of the life table illustrated in Table 7.4 can be extended to include other functions, L_{nx}, T_{nx}, and e_{nx} (i.e., functions analogous to the L_x, T_x, and e_x functions in the conventional life table). The L_{nx} column is derived by (linear) interpolation of adjacent entries in the l_{nx} column. For example,

$$L_{n45} = \frac{1}{2}(l_{n45} + l_{n46}) = \frac{1}{2}(89,799 + 89,486) = 89,642$$

The T_{nx} column is then derived by summing the L_{nx} column from the bottom up. Finally, the e_{nx} column is calculated by dividing T_{nx} by l_{nx}. The e_{nx} function tells us the average number of years, at a given age x, before first incarceration of *previously unincarcerated* survivors to age x. We can also compute the average years before first incarceration for *all* survivors (l_x) to age x (e_{gnx}) by dividing T_{nx} by the l_x function of the corresponding conventional life table. If we subtract the latter value (e_{gnx}) from total life expectation (e_x), we obtain a value for the average number of years at age x after a first incarceration (e_{gpx}), for all survivors to age x. Further algebraic manipulation of these expectancy values yields an estimate of the average years after first incarceration for persons not previously incarcerated: $(e_{nx} \star e_{gpx}) \div e_{gnx}$.

A somewhat different method of constructing a life table on institutionalization may be necessary when data on admissions per se are not available. Different products are also secured. We can derive approximate probabilities of entering an institution at each age by appropriate manipulation of the proportions of persons not institutionalized at each age (see equations for $_5r_{nx+2.5}$ and $_5r_{nx}$ in Appendix A). Alternatively, we can use the **prevalence-ratio method** of life table construction. In this method the observed proportion of persons confined at each age in a given year (P_{px}) is applied to the L_x function of the corresponding conventional life table to obtain the years of life lived in confinement at each age (L_{px}) and the years of life lived in confinement at each age and all later ages (T_{px}). By interpolating consecutive L_{px} values, we can obtain the number of survivors to each age who are being confined at that age (l_{px}). The quotient of T_{px} and l_{px} yields e_{px}, the average number of years a person *currently confined* at age x would be confined in his or her lifetime. If, however, we divide T_{px} by the number of survivors in the total population (l_x), taken from the conventional life table, we obtain the average number of years of confinement for *all persons* surviving to age x (i.e., e'_{gpx}). Subtracting e'_{gpx} from e_x, we obtain the average number of years of nonconfinement for all persons surviving to age x (e'_{gnx}). It should be evident that we can derive more than one estimate of institutional life expectancy (e.g., institutional life expectancy for the general population, institutional life expectancy for those who are currently institutionalized, and institutional life expectancy for those who have not previously been institutionalized).

Let us recap the discussion in terms of formulas for these relations. The stationary institutional population (L_{px}) in each 5-year age group is derived from the formula,

$$_5L_{px} = {}_5L_x \star {}_5P_{px} \tag{1}$$

Then,

$$T_{px} = {}^\omega\Sigma_x \, {}_5L_{px} \tag{2}$$

To calculate e'_{gpx}, the expected years of institutional life remaining for the general population, we divide T_{px} by l_x:

$$e'_{gpx} = T_{px} \div l_x \tag{3}$$

The expected years of *noninstitutional* life remaining for the general population can now be estimated by

$$e'_{gnx} = e_x - e'_{gpx} \tag{4}$$

These calculations assume that mortality levels are the same for both the noninstitutional and the institutional population. To carry out such calculations for the nation in 1990, we can use the U.S. life tables for 1989–1991 published by the National Center for Health Statistics and data on the population in institutions for April 1, 1990, from the 1990 Census of Population.[13]

The multistate life table represents an alternate way of measuring the lifetime chances of imprisonment or entering a nursing home. In the multistate life table, one computes transition probabilities representing the chance of moving from one state (or condition) to another. These probabilities are intended to cover all possible transitions during the year and enable one to track the movements of the population from "state" to "state." They would include "moving" from a nonprison state to a prison state, a nonprison state, or death, and then, for each of these first two states, to a prison state, a nonprison state, or death, and so on. To measure the chance of ever being a prison recidivist (i.e., confined in a prison for a second time), one would focus on the transitions from a nonprison state, after a previous first imprisonment, to a prison state for the second time, a nonprison state, or death. Prison records are probably not comprehensive and accurate enough to make the construction of a multistate life table possible, but the task is worthy of exploration.

Many studies developing measures of the lifetime chances of ever entering an institution, particularly a nursing home, in older age, have been made. They employ a variety of life-table methods and the results differ substantially, as illustrated by the following studies. Kemper and Murtaugh (1991) estimated, on the basis of data for 1990, that a 65-year-old has a 45% chance of ever entering a nursing home. McConnel (1984) maintained that this risk approaches and may exceed 50%, while Liang and Tu (1986) estimated the risk at 36%. These studies are included in the list of Suggested Readings given at the end of this chapter.

Application to Subnational Areas

To prepare life tables for states and substate areas analogous to those described above poses some additional problems. Decennial census data for 1990 on the different types of institutional population disaggregated by age of the resident or inmate for states are not available in printed reports, as for earlier censuses, but one can secure special tabulations of the institutional population from the U.S. Bureau of the Census on request. It would then be possible to prepare a multiple-decrement table by the prevalence-ratio method or a "conventional" multiple-decrement table by the event-exposure method from probabilities computed indirectly for the states. State departments of social welfare or corrections may have the necessary data on first admissions to prisons or nursing homes for their states. If such data are available from state offices, one could construct a multiple-decrement table on the basis of direct data for the state.

Jury Selection

The Sixth Amendment to the U.S. Constitution guarantees a person accused of a crime the "right to a speedy and public trial, by an impartial jury of the State and district wherein the crime shall have been committed." The Seventh Amendment guarantees the right to a trial by jury in civil cases. An impartial jury, interpreted as a jury of one's peers, should represent a demographic cross-section of the community, according to the decision of the Supreme Court in *Taylor v. Louisiana* (1975). In practice, the condition of representation by one's peers in the community stands as a very loosely defined principle to be given concrete shape through the composition of a source list of qualified persons, the composition of a jury pool or *venire*, and the competitive selections of the opposing attorneys (*voir dire*).[14] The selective process allows rejections of jury candidates for cause (e.g., when the candidate evidences favoritism for one side) and unchallenged rejections called peremptory challenges. The principle of representativeness is there to be called on when it serves the litigants' needs. The attorneys are interested in a jury of peers only if the principle leads to jury selections that will favor their client, or if it can be used to challenge the other side or to meet a challenge from the other side. The Court, however, is interested in a fair representation of citizens on juries.

Issues

The main demographic/statistical issues in jury selection are as follows:

1. From what geographic area should the jury be drawn? Some of the "demographic" controversy about juries has been concerned with the geographic area or community for selection of the source list and jury pool. The area may be defined in terms of a commuting radius around the courthouse specified in miles (e.g., 20 miles), in terms of political jurisdictions (e.g., counties), or in terms of some other principle. One court's area may, therefore, overlap with another court's area and citizens from the overlapping area may be called upon to sit on juries hearing cases in both areas. The lines may be drawn in a way that minimizes the representation of some interest group on the juries in both districts. Where the jurisdictional areas of different courts overlap, therefore, a special rule may be needed to assure adequate interest group representation in both courts. Jurors may have to be reassigned from one court to another to assure appropriate representativeness. Note that the Court has considerable leeway in defining the geographic area from which jurors are drawn.

2. Which interest groups, if any, should be represented on the jury? The defendant or plaintiff may argue that a particular interest group in the geographic area of the trial is underrepresented on the jury. The interest group named may be a subgroup of Hispanics, such as Puerto Ricans (e.g., in Jersey City), college graduates (e.g., in Bethesda, Maryland), or homosexuals (e.g., in San Francisco). The courts have provided a set of criteria for identifying the types of interest groups to be considered in jury selection. The broad definition, given in *Taylor v. Louisiana* (1975) and refined in *Duren v. Missouri* (1979), is that a jury is representative unless (1) the group alleged to be excluded or underrepresented is distinctive or cognizable, (2) the underrepresentation is not

reasonable given the number of such cognizable persons in the community, and (3) the underrepresentation is the result of some systematic bias in the jury selection process.[15]

A **cognizable group** is a group that is distinctive or identifiable in a given community. A cognizable group is defined as "a group of citizens who share a common perspective gained precisely because of membership in the group, which perspective cannot be adequately represented by other members of the community" (*Rubio v. Superior Court*, California, 1979). Groups that have been recognized as cognizable include ones defined by race, ancestry, socioeconomic or class status, sex, age, and geography.[16] Court decisions have regularly recognized blacks and Hispanics as cognizable groups. Although it has often been alleged that blacks were underrepresented on juries, the issue was tested only recently in court cases, among them *People v. Rhymes* (California, 1982). On appeal of a conviction for a crime, the black defendant argued in that case that blacks were underrepresented in the list of registered voters, the list from which the jurors were drawn, and that, as a result, blacks were underrepresented on the jury. In fact, the jury contained no blacks and the judge ordered a retrial with a new jury.

3. Who should be eligible to serve on juries? The basic requirements are attainment of age 18, United States citizenship, and proficiency in English.[17] The last of these, in principle, accompanies the requirement of citizenship, but often fails to attain a satisfactory level. Aliens—legal residents as well as illegal residents—are excluded. Yet aliens make up a substantial part of the population of some communities and are often defendants or plaintiffs in legal suits. The requirements of citizenship and proficiency in English are in conflict with the principle of representativeness of juries, particularly if the plaintiff or defendant is an alien.

4. What type of list should be used to select jurors? Special attention must be given to the basis for the development of the list from which the pool of potential jurors and then the actual jurors are drawn if the jury is to be representative of the community. The jurors are usually not selected from a list of all citizens of voting age for a specified area, but from a list of registered voters for the area. Lists of taxpayers, lists of motor vehicle registrants, lists of licensed drivers, special census lists, lists of welfare recipients, and city directories may also be used, following exclusion of aliens from the lists.

If the jury pool is drawn from a list of registered voters, then groups like blacks and Hispanics are likely to be underrepresented in comparison with the white non-Hispanic population because the former groups have higher proportions of children, and their members are less likely to be citizens (if Hispanic), to have registered to vote, and to be proficient in English. In 1996, for example, about 68% of whites 18 years and over (among civilians not in institutions) reported in the Current Population Survey that they were registered to vote in the presidential election, as compared with 63% of blacks and 36% of Hispanics.[18] Blacks and Hispanics would be less likely to appear on the voter registration lists, therefore, and hence would be less likely to be selected for jury duty in comparison with non-Hispanic whites. Use of lists of licensed drivers also poses serious problems. The list includes aliens, who must be weeded out, and excludes many citizens who lack drivers' licenses. Such citizens tend to be poor or of minority race/Hispanic origin and, therefore, would be underrepresented in the jury pool.

If the original list is a list created from a local census or a city directory, it is likely to be incomplete because lists made locally are not likely to meet recognized census standards and are likely to be more incomplete than the federal census. Like voter registration lists, a local census is likely to suffer from selective underenumeration of certain population groups. The studies of the U.S. Census Bureau have documented the greater relative underenumeration in our national censuses of blacks and Hispanics than non-Hispanic whites, of men than women, of adults 25 to 54 than other ages, particularly black men of these ages, and of the inner-city population than of the remainder of the urbanized areas (see Chapter 4). The local problem can be reduced by using experienced census takers and standard census methods and supplementing the basic list with information compiled from other local lists.

Mainly to deal with the problem of limited representation of some groups on voter registration lists, California and some other states have passed statutes requiring a merger of the voter registration lists and the motor vehicle registration lists (including persons with identification cards). Such a merged list would contain the names of aliens, who have to be expunged from the list for the purposes of jury selection. Many names would be duplicated. Because merger of lists alters the chances that a given person will be selected, it may reduce an existing bias in the jury pool, it may intensify an existing one, or it may create a new major bias.

5. By what method should the members of the jury be selected from the lists, **random** (probabilistic) selection, **systematic** selection (i.e., every nth name on the list), or some other device? However representative a selection is attempted, this goal is thwarted by various common legal practices. Some prospective jurors remove themselves by various "hardship" arguments. In various jurisdictions, prospective jurors can be excused for old age, physical handicap, economic hardship, and the pressure of other public or private activities. As a result, jurors tend to fall disproportionately in certain demographic categories: They tend to be younger, older, and more retired, unemployed, underemployed, female, uninformed, uneducated, and employed (rather than self-employed) than the general adult citizen population. Some jurisdictions (e.g., Montgomery County, Maryland) permit only age and handicap as bases of exclusion; one cannot avoid jury duty by claiming lack of time, economic hardship, or need to maintain a business. A daily pay of $15 for jury duty for all jurors makes jury service economically unattractive to all economic classes.

Superimposed on this self-selection and natural-selection process is the role of the attorneys in the selection process. Attorneys can remove prospective jurors for cause and have a specified number of peremptory strikes (i.e., opportunities to request that a prospective juror be exempted from a particular jury without giving a reason). The number varies with the nature of the offense and whether the case is a civil or criminal offense. In the case of a capital offense, the prosecuting attorney may have 10 strikes and the defense attorney 20 strikes. The underlying assumption in jury-selection challenges is that persons who share your demographic and socioeconomic characteristics are more likely than others to favor your side of the argument. The litigants make a strong effort, therefore, to have such persons well represented in the pool of potential jurors and to "engineer" their selection for jury service.

Race cannot be the basis of a peremptory challenge according to several rulings of the Supreme Court made between 1986 and 1992 (e.g., *Batson v. Kentucky*, 1986). The logic is that defendants are entitled to a jury selected without intrusion of race discrimination and prospective jurors have a right to be selected for jury service without such discrimination. The courts have not been as consistent with respect to peremptory challenges on the basis of sex, but the majority of courts has favored prohibiting them on the same grounds as race.[19]

Role of Demographers

The demographer may be called on to compile and analyze the data designed to show whether the composition of a proposed jury pool reflects the population of the community. The sources to be accessed could include census data for the local area relating to population composition and commuting. It may be necessary to ascertain the characteristics of the population within various specified radii of the courthouse by geometric retrieval methods and prepare the corresponding maps. Demographers may analyze the racial/ethnic composition of the community and its composition with respect to other cognizable groups, for comparison with the composition of jury pools and groups of jurypersons. The purpose may be to quantify the degree of underrepresentation of the cognizable groups on juries, and to probe its basis, whether in the selection of the source list, the jury selection process, or the geographic delineation of the "community." The demographer may need to use a PUMS file and/or an STF file to determine what percentage of each race/ethnic group is eligible to serve on juries (i.e., are citizens 18 years and over and are proficient in English) in a particular area. These percentages can be compared with those describing the jury pool and the crop of actual jurors in the specific area at the time. The differences between such percentages should be subjected to tests of statistical significance to determine the probability with which they could have occurred by chance alone.

In most cases jury composition will have no effect on the outcome, but in a few cases it can decisively affect it. It may contribute to a fairer outcome or to the opposite. In some recent cases, juries composed of mostly minority members have disregarded compelling evidence to exonerate minority defendants (a form of "nullification"), not unlike the practice of white juries in cases with white defendants and black plaintiffs in earlier decades in the South. The current process is a contest between adversaries calculated to create unrepresentative juries so as to achieve a victory for their particular side. In order to avoid bias in the membership of juries and to assure a jury of one's peers, a random selection of jury members from a comprehensive list of eligible jurors may be made. For this method of jury selection to work, the list must be a complete list of eligible jurors for the geographic area of the court's jurisdiction and persons eligible for jury duty must be allowed few excuses for not serving, as in the case of Montgomery County, Maryland, cited earlier. A random selection of prospective jurors from the list, properly executed, is necessarily representative of the population from which it was drawn. However, the actual composition of a particular jury drawn randomly from the list may still appear unrepresentative and be disputed, although it is in fact statistically representative.

COMPLIANCE WITH REGULATIONS RELATING TO THE CONDUCT OF PUBLIC AND PRIVATE NONPROFIT ORGANIZATIONS

Public and private nonprofit organizations as well as businesses are required to observe certain regulations in the treatment of their external clients or customers. Special regulations and laws may apply if these clients or customers fall into certain demographic groups such as those defined by sex, age, race/Hispanic origin, marital status, and family composition.

Some Issues in the Interface of Demography and Education

Three public programs supported by law and intended to reduce inequalities in educational and employment opportunities among racial and ethnic groups are discussed. They relate to public school racial integration, bilingual education in public schools, and affirmative action in admissions to public colleges and universities. The programs pose problems in educational administration, law, and applied demography.

Public School Racial Integration

There is much debate currently about the quality of public education as it differentially affects white non-Hispanics and racial/Hispanic minorities. Various programs have been instituted to remedy the problem. The practice of school busing, the allocation of reserved space in magnet schools, and modifying the delineation of public school districts are among these programs. Numerous disputes have arisen regarding their purpose, implementation, and effectiveness. Concentration of racial minorities and Hispanics in particular sections of cities and the assumption that this concentration adversely affects the quality of education they receive largely underlie attempts to achieve racial integration in public schools.

The debate regarding the delineation of the boundaries of school districts and the composition of the populations residing in them is viewed as important since the choices made affect the schools that children attend, the companions and teachers they have, and the content of their education. Such a device as redrawing school district boundaries tries to improve the quality of education for racial minorities by reducing overconcentration of racial minorities in the same schools and exposing them to new teachers, school environments, and curricula. Boundaries can sometimes be drawn in ways to concentrate racial minorities in a school district or they can be drawn to dilute their numbers. School districts can be modified in size and shape, subject to constraints for efficient administration. Demographers may be involved as expert witnesses in legal contests relating to the proper delineation of school districts but, more commonly, they may be asked to participate in the redrawing of school districts as communities grow or decline in population.

Efforts to improve the quality of public education for racial minorities have led also to busing students to other areas or districts in order to "redesign" school districts without redrawing their boundaries, and the use of affirmative action programs, including quotas, in the allocation of space to various race/Hispanic groups in magnet schools. Busing is intended to bring more racial minorities and Hispanic students into school districts dominated by white non-Hispanic students. Magnet schools pursue affirmative action programs, setting implicit or explicit quotas for racial minorities and Hispanics. The magnet-school program offers qualified minority students the opportunity to attend better schools in a different area of the city. Morrison (1998) has given an example of how arithmetic tightrope walking can obviate the criticism of a segregated admissions policy with quotas for racial minorities in magnet schools offering accelerated programs for gifted children.[20]

Active efforts to achieve racial integration in public schools began with the decision by the Supreme Court in 1954 in *Brown v. Board of Education of Topeka*. This decision led to widespread busing of students within and between school districts as the principal means of remedying the problem. The busing program succeeded in some areas, especially in the early years under court-ordered busing.[21] As opponents foresaw, however, busing has generally been a failure in the long run as an effective method of achieving racial integration, even in the areas operating under court orders. It could not overcome the considerable residential separation of the races and other serious problems associated with this separation. Residential separation of the races has changed only modestly since the 1954 decision, mainly because of the continuing out-migration of whites from the central cities to the suburbs at rates that exceeded the out-migration rates of blacks.

As the country forged ahead with the busing program, many private schools sprang up to accommodate white defections from the public schools. These were common, especially in the South. Sometimes whole communities defected by abolishing the public school system. Private schools that functioned as de facto public schools for whites emerged. Blacks, Asian Americans, and Hispanics are so dominant in many communities, being "majority minorities," that reshuffling the students racially/ethnically could accomplish little in the way of integration with white non-Hispanics in these communities. Such a goal becomes increasingly difficult to achieve statistically in terms of residential clustering of these groups measured by, say, the index of dissimilarity, as the proportion of nonwhites/Hispanics in the population rises above 70% or so, as it does in some large cities. Racial residential clustering is much greater than residential clustering of socioeconomic groups or white ethnic groups. Furthermore, school busing is an extremely costly program. Opponents of busing argue that it grossly abuses the time of parents and children and that the money and time can be spent more effectively at direct efforts to improve the quality of education in the schools that the students already attend.

After more than four decades of trying to desegregate public schools through busing, local jurisdictions appear to be abandoning this approach. The failure of the program and changes in the law both underlie this shift in the effort to achieve public school racial integration. The Supreme Court has ruled in a number of recent cases that using race as a sole criterion for delineating legislative districts (see Chapter 12) or admitting students to college is unacceptable. This interpretation of the Constitution may be carried over in the courts to the practice of busing, the delineation of school districts, and the use of quotas in the admissions to magnet schools.

Bilingual Education

Bilingual education refers to the programs in public schools by which instruction is given to immigrant children in their native language as a step toward their transfer to classes in English and other subjects taught in English. The programs are intended to integrate foreign-born children linguistically into the mainstream. They were initially (mid-1960s) justified by the high dropout rate of school-aged Spanish-speaking children. A rough indication of the school dropout rate for Hispanics at an earlier date is given by the proportion in 1981 of Hispanics 25 years old and over who were not high school graduates—56%. The corresponding figures for blacks and whites were 47% and 28%, respectively. In 1997 these figures were still far apart—45%, 26%, and 17%—although they were much lower. A more realistic measure is the proportion of youths 18 to 24 years of age who were not enrolled in school and were not high school graduates. In 1997, these figures were 35% for Hispanics, 14% for blacks, and 14% for whites.[22] We really need a cohort measure, preferably one based on matched cases, such as the proportion of enrollees in grade 8 in year y who are no longer enrolled in grade 12 in year $y+4$. However, it is difficult to construct an accurate measure of school attrition for Hispanic children since Hispanic cohorts have been augmented by many immigrant children whose education in their native countries is often unknown.

Programs of bilingual education are supported by federal funds made available under the Elementary and Secondary Education Act of 1965, as amended by the Bilingual Education Act of 1968, and are offered to states meeting specified requirements and choosing to implement such a program. Programs in bilingual education have been conducted for as much as three decades in some places. The efficacy of the programs in "mainstreaming" children has been widely challenged, however, especially by Hispanic parents.[23]

Bilingual education is intended to serve the children who do not speak English well or do not speak English at all by providing instruction in their native language first. How many children require this special instruction? The considerable growth in the volume of immigration since the 1960s from Mexico, India, Vietnam, and other countries of Latin America and Asia has greatly increased the number of young speakers of foreign languages in the country, especially in California, where a large share of the new immigrants reside. According to the 1990 decennial census, 70% of the students who speak a language other than English at home and do not speak English well or at all reside in only six states, namely California, Florida, Illinois, New Jersey, New York, and Texas. California alone has 1.4 million such students in its public schools, or one out of four in the total student body. In the nation only 2.5% of the children aged 5 to 9, 1.5% of the children aged 10 to 14, and 2% of the youngsters aged 15 to 17 speak a language other than English at home and do not speak English well or at all. If we base the percentages on the population speaking a language other than English at home, the percentages for those who do not speak English well or at all are much higher: 19% for ages 5 to 9; 11% for ages 10 to 14; and 13% for ages 15 to 17. These are national averages and the figures for states with large shares of recent immigrants, such as the six states named above, would be higher.

Bilingual education is justified on technical grounds by its advocates while its detractors see technical deficiencies in the program and political motives on the part of advocates. Supporters of bilingual education find evidence that, without prior training in their regular school subjects in their native languages, many of these limited-English children would not profit from their education and that an abrupt move to training in English only would be traumatic and counterproductive. Various linguistic theories have been propounded to support bilingual education (e.g., the greater the prior proficiency achieved in the native language, the greater the proficiency to be expected subsequently in English).

Opponents of bilingual education find evidence to support the position that bilingual training retards the progress of the students in learning English and that a course of total immersion in English would be more productive. They claim that bilingual education has produced a segregated class of non-English speaking students who remain for years in classes taught in Spanish. Opponents also maintain that supporters of bilingual training in Spanish in the Southwest have been using this training to promote a separate Hispanic monolingual culture in that area, not merely to provide a bridge to English proficiency. They point to the large body of research indicating that teaching children in their native language does not contribute to learning English or other subjects in English, and that children learn a foreign language most easily at the youngest ages. Moreover, opponents maintain, the overall dropout rate of school-aged Hispanics has not declined substantially in the past few decades when bilingual education programs have been "in force" and remains high in comparison with that for non-Hispanic whites and blacks.

There is probably some merit to all these arguments, and it is also probable that bilingual education works for some children under certain circumstances and not for these children under other circumstances, nor for others. In 1998, residents of California voted on Proposition 227, which calls for an end to bilingual education in public schools. Proposition 227 passed but it is being challenged in the courts. The state of California has decided to continue bilingual education but to limit such training to one year. It is likely that efforts to abolish bilingual education will spread to other areas of the country. A number of states have opted to reject the program and the federal funds that go with it.

The language situation in the United States has changed sharply since the passage of the Bilingual Education Act in 1968. In the early 1970s, all the classes in the bilingual education program were conducted in Spanish, but by the late 1990s, about one-third of the limited-English students in the public schools spoke one of a few hundred other languages. Hence, bilingual education has also become a major administrative problem.[24]

College Admissions

Since the mid-1960s colleges and universities have been subject to affirmative action guidelines in admitting students and, as a result, the share of racial minorities/Hispanics among the students rose. Even with an affirmative action program spanning many years, the enrollment at the University of Michigan was only 9% black in 1997 while the state's population was 14% black. By the criterion implied here, blacks are underrepresented in the student body of the university. The demographic analyst who may be enlisted to review such figures as they bear on the role of affirmative action in college enrollment is constrained to ask whether this is an appropriate standard for evaluating the share of blacks enrolled in a large state university. While use of data for the state of Michigan is one geographic criterion, others need to be considered. The educational qualifications of the candidates also should be considered in the standard. It is more reasonable to restrict the standard to high-school graduates or graduates in the upper third of the graduating classes in the state of Michigan. Since the university accepts students from the entire United States (and foreign countries), the entire United States, or some "weighted" geographic area (e.g., Michigan, the rest of United States), could be the geographic area employed as the standard against which the actual percentages of blacks and Hispanics enrolled should be measured. Any argument that the residential origins of the students currently enrolled in the university should be used as a standard may be countered by the argument that these origins are corrupted by past policies of adverse racial selectivity, and hence a different affirmative action standard is needed.

The admissions policy at any state university like the University of Michigan tends to seek diversity in enrollment as an end in itself by considering race, Hispanic ethnicity, and such other factors as rural background and parents who are alumni. Opponents of affirmative action claim to support diversity also, but only if it is achieved by outreach programs and other methods that do not rely on a different standard for non-Hispanic whites and others.

In the past decade, affirmative action in college admissions as a preference system for protected racial minorities/Hispanics has been challenged. The Regents of the University of California, following the terms of Proposition 209, a successful ballot initiative, have abolished the use of affirmative action in determining admissions to the public colleges and universities of the state. Affirmative action in admissions to the public colleges and universities of Texas was struck down in *Hopwood v. University of Texas Law School*, when in 1996 the U.S. Supreme Court let stand an appeals court decision of 1993 in favor of four white students who sued the University of Texas Law School for racial discrimination. While the Supreme Court's *Bakke* decision of the late 1970s (*Regents of the University of California v. Bakke*, 1978), allowing schools to use race as a factor in admissions but prohibiting racial quotas and separate tracks for the races, still stands as the rule in most of the United States, *Hopwood* appears to have undone *Bakke*.

The recent legal decisions resulted in sharp declines in applications and admissions of blacks and Hispanics, but notable increases for non-Hispanic whites and Asians, at some public colleges and universities in Texas and California for the fall of 1997. They resulted in even greater declines in black and

Hispanic enrollment at these schools inasmuch as the distribution of financial aid must also disregard race. At other public colleges and universities in these states, enrollments of blacks and Hispanics remained level or increased. These schools appear to have been able to maintain racial minority enrollment by changing their admissions policy, in particular by giving less weight to standardized tests and grades and giving more weight to other factors (excluding race). In order to achieve racial diversity in their student bodies, Texas colleges and universities are employing such criteria as high scholastic ranking among the graduates of the high schools of the state, disadvantaged family background, and special skills or accomplishments (e.g., leadership skills, community work). Studies are needed to analyze separately the records of black and Hispanic students (undergraduate, graduate, professional school) who would have been admitted if test scores and grades alone were used and the other black and Hispanic students who were admitted, and to compare the two groups of admittees in graduation rates and licensing and certification rates. Perhaps affirmative action has further support from this source.[25]

A more productive effort for the long term is to improve the quality of preparation of high school students applying for admission to colleges and universities by investing funds in the poorest school districts of each state.[26] Much progress has already been made in the educational attainment of racial minorities. Between 1960 and 1997 the share of blacks 25 years old and over who are college graduates rose steadily (from 3.1% to 13%), as did that for Hispanics between 1970 to 1997 (from 4.5% to 10%), but the gaps in the percentages between whites (25%) and the other groups remain large.[27]

Role of Demographers

Demographers can contribute to the debate on these controversial legal and educational issues by presenting appropriate census or other demographic data, interpreting them, and applying relevant analytic techniques, including the formal and systematic methods of demographic research. In this way demographers can help elucidate the nature and extent of the problem and, often, with computer simulation, geodemographic methods, and sensitivity analyses can set forth alternative scenarios that contribute to its management and resolution.

Demographic Targeting in Law Enforcement

The term **demographic targeting** refers to the practice of taking special action for or against a person's interests because of one or more of the person's demographic characteristics. The characteristics may be sex, age, race, ethnic origin, marital status, size of family, or socioeconomic status. When the action is adverse, the injured party may label it unfair and unjust, if not illegal. Such action is illustrated by the rejection of someone as an employee because of their age, charging customers differently for services performed because of their sex, treating customers in a store or restaurant differently because of their race, refusing to make deliveries or pickups because of the socioeconomic status of a neighborhood, and stopping suspects for alleged traffic violations on the basis of their racial or ethnic appearance. This last type of behavior is popularly referred to as **racial profiling**. It refers most commonly to the practice of some law enforcement officers of detaining blacks and Hispanics selectively for traffic violations, presumably without probable cause.

Racial profiling should be distinguished from criminal profiling. Criminal administration recognizes the principle of criminal profiling as a valuable tool of law enforcement. **Criminal profiling** seeks to maximize the probability of arresting the perpetrators of a crime by applying profiles of offenders based on previous experience with persons charged and convicted of particular types of crimes. Criminal profiling is viewed as absolutely essential in the enforcement of the drug laws, as well as in the efficient use of police resources in the handling of many other types of crimes. In the case of traffic offenses on highways, the record shows that the race of the probable offender varies depending on the part of the country, the particular highway, and the type of highway offense. Speeding offenders have different profiles from drivers involved in the drug trade. Some general factors at play are that the racial composition of a community affects the racial composition of persons detained for reported offenses, and the number of detentions by the police is influenced by the ratio of police officers to population and the ratio of crimes reported of a given type to population. What is important is that the race of the police officer and the race of the alleged offender should be statistically independent elements in the detention of alleged offenders.

Racial profiling is illegal on the highway as elsewhere since it is a violation of a person's civil rights ("equal treatment under the law") and since there must be probable cause to detain a person. Much anecdotal evidence supports the allegation that racial profiling does occur on the highway. However, the formal evidence to support this allegation is lacking at present.[28] A bill has been proposed in the Congress to support research to determine whether racial profiling goes on (HR 106-1443). Controlled studies are needed. These studies should compare the racial composition of motorists stopped on specific roadways with that of motorists at risk of being stopped on these roadways and, possibly, match the enforcement records of police officers of different races patrolling the same segments of the highway. The research may indicate that racial profiling is perpetrated by police officers of all races against black and Hispanic drivers because of a culture of racial profiling within a department or it may indicate that it is perpetrated by a few rogue white offenders in a department. It may prove to be only apparent and a function of the specific roadways, communities, and level of the local crime rate.

If we try to develop profiles of highway offenders, it is doubtful that we should find evidence that blacks are disproportionate offenders. On the other hand, the reports of the Federal Bureau of Investigation and the Bureau of Justice Statistics show that blacks had higher-than-average rates of arrests, convictions, and incarcerations for all serious crimes and most nonserious crimes.[29] Then, the question is properly raised whether justice has been even-handed in arresting, convicting, and incarcerating blacks and hence whether the crime statistics reflect the actual situation. In other words, the standard used as a basis for criminal profiling with respect to race may be tainted by past irregularities in the enforcement and administration of the law. More important, the practice of criminal profiling where race is an element, however justified by the statistical record and administrative efficiency, is fraught with the danger of perpetuating racial dissension and racial profiling itself. It has done and can do little to reduce the disparity in the crime records of the races. In sum, public policy supporting racial unity should override any consideration of the utility of the practice of criminal profiling with respect to race.

APPENDIX A: ALTERNATIVE LIFE-TABLE METHODS OF ESTIMATING THE CHANCE OF EVER ENTERING A NURSING HOME[30]

This appendix describes the steps in calculating the proportion of the population at age 45 expected to enter a nursing home at some time in the future. This exposition assumes that L_{nx}, the years of noninstitutional life lived in each age, was derived by the prevalence-ratio method. We can estimate $_5L_{nx}$ by multiplying the observed proportion of the noninstitutional population at each age ($_5N_x = 1 - {_5P_{px}}$) by the stationary population ($_5L_x$) taken from the corresponding general life table. Then, obtain T_{n45} by cumulating the $_5L_{nx}$ values from the final age up to age 45. Next, estimate the number of survivors to exact age 45 who have not yet entered a nursing home by interpolating on $_5L_{nx}$ as follows:

$$l_{n45} = {^1/_{10}}(_5L_{n45-49} + {_5L_{n40-44}})$$

Repeat this calculation of the number of survivors to age x (every fifth age) who have never spent time in a nursing home (l_{nx}) by the general formula:

$$l_{nx} = {^1/_{10}}(_5L_{nx} + {_5L_{nx-5}})$$

Now, we need to secure estimates of $_5i_{nx}$, the net number of persons entering nursing homes during the age intervals. We do this by subtracting the number of deaths in the age intervals from the age-to-age changes in the number of survivors who have never resided in a nursing home:

$$l_{n(x+5)} = l_{nx} - {_5d_{nx}} - {_5i_{nx}}, \quad \text{for } x = 45, 50, 55, \ldots$$
$$_5i_{nx} = l_{nx} - l_{n(x+5)} - {_5d_{nx}}$$

where l_{nx} is the number of survivors at exact age x who have never entered a nursing home, $_5d_{nx}$ is the number of persons dying between exact age x and exact age $x + 5$, and $_5i_{nx}$ is the net number of persons entering a nursing home between exact age x and exact age $x + 5$. The $_5d_{nx}$ values are obtained as the product of $_5q_x$, the probability of dying between exact age x and exact age $x + 5$, and l_{nx}:

$$_5d_{nx} = {_5q_x} \star l_{nx}$$

Values of $_5q_x$ are taken from the 1989–1991 U.S. life tables. Finally, the proportion of the population entering a nursing home at age x and all later ages ($\%I_{nx}$) is given by

$$\%I_{nx} = ({^\omega\Sigma_x}\, i_{nx} \div l_{nx}) \star 100$$

The proportion of the population entering a nursing home at age 45 or after (i.e., $\%I_{45}$) is derived by

$$\%I_{n45} = (^{\omega}\Sigma_{45}\ i_{nx} \div l_{n45}) \star 100$$

Alternatively, an estimate of $_5i_{nx}$ can be obtained by estimating the rate of entry into institutions between the midpoint ages of the institutional population ($_5r_{x+2.5}$) and then interpolating the $_5r_{x+2.5}$ values to derive the rate of change between exact age x and exact age $x + 5$:

$$_5r_{nx+2.5} = (_5N_x - _5N_{x+5}) \div _5N_x$$

It may be recalled that $_5N_x$ is defined as the proportion of the population between ages x to $x + 5$ not in nursing homes. The $_5r_{x+2.5}$ values need to be centered by interpolation:

$$_5r_{nx} = {}^1\!/_2(_5r_{(nx-2.5)} + _5r_{nx+2.5})$$

Finally, $_5i_{nx}$ is estimated by

$$_5i_{nx} = _5r_{nx}(1 - _5q_x/2)l_{nx}$$

where factor $(1 - _5q_x/2)$ is designed to take account of the duplication of deaths and entries within the age group (i.e., deaths occurring to persons who have entered a nursing home during the 5-year period).

We can calculate the noninstitutional life expectancy of survivors at age 45 not previously institutionalized (e_{n45}) with the values derived earlier:

$$e_{nx} = T_{nx} \div l_{nx}$$
$$e_{n45} = T_{n45} \div l_{n45}$$

where T_{n45} represents the cumulation of $_5L_{nx}$ from age 45 to the end of life and l_{n45} represents the number of survivors to age x not in institutions.

NOTES

1. Stella U. Ogunwalle, "Demographics in area ministry development planning of congregations," in K.V. Rao and Jerry W. Wicks (eds.), *Studies in Applied Demography: Proceedings of the International Conference on Applied Demgraphy*, Bowling Green, OH: Bowling Green State University, 1994.

2. Lists of indicators that focus on children and the elderly can be found in The Annie E. Casey Foundation, "1999 Kids Count Data Sheet" and "1999 Kids Count Data Book," Baltimore, MD: The Annie E. Casey Foundation (prepared for the Foundation by the Population Reference Bureau, Washington, DC); and the U.S. Federal Interagency Forum on Aging-Related Statistics, *Older Americans 2000: Key Indicators of Well-Being*, 2000.

3. Mean family or household income is the ratio of the total aggregate income of a group to the number of families or households. Per capita income is the ratio of the total aggregate income of a group to the total population of the group.

4. U.S. Bureau of the Census, "Dynamics of economic well-being: Poverty in 1990–92," *Current Population Reports*, Series P-70, No. 42.

5. Patricia Ruggles, *Drawing the Line: Alternative Poverty Measures and Their Implications for Public Policy*, Urban Institute, 1992.

6. In 1996 the program of Aid to Families With Dependent Children (AFDC) was converted to a state block-grant program, formally called Temporary Assistance to Needy Families (TANF).

7. See U.S. Bureau of the Census, "Income, poverty, and valuation of noncash benefits: 1994," *Current Population Reports*, Series P60–189, April 1996, esp. Table L, p. xxiv.

8. For purposes of poverty measurement, income is defined in the proposal of the National Academy of Sciences as disposable income plus "near-money" income. The value of certain non-cash benefits would be added to cash income; and certain expenses that cannot be used to purchase basic goods and services, such as income taxes, payroll taxes, child care costs, child support payments, transportation and other work-related expenses, and medical care payments, including health insurance payments, would be excluded. Recommended thresholds would be developed for a two-adult two-child family from consumer-expenditure data on food, clothing, and shelter, plus other needed expenditures. An equivalence scale would be used to adjust the reference family threshold for other family types, and a housing code index would be used to allow for differences in housing costs by region and size of metropolitan area. SIPP, the national survey, would be used to measure poverty. Under the proposed measure, more working families, but fewer families now receiving government assistance, would be counted as living in poverty. See Constance F. Citro and Robert M. Michael, *Measuring Poverty: A New Approach*, Washington, DC: National Academy Press, 1995.

9. Various specialized surveys, such as the National Survey of Adolescent Males, the National Longitudinal Surveys of Labor Market Experience, and the Survey of Income Dynamics, may also be useful here.

10. It is important that the data on abortions be tabulated by place of usual residence of the woman rather than by the location of the facility where the procedure was performed. Some states have only one facility of this kind.

11. Because estimates are obtained by this procedure for the last census date, they are rather dated. More current estimates of poor children can be developed on the basis of postcensal estimates of population for census tracts and survey estimates of poor children in families (see Chapters 9 and 11). The same sources as for 1990 can be accessed from the 2000 census when they become available.

12. U.S. Department of Justice, Bureau of Justice Statistics, "Lifetime likelihood of going to state or federal prison," by Thomas Bonczar and Allen Beck, NCJ-160092, March 1997.

13. U.S. National Center for Health Statistics, *U.S. Decennial Life Tables, 1989–91*, 1997. U.S. Bureau of the Census, *1990 Census of Population*, special tabulations on request, reports 1990 CP-1 and CP-2 (based on Summary Tape Files 1 and 3), and PUMS—5% sample on CD-ROM.

14. The qualified source list consists of the names of persons who are on a basic list from which prospective jurors can be called, such as a list of registered voters, but from which cases of hardship, old age, responsibility for child care, disability, and other disqualifying factors have been excluded. This list is further narrowed to a jury pool or *venire*, the panel of prospective jurors from which specific juries are selected. The size and nature of the jury pool varies from one court district to another, one type of court to another (e.g., state court versus federal court), and one type of offense to another. The jury pool in a capital offense with multiple defendants may number 600 to 800, but more commonly the pool numbers less than 100.

15. John R. Weeks, *Population: An Introduction to Concepts and Issues*, 6th ed., Belmont, CA: Wadsworth, 1996, pp. 572–574.

16. Andrew A. Beveridge, "Challenging jury pools, jury wheels and jury selection systems, Demographic and statistical approaches," paper presented at the 1999 annual meeting of the Population Association of America, New York, March 25 to 27, 1999.

17. Proficiency in English indicates that the individual speaks only English at home or, where a language other than English is spoken, English is spoken either "very well" or "well." This definition follows that given on the 1990 census questionnaire.

18. U.S. Bureau of the Census, *Statistical Abstract of the United States, 1998*, Table 483, and *Current Population Reports*, Series P20–466.

19. Jo Freeman, "The revolution for women in law and public policy," in Jo Freeman (ed.), *Women: A Feminist Perspective*, Mountain View, CA: Mayfield, 1995, p. 377.

20. Peter A. Morrison, "Charting alternatives to a segregated school admissions policy: Where demographic analysis fits in," paper presented at the annual meeting of the Population Association of America, Chicago, IL, April 2–4, 1998.

21. Reynolds Farley, "Residential segregation and its implications for school integration," *Law and Contemporary Problems* 39(1): 164–193 (Winter issue), 1975.

22. These estimates are based on the U.S. Census Bureau's Current Population Survey for the years noted.

23. See, for example, Rosalie Pedalino Porter, "The case against bilingual education," *Atlantic Monthly*, May 1998, p. 28 ff.

24. A related issue is the continuing national movement to make English the official language of the United States. Since the U.S. Constitution does not include a requirement that English must serve as the official language of the country, several congressional bills have proposed making English the official language. See, for example, S.356, 104th Congress, 1st Session, February 3, 1995. There have also been moves to pass a Constitutional amendment with this goal, one as recently as 1998. Since the 1980s, about half of the states have passed statutes declaring English as the official language. For example, this requirement is written into Florida's Constitution. States with laws mandating English as the official language may, in effect, be violating Civil Rights legislation prohibiting discrimination by states on the basis of race, color, or national origin (*Hagan v. Sandoval*, 11th Circuit). The Bilingual Education Act of 1968, which supports bilingual education in public schools, the Voting Rights Act of 1964, which makes obligatory the provision of ballots in languages other than English under specified "demographic" conditions in federal, state, and local elections, and the practice of providing decennial census questionnaires in languages other than English are all consistent with the idea of official multilingualism in the United States. However, the Congressional Record and the proceedings of the federal judiciary are printed only in English. This practice is consistent with the opposite public policy.

25. For a current news report on recent changes in the racial composition of college enrollments and programs to replace affirmative action where it has been outlawed, see Kenneth J. Cooper, "Colleges testing new diversity initiatives," *Washington Post*, April 2, 2000, p. A4.

26. See, for example, Stephan Thernstrom and Abigail Thernstrom, *America in Black and White: One Nation Indivisible*, New York: Simon and Schuster, 1997.

27. Figures are based on the decennial censuses of population and the Current Population Survey.

28. U.S. General Accounting Office, *Racial Profiling: Limited Data Available on Motorists Stops*, GGD—00-41, March 2000.

29. Based on data from the Federal Bureau of Investigation, *Crime in the United States*, and Bureau of Justice Statistics, *Prisoners in Federal and State Institutions* and *Prison and Jail Inmates at Midyear*. See, for example, U.S. Bureau of the Census, *Statistical Abstract in the United States*, *1998*, Table 354.

30. In the preparation of this appendix, the author benefited from an unpublished manuscript prepared by Ann E. Anderson (1979), then of the U.S. Bureau of the Census.

SUGGESTED READINGS

Social Indicators

Annie E. Casey Foundation. (1999). *Kids Count Data Book*. Baltimore, MD: Annie E. Casey Foundation.

Hauser, Robert M., Brown, Brett V., and Prosser, William (eds.). (1997). *Indicators of Children's Well-Being*. New York: Russell Sage Foundation.

U.S. Federal Interagency Forum on Aging-Related Statistics. (2000). *Older Americans 2000: Key Indicators of Well-Being*.

U.S. Federal Interagency Forum on Child and Family Statistics. (2000). *America's Children: Key National Indicators of Well-Being 2000*.

Equity in Education and Housing

Farley, Reynolds. (1975, Winter). "Residential segregation and its implications for school integration." *Law and Contemporary Problems* 39(1): 164–193.

Farley, Reynolds, and Taeuber, Karl. (1974). "Racial segregation in the public schools." *American Journal of Sociology* 79: 888.

Read, Frank T. (1975, Winter). "Judicial evolution of the law of school integration since *Brown v. Board of Education.*" *Law and Contemporary Problems* 39(1): 7–20.

Siegel, Jacob S. (1994). "The role of demographers in public and private suits of housing discrimination." In K. V. Rao and Jerry W. Wicks (eds.), *Studies in Applied Demography: Proceedings of the International Conference on Applied Demgraphy.* Bowling Green, OH: Bowling Green State University.

Yinger, John. (1995). *Closed Doors, Opportunities Lost: The Continuing Costs of Housing Discrimination.* New York: Russell Sage Foundation.

Lifetime Risk of Nursing Home Residency

Foley, D. A., Ostfeld, A. *et al.*(1992). "The risk of nursing home admission in three communities."*Journal of Aging and Health*: 155–173.

Kemper, P., and Murtaugh, C. (1991). "Lifetime use of nursing-home care." *New England Journal of Medicine* 32(9): 595–600.

Liang, J., and Jow-Ching Tu, E. (1986, October). "Estimating lifetime risk of nursing home residency: A further note." *Gerontologist* 26(5): 560–563.

Manton, K. G., Woodbury, M. A., and Liu, K. (1984). "Life table methods for assessing the dynamics of U.S. nursing home utilization: 1976–77." *Journal of Gerontology* 39(1): 79–87.

McConnel, C. E. (1984, April). "A note on the lifetime risk of nursing home residency." *Gerontologist* 24(2): 193–198.

Spence, D. A., and Wiener, J. (1990, February). "Nursing home length of stay patterns: Results from the 1985 National Nursing Home Survey." *Gerontologist* 30(1): 15–20.

Jury Selection

Detre, Peter A. (1994, May). "A proposal for measuring underrepresentation in the composition of the jury wheel." *Yale Law Review* 1994: 1913–1938.

King, Nancy J. (1993, October). "Racial jurymandering: Cancer or cure? A contemporary review of affirmative action in jury selection." *New York University Law Review* 1993: 707–776.

Weeks, John R. (1996). "The demographics of juries—A case study," pp. 572–574, in *Population: An Introduction to Concepts and Issues*, 6th ed. Belmont, CA: Wadsworth.

Other Applications

Pol, Louis G., and Thomas, Richard K. (2000). *The Demography of Health and Health Care.* 2nd ed. Norwell, MA: Kluwer Academic Publishers.

Poston, Dudley L., Jr. (1980). "The use of census data by social demographers." Chapter 14 in U.S. Bureau of the Census, *Census '80: Continuing the Factfinder Tradition*, by Charles P. Kaplan and Charles L. VanValey (eds.).

Smith, Stanley K., and McCarty, Christopher. (1996, May). "Demographic effects of natural disasters: A case study of hurricane Andrew." *Demography* 33(2): 265–275.

Thomas, Richard K. (1994). "Using demographic analysis in health services planning: A case study in obstetrical services," pp. 159–179. In Hallie J. Kintner *et al.* (eds.). *Demographics: A Casebook for Business and Government.* Boulder, CO: Westview Press.

U.S. Bureau of the Census. (1978). *Census Data for Community Action*, by Gary M. Young.

U.S. Bureau of the Census. (1989). *Census ABC's: Applications in Business and Community.*

U.S. General Accounting Office (March 2000). *Racial Profiling: Limited Data Available on Motorists Stops*, GGD—00-41.

U.S. General Accounting Office (March 2000). *Better Targeting of Airline Passengers for Personal Searches Could Produce Better Results*, GGD—00-38.

8

THE DEMOGRAPHY OF THE LABOR FORCE AND OF THE WORKFORCE OF ORGANIZATIONS

INTRODUCTION

Types of Workforces

There are many types of labor forces or workforces. The nation has its labor force, as does each region of the country, each state, and each metropolitan area. The workforce or labor force is also defined for a labor market area, the circumscribed geographic area within which workers are mainly recruited, work, reside, and hence commute to and from work. The workforce may also be defined for types of organizations (e.g., charitable organizations, professional associations), specific industries (e.g., construction industry), and specific companies (e.g., General Motors Corporation). Private nonprofit organizations, governments and government agencies, and businesses employ a corps of workers who do the work of the organization. Because the workforces of the various areas and types of organizations are similar in their general demographic characteristics and dynamics, they are considered together in this chapter.

Many other highly specific workforces, such as particular occupational groups, may be identified. Consider, for example, prison guards, the Catholic clergy, nurses, automobile plant workers, U.S. military personnel, homemakers, volunteer workers, and, more specifically, such workers at particular installations or in particular geographic areas. Note that some of these groups— homemakers and volunteer workers—are not part of the official labor force because they are not paid, but they contribute to the economy by virtue of their considerable volume of work. The retired population is another group that can be analyzed like the labor force. Although it is not part of the labor force in the usual sense, it is useful to consider the retired population of an organization, such as the U.S. government (federal retirees) or U.S. armed forces (veterans), like a workforce because the retirees often continue to work part-time or on contract for the organization, to receive benefits from it, or to work as volunteers for the same or other organizations.

The Labor Force Concept

Official national and subnational data on the working population are based on the labor force concept and many of our human resource policies reflect this concept. This is the concept used in the decennial census and national sample surveys, including the Current Population Survey, and hence in the reports of the Bureau of the Census and the Bureau of Labor Statistics. According to the labor force concept, the **labor force** includes all persons at work or with a job (i.e., employed and self-employed) and persons without a job but actively seeking work (i.e., unemployed) during a *designated period*. Hence, the total labor force consists of employed civilians, unemployed civilians, and members of the armed forces during a particular period.[1]

Participation in the labor force is determined by economic activity usually in the week preceding the date of the survey interview. Sometimes information on labor force participation relates to an entire year (as, for example, the year before the decennial census), as well as the week before the census (e.g., 1990 Census of Population). **Employed persons** include all persons (1) who did any work at all during the survey week as paid employees, in their own business, professional practice, or farm, or (2) who worked 15 hours or more as unpaid workers on a farm or in a business operated by a member of the family, or (3) who were not working but had a job or business from which they were temporarily absent. **Unemployed persons** are persons of working age who, in the reference period, (1) are without work, (2) are available for work, and (3) are taking steps to find work. These steps may involve submitting applications for jobs, registering with an employment agency, or calling prospective employers. All civilians who are not classified as employed or unemployed are described as "not in the labor force." The institutional population may be excluded from the population under study entirely or it may be counted among those "not in the labor force."

The official labor force concept is tied to the receipt of money income and excludes unpaid work (with the exception noted earlier). This is a narrow definition since, as was mentioned, many persons carry out productive activity without being paid (e.g., volunteer workers, home managers). There are other concepts for identifying the working population. A more comprehensive definition is used, for example, in the Health and Retirement Survey. The U.S. Census Bureau has been using the labor force concept since the 1940 census. The U.S. censuses of 1930 and earlier employed the "gainful worker" concept. According to the **gainful worker concept,** the gainful worker population consists of those persons who have a gainful occupation at which they *usually* work. The International Labor Office (ILO) seeks to compile data on the **economically active population** of various countries. The concept of economic activity is a broad term, encompassing both the labor force concept and the gainful worker concept. The Office of Economic Cooperation and Development (OECD) employs a labor force concept similar to that of the United States. Its data for the various countries differ as to the minimum age for tabulations (e.g., age 15 for Germany and Canada; age 16 for United States and France) and the inclusion or exclusion of the institutionalized population in the working-age population.

We have been viewing the workforce on the basis of data collected from households. Data on workers may also be collected from business establishments and other organizations. Establishment data differ from household data in two principal ways. In establishment data, an individual may be reported twice if he or she works in two locations and the geographic reference is the place of work rather than the place of residence. Generally, establishment data are available for employees of the government and employees of businesses, but not for employees of nonprofit organizations. The Census Bureau, the Bureau of Economic Analysis, and the Social Security Administration compile establishment data on civilian employees of businesses. The Census Bureau and the Office of Personnel Management compile establishment data on civilian employees of government and the Department of Defense compiles establishment data on the U.S. Armed Forces.

DEMOGRAPHIC PROCESSES AND CHARACTERISTICS

Basic Demographic Processes and Categories of Workers

Most persons become members of the labor force at an early adult age, remain in the labor force for varying periods of time, often several decades, and then usually leave by voluntary separation or less commonly by death or other involuntary separation. Some enter and leave the labor force several times during a lifetime. The labor force changes as a result of demographic processes analogous to those by which the general population changes. We can interpret the labor force as a population in itself, subject to the processes of birth, death, in-migration, and out-migration, or variants of them. Thus, the national labor force changes (L_1 to L_2) during a period (e.g., a year) as a result of labor force entries (E_{lf}) and exits (X_{lf}). The entries include entries of residents (ER_{lf}) and entries of immigrants (EI_{lf}), and the exits include deaths (D_{lf}) and other separations, consisting of separations of residents (XR_{lf}) and separations of emigrants (XE_{lf}):

$$L_2 = L_1 + E_{lf} - X_{lf} \tag{1}$$
$$L_2 = L_1 + ER_{lf} + EI_{lf} - D_{lf} - XR_{lf} - XE_{lf} \tag{2}$$

Regional labor forces change, in addition, as a result of internal migration of workers. In this case, we can extend the reference of ER_{lf} and XR_{lf} in the second equation above to include in-migrants and out-migrants of workers (i.e., movements between regions) or add terms for these movements. For birth cohorts, equations (1) and (2) takes on other forms, as illustrated later.

Labor force entries include rehires as well as new hires, and the separations include voluntary separations and involuntary separations in addition to deaths. The rehires are persons who worked in the nation's labor force or a particular area's labor force on a previous occasion, left it for one reason or another (e.g., to spend time at home, to work in another area), and then rejoined it. New hires are entering the labor force for the first time. Some of the in-migrants to an area are concurrently entries into the labor force of the area, having come to the area to take a job, and some of the out-migrants from an area are concurrently exits from the labor force of the area, having left their present job to take up a job in another area or to retire to another area.

Some of the members of the labor force are like persons with dual residences—that is, they hold a second, part-time job in addition to their principal full-time or part-time job. Some are like circulatory migrants—that is, they enter and exit the labor force or shift seasonally between two or more jobs on a regular basis.

The workforce of an *organization* also changes through processes resembling those of the general population. It grows through the addition of young first-time hires, other first-time hires, rehires (i.e., persons returning from nonwork to work in an organization that they previously left and workers returning from other organizations), and new hires of experienced workers (i.e., workers new to an organization). The workforce of an organization declines through voluntary separations (e.g., transfer to another organization or nonwork), deaths, and other involuntary separations (i.e., firings or terminations).

First-time workers may be either first-time workers who join an organization at a beginner's age, say age 18, or first-time workers joining an organziation at a later age. New hires are persons already in the labor force but are new to a particular organization; the rehires have previously worked for the organization. Separations include resignations (i.e., those who voluntarily transfer to another organization or to nonwork before late life), terminations (i.e., those who involuntarily transfer to another organization or nonwork before late life), voluntary retirements (i.e., those who voluntarily leave the organization for nonwork in late life), involuntary retirements (i.e, those who are forced into retirement by the organization), and deaths.

Basic Demographic Changes and Characteristics

A study by the Bureau of Labor Statistics/Fullerton (1994) provides some illustrative figures on the expected changes in the labor force of the United States.[2] The Bureau of Labor Statistics (BLS) projects that between 1992 and 2005 the civilian labor force will grow from 127.0 million to 150.5 million, reflecting a net absolute gain of 23.5 million and an average annual growth rate of 1.3%. About 51.2 million workers will enter the national labor force and about 27.7 million will leave it during this period. The entrants are almost equally divided among men and women, as is the population 16 to 24 years old, which provides the bulk of new entrants (or first-time hires). The leavers (or separations) are more likely to be men, who make up most of the older labor force. As a result of these prospective changes, particularly the relatively fewer women leaving the labor force, the share of the labor force represented by women is expected to rise from 45.5% in 1992 to 47.4% in 2005.

During this period, relatively fewer entrants into the labor force, and relatively more exits from the labor force, will be white non-Hispanic, compared with other race/ethnic groups—all consistent with the aging of the white male labor force. The white non-Hispanic labor force is expected to grow by only 0.8% per year—that is, much more slowly than the overall labor force (1.3% per year). This slower growth reflects the lower fertility and lower immigration of white non-Hispanics in comparison with other race/ethnic groups. As a result, the share of the labor force that is white non-Hispanic is expected to decline markedly between 1992 and 2005, from 78 to 73%. This change is almost the same as that for the white non-Hispanic population 16 years and over during this period, from 77 to 72% of the total population 16 years and over.

Factors in the Growth of the Labor Force

The growth in the labor force may be viewed as the joint effect of the change in population size and age distribution, on the one hand, and change in labor force participation, on the other. Population growth can account for an important part of future labor force growth. After reaching a peak in 1980, the share of the population in the ages entering the labor force, 16 to 24, has been dropping and is expected to continue dropping. Most of the baby-boom cohorts will be among the 45-to-64-year-olds in 2005—an age group that will account for one-quarter of the population in 2005. Accordingly, the share of the labor force in the ages 55 and over is expected to increase substantially between 1992 (12.2%) and 2005 (14.2%), while the share of the labor force in the ages 25 to 54 will fall by nearly the same number of percentage points in this period, from 71.7 to 69.8%.

The second primary element determining the size of the labor force, in addition to the numbers and age composition of the population, is the percentage of the population in each age group that is in the labor force (i.e., labor force participation ratios [LFPR]).[3] As Table 8.1 shows, from 1980 to 1997, LFPR of men declined at every age, from the early entry ages, 16 to 19, to the late retirement ages, 65 and over. The declines were particularly sharp at the entry and retirement ages. For the most part, women showed the opposite pattern, with large increases for every age from 20 to 24 to 55 to 64 and near stability at the fringe ages. Even women with young children have been entering the labor force in large numbers and, in general, women have been remaining in the labor force with few interruptions. As a result, the age pattern and level of LFPR of women have been shifting toward that of men. The general LFPR (ages 16 and over) for women in 1980 was one-third below that of men; by 1997 it was only one fifth lower.

To compare the labor force participation tendencies of two or more populations, we can compute age-adjusted general labor force participation ratios

TABLE 8.1   Labor Force Participation Ratios by Age and Sex, 1980, 1997, and 2006 (projections), and Calculation of Age-Adjusted Ratios for 1980 and 1997

Age (years)	Male 1980 (1)	Male 1997 (2)	Male 2006 (3)	Female 1980 (4)	Female 1997 (5)	Female 2006 (6)	Average population, 1980/1997[a] Male (7)	Average population, 1980/1997[a] Female (8)
16 and over	77.4	75.0	73.6	51.5	59.8	61.4	88,592	97,063
16–19	60.5	52.3	52.5	52.9	51.0	51.1	8,052	7,884
20–24	85.9	82.5	76.5	68.9	72.7	71.8	9,370	9,630
25–34	95.2	93.0	92.3	65.5	76.0	77.6	18,660	19,456
35–44	95.5	92.6	90.6	65.5	77.7	80.2	17,031	17,698
45–54	91.2	89.5	87.5	59.9	76.0	79.9	13,584	14,396
55–64	72.1	67.6	70.2	41.3	50.9	55.8	10,170	11,289
65 and over	19.0	17.1	17.8	8.1	8.6	8.7	11,725	16,710

Calculations for age-adjustment of general labor force participation ratios in 1980 and 1997:

$R_m^{80} = \Sigma r_{am}^{80} P_{am} \div \Sigma P_{am}$ $R_f^{80} = \Sigma r_{af}^{80} P_{af} \div \Sigma P_{af}$

$68,899 \div 88,592 = 77.7$ $49,791 \div 97,063 = 51.3$

$R_m^{97} = \Sigma r_{am}^{97} \div \Sigma P_{am}$ $R_f^{97} = \Sigma r_{af}^{97} \div \Sigma P_{af}$

$66,104 \div 88,592 = 74.6$ $57,684 \div 97,063 = 59.4$

Original difference: $75.0 - 77.4 = -2.4$ $59.8 - 51.5 = 8.3$
Adjusted difference: $74.6 - 77.7 = -3.1$ $59.4 - 51.3 = 8.1$
Allocation of difference: $-2.4 = -3.1 + 0.7$ $8.3 = 8.1 + 0.2$

Note: Percentage civilian labor force of civilian noninstitutional population in specified age group. Annual averages of monthly figures. Based on Current Population Survey. Data for 1980 and 1997 are not strictly comparable; see source.

   [a] Population in thousands.

Source: Basic data from U.S. Bureau of Labor Statistics, *Employment and Earnings*, January issues, 1981 and 1998; and *Monthly Labor Review*, November 1997. Calculations by author.

(see Chapter 1). Computation of such a measure eliminates differences in age composition underlying the general labor force ratios being compared, and hence permits (1) comparison of labor force participation unaffected by differences in age composition and (2) decomposition of the difference between the general labor force participation ratios into the part due to population age composition and the part due to labor force participation. Table 8.1 presents a summary of the calculations for deriving age-adjusted general labor force participation ratios in 1980 and 1997. The age-specific LFPR in each year are weighted by the average civilian noninstitutional population of the 2 years at each age to derive the adjusted values. The two sexes are treated separately. The original values for males for the 2 years are 77.4% and 75.0%, reflecting a loss of 2.4 percentage points. The adjusted values are 77.7% and 74.6%. The difference, a decline of 3.1 percentage points, represents the contribution of the changes in LFPR to the total change in the general labor force participation ratios between 1980 and 1997, and the remaining part of the difference, +0.7 percentage points, represents the contribution of the change in population distribution (i.e., −2.4 = −3.1 + 0.7). If the LFPR had not changed, changes in age distribution would have caused the overall LFPR to rise by 0.7 points, but the declines in LFPR completely offset the increase. The corresponding results for females are 8.3 = +8.1 + 0.2. That is, both factors, LFPR changes and age-composition changes, contributed to the rise in the overall LFPR between 1980 and 1997, but most of the overall increase resulted from increases in LFPR.

Age Composition of the Labor Force

Like the general population, the labor force of the nation and its regions have age structures, and the same measures of age composition used in analyzing general populations are applicable to the labor force. We can, for example, compute the median age of the labor force to summarize its age distribution and the index of dissimilarity to compare the labor force distributions by age for two areas or two dates.

The proportion of the population at the traditional ages of entering the labor force has been declining, the baby-boom cohorts are nearing the retirement ages, and the postwar decline in labor force participation ratios of men at the older ages is slowing. As a result, the median age of the labor force is rising. By 2006 it is expected to reach 40.3 years, about the same level as in 1962, before the baby-boom cohorts had started to enter the labor force. The median age of the labor force for men and women for 1980 and 1997 and projected values for 2006 are as follows:

| | Median age | | |
	1980	1997	2006
Total	34.7	38.6	40.3
Men	35.1	38.6	40.2
Women	34.0	38.5	40.5

Source: Based on U.S. Bureau of Labor Statistics, *Employment and Earnings*, January issues, 1981 and 1998, and *Monthly Labor Review*, November 1997.

Currently, male and female workers have about the same median age, as would be expected from the near-convergence of the labor force participation ratios of the two sexes.

The age structure of the labor force changes as a result of the aging of its members and the differences beween the initial age distribution and the age distributions of entries and exits. As in the case of the general population, after a sufficient number of years the age composition of the labor force will have redesigned itself. It will reflect mainly or solely the rates of entry, separation, and death of workers, the initial age composition having been largely or wholly "forgotten." This tendency of a population to forget its initial condition is called **ergodicity**. If the age-specific rates of entry, separation, and death do not change over time (**strong ergodicity**), the age composition of the workforce tends to converge to a distinctive form and remain there (i.e., it becomes stable). Since, in practice, these rates do change, particularly if the workforce of the organization is expanding or contracting (**weak ergodicity**), the age composition of the workforce of the organization tends to change also (i.e., it does not become **stable**). If the entry rates and separation rates are closely monitored and controlled by management to achieve stability, however, the planned workforce may attain a nearly stable condition (i.e., its age distribution would remain largely unchanged).

Economic Dependency

The state of the economy is a function of the balance of workers and nonworkers among other factors. Economic dependency ratios, which reflect this balance, are an indication of the burden that workers have in supporting the nonworkers in a population. An **economic dependency ratio** is defined as the number of persons not in the labor force per 100 persons in the labor force. The precise definition of the measure may vary, depending on whether the armed forces and the institutional population are included in the labor force and dependent population, respectively. If we include armed forces in the labor force, the overall economic dependency ratio was 109 in 1980, 98 in 1990, and 93 in 1997. Evaluation of the measure for three broad age segments of the population—children, the working ages, and the elderly—provides a useful partitionment of the total decrease:

Age group	1980	1990	1997
Total population	108.9	98.3	93.4
Under 16	50.7	45.8	44.2
16 to 64	37.4	30.5	28.2
65 and over	20.8	22.1	20.4

Source: U.S. Bureau of Labor Statistics, *Employment and Earnings*, January issues, "Another look at the labor force," Howard N. Fullerton, Jr., *The American Labor Force: 1992–2005*, 1994, Table 10; calculations by the author.

It is noteworthy that a large portion of the dependents are children and that the bulk of the dependents are persons under age 65. The time series shows a substantial decline in the child dependency ratio and the dependency ratio in the principal working ages and little change in the elderly dependency ratio since 1980. The share of all dependents who are elderly is rising, however. They constituted 19% of the total in 1980 and 22% in 1997; and their share of the total is expected to rise rapidly above 22% after 2010.

Other Characteristics

As suggested, workforces may differ with respect to other demographic and socioeconomic characteristics than age composition. They may differ, for example, with respect to sex composition, race/ethnic distribution, marital status, living arrangements, other socioeconomic characteristics (e.g., education, income, occupation), and health. All these factors may also be viewed as influencing labor force attachments—that is, they affect the chance of entering or leaving the labor force or a particular workforce.

The demographic and socioeconomic characteristics of the workforce of an organization change partly because it undergoes **demographic metabolism** by processes other than those analogous to births, deaths, in-migration, outmigration, and aging. These other processes—promotions, demotions, and lateral transfers—occur internally and are analogous to forms of nonmigrant mobility. They do not directly affect the overall size of the organization, but they do affect the internal composition of its workforce, particularly with respect to the socioeconomic status of the members. The internal mobility of the workers influences their income distribution, and in turn the income distribution of the workforce of the area and the socioeconomic status of the general population.

Tenure and Rank in Relation to Basic Demographic Characteristics

The length of time a worker has been a member of the labor force is designated **work experience**, while **tenure** refers to the period of time a person has been a member of the workforce of a particular organization (i.e., working under the same employer). **Rank** (or seniority) refers to the position a person has in the hierarchy of the workforce of an organization, as defined by occupation, grade, or wages/salary. As suggested, the rank reached through mobility in the organization may be seen as analogous to socioeconomic status in the general population.

The tenure and rank composition of workforces, in combination with their composition with respect to age, sex, and race/Hispanic origin are of considerable interest from the view of public policy. For the local area labor force, they can reflect, in a general way, compliance with statutory requirements on various personnel actions. Specifically, data on a labor force's rank and tenure distribution in association with its sex and race/ethnic composition, may give some clues as to compliance with regulations relating to equal treatment of the sexes and the races/Hispanics in hiring, firing, and promotions. Such an analysis can most effectively be conducted with respect to a particular industry or organization. An actionable suit would require a claim of unequal treatment in a *particular* organization of a *particular* individual.

These variables have other important administrative and fiscal implications and can affect the functioning and efficiency of particular organizations. They influence the organizations' programs of human resources management, worker production and productivity, costs and revenues, and retirement programs. For example, the age-tenure-rank structure of the workforce of an auto plant has important implications for the retirement-planning program of the auto company. Similarly, the proportion of women on the faculty of an educational institution and their distribution by rank may bear a relation to the attractiveness of the institution for female students, the nature of the curriculum, and the quality of the academic performance of the students of each sex.

The tenure distribution of the labor force of an organization tends to be correlated with its age distribution, especially for organizations that have been functioning for several years. One is not likely to find an organization staffed mostly by workers 45 to 54 years old with tenures typically under 10 years, or an organization staffed mostly by workers 25 to 34 years old with tenures typically over 10 years. The relationship between age and tenure is strengthened by the fact that older workers tend to shift jobs less than younger workers and, if terminated because of organizational restructuring ("downsizing"), they are not likely to be replaced. When older workers do shift jobs, they are less likely to be moving voluntarily than younger workers. Older workers are also less likely to leave the labor force than younger workers, except at retirement.

Older workers naturally tend to have longer cumulative work experience, but they also tend to have longer tenures per job. This is suggested by data for the national labor force from the Bureau of Labor Statistics on **median years of tenure** with the current employer for 1998, shown in Table 8.2. The median years of tenure for the entire workforce and at each age of the workforce is a useful measure summarizing the tenure distribution of the workforce of an area, organization, or industry. In 1998 the figure for all employed workers was 3.6 years. As expected, it was lower for females than males. The median years of tenure with the current employer rose steadily with advancing age, reaching a maximum of 10 years at ages 55 to 64, the highest "working ages." The average increase in tenure for a 10-year rise in age was 2.3 years. As expected, the increase varied over the age distribution, with the peak increase being between ages 40 and 50. As compared with the past, the future relation between age and tenure may be affected by the sharp changes in the age dis-

TABLE 8.2   Median Years of Tenure with Current Employer, by Sex and Age: 1998

Age (years)	Both sexes	Males	Females
Total, 16 and over	3.6	3.8	3.4
16–19	0.6	0.6	0.7
20–24	1.1	1.2	1.1
25–34	2.7	2.8	2.5
35–44	5.0	5.5	4.5
45–54	8.1	9.4	7.2
55–64	10.1	11.2	9.6
65 and over	7.8	7.1	8.7

Note: As of February. Relates to employed wage and salaried workers 16 years old and over. Based on tle Current Population Survey.
Source: U.S. Bureau of the Labor Statistics, "Employee tenure in 1998," *News*, USDL 98-387, September 23, 1998, Table 1.

tribution of the national workforce expected in the next few decades. Tenure may rise more rapidly with age as the labor force includes a larger share of older people.

Even given the same median or mean years of tenure for different dates, areas, or organizations, the dispersion of the tenure distributions may vary. One simple way of measuring dispersion is to calculate the proportion of the workforce having tenures above designated tenure markers at each age, such as 10 years or more, 15 years or more, or 20 years or more. These would indicate the share of the workforce of an organization having long tenures. These three levels of work longevity tend to exceed the median years of work for older workers in most organizations. In 1998 about one-quarter of employed workers had tenures with their current employers of 10 years or more. Another measure of the dispersion of the tenure distribution is the index of heterogeneity. The index of heterogeneity is defined as $1 - \sum p_i^2$, where p_i is the proportion of the workforce in each designated tenure category.[4] This index varies from 0 to 1 as asymptotes, depending on whether everyone is in one tenure category or the population is distributed evenly over all tenure categories. It has the disadvantage of being affected by the number of tenure categories into which the workforce is divided.

Irregularity in a tenure distribution or inequality between tenure distributions can be measured by the index of dissimilarity. In the former case, a second distribution is employed as a standard or basis of comparison. As the reader may recall, the formula is $1/2 \sum |p_i - p_s|$, where p_s represents the proportion in each (tenure) category in the standard labor force. This measure also varies between 0 and 1 and is affected by the number of categories in the distribution. Summary measures of tenure distributions are likely to vary according to the type of organization, its growth rate, and the number of years of its existence.

Knowledge of the factors affecting the tenure and rank of the workforce of an organization as well as its demographic characteristics is useful in projecting its demographic and related characteristics and in modelling the effects of demographic changes on organizational outcomes such as rank and tenure. For example, to analyze the tenure and rank structure of the workforce of an organization, in addition to its age and other basic demographic characteristics, we should consider a host of other factors, such as the rate of economic growth of the organization and the industry to which it belongs, its retirement patterns, personnel policies regarding hiring, promotions, transfers, and terminations, technological developments in the industry, the growth of the population of the area and the nation's population, and the growth rate of the economy of the local area as well as the growth rates of the regional and national economies.[5]

Some illustrations of the kinds of findings derived from such analyses may be listed.[6] While both age and rank are correlated with the tenure distribution, rank is a stronger explanatory variable than age for the distribution by tenure. Retirement age and the compulsory age of retirement are not important determinants of the tenure distribution as compared with hiring, firing, and promotion policies and the use of financial incentives such as pensions and buyouts. With a high growth rate, the local labor force or the workforce of an organization cannot be long-tenured even if young persons are hired and remain in the labor force a long time. A high rate of technological growth tends to be associated with the hiring of young, newly educated employees and hence with a lower average period of service. High growth in an industry tends to make the average tenure of the workforce in the industry lower also because the new hires tend to come from other firms in the same industry, not from outside the industry. The *Annual Report* for 1996 of the Aluminum Company of America notes, for example, regarding Alcoa's Fujikura Spartanburg, South Carolina, telecommunications facility: "Since the operation was in a high growth mode in 1996, roughly a third of the employees had less than one year of service."[7]

Employment Prospects and Promotions

The rates of growth of the population and of the labor force of an area have an important effect on the chances of upward mobility of individuals in a labor force characterized by a status hierarchy and a tapering of the organizational structure as one goes up the echelons of the hierarchy.

Effect of Population Growth and Mortality

Growth of an organization with a pyramidal or venturi-like shape has an important effect on the possibilities of upward mobility of individuals in the organization. According to Keyfitz (1973),[8] population growth triggers organizational growth and upward internal worker mobility and supplements such factors as ability, luck, and "connections" in affecting the opportunities for promotion. He maintains that population growth is a far more important factor than mortality among members of the labor force in providing opportunities for promotion. These opportunities result both from the direct effect of labor force growth and from the indirect effect of employees' being enticed to leave one employer in the industry for another.

Alternatively, vertical mobility is slowed in a population with no growth or modest change (i.e., little growth or decline)—that is, a near-stationary or stationary population in which there are only small differences in size between age groups. According to Keyfitz (1973, *op. cit.*), change from a 2% annual increase in population to a stationary condition implies a delay of $4^1/2$ years in reaching the middle positions of the average factory or office. Low population growth and population stationarity result from low fertility, low mortality, and low immigration. This would be the outlook for the United States in the next century, once the baby-boom cohorts aged into retirement, were it not for our currently massive immigration and the expectation of its continuing. This scenario is already the general experience of many industrialized countries of Europe that have not been receiving much immigration and that had less pronounced baby booms than the United States.

Note on Models

It is useful, for planning and policy analysis in human resources management, to develop models of worker mobility within organizational workforces. Like Keyfitz, Stewman (1981, *op. cit.*) developed a variety of demographic models of this type. To understand the relative role of various factors in modifying age-seniority profiles, he carried out simulations of the effect of hiring policies relating to age patterns of new hires, exit behavior relating to age-dependent worker decisions, and the growth rate of organizations over various periods of time, beginning with a "hodge-podge" age-seniority profile. For example, imposing the assumptions of "normal" hiring practices, "normal" exit behavior, and a growth rate of 6%, for a 20-year period, he derived the age-seniority profile depicted in the three-dimensional Lexis diagram as Figure 8.1. He found that very different profiles result from alternative management practices and worker exit decisions.

Retirement

The subject of retirement is of tremendous interest to economic demographers because of its role in the dynamics of the labor force, its importance as a socioeconomic status in our society, and its sizable impact on federal, state, and local budgets.

Definition of Retirement

First, an operational definition of retirement is needed. Different data sources suggest different definitions, and the increasing variability of post-career life suggests that the concept should take the form of a polytomous variable rather than a dichotomous variable, which is the way it is usually constructed. At least two definitions or concepts of retirement have emerged. One concept involves complete separation from the labor force in later life (i.e., after about age 50). The other involves receipt of a pension after a "career" in the labor force. A cross-classification of these two definitional concepts of retirement for the population 50 years and over identifies the following four

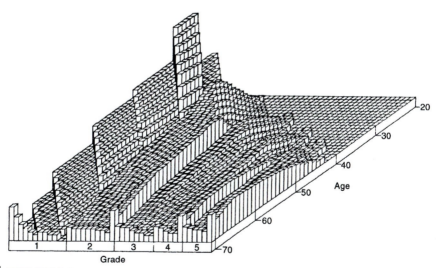

FIGURE 8.1   Age–seniority profile of the workforce of an organization: Assumptions of "normal" hiring policy, "normal" exit behavior, and a growth rate of 6%, for year 20. *Source:* Shelby Stewman, "The aging of work organizations: Impact on organization and employment practice," in Sara B. Kiesler *et al.* (eds.), *Aging: Social Change*, New York: Academic Press, 1981, Figure 10.3, p. 284. © Academic Press.

categories of older persons with respect to retirement status: Persons definitely retired, that is, those receiving a pension and not in the labor force; persons definitely not retired, that is, those not receiving a pension and in the labor force; persons "partially" retired, that is, those receiving a pension and in the labor force; and others, that is, those not receiving a pension and not in the labor force. The last of these groups consists mostly of women who have not been in the labor force for many years or ever, have no prospect of receiving a pension in their own right, and hence are not classifiable with respect to retirement status:

Labor force status

Pension status	Not in labor force	In labor force
With a pension	Definitely retired	Partially retired
Without a pension	Status indeterminate	Definitely not retired

Data to fill all the cells in this matrix are not available, but data to fill some parts of it can be secured from the records of the Social Security Administration and the Bureau of Labor Statistics. Definitions of retirement involving other variables (e.g., earnings) and more gradations in labor force attachments are possible but the various alternatives have not been fully evaluated.

Average Age of Retirement

The average age of retirement of the nation's labor force can be measured in two distinct ways, by analysis of aggregate data on new Social Security beneficiaries and by demographic analysis of data on the labor force at the older ages. These methods conform to the two different concepts of retirement described earlier. The first conforms to the definition of retirement based on the receipt of a pension following a work career; the second conforms to the definition of retirement as permanent withdrawal from the labor force at the older ages. The time series of data on new Social Security old-age beneficiaries requires adjustments for shifts over time in coverage and the ages included, and for the exclusion of retirements for disability. Because the receipt of a reduced Social Security benefit begins at age 62 and receipt of a full benefit begins at age 65, the data are subject to the further limitation that they set a lower limit on the age of retirement measured by them.

Estimates of the average (median) age of retirement derived by demographic analysis of labor force data do not have this limitation, but depend on the quality and consistency of labor force, population, and life table data from different sources and the validity of the assumptions made in the estimation formula. The method involves the calculation of retirements (R) as a residual from a special version of the component equation relating to the labor force at the older ages:

$$(-)R = (L_2 - L_1 s) \div \sqrt{s} \tag{3}$$

where L_1 and L_2 represent the labor force at the initial and terminal years 5 years apart for 5-year birth cohorts and s represents the 5-year life table survival rate for a particular birth cohort (see Chapter 1).[9]

The formula assumes that the mortality level of the labor force is the same as that for the general population and that there is zero net international migration. In general, the average age of retirement is calculated from age schedules of estimates of the labor force for 5-year birth cohorts at two successive dates 5 years apart. The steps are as follows. (1) Net retirements for each 5-year *birth cohort* at the older ages are calculated from the numbers in the labor force at the beginning and end of each 5-year period by use of the appropriate life tables, following the formula presented earlier; (2) the estimates of retirements for 5-year birth cohorts derived in step 1 are converted into estimates of retirements for 5-year *age groups* by an appropriate method of interpolation (e.g., Karup-King osculatory interpolation); and (3) an estimate of the median age of retirement for the 5-year period is computed from the estimates of retirements for 5-year age groups in step 2. [For further explanation of the method, refer to Gendell and Siegel (1992).[10]]

Calculations by the method of demographic analysis showed that the median age of retirement from the labor force declined about 5 years between the early 1950s and the early 1990s (i.e., from about 67.4 years to about 62.4 years).[11] Estimates of the median age of retirement for men and women from 1950–1955 to 1990–1995 are as follows:

Period	Men	Women
1950–1955	66.9	67.7
1960–1965	65.2	64.6
1970–1975	63.4	62.9
1980–1985	62.8	62.7
1985–1990	62.6	62.8
1990–1995	62.1	62.6

Source: Gendell and Siegel (1996, Table 2; 1992, Table 4); Gendell (1998, Table 1). Calculations based on data from the Current Population Survey. See note 11.

The general magnitude and pace of the decline were similar for men and women. Most of the decline occurred by the early 1970s, after which it continued at a slower pace. It appears that the median age of retirement is likely to level off at about age 62, the age of eligibility for reduced benefits under Social Security.

To determine the average (mean) number of years in retirement corresponding to a particular median age of retirement, we read off life expectation at the median age of retirement from the current life table. For example, with a median age of retirement of 62.1 years for men in 1990–1995, new male retirees could look forward to about 17 years of retirement according to the life table for 1993. With a median age of 62.6, women had 21 years. Both declining mortality and reduced age of retirement have contributed to the increase in the period of retirement in roughly equal proportions in the post–World War II period.[12]

There is a growing body of literature on the factors affecting the decision to retire. In brief, the average age of retirement has been falling because workers have been willing to trade additional income for leisure and the economic supports for achieving this goal are available. These economic supports include private pension plans, personal savings, family inheritance, Social Security, Medicare, and other government and private benefits. There is the possibility of supplementing these, if necessary, with part-time work. Moreover, a spouse may continue to work part or full time. Social Security benefits are adjusted for inflation, and so are some private benefits. It appears that the availability of benefits under Social Security at age 62, even though reduced, has considerable weight in the decision to retire early. Legislation calling for mandatory retirement at various ages and its repeal have apparently not been important in this decision.

TABLES OF WORKING LIFE

A table of working life, an extension of the conventional life table, is a valuable tool for analyzing labor force dynamics. It incorporates labor force entries and exits in addition to deaths as factors of change in the life table cohort as it ages. It provides measures of average length of working life and can be used to estimate time lost from work for various reasons, the proportion of a cohort that will never work, and rates and numbers of separations from the labor force due to death and retirement, as well as of accessions. The table is based on certain assumptions representing extensions of those applicable to conventional life tables. The rates of mortality and labor force participation are "frozen" as of a particular year or years, but yield estimates of "future" working life. Separation from the labor force is assumed to occur only through death or "permanent" withdrawal, not temporary separations.

The choice of death rates in calculations relating to the national labor force often arises, such as in model simulations of various future retirement rates, the construction of tables of working life, or the projection of the labor force by the cohort-component method. Death rates for persons in the labor force are lacking. Tables of working life usually employ a common set of death rates without distinction as to labor force status. Yet, it is aften assumed that the labor force tends to have lower mortality than persons not in the labor force. While this assumption is reasonable, in view of the fact that disability is a common basis for not entering the labor force or for leaving the labor force early, the degree of this advantage has not been closely established.

Methods of Construction

Tables of working life may be constructed as multiple-decrement tables by the prevalence-ratio method or the event-exposure method, or as multistate tables. The methods of construction have changed over time as new data became available, life table methods and applications were expanded, and computer technology developed. The newer tables employ the multistate method. Labor force changes, such as the net probability of entry or exit at each age are the direct inputs in the event-exposure method but have to be inferred in the prevalence-ratio method. In the multistate method they are represented explicitly by gross transition probabilities of moving between various labor force states and death at each age.

Prevalence-Ratio Method

The prevalence-ratio method, the simplest version of the multiple-decrement model, is employed in the absence of data for computing rates of entry into and rates of exit from the labor force directly. A portion of a table of working life based on the prevalence-ratio method is illustrated as Table 8.3. In this method, observed labor force participation ratios (i.e., observed labor force ÷ observed population) for 5-year age groups, w_x, are *assumed* to represent the labor force participation ratios at each age in the life table population (i.e., stationary labor force ÷ stationary population). The observed ratios are applied to the stationary population (L_x) of a conventional life table for the same general population, to derive the labor force stationary population (L_{wx}):[13]

$$L_{wx} = w_x \star L_x \tag{4}$$

The L_{wx} may be interpolated from 5-year data to single ages if they are not already in single ages, preferably by a form of osculatory interpolation. The l_{wx} function, representing survivors entering the labor force, can be derived approximately by linear interpolation of the single-year L_{wx}:

$$l_{wx} = 1/2 L_{wx-1} + 1/2 L_{wx} \tag{5}$$

By summing the L_{wx} from the bottom up, we can derive T_{wx} and then the average years of working life for the working population and the general population:

$$T_{wx} = {}_j\Sigma^{\infty} L_{wx=j} \tag{6}$$

$$e_{wx} = T_{wx} \div l_{wx} \tag{7}$$

$$e'_{wx} = T'_{wx} \div l_x \tag{8}$$

The calculations can then be extended to provide information at each age on rates of net entry into or rates of net exit from the labor force, disaggregated by death and other separations.[14]

In these calculations, the mortality rates of the general population are assumed to apply to the labor force and no allowance is made for the joint probability of dying and entering the labor force within a year of age. The method has not readily lent itself to the calculation of tables of working life for females because of the tendency of women to enter and leave the workforce several times in a working lifetime.[15]

Multistate Method

Tables of working life can be constructed by the multistate method using survey data on the labor force status of the same persons in 2 successive years. By matching records of the same individuals in the Current Population Survey in two successive years, gross probabilities of entering and exiting the labor force, expressed as transition probabilities from one labor force status to another, during the year can be developed.[16] This is the basis of the latest tables of working life published by the U.S. Bureau of Labor Statistics (BLS), those for 1979–1980.[17] Such tables are more accurate than prevalence-ratio tables and provide several additional measures, such as the chance of ever

TABLE 8.3 Illustrative Segment of a Table of Working Life Constructed by the Prevalence-Ratio Method: Males 1970

| | Number living of 100,000 born | | | Average number of remaining years at the beginning of the age interval | | | | |
| | In population | Percent of population | Number in labor force | Total | For those in the labor force | | For those in the labor force | For those in the population |
Year of age x to n (1)	$_nL_x$ (2)	$_nw_x$ (3)	$_nLw_x$ (4)	Life e_x (5)	Labor force activity ew_x (6)	Nonlabor force activity er_x (7)	Labor force activity ew_x^p (8)	Nonlabor force activity er_x^p (9)
16 to 19	385,892	57.96	223,668	53.3	45.2	8.1	41.4	11.9
16	96,710	40.69	39,357	53.3	45.2	8.1	41.4	11.9
17	96,565	53.50	51,668	52.3	44.2	8.1	41.1	11.2
18	96,399	64.88	62,549	51.4	43.3	8.1	40.6	10.8
19	96,218	72.85	70,094	50.5	42.4	8.1	40.0	10.5
20 to 24	477,977	85.15	407,010	49.6	41.5	8.1	39.4	10.2
20	96,029	78.62	75,503	49.6	41.5	8.1	39.4	10.2
21	95,819	81.78	78,369	48.7	40.6	8.1	38.7	10.0
22	95,598	85.22	81,473	47.8	39.6	8.2	38.0	9.8
23	95,374	89.68	85,539	46.9	38.7	8.2	37.2	9.7
24	95,156	90.50	86,125	46.1	37.8	8.3	36.4	9.7
25 to 29	472,842	94.40	446,373	45.2	36.9	8.3	35.6	9.6
25	94,952	92.97	88,285	45.2	36.9	8.3	35.6	9.6
26	94,755	93.77	88,854	44.2	36.0	8.2	34.7	9.5
27	94,566	94.49	89,361	43.3	35.1	8.2	33.8	9.5
28	94,379	95.12	89,781	42.4	34.1	8.3	32.9	9.5
29	94,190	95.64	90,091	41.5	33.2	8.3	32.1	9.4
30 to 34	467,867	96.44	451,236	40.6	32.3	8.3	31.2	9.4
30	93,994	96.05	90,286	40.6	32.3	8.3	31.2	9.4
31	93,792	96.35	90,374	39.7	31.3	8.4	30.3	9.4
32	93,583	96.55	90,360	38.8	30.4	8.4	29.4	9.4
33	93,364	96.64	90,229	37.8	29.5	8.3	28.5	9.4
34	93,134	96.62	89,987	36.9	28.5	8.4	—	9.3

(continues)

TABLE 8.3 *(continued)*

| | Number living of 100,000 born | | | Average number of remaining years at the beginning of the age interval | | | | |
| | In population | In labor force | | Total | For those in the labor force | | For those in the population | |
Year of age x to n (1)	$_nL_x$ (2)	Percent of population $_nw_x$ (3)	Number $_nLw_x$ (4)	Life e_x (5)	Labor force activity ew_x (6)	Nonlabor force activity er_x (7)	Labor force activity ew_x^p (8)	Nonlabor force activity er_x^p (9)
35 to 39	461,681	96.25	444,381	36.0	27.6	8.4	—	—
35	92,893	96.51	89,658	36.0	27.6	8.4	—	—
36	92,634	96.37	89,275	35.1	26.7	8.4	—	—
37	92,358	96.22	88,875	34.2	25.9	8.3	—	—
38	92,060	96.11	88,486	33.3	25.0	8.3	—	—
39	91,736	96.02	88,088	32.0	24.1	8.3	—	—
40 to 44	452,727	95.55	432,585	31.6	23.2	8.4	—	—
40	91,385	95.89	87,635	31.6	23.2	8.4	—	—
41	91,001	95.72	87,111	30.7	22.3	8.4	—	—
42	90,582	59.54	86,550	29.8	21.4	8.4	—	—
43	90,127	95.37	85,960	29.0	20.6	8.4	—	—
44	89,632	95.19	85,328	28.1	19.7	8.4	—	—
...								
65 to 69	291,854	40.33	117,733	13.1	5.7	7.4	—	—
65	63,104	48.79	30,794	13.1	5.7	7.4	—	—
66	60,821	43.40	26,398	12.6	6.1	6.5	—	—
67	58,453	39.14	22,882	12.1	6.0	6.1	—	—
68	55,999	35.65	19,966	11.6	5.8	5.8	—	—
69	53,478	33.08	17,693	11.1	5.5	5.6	—	—
70 to 74	227,840	23.90	54,470	10.6	5.4	5.2	—	—
70	50,899	28.09	14,299	10.6	5.4	5.2	—	—
71	48,276	25.92	12,513	10.1	5.4	4.7	—	—
72	45,610	23.48	10,713	9.6	5.2	4.4	—	—
73	42,902	22.21	9,528	9.2	4.9	4.3	—	—
74	40,153	18.47	7,416	8.8	4.7	4.1	—	—
75 and over	326,283	15.71	51,259	8.4	4.7	3.7	—	—

Note: The average remaining years of labor force activity and nonlabor force activity for the population is not calculated after the age of peak labor force participation—about age 33 for males—as indicated by the dashes.

Source: U.S. Bureau of Labor Statistics, *Length of Working Life for Men and Women, 1970,* by Howard N. Fullerton and James J. Byrne, Special Labor Force Report 187, 1977; reprinted from *Monthly Labor Review,* February 1976.

entering the labor force, the average number of entries into and exits from the labor force during a lifetime, and the expected duration in the labor force per entry. A portion of the BLS table for females in 1979–1980 is shown in Table 8.4.

Multistate life tables are based on the theory of **Markov chains**—that is, that the probability of "transitioning" from one state to another (defined by the initial and terminal state and age or duration) is based solely on the initial state. The states in the official tables of working life include two transitional states, "in the labor force" (L) and "not in the labor force" (NL), and one absorbing state, "death" (D). There are six possible transitions over a year, namely from L to L, L to NL, NL to NL, NL to L, L to D, and NL to D. As a practical matter, the last two transitions may be assumed to be the same in magnitude—that is, the probability of dying at any age is the same for persons in the labor force and those not in the labor force. (See Table 8.4, columns 8 to 12.)

A more elaborate version of the multistate table of working life can provide a rather comprehensive picture of the transitions among labor force states, including internal personnel shifts. The transitions can include, in addition to the basic ones of entry into and exit from the labor force and deaths, several specific types of entries and exits, such as first entries, second and later entries, voluntary withdrawals (quits), forced withdrawals (layoffs), and withdrawals due to disability. Theoretically, the multistate table can also describe internal worker movements such as promotions, demotions, and lateral transfers. The table could begin with a birth cohort and track the movements of the cohort over time through its various work transitions, as the members of the cohort enter the workforce for the first time, are promoted, are demoted, move laterally, leave the workforce (by choice, forced termination, death, or on becoming disabled), reenter the workforce, and partially or fully retire. Data for constructing such a table are not available at present, but tables with some of this detail can now be generated. A multistate table could also incorporate data on moves between occupations. However, the sample would be greatly fragmented and moves between occupations are difficult to measure satisfactorily. Very broad occupational categories could be employed, but the resulting information would be of limited value.

Availability of Tables

Only national tables of working life have been prepared. The Bureau of Labor Statistics (BLS) has produced a series of national tables for selected years covering the period from 1900 to 1979–1980. In the latest set, those relating to 1979–1980, separate tables are available for males and females, whites and nonwhites by sex, and four educational levels by sex. As explained earlier, these tables were constructed by the multistate method, as were two previous sets of tables, tables for 1970 and 1977. The earlier tables spanning several decades employed the prevalence-ratio method.[18] As of early 2000, the BLS has discontinued its life-table program. Recent tables of worklife expectancy have been published by Vocational Econometrics, Inc., and provide data on expected years of work for persons according to disability status, sex, race, and educational level for 1987, 1991, and 1995.[19]

TABLE 8.4 Illustrative Segment of a Table of Working Life Constructed by the Multistate Method: Females, 1979–1980 (Mortality Rates Used Are Those of the General Female Population)

| | | Expectation of active and inactive life by current labor force status | | | | | |
| | | Total population | | Currently active in labor force | | Currently inactive | |
Age x	Life expectancy $_*e'_x$	Active years remaining $_*e_x^a$	Inactive years remaining $_*e'_x$	Active years remaining $^ae_x^a$	Inactive years remaining $^ae'_x$	Active years remaining $^ie_x^a$	Inactive years remaining $^ie'_{xx}$
	(1)	(2)	(3)	(4)	(5)	(6)	(7)
16	62.9	29.3	33.6	30.1	32.9	28.7	34.3
17	61.9	28.8	33.1	29.6	32.4	28.0	33.9
18	61.0	28.3	32.7	29.0	31.9	27.4	33.5
19	60.0	27.7	32.3	28.5	31.5	26.8	33.2
20	59.1	27.2	31.9	27.9	31.2	26.1	32.9
21	58.1	26.6	31.5	27.3	30.8	25.4	32.7
22	57.1	25.9	31.2	26.6	30.5	24.7	32.4
23	56.2	25.3	30.9	26.0	30.1	24.0	32.2
24	55.2	24.6	30.6	25.4	29.8	23.3	31.9
25	54.2	24.0	30.2	24.8	29.4	22.6	31.7
26	53.3	23.3	29.9	24.2	29.1	21.9	31.4
27	52.3	22.7	29.6	23.6	28.7	21.2	31.1
28	51.3	22.0	29.3	22.9	28.4	20.5	30.8
29	50.4	21.4	29.0	22.3	28.0	19.8	30.5
...							
70	14.9	0.8	14.2	3.0	12.0	0.3	14.7
71	14.3	0.7	13.6	2.8	11.5	0.2	14.1
72	13.6	0.6	13.0	2.5	11.1	0.1	13.5
73	13.0	0.5	12.5	2.3	10.7	0.1	12.9
74	12.3	0.4	11.9	1.9	10.4	0.0	12.3
75	11.7	0.3	11.4	1.3	10.4	0.0	11.7

(*continues*)

TABLE 8.4 *(continued)*

Age x	Probability of transition between specified states during age interval x to x + 1					Age-specific rates of transfer per 1000 persons in initial status during age interval x to x + 1		
	Living to dead $*p_x^d$	Inactive to inactive $^ip_x^i$	Inactive to active $^ip_x^a$	Active to inactive $^ap_x^i$	Active to active $^ap_x^a$	Mortality $*m_x^d$	Labor force accession $^im_x^a$	Voluntary labor force separation $^am_x^i$
	(8)	(9)	(10)	(11)	(12)	(13)	(14)	(15)
16	0.00049	0.61018	0.38933	0.28459	0.71491	0.00050	0.58755	0.42949
17	0.00055	0.65845	0.34099	0.26841	0.73104	0.00058	0.49076	0.38629
18	0.00059	0.64144	0.35797	0.23074	0.76887	0.00059	0.50766	0.32722
19	0.00060	0.63368	0.36572	0.20738	0.79202	0.00060	0.51297	0.29088
20	0.00061	0.63680	0.36259	0.18972	0.80967	0.00061	0.50129	0.26230
21	0.00061	0.64831	0.35107	0.17552	0.82387	0.00062	0.47689	0.23842
22	0.00063	0.66119	0.33818	0.16608	0.83330	0.00063	0.45252	0.22223
23	0.00063	0.67430	0.32508	0.16070	0.83368	0.00064	0.42966	0.21241
24	0.00065	0.68760	0.31175	0.15478	0.84458	0.00065	0.40690	0.20202
25	0.00065	0.70299	0.29636	0.15125	0.84810	0.00065	0.38210	0.19501
26	0.00066	0.72078	0.27856	0.14873	0.85061	0.00066	0.35450	0.18928
27	0.00067	0.73299	0.26834	0.14524	0.85408	0.00068	0.33561	0.18302
28	0.00069	0.74023	0.25907	0.14177	0.85754	0.00070	0.32427	0.17744
29	0.00071	0.74635	0.25293	0.13723	0.86205	0.00072	0.31449	0.17063
...								
70	0.02178	0.94908	0.02915	0.28233	0.69590	0.02201	0.03536	0.34250
71	0.02388	0.94821	0.02791	0.29093	0.68520	0.02416	0.03409	0.35533
72	0.02614	0.94677	0.02709	0.29783	0.67604	0.02648	0.03330	0.36601
73	0.02857	0.94515	0.02629	0.29908	0.67235	0.02898	0.03240	0.36866
74	0.03121	0.94350	0.02530	0.29590	0.67289	0.03170	0.03120	0.36488
75	0.03411	0.94430	0.02157	0.34984	0.61603	0.03470	0.02752	0.44644

(continues)

TABLE 8.4 (continued)

Age x	Number surviving to exact age x, per 1000,000 persons born Labor force status			Number of status transfered during age interval x to x + 1				
	Total $*l_x$	Active $^a l_x$	Inactive $^i l_x$	Labor force entries $^i t_x^a$	Voluntary labor force exits $^a t_x^i$	Deaths by labor force status		
						Total $*t_x^d$	Active $^a t_x^d$	Inactive $^i t_x^d$
	(16)	(17)	(18)	(19)	(20)	(21)	(22)	(23)
16	98,357	42,096	56,261	30,133	20,207	49	23	25
17	98,308	51,999	46,309	22,270	20,435	55	29	25
18	98,253	53,804	44,449	21,671	18,173	58	33	25
19	98,196	57,270	40,926	20,195	17,103	59	35	24
20	98,137	60,326	37,811	18,381	16,116	59	37	22
21	98,078	62,555	35,523	16,580	15,087	60	39	21
22	98,017	64,007	34,010	15,188	14,317	61	40	21
23	97,956	64,839	33,117	14,150	13,805	62	41	21
24	97,894	65,143	32,751	13,296	13,169	63	42	21
25	97,831	65,229	32,602	12,492	12,696	64	42	21
26	97,767	64,982	32,785	11,713	12,245	65	43	22
27	97,702	64,407	33,295	11,252	11,739	66	43	23
28	97,636	63,876	33,760	10,994	11,303	68	44	24
29	97,568	63,522	34,046	10,720	10,826	70	45	24
...								
70	76,660	9,614	67,046	2,358	13,127	1,669	201	1,468
71	74,991	8,644	66,347	2,246	2,917	1,790	198	1,592
72	73,201	7,775	65,426	2,159	2,709	1,913	196	1,717
73	71,287	7,029	64,258	2,059	2,478	2,036	195	1,842
74	69,251	6,415	62,836	1,935	2,248	2,161	195	1,966
75	67,090	5,906	61,184	1,665	2,425	2,288	189	2,100

(continues)

TABLE 8.4 *(continued)*

Age x	Person years lived in each status during age x			Person years lived in each status beyond exact age x		
	Total L_x^*	Active $*L_x^a$	Inactive $*L_x^i$	Total $*T_x^*$	Active $*T_x^a$	Inactive $*T_x^i$
	(24)	(25)	(26)	(27)	(28)	(29)
16	98,333	47,048	51,285	6,188,267	2,880,000	3,308,267
17	98,281	52,902	45,379	6,089,934	2,832,952	3,256,982
18	98,225	55,537	42,688	5,991,653	2,780,050	3,211,603
19	98,166	58,798	39,368	5,893,428	2,724,513	3,168,915
20	98,107	61,440	36,667	5,795,262	2,665,715	3,129,547
21	98,047	63,281	34,766	5,697,155	2,604,275	3,092,880
22	97,986	64,423	33,563	5,599,108	2,540,994	3,058,114
23	97,925	64,991	32,934	5,501,122	2,476,572	3,024,550
24	97,862	65,185	32,677	5,403,197	2,411,581	2,991,616
25	97,799	65,105	32,694	5,305,335	2,346,395	2,958,940
26	97,735	64,695	33,040	5,207,536	2,281,290	2,926,246
27	97,669	64,141	33,528	5,109,801	2,216,595	2,893,206
28	97,603	63,700	33,903	5,012,132	2,152,454	2,859,678
29	97,534	63,447	34,087	4,914,529	2,088,754	2,825,775
...						
70	75,825	9,129	66,696	1,145,982	60,572	1,085,410
71	74,096	8,210	65,886	1,070,157	51,443	1,018,714
72	72,244	7,402	64,842	996,061	43,233	952,828
73	70,269	6,722	63,547	923,817	35,831	887,986
74	68,170	6,161	62,009	853,548	29,109	824,439
75	65,946	5,432	60,514	785,378	22,948	762,430

Source: U.S. Bureau ot Labor Statistics, *Worklife Estimates: Effects of Race and Education,* by Shirley J. Smith, Bulletin 2254, 1986; reprinted from *Monthly Labor Review,* August 1985.

Illustrative Results and Applications

Managers are very interested in the extent of movement into and out of the labor force because of the expenses associated with replacing exiting employees and the effect on production of early departures. According to the BLS tables of working life for 1979–1980, women move in and out of the labor force more frequently than men. Men had an average of 3.9 entries and 3.6 withdrawals over a worklife. Women had an average of 5.5 entries and 5.4 withdrawals (Table 8.5). Other measures of worklife show that the male labor force has generally experienced an increase in the period of nonwork over a lifetime and an increase in the share of total lifetime devoted to nonwork. For the female labor force the opposite is true; years of work and the share of total lifetime devoted to work have increased.

Educational attainment is among the factors strongly correlated with age of retirement. For both men and women, the most educated show the least inclination to retire. For the reference period, over a lifetime men with 15 years or more of schooling can expect to work 6.5 years longer than men who did not finish high school (41.1 years versus 34.6 years). (See U.S. Bureau of Labor Statistics/Smith *op. cit.*, Table 4.) Women falling in these two education

TABLE 8.5 Selected Worklife Measures by Sex, 1970 and 1979–1980, and by Sex and Race, 1979–1980 (in Years, Unless Otherwise Indicated)

Measure and age	Men[a] Total 1970	1979–1980	White	Black and other	Women[a] Total 1970	1979–1980	White	Black and other
Life expectancy								
At birth	67.1	70.0	70.7	65.3	74.8	77.6	78.3	73.9
At age 25	45.1	47.3	47.9	43.3	51.9	54.2	54.7	51.0
At age 60	16.1	17.5	17.6	16.5	20.8	22.4	22.6	21.0
Worklife expectancy[b]								
At birth	37.8	38.8	39.8	32.9	22.3	29.4	29.7	27.4
At age 25	34.0	33.1	33.6	28.6	19.0	24.0	24.1	23.5
At age 60	6.0	4.4	4.5	3.3	3.1	3.0	3.0	3.0
Percent worklife of total life[c]								
At birth	56.3	55.4	56.3	50.4	29.8	37.9	37.9	37.1
At age 25	76.3	70.0	70.6	66.1	36.6	44.3	44.1	46.1
At age 60	37.3	25.1	25.6	20.0	3.1	3.0	3.0	14.3
Labor force entries per:								
Person born	2.9	3.9	3.9	4.3	14.6	5.5	5.6	5.4
Person aged 25	1.2	1.5	1.5	1.8	2.8	3.0	3.0	3.1
Voluntary exits per:								
Person born	2.6	3.6	3.6	3.9	4.5	5.4	5.5	5.4
Person aged 25	1.6	2.3	2.3	2.4	3.3	3.8	3.8	3.7

[a] Data for race groups relate to 1979–1980.

[b] Population-based measure.

[c] Percent of worklife expectancy to total life expectancy at given age.

Source: U.S. Bureau of Labor Statistics, *Worklife Estimates: Effects of Race and Education*, by Shirley Smith, Bulletin 2254, 1986, Table 4.

categories show a much larger difference in duration of worklife, 12.6 years (34.9 versus 22.3 years). The earlier and more permanent retirement patterns of persons who have not graduated from high school may be due in part to differences in health among the various educational categories.

Race is another factor associated with duration of worklife, and for men the difference is striking. For the reference period, 1979–1980, worklife expectancy is nearly 7 years shorter for "blacks and others" than for whites (32.9 versus 39.8 years). (See Table 8.5.) "Blacks and others" are more likely than whites to exit the labor force early because of disability, selective termination, and education/occupation status, and are more likely to die before retirement.

Tables of working life can be used to determine casualty awards in court suits involving claims of wrongful injury, death, or disablement by providing information on the average years of working life lost, given the present age, sex, race, and educational level of the deceased, injured, or disabled person. In such a case, the tables of working life for the sexes, races, and educational levels are combined with information on current and lifetime income at each age for persons according to their sex, race, and educational level. This application will be discussed in more detail.

Experimental Tables of Employment Expectancies

Tables of employment expectancies may be viewed as a special type of worklife table. They are designed to provide information on the average number of years employees remain at a job in an industry or company, particularly where calculations are shown separately for major occupations and causes of separation. Such tables can guide company policy in deciding which cause of separation to modify or control if **employment expectancies**, or average years of employment at the company, are to be increased.

This type of multiple-decrement table is constructed by use of duration (i.e., years since the worker was hired) as the measure of time. The decrements are represented by the probabilities at each duration of dying, quitting, and being laid off. The probabilities of quitting and being laid off should be calculated as **dependent probabilities**—that is, as being in force at the same time.[20] Alternatively, the table may be contructed on the assumption that only layoffs occur or only quits occur. In this case, the probabilities of separation of each type are calculated as **independent probabilities**, with one cause acting in the absence of the other. Such tables are sometimes labeled "associated single" decrement tables.

The tables are constructed with data from company records on the work history of each employee. The data needed include the date the employee was hired, the age at time of hiring, subsequent separations and rehirings, initial occupation, and subsequent changes in occupation, with datas. In order to develop a multiple-decrement table for an industry or large company describing work duration, we need to compute central rates of dying, voluntary separation (quits), and involuntary separation (layoffs), for specific occupations, from data in company records and then to convert the central rates into the corresponding dependent and independent probabilities. The central rates relate the number of events at a given duration in years to the person-years of exposure (e.g., the number of layoffs at duration four divided by the midperiod worker population at duration four).[21]

An illustration of a multiple-decrement worklife table showing employment expectancies in which layoffs and quits are jointly in force is given as Table 8.6. An illustration of the associated decrement table showing employment expectancies on the assumption that quits are the only type of separation is given as Table 8.7. Both tables were prepared by Deardorff (1990) for his pilot study of employment expectancies in the construction industry.[22]

The table begins with a radix of 100,000 new workers at duration zero. The cohort is then subjected to the probabilities of dying, being laid off, and quitting until it is extinct. The usual life table functions, l_x, $_nd_x$, $_nL_x$, T_x, and e_x, are calculated, except that they represent specialized functions relating to the worker cohort, and $_nd_x$ in particular represents three columns of decrements, namely, numbers dying, being laid off, and quitting in a duration interval. The e_x column tells us the average number of years at duration x an employee can be expected to remain with the company. Separate tables can be calculated to obtain employment expectancies for different occupations and to measure the independent effect of one cause of separation as compared with another.

TABLE 8.6 Multiple Decrement Table of Employment Expectancies for Laborers in the SAE Construction Company (the Mortality Factor Has Been Excluded)

Duration (years)	Probability of separation			l_x	d_x	e_x
	By layoff[a]	By quits[a]	By layoff or quits			
0	.69232	.21963	.91195	100000	91195	0.63
1	.53272	.22113	.75385	8805	6638	1.01
2	.39185	.19593	.58778	2167	1274	1.56
3	.39390	.09847	.49237	893	440	2.07
4	.09202	.09202	.18405	453	83	2.59
5	.44467	.00000	.44467	370	164	2.06
6	.33680	.11224	.44904	206	92	2.30
7	.51169	.00000	.51169	114	58	2.75
8	.00000	.00000	.00000	56	0	4.09
9	.27534	.27534	.55067	56	31	3.09
10	.00000	.00000	.00000	25	0	5.32
11	.00000	.00000	.00000	25	0	4.32
12	.00000	.00000	.00000	25	0	3.32
13	.00000	.42097	.42097	25	10	2.32
14	.00000	.00000	.00000	15	0	2.53
15	.00000	.00000	.00000	15	0	1.53
16	.00000	.00000	.00000	15	0	0.53

[a] Probabilities are dependent.

Source: Kevin Deardorff, "Projected employment expectancies for employees of the SAE Construction Company, by occupation," unpublished paper prepared to fulfill the requirements of the MA degree in the Department of Demography, Georgetown University, 1990.

TABLE 8.7   Associated Table of Separations by Quits Only, for Laborers in the SAE Construction Company (the Mortality Factor Has Been Excluded)

Duration (years)	Prob. of separation by quits[a]	l_x	d_x	e_x
0	.44300	100000	44300	3.65
1	.33714	55700	18779	5.16
2	.25577	36921	9443	6.53
3	.12681	27478	3484	7.60
4	.09670	23994	2320	7.63
5	.00000	21670	0	7.40
6	.13843	21670	3000	6.40
7	.00000	18670	0	6.34
8	.00000	18670	0	5.34
9	.32968	18670	6155	4.34
10	.00000	12515	0	5.24
11	.00000	12515	0	4.24
12	.00000	12515	0	3.24
13	.42097	12515	5268	2.24
14	.00000	7247	0	2.50
15	.00000	7247	0	1.50
16	.00000	7247	0	0.50

[a] Probabilities are independent. Hence, they differ from those in Table 8.6.

Source: Kevin Deardorff, "Projected employment expectancies far employees of the SAE Construction Company, by occupation," unpublished paper prepared to fulfill the MA requirements of the Department of Demography, Georgetown University, 1990.

In his experimental calculations, Deardorff found that the rates of quits and layoffs of laborers and operators in the SAE Construction Company are quite high in the first few years of work, that the laborers and operators have low employment expectancies mainly because of layoffs, and that lowering quits among laborers and operators would result in much smaller increases in employment expectancies than lowering layoffs. For example, if layoffs were eliminated, the average length of employment of laborers with the company would increase greatly (from 0.63 years to 3.65 years), while the elimination of quits would hardly cause the average length of employment to change (from 0.63 years to 0.82 years). Hence, Deardorff concluded, the company would be strongly advised to spend its resources to reduce layoffs rather than quits if it wants to raise the duration of service of laborers and operators and reduce employee turnover and training costs.

Stationary Models for Staffing and Measuring Retirement Costs

The stationary model can be employed in other ways to illustrate demographic changes in the workforce of organizations and hence serve as a framework for managerial decisions. In addition to "modeling" average length of service, the stationary model may be used to develop such measures as the annual intake required to maintain a staff of a fixed size, the age distribution of the staff under a particular hiring formula and resignation pattern, and the number of retirees and retirement costs under specified intake and exit patterns.[23]

Adapting the stationary model of the conventional life table to the workforce of organizations, let us assume that a large organization hires 1000 new employees each year at age 18 (compare a life table radix of 1000 births) and that these new hires exit for whatever reason from the organization's workforce each year at the following rates: 25% for each of the first two ages (i.e., by age 20), 25% of the survivors over the next five ages, 25% of these survivors over the next five ages, and so on until age 75 and beyond, when the rest drop out (Table 8.8). The table is set up with $l_{18} = 1000$ as the annual number of new hires and $_nq_x = .25$ as the "mortality" rate for all intervals (n) except the terminal one (which is 1.0). The "survivors" (l_{x+n}) are derived by applying $1 - _nq_x$, or .75, to each prior l_x sequentially, beginning with 1000. The years of service in each age interval $(_nL_x)$ are calculated from the survivors (l_x) on the assumption that the departure times of employees who withdraw in each interval are spaced evenly throughout the interval—that is,

$$n/2(l_x + l_{x+n}) = _nL_x \tag{9}$$

Then, we derive $T_x = {}_j\sum^\infty {}_nL_{x=j}$ and $e_x = T_x \div l_x$, as in the conventional life table.

In this model, new employees stay with the organization an average of 11.0 years (e_0). At 2 years, or age 20, there is a peak of 16.9 years of service remaining (e_2). Then, "average remaining years" falls steadily until the end of the table. Under the assumptions made, the total number of employees in this work organization (i.e., T_0) is 11,010.

Alternative models that are more realistic involve fewer constraints, such as introducing new hires at any age and assuming a variety of withdrawal rates over the age scale. Let us assume that the organization has a constant annual

TABLE 8.8 Stationary Model for Maintaining a Fixed Distribution of Employees by Age and Corresponding Worklife Expectancies

Exact age x	$_nq_x$	l_x	$_nL_x$	T_x	e_x
18	.25	1000	875	11010	11.0
19	.25	750	656	10135	13.5
20	.25	562	2460	9479	16.9
25	.25	422	1845	7019	16.6
30	.25	316	1382	5174	16.4
35	.25	237	1037	3792	16.0
40	.25	178	778	2755	15.7
45	.25	133	582	1977	14.9
50	.25	100	437	1395	14.0
55	.25	75	328	958	12.8
60	.25	56	245	630	11.2
65	.25	42	185	385	9.2
70	.25	32	140	200	6.2
75	1.00	24	60	60	2.5

number of 1000 new hires at age 18, as before, but that the schedule of probabilities of withdrawal from work varies by age such that an employee would remain with the organization an average of 17.3+ years (e_0). The organization would then have 17,332 employees (T_0). Suppose management plans to raise the annual number of new hires to 1500 but to continue the schedule of variable probabilities of withdrawal. The size of the total workforce would then be 25,998 persons and the average tenure would remain at 17.3:

$$T_0' = (l_0' \div l_0) \star T_0 = (1500/1000) \star 17,332 = 25,998 \qquad (10)$$
$$T_0' \div l_0' = 25,998/1500 = 17.3 \qquad (11)$$

From the original model we can determine the approximate number of workers retiring each year and the costs of retirement programs administered by the organization. If the organization supports retirement for all persons at age 60 or on completion of 42 years of service, we select the figures of 56 persons retiring each year (l_{60}) and 630 retireees (T_{60}) in any year. If each of these retirees receives an annual pension of \$15,000, then the annual cost to the organization is \$9,450,000. If workers aged 18 to 59 ($T_0 - T_{60}$, or 10,380) contribute 5% of their salaries and the average salary is \$20,000, then the annual pool of funds equals \$10,380,000. Since this sum is far above the required payout amount, an ample sum is left as a reserve and to take account any change in the balance of retirees to workers. If the funds were out of balance, adjustments could be made in the contribution rate, the benefit rate, or the age of retirement for benefits.

SPECIAL WORKFORCES

Different workforces present interesting contrasts in their demographic characteristics and patterns of change. They may differ greatly from the general workforce with regard to their growth rates, sex and age structures, socioeconomic characteristics, health and longevity, patterns of retirement, and in other ways. Consider such specific workforces as the armed forces, the Catholic clergy, drug traffickers, folk artists, croupiers, and the workforce in particular industry groups (e.g., public safety, sports, public education, waste management). For some of these workforces, such as the armed forces and the Catholic clergy, there is a substantial body of data, but for others, particularly those engaged in illegal activities, such as drug traffickers, and those loosely defined, such as folk artists, there are few data. To illustrate the contrasts in special workforces, we will take a closer look at the armed forces and the Catholic clergy.

Armed Forces

Studies of the demographic characteristics and population dynamics of the armed forces and their families provide information useful for manpower planning, financial and retirement planning, and planning for social services for this special group of workers. Such studies aid in designing programs for recruitment, training, public relations, and family support. They contribute, for example, to an informed debate regarding the quality of life in the armed forces. Such a debate is critical to public support of the armed forces. Military service is viewed by a segment of the American public as an easy life supported by the taxpayer, while another segment, particularly the families of the servicemen and women, claim the opposite. Information regarding the armed forces is provided by the decennial census, current surveys taken by the U.S. Census Bureau, administrative records of the armed forces, and surveys taken by the armed forces command.[24]

The armed forces are heavily concentrated in the ages of youth (18 to 24), where they form about two-fifths of the total.[25] (See Figure 8.2.) Of the 1.5 million members of the armed forces on active duty in 1995, blacks comprised about 20%, a much higher proportion than in the general workforce (11%).[26] Women comprised 14% of the total and are, like the men, heavily concentrated in the ages under 25. Their occupational distribution is quite different from that of the men, in part because they are excluded from about 15% of the jobs, mostly those associated with direct ground combat. The members of the

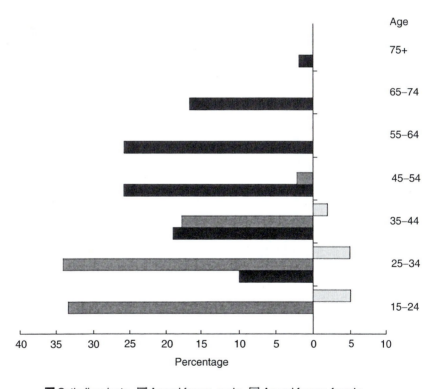

■ Catholic priests   ■ Armed forces, male   □ Armed forces, female

FIGURE 8.2   Age-sex structure of the armed forces, 1994, and of the Catholic priest population, 1995. *Note:* The armed forces includes both resident armed forces and armed forces overseas. The Catholic priest population includes only active diocesan priests. *Source:* U.S. Bureau of the Census, "Population projections of the United States by age, sex, race, and Hispanic origin: 1995 to 2050, by Jennifer C. Day, *Current Population Reports*, P25-1130, Tables D-1 and D-2, 1996; and Richard A. Schoenherr and Lawrence A. Young, *Full Pews and Empty Alters: Demographics of the Priest Shortage in the United States Catholic Dioceses*, Social Demography Series, Madison: University of Wisconsin Press, 1993.

armed forces tend to "retire" after completing their first or second tour of duty, usually as young adults. Attrition rates are high: nearly 32% of new recruits of 1993 failed to complete their 4-year terms. The leading reason for female attrition is pregnancy.

While geopolitical changes since 1990 have radically changed recruiting requirements, the military services at the beginning of the first decade of the 21st century have been experiencing a shortage of recruits. This is due to a number of factors, among which demographic and socioeconomic factors are prominant. The sharp drop in the size of the youth cohorts 16 to 18 years old resulting from the fertility declines in the 1970s and 1980s has reduced the available pool from which recruits can be drawn, greater racial and gender equity in the civilian workplace has lessened the attractiveness of the armed forces to racial minorities and women, and many civilian jobs are available because of a thriving civilian economy. The recruiting situation can change rapidly, however, as evidenced by the very different evaluation made by Klerman and Karoly in the early 1990s.[27]

Catholic Priests

Since the Catholic Church oversees religious activities in the dioceses, it manages the number and location of parish priests and parish churches. This oversight has been important to the Church because of the considerable change in the supply of priests in relation to the numbers of parishioners in the dioceses. The change in the numbers of parishioners is the result of changes in the ethnic and socioeconomic composition of neighborhoods, the shifting demand of the local population for church services, and the movement of population within and between metropolitan areas. All church organizations must deal with the shifts in the numbers and demographic characteristics of the populations they serve, whether they are ministering to the present membership, dealing with the needs of the surrounding community, or considering the prospective body of parishioners in a new location.

In the years following World War II, the Catholic population, consisting mainly of various white ethnic groups, moved in large numbers from the central cities to the suburbs as they achieved middle-class status, like other white middle-class Americans. The new suburbanites left most black, poor, and elderly Catholics behind. As a result, there was a relative deficit of Catholic churches and priests in the suburbs and a relative surplus of Catholic churches and priests in the cities. In time a better balance of parishioners and priests developed. More recently, however, the immigration of Hispanics and Eastern Europeans and their residential concentration in the central cities have renewed the demand for Catholic churches and priests in the central cities. Hispanics, who are mainly Catholic, have been growing rapidly as a consequence of high fertility and a steady large refugee, immigrant, and illegal movement into the United States.

Overall, there has been a shortage of priests in the country since the 1960s. Young men have been entering the priesthood in smaller numbers and older priests have been leaving the priesthood in larger numbers than in the past. The priest corps has been aging and, as a result, retirements have been relatively frequent. Fewer men enter the priesthood than in earlier decades because of the rule of celibacy, the requirement of a lifetime commitment, the reduced size of Catholic families, and the general secularization of our society. In the Chicago archdiocese, only one-sixth as many priests are ordained as die, retire, or resign at an early age.[28] As a result, the Archbishop of Chicago proposes to borrow priests from Latin America, Eastern Europe, and Africa. The problem of priest shortages is aggravated by the lack of priests who speak the language of the parishioners and know their culture. This shortage extends to the need for, say, Mexican rather than Guatemalan priests, or Haitian rather than Quebecan priests.

These changes have been subjected to formal demographic analysis by Schoenherr and Young (1993), who have prepared a comprehensive demographic study of the Catholic priest population.[29] It focuses on past and prospective changes among the priest population at the national, regional, and diocesan levels and applies a great variety of demographic measures in its analyses. The authors created their own data set equivalent to a population register covering the period 1966 to 1984.

Some of the findings of the study are presented in the following paragraphs. The U.S. diocesan priest population was estimated to number about 24,000 in 1995 and is expected to fall to approximately 21,000 by 2005 according to the "moderate" projection series. The median age of active priests was 47 years in 1975 and about 53 years in 1995 (projected), and it is expected to remain at about 53 years in 2005. The proportion of retired, sick, and absent priests has been growing. This segment is expected to rise from 11.3% of the total priest population in 1975 to about 20.1% in 2005. The median age of the total priest population (i.e, including inactive priests) in these years is expected to rise from 50 to 57. In 1995, half of the active priests were aged 53 or older. The contrast between the age distribution of the priest population and the military population is striking (see Figure 8.2).

Of the gross change in the number of priests during 1984, resignations, retirements, and deaths were all strong contributors, making up about 61% of the total, while ordinations made up only about 22%. Two decades earlier, in 1966, the shares were sharply different, 47% and 43%, respectively. U.S. diocesan priests tend to retire at a much older age than the labor force in general and, as a result, to spend many fewer years in retirement, as shown by the following figures:

| | | Mean ages | |
Period	At retirement	At death Preretirement priests	All priests
1966–1969	70.9	62.9	72.6
1970–1974	68.7	61.8	73.3
1975–1979	68.7	61.9	73.9
1980–1984	69.0[a]	61.9	73.8

[a] The median and mean ages of retirement from the total labor force are 62.6 years and 62.9 years, respectively, for this period.

Source: Schoenherr and Young (1993), Table 10.3. Weighted register counts.

TABLE 8.9   Annual Average Rate of Change in the Diocesan Priest Population by Period and Transition Event, 1966 to 1984, and Gross Change Rate by Transition Event, 1966–1984

Event	Average annual rate (percentage)				Gross change rate 1966–1984 (percentage)[a]
	1966–1969	1970–1974	1975–1979	1980–1984	
Gain					
Ordination	2.82	2.32	2.21	1.77	38.77
Incardination[b]	0.22	0.41	0.60	0.67	8.18
Other entrance[c]	0.10	0.15	0.20	0.23	2.89
Loss					
Resignation	1.32	1.71	0.85	0.65	19.50
Excardination[b]	1.08	0.18	0.30	0.37	3.97
Retirement	1.40	1.49	1.56	1.59	25.77
Death	1.19	0.94	0.77	0.77	15.58
Other exit[d]	0.27	0.28	0.30	0.29	4.86
Net decline	−1.13	−1.71	−.077	−0.99	−19.84

[a] Using 1966 active population for the denominator and the cumulative number of gains and losses for the numerator.

[b] Migration, mainly to and from abroad.

[c] Returns from leaves of absence, returns from sick leave, and awaiting assignment.

[d] Leave of absence, sick leave, and awaiting assignment.

Note: Number of gains and losses per 100 active priests. Number of priests registered in the 19-year period is 36,370.

Source: Adapted from Table 2.3 in Richard A. Schoenherr and Lawrence A. Young, *Full Pews and Empty Altars: Demographics of the Priest Shortage in United States Catholic Dioceses*, Madison: University of Wisconsin Press, 1993. Based on weighted register counts. Copyright © 1993. Reprinted by permission of the University of Wisconsin Press.

Tables 8.9 to 8.11 present additional data on various aspects of the past and prospective changes in the Catholic priesthood. Table 8.9 gives average annual rates of change in the number of priests for various periods between 1966 and 1984, separately for each component of change, or transition event. Over this 19-year period, the number of priests declined by 20%, and over the 40-year period, 1965–2005, the number is expected to decline by 40% (not

TABLE 8.10   Estimates of Lay Catholics, Diocesan and Religious Priests, and Layperson-to-Priest Ratios, 1975 and 1985, and Projections, 2005

Population or ratio	1975	1985	2005
Laypersons (thousands)	56,030	64,341	74,109
Active priests (thousands)			
Total	50,831	46,828	33,799
Diocesan	30,808	28,240	21,030
Religious	20,023	18,588	12,749
Layman/priest ratio			
Total	1,102	1,374	2,194
Diocesan	1,819	2,278	3,524
Religious	2,798	3,461	5,813

(*continues*)

TABLE 8.10 (*continued*)

Population or ratio	1975	1985	2005
Percent deficit[a]			
Total	—[b]	24.7[c]	99.0
Diocesan	—[b]	25.2	93.6
Religious	—[b]	23.7[c]	107.7

[a] Deficit of active priests as percent of active priests. The layperson/priest ratio in 1975 is taken as the standard for assessing the priest shortage in 1985 and 2005. Under this assumption, the percentage deficit is calculated indirectly as the ratio of the layman/priest ratio in 1985 or 2005 to the corresponding ratio in 1975.

[b] Under the assumption in ([a]), the percentage deficit in 1975 is zero.

[c] These figures are corrected figures and hence differ from those in the source.

Source: Adapted ftom Table 12.8 in Richard A. Schoenherr and Lawrence A. Young, *Full Pews and Empty Altars: Demographics of the Priest Shortage in United States Catholic Dioceses*, Madison: University of Wisconsin Press, 1993. Copyright © 1993. Reprinted by permission of The University of Wisconsin Press.

shown). The number of laypersons per priest is expected to rise sharply from about 1400 in 1985 to 2200 in 2005 as the number of laypersons rises and the number of priests falls. As a result, a steep rise is expected in the deficit of priests as a percentage of active priests, from 25% in 1985 to 99% in 2005 (Table 8.10). The data in Table 8.11 reflect the considerable regional variation in the increases in the parishioner/priest ratio in the 1970–1980 decade. The national figures for 1985 and for 2005 shown in Table 8.10 suggest that the increases in this ratio have generally continued throughout the country and that shortages of priests are now widespread.

TABLE 8.11 **Parishioners per Active Diocesan Priest, for Geographic Divisions: 1970 and 1980**

Geographic division	Parishioner/priest ratio		Percent increase, 1970–1980
	1970	1980	
United States	1328	1570	19
New England	1266	1535	21
Middle Atlantic	1268	1455	15
East North Central	1174	1424	21
West North Central	700	909	32
South Atlantic[a]	1238	1381	12
West South Central	1875	2017	8
Mountain	1385	1775	28
Pacific	1826	2291	25

[a] Includes one diocese from the East South Central division.

Source: Adapted from Table 4.2 in Richard A. Schoenherr and Lawrence A. Young, *Full Pews and Empty Altars: Demographics of the Priest Shortage in United States Catholic Dioceses*, Madison: University of Wisconsin Press, 1993. Copyright © 1993. Reprinted by permission of The University of Wisconsin Press.

DEMOGRAPHIC ASPECTS OF EMPLOYER ADMINISTRATIVE RECORDS

Types and Limitations

The administrative records of employers represent a major untapped resource for the demographic analysis and solution of a host of issues facing employers in the management of their business operations. Such files can provide employers with much information about their workforce and retirees that would prove useful in business decision making. Unlike the files with which demographers normally work, employer administrative files are kept for other than demographic purposes, so that it is not surprising that their utility has been overlooked, both by demographers and business managers. Recent interest in their use parallels the federal government's interest in public administrative records to supplement or replace the decennial population and housing censuses, and in private administrative records to supplement the national economic census.

Employers maintain several different types of records that may be exploited for the solution of their special problems. These include payroll records, benefits records, human resources records, and customer records. Only those files relating to employees and retirees are of interest at this juncture; customer records were discussed in Chapter 6. For demographic applications, some employer files may have to be used in combination. This is accomplished by matching the files on the Social Security number or, when the Social Security number is lacking, other identifying information such as birthdate or date of entry on duty.

Employer administrative files share some characteristics with administrative files in general, but they also have some special characteristics of their own. Like all administrative files, they are subject to errors of undercoverage or overcoverage. They carry some persons who should have been removed from the files for such reasons as death, resignation, and transfer to another location. The entries in the different fields of the record, such as employee promotions and dependents, may be of variable quality and currency. Employer administrative files tend to record incompletely those transitions (e.g., resignations) that occurred in the last months of each year because of processing delays. These status changes may then appear in the files of the following year. Deceased persons and persons with other status changes may be retained in some administrative files purposely until all the associated health claims are cleared.

Employer files are often updated continuously, whereas demographers need files that are "frozen" as of some date in the year, such as January 1, often for a series of years. Employer files may contain duplicate records for an individual if he or she has worked in different locations in the firm; for demographic purposes these duplications must be eliminated. Some files carry dummy entries on records for items that must be filled before the record is usable for business purposes (e.g., Social Security number); for demographic purposes such a record may be unusable. The quality of the records may vary greatly from one organization to another, with the size of the organization probably having a direct bearing on the usefulness of the records for demographic analysis.

Access to most company administrative records is on a need-to-know basis, and permission to use the records must be obtained for particular files. Organizations deal with the privacy and confidentiality issues by restricting use of the files in this way. There may be other restrictions on the use of administrative records, such as deletions of sections of the records, to preserve the privacy of individuals. Since administrative files are often not well adapted to demographic uses and have their individual characteristics, they must first be evaluated for a particular demographic application. It is important to learn how records enter and leave the file, what types of changes are recorded, and how often the file is updated.

Employers with sizable numbers of employees usually maintain all three types of files: payroll files, benefits files, and human resources files. The maintenance of a **payroll file** is nearly universal among employers, who require a system for paying employees and withholding taxes. The files contain a record for each employee at each place of employment in the firm and hence there may be multiple records for an employee in the files if he or she has worked in more than one plant during a pay period. These records contain such information as sex, Social Security number, birth date, wages or salaries, tax exemptions, amount of pay withheld for taxes, and hours worked.

A **benefits file** is used in the administration of a company's social insurance or fringe-benefit programs, including health benefits, life and accident insurance, and retirement plans. It includes such information as sex, Social Security number, birth date, number and characteristics of dependents covered by health, life insurance, and retirement plans, and name of insurance carrier. Companies may also maintain a **human resources file** in order to manage and plan a human resources program in the company. This file may be searched to locate a possible candidate within the company when a position requiring a specific level of education and skill is open in a part of a company. Like the other files, it contains information on sex, Social Security number, and birth date, but it also gives such information as job title and rank, work history, educational level, and skills.

Applications

Employer files can be exploited to develop a range of demographic data and measures, such as the growth rate, age-sex distribution and median age, age-specific death rates, and age-specific birth rates, for the covered population. These data and measures can then be elaborated in the form of life tables and projections of the employee and retiree populations. From these demographic projections, various socioeconomic projections, such as requirements for training, child care, and health services, can be derived. Additional steps convert these socioeconomic projections into projections of resources and funds required to plan for these services.

The cost of health and retirement benefits of a major company represents a significant part of the budget of the company. The company needs to have as accurate projections as possible of the number of surviving retirees from each cohort of workers and of their requirements for health services, including particularly use of hospitals. For this purpose, death rates and life tables must be developed for relevant groups.

Estimating Death Rates

It is important to emphasize that persons in an employer file are not representative of the total population or labor force in an area; rather, they are workers or retirees in a particular industry or company. To make projections for an industry or company, it is desirable to employ death rates and life tables specifically for this population, rather than ones for the general population. Mortality levels for the workforce of a particular industry or company are likely to be different from those of the general population. Employer administrative files can provide the data needed to derive death rates and life tables specifically applicable to the company.

In the following discussion, we draw on a study by Kintner and Swanson (1994), which recounts their experience with the administrative files of the General Motors Corporation (GMC) in developing death rates and life tables for the "salaried retirees" of the corporation.[30] The life tables are to be used in deriving projections of salaried retirees and their days of hospital care. Tapes for the salaried retirees eligible for health benefits were obtained for December 31, 1983 to 1987, to derive deaths and populations exposed to risk for calendar years 1984 to 1987.

The GMC files required some "cleansing" before the death rates could be calculated. The Social Security number was used to match a cohort member's records from year to year. Duplicate Social Security numbers in each year-end tape had to be removed so that matching to the cohort member's record of other years could be carried out and mismatching of records over the years could be avoided.[31] The final database includes information about all salaried retirees from December 31, 1983, to either December 31, 1987, or their date of death, whichever is earlier. Two files, the payroll file and the benefits file, were used to establish the number of deaths from 1984 through 1987. Deaths were identified by a change in the status code, by the replacement of an employee record by a surviving spouse record, or by cancellation of coverage.[32]

There are two approaches to deriving death rates from employer administrative files. They may be designated the period (cross-sectional) approach and the cohort (generational) approach. In the former, the deaths occurring to the population at a given age during a year are compiled according to age and then divided by the population at midyear. These are central death rates and must be converted to mortality rates (i.e., probabilities of dying) for use in life tables. In the generational approach, the population at each exact age (e.g., 55.0 years) is followed as a birth cohort over the year to identify deaths occurring to the cohort (e.g., at age 55) and these deaths are then related to the exposed population at each exact age.[33] In practice, variations of these two approaches are used. It is important in such a calculation to have a large enough group exposed to the risk of death and a sufficient number of deaths to reduce the effect of random fluctuations in the data. In the present illustration, data for the 4 years were combined to reduce the variance in the annual rates.

Kintner and Swanson adopted an estimation procedure for calculating mortality rates based on exact exposure. The resulting probabilities of dying

TABLE 8.12   Extract of an Unabridged Life Table for GM Salaried Male and Female Retirees: 1984–1987

Age (x)	q_x	d_x	$l_x{}^a$	L_x	T_x	e_x
Men						
50	.01746	1591	91104	90308	2420539	26.57
55	.01296	1094	84451	83904	1982776	23.48
60	.01385	1095	79108	78560	1573937	19.90
65	.01827	1337	73215	72546	1192677	16.29
70	.02844	1867	65645	64712	844550	12.86
75	.04678	2567	54879	53595	541846	9.87
80	.07379	3021	40946	39436	301229	7.36
Women						
50	.00342	326	95312	95149	3089230	32.41
55	.00547	511	93325	93070	2617275	28.04
60	.00888	802	90273	89872	2157749	23.90
65	.01214	1042	85793	85272	1717110	20.01
70	.01729	1383	79967	79276	1302058	16.28
75	.02550	1840	72173	71253	920808	12.76
80	.03964	2451	61824	60599	584633	9.46

[a] Life tables are based on a radix of 100,000 males and 100,000 females alive at birth. Prior to age 50, life table values were obtained from the 1984–1986 U.S. life tables for white males and white females.

Source: Hallie J. Kintner and David A. Swanson, "Estimating vital rates from corporate databases: How long will GM's salaried retirees live," in Hallie J. Kintner *et al.* (eds.), *Demographics: A Casebook for Business and Government*, A Rand Book, Boulder: Westview Press, 1994, Tables 16.4 and 16.5, pp. 274–275. © Copyright Rand 1994. Reprinted with permission.

between ages i and $i + 1$, q_i, had to be smoothed because they exhibited some unacceptable variability. The life table for salaried retirees was then constructed from these smoothed q_i, with imputed values from the U.S. Life Table for whites, 1984–1986, for ages 50 and under for men and ages 60 and under for women (Table 8.12). The resulting life expectancies proved to be more favorable than those of the white U.S. population, 1984–1986, and less favorable than those of the Group Annuitants Table for 1983 (GAM83) used by actuaries (Table 8.13). At age 50, life expectation for men is 25.9 years for U.S. whites, 26.6 years for GM salaried retirees, and 29.0 years for GAM 83. For women at age 60, the corresponding figures are 22.6, 23.9, and 25.0. This comparison lends support to the view that the salaried retirees of General Motors Corporation are a selected population with respect to mortality and that in making projections of this population, survival rates reflecting their distinctive mortality should be used.

Projections of Employees, Retirees, and Hospital Use

Projections of employees or retirees can now be prepared with the new life table. For projections of employees, whether we restrict ourselves to tracking cohorts of employees as they age after the base date or project employees over a specified age range, we have to make assumptions regarding new hires, resignations, and retirements after the base date. For projections of retirees, we

TABLE 8.13 Comparison of Life Expectation at Selected Older Ages for GMC Salaried Retirees and Two Selected Populations, for Mid-1980s

Age	U.S. whites, 1984–1986	GM salaried retirees, 1984–1987	GAM 83[a]
Men			
50	25.9	26.6	29.0
55	21.8	23.5	24.6
60	18.1	19.9	20.4
65	14.7	16.3	16.5
70	11.6	12.9	12.9
75	9.0	9.9	9.9
80	6.9	7.4	7.3
Women			
60	22.6	23.9	25.0
65	18.7	20.0	20.6
70	15.1	16.3	16.4
75	11.8	12.8	12.6
80	8.8	9.5	9.3

[a] Group annuitants, 1983; life table based on annuitants, not the general population or workers.

Source: Hallie J. Kintner and David A. Swanson, "Estimating vital rates from corporate databases: How long will GM's salaried retirees live," in Hallie J. Kintner *et al.* (eds.), *Demographics: A Casebook for Business and Government*, A Rand Book, Boulder; Westview Press, 1994, Tables 16.2 and 16.3, p. 273. © Copyright Rand 1994. Reprinted with permission.

can either follow only the current retiree population as a group of cohorts or "feed in" the new retirees as well. Kintner and Swanson did the former, tracking only retirees on the base date, December 31, 1983. Projections of salaried retirees were prepared for December 31, 1988, by applying single-age survival rates over each of the next 5 years, to the salaried population on the base date (Table 8.14).[34]

Next, projections of requirements for hospitalization for December 31, 1989 to 2000, in terms of the total number of days of hospital care, for General Motors salaried retirees, were derived by applying national rates of hospital utilization to the GMC population data. (See Table 8.15 for illustrative computations.) More specifically, rates of hospital discharge, representing hospital stays per 1000 population, and average days of hospital care per 1000 population, for sex and age groups, derived from the 1987 National Hospital Discharge Survey, were applied to the projections of GMC salaried retirees, disaggregated by age and sex, for each year, December 31, 1989 to 1999, to derive projections of hospital use for each year 1990 to 2000:

$$H_{ijy} = P_{ijy} \star R_{ijy} \qquad (12)$$

where H_{ijy} represents hospital discharges or days of care in year y for age-sex-group ij, P_{ijy} retirees in age-sex-group ij in year y, and R_{ijy} the rate of hospital use (whether discharges or days of care) for age-sex-group ij in year y. The

TABLE 8.14 Illustrative Calculations for Projecting GMC Male and Female Salaried Retirees from 1988 to 1989

Age	Male Retirees 12/31/88 (1)	Survival rate (2)	Survivors 12/31/89 (3) = (1) ★ (2)[a]	Female Retirees 12/31/88 (4)	Survival rate (5)	Survivors 12/31/89 (6) = (4) ★ (5)[a]
50	100	.98467	98	27	.98640	27
55	1413	.98743	1395	248	.99427	247
60	2458	.98562	2423	385	.99082	381
65	2719	.98064	2666	511	.98746	505
70	1938	.96986	1880	441	.98202	433
75	1311	.95160	1248	299	.97342	291
80	812	.92335	750	210	.95833	201
84+	1886	.82900	1563	482	.87200	420

[a] Survivors shown are for the following ages and not for the ages shown.

Note: Extract of calculations, omitting ages under 50 and ages not ending in 0 or 5 over age 50.

Source: See Table 8.12. Survival rates are based on the unabridged GMC life table for 1984–1987, calculated as L_{x+1}/L_x. Hallie J. Kintner and David A. Swanson, "Estimating vital rates from corporate databases: How long will GM's salaried retirees live?" in Hallie J. Kintner *et al.* (eds.), *Demographics: A Casebook for Business and Government*, A Rand Book, Boulder: Westview Press, 1994, Table 16.8, pp. 284–285. © Copyright Rand 1994. Reprinted with permission.

figures for individual age-sex groups were then combined to derive an overall total for each year:

$$H_y = \sum_{j=30}^{85+} \sum_{i=1}^{2} (P_{ijy} \star R_{ijy}) \tag{13}$$

where H_y is the total number of hospital stays or days of care for both sexes and all ages (30 years and over) in year y. The procedure assumes that these rates continue to apply in the future as in the past, although it would have been possible to project the usage rates.

Estimating Birthrates

It is possible that the crude birthrate and age-specific birthrates can be calculated for the employee population of a firm from its health benefits file. Moreover, since many of the employees are male, this line of research presents the possibility of deriving paternal as well as maternal birthrates. Covered mothers (i.e., female employees or wives of employees) usually bring their infants to a physician for care under the company's health plan or are required to report the birth of a child within a specified time period in order for the plan to cover the cost. Underreporting can be a serious concern, however. For example, if the infant dies very shortly after birth, the employee parent may fail to report the birth of the child. If a birth of a child occurs late in the year, the parent may delay reporting the birth until the following year. A year-end birth may also not be recorded in the year of occurrence because office operations have closed down in mid-December. It is important, therefore, to examine the

TABLE 8.15 Illustrative Projections of Hospital Utilization by GMC Male and Female Salaried Retirees for Year-end 1989

| Age[a] | Projected retirees, 12/31/89 (1) | U.S. hospitalization rates[b] | | Projected hospitalization | |
		Discharges (2)	Days of care (3)	Discharges (4) = (1) ⋆ (2)	Days of care (5) = (1) ⋆ (3)
Men					
50–54	917	128.7	828.0	118	759
55–59	8,208	200.4	1,394.1	1,645	11,443
60–64	11,543	200.4	1,394.1	2,513	17,486
65–69	12,789	308.7	2,445.2	3,948	31,272
70–74	8,709	308.7	2,445.2	2,688	21,295
75–79	5,719	491.2	4,263.7	2,809	24,384
80–83	2,715	491.2	4,263.7	1,333	11,576
84+	1,985	619.1	5,371.4	1,229	10,662
Total	53,585	NA	NA	16,285	128,877
Women					
50–54	231	133.6	853.7	31	197
55–59	1,321	169.2	1,232.4	224	1,628
60–64	2,057	169.2	1,232.4	348	2,535
65–69	2,688	258.8	2,174.3	696	5,845
70–74	1,990	258.8	2,174.3	515	4,327
75–79	1,284	387.8	3,531.8	498	4,535
80–83	684	387.8[c]	3,531.8	265[c]	2,416
84+	549	499.2	4,915.2	274	2,698
Total	10,804	NA	NA	2,851	24,181

NA: Not applicable.

[a] Ages under 50 in the source table have been omitted.

[b] Rates per 1000 population. Data from 1987 National Hospital Discharge Survey. This table follows the source table in assuming that hospitalization rates, both for discharges and days of care, were equal for the two 5-year age groups within each 10-year age group. This is a questionable assumption; preferably, the discharge rates and the rates for days of care should be graduated by an appropriate curve, such as a cubic polynomial fitted to the cumulative observations.

[c] Correction of error in the original table.

Source: Adapted from Hallie J. Kintner and David A. Swanson, "Estimating vital rates from corporate databases: How long will GM's salaried retirees live?" in Hallie J. Kintner *et al.* (eds.), *Demographics: A Casebook for Business and Government*, A Rand Book, Boulder: Westview Press, 1994, Table 16.9, pp. 286–287. © Copyright Rand 1994. Reprinted with permission.

file for a particular year to identify the births that occurred in the previous year. Death or divorce of the employed parent complicates the record-keeping operation.

In addition to problems of coverage and time reference, there are problems of age reporting. Age may be omitted for either father or mother or both, although the last is relatively rare. One of the parents may work elsewhere and have his or her own health insurance plan. The file may lack information about the parent who is carried under a different plan. If both parents work for the company, they have separate benefits records and their marital relation may not be known. Hence, in the event of a birth, the age of the other parent may not be known.

Birthrates are computed by relating the births occurring to persons at each age to males or females at each age at risk of having children. We can calculate age-specific birthrates either by the period method or the cohort method. Since the results are virtually the same for single ages, it is acceptable to take the conventional route and calculate only period or central rates.

Company fertility rates may be compared with national fertility rates to evaluate the accuracy of the fertility rates for the company and to establish differences in the fertility of socioeconomic groups within the population. Such a comparison may simply reveal that the fertility of the employee population is about the same as that of the general population, unless the discrepancy is large. Fertility rates for some companies may be substantially lower than those for the general population because their employee populations have much higher incomes and education. For example, when Kintner and Swanson (1994) compared their estimated birthrates for the employees of the General Motors Corporation (GMC) with those for the U.S. white married population in 1988, they found that the GMC birthrates were lower for all ages except those for the youngest ages, where there are few GMC employees. Their finding that the age *patterns* of paternal and maternal birthrates were the same gives some support to the validity of their results.

COMPLIANCE WITH REGULATIONS RELATING TO STAFF MANAGEMENT

Technological developments, changes in the structure of the economy, changes in views regarding personnel management, and particularly changes in the law have brought about major changes in human resources management in business, other private organizations, and government agencies since the 1960s. Prior to that decade, personnel decisions relating to hiring, promotion, transfer, firing, and retirement were largely made on the basis of practices and policies internal to the particular organization. They were viewed as the private business of the organization. However, several laws enacted since the 1960s and administrative regulations issued by various federal agencies relating to discrimination in employment practices have modified the "rules" by which employees are managed. As a result, the duties and responsibilities of personnel managers have changed greatly since that time. There are greater demands for internal record-keeping, the reporting of personnel practices and structures to government agencies, and use of public data. These public data are often demographic in nature and come from sources usually overseen by demographers. Furthermore, to accommodate to the new human resources environment, various types of demographic analyses have to be applied to the data.

Legislative Background

The new legislation includes principally the Equal Pay Act of 1963, Title VII of the Civil Rights Act of 1964, the Age Discrimination in Employment Act (ADEA) of 1967, and the Americans with Disabilities Act (AWDA) of 1990.

Another legislative initiative, the Equal Rights Amendment, would have added to the Constitution an amendment calling for equal rights specifically on the basis of sex, but it was ill-fated. It failed ratification by three-quarters of the states as required, after being passed by Congress in 1972. The Equal Pay Act provides that no employer shall discriminate with respect to pay scales between employees on the basis of sex. Title VII prohibits discrimination in the terms, conditions, and privileges of employment on the basis of sex, race, color, religion, or national origin. ADEA prohibits discrimination on the basis of age and is aimed at protecting older workers from being terminated and replaced by younger workers purely on the basis of age. AWDA requires employers recruiting employees to hire individuals with disabilities who can do the job with reasonable accommodations as well as nondisabled persons.

The Equal Employment Opportunity Commission (EEOC) and the Department of Labor have issued administrative regulations and guidelines to support the new legislation. The guidelines do not have any legal force, but the courts have taken EEOC's guidelines into account when ruling in discrimination suits. In effect, these laws, regulations, and guidelines ban discrimination in employment on the basis of certain personal (i.e., demographic) characteristics. Failure to adhere to them represents grounds for charges of discrimination in employment.

Industry's obligation to comply with the regulations has imposed on it the need to maintain detailed records relating to all personnel actions and the characteristics of its employees, and to be prepared to defend its personnel actions (or failures to act) against public and private complaints and legal suits. Personnel managers must also keep senior managers informed about changes in the company's workforce, the extent to which these changes comply with or fail to comply with existing requirements regarding discrimination in employment, and their plans to correct any evident problems vis-à-vis the requirements.

Race/Ethnic Discrimination in Employment

As mentioned, the Civil Rights Act of 1964 prohibits discrimination on the basis of race, color, religion, sex, or national origin. Section 703 states the following:

> (a) It shall be an unlawful employment practice for an employer—
> (1) to fail or refuse to hire or to discharge any individual, or otherwise to discriminate against any individual with respect to his compensation, terms, conditions, or privileges of employment, because of such individual's race, color, religion, sex, or national origin; or
> (2) to limit, segregate, or classify his employees in any way which would deprive or tend to deprive any individual of employment opportunities or otherwise adversely affect his status as an employee, because of such individual's race, color, religion, sex, or national origin.

Section 703 also states,

> Nothing contained in this title shall be interpreted to require any employer... to grant preferential treatment to any individual or to any group because of race, color, religion, sex, or national origin of such individual or group on account of any imbalance

which may exist with respect to the total number or percentage of persons of any race, color, religion, sex, or national origin employed by any employer..., in comparison with the total number or percentage of persons of such race, color, religion, sex, or national origin in any community, State, section, or other area, or in the available work force in any community, State, section, or other area.

The Civil Rights Act as amended in 1986 appears to qualify, if not abrogate, the latter stipulation of the 1964 act in providing for "affirmative action" when the former stipulation of the act is carried out. It also identifies certain "protected groups" in its oversight of racial discrimination. These groups are the racial/ethnic groups to be separately recognized in programs of "equal opportunity" and "affirmative action" for public and private employment. The following sections enumerate these protected groups and discuss some problems with the use of these categories in employment decisions.

Racial/Ethnic Classification in Civil Rights Programs

The classification of racial/ethnic groups promulgated in 1977 in Directive 15 of the U.S. Office of Management and Budget (OMB) was intended both for use in the statistical programs of the U.S. government and for use by state and local governments and private organizations in preparing reports required for compliance with fair employment laws. It is consistent with the Civil Rights Act as amended. Three broad race groups and one ethnic group, persons of Hispanic origin, were recognized as protected groups under this law. These race and Hispanic-origin groups were identified in the directive as follows:

American Indian, Eskimo, and Aleut—Persons having origins in any of the original peoples of North America and maintaining identification through tribal affiliation or community organization.

Asian and Pacific Islander—Persons having origins in any of the original peoples of the Far East, Southeast Asia, the Indian Subcontinent, or the Pacific Islands.

Black, not of Hispanic origin—Persons having origins in any of the black racial groups of Africa, excluding those of Hispanic origin.

Hispanic—Persons of Mexican, Puerto Rican, Cuban, Central or South American or other Spanish culture or origin, regardless of race.

The remaining members of the population, those not "protected," are *white, not of Hispanic origin,* persons having origins in any of the original peoples of Europe, North Africa, or the Middle East, excluding those of Hispanic origin.

This classification is a combination of racial, geographic, and ethnic classifications and maintains a separation between race and Hispanic ethnicity. In the 1990 decennial census, race and Hispanic origin were self-reported; the individual identified him or herself with respect to race and Hispanic origin but within guidelines set by the Census Bureau, which was acting in accordance with OMB Directive 15.

Numerous questions have been raised with respect to the use of this classification in civil rights cases. Some questions relate to the assumptions underlying the classification and the coverage of each of the groups; others relate to the purposes to be served by its use. The protected groups do not include some

ethnic groups which are disadvantaged (e.g., certain white ethnic groups originating in Europe, North Africa, and the Middle East, and the indigenous peoples of Central and South America). Most members of some Asian-American
groups (i.e., Japanese, Koreans, Chinese, and Asian Indians), Cubans (among
the Hispanics), and many individual blacks, Hispanics, and Asian Americans
of other national origins do not need the special protection afforded by the
law. Brazilians and Cape Verdians are defined as non-Hispanic and hence are
excluded from protection even though they are ethnically similar to Hispanics.
Blacks from the Caribbean area are often both black and Hispanic, but their
Hispanic origin takes priority in racial/ethnic tabulations of the data. Questions related to these anomalies of classification arise in legal applications of
the racial and Hispanic data.

Most members of some racial groups (e.g., blacks) and Hispanics are of
mixed race in reality and members of these groups differ widely in the degree
of the racial mixture. While other factors are involved, the degree of racial
mixture affects the extent to which members of the group experience discrimination in the workplace. The census classification does not take this factor
into account, however. Moreover, comparative analysis of the official racial
data in civil rights cases is distorted by the fact that the data incorporate a serious aberration in the racial reporting of many Hispanics. In 1990, as in 1980,
some 40% of Hispanics reported themselves as belonging to "other race"—
that is, a race other than the conventional ones and the national-origin groups
listed on the census questionnaire. The Hispanic count is not affected by this
misreporting of race, but the counts of whites, blacks, and other races, and
comparisons of the races with one another and with Hispanics, are distorted
by the misclassification.

The new directive on racial and ethnic classification for federal reporting
purposes issued by the Office of Management and Budget (OMB) in the fall
of 1997 may reduce the problem of race misreporting on the part of Hispanics in the 2000 census and later censuses. The new standards go into effect
in the census of 2000 and in other statistical operations in 2003 or earlier.
The principal changes are the placement of the Hispanic question before the
race question, the instruction to mark more than one race where appropriate, and the division of the "Asian and Pacific Islander" group into "Asian"
and "Native Hawaiian or other Pacific Islander." In addition, Central and
South American Indians are to be included in the "American Indian or Alaska
native" group and some changes in identifying names are to be made (e.g.,
"Hispanic or Latino," "black or African American"). The modification of the
census questions will present some difficult problems for classification and tabulation programs, considering the multiplicity of racial combinations that may
be tabulated and reported. The consequences of the new tabulation schemes,
particularly with respect to issues of civil rights, may be wide-ranging since the
integrity of the former distinctions between the races may be blurred and there
could be numerous disputes about the counts of particular races.[35]

Applications to Personnel Administration

The racial classification given in OMB Directive 15 was employed by private industry, government, and nonprofit organizations in their personnel prac-

tices and administration (i.e., financial aid and hiring, promotion, and firing practices) for the period 1977 to 1997.[36] Affirmative action programs based on the classification have been put in place and implemented widely in the workplace. Partly as a result of these programs, the race/ethnic composition of the workforce, particularly with respect to rank, has changed radically since the 1960s. Many legal contests have been successfully waged on the grounds of violation of Title VII of the Civil Rights Act.

In suits of racial discrimination in the workplace, the plaintiff in a protected group tries to show not only that he or she was discriminated against by an employer but also that the employing organization or its agents follow a *pattern* of discrimination against members of the racial group of the plaintiff. Such a pattern may be suggested to the court by demonstrating that the share of employees in the protected group employed by the defendant organization is below the share of such persons in the general community. Advocates of affirmative action maintain that personnel managers should take remedial action when the shares of workers in the protected groups in their organizations, and at various levels of responsibility in the organization, fall substantially below those in the general population of the commuting area or general service area for the organization. This position is logically and demographically naive, but politically persuasive. The Supreme Court as well as lower courts are beginning to recognize its weaknesses, as reflected in *Adarand Constructors v. Pena*, 1995, and *City of Richmond v. J. A. Croson Co.*, 1989.[37]

The standard selected for the comparison should be appropriately restricted or extended with respect to population, qualifications, geographic area, and time. The percentage of persons in the protected racial group employed by the defendant organization should be compared with the percentage of such persons in the working-age population who are able and available to perform the work, within a city, county, MSA, or other recognized recruitment area for the particular organization. Some guidelines are apparent. The applicants must be of working age, and the job to be filled may call for such qualifications as citizenship; a high school, college, or professional education; special physical characteristics; and a specified number of years of experience at a particular type of work. Even for many local civil service jobs, where requirements for entry are minimal and there is a public expectation that the workforce should reflect the racial/ethnic composition of the general population of the area, the standard should be limited to citizens of working age who meet the educational and physical requirements of the job. If the labor market for a particular occupational category is geographically extensive, as it is likely to be for a professional job, then the regional or national proportion in the labor force with the required qualifications should be used for the comparison with the company's performance record.

The plaintiff can be counted on to carry out the types of comparisons that serve his or her interests, and the defendant can be expected to do the same. Hence, there may be considerable argument about the delineation of the recruitment area for an organization, the appropriate population standard for judging its hiring practices, the qualifications for a job, and the type of comparative analysis to be conducted.

Those who support use of the area's total population as a standard for comparison, pursuing a liberal interpretation of the principal of affirmative action, may argue that the racial composition of the general labor force, and particularly the labor force in a given occupational field, is distorted by prior discriminatory practices, just as is the workforce of the organization. They may contend that these distortions can be corrected by use of a broader population base. The plaintiff may argue further that the general labor force in the designated area is unacceptable as the standard of comparison because many members of minority racial groups have opted out of the labor force as "discouraged workers." Moreover, it may be argued that, because of past geographic discrimination in the organization's search for new workers, the recruitment area should not be defined by the residential distribution of the present workforce of the organization.

Those holding the opposite position may argue that the Constitution calls for equal treatment of the races under the law, that the general population of an area does not represent an appropriate standard for determining the share of persons that should hold various jobs, and that, specifically, the proportion of the general population in a racial group is not a sound basis for determining the proportion of an organization's workforce qualified to perform particular lines of work. They may try to show that some workers of another race are more qualified and that their rights to the job are being denied by use of such loose standards. Their position is that the more defensible standard is the race/ethnic distribution of persons in the labor force having the qualifications required for the particular job and residing in an area represented by the current workforce of the organization holding similar jobs.

Numerous related issues may arise. In time, the racial/Hispanic composition of the area will shift, usually including a greater proportion of racial minorities. Should an organization be required continuously to modify the racial composition of its workforce on this basis? Where there are insufficient numbers of one racial group, can they be combined in ways to increase their bargaining strength (e.g., blacks and Hispanics)? Can they be divided to achieve their separate goals (e.g., Caribbean blacks, other blacks) or, alternatively, to diminish their strength (e.g., Puerto Ricans, Cubans, Mexicans, other Hispanics)? The grouping of the races and Hispanics in the pursuit of civil rights goals is a continuing issue. New categories of qualification, in addition to the traditional best-qualified category (e.g., qualified, qualifiable by appropriate in-house training or experience), have been implicitly or explicitly recognized under affirmative action programs with the express purpose of increasing the share of members of racial minorities being hired. This conceptualization widens the area of potential new hires and also the area of contention.

Analogous issues arise with respect to promotions and the distribution by rank.[38] The problem can be posed in terms of some questions. Should promotions be based on any considerations other than the needs of the organization and the qualifications of the applicant? Should the distribution by rank or grade of nonwhite workers in an organization reflect *at each level* the proportions in the community? Should racial minorities/Hispanics be represented as a group in these ranks or should the principal subgroups be represented as well? For example, if 65% of the police force in a city is black, should 65% of the sergeants or precinct captains be black? Should the percentages of sergeants or captains be based on the race distribution of the police force, the local labor force, the general population of the city, or some other group? What promotion plan should be employed to allow for changes over time in the racial composition of the police force, the labor force, and the general population of the area?

Special population and labor force data for the local area, the region, and the nation are needed to carry out these comparative studies. In particular, data from the Censuses of Population and Housing, its postcensal estimates program, and the Bureau of Labor Statistics' *Employment and Earnings* are indispensable. Some approximations may have to be made where data are lacking. For example, population estimates may have to be made to determine the actual recruitment area. Such research may involve studies of the commuting practices of the workforce of the organization and of the labor force of the area, distinguishing the various racial/Hispanic origin groups.

Racial Equity versus Racial Equality

A defining issue in the implementation of special treatment for protected minorities is whether the goal of the civil rights legislation is racial equity or racial equality. **Racial equity** calls for equality of opportunity in employment, education, housing, public services, and other areas where the individual confronts the institutions of the community. **Racial equality** calls for equality in outcomes, as measured by, say, equal proportions of the races employed in a particular skilled occupation or equal proportions employed at a given senior grade in an organization. Some interpret the legislation to support the concept of racial equity and others interpret the legislation to support the concept of racial equality. The legislation directly affirms the right of racial equity and calls for arrangements to assure the enjoyment of this right. Racial equality is not affirmed by these laws and cannot be enforced by them, although deficits in racial equality are widely used to suggest deficits in racial equity.

A study by Daymont (1980) examines the relationship between racial equity in labor market processes and racial equality in future labor market rewards.[39] He used a regression procedure to project the degree of racial equality in earnings that would prevail among men at various future dates, based on various sets of assumptions about progress among blacks in the labor market and in education. The results suggest that, even if racial discrimination is eliminated immediately in the labor market and in the schools (i.e., immediate racial equity), it would take several decades for the black-white earnings ratio to reach 0.95. The remaining wide gap between the achievement of equity and the achievement of equality, and the immense philosophical difference between them, must be considered in evaluating the associated legal positions, namely, advocacy of a colorblind society and advocacy of preferential treatment for blacks and other minority groups. The two views are virtually incompatible as goals and legal positions, at least in the short run.

Charges of preferential treatment of racial minorities have contributed to pressures to modify the legislation classifying nonwhite racial groups and Hispanics as protected groups and requiring affirmative action or preferential treatment in their behalf. Since about 1985, the judicial interpretation of affirmative action legislation has narrowed its scope. Federal courts and the Supreme Court have been moving toward a more colorblind approach, recognizing the argument of "reverse discrimination" (i.e., discrimination against unprotected groups) and decrying the use of race as the sole factor in defining the terms of the argument. The courts are generally shifting in the direction of championing racial equity above racial equality and "equal treatment under the law" above racial preferences.[40]

Some recent court decisions have interpreted the Civil Rights Act in favor of white males who argued that they were victims of racial discrimination in hiring practices. For example, in *Adarand Constructors v. Pena*, 1995, the Supreme Court decreed that affirmative action programs based on racial preferences in industry should seldom provide a basis for disparate treatment and should receive the strictest judicial scrutiny. The Court ruled that "a Federal program which provided general contractors a financial incentive to hire subcontractors controlled by 'socially and economically disadvantaged individuals,' particularly racial minorities, could be challenged by a majority-owned company and would be upheld only if it was narrowly tailored to serve a compelling governmental interest."[41]

Previously, in *City of Richmond v. J. A. Croson Co.*, 1989, the Court held that local governments may use racial classifications only to serve a compelling state interest, that a public employer must have a strong evidentiary basis to take remedial action, considering the relevant labor pool of available, qualified minority members, and that the impact of the remedy on the rights of third parties should be considered. As strong evidence, gross statistical disparities must be demonstrated to exist between the percentage of racial minorities being hired and the percentage of racial minorities who are qualified and available to perform the job. Affirmative action programs must set goals and must end when the goal is achieved.

Sex Discrimination in Employment

The same legislation guaranteeing racial minorities and Hispanics equal opportunity and fair treatment in the workplace guarantees such treatment to women. The basic principles are incorporated in the Fifth and Fourteenth Amendments to the Constitution, in effect calling for equal protection of the law as it pertains to the sexes. In spite of these Constitutional amendments, throughout the 19th century women generally could not hold office, serve on juries, convey property, or vote. The "big" changes occurred in the 20th century with the passage in 1920 of the Nineteenth Amendment (which gave women the right to vote), the Equal Pay Act of 1963 and the Civil Rights Act of 1964.[42]

The proposed Equal Rights Amendment would have made equal rights explicit for women, but it failed ratification by a sufficient number of states, even after an extension of time (from 1972 to 1982). The landmark Supreme Court cases of *Reed v. Reed* (1971) and *Frontiero v. Richardson* (1973) are important in workplace-discrimination law, even though they are not cases of workplace discrimination as such. They deal, respectively, with giving preference to males in the administration of estates and observing different legal requirements for husbands and wives with regard to spousal dependency. The

Court found, in the first case, that administrative convenience, the explanation given for the preference for males, had no rational basis. In the second case, the justices, applying the principle of strict scrutiny and equating discrimination based on gender with discrimination based on race, argued that sex is a suspect classification and bears no relation to individual responsibility or ability. Subsequent Supreme Court decisions have wisely backed away from the sex-equals-race approach. Since the relations between the races and the relations between the sexes are very different and the histories of these relations are distinctive, achieving equal treatment for women in the workplace presents rather different legal issues from those for racial minorities and Hispanics.

Fields of Work

The occupational distributions of women and men still differed sharply in 1996, although the differences have narrowed substantially since the late 1960s. Table 8.16 shows the occupational distributions of women and men in nine broad categories in 1970, 1983, and 1996. Women still tend to work in certain less skilled and less remunerative occupations, such as sales, clerical, and service work, and in certain more poorly paid professional occupations, such as elementary school teacher, librarian, social worker, and nurse. Well over half (55%) of working women were employed in sales, clerical, or service work in 1996, as compared with one quarter (27%) for men. The percentage of

TABLE 8.16 **Distribution of Employed Civilians by Major Occupational Group, for Men and Women: 1970, 1983, and 1996**

Occupation group	1996 Men	Women	1983 Men	Women	1970 Men	Women
Total, all occupations	100.0	100.0	100.0	100.0	100.0	100.0
Executives, administrative, and managerial	14.7	13.2	12.8	8.1	11.2	3.6
Professional specialty	12.8	17.1	11.7	14.0	14.3	15.7
Technicians and related support	2.7	3.5	2.8	3.3	—	—
Sales occupations	11.4	13.0	10.9	12.7	6.9	7.4
Administrative support, including clerical	5.6	24.8	5.8	29.7	7.6	34.9
Service occupations	10.2	17.5	9.7	18.9	8.2	20.4
Farming, forestry, and fishing	4.2	1.2	5.5	1.3	4.5	0.7
Precision production, craft, and repair	18.1	2.1	19.9	2.3	21.2	1.8
Operators, fabricators, and laborers	20.2	7.6	20.8	9.7	26.1	15.4

—: Zero or category not recognized.

Note: For 1996 and 1983, employed civilian noninstitutional population 16 years and over; annual average of monthly figures; based on Current Population Survey. For 1970, total resident population; based on sample data of 1970 Census of Population; categories approximated.

Source: For 1996 and 1983, U.S. Bureau of Labor Statistics, *Employment and Earnings*, January issues; unpublished data. See also U.S. Bureau of Census, *Statistical Abstract of the United States*, 1997, Table 645. For 1970, U.S. Bureau of the Census, *1970 Census of Population*, Vol. 1, Part 1, Section 2, Table 222.

women working in these occupations has been falling; in 1970 over three-fifths (63%) of the women followed these occupations. Sharp differences remain in other occupational groups. In 1996 over half (53%) of the men, but less than one quarter of the women (23%), were employed as managers, craftworkers, or operatives.

The concentration of women in certain occupations results from a combination of tradition, choice, and male dominance. The latter is reflected in discriminatory legislation, such as laws prohibiting women from working in certain types of jobs or laws restricting their work hours. Some of these occupations enable women to work part time, which they may choose to do for family reasons. Some of the less remunerative occupations (e.g., sales clerk, factory worker) were "assigned" to women because the women who worked had less education or were not viewed as the principal earner in the household. Women were thought of as better adapted to fill occupations that called for nurturing or supportive duties (e.g., elementary school teacher, social worker, and nurse) and were considered too weak or delicate to work in certain "male" occupations (e.g., construction worker, miner, bartender, police officer). The view was widely held that the man should be the family breadwinner and that "a woman's place is in the home." This regime was perpetuated by discouraging women from working outside the home and securing an advanced education, and encouraging them to marry and become "*only* housewives."

Earnings and Rank

The annual incomes of working women fall well below those of working men. A substantial pay gap between the sexes remains even after allowance is made for differences due to part-time work and part-year work. Consider the data on median weekly earnings of full-time wage and salary workers for men and women shown in Table 8.17. Although the earnings gap has been narrowing, in 1996 working women 25 years and over were still earning only

TABLE 8.17   Median Weekly Earnings of Full-time Wage and Salary Workers for Men and Women: 1984 and 1996

Year and age	Men	Women	Women as a percentage of men
1996			
16 years and over	557	418	75.0
16 to 24	307	284	92.5
25 and over	599	444	74.1
1984			
16 years and over	391	265	67.8
16 to 24	231	203	87.9
25 and over	422	282	66.8

Note: In current dollars of usual weekly earnings; annual averages of quarterly data. Based on the Current Population Survey.

Source: U.S. Bureau of Labor Statistics, *Employment and Earnings*, January 1986, Table 54, and U.S. Bureau of the Census, *Statistical Abstract of the United States, 1997*, Table 671.

three-quarters as much as men. The corresponding figure in 1984 was only 68%. Even if similar data for the same occupations are considered, there is a substantial gender earnings gap. For example, in 1996 the ratio (per 100) of female earnings to male earnings was 60% for sales personnel and 89% for mechanics and repairers. This suggests that women's work is undervalued not only in female-dominated jobs but even in male-dominated jobs. Moreover, women performing "women's work" earn less than women employed in low-paying male-dominated occupations.

There are many examples of pay discrepancies between "women's work" and "men's work" that cannot be accounted for by differences in job requirements, productivity, or responsibility. According to Sorensen (1994), lower pay for "women's work" accounts for approximately 27% of the total pay gap between men and women.[43] Note, however, that the gap can go in the other direction for some occupations; for example, male models are paid much less than female models.

In spite of the progress made by women in moving up the occupational ladder and entering the better paid occupations in the past few decades, they do not yet have the same effective opportunity for holding high-level positions in a variety of occupations as men. Consider the following two situations that raise some interesting issues relating to the advancement of the sexes in the workplace, one in the legal profession and another in an academic setting. The number of women graduating from law schools now equals that of men, but women have greater difficulty in joining prestigious law firms and in progressing through the organizational hierarchy. We can ask whether they are graduating from the wrong law schools or are graduating with less impressive academic records. Even if these conditions were true, however, they cannot fully explain the unequal outcome in work status. For the second situation, let us assume that there is found to be a relation between the proportion of women in the student body, the proportion of women on the faculty, and the quality of the academic performance of women students. The question is posed whether the proportion of women faculty members should be increased in institutions with large proportions of women students, with the prospect of raising the academic performance of women students. If the proportion of women faculty was increased for this reason, would this be considered a violation of the rights of men?

Comparable Worth

The legal foundation for monitoring fair payment of women on the job in relation to the payment of men is embodied in the Equal Pay Act of 1963. This act prohibits an employer from paying different wages to men and women if they are doing substantially equal work within the same establishment. Since most men and women work at different jobs, the applicability of this act is limited. Title VII of the Civil Rights Act of 1964 is more comprehensive in prohibiting discrimination on the basis of sex and other personal characteristics in all aspects of employment. In *County of Washington v. Gunther* (1981), the Court specifically extended the applicability of these two acts to different jobs if the jobs require equal skill, effort, and responsibility—a situation generally designated as **comparable worth**. Differences in pay are permitted when they are based on seniority, merit, productivity, or any factor other than sex. Various executive orders extended the acts to federal employees and employment under federal contracts. Executive Order 11246, for example, issued by President Lyndon Johnson, promoted affirmative action for protected groups among federal contractors. One major effect of the legislation has been to invalidate state labor laws that reserved the better-paying and more desirable jobs for men.

Part of the difference in the earnings of men and women results from the difference in the occupational distribution of the sexes, which results in part from differences in work experience. Women are more likely to have intermittent work histories as well as to have worked part time or part year, and this pattern can be accommodated better in the less skilled and hence less remunerative occupations. More important, the relation between the supply of and demand for women workers has exerted a downward pressure on women's earnings. Following this line of argument, the practice of unequal pay for comparable work is a result, in great part, according to Sorensen, of the limited job opportunities open to women in many occupations in the face of a large supply of willing and able women workers. However, since the process begins with the restriction of women to "women's jobs" and the exclusion of women from many jobs viewed as "men's jobs," part of the gap in earnings must be attributed to economic discrimination against women.[44]

Macpherson and Hirsch (1993) also saw a relation between the sex composition of occupations and the gap between the wages of men and women, but presented a different interpretation of the gender gap.[45] They concluded, on the basis of an analysis of Current Population Survey data for 1973–1992, that predominantly female occupations pay lower wages to women and men because they are more likely to have part-time workers, a lower level of worker tenure, and jobs requiring relatively less training to acquire proficiency. Hence, the direct effects of gender composition on wages is rather small and policies that eliminate only the part of the wage gap due to "female occupations" would have little effect on the sizable gender wage gap. According to Macpherson and Hirsch, once the effects of other factors are properly controlled, occupational wage differences correlated with gender are sufficiently small that they should not be a major focus of public policy.

The plaintiff in a suit alleging workplace sex discrimination can argue either disparate treatment or disparate impact. In an argument alleging disparate treatment, the plaintiff tries to prove that the employer treated her differently than others because of her sex (e.g., paid her less than men for equal work), while the defendant employer tries to show that the charge is false or that the unequal treatment was not the result of intentional discrimination but of market forces. In an argument alleging disparate impact, the plaintiff has to show that what appeared to be equal treatment of the sexes in the workplace had a different impact on the two sexes (i.e., an adverse impact on women). In the latter case, the employer tries to show that the practice had a significant business justification. So far, the lower courts have ruled that statistical evidence of unequal pay for comparable jobs is insufficient to establish a strong case of wage discrimination. Direct evidence of discriminatory intent is more probative. (See Sorensen, 1994.)

Assessing comparable worth is generally not a straighforward task. Where men and women work at the same occupation in the same industry, particularly for the same employer, and have the same assigned duties, it is not difficult to assess comparable worth. In general, however, this is not the case. Since men and women tend to work at different types of jobs, it is necessary to link various jobs typically held by men and various jobs typically held by women so as to establish job matches of comparable worth. Many of these job matches are subject to debate. The variety of factors accounting for differences between the sexes in occupations and incomes makes it extremely difficult to determine what "male" occupations and what "female" occupations should be seen as comparable in worth. The criteria of fairness relating to sex inequality in the workplace are controversial and are not easily established. It may be argued that comparable worth is too nebulous to pursue!

The various states have tended to deal with the issue of comparable worth in their own ways. As a result, there is a hodgepodge of rules intended to accomplish the purpose of the national legislation relating to comparable worth. By early 1999 many states and hundreds of smaller jurisdictions had enacted comparable-worth measures, but there is no provision for comparable worth affecting federal workers.

Discrimination for Age and Disability in Employment

We conclude this section on the problems facing organizational managers in complying with regulations relating to the demographic characteristics of their employees by briefly considering discrimination in employment for age and disability. These two characteristics are grouped here together for convenience and should not be assumed to bear any necessary relation to one another. While age discrimination usually affects persons in their later work years when disability is more common, generally a claim of age discrimination does not involve a counterclaim of inability to perform the duties of a job because of health reasons.

Age

The Age Discrimination in Employment Act (ADEA) of 1967 prohibited age discrimination in hiring, discharge, compensation, and other terms of employment for persons from age 40 through age 64. The law was amended in 1978 to include workers in private industry up through age 69 and in 1986 to prohibit mandatory retirement for age altogether.

Age discrimination in employment is an old practice, particularly in hiring, but because of reduced funding of and by government agencies and contracting markets in the early 1990s, organizations have been "retiring" older workers in disproportionate numbers. Both public and private organizations have also been restructuring ("downsizing"), mainly by reducing upper middle management staff. These older workers tend to be relatively high earners with expensive fringe benefits. Some have been persuaded to quit through very favorable offers or retirement packages, so-called buyouts; others have simply been forced to resign. Apart from organizational restructuring, age discrimination continues because of its perceived financial advantages to organizations and stereotypical attitudes about the productivity and technical adaptability of older persons.

It is difficult to prove age discrimination without internal documents showing that it was the explicit motive for the action taken or a younger person was hired at about the same time to perform the same duties as the older person terminated. The validity of comparing the share of workers in a given age group in the organization with the share in the population of the area or the general labor force of the area is doubtful because of the industry-occupation-specific character of each organization. However, age patterns specific to each industry/occupation can prove helpful in providing rough guides as to the share of persons expected in broad ages in the workforce of particular large organizations. If this information is presented in an appropriately qualified manner in a legal suit, it may be supportive of the plaintiff's or defendant's case, depending on the comparison made, but it cannot be probative.

Disability

In 1997 10% of the civilian noninstitutional population 16 to 64 years old had a physical, mental, or other health condition that had lasted 6 or more months and that limited the kind or amount of work the person could do at a job or prevented him or her from working at a job.[46] This proportion corresponds to the proportion of the working-age population reporting a serious disability. About half of the persons reporting a work disability are working. Two types of demographic variation in the proportions of the working-age population with work disability stand out: age and race. Work disability rises steadily with age, as expected. Across all age groups, the proportion of blacks with work disability far exceeds the proportions for other races and Hispanics.

The Americans With Diabilities Act (AWDA) of 1990, which makes it illegal to discriminate against the disabled, defines disability differently from the decennial census. Disability is defined in part as a physical or mental impairment that substantially limits participation in one or more of the major life activities. This definition raises many questions. For example, what is a "major life activity" and how substantially must it be "limited"? Can a disability be prospective (e.g., HIV infected, without evidence of AIDS)? In *Bragdon v. Abbott*, 1989, the Supreme Court held that people who test positive for HIV are covered under AWDA even if they exhibit no AIDS symptoms. If a prospective illness is a disabling condition, everyone with a genetic marker for some major disease must be considered legally disabled under the law. Persons with a major disease in remission could be presumed legally disabled. Clearly the Court's decision may initiate a new line of court contests.

The AWDA requires that reasonable accommodations be provided for disabled workers by employers of 15 workers or more and prohibits such employers from discriminating against employees with physical or mental impairments in hiring, discharge, compensation, or other terms of employment. Making reasonable accommodations in the workplace for disabled employees may involve installing wheelchair ramps, providing special chairs, desks, and other work equipment, remodeling washrooms, allowing alternative work schedules, and making other such adjustments. However, disabled workers need not receive any special priority in hiring or firing when others are being hired or fired.

The issue of employee qualifications is especially difficult in the case of employees with disabilities. The courts have held that an individual whose disorder interferes with his or her performance of the essential functions of a job is not qualified and is not protected by AWDA or the Rehabilitation Act (*Pesterfield v. TVA*, Sixth Circuit, 1991, and *Palmer v. Cook County Social Service Department*, U.S. District Court, 1995). On the other hand, failure on the part of employers to provide reasonable accommodations for employees with disabilities is to risk a charge of discrimination. The EEOC has issued guidelines to help employers interpret the law. Interpreting the law is especially difficult in the case of mental disabilities. The guidelines explain how employers should try "to accommodate to mental disabilities that do not directly compromise a worker's qualifications for the job."

ADJUDICATION OF CASUALTY CLAIMS

Money Value of Human Life

In the event of the death or serious injury of a worker, family income is often sharply reduced or completely eliminated. Responsibility for the death or injury may be attributable to another party and a suit for wrongful death or injury may be filed. In a suit for wrongful death, a monetary value must be placed on the prospective labor or services of the decedent in order to determine the amount of compensatory damages to be paid to the surviving members of his or her family. Similarly, in a suit for wrongful injury involving permanent work disability, a monetary value must be placed on the total or partial loss of the prospective labor or services of the disabled individual in order to determine the amount of compensatory damages to be paid to him or her. We are concerned here solely with the replacement in dollars of the income-producing capacity of a worker, not with other aspects of the loss.

In a liability claim for wrongful death, the expert must give his or her best projection of what an individual would have earned in his or her remaining lifetime had he or she lived.[47] While it is impossible to predict the future labor-force and earnings history of an individual decedent, values of future lifetime income or earnings can be estimated for aggregates of persons on the basis of such demographic and socioeconomic characteristics as age at death, sex, race, educational level, labor force participation, recent work experience, annual income, occupation, and continuity of lifetime work experience. It is apparent that the future lifetime earning capacity of a man 30 years of age is likely to be much greater than that of a man 55 years of age. Similarly, we may expect a large difference in prospective earnings for a college graduate and a high school dropout, or an accountant and an office clerk. While all the characteristics listed are important determinants of the earnings prospects of an individual, it is not possible to secure accurate estimates of lifetime earnings for some of the categories, such as occupation and continuity of lifetime work experience, particularly in cross-classification with race and educational level.

Future lifetime earnings, based on the "human capital" approach, is only one of several approaches to measuring a person's worth. Another approach that has been advanced is designated "willingness to pay." It is defined in terms of the amount people are willing to pay to reduce their risk of death or the amount they spend for life insurance. The human capital approach to the measurement of a person's worth has been most extensively studied and applied, however, and that is why it has been employed in this discussion.

Calculation of Lifetime Income/Earnings Lost

Several measures of future lifetime money income or earnings have been developed. They vary in their degree of precision and the type and detail of data required to derive them. Two principal data items are needed to make such estimates: annual income or earnings data for age groups and appropriate life tables. A large body of data is needed in addition to develop estimates that take account of the demographic and socieconomic characteristics of the decedent and to develop the necessary assumptions on prospective changes in the economy. The first major component, annual income or earnings for age groups, is required in the form of mean annual income or earnings at each of the working ages, preferably for such groups as males and females, race groups, educational-attainment groups, and labor-force status and experience groups. Data of this kind have been compiled from time to time from the Current Population Survey and the decennial census of population.

Official life tables are available that provide information for calculating cumulative risks of dying according to the age, sex, and race of the person. Some multiple decrement and multistate life tables that incorporate socioeconomic characteristics, such as labor force participation and educational attainment, are available and provide information for measuring the cumulative risk of dying according to educational level. The set of tables of working life for 1979–1980 published by the Bureau of Labor Statistics provide data on expected years of work for sex and race groups and for sex and educational-level groups.[48] For example, according to these tables, a male at exact age 30 (i.e., 30.0 years) who has completed 15 or more years of schooling and who is working may be expected to work an additional 31.6 years before leaving the labor force through death or retirement, whereas a male at exact age 30 who has not completed high school and who is working may be expected to work an additional 25.6 years. As noted earlier, tables of worklife expectancy have also been published by Vocational Econometrics, Inc., for 1987, 1991, and 1995. These add the variable of disability status to the variables of sex, race, and educational level.

A simple but rough method of calculating future lifetime earnings at a particular age for a designated group (e.g., white working males who dropped out of high school) is to sum the mean annual earnings for each successive age from the current age to the age corresponding to the expected working life for that class of persons:

$$L_a = \sum_{n=a}^{n=a+ewx} Y_n \tag{14}$$

where L_a is total lifetime earnings or liability at age a (plaintiff's age), n is the shifting age from the starting age a to each successive age until retirement age $a + ewx$, Y_n is mean annual earnings at each age, and ewx is expectation of working life at plaintiff's age a. Hence, using the figure for future working lifetime above, the future lifetime earnings of a 30.0-year-old male high school dropout would be approximated as the sum of mean annual earnings at each age from age 30 through age 55 (= sum of exact ages 30.0 + 25.6).

The formula used by the Census Bureau in a 1983 report to calculate lifetime earnings is much more elaborate and more realistic.[49] This formula calculates lifetime earnings for all persons at age a (L_a) as the cumulative product of (1) the mean annual earnings for all persons at each age n (y_n) for specialized aggregates of persons with different demographic and socioeconomic characteristics starting from a designated age a and continuing to age 64, (2) the probability of survival from starting age a to each later age n (p_n), and (3) the employment ratio at each age for a given starting age a (e_n). At each age n, this product is adjusted upward by an assumed (fixed) factor for the annual increase in earnings due to rising worker productivity $(1 + x)$ and adjusted downward by an assumed (fixed) discount rate representing the excess of the inflation rate over the interest rate $(1 + r)$.[50] The formula is as follows:

$$L_a = \frac{\sum_{n=a}^{n=64} y_n p_n e_n (1 + x)^{n-a+1/2}}{(1 + r)^{n-a+1}} \quad (15)$$

The method of calculation is illustrated in Table 8.18 for the simplified case where the workers are year-round, full-time workers (hence, the employment ratio can be disregarded), and the productivity rate and the discount rate are both 0.0 (hence, they can be disregarded). Illustrative results obtained from the Census Bureau formula for 1979 are shown in Table 8.19. They suggest wide differences in expected future lifetime earnings according to present age, sex, work experience, and years of school completed. As expected, lifetime earnings are much greater for a young person than for an older person because of the greater number of potential years lost. They are much greater for a man than a woman because of differences in the continuity of lifetime work experience, occupational distribution, pay scales for the same or similar work, and other factors. According to these tables, which assume a discount rate of 0.0% and an annual productivity increase of 0.0%, a 35-year old woman who did not finish high school would earn $134,000 in her remaining lifetime, whereas a 35-year old women who finished college (but no more) would earn $2^1/_2$ times as much, $335,000. According to these results, a male who did not finish high school would earn $441,000, much more than a female college graduate.

The gross figures for lifetime income lost assume that the decedent would have had an expense-free life. In a further refinement of the formula, mean annual earnings at each age should be reduced for expected taxes and living expenses, and the mean age of withdrawal from the labor force should be substituted for age 64. Optimally, allowance should be made for all costs incurred after retirement until death and burial.[51]

It is important to recognize the limitations of these measures even when all the adjustments described have been made. First and foremost, they attempt to predict the future, and to do so for an individual on the basis of aggregate data. The future is unpredictable, and aggregate data and average risks can be applied to an individual with limited confidence. The essential component, cross-sectional earnings data for ages, is employed as defining a syn-

■ **TABLE 8.18   Illustrative Calculation of Estimated "Lifetime" Earnings for a Male Year-round Full-time Worker from Age 55 to Age 64, with a High School Education, Assuming a Discount Rate and Annual Productivity Rate of 0.0% and Retirement at Age 64: 1979**

Age n (years)	Mean annual earnings[a] (1)	Survival rate[b] (2)	Earnings of survivors (3) = (1) ★ (2)
55	25,790	.99359	25,625
56	27,358	.98031	26,819
57	26,597	.96599	25,692
58	26,160	.95038	24,862
59	27,755	.93327	25,903
60	26,819	.91460	24,529
61	25,257	.89441	22,590
62	26,452	.87289	23,090
63	26,261	.85029	22,329
64	26,779	.82680	22,141
SUM	265,228		243,580[c]

[a] Mean earnings in 1979 in thousands of 1981 dollars. See U.S. Census Bureau source.

[b] Formula is $[1/2(L_{n+1} + L_n) \div L_{55}]$, that is, survival from age 55 to age $n + 1/2$. See National Center for Health Statistics source.

[c] $\sum(3) = \sum_{55}^{64}[(1) \star (2)] = 244,000$. Result in Table 8.19 = 249,000. The discrepancy between the figure calculated here and the figure in Table 8.19 cannot readily be explained; alternative acceptable survival calculations give a ceiling value of 246,000.

Source: Based on U.S. Bureau of the Census, "Lifetime earnings estimates for men and women in the United States: 1979," by Dan L. Burkhead, *Current Population Reports*, Series P-60, No 139, February 1983, Table B-1; and U.S. National Center for Health Statistics, "Life tables," Vol. II, Section 5, *Vital Statistics of the United States*, 1978, Table 5-2.

thetic cohort but interpreted as defining a real cohort. The main rates and ratios in the formula are "frozen" at the levels of the base year (i.e., mean annual earnings and survival rates). Other rates and ratios are projected (i.e., employment ratios) or fixed, model allowances (i.e., productivity, inflation, and interest rates). Consider the earnings data used in the 1983 publication. They are annual average cross-sectional data from sample surveys for 1978, 1979, and 1980. The accuracy of the estimates of lifetime earnings depends on how closely these current data reflect relationships that might be experienced in the next half century by the deceased worker.

It was assumed that persons did not begin working for pay until age 18 and ceased working when they reached age 65. Alternatively, the mean age of retirement according to current tables of working life or other sources could have been used. Generation (real cohort) life tables or generation tables of working life would be much more realistic than conventional life tables, but they are subject to considerable uncertainty because of the need for projecting the probabilities of dying and working.[52] The same mortality rates were

TABLE 8.19 Expected Lifetime Earnings for All Persons and for Year-round, Full-time Workers 18 to 64 Years old at Selected Ages, by Sex and Educational Attainment: 1979

Age and work experience	Less than 12 years	High school, 4 years	College 1 to 3 years	4 years	5 years or more
Males					
All persons					
18 years	$601	$861	$957	$1190	$1301
25 years	563	803	918	1165	1273
35 years	441	624	736	956	1065
45 years	283	401	483	639	715
55 years	121	178	230	298	352
Year-round, full-time workers					
18 years	$845	$1041	$1155	$1392	$1503
25 years	776	954	1075	1329	1444
35 years	614	750	864	1097	1196
45 years	410	501	586	762	820
55 years	203	249	297	388	422
Female					
All persons					
18 years	$211	$381	$460	$523	$699
25 years	188	330	411	474	673
35 years	134	235	293	335	512
45 years	77	145	175	207	316
55 years	30	61	77	93	132
Year-round, full-time workers					
18 years	$500	$634	$716	$846	$955
25 years	437	567	630	772	900
35 years	335	436	482	606	710
45 years	222	300	316	434	470
55 years	118	150	162	226	238

Note: In thousands of 1981 dollars. Based on discount rate and annual productivity rate of 0.0%. Earnings for *all persons* reduced by projected unemployment ratios.

Source: U.S. Bureau of the Census, "Lifetime earnings estimates for men and women in the United States: 1979," by Dan L. Burkhead, *Current Population Reports*, Series P-60, No. 139, February 1983, p. 3.

applied to persons of different educational levels and work experience, in spite of evidence to the contrary. Finally, since allowance for employment ratios, productivity, inflation rates, and interest rates requires anticipating the state of the future economy, several alternative allowances have to be made for these economic variables, with the attendant uncertainty.[53]

From time to time demographers may be called on to testify as expert witnesses in suits of wrongful injury or death. Their task is to become fully informed as to the basic materials available (i.e., earnings data, life tables, retirement-age studies, and measures of the economy), employ the most appropriate data and measures in their testimony, and be able to offer a reasoned statement of the limitations of the data and measures presented. The same types of tasks would devolve on demographers who testify in cases of alleged discrimination for race, ethnic origin, religion, age, gender, family composition, disability, or other legally recognized "demographic/socioeconomic" basis for legal action.

NOTES

1. While the Current Population Survey employs the labor force concept and is nominally restricted to the civilian noninstitutional population, it sometimes covers military personnel who live off post in addition to the civilian labor force.

2. U.S. Bureau of Labor Statistics, "Another look at the labor force," by Howard N. Fullerton, Jr., in *The American Workforce: 1992–2005*, Bulletin 2452, 1994, pp. 29–38.

3. The term *labor force participation ratio* is consistently used in this book instead of labor force participation rate, the term used by the Bureau of Labor Statistics and the Census Bureau. This practice is adopted in accordance with the accepted definitions of ratios, proportions, and rates, and the recommendations of the Committee on International Demographic Terminology of the International Population Union. See International Union for the Scientific Study of Population, *Multilingual Demographic Dictionary*, English Section, 2nd ed., adapted by Etienne van de Walle, Liege, Belgium: Ordina Editions, 1982. See pages 23 and 52.

4. Peter M. Blau, *Inequality and Heterogeneity*, New York: The Free Press, 1977, p. 78.

5. Jeffrey Pfeffer, "Some consequences of organizational demography: Potential impacts of an aging work force on formal organizations," pp. 291–329, in Sara B. Kiesler *et al.* (eds.), *Aging: Social Change*, New York: Academic Press, 1981; and Shelby Stewman, "The aging of work organizations: Impact on organization and employment practice," in Kiesler *et al.*, 1981.

6. Pfeffer (1981), *op. cit.* Jeffrey Pfeffer, "Organizational demography," in Larry L. Cummings and Barry M. Staw (eds.), *Research on Organizational Behavior*, Greenwich, CT: Jai Press, 1983, pp. 299–359.

7. Aluminum Company of America, *Alcoa Update 1996 Annual Report: It All Starts with Dirt*, 1997.

8. Nathan Keyfitz, "Individual mobility in a stationary society," *Population Studies* 27: 335–352, 1973.

9. An alternate, algebraically equivalent, form of the equation uses LFPR: $R = L_1(1 - r_2/r_1)\sqrt{s}$, where r_1 is the LFPR at the beginning of the 5-year interval and r_2 is the LFPR for the same cohort at the end of the 5-year interval.

10. Murray Gendell and Jacob S. Siegel, "Trends in retirement age by sex: 1950–2005," *Monthly Labor Review* 115(7): 22–29, July 1992.

11. Murray Gendell, "Trends in retirement age in four countries, 1965–1995," *Monthly Labor Review*, August 1998; Murray Gendell and Jacob S. Siegel, "Trends in retirement age in the United States, 1955–1993, by sex and race," *Journal of Gerontology: Social Sciences* 51B(3): S132–S139, May 1996; and Gendell and Siegel, 1992, *op. cit.*

12. To measure the relative contribution of the decline in the age of retirement and the decline in mortality to the increase in the average years of retirement during a period, a calculation akin to standardization is carried out. First, it is necessary to ascertain the increase in life expectation between the inital and terminal dates for the average of the median ages of retirement at the two dates. Then, we can derive the contribution of the decline in the age of retirement as the difference between the increase in average years in retirement (see text) and the increase in life expectation from the previous step.

13. The stationary population under the age for the peak worker ratio (w_{max}; e.g., w_{33}) must be adjusted upward to represent the stationary population that hypothetically would be working at each age if the worker ratio were the same as at the peak age (not shown in Table 8.3):

$$L'_{wx} = w_{max} \star L_x$$

The adjusted L'_{wx} values are then substituted for the L_{wx} values under the age with the peak worker ratio.

14. The partitioning of the total separation rate at each age into the part due to the mortality rate and the part due to the retirement rate can be carried out in more than one way. Rates of net entry or net exit and of retirement (r_{wx}) may be derived by calculating the relative changes in the 1-year l_{wx}'s (net entry/net exit) and then dividing by 1-year changes in l_x (survival) values:

$$1 - r_{wx} = (l_{wx+1}/l_{wx}) \div (l_{x+1}/l_x)$$

The l_x values are taken from the conventional life table corresponding to the population and year of the table of working life.

15. This limitation has decreasing relevance as the profile of the working life of men and women become increasingly similar. For a detailed description of the method of constructing a table of working life by the prevalence-ratio method, refer to *The Methods and Materials of Demography, Condensed Edition*, Academic Press, 1975.

16. Only a single survey is needed if there is a question on labor force status a year earlier. Matching of responses in two surveys permits more complete editing and an evaluation and adjustment of the responses.

17. U.S. Bureau of Labor Statistics, *Worklife Estimates: Effects of Race and Education*, by Shirley Smith, Bulletin 2254, 1986.

18. Tables of working life could be derived for the four regions using unpublished data from the Current Population Survey. The prevalence-ratio method and the multistate method could be tested for this purpose. Comparison of such regional tables of working life may reveal the extent of geographic variation in various labor force parameters.

19. A. M. Gamboa, Jr., "The new worklife expectancy tables: Revised 1995," Louisville, KY: Vocational Econometrics, 1995.

20. See A. H. Pollard, Farhat Yusuf, and G. N. Pollard, *Demographic Techniques*, 2nd ed., New York: Pergamon Press, 1981, Chapter 10.

21. Data for a company may have to be pooled over several years to record a sufficient number of worker events for deriving reliable rates, even when a conventional (i.e., cross-sectional) life table is to be constructed. In addition, the table may have to be abridged and the rates graduated in order to derive a stable set of duration-specific rates.

22. Kevin Deardorff, "Projected employment expectancies for employees of the SAE Construction Company, by occupation," unpublished paper prepared to fill the MA degree requirements of the Department of Demography, Georgetown University, 1990.

23. See Pollard *et al.*, 1981, *op. cit.*, Chapter 4, for several applications.

24. Jacob S. Siegel and Meyer Zitter (U.S. Census Bureau), "Demographic aspects of military statistics," unpublished paper presented at the 1958 annual meeting of the American Statistical Association, Chicago, IL, December 30, 1958.

25. U.S. Bureau of the Census, "Population projections of the United States by age, sex, race, and Hispanic origin: 1995 to 2050," by Jennifer C. Day, *Current Population Reports*, Series P25-1130, 1996, Tables D-1 and D-2.

26. U.S. Department of Defense, *Selected Manpower Statistics, 1995*, annual; U.S. General Accounting Office, GAO/NSAID-99-7, October 1998; GAO/NSAID-98-213, September 1998.

27. Jacob Alex Klerman and Lynn A. Karoly, "Trends and future directions in youth labor markets: Implications for army recruiting," Labor and Population Program, *Working Paper Series* 93-27, Santa Monica, CA: Rand Corporation, 1993.

28. Bill Dedman, "Chicago, in reversal, is now importing priests," *New York Times*, September 28, 1997, p. 13.

29. Richard A. Schoenherr and Lawrence A. Young, *Full Pews and Empty Altars: Demographics of the Priest Shortage in United States Catholic Dioceses*, Madison, WI: University of Wisconsin Press, 1993. See esp. Tables A-1, 2.3, 3.3, 4.2, and 12.8.

30. Hallie J. Kintner and David A. Swanson, "Estimating Vital Rates from Corporate Databases: How long will GM's salaried retirees live?" pp. 265–295, in H. J. Kintner *et al.*, *Demographics: A Casebook for Business and Government*, Boulder, CO: Boulder Press, 1994.

31. Records with duplicate numbers turned up in retirees' files as well as those of employees if they changed plants or received checks from more than one plant while working for the company. Tapes for pairs of years (e.g., 1983 and 1984) were used to determine the number of retirees at year-end (e.g., December 31, 1983) since some retirements occurring before the end of the year were not processed until the following year.

32. Kintner and Swanson examined the most recent status-change code to identify deaths, and then proceeded backward year by year. Some who were lost to follow-up in one database were searched for in the other database. For the few persons lost to follow-up in both files (0.13%), dates of death were obtained by an audit of the two files with the Social Security Administration's Death Master File.

33. In a generational calculation, the deaths of persons at age 55 to those celebrating their 55th birthday in a given year occur in part in the same year and in part in the following year. In the calculation of the central death rate, the exact person-years of exposure in a year is the sum of exposures of (1) persons 55 years of age at the beginning of the year until they reach their 56th birthday or die before their 56th birthday and (2) persons reaching their 55th birthday during the year until the end of the year or dying after their 55th birthday during the year.

34. This choice of dates permitted an evaluation of the projections for December 31, 1988, and of the death rates for 1984 to 1988. See Chapter 10 for a discussion of criteria for evaluation of population projections.

35. The Office of Management and Budget has issued its recommendations regarding the tabulations of data on race and Hispanic origin from the 2000 census. These call for showing the total numbers reporting more than one race and at least one tabulation showing the 63 possible categories of a single race and combinations of races.

36. The classification has been applied not only to issues of personnel administration but also to issues of legislative redistricting and voting representation, school district delineation, implementation of poverty programs, and compliance with requirements in housing accommodations and environmental protection. These issues are discussed in other chapters of this book.

37. For an illustration of a legal suit involving the delineation of qualified labor pools for affirmative-action goals, see Peter A. Morrison, "Applying demographic analysis in affirmative action disputes: An instructional case," *Population Research and Policy Review* 17(1): 1–22, 1998.

38. See Morrison, 1998, *op. cit.* for an example.

39. Thomas N. Daymont, "Race equity or race equality in labor market processes," *Demography* 13(4): 379–393, November 1980.

40. See Chapter 12 for a discussion of Supreme Court cases illustrating this trend in delineating legislative districts.

41. Quoted from Thomas E. Baker, *The Most Wonderful Work: Our Constitution Interpreted*, St. Paul, MN: West, 1996.

42. For a fuller discussion of the legal background on sex discrimination, see Jo Freeman, "The revolution for women in law and public policy," in Jo Freeman (ed.), *Women: A Feminist Perspective*, 5th ed., Mountain View, CA: Mayfield, 1995, pp. 365–404.

43. Elaine Sorensen, *Comparable Worth: Is It a Worthy Policy?* Princeton, NJ: Princeton University Press, 1994.

44. Sorensen, 1994, *op. cit.*

45. David A. Macpherson and Barry T. Hirsch, "Wages and gender composition: Why do women's jobs pay less? *Working Paper Series*, PI-93-20, Pepper Institute on Aging and Public Policy, Forida State University, Tallahassee, FL, 1993.

46. U.S. Bureau of the Census, *Statistical Abstract of the United States, 1998*, Table 222, 1998.

47. Louis I. Dublin, Alfred J. Lotka, and Mortimer Spiegelman, *Length of Life: A Study of the Life Table*, rev. ed., New York: Ronald Press, 1949, esp. pp. 274–279; Louis I. Dublin and Alfred J. Lotka, *The Money Value of a Man*, rev. ed., New York: Ronald Press, 1946; and Shirley J. Smith, "Liability cases: Use of working life tables in court," unpublished paper presented at the annual meeting of the Population Association of America, April 23, 1977.

48. U.S. Bureau of Labor Statistics, *Worklife Estimates, 1979–1980: Effects of Race and Education*, by Shirley Smith, Bulletin 2254, 1986.

49. U.S. Bureau of the Census, "Lifetime earnings estimates for men and women in the United States: 1979," by Dan L. Burkhead, *Current Population Reports*, Series P-60, No. 139, February 1983. "Lifetime earnings" does not include income other than actual earnings—that is, it excludes income derived from savings and investments based on earnings and it excludes the value of various noncash or "fringe" benefits received by many workers on the job.

The Census Bureau has published a number of reports on expected lifetime earnings or income, varying in their methodology and subject detail. The previous report, issued in 1974, was

Current Population Reports, Series P-60, No. 92. More recently, the Census Bureau has published estimates of lifetime earnings for educational-attainment groups (see *Statistical Briefs* SB/94-17, 1994, based on data in *Current Population Reports,* P20-476, "Educational Attainment in the United States: March 1993 and 1992." Calculations were based on mean annual earnings for 10-year age groups from ages 25 to 64 for educational-attainment groups. These estimates are too crude (e.g., age groups too broad, no allowance for mortality) and too general in their results (e.g., no sex) to be applied to individuals in liability cases.

50. The factor $1 + x$ allows for the real growth in productivity. The exponent assumes productivity growth for the number of years to age n, given starting age a. Assumed values for the annual productivity increase vary from 0.0 to 3.0%. The factor for the discount rate $(1 + r)$ converts future earnings to their present values. The exponent assumes that the discount rate applies to each year until age n, given starting age a. The discount rates assumed in the Census Bureau report for the different series are 0.0%, 3.0%, and 5.0%.

51. The modified formula would be,

$$L_a = \frac{\sum_{n=a}^{n=a+ewx}(y_n - t_n - l_n)p_n e_n (1 + x)^{n-a+1/2}}{(1+r)^{n-a+1}}$$

where t_n represents taxes, l_n living expenses, and the other symbols the same elements as noted earlier in the text.

It may be appropriate also to take into account the health or disability status (active life) of the person. A group in the aggregate will spend a number of years in a disabled state, some before and/or others after retirement. Tables of active/disabled life are becoming available for use in such calculations. Since expenditures for private-home care and nursing-home care are, for the most part, the responsibility of the family, some adjustment in the estimates should be made for money that would be spent on such care. Finally, there are expenses at death.

52. A composite set of projected survival rates, whereby 5-year survival rates for successive 5-year ages and 5-year time intervals are linked in a chain, is consistent with a generation life table based on the same historical and projected death rates.

53. The value of housewives' services have not been included in the formula when applied to women. This omission results in a serious underestimate of the lifetime money value of women. The earnings that would be imputed for women would represent the market value of the duties a housewife performs, based on her age, number of children, and age of children.

SUGGESTED READINGS

Demographic Processes and Characteristics of the Labor Force

Cantrell, R. Stephen, and Clark, Robert L. (1980, October). "Retirement policy and promotional prospects." *Gerontologist* 20(5): 575–580.

Ekerdt, David J., and DeViney, Stanley P. (1990). "On defining persons as retired." *Journal of Aging Studies* 4: 211–229.

Gendell, Murray, and Siegel, Jacob S. (1996). "Trends in retirement age in the United States, 1955–1993, by sex and race." *Journal of Gerontology: Social Sciences* 51B(3): S132–S139.

Keyfitz, Nathan. (1982). "Upward mobility in a stationary population." Chapter 5 in *Population Change and Social Policy.* Cambridge, MA: Abt Books.

Keyfitz, Nathan. (1973, July). "Individual mobility in a stationary population." *Population Studies* 27: 335–352.

Pfeffer, Jeffrey, 1981. "Some consequences of organizational demography: Potential impacts of an aging work force on formal organizations." Chapter 11 in Sara B. Kiesler, James N. Morgan, Valerie K. Oppenheimer (eds.), *Aging: Social Change*, New York: Academic Press.

Pfeffer, Jeffrey. (1983). "Organizational demography." *In* Larry L. Cummings and Barry M. Staw (eds.), *Research in Organizational Behavior* 5: 299–359. Greenwich, CT: JAI Press.

Stewman, Shelby. (1981). "The aging of work organizations: Impact on organization and employment practice." Chapter 10 in Sara B. Kiesler, James N. Morgan, and Valerie K. Oppenheimer (eds.), *Aging: Social Change.* New York: Academic Press.

Stewman, Shelby. (1986). "Demographic models of internal labor markets." *Administrative Science Quarterly* **31**: 212–247.

Stewman, Shelby. (1988). "Organizational demography." *Annual Review of Sociology* **14**: 173–202.

U.S. Bureau of Labor Statistics. (1994). *The American Work Force, 1992–2005.* Bulletin 2452.

U.S. Bureau of Labor Statistics. (1997). "Labor force 2006: Slowing down and changing composition," by Howard N. Fullerton, Jr., *Monthly Labor Review* **120**(11): 23–28.

U.S. Bureau of Labor Statistics. (1998). "Employee tenure in 1998." *News*, USDL 98-387.

Tables of Working Life

Gamboa, A. M., Jr. (1995). "The new worklife expectancy tables: Revised 1995." Louisville, KY: Vocational Econometrics.

Schoen, Robert, and Woodrow, Karen. (1980, August). "Labor force status life tables for the United States, 1972." *Demography* **17**(3): 297–322.

U.S. Bureau of Labor Statistics. (1976). *Length of Working Life for Men and Women: 1970.* By Howard N. Fullerton, Jr., and James J. Byrne. Special Labor Force Report 187.

U.S. Bureau of Labor Statistics. (1986). *Worklife Estimates: Effects of Race and Education.* By Shirley Smith. Bulletin 2254.

Special Groups and Workforces

Greenwood, Michael J., and Mehay, Stephen L. (1991). "Trends in regional patterns of migration, immigration, and economic activity: Implications for army recruiting." NPS-AS-91-015. Monterey, CA: Naval Postgraduate School.

Klerman, Jacob Alex, and Karoly, Lynn A. (1993). "Trends and future directions in youth labor markets: Implications for army recruiting," Labor and Population Program, *Working Paper Series* 93-27. Santa Monica, CA: Rand Corporation.

Schoenherr, Richard A., and Young, Lawrence A. (1993). *Full Pews and Empty Alters: Demographics of the Priest Shortage in the United States Catholic Dioceses.* Social Demography Series. Madison: University of Wisconsin Press.

Wagner, W. Gary, Pfeffer, Jeffrey, and O'Reilly III, Charles A. (1984, March). "Organizational demography and turnover in top-management groups." *Administrative Science Quarterly* **29**: 74–92.

Analysis of Employer Administrative Records

Kintner, Hallie J., and Swanson, David A. (1994). "Estimating vital rates from corporate databases: How long will GM's salaried retirees live?" *In* H. J. Kintner, T. W. Merrick, P. A. Morrison, and P. R. Voss (eds.), *Demographics: A Casebook for Business and Government*, pp. 265–297. Boulder, CO: Westview Press.

Morrison, Peter A. (1998). "Applying demographic analysis in affirmative action disputes: An instructional case." *Population Research and Policy Review* **1**(1): 1–22, esp. pp. 10–11.

Compliance with Regulations

Blau, Francine D., and Kahn, Lawrence M. (1992). "Race and gender pay differentials." *Working Paper* No. 4120. New York: National Bureau of Economic Research.

Daymont, Thomas N. (1980, November). "Racial equity or racial equality," *Demography* **13**(4): 379–393.

Ehrenberg, Ronald G. (1989). "Empirical consequences of comparable worth." *In* M. Anne Hill and Mark R. Killingsworth, *Comparable Worth: Analyses and Evidence*, pp. 90–106. Ithaca, NY: ILR Press.

England, Paula. (1992). *Comparable Worth: Theories and Evidence.* New York: Aldine de Gruyter.

Freeman, Jo. (1995). "The revolution for women in law and public policy." *In* Jo Freeman (ed.), *Women: A Feminist Perspective.* 5th ed., pp. 365–404. Mountain View, CA: Mayfield.

Hirsch, Barry T., and Schumacher, Edward J. (1992). "Labor earnings, discrimination, and the racial composition of jobs." *Journal of Human Resources* **27**: 602–628.

Macpherson, David A., and Hirsch, Barry T. (1993). "Wages and gender composition: Why do women's jobs pay less?" *Working Paper Series*, PI-93-20. Tallahassee, FL: Pepper Institute on Aging and Public Policy, Forida State University.

Michael, R. T., Hartmann, H. I., and O'Farrell, B. (eds.). (1989). *Pay Equity: Empirical Inquiries.* Washington, DC: National Academy Press.

Morrison, Peter A. (1993). "More than meets the eye." *Chance* **6**(2): 24–30.

Morrison, Peter A. (1998). "Applying demographic analysis in affirmative action disputes: An instructional case." *Population Research and Policy Review* **1**(1): 1–22.

Sorensen, Elaine. (1994). *Comparable Worth: Is It a Worthy Policy?* Princeton, NJ: Princeton University Press.

U.S. Bureau of the Census. (1987). "Male-female differences in work experience, occupation, and earnings: 1984." *Current Population Reports*, Series P-70, No. 10.

U.S. Bureau of the Census. (1997, August). "Americans with disabilities: 1994–1995," by John M. McNeil. *Current Population Reports* P70-61.

U.S. Bureau of the Census. (1999). "Work experience—Workers by Median Earnings and Gender: 1967 to 1997." Table P-34 based on Current Population Survey. Internet: www.census.gov/hhes/income/histinc/p34.html

U.S. General Accounting Office. (1997). "Statistical agencies: Collection and reporting of race and ethnicity data." Testimony by Bernard L. Ungar before the Subcommittee on Government Management, Information, and Technology, U.S. House of Representatives, April 23, 1997.

U.S. Office of Management and Budget. (1997). "Revisions to the standards for the classification of federal data on race and ethnicity." *Federal Register* **62**(210): 58,782–58,790. Notices, October 30, 1997.

Money Value of a Person

Alter, George C., and Becker, William E. (1985, February). "Estimating lost future earnings using the new worklife tables." *Monthly Labor Review*: 39–42.

King, Elizabeth M., and Smith, James P. (1988). *Computing Economic Loss in Cases of Wrongful Death.* Santa Monica, CA: Rand Corporation.

Nelson, David M. (1983, April). "The use of worklife tables in estimates of lost earning capacity." *Monthly Labor Review*: 30–31.

U.S. Bureau of the Census. (1967). "Present value of estimated lifetime earnings." By Herman P. Miller and Richard A. Hornseth. *Technical Paper* 16.

U.S. Bureau of the Census. (1979). "Lifetime earnings for men and women in the United States." *Current Population Reports*, Series P-60, No. 139.

U.S. Bureau of the Census. (1990). "Lifetime earnings by education," *Current Population Reports*, P-70, No. 32.

9

POPULATION ESTIMATES: BASIC DEMOGRAPHIC CHARACTERISTICS

INTRODUCTION

Censuses have major limitations in providing the basic data needed to conduct current public and private business. Their leading limitation is their lack of timeliness. U.S. censuses are taken every 10 years and, as we have seen, major changes in the numbers, distribution, and characteristics of the population can occur in short periods, such as a quinquennium, particularly at the local level. Several national sample surveys provide current data but have the limitations of lacking detail for subnational areas or of providing subnational data with unacceptably large sampling errors.

Part of the gap is filled by federal, state, and local programs of current population estimates derived by **demographic methods**. This rubric covers a wide range of computational designs. It encompasses the use of demographic data, techniques, and models, including the use of aggregate administrative data, but excludes direct estimation by censuses and sample surveys. Because these methods depend so heavily on the availability and quality of certain specialized types of data series, they can be applied effectively in the preparation of only a limited number of types of estimates. The accuracy of the estimates depends, however, not only on the type and quality of the data series employed but also on the adequacy of the specification of the estimating algorithms. The discussion of population estimates has been divided into two parts. This chapter is concerned with estimates of the total population and its basic demographic characteristics. More specifically, it deals with estimates of total population and estimates for age, sex, and race groups, for a broad range of geographic areas, from the nation to census tracts, generated typically by applying demographic and related techniques to demographic or quasi-demographic data. Chapter 11 deals with estimates of socioeconomic characteristics. A miscellaneous group of characteristics (e.g., education, income, poverty, health) is covered and, typically, demographic methods and sample survey data are combined in these estimates.

Uses of Estimates

Population estimates have countless uses. As we saw, the U.S. Census Bureau's national and state population estimates are employed as "controls" for several national sample surveys conducted by the federal government (Chapter 4). This step has the effect of reducing the bias and variance of the sample data, allowing partially or wholly for the net undercount of the sample data, and reducing discrepancies between various estimates series. The federal government uses official national and subnational estimates in calculating the distribution each year of many billions of dollars in the form of block grants to the states and jurisdictions within them (Chapter 12). Population estimates are needed as the denominators of many types of rates and ratios, such as birthrates, death rates, morbidity rates, and school enrollment ratios.

As we saw in Chapters 6, 7, and 8, population estimates play a central role in market analysis, public facility planning, environmental planning, and civil rights enforcement. They are often critical elements in the analyses leading to decisions whether or not to build a new library, fire station, hospital, or school, pass a tax measure, construct a shopping mall, build a new highway, or contruct a rapid-transit line. They are required information in the assessment of the environmental impact of an existing or proposed development and in the adjudication of civil rights legislation relating to employment, housing, age, sex, race, and disability. Decisions made on the basis of population estimates may lead to a change in the allocations of public and private funds, a change in the tax code, the passage of environmental regulations, and a limit on the construction of a business mall or residential housing development. Population projections complement postcensal estimates in these uses by extending their utility into the future.

Desiderata for Estimates

To serve their many uses effectively, population estimates should meet certain desiderata that are not unlike those demanded of population data in general. Of primary importance is the accuracy of the estimates. While the accuracy of any particular estimate is usually unknowable, there is a considerable and growing body of research identifying the better methods of deriving population estimates and the conditions under which more accurate estimates are obtained. Next is timeliness, or currency, and its concomitant requisite, the frequent revision and updating of the estimates. Frequent revision is necessary because substantial changes can occur in the local population situation in a short time. Periodic distribution of funds on the basis of allocation formulas with a population component adds to the need for frequent updating of the estimates as well as the need for accuracy.

The federalist form of our political system and the local administration of most of our social, health, and protective services create a demand for detailed population estimates for very small areas. Moreover, the estimates must be tailored to fit the particular application with respect to geographic detail. For example, local planning areas, administrative districts, or service areas designed to receive or provide specific goods or services may not correspond to any of the established Census Bureau geographic tabulation units or those used by state agencies, and the data may have to be geographically adapted to meet the purpose desired.

Next, users must have convenient and prompt access to the estimates. This desideratum calls for careful attention to the methods of data dissemination. Electronic access to data has been expanded immensely in the past few decades, affording currency in the receipt of the estimates for the user and cost reductions in their dissemination for the provider. Often, however, this is achieved at the expense of the convenience and time of the user. Finally, the estimates must be acceptable to the public if they are to be employed in programs that affect the public directly in important ways. The public must view the estimates as professional products that are not deliberately biased.

Availability of Estimates

The most extensive official program of population estimates is conducted by the U.S. Census Bureau. The current program of the Census Bureau encompasses annual estimates of the population of the nation, states, and counties, with detail for age, sex, race, and Hispanic origin, and components of change (births, deaths, and net migration), as well as annual estimates of the total population of metropolitan areas, cities of 10,000 or more, and minor civil divisions that are functioning general-purpose governmental units.[1] The part of the program consisting of annual estimates for counties with detail on population composition was added only in the mid-1990s as part of the Census Bureau's evolving program of continuous measurement, and is intended to complement and intersect with the American Community Survey.

The scope and role of the Census Bureau's population estimation program will change as a result of the gradual implementation of the American Community Survey, which is designed to replace the long, or sample, form of the census after 2000 (Chapter 3). This survey will produce many of the same types of population data as are now included in the population estimates program, for example, annual estimates of the total population and basic population characteristics of counties. Although the details of the relation of these two programs are still being worked out, it appears that the estimates of national, state, and county population from the population estimates program will be used as "controls" to adjust the American Community Survey results, in the manner that they have been used to adjust the Current Population Survey and other major national surveys.

The American Community Survey has some limitations as a source of population data. The first has already been implied. To control bias and variance, especially to reduce undercounts, the estimates from the survey require adjustment to independent population estimates derived by demographic methods. Next, for the smaller communities, the reference period is rather broad (i.e., 5 years) and hence the figures do not lend themselves easily to time series analysis. Several years of data (i.e., from 2003 to 2008) will have to be collected before usable estimates for small cities, census tracts, and other small areas will become available from the survey. Moreover, the survey figures, unlike census figures and the independent population estimates, are subject to sampling error. Since the long form will be eliminated from future censuses, there will be no easy way to evaluate much of the data from the American Community Survey.

The Bureau of Economic Analysis (BEA) also conducts a program of population estimates for states and substate areas. The program includes estimates for states, metropolitan statistical areas, and BEA economic areas. BEA economic areas are areas of economically related counties which, in total, cover the entire United States. Current estimates for these areas are available, at the time of this writing, on CD-ROM and on the Internet (www.bea.doc.gov).

All states have active population estimates programs and work cooperatively with the federal government in carrying out these programs. The familiarity of state and local analysts with the local population situation has aided them in developing the data and methods for making population estimates for their states and communities and in evaluating the estimates made. It has improved the quality and scope of state and local population estimates. State and local analysts have ready access to local records on building permits, school enrollments, vacancy/occupancy data on housing units, utility customers, and similar data for use in making or evaluating population estimates. In sum, necessity and experience have promoted the development of state and local statistical sources and the expertise of state and local population analysts.

METHODOLOGY OF NATIONAL ESTIMATES

The following discussion of the derivation of national population estimates is purposely brief, since the main interest of most applied demographers is in subnational demographic data. It is mainly concerned also with postcensal estimates, although some attention is given to intercensal estimates—that is, estimates which take account of a later census as well as an earlier one.

Postcensal Estimates

Currently the standard method for making national postcensal estimates is to apply the component estimating equation. Data on births, deaths, immigration, and emigration for the period from the previous census to the estimate date are combined with the counts from the previous census in a straightforward accounting equation.

Estimates of Total Population

The U.S. Census Bureau publishes estimates of the U.S. *resident* population annually, with detail for age, sex, race, and Hispanic origin. Estimates are also published for the *total population including U.S. armed forces abroad* and the *civilian* population in the same detail. The resident population includes only that portion of the armed forces stationed in the United States in addition to the civilian population.

Estimates must be made for part of the immigration flow and for all of the emigration flow because of the lack of adequate, recorded data on alien emigration, illegal immigration, net migration to and from Puerto Rico, and the net movement of other U.S. citizens. Sophisticated methods are being employed at the U.S. Census Bureau to fabricate these pieces of the equation, but they remain areas of great uncertainty. Although immigration and emigration are now substantial, they are numerically less important than births and deaths. The two components that are essentially "guessed," net illegal immigration and alien emigration, offset one another to some extent. For 1995 the annual allowance for net illegal immigration made by the U.S. Census Bureau in its official national estimates was 225,000, and the annual allowance for allien emigration was 222,000. Births and deaths are probably underreported by small amounts, but no allowance is made for these data errors, which also tend to offset one another to an unknown degree.

The official national postcensal estimates of the resident population are designed to be consistent with the last census counts. Since the census counts understate the actual population, postcensal estimates based on them also understate the actual population. In fact, the largest source of error in national postcensal estimates is the undercount in the last census (see Chapter 4). A full discussion of the derivation of national postcensal estimates is given in the annual reports of the U.S. Census Bureau presenting such estimates.[2]

Estimates for Age, Sex, and Major Race/Hispanic Origin Groups

In general, current official estimates for age groups are derived by carrying the census data forward by birth cohorts, allowing for deaths, immigration, and emigration. Postcensal births are introduced to represent the cohorts born between the census date and the estimate date. Because of the undercounts in the census and a policy of making the postcensal estimates "consistent" with the census counts, it is necessary to posit a criterion specifying the parameter of the postcensal estimates to be optimized while maintaining an undercounted total and undercounted figures for age, sex, and race groups. If the census figures and the postcensal estimates merely could be adjusted (i.e., corrected) for the net undercounts, age by age (sex and race), setting such a criterion would not be necessary. Among the possible optimizing criteria, the Census Bureau selected maximizing the accuracy of the postcensal *percent change in age groups*.

The criteria of consistency with the census level and optimizing postcensal age changes are essentially met by use of a procedure denoted as the **inflation-deflation procedure**. This procedure involves (1) adjusting the census figures for the estimated net undercount in each age-sex-race group, (2) carrying the adjusted census figures forward by birth cohorts to each successive age and calendar year by deducting deaths and adding net immigration in the appropriate cohorts, and (3) deflating the results in (2) by the estimated percentage of net census undercount at the *target* or terminal age. In this way, the age pattern and level of net undercounts at the last census are preserved, and the net undercount at one age is not shifted to a different age in the derivation of the postcensal estimates, as would occur if a special procedure were not applied.

Maximizing the accuracy of the postcensal percent changes at a given age is only one of several criteria for developing postcensal estimates consistent with the census counts. Others are maximizing the accuracy of the postcensal (percentage) age distribution and maximizing the accuracy of the change in the (percentage) age distribution between the census date and the estimate date.[3] Again, this must be achieved while maintaining the national census counts for age groups and a national postcensal total of all ages consistent with the level of the census counts. The inflation-deflation procedure does *not* meet the first of these two critera, and it meets the second criterion only roughly. Another criterion, maximizing the accuracy of the percentage changes for birth cohorts, is *not* of great interest or value to users.[4] Only the use of adjusted census figures and adjusted postcensal estimates would fully meet the various criteria. As we learned, such adjusted figures have been used in "controlling" the major national sample surveys since the 1980s.

Intercensal Estimates

Given the criterion that intercensal estimates should be consistent with the counts from both the earlier and later censuses, developing intercensal estimates presents the additional problem, as compared with postcensal estimates, of distributing the error of closure at each age. The **error of closure** is the gap between a postcensal estimate (i.e., an estimate based on the first census) and the count at the second census:

$$E_{10} = P_{10}^e - P_{10}^c \tag{1}$$

where E_{10} represents the decennial error of closure, P_{10}^e the postcensal estimate for the second census date, and P_{10}^c represents the count at the second census. In general, we can define an error of closure for each date as the difference between the postcensal estimate and the intercensal estimate:

$$E_t = P_t^e - P_t^c \tag{2}$$

where E_t is the error of closure at time t, P_t^c is the intercensal estimate at time t, and P_t^e is the postcensal estimate at time t. To achieve consistency between the two censuses and the estimates of postcensal change, it is customary to distribute the error of closure over the postcensal estimates. This can be done in several ways, and the analyst must choose one of them: in proportion to time, in proportion to the size of the postcensal estimate, or in proportion to time and the size of the postcensal estimate; as a linear function or a nonlinear function; and in other ways. Use of a linear function in proportion to time would assign one-tenth of the total error of closure, cumulated, to each successive year in the decade. The method used by the U.S. Census Bureau for the 1980s distributes the error of closure as a function both of time and the level of the postcensal estimate, following a geometric curve. The formula is

$$P_t^c = P_t^e (P_{10}^c \div P_{10}^e)^{t/10} \tag{3}$$

where P_{10}^c is the count at the second census date and P_{10}^e is the postcensal estimate at the second census date. For example, if the count of the population at the second census is 3,525,000, the postcensal estimate for this census date is 3,500,000, and the postcensal estimate for the fourth year in the decade is 3,375,000, the intercensal estimate for the fourth year (i.e., $t = 4$) would be

$$P_4^c = 3,375,000(3,525,000/3,500,000)^{4/10}$$
$$P_4^c = 3,375,000(1.002851)$$
$$P_4^c = 3,384,622$$

According to this formula, a larger part of the error of closure will be allocated to time intervals of more rapid change.

The problem of distributing the error of closure applies to intercensal estimates of all types (e.g., age, sex, race) and to all geographic levels (e.g., states, counties, cities)—that is, whenever the goal is to reconcile postcensal estimates with the two census counts. Whatever basic formulas are used to derive the postcensal estimates for subgroups (e.g., the inflation-deflation procedure for age groups) and to apply an intercensal adjustment (e.g., a formula taking time and population size into account), the estimates will still require adjustment to certain marginal totals (e.g., the all-ages intercensal estimates). For subnational estimates (e.g., states), an adjustment of the intercensal estimates to national totals is required to bring about consistency with the national intercensal estimates. For state-age estimates, for example, two-way proportionate adjustments to marginal totals for ages and states are required.[5]

METHODOLOGY OF SUBNATIONAL POSTCENSAL ESTIMATES

A great number and variety of methods of making postcensal estimates of population for subnational areas have been developed and applied. Figure 9.1 presents an outline of the leading methods. The methods listed may variously apply to states, counties, cities, and census tracts. In the following discussion, each principal method is described and its main assumptions are briefly noted.

■ **FIGURE 9.1**   Outline of Methods for Estimates of the Total
Population of Subnational Areas

Census and population registers
Direct estimates based on sample surveys
Mathematical extrapolation and proration/apportionment
Methods using demographic analysis
    Censal ratio methods
        Housing unit method
        Vital rates method
    Component methods
        Component method (tax returns)/administrative records method
        Component method (school enrollment)/Census Bureau's Method II
Ratio-regression and other regression methods
Composite estimates
Combinations of basic methods
    Averaging of basic estimates
    Use of basic estimates in ratio-regression

Censuses and Population Registers

Census counts are sometimes available for small areas for years other than the year of the decennial census. These censuses may have been taken by local authorities or by the Census Bureau at the request of a local authority. These are so-called special censuses. Another option is available in the several countries (e.g., Finland, Sweden, Denmark) that maintain a national **population register** (i.e., a continuous system of population accounting that incorporates data on both natural increase and internal migration). Population registers can provide population balances (i.e., population estimates) at any selected date for any designated area. The United States does not maintain a national population register, but it has several large administrative record files that can be viewed as partial population registers. Among these are the Social Security beneficiary and "covered" worker files, the Medicare file, and the Internal Revenue Service file of individual tax returns. Some of these play an important role in population estimates programs.

Sample Survey Estimates

The national sample surveys may be used as direct sources of estimates of the population of states and large metropolitan areas. These estimates may also be used as one of the independent variables in regression equations designed to estimate the total population (discussed later) or as elements in synthetic estimates of socioeconomic characteristics for subnational areas (Chapter 11). Sample surveys, even large ones, such as the Current Population Survey, SIPP, and the American Community Survey, are not mainly designed to provide estimates of the total population of areas, especially small areas. The biases and variances of the survey estimates of the total population of subnational areas may be so large as to preclude their direct use as estimates of absolute population size. Sample surveys are mainly designed to provide estimates of the *dis-*

tribution of the population by various demographic and socioeconomic characteristics.

Only the American Community Survey will be large enough to provide accurate estimates of total population for all the states. In view of the reservations about the sample survey estimates of total population, however, it is common practice to adjust such estimates in the final weighting stage to independent estimates of the total population and even selected basic demographic characteristics derived by demographic methods. This is being done for the surveys just cited.

Several devices can be employed to improve the accuracy of sample survey estimates for an area. These include oversampling, combining data for a few years or from two surveys, stratifying the sample, and increasing the number of primary sampling units. One way of enlarging a sample in effect is to employ **network sampling**—also called **multiplicity sampling**. This procedure involves securing information from respondents in the sample households about relatives, within a specified degree of consanguinity, who do not live in the sample households. Its use requires adjusting the sample weights for the probability that some individuals would be reported more than once.

Mathematical Methods and Ratio/Apportionment Methods

Several mathematical functions have been used to make postcensal estimates for subnational areas, for example, arithmetic extrapolation (i.e., assuming a constant amount of growth) and geometric extrapolation (i.e., assuming a constant growth rate). As evaluation tests have shown, these methods produce estimates that have rather large errors over a decade as compared with more analytic methods. In spite of their simplicity, they are not commonly used now because of their poor performance and the mechanical nature of their assumptions. They were widely used until the modern methods based on indicator data came into use after World War II.

Ratio/apportionment methods are essentially mathematical methods that employ an independent estimate for the grand total or "parent" population (e.g., state) of the set of areas (e.g., counties in the state) for which estimates are being made. The "typical" ratio estimate distributes the overall total among the constituent areas for the estimate date in proportion to their populations at a prior census date. Because this method makes the generally unrealistic assumption that the subareas have all grown at the same rate since the census date, the estimates are subject to substantial error. On the other hand, if the independent current estimate of the parent population is reasonably accurate, the estimates for the subareas as a group are likely to show an improvement over the prior census figures as estimates for the current date.

Alternatively, the overall postcensal change may be distributed in proportion to the gains among the subareas in the prior intercensal period. This method assumes that the subareas will each retain their share of the past growth; losses may or may not be continued, however. Again, the assumptions are unrealistic, but the estimates are presumably superior to those assuming that the population has not changed since the previous census.

Methods Using Demographic Analysis

Demographic methods of population estimation include those methods designated as censal ratio methods, component methods, and methods based on aggregate administrative data. All of these methods employ indicator data for the particular area under study to represent either total population change, total household change, or migration change for the postcensal period. **Indicator or symptomatic data** are data that can be used to measure changes in a demographic variable. Censal ratio methods employ indicator data to represent total change in households or population, depending on the choice of indicator data. Component methods vary on the basis of the type of indicator data employed to measure net migration. Use of aggregate administrative records is usually a part of a component method. Administrative data serve as indicator data to represent one or more of the components of change, the population in one or more age groups, or as a dependent variable in a regression equation.

Censal Ratio Methods: Housing-Unit Method

Censal ratio methods begin with the ratio of some indicator to the population at the census date and current data for the indicator. The indicator may be housing units, births, deaths, school enrollment, or other appropriate variable for which a postcensal time series can be assembled.

The simplest of the censal ratio methods is the housing-unit method. It is regarded as one of the most reliable methods for making local estimates and one of the easiest to apply. Since the necessary data for applying the housing-unit method are readily available at the local level and are often the only data readily available to local analysts, it is the most widely used method of making substate population estimates. Even the Census Bureau has initiated the use of the housing-unit method for preparing population estimates for areas within counties (i.e., places, remainder of counties, and minor civil divisions) that have governmental functions. Moreover, the Census Bureau has requested local governments to use the housing-unit method in preparing alternative postcensal population estimates if they wish to challenge the Census Bureau's estimates.[6]

The general design of the housing-unit method is to update the number of occupied housing units (i.e., households) from the previous census using data on building permits (new construction/conversion) and demolitions, certificates of occupancy, utility connections (mainly electric or water), or real and personal property tax information on residential units,[7] and then to convert this current estimate of households into a population estimate by use of a population-to-household ratio. The basic formula is

$$P_t = OH_t \star PPH_t + GQ_t \qquad (4)$$

where P_t repesents the total population at the estimate date t, OH_t is the occupied housing units at time t, PPH_t is the population per housing unit at time t, and GQ_t is the group quarters population at time t. This is a mathematical identity, but problems arise from the accuracy of the estimates of these elements, particularly the quality of the housing-unit indicator data, and the soundness of the assumptions used in extrapolating *PPH*. Worksheet 9.1 can be used to derive a housing-unit estimate for a local area using either building permits, utility connections, or certificates of occupancy.[8]

If the building-permit variant is applied, data are needed on residential demolitions and conversions as well as data on new construction. The combination of data on new construction, conversions, and demolitions during the postcensal period yields an estimate of change in the number of housing units:

$$TH_t = TH_0 + BP - D + C \tag{5}$$

where TH_t represents total housing units at time t, TH_0 represents total housing units at the census date, BP represents building permits between the census date and time t, D represents demolitions between the census date and time t, and C represents conversions between the census date and time t. In employing data on building permits to represent change in housing units, an allowance has to be made for the time lag between the issuance of the permit and completion of the unit for occupancy. A period of about 6 to 9 months is a common choice for this purpose. Since the time lag varies greatly from one region to another, however, this issue should be investigated locally. In addition, some (perhaps 2%) of the housing units are not completed. It is recommended further that the analysis and calculations be made separately for single units, multiunit structures, and mobile homes because the types of structures have different demographic characteristics and constitute different shares of the housing inventory from one area to another.

The postcensal estimate of total housing units must be converted into an estimate of occupied housing units, or households, by making an allowance for vacancies. For this purpose, an estimate of the current occupancy (or vacancy) ratio is needed:

$$OH_t = TH_t \star (OH \div TH)_t \tag{6}$$

The estimate of households must then be converted into an estimate of population using an appropriate ratio of population to households. A current estimate of population per household can be based on the figure for the local area at the previous census, current survey data on households for the United States and regions, or current Census Bureau estimates of population and households for states. One technique is to update the ratio of population to households for the local area from the previous census by applying (e.g., adding) the change in the ratio for the particular state, region, or the United States since the census date:

$$PPH_t = PPH_c + (PPH_t^S - PPH_c^S) \tag{7}$$

where PPH_c represents population-per-household at the previous census for the local area and the expression in the parentheses represents the postcensal change in population-per-household for the state. Finally, an estimate of the nonhousehold, or group quarters, population must be added.

In implementing the housing-unit method, the analyst must exercise care to assure that the geographic area and time period of the housing-unit data conform to the area and period required, that the data relate only to usual residents (that is, excludes temporary residents), that only residential (not commercial)

■ **WORKSHEET 9.1** Worksheet for Calculating a Postcensal Population Estamate by the Housing-Unit Method for a Hypothetical Subcounty Area: July 1, 1998.

Part A. Building-permit and demolition data

Census base (April 1, 1990)

	Single units/ nonspecific (a)	Multiple units (b)	Mobile homes (c)
1. Total population..			
2. Household population....................................			
3. Total housing units...			
4. Occupied housing units.................................			
5. Occupancy ratio.. $(5) = (4) \div (3)$			
6. Population per household............................... $(6) = (2) \div (4)$			

Data on change in housing units

7. Building permits (units).................................
   (Cumulated over a designated number of months allowing for a lag in construction, varying by region and structural type of housing unit. Refer to source document for cumulation period.)

8. Demolitions...
   (Cumulated from April 1990 to June 1998)

9. Completed structures.....................................
   $(9) = (7) * 0.98 - (8) + (3)$
   (The factor 0.98 allows for units not completed.)

10. Estimate of mobile homes, July 1, 1998.......
    (Refer to source document for alternative methods of estimation)

11. Occupied housing units, July 1, 1998...........
    $(11) = (5) * (9)$;
    $(11) = (5) * (10)$ for mobile homes

12. Region-specific factor of change in population-to-households ratio, 1990 to 1998.....................
    (See source document, or prepare an estimate.)

13. Population per household, July 1, 1998.......
    $(13) = (6) * (12)$

Population in households and total population, July 1, 1998

14. Persons in households....................................
    $(14a) = (11a) * (13a)$; $(14b) = (11b) * (13b)$
    and $(14c) = (11c) * (13c)$

(continues)

WORKSHEET 9.1 (*continued*)

15. Total persons in households......................... _____
    (15) = (14a) + (14b) + (14c)

16. Group quarters population........................... _____
    (See source document; use local sources)

17. Total resident population............................. _____
    (17) = (15) + (16)

Part B. Utility connections

Census base, April 1, 1990

1. Household population.................................... _____

2. Occupied year-round housing units................ _____

3. Persons per household.................................. _____
   (3) = (1) ÷ (2)

Change in housing inventory, 1990–1998

4. Active residential utility
   connections, April 1, 1990............................ _____

5. Active residential utility
   connections, July 1, 1998............................. _____

6. Ratio of change in connections,
   1990 to 1998... _____
   (6) = (5) ÷ (4)

7. Occupied units.. _____
   (7) = (6) * (2)

8. Region-specific factor of change in population-
   to-households ratio, 1990 to 1998.................. _____
   (See source document, or prepare an estimate.)

9. Persons per household, July 1, 1998............. _____
   (9) = (3) * (8)

Population in households and total population, July 1, 1998

10. Household population................................. _____
    (10) = (9) * (7)

11. Group quarters population.......................... _____
    (See source document; use local sources.)

12. Resident population.................................... _____
    (12) = (10) + (11)

(*continues*)

WORKSHEET 9.1 (*continued*)

Part C. Certificates of Occupancy

Census base, April 1, 1990

1. Total population...

	Single units/ nonspecific (a)	Multiple units (b)	Mobile homes (c)
2. Household population....................................			
3. Total housing units..			
4. Occupied housing units.................................			
5. Occupancy ratio.. (5) = (4) ÷ (3)			
6. Population per household............................... (6) = (2) ÷ (4)			

Change in housing units, April 1, 1990, to July 1, 1998

7. Certificates of occupancy.............................. (Cumulation of certificates issued in postcensal period.)			
8. Demolitions (units)... (Cumulation of demolition permits issued in postcensal period.)			
9. Housing structures.. (9) = (7) − (8) + (3)			
10. Mobile homes, July 1, 1998........................... (See source for alternative methods of estimation.)			
11. Occupied housing units, July 1, 1998............ (11) = (5) * (9); (11) = (5) * (10) for mobile homes			
12. Region-specific factor of change in population-to-households ratio, 1990 to 1998................. (See source document, or prepare an estimate.)			
13. Population per household, July 1, 1998......... (13) = (6) * (12)			

Population in households and total population, July 1, 1998

14. Persons in households.................................... (14a) = (11a) * (13a); (14b) = (11b) * (13b) and (14c) = (11c) * (13c)			
15. Total persons in households.......................... (15) = (14a) + (14b) + (14c)			
16. Group quarters population............................ (Refer to source document; use local sources.)			
17. Total resident population.............................. (17) = (15) + (16)			

Source: Based on U.S. Bureau of the Census, Population Division, *Review Guide for Local Population Estimates*, June 1995.

data are included, and that conversions from commercial to residential use or from residential to commercial use are properly included or excluded. As suggested earlier, it is recommended that the calculations be carried out separately for single units, multiunit structures, and mobile homes since the data for each of these structural types may require different adjustments for the occupancy ratio and the change in the population-per-household ratio as well as the lag between permit issuance and completion of the structure.

The estimating algorithm varies only a little if certificates of occupancy or utilities connections are used instead of building permits to estimate the current number of occupied housing units. Data on utility connections are required for both the census date and the estimate date to measure absolute or relative postcensal change in the number of occupied housing units. Postcensal change in the occupancy ratio is not a matter of concern in the utilities-connections variant of the housing-unit method. However, the data should be checked for any discrepancy between the number of customers and the number of occupied housing units at the census date, and for any shift in coverage of the data over the postcensal period. In general, postcensal series of housing-unit data should be maintained annually and scanned carefully for irregularities, and discrepancies with the census count should be fully investigated.

Censal Ratio Method: Vital Rates Method

The vital rates method involves calculating two censal-ratio estimates of population, one based on births as an indicator and the second based on deaths as an indicator. The ratio of births to population at the census date is extrapolated to the estimate date and *divided* into the current number of births to obtain the first population estimate. The second estimate is obtained in the same manner on the basis of the death rate and the number of deaths. The two population estimates are averaged. The averaging process tends to reduce the biases inherent in each of the estimates.[9]

The vital rates method is described here mainly for its historical interest, but not entirely. Formerly it was widely employed, mainly in combination with other methods, but it is little used now. Vital statisticians, who are often the analysts preparing local population estimates, may find the method logically troublesome since they must use the results to compute current birth and death rates. It may be worthy of resurrection, however, since it is easy to apply and test results were generally favorable. It is as defensible demographically as the housing unit method, but it has not been exploited as much, probably for the reason suggested.

Component Method (Tax Returns)/Administrative-Records Method

Another class of demographic methods is called component methods. Component methods are methods in which net migration is estimated separately from natural increase. Component methods differ mainly on the basis of the indicator data that are used to measure net migration. In the component (tax returns) method, Internal Revenue Service (IRS) data on individual tax returns are used to measure internal migration. This method was developed at the U.S. Census Bureau and carried the name administrative-records method for many years. In view of the general use of administrative records in population research, a more informative name, component method (tax returns), has been given to it here.

Annual files of individual tax returns, obtained under a restricted-use agreement with the IRS, serve as the basis by which the Census Bureau measures internal migration. The mailing address on the tax return is assigned to a specific area (that is, a state, county, remainder of a county, place, or minor civil division) by a geocoding program. The individual tax returns for the same households are then matched over a 1-year period, on the basis of the Social Security number (SSN) of the primary filer, in order to identify the nonmigrants, in-migrants, and out-migrants for each area over the 1-year period. The IRS tax returns distinguish persons under age 65 from those 65 years and over. Hence, it is possible to estimate the movements of the household population under age 65 separately.

The matched data are tabulated to provide estimates of internal migration and internal migration rates for each area over a year (e.g., July 1, 1997, to July 1, 1998) for persons (i.e., "exemptions") under age 65 at the end of the year (e.g., July 1, 1998). The migration rate is computed from the IRS matched exemptions by

$$(\text{Inmigrants} - \text{Outmigrants}) \div (\text{Nonmigrants} + \text{Outmigrants}) \qquad (8)$$

a formula designed to represent net migration divided by the population exposed to the risk of out-migration. The population to which this migration rate is applied is a little different—the household population under age 65 at the beginning of the estimate year (e.g., July 1, 1997), plus one-half the natural increase and net immigration under age 65 during the estimate year (e.g., July 1, 1997, to July 1, 1998), minus one-half the population 64 years of age at the beginning of the year (i.e., the cohort reaching age 65 during the year).

Estimates of the household population 65 years and over may be based on Medicare data, used either as an aggregate file for measuring total postcensal change in the elderly population since the census data or for inferring postcensal net migration in this population. Alternatively, the estimates may be obtained by a component method, incorporating estimates of net internal migration based on matched tax returns.

The estimates of total population are completed in two additional steps: first, combining the household population under age 65 at the previous census, natural increase under age 65, and net migration of the household population under age 65; and, second, combining the postcensal estimate of the household population under age 65 (from the first step), the household population 65 and over, and the group quarters population. Worksheet 9.2 presents a step-by-step illustration of the computation of an estimate of a county's population by the component (tax returns) method.[10]

The method has its limitations. These limitations result mainly from geocoding errors and the incomplete coverage of the population by the tax-return data. If household income is below the filing cutoff at the two dates, falls below the filing cutoff during the estimate year, or rises above it during the year, the migration status of the household cannot be ascertained from the IRS records. Then the data are used on the assumption that the nonfilers and unmatched filers have the same level and pattern of migration rates as the matched filers.

■ **WORKSHEET 9.2** Derivation of Postcensal Population Estimate by the Component (Tax Returns) Method for a Hypothetical County: 1998.

Item	Value	Derivation or source
Part A. Estimate of the population under age 65 on July 1, 1998		
Population on July 1, 1997		
1. Total population	93,401	Estimate on July 1, 1997
2. Population 65 years of age and over	9,021	Estimate on July 1, 1997
3. Group quarters population under age 65	5,660	Local records
4. Household populatian under age 65	78,720	(4) = (1) − (2) − (3)
Components of change for the household population under age 65, July 1, 1997 – June 30, 1998		
5. Population reaching age 65 (approximates population 64 years of age on July 1, 1997)	617	(5) = 0.06837 * (2)
6. Resident births	1,924	Local records/estimated
7. Resident deaths	233	Local records/estimated
8. Net immigration	164	Estimated/INS reports
9. Internal migration base on July 1, 1997	79,339	(9) = (4) + 0.5 * [−(5) + (6) − (7) + (8)]
10. Internal migration rate	−0.00943	Matching of tax returns
11. Amount of net in-migration	−748	(11) = (9) * (10)
Population on July 1, 1998		
12. Household population under age 65	79,210	(12) = (4) − (5) + (6) − (7) + (8) + (11)
13. Group quarters population under age 65	5,660	Line 3, Part A
14. Total population under age 65	84,870	(14) = (12) + (13)
Part B. Estimate of the population 65 years and over on July 1, 1998		
Population on July 1, 1997		
1. Total population 65 years and over on July 1, 1997	9,021	Line 2, Part A
2. Group quarters population 65 years and over	642	Local records
3. Household population 65 years and over	8,379	(3) = (1) − (2)
Components of change in household population 65 years and over, July 1, 1997 – June 30, 1998		
4. Population reaching age 65	617	Line 5, Part A
5. Resident deaths	701	Local records/estimated
6. Net immigration	21	Estimated/INS reports
7. Internal migration base on July 1, 1997	8,347	(7) = (3) + 0.5 * [(4) − (5) + (6)]
8. Internal migration rate	0.03172	Matching of tax returns
9. Amount of net in-migration	265	(9) = (7) * (8)
Population 65 years and over, July 1, 1998		
10. Household population 65 years and over	8,581	(10) = (3) + (4) − (5) + (6) + (9)
11. Group quarters population 65 years and over	586	Local records
12. Total population 65 years and over	9,167	(12) = (10) + (11)

(continues)

WORKSHEET 9.2 *(continued)*

Part C. Final total population, July 1, 1998

1. Preliminary total population under age 65	84,870	Line 14, Part A
2. Adjustment factor for population under age 65	1.000345	Adjustment to control total
3. Final estimate of population under age 65	84,899	(3) = (1) * (2)
4. Preliminary total population aged 65 years and over	9,167	Line 12, Part B
5. Adjustment factor for population 65 years and over	1.001068	Adjustment to control total
6. Final estimate of population 65 years and over	9,177	(6) = (4) * (5)
7. Final estimate of total population	94,076	(7) = (3) + (6)

Whether a serious bias results depends on whether there is a strong relation between low income and migration patterns. It is surmised that areas with many poor residents tend to have biased, especially understated, estimates of out-migration in the component (tax returns) method.

Component (School Enrollment) Method/Census Bureau's Method II

The Census Bureau's component Method II is a component method that features school enrollment as the indicator of net migration. In this method, as in the component (tax returns) method, the estimates of the components are added to the latest decennial census count to derive the postcensal estimate. Some of the component estimates—births, deaths, group quarters population, population over age 65—are the same as those calculated for the tax-returns method. Net internal migration of the household population under 65 years old in component Method II is derived in a series of steps that begins with an annual series of data on the number of children enrolled in elementary grades 1 to 8 (including private schools, ungraded and special classes) for the estimate area.

One choice of steps for deriving the estimated net migration of the household population for ages under 65 consists of (1) estimating the school-age population (*ca.* ages 6.25 to 14.25) from school enrollment data for grades 1 to 8; (2) determining the net migration of the cohorts of school age at the estimate date by the residual method, for the period between the census date and the estimate date; (3) converting the estimate in (2) into a net migration rate for the school-age cohorts; (4) converting the net migration rate for the school-age cohorts into a migration rate for the under-65 population on the basis of the past and current relationships of the migration rate for all ages under 65 to the migration rate for the school-age cohorts; and (5) applying the rate in (4) to the household population under age 65 at the previous census plus one half of the natural increase and one half of the net in-migration in the postcensal estimate period.

Step 4 is carried out jointly on the basis of the relationships between the national migration rates for various age groups shown by the Current Population Survey for postcensal years (e.g., 1997 to 1998) and on the basis of the state and county rates shown by the previous census for the years just preceding the census (e.g., 1985 to 1990).[11] It is assumed that legal immigration, as well as most illegal immigration, is reflected in the school enrollment statistics. Note that the base of component Method II is the most recent census counts, unlike the tax-returns method, which builds on the previous set of annual estimates.[12]

Ratio-Regression and Other Regression Methods

Regression methods incorporate indicator data as independent variables in a statistical equation designed to produce an estimate of the current population as a dependent variable.[13] In one form of the ratio-regression formula, the independent and dependent variables are expressed as the ratio of (1) the percentage share for a subarea to a parent area in the latest census year to (2) the corresponding percentage share at the previous census. In estimating the county populations of a state, a regression equation is prepared for the state using available symptomatic data for the counties in the state. The independent variables used in the regression equation may be such variables as elementary school enrollment in grades 1 to 8 (plus ungraded and special classes), state income tax returns, automobile registrations, births (2 or 3-year annual average), deaths (2 or 3-year annual average), births plus deaths (2 or 3-year annual average), drivers' licenses, federal tax returns, covered employment, voter registrations, sales taxes, and housing units.

In its current applications, the ratio-regression equation is designed to estimate the household population under 65 years old. The household population 65 years and over and the group quarters population are estimated separately, just as in the tax-returns method and school-enrollment method.

The general form of the multiple linear regression equation is

$$Y = b_0 + b_1X_1 + b_2X_2 + b_3X_3 + b_4X_4 + \epsilon \qquad (9)$$

The b's are the coefficients or weights to be assigned to the X (independent) variables, b_0 represents the Y-intercept, ϵ represents the random error of the observation for each subarea, and Y is the dependent variable. In estimating the population of the counties of Kansas for the 1970s, for example, the Census Bureau used the following independent variables: X_1, births (3-year average); X_2, deaths (3-year average); X_3, elementary school enrollment grades 1 to 8 (plus special and ungraded classes); and X_4, automobile and truck registrations. The equation was $Y_c = -0.0131 + 0.0788X_1 + 0.0404X_2 + 0.2563X_3 + 0.6328X_4$. In this case the variables are expressed as (1) the ratio of the share of the variable in the county to the state total in 1970 *to* (2) the corresponding ratio in 1960 for the counties in the state. The data for the independent variables for each county, transformed as just noted, are inserted into the equations for the counties of the state and then the coefficients are usually determined by a least-squares solution of the equations. The estimated population for the years in the next decade (1970s) is determined by inserting the values of each of the independent variables for the postcensal year (e.g., 1978) in the form described—that is, as ratios of county-to-state shares for the variables to the corresponding ratios in the base year (e.g., 1970). For another example, the state of Illinois is planning to use the following four independent variables in its year 2000 test of the ratio-regression method based on a regression equation reflecting experience in the 1980s: resident births (two-year average), school enrollment (grades 1 to 8), passenger car registrations, and federal income tax exemptions.[14]

The ratio-regression method is subject to several important limitations. It makes the questionable assumption that the statistical relationship between the change in the indicators selected and population change remains constant over time. The coefficients defining the relationship between the change in the indicators and the change in population for one decade may not apply to the following decade. Moreover, the relationship established over a 10-year period (i.e., between two census years) may not apply to the following 1-year, 2-year, ..., 8-year, and 9-year postcensal periods to which the estimating equation is applied. The ratio-regression method, like any regression procedure, entails the risk of **multicollinearity** (i.e., high intercorrelations between the independent variables). Multicollinearity makes it difficult to evaluate the relationship of any independent variable with the dependent variable in the multiple regression equation. As a result of multicollinearity, the coefficients are unstable. Finally, the coefficients and the population estimates are subject to sampling error if sample data are used in developing or evaluating the equation.

A number of proposals for varying the ratio-regression method of estimating population have been put forth. They include the use of difference-regression rather than ratio-regression, the use of dummy variables in the regression, the use of stratification, the use of ridge regression, and the averaging of simple regression estimates rather than using multiple regression. However, none of these has proven consistently superior to multiple linear ratio regression. The introduction of ridge regression has been a promising way of reducing the problem of multicollinearity. The bigger problems, however, such as temporal changes in the relationship between the change in indicators and change in population, remain unsolved.[15]

Composite Estimates

Composite estimates are estimates of the total population of an area that are based on different procedures for different segments of the age distribution. The method provides estimates both for age groups and the total population. The age segments usually chosen correspond to functional age groups for which there are suitable indicator data. For example, a composite estimate may be derived as follows:

Age group	Method and indicator
Under 5	Censal-ratio method (births)
5–17	Component method (school enrollment)
18–44	Censal-ratio method for females (births) and sex ratios for men
45–64	Censal-ratio method (deaths)
65 and over	Administrative records (Medicare)

Alternatively, the component method (school enrollment) may be used for the segment under age 15, ratio-regression for the segment aged 15 to 64 years, and administrative records (Medicare data) for the segment 65 years and over.

The sum of these estimates gives the figure for the total household population and an estimate of the group quarters population must be added. It is evident that the method lends itself readily to the calculation of estimates for age groups, whether 5-year groups or broader groups, as well as the total population.

There are many possible combinations of the censal-ratio method, component Method II, the ratio-regression method, and other methods, for deriving an estimate of the total population by this method. However, there is little empirical guidance as to the best choice to make for estimating each age group, whether the goal is to achieve the most accurate overall estimate or the most accurate estimate for a particular age group. In actual application, the composite method has commonly been averaged with other methods, such as the component (tax returns) method, when it has been used to derive estimates of total population.

Combination of Methods

Researchers have also experimented with ways of combining separate population estimates in the hope of reducing error. The advantage of combining estimates is that, if the estimates being combined are based on independent methods, data, and assumptions, they are likely to have opposing biases and combining the estimates is likely to reduce the biases. Furthermore, if the method with the greatest error is given the least weight, the level of accuracy is likely to be increased.

The simplest way of combining estimates is to average or weight two or three estimates directly. For example, estimates of the population derived by the component (tax returns) method can be averaged with estimates obtained by the ratio-regression method. The combination may be achieved by weighting the estimates with the same or different weights. If different weights are chosen, the choice of weights can depend on the analyst's judgment as to the relative accuracy of the estimates being combined or on more formal indices—e.g., the mean absolute percentage errors of the methods or the coefficients of variation (i.e., the relative variation) of the percentage errors of the methods, as indicated by evaluation tests.

A more complex device for combining estimates is to join population estimates from sample surveys such as the Current Population Survey and estimates based on demographic analysis as independent variables in a regression equation. The survey estimates for the primary sampling units (psu's) in the area of interest can be weighted together to develop an estimate for the area. This approach is suggested both because of the large variances of the sample survey estimates and the limitations of the individual estimates based on demographic methods, particularly for rapidly changing and small populations.[16]

Other Design Choices in Population Estimates

In the design of an estimation method, choices have to be made not only with respect to the general method but also with respect to a multitude of alternatives in its implementation. I consider two such issues here, referred to as the geographical direction of calculations and adjustment to marginal totals. They are closely linked.

Decisions have to be made as to the exact points in the calculations at which the figures will be adjusted to independently derived marginal totals. At one extreme, adjustments may be made to marginal totals for the components of change (e.g., births, deaths, net migration), geographic areas (e.g., states, counties), and characteristics (e.g., age) at each stage of the calculations and, at the other extreme, adjustments may be made only once to the total population of the broadest geographic area (e.g., United States). The adjustments to marginal totals may be carried out for one variable (e.g., geographic levels) or for two variables (e.g., age groups and geographic levels).

In considering the geographic direction of calculations, we distinguish a "bottom-up" design from a "top-down" design. In a bottom-up design, the population estimate of a parent area (e.g., state) is derived by summing the estimates for the constituent areas (e.g., counties). In a top-down design, the population estimates of the parent area are derived first and serve as "controls" (i.e., marginal totals) to which the estimates of the constituent areas are adjusted. In practice, such designs are commonly mixed, as when state estimates are obtained as the sum of county estimates (bottom-up), state estimates are adjusted to the United States population totals (top-down), and subcounty estimates are adjusted to the final county estimates (top-down).

The Census Bureau has been preparing population estimates for states, counties, and subcounty areas on a regular basis since the mid-1970s. During this period, the methological design of the program has changed more than once, as test results and refinements in data and methods recommended a shift in method. At one period, state totals were derived by an average of the composite method (two age groups under age 65, each with its associated method) and the component (tax returns) method but, more recently, the state totals have been derived as the sum of county estimates prepared by the component (tax returns) method. The principal method for counties was once the component (school enrollment) method but, more recently, the component (tax returns) method has been preferred for counties. Subcounty estimates (36,000 or so general-purpose governmental units) were derived by the component (tax returns) method from the mid-1970s to the mid-1990s, but the housing-unit method is applied currently for these areas. Building-permit data serves as the basis for updating the census counts of housing units for places, remainders of counties, and minor civil divisions.

Estimation of Population Characteristics: Age, Sex, and Race Groups

Earlier we alluded to various calculations that would produce estimates of the age, sex, and race distribution of the population of states and counties. The composite method, described previously, is one such method. A simpler one is the proration method and a more elaborate one is the cohort-component method.

Overview of Methods

We may dismiss the proration method quickly at this point. It is akin to the ratio/apportionment method mentioned earlier in this chapter and discussed briefly again in Chapter 10 as a projection device. In the proration method, the estimated total population of an area is distributed by age, sex, and race according to the distribution recorded at the previous census for the area, or according to an estimated distribution based on the change in the distribution for some parent area (e.g., the state or United States) in relation to the area's previous intercensal change. The prorated figures may need to be adjusted to control totals for age, sex, and race for the parent area.

The composite method can be designed to produce separate estimates for the races and separate estimates for age-sex groups by use of appropriate indicators and computational algorithms for age groups, as suggested earlier. These methods (indicators) may be the censal-ratio method (births, deaths), the cohort-component method (school enrollment, federal tax returns), the ratio-regression method (federal tax returns, school enrollment, housing units), and administrative records (Medicare data), for one age group or another.

The most widely used method for developing age estimates for subnational areas is the cohort-component method and, hence, we examine this method in greater detail. The component (school enrollment) method/component Method II can readily be extended beyond its conventional form to produce estimates for sex, race, and age groups. The component (tax returns) method can also be extended to produce estimates for sex, race, and age groups, but the process is more complex.

Cohort-Component Method

In its general form, the cohort-component method of estimating population makes separate allowance for births, and for deaths and net migration of birth cohorts. To prepare a postcensal estimate for a county by the cohort-component method, data on births, and data on deaths and net migration for age groups, are needed. Estimates of these components may be prepared by use of data on births or birthrates, deaths or survival rates, and migrants or migration rates. Estimates of net migration can be developed for 5-year age groups or single ages on the basis of the net migration rates of school-aged children. The school-age migration rate can be transformed to represent the net migration rate for each age group. This transformation should take into account the variation in migration rates for age-sex-race groups in the census (e.g., for 1985–1990) for the particular state or county and the postcensal gross migration rates for the United States for broad age groups given by the Current Population Survey. Estimates for the male and female populations can be derived by employing the change since the previous census in age-specific sex ratios for the United States, in combination with sex ratios for each estimate area at the last or last two census dates. The estimates for race groups can be developed by carrying out the calculations separately for each principal race.

As an example of cohort-component estimates for counties, we examine the procedure employed by the Bureau of Economic and Business Research of the University of Florida to develop postcensal estimates for the counties of Florida for age, sex, and race groups during the 1980s, in connection with an evaluation of the method against the 1990 census results.[17]

The base population was the 1980 census data for 5-year age groups, males and females, and white and nonwhites. The estimates for the sexes and races were made separately. The base population was carried forward over two 5-year intervals, first to 1985 and then to 1990. In general, estimated births and in-migrants were added to the base population and estimated deaths and out-migrants were subtracted. For the mortality allowance, 5-year survival rates, specific by sex and race, from 1980 life tables for Florida, were applied to the base population:

$$ {}_5^5 S_x^{x+5\ 80} = ({}_5L_{x+5} \div {}_5L_x)^{80} \tag{10} $$

where ${}_5^5 S_x^{x+5\ 80}$ refers to a 5-year survival rate for 1980 and ${}_5L_x$ to the life table stationary population in ages x to $x + 5$. These were provided by the Florida State Department of Health and Rehabilitative Services.[18] To allow for the improvements that took place after 1980, the survival rates from the state life table were adjusted upward on the basis of changes in the survival rates for the United States in each age, sex, and race group. This adjustment should be carried out entirely on the complements of the survival rates $(1 - S)$ to avoid results exceeding 1. Separate life tables for the counties were not available. Use of state life tables is generally an acceptable shortcut, given the fact that the calculations were carried out separately for the races.

Migration was estimated by applying separate migration rates to the population at risk of in-migration and out-migration. The migration rates were based on the 1980 census data on intercounty migration patterns for the period 1975 to 1980. In calculating the rates, in-migrants to a given county in 1975–1980 were divided by the population of the United States (excluding the given county) in 1975 and out-migrants in 1975–1980 were divided by the population of the given county in 1975. The general formula for both calculations is

$$ r_m^{75-80} = {}_5 m_x^{x+5\ 75-80} \div {}_5 P_x^{75} \tag{11} $$

where r_m represents the in- or out-migration rate for a 5-year birth cohort for 1975–1980, m represents migrants in this cohort, and P represents the starting population at risk in 1975. The estimates of in-migration for each age/sex/race group for the 5-year postcensal periods were then derived by applying the in-migration rates to the population of the United States (excluding the population of the given county) at the beginning of the 5-year estimation period (i.e., 1980 or 1985), and the estimates of out-migration for the 5-year postcensal periods were derived by applying the out-migration rates to the population of the given county at the beginnning of the 5-year estimation period.

The general equation for deriving both in-migrants and out-migrants for a 5-year birth cohort during 1980–1985 is

$$ {}_5 m_x^{x+5\ 80-85} = r_m^{75-80} \star {}_5 P_x^{80} \tag{12} $$

where ${}_5 P_x^{80}$ corresponds to the type of population used in calculating r_m^{75-80}. The group quarters population was given separate attention in many counties because of its large size and distinctive mobility patterns. It may be noted that the Florida procedure fails to take account of migration indicators for the actual period of estimation. For this purpose, use could be made of school enrollment data at the local level available from local school districts, Medicare data for counties available from the Health Care Financing Agency, and intercounty migration data for age groups at the national level available from the Current Population Survey.

To estimate fertility, calculations with age-specific birthrates were unnecessary since the numbers of births for the two postcensal periods are known. The estimates for children under 5 in 1985 and 1990 were based on the actual number of births between 1980 and 1985 and between 1985 and 1990 for each county. The ratio of the population under 5 in 1980 to births between 1975 and 1980 was applied to the number of births between 1980 and 1985 to derive estimates of children under 5 in 1985 and to births between 1985 and 1990 to derive estimates of children under 5 in 1990. This procedure presumably accounts for mortality and migration of the young children between birth and the end of the 5-year period. Another procedure is to treat the births like other age groups, applying appropriate survival rates to the births, and adding estimated net in- or out-migration. State-of-birth data from the 1980 census, postcensal school-age migration for 1980–1985 and 1985–1990, net migration for the counties for 1970–1980, and a residual estimate of net migration for the birth cohort, 1975–1980 may be useful for this purpose.

Like school-age children, the population 65 years and over was estimated by a ratio method. The ratio of the population 65 years and over to Medicare enrollments in 1980 was applied to the Medicare data in 1990 to derive the estimated population 65 years and over in 1990. The Medicare data could also be used like the school-enrollment data—that is, as a basis for a residual estimate of net migration. The resulting migration rate for the elderly could be joined with the migration rate for school-age children to develop migration rates for other age groups.

We now have the pieces for composing age groups in 1985:

$$_5P^{85}_{x+5} = {}_5P^{80}_x \; _5S^{x+5 \; 80-85}_x + {}_5{}^5m^{x+5 \; 80-85}_x \tag{13}$$

Since the migrants were exposed to the risk of dying about half the period, it is desirable to reduce the number of migrants employed in equation (13) by multiplying it by $\sqrt{S}$ (e.g., $S = .95$; $\sqrt{S} = .9747$). The final estimates of the population of Florida counties distributed by age, sex, and race were derived by adjusting the cohort-component estimates to estimates of the total population prepared by the housing-unit method.[19]

Note that the cohort-component method at the local level may profit from supplementary techniques or data, such as adjustment to independent estimates of the total population for the area, special handling of the group quarters population (military, institutional), and use of appropriate currrent indicator data (school enrollment, Medicare data). While the cohort-component method is the most logical method of making estimates of the age, sex, and race distribution of the population of counties, there are simpler, cheaper, and speedier ways to derive useful results. They include a combination of the housing-unit method for the area total, the proration method for the distribution of characteristics, and adjustment of these preliminary results to control estimates for age, sex, and race for the parent area (e.g., states).

The Census Bureau has experimented with an extension of the component (tax returns) method/administrative records method to derive estimates of the demographic characteristics of state and county populations.[20] The basic method of measuring migration is the matching of addresses on federal tax returns in two successive years for the same primary taxfiler identified by Social Security number. The demographic characteristics of the taxpayer and the taxpayer's dependents (i.e., their age, sex, and race/Hispanic origin) are obtained or inferred from a 20% sample of applications for Social Security numbers. The linkage, as before, is based on Social Security number, but in this case only a sample of applications is matched and hence estimates for many counties cannot be made.

In the current estimates program of the Census Bureau, the estimates of the total population of states and counties are derived by the component (tax returns)/administrative records method and the age-sex distribution of the population for states are derived by an extension of the component method (school enrollment)/component Method II. The detailed figures for states are then used as "controls" for the county estimates for these demographic groups, which have been derived by the proration method. In this version of the proration method, (1) county figures for the demographic groups from the 1990 census are adjusted proportionally ("raked") to agree with the county totals for the current date, obtained by the component (tax returns)/administrative records method, and (2) the results for the counties in step (1) are adjusted to agree with the corresponding state figures for the various demographic groups. The schema for these calculations may be represented as follows:

	States	Counties
Total	↑ "AR" method ←	↑ "AR" method
Age-sex distribution	↑ "Method II" ←	↑ Proration of county total from previous census

The arrows indicate the direction of adjustment to marginal "controls."

EVALUATION OF METHODS OF SUBNATIONAL POPULATION ESTIMATION

Much research has been carried out at the U.S. Census Bureau, state agencies, and universities to measure the accuracy of the various methods of making postcensal population estimates for subnational areas. The results of these studies provide guidance to research and administrative organizations in the choice of methods for use in research and planning, inform users about the accuracy of various methods, and serve as important material for use in litigation involving questions of population size, growth, and distribution.

Design of Evaluation Studies

We may classify the ways of evaluating the accuracy of postcensal population estimates in three categories: comparison of postcensal estimates for a set of areas, prepared by common methods, with an established standard, such as a decennial census or special censuses; comparison of a set of postcensal estimates, prepared by a variety of methods in a variety of working situations by a number of different analysts, with a census as standard; and comparison of postcensal estimates with later intercensal estimates, later postcensal estimates, or socioeconomic correlates of population change during the postcensal period. Here we deal mainly with the first type of evaluation study—the type that has been carried out most commonly and for which we have the most results. Secondary consideration is given to the third type of evaluation method.

Comparison with Census Counts

The most systematic and straightforward design for an evaluation program is to prepare a set of postcensal population estimates for the census date on the basis of the prior census by various methods and to compare the estimates with the census counts. The Census Bureau has conducted several such tests, comparing postcensal estimates based on the census counts for 1960 to 1980 with the census counts for 1970 to 1990. Four relatively standard measures and a variety of less standard ones have been used to evaluate postcensal estimates against decennial census figures. The standard ones are mean absolute percent error, mean algebraic percent error, proportion of positive differences, and number of errors of 5 percent or 10 percent or more.

1. *Mean absolute percent error (MAPE)*. This is the most common measure used for evaluation of postcensal population estimates. It is the mean of the absolute percent differences (i.e., disregarding signs) between the estimates and the census counts over all the areas in a set. Specifically, the percentage difference between each postcensal estimate and the corresponding census count is calculated, using the census counts as the standard, the signs are disregarded, and then the mean of the percents over all areas in the set is calculated. This measure gives equal weight to each percentage in the set; hence, it is described as an *unweighted* mean.

$$P_u = \Sigma |P_i| \div n \qquad (14)$$

where P_u denotes the mean absolute percent error for a particular method, $|P_i|$ denotes the absolute percent error for the method for each area in the set, and n is number of areas in the set. Each P_i is computed as

$$P_i = [(p_i - p_c) \div p_c] \star 100 \qquad (15)$$

where p_i and p_c are the population estimate and the census count for a particular area, respectively.[21]

A *weighted* mean absolute percentage error can be calculated by adding the absolute errors (i.e., disregarding signs) over the data set and dividing by the total census population for all areas in the set. Such a measure can be larger or smaller than the unweighted mean absolute percentage error (MAPE), depending on the relation between the size of the error and the size of the area. The weighted mean is usually smaller because, as will be shown, the larger areas tend to have the smaller errors. The equation for the weighted mean absolute percent error is

$$P_v = \sum \left| \frac{p_i - p_c}{p_c} \right| p_c \div \sum p_c \star 100 = \sum \frac{|p_i - p_c|}{\sum p_c} \star 100 \qquad (16)$$

2. *Mean algebraic percent error* (MALPE). This measure differs from the mean absolute percent error in taking account of the signs of the percent differences. Both an unweighted and a weighted mean can be computed. The unweighted measure, which gives each percent equal weight, is the common form of the measure:

$$P_w = \left[\sum (p_i - p_c) \div p_c \right] \div n \star 100 = \sum P_i \div n \qquad (17)$$

The weighted mean algebraic percent error can be derived by summing the postcensal estimates and summing the census counts over all areas in the set, taking the difference between them, and dividing by the sum of the census counts. It weights the percent differences according to the size of the population.

Much of the error is "washed out" by this measure, since positive errors (i.e., an excess of the estimate over the census count) and negative errors (i.e., an excess of the census count over the estimate) offset one another to a large degree. The value of P_w is always algebraically less than the value of P_u. P_w may be seen as a measure of net error or bias in the estimates. If the sign of the result is positive, the method has an upward bias, and if the sign of the result is negative, the method has a downward bias.[22]

3. *Proportion of positive differences.* The simplest way to determine whether a particular method is biased upward or downward is to count the number of areas with positive errors and divide it by the total number of areas in the set. For 50 states and the District of Columbia, more than 25 positive differences suggest that a method is biased upward, and 25 or fewer positive differences suggest that a method is biased downward. Bias is assumed not to exist if the positive and negatives differences are about equally distributed among the areas in a set.

4. *Number of errors of 5% or more, or 10% or more.* This measure indicates whether there is a tendency for a method to produce extreme errors. Extreme errors are a cause for concern even if there are only a few in a data set and the mean absolute percentage error is small or modest. An alternative measure of the number of extreme errors is the number of absolute percentage errors that are greater than one standard deviation above or below the (unweighted) mean absolute percentage error.

5. *Quadratic mean percent error.* Another measure, the quadratic mean percent error, or the root mean squared error (*RMSE*), tends to give greater weight to the large errors and lesser weight to the small errors. As the name of the measure suggests, the percentages of error are squared, the mean of the squared percentage errors is taken, and then the square root is calculated:

$$RMSE = \sqrt{\left[\sum \left(\frac{p_i - p_c}{p_c} \right)^2 \div n \right]} = \sqrt{\sum (P_i)^2 \div n} \qquad (18)$$

The *RMSE* will always be larger than the mean absolute percentage error. It is intended at once to give a sense of the average percentage error while reflecting the tendency of a method to have large errors. Note that the *RMSE* defined here is a different measure than the *RMSE* discussed in connection with sampling error in Chapter 4, although the form of the measure is the same.

Census Standard Lacking

Some guidelines are needed for evaluating postcensal estimates where a standard in the form of a census count is lacking. This is the case for most estimates since they are prepared during the postcensal period (i.e., for the first, second,..., eighth, and ninth years after a census). The following guidelines can be applied. First, the estimate series should reflect a considerable degree of continuity, since population does not usually change erratically, even as a result of net migration. If there are erratic changes, these changes must be probed and explained. Second, the estimate series should be reasonably consistent with alternative estimates that have been prepared by independent and reliable methods. Third, the estimates should appear logical in the light of data on various demographic, social, and economic characteristics of the areas for which the estimates are made. Finally, the "confidence interval" of the estimates should be acceptably narrow in percentage terms. To the extent possible, an effort should be made to calculate a limited type of confidence interval for the postcensal estimates by analysis of the errors of a group of estimates calculated by a similar method for a similar length-of-estimation period in the past.[23] Since sampling is not generally involved in such estimates, the confidence intervals are not to be interpreted in the same way as those used in evaluating sample data.

The measures of error enumerated earlier can be adapted for use in connection with estimates for age, sex, and race groups. Demographic logic provides additional guidelines for evaluating postcensal estimates for age-sex groups. Cohort analysis and sex ratio analysis can serve as powerful tools for reviewing a time series of estimates for sex-age groups. The estimates should be evaluated in terms of the implied cohort changes and changes in the level and trend of sex ratios, and they should pass demographic scrutiny. If there are irregularities in cohort changes or sex ratios, any explanation is called for. Net migration may account for some or all of these irregularities.

Evaluation of Other Parameters

The total population of an area is not the only parameter of population estimates that we should try to evaluate. A parameter of special interest is the percentage that the area's population represents of the total population over all areas in the set. The index of dissimilarity can be used as the formula for evaluating this parameter:

$$ID = 1/2\left(\sum |s_i - s_c| \div n\right) \tag{19}$$

where s is the percentage of the total, either estimated (s_i) or "counted" (s_c). (For further discussion of the index of dissimilarity, see Chapter 1.) Some users have particular interest in the postcensal shifts in the age distribution of an area's population. The index of dissimilarity can also be adapted for use in comparing estimates of postcensal shifts in the age distribution of an area with the change in the census age distribution of the area (discussed later).

We should also extend our measures of error to include the estimated *postcensal population change* and the estimated *postcensal net migration*, inasmuch as the bulk of the population is "known" from the census or from the census plus postcensal natural increase. Net migration is the main component contributing uncertainty to the estimate. For some users, principal interest lies specifically in these parameters—postcensal population change and postcensal net migration.[24] While these standards are more stringent than those for total population size, they are also more realistic measures of our ability to estimate postcensal population changes.

Particular measures that could be evaluated are the average annual rate of postcensal change and the annual average rate of postcensal net migration. The mean error in the average annual rate of postcensal change may be derived as follows: (1) calculate the ratio of the postcensal estimate to the previous census count for each area; (2) obtain the natural logarithm of this ratio; (3) divide by the number of years in the postcensal period (typically 10 years for the postcensal test population); (4) calculate the amount of difference between the average annual rate of change based on the postcensal estimate obtained in (3) and the average annual rate of change between the two census counts for each area; and (5) take the mean of the differences in (4) for all areas in the set without regard to sign:

$$r_i = \ln(p_i \div p_{1c}) \div t \tag{20}$$

$$r_c = \ln(p_{2c} \div p_{1c}) \div t \tag{21}$$

$$\bar{r}_{pe} = \sum |r_i - r_c| \div n \tag{22}$$

where $\bar{r}_{pe}$ represents the mean error in the annual average rate of postcensal change, r_i represents the rate of change in the postcensal estimate, and r_c represents the rate of change in the census population.

The mean error in the average annual rate of net migration is derived in a parallel fashion. The formula for the annual average rate of net migration for the 10-year postcensal estimate period is

$$r_{mi} = r_i \sum(m) \div (P_1 - P_0) \tag{23}$$

where r_{mi} is the estimated annual average rate of net migration, r_i is the estimated annual average rate of population change, Σm is the amount of net migration for the decade, and P_1 and P_0 are the initial and terminal populations. (For the derivation of formula (23) for the postcensal average annual rate of net migration, see Chapter 1.) For example, if the population increased during a decade by 1500, or 22.64%, and net migration amounted to 500, the calculation for the estimated average annual rate of net migration is

$$.00680 = .02041(500) \div 1500$$

The mean error in the average annual rate of net migration without regard to sign is derived as follows:

$$\bar{r}_{me} = \sum |r_{mi} - r_{mc}| \div n \tag{24}$$

where r_{mi} is the average annual rate of postcensal net migration and r_{mc} is the average annual rate of net migration consistent with the census figures. To derive this measure, for each area, (1) adjust the difference between the two censuses to include an allowance for net census undercount to the extent possible (see Chapter 4); (2) calculate the annual average rate of net change from the results in step (1); (3) derive the amount of net migration by removing natural increase from the amount of decennial change implied in step (1); (4) calculate the average annual rate of net migration for the intercensal period by formula (24) from the results in steps (1), (2), and (3) for each area in the set; (5) repeat the calculations in steps (1) through (4) for the postcensal estimates of population and net migration; and (6) take the mean of the differences between the two annual average migration rates, r_{me} in step (5) and r_{mc} in step (4), disregarding the signs of the differences.

The contribution of undercoverage in the censuses to the accuracy of postcensal estimates and the contribution of the inconsistency of coverage of successive censuses to the evaluation standards are special issues. In general, in evaluating postcensal estimates, the census counts are assumed to be fully accurate and consistent in coverage with one another. As described in Chapter 4, these assumptions are problematic and hence the results of the tests are subject to error. Consistency in the amount of net undercount for each area in the two paired censuses involved in the evaluation would reduce the errors in the evaluation results, but the postcensal estimate would still be in error if the initial census is not complete.[25]

Results of Evaluation Studies

Because of the widespread use of postcensal population estimates for subnational areas, the accuracy of such estimates is a matter of considerable interest and importance. An empirical basis for selecting a method among the several alternatives is needed. Moreover, users and practitioners must be given an indication of the probable accuracy of the estimates with which they are working. For measuring the nature and extent of the errors in postcensal population estimates, it is useful to group the estimates according to method of estimation, type of area (i.e., geographic and political status), size of population, and rate of growth. These evaluations relate entirely to the total population with an occasional test of demographic characteristics. While evaluation of the postcensal rate of growth or rate of net migration in addition to the total population and its age-sex-race components would be of interest, studies of this kind are not available. Studies of the effect of the length of the estimation period are also lacking, since most evaluations involve comparisons with a later census. Thus, they usually cover a 10-year postcensal period. It is widely and reasonably assumed that estimation errors increase with the length of the estimation period.

Numerous tests of the accuracy of state and local population estimates for particular states have been carried out. The U.S. Census Bureau has conducted a number of geographically comprehensive tests of the leading methods. These tests have been conducted in connection with each census from 1970 to 1990 covering states, counties, and subcounty areas.

State Estimates

A study evaluating sets of state estimates against the 1990 census has not been published. A comparison merely of a single set of 10-year postcensal state estimates with the census would yield little information since we would not have a comparison of errors according to different methods for the same state and there are too few observations to compare the errors according to other characteristics of the estimates. Hence, we turn to the Census Bureau's study comparing 10-year postcensal estimates for 1980 with the 1980 census figures as standards. In that test, several sets of state estimates, differing by method and the inclusion/exclusion of an adjustment for the undercount in the 1970 census, were prepared. The methods tested were Component Method II/school enrollment, the ratio-regression method (with federal tax returns, school enrollment, and housing units), the component (tax returns) method/administrative records, the composite method (combining the Component Method II/school enrollment and ratio-regression), and various combinations of these methods. Measures of evaluation included the mean absolute percentage error (MAPE, unweighted and weighted), the number of positive errors, and the number of errors of 3%, 5% or more.

By 1980, errors for 10-year state estimates had fallen to impressively low levels (Table 9.1).[26] When the three basic methods—ratio-correlation, Component Method II/school enrollment, and administrative records/tax returns—were tied to 1990 census figures adjusted for net undercounts and the results averaged, the unweighted mean absolute percentage error was 1.46%, about equal to the best of the individual methods (administrative records) and the best of the paired methods. Component Method II as a single method gave the highest average error, 1.85%. Regardless of method, the estimates adjusted for the 1970 census undercount showed a nearly equal number of positive and negative errors—that is, they were generally unbiased, but the estimates based on unadjusted 1970 census counts were consistently biased downward, a result of the greater undercount in the 1970 census than in the 1980 census. In a later evaluation study with different data and methods, the best result came from an average of the composite method and the administrative records method—1.05%.

County Estimates

The Census Bureau/Davis (1994) conducted a systematic evaluation of postcensal estimates for counties against the 1990 census.[27] Since the estimates were published in connection with the Federal-State Cooperative Program (FSCPPE), different methods were used to develop the county estimates for different states. Three basic methods were employed: The administrative records/component method (tax returns), Component Method II (school enrollment), and ratio-regression. Most states used a combination of two or three methods. According to the study, county population estimates as a group for the 10-year period 1980–1990 had an unweighted mean absolute percentage error (MAPE) of 3.6%.

Since six basic methods or averages of them were used to derive the estimates for different states, interpretation of the results must be qualified. Even when a method was applied in only a few states, however, there are numerous county observations. Table 9.2 gives selected results of the tests for counties for 1990, with comparative data for 1980. Counties for which all three of the basic methods were averaged had the lowest MAPE (3.3%), but this result is

■ **TABLE 9.1   Measures of Error for Population Estimates of States, by Method: 1980**

Method[a]	New procedure Mean absolute percent error[b] (MAPE)	Old procedure Mean absolute percent error		Number of errors		
		Unweighted	Weighted[c]	Positive	3% or more	5% or more
Unadjusted						
Component II	NA	2.92	2.42	11	21	7
Ratio-correlation	NA	2.82	2.31	9	22	8
Administrative records	2.18	2.47	2.43	6	20	3
Composite[d]	2.61	NA	NA	NA	NA	NA
Averages						
CMII, RC, and AR	NA	2.48	2.31	10	19	5
CMII and RC	NA	2.74	2.33	10	23	6
CMII and AR	NA	2.42	2.33	11	18	5
RC and AR	NA	2.52	2.32	8	21	4
Composite and AR	2.22	NA	NA	NA	NA	NA
Adjusted for 1970 undercount						
Component II	NA	1.85	1.34	25	11	2
Ratio-correlation	NA	1.77	1.12	25	7	2
Administrative records	1.36	1.45	1.18	23	4	2
Composite[d]	1.19	NA	NA	NA	NA	NA
Averages						
CMII, RC, and AR	NA	1.46	0.98	23	5	1
CMII and RC	NA	1.67	1.11	23	5	2
CMII and AR	NA	1.43	1.00	25	5	3
RC and AR	NA	1.47	1.03	24	5	2
Composite and AR	1.05	NA	NA	NA	NA	NA

NA: Not available.

[a] The methods are identified differently elsewhere in this chapter. The ratio-correlation method (RC) is identified as the ratio-regression method, the administrative-records method (AR) is identified as the component (tax returns) method, and Component Method II (CMII) is also called the component (school enrollment) method.

[b] Mean absolute percent error, unweighted.

[c] Weighted by population size.

[d] Ages under 15, component method; age 15 to 64, ratio-correlation method.

Note: Base of estimates is 1970 census population or 1970 adjusted census population as indicated; estimates are 10-year extensions; and standard for comparison is 1980 census population.

Source: U.S. Bureau of the Census/Starsinic, 1983, Table B; and U.S. Bureau of the Census/Byerly, 1984, Table D.

only slighly lower than for the counties for which the average of the component (tax returns) method and the ratio-regression method was used (3.5%). Component Method II appeared to augment the level of error for the paired methods; when it was combined with ratio-regression, the MAPE was 7.2%.[28]

In general, the magnitude of the errors for county estimates is heavily affected by the population size of the county. Counties with larger populations tend to have lower errors than counties with smaller populations. Counties with populations of 100,000 or more had a MAPE of 2.0%, while those with populations under 2500 had a MAPE of 7.7% (Table 9.3). The magnitude of the errors for county estimates is also heavily affected by the rate of growth of

■ **TABLE 9.2   Measures of Error for Population Estimates of Counties, by Method: 1990 and 1980**

Measure[a]	Component Method II (CII)	Ratio-regression method (RR)	Component (tax returns) method (CTR)	Average of methods			
				CII and RR	CII and CTR	RR and CTR	CII, RR, and CTR
1990							
MAPE[b]							
Unweighted	X	X	3.7	7.2	4.4	3.5	3.3
Weighted	X	X	2.8	4.4	12.8	2.2	2.2
MALPE[c]	X	X	1.7	−4.7	—	2.2	0.9
90th percentile[d]	X	X	8.3	15.7	9.6	7.0	6.6
1980							
MAPE[b]							
Unweighted	5.8	4.9	4.3	4.6	4.5	4.1	4.2
Weighted	3.7	3.9	3.2	3.3	3.2	3.2	3.1
Percentage of counties with—	34.8	35.3	27.8	33.5	30.5	30.4	31.0
Positive errors							
Errors of 10% or more	15.7	10.2	6.5	9.6	8.4	6.5	7.1

X: Not applicable; method not used alone.

—: Zero or rounds to zero.

[a] Test results in 1990 relate only to states that used these methods. For example, the CTR results are for two states only, while the results of the average of CTR and RR relate to 32 sates. Test results in 1980 relate to all states for all methods.

[b] Mean absolute percent error. Weighted MAPEs are weighted by population size of county.

[c] Mean algebraic percent error.

[d] Value in rank order above which 10% of all the values fall.

Source: Based on U.S. Bureau of the Census/Davis, 1994, Table 8; and U.S. Bureau of the Census/Felton, 1986, Table E.

the population. Counties that grew rapidly or declined during the 1980s had greater errors than those that grew moderately in population size. For example, counties that grew between zero and 5% had a MAPE of 3.0%, while those that grew over 25% had a MAPE of 4.9% and those that declined more than 5% had a MAPE of 3.8% (Table 9.4).

A more comprehensive evaluation of postcensal population estimates for counties was carried out in connection with the 1980 census.[29] The same three basic methods, namely, Component Method II, ratio-regression, and the component method (tax returns), and averages of them, were tested for all counties. The unweighted mean absolute percentage error (MAPE) for the average of the three methods was 4.2%, a result equal to or better than those for the paired or individual methods (Table 9.2). All methods gave results that were sharply biased downward, apparently because of the relatively greater undercount in the 1970 census than in the 1980 census. When the 1970 census was adjusted for the undercount, the value of MAPE for the average of the three methods fell to 3.8%, again a value equal to or better than the paired or individual methods.

TABLE 9.3   Measures of Error for Population Estimates of Counties, by Size: 1990

Size in 1980	Mean absolute percent error[a]		Mean algebraic percent error[a]	Root mean squared error[b]	Median absolute percent error
	Unweighted	Weighted[c]			
All counties	3.6	2.3	1.8	4.9	2.7
100,000 and over	2.0	1.8	0.6	2.8	1.6
50,000–100,000	2.8	2.8	1.2	3.8	2.1
20,000–50,000	3.4	3.3	2.2	4.5	2.8
10,000–20,000	3.9	3.9	2.2	5.1	3.3
5,000–10,000	4.2	4.2	1.8	5.5	3.5
2,500–5,000	4.6	4.6	1.2	5.9	3.7
Less than 2,500	7.7	7.3	2.7	10.4	5.5

[a] Arithmetic mean.
[b] Quadratic mean.
[c] Weighted by population size of county.
Source: U.S. Bureau of the Census/Davis, 1994, Table 1.

The U.S. Census Bureau/Davis' test results for county estimates in 1980 show the same patterns of variations in MAPEs according to size of population and rate of population growth as in 1990 (Table 9.5). Since these two factors operate independently to a fair degree, the cross-classification of the factors results in a nearly 12% error for counties with the smallest population (under 2500) and the highest growth rate (25% or more) both in 1990 and 1980.

Subcounty Areas

A general evaluation study for subcounty population estimates for the 1980s has not been conducted. For information on the accuracy of subcounty

TABLE 9.4   Measures of Error for Population Estimates of Counties, by Rate of Growth: 1990

Growth rate	Mean absolute percent error[a]		Mean algebraic percent error[a]	Root mean squared error[b]	Median absolute percent error
	Unweighted	Weighted[c]			
All counties	3.6	2.3	1.8	4.9	2.7
<−5%	3.8	2.4	1.6	4.9	3.2
−5 to 0%	3.3	2.2	1.8	4.2	2.6
0 to 5%	3.0	2.1	1.7	4.1	2.3
5 to 10%	3.4	2.0	2.0	5.0	2.4
10 to 15%	3.4	2.3	1.5	4.4	2.7
15 to 25%	3.9	2.2	1.9	5.4	2.9
25% and over	4.9	2.6	2.2	7.1	3.5

[a] Arithmetic mean.
[b] Quadratic mean.
[c] Weighted by population size of county.
Source: U.S. Bureau of the Census/Davis, 1994, Table 1.

TABLE 9.5   Mean Absolute Percent Error for Population Estimates of Counties, by Size of County and Rate of Growth: 1990 and 1980

Year and growth rate	All counties	100,000+	50,000–100,000	20,000–50,000	10,000–20,000	5,000–10,000	2,500–5,000	<2,500
1990								
All counties	3.6	2.0	2.8	3.4	3.9	4.8	5.1	7.8
<−5%	3.8	2.0	3.0	3.2	3.7	4.0	3.7	5.6
−5 to 0%	3.3	1.9	2.3	2.9	3.5	4.1	4.3	8.7
0 to 5%	3.0	1.9	2.3	3.1	2.9	4.3	4.7	5.1
5 to 10%	3.4	1.8	2.5	3.1	4.0	5.3	5.7	6.6
10 to 15%	3.4	2.1	3.1	3.7	4.0	5.1	4.0	5.2
15 to 25%	3.9	2.1	2.8	3.7	4.6	4.7	5.1	9.5
25%+	4.9	2.5	4.1	5.0	7.0	5.5	7.5	11.7
1980								
All counties	4.1	2.7	3.7	3.7	4.0	4.8	5.1	7.8
<−5%	3.9	2.3	7.6	4.2	4.0	4.0	3.7	5.6
−5 to 0%	3.6	2.0	2.7	2.9	4.1	4.1	4.3	8.7
0 to 5%	3.5	1.9	2.3	3.6	4.3	4.3	4.7	5.1
5 to 10%	3.8	2.6	3.6	3.4	5.3	5.3	5.7	6.6
10 to 15%	4.0	2.4	3.5	3.5	5.1	5.1	4.0	5.2
15 to 25%	4.4	2.8	3.8	3.9	4.7	4.7	5.1	9.5
25%+	5.3	4.3	4.5	4.7	5.5	5.5	7.5	11.7

Source: U.S. Bureau of the Census/Davis, 1994, Table 5.

estimates, we turn to a study, conducted by the Bureau of the Census, of errors in 10-year estimates for 1970–1980 for the 36,000 incorporated places and minor civil divisions with governmental functions.[30] The mean absolute percentage error for all areas was 15.2% (Table 9.6). The average error varied inversely, and sharply so, according to size of area, from a low of 3.9% for areas with a population of 100,000 or greater to a high of 35% for areas with a population less than 100. Nearly one-quarter of the areas had extreme errors of 20% or more; most of these occurred in small areas (not shown). The degree of error in the estimates also varied with the area's rate of change, negative or positive, between 1970 and 1980. As with counties, these two variables operated independently to widen the error band. Estimates for areas with large increases in population tended to be biased downward and estimates with large decreases in population tended to be biased upward.

Housing-Unit Method

The housing-unit method, the most widely used of the methods, has not been included in the national tests, but a number of tests of this method have been carried out by federal, state, and university researchers for the counties and subcounty areas within particular states. Recent tests provide evidence that the housing-unit method produces relatively accurate results when applied carefully (i.e., with attention to the type and quality of the data and the choice of assumptions). Moreover, it is conceptually simple and easily explained, and it is extremely flexible in that it is not confined to a single technique or type of data and it can be applied at most geographic levels.[31]

TABLE 9.6 Mean Absolute Percent Error and Percentage of Positive Errors for Population Estimates of Subcounty Areas, by Size of Area and Rate of Growth: 1980

Size of area	Total	Percent change in population, 1970–1980									
		−15.0 or more	−10.0 to −14.9	−5.0 to −9.9	−0.0 to −4.9	+0.0 to 4.9	5.0 to 9.9	10.0 to 14.9	15.0 to 24.9	25.0 to 49.9	50.0 or more
Total											
Percentage error	15	36	16	12	11	10	10	10	11	13	22
Number of areas	35,644	3,789	2,163	2,916	3,624	3,833	3,638	2,983	4,304	4,980	3,414
Percentage positive	48	85	73	67	59	51	54	37	37	28	23
Less than 100											
Percentage error	35	47	26	21	22	24	21	24	23	24	40
Percentage positive	55	83	58	61	48	44	36	36	31	19	16
100 to 499											
Percentage error	20	34	19	16	14	14	13	14	15	16	26
Percentage positive	53	87	74	68	58	52	46	40	37	28	18
500 to 999											
Percentage error	13	33	14	13	11	11	10	11	10	13	2
Percentage positive	46	88	81	72	63	53	44	34	38	27	20
1,000 to 2,499											
Percentage error	12	34	12	10	9	9	9	9	10	12	17
Percentage positive	44	84	81	73	60	51	45	37	34	28	27
2,500 to 4.999											
Percentage error	10	19	12	9	8	8	8	8	8	11	14
Percentage positive	43	84	77	68	60	48	38	34	34	28	30
5,000 to 9,999											
Percentage error	8	20	9	7	7	7	7	7	8	8	12
Percentage positive	46	80	66	61	57	40	42	43	39	31	32
10,000 to 24,999											
Percentage error	6	12	7	6	6	6	6	6	6	7	7
Percentage positive	52	69	64	62	55	54	49	43	50	40	37
25,000 to 49,999											
Percentage error	6	7	7	5	6	6	5	6	4	5	5
Percentage positive	53	56	67	61	58	56	52	46	34	37	32
50,000 to 99,999											
Percentage error	4	6	4	4	4	5	4	4	4	6	6
Percentage positive	46	57	68	59	54	45	34	10	41	24	27
100,000 and over											
Percentage error	4	3	4	3	3	5	4	4	4	6	X
Percentage positive	37	64	48	39	36	47	12	29	25	17	X

X: Not applicable.

Note: Base of estimates is 1970 census population; estimates are 10-year extensions; and standard of comparison is 1980 census population.

Source: U.S. Bureau of the Census/Galdi, 1985, Table 2.

Studies of the accuracy of population estimates prepared by the housing-unit method for counties and subcounty areas in Florida for 1980 and 1990 were reported by Smith (1986) and Smith and Cody (1992, 1999).[32] Smith and Cody found a MAPE of 5.5% for the counties of Florida in 1990, a result substantially higher than the 3.6% for all counties in U.S. Census Bureau/Davis'

TABLE 9.7   Measures of Error for Population Estimates of Florida
Counties Prepared by the Housing-Unit Method and the Census Bureau
Average Method, by Size of County: 1980

Size in 1970	No. of areas	Mean absolute percent error	Mean algebraic percent error	Percent error	
				5% or less	10% or more
Housing-unit estimates					
<15,000	25	5.6	−1.1	52.0	16.0
15,000–49,999	18	7.2	−5.7	33.0	27.8
50,000–99,989	9	4.7	−4.0	55.6	0.0
100,000+	15	3.1	−1.8	80.0	0.0
Total	67	5.4	−2.9	53.7	10.4
Weighted average[a]		3.9	−2.7		
Census Bureau estimates[b]					
<15,000	25	4.8	−3.1	56.0	8.0
15,000–49,999	18	6.8	−6.8	38.9	16.7
50,000–99,999	9	6.9	−6.9	33.3	22.2
100,000+	15	5.4	−5.4	33.3	6.7
Total	67	5.7	−5.1	43.3	11.9
Weighted average[a]		5.6	−5.6		

[a] Weighted by population size.

[b] Average of ratio-regression method, component (tax returns) method, and Component Method II.

Note: Base of estimates is 1970 census population; estimates are 10-year extensions; and standard of comparison is 1980 census population.

Source: Stanley K. Smith, "A review and evaluation of the housing-unit method of populatian estimation," *Journal of the American Statistical Association* 81(394): 287–296, 1986, Table 2. Reproduced with permission from the *Journal of the American Statistical Association.* © 1986 by the American Statistical Association. All rights reserved.

work. Some of the specific findings reported by them echo those reported in other small-area estimates research, namely that the percentage error (disregarding sign) is inversely related to population size and that errors (disregarding signs) according to growth rates follow a U-shaped curve. They found that electric-customer data provide more accurate household estimates than building-permit data and that errors in the estimates for households contribute more to the overall error in population estimates than do errors in average household size or group quarters population. For the counties of Florida in 1980, Smith obtained a MAPE of 5.4%, but for the largest counties (population 100,000 and over), he obtained a MAPE of only 3.1% (Table 9.7). The Census Bureau estimates, based on an average of three leading methods, had about the same MAPE for all counties as Smith's housing-unit method.

Overall, the MAPEs for subcounty areas in the Smith and the Census series (component/tax returns method) are similar—14% and 16%, respectively— but the figures for the largest areas, 100,000 and over, are far apart, 3.8% and 9.8% (Table 9.8). Both the housing-unit method and the component (tax

TABLE 9.8   Measures of Error for Population Estimates of Florida Subcounty Areas Prepared by the Housing-Unit Method and the Component (Tax Returns) Method, by Size of Area: 1980

Size in 1980	No. of areas	Average percentage error		Percentage positive errors	Percentage errors 10% or more
		Unweighted	Weighted[a]		
		Housing-unit estimates			
<100	13	74.4	76.5	46.2	100.0
100–499	46	32.4	29.5	50.0	76.1
500–999	49	16.0	18.1	49.0	57.1
1,000–2,499	75	15.7	15.7	45.3	50.7
2,500–4,999	59	8.9	8.6	57.6	40.7
5,000–9,999	70	7.9	8.0	54.3	25.7
10,000–24,999	64	8.3	8.1	39.1	37.5
25,000–49,999	43	6.7	6.7	41.9	18.6
50,000–99,999	20	6.7	6.5	40.0	25.0
100,000+	21	3.8	3.8	23.8	9.5
Total	460	14.4	5.6	46.7	42.4
		Administrative-records estimates[b]			
<100	13	91.5	83.4	38.5	92.3
100–499	46	29.5	26.8	52.2	63.0
500–999	49	15.3	14.9	59.2	51.0
1,000–2,499	75	15.1	16.2	52.0	46.7
2,500–4,999	59	11.1	10.7	55.9	42.4
5,000–9,999	70	10.4	10.7	51.4	38.6
10,000–24,999	64	9.4	9.5	37.5	39.1
25,000–49,999	43	8.8	8.8	30.2	37.2
50,000–99,999	20	10.7	10.9	15.0	55.0
100,000+	21	9.8	9.1	4.8	47.6
Total	460	15.7	9.6	45.0	46.7

[a] Weighted by population size of subcounty area.

[b] The administrative-records method is generally identified as the component (tax returns) method in this chapter.

Note: Base of estimates is 1970 census population; estimates are 10-year extensions; and standard of comparison is 1980 census population.

Source: Stanley K. Smith, "A review and evaluation of the housing-unit method of population estimation." *Journal of the American Statistical Association* 81(394): 287–296, 1986, Table 3. Reproduced with permission from the *Journal of the American Statistical Association*. © 1986 by the American Statistical Association. All rights reserved.

returns) method tend to show large errors for subcounty areas, but in this comparison the housing-unit method generally gives better results.

Demographic Characteristics

Population estimates are frequently prepared at the state and local level for such characteristics as age, sex, and race, but there are few formal studies evaluating this work. Table 9.9 illustrates the results of one such evaluation. The study, carried out by Shahidullah (1994, *op. cit.*), shows mean absolute percentage errors for estimates of age, sex, and race groups for Florida's counties in 1990. It may be recalled that the estimates were developed by a

■ **TABLE 9.9** **Mean Absolute and Mean Algebraic Percent Error for Population Estimates of Florida Counties, by Age, Sex, and Race: 1990**

Age group	White Both sexes	Male	Female	Nonwhite Both sexes	Male	Female
Mean absolute percent error						
All ages	5.5	5.5	5.9	116.1	19.4	14.0
0–14	8.2	8.0	9.8	112.5	13.9	13.5
15–24	10.0	11.3	12.2	23.6	28.7	23.3
25–44	9.2	9.7	10.3	12.1	30.1	19.4
45–64	9.1	8.2	10.1	14.6	16.2	17.5
65 and over	5.6	6.5	6.9	19.3	23.2	19.8
Mean algebraic percent error						
All ages	2.1	1.8	2.3	6.2	7.1	5.1
0–14	5.1	4.2	6.2	−0.3	0.1	−0.3
15–24	5.3	5.3	5.3	4.5	6.0	13.0
25–44	1.5	1.0	1.9	9.8	3.4	7.2
45–64	2.6	2.3	2.7	0.1	3.1	3.3
65 and over	−3.2	−2.7	−3.4	12.6	15.8	11.2

Note: Some values for nonwhites in the original table had to be modified because they were inconsistent with the values for the same category in other tables or with other cells in the same table.

Source: Adapted from Mohammed Shahidullah, "An evaluation of the accuracy of 1990 population estimates by age, sex, and race for Florida and its counties," pp. 109–120, in K. V. Rao and Jerry W. Wicks (eds.), *Studies in Applied Demography: Proceedings of the International Conference on Applied Demography*, Population and Society Research Center, Department of Sociology, Bowling Green, OH: Bowling Green State University, 1994, Table 7. © Copyrighted by the Population and Society Research Center, Bowling Green State University. Reprinted with permission.

cohort-component method in which the variations in rates of internal migration according to age, sex, and race were derived from the 1980 census. Such estimates were then "controlled" to estimates of the total population for counties developed by the housing-uinit method. The estimates reflect higher errors for young adults than other age groups and higher errors for nonwhites, especially males, than whites.

Choice of Method

Selection of methods for practical use cannot be made only on the basis of the relative rank of the methods in evaluation studies measuring accuracy and bias. Other factors—such as the robustness of the method, the logic of the method, the availability and quality of basic data, the availability of resources in time, money, and trained personnel, the ease of explaining the method, and its acceptability by users—must also be considered. A method may be precisely specified by the estimating formula, but the results, and hence the level of error, may differ substantially depending on how the general method is implemented with respect to the selection and use of the basic data, the specific steps in calculation, and the choice of assumptions. When, as for the state estimates, the measured errors of the various methods tested in the evaluation studies have fallen to relatively modest levels but censuses continue to experience undercounts in varying degrees, the true rank order of these methods is increasingly in doubt. Accordingly, for such areas, if the census undercount cannot be built into the evaluation studies, the method of choice among the preferred methods should depend as much on such factors as the availability and quality of the basic data and the practicality of applying a method as on the results of the tests.

SOME APPLICATIONS

General Applications

Population estimates are used to delineate school districts, legislative districts, traffic analysis zones, health districts, water and sewer districts, airport noise contours, trading areas, and other special-purpose areas. To develop estimates for such areas, data for microgeographic areas within census tracts that do not correspond to census standard tabulation areas usually have to be developed and then combined into totals for the appropriate areas. The housing-unit method in one of its many versions is typically the method chosen to make such estimates. There are many illustrations of programs of this kind. I cite two of them. Serow *et al.* (1994) described the development of population estimates for traffic analysis zones in connection with the legislative redistricting of Palm Beach County, Florida.[33] Tayman (1994) described the program of the San Diego Association of Governments for preparing population estimates for microgeographic areas within San Diego County.[34] These areas are small enough that they can be aggregated approximately to represent traffic analysis zones, school districts, water and sewage districts, trading areas, and other areas as required.

There are countless cases where population estimates for governmental jurisdictions within states are used to carry on the regular business of government. Commonly, they are the basis for the distribution of tax revenues. For example, the population estimates for counties made by the Population Research Unit of the Department of Finance, State of California, are the basis for the allocation of gasoline and liquor taxes to the counties of the state.

Legal Applications

From time to time, postcensal population estimates are introduced by plaintiffs or defendants as a central element in legal contests. In these contests, the side presenting the estimates may have to defend their accuracy and it may be necessary in the exchange to give an exposition of the method and of the relative accuracy of various estimation methods based on evaluation studies. We illustrate this application of population estimates with two legal contests, one relating to the use of population estimates in the distribution of state funds to the cities of Clark County, Nevada, and the other relating to the delineation of supervisorial districts in Los Angeles County, California. We will then consider another type of litigation relating to claims of survivors of cohorts that had some type of adverse experience in common at an earlier date.

Henderson City v. Clark County, Nevada

In 1987–1988, the city of Henderson in Clark County, Nevada, sued Clark County on the ground that the county had underestimated the population of the city relative to that of the other cities in the county, mainly Las Vegas, and that, as a result, had allocated too few funds to Henderson in that year. Nevada state law calls for the annual distribution of liquor taxes among the cities of each county according to population size. The relative size of the cities in each county is at issue since the total funds to be distributed to the counties are predetermined. Henderson had grown very rapidly—49% as compared with 31% for Las Vegas—in the previous intercensal decade, the 1970s, and the indications were that the city was continuing to grow more rapidly in the current decade, the 1980s.

In this case the task of the demographer/consultant retained by the city of Henderson was to advise the plaintiff's attorney about population trends in Henderson, Las Vegas, and the other cities in Clark County. This would involve the preparation of a set of up-to-date population estimates for these areas, and testifying before the appropriate judicial bodies about the methodology, results, and limitations of the estimates. Accordingly, the demographic consultant prepared a special set of population estimates for Henderson, Las Vegas, and the other cities in Clark County for 1986 by the housing-unit method, using building-permit data. Data on certificates of occupancy were also available but proved to be inadequate because of the evidence of variable completeness of the files during the 1980s. The governments of Las Vegas and the other cities in the county prepared their own estimates of the populations of the cities in the county.

The population analysts then presented their materials before the Clark County commissioners, who were acting as a quasi-judicial body. The presentation of Henderson's consultant included a description of the estimates proposed and the method used, and a summary analysis of the research findings relating to the accuracy of the housing-unit method. The commission ruled in favor of Henderson, Henderson's estimate for the city was accepted for official use by the county, and funds were reallocated according to the revised estimates. In a similar complaint by the city of Henderson in the following year, presented before a state administrative law judge, Henderson lost its case. The 1990 census later confirmed the merits of Henderson's claim, however.

A demographic expert is only an aide to one side in an adversarial contest and should not expect to be on the winning side every time. There are other considerations in such contests. The other side also has its demographic experts, who may be just as competent and zealous in the defense of their work. Furthermore, cases are not always decided "on the merits."

Garza v. County of Los Angeles

The case of *Garza v. County of Los Angeles* involved the presentation of estimates of the total population and special subgroups in the population for a proposed supervisorial district in Los Angeles County, California. In 1989, MALDEF[35] and the U.S. Department of Justice sued the county of Los Angeles in the U.S. District Court in Los Angeles on the ground that Hispanics in Los Angeles County had regularly been denied the opportunity to have a member on the county's five-member board of supervisors. The plaintiffs claimed that it was possible to delineate a supervisorial district in the county with a compact Hispanic voting majority.

Changes in the size, distribution, and composition of the population of Los Angeles County were considerable between 1980 and 1989. The 1980 census was out of date and the 1990 census was not yet available. Postcensal estimates had to be employed instead. The Supreme Court had ruled in *Kirkpatrick v. Preisler* (1969) that, if population change was substantial and could be accurately measured, postcensal population estimates and projections could be employed in place of the census. Accordingly, the plaintiff used estimates and short-term projections for the county and its census tracts for 1990, prepared by the Department of Health of the county, to delineate a proposed "Hispanic" district and submitted the results to the Court. The Health Department had prepared estimates for the county as a whole for age and race groups, and Hispanics, by averaging two sets of estimates for 1987, one based on demographic analysis and the other based on the Current Population Survey, after the individual estimates were adjusted to agree with California Department of Finance estimates of the total population of the county.[36] Estimates for census tracts for 5-year age groups, race groups, and Hispanics were then prepared by linear regression using vital records, drivers licenses, and housing-unit counts. Next, the census tract estimates were "controlled" to the county-wide estimates for the particular population subgroup. Finally, the estimates for 1987 were projected to 1990 by the cohort-survival method. The plaintiff used these census-tract estimates to draw the boundaries of a proposed "Hispanic" district.

To qualify as a supervisorial district, among other criteria, the proposed district's population had to be equal to that of the other four districts (i.e., 20% of the total population of the county), in accordance with the principle of population equality, and over half the citizens of voting age in the proposed district had to be Hispanic, in accordance with the principle of political equality.[37] The defendants argued in favor of the use of the latter criterion in delineating the new district, following the decision in *Thornburg v. Gingles* (1986), on the ground that use of the total population instead of the citizen population of voting age would result in citizens' having more political power in some districts than citizens in other districts. The plaintiffs argued in favor of the use of the total population on the ground that all residents are entitled to equal protection of the law under the Constitution.

Much of the debate in the trial revolved around the question whether the proposed district had reached the 50% mark for Hispanic citizens 18 years of age and over. In one construction of the district, based in part on census-sample tabulations, the proportion of Hispanics of voting age appeared to exceed 50%. The excess over 50% was not statistically significant, however, since the 90% confidence interval on one side fell below 50%. A major difficulty in delineating a legally acceptable "Hispanic" district is that a disproportionately large share of Hispanics are aliens or are under age 18.

The Court ruled in favor of the plaintiff, accepting the estimates and projections prepared by the Los Angeles County Health Department and the district delineated by the plaintiff. The ruling was subsequently sustained by the

U.S. Court of Appeals. On further appeal, the U.S. Supreme Court refused to review this decision. A subsequent comparison of the projections with the 1990 census counts revealed that the new district was technically illegal since its population in fact deviated by a considerable amount from 20% of the county's total population and less than 50% of the citizen population of voting age was Hispanic.

This high-profile case raised numerous demographic issues in relation to the law. It reaffirmed the acceptability of demographic analysis and postcensal population estimates in litigation. It initiated the use of postcensal population estimates in court contests relating to legislative redistricting, with the sole requirements that the latest census counts for the area were no longer adequate and that evidence was available that the area's population was growing rapidly. In addition, the case involved the use of postcensal population estimates and short-term projections for very small areas (i.e., census tracts) and for small demographic components of the population (i.e., age, Hispanic, race, and citizenship cross-classified), and the blending of census sample data with independent population estimates at various levels.

The case raised other interesting demographic issues, in addition to the questions relating to the use of postcensal population estimates for small population groups and their accuracy. They included the concepts and census measurement of the Hispanic population, the measurement and extent of census undercount for local areas, and reporting errors in data on nativity and Hispanic ethnicity. Other issues that were debated included the validity of ecological correlation in measuring racial polarization in voting and the applicability of measures of geographic compactness to legislative districts.

Cases Relating to Cohort Survivors

Many legal issues revolve around the use of estimates of survivors of a population, a particular cohort, or group of cohorts, after a specified period of time (e.g., a decade) for a local area, and the share that the survivors constitute of the total current population or of the original cohort(s) at the current date. The lawsuits are typically **class-action suits**—that is, suits in which a group of people claim to be victims of injury resulting from a common cause at a common time and place. Legal redress may be sought for this shared injury at an early date, but often court adjudication and imposition of any penalty do not take place until substantial time has passed.

The original population may have been subject to a noxious agent, discrimination in the schools, price or rent overcharges, or product irregularities up to a particular date. We may want to know how many members of this original population are still alive 5 or 10 years later as a measure of the residual extent of the problem or the possible number of claimants and beneficiaries in any legal suit. We may want to determine how many of the members of the original population are still alive and living in the original area, how prevalent these survivors are in the current total population of the area, and how feasible it is to redress them at the current date.

Turning to other more specific cases, we may want to know the efficacy of a treatment protocol for a particular disease in terms of survival or death after a specified period, or the number of survivors of a cohort of drug addicts or smokers. We may simply need an independent estimate of the expected number of survivors of a longitudinal study of older persons as a check or control on the number of survivors found by the follow-up survey.

The specific details of the problems may vary, but their general outlines are the same. A population is reduced by mortality, out-migration, or emigration, and augmented by in-migration, immigration, and births. If a cohort is being tracked and intercohort events are not an issue, births are not involved and the events of interest are restricted to those occurring to the original cohort. We need to estimate the many demographic changes that have occurred in the original cohort. The task involves developing estimates of turnover in local populations by making effective use of vital statistics, census data, and administrative records. The allowance for mortality is the simplest of these to make since mortality is relatively invariant across geographic areas once race is taken into account. As noted earlier, national abridged life tables are available annually, and national and state unabridged life tables are available decennially for the sexes and major races, and state health agencies often construct life tables for their states. The greater problem is the measurement of in-migration and out-migration. For this purpose, we have the gross migration data for each county for the 5-year period before each census date from the census, and we have a variety of administrative data sets available for each state from which migration can be estimated (e.g., school enrollment, drivers licenses).

Morrison (1999) presents two examples of such legal cases, one involving a claim of price overcharges for orange juice in a particular group of stores in Los Angeles County a decade earlier and the other involving a claim of educational deprivation by the children of parents who attended segregated public shools in the city of St. Louis.[38] Morrison's conclusions in these cases will illustrate the type of information that the court can be furnished to make its decision on restitution. In the Los Angeles County case, Morrison concluded that relief in the form of a price cut 10 years after the injury would fail to reach most of those originally overcharged and would bestow an unwarranted windfall on nearly two-fifths of those favored by the reduction. In the second case, most of the offspring of the victims of St. Louis' once-segregated schools now live elsewhere and one-fifth or more of the black students now attending St. Louis' public schools cannot themselves be victims of the intergenerational effect being claimed.

NOTES

1. U.S. Bureau of the Census, Population Division, "Paper Listings and Electronic Products Available from the Population Division," Revised 2000.

2. See U.S. Bureau of the Census/Deardorff, Hollmann, and Montgomery, 1996; U.S. Bureau of the Census/Hollmann, 1993.

3. The first criterion would be met by carrying adjusted census figures forward by birth cohorts and then deflating them pro rata to agree with the all-ages unadjusted postcensal total.

4. This criterion is roughly approximated by working with unadjusted figures entirely in the estimation process. It is the way the analyst would proceed if he or she posited no prior conditions (i.e., in the absence of adjusted counts) and is the way the Census Bureau prepared its postcensal population estimates prior to the 1970s, when the "inflation-deflation" procedure was introduced.

5. For a discussion of such an adjustment procedure, see *The Methods and Materials of Demography: Revised Condensed Edition*, Academic Press, 2002.

6. U.S. Bureau of the Census, Population Division, *Review Guide for Local Population Estimates*, June 1995. The report lays out a complete series of worksheets for use by a local government in developing a housing-unit estimate for a local area in a challenge to the Census Bureau's estimate for the area.

7. Becker has been investigating the possible use of the U.S. Census Bureau's Master Address File as a basis for securing housing unit counts for any selected area. See Patricia C. Becker, "Using the Master Address File to estimate population for small areas," paper presented at the U.S. Census Bureau, Population Estimates Methods Conference, Suitland, MD, June 8, 1999.

8. These worksheets are adapted from U.S. Bureau of the Census, Population Division, *Review Guide for Local Population Estimates*, June 1995. Only summary worksheets are shown in Worksheet 9.1.

9. For a complete exposition of the method, see Donald J. Bogue, "A technique for making extensive population estimates," *Journal of the American Statistical Association* 45(250): 149–163, June 1950.

10. This illustration of the method adapts and modifies the illustration given in U.S. Bureau of the Census, "National and state population estimates: 1990 to 1994," by Edwin Byerly and Kevin Deardorff, *Current Population Reports*, Series P25-1127, 1995, appendix Tables 1, 2, and 3. Pages *xi–xv* of this report give a rather complete description of the component (tax returns) method.

11. Both state variations in the age pattern of migration and contemporary data from the Current Population Survey should be taken into account in preparing current subnational estimates of net migration. Each state has its own pattern of net migration for age groups over any particular time period, such as 1985–1990, as observed in the census. In applying the national data from the Current Population Survey, it is important to note that, as the estimation period following the census lengthens, the migration rates must be modified to reflect the actual ages involved. For example, the cohorts 6.25 to 14.25 years old on July 1, 1995, were 1 to 9 years old in April 1, 1990. A $1^{1}/_{4}$-year migration rate for the cohorts aged 5 to 13 in 1990 and 6.25 to 14.25 in 1991 is different from a $5^{1}/_{4}$-year migration rate for the cohorts aged 1 to 9 in 1990 and 6.25 to 14.25 in 1995, and their ratio to the all-ages migration rate in these periods differs.

12. For a fuller description of Component Method II, see "Estimates of the population of states with components of change: 1970 to 1975," by David L. Word, *Current Population Reports*, Series P-25, No. 640, November 1976. For a step-by-step outline of Component Method II, see "Methods of population estimation: Part 1: Illustrative procedure of the Census Bureau's component Method II," *Current Population Reports*, Series P-25, No. 339, June 1966.

13. For an introduction to multiple regression, see Rudolf J. Freund and William J. Wilson, *Statistical Methods*, rev. ed., San Diego, CA: Academic Press, 1997.

14. See Mohammed Shahidullah and Mark Flotow, "Review of administrative records and ratio-correlation methods for producing post 2000 county population estimates in Illinois," paper presented at the U.S. Bureau of the Census, Estimates Methods Conference, Suitland, MD, June 8, 1999.]

15. See David A. Swanson and Lucky Tedrow, "Improving the measurement of temporal change in regression models used for county population estimates," *Demography* 21(3): 373–382, 1984.

16. Eugene P. Ericksen, "A method for combining sample survey data and symptomatic indicators to obtain population estimates for local areas," *Demography* 10(2): 137–160, May 1973; and "A regression method for estimating population changes of local areas," *Journal of the American Statistical Association* 69(348): 867–875, December 1974.

17. Mohammed Shahidullah, "An evaluation of the accuracy of 1990 population estimates by age, sex, and race for Florida and its counties," in K. V. Rao and Jerry W. Wicks, *Studies in Applied Demography: Proceedings of the International Conference on Applied Demography*, Bowling Green, OH: Bowling Green State University, 1994, pp. 109–120.

18. Life tables for Florida for 1979–1981 and 1989–1991 are also available from the National Center for Health Statistics. U.S. National Center for Health Statistics, *U.S. Decennial Life Tables for 1979–1981*, Vol. II, No. 10, 1987, and 1989–1991, Vol. II, No. 10, 1999.

19. For a fuller description of the cohort-component methodology, see U.S. Bureau of the Census, "State population and household estimates, with age, sex, and components of change: 1981–1986," *Current Population Reports*, Series P25-1010, September 1987. For a description of a component method of making county population estimates based on census 5-year migration data for sex and age groups, see U.S. Bureau of the Census, "County intercensal estimates by age, sex, and race: 1970–1980," by Richard Irwin, *Current Population Reports*, Series P-23, No. 139, 1985; and "Methodology for experimental county population estimates for the 1980s," by Richard Irwin, *Current Population Reports*, Series P-23, No. 158, 1988.

20. U.S. Bureau of the Census, "Population estimates by race and Hispanic origin for states, metropolitan areas, and selected counties: 1980 to 1985," by David L. Word, *Current Population Reports*, Series P-25, No. 1040-RD-1, May 1989.

21. The mean absolute percentage error has an upward bias resulting from the effect of outliers, or extreme errors. Such outliers produce an asymmetrical distribution of the percentage errors. Accordingly, other measures have been developed to reduce this bias. One such measure is the median absolute percentage error (i.e., the percentage error falling at the 50-percentile mark when the percentage errors are ranked in order of size without regard to sign). These measures have more relevance to the evaluation of population projections than postcensal estimates since the discrepancies between projections and census counts for a designated projection period tend to be much greater than for postcensal estimates. Hence, we will consider these additional measures mainly in Chapter 10.

22. There are several other ways of measuring bias in the estimates that take the entire distribution into account. One unweighted measure is to add the percentage errors, taking account of signs; a positive sum indicates an upward bias and a negative sum indicates a downward bias. A weighted measure of bias is the percentage that the populations in the areas with positive errors constitute of the total population in the set of areas.

23. See David A. Swanson, "Confidence intervals for postcensal population estimates: A case study for local areas," *Survey Methodology* 15: 271–280, 1989.

24. Demographers have often been engaged in the estimation of net migration per se and some users, for example labor market analysts, have an explicit interest in these data. For this reason, much effort has been invested in refining the methods of measuring internal migration, both by census and survey methods and by demographic analysis. See, for example, Hallie J. Kintner and David A. Swanson, "Measurement error in census counts and estimates of intercensal net migration," *Journal of Economic and Social Measurement* 19: 97–120, 1993; and David A. Swanson, Hallie J. Kintner, and Mary McGehee, "Mean square confidence intervals for measuring uncertainty in intercensal net migration estimates: A case study of Arkansas, 1980–1990," *Journal of Economic and Social Measurement* 21: 85–126, 1995.

25. This concern suggests adjusting the census data for net undercount to the extent possible. D. H. Judson, Carole L. Popoff, and Michael J. Batutis (1999) report, however, in connection with their evaluation of the Census Bureau's county population estimates for 1990, that even when they correct the census data for net undercounts, none of their conclusions with respect to the sources of bias in the estimates change. See "An evaluation of the accuracy of the U.S. Bureau of the Census county population estimates," paper presented at the U.S. Census Bureau, Population Estimates Methods Conference, Suitland, MD, June 8, 1999. The evidence on the inconsistency in coverage of the 1970 and 1980 censuses suggests larger errors in the results of evaluation studies for this decade unless the 1970 census data are adjusted for net undercounts.

26. U.S. Bureau of the Census, "Evaluation of population estimation procedures for states, 1980: An interim report," by Donald E. Starsinic, *Current Population Reports*, Series P-25. No. 933, 1983; "Estimates of the population of states: 1970 to 1983," by Ed Byerly, *Current Population Reports*, Series P-25, 957, 1984.

27. U.S. Bureau of the Census, "Evaluation of postcensal county estimates for the 1980s," by Sam T. Davis, *Technical Working Paper Series*, No. 5, Population Division, U.S. Bureau of the Census, 1994.

28. The 2591 counties in 45 states where ratio-regression was used alone or in combination with another method showed lower errors (3.5%) than the 549 counties in five states where the method was not used (4.1%) (not shown in table). Inclusion of Component Method II in the combination did not help. The 619 counties in 13 states where Component Method II was used had a MAPE of 4.0% while the remaining 2521 counties in 37 states where Component Method II was not used had a MAPE of 3.5%.

29. U.S. Bureau of the Census, "Evaluation of population estimation procedures for counties: 1980," by Gilbert R. Felton, *Current Population Reports*, Series P-25, No. 984, September 1986.

30. U.S. Bureau of the Census, "Evaluation of 1980 subcounty population estimates," by David Galdi, *Current Population Reports*, Series P-25, No. 963, February 1985.

31. Stanley K. Smith, "A review and evaluation of the housing unit method of population estimation," *Journal of the American Statistical Association* 81(394): 287–296, June 1986.

32. Stanley K. Smith and Scott Cody, "Evaluating the accuracy of 1990 population estimates in Florida," *Special Population Reports*, No. 3, Bureau of Economic and Business Research, University of Florida, Gainesville, 1992; Stanley K. Smith and Scott Cody, "Evaluating the housing unit method: A case study of 1990 population estimates in Florida," paper presented at the U.S. Bureau of the Census, Population Estimates Methods Conference, Suitland, MD, June 8, 1999; and Stanley K. Smith, "A review and evaluation of the housing unit method of population estimation," *Journal of the American Statistical Association* 81(394): 287–296, June 1986.

33. William J. Serow *et al.*, "The use of intercensal population estimates in political redistricting," in Hallie J. Kintner *et al.* (eds.), *Demographics: A Casebook for Business and Government*, A Rand Book, Boulder, CO: Westview Press, 1994.

34. Jeff Tayman, "Estimating population, housing, and employment for micro-geographic areas," in K. V. Rao and Jerry W. Wicks (eds.), *Studies in Applied Demography: Proceedings of the International Conference on Applied Demography*, Population and Society Research Center, Bowling Green, OH: Bowling Green State University, 1994.

35. MALDEF is the acronym for Mexican-American Legal Defense and Education Fund.

36. Nancy Bolton, "The use of population estimates and projections in the court-mandated reapportionment of Los Angeles County," in Hallie J. Kintner *et al.*, *Demographics: A Casebook for Business and Government*, Boulder, CO: Westview Press, 1994, pp. 55–69.

37. In general, the proposed district should meet certain criteria, among them, population equality, political equality, geographic compactness, and racial compactness. See Chapter 12 and Jacob S. Siegel, "Geographic compactness vs. race/ethnic compactness and other criteria in the delineation of legislative districts," *Population Research and Policy Review* 15: 147–164, April 1996, esp. pp. 149–153.

38. Peter Morrison, "Unveiling the demographic action in class-action lawsuits: Two instructional cases," *Population Research and Policy Review* 18(5): 491–505, October 1999.

SUGGESTED READINGS

Recent Official National Estimates

U.S. Bureau of the Census. (1993). "U.S. population estimates, by age, sex, race, and Hispanic origin: 1980 to 1991," by Frederick W. Hollmann. *Current Population Reports*, Series P25-1095.

U.S. Bureau of the Census. (1996). "U.S. population estimates by age, sex, race, and Hispanic origin: 1990 to 1995," by Kevin E. Deardorff, Frederick W. Hollmann, and Patricia Montgomery. PPL-41. Population Division, U.S. Bureau of the Census.

U.S. Bureau of the Census. (1999a). "U.S. population estimates by age, sex, race, and Hispanic origin: April 1, 1990 to November 1, 1998. PE-61. *Electronic Products*, Population Division, U.S. Bureau of the Census.

U.S. Bureau of the Census. (1999b). Proceedings of the Population Estimates Methods Conference. June 8, 1999. Suitland, Maryland. www.census.gov/population/www/estimates/popest.html.

Subnational Estimates

Recent Official Estimates

U.S. Bureau of the Census. (1998a). "Estimates of the population of counties by age, sex, race/Hispanic origin: 1990 to 1997." PE-64. *Electronic Products*, Population Division, U.S. Bureau of the Census.

U.S. Bureau of the Census. (1998b). "Estimates of the population of counties for July 1, 1997, and population change: April 1, 1990, to July 1, 1997." PPL-94. Population Division, U.S. Bureau of the Census.

U.S. Bureau of the Census. (1998c). "Estimates of the population of states by age groups and sex: 1990 and 1997." PPL-109. Population Division, U.S. Bureau of the Census.

U. S. Bureau of the Census. (1997a). "Estimates of the population of minor civil divisions: July 1, 1996, and population change, April 1, 1990, to July 1, 1996." PPL-85. Population Division, U.S. Bureau of the Census.

U.S. Bureau of the Census. (1997b). "Estimates of the population of places: July 1, 1996, and population change, April 1, 1990, to July 1, 1996." PPL-84. Population Division, U.S. Bureau of the Census.

U.S. Bureau of the Census. (1997c). "Population estimates for states, counties, minor civil divisions, and incorporated places: April 1, 1990, to July 1, 1996." PE-59. *Electronic Products*, Population Division, U.S. Bureau of the Census.

General Methods

Canada, Statistics Canada. (1987). *Population Estimation Methods, Canada.* Ottawa, Canada.

Martindale, Melanie. (1999). "Overview of California's county population estimating methods," Paper presented at the Population Estimates Methods Conference, Suitland, MD, June 8, 1999.

Morrison, Peter. (1971). *A Manual for Estimating and Projecting Local Population Characteristics.* R-618-HUD. A Report prepared for the Department of Housing and Urban Development. Santa Monica, CA: Rand Corporation.

Murdock, Steve H., and Ellis, David R. (1991). *Applied Demography: An Introduction to the Basic Concepts, Methods, and Data.* Boulder, CO: Westview Press. See Chapter 5.

National Academy of Sciences, National Research Council. (1980). *Estimating Population and Income for Small Areas.* Washington, DC: National Academy Press.

Rives, Norfleet W., Jr., and Serow, William J. (1984). *Introduction to Applied Demography: Data Sources and Estimation Techniques*, Quantitative Applications in Social Sciences 39. Beverly Hills, CA: Sage. See Chapters 5 and 6.

Shryock, Henry S., Siegel, Jacob S., and Associates. (1980). *The Methods and Materials of Demography.* Washington, DC: U.S. Bureau of the Census. See Chapter 23. See also Revised Condensed Edition, Chapter 20, Academic Press, 2002.

Simpson, Stephen (ed.). (1998). *Making Local Population Statistics: A Guide for Practitioners.* Wokingham, United Kingdom: Local Authorities Research and Intelligence Association.

U.S. Bureau of the Census. (1993). "Postcensal population estimates: States, counties, and places," by John F. Long. *Working Paper Series,* No. 3. Population Division, U.S. Bureau of the Census.

U.S. Bureau of the Census. (1999). Proceedings of the Population Estimates Methods Conference, June 8, 1999. Suitland, MD, Papers available at Internet site: www.census.gov./population/www/estimates/popest.html.

Exposition and Application of Specific Methods

Sample Survey Methods

Ericksen, Eugene P. (1974). "A regression method for estimating population changes of local areas." *Journal of the American Statistical Association* 69(382): 867–875.

Sirken, Monroe G. (1970). "Household surveys with multiplicity." *Journal of the American Statistical Association* 65(378): 257–266.

Smith, Stanley K., and Christopher McCarty. (1996, May). "Demographic effects of natural disasters: A case study of Hurricane Andrew." *Demography* 33(2): 265–275.

U.S. Bureau of the Census. (1998). "The American Community Survey and Intercensal Population Estimates: Where are the Crossroads?" by Amy Symens Smith. *Working Paper Series*, No. 31. Population Division, U.S. Bureau of the Census.

Housing-Unit Method

Serow, William J., Terrie, E. Walter, Weller, Bob, and Wichmann, Richard W. (1994). "The use of intercensal population estimates in political redistricting." In Hallie J. Kintner, Thomas W. Merrick, Peter A. Morrison, and Paul R. Voss (eds.), *Demographics: A Casebook for Business and Government*, pp. 33–54. A Rand Book. Boulder, CO: Westview Press.

Smith, Stanley K., and Lewis, Bart B. (1983, November). "Some new techniques for applying the housing unit method of local population estimation: Further evidence." *Demography* 20(3): 407–413.

Tayman, Jeff. (1994). "Estimating population, housing, and employment for micro-geographic areas." In K. Vaninadha Rao and Jerry W. Wicks (eds.), *Studies in Applied Demography: Proceedings of the International Conference on Applied Demography*. Bowling Green, OH: Bowling Green State University.

U.S. Bureau of the Census. (1995). *Review Guide for Local Population Estimates*, pp. 1–16. Population Estimates Branch, Population Division, U.S. Bureau of the Census.

Regression Methods

Bolton, Nancy. (1994). "The use of population estimates and projections in the court-mandated reapportionment of Los Angeles County." In H. J. Kintner, T. W. Merrick, P. A. Morrison, and P. R. Voss (eds.), *Demographics: A Casebook for Business and Government*, pp. 55–69. A Rand Book. Boulder, CO: Westview Press. See the appendix of the article.

Ericksen, Eugene P. (1973, February). "A method for combining sample survey data and symptomatic indicators to obtain population estimates for local areas." *Demography* 10(2): 137–160.

Ericksen, Eugene P. (1974). "A regression method for estimating population changes of local areas." *Journal of the American Statistical Association* 69(382): 867–875.

O'Hare, William P. (1976, November). "Report on a multiple regression method for making population estimates." *Demography* 13(3): 369–379.

O'Hare, William P. (1980, August). "A note on the use of regression methods in population estimates." *Demography* 17(3): 341–343.

Serow, William J., *et al.* (1994). *op. cit.*

Spar, M. A., and Martin, J. H. (1987, December). "Refinements to regression-based estimates of postcensal population characteristics." *Review of Public Data Use* 7(5/6).

Swanson, David A., and Tedrow, Lucky M. (1984, August). " Improving the measurement of temporal change in regression models used for county population estimates." *Demography* 21(3): 373–382.

Component Methods

U.S. Bureau of the Census. (1966, June). "Methods of population estimation: Part 1: Illustrative Procedure of the Census Bureau's Component Method II." *Current Population Reports*, Series P-25, No. 339.

U.S. Bureau of the Census. (1980). "Population and per capita money income estimates for local areas: Detailed methodology and evaluation," Chapter 2. *Current Population Reports*, Series P-25, No. 699.

U.S. Bureau of the Census. (1995). *Review Guide for Local Population Estimates*. Appendices A and B, pp. 1–17. Population Estimates Branch, Population Division, U.S. Bureau of the Census.

Evaluation of Subnational Estimates

Kintner, Hallie J., and Swanson, David A. (1994). "Confidence intervals of net migration estimates that incorporate measurement errors in census counts." In K. Vaninadha Rao and Jerry W. Wicks (eds.). *Studies in Applied Demography: Proceedings of the International Conference on Applied Demography*, pp. 121–141. Bowling Green, OH: Bowling Green State University.

Shahidullah, Mohammed. (1994). "An evaluation of the accuracy of 1990 population estimates by age, sex, and race for Florida and its counties." In K. Vaninadha Rao and Jerry W. Wicks, *Studies in Applied Demography: Proceedings of the International Conference on Applied Demography*, pp. 109–120. Bowling Green, OH: Bowling Green State University.

Smith, Stanley K. (1986). "A review and evaluation of the housing-unit method of population estimation." *Journal of the American Statistical Association* 81(394): 287–296.

Smith, Stanley K., and Cody, Scott. (1992). "Evaluating the accuracy of 1990 population estimates in Florida." *Special Population Reports*, No. 3. Bureau of Economic and Business Research. Gainesville: University of Florida.

Smith, Stanley, and Cody, Scott. (1999, June 8). "Evaluating the housing-unit method: A case study of 1990 population estimates in Florida." Paper presented at the U.S. Bureau of the Census, Population Estimates Methods Conference, Suitland, MD.

Smith, Stanley K., and Mandell, Marylou. (1984). "A comparison of population estimation methods: Housing unit versus Component II, ratio correlation, and administrative records." *Journal of the American Statistical Association* 79(386): 282–289.

Swanson, David A. (1989). "Confidence intervals for postcensal population estimates: A case study for local areas." *Survey Methodology* 15: 271–280.

Swanson, David A., Kintner, Hallie J., and McGehee, Mary. (1995). "Mean square confidence intervals for measuring uncertainty in intercensal net migration estimates: A case study of Arkansas, 1980–90." *Journal of Economic and Social Measurement* 21: 85–126.

U.S. Bureau of the Census. (1980). "Population and per capita money income estimates for local areas: Detailed methodology and evaluation," Chapter 3. *Current Population Reports*, Series P-25, No. 699.

U.S. Bureau of the Census. (1983). "Evaluation of population estimation procedures for states, 1980: An interim report," by Donald E. Starsinic. *Current Population Reports*, Series P-25, No. 933.

U.S. Bureau of the Census. (1984). "Estimates of the population of states: 1970 to 1983," by Edwin Byerly, *Current Population Reports*, Series P-25, 957.

U.S. Bureau of the Census. (1985). "Evaluation of 1980 subcounty population estimates," by David Galdi. *Current Population Reports*, Series P-25, No. 963.

U.S. Bureau of the Census. (1986). "Evaluation of population estimation procedures for counties: 1980," by Gilbert R. Felton. *Current Population Reports*, Series P-25, No. 984.

U.S. Bureau of the Census. (1994). "Evaluation of postcensal county estimates for the 1980s," by Sam T. Davis. *Working Paper Series*, No. 5. Population Division, U.S. Bureau of the Census.

Role of Demographer in Court

Bolton, Nancy. (1984). *op. cit.*

Clark, W. A. V. (1994). "Evaluating boundary changes for discriminatory effect." In Hallie J. Kintner, Thomas W. Merrick, Peter A. Morrison, and Paul R. Voss (eds.), *Demographics: A Casebook for Business and Government*, pp. 70–88. A Rand Book. Boulder, CO: Westview Press.

Clark, W. A. V., and Morrison, Peter A. (1991a). "Demographic paradoxes in the Los Angeles Voting Rights Case." *Evaluation Review* 15: 712–726.

Clark, W. A. V., and Morrison, Peter A. (1991b). "Postscript: Should the court rely on postcensal estimates for redistricting?" *Evaluation Review* 15: 727–728.

Morrison, Peter A. (1999, October). "Unveiling the demographic 'action' in class-action lawsuits: Two instructional cases." *Population Research and Policy Review* 18(5): 491–505.

Pendleton, Brian F. (1987). "Opinions concerning the use of census data when consulting on the use of statistics in law." In David A. Swanson and Jerry Wicks (eds.), *Issues in Applied Demography: Proceedings of the 1986 National Conference*, pp. 75–80. Bowling Green, OH: Bowling Green State University.

Smith, Stanley K. (1993). "Expert testimony in adversarial legal proceedings: Some tips for demographers." *Population Research and Policy Review* 12(1): 43–52.

Smith, Stanley K. (1994). "Population estimates, projections, and expert testimony in adversarial legal proceedings: A case study of automobile dealerships." In Hallie J. Kintner *et al.* (eds.), *Demographics: A Casebook for Business and Government*, pp. 180–202. Boulder, CO: Westview Press.

10

POPULATION PROJECTIONS: BASIC DEMOGRAPHIC CHARACTERISTICS

INTRODUCTION

Uses

Population projections are essential tools in national government planning, local community planning, and business planning. Population projections are needed by agencies and organizations engaged in private activities (e.g., Verizon Communications) as well as public activities (e.g., New York State Health Department), and for small areas (e.g., Howard County, MD) as well as large areas (e.g., the South region). While we may readily appreciate the use for projections of the total population, there is almost equal need for figures on the age–sex distribution of the population. Such figures are important in themselves, but they are also the starting point for many other types of projections, in particular projections of the socioeconomic characteristics of the population. The latter in turn are the basis for many types of projections relating to requirements for community services and facilities. Projections of the total population and its age–sex distribution underlie all types of government, social, and business planning at every geographic level.

Public administration has as a primary task designing a livable future for the population of a community. To achieve this, population projections must ultimately be converted into measures of the future need for water and sewage facilities, housing, hospitals, post offices, schools, recreational space and facilities, libraries, fire and police stations, and other community facilities. The development of such figures may entail, as an intermediate step, the preparation of projections of households, families, income distribution, educational level, and the labor force. Projections of population are critical when projections or forecasts, as they are usually called, of the use of or the need for a facility (e.g., hospital, schools), service (e.g., police protection, health services), or product (energy, fuel) are derived by a method involving per capita demand (i.e., the so-called ratio method). In this method, projections of per capita demand for, or utilization of, services, facilities, or products are applied to projections of population as a starting point, as described in Chapter 11.

As we saw in Chapter 6, businesses depend on the availability of accurate projections of the population and its socioeconomic characteristics to plan their expansion, consolidation, and other organizational changes. Population projections are required for the assessment of the future environmental impact of existing or proposed developments. The results of demographic studies may support the expansion of the construction of highways, commercial building, or residential developments, or dictate the imposition of a limit on such construction. The U.S. Environmental Protection Agency requires the use of official population projections for regional planning of air and water quality. The consequences of this planning are significant. For example, they affect the timing and location of sewer hookups in areas under development and thereby affect housing and industrial growth in these areas.

Definition and Characteristics of Projections

As used here, the term **projection** refers to any carefully constructed approximation to the future size and characteristics of the population of an area. Some projections are intended by the analyst to represent merely the consequences for population size and characteristics of the application of a set of demographic or mathematical assumptions to population census figures or postcensal estimates. Many projections, however, are intended as forecasts or can reasonably be interpreted as **forecasts**—that is, predictions of population numbers. Here we follow the practice of using *projections* as a general term but, when a set of alternative projections is presented, as is often the case, we interpret the middle or intermediate series in the set as forecasts or predictions. Consumers generally interpret and use the terms *forecasts* and *projections* in this way.

Population projections for a particular area usually encompass figures on age, sex, and race, but they may also relate to such social and economic characteristics as household status and living arrangements, labor force status, educational level, and income status. The discussion in this chapter is restricted to the total population, age, sex, and race—the basic demographic items—and projections of socioeconomic characteristics are considered in Chapter 11. Projections for the former items underlie those for the latter. The utility of projections for age and sex groups is virtually self-evident. There is need, for example, for projections of the numbers of infants, working-age population, and elderly persons, and ratios of numbers in different age groups (e.g., persons 65 and over to persons in the principal working ages; women 65 to 79 years of age to women 45 to 49 years). Projections of the principal race groups and Hispanics are useful both in themselves for planning many social programs and as methodological scaffolding for the calculation of other projections.

National population projections prepared by official agencies may extend 75 or more years into the future, but projections for states tend to have a much shorter time horizon. The types of facilities and services to be provided in large part determine the length of the period for which population projections are required. Building major capital projects and planning for the funding of grand social programs such as Social Security require long-term projections. In view of the wide variety of services and facilities for which plans must be made by a typical community, it needs both short and long-term population projections. The planning of schools and libraries is short-term in comparison with the planning of an airport or an atomic plant, and the planning of the latter facilities is short-term in comparison with the planning of a nuclear-waste dump site.

The type of facilities and services to be provided in large part also determines the demographic characteristics and detail required in the projections. Planning of schools calls for projections of the age-sex distribution of the child and teenage population in fine age detail for small geographic areas, as does planning for the number and types of teachers. Planning for housing and water/sewage facilities calls for projections of the marital status and living arrangements of the local population along with projections of the number of households disaggregated by size and type.

The type and time horizon of projections influence the level of accuracy that is achieved and that can be achieved. Appropriate evaluation techniques have been developed and many studies have been conducted that inform us about the extent of error of projections of different types. These studies show that, in general, the smaller the area and the longer the projection period, the larger the forecasting error.

NATIONAL PROJECTIONS

National population projections are considered rather briefly here compared with subnational projections, since the latter are of much greater concern to most applied demographers. However, national projections are also an important concern of many applied demographers, especially those who work for the federal government. National population projections serve as tools in national planning, as the framework for many other types of projections, and as tools in the derivation and evaluation of state and other subnational population projections.

Availability of Official Projections

There are two sources of periodic and comprehensive national population projections for the United States: the U.S. Census Bureau and the Actuary's Office of the U.S. Social Security Administration (SSA). The two sets of projections differ in several respects, namely, the geographic area of reference, the underlying assumptions, the substantive detail, the time horizon, the time detail, and the frequency of publication. The Census Bureau projections are designed as a general-purpose set of projections. They relate to the 50 states and the District of Columbia. The latest set of projections, released in 1996, are disaggregated by age (single ages to age 64; 5-year age groups 65 and over), sex, race, and Hispanic origin, and extend to 2050 at 1- and 5-year time intervals.[1] The Census Bureau has been revising its projections every several years, or about twice a decade.

The SSA projections are designed especially for use in planning the Old-Age and Survivors Insurance program, particularly its financing. They relate to the combined population of the United States, the outlying areas, and U.S. civilians abroad. The latest projections include detail by age (5-year groups), sex, and marital status, and extend to 2080, at 1-, 10-, or 20-year time intervals. The SSA revises its projections every few years for use in the annual review of the Social Security Trust Funds by the Board of Trustees of the funds. At this writing, the latest SSA figures were released in 1997.[2]

Comparison of Projections

The Census Bureau's "middle" population projection for 2030 is 346.9 million, with alternative "lowest" and "highest" projections of 291.1 million and 405.1 million, respectively (Table 10.1). The SSA's "intermediate" projection, 343.4 million, is about the same as the Census Bureau's "middle" figure, but the SSA range is substantially narrower. The range widens greatly for both sets of projections between 2030 and 2050. The Census Bureau's "middle" forecast for 2050 is 393.9 million, with a "lowest" figure of 282.5 million and a "highest" figure of 518.9 million. The Census Bureau's alternative figures continued to straddle the SSA's figures to 2050.

National population projections have been prepared by other researchers, usually as critiques of the official series, which were viewed as being too sanguine or too conservative with respect to one or another of their assumptions. Olshansky and Furner, as well as Lee and Tuljapurkar, prepared other sets of U.S. projections in the early 1990s.[3] The Olshansky/Furner projections, like the SSA figures, fall well within the range of the latest Census Bureau figures for 2050, but the Lee/Tuljapurkar figures are somewhat broader (Table 10.1). The Lee/Tuljapurkar projections range from 251.9 million to 562.5 million in 2050. Other analysts, such as Ahlburg and Vaupel, Guralnik *et al.*, and Manton *et al.*, employ more extreme or speculative assumptions, particularly with respect to mortality.[4] The high figure in the Ahlburg/Vaupel set (811 million) is far above the Census Bureau and SSA figures, although their medium figure (402 million) is roughly the same as the medium figures in the other sets. The Census Bureau projections are by far the most widely used, so that the other projections are not to be viewed as practical alternatives to the Census Bureau projections but only as guides for interpreting them.

TABLE 10.1 Comparison of Various National Projections of Total Population: 1990 to 2050 (Numbers in Thousands)

Source and series	1990	2010	2030	2050	Percentage change 1990 to 2050
Bureau of the Census[a]					
Lowest		281,468	291,070	282,524	13.2
Middle	249,402	297,716	346,899	393,931	58.0
Highest		314,571	405,089	518,903	108.1
Social Security Administration[b]					
High cost (low)		300,921	325,194	324,579	25.5
Intermediate (middle)	258,681	305,924	343,389	361,923	39.9
Low cost (high)		311,247	364,576	409,117	58.2
Olshansky and Furner					
Lowest		281,768	299,235	NA	
Low		281,938	302,451	318,946	28.2
Middle	248,710	288,972	320,884	343,537	38.1
High		298,769	350,902	411,413	65.4
Highest		298,930	351,268	NA	
Lee and Tuljapurkar[c]					
Low		267,200	266,398	251,940	1.5
Middle	248,249	293,595	332,995	365.702	47.3
High		331,445	438,775	562,450	126.6

NA: Not available.

[a] Excludes U.S. armed forces overseas and other U.S. citizens abroad. Armed forces overseas numbered 310,000 in 1994.

[b] Includes outlying areas, U.S. citizens abroad, and an adjustment for net census undercount. These totaled 9,616,000 in 1990.

[c] Base estimates relate to 1989.

Source: Bureau of the Census/Day, 1996; Social Security Administration/Bell, 1997; Olshansky, 1987; and Lee and Tuljapurkar, 1996; Interagency Forum on Aging-Related Statistics, Occasional Paper from the National Center for Health Statistics, *Projections of Health Status and Use of Health Care of Older Americans,* 1996.

Methods

The standard method of making national population projections is the cohort-component or cohort-survival method. As we saw, this method carries the age-sex distribution of the population forward by birth cohorts on the basis of separate assumptions relating to fertility, mortality, and net immigration. The Census Bureau and the Social Security Administration have employed this method for preparing national population projections for more than half a century. Before the cohort-component method was introduced in the early 1930s, mathematical extrapolation was common. In that era, various growth curves, such as exponential curves or logistic curves, were used to project the population. Mathematical and statistical methods have reappeared in recent decades in more sophisticated forms as time-series modeling and stochastic demographic forecasting, as described later.

Demographic Methods: Cohort-Component Method

The **cohort-component method** begins with the latest age-sex distribution of the population and "ages" these birth cohorts with appropriate survival rates.[5] Estimates of net immigration are added to the survivors and estimates of new birth cohorts are generated from projected age-specific birthrates and the survivors. The Census Bureau and the Social Security Administration (SSA) regularly produce sets of projections with alternative series in each set, based on different combinations of assumptions relating to fertility, mortality, and net immigration (also marriage and divorce for the SSA projections). The Census Bureau product features three series—designated highest, middle, and lowest—while the SSA product offers three series designated high-cost alternative, intermediate alternative, and low-cost alternative.[6] The different series in a given set of Census Bureau or SSA population projections differ on the basis of the terminal levels of fertility and mortality, the assumed levels of net immigration, and the paths by which the terminal levels are reached.

The latest set of Census Bureau projections is based on postcensal estimates of the age, sex, and race/Hispanic distribution of the U.S. resident population for 1994, data on the level of fertility, mortality, and net immigration for 1995 and earlier, and projected terminal levels of the total fertility rate, life expectancy, and annual net immigration for 2050. These assumptions are as follows:

Component	1995	2050 Low	Middle	High
Total fertility rate[a]	2055	1910	2245	2580
Life expectancy (years)	75.9	74.8	82.0	89.4
Annual net immigration (thousands)	820	300	820	1370

[a] The number of children a woman would have in her lifetime according to the age-specific birthrates of the year shown (expressed per 1000).

A distinctive feature of these projections is the separate treatment of the several races in all the calculations. Current age-specific birthrates are merged with target age-specific birthrates consistent with the assumed terminal total fertility rate. Similarly, current survival rates are merged with target survival rates consistent with the assumed terminal levels of life expectancy. While the highest and lowest series provide a rough indication of the possible error in the middle series, they are not to be interpreted as confidence intervals for this series. The method does not lend itself to the calculation of a probability distribution that can be associated with the alternative series of projections in each set.

In the SSA projections, the population of the Social Security Area on January 1, 1995, disaggregated by age, sex, and marital status, is carried forward with assumed age-specific birthrates, death rates, marriage rates, divorce rates, and net immigration. The SSA mortality projections are based on death rates for 10 classes of causes of death for age/sex groups, assumptions as to the percentage reductions in these age-sex-cause-specific death rates by the terminal date (2080), and interpolations of the values for these categories for the intermediate years. The SSA fertility projections set terminal levels of the total fertility rate in 2021, interpolate current age-specific birthrates with the terminal levels of such rates consistent with the total fertility rates assumed, and then hold the rates constant. These assumptions are designed with the view of anticipating the future costs of the SSA retirement system. Accordingly, its high-cost alternative, based on low fertility, low mortality, and low immigration, shows the highest proportion of elderly persons, and its low-cost alternative, based on the high assumptions for each component, shows the lowest proportion of elderly persons.

Statistical Methods: Time-Series Modeling

A variety of statistical methods have also been employed to make population projections. Statistical methods commonly use time-series analysis or regression analysis to project a series of data. **Time-series forecasting** refers to the prediction of a variable on the basis of an analysis of past observations of the variable. Use of mathematical curves, such as a third-degree polynomial or a growth curve, for forecasting population is a simple form of time-series forecasting.

In the past few decades, elaborate forms of time-series forecasting have been especially adapted to demographic phenomena. In a demographic context, time-series forecasting analyzes the structure of past changes in the total population, birthrates, or death rates for the purpose of extending each series into the future. Complex statistical time-series methods have been applied to changes in the nation's total population, birthrates, and death rates. These methods include so-called Box-Jenkins methods. One class of time-series models incorporated in the Box-Jenkins methods is designated by the acronym ARIMA (i.e., autoregressive integrated moving-average). They involve such procedures as differencing of the series to various orders (e.g., first differences, second differences, and so on), transformation of the series to logarithmic form or moving averages, and autoregressive processes.[7] Box-Jenkins methods have the advantage of making possible the description of the uncertainty of population forecasts in terms of confidence intervals. Some methods of time-series forecasting correspond over long periods to simple polynomials or growth-rate models.

Time-series models have generally been limited to short-term projections of the total population (i.e., less than 10 years). While they have also been used for longer-term projections, they have not proved useful for this purpose.[8] This is partly because of the impractically wide confidence intervals in the resulting projections after a handful of decades and partly because they are not suitable for projections of age-sex distributions. Actual application of ARIMA time-series analysis to the U.S. total population by Pflaumer (1992) gives extremely broad confidence intervals by the middle of the 21st century.[9] For example, depending on the choice of ARIMA models, the 95% confidence limits are 277 million and 526 million corresponding to the point projection of 402 million in 2050, and 465 million and 667 million corresponding to the point projection of 557 million in 2050. In this respect, the projections are not different from the cohort-component projections prepared by the U.S. Census Bureau (1996, *op. cit.*) and by Ahlberg and Vaupel (1990, *op. cit.*), which show rather broad ranges in the alternative series. Time-series methods for the total population of the nation may be as accurate as, or more accurate than, the more demographically elaborate methods. Hence, Pflaumer suggests that time-series models should be used as a type of standard against which to evaluate the more complex demographic methods, particularly the plausibility of the assumptions in the cohort-component method.

Stochastic Demographic Forecasting

For population forecasting, it is now more common to apply time-series analysis to age-specific birthrates, death rates, and migration rates than to the total population. When time-series analysis with stochastic (probabilistic) modeling is applied to the components of change within the framework of a cohort-component method of projecting the population, the method is called **stochastic demographic forecasting.** In this method, stochastic modeling of time-series processes is applied to historical series of birthrates, death rates, and migration rates.[10] Fertility, mortality, and migration vary greatly according to age, so that it is necessary to model age-specific rates. The fitted time-series models are then used to project the rates and to provide confidence intervals for them for each forecast year. Stochastic demographic forecasting uses errors in past projections to develop probabilistic statements about errors in future projections. The forecasts of the probability distributions of the birth, death, and migration rates are subsequently used in stochastic Leslie matrices to generate probability distributions for the population forecasts. **Leslie matrices** are expressions of the equations for projecting population by the cohort-component method in the highly compact form of matrix algebra notation. The matrices are designed to project a base population with schedules of birth, death, and migration rates.

Stochastic demographic forecasting has performed as well as more conventional demographic methods in forecasting the population and, in addition, it can specify a confidence interval.[11] A somewhat narrower band of projections can be obtained by stochastic demographic forecasting than time-series analysis alone and cohort-component analysis alone (Lee and Tuljapurkar, 1994, *op. cit.*). Hence, this method may usefully supplement the conventional cohort-component method.

Uncertainty and Its Management

A number of devices have been used to reflect and assess the uncertainty of population forecasts. Basically they fall into four classes. These are the systematic analysis of errors in past forecasts, simulations of population growth based on stochastic modeling of the components of growth, development of alternative population series based on alternative assumptions relating to the components of growth, and preparation of alternative projections by independent methods.

The agencies of the federal government issuing national projections—the National Resources Board and the National Resources Committee in the 1930s and early 1940s, and the Census Bureau and the Social Security Administration from the early 1940s—have presented the projections in sets, each series in the set representing the outcome of a different combination of assumptions on fertility, mortality, and net immigration. Each series in the set of projections was offered as a realistic approximation to the future size of the nation's population but not with the same likelihood of realization. Alternatively viewed, the presentation of several series in each set reflected the demographer's uncertainty about future population size. However carefully conceived the assumptions about fertility, mortality, and net immigration may be, judgment is involved in designing them and a given series of projections is subject to error. This error is suggested by the gap between the various series of projections in each set. By comparing the lowest, middle, and highest series among the latest Census Bureau projections, we have one measure of this uncertainty:

Year	Absolute range[a]	Relative range[b]
2000	6.9	2.5
2010	33.1	11.1
2020	68.9	21.3
2030	114.0	32.9
2040	170.8	46.2
2050	236.4	60.0

[a] Difference between highest and lowest series in millions.
[b] Difference between highest and lowest series as a percentage of the middle series.

If we reinterpret these ranges as the range in the amount of growth projected since 1994 and the growth in the middle series as the predicted amount of growth since 1994, the relative "error" in the amount of projected growth (i.e., the range of projected growth as percent of middle growth) is 89% for 2010 and 177% for 2050. These figures suggest that any series of projections is less and less dependable as the projection period lengthens and that, after a half century, the projection of the total population may be very wide of the mark.[12] The wide range in the amount of growth in 2050 suggests that we do not know, even approximately, how much our population will grow by 2050. Many of the forces that will influence population change in 2050 have not even emerged yet.

Similar calculations relating the values for the extreme series to the middle series of Census Bureau population projections for age groups in the years to 2030 suggest how the components of change contribute to the degree of error in different age groups (Table 10.2). For the population not born by the jump-off or base year, uncertainty about fertility dominates the error structure and causes large errors in the new birth cohorts. For the population alive at the base date, mortality and immigration mainly account for the errors in the projections. The projections of these age segments of the population, especially the population in the main working ages, are much more reliable than those for the newborn population, at least in the early decades. After a few decades, however, the cumulative effect of assumed immigration and mortality substantially reduces the reliability of the projections of the cohorts alive at the start as well. Because of the age concentration of mortality, the errors are especially large at the oldest ages after a few decades.[13] From the start, the projected percentage distribution of the population by age is affected by the large errors in the newborn population and the rapidly increasing error in the total population.

▆ **TABLE 10.2   Difference between the Highest and Lowest Series of Current Census Bureau National Population Projections as a Percentage of the Middle Series, by Age Groups: 2000, 2010, and 2030 (as of July 1, Resident Population of the United States)**

Age (years)	2000	2010	2030
All ages	2.5	11.2	32.9
0 to 4	<u>10.6</u>	35.4	62.3
5 to 9	1.4	24.7	63.9
10 to 14	1.6	<u>14.1</u>	48.2
15 to 19	2.2	5.9	45.6
20 to 24	3.2	7.8	42.5
25 to 29	3.1	9.7	34.3
30 to 34	2.5	10.7	<u>25.7</u>
35 to 39	1.8	9.5	18.3
40 to 44	1.3	7.4	19.3
⋮			
60 to 64	1.3	4.8	16.8
65 to 69	1.5	6.2	16.8
70 to 74	1.7	7.9	19.7
75 to 79	2.4	10.7	26.7
80 to 84	3.0	14.1	36.9
85 to 89	4.6	19.6	52.2

Source: Based on U.S. Bureau of the Census, "Population projections of the United States by age, sex, race, and Hispanic origin: 1995 to 2050," by Jennifer C. Day, *Current Population Reports*, Series P25-1130, 1996, Table S.

The results of the limited efforts to derive confidence limits for forecasts of the national population are consistent with the view that the ability to forecast national population declines with the length of the forecast period. One general design for deriving confidence limits is to calculate the **root-mean-square error** (RMSE) of the annual average growth rates of a set of prior national projections, stratifying the results in terms of the length of the projection period. These figures are based on the deviations of the average annual growth rates in various sets of projections from the average annual growth rates of the best (or latest) figures available for the projection periods.

The results of such calculations are shown in Table 10.3. If the RMSE can be interpreted as estimates of the standard error around the growth rate of the middle series of the latest projections, then there would be roughly a two-thirds chance that the highest and lowest projected growth rates contain the actual growth rates. For example, at 20 years the projected middle rate of growth of the population plus 0.47 and minus 0.55 represents the bounds with a two-to-one odds ratio (i.e., a two-thirds chance) that the projected range straddles the actual population. The projected difference in growth rates—+0.47 and −0.55—approximates the RMSE (two-thirds chance) of past projections—

■ **TABLE 10.3 Root-Mean-Square Error of Past Projections of National Growth Rates, Compared with Differences between Annual Growth Rates in the Current Set of National Projections, by Length of Projection Period (Errors and Variations in Growth Rates Expressed per 100)**

Number of years in projection period	Root-mean-square error of past projections						Difference in growth rates	
	All	(n)	1950–1971	(n)	1972 and after	(n)	Highest and middle	Middle and lowest
1	0.15	(14)	0.15	(7)	0.14	(7)	0.08	0.07
2	0.16	(14)	0.18	(7)	0.14	(7)	0.17	0.17
3	0.15	(14)	0.16	(7)	0.14	(7)	0.23	0.23
4	0.17	(13)	0.18	(7)	0.17	(6)	0.29	0.29
5	0.17	(12)	0.18	(7)	0.15	(5)	0.33	0.32
6	0.24	(12)	0.29	(7)	0.17	(5)	0.34	0.35
7	0.24	(12)	0.29	(7)	0.14	(5)	0.37	0.36
8	0.24	(12)	0.29	(7)	0.14	(5)	0.38	0.38
9	0.27	(12)	0.32	(7)	0.17	(5)	0.40	0.40
10	0.31	(11)	0.36	(7)	0.18	(4)	0.41	0.42
15	0.40	(10)	0.46	(7)	0.19	(3)	0.48	0.51
20	0.45	(9)	0.49	(7)	0.22	(2)	0.47	0.55

(*n*): Number of reports.

Note: Past projection data from the middle series given in reports Nos. 601, 704, 952, 1018, 1092, and 1104 of Series P-25, *Current Population Reports*. For earlier reports, a middle series was constructed by averaging the middle two of four series.

Source: U.S. Bureau of the Census, Series P-25, Nos. 78, 123, 187, 286, 381, 448, 470, 493, 601, 704, 952, 1018, 1092, and 1104. Adapted from U.S. Bureau of the Census/Day, 1996, Table R.

+0.45 and −0.45. Such exploratory calculations suggest that the national projections cover too narrow a range since they do not represent 95% confidence limits.

Keyfitz (1981) and Stoto (1983) have analyzed the use of past errors in projections for making probabilistic statements about the errors in current official projections.[14] Keyfitz concluded that, if the standard error (RMSE) of future projections of U.S. population growth is similar to that of the past and if future projections are as good in quality as, but no better than, those of the past, the chance that the range of U.S. population projections will encompass the actual population is about two-thirds. Stoto also found that the Bureau of the Census' high and low series correspond approximately to a 68% confidence interval rather than a 95% one.

Given the evidence of increases in RMSEs with the increase in the length of the projection period and given the wide range of the national population projections after a few decades, it is doubtful that the projections of total population have any predictive value in 30 to 50 years. However, if we judge from the data in Table 10.3, showing RMSEs for projection periods up to 20 years for two base periods, the official projections for the nation appear to be improving in accuracy. Whether this is a result of improvements in method or data or reduced variability in population trends, making it easier to forecast population changes, is not known.

SUBNATIONAL PROJECTIONS

Availability of Official Projections

Two federal agencies have been publishing complete sets of projections of the population of states: the U.S. Bureau of the Census and the U.S. Bureau of Economic Analysis. The Census Bureau projections have been issued on an irregular schedule. New projections have appeared in recent decades with about the same frequency as the national projections (i.e., twice a decade). The Census Bureau's state population projections are designed to be consistent with its national population projections. The projection period has varied from 15 to 30 years. At this writing, the latest set of Census Bureau projections of state populations was published in 1996 and extends to the year 2025 at one-year time intervals.[15] The set consists of two series of projections, designated A and B. The projections include age/sex and race/Hispanic detail and were prepared by the cohort-component method, as described later in this chapter.

Reports presenting projections of state population were published by the U.S. Bureau of Economic Analysis (BEA) at five-year time intervals from 1975 to 1995. Only one series of state population projections was shown in the 1995 report;[16] it is consistent with the Census Bureau's middle series of national population projections. Figures were given for three broad age groups (under 18 years, 18 to 64 years, and 65 years and over) for a period of about 50 years (i.e., to 2045). They were prepared by the method of economic analysis, as described in this chapter. BEA terminated its program of population and economic projections in the late 1990s; hence, we have seen the last of their state population projections.

Typically, state agencies or state university bureaus or institutes also prepare population projections for their states. The analyst who prepares the projections is usually a member of the Federal-State Cooperative Program for Population Projections, a semi-formal union of state statisticians and demographers engaged in research on and production of state and local population projections. The group has met annually since 1979 to exchange information on data and methodology, with the goal of improving the availability and quality of state and local population projections, particularly for counties. The program is sponsored and supported in part by the U.S. Bureau of the Census.

Methods

The methods of developing population projections for subnational areas parallel those for subnational population estimates. They range from mathematical extrapolation and proration to statistical, demographic, and economic analysis, and methods that combine or integrate them, called structural equation or demographic-economic models.

Mathematical Extrapolation and Proration

A variety of methods of mathematical extrapolation have been employed for subnational projections, including several types of growth curves. This simple form of time-series forecasting is infrequently employed now, having been replaced by more complex methods of time-series forecasting (e.g., Box-Jenkins models using ARIMA methods) and by demographic and econometric methods.

The proration method employs independent projections of population for a parent area (e.g., a state) in the derivation of projections for a set of subareas (e.g., counties). In one variation of this method, the subareas' shares of the population in the parent area at the current date are applied to the projected totals for the parent area. In another variation, the population gain in the parent area following the base date of the projections is distributed among the subareas according to the gains in an earlier intercensal period. In a third variation, the subareas' shares of the population in the parent area are projected according to some mathematical formula before being applied to the projected totals for the parent area.[17] These methods are simple to apply and to understand. However, they are used now only in the absence of historical data on the components of change and other indicator data, since they provide little information about how the future population of an area develops and, hence, have little or no analytic utility.

Demographic Methods: Cohort-Component Method for States

Among demographers the cohort-component method, or the cohort-survival method, is now the preferred method of preparing population projections for states and probably for substate areas as well. In applying the cohort-component method to states, the analyst must develop historical and projected series of rates of fertility, mortality, internal migration, and immigration for the state. For this purpose, he or she must make choices with regard to the specific types of rates to be used, the extent of disaggregation of the rates (e.g., age, sex, race), and the method of extending the rates into the future. A choice has to be made, for example, between holding the latest rates of fertility, mortality, and internal migration for the state constant for future years and projecting them.

The total fertility rate may be used to summarize the past and projected level of fertility. It can be computed directly from a schedule (or set) of age-specific birthrates, or by indirect "standardization" for any area for which the total number of births and the age distribution of the population are known. Projected total fertility rates may be assumed to be higher than, the same as, or lower than the present rates. Preestablished projections of national fertility could be a useful guide for the state projections. The total fertility rates for the state may then be disaggregated in the form of age-specific birthrates and projected on the basis of some assumption regarding the stability or change in the age pattern of birthrates.

Projected life table survival rates, based on death rates for the state, are needed for carrying forward the cohorts alive at the beginning of the projection period and the births occurring during the projection period. Official life tables are available for states, with detail on race or color covering several decades (1929–1931 to 1989–1991). The state health department may have prepared a current life table for the state, or a current life table can be constructed for the state from estimated age-specific death rates. For small states, it may be necessary to group deaths for two or three calendar years in constructing the table. The method of projecting survival rates for the states could usefully take into account the projections of national survival rates.

In designing a methodology for projecting internal migration among the states, the analyst has to consider the types and forms of data available, the degree of disaggregation of the migration measure both with respect to demographic detail and form, and the way the migration rates will be projected. The sources of internal migration data for developing projections of state population may be enumerated and classified as follows:

> *Censuses and surveys (direct data)*. Decennial census data on state-to-state gross migration flows for age, sex, and race/Hispanic groups (5-year data; e.g., 1985–1990); annual national current data on interstate migration for broad age, sex, race/Hispanic groups provided by the Current Population Survey (1-year data; e.g., 1996–1997).
>
> *Administrative records (direct data)*. Current data on annual state-to-state gross migration flows derived by matching individual federal tax returns for paired calendar years (1-year data), for the population under 65 years of age and the population 65 years and over (covering 1975 to 1994); possible use of other administrative records to derive annual state-to-state gross migration flows on the basis of change of address (e.g., drivers' licenses) or change of place of work (e.g., SSA Continuous Work History File).
>
> *Intercensal estimates from censuses (indirect data)*. Estimates of net migration during the prior 10-year intercensal period for 5-year birth cohorts and sex/race groups derived by the residual method from pairs of censuses.
>
> *Postcensal estimates from administrative records (indirect data)*. Estimates of net migration for the school-age population and the elderly population for age/sex/race groups for the postcensal period derived by the residual method.

There is no single ideal source of migration data for projecting state populations since each source is deficient in some respect, either the area of reference, currency, population detail, or frequency.

Gross migration data as used here refers to separate data on in- and out-migration for an area. The detail may include identification of the areas of origin and destination for each migration stream, as in the 1990 census data on migration, 1985–1990, and on state of birth. The term **net migration** indicates the balance of in- and out-migration for an area. As the reader may have noted, gross migration data are typically available from censuses and surveys, but they can also be obtained from administrative records that can be matched to indicate change of address. Net migration data are typically obtained as residual estimates after removing natural increase from total population change; this method cannot provide in-migration and out-migration separately.

The most elaborate method of projecting internal migration for states is based on a **multiregional model**, the model used by the Census Bureau in its recent sets of state population projections. It involves the techniques of multiregional mathematical demography. **Multiregional mathematical demography**

is a branch of multistate mathematical demography that considers simultaneously the population dynamics of sets of geographic regions.[18] Other applications of multistate mathematical demography are concerned with other demographic or socioeconomic **states** (i.e., statuses, conditions, or characteristics),
such as marital status, labor force participation, and school enrollment. The
specific device employed in the analysis of interstate migration and in the projection of state populations is a multiregional life table. The **multiregional life
table** is a multistate life table describing the survival and migration history of
a hypothethical cohort of births subject to observed mortality and migration
rates.[19] These rates are converted to transition probabilities, which are the elements carrying the population forward from birth to death and transferring
the population from state to state. For example, if we assume that a country
has merely two geographic parts, area 1 and area 2, four sets of rates (migration from area 1 to area 2, migration from area 2 to area 1, dying in area 1,
dying in area 2) are converted to six sets of transition probabilities (staying in
area 1, moving from area 1 to area 2, dying in area 1, staying in area 2, moving
from area 2 to area 1, and dying in area 2).

In developing the latest projections of state population, the Bureau of
the Census employed the cohort-survival method and projected the rates for
each component in relation to the projected national rates for them (excepting
internal migration), as it had done in several previous rounds of state projections. Survival rates and birthrates for each age, sex, and race/Hispanic group
were assumed to converge to the national middle-series value for the group in
2025.[20] The Census Bureau continued its practice of projecting migration rates
that are highly disaggregated both with respect to their demographic detail and
their structure. The projected rates were applied to the base population disaggregated by age, sex, and race/Hispanic origin.

A history of the state population projections of the Census Bureau shows
the use of increasingly complex methods of deriving the migration component.
In 1965, calculations in terms of net migration were replaced by calculations
in terms of gross migration as an element in a component method. In 1986
the latter method was elaborated into a full-scale multiregional model, using a
matrix of state-to-state gross migration flows disaggregated by age, race, and
sex. In earlier work, regression analysis was employed to project the series of
annual migration rates. For the latest set of state population projections, the
projections of migration were derived by time-series modeling applied to the
gross migration data.

In more specific terms, the projections of internal migration for Series
A of the latest state projections were developed from the internal migration
rates computed on the basis of data on state-to-state gross migration flows for
age, sex, race/Hispanic groups recorded in the 1990 census (5-year data), and
the annual state-to-state gross migration rates derived by matching federal tax
returns (1-year data). First, the state-to-state migration rates based on matched
tax returns were projected by a time-series model, using data for 1975–1976
to 1993–1994:

$$_{i,j}Y_t = b \, _{i,j}Y_{t-1} \tag{1}$$

where the Y values represent the first differences of the natural logarithms of
the rates of migration from state i to state j in time periods t and $t-1$, and

b is a constant estimated by regression from the time series of rates. Next, the migration rates for 1985–1990 were used to disaggregate these projected rates by age, sex, and race/Hispanic origin. The disaggregated state-to-state migration rates were applied to the annual survivors of each birth cohort for each state to obtain the numbers of out-migrants and in-migrants for each state. The projected out-migrants were subtracted from the survivors in the state of origin and added to the state of destination as in-migrants.

In Series A, the preferred series in the set of state population projections, time-series modeling was applied exclusively to the historical migration series for the first 5 years of the projection period. Over the next 10 years the projections of migration were interpolated toward the mean of the series, and in the last 15 years the mean of the series was used exclusively. Series B uses an economic model to project state-to-state migration. Migration is the dependent variable in regression equations with changes in employment in the areas of origin and destination and in the nation as the independent variables. The required projections of employment in the states were obtained from the Bureau of Economic Analysis.

Demographic Methods: Cohort-Component Method for Counties

Neither the Census Bureau nor the Bureau of Economic Analysis (BAE) has published population projections for counties. The BEA published projections for Metropolitan Statistical Areas (MSAs) and BEA economic areas until 1996, but it has discontinued this program. For the latest BAE projections of MSAs and BEA economic areas, refer to the BEA Web site (www.bea.doc.gov).

The cohort-component method is a common, if not the most common, way of making projections for substate areas. It is *the* way to make projections of the age distribution of such areas, although the proration method is also available for this purpose These areas may correspond to political units such as counties, or they may be statistical units combining counties and portions of counties (e.g., wiring or service areas of the regional telephone company). In preparing projections of the population for counties or groups of counties by the cohort-component method, compilation of appropriate data on the components and making projections of them, especially net migration, are more problematic and difficult. However, the method used for states can be replicated roughly at the county level. Recall that the Census Bureau now prepares current estimates of county population with age, sex, and race detail annually that can serve as the base population for such projections.

Current and projected life table survival rates, based on death rates for the area under study or borrowed from other areas, are needed for carrying forward the cohorts alive at the beginning of the projection period and the births occurring during the projection period. In the selection of the life tables or sets of death rates for a current year, it is wise to treat the black and nonblack populations separately, or to weight the state mortality data for blacks and nonblacks according to the race distribution of the population in the specific area. This approach is suggested because the race distribution of the population can vary greatly from area to area and the mortality levels of the races are rather different.

The geographic variation in mortality among the states in recent decades is moderate or small within the major racial categories. For example, in 1989–1991, the range from highest to lowest life expectancy among the states was as follows:

| | Life expectancy at birth | | | |
| | White | | Black | |
Area[a]	Male	Female	Male	Female
Highest	75.1[b]	81.6[c]	69.0[d]	76.5[e]
United States	72.7	79.4	64.5	73.7
Lowest	70.7[f]	78.0[f]	62.4[g]	72.4[g]

[a] Except for the United States figures, excludes the District of Columbia and excludes 18 states for blacks, for which figures are not available. [b] Hawaii; [c] South Dakota; [d] Colorado; [e] Massachusetts; [f] West Virginia; [g] Illinois.

The mean deviations (around the unweighted average) in life expectation at birth for whites and blacks, for each sex, among the states, for 1959–1961 to 1989–1991, are as follows (in years):

| | White | | Black | |
Period	Male	Female	Male	Female
1989–1991	0.91	0.63	1.26	0.76
1979–1981	0.75	0.57	0.99	0.66
1969–1971	0.80	0.58	1.09	0.93
1959–1961	0.68	0.62	1.13	0.90

Source: Calculated by the author on the basis of U.S. National Center for Health Statistics, *U.S. Decennial Life Tables for 1989–1991*, Vol. II, "Alaska through Wyoming, State Life Tables," 1998; earlier years from Jacob S. Siegel, *A Generation of Change: A Profile of America's Older Population*, Russell Sage Foundation, 1993, Table 4.15.

In 1989–1991, the mean deviation in life expectation at birth among the states was less than 1 year for whites and about 1 year for blacks. Generally, over the two decades from 1959–1961 to 1979–1981 the geographic differences remained unchanged or narrowed, but they appear to have widened somewhat in the 1980s.

Mortality varies among the geographic sections of a state as well as among states, and state values, even for blacks and nonblacks separately, may not apply very well to some areas within a state. It is prudent, therefore, to evaluate the mortality situation in the areas under study. A simple comparison of death rates for three key age groups (e.g., under 1, 40 to 44, and 65 and over) will provide an indication of the extent of geographic variation in mortality among the counties in a state. In the absence of mortality data for the specific areas desired, however, it may be acceptable to employ mortality data for some broader geographic area for which such data are available, preferably disaggregated by race.[21]

As with states, there are at least five sources of county migration data. The first is the decennial census, which gives data, for the 5-year period preceding the census, on total in-migration and out-migration for each county (i.e., without identification of the origin or destination of the migrant streams and without age, sex, or race detail). Current estimates of annual migration for counties can be developed by the Census Bureau by matching individual federal tax returns in successive years for the same tax filer (without age, sex, or race detail). National intercounty migration data for age/sex/race groups for post-censal years can be obtained from the Current Population Survey for 1-year periods. Administrative records can be exploited to provide current direct estimates of total in- and out-migration (e.g., drivers' licenses) or current indirect estimates of net migration for selected age groups (e.g., school-age population, the elderly). Finally, estimates of net migration for age, sex, and race groups for counties can be derived for 10-year intercensal periods by the residual method (e.g., 5-year birth cohorts for 1990–2000).

A common procedure for developing projections of migration for a county begins with the derivation of estimates of 10-year net migration for 5-year birth cohorts, by sex and race, as a residual for the prior intercensal period:

$$\, {}_5^5 M_a^{a+10} = ({}_5 P_{a+10}^2 - {}_5 P_a^1 S) \div \sqrt{S} \qquad (2)$$

where M is migration, P is population, S is a 10-year survival rate for a 5-year birth cohort, 1 and 2 refer to the first and second census, and a refers to age (see Chapter 1). The more refined calculations can be based on census data adjusted for net census undercounts.[22]

These 10-year estimates for 5-year birth cohorts now need to be decomposed into estimates for two 5-year time periods.[23] In the following diagram, the cohorts of migrants labeled A must be separated into the parts A_1 and A_2, B into B_1 and B_2, and so on. Each part represents the younger and older part of the 10-year cohort:

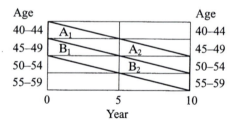

Next, we must evaluate the net migration estimates for the second 5-year period against the 5-year census migration data, adjusting the former as necessary, and then extend the data for 5-year time periods for 5-year birth cohorts into the future, preferably in the form of migration rates. The rates can be held constant or extrapolated on the basis of the two-or-more (e.g., B_1 and A_2) 5-year periods of data available.

The cohort-component method makes possible the direct calculation of demographically consistent population projections among demographic categories and among areas. As explained later, use of such a highly disaggregated method is not only an effective means for making projections for age groups but it can add considerable analytic and interpretive utility to the results. There is no evidence, however, that it adds to the accuracy of the figures, either for the total population or age groups.

A description of the cohort-component method as applied to projections for subnational areas is given in the Census Bureau's detailed guide for preparing projections of county population (U.S. Bureau of the Census/Irwin, 1977) as well as in the latest report on state projections (U.S. Census Bureau/Campbell, 1996, *op. cit.*).[24] The former report sets forth paradigms for applying the method. The cohort-component method can be applied by computer program, using a spreadsheet, and directly produces the age detail desired, with the ready addition of sex/race detail.

Economic Analysis/Econometric Methods

For our purpose, **economic analysis** refers to any method that employs economic variables in the derivation of population projections. The **econometric method** is a type of economic analysis that uses economic indicators as independent variables in a regression equation, with population or migration as the dependent variable (as, for example, in the Census Bureau's latest state projections, Series B). The basic regression equation links the independent economic variables and dependent demographic variables on the basis of data for a past period. Some econometric models use a log-linear regression equation (i.e., a linear equation with the variables expressed in logarithms), with numerous economic and demographic inputs to measure net migration. To solve for future population size or change with the regression equation, the economic indicators must be projected and the projected values must then be inserted into the basic regression equation. The most difficult task is to project the economic indicators for the particular set of subnational areas under study.

The economic indicators may be such variables as employment, unemployment, labor force participation, earnings or wages, labor supply, income, and even migration. They may be expressed in the form of ratios or rates, such as labor force participation ratios, unemployment ratios, wage rates, per capita income, and migration rates, as well as absolute numbers. The indicators may be quasi-economic variables, such as college or military population, the number of colleges by type and size, number of highways by type, number of cities by size, radial distance from a large metropolitan area, and population density of the area.

In its last set of population projections for states, those for 1995, the U.S. Bureau of Economic Analysis (1995, *op. cit.*) used a combination of the econometric method and other types of economic analysis. Short-term projections, those for 1995–2000, were prepared by the econometric method,[25] long-term projections, those for 2000–2040, were prepared by a simpler type of economic analysis, and the results were adjusted for consistency in 2000. The long-term population projections for each state were developed from projected changes in total employment, derived on an industry-by-industry basis. Three age groups were delineated and treated separately: (1) labor-force ages (18 to 64), (2) pre-labor-force ages (under 18), and (3) post-labor-force ages (65 and over). The population in the labor-force ages was projected as a function of employment in the area; the pre-labor-force ages were projected as a function of the labor force; and the post-labor-force ages were projected independently since population changes in these age groups are not reflected well by changes in employment. The key projection parameter was ratio of the employment ratio for ages 18 to 64 in the state to the corresponding employment ratio for the United States.[26]

Demographic–Economic/Structural Equation Models

There is theoretical and, potentially, practical merit in projecting subnational populations by merging the method of economic analysis and the method of demographic analysis into a single method. In the merger, the demographic model provides the essential pattern of changes in population and population structure, while economic analysis, particularly econometric analysis, provides possible explanations for the population changes and may dictate adjustments in the basic pattern of changes.

The combination may be illustrated by a projection of the population of states made by the National Planning Association (1982).[27] The method is based on the premise that the magnitude of the migration component is strongly affected by the amount of employment. First, a cohort-component projection of the population assuming zero net migration is made for each state. Such a "no-migration" population is called a **closed population**. Second, labor force participation ratios (LFPR) for age-sex groups are projected. Third, the projected closed population is multiplied by the projected LFPR to derive projections of labor supply for the no-migration population. Fourth, the projected actual labor supply is calculated from an economic model and compared with the labor supply for the closed population. The difference represents net migration of the labor force into the state. Fifth, the age-sex distribution of worker migrants for the projection period is obtained from estimates for the previous intercensal decade by the residual method. Finally, the migration projections, inflated to include other family members, are combined with the projections of the closed population to derive projections of the total population distributed by age and sex.

Structural equation/demographic–econometric models are specifically designed to identify and quantify the demographic, economic, and social factors that influence the components of population change, especially the migration component (Ahlburg, 1998; Ahlburg and Land, 1992, *op. cit.*).[28] In an integrated demographic-econometric model, the migration component of the cohort-component calculations is projected on the basis of the relation between migration and economic (and related) indicators, expressed in terms of regression equations. The methods vary mainly in the detail and form of the migration data, the choice of the economic indicators, and the form in which the relation is expressed. Migration streams are known to be related to unemployment ratios, wage rates, labor force participation ratios, and the distance between origin and destination.[29] The evidence is that in-migration to an area is strongly affected by unemployment ratios, demand for labor, and wage rates in the area. Even though a causal relationship may not have been proven or the causal nexus may flow in both directions, the relation between in-migration and these variables can be useful in making projections of population.

The form of the migration data in the regression equation may vary greatly. Projections of total net migration may be obtained as the dependent variable from the regression equation. In-migration and out-migration as well as area-to-area migration flows can be projected. The model may project in-migration and out-migration separately for age-sex groups, or it may project all-ages migration and the age-sex distribution may be determined independently. The regressions can be expressed separately for each origin with indicator variables for each origin and destination.

One possibility is to set up several regression equations, separating the noncollege civilian population of labor-force age, the college population, the military population, and the retired population. The first and largest group, the noncollege civilian population of labor-force age, can be linked to economic and demographic factors in a log-linear regression equation to project migration, as follows:

$$\text{Ln}\, M_{ij} = b_0 + b_1 \ln P_i + b_2 \ln P_j - b_3 \ln D_{ij} + b_4 \ln U_i - b_5 U_j - b_6 I_i + b_7 I_j \quad (3)$$

in which M_{ij} represents migration of the noncollege civilian population in the labor-force ages from area i to area j, i and j represent the areas of origin and destination, respectively, b represents the constants or weights associated with each independent variable, P_i and P_j represent the populations in the areas of origin and destination, respectively, D_{ij} represents the distance between the areas of origin and destination, U represents unemployment in each area, and I represents per capita income in each area. These factors borrow from so-called gravity models and economic attractiveness models. Equation (3) can be supplemented by parallel equations that represent the other types of migration. For example, migration of children can be linked to the migration of noncollege civilian population in the labor force ages.

Structural equation/economic-demographic models have been criticized on several grounds. They may hypothesize causal relationships between economic and demographic factors that are not firmly founded. As a result of high auto-correlations between demographic and economic series, spurious causal relationships with poor predictability may be posited. Moreover, these complex models have not produced substantially more accurate population forecasts than simpler ones. A special difficulty has been the failure of economic-demographic models to take account of the migration of three special population groups whose moves are not directly related to labor market factors, namely college students, military personnel, and retired persons. In spite of these and other limitations, the method has proved useful in identifying some of the major causal factors that influence population change. Analysts have worked on the integration of demographic and economic methods in preparing subnational population projections for a long time, but it remains a work in progress, largely because of the lack of data to fit the theoretical requirements of the models.[30]

Geodemographic Methods

Geodemographic methods are based on the assumption that a specified area has a determinate maximum population capacity that the area cannot reasonably exceed. The method is applicable principally to densely populated urban areas. The maximum is set in terms of either housing units or population density (i.e., population per square mile). If a maximum for housing units is established, then it is necessary to project maximum figures for persons per housing unit for different types of units. If a maximum density is established, no additional parameter has to be determined, since it can be combined with the area figure to derive the population projection. Alternative projections vary as a result of the assumptions relating to the period during which the maximum will be reached and the trajectory for arriving at it.

One form of applying the method to local areas is to determine the future planned availability of housing units and then to convert these numbers into short- or intermediate-term projections of total population. Net in-migration is calculated such that it is able to fill the expected number of housing units when allowances are made for vacancies, shared quarters, second-homes, and so on.

This method is quite limited in the type of area to which it is applicable and provides projections only of the total population. Once a maximum population for some year and consistent projections for intermediate years have been determined, other methods must be used to secure projections of age, sex, and race groups. The method is particularly useful as an evaluative tool for projections made by other methods. It is not frequently employed now as the principal method of projection, as it often was in the past, particularly by urban land economists.

Evaluation

Relatively few studies have been made of the accuracy of subnational population projections as compared with studies of the accuracy of subnational postcensal estimates. The task of conducting evaluation studies of subnational projections is made difficult by the many variations in the methods of projection and the great variety of areas, in terms of political status, geographic level, size, and other characteristics, for which subnational projections are made.

Design of Evaluation Studies

For evaluating the accuracy of population projections, the projections are usually compared with other figures presumed to be more accurate. The quality of the test results depends in part on the quality of the standard for the test. That standard may be adjusted census counts, census counts, postcensal estimates, or revised projections, available after appropriate time lags. The type of standard selected depends mainly on the timing and length of the projection period. For example, consider a set of projections extending to the year 2000, prepared just after the 1980 census. In 1997, the 1990 census counts or adjusted census counts may be used to evaluate the projections for 1990 (i.e., after 10 years), postcensal estimates for 1995 may be used to evaluate the projections for 1995 (i.e., after 15 years), and revised projections prepared in 1995 for the year 2000 may be used to evaluate the projections for 2000 (i.e., after 20 years). As an improved standard becomes available, the test can be repeated in order to obtain an improved measure of error.

Another factor affecting the quality of the evaluation results is the grouping of the test populations. Evaluation studies should group projections on the basis of factors that identify possible sources of variations in error. The list may include geographic region, geographic type, political status, method of derivation, size of population, growth rate, base year, and length of projection period. Accordingly, for example, a study might separately evaluate a set of projections identified by a particular base year (e.g., 1980), method (e.g., simple variation of the cohort-component method), geographic area (e.g., counties in three states), and population-size group (e.g., counties under 25,000). Such disaggregation aids in identifying the correlates of error and in making decisions as to the future choice of data, methods, and assumptions.

Another important factor affecting the quality of test results is the selection of the measures of error. Many measures have been devised and each gives the analyst different information about the quality of the projections. The design of the test of accuracy also may have an impact on the quality of test results. The projections to be evaluated may have been especially developed for the test following uniform guidelines—that is, sets of projections were constructed systematically by analysts in connection with an evaluation program. Alternatively, the projections may have been developed as actual working data by a great variety of analysts in many different milieus—that is, the projections were prepared in the "course of business." Artificially constructed projections are easier to compare and evaluate since they can be designed to fit the evaluation plan in terms of methods, starting year, grouping of test populations, and geographic types. The results of the evaluation may not be as informative as those for real-world projections, however. Most of the evaluation studies of subnational population projections that are available to us conform to the former design.

Comparisons of population projections with some standard such as a census are tests of *accuracy* (i.e., either precision or bias) only, but this is not the sole guide to the merits of projections. Equally, if not more, important is their *analytic utility*—that is, their value in informing the researcher or planner as to the future implications for population size of the assumptions made in designing the projections. Projections can answer such questions as how population size and structure will change under specified demographic conditions and, in particular, how they will change if recent population trends continue. Population projections may serve a normative role, identifying the demographic conditions under which the population will reach or exceed some desired level, or as crisis prognosticators, alerting the planner to the demographic conditions that will lead to intolerable population size (e.g., an oversized school-age population). Most users interpret population projections primarily, if not solely, as forecasts, however, and hence put greatest weight on accuracy as the measure of utility.

Measures of Accuracy

The basic measures that have been described as useful for evaluating a set of postcensal population estimates are also useful for evaluating population projections, namely, the mean absolute (unweighted) percent error (MAPE), mean algebraic (unweighted) percent error (MALPE), the proportion of positive errors, and the number of errors of 5% or more and 10% or more. As we may recall, the first is a measure of precision, the second and third are measures of bias, and the last is a general measure of precision.

Other measures have been proposed for evaluating population projections. Some are intended to adjust for what is viewed as an upward bias in the mean absolute (unweighted) percent error resulting from the effect of outliers (i.e., extreme errors, or errors that depart from the bulk of the observations). The distribution of absolute percentage errors for any set of projections tends to be asymmetrical, having a lower limit of zero while being skewed to the right. Since the mean absolute percent error is pulled to the right from the center or typical level of the percentages, it has been described as overstating the level of error in a set of projections.[31] This is not necessarily a shortcoming, since the analyst may want to give equal weight to all the values observed, even the very large ones, as this measure does, assuming that the large values are not contaminated by large measurement errors. Moreover, the simple arithmetic mean has the advantage of being easily understood and a fundamental element in higher statistical analysis of the distribution. Other measures should be applied if the analyst believes that MAPE is too affected by outliers, but it should not be abandoned or displaced.

One solution to the problem is to compute the **median absolute percent error**. This measure is not pulled from the center to the right of a skewed distribution as much as the mean and is not directly affected by outliers or extreme errors. For example, the value for this measure in 1990 for 10-year postcensal estimates for counties was 2.7%, as compared with 3.6% for the mean absolute percent error (U.S.Bureau of the Census/Davis, 1994, *op. cit.*, Chapter 9). On the other hand, since it is a measure of rank order, it neglects much of the information in the distribution. Another possible solution is to calculate the **weighted mean absolute percent error**:

$$\text{WMAPE} = \sum [|(p_i - p_c) \div p_c| \star p_c] \div \sum p_c = \sum |p_i - p_c| \div \sum p_c \star 100 \quad (4)$$

where p refers to the population estimate (i) or count (c) for each area in the set. With this measure, the largest errors tend to receive a reduced weight, in effect, since, as test results show, larger errors tend to be associated with the smaller populations. This is demonstrated conclusively in U.S. Bureau of the Census/Davis (1994), which gives the following mean absolute percent errors, unweighted (UMAPE) and weighted (WMAPE), for postcensal estimates of U.S. counties in 1990, according to population size:

Size in 1980	UMAPE	WMAPE
All	3.6	2.3
100,000 and over	2.0	1.8
50,000 to 100,000	2.8	2.8
20,000 to 50,000	3.4	3.3
10,000 to 20,000	3.9	3.9
5,000 to 10,000	4.2	4.2
2,500 to 5,000	4.6	4.6
Under 5,000	7.7	7.3

Source: U.S. Bureau of the Census, "Evaluation of postcensal county estimates for the 1980s," by Sam T. Davis, Working Paper Series, No. 5, Population Division, U.S. Bureau of the Census, 1994, Table 1.

As a result of weighting the percentage errors by population size, the overall error drops from 3.6% to 2.3%. The weighted MAPE is close to but below the median absolute percent error and may have made an excessive correction.

A variety of **symmetrical mean absolute percent errors** (SMAPE) can be derived by a transformation of the percentage errors used in calculating MAPE. A linear transformation may attempt to reduce the bias resulting from outliers by dividing the absolute amount of error for each area in the set by an average of the projection and the standard (e.g., census count) rather than the standard alone:

$$P_{su} = \frac{|p_i - p_c|}{(p_i + p_c) \div 2} \star 100 \tag{5}$$

$$SMAPE_1 = \sum |P_{su}| \div n \tag{6}$$

where P_{su} represents the modified absolute percentage error and the other symbols are the same as defined previously. For example, a projection of 11,000 for a census date and a census value of 10,000 yield a percentage error of +10.0%. The averaging of the estimate and the census count in the base of the measure yields a percentage error of 9.5%. However, such averaging reduces only those percentage errors where the projection exceeds the census. Hence, it is not a dependable measure for achieving a symmetrical distribution of errors. Moreover, it appears to involve an arbitrary tampering with the basic results.

Other measures designed to reduce the value of MAPE involve a nonlinear transformation (e.g., logarithmic, square root, cube root) of the projections and the standard figures before the percentage error is computed. The SMAPE formula for the logarithmic transformation is as follows:

$$SMAPE_2 = e^{\sum [|(\ln p_i - \ln p_c)| \div \ln p_c] \div n} \tag{7}$$

This and the other nonlinear transformations compress the individual errors while maintaining their original rank order. The process produces a more typical, or "valid," mean absolute percentage error according to Tayman and Swanson (1999, *op. cit.*) and Tayman *et al.* (1999, *op. cit.*).[32]

As was the case for national population projections, proposals have been made to apply more stringent tests in measuring the accuracy of subnational projections (Keyfitz, 1972; Stoto, 1983; and Stoto and Schrier, 1982).[33] Such tests focus on the *change* in the population since the base date on the ground that it is this change that the analyst has as his or her task to forecast. The change can be evaluated as an overall percentage or as an average annual rate. One way of focusing on the projected change in measuring error is to take the difference (Δr_i) between the projected average annual rate of increase (r_i) and the actual average annual rate of increase (r_c) for a projection period:

$$\Delta r_i = r_i - r_c \tag{8}$$

Stoto (1983, *op. cit.*) and Stoto and Schrier (1982, *op. cit.*) employed this measure in evaluating projections of state populations.

Alternatively, the amount of improvement in the projection achieved by careful analysis over merely accepting the last census figure or postcensal estimate as the projection can be compared with the actual change since the last census or postcensal estimate. Tayman and Swanson (1996) applied such a measure to the evaluation of projections for counties and census tracts in a selected number of states and SMSAs.[34] Their measure is called the **proportionate reduction in error** (PRE). It is calculated as the percentage deviation of (a) the percentage error in the base population (i.e., census or postcensal estimate) considered as the forecast, from (b) the percentage error in the actual forecast. The denominator of their measure is (a), the percentage error in the base population considered as the forecast. The formula is

$$\text{PRE} = [(a) - (b)] \div (a) = [(C_0 - C_1) \div C_1]$$
$$- [(P_1 - C_1) \div C_1] \div [(C_0 - C_1) \div C_1] \tag{9}$$

where C_0 represents the last census count assumed to be the forecast, C_1 the actual population, and P_1 represents the actual forecast. The formula reduces to

$$\text{PRE} = (C_0 - P_1) \div (C_0 - C_1) \tag{10}$$

Because the denominator can be extremely small, even approximating zero, a more stable measure is needed. We can simply take the difference between the base estimate or assumed forecast (C_0) and the actual forecast (P_1) as a percent of the actual population (C_1):

$$\text{Adjusted PRE} = (C_0 - P_1) \div C_1 \tag{11}$$

Such a measure captures the gain in accuracy, if any, of the analytic forecast over the "nonforecast" forecast and avoids the instability of the Tayman/Swanson measure.

Results of Evaluation Studies

In 1982, Stoto and Schrier carried out a comprehensive evaluation of projections of state population. The study covers several sets of projections for states from 1950 to 1980, including sets of economic projections prepared by the Bureau of Economic Analysis, sets of demographic projections prepared by the Bureau of the Census, and sets of mathematical projections prepared by Stoto and Schrier themselves. The latter are geometric extrapolations of total population (i.e., they assume that the recent rate of population growth will remain constant). The measure of error is the difference (Δr_i) between the projected growth rate and the actual growth rate, as described earlier.

Summary measures of error, based on Δr_i, for 5- and 10-year Census Bureau projections and geometric projections of state population, are as follows:

Projection method	Duration	N	Bias	RMSE
Geometric	5 years	240	−0.067	1.032
Geometric	10 years	192	+0.252	0.906
Census	5 years	288	−0.200	0.896
Census	10 years	192	−0.143	0.861

Source: Stoto and Schrier (1982, *op. cit.*).

For the 5- and 10-year periods from 1955 to 1980, the census projections and the geometric projections are relatively unbiased and the root mean square errors (RMSE) are rather similar. With the removal of two outlier points, the 5- and 10-year projections are about equally accurate. In terms of summary measures based on Δr_i, simple geometric extrapolation is almost as accurate as the more complex Census methodology.

Summary measures based on Δr_i for two (merged) 5-year OBERS (BEA) projections and for the corresponding Census and geometric projections are as follows:

Projection method	Duration	N	Bias	RMSE
Geometric	5 years	96	−0.251	0.816
Census	5 years	192	−0.318	0.832
OBERS	5 years	96	−0.465	1.798

Source: Stoto and Schrier (1982, *op. cit.*).

On the basis of Δr_i, the OBERS (BEA) projections are more biased, on average, than the other two sets of projections and the RMSE for the OBERS projections is more than twice as large as for the other sets. Evidently, the added economic detail in the OBERS model did not increase, but substantially decreased, the accuracy of the model for population projections.

In addition to methodology, other factors appear to be associated with bias and variance in population projections in the Stoto-Schrier study. One factor is the rate of growth; large errors are associated with rapidly growing geographic areas for all three projection methods. A second factor, closely linked to the first, is geographic "region." There are significant differences in accuracy among the nine geographic divisions for all three projection methods, associated presumably with the very different amounts and patterns of migration and population growth of the divisions. A third factor is jump-off or base year; all the projections made at a certain time tend to err in the same direction.

Stoto presented an analysis (1983) of Long's data (1977), which consist of four sets of population projections for the 50 states from 1970 to 1975.[35] The first set was prepared at the U.S. Census Bureau by the method of demographic analysis. Two sets, those of the National Planning Association and those of the Bureau of Economic Analysis, employ economic variables and assumptions, and the fourth set, also prepared by the Census Bureau, was developed by the method of demographic analysis but assumes no internal migration. The algebraic mean of the Δr_i's, measuring bias in the projected annual average growth rates, and the standard deviation of the rates, measuring precision, for each of these sets of projections, are as follows:

Set of projections	Bias	Standard deviation	Sample size
Census, series I-E	−.23	.92	50
National Planning Association	−.09	.76	50
Bureau of Economic Analysis	−.41	.93	50
Census, series III-E	−.16	.95	50

Source: Stoto (1983, *op. cit.*).

These projections are all biased downward and are much less accurate than projections for the United States as a whole, according to Stoto's test calculations. Subnational projections are one-half to one-third as accurate (in terms of standard deviation) as national projections.

We turn next to Long's evaluation (1994) of a historical series of state population projections, with various base years from 1965 to 1986, in terms of the mean absolute percent error (Table 10.4).[36] The results distinguish the

■ **TABLE 10.4   Mean Absolute Percent Error of Census Bureau State Population Projections, with Base Years, 1965 to 1986, by Length of Projection Period**

Base year and series	Length of projection period			
	5	10	15	20
1965				
Constant growth (1960–1965)	4.12	6.55	10.88	14.67
Census projections—migrant pool method				
P-25, No. 375, Series I-B	3.19	5.35	9.62	13.37
P-25, No. 375, Series II-B	3.20	5.32	9.85	11.96
P-25, No. 375, Series I-D	3.1	5.8	9.2	11.6
*P-25, No. 375, Series II-D	3	5.6	8.9	11.2
1970				
Constant growth (1960–1970)	4.53	8.17	10.64	11.41
Census projections—migrant pool method				
P-25, No. 477, Series I-C	5.00	9.32	12.29	14.02
P-25, No. 477, Series III-C	4.63	8.99	13.06	17.02
*P-25, No. 477, Series I-E	5.18	9.72	12.54	13.86
P-25, No. 477, Series III-E	4.74	8.95	11.67	14.37
1975				
Constant growth (1970–1975)	3.12	3.43	6.20	
Census projections–migrant pool method				
P-25, No. 796, Series II-A	4.7	6.4	6.5	
*P-25, No. 796, Series II-B	3.8	4.5	5.6	
1980				
Constant growth (1970–1980)	3.79	8.18		
Census projection—net migration method				
*P-25, No. 397	3.2	6.7		
1986				
Constant growth (1980–1986)	3.74			
Census projection—multistate method				
*P-25, No. 1017	2.6			

* The "preferred" series as indicated in the original text.

Source: John Long, "Complexity, accuracy, and utility of official population projections," *Mathematical Population Studies* 5: 203–216, 1995.

length of the projection period and include comparative data using the geometric method. This study shows that, as expected, as the length of the projection period increases, the accuracy of the projections declines sharply. Furthermore, complexity does not consistently add to accuracy and in some cases simple geometric projection is superior to complex cohort-component projections. Long surmises that data lag—that is, the lengthy delay in securing and incorporating decennial census data on migration into the demographic projections—is one possible explanation for this pattern of results. However, the geometric method is useful only for forecasting total population, not age composition. For the latter, the component method, or at least a proration method in combination with national age totals, is necessary. A possible conclusion is that, if one is interested only in the total population or the population growth rate, and in the accuracy of the results, a complex model is not necessary. After a short time lag, the same is likely to be true for age groups because of the major role of migration, although formal evidence is lacking. For many of the analytic and managerial purposes that official population projections are intended to serve, however, the complex models are quite useful, even if they are not more accurate.

Smith and Sincich (1992) evaluated a number of different methods of making state population projections according to the length of the projection period, using MAPE and MALPE with the 1990 census as the standard.[37] The methods included mathematical extrapolation, proration methods, time-series analysis, the cohort-component method, and economic analysis. Some sets of projections were drawn from official studies and others were prepared by the authors. The results regarding precision are strikingly clear. All methods showed about the same level of error within each length-of-projection period from 5 to 20 years (except exponential growth in 20 years), and the errors increased progressively with the length of the projection period (Table 10.5). In 20 years exponential extrapolation was biased sharply upward and time-series analysis was biased sharply downward.

For evaluation results relating to counties and census tracts, we consider a study conducted by Tayman and Swanson (1996, *op. cit.*) that summarizes errors for census tracts in three SMSAs and for counties in seven states, in terms of MAPE and MALPE. As shown in Table 10.6, according to MALPE the bias is low in all areas except Detroit's census tracts and the counties in Wyoming and North Dakota. In areas with the highest growth rates (counties in Washington and Florida; census tracts in the San Diego SMSA), the MALPEs are negative. This indicates that the analysts could not anticipate the full extent of the population increase. The level of the bias is not related to whether the area is a county or a census tract.

When MAPE is considered, the forecasts for counties are more precise than the forecasts for census tracts (except the counties in North Dakota). On measuring the relative improvement in the forecasts for 1990 over holding the 1980 census constant, the results show that the efforts to make actual projections usually paid off (e.g., counties in Washington), but not always (e.g., census tracts in Detroit). In 3 of the 10 comparisons, making "designer" forecasts reduces forecast precision, and in 6 of the 10 comparisons, making "designer" forecasts increases forecast bias! This occurs both for the counties and the census tracts. For both counties and census tracts, a strong direct relationship emerges between population size and the contribution of the forecast to the reduction of forecast error as compared with holding the last census constant (not shown in table). Forecasting did not do well when the areas had low, zero, and negative growth rates.

Analytic Utility of Projections

As noted earlier, accuracy of forecasts is only one criterion for judging the merits of a set of population projections for small areas. Subnational projections generally have a questionable, if not a poor, record on accuracy as shown by the standard evaluation measures. Yet they can be very valuable tools for understanding future population changes and hence for planning area facilities

TABLE 10.5 Mean Absolute Percent Error (MAPE) and Mean Algebraic Percent Error (MALPE) for State Population Projections, by Method and Length of Projection Period (Standard = 1990 Census)

Measure and method	Length of projection period (years)			
	5	10	15	20
MAPE[a]				
Line	3.5	6.0	8.0	11.3
Expo	3.9	7.0	10.6	16.2
ARIMA	3.3	6.3	9.1	11.5
Shift	3.8	6.4	9.2	13.4
Share	3.6	6.0	8.2	11.7
Census Bureau	3.7	6.1	8.3	12.4
NPA	4.3	6.8	8.4	NA
OBERS	4.0	6.5	9.1	12.8
MALPE[b]				
Line	0.1	−0.5	−1.1	−1.9
Expo	1.2	2.4	4.3	7.8
ARIMA	−1.1	−2.8	−4.4	−6.0
Shift	0.4	0.2	−0.2	−0.8
Share	0.4	0.2	0.2	0.4
Census Bureau	−0.7	−1.1	−0.4	2.4
NPA	−2.4	−0.9	−0.6	NA
OBERS	1.7	−3.6	−2.6	−4.9

NA: Not available.

[a] Unweighted mean disregarding signs.

[b] Unweighted mean regarding signs.

Definitions: Base periods vary from one set of projections to another.

Line: Linear extrapolation (constant amount of change)

Expo: Exponential extrapolation (constant rate of change)

ARIMA: Autoregressive integrated moving-average time-series model of population change

Shift: Constant annual average amount of change in each state's share of national population

Share: Constant state share af national growth

Census Bureau: Cohort-component method

NPA: National Planning Association structural model relating migration to projections of employment

OBERS: Office of Business Economics (Department of Commerce) and Economic Research Service (Department of Agriculture) structural model relating migration to projections of employment

Source: Adapted from Exhibit 2 and text in Stanley K. Smith and Terry Sincich, "Evaluating forecast accuracy and bias of alternative population projections for states," *International Journal of Forecasting* 8(3): 495–508, Special Issue, Dennis A. Ahlburg and Kenneth C. Land (eds.), *Population Forecasting*, November 1992. © 1992. Reprinted with permission from Elsevier Science.

and services. Earlier we referred to this use of projections as their analytical utility—a concept explored further in this section.

Preparation of projections continuing recent growth trends for a set of areas and preparation of alternative series of projections are ways of exploiting projections for their analytical utility. A set of projections continuing recent growth trends, carefully defined, may focus attention on the probable pressure on existing resources in the years to come unless the available resources

■ **TABLE 10.6** Measures of Precision (MAPE), Bias (MALPE), and Error Reduction (ER) for 10-Year Population Projections for Census Tracts in Three SMSAs and for Counties in Seven States 1990

Area	MAPE Actual projection[a]	MAPE Base population as projection[b]	MAPE Error reduction[c]	MALPE Actual projection[a]	MALPE Base population as projection[b]	MALPE Error reduction[c]
Census tract						
Detroit	28.5	23.3	−5.2	+20.1	+9.4	−10.7
Dallas-Ft. Worth	18.6	25.3	+6.7	+5.8	−3.3	−9.1
San Diego	20.9	21.5	+0.6	−3.6	−18.9	−15.3
County						
Iowa	8.0	10.0	+2.0	+7.4	+9.4	+2.0
Wyoming	15.1	14.2	−0.9	+15.1	+6.0	−9.1
North Dakota	19.2	14.4	−4.8	+19.2	+12.8	−6.4
Ohio	3.2	5.0	+1.8	−1.4	−1.1	+0.3
Arkansas	4.1	7.6	+3.5	+3.5	+0.7	−2.8
Washington	4.3	11.1	+6.8	−2.0	−9.0	−7.0
Florida	9.8	24.8	+13.0	−5.3	−24.8	−19.5

Note: See text for further explanation. MAPE (mean absolute percent error) is an unweighted measure of precision; MALPE (mean algebraic percent error) is an unweighted measure of bias.

[a] Projections for 1990 were prepared in the early 1980s using cohort-component (county) and land-use models (census tracts).

[b] The 1980 census count is assumed to be the projection for 1990.

[c] Amount of excess or deficit of "percent error of base population as projection" from "percent error of actual projection." A minus sign (−) indicates that the percentage error from using the 1980 census as the projection was smaller; a plus (+) sign indicates that the percentage error from using the 1980 census as the projection was larger. This is not the PRE (proportionate reduction in error) given in the source table.

Source: Based on Jeffrey Tayman and David Swanson, "On the utility of population forecasts," *Demography* 33(4): 523–528, November 1996, Table 2. © Population Association of America. Reprinted with permission.

are expanded or the growth rate declines. Additional series varying the fertility, mortality, or migration assumptions can provide useful indications of the effect of a shift in one of these variables on population size and structure. An unrealistic series of projections can have analytic utility also. A comparison of projections assuming no internal migration with projections assuming a continuation of recent levels of internal migration provides one measure of the effect of migration on future population growth and age structure, and on the future growth of the labor force. Land-use modeling, a very different methodology from the cohort-component method, can provide an indication of the reasonable maximum population that an area can physically support.

Assuming that the alternative series of population projections in a set, designated variously as high, medium, and low, or I, II, and III, are realistic possibilities for a set of areas, the range of such alternative series can suggest roughly the degree of uncertainty in the middle series. This conclusion assumes that the middle series was designed to be the forecast series. As a practical matter, the user often has to choose a single series among the alternative series and selects the middle series for this purpose. The middle series may or may not be described as a prediction or forecast, but it is interpreted as such by most users and it should be so regarded unless there is reason to dispute this choice.

Loss Functions and Confidence Intervals

Some users may prefer the higher or lower series because it meets their needs for an acceptable level of risk better than the middle series. How does one proceed to select one of the series in a set of projections? First, recognize that the range of the projections from the low to the high series does not represent a confidence interval with a known probability, such as is associated with a survey estimate based on a probability sample. For this purpose the demographer has to link a probability distribution with the projected population series. However, this linkage is also not enough to make a selection of one of the series in the practical case. According to Muhsam (1956), to make a formal selection of a series, three elements have to be taken into account, the probability distribution, a loss function, and a policy criterion:[38]

> (a) The loss function, i.e, a rule which permits [one] to compute or estimate, for any deviation—positive or negative—of the actual population from the forecast, the loss caused to the person who followed the planner's advice by such a deviation;
> (b) The probability distribution of the population forecast, i.e., a function which shows the probability of the population to reach, at the period under consideration for the planning problem, any figure or to fall within certain limits;
> (c) A policy criterion, which defines the risks the planner is ready to run, and which he wishes to avoid or prefers to minimize.

The policy criterion takes the form of "minimizing loss," "avoiding maximum loss," "maximizing gain," "securing some gain," and so on. The basis for the establishment of a policy criterion is purely subjective and every policy criterion cannot be translated into a mathematical formula.

For the user to make a choice among alternatives series so as to experience the least loss or the maximum gain in a given application of the projections, he or she needs to calculate the **loss function** associated with a particular series and with a particular application.[39] The cumulative product of the values of the loss function ($L(x_0, x)$) and the associated probabilities ($P(x)$) yields the expected gain or loss (R) from the choice of a particular population projection x_0:

$$R = \int_{-\infty}^{+\infty} P(x)L(x_0, x)\mathrm{d}x \doteq \sum_{-\infty}^{\infty} P_x L_{x_0, x} \qquad (12)$$

If the policy criterion is to minimize loss, we need to find the value of the population x_0 for which the total loss (R) is a minimum. The value of the population x_0 for which R is a minimum is obtained by setting the derivative (slope) of $R(x_0)$ at zero and solving the resulting (differential) equation for x_0:

$$\frac{\partial R(x_0)}{\partial x_0} = 0 \qquad (13)$$

Consider the building of public works, such as dams, waste disposal dumps, or water filtration plants. A policy may be based on the criterion of building a capital project to fit the "best" forecast exactly or avoiding the maximum loss. Often it is more important to avoid underbuilding than overbuilding since it is more costly to reconstruct the plant if more capacity is needed later than to have excess capacity that is available for expanded use at a later date. Hence, usually, in planning public works, the high series is the preferred series to use. To a lesser degree, this applies also to building schools, fire stations, and police stations.

At other times, it is more important to avoid an overestimate, and in this case the lower projection series should be selected. This policy is usually applicable in planning labor supply, as in hiring teachers or other public workers, or in planning the manufacture and distribution of consumer goods. Here managers tend to feel that making up for an underestimate of population, if necessary, is not as expensive an operation as overbuilding plants and overproducing the company's products.

Demographers cannot generally provide probability distributions for state and local population projections, but some progress has been made in this direction. To formalize the statement of error in projections of state populations, some efforts have been made to develop confidence intervals for them. Population projections for a set of areas have error structures that can be specified on the basis of an analysis of prior performance in preparing such projections, given certain conditions. Use of the past error record assumes not only that the chances of error in the future resemble those of the past but also that projections have measurable confidence intervals even if they were not produced by a stochastic (probabilistic) process. If high, medium, and low series of population projections are calculated, one can try to assign probabilities to the range so delimited, but it is more useful to determine the confidence interval of the middle series or forecast series with a specified probability (e.g., 67% or 95%).

Accompanying subnational population forecasts with statements of uncertainty and establishing a confidence interval around them help make them more useful tools for decision making. Comparison of forecasts for various dates with the subsequent, measured level of the population for these dates provides the basis for developing a summary of errors and inferring the confidence level of current forecasts. As suggested, the set of population projections from the past must "resemble" the set for the future for the comparison to have merit. It is important that the projections anticipate similar population growth patterns as in the past. This is much less likely for subnational areas than for the country as a whole. Preferably the two sets should resemble one another in terms of the method employed and in terms of other variables that could affect the level of error, such as the length of the projection period, type and size of area, and the growth rate. In view of the differences in bias and variability with respect to certain characteristics (e.g., region, method, jump-off year), it is wise to construct different confidence intervals for sets of projections with these characteristics. Current forecasts may employ an improved version of a method for which test results are available; hence, estimates of error based on past comparisons may tend to be too high.

As noted earlier, a measure providing an indication of the confidence interval of a projection is the **root mean square error** for a past set of projections—that is,

$$\text{RMSE} = \sqrt{\left(\sum P_i^2 \div n \right)} \tag{14}$$

where P_i represents the percentage deviation of the projected population from the actual population. The RMSE corresponds approximately to the 67%

probability range around a forecast if (1) about two-thirds of the test results fall in the range defined by +/− one standard deviation (approximating the RMSE) around the actual population, (2) the test results are symmetric (just as likely to be too high as too low), and (3) the distribution of the results follows the normal curve.

The RMSE may serve as a good measure for constructing confidence intervals in the evaluation studies of subnational population projections since the bias component of RMSE is generally very small and the standard deviation may approximate the RMSE.[40] The few evaluation studies conducted indicate that published ranges of projections (i.e., low and high series) are substantially narrower than suggested by calculations of confidence intervals at the 95% level.

If, alternatively, we think in terms of the amount of error in the average annual growth rate (Δr_i) of the population projections rather than the error in the population projections, we assume that the true, but currently unknown average annual growth rate, r, has a normal distribution with mean r (the projected average growth rate) and standard deviation σ_r. We also assume that the previously observed r's are like a random sample of what is expected in the future.

As noted earlier, time-series analysis using Box-Jenkins methods and stochastic demographic forecasting can provide confidence intervals for the quantities forecast. Stochastic demographic forecasting has not been applied to subnational projections, however. Both Voss and Palit (1981) and Smith and Sincich (1992) have made forecasts of state population using Box-Jenkins methods with ARIMA time-series techniques.[41] They showed that ARIMA models could produce population forecasts at least as reliable as demographic models and suggested that the method could be used in the evaluation of demographic projections. They did not provide probability distributions for their projections, however.

There are costs to making poor decisions on the basis of inaccurate projections or a wrong choice among a set of projections. There are also costs to generating different types of projections, particularly the more complex ones. We are seeking a method consistent with the minimal cost of generating projections that have the accuracy required to make the right decisions. Because of the great variability of population changes and our inability to predict the underlying factors influencing population change, the most careful projection work has not produced very accurate results for subnational areas. Given the task of projecting fertility, mortality, and internal migration as well as immigration for a group of areas, after a decade or so projections of total population for such areas have large errors and errors for age groups may be nearly as great. Test results for age groups are lacking, however. On the other hand, even a simplistic method of projecting total population that differentiates the growth rate among the individual units in a set adds some improvement in accuracy over holding the most recent census figures constant. For projections of total population, therefore, simple methods may be as accurate as more complex methods. The former are not designed to produce projections of age composition and other characteristics, however.

NOTES

1. U.S. Bureau of the Census, "Population projections of the United States by age, sex, race, and Hispanic origin: 1995 to 2050," by Jennifer C. Day, *Current Population Reports*, P25–1130, February 1996. When this book was in the final stages of preparation, the Census Bureau issued a revised set of national projections, dated January 2000; these figures have not been integrated into the body of the text (Population Division, U.S. Bureau of the Census, 2000b).

2. Office of the Chief Actuary, U.S. Social Security Administration, "Social Security area population projections: 1997," by Felicitie C. Bell, *Actuarial Study* No. 112, August 1997.

3. Interagency Forum on Aging-Related Statistics, *Projections of Health Status and Use of Health Care of Older Americans*, U.S. National Center of Health Statistics, January 1996. See also S. Jay Olshansky, "Simultaneous/multiple cause delay (SIMCAD): An epidemiological approach to projecting mortality," *Journal of Gerontology* 42(4): 358–365, 1987; and Ronald D. Lee and Shripad Tuljapurkar, "Stochastic population projections for the United States: Beyond high, medium, and low," *Journal of the American Statistical Association* 89(428): 1175–1189, 1994.

4. Dennis A. Ahlburg and James W. Vaupel, "Alternative projections of the U.S. population," *Demography* 27(4): 639–652, 1990. Jack M. Guralnik et al., "Projecting the older population of the United States: Lessons from the past and prospects for the future," *The Milbank Quarterly* 66: 283–308, 1988 and Kenneth G. Manton et al., "Projecting the future size and health status of the U.S. elderly population," *International Journal of Forecasting* 8(3): 433–458, November 1992.

5. See Kenneth C. Land, "Methods for national population forecasts: A review." *Journal of the American Statistical Association* 81(396): 888–901, 1986; and *Methods and Materials of Demography*, Revised Condensed Edition, Academic Press, 2002.

6. In the Census Bureau projections, highest series and lowest series refer to combinations of assumptions that produce the highest and lowest population totals:

Component	Highest	Middle	Lowest
Fertility	High	Middle	Low
Mortality	Low	Middle	High
Immigration	High	Middle	Low

In the Social Security Administration projections, the terms *high-cost alternative* and *low-cost alternative* refer to projection series that, if realized, would be the more costly and the less costly, respectively, for the OASDI program. Accordingly, the combinations of assumptions for the alternative series are as follows:

Component	High-cost	Intermediate	Low-cost
Fertility	Low	Middle	High
Mortality	Low	Middle	High
Immigration	Low	Middle	High

7. Differencing of a series refers to the operation of taking the algebraic differences between adjacent members of the series. First-order differences represent the algebraic differences between the members of the original series. Second-order differences are the algebraic differences of the first-order differences. When nth-order differences are constant, an nth-degree polynomial would fit the original data exactly.

Autoregression refers to regression in which the variable (e.g., population, second differences of the population, first differerences of the logarithms of the population) are regressed on lagged values of itself (y_t and $y_{t-1,2,3,...}$).

For a description of various statistical forecasting techniques, see Francis X. Diebold, *Elements of Forecasting*, 2nd ed., Cincinnati, OH: South-Western, 2001.

8. Dennis A. Ahlburg and Kenneth C. Land, "Population forecasting: Guest editors' introduction," *International Journal of Forecasting* 8(3): 289–299, November 1992.

9. Peter Pflaumer, "Forecasting U.S. population totals with the Box-Jenkins approach," *International Journal of Forecasting* 8(3): 329–338, November 1992.

10. Ahlburg and Land, 1992, *op. cit.*; and Ronald D. Lee, "Stochastic demographic forecasting," *International Journal of Forecasting* 8(3): 315–327, November 1992.

11. Shripad Tuljapurkar, "Stochastic forecasts and their uses," *International Journal of Forecasting* 8(3): 385–391, November 1992.

12. Lee, 1992, *op. cit.* See also Jacob S. Siegel, "Development and accuracy of projections of population and households in the United States," *Demography* 9(1): 51–68, 1972.

13. The proportion of persons 65 years and over is of special interest. In 2030 the middle series, the lowest series, and the highest series all show 20% for the proportion, representing a remarkable convergence of the three series. This convergence results from the offsetting impact of the fertility and mortality assumptions on the age distribution in both the highest series and lowest series. It may give a misleading view of the confidence one should have in the middle figure. If we combine high fertility, high mortality, and high immigration, the figure is about 17%, and if we combine low fertility, low mortality, and low immigration, the figure is about 23%.

14. Nathan Keyfitz, "The limits of population forecasting," *Population and Development Review* 7(4): 579–593, 1981; and Michael S. Stoto, "The accuracy of population projections." *Journal of the American Statistical Association* 78(381): 13–20, March 1983.

15. U.S. Bureau of the Census, "Population projections for States, by age, sex, race, and Hispanic origin: 1995 to 2025," by Paul R. Campbell, PPL-47, 1996.

16. U.S. Bureau of Economic Analysis, *BEA Regional Projections to 2045*, Vol. I, *States*, 1995.

17. Possible steps in applying the third version of the proration method are as follows:

(1) the current populations and those at an earlier date (defining a base period) for the subareas (e.g., counties) are converted to percentage distributions, totaling 100% for the parent area (e.g., state) for each year,

(2) the average annual changes in the percentages in (1) over the base period are calculated,

(3) the average annual changes in (2) are projected to selected future dates by some formula (e.g., that the average annual change will approach zero or other value at some specified future date by linear extrapolation),

(4) the projected average annual changes in (3) are sequentially applied to the current percentages of area totals in each subarea in (1) to derive the percentages for each subarea for each future year,

(5) the projected percentages over all subareas for each year in (4) are adjusted pro rata to 100%, and

(6) the adjusted percentages in (5) are applied to the independent projected population totals for the parent area.

18. Methods and computer programs for multiregional projections are described in Frans Willekens and Andrei Rogers, *Spatial Population Analysis: Methods and Computer Programs,* RR. 78-18. Laxenburg, Austria: International Institute for Applied Systems Analysis, 1978. See also Andrei Rogers and Frans Willekens (eds.), *Migration and Settlement: A Multiregional Comparative Study*, Dordrecht, Netherlands: Reidel, 1986; and F. Willekens and J. Drewe, "A multiregional model for demographic projection," in F. Willekens (ed.), *Multistate demography: New Methods and Applications*, Amsterdam: Reidel, 1990.

19. As in the basic life table, the stationary population of the multiregional life table is a zero-growth population, derived by holding constant the observed migration rates in addition to the observed mortality rates. The functions of the table are not affected by the regional distribution and age distribution of the *observed* population. For more information, see Shiva S. Halli and K. Vaninadha Rao, *Advanced Techniques of Population Analysis*, New York: Plenum Press, 1992, Chapter 9; Robert Schoen, Modeling Multigroup Populations, New York: Plenum Press, 1988, pp. 96–98; and Krishnan Namboodiri, *Demographic Analysis: A Stochastic Approach*, San Diego, CA: Academic Press, 1991, pp. 147–150.

20. The assumption is that state variation in birthrates and survival rates will be eliminated within each projection category—age, sex, race, and Hispanic origin—by 2025. It does not mean that the overall fertility and mortality of each state will be the same. This assumption causes the growth rates of the states to become more similar, but not the same.

21. If projections of the population of a single county are to be prepared, it is desirable to combine mortality data for a number of years—say, 3 years centered on the census year—or for a group of counties. If areas smaller than counties are the geographic units for projection, the same guidelines can be followed. For even greater stability of the mortality indicators, data for years and areas may be combined. To the extent possible, the populations of the areas combined should be similar in socioeconomic characteristics.

22. Alternative procedures are to use national census survival rates in lieu of life tables for the specific area or in lieu of adjusting the census data for net census undercounts. For a discussion of residual estimates of net migration and the computation and use of national census survival rates, see *The Methods and Materials of Demography, Condensed Edition*, Academic Press, 1976.

23. One method of accomplishing this is to calculate (one plus) the 10-year percent change due to net migration for the 5-year birth cohort, take the square root of this value, calculate the number of net migrants for a 5-year period as shown in the following formula, and assign the result to the first half of the decade:

$$_5^5M_a^{a+5} = \sqrt{\left[\left(_5P_a + {}_5^5M_a^{a+10}\right) \div {}_5P_a\right]} \star {}_5P_a - {}_5P_a$$

The figures for the second half of the decade can be derived by subtraction from the 10-year figures for the birth cohorts. Alternatively, the 10-year amounts of net migration obtained by formula (2) can be subdivided into two parts by the Karup-King interpolation formula. Each part represents an estimate of 5-year migration for a 5-year birth cohort. See *The Methods and Materials of Demography: Revised Condensed Edition*, Academic Press, 2002.

24. U.S. Bureau of the Census, "Guide for local area population projections," by Richard Irwin, *Technical Paper* 39, July 1977.

25. The projections of state population for 1995–2000 were based on a econometric model for each of the states, the District of Columbia, and the nation. A typical state model is summarized in the following equation:

$$X_j = A_jX_j + B_jZ_j + C_jQ_j + U_j$$

where j denotes the state, X denotes the economic and demographic variables determined in the state model, Z denotes the exogenous variables (e.g., the minimum wage), Q denotes the variables determined in the national model, U denotes the error term, and A, B, and C are state-specific coefficients.

26. For the long-term projections, "The labor-pool population for each state was projected in three steps. First, the ratio of the labor-pool population to employment for the state, as a percentage of the ratio of the labor-pool population to employment for the nation, was projected on the basis of historical trends in the percentage. Second, this projected percentage was multiplied by the projected national ratio, to yield the projected ratio for the state. Finally, the projected ratio for the state was multiplied by the projected state employment to yield the projected labor-pool population for the state."

The pre-labor-pool-aged population for each state was projected in three similar steps. The basic ratio related the prelabor-pool-aged population to the labor-pool-aged population. The postlabor-pool-aged population for each state was projected as a share of the corresponding national population on the basis of dampened historical rates of change in its share. U.S. Bureau of Economic Analysis, 1995, *op. cit.*, page M-9.

27. National Planning Association, *Regional Economic Projection Series*, Report No. 81-R-1, Washington, DC, National Planning Association, 1982.

28. For a review of the method, see Dennis A. Ahlburg, "Modeling macro economic-demographic linkages: A study of models of national and regional economies," pp. 287–336, in Kenneth C. Land and S. Schneider (eds.), *Forecasting in the Natural and Social Sciences*, Boston: D. Reidel, 1987.

29. Ira S. Lowry, *Migration and Metropolitan Growth: Two Analytical Models*, San Francisco, CA: Chandler Publishing Company, 1966.

30. John F. Long, "Prospects for a composite demographic-economic model of migration for subnational population projections," pp. 153–165, in American Statistical Association (eds.), *Report of the Conference on Economic and Demographic Methods of Projecting Population*, Alexandria, VA, October 3–4, 1977. See also the papers by Pittenger, Greenwood, and Birch in this volume.

31. Jeff Tayman and David A. Swanson, "On the validity of MAPE as a measure of population forecast accuracy," *Population Research and Policy Review* 18(4): 299–322, August 1999. See also Jeff Tayman, David A. Swanson, and Charles F. Barr, "In search of the ideal measure of accuracy for subnational demographic forecasts," *Population Research and Policy Review* 18(5): 387–409, October 1999.

32. These authors describe another class of measures, M-estimators of location, that were designed to overcome the upward bias in the mean absolute percentage error. They are derived through an iterative process based on the median absolute deviation from the median percentage error. They have as their main disadvantages the complexity of their method of derivation and the difficulty of explaining how they are derived and to be interpreted.

33. Nathan Keyfitz, "On future population," *Journal of the American Statistical Association* 67: 347–362, 1972; Michael S. Stoto, "The accuracy of population projections," *Journal of the American Statistical Association* 78(381): 13–20, 1983; and Michael S. Stoto and Alicia P. Schrier, "The accuracy of state population projections," pp. 177–182, in American Statistical Association (eds.), *Proceedings of the Social Statistics Section*, Alexandria, VA: American Statistical Association, 1982.

34. Jeff Tayman and David A. Swanson, "On the utility of population forecasts," *Demography* 53(4): 523–528, November 1996.

35. Michael Stoto, "The accuracy of population projections," *Journal of the American Statistical Association* 78(381): 13–20, March 1983; based on data in John Long, "Prospects for a composite demographic-economic model of migration for subnational population projections," in American Statistical Association (eds.), *Report of the Conference on Economic and Demographic Methods for Projecting Population*, October 1977.

36. John F. Long, "Complexity, accuracy, and utility of official population projections," *Mathematical Population Studies* 5: 203–216, 1995.

37. Stanley K. Smith and Terry Sincich, "Evaluating the forecast accuracy and bias of alternative population projections for states," *International Journal of Forecasting* 8(3): 495–508, November 1992.

38. Helmut Muhsam, "The utilization of alternative population projections in planning," *Bulletin of the Research Council of Israel* 5(2–3): 133–146, March/June 1956.

39. For a mathematical discussion of loss functions, see Muhsam (1956, *op. cit.*) and John E. Freund, *Mathematical Statistics*, 5th ed., Englewood Cliffs, NJ: Prentice-Hall, 1995, Chapter 9, "Decision Theory."

40. Nathan Keyfitz, "The limits of population forecasting," *Population and Development Review* 7: 579–593, 1982.

41. Paul R. Voss and C. D. Palit, "Forecasting state population using ARIMA time series techniques," *Technical Series* 70-6, Madison, WI: University of Wisconsin, 1981; and Smith and Sincich, 1992, *op. cit.*

SUGGESTED READINGS

General

Ahlburg, Dennis A., and Land, Kenneth C., eds. (1992, November). *Population Forecasting*. Special Issue of *International Journal of Forecasting* 8(3): 289–542.

Lutz, Wolfgang, Vaupel, James W., and Ahlburg, Dennis A., eds. (1998). *Frontiers of Population Forecasting*. A supplement to Vol. 24 of *Population and Development Review*. New York: Population Council.

National Projections: Methods and Evaluation

Ahlburg, Dennis A. (1992). "Error measures and choice of a forecast method." *International Journal of Forecasting* 8(1): 99–100.

Ahlburg, Dennis A., and Vaupel, John W. (1990). "Alternative projections of the U.S. population." *Demography* 27(4): 639–652.

Alho, Juha. (1990). "Stochastic methods in population forecasts." *International Journal of Forecasting* 6: 521–530.

Carter, Larry, and Lee, Ronald D. (1986). "Joint forecasts of U.S. marital fertility, nuptiality, births, and marrriage using time series models." *Journal of the American Statistical Association* 81(396): 902–911.

Guralnik, Jack M., Yanagishita, M., and Schneider, E. L. (1988). "Projecting the older population of the United States: Lessons from the past and prospects for the future." *Milbank Quarterly* 66: 283–308.

Haub, Carl. (1987, December). "Understanding population projections." *Population Bulletin* 42(4).

Keyfitz, Nathan. (1972). "On future population." *Journal of the American Statistical Association* 67: 347–363.

Keyfitz, Nathan. (1981). "The limits of population forecasting." *Population and Development Review* 7(4): 579–593.

Land, Kenneth C. (1986). "Methods for national population forecasts: A review." *Journal of the American Statistical Association* 81(396): 888–901.

Lee, Ronald D., and Tuljapurkar, Shripad. (1994). "Stochastic population forecasts for the United States: Beyond high, medium, and low." *Journal of the American Statistical Association* 89(428): 1175–1189.

Manton, Kenneth G., Stallard, Eric, and Singer, Burt. (1992, November). "Projecting the future size and health status of the U.S. elderly population." *International Journal of Forecasting* 8(3): 433–458.

Olshansky, S. Jay. (1987). "Simultaneous/multiple cause delay (SIMCAD): An epidemiological approach to projecting mortality." *Journal of Gerontology* 42(4): 358–365.

Pflaumer, Peter. (1992, November). "Forecasting U.S. population totals with the Box-Jenkins approach." *International Journal of Forecasting* 8(3): 329–338.

Siegel, Jacob S. (1972). "Development and accuracy of projections of population and households in the United States." *Demography* 9(1): 51–68.

Stoto, Michael S. (1983, March). "The accuracy of population projections." *Journal of the American Statistical Association* 78(381): 13–20.

Tuljapurkar, Shripad. (1992, November). "Stochastic population forecasts and their uses." In Dennis Ahlburg and Kenneth Land (eds.), *International Journal of Forecasting* 8(3): 385–391.

U. S. Bureau of the Census. (1996). "Population projections of the United States by age, sex, race, and Hispanic origin: 1995 to 2050," by Jennifer C. Day. *Current Population Reports*, Series P25-1130.

U.S. Bureau of the Census. (2000a). "Accuracy of the U.S. Census Bureau's national population projections and their respective components of change." By Tammany J. Mulder. Population Projections Program, Population Division, U.S. Bureau of the Census.

U.S. Bureau of the Census. (2000b). "Population projections of the United States, by age, sex, race, Hispanic origin, and nativity: 1999–2000." Report of the Population Projections Program, Population Division, U.S. Bureau of the Census.

U.S. Social Security Administration, Office of the Actuary. (1997). "Social Security area population projections: 1997," by Felicitie C. Bell. *Actuarial Study*, No. 112.

Subnational Projections

Methods

American Statistical Association, eds. (1977, October 4–7). *Report of the Conference on Economic and Demographic Methods for Projecting Population*. Alexandria, VA.

American Statistical Association, eds. (1983). *International Conference on Forecasting Regional Population and its Economic Determinants and Consequences*, May 1982, Airlie, VA. Sponsored by the American Statistical Association and U.S. Bureau of the Census.

Frees, Edward. (1992). "Forecasting state-to-state migration rates." *Journal of Business and Economic Statistics* 10(2): 153–167.

Johnson, Kenneth P., and Phillips, Bruce D. (1977, October 4–7). "Economic based populations projections," pp. 117–133. In American Statistical Association (eds.), *Report of the Conference on Economic and Demographic Methods for Projecting Population*. Alexandria, VA.

Long, John F. (1977, October 4–7). "Prospects for a composite demographic-economic model of migration for subnational populations." In American Statistical Association (eds.), *Report of the Conference on Economic and Demographic Methods for Projecting Population*. Alexandria, VA.

National Planning Association. (1982). *Regional Economic Projection Series*, Report 81-R-1. Washington, DC: National Planning Association.

Shryock, Henry S., Siegel, Jacob S., and Associates. (1976). *The Methods and Materials of Demography*, Condensed Edition, by Edward G. Stockwell, Chapter 23. New York: Academic Press.

Statistics Canada. (2000). *Population Projections for Canada, Provinces, and Territories: 2000–2006* by M. V. George *et al*. Ottawa, Canada: Demography Division, Statistics, Canada.

U.S. Bureau of the Census. (1977). "Guide for local area population projections," by Richard Irwin. *Technical Paper*, No. 39.

U. S. Bureau of the Census. (1996). "Population projections for states, by age, sex, race, and Hispanic origin: 1995 to 2025," by Paul R. Campbell. *Current Population Reports*, Series PPL-47.

U.S. Bureau of Economic Analysis. (1995). *BEA Regional Projections to 2045*. Vol. I, *States*, Vol. II, *Metropolitan Statistical Areas*, and Vol. III, *Economic Areas*.

Voss, Paul C., and Palit, C. D. (1981). "Forecasting state population using ARIMA time series techniques." *Technical Series* 70-6. Madison, WI: University of Wisconsin.

Limitations and Evaluation

Murdock, S. H., Leistritz, F. L., Hamm, R. R., Hwang, S. S., and Parpia, B. (1984). "An assessment of the accuracy of a regional economic-demographic projection model." *Demography* 21(3): 383–404.

Murdock, S., Hamm, R., Voss, P., Fannin, D., and Pecotte, B. (1991). "Evaluating small-area population projections." *Journal of the American Planning Association* 57: 432–443.

Siegel, Jacob S. (1953, February). "Forecasting the population of small areas." *Land Economics* 29(1): 73–87.

Smith, Stanley K. (1987). "Tests of forecast accuracy and bias for county population projections." *Journal of the American Statistical Association* 82(429): 991–1003.

Smith, Stanley K., and Shahidullah, M. (1995). "An evaluation of population projection errors for census tracts." *Journal of the American Statistical Association* 90: 64–71.

Smith, Stanley K., and Sincich, Terry. (1991). "An empirical analysis of the effect of the length of the forecast horizon on population forecast errors." *Demography* 28(2): 261–274.

Smith, Stanley K., and Sincich, Terry. (1992, November). "Evaluating the forecast accuracy and bias of alternative population projections for states." *International Journal of Forecasting* 8(3): 495–508.

Stoto, Michael A., and Schrier, Alicia P. (1982). "The accuracy of state population projections" (pp. 177–182). In American Statistical Association (eds.), *Proceedings of the Social Statistics Section*. Alexandria, VA: American Statistical Association.

Tayman, Jeff. (1996). "The accuracy of small area population forecasts based on a spatial interaction land use modeling system." *Journal of the American Planning Association* 62: 85–98.

Tayman, Jeff, and Swanson, David A. (1996, November). "On the utility of population forecasts." *Demography* 33(4): 523–528.

Tayman, Jeff, and Swanson, David A. (1999, August). "On the validity of MAPE as a measure of population forecast accuracy." *Population Research and Policy Review* 18(4): 299–322.

Tayman, Jeff, Swanson, David A., and Barr, Charles F. (1999, October). "In search of the ideal measure of accuracy for subnational demographic forecasts." *Population Research and Policy Review* 18(5): 387–409.

General Statistical Methods

Diebold, Francis X. (2001). *Elements of Forecasting*. 2nd ed. Cincinnati, OH: South-Western (Thomson Learning).

Yaffee, Robert A. with M. McGee. (2000). *An Introduction to Time Series Analysis and Forecasting: With Applications of SAS and SPSS*. San Diego, CA: Academic Press.

11

ESTIMATES AND PROJECTIONS OF SOCIOECONOMIC AND HEALTH CHARACTERISTICS

INTRODUCTION

The previous chapters on estimates and projections have been concerned with basic demographic characteristics—the total population and its age-sex-race distribution—both for the nation and the areas within it. This chapter explores estimates and projections of the socioeconomic and health characteristics of the population. The list of such characteristics is long and includes nativity, religion, ancestry and language, educational attainment and school enrollment, marital status, household characteristics and living arrangements, labor force participation and employment, income and wealth, and health and disability status. This chapter deals illustratively with only some of these, mainly households, labor force, school enrollment, and health status.

Social scientists, administrators, and planners have a critical need for current estimates and projections of socioeconomic and health characteristics of the population, in addition to estimates and projections of the basic demographic characteristics. Such figures not only have their own direct uses, as in

489

the administration of federal block grants, but also are useful in the administration of programs relating to public welfare, education, health, public safety, and transportation. For the latter purpose, various types of applied projections, such as projections for occupational categories and community facilities, are needed. Consider the field of educational administration. Projections of school enrollment for local areas are essential for planning the number of classrooms, schools, and teachers. Such figures are required for counties and subcounty areas because school administration is local. Consider also the field of health administration. In addition to data on health conditions at all geographic levels, data are needed on the demand for health care and use of health care services and facilities. Local figures are needed because much health care planning, as educational planning, occurs at the local level and health conditions vary from one local area to another. Moreover, states need to measure the degree to which they are meeting the health guidelines for the year 2000, as promulgated in U.S. Public Health Service, *Healthy People: National Health Promotion and Disease Prevention Objectives,* and to plan how they will meet the new guidelines for 2010.

NATIONAL ESTIMATES OF CHARACTERISTICS

In this discussion, national estimates for socioeconomic characteristics are treated separately from subnational estimates because the sources of data, methods of generating the estimates, and the error patterns of the two types of estimates are generally different. National estimates on many subjects are readily available from various national surveys. For example, national estimates of nativity, marital status, living arrangements, households, labor force, disability, educational level, school enrollment, individual and household income, and poverty—all disaggregated by age, sex, and race/Hispanic origin—are provided frequently, if not annually, by the Current Population Survey (CPS). Similarly, the Survey of Income Programs and Participation (SIPP) furnishes national data on income, poverty, assets, participation in public benefits programs, health insurance, and related economic subjects. The National Health Interview Survey is the source for national data on health conditions, use of health services, and other health-related items. Health information focused on elderly persons is provided by the Health and Retirement/AHEAD Survey. The American Community Survey is designed to produce continuing national and subnational estimates on the socioeconomic characteristics of the population, corresponding to the items on the long form of the census, beginning in the period 2003 to 2008.[1]

The national estimates of socioeconomic characteristics from the surveys are of use in themselves in describing the state of the American population and in giving direction to a myriad of public and private programs. In addition, they can be used in combination with independent estimates of state and county population disaggregated by age, sex, and race in the preparation of "synthetic" estimates of socioeconomic characteristics for these subnational areas (as will be discussed further).

Alternatively, we may prepare national estimates of some socioeconomic characteristics by demographic analysis for the purpose of evaluating the survey estimates, testing the possibility of making such estimates in the absence of current survey data, or generating estimates for intermediate years. We may wish, for example, to evaluate the CPS estimate of the number of married men in the United States for a current date by preparing an independent estimate of the number of married men by the method of demographic analysis and comparing the two estimates. One could proceed as follows. To the census count of married men, add the number of marriages (including remarriages) and the number of married male "net immigrants" in the postcensal period, and then subtract the number of divorces, widowings of married men, and deaths of married men. The calculations are carried out most efficiently for birth cohorts, but the model can be expressed simply as

$$MM_e = MM_c + m - v - d_{mm} - w_{mm} + i_{mm} - e_{mm} \tag{1}$$

where MM and mm represent married men, e refers to the estimate, c refers to the census count, m refers to marriages, v refers to divorces, d refers to deaths, w refers to widowings, i refers to immigrants, and e refers to emigrants. The components relate to the postcensal period. To estimate each component, it is necessary to take a number of subsidiary steps and to refer to several data sources. To estimate the number of immigrants who are married, for example, it may be necessary or useful to refer to the Immigration and Naturalization Service data on the marital status of immigrants, decennial census data on the marital status of persons living abroad 5 years earlier, and CPS data on the marital status of persons living abroad 1 year earlier. The sources of the basic data for estimating all the components may be quite varied: the decennial census, the CPS, the (former) marriage and divorce registration systems, the vital registration system, life tables (including possibly marriage formation and dissolution tables) from the National Center for Health Statistics, and the immigration registration system.

STATE AND LOCAL ESTIMATES OF CHARACTERISTICS

Outline and Description of Methods

The principal methods of preparing state and local estimates of socioeconomic characteristics may be enumerated as follows:

> Direct survey estimates
> Demographic analysis
>> Censal-ratio methods
>> Prevalence-ratio methods
>> Component and cohort-component methods
>> Cohort-progression
>> Use of administrative record data
> Economic analysis
> Synthetic estimates
> Regression methods
> Combinations of methods

While this list enumerates the methods as if they are distinctive, the classification is merely a heuristic device. The categories are imprecisely defined and the methods may be combined or applied only in part. The principal features of many of these methods are described next.

Direct Survey Estimates and Variations

While the federal government conducts several surveys representative of the U.S. population, with the notable exception of the American Community Survey, these surveys are designed to produce estimates primarily for the United States as a whole and only secondarily for the larger subnational areas (i.e., larger states and SMAs)—a fact noted earlier. Because of their design and cost structure, the present surveys cannot provide usable estimates for the smaller states, smaller metropolitan areas, and other types of small areas. Precise estimates of characteristics cannot be obtained for many states because the sample size is too small or the sample strata cross state lines. Postcensal estimates from a survey also have to be accurate enough to distinguish change in the characteristics of the states since the previous census, but this is not generally the case, even over a decade (discussed later). Even estimates of socioeconomic characteristics for the larger states and metropolitan areas, and their measured changes since the previous census, should be viewed with caution because of the possibly large variances associated with them.

States may consider taking censuses or surveys of their own in the hope of securing direct estimates for the socioeconomic characteristics of the state and its subareas. Generally, however, the states do not have the financial and technical resources to conduct censuses or surveys that would produce reliable and valid estimates of this kind. When the goal is securing estimates for particular local areas, it is generally not feasible to conduct a local sample survey. It is a false but widespread presumption that surveys always give results superior to alternatives such as indirect estimation. On the contrary, it may be desirable to forstall the conduct of underfinanced, poorly planned, and inexpertly executed surveys and to employ alternatives to the use of a single, locally conducted sample survey.

Many alternative estimation devices may be tried. They include the averaging of direct estimates from national surveys over groups of years, supplementation or stratification of the sample, the use of national survey estimates in combination with local nonsurvey data in a synthetic approach, the use of the direct survey estimate as an independent variable along with other variables in a regression estimate, the averaging of direct survey estimates with other estimates, as well as the use of estimates derived entirely by nonsurvey methods.

To reduce the sampling errors of estimates for states from the national surveys, 2-year, 3-year, and even 5-year averages of the survey data may be calculated. While this maneuver increases the accuracy of the estimates, it makes them less timely. Five-year averages, especially, lack timeliness and confuse the time references for measurement of change, even though they may provide the most accurate and stable indications of level for the indicated period. Two or 3-year averages may prove to be the preferred choice, once the sampling errors are evaluated. The American Community Survey has the strengths and weaknesses identified; while it will provide direct estimates for most areas of interest on a continuous basis, the grouping of years of data limits its timeliness and estimates cannot be provided for all areas of interest.

To illustrate the effect of averaging sample survey estimates for varying numbers of years on the variance of the estimates, consider a report prepared by the Population Reference Bureau (Pollard and Riche, 1994).[2] A comparison of the accuracy of CPS estimates, based on 1-year, 3-year, and 5-year data for states, for six socioeconomic indicators, shows how the variance of the estimates increases as the number of years in the average is reduced. However, whether we examine 5-year estimates, 3-year estimates, or 1-year estimates, the ten most populous states and Massachusetts generally have the smallest standard errors for the six socioeconomic characteristics. In the comparison of CPS figures for the census year with the census sample figures—a comparison affected by the differences in survey design—the large states have smaller deviations from the census than the small states.

In the Pollard/Riche study, for each of the six variables, the ratios of single-year state standard errors to 5-year state standard errors were appreciably larger than the ratios of 3-year errors to the 5-year ones. The latter ratios approximated 1.25 for each variable, while the former ranged from 1.62 to 1.83. That is, when the number of years being averaged is reduced from 5 to 3, the standard errors increased about 25% for each variable, but when the number is reduced from 5 to 1, the standard errors increased by 62 to 83%. Table 11.1 illustrates these results in terms of a distribution of standard errors of CPS data on teens not in school and not in the labor force in 1991. Only 17 of the states have standard errors under 1.5% for single-year estimates, but 46 states fall in this range for 5-year estimates.

Furthermore, sample survey estimates for 1 year do not provide a sound basis for making accurate estimates of change over time for most states. According to a study of the quality of the current estimates of poverty for states based on the CPS, Pollard (1989) found that the CPS for a single year (1987)

TABLE 11.1 Number of States by Size of Standard Error, According to Number of Survey Years, for Percentage of Teens Not in School and Not in the Labor Force: Current Population Survey, 1991, 1990–1992, 1989–1993

Percentage	Single-year estimate	3-year estimate	5-year estimate
Total[a]	51	51	51
Less than 1.0	4	11	19
1.00 to 1.49	13	16	27
1.50 to 1.99	9	21	4
2.00 to 2.49	12	2	—
2.50 or greater	13	1	

Source: Kelvin M. Pollard and Martha Farnsworth Riche, "The CPS and kids count," a report to the Annie E. Casey Foundation, submitted by the Population Reference Bureau, Washington, DC; 1994, Supplementary Table 1. © Population Reference Bureau. Reprinted with permission.
[a] Includes the District of Columbia.

does not provide useful indications of postcensal change (1979–1987) in the extent of poverty for states.[3] He found that the CPS estimates of poverty ratios for most states in 1987 were not significantly different from the 1980 census sample figures (for 1979). Specifically, he found that, for 39 states, the change in the proportion poor between 1979 and 1987 was not different from zero at the 10% level of significance. Ross and Danziger (1987) reached a similar conclusion with reference to the period 1980–1986.[4] Changes over time are more likely to be significant if 5-year average estimates or 3-year average estimates are employed, but then the time reference for the change and the timeliness of the figures become matters of concern.

It is possible that adequate estimates of the level of poverty at a postcensal date for states and adequate estimates of postcensal change in poverty for states could be based on an average of two comparable (CPS) sample surveys for the current "year" and an average of two comparable (CPS) sample surveys for the census "year." The following equations express the estimated level of poverty at the postcensal date in a state in terms of the census figure and the postcensal change shown by the two pairs of surveys:

[1] $^tP'_e = {}^cP_c + ({}^tP_e - {}^cP_e)$,

for deriving postcensal change by addition, or   (2)

[2] $^tP'_e = {}^cP_c({}^tP_e \div {}^cP_e)$,

for deriving postcensal change by a factor   (3)

where $^tP'_e$ is the 2-year average estimated population at the postcensal date, ^cP_e is the 2-year average population from the surveys at the census date, ^tP_e is the 2-year average population from the surveys at the current date, and ^cP_c is the census sample count of the number in poverty. Change since the census date is measured on the basis of comparable sample survey estimates of the characteristic under study. This procedure takes advantage of the greater precision of the census figure for the characteristic at the time of the census while measuring change on the basis of a consistent survey instrument.

A problem of bias in the estimates for states arises when the component primary sampling units of sample strata cross state lines and hence do not represent a single state. Under these circumstances, it is impossible to combine the unbiased estimates for strata into unbiased estimates for states. To reduce the bias in estimates for states based on the National Health Interview Survey, the National Center for Health Statistics developed the **nearly unbiased estimator**.[5] It yields an estimate for a state that is technically nearly unbiased. The corrective procedure provided by the nearly unbiased estimator allocates the aggregate stratum estimate in the survey to a state in relation to the proportion of the total stratum population coming from the state.[6]

Such design problems have been overcome by the American Community Survey (ACS), the new national sample survey that will provide annual data on social and economic characteristics of the population for states and many substate areas from 2003 on. As mentioned in Chapter 3, the ACS is a rolling sample and data will be averaged for either 3 or 5 years depending on the size of the area. It will produce annual estimates centered $1^1/_2$ or $2^1/_2$ years prior to the end of the previous survey year for most substate areas. In 2010, the ACS is expected to replace the census long form, which provided data on socioeconomic characteristics in prior censuses.

Censal-Ratio Method and Prevalence-Ratio Method

Demographic analysis may be defined broadly to include the whole array of estimating methods listed earlier except direct survey estimates. One simple demographic device for estimating socioeconomic or health characteristics in a local area is to calculate the proportion of the total population having the characteristic, or preferably the proportion of each age-sex-race group having the characteristic, for the local area at the previous census, assume that the proportions remain unchanged to the estimate date, and apply them to the postcensal estimates of the corresponding population groups (i.e., total population, age, sex, and race) in the local area. Alternatively, the census proportions may be extrapolated to the estimate date on the basis of their record of change for the last intercensal decade in the specific area, the record of change during the postcensal period in the parent area, or a combination of these changes. Such a method can be used to estimate, for example, for a state and its counties, the number of households, the number and proportion of high school graduates, the number and proportion of disabled persons, and the prevalence of other socioeconomic or health characteristics. The names—censal-ratio method and prevalence-ratio method—indicate that the method is a ratio method; the first relates the variable of interest to the total population, and the second relates the values of the variable in each age group to the population in each age group.

Sometimes special indicator data are available for improving the estimates of the postcensal proportions or other estimating ratios. The postcensal estimates of households for states published by the Census Bureau can be used to make estimates of households for counties or other substate areas. The postcensal percentage change in the ratio of households to population for the counties in a state can be assumed to be the same as the postcensal percentage change in the household-to-population ratio for the state. After the census ratios for counties are "projected" to the estimate date with the state ratios, they would then be multiplied by an independently derived estimate of the county population total to derive estimates of households for the counties:

$$(^eH_{co} \div ^eP_{co}) = [(^eH_s \div ^eP_s) \div (^cH_s \div ^cP_s)] \star (^cH_{co} \div ^cP_{co}) \qquad (4)$$

$$^eH_{co} = (^eH_{co} \div ^eP_{co}) \star ^eP_{co} \qquad (5)$$

where subscript s represents state, subscript co represents county, superscript e represents postcensal estimate, superscript c represents the census figure, and H and P represent households and population, respectively. Note again that to apply this method, independent current estimates of the total population are required.

Use of Administrative Records

The availability of several types of administrative data makes possible the preparation or improvement of estimates for some socioeconomic and health characteristics. More accurate postcensal estimates of households for substate areas can be prepared by the use of administrative records to update the number of housing units recorded at the previous census than by the ratio method described earlier.[7] As we recall, the number of housing units may be updated on the basis of data on residential building permits issued and residential demolitions recorded. Change in the vacancy ratio needs to be considered as well. There are several ways of getting a handle on the change in the local vacancy ratio. It may be assumed to be the same as it was at the previous census for the particular area. The local census ratio may be adjusted for postcensal change on the basis of the change in the national, regional, or state ratio as reported in the American Housing Survey, or a current estimate for the local area may be available from the records of the area Federal Home Loan Bank.

Data on covered employment (SSA Work History File), data on elderly Social Security beneficiaries (SSA Master Beneficary File), Medicare and Medicaid data, IRS individual income tax returns, state automobile registrations, and lists of food stamp recipients are other types of administrative record data that may be used in estimating socioeconomic characteristics for subnational areas. State health officials maintain various registries, including ones for cancer and immunization, and lists of Medicaid recipients. Data on food stamp recipients and Medicaid eligibles are useful as proxies for measuring the number of poor persons by indirect techniques for various small areas.

Administrative files represent an important source of demographic data, but they suffer from certain limitations. The content is relatively inflexible and new inquiries cannot be readily added when needed. The files are often incomplete, and they may contain duplicate records or other records that should be removed. Duplicates are likely to result when securing information from more than one source on certain topics (e.g., health insurance). The individual records may be incomplete and are subject to confidentiality regulations. Finally, the data vary in quality from state to state, since data collection procedures and maintenance of the records differ greatly from state to state.

Component and Cohort-Component/Cohort Progression Methods

Current estimates of the population having a particular socioeconomic characteristic, for subnational areas, can sometimes be made by the component or cohort-component methods. The use of these methods for this purpose is limited because the necessary data are often not available. The calculations may be carried out at the all-ages level, as in the component method, or designed to incorporate age duration, or grade detail, as in the cohort-component method. Such estimates may be useful in evaluating survey estimates for the same characteristic. They may also be averaged with alternative estimates, in the hope of increasing the accuracy of the final estimates. A few general illustrations of applications of the component and cohort methods are given here.

Estimates of school enrollment by grade or age for any specified area for a current date can be made from census data on enrollment by grade and age and school records on enrollment by grade and age. We are assuming that school records have not been compiled for our particular area of interest, but for some similar area (i.e., a larger or smaller area), from which we will "borrow" the data. We propose to carry the census enrollment figures forward with **grade-progression ratios** calculated from the borrowed school records. Such ratios represent the number of students in a grade in a given year to the number in the prior grade 1 year earlier. Another way of proceeding is to carry forward grade-specific ratios of enrollment within each age group—that is, in the form of prevalence ratios. Estimates of new enrollees in the starting grade may be based on the number of births 5 or 6 years earlier.

Suppose we wish to prepare postcensal estimates of the number of widows for states and counties by the component method. We would reduce the latest census figures for the numbers of widows in the area by deaths and remarriages of widows and add the number of deaths of married men and the number of widowed "net interstate migrants" or "net intercounty migrants." The estimation of the interstate or intercounty migration of widows is the most difficult part. It may be accomplished by use of postcensal estimates of total in- and out-migration, or net migration, for states or counties; census data on the marital status of interstate migrants for the 5-year period preceding the previous census (e.g., 1985–1990), and 1-year estimates of the marital status of in- and out-migrants for regions from the Current Population Survey. Estimates of persons in other marital statuses may be prepared in a similar fashion.

Synthetic Methods

The **synthetic method** usually involves the estimation of the population having a socioeconomic or health characteristic for a subarea by applying proportions of the population having the socioeconomic or health characteristic in one or more demographic categories (age, sex, race, etc.) at a higher geographic level to population figures for these demographic categories at the lower geographic level. It may be thought of demographically as a prevalence-ratio method that projects the ratios from a parent area on to its geographic subareas, thus assuming invariance of these ratios within the parent area.[8] The method may be defined statistically as the weighted average of the proportions of designated subgroups (e.g., race/Hispanic groups) having the socioeconomic characteristic (e.g., income category) in a parent population, the weights being proportional to the distribution of the subgroups (e.g., race/Hispanic groups) in a subarea of the parent population:

$$p_a = \sum_n [(P_{an} \div P_{tn}) \star p_{tn}] \tag{6}$$

$$p_a/p_t = \sum_n [(P_{an} \div P_{tn}) \star p_{tn}] \div p_t \tag{7}$$

where p_a is the estimate of the population with the socioeconomic characteristic a in the subarea, P_{an} is the population with the characteristic a in the parent area in a specific category n, P_{tn} is the total population t in the specific category in the parent area, p_{tn} is the total population in the specific category in the subarea, and p_t is the total population of the subarea.

Typically in this method, national or regional survey estimates of the proportions in specified demographic categories n (e.g., age, sex, race, income), having the socioeconomic or health characteristic a (e.g., poverty) being measured, are applied to similar data on the population composition of subareas (e.g., states or counties). For example, we may use the national survey estimates (e.g., Current Population Survey estimates) of the population of a region having a socioeconomic or health characteristic of interest, within the demographic categories of age, sex, and race, in combination with independent estimates of the age, sex, and race distribution of the state's population. Here is a simplified hypothetical illustration, using race and Hispanic origin as the "symptomatic" variables to develop a synthetic estimate of the proportion of poor persons for a state on the basis of the regional proportions of poor persons for each race/Hispanic origin group:

Race/Hispanic Origin	Proportion poor of race group: Region R (1)	Proportion of total population: State S (2)	Proportion poor of total population: State S (3) = (1) ⋆ (2)
White non-Hispanic	.141	.682	.096
Black non-Hispanic	.309	.207	.064
Other races	.126	.061	.008
Hispanic	.267	.050	.013
All races	.163	1.000	.181

The synthetic estimate of the proportion of poor persons in state S is 18.1%, compared to the observed value of 16.3% for region R. Recall the calculation of the fetal loss rate for a hypothetical county by the synthetic method in Chapter 7.

It is desirable to extend the list of variables used as weights in synthetic estimates by including other variables in addition to age, sex, and race/Hispanic origin. For this purpose, estimates for these additional variables (e.g., income, educational level) must be available for the subnational areas and they must be associated with variation in the characteristic of interest (e.g., net worth). Appropriate data may be available from the latest census or sample survey. For example, if we want to estimate the distribution of the population of a state by net worth, we may be able to apply the percentage distribution of the population by net worth within each age and household-income group for the nation from SIPP to independent estimates of the population of the state for each age and income group.[9] It is assumed that estimates of the income distribution of the population in each age group for the state are available from some independent source, including a census.

The National Center for Health Statistics (NCHS) has conducted considerable research on the synthetic method since the mid-1960s in connection with making estimates of persons with various health conditions for states.[10] The use of the synthetic method to derive local estimates of health characteristics for decennial census years is particularly appropriate since the National Health Interview Survey (NHIS) produces data for the nation as a whole on a great variety of health characteristics for many population groups and the decennial census also provides data for subnational areas for these population groups. The health characteristics that the NCHS has measured by the synthetic method include such items as restricted activity days, bed-disability days, work-loss days, hospital discharges, length of hospitalization, number of physician visits per year, number of dental visits per year, percentage of persons limited in activity, and percentage of persons unable to carry on major activity.

WORKSHEET 11.1 Illustration of the Computation, by the Synthetic Method, of Estimates of the Percentage of Live Births That Are Jaundiced, for Pennsylvania: 1980

Race, age, and live-birth order	NNS [a] percentage jaundiced, U.S. (1)	Hospital births, Pennsylvania (2)	Estimated number of jaundiced births (3) = (1) ⋆ (2)
Total[a]		156,799	33,806
White			
Under 20, 1	.205	13,484	2,764
Under 20, 2+	.265	2,898	768
20–24, 1	.228	23,739	5,412
20–24, 2	.200	15,005	3,001
20–24, 3+	.189	5,356	1,012
25–29, 1	.231	17,664	4,080
25–29, 2	.222	17,877	3,969
25–29, 3	.232	7,959	1,846
25–29, 4+	.139	2,921	406
30–34, 1	.223	4,889	1,090
30–34, 2	.199	8,115	1,615
30–34, 3	.263	5,768	1,517
30–34, 4+	.219	3,628	795
35 and over, 1–3	.284	3,445	978
35 and over, 4+	.188	2,451	461
All other races			
Under 20, 1	.191	4,208	804
Under 20, 2+	.114	1,285	146
20–24, 1	.187	3,174	594
20–24, 2	.149	2,704	403
20–24, 3+	.158	1,779	281
25–29, 1	.215	1,390	299
25–29, 2	.176	1,674	295
25–29, 3+	.185	1,999	370
30+, 1–2	.257	1,535	394
30+, 3+	.273	1,852	506

Synthetic state estimate = 33,806 ÷ 156,799 = 21.6%

[a] National Natality Survey.

Source: Joe Fred Gonzalez, Jr., Paul J. Placek, and Chester Scott, "Synthetic estimation in followback surveys at the National Center for Health Statistics," in U.S. Office of Management and Budget, *Indirect Estimators in Federal Programs*, Statistical Policy Working Paper 21, July 1993.

They are cross-classified for such population groups as race, sex, age group, family income, family size, and industry of head of family.

Similarly, the data on the birth certificate and data obtained from the National Natality Survey of 1980 (a followback survey based on a sample of births and designed to secure additional information about the birth) provides the basis for synthetic estimates for states on a variety of health characteristics of mothers and infants.[11] Worksheet 11.1 illustrates the calculation of a synthetic estimate based on the 1980 survey with the derivation of the number and percentage of infants with jaundice in Pennsylvania in 1980. For this purpose, some 96 cells describing race (2), age of mother (6), and live birth order of child (8) were collapsed into 25 cells. Table 11.2 presents synthetic estimates

TABLE 11.2 **Synthetic Estimates of Selected Health Characteristics of Infants, for Five States: 1980 (Percent of Total Live Births)**

Characteristic	Pennsylvania	Indiana	Tennessee	Kansas	Montana
Caesarian delivery	17.3	16.7	17.0	16.8	16.8
Respiratory distress	3.9	4.0	4.1	3.9	3.9
Infant jaundiced	21.6	21.4	21.1	21.5	21.5
Low birth weight	6.5	6.5	7.2	6.4	6.3
Late[a] or no prenatal care	4.3	4.7	5.0	4.5	4.3
Low 1-minute Apgar score[b]	9.4	9.4	9.7	9.4	9.4

[a] Prenatal care beginning in the third trimester.

[b] A score of less than seven out of ten (optimum). A 1-minute Apgar score is a measure of the physiological condition of the infant one minute after birth.

Source: Based on Gonzalez et al., 1993. Calculated from U.S. data from the National Natality Survey and from state registration data on the distribution of births by race, age of mother, and live-birth order.

for five states for a variety of characteristics of infants from the 1980 National Natality Survey. The U.S. Census Bureau and others have prepared synthetic estimates of unemployment and delapidated housing units for states, SMSAs, and counties, and of census undercounts for states, on the basis of national indicator ratios.[12]

In the form described, synthetic estimation has the advantages of simplicity of interpretation, ready availability of the necessary data, ease of calculation, and low cost, as compared with a direct survey of the population. Synthetic estimates have important limitations, however. The types of socioeconomic and health characteristics for which a national sample survey can provide useful estimates are limited. Synthetic estimates are subject to error both as a result of the inadequacies of the basic assumptions and the sampling error of some of the input data. The synthetic method tends to take insufficient account of local variations in the prevalence of the characteristic being measured (e.g., poverty); and the prevalence of the characteristic may vary for categories other than those accounted for. We are limited to variables for which reasonably accurate independent estimates are available for the target areas. Finally, the sampling error of the estimates may be large and difficult to measure. Much of the research on the synthetic method has dealt with the measurement of the sampling error of the estimates and ways of reducing it, although the method is subject to substantial bias as well.[13]

Comparison of synthetic estimates with census or registration data provides the most accurate indication of the quality of the synthetic estimates. Table 11.3 presents a three-method comparison of the percentage of babies with low birth weight and the percentage of mothers with late or no prenatal care for five states in 1980. Synthetic estimates are compared with "true" values from the vital registration system and with direct survey estimates. In general, the synthetic estimates are closer to the true values than the direct estimates and have lower relative mean square errors.

In applying the synthetic method, it is necessary to select variables as weights, first, whose distribution varies substantially or widely from area to area *and*, second, for which the prevalence or incidence of the characteristic

TABLE 11.3   Comparison of "True" Values, Synthetic Estimates, and Direct Survey Estimates of the Percentage of Births with Low Birth Weight and the Percentage of Mothers with Late or No Prenatal Care, for Five Selected States: 1980

Characteristic and state	"True" percent[a]	Synthetic estimate					Direct estimate[e]	
		Percentage[b]	Standard error	Bias	MSE[c]	RRMSE[d]	Percent	RRMSE[d]
Low birth weight								
Pennsylvania	6.5	6.5	0.2	0.0	.00	.00	6.6	.00
Indiana	6.3	6.5	0.2	0.2	.04	.03	6.8	.22
Tennessee	8.0	7.2	0.2	−0.8	.64	.10	8.5	.23
Kansas	5.8	6.4	0.2	0.6	.36	.10	6.8	.36
Montana	5.6	6.3	0.2	0.7	.49	.13	9.2	.71
Late[f] or no prenatal care								
Pennsylvania	3.9	4.3	0.2	0.4	.16	.10	4.3	.21
Indiana	3.8	4.7	0.2	0.9	.81	.24	2.0	.21
Tennessee	5.4	5.0	0.2	−0.4	.16	.07	4.7	.26
Kansas	3.4	4.5	0.2	1.1	1.21	.32	2.1	.35
Montana	3.7	4.3	0.2	0.6	.36	.16	3.0	.62

[a] Based on vital registration data. No standard error; the bias is assumed to be negligible.

[b] Based on the U.S. data from the National Natality Survey and state data on the distribution of births by race, age of mother, and live-birth order.

[c] Mean square error. The MSE of an estimate x is the variance (i.e., square of standard error) of x plus the square of the bias.

[d] Relative root mean square error, calculated as the square root of the mean square error divided by the "true" percentage.

[e] Based on the state portion of the National Natality Survey sample.

[f] Prenatal care beginning in the third trimester.

Source: Based on Gonzalez *et al.*, 1993.

of interest varies substantially or widely among the categories of the variable. Weighting the national or regional proportions of the population having some socioeconomic or health characteristic of interest in age-sex groups by the age-sex distribution in each state cannot effectively reveal the variation from state to state in the proportion of the total population of the state having the characteristic, given the relative geographic invariance of age-sex distributions. Race/Hispanic origin is an indicator variable that can provide the desired variation. The national percentage of blacks was 13% in 1997, but in some states it was near or over one-third. In the nation as a whole 27% of the population was "other than non-Hispanic white" (i.e., "racial/ethnic minority"), but in California the figure was 49%, in New York 34%, and in Texas 44%. Second, using disability as an example, its prevalence among blacks greatly exceeds its prevalence among whites. The percentage of work-disabled in 1997 was 16% for blacks, 9% for whites, and 9% for Hispanics.[14]

Moreover, synthetic estimation provides no information for the subarea about the category-specific *proportions*, which are adopted from the parent area. For example, if we assume that the proportion of white males disabled at ages 45 to 54 in the United States applies to Minnesota, we have learned nothing special about the proportion of persons in this age/sex/race group who are disabled in Minnesota. Synthetic estimation does provide a crude estimate of the *absolute* number of persons or events in a demographic category (e.g., age) having the characteristic (e.g., disability). The sum of the numbers over all categories (e.g., all ages, sexes, and races) would be a useful rough estimate of the total number of disabled persons in the state. The accuracy of the overall proportion of disabled persons for the state depends mainly on the degree to which the proportions for the individual categories for the United States apply to the state and on the adequacy of the estimates of the weighting variables for the state. If these conditions are favorably met, the synthetic estimate is said to be unbiased. If, in addition, a large enough sample is selected for each category, the variance of the estimate will be small.

When direct survey estimates for a region can be obtained, synthetic estimates for the states composing the region may be adjusted proportionately to be consistent with the regional figures. Assuming that the figure for the region is unbiased, this procedure results in some reduction in bias in the state estimates.[15] The estimator—that is, the algorithm for arriving at an estimate—is

$$^sp_{va} = \left[\left({}^rP_{da} \div \sum{}^s p_{ea} \right) \star {}^s p_{ea} \right] \tag{8}$$

where $^sp_{va}$ is the ratio-adjusted synthetic estimate for the state in category a, $^rP_{da}$ is the direct estimate for the region in the category, and $^sp_{ea}$ is the initial synthetic estimate in the category for the state. Such **ratio-adjusted synthetic estimates** for states sum to the direct estimate for the region.

Regression Methods

As we may recall, in the regression method, national, regional, or local data from surveys, administrative records, and other sources are used in a mathematical equation that relates one or more independent variables from these sources to the characteristic under study or some simple function of it. The regression method offers a way of employing a wider variety of indicator or symptomatic data ("covariates") than the synthetic method in making estimates of socioeconomic characteristics for subnational areas.[16]

The symptomatic variables selected for use in the regression equation are believed to be correlated with the characteristic being estimated. The independent variables may be estimates derived from a number of sources, such as a direct survey estimate for the area, an estimate based on demographic analysis, the components of change underlying the latter estimate, and a synthetic estimate. The independent variables may be estimates of such variables as per capita income, percentage of the adult population completing high school, and percentage foreign-born, depending on the socioeconomic characteristic (i.e., the dependent variable) to be estimated. The form of the dependent variable may be, for example, the number with the characteristic, the percentage of the population with the characteristic, or the percentage difference between the true number with the characteristic and a synthetic estimate of it. The form of the regression equation may vary from ordinary least squares (linear, polynomial) to logistic regression to locally weighted regression.[17] The analyst will have to experiment with the alternatives suggested and others to arrive at an optimum procedure for making regression estimates for particular socioeconomic characteristics for particular areas. Statistical software packages commonly contain procedures for solving various types of regression equations (e.g., SAS, SPSS, SUDANN).

To compute estimates of health conditions in states, the NCHS has employed a **regression-adjusted synthetic estimator** in addition to the basic synthetic estimator. This estimator relates the synthetic estimate in the form of its percentage error as the dependent variable to a set of independent variables in the regression equation.[18] The equation follows the conventional linear model but Y, the dependent variable, requires further definition:

$$Y = \alpha + \beta_1 z_1 + \beta_2 z_2 + \cdots + \beta_{m-1} z_{m-1} + \beta_m z_m + e \tag{9}$$

$$Y = [(X_s - X_t) \div X_t] \star 100 \tag{10}$$

Y is the percentage difference between the synthetic estimate (X_s) and the estimated true value (X_t) (e.g., for a state), e represents random error, z represents the value of independent variables $z_1, \ldots, z_m$ (e.g., for the state), and $\beta_1, \beta_2, \ldots, \beta_m$ are regresssion coefficients to be estimated. If the two equations are combined and solved for X_t, the following estimator is obtained:

$$X_t = X_s[1 + 0.01(\alpha + \beta_1 z_1 + \cdots + \beta_m z_m)] \tag{11}$$

This equation suggests how the combination of the synthetic estimate and the regression estimator makes an adjustment for the bias in the synthetic estimate. Note, however, that the method described is only one of many ways to combine covariates with the synthetic estimator.

Combinations of Methods

As suggested by the last example, the various methods may be combined. A direct survey estimate may be combined with other variables in the regression method. The synthetic method may be used in a regression equation, either as a part of the dependent variable (as in the regression-adjusted synthetic method) or as an independent variable (in a combined synthetic-regression method). Methods may be averaged, as in the **composite synthetic method**; here a direct sample survey estimate is averaged with the synthetic estimate. The direct sample survey estimate is generally unbiased but has a relatively large variance, while the synthetic estimate is generally biased but has a relatively small variance. A weighted average of the two estimates will yield an estimate with bias and variance between those of the original estimates. Direct estimates may be combined with ratio-adjusted synthetic estimates in a weighted average to form another type of composite synthetic estimate (Malec, 1993, *op. cit.*).

Illustrations of Methods

To illustrate further the possibilities for combining methods, we consider a few current programs involving estimates of socioeconomic characteristics for subnational areas. These are the Census Bureau estimates of households for states, the Census Bureau estimates of child poverty for states and counties, the U.S. Department of Agriculture (USDA) estimates of infants and children income-eligible for the Women, Infants, and Children (WIC) program for states, and the NCHS estimates of the percentage of persons in a state or county who have visited a physician in the past year.

Households for States

The U.S. Census Bureau prepares postcensal estimates of households for states by the prevalence-ratio (i.e., householder-ratio or headship-ratio) method.[19] An age-specific **householder ratio**, or **headship ratio**, is the ratio of the number of heads of households in a given age group to the population in that age group. In the Census Bureau application of the method, the headship ratios shown by the 1990 census for states are extended to the estimate date on the basis of the change in national headship ratios shown by the Current Population Survey (CPS). Next, the estimated headship ratios for states for the current year are applied to population estimates in the corresponding age groups in the current year to derive estimates of households for each age group of householder. The total number of households for a state is then obtained by summing the estimates of households for the various age groups of householders. The following equations show the derivation of the estimates for postcensal year t:

$$_sH_j^t = (_{U.S.}HR_j^t \div _{U.S.}HR_j^c) \star _sHR_j^c \star _sP_j^t \tag{12}$$

$$_sH^t = \sum _sH_j^t \tag{13}$$

where j represents an age group, H^t represents estimated households, HR^t represents the estimated headship ratio from CPS, HR^c represents the headship ratio from the census, P represents the population, s represents the state, and $U.S.$ represents the nation.[20]

In applying this method, it may be useful to disaggregate the ratios of householders to population for characteristics in addition to the age of the householder, such as the sex and marital status of the householder and the type of household. If this refinement is employed, it is necessary to have current population estimates for the state, disaggregated by these variables, in addition to age. This degree of disaggregation is employed in making the official estimates of households.

Estimates of Poor Children for States and Counties

Many federal programs use income or poverty criteria in formulas for allocating funds to local jurisdictions. In response to the need for current data of this kind on the part of several federal agencies and, in particular, in response to the requirements of Title I of the Elementary and Secondary Education Act (1994), during the mid-1990s the Census Bureau began preparing estimates for states and counties of (1) poor children under age 5 (states only), (2) related children aged 5 to 17 in poor families (school districts also), (3) poor children under age 18, (4) the total number of poor persons, and (5) median household income. The estimates for counties and school districts are prepared biennially and published with a lag of 3 years after the reference year. A description of the SAIPE program, and its methodology, along with the estimates are available at census Web site *www.census.gov/ftp/pub/hhes/www/SAIPE.html*.

In general, the method of developing the current estimates of poor children and all poor persons for states and counties combines the direct survey method and the regression method. The estimates are based on the March Current Population Survey (CPS), data on federal income tax returns, data on participation in the Food Stamp program, current independent population estimates, and data from the 1990 census.

In developing the estimates for states, the direct estimates from the CPS for the reference year are weighted with estimates based on a regression equation in which the CPS estimates are the dependent variables and the independent variables are (1) the percentage of poor persons as represented by tax returns, (2) the percentage of the population receiving food stamps, (3) the percentage of persons under 65 for whom tax returns were not filed, and (4) the results of a regression analysis of poverty from the 1990 census. The weighting procedure is designed to improve the estimates from the March survey for states with small sample sizes. The greater the relative variance of the state CPS estimate, the greater the weight given to the regression estimate. The resulting state estimates are then adjusted pro rata to the national CPS estimates for the particular age/poverty category. These adjusted state estimates are then employed as "controls" for the county estimates.

The estimates for counties are also based on a weighted average of direct survey estimates (where available) and a regression estimate.[21] The survey estimates are 3-year average CPS figures centered on the reference year. The regression equation is a log-linear equation employing similar elements as for the state estimates. The dependent variable is the CPS estimate and the independent variables are (1) poor persons included as "exemptions" in the tax returns, (2) all persons included as "exemptions" in the tax returns, (3) food stamp recipients, (4) estimates of the population in the relevant age group, and (5) poor persons in the relevant age group from the 1990 census. For those counties not represented directly in the CPS—about two-thirds of them—the regression estimate receives 100% of the weight. The resulting estimates for counties are then adjusted pro rata to the final estimates for the states.

The American Community Survey will begin providing current direct survey estimates for states, counties, and school districts late in the first decade of the 21st century with much smaller variances than the CPS. The availability of new survey estimates will call for an entirely new design for deriving the small area poverty estimates.

Infants and Children Income-Eligible for the WIC Program for States

Estimates of infants and children who are income-eligible for the Special Supplemental Nutrition Program for Women, Infants, and Children (WIC), administered by the U.S. Department of Agriculture (USDA), are prepared by Mathematica Policy Research for the Food and Consumer Service, USDA. The method of deriving the estimates essentially involves averaging (1) CPS-sample estimates and (2) estimates of WIC-eligibles based on a regression equation employing data on participation in selected government programs and per capita income. These estimates are more current than census-sample data and more precise than CPS-sample estimates taken alone. As described in a report submitted by Mathematica Policy Research, Inc., to the Food and Consumer Service, USDA, the steps in the method for making estimates for 1992 are as follows:[22]

1. Calculate the percentage of infants and children who were income-eligible for each state from the 1990 census.

2. Derive sample estimates of the percentage of infants and children who were income-eligible for each state from the most recent CPS (March 1993 for 1992 income data).

3. Calculate the change in the percentage eligible between 1989 and 1992 on the basis of the figures in (1) and (2).

4. Prepare a second estimate of the change in the percentage eligible for each state using a regression equation based on changes in participation in the food stamp program, changes in participation in the unemployment insurance program, and changes in per capita income.

5. Calculate a weighted average of the results in (3), the estimates of change based on the CPS/census-sample data, and the results in (4), the estimates of change based on the regression equation, with weights based on the precision of the sample estimates and the fit of the regression line.

6. Derive an improved estimate of the percentage eligible in 1992 by adding the results in (5), the average estimate of change in the percentage eligible between 1989 and 1992 based on the two methods, to the results in (1), the estimate of the percentage eligible in 1989 calculated from the census.

7. Obtain preliminary estimates of the number of eligible infants and children for each state in 1992 by multiplying the results in (6), the percentages eligible in 1992, by the number of infants and children in each state in 1992.

8. Adjust the results in (7), the preliminary estimates of the numbers of eligible infants and children in each state, so that the state figures sum to the national totals for eligible infants and children shown by the CPS.

Note certain features of this method, designed to improve the quality (i.e., reduce variance and bias) of the estimates for states over a simple use of CPS sample figures. These are the use of a second estimator, namely a regression equation incorporating several symptomatic variables; anchoring the estimate of change to the census figures, not the CPS sample figures; and adjusting the preliminary estimates for the states to the national totals. The process of modifying the initial survey estimates in these ways is referred to by some statisticians as **shrinkage**. In general, shrinkage refers to the imposition of restrictions on estimates with the goal of improving the results. These restrictions may be of several kinds and may be used alone or in combination. The most common are the weighting of survey estimates with estimates derived from a regression equation or a synthetic estimate and the adjustment of survey estimates to control totals for larger geographic areas.

Occurrence of a Single Doctor's Visit for States

Malec (1997) and Malec *et al.* (1993) maintain that there are many situations where the simpler synthetic and related procedures are inadequate to produce accurate estimates for states.[23] They devised a method whose major aim is to take account of variation among the states that is not encompassed by synthetic estimates. To illustrate the method, they used data from the National Health Interview Survey to measure the occurrence of at least one visit to a doctor during the preceding year for states. This item is a **binary random variable**—that is, one with a simple yes-no answer. Their analysis was hierarchical. Two regressions were employed sequentially: first, a logistic regression relating the probability of making a doctor's visit to the individual's characteristics for a county or groups of counties; then, a multivariate linear regression relating the parameters of the logistic regression to covariates measured at the county level.

Evaluation of Methods

Estimates of socioeconomic characteristics are subject to error as a result of the inadequacies of the method used to derive them, the assumptions associated with the method, and the sampling error of the sample data. As with estimates and projections of the total population, estimates of socioeconomic characteristics can be evaluated against various types of independent data. These may be counts or estimates from the decennial census; direct sample survey estimates for large states, groups of small states, or groups of years; vital registration; and other data. Measures of error for a set of estimates include the measures described in Chapters 9 and 10 and, where the estimates are based directly or indirectly on a sample, the mean square error, the average mean square error, and the relative mean square error.

Before we define the new measures mentioned, recall that the root mean square error ($RMSE$) cited in the previous chapter is defined as

$$RMSE = \sqrt{\left[\sum_{i}^{n} (u_i - U_i)^2 \div n \right]} \tag{14}$$

where u_i is an estimate for area i, U_i is the "true" value for area i, and n is the number of areas in the set. Two attributes of this measure are evident. It is a measure of error for a *set* of data and, in effect, it gives extra weight to the large errors by squaring the amount of error. It is statistically equivalent to the quadratic mean of the errors in the set.

This measure should be distinguished from the **mean square error** (MSE) and the **relative root mean square error** ($RRMSE$). These measures refer to the *total error* of an *individual* estimate based on *sample* data. The mean square error (MSE) of an estimate x has an established definition in sampling theory. It is equal to the variance of x plus the square of the bias of x:

$$MSE(x) = VAR(x) + [BIAS(x)]^2 \tag{15}$$

The precision of sample estimates derived by different methods may be compared on the basis of the relative root mean square error ($RRMSE$) of the estimate—that is, the ratio of the square root of the mean square error of an estimate to the true value:

$$\frac{\sqrt{MSE(x)}}{E(x)} \tag{16}$$

A measure, useful particularly for evaluating synthetic estimates based on sample data, is the **average mean square error** (AMSE). This measure evaluates synthetic estimates by averaging the individual mean square errors of a set of synthetic estimates.[24] Accordingly, this measure can be applied and interpreted for grouped data.

As part of its long-time research on synthetic estimation, beginning in the late 1960s, the NCHS compared basic and adjusted synthetic estimates of death rates for four causes of death for each state in 1960 with the actual death rates for each state from the registration system (Levy, 1971).[25] The quality of the synthetic estimates was only good or fair for two of the causes of death and poor for the other two. The study showed that the accuracy of synthetic estimates may differ considerably from state to state and from subject to subject. Namekata, Levy, and O'Rourke (1975) compared basic synthetic estimates of complete and partial work disability for states with the direct estimates available from the 1970 census for each state.[26] The test results showed that the quality of the estimates varied for the two classes of disability. An evaluation of a set of "nearly unbiased synthetic estimates" of deaths in 42 states in 1960, using as a measure of error the median absolute percent difference, showed that the estimates had only a small bias but that their sampling variance could be quite large (Levy and French, 1977).[27] Schaible *et al.* (1977) found that composite estimates (discussed earlier) were much more accurate than either the synthetic estimates or the direct sample estimates in a comparison of state unemployment ratios and percentages completing college based on the National Health Interview Survey with 1970 census data as the standard.[28]

Table 11.3 presents a limited evaluation of synthetic estimates of infant health characteristics based on the National Natality Survey of 1980. This table compares the true values, the synthetic estimates, and the direct survey estimates, for the percentage of infants with low birth weight and the percentage of infants with late or no prenatal care, for five states. Several measures of error are shown. Judging by the relative root mean square error, the direct estimates for these health markers are less accurate in the small states than in the large states and the synthetic estimates are more accurate than the direct estimates.

Many of these evaluation studies were conducted when the synthetic method was first introduced. Research on the methodology of small area estimates for socioeconomic characteristics has been continuing, as we saw with the SAIPE program of the Census Bureau and the WIC estimates program of the U.S. Food and Consumer Service. The relative accuracy of direct survey methods and indirect methods, including various versions of the synthetic and regression methods, remains to be established. We already have some evidence of a gain in combining individual estimates made by different methods. Users should be critical of any subnational estimates offered and seek to be informed as to the methods and assumptions employed in their derivation.

PROJECTIONS OF SOCIOECONOMIC CHARACTERISTICS

Federal Programs

Given the vast array of public programs that the federal government administers or supports, it should not be surprising that it prepares a wide variety of projections of the socioeconomic characteristics of the population. A current review shows that indeed the federal government is deeply involved in the business of making national and even state projections of various socioeconomic characteristics that have specific programmatic applications. In fact, so widespread is the activity of forecasting in the federal government that the analysts have organized themselves into a federal forecasters group and sponsor an annual conference (since 1988). The program of the conference held in 1999 suggests the range of subjects for which projections are prepared.[29]

In addition to the basic projections of national and state population prepared by the Bureau of the Census and the Bureau of Economic Analysis, and the national projections of population of the Social Security Administration, national and occasionally subnational projections on the following socioeconomic subjects and others are prepared by various federal agencies:

Subject	Federal agency
Marital status	Census Bureau
	Social Security Administration
Households	Census Bureau
Educational attainment	Census Bureau
Labor force	Bureau of Labor Statistics
	Social Security Administration
Employment	Bureau of Labor Statistics
	Bureau of Economic Analysis*
School enrollment	National Center for Education Statistics*
Teachers	National Center for Education Statistics
Farm population	Economic Research Service, USDA
Farm employment	Economic Research Service, USDA
Health manpower	Bureau of Health Professions, HHS
Physicians by specialty	
Nurses	
Income and earnings	Bureau of Labor Statistics
	Bureau of Economic Analysis*
Veteran population	Dept. of Veterans Affairs
VA beneficiaries	Dept. of Veterans Affairs

    * These agencies have published projections for states as well as projections for the nation.

Projections of many nondemographic series requiring projections of population as exogenous (i.e., independently derived) variables for their calculation are also prepared by federal agencies for use in administering public programs. Some projections of this kind are listed here:

Subject	Federal agency
Energy demand	Energy Information Administration
Hospital construction	Health Resources and Services Administration
Volume of mail	U.S. Postal Service
Agricultural consumption	Economic Research Service, USDA
Farm land values	Economic Research Service, USDA
Tax forms	Internal Revenue Service
Airline passengers	Federal Aviation Administration
Caseload filings	Administrative Office of the U.S. Courts

General Methods

The principal methods of preparing projections of socioeconomic and health characteristics may be outlined as follows:

Name	Alternate name
General analytic methods	
Prevalence-ratio method/event-exposure method	Participation-ratio method/incidence rate method
Cohort-component method	Cohort-survival method
Cohort-progression method/grade progression method	Macrosimulation
Stochastic demographic forecasting	Probabilistic demographic forecasting, microsimulation
Specific statistical methods	
Time-series methods	Box-Jenkins methods
Regression methods	Econometric methods

While some of these methods were described briefly in the previous two chapters, the material is partly repeated in this chapter with a focus on its application to socioeconomic and health characteristics. The several methods enumerated can be applied, usually in combination, to the preparation of national *and* subnational projections of socioeconomic characteristics of the population. The most common analytic methods of making such projections are the prevalence-ratio method and the cohort-progression method. These methods have also been called the participation-ratio method and macrosimulation, respectively, although these alternate names usually refer to special applications of the methods. All the analytic methods listed, except stochastic demographic forecasting, deal with aggregate data and produce deterministic results.[30]

Stochastic demographic forecasting employs microsimulation and combines both analytic and statistical approaches. Because stochastic forecasting produces probabilistic results, it can provide confidence intervals for the resulting forecasts. The two other methods, time-series analysis and regression, are classified as statistical methods, and can be applied as independent methods or as supporting methods within the framework of demographic analysis.

Prevalence-Ratio Method

In the prevalence-ratio method, projected prevalence ratios for a socioeconomic or health characteristic—that is, projected proportions of the population at each age or age group participating in some activity or having a given characteristic—are applied to population projections for the corresponding ages. Illustrative formulas for 5-year age groups are as follows:

$$\text{Current prevalence ratio } = CPR = {}^{y}_{5}P^{c}_{a} \div {}^{y}_{5}P^{t}_{a} \tag{17}$$

$$\text{Projected prevalence ratio } = PPR = ({}^{y+n}_{5}P^{c}_{a} \div {}^{y+n}_{5}P^{t}_{a}) \tag{18}$$

$$\text{Projection of the number with the characteristic } = PPR \star {}^{y+n}_{5}P^{t}_{a} \tag{19}$$

where (1) the projected proportion of (a) the population P in age group $a/a+4$, with characteristic c in future year $y + n$, $({}^{y+n}_{5}P^{c}_{a})$, of (b) the total population t in age group $a/a + 4$, in year $y + n$, $({}^{y+n}_{5}P^{t}_{a})$, is multiplied by (2) the projected total population t in age group $a/a + 4$, in year $y + n$, $({}^{y+n}_{5}P^{t}_{a})$. Hence, the method calls for prior projections of an age schedule of prevalence ratios and of the age distribution of the population. The method of projecting a time series of prevalence ratios may vary from informal generalization on the basis of a few recent observations to complex time-series methods where annual observations are available, such as the Box-Jenkins methods. One common technique of extrapolation is to apply the average annual rate of change in the prevalence ratios over some prior period, such as the previous decade or two. Box-Jenkins methods may involve a variety of techniques, including conversion of the data to natural logarithms or taking first or second differences of the series.

Cohort-Progression Method

The conventional form of the cohort-progression method uses ratios of the number of persons in age or grade a in year y to the number of persons in age or grade $a - t$ in year $y - t$, for a birth, school grade, or other type of cohort: $^yP_a \div {}^{y-t}P_{a-t}$ or, for one-grade one-year change, $^yP_a \div {}^{y-1}P_{a-1}$. Assuming that these ratios describe the situation in the latest observed period and that they are held constant for the projection period, they would be applied to $^yP_{a-t}$ in the current year to derive $^{y+t}P_a$ and to $^{y+t}P_{a-t}$ to derive $^{y+2t}P_a$, and so on:

$$^{y+t}P_a = ({}^yP_a \div {}^{y-t}P_{a-t}) \star {}^yP_{a-t} \qquad (20)$$

$$^{y+2t}P_a = ({}^yP_a \div {}^{y-t}P_{a-t}) \star {}^{y+t}P_{a-t} \qquad (21)$$

Diagrammatically, for birth or grade cohorts, we have

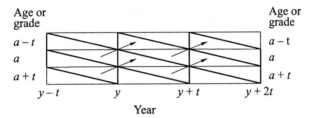

Arrows link different cohorts with the same initial and ter-minal ages or grades.

These ratios represent *net* cohort changes, but they could theoretically be dis-aggregated into components such as deaths, marriages, divorces, promotions, demotions, and so on, depending on the nature of the cohort changes and the availability of data.

Macrosimulation is a more elaborate form of the cohort-progression method, employing transition probabilities to shift groups of individuals from one state to another. **Macrosimulation** refers to the calculation of artificial data for population aggregates resembling those that would be observed in real life. For example, in making projections of marital status or households, this model begins with current estimates of the marital status or household status of the population and employs transition probabilities to update their characteristics in future years.[31] Transition probabilities for marital status may shift the married population to the states of divorced, widowed, married, or dead; the divorced population to married, divorced, or dead; and so on. For household status, a family "married-couple" householder may shift to "other family" householder, nonfamily householder, and married-couple householder, or dead. Macrosimulation has not often been used to make household projections.

Microsimulation

The stochastic (probabilistic) method, also called microsimulation, has also not been widely used for making projections of socioeconomic characteristics. **Microsimulation** refers to the probabilistic generation of artificial data on a individual basis of the kind that would be observed in real life.[32] The method is complex, difficult to implement, difficult to describe to users, and computer costs are high. It is more informative, however, than the other methods for studying the interaction between the various factors affecting the life cycle and its changes. The microsimulation method simulates life course events and generates detailed records of demographic status transitions for each *individual*.

National Projections

The official national projections of various socioeconomic characteristics have usually employed combinations of the analytic and statistical methods enumerated. Typically an analytic measure expressed in a time series is projected by a statistical method. For example, the official national projections of households and the labor force are currently prepared by extending a series of prevalence ratios by formal or informal time-series analysis. The projections of annual high school graduates are prepared by extending a series of event-exposure rates by the methods of time-series analysis, and the projections of enrollment at the college level are derived by extending a series of enrollment ratios by a regression method.

Household Projections

In the prevalence-ratio/time-series method of preparing household projections, household-to-population ratios (or headship ratios) must be extended into the future according to some statistical formula. In a more refined design, projections of the marital distribution of the population are first prepared, and then ratios of households-to-ever-married population and ratios of households-to-never-married population are projected separately by a statistical formula. The Census Bureau (1996) employed such a method in preparing its latest national projections of households.[33] The projections are based on current estimates of households for 1994, which were derived by extending the 1990 census counts of households with (1) administrative-record data on building permits and other data on housing-unit changes, and (2) the changes since 1990 according to type of household recorded in the Current Population Survey.[34] Three series of projections of households classified by type of household were developed for the years 1995 to 2010. The household-type matrices consisted of five household types and two marital-status types (never married, ever married), classified by the age, sex, race, and Hispanic origin of the householder. The results include projections of these same household-types and marital-status categories.

The projected number of households in the various categories is the product of (1) the proportions of the household population by type of household and other demographic characteristics and (2) the household population disaggregated by these demographic characteristics. The time-series model used in the preferred series of projections, Series 1, was based on estimates of annual changes in householder proportions for 1959 to 1993 derived from the Current Population Survey. After a logistic transformation of the proportions (p)—that is, conversion from p to $\ln[p \div (1-p)]$—and some adjustments to remove outliers, an ARIMA (type 0, 2, 1) model was fitted to the historical data.[35] Projections of married-couple households require prior projections of the marital status of the household population; these were derived by applying a simple time-series model to the proportions of the population in marital categories. Series 2 projections fixes the age-sex specific proportions in various household and marital categories as of 1990, while series 3 adds race/Hispanic detail to the design of series 2. That is, series 2 and 3 allow only for changes in future population composition.

Labor Force and Employment Projections

The prevalence-ratio/time-series method is also employed by the Bureau of Labor Statistics (BLS) in projecting the national labor force. The specific measure used is the labor force participation ratio (LFPR), or the proportion of an age group in the labor force. For the projections of the labor force published in 1999, future LFPR for the period 1998 to 2008 were developed on the basis of an informal application of time-series analysis. The trends in LFPR during the 1978–1998 period were analyzed, the time series of LFPR were projected to future dates, and the resulting projections of LFPR were applied to the middle series of projections of the civilian noninstitutional population prepared by the Census Bureau.[36] The BLS projected participation ratios for 136 separate demographic groups (age/sex/race/Hispanic), both to refine the projection process and to obtain the detailed projections desired. The figures are revised every 2 years.

It was assumed that the LFPR would generally continue to increase or fall during the 1998–2008 period as they had done during the 1978–1998 period, but at a slower place. For men in the peak age band of labor force participation, ages 25 to 54, and at ages 55 to 64, the rates for 5-year age groups are expected to remain unchanged, or to rise or fall slightly. Older men, especially men 65 to 74, are expected to show a large increase in participation ratios. The LFPR of all age groups of women are expected to increase, but the general increase in participation is expected to continue slowing down. The largest increase is expected for women 55 to 64 years of age. The changes for women reflect two important developments: slower increases in labor force participation of younger women and greater stability of labor force participation of the baby-boom cohorts during 1998–2008 than during 1988–1998.

Projections of the labor force based on population may be described as projections of **labor supply** (i.e., the number of persons available for work). By its nature this number combines employed persons and persons seeking work. Alternatively, projections of employment based on requirements for labor by industry (i.e., the number of jobs industry can offer) are projections of **labor demand**. Any discrepancy between projections of labor supply and labor demand should be reconciled. It may indicate the prospect of a surplus of labor or the prospect of a shortage of labor. A large discrepancy may suggest the need to expand job opportunities or plan for a labor shortage.

The national projections of employment made by the Bureau of Economic Analysis (BEA) in 1995[37] and the Bureau of Labor Statistics (BLS) in 1999[38] are projections of labor demand. The BLS national projections of employment are prepared in terms of major industry categories on the basis of a macroeconomic projection of the U.S. economy. The BEA national projections of employment are calculated as the sum of state projections of employment and are modified to be consistent with the BLS national "supply-side" projections of the labor force. The latter have been adjusted to allow for unemployment (using projections of "full-employment" unemployment ratios).

School Enrollment Projections

It is convenient to use the projections of public elementary and secondary school enrollment according to grade prepared by the U.S. National Center of Education Statistics (NCES) to illustrate the cohort-progression method.[39] The steps in the progression are easily identified—school grades. In this application we call the method the **grade-progression method**, but it has also been called the grade-retention method. First, enrollment data for each grade over a series of years are assembled, as illustrated in Table 11.4. Grade-progression ratios (GPR) are then calculated as the ratio of enrollment (E) in one grade (g) in a given year (y) to enrollment in the prior grade (g − 1) in the preceding year (y − 1).

$$GPR = {}^{g}E_y \div {}^{g-1}E_{y-1} \tag{22}$$

TABLE 11.4 National Public Elementary and Secondary School Enrollment, by Grade: 1992 to 1995 (Figures in Thousands)

Grade	1992	1993	1994	1995
Kindergarten and grades 1 to 8	31,088	31,504	31,898	32,341
Kindergarten	3,817	3,922	4,047	4,173
First	3,542	3,529	3,593	3,671
Second	3,431	3,429	3,440	3,507
Third	3,361	3,437	3,439	3,445
Fourth	3,342	3,361	3,426	3,431
Fifth	3,325	3,350	3,372	3,438
Sixth	3,303	3,356	3,381	3,395
Seventh	3,299	3,355	3,404	3,422
Eighth	3,129	3,249	3,302	3,356
Unclassified[a]	539	515	494	502
Grades 9 to 12	11,735	11,961	12,213	12,500
Ninth	3,352	3,487	3,604	3,704
Tenth	3,027	3,050	3,131	3,237
Eleventh	2,656	2,751	2,748	2,826
Twelfth	2,431	2,424	2,488	2,487
Unclassified[a]	269	248	242	245

[a] Includes ungraded and special education.
Source: U.S. Office of Education, National Center for Education Statistics, *Digest of Education Statistics*, Annual.

TABLE 11.5 National Grade-Progression Ratios for Public Enrollment, 1988–1989 to 1995–1996, and Projections, 2008–2009

Grade progression	1988–1989	1989–1990	1990–1991	1991–1992	1992–1993	1993–1994	1994–1995	1995–1996	2008–2009
KG to Gr.1	1.015	1.003	.984	.961	.925	.916	.907	NA	X
Gr.1 to Gr.2	.941	.955	.959	.965	.968	.975	.976	.980	.974
Gr.2 to Gr.3	1.004	1.002	1.001	1.000	1.002	1.003	1.001	1.003	1.002
Gr.3 to Gr.4	1.005	1.004	1.007	1.002	1.000	.997	.998	1.001	1.000
Gr.4 to Gr.5	1.005	1.005	1.005	1.003	1.002	1.003	1.004	1.005	1.004
Gr.5 to Gr.6	1.014	1.014	1.012	1.011	1.009	1.009	1.007	1.014	1.001
Gr.6 to Gr.7	1.031	1.059	1.022	1.019	1.016	1.014	1.012	1.018	1.007
Gr.7 to Gr.8	.982	.984	.984	.984	.985	.984	.986	.993	.988
Gr.8 to Gr.9	1.101	1.111	1.112	1.110	1.114	1.109	1.122	1.130	1.121
Gr.9 to Gr.10	.923	.922	.920	.914	.910	.898	.898	.895	.901
Gr.10 to Gr.11	.908	.911	.913	.911	.909	.901	.903	.904	.904
Gr.11 to Gr.12	.900	.906	.916	.919	.913	.904	.905	.914	.910

NA: Not available. X: Not applicable.

Note: KG to Gr.1 denotes the ratio of enrollment in grade 1 in the second year shown to enrollment in kindergarten in the first year shown. Other grades paired denote the ratio of enrollment in the second year and grade shown to enrollment in the first year and grade shown. Enrollment figures in the source have intentionally not been adjusted to include persons unclassified by grade and in special education.

Source: 1988–1989 to 1995–1996: Based on U.S. Office of Education, National Center for Education Statistics, *Digest of Education Statistics,* annual. 2008–2009: Based on National Center for Education Statistics, *Projections of Education Statistics to 2009,* by Debra E. Gerald and William J. Hussar, 1999.

A historical series of such ratios is shown for the grades from kindergarten to high school for national public enrollment from 1988–1989 to 1995–1996 in Table 11.5. For example, the grade-progression ratio from grade 7 to grade 8 for 1994 to 1995, .986, is calculated by dividing enrollment in grade 8 in 1995, 3,356,000, by enrollment in grade 7 in 1994, 3,404,000.

The array of grade-progression ratios shown in Table 11.5 reflects the very high degree of grade retention in the elementary or "compulsory" grades, the reduced grade retention in the secondary grades, the trend of falling grade retention between kindergarten and grade 1, the excess grade "retention" in the ninth grade resulting from the entry of large numbers of new enrollees from outside the system, and the nearly stationary pattern of the grade-progression ratios at every grade. Such grade-progression ratios are net ratios, allowing at once for deaths in the cohort, grade promotion and demotion, institution-alization and deinstitutionalization, other dropouts and reinstatements, and immigration and emigration. Separate allowance can be made for some or all of these components, particularly for mortality, net promotions, and net immi-gration, but the relative stability of the grade-progression ratios suggests that this disaggregation would not contribute much to the accuracy of the projec-tions. The disaggregation would be of analytical and administrative interest, however.

The resulting time series of grade-progression ratios can be projected ac-cording to any of a variety of projection methods or simply held constant at the latest level. With the latter assumption, enrollment in grade g for the year $y + 1$ is calculated as follows:

$$^{g}E_{y+1} = {}^{g-1}E_y \star ({}^{g}E_y \div {}^{g-1}E_{y-1}) \tag{23}$$

Alternatively, the series can be extended to future years by a variety of meth-ods of statistical time-series analysis. The official national projections of ele-mentary and secondary enrollment by grade used **exponential smoothing** for this purpose. In this method, the members of the series are averaged with shift-ing weights, the greater weights being given to the later ratios. Specifically, in exponential smoothing the weights for observations decrease exponentially as the observations recede farther into the past:

$$P = aX_t + a(1-a)X_{t-1} + a(1-a)^2X_{t-2} + a(1-a)^3X_{t-3} + \cdots \tag{24}$$

where P is the projection, a is the smoothing constant, and X_t is the past obser-vations at time t. (The sum of the weights applied to the X's in the exponential smoothing formula is 1.000.) The specific rate at which the weights of prior observations decrease is determined by a smoothing constant selected by the analyst after some experimentation. In the projections, the smoothing constant selected was 0.4. In addition, since the historical series had an essentially level or **stationary** pattern, single exponential smoothing (as compared with double exponential smoothing) was applied. Once the smoothed grade-progression ratios are determined by the formula, they are held constant for all future years.

The derivation of projections for kindergarten or first grade present a spe-cial problem because data for a prior grade are lacking. Such enrollments can be linked to births several years earlier or to the population in the appropriate ages or combination of ages at a current date (ages 5 and 6). These projections then become the basis for deriving the enrollments in the higher grades by grade-progression ratios. In the calculations made by the National Center for Education Statistics, kindergarten enrollment was projected on the basis of its ratio to the estimated population for age 5, and first-grade enrollment was projected on the basis of its ratio to the estimated population for age 6.

In effect, for its enrollment projections by grades, the NCES employed a combination of two basic analytic methods—the prevalence-ratio method for kindergarten and grade 1 and the cohort-progression method for all other grades. It then derived projections for enrollment in the elementary and secondary grades by applying a single set of smoothed grade-progression ratios repetitively to the grade projections of the prior year.[40]

The latest projections of enrollment by grades at the elementary and secondary levels prepared by the NCES were based on an annual series of grade-progression ratios from 1970–1971 to 1995–1996. The projections extend to 2008–2009 in single calendar years and are available for single school grades for public schools and for two broad grade groups for private schools. Projections are revised annually.

The NCES also prepares national projections of college enrollment for age/sex groups. Its latest projections, extending from 1996 to 2009, were based on a combination of the prevalence-ratio method and the regression method. The regression equations are designed to estimate the enrollment ratio at each age from data for the period 1970 to 1996. The independent variables include disposable income per capita and unemployment ratios. The regression model is a multiple multiplicative model (i.e., a nonlinear regression model):

$$Y = aX_1^{b1} X_2^{b2} \tag{25}$$

This equation can easily be transformed into linear form by taking the natural logarithms (ln) of both sides of the equation:

$$\ln Y = \ln a + b_1 \ln X_1 + b_2 \ln X_2 \tag{26}$$

In this formulation a 1% change in $\ln X_1$, the ln of disposable income per capita, will cause a percentage change in $\ln Y$, the ln of the enrollment ratio, equal to b_1. Other categories of enrollment, for example, level enrolled, were estimated by distributing the total for each age/sex group proportionately according to prior distributions of enrollment in these categories.

Projections of Educational Attainment

In designing a method of projecting educational attainment, there are several alternatives with respect to the form of the analytic measure used and several alternatives with respect to the way the basis time series is arrayed. The measure may be (1) the percentage of an age group completing each educational level, (2) the continuation ratio, that is, the ratio of (a) the percentage of an age group completing an educational level (e.g., college) to (b) the percentage completing or attending a prior level (e.g., completing high school or attending college), or (3) the logits of these measures. The time series for the measure for a particular educational level may be arrayed in several ways: (1) a particular *age group* for a series of birth cohorts (i.e., calendar years); (2) a particular *birth cohort* for a series of age groups; and (3) a series representing different age groups and birth cohorts.

The "same-cohort" method using prevalence ratios has been the method of choice for preparing national projections of educational attainment because this array of the educational attainment ratios is most likely to show stability in the original data. The prevalence ratios may be held unchanged from age to age at the last observed level:

$$ (^{y+5}p_{(a+5)ae} \div {}^{y+5}p_{(a+5)at}) = (^{y}p_{ae} \div {}^{y}p_{at}) = (^{y-5}p_{(a-5)e} \div {}^{y-5}p_{(a-5)t}) \quad (27) $$

where p represents population, a represents age group, at represents total population in an age group, e represents educational level, and y represents year. After age 35 for all levels of schooling and after age 25 for high school graduates, the proportion of the population at a given educational level for a birth cohort hardly changes with time—that is, few persons add to their accumulation of school grades at the higher ages. For example, the proportion of high school graduates in ages 30 to 34 in 1990, ages 35–39 in 1995, ages 40–44 in 2000, and so on, would tend to be nearly the same.

Any projection of the proportions of an age group attaining any level (e.g., high school graduates) would be carried out along cohort lines and the changes made should be rather modest. If necessary, the series can be smoothed before projection. One source of variation in educational attainment ratios for a birth cohort at various ages is the changing distribution of the population within each age group by race, Hispanic origin, and nativity resulting from differential mortality and immigration, factors inversely correlated with educational level.

Projections made in this way are based on several assumptions. With reference to high school graduates, for example, the assumptions are (1) that there is no increase in schooling after age 25, (2) that the survival rate of high school graduates in a particular birth cohort is the same as that of the rest of the population in the cohort, (3) that the relative numerical effect of net immigration on high school graduates and non-high school graduates is equal during the forecast period, and (4) that the relative change in the net undercount or underestimate of high school graduates and the rest of the population in the birth cohort is the same. The evidence on educational or other socioeconomic differentials in mortality rates clearly contradicts the second of these assumptions. Adjustments can be made in the educational-level-specific proportions for projection purposes by applying the findings on socioeconomic differentials on mortality. The third and fourth assumptions are also not supportable. Nevertheless, the impact of these assumptions is not great (i.e., the method is rather robust against the assumptions), as is suggested by the record of decennial census data on educational attainment for age groups. Projections of high school graduates in the population have been made from time to time by the same-cohort method using prevalence ratios.[41]

The NCES does not prepare projections of the population according to educational attainment, only the number of persons graduating high school each year. The projections of annual high school graduates are made by extending a time series of rates representing the ratio of the number of students graduating high school to the number of students enrolled in grade 12. The method of extending the rates is to derive the exponentially smoothed rate for the series, as described earlier, and then fixing this rate for the projection period.

Evaluation of Projections

The principal standards for the evaluation of national projections of socio-economic series are censuses, the Current Population Survey and other national surveys, and projections for the same date, with an appropriate time lag. The parameters of the projections evaluated may be the number with the characteristic, the amount or rate of change in the number since the base or jump-off date, the percentage distribution of the characteristic, or some other aspect of the characteristic of interest. The specific measures of evaluation are those already described in this and the previous chapter.

One useful type of evaluation is to disaggregate the total error of the projections derived by the prevalence-ratio method into the error resulting from the age schedule of prevalence ratios and the error resulting from the population projections. A variation of the method of standardization can be used to separate the contribution of these two factors to the total error in the projections. The contribution of error by the population component may be sharply limited in some cases. These are cases in which the population component is expected to be relatively accurate. For example, household and labor force projections deal with householders or workers, and the underlying population projections do not involve projections of births for the first 15 to 20 years into the future. Moreover, the error in projections of mortality, and possibly net immigration, affecting the ages from 20 to 59 could be minimal. Hence, the error in the prevalence ratios would dominate the total error. For enrollment projections, the opposite is true. Enrollment ratios for the elementary and secondary grades can vary little, but the population at the younger ages after several years is subject to considerable error.

Just as alternative projection series are commonly prepared for the basic demographic characteristics, alternative series are usually prepared for one or more of the components in projections of socioeconomic characteristics. A wide range between series is to be expected in all projections where the segment of the population yet to be born is a major component or where prevalence ratios can vary widely. Projections of elementary and secondary enrollment illustrate the former situation after 5 to 10 years. Reasonable variations in enrollment ratios for the ages that attend these grades add very little to the range, since enrollment ratios at these ages are already near 100%; the population component contributes great uncertainty, however. After about 18 years or so, variations in the size of the new birth cohorts begin to affect college enrollment; here there is great uncertainty about both enrollment ratios and population size. Projections of labor force and households begin to have a high degree of uncertainty after about 18 years also, matching that of the total population and college enrollment. On the other hand, for relatively closed populations such as educational-level categories above age 25 or 35, the picture is different. Inasmuch as nearly all persons have completed their education by age 35, projections of the distribution of the population by educational level above this age for the same cohort are relatively dependable for many years.

The same is true of the distribution of women over age 50 by the number of children they have had (e.g., proportion childless).

Relatively few systematic studies of the accuracy of projections of the socioeconomic characteristics of the population have been conducted. There are some studies of the accuracy of projections of households, the labor force, and school enrollment.[42] The errors in projections of households and labor force tend to exceed the error in the population 18 years and over. This is as expected, because projections for the former items are subject to error both from population and prevalence ratios. When attention is focused on projections of the increase in households or labor force, the percentage errors become considerable after merely a decade. As in studies evaluating population totals, in general in these studies also, the size of the errors varies directly with the length of the projection period. Fullerton's evaluation of six projections of labor force to 1995, prepared from 1980 to 1991, showed that the errors in the total labor force decreased as the target date grew nearer and that, in percentage terms, the errors were relatively small even after 15 years, being only about 3.5% for the 1980 projections. With respect to enrollment, the National Center for Education Statistics found, as expected, that the mean absolute percent errors of its projections of enrollment at the elementary and high-school level were relatively small, even for 10-year projections, but its projections of college enrollment were large after only 5 years (6%).

State and Local Projections

The uncertainties in projecting the characteristics of the population increase as the size of the area falls, since there is greater volatility in living arrangements and employment opportunities and greater relative turnover in population through migration in particular areas of the country than in the nation as a whole. The prevalence-ratio method and the cohort-progression method, combined with statistical time-series analysis and regression analysis, can be employed to prepare projections of socioeconomic or health characteristics for subnational areas as for the nation. In view of the greater availability of the required data and the greater simplicity of the method, the prevalence-ratio method, combined with time-series analysis, is the most commonly applied method of making projections of this kind.

Projections of Households

Projections of households for states or subdivisions of states are not available, except commercially. To develop projections of households for states, the prevalence-ratio method may be applied in the usual way—that is, by projecting headship (or householder) ratios on a period basis and multiplying the projected ratios against projected population figures, disaggregated by age and sex. A more refined approach is to construct the prevalence ratios in the form of ratios of household heads to the ever-married and never-married population. This approach requires prior projections of the marital status of the population for states.

Another approach is to apply the cohort-progression concept, carrying forward the number of household heads for each age-sex group to the next age group and date by relating household heads, say, at ages $a/a + 4$ in year y to household heads at ages 5 years younger 5 years earlier. When the cohort-progression ratio is held constant, we have

$$^{y+5}_5H_a = (^y_5H_a \div ^{y-5}_5H_{a-5}) \star ^y_5H_{a-5} \qquad (28)$$

Alternatively, headship ratios may be linked in cohort form between adjacent ages and adjacent years, and then projected on a period basis. The calculation of a projected headship ratio, assuming that the 5-year cohort-change ratio in headship ratios remains constant in the projection period, is symbolized by:

$$(^{y+5}_5H_a \div ^{y+5}_5P_a) \\ = (^y_5H_a \div ^y_5P_a) \div (^{y-5}_5H_{a-5} \div ^{y-5}_5P_{a-5}) \star (^y_5H_{a-5} \div ^y_5P_{a-5}) \qquad (29)$$

The resulting headship ratio would be multiplied against the projected population at ages a to $a + 4$ in year $y + 5$. A simple basis for projecting the cohort-change ratio in headship ratios for states or local areas is to use the pattern of change in the cohort-change ratio for the United States.

Projections of the Labor Force and Employment

The prevalence-ratio method can also be conveniently employed in the preparation of labor force projections for states and local areas. To compile the time series of labor force participation ratios (LFPRs), a historical series of state and local labor force data is needed. In general, they may be obtained from the decennial census, publications of the Bureau of Labor Statistics, various state agencies, and, within a decade, the American Community Survey. The Bureau of Labor Statistics publishes LFPRs from time to time for states. These can be employed either to make state labor force projections or as bases for projecting LFPRs for areas within the states. The Bureau of Economic Analysis (BEA) has periodically published projections of employment for states, metropolitan areas, and BEA economic areas, but the program has been discontinued (BEA, 1995, *op. cit.*). State employment security offices or other state agencies (e.g., Bureaus of Business Research) commonly make labor force and employment projections for their states.

The BEA "midterm" projections of employment for states were prepared on the basis of economic and demographic relationships for each state and between each state and the nation, summarized in a regression equation for each state. The structure of a typical state model is given by

$$X_j = A_j X_j + B_j Z_j + C_j Q_j + U_j \qquad (30)$$

where X denotes the economic and demographic variables determined in the individual state model, Z denotes the exogenous variables (e.g., minimum wage), Q denotes the variables that measure interstate activities, j refers to a state, A, B, and C are state-specific coefficients, and U is an error term. The projections are based on the premise that employment in each state affects employment in all other states and in the nation. "Long-term" projections of employment for each state to 2045 were prepared in terms of major industries, separating "basic" and "nonbasic" industry. The projections of employment in each nonbasic industry were tied to basic-industry employment by the nonbasic industry location quotient. The **location quotient** for a state is the ratio of

(1) an industry's employment in a state as a share of total employment in the state to (2) the industry's employment in the nation as a share of total national employment. Analysis of historical trends in each industry formed the foundation of these projections.

Projections of Public School Enrollment

As with national projections of school enrollment, both the prevalence-ratio method and the cohort-progression method can be used for preparing projections of school enrollment for states and local school districts. Statistical time-series analysis and regression can then be employed as the specific techniques of projection. The prevalence-ratio method requires prior projections of children and youth in single ages, and the grade-progression method requires prior projections of births or children aged 5 and 6 years. To calculate the entrants into the school system, kindergarten and first-grade pupils could be linked to the numbers of births 5 and 6 years earlier. Preferably, however, if projections of population in single ages are available, enrollment in the starting grades should be linked to population projections for the appropriate ages in the same calendar year. For example, the ratio of first graders to children aged 6 years, or a weighted average of children aged 5 and 6 years (with weights determined from the actual age distribution of children in grade 1), can be used to derive the projected number of pupils in grade 1. Then, the first graders and those in other grades can be carried forward by projected grade-progression ratios to future school years.

Two illustrations relating to subnational projections of school enrollment are briefly described in this and the following paragraphs. The first illustration concerns work of the U.S. National Center for Education Statistics (NCES). In 1999 the NCES published projections of public elementary and secondary enrollment for states from 1998 to 2009 (NCES/Gerald and Hussar, 1999, *op. cit.*). Public school enrollment data from the NCES Common Core of Data Survey for 1970 to 1996, along with population estimates from 1970 to 1997 and population projections from 1998 to 2009 for children, from the Bureau of the Census, were used to develop these projections. Elementary and secondary enrollments for individual grades 2 to 12 were projected by the grade-progression method. Kindergarten and first-grade enrollments were projected on the basis of enrollment ratios and the Census Bureau's projections of 5 and 6-year olds (e.g., first-grade enrollment in ratio to 6-year olds). The time series of grade-progression ratios were projected to 1997 by exponential smoothing and then the ratios were assumed to remain constant in all future years. The method assumes that future patterns of change in school enrollment will replicate those of the past and that there will not be any sharp changes in school policy.

Morrison (2000) presents the special case of forecasting enrollments for "entry-port" school districts—that is, school districts receiving large numbers of immigrant children.[43] Specifically, forecasts of school enrollment for elementary and secondary grades from fall 1997 and beyond were prepared from historical data from fall 1988 to fall 1996 by the grade-progression method for the Santa Ana Unified School District, Orange County, California, a principal region of immigrant settlement. In addition to the usual factors of deaths, promotions, demotions, dropouts, and interdistrict transfers, other special factors operated here to produce somewhat more erratic and irregular grade-progression ratios and to make the task of projecting them extremely uncertain. According to Morrison, although the area was nearly physically saturated and the level of residential density was high, it was experiencing an influx of immigrants, with potential future multiplier effects, and circular transnational student migration to and from Mexico that induced seasonal enrollment changes. Under such circumstances the task becomes one not so much of forecasting enrollment to anticipate actual changes as of forecasting enrollment to develop an early warning system that may dictate a change of course in school planning.

The historical array of grade-progression ratios, from kindergarten to grade 12 for the period from fall 1988–1989 to fall 1995–1996, shown in Table 11.6, reflects the turbulence in grade-to-grade changes in this school district. For example, the ratios of kindergarten enrollment to births showed a pronounced general decline, possibly because of the movement of young families out of the Santa Ana district or transfer to parochial schools in the district. The massive gain from eighth to ninth grade results in large part from the assignment of overage children with an English language deficiency to the ninth grade.

Projected kindergarten enrollment was derived from historical birth-to-kindergarten ratios in combination with estimates and projections of births 5 years earlier. It was assumed that the projected ratio for births to kindergarten equals the average ratio for the 4 most recent years. Projected grade-progression ratios were assumed to be the weighted average of the ratios for the 4 most recent paired years, and then plausible low and plausible high values were set for certain grade sequences. The projected ratios are included in Table 11.6 with the historical series.

PROJECTIONS OF PERSONNEL, FACILITIES, AND SERVICE REQUIREMENTS

Projections of demographic and socioeconomic entities or groups such as households, labor force, school enrollment, educational-attainment classes, and income groups underlie a wide range of applied projections required for planning and administering many public and private programs. These applied projections pertain to personnel, physical facilities, and services of various types, and they are needed for advance budget and other administrative planning. The nation, states, and other jurisdictions have to anticipate their needs for workers in various occupational specialties, to assure that a sufficient number will be trained and available for service. Communities need projections of hospitals and hospital beds, schools and classrooms, and housing, as well as of waste disposal services, health services, financial services, and a whole range of other types of projections as tools of community planning. Projections of hospitals and hospital beds can be tied in with prior projections of health conditions and average bed use. Projections of teachers, schools, and classrooms can be linked to prior projections of school enrollment and average class size.

TABLE 11.6 Grade-Progression Ratios, 1988–1989 to 1995–1996, and Projections, 1996–1997 and Beyond, for the Santa Ana Unified School District (Some School Years Have Been Selectively Omitted)

Grade progression	1988–1989	1990–1991	1992–1993	1994–1995	1995–1996	1996–1997 onward		
						Forecast	Plausible high	Plausible low
B to KG	NA	.772	.738	.631	.669	.674	.778	.631
KG to Gr.1	1.035	1.051	1.012	1.012	1.039	1.018		
Gr.1 to Gr.2	.939	.940	.950	.946	.962	.954		
Gr.2 to Gr.3	1.005	.968	.967	.952	.970	.965		
Gr.3 to Gr.4	1.031	.981	.978	.964	.965	.970		
Gr.4 to Gr.5	.991	.977	.988	.966	.984	.971		
Gr.5 to Gr.6	1.082	.986	1.006	1.005	.980	.996		
Gr.6 to Gr.7	.984	.961	.963	.973	.993	.972		
Gr.7 to Gr.8	1.011	.956	.965	.956	.936	.947		
Gr.8 to Gr.9	1.418	1.314	1.144	1.172	1.119	1.142	1.142	1.119
Gr.9 to Gr.10	.859	.913	.831	.831	.844	.832		
Gr.10 to Gr.11	.762	.742	.791	.846	.856	.824	.856	.824
Gr.11 to Gr.12	.678	.801	.757	.789	.782	.772		

Note: B to KG denotes the ratio of enrollment in kindergarten in the second year shown to births 6 years earlier. Other grades paired denote the ratio of enrollment in the second grade and year shown to enrollment in the first grade and year shown.

Source: Peter A. Morrison, "Forecasting enrollments for immigrant entry-port school districts," *Demography* 37(4): 499–150, November 2000. © Population Association of America. Reprinted with permission.

In our discussion of labor force projections, a distinction was made between demand and supply projections. The same type of distinction can be made with respect to projections of personnel, facilities, and services. A discrepancy between projected demand and projected supply for the same category suggests the prospect of either a shortage or a surplus. If such projections can be accepted as accurate forecasts, to avoid *either* costly, disruptive eventuality, the forecasts suggest that special action should be taken to reduce the demand or increase the supply, or vice versa.

The projection of specialized occupational personnel is illustrated for three occupational groups, namely, public schoolteachers, dentists, and research librarians. The projections illustrate three different methods. The National Center of Education Statistics (NCES/Edgar and Hussar, 1999, *op. cit.*) projects the demand for public elementary and secondary teachers from 1995 to 2009 by regression equations that link the number of public classroom teachers (T) to enrollment at the corresponding educational level (X_1) and to educational revenue receipts per capita from state sources (at 1986–1987 dollars) (X_2). The regression equations are linear multiple-variable equations:

$$T = b_0 + b_1 X_1 + b_2 X_2 \tag{31}$$

In the equation for secondary enrollment, the state revenues are lagged 3 years. The regression equation expresses the relation that, as the state spends more money on education and as enrollment increases, the number of elementary and secondary teachers to be hired increases. As in all regression analyses, the method yields accurate forecasts only if the relationships that existed among the variables in the past period continue throughout the projection period and if accurate forecasts of the independent variables (i.e., enrollments and state revenues) are available. The forecasts of enrollment at the elementary and secondary levels needed for this calculation were derived as described earlier.

Projections of the number of dentists for the period 1995 to 2020 have been prepared by the cohort-component method by the Bureau of Health Professions of the U.S. Health Resources and Services Administration.[44] The method yields a set of supply-side projections. The calculations begin with (1) the number of active dentists disaggregated by age and gender, as shown in the master file of the Amercan Dental Association and (2) data on (a) current graduates of dental schools and (b) current enrollment in dental schools, provided by the American Association of Dental Schools. The number of active dentists was "survived" to the projection dates with the mortality rates of white males obtained from the reports of the National Center of Health Statistics. Allowance for the retirement of dentists was based on data on retirement of physicians available from the Bureau of Labor Statistics. Special allowance was made for the lag between graduation from dental school and active practice, temporary separations from active practice, and returns to active practice. Three series of projections were developed, varying on the basis of the level of enrollment assumed for the first year in dental schools. No allowance was made for immigration and emigration of dentists nor for the differences in survival patterns among the sexes and races. The methodology is being refined to make allowances for these limitations.

The Association of Research Libraries prepares forecasts of the number of research librarians on the basis of a quadrennial survey of its members.[45] Currently the association has survey results for 1990, 1994, and 1998. The survey secures data for single years of age and years of experience. A substantial share of the librarians fail to report their age in the surveys (about 16% in the 1994 survey), and their ages have to be allocated. It is not known how the results would vary if alternative allocations of age were made, since sensitivity tests of the procedure for allocating nonreports of age have not been conducted.

Forecasts have been made on the basis only of the 1990 and 1994 surveys. The joint use of the 1990, 1994, and 1998 surveys would make it possible to calculate progression ratios for birth cohorts for the "experienced" research librarians for two 4-year periods. The ages could be combined in 4-year groups, which would match exactly the time interval between the surveys. Progression ratios between pairs of surveys (year $y - 4$ and year y, and year y and year $y + 4$) can be calculated as follows: $^{y}L_{24-27} \div {}^{y-4}L_{20-23}$, $^{y}L_{28-31} \div {}^{y-4}L_{24-27}$, and so on; and $^{y+4}L_{24-27} \div {}^{y}L_{20-23}$, $^{y+4}L_{28-31} \div {}^{y}L_{24-27}$, and so on. Such ratios incorporate the net effect of mortality, international migration, dropouts, and returns to practice in the 4-year period. "Inexperienced" librarians, or librarians with less than 1 year of experience, can be estimated by use of the ratio of 20- to 23-year-old librarians to the population in that age group: $^{y-4}L_{20-23} \div {}^{y-4}P_{20-23}$, $^{y}L_{20-23} \div {}^{y}P_{20-23}$, and $^{y+4}L_{20-23} \div {}^{y+4}P_{20-23}$. Projections of population in single ages are available from the Census Bureau. The future number of experienced librarians in 4-year age groups can be derived by applying the latest cohort-progression ratios to the number of librarians at the younger ages in the later year. For example, projections of librarians aged 24 to 27 and 28 to 31 years 4 years ahead ($y + 4$) can be obtained by

$$^{y+4}L_{24-27} = (^{y}L_{24-27} \div {}^{y-4}L_{20-23}) \star {}^{y}L_{20-23} \qquad (32)$$

$$^{y+4}L_{28-31} = (^{y}L_{28-31} \div {}^{y-4}L_{24-27}) \star {}^{y}L_{24-27} \qquad (33)$$

Alternatively, the cohort-progression ratios can be projected on the basis of the observations for the two past 4-year periods.

Projections of librarians in the conventional 5-year age groups in the calendar years ending in zero and five (e.g., 25–29 years in 2005) can be obtained by interpolation. Interpolation is needed both for the age grouping and the calendar year. In general, osculatory interpolation could serve for the ages and linear interpolation for the time intervals.[46]

NOTES

1. The reader may recall that the estimates from these surveys are adjusted to independent current estimates of the national population and its distribution by age, sex, and race/Hispanic origin, and estimates of state total population, derived by demographic analysis. They are further adjusted for net undercount of the population in these categories at the national level in the last census.

2. Kenneth M. Pollard and Martha F. Riche, "The CPS and kids count," a report to the Annie E. Casey Foundation prepared by the Population Reference Bureau, Washington, DC, 1994.

3. Kevin M. Pollard, "The dilemma in estimating postcensal state poverty rates," *Population Today* 17(10): 6–7, 10, October 1989, Washington D.C.: Population Reference Bureau.

4. Christine Ross and Sheldon Danziger, "Poverty rates by state, 1979 and 1985: A research note," *Focus* 10(3): 1–5 (Fall 1987).

5. U.S. National Institute on Drug Abuse, "Small area estimation—synthetic and other procedures, 1968–78," by Paul S. Levy in Joseph Steinberg (ed.), *Synthetic Estimates for Small Areas: Statistical Workshop Papers and Discussion*, NIDA Research Monograph 24, February 1979.

6. If there is little variation within strata with respect to the characteristic being measured, the bias in the nearly unbiased estimate is likely to be small. The nearly unbiased estimate is more likely to have a large variance than a large bias since the sample size of any one stratum is likely to be small. If the national surveys could be redesigned so that all sample strata were confined to individual states, the bias in direct estimates of states would be reduced and the direct estimates and other estimates based on them would be improved.

7. The procedures for preparing current estimates of households from administrative records were described in more detail in Chapter 9 in connection with the housing-unit method of estimating population.

8. In a broader interpretation, synthetic estimation is a type of indirect estimation employing statistical relationships from a different geographic domain or a different date than the area or date for which estimates are sought.

9. See, for example, Edmond Ting and Joan Wathen (CACI Inc.), "Estimation of net worth," paper presented at the annual meeting of the Population Association of America, Baltimore, MD, March 30–April 1, 1989.

10. U.S. National Center for Health Statistics, "Synthetic state estimates of disability," PHS Publication No. 1759, 1968; "State estimates of disability and utilization of medical services, United States, 1969–71," DHEW Pub. No. (HRA) 77-1241, January 1977; and "Synthetic estimation of state health characteristics based on the Health Interview Survey," by Paul S. Levy and Dwight K. French, *Vital and Health Statistics*, Series 2, No. 75, 1977.

11. J. F. Gonzalez, P. J. Placek, and Chester Scott, "Synthetic estimation in followback surveys at the National Center for Health Statistics," in U.S. Office of Management and Budget (eds.), *Indirect Estimators in Federal Programs,* Statistical Working Paper 21, 1993.

12. Maria E. Gonzalez, "Use and evaluation of synthetic estimates," pp. 46–50, in U.S. Bureau of the Census, *Statistical Methodology of Revenue Sharing and Related Estimates Studies,* Census Tract Papers, Series 40, No. 10, 1974; Maria E. Gonzalez and Christine Hoza, "Small area estimation with application to unemployment and housing estimates," *Journal of the American Statistical Association* 73: 7–15, 1978; A. P. Dempster and T. J. Tomberlin, "The analysis of census undercount from a postenumeration survey," in U.S. Bureau of the Census, *Proceedings of the 1980 Conference on Census Undercount,* pp. 88–94, 1980; and Allen L. Schirm and Samuel H. Preston, "Census undercount adjustment and the quality of geographic population distributions," *Journal of the American Statistical Association* 82(400): 965–978, 1987.

13. For a discussion of sampling error in synthetic estimates, see U.S. National Center for Health Statistics, "Synthetic estimation of state health characteristics based on the Health Interview Survey," by Paul S. Levy and Dwight K. French, *Vital and Health Statistics, Series* 24, No. 75, 1977.

14. U.S. Census Bureau, *Statistical Abstract of the United States, 1998*, Tables 34 and 622.

15. Donald Malec, "Model-based state estimates from the National Health Interview Survey," in Office and Management and Budget, *Indirect Indicators in Federal Programs,* pp. 8-1 to 8-21, Statistical Policy Working Paper 21, 1993.

16. Synthetic estimation may be viewed as a simplified or reduced form of multiple regression estimation. See U.S. Institute on Drug Abuse/Levy, 1979, *op. cit.*

17. Ordinary least squares and logistic regression were defined in an earlier chapter. Locally weighted regression is a type of nonparametric regression. It gives greater flexibility in fitting a regression equation to the data than the ordinary least squares method and is a good substitute for nonlinear regression. For further discussion of this method, refer to the following sources: W. S. Cleveland and S. J. Devlin, "Locally weighted regression: An approach to regression analysis by local fitting," *Journal of the American Statistical Association* 83(403): 596–610, 1988; and W. S. Cleveland, S. J. Devlin, and E. Grosse, "Regression by local fitting: Methods, properties, and computational algorithms," *Journal of Econometrics* 37: 87–114, 1988.

18. U.S. National Center for Health Statistics, "Synthetic estimation of state health characteristics based on the Health Interview Survey," by Paul S. Levy and Dwight K. French, *Vital and*

Health Statistics, Series 2, No. 75, October 1977; and Paul S. Levy, "The use of mortality data in evaluating synthetic estimates," pp. 328–331, in *Proceedings of the Social Statistics Section, 1971*, Washington, DC: American Statistical Association, 1971.

19. U.S. Bureau of the Census, "Estimates of housing units, households, and persons per household for the United States, regions, and states: 1990 to 1996," *PPL-73*, 1997.

20. Alternatively, the estimates can be prepared by (1) extrapolating the ratio of (a) the total number of households to (b) the total adult household population (18 years and over) for states from the census on the basis of the change in this ratio at the national level from the CPS and (2) multiplying the extrapolated ratios by the estimated population 18 years and over for states.

This procedure, which disregards age groups, was essentially used to prepare intercensal estimates of households for states during the 1980s. For this purpose, state data for the ratio of households to the adult population came from the two censuses and annual intercensal trends in this ratio were based on the national CPS data. As a last step, the state intercensal estimates of households were adjusted pro rata to national intercensal estimates of households.

21. National Research Council, *Small Area Estimates of School-Age Children in Poverty. Interim Report 3. Evaluation of 1995 County and School District Estimates for Title I Allocation*, Washington, DC: National Academy Press, 1999.

22. Allen L. Schirm, "State estimates of infants and children income-eligible for the WIC program in 1992," Mathematica Policy Research, Inc., report submitted to the Food and Consumer Service, USDA, May 15, 1995.

23. Donald Malec, "Model-based state estimates from the National Health Interview Study," pp. 8-1 to 8-21, in U.S. Office of Management and Budget, *Indirect Indicators in Federal Programs*, Statistical Policy Working Paper 21, 1993; and Donald Malec, J. Sedransk, Chris Moriarity, and Felicia LeClere, "Small area inference for binary variables in the National Health Interview Survey," *Journal of the American Statistical Association* 92: 815–826, 1997.

24. Maria E. Gonzalez and Joseph E. Waksberg, "Estimation of the error of synthetic estimates," paper presented at the first meeting of the International Association of Survey Statisticians, Vienna, Austria, August 18–25, 1973; and U.S. Bureau of the Census, "Use and evaluation of synthetic estimates," by Maria E. Gonzalez, in *Statistical Methodology of Revenue Sharing and Related Estimates Studies*, pp. 46–50, Census Tract Papers, Series GE-40, No. 10, 1974.

25. Paul S. Levy, "The use of mortality data in evaluating synthetic estimates," American Statistical Association (eds.), *Proceedings of the Social Statistics Section, 1971*, Washington, DC: American Statistical Association, 1971.

26. T. Namekata, P. S. Levy, and T. W. O'Rourke, "Synthetic estimates of work loss disability for each state and the District of Columbia," *Public Health Reports* 90: 532–538, 1975.

27. U.S. National Center for Health Statistics, "Synthetic estimation of state health characteristics based on the Health Interview Survey," by Paul S. Levy and Dwight K. French, *Vital and Health Statistics*, Series 2, No. 75, October 1977.

28. W. L. Schaible, D. B. Brock, and G. A. Schnack, "An empirical comparison of the simple inflation, synthetic, and composite estimators for small area statistics," in American Statistical Association (eds.), *Proceedings of the Social Statistics Section, 1977*, pp. 1017–1021, Washington, DC: American Statistical Association, 1978.

29. U.S. Department of Education, National Center for Education Statistics, *The 10th Federal Forecasters Conference—1999*, edited by Debra E. Gerald, 2000.

30. Mathematical models of social processes may be either deterministic or stochastic. If the effect of a change in the system can be predicted with certainty, the system is said to be deterministic. Since, however, we cannot predict the future behavior of individuals with certainty or the system is not fully specified, there is uncertainty in any prediction. We should, and may attempt to, attach probabilities to possible future states. The associated model is then described as stochastic. Deterministic models, employing aggregate data, are statistical approximations to stochastic models. When deterministic models are employed, indications of uncertainty have to be derived in nonstochastic ways. See Chapter 1 in D. J. Bartholomew, *Stochastic Models for Social Processes*, 2nd ed., New York: John Wiley and Sons, 1978.

31. The number of households and their distribution by size and structure are derived from the characteristics of reference persons in the household. A detailed description of the application of this method for projecting households is given in Yi Zeng et al., "Household projection using conventional demographic data," pp. 59–87, in Wolfgang Lutz et al. (eds.), *Frontiers of Population*

Forecasting, A Supplement to Vol. 24, 1998, *Population and Development Review,* New York: Population Council.

32. Bartholomew (1978, p. 9). U.S. Bureau of the Census, *Guide for Local Area Population Projections,* by Richard Irwin, Technical Paper 39 (p. 29) describes the method as follows:

> One hypothetical person at a time is processed through a series of probabilities (by computer necessarily) which approximate a life cycle. In projections of marriages and families, for example, the first "person" processed may never marry, since there is a chance at every age of remaining single. The next "person" run through the schedule probably will marry, since the probabilities of marrying, to which each indivdual is subjected at each age, are high in the young adult years. After the required number of individuals are processed, based on the needed sampling confidence limits, a population takes form… [for each date], classified by all the characteristics which were included in the model. This distribution is then superimposed on the actual population to obtain the final projections.

33. U.S. Bureau of the Census, "Projections of the number of households and families in the United States: 1995 to 2010," by Jennifer C. Day, *Current Population Reports* P25-1129, April 1996.

34. The current estimates used in projecting the number of housholds are not based directly on the Current Population Survey, the American Housing Survey, or the Housing Vacancy Survey, each of which provides a different current estimate of households.

35. William R. Bell, J. E. Bozik, S. K. McKenzie, and H. B. Shulman, "Time series analysis of household headship proportions: 1959–1985," Research Report Number 86/01, Statistical Research Division, U.S. Bureau of the Census, 1986.

36. U.S. Bureau of Labor Statistics, "Labor force projections to 2008: Steady growth, changing composition," by Howard N. Fullerton, Jr., *Monthly Labor Review* **122**(11): 19–32, November 1999. See also U.S. Bureau of Labor Statistics, "Labor force participation: 75 years of change, 1950/1998 and 1998/2025," by Harold N. Fullerton, Jr., *Monthly Labor Review* **123**(12): 3–12, November 1999.

37. U.S. Bureau of Economic Analysis, *BEA Regional Projections to 2045,* Vol. 1, *States,* July 1995.

38. U.S. Bureau of Labor Statistics, "Industry output and employment," by Allison Thomson, *Monthly Labor Review* **122**(11): 33–50, November 1999.

39. U.S. National Center for Education Statistics, *Projections of Education Statistics to 2009,* NCES 1999-038, by Debra E. Gerald and William J. Hussar, 1999.

40. A much different method, used by the Census Bureau in making enrollment projections for school levels, is to project enrollment ratios for each age/sex group (r) according to the annual average change in nonenrollment ratios ($1 - r$) during the previous decade or two, calculate the corresponding numbers enrolled at each age, then distribute these numbers according to grade levels as recorded in the latest year. See U.S. Bureau of the Census, "Demographic projections for the United States," *Current Population Reports,* Series P-25, No. 476, February 1972, pp. 5–6.

41. For projections of educational attainment prepared by the method described, see Samuel Preston, "Cohort succession and the future of the oldest-old," Chapter 3 in Richard M. Suzman, David P. Willis, and Kenneth G. Manton (eds.), *The Oldest-Old,* New York: Oxford University Press, 1992; Jacob S. Siegel, *A Generation of Change: A Profile of the Older Population,* New York: Russell Sage Foundation, 1993, Chapter 7; and U.S. Bureau of the Census, "Demographic projections for the United States," *Current Population Reports,* Series P-25, No. 476, February 1972, pp. 6–8.

42. See, for example, Jacob S. Siegel, "Development and accuracy of projections of population and households in the United States," *Demography* **9**(1): 51–68, February 1972; U.S. Bureau of Labor Statistics, "An evaluation of labor force projections to 1995," by Howard N. Fullerton, Jr., *Monthly Labor Review* **120**(9): 5–9, September 1997; Howard N. Fullerton, Jr., "Evaluating the 1995 BLS labor force projections," in American Statistical Association (eds.), *Proceedings of the Section on Government Statistics and the Section on Social Statistics,* pp. 394–399, Alexandria, VA: American Statistical Association, 1999; and NCES/Gerald and Husssar, 1999, *op. cit.*

43. Peter Morrison, "Forecasting enrollments for immigrant entry-port school districts," *Demography* **37**(4): 499–510, November 2000.

44. Stuart Bernstein, U.S. Bureau of Health Professions, "Forecasting workforce supply: Dental personnel and dentists," in Debra E. Gerald (ed.), *The 10th Federal Forecasters Conference— 1999: Papers and Proceedings*, Washington, DC: U.S. National Center for Education Statistics, 1999.

45. Stanley J. Wilder, *The Age Demographics of Academic Librarians: A Profession Apart*, A report based on data from the annual ARL salary survey, 1995, Washington, DC: Association of Research Libraries.

46. For further guidance regarding methods of interpolation, refer to the Revised Condensed Edition of *The Methods and Materials of Demography*, Academic Press, 2002.

SUGGESTED READINGS

Estimates

Official National Estimates

U.S. Bureau of the Census annual or occasional reports on marital status, living arrangements, households, income, poverty, educational level, enrollment, nativity, and citizenship; U.S. Bureau of Labor Statistics monthly reports on labor force, employment, unemployment, and earnings; and U.S. Bureau of Economic Analysis annual reports on employment and personal income.

Subnational Estimates

Cleveland, W. S., and Devlin, S. J. (1988). "Locally weighted regression: An approach to regression analysis by local fitting." *Journal of the American Statistical Association* 83(968): 596–610.

DiGaetano, Ralph, Mackenzie, Ellen, Waksberg, Joseph, and Yaffe, Richard. (1981). "Synthetic estimates for local areas from the Health Interview Survey." In U.S. Bureau of the Census, *Small-Area Population Estimates—Methods and Their Accuracy, and New Metropolitan Area Definitions and Their Impact on the Private and Public Sector*, pp. 61–79. Small-Area Statistics Papers Series GE-41, No. 7.

Elston, Jennifer M., Koch, Gary G., and Weissert, William G. (1991, March). "Regression-adjusted small area estimates of functional dependency in the noninstitutionalized American population aged 65 and over." *American Journal of Public Health* 81(3): 335–343.

Fay, Robert E. (1979). "Some recent Census Bureau applications of regression techniques to estimation." In U.S. National Institute on Drug Abuse, *Synthetic Estimates for Small Areas: Statistical Workshop Papers and Discussion*, pp. 155–184. Joseph Steinberg (ed.). Research Monograph 24.

Fay, Robert E., and Herriot, Roger. (1979). "Estimates of income for small places: An application of James-Stein procedures to census data." *Journal of the American Statistical Association* 74(366): 269–277.

Gonzales, Maria E., and Hoza, Christine. (1978). "Small-area estimation with application to unemployment and housing estimates." *Journal of the American Statistical Association* 73(361): 7–15.

Gonzalez, J. F., Placek, P. J., and Scott, C. (1993). "Synthetic estimation in followback surveys at the National Center for Health Statistics." In U.S. Office of Management and Budget, *Indirect Estimators in Federal Programs*, pp. 2-1 to 2-11. Statistical Policy Working Paper 21.

Gonzalez, Maria E., and Waksberg, Joseph. (1973, August). "Estimation of the error of synthetic estimates." Paper presented at the first meeting of the International Association of Survey Statisticians, Vienna, Austria.

Levy, Paul S. (1974). "The use of mortality data in evaluating synthetic estimates." In American Statistical Association (eds.), *Proceedings of the Social Statistics Section, 1971*, pp. 328–331. Alexandria, VA: American Statistical Association.

Levy, Paul S. (1979). "Small area estimation—synthetic and other procedures, 1968–78." In U.S. National Institute on Drug Abuse, Joseph Steinberg (ed.), *Synthetic Estimates for Small Estimates: Statistical Workshop Papers and Discussion*, pp. 4–19. NIDA Research Monograph 24.

Malec, Donald. (1993). "Model-based state estimates from the National Health Interview Survey." In U.S. Office and Management and Budget, *Indirect Indicators in Federal Programs*, pp. 8-1 to 8-21. Statistical Policy Working Paper 21.

Namekata, T., Levy, P. S., and O'Rourke, T. W. (1975). "Synthetic estimates of work loss disability for each state and the District of Columbia." *Public Health Reports* 90: 532–538.

O'Hare, William P. (1993, June). "Assessing post-census state poverty estimates." *Population Research and Policy Review* 12(3): 261–275.

Reder, Stephen. (1997). "Synthetic estimates of literacy proficiency for small census areas." Report prepared for the Office of Vocational and Adult Education, U.S. Department of Education, by Portland State Univerity.

Reznek, Arnold P., and Spoeri, Randall K. (1981). "A local-area application of methodologies for estimating and projecting socioeconomic data items." In U.S. Bureau of the Census, *Small-Area Population Estimates: Methods and Their Accuracy, and New Metropolitan Area Definitions and Their Impact on the Private and Public Sector*, pp. 41–55. Small-Area Statistics Papers Series GE-41, No. 7.

Schirm, Allen L. (1994). "The relative accuracy of direct and indirect indicators of state poverty rates." American Statistical Association (eds.), *1994 Proceedings of the Section on Survey Research Methods*. Alexandria, VA: American Statistical Association.

Schirm, Allen L. (1995). *State Estimates of Infants and Children Income-Eligible for the WIC Program in 1992*. Report prepared by Mathematica Policy Research, Inc., Washington, DC, for the U.S. Food and Consumer Service, Department of Agriculture.

Sigmund, Charles L., Popoff, Carole, and Judson, D. H. (Decision Analytics, Reno, Nevada). (1999, March 25–27). "A system for synthetic estimates of health-related characteristics: Linking a population survey with local data." Paper presented at the annual meetings of the Population Association of America, New York City.

U.S. National Center for Health Statistics. (1977a). *State Estimates of Disability and Utilization of Medical Services: United States, 1969–71*. DHEW Publication No. (HRA) 77–1241, Health Resources Administration.

U.S. National Center for Health Statistics. (1977b). "Synthetic estimation of state health characteristics based on the Health Interview Survey." By Paul S. Levy and Dwight K. French. *Vital and Health Statistics: Data Evaluation and Methods Research* 2 (75). DHEW Publication No. (PHS) 80-1356.

U.S. National Center for Health Statistics. (1979). "Small area estimation: An empirical comparison of conventional and synthetic estimators for states." By W. L. Schaible, D. B. Brock, R. J. Casady, and G. A. Schnack. *Vital and Health Statistics: Data Evaluation and Methods Research* 2 (82).

U.S. National Institute on Drug Abuse. (1979). Joseph Steinberg (ed.), *Synthetic Estimates for Small Areas: Statistical Workshop Papers and Discussion*. NIDA Research Monograph 24.

U.S. Office of Management and Budget. (1993). *Indirect Indicators in Federal Programs*. Statistical Policy Working Paper 21. See esp. Chapters 2, 3, 5, 8, and 9.

Projections

Official National Projections

U.S. Bureau of the Census. (1996). "Projections of the number of households and families in the United States: 1995 to 2010," by Jennifer C. Day. *Current Population Reports*, P25-1125.

U.S. Bureau of the Census. (2000). "Population Projections of the United States, by age, sex, race, Hispanic origin, and nativity: 1999–2100." Population Projections Program, Population Division, U.S. Bureau of the Census.

U.S. Bureau of Labor Statistics. (1999, November). "Labor force projections to 2008: Steady growth and changing composition," by Howard N. Fullerton, Jr. *Monthly Labor Review* 122(11): 19–32.

U.S. Bureau of Labor Statistics. (1999, November). "Industry output and employment," by Allison Thomson. *Monthly Labor Review* 122(11): 33–50.

U.S. Bureau of Labor Statistics. (1999, December). "Labor force participation: 75 years of change, 1950/1998 and 1998/2025." By Howard N. Fullerton, Jr. *Monthly Labor Review* 123(12): 3–12.

U.S. National Center for Education Statistics. (1999). *Projections of Education Statistics to 2009*, by Debra E. Gerald and William J. Hussar. NCES 1999-038.

U.S. National Center for Education Statistics. (2000). *Projections of Education Statistics to 2010*, by Debra E. Gerald and William J. Hussar. NCES 2000-071.

U.S. Social Security Administration, Office of the Actuary. (1992). *Economic Projections for OASDHI Cost and Income Estimates: 1992*. By Eugene B. Yang and Stephen C. Goss. Actuarial Study No. 108.

U.S. Social Security Administration, Office of the Chief Actuary. (1997). *Social Security Area Population Projections: 1997*. By Felicitie C. Bell. Actuarial Study No. 112.

National Projections Studies

Aprile, R., and Palombi, M. (1998). "Demographic trends and teaching staff costs: The case of Italy." *Genus* (Italy) 54(3–4): 265–284.

Edmonston, Barry, and Passel, Jeffrey S. (1992). "Immigrants and immigrant generations in population projections." *International Journal of Forecasting* 8(3): 459–476.

Fullerton, Howard N., Jr. (1997). "Evaluating the 1995 BLS labor force projections." *American Statistical Association, Proceedings of the Section on Government Statistics and the Section on Social Statistics*. Alexandria, VA: American Statistical Association.

Kono, Shigemi. (1987). "The headship rate method for projecting households." In John Bongaarts, Thomas Burch, and Kenneth W. Wachter (eds.), *Family Demography: Methods and Their Application*, pp. 287–308. Oxford: Clarendon Press.

Manton, Kenneth G., Singer, Burt, and Suzman, Richard. (eds.). (1993). *Forecasting the Health of Elderly Persons*. New York: Springer-Verlag.

Manton, Kenneth G., Stallard, Eric, and Singer, Burt. (1992). "Forecasting the future size and health status of the U.S. elderly population." *International Journal of Forecasting* 8(3): 433–458.

Mason, Andrew, and Racelis, Rachel. (1992). "A comparison of four methods for projecting households." *International Journal of Forecasting* 8(3): 509–527.

Siegel, Jacob S. (1972, February). "Development and accuracy of projections of population and households in the United States." *Demography* 9(1): 51–68.

U.S. National Center for Health Statistics, Centers for Disease Control and Prevention. (1996). *Projections of health status and use of health care of older Americans*. Occasional Paper from the National Center for Health Statistics, with collaboration of the University of Illinois at Chicago and the University of Chicago and support from the Interagency Forum on Aging-Related Statistics. Unpublished study.

Zeng, Yi, Vaupel, James W., and Wang, Zhenglian. (1998). "Household projection using conventional demographic data." In Wolfgang Lutz, James W. Vaupel, and Dennis A. Ahlburg (eds.), *Frontiers of Population Forecasting*, pp. 59–87. New York City: Population Council.

Subnational Projections

Brown, Warren A. (Cornell University). (1994, September 22–24). "Tools and methods for improving school enrollment forecasting." Paper prepared for the International Conference on Applied Demography, Bowling Green State University, Bowling Green, OH.

Dunton, Nancy. (1994). "Planning for children's residential care." In Hallie J. Kintner, Thomas W. Merrick, Peter A. Morrison, and Paul R. Voss (eds.), *Demographics: A Casebook for Business and Government*, pp. 327–342. Boulder, CO: Westview Press.

Fishlow, Harriet. (1994). "Enrollment projection in a multicampus university system." In Hallie J. Kintner et al. (eds.), *Demographics: A Casebook for Business and Government*, pp. 298–306. Boulder, CO: Westview Press.

McKibben, Jerome N. (1996, December). "The impact of policy changes on forecasting for school districts." *Population Research and Policy Review* 15(5–6): 527–536.

McKusick, David R., Wrightson, William, and Wilkin, John C. (Actuarial Research Corporation, Columbia, MD). (1999, March 25–27). "Model for long-range population projection by disability status." Paper presented at the annual meeting of the Population Association of America, New York City.

Morrison, Peter A. (1996, April). "Forecasting enrollments during court-ordered desegregation." *Population Research and Policy Review* 15(2): 131–146.

Morrison, Peter A. (2000, November). "Forecasting enrollments for immigrant entry-port school districts." *Demography* 37(4): 499–510.

New York State Council on Children and Families. (1985). *1985–90 Statewide Comprehensive Plan for Residential Child Care.* By Gail Koser, Nancy Dunton, and Laura Lippman.

Opitz, Wolfgang, and Nelson, Harold. (1996, December). "Short-term, population-based forecasting in the public sector: A dynamic caseload simulation model." *Population Research and Policy Review* 15(5–6): 549–563.

U.S. Bureau of Economic Analysis. (1995). *BEA Regional Projections to 2045.* Volume 1. *States.*

12

▮ SOME POLITICAL APPLICATIONS OF DEMOGRAPHIC DATA AND METHODS

INTRODUCTION

Demographic Changes and the Political Landscape

Demographic changes are certain to be associated with and result in changes in the political landscape. The political landscape encompasses the variety of populations involved in political representation and the allocation of public

535

funds. It encompasses the content of political debate and the positions on public issues taken by political parties. Illustrative demographic-political aggregates constituting the political landscape include the state populations involved in congressional apportionment, local populations involved in redistricting for the Congress and state and local legislative bodies, persons of voting age, citizens of voting age, persons registered to vote, persons who have actually voted in local areas, and the constituencies of local, state, and national elected officials. Accordingly, the political landscape encompasses virtually the entire range of general and special populations in every political jurisdiction, large and small. Population changes can have a profound effect, therefore, on the character of our politics at every level of government, including the number and political party of elected officials, the public issues raised, the solutions proposed and implemented, and the forms of government administration. For example, one reason for the more reasoned and balanced political views of U.S. senators than members of the U.S. House of Representatives is that the former necessarily represent a much more demographically diverse population.

The leading national and regional population changes were described in some detail in Chapter 2 of this book. I highlight some of them here because of their special importance in affecting the political landscape. The U.S. population has been shifting to the South and West. The five fastest growing states during the 1980s and 1990s are located in the South and West. Post-1960s immigration is much greater in volume and very different in racial/ethnic composition from the pre-1960 immigration and, especially, the pre–World War II immigration. A sizable immigration of persons from Asia, Africa, and, especially, Latin America has replaced the streams from Europe. The immigrants, particularly the Hispanic immigrants, have very high fertility. Earlier geographic concentrations of the immigrants are being intensified as the new immigrants settle, as before, in New York, New Jersey, and Illinois, but they are also settling in Florida, California, and Texas. Blacks are "returning" in large numbers to the South. Whites are moving to the South as well, but they are also relocating to the Western states (except California).

As a result of these trends in immigration, internal migration, and fertility, the racial/ethnic complexion of the population is rapidly changing, especially in many coastal states and old industrial states. As these population shifts occur, they are changing the geographic base of support of the two principal political parties, the areas of origin of the nation's political leaders, and the views taken by them on critical public issues. Population shifts combined with identity politics (i.e., the politics of a devalued community of interest responding to their selection-out by more privileged communities of interest) are shaping the political agenda for better or worse. Recent population changes may even lie behind the silence of the main political parties regarding immigration. Considering its wide-ranging influence on American society and its prospective lead role in the growth of the population in the 21st century, immigration matters merit active public attention. Review and reform of our immigration policy, laws, and programs appear, however, to have become the "third rail of politics," replacing reform of the Social Security program in this regard.

Recent changes in the age structure, household composition, and economic status of the population also have their political fallout. The population is aging and the shares of households consisting of individuals living alone and single-parent families have sharply increased. Older persons vote in disproportionately large numbers and represent an important voting bloc, particularly with respect to issues directly affecting them, such as the financial status of the Social Security system, the Medicare program, and the cost of prescription drugs. Single parents have distinctive positions on issues such as child care, parental work-leave, the quality of public schools, and parents' and grandparents' rights, and politicians have been forced to confront them.

The economic boom of the 1990s continued to the end of the decade as unemployment fell to historically low levels, inflation was contained, and real median household income rose. The boom has been achieved at a price, however. Many of the additional jobs are low paying and relatively unskilled as the better-paying manufacturing jobs have been disappearing, both parents in many two-parent families feel that they have to work full time, income and asset disparity in the population have been rising, and the share of children in poverty remains high. These conditions affect racial/ethnic minorities more adversely than they do others. Discussion of these demographic/economic matters has entered into the political debate associated with the elections of 2000, and many voters align themselves with the political parties on the basis of their demographic/economic status.

Judicial Review of Census Data and Their Use in the Courts

Demographic concepts, data, and methods are often introduced in litigation where government activities or political operations are under administrative or legal review. Among these activities are the apportionment of the Congress, the delineation of election districts, including congressional redistricting of states, adjustment of the decennial population census results for undercounting, and census practices in assigning usual residence to persons with ill-defined or dual residences. In Chapter 9 we considered two cases in which there were legal challenges to population estimates for local jurisdictions made by local governments (i.e., cities in Clark County, Nevada, and supervisorial districts in Los Angeles County, California). Court-ordered desegregation has expectedly been associated with a host of demographic questions. As noted in Chapter 7, the practices of federal and local government housing authorities have been legally challenged on the grounds of racial discrimination and demographic analysis proved valuable in resolving the issues. There have been legal challenges to the delineation of school districts, revolving around the question of the over- and underconcentration of black and Hispanic households in particular school districts. While there are numerous possible issues linking demography and the law, this chapter deals with only a few narrowly political matters, namely, congressional apportionment, legislative redistricting, and use of population census data for political representation and the allocation of federal funds.

CONGRESSIONAL APPORTIONMENT

Legal Basis

The framers of the Constitution voted to apportion representation in the new government on the basis of population. They believed that to assure fair representation, a periodic count of the population was necessary. Accordingly, the Constitution mandated a census every 10 years, stating that (Article I, Section 2):

> Representatives ... shall be apportioned among the several States which may be included within this Union, according to their respective Numbers.... The actual Enumeration shall be made within three years after the first Meeting of the Congress of the United States, and within every subsequent Term of ten years in such Manner as they shall by Law direct... each State shall have at Least one Representative....

While the essential intent of this section is clear, it has been subject to question and alternative interpretation in several respects. Four demographic issues relating to Section 2 have been covered in federal legislation or contested in the courts. They hinge on the meaning of the words *apportioned*, *numbers*, and *enumeration*. More specifically, the issues concerned the questions, who should be counted, how should the population be counted, how should the representatives be apportioned on the basis of the counts, and what specific geographic areas should the apportioned representatives represent? We consider these questions in the following sections.

Apportionment Population

The Constitution does not specify exactly who should be counted in each state for purposes of the apportionment. In each state there are groups ineligible to vote, such as children under voting age, legally resident aliens, convicts, unregistered persons, illegally present aliens, and persons whose state of usual residence is not uniquely defined and who, as a result, may be ineligible to vote in their current "residence," such as college students, military personnel, and persons with dual residences. Moreover, there is more than one way of assigning people to a residence. For example, we distinguish between the *de facto* population (i.e., persons physically present) and the *de jure* population (i.e., usual residents).

In defining the population to be counted for the apportionment of the Congress, we can consider the issue in terms of the inclusion or exclusion of five groups: (1) children under voting age, legally resident aliens, and other legally resident persons ineligible to vote, such as convicts or unregistered voters; (2) military personnel stationed overseas and their dependents living overseas, and federal employees and their dependents living overseas; (3) illegally present aliens; (4) other U.S. citizens living overseas; and (5) the population of the District of Columbia. In general, the apportionment population includes, as a base population, all citizens and legally resident aliens who are "permanent" residents of the United States, legally present aliens "temporarily" here (e.g., foreign students) other than short-time foreign visitors (e.g., tourists), and illegally present aliens. Foreign diplomatic and military personnel in the

United States and residents of the District of Columbia, in addition to tourists and other short-term visitors, are excluded.

The first group listed here, consisting of legal residents ineligible to vote, has been included in the apportionment population without issue. The second group, the overseas "federal" population, has been the subject of judicial and administrative rulings, which led to their inclusion in some recent censuses (e.g., 1970 and 1990) and not in others (e.g., 1980). The third group, the illegally present aliens, has been included but not without congressional wrangling and court contests in 1980 and 1990. The fourth group, "other U.S citizens living overseas," however, has never been included in the apportionment population or the resident population of the United States although it was covered in several censuses in the previous century. Finally, the population of the District of Columbia has regularly been excluded from the apportionment population although it has been included in the resident population of the United States. It is apparent that this definition of the apportionment population can provoke many questions, some of which are discussed later.

The Constitution as framed specifically named two groups to be excluded from the census and hence from the count of the apportionment population, Indians not taxed and two-fifths of the slaves. The 14th Amendment later removed these exclusions. In 1988 an administrative ruling of the Department of Commerce, issued in cooperation with the Department of Defense, ordered the inclusion of overseas civilian employees of the Federal government and overseas military personnel, and their dependents, in the apportionment population of the 1990 census. These groups would be assigned to their "home-of-record" in the states. This was done previously in 1970. A similar step has been taken with respect to the year 2000 census. The integrity of our government structure and political equity would appear to justify the inclusion of U.S. military and federal civilian personnel overseas and their dependents in the apportionment population although this step is demographically hard to defend and operationally difficult to implement. Moreover, it favors the states with large military installations. In *Franklin v. Massachusetts* (1992) the Supreme Court ruled that the inclusion of overseas U.S. armed forces and U.S. civilian employees, and their dependents, in the apportionment population was constitutional.

Foreign diplomatic and military personnel posted in the United States and private U.S. citizens living overseas are excluded from the enumeration. The same logic suggests the exclusion of illegally present aliens from the apportionment population. In *Ridge v. Verity* (U.S. District Court, Western District of Pennsylvania, 1989), several members of Congress sued the U.S. Department of Commerce in order to stop the inclusion of illegally present aliens in the forthcoming 1990 census. Even granting the philosophical and legal justifiability of excluding illegal aliens from the census, it would be operationally difficult to implement. The Census Bureau would have a serious problem in accurately identifying illegal aliens in collecting the data or in processing the completed questionnaires. Legality of residence is not a feasible subject of inquiry on the census just as legality of income is not a feasible matter of inquiry.

The presentation of the plaintiffs in *Ridge v. Verity* included the calculation in 1988 of alternative series of population projections for states for 1990 including and excluding illegal aliens, in order to evaluate the effect on congressional apportionment of each of these conditions. The court ruled against the plaintiffs, mainly on the grounds of **standing**. As the legal principle of standing was applied in this case, the plaintiffs could not demonstrate *past harm to themselves inflicted by the defendant*. The plaintiffs could only show a loss of congresspersons from their states (not *their* seat) after 1990 as a result of including illegal aliens in the *projected* apportionment population, and the alternative projections showed different states winning and losing seats.

The decision of the court illuminates the conflict between an effective legal case and good demographic practice. The very presentation of alternative projections, however carefully framed, dooms the plaintiff's argument to the charge of the lack of standing. There is little precedent in case law for standing based on *future* injury, *alternative* degrees of possible injury, and loss to impersonal entities. The issue of the exclusion of illegal aliens from the apportionment population was subsequently brought before the House of Representatives in the Census Equity Act, H.R. 2661 (1989), but since a similar bill was not brought before the Senate, the Congress dropped the matter.

Accordingly, in 1990, membership in the House of Representatives was apportioned among the 50 states on the basis of the total resident population of the 50 states (i.e., including illegal aliens but excluding residents of the District of Columbia), plus the "home" population serving overseas (i.e., U.S. armed forces and federal civilian personnel assigned overseas, and their dependents). In 1990 the apportionment population numbered 249.0 million; it included 0.9 million overseas military personnel and federal civilian employees and their dependents, and it excluded the 0.6 million residents of the District of Columbia.

Several proposals have been made to amend Article I, Section 2, for the purpose of establishing a different basis for apportioning the Congress. Among these are the use of federal income tax returns, which provide data on the number and state residences of "exemptions" (i.e., filers and their dependents). It is argued in support of this proposal that it would dispense with the need to take an expensive census and that the apportionment could be updated frequently. On the other hand, it would penalize states with disproportionately large shares of persons who are not required to file—that is, mainly low-income persons.

Several proposals aim to limit the apportionment population more closely to those who have the right to vote, such as persons of voting age, the registered population, or the number of persons voting for presidential electors. The last of these proposals, it is argued, would eliminate the need for a census, make more frequent apportionments possible, take into account more current population trends than the present procedure using the decennial census, meet the test of political equality (i.e., equality in numbers qualified to vote) among legislative districts more closely, and serve as an incentive for people to register and vote. Since the number of votes cast in a presidential election is known nationwide at the precinct level a few weeks after the election, reapportionment could take place every 4 years within a year or so after each presidential election. On the other hand, states with relatively large shares of children and recent immigrants would be underrepresented in the apportionment, as would states with relatively large shares of persons in the lower educational and economic classes, including many members of racial minorities and Hispanics, given present patterns of voter participation. Political power would shift regionally as a result both of differences in population composition and differences in voter participation.

Table 12.1 illustrates the effect of the proposal to base the apportionment of the Congress on the presidential vote. It displays a comparison of the distribution of the 435 congressional seats among the nine geographic divisions of the United States according to (1) the estimated total resident population in 1996 and (2) the popular vote cast for president in 1996. This comparison suggests the direction and general magnitude of the changes in the geographic distribution of seats if the proposal was implemented. The states in the Northeast and Midwest would gain about 15 seats, while the states in the the South and West would lose an equal number. This would mean a tremendous geographic shift in political power, reversing the geographic redistribution of political power during the post–World War II years.

Apportionment Process

The required census figures on the total resident population of the states, adjusted to include the overseas population, must be available for the calculation of the apportionment of the Congress and transmitted to the president

TABLE 12.1 Illustrative Comparison of the Distribution of 435 Congressional Seats among the Geographic Divisions Based on the Estimated Population in 1996 and the Popular Vote Cast for President in 1996

Division	Population (1)	Presidential vote cast (2)	Difference (3) = (2) − (1)
United States	435.0	435.0	—
New England	21.9	25.8	+3.9
Middle Atlantic	62.7	62.8	+0.1
East North Central	71.5	76.9	+5.4
West North Central	30.3	35.8	+5.5
South Atlantic	78.1	74.8	−3.3
East South Central	26.6	25.8	−0.8
West South Central	48.0	42.9	−5.1
Mountain	26.4	25.8	−0.6
Pacific	69.5	64.4	−5.1

—: Zero

Note: These figures were not derived by the apportionment formula. In deriving them, the population of the District of Columbia and the vote cast by residents of the District of Columbia were included in the United States total and in the figures for the South Atlantic states.

Source: Based on U.S. Bureau of the Census, *Statistical Abstract of the United States, 1998*, Tables 26 and 462, 1998. The data on popular vote cast for president in states, 1996, given in Table 462, are taken from Congressional Quarterly, Inc., Washington, DC, *America Votes*.

within 9 months of the official census date (e.g., December 31, 2000). Congressional **apportionment** refers to the process by which seats in the House of Representatives are assigned to the states as well as to the resulting distribution of such seats. Since congressional seats must be apportioned among states in whole numbers, some way has to be found to deal with fractional shares of population, seats, or congresspersons. It should be clear that the 435 congressional seats cannot be allocated among the 50 states on the basis of a single national average, the population per congressperson (about 647,000 in 2000, 572,466 in 1990, and 519,235 in 1980). The task is to choose the formula for apportionment that will achieve the most equitable distribution among the states of the 435 seats in the House of Representatives.

According to the Constitution and congressional law, every state must have at least one representative, representatives shall be elected only from districts (not at large), no district can elect more than one representative, and each member of Congress must represent only one district and state.[1] It has been deemed impractical to assign a fractional representative to a state or to give the representatives of a state fractional votes.[2] Within these constraints, a variety of methods of apportioning the Congress are possible. The method of apportionment used to meet the required conditions for the past several censuses is the **method of equal proportions**. Congress adopted the method of equal proportions in 1941. By this method the proportional differences in the number of persons per representative and the number of representatives per person for any pair of states is reduced to a minimum, as explained here.

To make the computations according to the method of equal proportions, we first allot one seat to each state, as the Constitution requires, and then assign the remaining 385 seats to the states according to "priority values." These priority values determine a state's claim for each new seat—its second, third, and so on. To determine the priority values, the apportionment population (P) in each state is multiplied by the factor $1 \div \sqrt{n(n-1)}$, where n is the number of the seat:

$$\text{Priority value} = P \star \left[1 \div \sqrt{n(n-1)} \right] \qquad (1)$$

For example, in 1990 the priority value for the second seat for California was determined by multiplying the apportionment population of the state for that year, 29,839,250, by $1 \div \sqrt{2(2-1)}$, or 0.7071068. The product of these numbers is 21,099,537. The same computation was then made for New York, the next most populous state. When the apportionment population of New York, 18,044,505, was multiplied by the factor 0.7071068, the result was 12,759,392. The same calculation was carried out for each state. So far, a second seat went to California, then a second seat to New York.

The priority value for each state's claim to a third seat is calculated by multiplying the apportionment population by $1 \div \sqrt{3(3-1)}$, or 0.4082483. The result for California is 12,181,823, and a third seat went to California, following the rank order of the priority values. This process is repeated for every state for any desired number of seats. Thus, to determine Pennsylvania's claim to a 21st seat, the multiplier is $1 \div \sqrt{21(21-1)}$, or 0.04879500, and, given an apportionment population of 11,924,710, the priority value is 581,866. In short, when the required priority values for all the states have been calculated,

TABLE 12.2   Priority Values for Applying the Method of Equal Proportions to Determine Congressional Seats in Sequence 51–60 and 426–435 on the Basis of the 1990 Population Census

Sequence	State	Seat	Priority value	Sequence	State	Seat	Priority value
51	CA	2	21099536	426	PA	21	581866
52	NY	2	12759392	427	NC	12	579472
53	CA	3	12181822	428	CA	52	579430
54	TX	2	12063104	429	TX	30	578382
55	FL	2	9194765	430	MS	5	578346
56	CA	4	8613849	431	WI	9	578265
57	PA	2	8432043	432	FL	23	578070
58	IL	2	8108168	433	TN	9	577075
59	OH	2	7698501	434	OK	6	576497
60	NY	3	7366638	435	WA	9	576049

Source: Unpublished records of the U.S. Census Bureau.

they are ranked from the largest to the smallest and this rank order determines the assignment of seats from the 51st to the 435th.

The multipliers drop off sharply as the seat number rises, as illustrated by the following array of multipliers for seats 2 to 4, 20 to 22, and 30 to 32:

Seat	Multiplier	Seat	Multiplier	Seat	Multiplier
2	.70710678	20	.05129892	30	.03390318
3	.40824829	21	.04879500	31	.03279129
4	.28867513	22	.04652421	32	.03175003

Table 12.2 shows the priority values for seats of order 51 to 60 and 426 to 435, and the corresponding states, as calculated by the Census Bureau on the basis of the 1990 census data. Seat number 435 went to Washington with a priority value of 576049. By extending the calculations to a hypothetical 436th seat, we could determine the state that barely missed getting an additional representative.

We can now test whether the method of equal proportions produces the smallest possible proportional difference in population per representative between any pair of states, as claimed. The criterion may be tested for Minnesota and Maryland with 1990 apportionment populations. With eight seats for Minnesota, the average number of persons per seat is 548,379. The state of Maryland was also allocated eight seats. The average number of persons per seat is 599,828, 9.4% more than the average for Minnesota. If a seat was taken from Minnesota and given to Maryland, the difference in the number of persons per representative would have been 15%. The test is met. The proportional difference between the numbers per representative is smaller for the original apportionment than would be the case with an alternative apportionment. A similar test can be applied to any two states, including those with initially different numbers of representatives (e.g., Idaho, 2, North Dakota, 1).

Alternative formulas are possible and many have been proposed. Four other proposed methods are compared in terms of their formulas and mathematical basis, with the method of equal proportions in the following list:

Method	Divisor in formula	Test
Equal proportions	$\sqrt{n(n-1)}$	Smallest percentage difference between number of persons per representative and between number of representatives per person
Major fractions	$(n-1) \div 2$	Smallest absolute difference between number of representatives per person
Harmonic means	$[2(n-1)n] \div [(n-1)+n]$	Smallest absolute difference between number of persons per representative
Smallest divisors	$n-1$	Smallest absolute "representation surplus"
Largest divisors	n	Smallest absolute "representation deficiency"

Source: U.S. Bureau of the Census, "Counting for representation: The census and the Constitution," 1987.

In *U.S. Department of Commerce v. Montana* (1992), the Supreme Court declared the method of equal proportions constitutional and affirmed that Congress had properly exercised its authority in selecting this method for the apportionment.[3]

Apportionment Trends

Population trends from one decennial census to the next are great enough to cause major shifts in the apportionment of the Congress, with consequent shifts in the locus of political power. Table 12.3 compares the apportionment of the Congress in 1990 and 1980. (In 1990, unlike 1980, the overseas population was included in the apportionment population.) Nineteen congressional seats were shifted to other states, but only 21 states were involved in the exchange. This is because California, Florida, and Texas each gained several seats and New York lost several. Except for New York, the losses were rather dispersed among the states. States in the Northeast and Midwest lost seats and states in the South and West gained seats. This was the pattern between 1970 and 1980. The trends of the past few decades have continued into the 1990s. Eighteen states would gain or lose seats in 2000 on the basis of the postcensal population estimates for 1998.[4] This number is about the same as the projections for 2000. Bureau of the Census projections for 2000 suggest that 17 states would gain or lose congressional seats in that year (Table 12.3).

REDISTRICTING

U.S. Congress

When the governors of the states are informed as to the numbers of representatives their state has been allotted by the apportionment formula, it becomes the responsibility of the state legislatures (commissions in several states) to redraw the boundaries of the congressional districts in their states according to the allotted number of districts and the population counts in the recent census. If a congressperson does not represent the entire state, a way has to be found to divide the state geographically into separate representative districts that conform to specified legal, traditional, demographic, and other requirements. The Constitution does not specify that there should be districts within the states to

TABLE 12.3 Congressional Apportionment among the States in 1980, 1990, and as Projected for 2000, and Changes in Apportionment, 1980–1990 and 1990–2000

State	Apportionment 1980	1990	2000	Change 1980–1990	1990–2000
United States	435	435	435	—	—
Alabama	7	7	7	—	—
Alaska	1	1	1	—	—
Arizona	5	6	8	+1	+2
Arkansas	4	4	4	—	—
California	45	52	52	+7	—
Colorado	6	6	7	—	+1
Connecticut	6	6	5	—	−1
Delaware	1	1	1	—	—
Florida	19	23	24	+4	+1
Georgia	10	11	13	+1	+2
Hawaii	2	2	2	—	—
Idaho	2	2	2	—	—
Illinois	22	20	19	−2	−1
Indiana	10	10	10	—	—
Iowa	6	5	5	−1	—
Kansas	5	4	4	−1	—
Kentucky	7	6	6	−1	—
Louisiana	8	7	7	−1	—
Maine	2	2	2	—	—
Maryland	8	8	8	—	—
Massachusetts	11	10	10	−1	—
Michigan	18	16	15	−2	−1
Minnesota	8	8	8	—	—
Mississippi	5	5	4	—	−1
Missouri	9	9	9	—	—
Montana	2	1	2	−1	+1
Nebraska	3	3	3	—	—
Nevada	2	2	3	—	+1
New Hampshire	2	2	2	—	—
New Jersey	14	13	13	−1	—
New Mexico	3	3	3	—	—
New York	34	31	29	−3	−2
North Carolina	11	12	12	+1	—
North Dakota	1	1	1	—	—
Ohio	21	19	18	−2	−1
Oklahoma	6	6	5	—	−1
Oregon	5	5	5	—	—
Pennsylvania	23	21	19	−2	−2
Rhode Island	2	2	2	—	—
South Carolina	6	6	6	—	—
South Dakota	1	1	1	—	—
Tennessee	9	9	9	—	—
Texas	27	30	32	+3	+2
Utah	3	3	4	—	+1
Vermont	1	1	1	—	—
Virginia	10	11	11	+1	—

(*continues*)

TABLE 12.3 (*continued*)

State	Apportionment 1980	1990	2000	Change 1980–1990	1990–2000
Washington	8	9	9	+1	—
West Virginia	4	3	3	−1	—
Wisconsin	9	9	8	—	−1
Wyoming	1	1	1	—	—

—: Zero (i.e., no change).

Note: The actual apportionment in 2000 differed from the CRS/Huckabee projections as follows: California and North Carolina each gained a seat, Florida gained two seats rather than one, Indiana lost a seat, and Utah and Montana did not gain a seat.

Source: 1980 and 1990: U.S. Bureau of the Census, 1990 Census of Population, *U.S. Summary,* Table 3. Projections of population for 2000: U.S. Bureau of the Census, "Population projections for states by age, sex, race, and Hispanic origin: 1995 to 2025," by Paul R. Campbell, *PPL-47*, 1996; seat allocations for 2000 computed and published by the U.S. Congressional Research Service, "Apportionment impact of applying 1992 census adjustment factors to projections of state populations in 2000," by David C. Huckabee, Memorandum, May 19, 1997.

be represented by the elected members of the House; hence, it does not specify standards to be used in delineating district boundaries.

Criteria for Redistricting

It was long after the Constitution was ratified by the Constitutional Convention that the Congress and the Supreme Court ruled on the matter of members representing specific districts and on the criteria that federal and state legislative districts should meet. In accordance with various federal laws, Supreme Court decisions, and established tradition, a number of criteria have evolved governing the delineation of legislative districts, with no clearly defined priority. There are four basic ones. The first is the one-district–one-representative rule, requiring one and only one representative per district. The second is the "one-person–one-vote" rule, or, more appropriately, the one-person–one-constituent rule, requiring **population equality** among congressional districts within a state, following *Wesberry v. Sanders* (1964) and population equality among state legislative districts, following *Baker v. Carr* (1962). The third is maximizing the representation of minority races/Hispanics through the delineation of **racially defined** or **racially compact** districts (i.e., districts in which a racial minority/Hispanics have a large contiguous population), following the Voting Rights Act of 1965, as amended in 1970, 1975, and 1982. Maximization of minority representation can be achieved in some cases by dividing the population into two sizable groups instead of "packing" the entire group into one district. The racial definition of districts is, as explained later, supported by political compactness, bloc voting, and polarization in voting. Other redistricting criteria are **geographical compactness** (i.e., having relatively regular boundaries), **political equality** (i.e., approximate equality in the population eligible to vote in the districts of a state), appropriately designated the one-person–one-vote rule. Finally, the criteria include protection of existing political boundaries and incumbents and maintainence of communities of interest (e.g., coastal areas, rural areas).

A string of recent court decisions have sharply qualified some of these criteria. Only the first two of them, district/representative equality and population equality among districts, are "non-negotiable." Maximizing racial representation has a strong legal basis, but its priority has been lowered, with the result that the principle of maximization no longer has the same legal primacy or independent legal force. While accepting the maximization principle, *Thornburg v. Gingles* (1986) set political compactness, political cohesiveness, and polarization in voting as joint conditions for delineation of majority-minority districts. A **majority–minority district** is one in which a majority of the population of a district belongs to a particular racial/Hispanic minority. **Political compactness** exists when over 50% of the eligible voters belong to a particular racial/Hispanic group. **Political cohesiveness** refers to a consistent record of a minority group's voting as a bloc, and **polarization in voting** refers to a consistent record of the majority's voting for majority candidates in opposition to any minority candidate.

Thornburg v. Gingles established, in effect, the legality of applying the concept of racial/Hispanic compactness in the delineation of legislative districts, but compactness appears to mean only the contiguity of the members of the group, not necessarily a geographically compact district. The requirement to observe geographic compactness, previously established by several expired acts of Congress, was strongly reaffirmed in *Shaw v. Reno* (1993), even though the district in question (North Carolina, 12th District) was racially compact. In other words, it was unlawful to draw districts with bizarre shapes just to pull in a large minority population.

Several recent Supreme Court decisions (*Shaw v. Reno,* 1993; *Miller v. Johnson,* 1995; *Bush v. Vera,* 1996; and *Shaw v. Hunt,* 1996) prohibit dependence solely or even predominantly on one criterion to delineate legislative districts and, instead, seek "value pluralism." This concept means applying several criteria in combination, such as political equality, racial compactness, political cohesiveness, and geographic compactness.[5] The other criteria named earlier (i.e., those relating to preserving incumbencies, political boundaries, and communities of interest) rest in tradition and have been less involved in legal conflict.

Malapportionment (really maldistricting, i.e., districts with grossly unequal populations) was a common occurrence up to the 1960s. Malapportionment could arise from two situations. One was in connection with the establishment of new districts. The second and more common reason for legislative districts of vastly different populations was the failure of the states to redraw district boundaries after major population shifts. The 1964 Supreme Court ruling in *Wesberry v. Sanders* extended the "one-person–one-vote" rule to congressional redistricting after previously ruling on it in state contests in *Baker v. Carr* (1962) and declaring in *Reynolds v. Sims* (1964) that a citizen had a right to "fair and effective representation." Congressional districts must be substantially equal in population. According to the Court, "as nearly as practicable, oneman's vote in a congressional election is to be worth as much as another's…. While it may not be possible to draw Congressional districts with mathematical precision, that is no excuse for ignoring our Constitution's plain objective of making equal representation for equal numbers of people the fundamental goal for the House of Representatives."

At the time of the 1964 court decision, several states had not redistricted for decades and in many others there were numerous districts with far greater populations than others, with vastly different "political representation per person." The consequences of perpetuating ancient district boundaries was to penalize, through underrepresentation, residents living in parts of states that had been growing in population. Hence, the decision in *Wesberry v. Sanders* forced a major redistricting of most states after the 1970 census, although some states resorted to the expedient of electing members at large—a legally questionable practice. The census counts of 1980 for the congressional districts of 1970 showed that extensive redrawing of district boundaries was needed again. This experience was repeated in 1990. Numerous districts were redrawn in 1990 to ensure that all districts within the state were approximately equal in population. Since the courts decreed that a district's population should not deviate by more than 1% from the average district population for the state— a stringent criterion to meet—and since even small population changes could affect prior conformity to this criterion, few districts could meet the criterion in 1990 (*Karcher v. Daggett*, 1983). Yet nearly all had been made to conform after the 1980 redistricting. The 21 states with changes in the number of seats allocated to them necessarily had to be redistricted in 1990, but so did many others because of population changes within them.

Geographic Compactness and Gerrymandering

The requirement of geographic compactness has a long history in law but has been violated regularly and gone unenforced (Siegel, 1996, *op. cit.*). The drawing of extremely misshapen legislative districts is known as **gerrymandering**, a term that goes back to 1812. (See Figure 12.1.) Specifically, gerrymandering refers to the excessive manipulation of the shape of districts for politically or racially partisan purposes. Gerrymandering is practiced both by political parties and by the principal racial/ethnic groups. In **political gerrymandering** the basic intent is to delineate legislative districts so as to maximize the chance of the party's candidates being elected. The effect of redrawing congressional and state legislative districts is almost always to increase the political power of the already dominant political party in the state since this party controls the redistricting process in the state. In **racial gerrymandering**, malcompact districts are designed to assure the dominance of one racial group in a district and, given a racially polarized political environment, the election of its candidates. Such gerrymandering can concomitantly result in the geographic malcompactness of adjacent districts, which may be dominated by another racial group or political party.

Examples of gerrymandering still abound, with many districts being shaped like forms of animal life, both extinct and contemporary, such as snakes, tadpoles, and pterosauruses. They are especially common in North Carolina, Louisiana, Georgia, and Texas, as shown in Figure 12.1 for District 12 of North Carolina. In *Shaw v. Reno* (1993), the Supreme Court called for the redrawing of the boundaries of those districts in North Carolina where racial

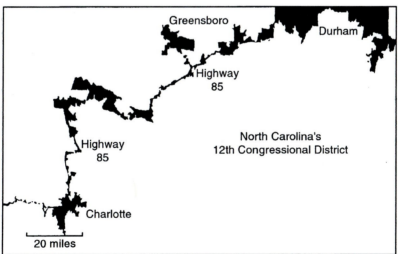

FIGURE 12.1   The original political gerrymander, Massachusetts, Essex County, 1812, and a modern racial gerrymander, North Carolina, 12th Congressional District, 1992. *Note:* The district that the Massachusetts legislature carved out of Essex County in 1812 had a "dragonlike contour" according to historian John Fiske. The district looked as shown in the drawing after printer Gilbert Stuart pencilled in a head and claws. The word *gerrymander* is a fusion of the word *salamander* and the name Elbridge Gerry, then governor of Massachusetts. North Carolina's 12th Congressional District follows Highway 85 for about 150 miles and includes residential concentrations of blacks in several leading cities of North Carolina.

compactness was the sole criterion used in drawing the boundaries and where the districts were grossly distorted in shape. On the other hand, in *Miller v. Johnson* (1995), the Court rejected a district in Georgia drawn solely with race as a criterion, even though the district was not geographically malcompact. Several measures of geographic compactness of legislative districts have been developed, but they have rarely been implemented in practice or considered in court contests relating to the delineation of legislative districts. Two measures that have been proposed are the perimeter/area method and the circumscribed circle/area method. The first is the ratio of the area of the district to the area of the circle with the same perimeter as the district, and the second is the ratio of the area of the district to the area of the smallest circle that circumscribes it. Since the circle is used as a standard of compactness, a congressional district shaped like a circle would has a compactness measure of one. Table 12.4 presents some illustrative results for these measures based on 1990 census data. Taking an average of the two measures is suggested as a way of reducing the biases of each measure or combining their strengths. Another measure proposed is the complement of the coefficient of variation of the radials of the district.[6] This measure has advantages, such as a natural standard of one and dependence on the entire boundary of the district, but it has a notable disadvantage, namely not having a unique result because the district does not have a unique center.

Current Issues in Redistricting

Redistricting has become a very problematic task since the Supreme Court ruled that districts with bizarre shapes might violate the Constitution (*Davis v.*

TABLE 12.4   Three Measures of Geographic Compactness of Congressional Districts for Selected States: 1990

State	A_{DP}/A_{CP} [a]	A_D/A_{CC} [b]	Average
United States[c]	0.24	0.36	0.30
Arkansas	0.27	0.44	0.36
Georgia	0.18	0.34	0.26
Iowa	0.41	0.43	0.42
Maryland	0.18	0.32	0.25
Missouri	0.32	0.44	0.38
New Mexico	0.33	0.44	0.38
Oregon	0.27	0.37	0.32
Texas	0.13	0.31	0.22
Wisconsin	0.33	0.39	0.36

[a] Perimeter/area index. Ratio of the area of the district to the area of the circle that has the same perimeter.

[b] Circumscribed circle/area index. Ratio of the area of the district to a circumscribed circle.

[c] The mean of the measures over all congressional districts excluding states with only one congressional district.

Source: Basic data prepared by Election Data Services, Inc., and reprinted with permission. Adapted from Richard H. Pildes and Richard G. Niemi, "Expressive harms, 'bizarre districts,' and voting rights: Evaluating election-district appearances after Shaw," *University of Michigan Law Review* 92(3): 483–587, December 1993, Table 6.

Bandemer, 1986), that there was a limit to the malcompactness of legislative districts that is acceptable, even to carry out the affirmative-action goals of the Voting Rights Act (*Shaw v. Reno*, 1993), and that race could not be the sole factor in delineating legislative districts, however geographically compact the area (*Miller v. Johnson*, 1995). The provisions of the Voting Rights Act relating to legislative districts were further qualified in *Johnson v. DeGrandy* (1994), which ruled that, in the drawing of district boundaries, state legislatures do not have to increase the overall number of districts represented in the legislature in order to maximize the number of minority districts, and in *Holder v. Hall* (1994), which ruled against a demand for the delineation of single-member districts in Bleckley County, Georgia. The decisions in *Miller v. Johnson* (1995) and *Shaw v. Reno* (1993) seem to indicate that it is not shape per se but race considered to the exclusion of other criteria that is offensive and a violation of the Equal Protection Clause of the Constitution. Legal scholars interpret this to mean that the Supreme Court is seeking the use of an appropriate combination of criteria (i.e., "value pluralism") in delineating congressional districts.[7]

Case law applicable to the delineation of legislative districts at all levels of government is evolving rapidly and must be followed closely in order to make the most judicially defensible decisions. The legal situation appears confusing, but it may be summarized as follows.

1. Redistricting can take race into account but race cannot be the sole criterion or even the predominant one, barring a compelling state interest.
2. A delineation that appears race-neutral or that takes race into account along with a variety of other criteria will be less subject to legal challenge.
3. Forcing a legislative body to increase its size in order to add minority representation and maximizing the number of minority districts on essentially racial/ethnic grounds are unacceptable.
4. The Voting Rights Act merely requires proportionality of representation, not its maximization, for protected groups.
5. Extreme geographic malcompactness is unacceptable, as is racial gerrymandering.
6. A racial/ethnic group is not considered a community of interest like a rural area, a coastal area, or a mountainous area. (This interpretation is a legalism that defies sociological canon.)

The legal definition of malcompactness and the legal use of measures of malcompactness remain unresolved.

Role of Technology

Recent advances in computer technology and applications have changed the environment in which redistricting is done. These advances include the capabilities of the personal computer and the availability on compact laser disks of TIGER, the Census Bureau's automated geographic information system for the United States. A multitude of alternative delineations of the districts in a state can be drawn quickly using the computer programs for TIGER on a personal computer. After accessing TIGER and the TIGER map of the area and identifying the boundaries of the proposed districts in terms of counties, towns, or precincts, maps of the specified areas may be drawn by the computer, which can then provide information on the demographic, housing, and socioeconomic characteristics of the proposed districts.

This development has made redistricting more democratic, more competitive, and technically more simple, but it has also made the redistricting situation more complex politically. When "everyone" is able to design a redistricting plan and numerous plans can be quickly produced, the possibility of abuse in the form of extreme political or racial gerrymandering or in the form of efforts to gain a party or racial advantage is increased.

If we add the unsettled legal situation regarding redistricting to the technological developments, we have the ingredients for endless litigation. Consider the case of the Third District of Virginia. A panel of federal judges declared this district unconstitutional on the ground that race was the predominant factor in its design and other important criteria in redistricting, such as geographic compactness and respect for communities of interest, were neglected. Yet, the state legislature had created this black-majority district expressly in response to the Voting Rights Act and the political pressure to create a black-majority district, which could elect the state's first black member of Congress. The state of Virginia appealed to the U.S. Supreme Court to permit the state to keep the original Third District on the ground that there was a "compelling interest" in the state's creation of such a district in order to comply with the Voting Rights Act. Although the state had little expectation that the Court would support its claim, it was also asking the Court for guidance as to how to draw new districts as it proceeded to redesign the districts in the state. The Court had already ruled in 1996 that such majority-minority districts in Texas and North Carolina were unconstitutional.

Availability of Data

Recognizing the importance of the census of population in redrawing the boundaries of legislative districts, Congress enacted PL 94-171 in 1975. This act sets up a voluntary program by which those officials in each state responsible for redistricting could submit to the Secretary of Commerce a plan identifying the geographic areas for which tabulations of population were desired in order to implement their redistricting programs. For example, states could request census data on the total population and the population 18 years old and over disaggregated by major racial group and Hispanic origin, for local election precincts. The plan must be submitted to the Commerce Department no later than 3 years prior to the census date (e.g., by April 1, 1997) and the Census Bureau must provide the tabulations to the state within a year after the census date (e.g., by April 1, 2001). On this basis, the redistricting process could be completed by the state legislatures and local governing bodies in time for the congressional and other elections scheduled for the second year following the census (e.g., November 2002).

State Legislatures and Local Councils

The term *redistricting* is also used to refer to the delineation of the boundaries of legislative districts for representation in state legislatures, county councils, and city boards and councils. The state legislature may require a different type of population for the delineation of state legislative districts, such as persons of voting age or citizens of voting age, but the same criteria for delineation as enumerated earlier generally apply in this case.

State legislative districts, for example, must still conform to the principle that politically coordinate legislative districts must be equal in population size. In *Baker v. Carr* (1962), a group of Tennessee citizens claimed that they were denied equal representation in the state legislature because of the way the district boundaries were drawn. The Supreme Court ruled in their favor. This ruling came to be known as the one-person–one-vote rule. The court did not go so far as to say how "equal" participation had to be. Rather, it handed this question over to the lower courts. Later, in *White v. Regester* (1973), the Supreme Court ruled that districts in a given state had to be only approximately equal in population. This ruling has been interpreted by lower courts to mean that the populations of the districts in a state must have a total range of less than 10% (*Gaffrey v. Cummings*, 1973).

The same principles apply in the delineation of legislative districts of cities and counties. For example, councilmanic districts may be delineated in terms of a specially defined population, not necessarily the total resident population. Yet, the population numbers for the districts following this definition must be approximately equal as well as conform to the other guidelines for district delineation. If, for example, a city council has voted to increase the number of wards in the city, all ward boundaries may have to be redrawn to achieve approximate population equality, geographic compactness, and racial/ethnic compactness, and to recognize communities of interest and the interests of incumbents.[8]

Legal Contests on Delineation of Legislative Districts

As we have seen, the need to conform to federal laws, and Supreme Court and lower court decisions, has imposed on state and local governmental bodies a set of requirements for the delineation of legislative districts that have been difficult to observe because of their indefiniteness, inconsistency, and lack of specified priority. These problems have precipitated many court contests relating to the delineation of state and local legislative districts. State and local jurisdictions have called on applied demographers to assist in their suits. The demographers may be called on to compile the appropriate demographic data in connection with the redrawing of district boundaries, to clarify demographic concepts for extracting the necessary data, to apply appropriate forms of demographic analysis to the proposed areas, to make alternative estimates of population, and otherwise participate in delineating districts that may comply with legal requirements. A few illustrations of such cases are given in the discussion that follows.

Garza/Department of Justice v. County of Los Angeles

In the case of *Garza/Department of Justice v. County of Los Angeles* (*DOJ v. COLA*, 1989), MALDEF[9] and the Department of Justice sued the County of Los Angeles on the ground that the county failed, as required by the Voting

Rights Act, to delineate a "Hispanic opportunity district" as one of the five supervisorial districts in the county. Such a district would be one in which Hispanics were concentrated and from which they could elect a candidate of their choice in a contest for the board of supervisors of the county of Los Angeles. The plaintiffs argued that it was possible to draw such a district since over one-fifth of the population of the county was Hispanic and there was a heavy concentration of Hispanic residents in the central part of the county. In addition, there was evidence of deliberate exclusion of Hispanics from the board, since no Hispanic had ever served on the board. Moreover, the pattern of majority bloc voting enabled the majority to defeat any Hispanic candidate and to exclude Hispanics from public office, while a pattern of Hispanic bloc voting demonstrated that Hispanics preferred to elect Hispanics.

Associated with the main question raised by this case, the possible delineation of a Hispanic supervisorial district in the county of Los Angeles, are a number of demographic questions and issues. These include the acceptability in a federal court of postcensal population estimates and projections for small areas such as census tracts, the accuracy of such estimates, the derivation and accuracy of estimates of Hispanic citizens of voting age for parts of a county, estimation of persons of Hispanic origin by use of a list of Spanish surnames, the quality of self-reported data on citizenship, the use of ecological correlation to measure polarization in voting, the conceptual boundaries of the minority groups represented in voting rights legislation, and measurement of the racial and geographic compactness of proposed districts. Only some of these issues, namely, the acceptability of postcensal estimates and projections in local redistricting, the estimation of the share of citizens among Hispanics of voting age within the county, surname analysis, and the use of ecological correlation to measure polarization in voting, are discussed further here.

Use of Postcensal Estimates and Projections in Redistricting

From a demographer's point of view, perhaps the most important issue in *DOJ v. COLA* is the plaintiffs' use of postcensal estimates and short-term projections in their plan to construct a legally acceptable majority-minority district. The Constitution mandates that the decennial census must be employed for apportioning Congressional representation among the states, but it is silent on the numbers to be used in redistricting the states for election of the Congress. There is the presumption, supported by long tradition, that the decennial census counts should be used for the latter purpose also. In the present case the legal acceptability of postcensal estimates and short-term projections for delineating legislative districts for an area within a State is in question. In 1989 the plaintiffs in *DOJ v. COLA* could make an excellent case for the tremendous population changes in Los Angeles County since the last census in 1980. These rendered the 1980 census figures for the county obsolete as measures of current population size, distribution, and racial/ethnic composition. The next election of county supervisors was imminent, predating the availability of 1990 census figures. Since the plaintiffs were unwilling to wait for the 1990 census and could not depend on 1980 census figures to meet the legal/demographic requirements for delineating a "Hispanic" district, as noted below, they turned to the postcensal estimates and short-term projections of the County's Department of Health Services. In the present case the available figures were two-year projections for the census tracts of Los Angeles County for 1989 built on postcensal estimates for 1987.[10]

Although questions were raised about the legal acceptability of the estimates and short-term projections introduced by the plaintiff, much of the debate revolved around the accuracy of the figures. The court was willing to accept the use of the figures if it was convinced that they were sufficienctly accurate. Alternatively it could recommend that the plaintiffs wait until the 1990 census results were available. In short, the court allowed their use in the suit and the defendant did not offer a strong legal argument in opposition. An important prior decision of the Supreme Court (*Kirkpatrick v. Preisler*, 1969), later recognized by the Court of Appeals, supported the use of estimates and projections by states when population shifts can be "predicted with a high degree of accuracy." The test of a "high degree of accuracy" has to be met by the plaintiff but its definition has not been established.

Measuring the Share of Hispanic Citizens of Voting Age

The decision in *Thornburg v. Gingles* (1986) was very influential in the arguments presented in *DOJ v. COLA*. Recall that *Thornburg v. Gingles* set up three conditions for a protected group to prove a violation of the Voting Rights Act in connection with redistricting. The plaintiff had to show (1) that the protected group is sufficiently large and geographically compact to constitute a majority of eligible voters in a single-member district, (2) that it is politically cohesive, and (3) that the majority votes sufficiently as a bloc to enable it readily to defeat the minority-preferred candidate.

The requirement of population equality would be met if the proposed district contained 20% of the county's population—not more or less. The 1980 census showed that the figure was 18.6%. The requirement of racial/Hispanic compactness would be met if it could be shown that more than 50% of the citizens of voting age in the proposed area were Hispanic. To meet the latter requirement, the plaintiff employed data from the Census Bureau's Public Use Microdata Sample (PUMS) for 1980. PUMS gave only countywide data on the proportion of voting-age citizens who were Hispanic, however, and use of countywide data fails to take account of variations in the distribution of citizens among Hispanics of voting age within the county. The key problem arises, however, from the large percentages of Hispanics who are under voting age, who are of voting age but not citizens, or who are citizens but are not registered to vote. The proportion of citizens among the voting-age population is far lower in Hispanic areas than in non-Hispanic areas (Clark and Morrison, 1992, *op. cit.*). The plaintiffs' estimate of the percentage of voting-age citizens who were Hispanic in the proposed Hispanic district, based on the PUMS data, barely exceeded 50% and its 95% confidence interval straddled the 50% mark. When the exact figure for the proposed area was determined on the basis of special (1980) census tabulations, it clearly failed the test—46.9%. This figure still has to be adjusted downward for the evident overreporting of citizenship by Hispanics. On the other hand, allowance should be made for the relative undercount of Hispanics in the census.

Given these uncertainties, the plaintiffs introduced as evidence postcensal estimates and projections for census tracts by race/Hispanic origin for 1989 prepared by the Los Angeles County Department of Health Services. The acceptability of postcensal estimates and projections in supporting the claim of the plaintiff and the methodology and accuracy of the estimates became issues of debate. These estimates were used to show that the proposed district passed the Thornburg-Gingles test by the current date.[11]

Ecological Correlation

In the delineation of legislative districts, following the requirements of the Voting Rights Act and the Supreme Court's ruling in *Thornburg v. Gingles*, political cohesiveness among a racial minority and polarization in voting by the majority must be demonstrated in order to support the choice of a proposed legislative district. For the purpose of proving polarization in voting, the method of ecological correlation is commonly applied. Specifically, **ecological correlation** is a method of determining the strength of the relation between two or more variables on the basis of a regression between these variables, using geographic areas as units of observation. The results are usually interpreted to apply to all the individuals in a geographic area taken as an observation unit. Ecological correlation is employed in these cases because the necessary data may not be available for individuals or the use of geographic units greatly reduces the volume of data to be manipulated. Ordinarily information is not available as to how each person voted with respect to a slate of candidates. We know only the voting counts for entire precincts and the names of the registered voters listed for each voting precinct.

In *DOJ v. COLA*, the plaintiffs tried to show the relationship between the Hispanic/non-Hispanic composition of registered voters in various voting precincts based on their surnames, on the one hand, and their voting behavior (i.e., preference for Hispanic and non-Hispanic candidates), on the other. The number and proportion of registered voters with Spanish surnames can be ascertained by means of **surname analysis**, a systematic matching of the surnames of persons on the voting list and a list of specially compiled Spanish surnames (considered further later). The percentage of registered voters with Spanish surnames in the voting precincts of the proposed supervisorial district was correlated with the percentage of persons in these precincts voting for Hispanic candidates. Such calculations were intended to provide measures of political cohesiveness and polarization in voting practices on the part of Hispanics and non-Hispanics. By employing data on the relation between Spanish surnames and Hispanic origin at the county level, the results of the correlation were transformed into a measure of the relation between the Hispanic origin of voters and voting for an Hispanic candidate. In the present case, the plaintiffs maintained that Hispanic voters heavily favored Hispanic candidates and that non-Hispanic voters gave little support to Hispanic candidates. In more general terms, political cohesiveness and polarization in voting were claimed on the basis of the ecological correlation between data on voting behavior for election precincts and data on the ethnic makeup of the voters in election precincts.

Ecological correlation has been the standard procedure for demonstrating political cohesiveness and polarization in voting in litigation based on the Voting Rights Act of 1965 and its later amendments. The appropriateness of ecological correlation for such uses has been challenged and hotly debated, even in the courts, as in this case, on the ground that erroneous conclusions can be reached about individuals when data for geographic areas as units are correlated. Robinson (1950) called attention to the possibility long ago that ecological correlation may give fallacious results, as did Blalock (1964; 1989).[12] Robinson illustrated his conclusion by comparing Pearsonian coefficients of correlation for nine geographic divisions and for individuals, based on data relating color and illiteracy in 1930. The two procedures led him to opposite conclusions. Grofman (1991) and Lichtman (1991) have been the principal spokesmen for the use of the method in measuring racial bloc voting and polarization in voting.[13] An alternative "neighborhood model," claimed to be more plausible, has been proposed by Freedman *et al.* (1991), and Klein and Freedman (1993) have criticized the use of ecological correlation by plaintiffs' experts in voting rights cases on the ground that it rides on the implausible assumption that voting behavior is determined solely by race and Hispanic origin.[14] They maintain that the constancy assumption behind the ecological regression model—that is, that a group's voting behavior does not vary from area to area and is not affected by the strength of the other groups in an area—cannot be validated.

In general, bias in the results from ecological correlation arises from the assumption that the observation for a geographic unit represents the individuals in the area closely, without regard to the variation in the characteristics of the individuals in the geographic unit. The bias can be reduced if certain requirements are met.[15] These requirements relate to the number of geographic units of observation, the population size of the units, and the internal homogeneity of the units. Homogeneity in the demographic and socioeconomic characteristics of the units being observed, particularly with respect to the characteristics being correlated, is an important desideratum. Reducing the size of the units and increasing their number contribute to the stability of the results, the homogeneity of the population in the units, and the degree to which the area results represent the individuals within them. Weighting of the geographic units on the basis of population size or on the basis of the numbers having the characteristics being analyzed is needed to assure reasonable representation of individuals in the analysis.

There are also problems in the use of very small areas as units of analysis. The boundaries of such areas are more likely to change over time, the data are subject to larger sampling errors, and the necessary cross-tabulations may not be available.

Surname Analysis

Surname analysis was devised as a way of approximating the number and characteristics of persons of Hispanic origin in files that did not identify persons in terms of Hispanic origin. It was used in connection with earlier censuses to identify the Hispanic population in the Southwestern part of the United States. Spanish surnames may be a more consistent identifier than self-reported

Hispanic origin, which is affected by respondent variability. Files from different sources (e.g., counties in a state) may encode Spanish origin differently, and use of the Spanish surname list in identifying Hispanic persons for all the records in all the areas may resolve this problem.

To conduct a surname analysis, an acceptable list of surnames for an ethnic group and a list of individuals in a specified population of interest must be available. A manual or computer match of the two lists must then be carried out. Individual names are listed in many administrative files—for example, registered voters, licensed drivers, vital records, jury pools, persons arrested, employee files, company beneficiaries, crime victims, and airline ticket buyers. By matching the names in these lists with a list of Spanish surnames, the number and proportion of Hispanics in the lists can be approximated. Surname analysis has many practical applications. As we saw, it was used in *DOJ v. COLA* to estimate the proportion of Hispanics among registered voters in connection with delineating a proposed majority-minority legislative district, and it has been used in other voting rights litigation.[16]

The most widely used list of Spanish surnames for identifying persons of Hispanic origin was developed at the Census Bureau in the late 1970s by Passel, Word, and associates.[17] It contains about 12,500 Spanish surnames. The method of developing the list is essentially objective and reproducible. It is based on the fact that the Hispanic population of the United States shows extreme geographic concentration. For a name to be considered Spanish and included on the list, it must be distributed geographically in the file of federal tax returns for 1977 like the population of Hispanic origin in the United States as shown by the March 1976 Current Population Survey.

Theoretically, a list of surnames could be developed for other ethnic, racial, and language groups in addition to Hispanics. Some exploratory work has been done to develop an Asian surname list.[18] The use of surnames to identify individuals' ethnic origins has some obvious limitations. Not all persons with Spanish surnames are of Hispanic origin and not all persons of Hispanic origin bear Spanish surnames. Married women commonly take on the surnames of their husbands, losing an old surname and gaining a new surname or adopting a joint name. Some names of Filipinos are Spanish (e.g., Escober), but the ethnic origin of the person is Asian. Some common Chinese and Korean names are common "American" names (e.g., Lee). Clearly a surname is only an approximate identifier of a person's ethnic affiliation and can be misleading. However, a carefully constructed and validated list can identify a high proportion of the target ethnic group, with only a small balance of false positives and false negatives.

Romero v. City of Pomona

Romero v. City of Pomona (U.S. Ninth Circuit, 1989) illustrates a few other demographic issues in connection with the delineation of legislative districts. In this case, the plaintiffs sought to end the at-large system of electing members to the city council of Pomona and to replace it with a single-district system. They argued this position on the ground that it unlawfully diluted Hispanic and black voting strength and prevented these groups from electing candidates of their choice to the council. Although 31% of the population was Spanish-surnamed and an additional 19% was black, the minority voters were not very concentrated and it proved to be impossible to draw a "safe" district for either Hispanics or blacks. Further, the defendant maintained that the at-large system was not necessarily prejudicial to the election of minority candidates. In fact, the court found that the city of Pomona did not discriminate against minority candidates in its electoral practices and that its electoral practices actually encouraged the election of minority candidates.

The defendant widened the argument to show that all three threshhold tests of *Thornburg v. Gingles* (1986) regarding the delineation of a proposed electoral district—(1) "geographic" (i.e., racial) compactness, (2) bloc voting by the majority, and (3) minority group cohesion—were not met. Neither blacks nor Hispanics constituted a majority of the eligible voters (i.e., citizens 18 years old and over) of any proposed single-member district. The court rejected the claim of compactness based on the fact that 65% of the total population of a proposed district was *either black or Hispanic*. Blacks and Hispanics did not constitute a *single* politically cohesive group since the evidence showed that blacks and Hispanics did not commonly vote against white candidates, but often preferred the white candidate to the candidate of the other minority group.

We see that, in effect, this case tested the propriety of combining minorities (here blacks and Hispanics) as a single protected group under the Voting Rights Act. The question whether Hispanics as a whole or each of its major national ethnic components (i.e., Mexican-Americans, Cuban-Americans, and Puerto Ricans) should be considered a separate protected group did not arise here, as in *DOJ v. COLA*. The case also tested the acceptability of exit polls as a means of measuring patterns of polarization in voting. Ecological correlation and other methods were also used for this purpose, however.

MEANING OF ENUMERATION AND ADJUSTMENT OF CENSUS DATA

Meaning of Enumeration

Debates over the meaning to be attached to the words "actual enumeration" in Article 1, Section 2, of the Constitution have been concerned with the legally acceptable ways by which the decennial census can be taken. Traditionally, the phrase has meant a direct "door-to-door" or "person-by-person" count of the population, even though in all censuses some use has been made of judgment and estimation because not every member of the population can be interviewed or represented by a member of his or her own household. With developments in statistical methods, some have urged that "enumeration" should be given a broader interpretation and not be restricted to door-to-door counting procedures. It has been maintained, for example, that the use of sampling as a supplementary procedure would save money and aid in securing a more complete count of the population for apportionment of the Congress, fund allocation, and other purposes.

Formal estimation devices ("Coverage Improvement Procedures"), involving sampling and other nonenumerative procedures, have been employed in taking decennial censuses since 1970 (see Chapter 4). In the 1990 census some 3.9 million persons, or 1.6% of the population, were added to the basic count through Coverage Improvement Procedures. Many of the same procedures were employed in 1980 and 1970. The historical mixing of counting and estimation has opened the door to a defense for the broader use of estimation procedures in taking the census in order to arrive at a more complete count of the population at less cost.

Adjustment of Census Counts

The issue of census coverage and the related issue of census adjustment for undercoverage are important for several reasons. A modification of census data as enumerated can affect the apportionment of the Congress, the shape and size of congressional districts, and the balance of political power in the House of Representatives, as well as the political character of other legislative bodies. Adjustment of the 1990 census counts of state population for the net undercount, using alternative estimates from the Post-Enumeration Survey (PES), would have resulted in a shift of two seats affecting four states or a shift of one seat affecting two states.[19] (See Table 12.5.) Adjustment of census data can affect the allocation of federal funds to states and units of local government directly, and indirectly through the distribution of state funds to their constituent jurisdictions. Federal grant funding to the states obligated $185 billion on the basis of population census counts in fiscal year 1997–1998, although the census undercount would affect only a portion of the funding under these programs.[20]

Given the role of the census in the apportionment and redistricting processes and in the allocation of federal, state, and local funds, the accuracy and completeness of the census take on special importance. The more complete and accurate the census figures are, the more likely it is that each district and each resident will have equal representation in Congress and in state and local legislative bodies. The completeness and accuracy of the population count directly affect the voting power of each resident. Moreover, the more complete and accurate the census figures are, the more likely it is that the states and the jurisdictions within them will receive their just shares of public funds for providing services to the public.

Legal Contests on Adjustment of Census Counts

Given the measured levels of the gross estimates of census undercounts and the wide differences in recent censuses between the estimated net undercounts of blacks and Hispanics, on the one hand, and non-Hispanic whites, on the other, demands have come from many quarters to adjust the census figures for the omissions. From *East Chicago v. Stans* (Dept. of Commerce) in 1970 to *Wisconsin v. City of New York* in 1996, the courts have heard a steady clamor for adjustment. New York City, joined by a coalition of other cities and states, took the Commerce Department and the Census Bureau to court during the 1980s and the 1990s because of the census undercount issue. In brief, these suits charged that the use of unadjusted census counts by the Census Bureau violated the intent of Article 1, Section 2, of the Constitution and the guarantee

TABLE 12.5   Illustrative Apportionments Based on Adjusted 1990 Population Census Counts and Adjusted 2000 Population Projections

State	Apportionment 1990	2000	State	Apportionment 1990	2000
AL	7	7	MT	1	2
AK	1	1	NE	3	3
AZ	6	8	NV	2	3
AR	4	4	NH	2	2
CA	53 (+1)	52	NJ	13	13
CO	6	7	NM	3	3
CT	6	5	NY	31	29
DE	1	1	NC	12	12
FL	23	24	ND	1	1
GA	11	13	OH	19	18
HI	2	12	OK	6	5
ID	2	2	OR	5	5
IL	20	19	PA	21	19
IN	10	9 (−1)	RI	2	2
IA	5	5	SC	6	6
KS	4	4	SD	1	1
KY	6	6	TN	9	9
LA	7	7	TX	30	32
ME	2	2	UT	3	4
MD	8	8	VT	1	1
MA	10	10	VA	11	11
MI	16	15	WA	9	9
MN	8	8	WV	3	3
MS	5	5 (+1)	WI	9 (−1)	8
MO	9	9	WY	1	1

Note: Number in parentheses following number of seats represents gain or loss as a result of the undercount adjustment.

Source: 1990 data: U.S. Bureau of the Census, 1990 Census of Population, *U.S. Summary*, Table 3, supplemented by information in U.S. Congressional Research Service, "Census adjustment: Impact on reapportionment and redistricting," by David C. Huckabee, 94-649 GOV, Oct. 12, 1995. 2000 data: Based on U.S. Bureau of the Census projections of state populations (PPL-47), adjusted by the Post Enumeration survey results released in July 1992. The adjustment and the calculation of the apportionment were carried out by the U.S. Congressional Research Service: "Apportionment impact of applying 1992 census adjustment factors to projections of state populations in 2000," Memorandum by David C. Huckabee, May 19, 1997.

of equal protection in the Fourteenth Amendment. The U.S. Census Bureau prevailed in 1970 and the 1980s. The courts ruled that the Census Bureau had not acted "arbitrarily and capriciously" but according to the "state of the art," or that the plaintiff had no "standing"—that is, the plaintiff could not show that it had been injured by the Census Bureau and that the Census Bureau had a reliable method to remedy the alleged injury.

During the 1980s the Census Bureau worked on improving the Post-Enumeration Survey/dual-systems estimation method of census adjustment with the expectation that it would be adjusting the 1990 counts, but Commerce Department officials vetoed the adjustment plan. New York City and a coalition of other litigants went to court again (*New York City et al. v. U.S. Department of Commerce, 1988*), demanding the statistical adjustment of the 1990 census. As a result, the Census Bureau was directed to continue its plans for adjustment and the Secretary of Commerce was directed to appoint an advisory committee to advise him on the action to be taken. Even though the Census Bureau now favored adjustment and felt technically prepared to implement it, the secretary's advisory committee was evenly divided on the issue and in July 1991 the secretary ruled against adjustment again. In his decision he acknowledged that the adjusted counts could be more accurate than the basic counts at the national level, but he also argued that dual-system estimation, the method of deriving the adjustments, would not necessarily improve the 1990 census counts for small areas and that the use of estimation methods would put the credibility of the census in jeopardy. On the other side, his decision also approved incorporating data from the PES into the Census Bureau's postcensal population estimates program.

Following further litigation in the lower courts and the decision of an appeals court (Second Circuit, 1994) to require the Census Bureau to adjust the 1990 census, the matter reached the Supreme Court in 1996 (*Wisconsin v. City of New York et al.*). New York City argued that the secretary's decision not to adjust the census was not consistent with the principle of equal representation under the law and hence was unconstitutional. Furthermore, adjustment of the census was a logical next step in the evolution of census-taking procedures. Just as the Second Circuit had ruled in 1994, so the secretary's decision should be subject to strict scutiny and not be accepted as inviolable. The federal government argued that the Secretary of Commerce acted within the range of discretion afforded to him by the Constitution in declining to make a statistical adjustment. The State of Oklahoma, also opposing adjustment, argued that Title 13 of the U.S. Code expressly prohibits the use of sampling to derive the figures used in the apportionment of congressional representatives and that the Constitution does not guarantee census accuracy. Joining it, the state of Wisconsin argued that, according to the Constitution, Congress had the authority to direct the manner of taking the census and that the courts could not grant a plaintiff an enforceable right to a precise census. Wisconsin further argued that the use of statistical estimation to correct the census would penalize states like Wisconsin that had a high rate of participation in the census.

In its decision on the 1996 suit, the Supreme Court held that the secretary's decision conformed to applicable constitutional and statutory provisions and was not subject to heightened scrutiny. In effect, the Court ruled that the unadjusted counts would be the official counts for 1990. The opinion acknowledged the use of adjustments in the form of imputations and substitutions in the 1970, 1980, and 1990 censuses but argued that this use of adjustments was far more limited than the undercount adjustment proposed for 1990.

Changes in the Administration and in the political composition of the Congress in the 1990s modified the character of the debate. The new conservative Congress resisted the idea of census adjustment, while the new Democratic administration favored it. As the Census Bureau proceeded with plans to develop an "integrated" 2000 census count (that is, to use sampling to supplement the basic count, or employ "Integrated Coverage Measurement"), the House of Representatives sued the Department of Commerce *(U.S. House of Representatives et al. v. Department of Commerce,* 1998) before a three-judge federal appeals court on the principal ground that the Census Bureau's plan to use adjusted counts for apportioning representation in the Congress violated federal law (Title 13 U.S.C.). The Court accepted the argument of the plaintiffs that the Census Bureau's plan violated federal law. It did not rule specifically on the constitutionality of the use of sampling.

The Department of Commerce appealed the decision to the Supreme Court *(U.S. Department of Commerce v. House of Representatives et al.,* 1998). The plaintiffs argued before the Court that no census can be successful without the use of nonenumerative procedures. They maintained further that a malapportionment of representation tends to occur when some groups are more completely enumerated in the census than other groups. In addition, the plaintiffs argued, the Census Act permits discretionary use of sampling in deriving the apportionment population. Finally, the plaintiffs maintained, the House of Representatives had no legal standing to pursue the matter. The defendants argued that use of sampling would lead to additional errors and be subject to political manipulation. With a more legal focus, they argued that the use of sampling would violate federal law and the Constitution, which calls for an "actual enumeration." It should be evident that the essential reason for the positions taken by the litigants in the case is that the adjustment would strengthen Democratic constituencies and weaken Republican ones, given that the uncounted persons tend disproportionately to be members of racial minorities, Hispanics, and lower income persons (i.e., groups that tend to vote Democratic).

The Supreme Court rendered its decision in early 1999. It upheld the decision of the appeals court, finding that federal law does not allow use of sampling as a method of adjusting the census for apportionment purposes.[21] The decision did not address (i.e., allow or disallow) the use of adjusted census figures for other purposes such as redistricting and the allocation of federal funds subsequent to the completion of the conventional census. As a result of the decision, the Census Bureau was forced to reduce the planned size of the Post-Enumeration Survey from 750,000 households to 300,000 households and to use traditional methods of follow-up for nonresponse in the 2000 census. It appears that the decision as to how to conduct the census has been taken from the hands of the technical experts and placed in the hands of the politicians and the courts.

Criteria for Adjusting the Census

As we have seen, both the case for adjusting the census to apportion the Congress and the case for not adjusting it are strong. That may be why it has been such an agonizingly difficult issue to resolve. Interim decisions have been made by the courts because the Congress, the Administration, the Census Bureau, and other stakeholders (e.g., New York City, Wisconsin) could not agree on how to take the census. As suggested, however, political considerations and team loyalty on the part of these stakeholders have tended to influence the positions taken at every juncture. The decision to adjust or not to adjust the census must be based on more than its political utility or acceptability although this may serve as one criterion. The general criteria for adjusting the census may be presented in terms of the following series of abbreviated captions and questions:

1. *Legality*. Does it conform to Constitutional and other statutory requirements, such as those relating to the process (i.e., enumeration), the authority to determine how it shall be conducted (i.e., U.S. Congress), and its political consequences (e.g., equal protection of the laws)?

2. *Technical feasibility*. Is there a method that can provide sufficiently reliable adjustment factors not only for the nation and states but for all geographic units, and not only for the counts of total population but for the data on demographic, socioeconomic, and housing characteristics as well?

3. *Operational feasibility*. Can the adjustment operation—developing the adjustments, applying them to the raw census data, and publishing the results—be carried out in the time set for the operation by law and within other reasonable administrative bounds?

4. *Consequentiality*. Are the census coverage errors, and the differences in coverage errors among areas and among major social groups, of sufficient magnitude to justify modification of the basic counts or the conventional census-taking method, recognizing the attendant risk of degrading some or many of the counts and diminishing public credibility in the census? Will an adjustment significantly affect the number and apportionment of representatives and the allocation of public funds?

5. *Financial feasibility*. Can the census and adjustment operations be carried out at a sufficiently economical cost to make them feasible under the limited budgets available for this purpose?

6. *Political feasibility*. Would knowledge of the plan to adjust the census on so grand a scale be acceptable to the public, or would it reduce the public's confidence in the process, its willingness to cooperate in the enumeration, and its readiness to accept the results? Given the fact that there would be many losing as well as winning constituencies, would the plan to adjust the census still be acceptable to politicians, including members of the U.S. Congress?

Summary of the Adjustment Situation

Adjusted census data were not used in the apportionment or redistricting following the 1990 census. As of early 1999, the Census Bureau is prohibited from adjusting the 2000 census counts for the apportionment of the Congress. Presumably adjusted figures may be used in the redistricting of the states for the Federal Congress and in allocating federal funds to the states, but these matters are still in legal limbo. One may expect the Republican-dominated Congress to oppose any attempt by the states to use adjusted figures for congressional redistricting. It may even move to prohibit it, as some states (e.g., Alaska, Arizona, Colorado, Kansas, and Virginia) have already done. The use of adjusted counts for redistricting may have to be resolved by the Supreme Court.

With the acquiescence of the federal courts, the U.S. Congress, and the Administration, the Census Bureau instituted the practice of adjusting its national sample surveys taken during the 1990s by the undercount measures shown by the 1990 census PES. This is accomplished by the use of adjusted independent postcensal population estimates in the processing of the sample surveys. This process most likely will be continued into the 2000s. In addition, the Congress will probably not interfere with the use of postcensal population estimates adjusted for census undercounts for allocating federal funds. The Congress would be expected to place more political weight on the figures used for apportionment and redistricting than on the figures employed in allocating funds.

Census plans that produce two sets of census numbers—the unadjusted counts and adjusted counts—present problems beyond the decision as to which set of numbers to use in redistricting and allocation of Federal funds. Some allocation programs call for the use of census data or data available only from the census. Presumably, both sets of numbers, the unadjusted and the adjusted numbers, would be official. In order to deal with this problem, the applicable laws would have to be reviewed and possibly changed, and the postcensal estimates program would have to be expanded to reflect the double accounting system.

USE OF POPULATION STATISTICS IN THE ALLOCATION OF PUBLIC FUNDS

Population census data, postcensal population estimates, and population projections, whether generated by federal, state, or county governments, are used by these entities to allocate billions of dollars in total each year to constituent governmental units for many public programs. Population data are used to determine eligibility for grants under various programs, to determine the share of the grants under apportionment formulas, and to determine the size of the grants under entitlement programs. If there is an eligibility requirement for federal grants, usually the jurisdiction has to meet certain threshholds with respect to total population or urban, rural, or metropolitan status to qualify, or it has to show a specified proportion of housholds with a household income below a specified level (e.g., the poverty level).

Considerable amounts of federal money are distributed to state and local governments on the basis of formulas that use official data, provided mostly by the Bureau of the Census. When federal funds are allocated, the federal government has a large hand in determining the allocation formula, the type of population used in figuring the allocation, the level of government to receive the funds, and, to a limited extent, the use to which the money can be put. While the form of these allocations has shifted greatly over the past several decades, they remain a characteristic feature of the federal role. Sometimes the federal agency administering the program determines the factor or set of factors to be used in the allocation formula. On the other hand, the program may be a purely state or local program financed by federal funds, as in the case of Medicaid.

A shift in the early 1970s from categorical grants to block grants and revenue-sharing contributed to the development of local statistical sources and to the growth of statistical and demographic programs at the state and local levels. **Categorical grants** are awarded to local entities for specific programs defined by federal agencies, while **block grants** and revenue sharing are based on formulas without specification of the programs to be supported. A wide array of categorical programs were collapsed into block funding in the 1970s, and statistical formulas requiring census and other data on population, income, housing, and related items determined the allocation to each jurisdiction. The shift to block grants led to the use of annual estimates of population, rather than merely decennial census data, in the formulas and for other purposes. The shift from categorical grants to block funding also led to close scrutiny by the states and local jurisdictions of the estimating methods used by federal statistical agencies, particularly the Census Bureau, and to legal challenges of the 1980 census counts and the population estimates made for grant allocations.[22] State and local governments have increased their capacity to produce and use population estimates and other statistics, and this has been associated with an expanding role of professionally trained demographers in state and local settings.

Federal Programs with Population as a Factor in Allocation Formulas

Most formula-grant programs rely on census data to apportion federal funds. Population, either in the form of the total population of an area, some age group (e.g., population under 18 years old), or a geographic component (e.g., rural population), is one of the most common factors incorporated in formulas for distributing federal funds. The formulas may also incorporate population indirectly, as in per capita income. The formulas may call for population alone or population in addition to other factors.

The U.S. General Accounting Office (GAO) reported that there were 100 federal programs providing grants to state and local governments on the basis of formulas incorporating population-related data in 1998.[23] Population-based grant funding has been growing. In 1990–1991 total obligations for these programs amounted to more than $116 billion, although some of the programs allocated only a portion of their funds on the basis of population and other factors were involved in the formulas in addition to population. Federal funding for population-based grants amounted to $185 billion in fiscal year 1997–1998.

Federal departments that make the greatest use of population data in their grant funding include, in rank order, the Department of Health and Human Services (HHS), the Department of Education, the Department of Transportation, the Department of Labor, the Department of Agriculture, and the Department of Housing and Urban Development. By far the largest single program is the Medicaid program (Dept. of HHS), followed by Highway Planning and Construction (Dept. of Transportation) and Family Support Payments to States (Dept. of HHS). Figure 12.2 presents a list of federal departments that will be conducting grant programs in fiscal year 1990–1991, the major programs administered by these departments, and the databases used to allocate funds for each program.

Most programs use current population estimates, but 31 of the 100 programs authorized for 1990–1991 use some data in their formulas for which

FIGURE 12.2   Selected Federal Programs Using Population-Related Data, in Whole or Part, to Allocate Funds: Fiscal Year, 1990–1991

Department and CFDA No.	Program name	Estimated obligations ($ in millions)	Code
Department of Agriculture			
10.557	Special supplemental food program for women, infants and children	2,345.1	D
Department and Housing and Urban Development			
14.218	Community development block grants: Entitlement grants	1,982.1	
Department of Labor			
17.250	Job training partnership act	2,461.4	D
Department of Transportation			
20.106	Airport improvement program: State apportionments	1,800.0	R
20.205	Highway planning and construction	15,432.0	D, R
20.507	Urban mass transportation capital and operating assistance formula grants	1,941.7	D, R
Department of Education			
84.010	Chapter 1 programs—local educational agencies	5,557.8	D
84.126	Rehabilitation services: Basic support	1,628.5	
Department of Health and Human Services			
93.020	Family support payments to states— assistance payments	12,699.1	
93.600	Administration for children, youth and families—head start	2,055.5	D
93.658	Foster care—Title IV-E	2,334.1	
93.667	Social Services Block Grant	2,800.0	
93.778	Medical Assistance Program (Medicaid)	51,555.0	
93.992	Alcohol, drug abuse, mental health services block grant	1,205.2	D
Total	All programs using population-related data	$116,052.3	

Codes: CFDA: Catalogue of Federal Domestic Assistance D: The decennial census is the only source for some or all of the data elements used in the program's allocation formula R: Use of decennial census data in the program's allocation formula(s) is required by statute. All other programs can use the most current populatian or per capita income estimates available.

Source: U.S. General Accounting Office, *Formula Programs: Adjusted Census Data Would Redistribute Small Percentages of Funds to States*, GAO/GGD-92-12, 1991.

the decennial census was the only source, such as rural and urban populations and families below the poverty level. An additional handful of programs (about 12) use state population data from the decennial census, even though the Census Bureau has more current estimates. The programs depending on the decennial population census for some or all of their data (i.e., that require state and substate data on populations that are not estimated for current years) had estimated 1990–1991 fiscal year obligations of $33.4 billion.

Usually the grant formulas require a combination of total population data and other population-related data. Very few programs use the total population of an area as the sole factor in the allocation of funds. Of the programs allocating grant funds, only four use total population as a sole determinant. Social Services Block Grant, for example, bases funding levels solely on a state's proportion of the total U.S. population. Population and population-related data may be used in only part of the formulas. In addition to direct use of population in the formulas in the form of total population, population in some age group, or population in nonurbanized areas or rural population, and indirect use of population in ratios such as per capita income, the formula may include school enrollment, number of rental units in urban areas, children in low-income families, public road mileage, number of handicapped children, families in poverty, and other such factors.[24]

Grant formulas tend to incorporate one or more of three types of elements. The first is an element representing the gross demand for federal support under the grant program, the second is an element representing the need for federal support, and the third is an element representing the jurisdiction's own efforts to pay for its programs. The statistical proxy for gross demand in the formula is population size in some form, the proxy for need may be per capita income or poor families, and a jurisdiction's effort to handle its own financial burden may be represented by taxes collected in relation to individual or household income ("tax effort"). The formula of the Revenue Sharing Program of the 1970s and 1980s (1972–1986), which required the distribution of several billion dollars each year to 39,000 general-purpose governmental units, included these three elements in the form of total population, per capita income, and the ratio of taxes to personal income. The funds were distributed directly on the basis of total population and tax effort and inversely on the basis of per capita income, as suggested by the following formulas:

$$F = P \div (I_a/P) \star (T/I_b) \tag{2}$$

$$\therefore F = P \star (P/I_a) \star (T/I_b) \tag{3}$$

$$\therefore F \simeq (P/I)^2 \star T \tag{4}$$

where F represents the amount for a particular governmental unit entering into the apportionment calculations for all governmental units, and P, I, and T represent population, income, and taxes, respectively. I_a and I_b distinguish two measures of income, total money income (Census Bureau) and personal income (Bureau of Economic Analysis), that are only modestly different.

The Community Development Block Grant program, initiated in 1972 with the Revenue-Sharing program, continued after the demise of the Revenue-Sharing program in 1986. This program divided funds between metropolitan and nonmetropolitan areas, then between cities and "urban counties."[25] (An "urban county" is a county with 200,000 or more residents.) For the central cities of SMSAs, the formula used three main factors: population, overcrowded housing, and poverty (double weighted). A dual approach was introduced later, allowing the use of either a formula with age of housing (number of pre-1940 housing units) or the original formula with overcrowded housing, whichever is more favorable to the area. The use of age of housing was intended to recognize the needs of older industrial cities which have aging infrastuctures and a declining manufacturing base.

Grant legislation tends to include a variety of provisions or elements, other than data, that influence the size of allotments to states and local areas under the formulas. These elements relate to maximum and minimum grants, set-aside portions for specific grantees, hold-harmless allotments to assure that states receive at least a percentage of a prior year's funding, equal distributions among states for at least a portion of the available funds, and matching requirements at state and local levels.

Use of Adjusted Census Counts

Because of the evidence of undercounting in the 1980 and 1990 population censuses, claims have been made that the federal allocations of funds based on the census counts fall short of the true amounts required by law for many jurisdictions. These claims were expressed most vigorously by certain cities with large racial minority populations and Hispanics (e.g., New York City, Detroit, Los Angeles) and the states in which these groups make up a large share of the population (e.g., New York, Michigan, California). As noted earlier, these jurisdictions have combined the claim of political underrepresentation with the claim of underfunding as a basis for several suits against the Department of Commerce and the Bureau of the Census, demanding an adjustment of the census population. As we have seen, federal fund allocations are made to states and local areas on the basis of a variety of formulas, so that the effect of the adjustment for population undercount varies depending on the way the formulas incorporate the population element.

Adjustment for Total Population Only

Even for the several programs where the allocation of funds is based on population only, the adjustment process is not straightforward. A serious problem in evaluating the effect of an undercount adjustment is the difficulty of deriving sufficiently accurate estimates of the undercount for all relevant areas, especially small geographic units. As noted earlier, there are 39,000 general purpose governments in the United States and, of these, over 50% have less than 1000 inhabitants. While estimates of the net undercount for small areas can be derived by applying the synthetic method to the evaluation results for larger areas, or combinations of sample areas of the same class or with similar characteristics, obtained from the PES ("post-strata"), estimates based on such samples tend to have very large sampling errors. Hence, adjusted estimates for small areas tend to be very imprecise. Furthermore, alternative PES-based estimates of the undercounts for a given set of areas do not yield consistent differences in fund allocations from the allocations based on unadjusted data. In sum, the development of adequate estimates of coverage at the substate geographic level remains a difficult and elusive goal. (See Chapter 4 for a discussion of the results of the PES and adjusted census data in 1990.)

Adjustment for Population and Population-Related Factors

The decision to adjust the population factor in an allocation formula should encompass the adjustment of this element not only when it stands alone, but also when it is a component in a ratio such as per capita income.

If the grant-funding formula involves both population per se and some other population-related factor(s), such as per capita income, evaluation of the effect of the population adjustment is more complex. In a formula where funds are distributed in direct relation to population and inversely in relation to per capita income, an adjustment of the population element in both factors intensifies the positive effect of adjusting population on the fund allocation (see formulas 2, 3, and 4).

In an allocation of funds among states under an apportionment formula, however, many states would lose money as a result of the adjustment, even though they may have gained population from the adjustment. Whether there is actually a loss or gain in funds allotted by an apportionment formula depends only in part on the size of the undercount adjustment for a state, however. Multiple interdependent conditions and adjustments produce gains and losses of allocated funds that can be determined only by carrying out the entire body of calculations for a set of coordinate governmental units (e.g., states, counties). It is not possible, therefore, to predict the effect—either direction or amount— of an undercount adjustment, especially when both a population factor and a per capita income factor are combined in the grant formula. The requirement that the formula must be applied to all coordinate political units before a judgment can be made about the effect on any one of them applies even more strongly to formulas involving both population, per capita income, and other factors. The results are often completely unpredictable and counterintuitive, and jurisdictions expecting to gain money may very well lose money.[26]

If the population element in the formula is to be adjusted for census undercount, we should also consider adjusting the other elements in the formula (e.g., income) in addition to population. Adequate estimates for a formula adjustment of money income are not available, although match studies and comparison of administrative records have provided us with some information about the accuracy of reporting of money income.

Effect of Adjustment on Fund Allocations

Several studies have been conducted to measure the effect of a population adjustment on fund allocations. Some use hypothetical data and others use actual program data.[27] These studies demonstrate that when, as is often the case, the grant money is distributed on the basis of an **apportionment formula** (that is, a fixed total sum of money is prorated among the constituent governmental units), the funds lost as a result of the undercount tend to be far smaller in percentage terms than the undercount adjustment and that a large share, possibly exceeding half, of the coordinate governmental units receiving funds lose money as a result of the adjustment. The studies conclude that the claims of funds lost tend to be greatly exaggerated.

We can anticipate such an effect. Necessarily, under a simple apportionment formula—that is, under a zero-sum game—if some government units gain money, others must lose money, even though their population has been increased by an adjustment for census undercount. The effect of the adjustment of the population of the constituent governmental units is attenuated greatly in the redistribution of the same total amount of dollars as before the adjustment.

Table 12.6 illustrates these characteristics of apportionment formulas. It shows the distribution of $100 million to the states (only 20 states are displayed) according to the census counts of 1990 and according to the 1990 census figures adjusted for the undercount. It is apparent that the percentage adjustment of funds distributed to each state is much smaller than the percentage adjustment of population and that any state with a percentage undercount less than the national average percentage undercount loses money.

Using 1990 adjusted population counts instead of the actual census counts, GAO (1991, *op. cit.*) simulated allocations for three major federal programs: Social Services Block Grant, certain Federal Aid-Highway programs, and Medicaid. Table 12.7 summarizes the results for the three federal programs by grouping the states on the basis of the percentage shift in allocations from the adjustment. Tables 12.6 and 12.7 show similar patterns of results. While the population of every state moves upward from the adjustment for the undercount, many states lose money as a result of it. For example, 25 states lose money in GAO's simulation of the Social Services Block Grants and 24 states

TABLE 12.6   Results for 20 States of the Distribution of $100 million over 50 States and District of Columbia According to 1990 Census Population Counts and Adjusted Census Counts

State	Population Census count[a]	Census adjusted[a]	%[b]	Distribution of $100 million Census count[c]	Census adjusted[c]	%[b]
United States	248,710	252,723	1.6	100,000	100,000	—
Arizona	3,665	3,754	2.4	1,474	1,485	0.7
California	29,760	30,595	2.7	11,966	12,107	1.2
Delaware	666	678	1.8	268	268	—
Florida	12,938	13,197	2.0	5,202	5,222	0.4
Idaho	1,007	1,029	2.2	405	407	0.5
Indiana	5,544	5,572	0.5	2,229	2,205	−1.1
Kentucky	3,685	3,746	1.6	1,482	1,482	—
Maine	1,228	1,237	0.7	494	489	−1.0
Michigan	9,295	9,361	0.7	3,737	3,704	−0.9
Mississippi	2,573	2,629	2.1	1,035	1,040	0.5
Nebraska	1,578	1,589	0.6	634	629	−0.8
New Hampshire	1,109	1,119	0.8	446	443	−0.7
New York	17,990	18,262	1.5	7,233	7,226	−0.1
North Dakota	639	643	0.7	257	254	−1.2
Oregon	2,842	2,896	1.9	1,143	1,146	0.3
Rhode Island	1,003	1,005	0.1	403	398	−1.2
Tennessee	4,877	4,964	1.7	1,961	1,964	0.2
Utah	1,723	1,753	1.7	693	694	0.1
Washington	4,867	4,958	1.8	1,957	1,962	0.3
Wisconsin	4,892	4,922	0.6	1,967	1,948	−1.0

[a] Population figures in thousands.
[b] Ratio of [(adjusted census count − census count) to census count] per 100. Plus signs are omitted.
[c] Dollars in thousands.
Source: Based on data in Howard Hogan, "The 1990 Post-Enumeration survey: Operations and results," *Journal of the American Statistical Association* 88(423): 1047–1060, Table 5. Population data reproduced with permission from the *Journal of the American Statistical Association*. Copyright 1993 American Statistical Association. All rights reserved.

lose money or receive the same money in GAO's simulation of the Federal Highway-Aid programs. Many more states gain under Medicaid than lose because Medicaid's minimum reimbursement provisions limit the federal funding losses from the undercount.

Murray (1992, *op. cit.*) estimated that if, in the allocation of federal funds, the 1990 census had been adjusted for the uncounted population, the states would have gained an additional $56 per uncounted person. This estimate applies only to the states gaining funds and is not applicable to the remaining states. (Use of a later revision of the estimated undercount made by the Census Bureau would lower Murray's estimate of average costs.) A GAO (1998, *op. cit.*) review of Murray's study confirmed his findings and, in effect, the earlier findings of the Census Bureau/Siegel (1975) that claims of underfunding have been greatly exaggerated, except for a few areas when a whole decade was considered. Both GAO (1991, *op. cit.*) and Murray estimated that adjusting census population data for net undercounts in the 1990 census would redistribute only a fraction of 1% of total net federal funds allocated through formulas.

The GAO has reexamined this issue more recently, measuring the effect of the 1990 census undercount on funding to states under 15 federal grant

TABLE 12.7   Distribution of States According to Change in Fund Allocations from Use of 1990 Population Census Counts to Use of Adjusted Census Counts, for Three Federal Programs: Fiscal Year 1990–1991

Percentage change	Social services block grants	Federal-aid highway programs	Medicaid	Percentage adjustment[a]
Total	51	51	50[b]	51[c]
Loss				
More than 2%			2	
1 to 2%	12	3	10	
Less than 1%	13		5	
0.5 to 1%		4		
Less than 0.5%		13		
No change		4	10	
Gain				
Less than 1%	21		20	
Less than 0.5%		25		4
0.5 to 1%		2		13
1 to 2%	3		3	16
More than 2%	2			18

[a] Revised estimates of census undercounts, based on the 1990 Post-Enumeration Survey.

[b] Arizona does not participate in the Medicaid program.

[c] The national estimate of the percent undercount based on the PES is 1.6%.

Source: U.S. General Accounting Office, "Formula programs: Adjusted census data would redistribute small percentage of funds to states," GAO/GGD-92-12, November 1991, Tables II-1, II-2, and II-3. Based on population data in Howard Hogan, "The 1990 Post-Enumeration Survey: Operations and Results," *Journal of the American Statistical Association* 88(423): 1047–1060, September 1993. Population data reproduced with permission from the *Journal of the American Statistical Association*. Copyright 1993 American Statistical Association. All rights reserved.

programs in fiscal year 1997–1998 (GAO, 1999, *op. cit.*). These 15 programs were among the 25 largest formula-grant programs and represented $147 billion, or 79%, of population-based grant programs. GAO found, as before, that adjusting population counts would redistribute only a small fraction of formula-grant funding. The 1990 undercount would cause a loss of $449 million in federal funding for 1997–1998, or 0.33% of the $138 billion in funds apportioned to the states by formula. This amounted to $145 per omitted person in the 27 states with funding losses and the District of Columbia.

Only 8 of the 15 programs were responsible for all of the reallocation and Medicaid accounted for 90% of all funds reallocated. Table 12.8 lists these federal grant programs, the fiscal year 1997–1998 obligations, and the change in formula funding required by the undercount adjustment. Figure 12.3 depicts the shift in funding among the states that would result from the use of adjusted population counts in the eight programs accounting for the reallocation of funds. California would be the leading percentage gainer in grant funding, with a 1.62% increase, and Rhode Island would experience the largest percentage reduction, with a 1.80% decrease.

Additional measures of the effect of the undercount on federal funding programs, with a prospective dimension, are set forth in the report of the U.S. Census Monitoring Board (2000, *op. cit.*), prepared by PricewaterhouseCoopers for the Board. The report analyzes the effect, on federal funding of the estimated census 2000 undercount, for the same eight federal grant programs examined by GAO in 1999 that accounted for the reallocation of funds. The total for the eight programs included in the study is $112.6 billion, of which Medicaid makes up the bulk with $100.5 billion. In carrying forward the study, undercounts for states in 2000 were first estimated on the basis of the projected 2000 population and percentage undercounts in 1990 from the PES, disaggregated for 16 groups (four race groups, two Hispanic/non-Hispanic,

TABLE 12.8 Eight Large Formula-Grant Programs, Formula Funding, and Change in Formula Funding from Use of Adjusted Population Census Data: Fiscal Year, 1997–1998

Formula grant programs	Formula funding[a]	Change in formula funding Amount[a]	Percentage
Total	$105,363	$449.0	0.43
Medicaid	$93,789	$402.4	0.43
Other grant programs	11,574	46.5	0.41
Rehabilitation services: Basic support	2,166	12.7	0.59
Foster care	3,106	11.1	0.36
Social services block grant	2,286	8.5	0.37
Prevention and treatment of substance abuse	1,483	6.0	0.40
Child care and development block grant	949	5.5	0.58
Adoption assistance	590	1.6	0.27
Vocational education: Basic grants	994	1.2	0.12

[a] Dollars in millions.

Source: U.S. General Accounting Office, *Formula Grants: Effects of Adjusted Population Counts on Federal Funding to States*, GAO/GEHS-99-69, 1999, Table 3.

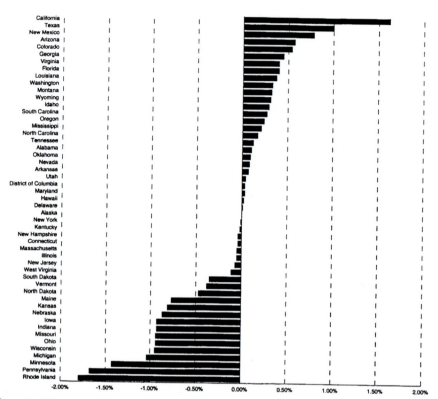

FIGURE 12.3 Percentage shift in funding that would result from the use of adjusted population census data in eight federal grant programs, for states in rank order: fiscal year, 1997–1998. *Source:* U.S. General Accounting Office, *Formula Grants: Effects of Adjusted Population Counts on Federal Funding to States,* GAO/HEHS-99-69, 1999, Figure 1.

and two age groups) within each state and the District of Columbia. Next, budget projections were made for the eight federal grant programs for each year 2002–2003 to 2011–2012. The effect of the census 2000 undercount on the allocation of federal funds to states initially was calculated for the base year and "then extrapolated to the 2002–2012 period."[28] State funding allocations were calculated using both official and adjusted 2000 state population projections. These calculations take into account all elements of the current funding formulas, including hold-harmless and minimum-share provisions.

The results of the adjustment for undercount on allocations of funds are consistent with those previously described. Table 12.9 displays a comparison of the estimated 2000% undercount of population and the percentage of total funding resulting from the undercount adjustments for states. (The funding gains and the funding losses are not equal because of the inclusion of Medicaid.) The compression of the funding changes, as compared with the population adjustments, can be illustrated at both national and state levels. The national net undercount of the population for 2000 is 1.75%. The losses amount to only 0.4% of the total funds obligated, approximately the same as for the gains. California has an estimated net undercount of 3.0% but an

■ **TABLE 12.9   Estimated Percentage Net Undercount in Census 2000 and Projected Change in Funding of Eight Federal Grant Programs from Use of Adjusted Population Census Data, for 20 Selected States: 2002 to 2012 (Fiscal Years from 2002–2003 to 2011–2012)**

State	Estimated 2000 census percentage undercount[a]	Change in formula funding[b] Amount[c]	Percentage of total funding
United States	1.75	−$721.9	−0.03
Funding gains	NA	$8396.3	0.38
Funding losses	NA	−$9118.2	−0.42
Arizona	2.49	−$205.8	−0.71
California	3.01	−5047.8	−2.15
Delaware	1.90	−0.4	−0.01
Florida	2.16	−509.3	−0.61
Idaho	2.23	−29.1	−0.37
Indiana	0.52	529.3	1.50
Kentucky	1.58	52.3	0.13
Maine	0.73	152.8	1.01
Michigan	0.75	1116.5	1.50
Mississippi	2.10	−62.2	−0.21
Nebraska	0.71	171.2	1.26
New Hampshire	0.86	3.1	0.04
New York	1.78	−1.8	—
North Dakota	0.75	40.1	0.77
Oregon	1.94	−56.4	−0.24
Rhode Island	0.41	248.8	2.20
Tennessee	1.77	−16.2	−0.03
Utah	1.76	0.8	0.01
Washington	1.93	−125.1	−0.32
Wisconsin	0.70	488.9	1.38

NA: Not available.

—: Less than 0.005%.

[a] Undercount as a percentage of adjusted population. See text for method of derivation. For most states, the estimated undercount percentage for 2000 is slightly higher than in 1990.

[b] Plus signs are omitted.

[c] In millions of dollars.

Source: U.S. Census Monitoring Board, *Effect of Census 2000 Undercount on Federal Funding to States and Local Areas, 2002–2012*, prepared by PricewaterhouseCoopers, March 9, 2000, Tables 2 and 7.

estimated funding loss of 2.2%. New York's figures are 1.8% and 0.0% (i.e., less than 0.005%). Over all states the losses amounted to $9.1 billion for the 10-year period. The funding loss in the states that would lose funds in 2002–2003 averages $159 per uncounted person, compared to GAO's 1997–1998 estimate of $145 per uncounted person.

The losses are more concentrated in the MSAs and, within them, in the central counties of MSAs, where the groups most likely to be omitted from the census reside. The three counties that are expected to suffer the greatest loss in federal funds over the 2002–2012 period as a result of the census 2000 undercount are Los Angeles County, California ($1.8 billion), Kings County, New York ($1.0 billion), and Bronx County, New York ($0.8 billion).

Standardized Population Estimates and Projections

Since many federal grant programs require distribution of funds to states on the basis of population, it is useful to consider whether a standard set of population estimates and projections should be developed and employed for federal fund allocations. The same general arguments for doing this would apply to both estimates and projections, but the need for federal oversight would appear to apply more forcefully to projections. Estimates of state population made by the federal government and state agencies are not likely to differ much from one another. The population estimates prepared by the Census Bureau use current data provided by the states and methodologies developed in cooperation with them, and hence the estimates prepared by the Census Bureau are usually acceptable to the states. Population estimates prepared by the Census Bureau have long been used in formulas for fund allocations and have presented few problems from this point of view.

In the late 1970s, the Office of Management and Budget began exploring the idea of using population projections in some formulas for allocating federal funds to the states and, by extension, the idea of using a standard set of population projections in these formulas.[29] The rationale for this plan was multifaceted. One purpose was to use data more appropriate to the object of the legislation. Another was to prevent the manipulation of the figures by the states and to avoid serious inconsistences in the figures used by the federal government to distribute funds to the states. Individual states making their own projections could manipulate the assumptions so as to overstate their populations and hence increase their share of apportioned funds. Even without manipulation of the figures, population projections made by 50 states could be seriously inconsistent. If 50 states prepare their own projections, it is quite possible that the sum would sharply deviate from a reasonable independently calculated national total.

The proposal was that the federal government would prepare projections of state population and that the states would prepare projections for the smaller geographic areas by disaggregating the state figures. The state projections would be prepared by a combination of the methods of the Census Bureau (demographic analysis) and OBERS (economic analysis) methodology. The objections made to the plan related in particular to the methodology proposed and the implications of accuracy in the method. The idea of standard population projections was not generally opposed.[30] A combination of the Census Bureau method and the OBERS method, with their different approaches and data requirements, would result in considerable complexity in the method. As the evaluation tests have shown, complexity does not necessarily result in increased accuracy of state projections. Moreover, it may inhibit general acceptance of the proposed set of projections.

As we have seen, simple geometric extrapolation is as accurate for making projections of state population as the more complex methods. Moreover, it is adaptable at all geographic levels, is inexpensive to apply, and, by limiting the judgment of the analyst, is essentially free of political pressure. For these reasons, Stoto and Schrier, who carried out the probative evaluation tests for state population projections, support the use of geometric extrapolation in preparing standardized population projections for states.[31]

The idea of standard population projections was never implemented because many believed that the federal government would be playing too paternalistic a role in developing the projections and that an acceptable means of combining the demographic and economic approaches to the methodology could not be found. Funding formulas continue to depend on census and current population figures. There is, however, an active Federal-State Cooperative Program on Population Projections, as well as an active Federal-State Cooperative Program on Population Estimates, and their work may lay the groundwork for a possibly limited use of standard population estimates and projections for states for fund allocation.

NOTES

1. 81Stat. 581. (Public Law 90-196). See also U.S. Congressional Research Service, "Census Adjustment: Impact on apportionment and redistricting," by David C. Huckabee, *CRS Report for Congress*, 94-649GOV, October 12, 1995.

2. This alternative could theoretically satisfy the requirements of at least one representative from each state and equal representation for each person across the United States. Another alternative is to let the state decide how to allocate its noninteger vote among its districts. Such methods could be construed as conforming to the Constitution but, admittedly, they would defy tradition and practicality. In addition, the small states could lose their disproportionate representation in the House of Representatives.

3. It can be shown that the method of equal proportions is biased in favor of the smaller states and that the method of major fractions is the most unbiased method. Yet the various division methods differ little in their results. See D. L. Poston, Jr., L. F. Bouvier, and H. Dan, "The impacts of apportionment method and legal and illegal immigration on congressional apportionment in the year 2000," *Population Research and Policy Review* 18(5): 507–524, October 1999.

4. Mark Mather, "Reapportionment headed South, West," *Population Today* 27(2): 3.

5. See Jacob S. Siegel, "Geographic and racial/ethnic compactness in the delineation of legislative districts," *Population Research and Policy Review* 15(2): 147–164, 1996; and E. Walter Terrie, "Several recent Supreme Court decisions and their implications for political redistricting in Voting Rights Act context," *Population Research and Policy Review* 15(5–6): 565–578, 1996.

6. The formula is $1 - CV_r = 1 - (\sigma \div \bar{r}) = 1 - [\sqrt{\Sigma(r_i - \bar{r})^2 \div n}/\bar{r}]$, where r_i represents radials, n represents the arbitrary number of radials selected (e.g., 6 or 12), and $\bar{r}$ represents the mean of the radials. See Siegel, 1996, *op. cit.*

7. Richard A. Pildes and Richard G. Niemi, "Expresssive harms, 'bizarre districts,' and voting rights: Evaluating election-district appearances after Shaw," *University of Michigan Law Review* 92(3): 483–587, December 1993.

8. See the discussion of this type of problem in U.S. Bureau of the Census, "Applications in the public sector: Wards for Abbeyville," pp. 65–75, in *Census '80: Projects for Students*, 1981; William A. V. Clark and Peter A. Morrison, "Gauging Hispanic voting strength: Paradoxes and pitfalls," *Population Research and Policy Review* 11(2): 145–156, 1992; Peter A. Morrison, "Empowered or disadvantaged? Applications of demographic analysis to political redistricting," in Hallie J. Kintner *et al.* (eds.), *Demographics: A Casebook for Business and Government*, Boulder, CO: Westview Press, 1994; and Peter A. Morrison, "Demographic influences on Latinos' political empowerment: Comparative local illustrations." *Population Research and Policy Review* 17(3): 223–246, 1998.

9. MALDEF is the acronym for the Mexican-American Legal Defense and Education Fund.

10. Nancy Bolton, "The use of population estimates and projections in the court-mandated reapportionment of Los Angeles County," in Hallie J. Kintner *et al.* (eds.), *Demographics: A Casebook for Business and Government,* pp. 55–69, A Rand Book, Boulder, CO: Westview Press, 1994.

11. In *DOJ v. COLA*, the court ruled in favor of the plaintiff not on the basis of the many technical arguments presented to the court but on the ground that the board of supervisors had systematically tried to prevent the creation of a Hispanic district. As a result of the suit, a Hispanic district was created and a Hispanic was elected to the board of supervisors early in 1990. Subsequently, the 1990 census established the fact that the new district had no legal basis: It lacked sufficient population to meet the population-equality criterion and a sufficient share of Hispanics among the citizens of voting-age to meet the political compactness criterion.

12. Warren S. Robinson, "Ecological correlation and the behaviour of individuals," *American Sociological Review* 15: 351–357, June 1950; H. M. Blalock, Jr., *Causal Inference in Nonexperimental Research,* Chapel Hill: University of North Carolina Press, 1964, pp. 87–98; H. M. Blalock, Jr., "Comparing individual and structural levels of analysis," pp. 57–86, in K. Namboodiri and R. G. Corwin (eds.), *Research in Sociology of Education and Socialization,* Vol. 8, *Selected Methodological Issues,* Greenwich, CT: JAI Press, 1989.

13. Bernard Grofman, "Statistics without substance: A critique of Freedman *et al.* and Clark and Morrison," *Evaluation Review* 15(6): 746–769, 1991; and Allen Lichtman, "Passing the test: Ecological regression analysis in the Los Angeles County case and beyond," *Evaluation Review* 15(6): 770–816, 1991.

14. David A. Freedman *et al.,* "Ecological regression and voting rights," *Evaluation Review* 15(6): 673–711, 1991; and Stephen P. Klein and David A. Freedman, "Ecological regression in voting rights cases." *Chance* 6(3), Summer 1993.

15. See Glen Firebaugh, "A rule for inferring individual-level relationships from aggregate data," *American Sociological Review* 43: 557–572, August 1978, for a theoretical analysis of conditions under which aggregate-level data provide unbiased estimates of individual-level relationships.

16. See, for example, Allan F. Abrahamse, Peter A. Morrison, and Nancy Minter Bolton, "Surname analysis for estimating local concentration of Hispanics and Asians." *Population Research and Policy Review* 13(4): 383–398, 1994.

17. Jeffrey S. Passel and David L. Word (U.S. Bureau of the Census, Population Division), "Constructing the list of Spanish surnames for the 1980 census: An application of Bayes theorem," paper presented at the annual meeting of the Population Association of America, Denver, CO, April 10–12, 1980.

18. J. S. Passel, D. L. Word, N. D. McKenney, and Y. Kim (U.S. Bureau of the Census, Population Division), "Postcensal estimates of Asian populations in the United States: A description of methods using surnames and administrative records," paper presented at the annual meeting of the Population Association of America, San Diego, CA, 1982.

19. U.S. Congressional Research Service, "Census adjustment: Impact on reapportionment and redistricting," by David C. Huckabee, *CRS Report for Congress,* 94-649 GOV, October 12, 1995.

20. U.S. General Accounting Office, *Formula Grants: Effects of Adjusted Population Counts on Federal Spending to States,* GAO/HEHS-99-69, February 1999.

21. Instead of ruling on the merits of the case, the Supreme Court could have urged the parties to settle the dispute among themselves, observing that Congress has a remedy it can apply (i.e., to grant or withhold funds for the census). The Congress has another remedy. If the adjustment process awards an additional seat to a state, the Congress could choose not to remove that seat from another state, but temporarily to increase the size of the House by the necessary member. This solution has a precedent in the way the apportionment was handled after Alaska and Hawaii became states in 1959.

22. See Judith Innes de Neufville, "Federal statistics in local governments," in William Alonso and Paul Starr (eds.), *The Politics of Numbers,* pp. 343–362, New York: Russell Sage Foundation, 1987.

23. U.S. General Accounting Office, *Using Census Data for Fund Allocations.* GGD-98-132R, May 1998; and U.S. General Accounting Office, *Formula Programs: Adjusted Census Data Would Redistribute Small Percentage of Funds to States,* GAO/GGD-92-12, November 1991.

24. For further information on the programs using population data to distribute federal funds, see U.S. General Accounting Office, *Federal Formula Programs: Outdated Population Data Used to Allocate Most Funds*, GAO/HRD-90-145, September 1990; GAO, 1991, *op. cit.*; GAO, 1998, *op. cit.*; U.S. General Accounting Office, *Formula Grants: Effects of Adjusted Population Counts on Federal Spending to States*, GAO/HEHS-99-69, February 1999; and U.S. Census Monitoring Board, *Effect of Census 2000 Undercount on Federal Funding to States and Local Areas*, 2002–2012, prepared by PricewaterhouseCoopers, March 2000.

25. Richard P. Nathan, "The politics of printouts: The use of official numbers to allocate federal grants-in-aid," in William Alonzo and Paul Starr (eds.), *The Politics of Numbers*, pp. 331–342, New York: Russell Sage Foundation, 1987.

26. For a discussion of this problem and illustrative calculations of the effect of an adjustment of both the population factor and the per capita income factor in a grant formula, see Jeffrey S. Passel and J. Gregory Robinson (U.S. Census Bureau, Population Division), "The effect of data errors and census undercount on General Revenue Sharing Allocations," paper presented at the annual conference of the American Planning Association, Minneapolis, MN, May 5–9, 1984; J. Gregory Robinson and Jacob S. Siegel, "Illustrative assessment of the impact of census underenumeration and income underreporting on revenue-sharing allocations at the local level," *Proceedings*, *American Statistical Association*, Annual Meeting, August 1979; and U.S. Bureau of the Census, "Coverage of population in the 1970 census and some implications for public programs," by Jacob S. Siegel, *Current Population Reports*, Series P-23, No. 56. 1975.

27. U.S. Census Monitoring Board/PricewaterhouseCoopers, 2000, *op. cit.*; Michael Murray, "Census adjustment and the distribution of federal spending," *Demography* 29(3): 319–332, 1992; U.S. General Accounting Office, 1991, *op. cit.*; Arthur J. Maurice and Richard P. Nathan, "The census undercount: Effect on federal aid to cities," *Urban Affairs Quarterly* 17(3): 251–284, 1982. GAO, 1999, *op. cit.*; GAO, 1998, *op. cit.*; U.S. Bureau of the Census/Siegel, 1975, *op. cit.*; Robinson and Siegel, 1979, *op. cit.*; and Passel and Robinson, 1984, *op. cit.*

28. It is not clear from the statement whether allowance was made for the growth in population over the 2002–2012 decade or whether the census 2000 population projections were frozen for this period.

29. Norfleet W. Rives, Jr., "The use of population projections to distribute public funds, *Rand Paper Series* P-6584, Rand Corporation, 1981.

30. Jeanne E. Griffith, "Standardizing population projections required in federal fund allocations," *Statistical Reporter* 80-4: 57–63, 1980.

31. Michael A. Stoto and Alicia P. Schrier, "The accuracy of state population projections," in American Statistical Association (eds.), *Proceedings of the Social Statistics Section*, pp. 177–182, Alexandria, VA: American Statistical Association, 1982.

SUGGESTED READINGS

General

Alonzo, William, and Starr, Paul (eds.) (1989). *The Politics of Numbers*. New York: Russell Sage Foundation.

Anderson, Margo, and Fienberg, Stephen E. (1999). *Who Counts? The Politics of Census-Taking in Contemporary America*. Vol. V, in the 1990 Census Research Series. New York: Russell Sage Foundation.

Bryant, Barbara, and Dunn, W. (1995). *Moving Money and Power: The Politics of Census Taking*. Ithaca, NY: New Strategist Publications.

Entin, Jonathan L. (1993), "Legal considerations in census planning." In International Union for the Scientific Study of Population, International Population Conference, Montreal, 1993. Liège, Belgium: IUSSP.

Adjustment for Census Undercount

Anderson, Margo, and Fienberg, Stephen E. (1996, Summer). "An adjusted census in 1990: The Supreme Court decides." *Chance* 9(3): 4–9.

Choldin, Harvey. (1994). *Looking for the Last Percent: The Controversy over Census Undercounts.* New Brunswick, NJ: Rutgers University Press.

Darga, Kenneth. (1999). *Sampling and the Census: A Case Against the Proposed Adjustments for Undercount.* LaVergne, TN: The AEI Press.

Ericksen, Eugene P., and Kadane, Joseph B. (1985). "Estimating the population in a census year: 1980 and beyond." *Journal of the American Statistical Association* 80(389): 98–109.

Fienberg, Stephen. (1996, March 23–26). "Adjusting the census: Statistical methodology for going beyond the count," in U.S. Bureau of the Census, *Second Annual Research Conference,* Reston, VA.

Freedman, David. (1991, May 31). "Adjusting the census." *Science,* pp. 1233–1236.

Schirm, Allen L., and Preston, Samuel H. (1987). "Census undercount adjustment and the quality of geographic population distributions." *Journal of the American Statistical Association* 82(400): 965–983.

U.S. Bureau of the Census. (1996). *1990 Census of Population and Housing, History,* Part D. Chapter 12, "Legislation and litigation."

Redistricting and Political Empowerment

Clark, William A. V., and Morrison, Peter A. (1991a). "Demographic paradoxes in the Los Angeles Voting Rights case." *Evaluation Review* 15: 712–726.

Clark, William A. V., and Morrison, Peter A. (1991b). "Postscript: Should the court rely on postcensal estimates for redistricting." *Evaluation Review* 15: 727–728.

Clark, William A. V., and Morrison, Peter A. (1992). "Gauging Hispanic voting strength: Paradoxes and pitfalls." *Population Research and Policy Review* 11(2): 145–156.

Clark, William A. V., and Morrison, Peter A. (1995). "Demographic foundations of political empowerment in multiminority cities." *Demography* 32(2): 183–201.

Grofman, Bernard, and Davidson, C., eds. (1992). *Controversies in Minority Voting: The Voting Rights Act in Perspective.* Washington, DC: The Brookings Institution.

Hill, David B., and Kent, Mary M. (1988). "Election demographics." *Population Trends and Public Policy,* No. 14. Washington, DC: Population Reference Bureau.

Morrison, Peter A. (1994). "Empowered or disadvantaged? Applications of demographic analysis to political redistricting." In Hallie J. Kintner *et al.* (eds.), *Demographics: A Casebook for Business and Government.* Boulder, CO: Westview Press.

Morrison, Peter A. (1998). "Demographic influences on Latinos' political empowerment: Comparative local illustrations." *Population Research and Policy Review* 17(3): 223–246.

National Conference of State Legislatures, NCSL Reapportionment Task Force. (1989). *Reapportionment Law: The 1990s.* Washington, DC: National Conference of State Legislatures.

National Conference of State Legislatures, NCSL Reapportionment Task Force. (1989). *Redistricting Provisions: 50 State Profiles.* Washington, DC: National Conference of State Legislatures.

Niemi, Richard G., Grofman, Bernard, Carlucci, Carl, and Hofeller, Thomas. (1990, November). "Measuring compactness and the role of compactness standard in a test for partisan and racial gerrymandering." *Journal of Politics* 52(4): 1155–1181.

Pildes, Richard H., and Niemi, Richard G. (1993). "Expressive harms, 'bizarre districts,' and voting rights: Evaluating election district appearances after Shaw." *Michigan Law Review* 92(3): 483–587.

Poston, Dudley L., Jr., Bouvier, Leon F., and Dan, Hong. (1999, October). "The impact of apportionment method, and legal and illegal immigration, on congressional apportionment in the year 2000." *Population Research and Policy Review* 18(5): 507–524.

Serow, William J., Terrie, E. Walter, Weller, Bob, and Wichmann, Richard W. (1994). "The use of intercensal population estimates in political redistricting." In Hallie J. Kintner *et al.* (eds.), *Demographics: A Casebook for Business and Government,* Boulder, CO: Westview Press.

Siegel, Jacob S. (1996). "Geographic and racial/ethnic compactness in the delineation of legislative districts," *Population Research and Policy Review* 15(2): 147–164.

Terrie, E. Walter. (1996). "Several recent Supreme Court decisions and their implications for political redistricting in Voting Rights Act context." *Population Research and Policy Review* 15(5–6): 565–578.

Thernstrom, Abigail M. (1987). "Statistics and the politics of minority representation: The evolution of the Voting Rights Act of 1965." In William Alonzo and Paul Starr (eds.), pp. 303–328. *The Politics of Numbers* New York: Russell Sage Foundation.

U.S. Bureau of the Census. (1980). "Apportionment and redistricting." In Charles P. Kaplan and Thomas L. VanValey, pp. 114–127. *Census '80: Continuing the Factfinder Tradition.*

U.S. Bureau of the Census, Geography Division. (1989). "The TIGER file and redistricting," by Robert L. Lamacchia, unpublished paper.

U.S. Bureau of the Census. (1991, March). "Population trends and Congressional apportionment." *1990 Census Profile*, No. 1.

U.S. Congressional Research Service. (1995). "Census adjustment: Impact on reapportionment and redistricting," by David C. Huckabee. *CRS Report for Congress* 94-649 GOV.

Allocation of Public Funds and Effect of Undercount

de Neufville, Judith Innes. (1987). "Federal statistics in local governments." In William Alonso and Paul Starr (eds.), pp. 343–362. *The Politics of Numbers.* New York: Russell Sage Foundation.

Maurice, Arthur J., and Nathan, Richard P. (1982). "The census undercount: Effect on federal aid to cities." *Urban Affairs Quarterly* 17(3): 251–284.

Murray, Michael. (1992). "Census adjustment and the distribution of federal spending." *Demography* 29(3): 319–332.

Nathan, Richard P. (1987). "The politics of printouts: The use of official numbers to allocate federal grants-in-aid." In William Alonzo and Paul Starr (eds.), pp. 331–342. *The Politics of Numbers.* New York: Russell Sage Foundation.

Passel, Jeffrey, and Robinson, J. Gregory (U.S. Bureau of the Census, Population Division). (1984, May 5–9). "The effect of data errors and census undercount on General Revenue Sharing Allocations." Paper presented at the annual conference of the American Planning Association, Minneapolis, MN.

Robinson, J. Gregory, and Siegel, Jacob S. (1979). "Illustrative assessment of the impact of census underenumeration and income underreporting on revenue-sharing allocations at the local level." *Proceedings of the Social Statistics Section.* Washington, DC: American Statistical Association.

U.S. Bureau of the Census. (1975). "Coverage of population in the 1970 census and some implications for public programs," by Jacob S. Siegel. *Current Population Reports*, Series P-23, No. 56.

U.S. Congress. (1975). "Federal formula grant-in-aid programs that use population as a factor in allocating funds." 94th Congress, 1st Session. Compiled by Congressional Research Service, Library of Congress.

U.S. General Accounting Office. (1990). *Federal Formula Programs: Outdated Population Data Used to Allocate Most Funds.* GAO/HRD-90/145.

U.S. General Accounting Office. (1991). *Formula Programs: Adjusted Census Data Would Redistribute Small Percentage of Funds to States.* GAO/GGD-92-12.

U.S. General Accounting Office. (1998). *Using Census Data for Fund Allocations.* GGD-98-132R.

U.S. General Accounting Office. (1999). *Formula Grants: Effects of Adjusted Population Grants on Federal Funding to States: Report to Congressional Requesters.* GAO/HEHS-99-69.

Ecological Regression

Blalock, H. M. (1989). "Comparing individual and structural levels of analysis." In K. Namboodiri and R. G. Corwin (eds.), *Research in Sociology of Education and Socialization,* Vol. 8, pp. 57–86. *Selected Methodological Issues.* Greenwich, CN: JAI Press.

Freedman, D. A., Klein, A., Sacks, J., Smythe, C., and Everett, C. (1991). "Ecological regression and voting rights." *Evaluation Review* 15(6): 673–711.

Grofman, Bernard. (1991). "Statistics without substance: A critique of Freedman *et al.* and Clark and Morrison." *Evaluation Review* 15(6): 746–769.

Klein, Stephen P., and Freedman, David A. (1993, Summer). "Ecological regression in voting rights cases." *Chance* 6(3).

Lichtman, Allan. (1991). "Passing the test: Ecological regression analysis in the Los Angeles County case and beyond." *Evaluation Review* 15(6): 770–816.

Surname Analysis

Abrahamse, Allan F., Morrison, Peter A., and Bolton, Nancy Minter. (1994). "Surname analysis for estimating local concentration of Hispanics and Asians." *Population Research and Policy Review* 13(4): 383–398.

Passel, Jeffrey S., and Word, David L. (U.S. Bureau of the Census, Population Division). (1980, April 10–12). "Constructing the list of Spanish surnames for the 1980 census: An application of Bayes theorem." Presented at the annual meeting of the Population Association of America, 1980, Denver, CO. Distributed the U.S. Bureau of the Census as documentation for the 1980 List of Spanish Surnames.

Passel, Jeffrey S., Word, D. L., McKenney, N. D., and Kim, Y. (U.S. Bureau of the Census, Population Division). (1982). "Postcensal estimates of Asians populations in the United States: A description of methods using surnames and administrative records." Paper presented at the annual meeting of the Population Association of America, San Diego, CA.

Shin, E.-H., and Yu, E.-Y. (1984). Use of surnames in ethnic research: The case of Kims in the Korean-American population. *Demography* 21(3): 347–359.

U.S. Bureau of the Census, Population Division. (1996). "Building a Spanish surname list for the 1990s—a new approach to an old problem," by David L. Word and Colby Perkins. *Population Division Working Papers*, No. 13.

13
DEMOGRAPHIC ASPECTS OF SELECTED PUBLIC POLICY ISSUES

INTRODUCTION

Demographic data, methods, and perspectives can contribute to the clarification, analysis, and solution of a wide array of public policy issues and other issues of public interest. The list of public policy issues with demographic dimensions is as broad as the list of public policy issues, because demographic elements are involved in some way in all public policy issues. Whether it is a question of environmental protection, reparations to survivors of a riot, the evolution of an epidemic, the rights of family members, the relative allocation of public funds for research on various health conditions, the restructuring of our educational system, or delineating school districts, there is a role for demographic expertise. The discussion of public policy issues in this chapter supplements the discussion in earlier chapters of such issues as political representation and the allocation of public funds, the delineation of legislative districts, discrimination of racial minorities in housing, bilingual education, jury selection, sex differences in work compensation, and human resources planning under affirmative action.

This chapter will explore five other issues of broad public concern. They are the economic impact of immigration, sex differences in premiums and benefits under insurance and retirement programs, the outlook for the Social Security retirement program, the relative cost of supporting a child and an elderly person, and the role of population growth in the increasing costs of health care. These issues clearly cross disciplinary lines, involving, as the case may be, economics, actuarial science, social work, and health administration. Public policy issues are rarely simply demographic and demographers are accustomed to "hyphenated" research interests. These five topics were selected in part because they illustrate further the range of issues and the range of disciplines in which demographers may be involved. The citations given here are mainly the work of demographers. The demographer's primary role in these public policy debates is not to take policy positions or even to define policy positions, but to provide the information that policy makers need to make informed decisions on the issue at hand. The brief treatment of these topics is intended to be more suggestive than comprehensive, given the complexity of the subjects.

Economic Impact of Immigration

The public's perception is that new immigrants, especially illegal immigrants, take jobs away from natives and permanent immigrants, contribute to local unemployment, and lower wage rates in the occupations at which they work. Moreover, the public generally believes that new immigrants are more likely to receive public welfare payments and, in general, to constitute a net financial burden on the rest of the population by receiving more in social services than they pay in taxes.[1]

To say whether the financial charges are true, we need a general framework for considering the fiscal costs and returns of immigration. Fiscal costs include transfer payments (e.g., welfare), public education, use of public transportation, police protection, and other activities for which the expenditures benefit an individual, and fiscal revenues comprise the body of funds that have moved from an individual to the government, such as sales and income taxes and tuition for public education. From a financial point of view, if the public costs of supporting a specified group of persons exceed the revenues obtained from them, the group is a net burden to the community; if revenues from the group exceed costs, then the group is a net asset to the community.

Research studies on the fiscal impact of immigration must balance revenues against costs but, to be meaningful, they must also have a control group to evaluate the immigrant record (e.g., native residents). The issue is best analyzed separately for legal and illegal entrants, and separately for the nation, and states and localities within the nation, both because of differences in data and methods but also because of possible differences in fiscal impact and policy implications. The design of most past studies probing the fiscal impact of immigration has been to treat legal and illegal immigration in combination and to aggregate the fiscal effects of immigration across all levels of government. Making these distinctions would add to both the quality of the studies and their policy usefulness. This discussion of the costs of immigration draws particularly on the summary analysis of the fiscal effects of immigration presented by Rothman and Espenshade (1992), a report of the National Academy of Sciences (Smith and Edmonston, 1997) on the economic effects of immigration, testimony given before the Commission on Immigration Reform (1997), and a book by Borjas (1999) on the economic effects of the post-1965 immigration.[2] Discussions of this subject should be guided in large part by the view of Borjas that immigration policy should be used to maximize the economic well-being of the resident population of the United States, defined in such terms as per capita income and income inequality.[3]

One-third of all U.S. immigrants live in California, and another two-fifths live in New York, Florida, Texas, New Jersey, Illinois, and Massachusetts. The immigrants are also heavily concentrated in certain unskilled occupations, such as agricultural labor, janitorial service, and domestic service, and hence have major impacts on a few labor markets. A disproportionate number also work in some highly skilled jobs, such as college instruction and medical research. It is difficult to measure these area-specific and job-specific effects. They are the joint result of events in these states and occupations as well as events in the rest of the country and abroad (e.g., job displacement in the states, international competition).

Total Immigration

Rothman and Espenshade reviewed the available studies on the labor market effects of immigration and concluded that the empirical evidence does not support the view that immigrants depress wages or raise unemployment ratios of native workers. Moreover, they maintain that there is insufficient evidence to support the view that immigrants are a net fiscal burden on the American population and try to show that no universal conclusion about the fiscal impact of immigration on government budgets is possible. When the available studies were grouped according to the level of government to which they pertain, they found that the fiscal burden of immigration fell more heavily on states and, especially, on local governments than on the national government. The impact is always negative for local governments, while the results for states are mixed. The federal government has passed the burden and responsibility for the conduct and financing of social programs on to states, which in turn have passed them largely on to local governments. Since the national figure includes the figures for state and local governments, the United States balance *taken alone* must be seen as consistently positive.

The hearings of the U.S. Commission on Immigration Reform appear to confirm the Rothman-Espenshade findings. The commission found that, while the overall national impact of immigration is small in relation to the national economy, there are notable effects in the handful of states where immigration is concentrated. Its general conclusion is that immigration accounts for only a small part of the decline in jobs and earnings for native unskilled workers and immigrants previously here.

The Smith and Edmonston/National Academy of Sciences study concludes that immigration produces net economic gains for U.S. residents. Immigration results in an increase in the supply of labor, which helps to produce new goods and services and augments the Social Security Trust Fund. Immigration also allows native workers to be used more productively, permitting them to specialize in producing goods at which they are relatively more efficient. Different groups in the population may lose or gain from the presence of immigrants, however. The more highly skilled workers will gain in that their incomes may be expected to rise. The buyers of the goods and services produced by immigrant labor will also benefit from lower prices. On the other hand, the less skilled native workers who compete with immigrants are likely to experience falling wages. The small (4%) increase in the labor supply from immigration during the 1980s may have reduced the wages of competing native workers by about 1 or 2%, while the wages of noncompeting native workers increased.

According to the Smith-Edmonston study, the small adverse impact on the wage and employment opportunities of competing native groups is not confined to the areas of immigrant settlement but is dispersed over the country. The massive immigration to some states has led to significant displacement of the population from those states, particularly of native low-wage and blue-collar workers who must compete with the new immigrants. They have moved into neighboring states, which, as a secondary effect, have experienced some depression of wages. Another group that appears to be adversely affected by the new immigration is the group of immigrants that came just before, for whom the new immigrants are a ready substitute in the labor market. On the other hand, the study maintains that there is no evidence at the national level for the widely held presumption that blacks have been adversely affected by the influx of low-skilled immigrants. Most blacks live in different areas than those where immigrants are concentrated, and their economic fate is affected by other factors.[4]

The National Academy study also found that, while immigration may have much larger effects on certain parts of the labor market than on others, there is only a weak relationship between the amount of immigration for a city or state and the wages of natives. The study concludes that, given the massive size of the U.S. economy, immigration is unlikely to have had a very large effect on relative earnings or on gross domestic product per capita nationally. Many other factors are more critical.

Immigrants improve their economic status by immigration because of the higher wage levels in the United States than in the less developed countries from which they come. The wider spread of wages here is also attractive to skilled workers from many more developed countries. Immigrant wages in the United States are lower than those of natives, however, and the gap has been widening because of the low level of skill of the new arrivals and the greater improvement in the education of natives than of immigrants. Rothman and Espenshade suggested that part of the growing gap in wage levels is due to the influx of illegal immigrants, who are generally ill educated, but part is also due to the change in the immigrants' countries of origin and the decline in the educational level of refugees and legal immigrants. The country-of-origin change was brought about by the Amendment of the Immigration and Nationality Act of 1965 and favors immigration from less developed countries. Borjas (1999, *op. cit.*) also noted that the new immigrants show a declining economic performance and skill relative to that of natives and that this increasing skill gap can be explained by the change in the immigrants' countries of origin.

In its detailed analysis of the fiscal impact of immigration, the National Academy of Sciences examined data for New Jersey (1989–1990) and California (1994–1995). The review found that in both states the presence of immigrant-headed households caused a net fiscal burden[5] on native-headed households and that the per capita figure for California ($1174) was five times greater than that for New Jersey. Since these states have large numbers of immigrants, the fiscal burden on native residents is relatively high. If the burden were spread over all U.S. native households, however, it would be far lower—$166 to $226 in 1996 dollars per native household. Latin American immigrant households create by far the heaviest burden on native households. The reasons are manifold. Their households tend to have lower incomes and hence pay lower state and local taxes; they include more school-age children than other immigrant households and hence consume more educational services; and since they are poorer, they receive more public transfer funds.

On the basis of an analysis of recent immigration to California, Clark and Schultz conclude that immigration is creating substantial burdens for local communities in the state and that there is a strong potential for an intensification of these local burdens.[6] They compare the distribution of the population by nativity and race with the distribution of welfare allocations. Immigrants made up 26% of the population in 1994 but received 44% of the welfare payments (Table 13.1). Immigrants who entered before 1980 were particularly likely to become a public burden; they made up 10% of the population but received 28% of the welfare funds.

Illegal Immigration

When illegal immigration is considered separately, the cost-benefit balance appears to be less favorable than for legal immigrants at all levels of government, but the studies are conflicting. The measurement of the economic impact of illegal immigration depends on estimates of their numbers, both nationally and locally. According to the Immigration and Naturalization Service, an estimated 5 million illegal aliens resided in the United States in 1996.[7] While they constitute a small percentage of the U.S. population (1.9%), they are, like legal

■■■■ **TABLE 13.1** **Comparative Distribution of Population and Welfare Payments by Nativity and Race, for California: 1994**

Nativity and race	Population	Welfare payments[a]
Total	100.0	100.0
Native[b]	74.5	55.7
White, non-Hispanic	47.8	26.5
Black	5.5	12.0
Hispanic	17.5	14.9
Asian	2.9	0.6
Other	0.8	1.7
Foreign born	25.5	44.2
Immigrating before 1980	10.1	27.6
Immigrating 1980–1994	15.4	16.6

[a] AFDC (Aid to Families with Dependent Children), SSI (Supplementary Security Income), and other public assistance.

[b] For natives, race and Hispanic origin are cross-classified; the vast majority of Hispanics are classified as white.

Source: Based on W. A. V. Clark and Freya Schultz, "Local impacts of recent immigration to California: Realism vs. racism," *Population Research and Policy Review* 16(5): 475–491, October 1997, Table 3, p. 487. *Primary source*: Current Population Survey, 1994. © 1997. Reprinted with kind permission of Kluwer Academic Publishers.

immigrants, concentrated in a handful of states. About 40% of all illegal aliens live in California. Over half of the total had Mexico as their country of origin.

The public has been concerned with the costs associated with the illegal aliens' receipt of public benefits, especially since it could be an inducement for further immigration. The limited access to federal public benefits that illegal aliens had was further restricted in 1996 by the Personal Responsibility and Work Opportunity Reconciliation Act (WORA)[8] and by the Immigration Reform Act (IRA). These acts also limited their access to state and local public benefits. Under the WRA, illegal aliens remain ineligible for nearly all social programs. They continue to be eligible for emergency medical assistance under Medicaid. Although illegal aliens are not eligible for federal welfare benefits, children born to illegal aliens in the United States are U.S. citizens and can receive such benefits. In fiscal year 1995, about $1.1 billion in Aid to Families with Dependent Children (AFDC) and Food Stamp benefits went to households with an illegal alien parent to assist their citizen children (U.S. Government Accounting Office, 1997).[9] Illegal aliens also receive Supplementary Security Income and housing assistance for their citizen children. When a citizen child of an alien parent receives assistance, the aid also helps support the child's family and so a question is raised about use of public assistance by illegal aliens.

A General Accounting Office (GAO) report published in 1993 concluded that education, emergency services, Medicaid, and incarceration for illegal aliens would cost the state of California $2.5 billion in fiscal year 1995.[10] Senator Barbara Boxer (D-CA) used the report's findings to calculate that, with an allowance for taxes paid to the federal and state governments by illegal immigrants, the net cost to the state would be about $1.4 billion.[11] Rea and Parker (1993) reported that in San Diego County, illegal aliens pay $59.7 million annually in state and local taxes but use $244.2 million in public services each year.[12] Illegal immigrants also pay $162.6 million in federal taxes, a part of which is returned to the state.

On the other side, Marcelli and Heer (1997) concluded from an analysis of data for Los Angeles County, California, that illegal aliens do not use a disproportionate share of public assistance.[13] In a comparison of Mexican illegal aliens, other non-U.S. citizens, and U.S. citizens with respect to their use of seven welfare programs in the county in 1994, they found that illegal aliens were 11% less likely than other noncitizens, and 14% less likely than U.S. citizens, to have received welfare payments. When the illegal aliens received welfare payments, they tended to receive less. These results were based on a special 1994 Los Angeles County Household Survey of foreign-born Mexicans and the Current Population Surveys of March 1993 and 1994.

Conclusion

Under most scenarios the long-run fiscal effect of immigration is strongly positive at the federal level, but substantially negative at the state and local levels. The federal effect is shared equally across the nation, but the negative state and local effects are concentrated in a few states and localities that receive most of the new immigrants. The residents of some states, such as California, may incur net fiscal costs from immigration, while the residents of most states reap net fiscal benefits.

Whether there is a net economic gain or net economic loss through immigration as measured by government receipts and outlays, society secures many economic benefits from the presence of immigrants. Among the benefits are the following: The employment of immigrants benefits natives by maintaining the viability of companies that employ natives as well as immigrants. Immigrants contribute to local employment growth since some become entrepreneurs and establish businesses (Enchautegui, 1997).[14] The presence of immigrants contributes to lower prices for farm products by serving as an economical source of farm labor (U.S. Bureau of International Labor Affairs/Greenwood and McDowell, 1990).[15] Immigration helps to support beneficiaries under Social Security by offsetting the demographic effect of past low fertility on population growth and by augmenting the labor force. Low-wage immigrant workers support higher-income households by providing services such as gardening, housecleaning, and child care at low cost and by affording members of these households more time for work.

The costs of immigration remains a controversial public issue, particularly in the states with heavy influxes of both legal and illegal immigrants.[16] Immigration has become such a sensitive issue that the leading politicians, especially at the national level, refrain from dealing with it. This is unfortunate since a revised national immigration policy setting new goals as to numbers and types of immigrants is urgently needed and research on the costs of immigration should be essential elements in developing such a policy.

SEX DIFFERENCES IN COSTS AND BENEFITS OF INSURANCE AND RETIREMENT PROGRAMS

A public policy issue much debated in recent decades concerns whether there should be differences between men and women in premiums (or contributions) and benefits (or annuities) for various types of insurance, including life insurance, retirement insurance, long-term-care insurance, disability insurance, and health insurance. For simplicity this discussion is restricted mainly to life insurance and retirement insurance. The policy issue pits the principle of fairness or equity against the principle of equality. The demographic considerations are rather similar for life insurance and retirement insurance, but they "play out" differently for the two programs. Because of the well-established difference in longevity between the sexes (i.e., the much greater longevity for women than men), it has been common practice for insurance companies to charge men higher monthly premiums for life insurance than women and to charge women higher monthly contributions than men under retirement annuity programs. The issue is whether these practices are justified in view of the laws and court decisions calling for equal treatment of the sexes. These judicial decisions have been made in spite of the strong demographic evidence that the sexes are not equal. A sex-differentiated handling of the matter may appear fair, but legal, social, and political considerations have led in the opposite direction.

Demographic Background

The principal demographic facts underlying the issue are the greater mortality of men than women at every age of life and the resulting advantage in life expectancy of women over men at every age. In 1997 life expectancy at birth was 73.6 years for males and 79.4 years for females; at age 65 the figures were 15.9 years for men and 19.2 years for women (Table 13.2). As a consequence, the surviving beneficiaries of men, usually their wives, are likely to start collecting benefits at an earlier age (i.e., after fewer years of coverage), and hence to collect them over a much longer period, than the surviving beneficiaries of women, who are usually their husbands. On the other hand, male retirees will, on average, receive monthly retirement benefits for fewer months or years than female retirees who retired at the same age.[17]

To determine the relevance of the sex gap in longevity to sex-differentiated premiums and benefits, we need to consider whether the tools we have to measure the longevity differences are adequate for this purpose and whether the differences in longevity are transitory or "permanent." We can dismiss the first question regarding the adequacy of the data on sex differences in longevity very quickly. While the current life tables for males and females may be affected by errors in the basic data, these errors are believed to be of little consequence for the essential findings regarding the sex difference in longevity.[18] Moreover, the quality of the segment of the life tables over age 65, the segment that has been of most concern, has been greatly improved by the use of mortality rates from the Medicare record system. These rates have some advantages over the rates from the vital registration system, in particular the fact that their numerators and denominators have a common source and the data are subject to validation.

TABLE 13.2 Sex and Race Differences in Expectation of Life in Years and Survival Rates, for Selected Ages: 1900–1902 to 1997 (Death Registration States, 1900–1902 and 1919–1921; United States, 1939–1941 to 1997)

	Life expectation				Survival rate			
	Sex		Race		Sex		Race	
Year	Male	Female	Black	White	Male	Female	Black	White
	At birth							
1900–1902	47.9	50.7	33.8	49.6				
1919–1921	55.5	57.4	47.0	57.4				
1939–1941	61.6	65.9	53.8[a]	64.9	(Not applicable)			
1959–1961	66.8	73.2	63.9	70.7				
1979–1981	70.1	77.6	68.5	74.5				
1997	73.6	79.4	71.1	77.1				
	At age 65				Birth to age 65[b]			
1900–1902	11.5	12.2	10.9	11.9	.387	.432	.205	.415
1919–1921	12.2	12.7	12.2	12.5	.492	.521	.327	.524
1939–1941	12.1	13.6	13.0[a]	12.8	.558	.655	.378[a]	.632
1959–1961	13.0	15.8	14.0	14.4	.642	.785	.560	.731
1979–1981	14.2	18.4	15.4	16.6	.706	.835	.644	.786
1997	15.9	19.2	16.1	17.8	.770	.860	.697	.829
	At age 85				Age 65 to age 85[c]			
1900–1902	3.8	4.1	4.6	4.0	.134	.163	.136	.149
1919–1921	4.1	4.3	4.9	4.2	.161	.183	.177	.173
1939–1941	4.1	4.5	5.9[a]	4.2	.156	.213	.220[a]	.182
1959–1961	4.4	4.7	5.3	4.5	.200	.322	.274	.260
1979–1981	5.1	6.4	6.5	5.9	.255	.452	.310	.366
1997	5.5	6.6	6.4	6.2	.333	.491	.346	.424

[a] For the entire nonwhite population.
[b] Survival from birth to exact age 65.
[c] Survival from exact age 65 to exact age 85.
Source: Based on U.S. National Center for Health Statistics, "U.S. life tables, 1997," *National Vital Statistics Reports* 47(28), December 1999, Table 11.

In part, the likelihood that the sex differences in longevity will persist depends on the extent to which they can be accounted for by genetic factors as compared to nongenetic factors. The nongenetic factors include such lifestyle or behavioral practices as those relating to diet, exercise, smoking, sleep, and engaging in risky behavior; access to and use of health resources; and conditions in the living, working, and recreational environments. In addition to the direct role of genetic factors, the nongenetic factors, including both lifestyle and the environment, strongly influence the expression of the genetic component. If the sex difference in longevity has a strong biological basis, it may be expected to persist; nongenetic influences are more amenable to change.

A meritorious case can be made for the view that the mortality advantage of females over males has a substantial genetic component. The female advantage is pervasive over the age scale and applies to many of the leading causes of death, including the endogenous ones (i.e., chronic diseases typically resistent to treatment or cure). Several physiological factors appear to favor women. The difference has persisted over many decades. A difference in life expectancy at birth equaling or exceeding 7 years prevailed over the 15 years from 1970 to 1986, and a difference exceeding 5 years has prevailed in all the years since the 1940s. However, the change in the size of the sex difference as longevity has increased suggests that there is an important nongenetic component. The sex difference in life expectancy at birth was only 3 years in 1900–1902, reached a maximum at 7.8 years in 1979, and then fell to 5.8 years in 1997. At age 65, the difference now stands at 3.3 years, while in 1900–1902 it was less than 1 year.

The evidence regarding the relative roles of genetic and nongenetic factors in the female longevity advantage is inconclusive. Even if nongenetic influences are dominant in explaining the sex difference in longevity, it may persist because the male-female differences in lifestyle and behavior are expected to continue. Leading analysts posit a continuation of the longevity gap. Actuaries at the U.S. Social Security Administration (SSA, 1997), demographers at the U.S. Census Bureau (1995), demographers Carter and Lee (1993), and Ahlburg and Vaupel (1990) all project a continuation of substantial differences in the life expectancy of the sexes.[19] For example, in the intermediate SSA series, the sex difference in life expectancy at birth in the year 2050 is 5.5 years; at age 65 it is 3.4 years. The corresponding figures in the Carter-Lee set of projections are much larger, about 12 years at birth and 6 years at age 65. The Ahlburg-Vaupel projections show a difference in life expectancy at birth of 4 to 5 years in the middle of the 21st century.

Whatever the cause or causes of the sex gap, if the gap persists, the demographic basis for differential treatment of the sexes in insurance and annuity programs remains. Moreover, the tools in the form of regular official life tables and annuity tables to implement and monitor the use of different rates for the sexes are available. The fact that there is a demographic basis for treating the sexes differently may be considered insufficient to justify disparate treatment, however. Different types of insurance contracts may require a different disposition of the question and there are legal and other aspects of the issue to be considered, as discussed next.

Legal Background

One view argues that, in spite of the demographic evidence, the two sexes should be treated *equally* with regard to premiums/contributions and benefits/annuities in insurance and annuity programs. In this view, the definition of equality is equal *monthly* premiums or contributions and equal *monthly* benefits or annuities. In another view, the guideline should be equal *lifetime* premiums or contributions and equal *lifetime* benefits or annuities.[20] The former criterion may be called equality and the latter one fairness or equity. The equality concept has been written into law with respect to *employer-sponsored* insurance and annuity programs, while the states follow their own rules with respect to *individual* insurance and annuity contracts. In the insurance programs conducted by the federal government for its employees and retirees (life, retirement, and health), monthly premiums and benefits are the same for the sexes (as well as ages and races), but differ on the basis of salary and, in the case of life insurance, on the basis of family composition. This is a variation on the equality principle.

Insurance Purchased by Groups

A considerable body of law has accumulated since the 1960s calling for equal treatment of the sexes with respect to fringe benefits and compensation in employer-sponsored programs. The legal arguments have been made in defiance of the statistical evidence while acknowledging it. Title VII of the Civil Rights Act of 1964 bars discrimination with respect to the privileges of employment on the basis of sex, and the Equal Pay Act of 1963 calls for equal pay for equal work. They raise the spectre that requiring different premiums or contributions from the sexes, or awarding different benefits or annuities to them, is a violation of law. In effect, they require equalization of all benefits in retirement programs since these programs can be interpreted either as compensation or as fringe benefits (i.e., privileges of employment). Use of sex-specific annuity tables results in the payment of different periodic pension benefits to men and women. Failure to equalize benefits and to use the rate of the higher-paid sex in doing so would constitute a prohibited reduction in rates of compensation. In sum, differentiating between men and women in annuity payments on the basis of sex-specific mortality tables would constitute disparate treatment with regard to compensation in violation of Title VII.[21]

The U.S. Supreme Court addressed the question of the use of sex-differentiated life tables in determining annuity benefits derived from public and private employer-sponsored pension and tax-deferred plans in *Arizona Government Committee v. Norris* (1983) and *City of Los Angeles v. Manhart* (1978). In *Manhart*, an employer-sponsored plan used sex-differentiated actuarial tables to determine employee contributions. The benefits were equal, but the costs of obtaining the benefits were greater for women. The Court held that Title VII prohibits the practice of requiring higher contributions from female employees based on statistical averages for women. The Court noted that the statute's focus on the individual was unambiguous and that "even a true generalization about the class is an insufficient reason for disqualifying an individual to whom the generalization does not apply." The Court would have been more correct to say "may not apply."

The Supreme Court also refused to review a lower court decision (U.S. Court of Appeals for the Second Circuit) in *Spirt v. TIAA-CREF and Long Island University* (1984), when the *Spirt* decision was appealed by TIAA-CREF.[22] This decision stands, therefore, and requires that all retirement benefits derived from contributions made after May 1, 1980, be calculated without regard to the sex of the beneficiary.[23]

The change to unisex premiums with a single-sex life table from separate-sex life tables under an employer-sponsored life insurance program would be in the opposite direction to the change to unisex contributions under an employer-sponsored retirement program:

Program	Men	Women
Retirement	Monthly contributions higher	Monthly contributions lower
Life insurance	Monthly premiums lower	Monthly premiums higher

After its setback in *Spirt*, the TIAA-CREF benefits were based on a life table that averaged male and female mortality levels from the sex-distinct life tables previously used by the association. This averaging was based on the distribution of the annuitant population by sex, an income option, and other relevant factors. The benefits of men for several income options were decreased substantially and the benefits of women in the same categories were raised by the same percentage. TIAA-CREF also has gender-merged rates for purchased life insurance. Such new rates resulted in lower premiums for men and higher premiums for women.[24]

Insurance Purchased by Individuals

There is no federal law or Supreme Court decision mandating unisex rates for insurance purchased by *individuals*. In general, states regulate insurance practices, and they may choose whether or not to allow sex-differentiated life insurance or annuity rates. About one-third of the states have Equal Rights Amendments, but only Montana mandates unisex rates for life insurance. In all other states, the rates charged are based on the actual losses of specific groups of individuals. The companies operating in these states have different life insurance rates and annuity rates for men and women and possibly other groups (e.g., smokers and nonsmokers). While insurance companies in all states except Montana may employ unisex rates for any of their programs, in general they are opposed to levying unisex rates on the grounds that their rates must reflect the potential for loss as shown by their experience records and the statistical record. Leading insurance companies, such as New York Life, John Hancock, and TIAA-CREF, continue to employ sex-differentiated tables for all types of insurance in all but a few states.

Actuarial Considerations

The whole concept of insurance involves the sharing of risk by individuals in groups of policyholders whose risk is relatively similar, called risk classification. Age, sex, and health are accepted factors in setting insurance rates, because risk varies with these factors according to well-documented experience. Age has always been used in this way, given the demonstrated differences in risk of death at different ages. In many rate tables, there is an age cutoff for purchasing insurance or the amount of insurance is limited at the older ages. No one has argued that these variations for age constitute an act of age discrimination, as has been done for sex. Other bases of differentiated risks may be taken into account. All three of the companies cited have different rate tables for smokers and nonsmokers (after applicants have passed the health examination). Additional health criteria may be taken into account in setting rates, such as driving record, health condition, and family health history.

The basis for incorporating sex differences in premiums or benefits is as strong as that for distinguishing smokers from nonsmokers, or persons with previous or current health conditions from those free of such conditions. Race is another candidate for inclusion in this group of factors. The difference in longevity between whites and blacks is strong and persistent, and remains generally greater than the sex difference at all ages below age 75 (Table 13.2).

It has, however, diminished sharply with the passage of time. Different rates for the races are still in force in old policies in some Southern states even though equal rates have been applied in new policies. Taking account of the race difference in longevity in insurance and annuity programs, whatever its demographic merits, would create a political storm and outcry today. It has long been prohibited by the courts.

OUTLOOK FOR THE SOCIAL SECURITY RETIREMENT SYSTEM

Nature of the Social Security System

The Social Security program has provided older persons with a modicum of retirement income security since 1935. Contributions to Social Security are made by workers and benefits are paid to disabled and retired workers, and to their spouses and children in the event of the worker's death. Benefits are adjusted ("indexed") for changes in the Consumer Price Index. Currently over 90% of "aged units"—couples and single persons—receive Social Security benefits. For about half of these households, Social Security is the source of their only retirement income and for about 15 million persons it is the means to remain above the poverty line. It has been a key factor in the sharp decline in the extent of poverty among the elderly since 1959, when data on poverty first became available.[25]

The Social Security program has some elements of an insurance or funded system but it is primarily financed as a pay-as-you-go system. In a pay-as-you-go system, the payments made to current beneficiaries come from tax deductions taken from the earned income of current workers, and there is only a small reserve fund for contingencies. The costs of the generations that became beneficiaries when the system was first established in the 1930s and that could not "afford" to pay for their retirement, and the income-redistribution aspects of the program, gave it the character of a pay-as-you-go system. In a funded system, however, the taxes or contributions may be accumulated either in individual accounts or a general fund, but distributions from the accounts or fund occur usually after a long period of accumulation to allow the fund or accounts to grow sufficiently.

The amount of the benefit paid to a beneficiary is determined by several factors, principally the contributions paid by the individual worker, the number of years the contributions were paid, the age and disability status of the beneficiary on first receipt of a benefit, and in the event of death of the worker, the relationship of the beneficiary to the worker. The current issue is that within a generation or so the Social Security Trust Fund will be unable to pay full benefits as required under the law.[26] The task is to restore the fund to complete viability through much of the 21st century.

Basic Demographic Factors

From a demographic point of view, the funding of the Social Security System is basically dependent on the age distribution of the population and, more exactly, on the relative numbers of elderly persons and persons of working age (i.e., the **elderly age-dependency ratio** or, as it is more commonly called, the aged dependency ratio). It should be recognized at the outset that this measure reflects essentially the role of age structure in elderly dependency and is therefore a measure only of *potential* elderly dependency. Table 13.3 shows the past and prospective trend of the elderly age-dependency ratio, in the form of the population aged 65 and over per 100 persons 18 to 64 years of age, from 1950 to 2030. The ratio rose from 13.4 to 20.9 between 1950 and 1995. It will change little from 1995 to 2010 but, then, in the two decades from 2010 to 2030, it is expected to show an explosive rise to 36. The ratio should remain fairly steady in the following two decades, from 2030 to 2050, as the baby-boom cohorts move up *within* the elderly age band. Figure 13.1 illustrates the trend over a longer period, with alternative projections, in terms of the ratio of the population 65 years and over to the population 20 to 64 years of age, for the Social Security area.[27]

The age distribution and the dependency ratio are products of past trends in fertility, mortality, and net immigration. These factors, especially fertility, will shape the age distribution of the population in the future as in the past. Fertility is the principal determinant of the age structure of a population, and hence it plays a major role in determining the demographic inputs affecting the financial viability of the Social Security program. The general decline in fertility rates in the past century, with the notable exception of the baby-boom period, and the persistence of low, near-replacement-level or replacement-level fertility (i.e., an average of 2.1 children per woman in her lifetime) since the early 1970s have contributed to producing an age structure with a relatively low proportion of children and young adults and a high proportion of elderly

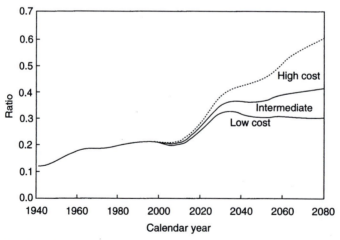

FIGURE 13.1   Elderly age-dependency ratios, estimated 1940 to 1995 and projected 1996 to 2080. *Note:* Ratio of population 65 years old and over to population 20 to 64 years old. Lines for 1996 to 2080 correspond to three alternative projected series. *Source:* U.S. Social Security Administration, Office of the Chief Actuary, "Social Security Area population projections: 1997," by Felicitie C. Bell, *Actuarial Study No. 112,* 1997, Figure 8.

█ **TABLE 13.3 Past and Prospective Trends in Three Measures of Elderly Dependency: 1950 to 2030**

Year	Ratio 1[a]	Ratio 2[b]	Ratio 3[c]
1950	13.4	13.4	
1975	18.2	19.8	
1995	20.9	22.9	23.8
Ratio, 1975/1950	1.36	1.48	
Ratio, 1995/1975	1.15	1.16	
2010	21.2[d]	23.2[e]	24.4
2030	35.7[d]	39.0[e]	40.0
Ratio, 2010/1995	1.01	1.01	1.03
Ratio, 2030/2010	1.68	1.68	1.64

[a] Number of persons 65 years old and over per 100 persons aged 18 to 64.

[b] Number of persons not in the labor force 65 years old and over per 100 persons in the labor force 16 years old and over.

[c] Number of beneficiaries per 100 contributors.

[d] Middle series of projections.

[e] B series of projections.

Source: Compiled from Murray Gendell, "Trends in retirement age in four countries, 1965–1995," *Monthly Labor Review*, August 1998, pp. 20–30, Table 6; Jacob S. Siegel, *A Generation of Change: A Profile of America's Older Population*, New York: Russell Sage Foundation, 1993, Table 7.23; and U.S. Bureau of the Census, "Population Projections of the United States by age, sex, race, and Hispanic origin," by Jennifer C. Day, *Current Population Reports* P25-1130, 1996, Table E.

persons. The baby boom of the late 1940s, 1950s, and early 1960s swelled the share of persons 33 to 52 years of age in 1998, and will swell the share of persons 62 and over beginning about 2007 and 65 and over about 2010. The arrival of the baby-boom cohorts at age 65 will have a profound impact on the elderly dependency ratio. By 2030 the baby-boom cohorts, at ages 65 to 84, will all be elderly, and their influence on the elderly dependency ratio will be nearly at a maximum.

Declines in mortality have reinforced the effects of fertility in raising the number and share of older persons since the late 1960s. Mortality changes in the pre-1965 era were mostly concentrated in the ages of childhood and youth, thus *tending* to increase the share of young persons in the population. In more recent decades, however, substantial declines in mortality have also occurred in the later adult ages, resulting in substantial increases in survival within the 65-and-over age group (Table 13.2). This turn in the mortality trend contributed to a rapid increase in the share as well as the number of elderly persons in the population. The declines in mortality in the upper ages are expected to continue, albeit at a slower pace (Table 13.4).

Between 1935, when the Social Security Act was passed, and 1997, life expectancy at birth rose from 59.9 years to 73.6 years for men and from 63.9 years to 79.4 years for women. In 1935 the life expectancies for men and women were below the "normal" retirement age of 65; now they exceed it by many years—some 13.7 years for men and 15.5 years for women. With expected future gains in life expectancy, the added years will be even greater.

■ **TABLE 13.4   Expectation of Life in Years at Birth and at Age 65, by Sex: 1935 to 2045**

Year	At birth Both sexes	Male	Female	At age 65 Both sexes	Male	Female
1935	61.7	59.9	63.9	12.6	11.9	13.2
1965	70.2	66.8	73.7	14.6	12.9	16.2
1995	75.8	72.5	78.9	17.3	15.6	19.0
1997	76.5	73.6	79.4	17.7	15.9	19.2
Projections[a]						
2015	78.0	75.1	80.8	18.1	16.4	19.8
2025	78.7	75.8	81.5	18.5	16.8	20.2
2035	79.3	76.5	82.1	19.0	17.2	20.7
2045	79.9	77.2	82.6	19.4	17.6	21.1

[a] Intermediate projections published by the U.S. Social Security Administration (1997), based on data through 1995. These projections are nearly the same as those of the U.S. Bureau of the Census (1996) middle series.

Source: U.S. National Center for Health Statistics, "Life tables," various issues *Vital Statistics of the United States*; "Deaths: Final data for 1997," *National Vital Statistics Reports* 47(19), June 30, 1999; and U.S. Social Security Administration, Office of the Chief Actuary, "Social Security Area Population Projections: 1997," by Felicitie C. Bell, *Actuarial Study* No. 112, 1997, Table 9.

Most workers of today will be collecting Social Security benefits for many years after the normal retirement age—unlike the situation of the late 1930s. As we saw, some analysts characterize the projections of mortality made by the Social Security Administration as much too conservative. If realized, their mortality projections would require larger outlays of public funds for Social Security benefits than currently envisaged.

The *share* of elderly persons will rise sharply after 2010 as a joint result of past and expected continuing low fertility, the arrival of the members of the baby-boom cohorts at the elderly ages, and the recent and prospective declines in mortality rates at the older ages. Although immigration will augment greatly the *numbers* of elderly persons in the next several decades, mostly from the aging of younger immigrants, it is not expected to contribute much to the increase in the *share* of elderly persons, as the SSA and Census Bureau population projections demonstrate.

Demographic Characteristics of Contributors and Beneficiaries

The demographic characteristics such as sex and race influence the contributions and costs of the Social Security program. Differences in the pay levels, work history, and longevity of men and women affect how much they contribute to the Social Security program and receive in benefits. Most older persons are women, so that women are the principal beneficiaries of the program. Women make up less than half of the beneficiaries who are receiving retired worker benefits but 99% of those beneficiaries who receive spouse or survivor benefits. Elderly single women are likely to be receiving retired workers benefits, but elderly married and widowed women are likely to be receiving spouse or survivor benefits. Though the provisions of the Social Security Act do not distinguish between men and women, women tend to receive lower (monthly) benefits than men. This is so because women's lifetime earnings are smaller, as a result of the fact that they tend to receive lower wages and have less work experience.

On the other side, women have been entering the labor force at most ages in large numbers. A few measures of the diminishing gap in the labor force participation of the sexes will remind the reader of the magnitude of the change. Around 1950 women's labor force participation ratio (LFPR) was about one-third of that for men, but by 1997 it was about four-fifths of that for men. The LFPR for women 55 to 64 years of age in 1997 was 41% when they were 25 to 34 years of age, while the LFPR for age group 25 to 34 years of age in 1997 is 76%. As a result, increasing proportions of women are receiving Social Security benefits on the basis of their own work history. The percentages of women 62 years and over receiving such benefits for various dates are as follows:

Year	Percentage
1960	43.3
1970	50.6
1980	56.9
1988	59.7

Source: Barbara A. Lingg, "Women beneficiaries aged 62 or older, 1960–1988," *Social Security Bulletin*, July 1990. Reproduced as Table 6.1 in Employee Benefit Research Institute, *Pension Funding and Taxation: Implications for Tomorrow*, 1994.

The significance of this trend is that women will not need to depend as much as in the past on the benefits of husbands or on survivors insurance in their old age.

Women's history of lower labor force participation has resulted in fewer years with covered earnings on which Social Security benefits are based, and lower earnings levels of women have tended to limit the lifetime earned income on which benefits are based. Median earnings of women working full-time and year-round are still well below those of men, although the earnings of men and women have been converging. Fewer years with covered earnings and lower annual earnings result in lower monthly retired worker benefits. On average, the retired worker benefits received by women are about 75% of those received by men.[28] Expected changes in the labor force participation of women and increased earnings will reduce the differences in Social Security benefits but they will not eliminate them soon.

Women's experience under Social Security differs from men's not only because of earnings differences but also because of differences in longevity. Women now outlive men by about 4 years at age 65, and married women outlive their 65-year-old husbands by about 7 years, assuming a three-year difference in the age of spouses. The consequence is that Social Security must pay benefits for many more years to women, even if at lower monthly benefits, because they are the survivors rather than men. The difference in longevity may not affect the receipt of *monthly* benefits under Social Security, but *lifetime* benefits may be considerably greater for women because of it.

The sexes may be affected in different ways financially by any changes in the Social Security program. The three alternative proposals of the 1994–1996 Social Security Advisory Council, convened to advise the Congress on ways of "fixing" Social Security, would make changes that could affect the relative levels of benefits received by men and women. Each of the proposals has the potential to exacerbate the current differences between the benefits of men and women (GAO/Ross, 1997, *op. cit.*).

The black population has a much lower median age and a much smaller proportion at ages 65 years and over than the white population. Its fertility rates and mortality rates are generally higher than those of whites. Hence, the old-age beneficiary population includes a relatively small proportion of blacks. This may not be true of the disability beneficiary population, since many of the people who have retired early have done so for health reasons and blacks report a work disability (i.e., a health condition or impairment that limits the amount or type of paid work one can do) relatively more often than whites at the pretirement ages. Blacks receive disability awards much more often than whites from the Social Security Administration at ages 55 to 64 years.[29] This is not readily apparent from estimates of the median age of retirement, which are only modestly lower for blacks than for whites (Table 13.5).

Blacks have a higher recorded chance of dying before reaching the normal age of retirement than whites. According to the life tables for 1997, the survival rate from birth to age 65 is 70% for blacks and 83% for whites (Table 13.2).

TABLE 13.5 Median Age at Retirement, by Sex and Race, and Mean Age of Persons Initially Awarded Social Security Retirement Benefits, by Sex, 1950–1955 to 2000–2005

Period	Median age[a] All races		Black		Mean age All races	
	Men	Women	Men	Women	Men	Women
1950–1955	66.9	67.7	NA	NA	68.5	67.9
1960–1955	65.2	64.6	64.3	63.3	66.3	65.7
1970–1975	63.4	62.9	62.9	61.9	63.4	63.1
1980–1985	62.8	62.7	62.0	62.8	62.9	62.9
1985–1990	62.6	62.8	61.7	61.7	62.7	63.1
1990–1995	62.1	62.6	NA	NA	62.2	62.7
2000–2005[b]	61.7	61.2	NA	NA	NA	NA
Decrease, 1950–1955 to 1990–95 (years):	4.8	5.1	NA	NA	6.3	5.2

NA: Not available.

[a] Estimated from 5-year age-specific labor force data obtained from the Current Population Survey and life table survival rates; and projections of the labor force published by the U.S. Bureau of Labor Statistics.

[b] Based on projected data for 2000 and 2005.

Source: Murray Gendell, "Trends in retirement age in four countries, 1965–1995," *Monthly Labor Review* **121**(8): 20–30, August 1998, Table 1; M. Gendell and J. S. Siegel, "Trends in retirement age in the United States, 1955–1993, by sex and race," *Journal of Gerontology: Social Sciences* **51B**(3): S132–S139, 1996, Table 2; and M. Gendell and J. S. Siegel, "Trends in retirement age by sex, 1950–2005," *Monthly Labor Review* **115**(7): 22–29, July 1992, Tables 1 and 4.

This fact has become the basis for the argument that blacks fail to secure a fair return from their contributions to the Social Security program because they do not live long enough to receive benefits. One solution proposed is to assign a different age of normal retirement for whites and blacks by ascertaining the age for each group corresponding to a life expectancy of a preset number of years, such as 10 or 15 years. The concept may be labeled "the age with 10 years until death" or "the age with 15 years until death." The counter argument is that blacks benefit disproportionately from disability retirement and from lower recorded death rates at the oldest ages (i.e., 85 and over). Moreover, correction of death rates for census undercounts suggest that the reported death rates overstate the actual mortality of blacks relatively more than for whites.[30]

Economic Dependency/Support of the Elderly

Since not all persons in the principal working ages work and not all elderly persons are retired, the age-dependency ratio is not the best indicator of economic dependency. For a more appropriate measure, data on elderly persons not in the labor force and data on persons in the labor force regardless of age may be substituted for the elements in the age-dependency ratio. The modified measure is the **elderly economic dependency ratio.** The elderly economic dependency ratio can be computed as the ratio (per 100) of persons 65 years and over not in the labor force to all persons in the labor force. The number of workers has been rising much more slowly than the number of elderly nonworkers for many decades and is expected to continue doing so. As a result, the ratio of elderly persons not in the labor force to persons in the labor force has been rising steadily and is expected to continue in this direction. Changes in this measure parallel those for the elderly age-dependency ratio (Table 13.3). It is also informative to examine the relative number of contributors and elderly beneficiaries under Social Security. The projected trend in this measure also resembles the trends of the age-dependency ratio and the economic dependency ratio. All three measures agree that elderly dependency will hardly change between 1995 and 2010 but will rise sharply between 2010 and 2030.

The population burden on the Social Security system is often also expressed in terms of the reciprocal of the economic dependency ratio, or the **economic support ratio.** This measure shows that in 1960 there were 5.7 workers for every elderly nonworker, and in 2030 there are expected to be only 2.6 workers for every elderly nonworker. The decline in the economic support ratio results both from the rapid rise in the number of elderly persons as compared with persons in the principal working ages, and from the general decline in labor force participation among the elderly and younger men. Labor force participation ratios at ages 65 years and over have been declining steadily in the past several decades for both men and women. (Since 1995, the labor force participation of men and women at the older ages appears to have been leveling off or increasing.) Moreover, the growth of the labor force has been restrained in recent decades because of the smaller birth cohorts entering the working ages.

The trends in labor force participation are associated with a substantial decline since 1950 in the average age of retirement of both men and women (Table 13.5). The decline, as measured by demographic analysis of Current

Population Survey data on labor force participation, was about 5 years for both men and women between 1950–1955 and 1990–1995. The fall in the retirement age and the increase in longevity have led to impressive increases in the number of years of nonworking life after retirement and the share of total adult life devoted to nonwork rather than work. The median retirement age of 66.9 years for men in 1950–1955 corresponds to a life expectancy (i.e., retirement period) of 12.0 years, and the median retirement age of 62.1 years for men in 1990–1995 corresponds to a retirement period of 17.4 years.[31] For women the corresponding figures are, for 1950–1955, 67.7 years and 13.6 years, and, for 1990–1995, 62.6 years and 21.1 years. These figures represent increases in the retirement period of 5.4 years for men and 6.5 years for women over these four decades. Of the increase in the years of retirement, about half is accounted for by the increase in longevity and about half is accounted for by the fall in retirement age.

The decline in retirement age may have run its course, but there are no signs of the trend's reversal. This assessment is based not on a formal calculation of the retirement age from labor force participation ratios but on the possible influence of a number of emergent trends affecting labor force participation. As stated, the declines in the labor force participation of older men and women have been leveling off. Declines in the rate of disability among older persons have been recorded. Service-sector jobs have been replacing the more physically demanding jobs in manufacturing. More flexible work schedules, including part-week or part-year employment and home work, are being offered, and many older men are leaving full-time work and taking on part-time work. Changes in pension arrangements allow more workers to work part-time and receive a retirement pension.

Analysis of Effects of Demographic Factors

Current proposals for financially strengthening the Social Security program include raising the "normal" retirement age faster and further than the 67 already mandated by the year 2027 and "indexing" the changes in normal retirement age to changes in life expectancy. A rise in the normal retirement age could have substantial net positive effects on the financial integrity of the Social Security Trust Fund.[32] A rise in the retirement age could boost the number of older workers, reducing the retirement benefits paid out and increasing the payroll taxes collected. Even if more older workers do not continue to work and retire before they reach the higher normal retirement age, they would receive much reduced retirement benefits. However, as we saw, the average worker today is not "responding" to the normal retirement age and retires a few years before reaching that age. Elimination of the mandatory retirement age appears to have made no difference. Whether the recent elimination of the financial penalty for working at ages 65 to 70 will make a difference remains to be seen. It would appear that the age for receiving *reduced* benefits must be raised or eliminated to effect a substantial difference in retirement-age patterns of workers.[33]

The proposal to link normal retirement age to life expectancy can be justified by actuarial fairness. Cohorts that live longer should pay the costs of a lengthier retirement. Payroll tax rates or benefits could be adjusted to allow for changing longevity. Lee and Tuljapurkar (1997) estimate that each additional year of life expectancy requires a 3.6% increase in the payroll tax rate or a 3.6% reduction in benefits, in relation to their initial levels.[34]

Keyfitz (1985) carried out an array of simulation exercises designed to show how demographic and socioeconomic factors affect the implicit rate of return, or the implicit annual rate of interest, to successive cohorts from participating in a retirement program.[35] The implicit rate of return is the rate of interest that makes contributions equal to benefits in a retirement system when both are discounted back to given date. Keyfitz explored the effect on the rate of return of shifts in fertility, mortality, immigration, labor force participation, and retirement age. The analysis supposes that an individual goes through working life making his or her contribution to the support of the elderly people in the same years as the money is distributed—that is, it assumes a pay-as-you-go retirement system.

Given a retirement system with a fixed pension schedule, Keyfitz found that higher fertility would have a major effect in increasing the rate of return from participating in a retirement program. Table 13.6 shows Keyfitz's results for the percentage rate of return on Social Security contributions for successive birth cohorts for five levels of fertility, assuming fixed annual pensions, the mortality and immigration levels of 1979, and the labor force participation ratios of the early 1980s. For example, the rate of return on the contributions of the birth cohorts of 1980–1985, with birthrates at the level of those of 1979, would be 0.36%, while with birthrates 50% over those of 1979, the rate of return would be 1.86%. All the cohorts born in the 21st century will get a negative return on their contributions unless birthrates are well above those of 1979. The movement of the baby-boom cohorts through the age cycle helps

TABLE 13.6 Annual Rate of Interest on Social Security Contributions for Birth Cohorts, 1960–1965 to 2050–2055, for Various Levels of Fertility

| Birth cohort | Fraction of 1979 birthrates | | | | |
	0.50	0.75	1.00	1.25	1.50
1960–1965	0.00	0.40	0.57	0.58	0.48
1970–1975	−0.72	0.18	0.89	1.43	1.84
1980–1985	−1.73	−0.58	0.36	1.16	1.86
1990–1995	−2.59	−1.33	−0.32	0.53	1.28
2000–1905	−2.95	−1.75	−0.77	0.05	0.78
2010–2015	−3.03	−1.96	−1.05	−0.26	0.41
2020–2025	−2.94	−1.99	−1.11	−0.34	0.34
2030–2035	−2.73	−1.93	−1.09	−0.33	0.34
2040–2045	−2.53	−1.87	−1.10	−0.35	0.32
2050–2055	−2.34	−1.82	−1.09	−0.36	0.32

Note: See text for explanation. Initial population is United States population, by age, in 1980. Projections assume fixed mortality rates, fixed amounts of immigration, and fixed labor force participation ratios at base-period levels. Assumes fixed pensions.

Source: Nathan Keyfitz, "The demographics of unfunded pensions," *European Journal of Population* 1: 5–30, 1985, Table 10, p. 20. © 1985. Reprinted with kind permission of Kluwer Academic Publishers.

to explain the shifts in these rates of return for any particular level of fertility. Small cohorts are paying for large ones retiring in the 2010s and later. At all assumed ages of retirement, the ratio of premiums per 100 units of pension rises sharply when the baby-boom cohorts retire. According to the Keyfitz simulations, contrary to expectation, mortality shifts, even if confined to the older ages, and immigration would make little difference and, also contrary to expectation, a lower age of retirement tends to give slightly higher rates of return on the "investment." The simulations demonstrate the paramount role of fertility in molding the age-dependency structure of the population.

Other Economic Factors

The viability of the Social Security program is affected by other factors than the demographic and socioeconomic ones noted. The other factors are essentially financial. Principal among them are the contributions of workers and the amount of benefits paid. The former depends on the tax rate, the amount of wages or salary subject to tax, the inflation rate, and the wages or salaries of workers. The latter—that is, benefits paid—depends on the numbers retiring, the ages of persons retiring, the basis of retirement (disability, early retirement, normal retirement), and the inflation rate. The wages and salaries of workers, in turn, depend on worker productivity, hours worked, and the unemployment ratio.

To project the future costs of the Social Security program, the Social Security Administration prepares a set of economic projections in combination with the set of population projections. The series of population projections are defined in terms of three alternative cost scenarios ("low cost," "intermediate," and "high cost"), but are not based on any explicit economic variables. (See Chapter 10.) The important variables in the economic projections are changes in wages and prices or, more specifically, the difference in the growth of covered wages and the rise in the Consumer Price Index (the so-called real-wage differential). This measure is closely linked to the growth of worker productivity. Assumptions regarding the real-wage differential or productivity are subject to substantial error as are the assumptions underlying the population projections. Errors in the population assumptions and economic assumptions may offset one another or intensify one another.[36]

Currently, the baby-boom cohorts are in or near their years of highest earnings. As a result, payroll and income tax revenues have been swelling. At the same time, the nation has been experiencing an economic boom, with low unemployment, low inflation, and rapid growth in the gross domestic product and worker productivity. This combination of factors has caused revenues to swell further and to produce large budget surpluses, particularly at the federal level. The enhanced payroll-tax receipts are deposited in the Social Security Trust Fund, increasing the reserves that provide funds for retirement and the support of survivors of deceased workers. Though these reserves will continue growing for some years, the demands on them following the retirement of the baby-boom cohorts will cause an erosion of the reserves, even assuming economic stability. The assumptions include an orderly development of the economy as projected, no increase in the payroll tax, no reduction in benefits, no further increase in the age of retirement, and no new infusion of income from private investment of the funds. With this scenario, the current benefits that the trust fund will be obligated to pay will exceed the current payroll tax revenues and gradually the reserves will be depleted.

It should be apparent that the solvency of the Social Security system is closely linked to the health of the economy. Economic growth exceeding the assumptions underlying the present projections would improve the outlook for the financial condition of the Social Security program. The effect of economic growth on the Social Security system resembles that of population growth, with the difference that the country can experience much faster economic growth than population growth. When economic growth is low, population growth takes on greater importance in its effect on the Social Security system. When the economy is performing superbly well, as in the late 1990s, relatively low growth rates in population become secondary.[37]

ALLOCATION OF PUBLIC FUNDS BETWEEN CHILDREN AND THE ELDERLY

Shifting Balance of Public Support between the Groups

A major public policy issue has been the appropriate allocation of public funds between programs for children and programs for the elderly. Changes in age structure, the state of the economy, changing perceptions as to the needs of the two groups, the law, and budgetary and political pressures may be expected to cause shifts in the balance of public funds spent for the support of children and the support of elderly persons. These two age segments of the population are generally dependent on resources other than their own, receiving them either by direct public transfers or transfers within the family. For the most part, children and the elderly depend greatly on public support for their well-being, even though some elderly persons get along with little such support and the costs of supporting children are considered to be mostly private family responsibilities.

The costs of supporting the elderly have been largely public responsibilities since the passage of the Social Security Act in 1935. By that time the family had already begun to withdraw from its responsibility in this regard. In more recent decades, the family has also begun to withdraw from its responsibility for the care of children. This is evidenced by a number of trends. Among them are the rise in the percentage of births occurring out of wedlock, the rise in the rate of divorce in marriages with children, the frequent "disappearance" of the nonresidential father, the frequent nonpayment of child support, and the mass entry of women into the labor market. The final item listed has resulted in the prevalence of the dual-earner urban family and the growth of the private child-care industry. Couples now feel less obligated to remain in a marginal marriage and choose to take advantage of the greater opportunity and ease of "marital mobility," with generally negative consequences for their children.[38]

The rapid growth in the size of the elderly population, its widespread poverty, its social activism, and its high level of voter participation between the two world wars led to the passage of the Social Security Act in 1935 and a new predilection for political support of elderly causes. The conditions were ripe. As recently as 1959, over one-third of the elderly were poor as compared with about one-quarter of the children under 18 years of age. About 64% of the population 65 and over reported that they had voted in the 1972 presidential election compared with only about 55% of the population under 35 years old. Children have a declining constituency and the interests of children are represented by an increasingly smaller segment of the population. As the share of children in the population levels off or declines and the child population becomes racially more variegated, the older, racially more homogeneous population is becoming less interested in supporting "other people's" children. Children under age 18 are less and less likely to live with their parents. As the ratio of elderly dependents to children rises, the care of elderly parents instead of children is demanding the time and attention of more and more middle-aged women.

The largest publicly financed social program for children is the program of public education. For the elderly, two public programs dominate, one for economic support and the other for health, namely, the Social Security program and the Medicare program. The Supplementary Security Income and Medicaid programs are, respectively, also programs of economic support and health, but they are available to both age segments of the population. The two age groups in effect compete with one another for the funds available for these and other public human services programs. It is clear, however, that Congress and the public have favored the elderly as opposed to children in the allocation of public funds over the past several decades. The perception of unfair differences in the treatment of different age groups could bring about intergenerational strife and the erosion of our system of social insurance.

Mere population numbers today would suggest that children would be the winner in this contest of the age groups. In 1997 the population under age 18 was twice as large (69.5 million) as the population 65 years and over (34.1 million). A major shift in numbers is expected to occur soon, however. According to the medium projection series of the U.S. Census Bureau, between 1997 and 2010 the numbers of children and the elderly will begin to converge. The older age group shows a large increase (3.0 million) and the younger age group shows a decline (4.6 million). The difference in the changes for the two groups will become quite pronounced between 2010 and 2030, the period when the baby-boom cohorts enter the 65-and-over population. In this period the number of elderly persons is expected to increase by 22 million as compared with a decline of 2.3 million for children. Another way of considering the relative growth of the two groups is to compare shifts in the proportion of children in the population with shifts in the proportion of elderly persons. Since the 1960s, these proportions have tended to converge as the proportion of children declined and the proportion of elderly persons increased. Their convergence is expected to continue in the future, accelerating after 2010. Between 1997 and 2010, the proportion of children under 18 is expected to drop from 26% to 24%, while the proportion of elderly persons is expected to rise modestly to a little over 13%. In the following two decades, we may expect little change in the proportion of children, but a steep rise in the proportion of elderly persons to 20% in 2030.

It has been suggested that the slower growth in the share of children in the population recorded in recent decades will permit the conversion of some public funds from use for children to the service of the elderly, thereby ameliorating the impending problems brought on by the tidal wave of baby-boom cohorts. At the same time, the charge is often made that too much public money is already being allocated to the elderly at the expense of children and that, as a result, the welfare of children is being neglected. It has been argued that the diversion of funds from programs for children has led to a slowing of the efforts to reduce child poverty and a deterioration in the quality of public education.[39] Millions of children still live in poor households (13.8 million, or 19.8% of all children, in 1996) and there are many indications of a decline in the scholastic performance of children.

Relative Cost of Supporting a Child and an Elderly Person

Even if the absolute and proportional size of the the child population and the elderly population were equal, the costs of publicly supporting older persons and children would not be the same because the per capita cost of supporting an older person does not equal that of supporting a child. Several researchers have developed estimates of the relative costs of supporting a child and an older person. Sauvy (1969)[40] estimated that, in 1950, the support costs of a child under age 18 were 27% lower than the support costs of a person aged 65 or over. Clark (1977)[41] and Clark and Spengler (1980)[42] estimated that during the 1970s the yearly public cost of supporting a dependent 65 years or over greatly exceeded that of supporting a dependent under 18. Clark and Spengler calculated, on the basis of expenditures on major public social programs for children and the elderly, that about three times as much public money was spent, on the average, on elderly dependents as was spent on children. They divided estimated government expenditures for the age group by the size of the group and obtained estimates of $3721 for each elderly person and $1215 for each child dependent.

An indication of the relatively greater support cost of the elderly than of children may be obtained by comparing per capita (1) (a) federal, state, and local expenditures on elementary and secondary education and (b) selected federal expenditures on income security, with (2) (a) federal expenditures on Medicare, Social Security, general retirement and disability insurance and (b) federal employee retirement and disability. The former funds are dedicated almost entirely to children under 18 and the latter funds are dedicated almost entirely to persons 65 and over. Table 13.7 presents the data and calculations for 1990 and 1995. Both in 1990 and 1995, per capita public expenditures for the elderly were three to four times as great as expenditures for children. Moreover, expenditures for the elderly were one-and-a-half to twice as great a proportion of the gross domestic product as expenditures for children in 1990 and 1995. The evidence of greater public support for elderly persons than children over the later decades of the century is strong.

Estimates of support costs are sensitive to the age of entry into and age of exit from the labor force. Raising the normal age of retirement gradually to 67 years, as is now mandated for the early decades of the 21st century,

TABLE 13.7 Estimates of Relative Public Expenditures on Children and the Elderly: 1995 and 1990

Item	1995 Children under 18	1995 Persons 65 years and over	1990 Children under 18	1990 Persons 65 years and over
Expenditures (mil. of dollars)				
Federal				
Elementary, secondary, and vocational education	14,694		9,918	
Medicare		159,855		98,102
Social Security		335,846		248,623
Income security (part)	98,347[a]	70,988[b]	55,111[a]	57,185[b]
State and local				
Elementary and secondary education	264,240		202,009	
Federal, state, and local				
Total	377,281	566,689	267,038	403,910
Total, excluding income security (part)	278,934	X	211,927	X
Per capita expenditures				
Total	5,512.7	16,885.8	4,176.3	12,995.4
Total, excluding income security (part)	4,075.7	X	3,314.4	X
Percentage of gross domestic product				
Total	5.2	7.8	4.6	7.0
Total, excluding income security (part)	3.8	X	3.7	X

X: Not applicable.

[a] Food and nutrition assistance and miscellaneous income security programs.

[b] General retirement and disability insurance, and federal employee retirement and disability.

Source: Derived by the author on the basis of data in U.S. Bureau of the Census, *Statistical Abstract of the United States, 1998*, Tables 14, 506, 543, and 715.

should reduce the gross cost of supporting the dependent elderly. (On the other hand, it may induce many workers to opt for retirement at an earlier age with reduced benefits.) Some money should be also saved because of the generally declining or stable proportion of children. These two factors should reduce the relative per capita cost of supporting the dependent elderly as compared to children. These savings are not expected, however, to be sufficient to offset fully the rise in the costs of supporting the sharply increasing proportion of elderly persons after 2010. If reasonable relative per capita costs of public support are applied to the three age segments—children, working-age adults, and the elderly—the elderly will account for the largest share of the total public support costs from 1997 to 2030. Aggregate public support costs for elderly dependents may already be greater than those for working-age dependents and children combined and will almost certainly be far greater by 2030.

POPULATION FACTOR IN RISING COSTS OF HEALTH CARE

Health care costs have been rising sharply in recent decades in percentage terms and as a share of the gross domestic product (GDP). There is a widespread view that the increase in the number and proportion of elderly persons in the population is the primary factor accounting for the increase in health care costs.[43] Others have offered the view that population size and aging are minor factors in the total increase.[44] This section briefly explores the question of the relative importance of population and other factors in accounting for the increase in health care costs.

Trends in the Cost of Health Care

In 1995, personal health care expenditures amounted to $869.0 billion, or 12% of GDP (Table 13.8). Ten years earlier, in 1985, the bill amounted to only $376.4 billion, or 9% of GDP. Thus, health care expenditures rose sharply in these 10 years both in relative numbers (131%) and as a percentage of GDP (3 percentage points). Per capita costs doubled in this period. Persons 65 years and over accounted for a disproportionately large share of total personal health care expenditures. About one-third of the total personal health care bill in 1995 was spent in their behalf, while they made up only 13% of the total population. Moreover, per capita spending for the elderly has been steadily increasing. It is now considerably greater than for the rest of the population. As explained later, however, it is fallacious to infer from these facts that population increase and population aging account for a large share of the increase in health care costs.

In an in-depth analysis of the role of population factors in the changing costs of health care, it is useful to separate the major sources of health care expenses, since they may constitute a changing part of the health care bill

TABLE 13.8 Gross and Per Capita Costs in Personal Health Care Expenditures According to Object: 1995 and 1985 (in Billions of Dollars; Includes Puerto Rico and Outlying Areas)

Object	1995 Gross costs		Per capita costs[a]	1985 Gross costs		Per capita costs[a]
Total	878.8	100[b]	3,221	376.4	100[b]	1,523
Hospital	350.1	40	1,283	168.3	45	681
Physician	201.6	23	739	83.6	22	338
Other professional services	98.4	11	361	38.3	10	155
Drugs/other medical nondurables and durables	97.2	10	356	43.8	12	177
Nursing home	77.9	9	285	30.7	8	124
Other	53.6	6	197	11.7	3	48

[a] Based on population estimates as of July 1 for the United States and outlying areas prepared by the Social Security Administration.

[b] Percentage distribution.

Source: U.S. Health Care Financing Administration, *Health Care Financing Review*, Fall 1996. See also U.S. Bureau of the Census, *Statistical Abstract of the United States: 1997*, Tables 154 and 155.

and population changes may play a different role in each of them. Hospital care and physicians' services account for the major health care expenses. Of total health care expenditures in 1995, about 40% went for hospital care, about one-quarter went to physicians, and about one-tenth each went to other professional services, drugs, and nursing homes (Table 13.8).

Factors Affecting Change in the Cost of Health Care

The factors that affect change in the costs of health care include general economy-wide inflation, excess inflation in the health care industry, increase in population size, and changes in the quantity and intensity of health care delivered per capita, including technological developments, changing per capita demand for health care, and changes in the age composition and other characteristics of the population.

An increase in the size of the population, as well as an increase in the proportion of elderly persons in the population, *tends* to cause an increase in the overall demand for health care and hence in its costs. The aging of the population *tends* to cause a rise in health care costs because health care costs rise with increasing age above the early childhood years and per capita costs are much greater for the older ages than for the younger ages. Changes in the sex composition of the population, as well as in the race/ Hispanic origin, marital status, educational level, and income composition of the population, also affect health care costs since per capita demand and use of health care services vary with these characteristics. The untested proposition here is that changes in age composition have a more pronounced effect on costs than changes in these other characteristics.

Economy-wide inflation may be measured in different ways, but its essential meaning is reasonably well understood and there are established instruments for measuring it, namely, the Consumer Price Index and price-adjusted per capita gross domestic product. The scope of excess inflation in health care is much less clear. Shi and Singh (1998) defined it as including the costs of practicing overly defensive medicine (i.e., in a way expressly to avoid malpractice suits), pursuing a medical model of health care delivery (i.e., emphasizing the treatment of illness, not the prevention of disease), waste and abuse, and the tendency to employ various unnecessary and costly procedures in certain geographic areas.[45] Even though many alternative definitions may be offered, this one conveys the essential elements.

Technological developments often result in the introduction of new and expensive medical equipment. Examples are the use of computer automated tomography (CAT) and magnetic resonance imaging (MRI). This process tends in the short run to drive up the costs of health care, although, in the long term, use of such equipment may help to reduce health care costs. Since the passage of Medicare and the growth of private health insurance programs, the populace has become relatively well informed as to the diagnostic and therapeutic modalities available, including the most intensive and expensive ones, and seeks these when it feels that they may be helpful. As a consequence, not only are affluent patients asking for costly diagnostic and therapeutic health care but persons of modest means as well. The demand for health care is relatively elastic and has no obvious limit.

Relative Role of Population Changes

The contribution of overall population growth to the change in personal health care expenditures during some period is represented simply by the population growth rate during the period. Alternatively, it can be measured as the difference between the percentage change in per capita health care expenditures and the percentage change in the gross amount of health care expenditures during the period. The population increased by about 10% between 1985 and 1995, and per capita health care expenditures rose about 10% less steeply than gross health care expenditures during this period. Per capita health care costs rose 109% compared with the 131% rise in gross health care costs [(2.31 ÷ 2.09) − 1]. (See Table 13.8.)

If we then adjust the change in per capita health care costs (109%) for general price inflation, using the change in "real" per capita gross domestic product (14.8%),[46] we obtain 82% as the change in the per capita cost of health care adjusted for general price inflation between 1985 and 1995 [(2.09 ÷ 1.148) − 1]. The 82% increase accounts for two main factors—changes in medical-specific price inflation in excess of economy-wide inflation and the intensity and use per capita of health care services, including technological developments, changes in population composition, particularly age composition, and other changes in per capita demand.

To get a handle on the contribution of aging, we may refer to figures on the increase in the percentage of the population 65 years and over in the 1985–1995 decade (0.83 percentage point) and the relative per capita costs of health care for the elderly and the total population (e.g., 2.5 times). They suggest that the estimated contribution of the aging of the population to the total percentage change in health care costs during the 1985–1995 decade was a few percentage points at most (0.83 ⋆ 2.5 = 2.1). Alternatively, we can measure the effect of the change in age composition by applying the method of standardization to per capita health care expenditures. Using two age groups, under 65 and 65 and over, we hold constant the estimates of per capita health care expenditures for the two age groups while weighting them by the proportions of elderly persons and nonelderly persons in 1985 and 1995 (see further explanation presented later). On this basis, the estimated contribution of age composition is 1 1/2 to 2 percentage points. Thus, population increase and the aging of the population together account for only a small part of the total increase in health care costs during the 1985–1995 decade—perhaps 12 to 13 percentage points out of the total percentage increase of 131%. Most of the change is explained by general inflation, excess inflation in the health care industry, and the change in per capita demand (excluding the part due to change in age composition).

The Actuary's Office of the Health Care Financing Agency (HCFA) prepares estimates of the components of the increase in personal health care expenditures annually. Its analysis identifies separately the contribution of total population growth, economy-wide inflation, excess medical inflation, and a residual that represents the growth in the quantity of health services delivered per capita, including changes in per capita demand, changes in age composition, and other changes in the composition of the population. According to

TABLE 13.9 Contribution of Population Growth and Other Factors to the Increase in Personal Health Care Expenditures: Historical Series of Annual Averages, 1960–1970 to 1990–1998

Period	Health care expenditures	Percentage increase			Percentage of total increase			
		Population	Prices[a]	Residual[b]	Total	Population	Prices[a]	Residual[b]
1990–1998	6.5	1.0	3.9	1.7	100	15	60	26
1980–1990	11.0	1.0	7.7	2.3	100	9	70	21
1970–1980	13.0	0.9	8.1	4.0	100	7	62	31
1960–1970	10.5	1.3	4.0	5.2	100	12	38	50

[a] Represents sum of economy-wide inflation and excess medical inflation.

[b] Growth in quantity of health care services delivered per capita, including use of new technology, changes in age-sex composition, and any other changes in quantity of health care services delivered per person.

Source: Cathy A. Cowan *et al.*, "National health expenditures, 1998," *Health Care Financing Review* 21(2), Winter 1999; and unpublished data provided by Anne Martin of the U.S. Health Care Financing Administration, Office of the Actuary, National Health Statistics Group.

HCFA, the contribution of total population growth has fluctuated around 1% on an annual average basis for each of the last four decades (Table 13.9). In each decade, population growth made up 15% or less of the total increase in the personal health care bill. In the latest period, 1990–1998, total population growth contributed 15%, inflation contributed 60%, of which excess medical inflation was 23%, and the residual amounted to 26%:

	Annual average percentage increase	Percentage of total increase
Total, by components:	6.5	100
Population	1.0	15
Economy-wide inflation	2.4	37
Excess medical inflation	1.5	23
Residual[a]	1.7	26

[a] Includes changes in per capita demand, changing population composition, and technological developments.

Source: Cathy A. Cowan *et al.*, "National health expenditures, 1998," *Health Care Financing Review* 21(2), Winter 1999; and unpublished data provided by Anne Martin of the U.S. Health Care Financing Administration, Office of the Actuary, National Health Statistics Group.

Hence, in the 1990–1998 period, population growth and population aging had only a small effect on the growth of the personal health care bill compared with inflation.

Serow (1993) has also considered this issue and found that, on average over the period since 1960, price increases accounted for more than half the total increase in per capita health expenditures, "intensity" in the provision of health care (e.g., office visits, admissions to nursing homes) accounted for about one-third, and the remaining one-tenth was due to the changes in population composition, including the aging trend.[47] In 1990 the contribution of inflation was somewhat higher (about 62%), intensity somewhat lower (29%), and the share of population composition about the same (9%).

The Alliance for Aging Research has summarized several studies concerned with the contribution of population aging to total costs (1997, *op. cit.*). All these studies conclude that contributions from population increase, population aging, and other changes in population composition account for only a small part of the total increase. Burner and Waldo (1995), for example, show that between 1973 and 1983 general price inflation accounted for about 60% of the rise in national health expenditures, and excess inflation in the health care industry accounted for another 10%.[48] Between 1983 and 1993 the role of general price inflation diminished somewhat. In this more recent period, general price inflation accounted for about 40% of the rise in health care expenditures while inflation specific to the health sector accounted for another 20%.

An important policy implication of these findings is that rising health care costs are not the inevitable consequences of population movements. Rather, they can be attributed to general movements in the economy and specific industries and institutions, such as physicians, insurance companies, pharmaceutical firms, and so on. Hence, action can be taken to control these costs (Getzen, 1992, *op. cit.*)

Similar considerations suggest a larger role of the change in population numbers and age composition in health care costs between 1998 and 2030. The total population is projected to grow over 28% in this period. The analysts of the Health Care Financing Administration as well as other analysts predict that, after the baby-boom cohorts arrive at the elderly ages in 2010 or so, population aging will have a major effect on health care expenditures. To speculate on the possible contribution of aging to the increase in health care expenditures during the expected elderly boom, we apply the standardization method here also. We compare health care costs at the beginning of the period with the expected costs at the end of the period on the assumption that per capita expenditures in each age group at the beginning date will remain unchanged through the period but that the age distribution will continue to change through the period. The following simplified example is adapted from Getzen (1992, *op. cit.*): (1) First, the per capita expenditure over all ages (equivalent to age-specific per capita expenditures weighted by the share of the population in each age group) in the initial year is calculated; (2) next, the age-specific per capita expenditures in the initial year are weighted by the share of the population in each age group in the terminal year; and (3) the difference between the initial and terminal per capita figures over all ages is calculated as an estimate of the effect of age composition. For example, given 13% of the population 65 and over with per capita expenditures of $8000 and 87% of the population under age 65 with per capita expenditures of $2000 for the base year, the average per capita expenditure over all ages is $2780:

$$.13 \times \$8000 + .87 \times \$2000 = \$2780$$

Now suppose we have a rise in the percentage of elderly to 20%, as envisaged for 2030:

$$.20 \times \$8000 + .80 \times \$2000 = \$3200$$

The difference in the results represents a rise of 15% in average costs due to the shift in age composition (i.e., $3200 ÷ $2780), that is, 2.1% for each point rise in the percentage of elderly (15 ÷ 7).

Aging may tend to increase the demand for health care, but concessions to budget realities may limit that increase and reduce the effect of aging on costs. Hence, the effect of the baby-boom increase on health care costs could be restrained by the slower growth in gross domestic product and budgetary ceilings.[49] Moreover, age-specific rates of serious illness could fall and so the need for a large rise in health expenditures would be reduced.

NOTES

1. This discussion is not concerned with the types of public benefits immigrant aliens or illegal aliens should receive.

2. Eric S. Rothman and Thomas J. Espenshade, "Fiscal impacts of immigration to the United States," *Population Index* 58(3): 381–415, 1992; James P. Smith and Barry Edmonston (eds.), *The New Americans: Economic, Demographic, and Fiscal Effects of Immigration*, Washington, DC: National Academy Press, 1997, esp. Summary Chapter; U.S. Commission on Immigration Reform, *Becoming an American: Immigration and Immigrant Policy, Report to Congress*, No. 98-0053-P, 1997; and George J. Borjas, *Heaven's Door: Immigration Policy and the American Economy*, Princeton, NJ: Princeton University Press, 1999.

3. Beyond economic criteria, public policy should be used to maximize well-being in other spheres of community and personal life, including health, welfare, conservation of time, a livable environment, and general tranquility. Immigration policy should also support our foreign policy goals of protecting our national security interests and serving as a model of humanitarian and moral international behavior. While the focus here is on economic balance sheets, this alone should not be determinative of our immigration policy.

4. Hammermesh and Bean come to a different conclusion. They maintain that immigration has had a cumulatively negative effect on the economic prospects of blacks, and specifically that it has contributed to the widening gap between the annual earnings of black and white males. See Daniel S. Hammermesh and Frank D. Bean (eds.), *Help or Hindrance? The Economic Implications of Immigration for African Americans*, New York: Russell Sage Foundation, 1998.

5. A net fiscal burden means that there is an excess of the cost of government services and benefits provided over taxes paid.

6. See W. A. V. Clark and Freya Schultz, "Evaluating the local impacts of recent immigration to California: Realism versus racism," *Population Research and Policy Review* 16(5): 475–491, October 1997.

7. The Immigration and Naturalization Service has no separate data system for counting the illegal alien population or its total annual flow. Numerous estimates have been prepared using a great variety of methods. Because of the difficulties in estimating a clandestine population of this type, any estimates have a considerable degree of uncertainty. See U.S. Immigration and Naturalization Service, *1997 Statistical Yearbook of the Immigration and Naturalization Service*, 1999, Chapter VII. For a review of the methods of developing estimates of illegal aliens, see U.S. General Accounting Office, *Illegal Aliens: Despite Data Limitations, Current Methods Provide Better Population Estimates*, GAO/PEMD-93-25, August 1993. The serious attempts to estimate the illegal alien population in the United States and their state and local distribution have been made almost exclusively by applied demographers.

8. The WORA program replaced the AFDC program in 1996.

9. U.S. General Accounting Office, *Illegal Aliens: Extent of Welfare Benefits Received on Behalf of U.S. Citizen Children*, GAO/HEHS-98-30, November 1997.

10. Reported in the *Los Angeles Times*, December 1994. See U.S. General Accounting Office, *Benefits for Illegal Aliens: Some Program Costs Increasing, but Total Costs Unknown*, GAO-HRD-93-33, September 1993, and U.S. General Accounting Office, *Illegal Aliens: Assessing Estimates of Financial Burden on California*, GAO/HEHS-95-22, November 1994.

11. Reported in the *San Diego Union-Tribune*, October 9, 1993.

12. Louis Rea and Richard A. Parker, "Illegal immigration in San Diego County: An analysis of costs and revenues," Sacramento, CA: California Legislature, 1993.

13. Enrico A. Marcelli and David M. Heer, "The unauthorized Mexican immigrant population and welfare in Los Angeles County: A comparative statistical analysis," *Sociological Perspectives* **41**(2): 279–302, 1997.

14. Maria E. Enchautegui, "Immigration and county employment growth," *Population Research and Policy Review* **16**(5): 493–511, 1997.

15. U.S. Bureau of International Labor Affairs, Department of Labor, "The labor market consequences of U.S. immigration: A survey," by Michael J. Greenwood and John M. McDowell, *Immigration Policy and Working Paper* 1, 1990.

16. The current conflict between certain states and the federal government regarding the public costs of immigration has moved into the courts. Florida, California, and Arizona have sued the federal government to recover immigration-related costs.

17. A note on two other types of insurance, disability insurance and long-term-care insurance, may be of interest. Since women have higher short-term disability rates than men, women would receive more benefit days for the same premiums than men. The figures for work-loss days per person in 1995 are 6.1 days per woman and 4.5 days per man. The sex difference applies also to the more general measure, restricted-activity days per person, which includes work-loss days, bed-disability days, and school-loss days. Although women have greater longevity than men, they are more likely to have worse health and functioning at the older ages. According to multistate life tables developed by Crimmins *et al.*, the percentage of life expected to be inactive (i.e., disabled) is higher at every age for females. See Eileen M. Crimmins, Mark D. Hayward, and Yasuhiko Saito, "Differentials in active life expectancy in the older population of the United States," *Journal of Gerontology: Social Sciences* 51B(3): S111–S120, May 1996. Sex differences in long-term disability and in the need for long-term care have an effect on costs similar to the effects for annuitants. Because of higher disability rates at the older ages, women are likely to begin collecting disability payments at an earlier age and to collect them over a longer period of time than men, and to require long-term care over a longer period than men. Women who start long-term care at the same age as a group of men are likely to require greater periods of care because of their greater longevity.

18. See, for example, U.S. Bureau of the Census, "The coverage of population in the 1980 census," by Robert E. Fay, Jeffrey S. Passel, and J. Gregory Robinson, *1980 Census of Population and Housing*, PHC80-E4, 1988, esp. Table 4.4.

19. U.S. Social Security Administration, Office of the Chief Actuary, "Social Security Area Population Projections: 1997," by Felicitie Bell, *Actuarial Study* No. 112, August 1997; U.S. Bureau of the Census, "Population projections of the United States by age, sex, race, and Hispanic origin: 1995 to 2050," by Jennifer C. Day, *Current Population Reports*, Series P25-1130, 1996; Lawrence R. Carter and Ronald D. Lee, "Modeling and forecasting U.S. sex differentials in mortality," *International Journal of Forecasting* 8(3): 393–411, November 1992; and Denis A. Ahlburg and James W. Vaupel, "Alternative projections of the United States population," *Demography* 27(4): 639–652, 1990.

20. See Nathan Keyfitz, "Equity between the sexes: The pension problem," *Population Change and Social Policy*, Cambridge, MA: Abt Books, 1982.

21. In 1972 the U.S. Equal Employment Opportunity Commission issued guidelines relating to discrimination on the basis of sex, making it an unlawful employment practice for an employer to have a pension or retirement plan that provided different benefits to men and women.

22. *Source*: Teachers Insurance and Annuity Association, "The Norris decision and gender-merged annuity rates for future TIAA-CREF premiums," *Notice to Annuity Owners*, New York, August 1983.

23. This change had little or no effect on most people receiving annuity incomes under joint, or two-life, payment methods. For those receiving annuity payments under one-life methods, the change caused increases in women's benefits and reductions in men's benefits.

24. There are actually several alternatives for building the same premiums and benefits for the two sexes into the system, assuming the same face value of the policy. In life insurance, the monthly premiums for women could be raised to meet the rates for men, the rates for men could be lowered to meet those for women, or the rates for both sexes could be shifted to an intermediate level (possibly taking account of the sex distribution of policyholders). Similarly, in retirement programs, the monthly contributions of women could be lowered to those for men, those for men could be raised to those for women, or the rates for both sexes could be shifted to an intermediate

level (possibly taking account of the sex distribution of annuitants). Alternatively, in retirement programs annuities for men could be raised, the annuities for women could be lowered, or the annuities could be set at an intermediate level.

While the simplest and fairest course might seem to be to average either the actuarially determined premiums or the actuarially determined benefits of the sexes in order to achieve equality, there is some social justice in not raising the premiums and not lowering the benefits of women, but in raising the premiums and lowering the benefits of men. The justification for this course is the fact that women typically have received lower wages and salaries for the same work or have been segregated in various lower-paid jobs (see Chapter 8). The "favors" bestowed on women and the "sanctions" applied against men by equalizing the premiums and benefits in this way could be incorporated in both life insurance and retirement programs.

25. A broad program of retirement income security would also include private savings, private pension income, income from assets, income from continuing employment, and use of the reverse home mortgage program. See, for example, Yung-Ping Chen, "Racial disparity in retirement income security: Directions for policy reform," in Toni P. Miles (ed.), *Full-Color Aging: Facts, Goals, and Recommendations for America's Diverse Elders*, Washington, DC: Gerontological Society of America, 1999.

26. According to the forecasts of the financial status of the Social Security system given in the Trustees' *Annual Report* for 1997, barring changes in the law, federal expenditures for programs that cover the retirement of the elderly (OASI) will rise very rapidly after 2010 or so, principally because of the advent of the baby-boom cohorts. By 2014, expenditures are expected to exceed income, and from then until 2031, the fund would have to draw on its current income and rapidly diminishing reserves. After about 2031, Social Security (SS) cannot pay full benefits. Then, it can pay only about 75% of promised benefits and by 2071 it can pay only 67%. See Social Security and Medicare Boards of Trustees, "Status of the Social Security and Medicare Programs: A summary of the 1997 annual reports," April 1997; and U.S. General Accounting Office, *Social Security: Different Approaches for Addressing Program Solvency*, GAO/HEHS-98-33, July 1998.

It is desirable, in reviewing the options for extending the solvency of the Social Security Trust Fund, to consider jointly all the federal programs that provide income support to elderly persons. The federal budget will be strained much more by the increases in the costs of the Social Security Disability program, the hospital insurance part of Medicare, and Medicaid than by the increases in the costs for old-age retirement. Federal outlays on the Social Security Old-Age and Disability (OASDI) programs and the two parts of Medicare (hospital insurance and supplementary medical insurance) will rise sharply from 7.4% of gross domestic product (GDP) in 1997 to 15.1% in 2071. If we include Medicaid, the figure rises from less than 9% of GDP in 1997 to roughly 19% in 2050, while federal revenues may be only about 18% of GDP in 2050. Thus, these entitlement programs have to be reformed if they are not to consume all government revenues by 2050. See U.S. Council of Economic Advisors, *Annual Report, 1997*.

27. Note that the elderly dependency ratio may be variously defined with respect to the age bands selected for the principal working and nonworking ages.

28. U.S. General Accounting Office, *Social Security Reform: Implications for the Financial Well-Being of Women*, Statement by Jane L. Ross, GAO/T-HEHS-97-112, April 1997.

29. Murray Gendell and J. S. Siegel, "Trends in retirement age in the United States, 1955–93, by sex and race." *The Journal of Gerontology: Social Sciences* 51B(3): S132–S139, May 1996.

30. Gendell and Siegel, 1996, *op. cit.*; Table 13.2; U.S. National Center for Health Statistics, "Quality of death rates by race and Hispanic origin: A summary of current research, 1999," *Vital and Health Statistics* 2(128), September 1999, Tables A and 6; and Irma T. Elo, "New African-American Life Tables from 1935–1940 to 1985–1990," *Demography* 38(1): 97–114, February 2000.

31. Murray Gendell, "Trends in retirement age in four countries, 1965–95," *Monthly Labor Review*, August 1998, pp. 20–30, Table 3 and text.

32. U.S. General Accounting Office, "Social Security reform: Implications of raising the retirement age." GAO/HEHS-99-112, 1999.

33. Richard V. Burkhauser, "Touching the third rail: Time to return the retirement age for early Social Security benefits to 65," *Gerontologist* 36(6): 726–727, December 1996; David A. Wise, "Retirement against the demographic trend: More older people living longer, working less, and saving less," *Demography* 34(1): 83–95, February 1997.

34. Ronald Lee and Shripad Tuljapurkar, "Death and taxes: Longer life, consumption, and Social Security," *Demography* 34(1): 67–81, February 1997.

35. Nathan Keyfitz, "The demographics of unfunded pensions," *European Journal of Population* 1: 5–30, 1985.

36. Tuljapurkar has suggested how the variance of population projections can be used in a set of equations with the economic variables affecting Social Security to model the solvency of the system. See Shripad Tuljapurkar, "Stochastic forecasts and their uses," *International Journal of Forecasting* 8(3): 385–391, November 1992.

37. See Robert B. Friedland and Laura Summer, *Demography Is Not Destiny*, Washington, DC: National Academy on an Aging Society, 1999, esp. Chapters III and V.

38. Preston presents a comprehensive and well-documented analysis of the decline in the responsibility of the family for the care of children. See Samuel H. Preston, "Children and the elderly: Divergent paths for America's dependents," *Demography* 21(4): 435–458, November 1984. See also Lenore J. Weitzman, *The Divorce Revolution: The Unexpected Social and Economic Consequences for Women and Children in America*, New York: The Free Press, 1985; and Andrew J. Cherlin, "Going to extremes: Family structure, children's well-being, and social science," *Demography* 36(4): 421–428, November 1999.

39. Preston, 1984, *op. cit.*; June Axinn and Mark J. Stern, "Age and dependency: Children and the aged in American social policy," *Milbank Memorial Fund Quarterly: Health and Society* 63(4): 648–670, Fall 1985.

40. Alfred Sauvy, *General Theory of Population* (translated by Christophe Campos), New York: Basic Books, 1969.

41. Robert Clark, "The influence of low fertility rates and retirement policy on dependency costs," prepared for the American Institutes for Research in the Behavioral Sciences, Washington, DC: 1976. Summarized in Harold Sheppard and Sara Rix, *The Graying of Working America: The Coming Crisis of Retirement-Age Policy,* New York: The Free Press, 1977, Chapter 2.

42. Robert L. Clark and Joseph J. Spengler, "Dependency ratios: Their use in economic analysis," p. 72, in Julian Simon and Julie DaVanzo (eds.), *Research in Population Economics*, Vol. 2, Greenwich, CT: JAI Press, 1980. See also James S. Schulz, *The Economics of Aging*, 3rd ed., New York: Van Nostrand Reinhold, 1985.

43. See, for example, Philip Longman, *Born to Pay: The New Politics of Aging in America,* Boston: Houghton Mifflin, 1987; and Edward L. Schneider and Jack M. Guralnik, "The Aging of America: Impact on health care costs," *Journal of the American Medical Association* 263: 2335–2340, 1990.

44. See, for example, Alliance for Aging Research, *Seven deadly myths: Uncovering the facts about the high cost of the last year of life*, Washington, DC: Alliance for Aging Research, 1997; Daniel L. Waldo, S. T. Sonnefeld, D. R. McKusick, and R. H. Arnett, III, "Health care expenditures by age group, 1977 and 1987." *Health Care Financing Review* 10(4): 111–120, 1989; Jack Habib, "The economy and the aged," in Robert H. Binstock and Ethel Shanas (eds.), *Handbook of Aging and the Social Sciences*, 2nd ed., New York: Van Nostrand Reinhold, 1985.

45. Leiyu Shi and Douglas A. Singh, *Delivering Health Care in America: A Systems Approach,* Gaithersburg, MD: Aspen Publishers, 1998, esp. pp. 451–457.

46. Real costs are costs after an adjustment for price inflation; current costs are costs before an adjustment for price inflation. Change in the real or price-adjusted per capita gross domestic product is viewed as a better measure of price inflation for the economy as a whole than the Consumer Price Index. The Consumer Price Index does not adequately reflect changes in the cost of hospital care and nursing-home care, which together make up about half of the personal health care bill. The Health Care Financing Administration uses the GDP procedure for the deflation of the costs of health care.

47. William J. Serow, "Demographic aspects of health care access: 1990–2020," *Working Paper Series*, PI-93-6, Pepper Institute on Aging and Public Policy, Florida State University, Tallahassee, FL, pp. 20–21.

48. S. T. Burner and D. R. Waldo, "National health expenditure projections, 1994–2005," *Health Care Financing Review* 16: 221–242, 1995; Thomas E. Getzen, "Population aging and the growth of health expenditures," *Journal of Gerontology: Social Sciences* 42(3): S98–S104, 1992; and Daniel N. Mendelson and William B. Schwartz, "The effects of aging and population growth on health care costs," *Health Affairs*, Spring 1993, pp. 119–125.

49. William B. Schwartz, "The inevitable failure of current cost containment strategies," *Journal of the American Medical Association* 257: 220–224, 1987.

SUGGESTED READINGS

General

Davis, Kingsley, and van den Oever, P. (1981). "Age relations and public policy in advanced industrial societies." *Population and Development Review* 7: 1–18.

Espenshade, Thomas J., and Serow, William J., eds. (1978). *The Economic Consequences of Slowing Population Growth*. New York: Academic Press.

Keyfitz, Nathan. (1982). *Population Change and Social Policy*. Cambridge, MA: Abt Associates.

Kingsley Davis, Bernstam, Mikhail S., and Ricardo-Campbell, Rita (eds.) (1986). *Below-Replacement Fertility in Industrial Societies: Causes, Consequences, and Policies*, a Supplement to *Population and Development Review* 12.

Economic Costs of Immigration

Borjas, George J. (1999). *Heaven's Door: Immigration Policy and the American Economy*. Princeton, NJ: Princeton University Press.

Butcher, Kristin F., and Piehl, Anne Morrison. (1996). "Immigration and the wages and employment of U.S.-born workers." In Thomas J. Espenshade (ed.), *Keys to Successful Immigration: Implications of the New Jersey Experience*. Washington, DC: Urban Institute Press.

Clark, Rebecca L., and Zimmermann, Wendy N. (1996). "Undocumented immigrants in New Jersey: Numbers, impacts, and policies." In Thomas J. Espenshade (ed.), *Keys to Successful Immigration: Implications of the New Jersey Experience*. Washington, DC: Urban Institute Press.

Clark, W. A. V., and Schultz, Freya. (1997). "Evaluating the local impacts of recent immigration to California: Realism vs. racism." *Population Research and Policy Review* 16(5): 475–491.

Enchautegui, Maria E. (1997). "Immigration and county employment growth." *Population Research and Policy Review* 16(5): 493–511.

Espenshade, Thomas J. (1994). *A Stone's Throw from Ellis Island: Economic Implications of Immigration to New Jersey*. Lanham, MD: University Press of America.

Fix, Michael, and Passel, Jeffrey S. (1994). *Immigration and Immigrants: Setting the Record Straight*. Washington, DC: The Urban Institute.

Huddle, D. (1993). The Costs of Immigration." Washington, DC: Carrying Capacity Network.

Los Angeles County, Internal Services Division. (1992). *Impact of Undocumented and Other Immigrants on Costs, Revenues, and Services in Los Angeles County*. Los Angeles County, CA.

Marcelli, Enrico A., and Heer, David M. (1997). "The unauthorized Mexican immigrant population and welfare in Los Angeles County: A comparative statistical analysis." *Sociological Perspectives* 41(2): 279–302.

Passel, Jeffrey S. (1994). "Immigrants and taxes: A reappraisal of Huddle's 'The costs of immigrants.' " Washington, DC: The Urban Institute. *Policy Discussion Paper* PRIP-UI-29.

Rea, Louis, and Parker, Richard A. (1993). "Illegal immigration in San Diego: An analysis of costs and revenues." Sacramento: California Legislature.

Rothman, Eric S., and Espenshade, Thomas J. (1992). "Fiscal impacts of immigration to the United States." *Population Index* 58(3): 381–415.

Smith, James P., and Edmonston, Barry, eds. (1997). *The New Americans: Studies on the Economic, Demographic, and Fiscal Effects of Immigration*. Washington, DC: National Academy Press.

Smith, James P., and Edmonston, Barry, eds. (1998). *The Immigration Debate: Studies on the Economic, Demographic, and Fiscal Effects of Immigration*. Washington, DC: National Academy Press.

U.S. Bureau of International Labor Affairs, Department of Labor. (1990). "The labor market consequences of U.S. immigration: A survey." By Michael J. Greenwood and John M. McDowell. *Immigration Policy and Working Paper* 1.

U.S. Commission on Immigration Reform. (1997). *Becoming an American: Immigration and Immigrant Policy, Report to Congress,* No. 98-0053-P.

U.S. General Accounting Office. (1994, November 28). *Illegal Aliens: Assessing Estimates of Financial Burden on California.* GAO/HEHS-95-22.

U.S. General Accounting Office. (1995, July 25). *Illegal Aliens: National Net Costs Vary Widely.* GAO/HEHS-95-133.

Vernez, Georges, and McCarthy, Kevin F. (1996). *The Costs of Immigration to Taxpayers: Analytical and Policy Issues.* Santa Monica, CA: The Rand Corporation.

Sex Differences in Premiums and Benefits in Insurance and Retirement Programs

Abraham, Kenneth S. (1986). *Distributing Risk: Legal Theory and Public Policy.* New Haven, CT: Yale University Press.

Brilmayer, Lea, Hekeler, Richard W., Laycock, Douglas, and Sullivan, Teresa A. (1979–1980). "Sex discrimination in employer-sponsored insurance plans: A legal and demographic analysis." *University of Chicago Law Review* **47**: 505–560.

Caddy, Douglas. (1986). *Legislative Trends in Insurance Regulation.* College Station: Texas A&M University Press. Chapter 4.

Keyfitz, Nathan. (1982). "Equity between the sexes: The pension problem." Chapter 16 in Nathan Keyfitz, *Population Change and Social Policy.* Cambridge, MA: Abt Books.

Lencsis, Peter M. (1997). *Insurance Regulation in the United States: An Overview for Business and Government.* Westport, CT: Quorum Books. Chapter 2.

Demographic Factors in Outlook for Social Security

Burkhauser, Richard V. (1996, December). "Touching the third rail: Time to return the retirement age for early Social Security benefits to 65." *Gerontologist* **36**(6): 726–727.

Clark, Robert L., and Spengler, Joseph J. (1979). *The Economics of Individual and Population Aging.* Cambridge: Cambridge University Press.

Gendell, Murray. (1998, August). "Trends in retirement age in four countries, 1965–95." *Monthly Labor Review* **121**(8): 20–30.

Gendell, Murray, and Siegel, Jacob S. (1996). "Trends in retirement age in the United States, 1955–1993, by sex and race." *Journal of Gerontology: Social Sciences* **51B**(3): S132–S139.

Keyfitz, Nathan. (1985). "The demographics of unfunded pensions." *European Journal of Population* **1**: 5–30.

Lee, Ronald, and Skinner, Jonathon. (1996). "Assessing forecasts of mortality, health status, and and health care costs during baby boomers' retirement." In Eric A. Hanushek and Nancy L. Maritato (eds.), pp. 195–243, *Assessing Knowledge of Retirement Behavior.* Washington, DC: National Academy Press.

Lee, Ronald, and Tuljapurkar, Shripad. (1999, February). "Death and taxes: Longer life, consumption and Social Security." *Demography* **34**(1): 67–81.

Manton, Kenneth G., and Corder, Larry. (1998). "Forecasts of future disabled and institutionalized populations, 1995 to 2040." In Theodore R. Marmor and Philip R. DeJong (eds.), *Ageing, Social Security, and Affordability.* Aldershot, England: Ashgate.

Quinn, Joseph F., and Burkhauser, Richard V. (1994). "Retirement and labor force behavior of the elderly." In Linda G. Martin and Samuel H. Preston (eds.), pp. 50–51, *Demography of Aging.* Washington, DC: National Academy of Sciences.

Ricardo-Campbell, Rita. (1986). "U.S. Social Security under low fertility." In Kingsley Davis, Mikhail S. Bernstam, and Rita Ricardo-Campbell (eds.), pp. 296–312, *Below-Replacement Fertility in Industrial Societies: Causes, Consequences, and Policies.* A Supplement to *Population and Development Review* 12.

U.S. Advisory Council on Social Security. (1997, March). *1994–96 Report.* "Social Security and the future of U.S. fertility." Reproduced in *Population and Development Review* **23**(1): 208–213.

U.S. Council of Economic Advisors. (1999, March). "The Council of Economic Advisors on work and retirement among the elderly." *Population and Development Review* 25(1): 189–196. Excerpts from the *1999 Annual Report of the U.S. Council of Economic Advisors.*

U.S. Social Security Advisory Board. (1999). *The 1999 Technical Panel on Assumptions and Methods: Report to the Social Security Advisory Board.*

Weaver, Carolyn. (1986). "Social Security in aging societies." In Kingsley Davis, Mikhail S. Bernstam, and Rita Ricardo-Campbell (eds.), pp. 273–295, *Below-Replacement Fertility in Industrial Societies: Causes, Consequences, and Policies.* A Supplement to *Population and Development Review* 12.

Wise, David A. (1997, February). "Retirement against the demographic trend: More older people living longer, working less, and saving less." *Demography* 34(1): 83–95.

Relative Cost of Raising a Child and an Elderly Person

Axinn, June, and Stern, Mark J. (1985, Fall). "Age and dependency: Children and the aged in public policy." *Milbank Memorial Fund Quarterly: Health and Society* 63(4): 648–670.

Clark, Robert. (1976). "The influence of low fertility rates and retirement policy on dependency costs." Prepared for the American Institutes for Research in the Behavioral Sciences, Washington, DC. Summarized in Harold Sheppard and Sara Rix, *The Graying of Working America.* New York: The Free Press, 1977.

Clark, Robert, and Spengler, Joseph J. (1978). "Changing demography and dependency costs: The implications of new dependency ratios and their composition." In Barbara Herzog (ed.), *Income and Aging: Essays on Policy Prospects.* New York: Human Science Press.

Preston, Samuel H. (1984). "Children and the elderly: Divergent paths for America's dependents." *Demography* 21(4): 435–458.

Population Factor in Increase in National Health Expenditures

Alliance for Aging Research. (1997). *Seven Deadly Myths: Uncovering the Facts about the High Cost of the Last Year of Life.* Washington, DC: Alliance for Aging Research.

Burner, S. T., and Waldo, D. R. (1995). "National health expenditure projections, 1994–2005." *Health Care Financing Review* 16: 221–242.

Cowan, Cathy A., *et al.* (1999, Winter). "National health expenditures: 1998." *Health Care Financing Review* 21(2).

Fisher, Charles R. (1980). "Differences by age groups in health care spending." *Health Care Financing Review* 1(4): 65–90.

Getzen, Thomas E. (1992). "Population aging and the growth of health expenditures." *Journal of Gerontology: Social Sciences* 42(3): S98–S104.

Levit, Katherine, *et al.* (2000, January/February). "Health spending in 1998: Signals of change." *Health Affairs* 19(1): 124–132.

Mendelson, Daniel N., and Schwartz, William B. (1993). "The effects of aging and population growth on health care costs." *Health Affairs* (Spring): 119–125.

Schneider, Edward L., and Guralnik, Jack M. (1990). "The aging of America: Impact on health care costs." *Journal of the American Medical Association* 263: 2335–2340.

Waldo, Daniel L., Sonnefeld, S. T., McKusick, D. R., Arnett III, R. H. (1989). "Health care expenditures by age group, 1977 and 1987." *Health Care Financing Review* 10(4): 111–120.

14
THE DEMOGRAPHY OF ORGANIZATIONAL POPULATIONS

DEMOGRAPHIC ASPECTS OF ORGANIZATIONS AS A SET

Whether they are businesses, colleges, professional or trade associations, churches, or charitable organizations, each individual organizational unit may be viewed as an element in a set or "population" of organizational units of the same general type. While the term *population* is generally used to refer to groups of persons, and sometimes to groups of animals and plants of the same order, family, genus, or species (e.g., whale population, Dutch elm population) and groups of manufactured products of a particular type (e.g., automobiles, television sets), its usage may be extended to encompass a set of organizations. These sets may be relatively broad in coverage, such as retail businesses, liberal arts colleges, philanthropic foundations, or Protestant churches, or they may be relatively limited in coverage, such as men's retail clothing stores in Minnesota, community colleges in the South Atlantic states, and Catholic parish churches in New York City. Such sets of organizations are subject to many of the types of demographic analyses that are commonly applied to human populations or the collective membership of individual organizations (e.g., workforce of General Motors Corporation, policyholders of Metropolitan Life Insurance Company, members of the Population Association of America).

The demographic analogy is really closer when we liken organizations to households rather than to individuals. Both households and individuals have demographic characteristics, but households also have a "demographic composition" of their own. For example, a household has a size, internal relationships, age-sex structure, and an ethnic composition. Some of its characteristics are based on those of a reference person or householder. It can lose members and take on members, so that its identity as a distinctive unit comes into question in longitudinal/panel studies. Accordingly, rules have to be fashioned to establish when a household comes into existence, remains the same household or becomes a different household, and dissolves under circumstances of changing membership and changing location. Similarly, an organization has a size, as measured, for example, by the number of its employees, stockholders, enrollments, or members, and it may experience a variety of changes, such as an expansion or contraction of its component units or a relocation.

A basic issue to be resolved, then, is the definition of the organizational unit and the rules by which it maintains its identity. Organizations are dynamic and change in structure, location, and ownership. Organizations may have component units that produce different products, provide different services, serve different clients, and are managed independently. A business may have several scattered plants at different locations, a university may have several colleges on different campuses, and a church may have several buildings in different neighborhoods. The organization may be a new entity, the product of a merger of two other organizations, or the result of a spinoff from another organization. A specific definition of organizational identity has to be formulated for each type of organization, taking into account the complexity and variability just noted.

An associated issue to be resolved in determining the number of organizational units at any time is the date of formation (birth) and the date of dissolution (death) of each organization. The definitions of the birth and death of an organization must be consistent with one another and with the definition of the organization itself. These depend, in part, on the basis of the organization's formation and dissolution and the types of analysis to be applied to it. These issues are discussed further in this chapter.

Once a definition for the existence of a set of organizations is determined, we can count or estimate their numbers and measure their changes over some designated period. We can then determine the contribution of the components of change and make projections of the class of organizations by demographic or other techniques. These forms of analysis require accurate data on the demographic events affecting the set of organizations under study—that is, the number of births, deaths, and other changes (e.g., migrations, particularly for subnational studies)—and a life table tracking the survival history of the members of the set. The sources of data, the types of data files, and the problems of data quality are largely specific to each class of organizations and analytic task.

Since organizational units may be formed, terminated, moved to new locations (even moved abroad), merged with or acquired by other organizational units, and separated or spun off from parent units, we may speak, by analogy, of birth, death, in-migration, out-migration, marriage, divorce, parent-hood, and child status of organizational units. Each organizational unit has an age (i.e., time in years since its original formation or its formation by indus-trial transformation, merger, or spinoff), depending on the definition of birth employed. Hence, each group of organizations forming a set has an age dis-tribution and an average age. Births, deaths, and other events bring about changes in the age distribution of the set of organizations and its average age over time. These data and measures are often extremely difficult to develop, given the limited material currently available.

In the remainder of this chapter, the broad categories of organizations are treated separately, beginning with businesses, which are discussed in relatively great detail. This is followed by a discussion of nonprofit organizations (i.e., colleges, churches) and nations, interpreted as quasi-organizations.

BUSINESSES

Economic censuses and surveys distinguish establishments from firms, or com-panies, among business units. An **establishment** as defined in these censuses and surveys is a business or industrial unit at a single geographic location that produces or distributes goods or performs services. Examples are a sport-ing goods store in Rockville, Maryland, a fertilizer plant in Ames, Iowa, and a television repair shop in San Francisco, California. A **company** or **firm** is a business organization consisting of one or more establishments in differ-ent geographic locations under common ownership or control. Establishments within the same company can be engaged in the same or different kinds of busi-nesses. Examples of firms are Office Depot, Safeway Foods, Kinko's Copies, R. J. Nabisco, and Nations Bank, although a firm may be a local business with a few branches. If a company or firm controls one or more establishments, all of the subsidiary establishments are included as part of the owning or controlling company. Thus, the data for firms represent summaries of data for establish-ments under common ownership. In 1996 there were 5.5 million firms with payroll (i.e., with employees) but 6.7 million establishments, implying that each firm had an average of 1.23 establishments.[1] This mean size is rather unrepresentative of the number of establishments associated with the typical firm, since most firms have fewer than 10 employees and nearly all of these small firms have only one establishment. That is to say, the distribution of firms by size is heavily weighted by a relatively small number of large firms.

Sources of Data

We can secure counts of business and industrial units from censuses, surveys, administrative records, and special lists, or we can estimate their numbers on the basis of counts or estimates at prior dates and supplementary informa-tion. As described in Chapter 3, the economic censuses provide counts of busi-ness and industrial units at 5-year time intervals for the years ending in "2" and "7." The economic censuses include censuses of retail trade, wholesale trade, manufactures, services, construction, mineral industries, and tranportation. Censuses of agriculture and governments are taken concurrently. The censuses provide information on the numbers and characteristics of business units, farms, and governments. The tabulations of the economic censuses include the size of the business (e.g., number of employees, annual payroll), the legal form of ownership (i.e., sole proprietorship, partnership, or corporation), and **affiliation status** (i.e., single establishment, two or more establishments). Estimates of the characteristics of business units are also obtained from surveys based on samples of units selected from the economic censuses. The U.S. Census Bureau conducts a Company Organization Survey annually by mail covering a sample of businesses operating at more than one location. Special surveys linked to part of the economic censuses are conducted every 5 years to determine the extent of ownership of businesses by racial minorities and women.

The Census Bureau has maintained a master list of businesses called the Standard Statistical Establishment List (SSEL) since 1973.[2] This is a list of all establishments with payroll (i.e., having employees), operating in the 50 states and the District of Columbia in private, nonagricultural industries. Current information about businesses operating at more than one location is obtained from the annual mail survey. Current information about businesses operating at a single location is obtained from federal administrative records, such as the tax records of the Internal Revenue Service and the establishment lists of the Social Security Administration. The SSEL files contain information on affiliation status, industry, geographic location, and size (i.e., employment and wages). For example, the 1992 list contains records with such information on establishments that were active in the year 1992. A set of consecutive SSELs, in effect, constitutes a continuous business population file recording the formation, reorganization, and dissolution of business units over a designated time period. An alternative business register, called Dun's Market Identifier (DMI) is maintained by Dun and Bradstreet Corporation of Murray Hill, New Jersey.

Of the numerous other sources, only a few are cited here. The annual compilation *County Business Patterns*, published by the U.S. Census Bureau, presents data on numbers of establishments distributed by major industry and size. As suggested earlier, two federal agencies, the Social Security Administration (SSA) and the Internal Revenue Office (IRS), maintain records of business establishments for tax collection and other purposes. The IRS data on tax returns filed provides annual data on nonfarm businesses according to form of ownership. The Office of Advocacy, U.S. Small Business Administration, maintains a small business database and prepares analyses of business and employment patterns. States maintain records of employment, unemployment insurance tax liabilities, sales tax registration, and other tax files of business units in their states. The states report the number and size of new businesses with employees to the U.S. Department of Labor.

The federal economic census data have several deficiencies. Like all census data, they suffer from coverage errors (i.e., omission of some units and erroneous inclusion of others) as well as errors of misreporting and nonreporting, and sampling errors for the sample data. The economic censuses do not cover all sectors of the economy. Specifically, they do not cover communications, finance, insurance, real estate, and utilities. Several censuses exclude firms without employees. Only a sample of smaller firms, mainly firms with at least four employees, is included. The sample is designed to yield 90% or more of the business activity in each industry. Information for firms with no employees and for small firms not in the sample is obtained for some censuses (e.g., retail trade and service industries) from the administrative records of the Internal Revenue Service and the Social Security Administration. Many applications of the economic censuses require data at more frequent intervals than 5 years, and estimating methods have been developed and implemented to fill this gap.

The principal weakness of the SSEL files is their omission of establishments without payroll (i.e., without employees). Next, it is not possible to follow many reorganizations from year to year, particularly with respect to ownership and affiliation status and, as a result, the age, birth, and death tabulations that may be made from the files tend to be biased. The brief history of the SSELs (from 1973) sets limits on the age categories of establishments that may be used in any analysis.

Data from state and private sources (e.g., the DMI file), designed for administrative and business purposes, are replete with problems from a demographic point of view (e.g., coverage, reporting errors, currency) although they have been employed in many studies. The counts of businesses, especially new businesses, available from the Census Bureau, the IRS, and the states differ greatly from one another.

Demographic Characteristics

Like households, businesses can be described demographically in terms of both the characteristics of the owner of the business (*cf.*, householder) and the characteristics of the business itself (*cf.*, household). Owners differ, for example, with respect to age, sex, race, educational level, income, and net worth. Businesses differ with respect to age (i.e., the number of years since the business was founded) and various socioeconomic and geographic characteristics (e.g., major industry group, form of ownership, affiliation status, size, and geographic region). The demographic characteristics of businesses are considered from both these points of view in varying degrees of detail in subsequent sections.

Beyond the demographic analogy between businesses and households, there is a measurable relationship between these two types of units. The question of interest is, how widespread is household involvement in the conduct of businesses? According to Reynolds (1998), pilot studies based on a nationally representative sample survey in 1996–1997 showed that participation in a new or small business is a common experience among households.[3] A substantial share of households (about 40%) are or have been involved in business operations. One out of thirteen households (8%) includes at least one adult member trying to start a new business. One out of five households includes a member who is an active manager of a firm that he or she owns. If we add the cases where people invested in another's new firm, tried to start a new business and quit, or operated a business that was shut down, two out of five households have one or more members with current or past experience with new businesses.

Ownership by Age and Sex

Little is formally known of the age of the owners of businesses. For sole proprietorships and partnerships, the type of information sought is apparent although, for those partnerships with several members, it would be difficult to assign an age to the owners of the business. For corporations, we are seeking, in effect, the age distribution of the numerous shareholders of the business or, at least, their average age. Such information is unavailable, however.

Women own a relatively small share of all firms and an especially small share of large firms. In 1992 women owned 34% of all firms (Table 14.1) and about 16% of employer firms (i.e., with paid employees). The share of women-owned businesses has been growing; in 1987 only 30% of firms were owned by women (Table 14.1).[4] By way of comparison, over half of all potential owners (i.e., adult women 25 years and over) are women. Nine out of ten women-owned firms have few or no employees and two out of five firms without employees are women-owned firms.

Race/Hispanic Ownership

A disproportionately small share of firms are owned by racial minorities or Hispanics. In 1992, 11% of all firms were racial-minority/Hispanic-owned

TABLE 14.1 Distribution of Firms by Sex and Race/Hispanic Origin of Owners: 1987 and 1992

Sex and race of owner	Number of firms (in thousands)		Percent increase	Percent of total: 1992	
	1992	1987	1987–1992	Of all firms	Of minority firms
All races	17,253.1	13,695.5	26.0	100.0	(X)
Men	11,364.2	9,590.7	18.5	65.9	(X)
Women	5,888.9	4,114.8	43.1	34.1	(X)
Racial/Hispanic groups, total	1,965.6	1213.8	61.9	11.4	100.0
Men	1,248.1	825.4	51.2	7.2	63.5
Women	717.4	388.3	84.8	4.2	36.5
Black	620.9	424.2	46.4	3.6	31.6
Men	343.7	265.9	29.3	2.0	17.5
Women	277.2	158.3	75.2	1.6	14.1
Hispanic	771.7	422.4	82.7	4.5	39.3
Men	525.3	307.3	70.9	3.0	26.7
Women	246.4	115.0	114.2	1.4	12.5
A/PI/AI/AN[a]	606.4	376.7	62.1	3.5	30.9
Men	397.8	258.5	53.9	2.3	20.2
Women	208.6	118.2	76.5	1.2	10.6

X: Not applicable.

[a] Asian, Pacific Islander, American Indian, and Alaska native.

Note: A women-owned or minority-owned business is one in which the person (or persons) owning the majority interest in the business is a women or a member of a racial minority or Hispanic, respectively.

Source: U.S. Bureau of the Census, *Survey of Minority-Owned Businesses, Summary 1992*, Series MB92-4; U.S. Bureau of the Census, *1987 Economic Censuses, Women-Owned Businesses*.

(Table 14.1), while 25% of all adults 25 years and over were members of racial minorities/Hispanic groups. Asians show up prominently as owners, controlling 31% of the minority-owned businesses while making up only 15% of the adult minority population. Like minorities in general, minority women owned a small share of all women-owned firms—only 12%. Minority women stood out as owners among minority owners, however; well over one-third of minority-owned firms were owned by women. This is impressive even though over half of all minority adults (25 and over) are women. Recall, however, that only one-third of all firms are owned by women, regardless of race.[5]

In every racial/Hispanic/sex category, the growth rate of minority-owned businesses between 1987 and 1992 far exceeded the growth rate of businesses in general. Consider one group, Hispanic women. The 5-year growth rate was 114% compared to 43% for all women-owned businesses and 26% for businesses without regard to race or sex.

Age of Businesses

Theoretically, the age or date of birth of a business can be ascertained by direct inquiry in a census or survey. Efforts to secure data on age of businesses in this way have not proven successful. A survey of a sample of businesses in 1995, conducted by the U.S. Bureau of the Census, asked for date of birth and the nonresponse rate was about 50%. Given the variety of forms of births of businesses, there are immense difficulties in operationally defining and ascertaining the date of birth of a business by direct inquiry, even greater ones than there are in operationally ascertaining the number of different businesses.

Alternatively, age of businesses can be measured by the number of years a given establishment can be identified as the same establishment in successive annual lists of business establishments. Matching the entries in the Census Bureau's Standard Statistical Establishment Lists (SSELs) from one annual list to the next on the basis of the business identification number can provide this information. Recall that the SSELs covers only private nonagricultural establishments having employees. Because it was first compiled in 1973, it is not possible to distinguish ages for establishments founded in years prior to 1973. Excluding the early years 1973–1975, when the data were of questionable quality, the age categories are limited, therefore, to values from zero to about 10-or-more in the 1987 SSEL. The birth year is the year in which the business first appeared in the SSEL and reported a payroll. If the year of study is 1987, age under 1 year corresponds to formation in the year 1987, and age at 1 year corresponds to formation in year 1986. Ages 10-and-over represents businesses formed in year 1977 or earlier.

The ages so determined are either exact ages or completed ages (e.g., births versus under age 1; reaching age 1 versus age 1, and so on), depending on the frequency with which the businesses are "canvassed" during the year. If the canvas is taken once for the entire year, they are completed ages. If it is taken continuously and includes *all* businesses that were active at any time during the year, they are exact ages. The latter numbers are not affected by deaths of businesses to the birth cohort within the year of age. Because the SSEL was apparently able to cover some but not all businesses active during each year, the age reference for the data is probably somewhere between exact age and completed age.

In view of the exclusion of (young) businesses without employees and the likelihood that failure to match establishments correctly exceeds the likelihood of matching establishments erroneously, the measurement of age is probably biased downward. Moreover, it is difficult to follow establishments that change identification numbers between annual lists because of a change in affiliation status, physical location, ownership, or other reason. In carrying out such a match operation, the age of a business must be determined in a way that is consistent with the way its dates of birth and death, and its identity for inclusion and continuation in the list, were determined.[6]

The age distribution of establishments follows a parabola with an asymmetric U-shape or a lower right asymptote. The distribution reflected in the SSEL for 1992 shows that the percentage of establishments declines irregularly from the first year (12%) to age 6 (4%) and then hardly changes up to age 9 (4%). (See Table 14.2.) No information is available on the age distribution of the nearly one-third of establishments at ages 10 and over. The median age is 6.2 years. The age distribution for 1987 resembles an asymmetric parabola more closely. The share at each age drops from 15% at age under 1 to 3% at age 6, and then rises to 5% at age 9, leaving nearly one-third of the "popu-

TABLE 14.2 Percentage Distribution of Private Nonagricultural Establishments with Payroll by Age: 1987 and 1992

Age (years)[a]	1992	1987
Total		
Number	6,137,905	5,727,985
Percent	100.0	100.0
Under 1	11.9	14.7
1	10.0	8.8
2	7.9	8.4
3	6.0	7.8
4	5.8	6.8
5	7.4	6.8
6	4.1	2.8
7	4.1	3.6
8	4.2	3.6
9	3.8	5.3
10 and over	35.0	31.3
Median age	6.24	5.51

[a] Year in which the business first reported payroll and appeared on the Standard Statistical Establishment List file is taken as birth year.

Note: Excludes most establishments that do not have employees. In 1992 there were 17.3 million firms representing over 18.5 million establishments.

Source: Alfred R. Nucci, "Comparison of 1987 and 1992 establishment life table survival distribution," presented at the Annual Meeting of the Southern Demographic Association, Annapolis, MD, October 29–31, 1998. *Basic source*: U.S. Bureau of the Census, Center for Economic studies, 1987 and 1992 Standard Statistical Establishment List files, special tabulations.

lation" at ages 10 and over. On the average, business establishments became "older" as a class in this 5-year period. In 1987 the median age was 5.5 years.

Socioeconomic Characteristics of Businesses

Size is one of the most informative variables characterizing a business since it is correlated with form of ownership and longevity. The great majority of firms are very small in size, having few or no employees. In 1996 three-fifths of all firms with payroll had fewer than five employees and only 1.7% had 100 employees or more (Table 14.3). If we include an estimate of the large number of firms that have no employees, numbering several million, the concentration of small businesses is far greater. About four out of five firms have no employees or fewer than five employees, and only about one-half of 1% of all firms have 100 employees or more. An even greater proportion of the firms that close their doors in any year are small. Similarly, the vast majority of establishments are autonomous (i.e., not associated with another establishment in the same firm). At least four out of five establishments with payroll are autonomous and the share is much higher if we allow for firms without employees (Table 14.3).

Firms are heavily concentrated in two economic sectors, services and retail trade. These sectors make up 6 out of ten firms (Table 14.4). Next in order are construction, and finance/insurance/real estate (FIRE), each of which represents about 11% of the total. The majority of women-owned firms are engaged in services, and more than four out of five women-owned firms are engaged in services, retail trade, or FIRE. The small number of women-owned firms with

TABLE 14.3 Percentage Distribution of Firms and Establishments with Payroll by Size of Firm: 1990 and 1996

Size of firm (employees)	Firms		Establishments	
	1996	1990	1996	1990
Total				
Number	5,478,047	5,073,795	6,738,76	6,175,559
Percent	100.0	100.0	100.0	100.0
0–4	60.7	59.5	49.5	49.1
5–9	18.2	18.8	15.0	15.7
10–19	10.7	11.1	9.3	9.7
20–99	8.7	8.9	9.4	9.6
100–499	1.4	1.4	4.2	4.1
500 or more	0.3	0.3	12.5	11.8
Median size	Less than 5	Less than 5	5.17	5.29

Note: Firms are an aggregation of all establishments in different locations owned by a parent company. Employment is measured in March and payroll is reported for the year; hence, some firms reporting a payroll may have reported no employees. Excludes most firms and establishments that do not have employees. In 1992 there were 17.3 million firms representing over 18.5 million establishments.

Source: U.S. Office of Advocacy, U.S. Small Business Administration; based on unpublished data provided by the U.S. Bureau of the Census. See also U.S. Bureau of the Census, *Statistical Abstract of the United States, 1999*, Table 878.

TABLE 14.4 Percentage Distribution of All Firms and Women-Owned Firms by Major Industry Group, 1992, and Percentage Distribution of Firms with Payroll by Size, for Major Industry Groups, 1996 (Numbers in Thousands, Major Industry Group based on the 1987 SIC System)

Major industry group	1992		1996 – Percentage by size of firm[a]						
	All firms [b]	Women-owned[c]	Total no.[d]	Under 5	5–9	10–19	20–99	100–499	500 or more
Total									
Number	17,253.1	5,888.9	5,478.0	60.7	18.2	10.7	8.7	1.4	0.3
Percent	100.0	100.0							
Agric. services, forestry and fishing	2.5	1.4	111.5	68.2	17.7	9.5	4.2	0.4	0.1
Mining	0.9	0.6	21.1	57.8	15.2	11.4	10.9	2.4	1.9
Construction	10.6	3.1	651.9	65.0	17.4	9.9	6.9	0.7	0.1
Manufacturing	3.0	2.6	332.6	39.1	18.4	15.9	20.2	5.0	1.5
Transportation, communications, and public utilities	4.1	2.4	217.7	61.0	16.4	10.5	9.6	1.8	0.8
Wholesale trade	3.1	2.6	417.0	54.0	18.9	13.1	11.3	2.0	0.8
Retail trade	14.4	18.6	1,103.5	54.7	20.4	12.9	10.5	1.2	0.3
Finance, insurance, and real estate	11.3	10.2	453.3	72.7	13.4	6.5	5.4	1.3	0.7
Services	45.1	53.6	2,175.6	62.9	18.3	9.6	7.3	1.5	0.4
Unclassified	5.1	4.8	29.0	92.1	5.2	1.7	0.7	—	—

—: Rounds to zero.

[a] Size in terms of number of employees.

[b] Individual propietorships, partnerships, and subchapter S corporations.

[c] A women-owned business is one in which the person or persons owning a majority interest in the business is a women.

[d] Firms with payroll (i.e., mainly employer firms).

Source: U.S. Bureau of the Census, 1992 Economic Censuses, *Survey of Minority-Owned Business Enterprises, Summary,* Table 10. Office of Advocacy, U.S. Small Business Administration, based on data provided by U.S. Census Bureau, *Statistics of U.S. Businesses,* 1996.

employees are less concentrated in these industries; only two-thirds of firms with employees are engaged in services, retail trade, or FIRE. Nearly half of minority-owned firms are engaged in services, and over 70% are engaged in services, retail trade, and construction.[7] Minority-owned firms with employees are even more concentrated in these industries.

Net Change and Components of Change

From two counts or estimates of a given set of businesses, we can determine the net increase or net decrease and the average annual rate of change in the set of businesses during the intervening period. National counts of business units may be secured, for example, from the Census Bureau's Standard Statistical Establishment Lists (SSELs). Between 1990 and 1996, the number of firms and the number of establishments (with payroll) increased at an annual average rate of 1.3% and 1.4% per year, respectively:

| Year | Number (thousands) | | Rate[a] | |
	Firms	Establishments	Firms	Establishments
1996	5478	6738	1.3	1.4
1990	5074	6176	(NA)	3.1
1980	(NA)	4543	(X)	(X)

NA: Not available. X: Not applicable.

[a] Annual average rate of increase in preceding period in percentage.

Source: U.S. Small Business Administration, based on data provided by the U.S. Census Bureau.

The small difference in the rate for 1990–1996 between firms and establishments implies that there was little or no change in the average number of establishments per firm in this 6-year period. The growth rate of businesses can be quite variable, as suggested by the much larger growth rate during the 1980s than the 1990s. The accuracy of the figures on net change depends on the completeness and consistency of coverage of the various files on establishments at the different dates.

It is next of interest to decompose the net change in the number of business units during a period into births and deaths of the businesses. Births and deaths may enter into net change during a period in different ways depending on whether the business change is a formation *de novo*, a dissolution, a merger of two businesses, the acquisition of one business by another, a breakup of a business into parts, a spinoff of a part of a business from a parent business, or an industrial transformation. The different roles for births and deaths in connection with these types of business changes may be identified as follows:

Type of change	Gross change	Net change
Formation (no prior business)	One birth	+1
Dissolution (original business)	One death	−1
Merger of two businesses	Two deaths and one birth	−1
Acquisition of a business	Two deaths and one birth	−1
Breakup	One death and two births	+1
Spinoff	One death and two births	+1
Industrial transformation	One death and one birth	—
New ownership	One birth and one death	—

One may identify six or so types of births of business units: (1) the formation of a new business, (2) the creation of a new business when two existing businesses are merged, (3) the creation of an enlarged business when an existing business acquires another existing business, (4) the creation of two new businesses when an existing business is broken up or when a part of an existing business is spun off, (5) the transformation of a business from one industry to another, and (6) the opening of the same business under new ownership. There are also several types of business deaths: (1) dissolution or closing of an existing business, (2) the closings of two existing businesses when they merge, (3) the closing of an existing business when it is acquired by another business, (4) the termination of a business in its original form when it acquires another business, breaks up into parts, or spins off a part, (5) the termination of a business when it wholly changes its industrial product or service, and (6) the termination of a business in its original identity when it changes ownership.

One may reasonably exclude changes of ownership as a basis for counting business births and deaths if no other change is involved. Births of type five and deaths of type five are relevant only in connection with counts of births and deaths for particular industrial categories (e.g., automobile companies), not for births and deaths overall. As the reader may have surmised, alternative events or statuses may be assigned here, such as marriage in the case of merger and acquisition, and divorce in the case of breakup and spinoff. Parenthood and childbirth are alternative statuses in the case of breakups and spinoffs. These conceptual translations have yet to be tested and measured with actual data.

Since demographers are not normally familiar with these business changes, it seems useful to explain them further. Business **dissolution** refers to business closings for such reasons as failure, bankruptcy, owner retirement, and owner desire to change to a different work activity. In an **acquisition** or **buyout**, one company buys another company, which becomes a subsidiary of the buyer company, whereas in a **merger** the two companies join as equals. In a **divestiture** or **spinoff** a firm divests itself of a part of its assets, usually a subsidiary, and a new firm is born. **Breakups** involve the dissolution of a company and the division of its assets and structural parts into two or more companies. **Industrial transformations** occur when businesses change their affiliation from one industry to another. This process may be seen as involving the dissolution of a business and its rebirth, with no net change or, alternatively, as a change in classification only. "Demographic" changes of these types have affected many large, well-known companies in recent decades.[8]

Table 14.5 presents the distribution of births and deaths of U.S. automobile firms by type of starting and ending event during the period 1885 to 1981. This table was adapted from a study by Hannan *et al.* (1997) employing intensive historical analysis, and it follows essentially the categories of starting and ending events enumerated earlier, with some minor exceptions. The leading types of events are formations of new auto companies (45%) and dissolutions of auto companies (42%). These changes, together with transformations from or to other industries (33 and 31%, respectively), cover about three-quarters of the starting events and three-quarters of the ending events. These percentages would probably be higher if the large proportions of unknowns (18%) could be assigned to specific event categories. A small proportion of firms that were still active in 1981 are labeled "right-censored" since their final fate had yet to be determined.

There is a dynamism in the business world that results in frequent restructuring of companies but it complicates analysis of their demographic changes. For example, a company spun off (i.e., birth) is commonly bought up in an acquisition (i.e., death) after a short while. Spunoff companies are several times more likely to be bought up in an acquisition than the average firm. It would be an interesting demographic exercise to calculate the probability that companies that are born by spinoff will die by acquisition within a specified period (e.g., 5 years). Spunoff companies may also grow rapidly and acquire other companies.[9] Spinoffs (or divestitures), mergers, and acquisitions have been common in recent years. Between 1990 and 1996, the number of acquisitions and mergers involving U.S. companies increased by nearly two-fifths:

	Mergers and acquisitions	Divestitures
1996	3216	2423
1990	2332	1907
Percentage increase	38	27

Source: Derived from data compiled by Securities Data Company, Newark, NJ, Merger and Corporate Transactions Database. See also U.S. Bureau of the Census, *Statistical Abstract of the United States, 1998*, Tables 884 and 885.

Three industries—radio and television broadcasting companies, business services, and commercial banks and bank holding companies—accounted for nearly one-quarter of the mergers and acquisitions in 1996.

As we have seen, the analysis of component changes for business establishments can be complex. The analysis is usually more complex for subnational areas than for the nation, since the component of migration must be considered. For example, if a business moves to a new location, such as a different state, the move may be considered as a death or out-migration for the area of origin and birth or in-migration for the area of destination. More commonly, an existing business expands and sets up an additional facility in the other state. When a business expands for the first time to a new area, such a change may be considered zero net change for the original area, but for the new area the event is a birth or in-migration. These complexities suggest an alternative simplified definition of births and deaths of businesses, namely those events that occur to new firms at their original location and those that occur to existing firms at a secondary location. Mergers and acquisitions, and breakups and

TABLE 14.5 Percentage Distribution of Births and Deaths of U.S. Automobile Firms by Type of Starting or Ending Event: 1885–1981

Starting event	Percentage	Ending event	Percentage
Total		Total	
Number	2197	Number	2197
Percent	100.0	Percent	100.0
Formation de novo	44.8	Dissolution	41.8
Transformation [a]	32.9	Transformation [b]	30.5
Merger	0.9	Merger with another firm	1.5
Acquisition	0.9	Acquisition by another firm	3.6
Spin-off from an automaker	0.7		
Restart with assets of a bankrupt firm	1.5	Takover by creditors	—
Reentry	—	Nationalization	—
		Ended by war—no reentry	0.1
Unknown	18.3	Unknown	17.8
		Right-censored in 1981	4.8

—: Rounds to zero.
[a] Entry from another industry.
[b] Exit to another industry.
Source: Based on Tables 1 and 2 (pp. 288–289) in Michael T. Hannan *et al.*, "Organizational mortality in European and American automobile industries, Part I: Revisiting the effects of age and size," *European Sociological Review* 14(3): 279–302, 1997. © 1997 Oxford University Press. Reproduced by permission.

spinoffs, would then belong to a supplementary classification scheme. This is the concept of birth and death that is used in the subsequent discussion.

Data on births, deaths, and migrations of any set of businesses during a period are not directly available from censuses, surveys, lists, or administrative files. Data on these events have to be obtained indirectly using these sources. Consider the use of SSEL files for this purpose. A series of SSEL files constitutes, in effect, a continuous population register and thus incorporates information on the formation, dissolution, and reorganization of establishments in any given period. In the analysis of the SSEL files, a business dissolution or death during a year is defined as occurring when an establishment active in the year does not match an establishment in the next year on the basis of a business identification number, or matches an establishment in the next year that reports no payroll. The figure so obtained is intended to cover all the dissolutions occurring to businesses active in the year, but it understates the number of dissolutions in the year in failing to include some or all of those occurring to businesses formed between these two years. A business formation or birth is determined on the basis of the opposite experience, that is, the failure of an establishment in one year to match an establishment in the prior year on the basis of its identification number, or a match of an establishment in the prior year that reported no payroll in that year. Annual matching of this kind yields a series of annual births and deaths, permitting an analysis of the annual fluctuations in the number of business establishments in terms of these components. The figure on nonmatches is intended to cover all the business formations in the year except that it misses some or all of those that were dissolved after being started during the year. Hence, the numbers of births and deaths in the observation periods are understated by the number of such business units. Natural increase, the balance of births and deaths, during the period is not affected.[10]

The crude birthrate and the crude death rate of a set of business units in a given year may be computed by the usual formula, the ratio of events (formations or dissolutions) in the year to the midyear population of businesses. The difference between the crude birthrate and the crude death rate of business units represents their rate of natural increase or decrease. The sum of the birth and death rates may be interpreted as a measure of gross turnover or durability of the business units.

These calculations are illustrated by the following data on the changes in the number of establishments between 1994 and 1995, based on March 1994 to March 1995 business activity:

Establishments, 1994	5,770,090
Births, new firms (original locations)	594,369
Births, existing firms (secondary locations)	101,288
Deaths, original locations	(−)497,246
Deaths, secondary locations	(−)90,091
Establishments, 1995	5,878,410
Net change, 1994–1995	
Amount	108,320
Percent[a]	1.9
Due to births	12.1
Due to deaths	(−)10.2

Gross change (percent), 1994–1995	22.3

a Based on population in 1994, not the average population in 1994 and 1995.

Source: A Report of the President, *The State of Small Business, 1997*, and Office of Advocacy, U.S. Small Business Administration, *Report on Small Business and Competition*, 1998, Table A.15. Basic data provided by the U.S. Bureau of the Census.

Analysis of the data from the SSELs of 1987 and 1988 yields a dissolution rate of 12.2% for the establishments in the 1987 list between 1987 and 1988, and a dissolution rate of 11.8% for the establishments in the 1992 list between 1992 and 1993:

Item	1987	1992
Total active estab.	5,727,984	6,137,905
Closed[a]	701,367	721,619
Aged under 1[b]	844,616	728,342
Death rate	12.2	11.8
Birth rate	14.7	11.9
Rate of natural increase	2.5	0.1

a Closings in the year. Establishment is included in the 1987 list but is not matched in the 1988 list, or in the 1992 list but not in the 1993 list.

b Born in year. Establishment is included in the 1987 list but is not matched in the 1986 list, or in the 1992 list but not in the 1991 list.

Source: Alfred R. Nucci, "Preliminary evidence on establishment dissolution by age during expansions and contractions," presented at the annual meeting of the American Statistical Association, Anaheim, CA, August 10–14, 1997.

These birth and death rates are not conventional (central) rates. They are cohort rates and omit some or all of the births dying as infants during the observation year.

According to the figures assembled here, the rate of natural increase was much higher in 1987 than in 1992. In economically favorable times, the birthrate of businesses exceeds their death rate—that is, more businesses open than close. Even in unfavorable times, however, when many businesses close, other prospective entrepreneurs are ready to take over the same businesses that have just been closed and there may be only a negligible natural decrease and even a small natural increase, as in this case.

Establishments that differ with respect to form of ownership, size, type of industry, affiliation status, and specific line of business tend to differ also with respect to their growth patterns. We consider two of these variables—ownership and specific line of business—to illustrate this variation. For this purpose we first examine crude birthrates and crude death rates compiled by King and Wicker (1993), for various types of retail and service establishments active in 1985 and 1986 in the Los Angeles area.[11] These data show a birthrate of 213 per 1000 establishments and a death rate of 180 per 1000 establishments, implying a natural increase rate of 33 and a gross turnover rate of 393. Corporations show lower birth, death, and natural increase rates than sole proprietorships and partnerships:

Ownership form	Birthrate	Death rate	Rate per 1000 establishments Natural increase rate[a]	Gross turnover rate[b]
All forms	213	180	33	393
Sole proprietorship	238	200	38	438
Partnership	268	234	34	502
Corporation	141	117	24	258

[a] Difference between birthrate and death rate.
[b] Sum of birthrate and death rate.
Source: King and Wicker (1993).

Accordingly, the gross turnover rate is also lower for corporations. It is not unexpected to find that sole proprietorships and partnerships, particularly the latter, come into existence and pass out of existence more readily than corporations, and that corporations have more stable and durable lives than individuals and partners as business owners.

According to the King/Wicker data, the types of retail businesses that have high rates of natural increase (e.g., full-time specialty shops, clothing stores, specialty foods, personal services) tend to show high birthrates, high death rates, and high gross turnover rates (Table 14.6). The types of retail businesses that have negative change or low rates of net increase (e.g., service stations, department stores, drugstores, recreational-vehicle dealers) tend to show low birthrates, low death rates, and low gross turnover rates.

Mortality

To study the mortality experience of businesses more closely, it is necessary to secure data on the ages of the businesses that closed during a year as well as data on the ages of all the businesses active in the year. With such data, age-specific death rates for a set of businesses can be computed, their survival history can be described, and a life table for them can be constructed. If age could be secured by direct inquiry in a census or survey of establishments, or extracted from current lists that also provide counts of the number of establishments, and if the numbers of births and deaths could be secured through a registration or similar system, age-specific death rates and the infant mortality rate could readily be calculated. However, it is difficult to apply this approach to business organizations except on a limited scale (i.e., either covering only a small geographic area or canvassing a small sample).

Rather, indirect methods have to be applied to lists of tax filers, state reports of employment insurance tax liabilities, or establishment lists. As may be recalled, age can be measured from the SSELs as the number of years an establishment appears in the lists with the same business identification number and reports a payroll, death during a period is measured by the omission from a list of an establishment that appeared in prior lists, and birth is measured as the inclusion on a list of an establishment that did not appear on prior lists.

Age-Specific Death Rates

Age-specific death rates for business establishments are computed by dividing the number of deaths of businesses of a given age during a year by the

■ **TABLE 14.6 Birthrates, Death Rates, and Related Measures, for Selected Types of Retail and Service Establishments in the Los Angeles area: 1985–1986 (a Minus Sign Denotes Natural Decrease)**

| | Rates per 1000 establishments | | | |
Type of establishment	Birthrate	Death rate	Natural increase rate[a]	Gross turnover rate[b]
All types, mean[c]	213	180	33	394
All types, median[c]	188	165	26	367
Full-time specialty shop	304	196	108	500
Clothing store	275	218	57	493
Eating/drinking place	256	225	31	481
Specialty food shop	253	216	37	469
Packaged liquor store	189	194	−5	383
Florist shop	212	170	42	382
Grocery store	191	179	12	370
Jewelry store	203	165	38	368
Personal services	210	157	53	367
Home furnishings store	179	158	21	337
Service station	153	178	−25	331
Sporting goods store	170	144	26	314
Recreational vehicles dealer	139	140	−1	279
Drug store	122	117	5	239
Department store	93	105	−12	198

[a] Difference between birthrate and death rate.
[b] Sum of birthrate and death rate.
[c] Mean and median of the array of rates for all establishments.
Source: Adapted from Jeanne C. King and Allan W. Wicker, "Demography for organizational populations: Methodological review and application," pp. 83–143, in *Advances in Entrepreneurship, Firm Emergence, and Growth*, Vol. 1. Greenwich, CT: Jai Press, 1993, Table 5. © 1993 Elsevier Science. Reproduced by permission.

midyear population of establishments of that age:

$$m_x = \frac{D_x}{P_x} \times 1000 \tag{1}$$

where x refers to age. Figure 14.1 shows a set of age-specific death rates, based on the King/Wicker data. They relate to retail and service establishments in the Greater Los Angeles area in 1985 and 1986 and cover ages from under 1 to 25 and over as a group. The first few years are especially risky for these businesses. The rate is high and rises between the first year (200 per 1000 establishments at age under 1) and second year (292 at age one). Thereafter, the rates decline with increasing age of the business unit until about ages 14 to 15 (100), when the rate is only one-third the level at age 1. From there the rates begin to level off. What happens after age 25, we do not know because we do not have the necessary data. Mortality tends to rise in the first year of life as the initial resources of foundering businesses are exhausted and then to decrease in subsequent years as the new businesses that are stronger become fully established and grow.

Two other illustrative sets of age-specific death rates are shown in Table 14.7 and Figure 14.1. They are based on the SSELs and hence relate to estab-

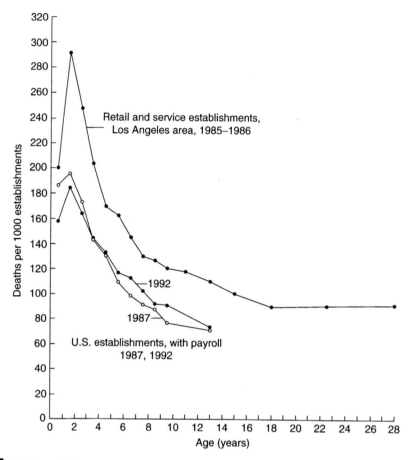

FIGURE 14.1   Age-specific death rates for U.S. establishments with payroll, 1987 and 1992, and for retail and service establishments in the Los Angeles area, 1985–1986, by age. *Source:* Adapted from data in the text and Figure 1 of Jeanne C. King and Allan W. Wicker, "Demography for organizational populations: Methodological review and application," in *Advances in Entrepreneurship, Firm Emergence, and Growth,* Vol. I, pp. 83–143, Greenwich, CT: JAI Press, 1993; and Alfred R. Nucci, "Comparison of 1987 and 1992 establishment life table survival distribution," presented at the Annual Meetings, Southern Demographic Association, Annapolis, MD, October 29–31, 1998.

lishments with employees operating in the 50 states and the District of Columbia in private nonagricultural industries. They make use primarily of the SSELs of 1991, 1992, and 1993 and the SSELs of 1986, 1987, and 1988 to obtain the birth, death, and population data although, to determine age of the establishments, the entire file of SSELs had to be examined. As explained later, the rates are not exactly central death rates, but they are reasonable representations of the level and age pattern of the mortality of private establishments with employees in these calendar years. These rates cover a narrow age range— from age under 1 to ages 10 and over as a group. For the ages covered in common by the U.S. data and the Los Angeles data, the age patterns of mortality are similar. As was true of the Los Angeles data, the set of national rates for 1992 shows lower mortality in the first year of life (158) than in the sec-

TABLE 14.7 Age-Specific Death Rates of Private Nonagricultural Establishments with Payroll: 1987 and 1992

Age (years)	1992	1987	Change, 1987 to 1992
Total	0.1176	0.1225	−0.0049
Under 1	0.1576	0.1867	−0.0291
1	0.1851	0.1961	−0.0110
2	0.1649	0.1735	−0.0086
3	0.1465	0.1424	+0.0041
4	0.1347	0.1310	+0.0037
5	0.1174	0.1090	+0.0084
6	0.1130	0.0980	+0.0150
7	0.1032	0.0915	+0.0117
8	0.0919	0.0883	+0.0036
9	0.0915	0.0770	+0.0145
10 and over	0.0744	0.0715	+0.0029

Note: Covers 6.1 million private nonagricultural establishments with payroll in 1992 and 5.7 million in 1987. Excludes most establishments that do not have employees. In 1992 there were 17.3 million firms representing over 18.5 million establishments. As explained in the text, these rates are not central rates, but cohort rates. However, for single ages they approximate central rates.

Source: Alfred R. Nucci, "Comparison of 1987 and 1992 establishment life table survival distribution," presented at the Annual Meeting of the Southern Demographic Association, Annapolis, MD, October 29–31, 1998. *Basic source*: U.S. Bureau of the Census, Center for Economic Studies, 1992 and 1987 Standard Statistical Establishment List files, special tabulations.

ond year (185), and then a steady decline over all subsequent years up to the eleventh year and over (92). The set of death rates for 1987 shows a general pattern similar to that of 1992, even though the two sets of rates cross over one another in midstream (at age 3). As with retail establishments in Los Angeles, so the greatest problem of survival for most types of business units occurs in the earliest years. With a short lag, possibly a year, the longer a business lasts, the smaller is its chance of failing.

The curve of business mortality resembles the curve of radioactive decay, which follows a negative exponential model of failure. That is, the conditional probabilities of failure decline at a constant rate. The age pattern of the mortality of businesses is both similar to and yet sharply different from the curve of human mortality. Like businesses, humans experience high mortality in infancy and a decline in mortality to about age 10 but, unlike businesses, they do not experience a rise in the first few years or a leveling off of mortality after reaching maturity. Instead, human mortality rises at about a constant rate from young adulthood to very old age after declining in early childhood, with a deceleration of the rate of increase after about age 90. The two mortality patterns are essentially different in that after the earliest years the mortality curve of humans has a generally rising course and that of businesses a generally declining or constant course. The age pattern of business mortality typically involves monotonically decreasing conditional probabilities of dissolution after the second year, while the pattern of many other types of survival or failure data, such as product survival, involves essentially constant or increasing conditional probabilities of failure. Since little is known empirically about the longer-term mortality of businesses and their life span is indeterminate, meaningful comparisons among various populations are difficult to make.

There is special interest in the mortality of business units in the first few years of life because the rate tends to be highest at these ages, moves in a direction contrary to that for many, if not all, the later ages, and shows great variation from one type of business to another. There is evidence that the infant mortality of businesses varies by a number of characteristics, including the form of ownership, affiliation status, type of industry, specific line of business, region of country, and employment-size class. Infant mortality of businesses, as for humans, can be measured by relating the number of deaths of infant businesses during a year to the number of births of businesses during the same year:

$$IMR_a = \frac{D_{0,y}}{B_y} \times 1000 \tag{2}$$

where y represents year and 0 represents age under 1. This measure is structured more like a real cohort rate or a probability than a central rate based on the midyear number of businesses. King and Wicker calculated an infant mortality rate from their data by this formula and obtained a figure of 173 deaths per 1000 newborn establishments:

$$IMR_a = \frac{5,697}{32,928} \times 1000 = 173 \tag{3}$$

The corresponding central death rate at age under 1 based on the lower midyear population under age 1 is much higher:

$$IDR = \frac{5,697}{28,548} \times 1000 = 200 \tag{4}$$

At every age, including infancy, some deaths in each year occur to the birth cohort of one year and the remaining deaths occur to the birth cohort of the prior year. If the number of births changes sharply from year to year, the conventional infant mortality rate may be misleading. It can be refined by taking a weighted average of the births in the current year and the births in the previous year to represent the number of business units exposed to the risk of dying in infancy in the current year. To determine such **separation factors**, we need to know the course of mortality of businesses *within* the first year or two of life. The appropriate data on quarterly or monthly changes in death rates are not available, however.

Apparently business dissolutions are not so sharply concentrated in the first few months of life as human mortality, as suggested by the rough similarity of death rates of businesses at ages under 1, 1, and 2. To calculate an adjusted infant mortality rate for the U.S. population in 1997, one would use 0.13 and 0.87 as separation factors to be applied to the births of the previous year and the births of the current year, respectively. In the life table for businesses shown

TABLE 14.8 Life Table for Private Nonagricultural Establishments with Payroll: 1992 (See Text for Meaning of Functions and Method of Calculating Them)

Age[a]	$_nq_x{}^b$	l_x	$_nd_x$	$_nL_x{}^c$	T_x	e_x
0.0–1.0	.15765	100,000	15,765	91,892	819,561	8.20
1.0–2.0	.18514	84,235	15,595	76,172	727,669	8.64
2.0–3.0	.16492	68,640	11,320	62,810	651,497	9.49
3.0–4.0	.14647	57,320	8,396	53,012	588,687	10.27
4.0–5.0	.13466	48,925	6,588	45,551	535,675	10.95
5.0–6.0	.11738	42,336	4,969	39,800	490,124	11.58
6.0–7.0	.11302	37,367	4,223	35,213	450,324	12.05
7.0–8.0	.10318	33,144	3,420	31,403	415,111	12.52
8.0–9.0	.09188	29,724	2,731	28,336	383,708	12.91
9.0–10.0	.09153	26,993	2,471	25,738	355,372	13.17
10.0 and over	1.00000	24,522	24,522	329,634	329,634	13.44

[a] Period between two exact ages.

[b] Assumed to be the same as the death rates calculated directly from the source (see Table 14.7). These rates are cohort rates assumed to approximate conditional probabilities of dying between the exact ages shown.

[c] The separation factors used are assumed to be different from 0.5 and 0.5, but approximate these values. They give slightly greater weight to the cohort reaching the indicated age in the current year than to the cohort reaching the indicated age in the previous year.

Source: Adapted from Alfred R. Nucci, "Preliminary evidence on establishment dissolution by age during expansions and contractions," presented at the Annual Meeting of the American Statistical Association, Anaheim, CA, August 10–14, 1997. Basic source of age-specific death rates: U.S. Bureau of the Census, Center for Economic Studies, 1992 Standard Statistical Establishment List file, special tabulations.

in Table 14.8, weights of .486 and .514 are assumed:

$$IMR_b = \frac{D_{0,y}}{.486B_{y-1} + .514B_y} \qquad (5)$$

Such a choice of factors implies that a slightly smaller share of deaths of infant businesses in the current year occurs to the "older" businesses (i.e., those founded in the previous year) than to the "younger" ones (i.e., those founded in the current year). The pattern of monthly death rates in the first year of life may differ for various types of businesses and the separation factors would then be varied according to the type of businesses being studied. In the absence of empirical evidence, however, one could simply use 0.5 and 0.5 as separation factors or, if births do not change much from year to year, calculate the infant mortality rate in the conventional manner.

Life Table Analysis

The preceding discussion of age-specific death rates and infant mortality rates of businesses leads directly to the calculation of life tables for businesses. The survival history of a set of business units can be analyzed by a life table, which follows a cohort of businesses from birth to extinction by tracking the survival of the group of businesses to each successive age. Three main functions (i.e., interdependent columns of data) shown in a life table are the probability of dissolution of a business between successive exact ages, the number of businesses surviving to each exact age from a hypothetical cohort of 100,000 newborn businesses, and the life expectancy of the businesses at each exact age. Life table analysis applied to business data is also called **business failure analysis**. The life table can be constructed as a conventional (i.e., period) life table, a generation life table, a multistate life table, or as part of a longitudinal event-history analysis. The analysis of the life histories of businesses and, particularly, the construction of life tables for businesses, has a relatively recent history, with pertinent studies first appearing in the second quarter of the 20th century.

The calculation of a life table typically begins with a set of observed age-specific central death rates. These age-specific death rates (m_x) have to be converted to **conditional probabilities of dying** (q_x), which can be used to carry the initial cohort from one exact age to the next. Conditional probabilities of dying for businesses at each age are rates of dying between exact ages that are conditional on survival of the businesses to the age in question:

$$\lambda(x) = f(x) \div [1 - F(x)] \tag{6}$$

where $f(x)$ is the probability of business failure at age x and $F(x)$ is the cumulative probability of failure, or nonsurvival, up to age x.

The elements in the preceding formula may be represented term for term, in effect, by the usual life table formula for the conditional probability of dying:

$$q_x = d_x \div l_x \tag{7}$$

where, assuming a radix of 100,000 newborn businesses, d_x represents the probability of dying in the age group, and l_x represents the cumulative probability of surviving to age x. If we have no independent information on the distribution of the deaths within each year of age, we can assume a rectangular distribution of deaths within single ages over time and use the standard formula for converting m_x to q_x [$= 2m_x \div (2 + m_x)$]. This formula implies separation factors of .5 and .5. We can then proceed to construct the rest of the life table by the usual formulas. Starting with $l_0 = 100,000$:

$$
\begin{aligned}
d_0 &= l_0 q_0 \\
l_1 &= l_0 - d_0 \\
d_x &= l_x q_x \\
l_{x+1} &= l_x - d_x \\
L_x &= 1/2 l_x + 1/2 l_{x+1} \\
T_x &= \sum_{a=x}^{a=\infty} L_a \\
e_x &= T_x \div l_x
\end{aligned}
\tag{8}
$$

where

q_x is the conditional probability of dissolution of establishments from exact age x to exact age $x + 1$, given survival to age x.

d_x is the number of dissolutions of establishments at each age.

l_x is the number of establishments surviving to each exact age from a hypothetical cohort of 100,000 newborn establishments (at exact age 0).

L_x is the number of active years of establishment life in each age.

T_x is the total number of active years of establishment life from age x on.

e_x is the life expectancy of the establishments at each exact age.

This calculation presents some serious problems of data availability, as already suggested. An accurate set of age-specific central death rates covering a wide range of ages and data for determining the appropriate separation factors are needed. Even though we may not be able to secure accurate age-specific death rates for very old businesses, we need to determine as much of the age pattern of mortality as we can in order to calculate the proportion of businesses surviving to various older ages and the life expectancy of the businesses. We do not know the pattern of death rates and survivors within the terminal age group, so that it must be narrowed as much as possible. Since businesses as a set have an indeterminate life span, their death rates can cover only a limited age range of business lives. A table covering only the first 10 or 15 ages may have too large a proportion of surviving businesses at the terminal age and hence may yield distorted values for life expectancy, particularly at the higher ages. If the number of survivors has not been reduced to a relatively small proportion of the initial cohort of 100,000 businesses by the terminal age group, a distorted terminal value for T_x and hence for all the e_x's would be obtained.[12]

As with conventional life tables in general, life tables for business establishments are based on the assumptions that there is no migration of establishments, that the annual numbers of births (openings) and deaths (closings) are equal, and that age-specific dissolution rates remain unchanged for the life of the cohort at the observed annual level. The construction of the table produces a stationary population of a set of business units at each age of life and estimates of life expectation of this set of units at each age.

Nucci (1997) developed the only recent national life tables for business establishments.[13] They relate to 1992 and 1987 and are based on data in the Census Bureau's SSELs for these and the adjacent years. His life tables are derived from the series of death rates shown in Table 14.7 and extend from age under 1 to ages 10 and over as a terminal group. While the death rates used in constructing the life tables were based on the SSELs, we cannot be certain exactly how to interpret them. They are clearly not central rates, because the deaths pertain to birth cohorts and the base of the rates is the population at the start of the year. If this is so, the conventional conversion of m_x to q_x made in life table construction is not appropriate.

At the same time, the population at age zero is not the number of births and some or many, if not most, of the deaths occurring to infant businesses are omitted. One interpretation is that the age-specific death rates computed from the data in the SSELs, symbolized in this discussion by q'_x rather than m_x, represent the life-table equivalent of

$$q'_x = q_{x+1/2} = (L_x - L_{x+1}) \div L_x \qquad (9)$$

a cohort mortality rate applicable to an age one-half year higher than the required q_x:

$$q_x = (l_x - l_{x+1}) \div l_x \tag{10}$$

Hence, averaging the calculated q'_x at adjacent ages could provide more accurate probabilities of dying than accepting the q'_x as q_x or deriving them by the m_x-to-q_x conversion formula:

$$q_x = (q'_{x-1} + q'_x) \div 2 \tag{11}$$

This formulation leaves the path from l_0 to l_1, the probability of dying between birth and the first birthday, unaccounted for:

$$q_0 = (l_0 - l_1) \div l_0 \tag{12}$$

In this case, q'_0 may be a useful approximation for q_0. The life tables developed by Nucci make q_x equal to q'_x on the assumption that all births and deaths are "captured" in the match operations of the SSELs and the data refer to population and events between two exact ages.

Nucci's life table for 1992 is presented in Table 14.8. The number of surviving businesses drops sharply between age under 1 year and age 1. By age 2 one-third of the initial businesses have closed, by age 4 one-half of them have closed, by age 7 two-thirds have closed, and by age 10 three-quarters have closed. These observations also apply to the 1987 life table (not shown). Life expectation (e_x) in 1992 rises steadily from birth (8.2 years) to age 10 (13.4 years). In 1987, the rise in life expectation is more rapid with increasing age; it starts with essentially the same initial value at age under 1 but rises to 14 at age 10.

There is a question whether, apart from the usual limitations applicable to period life tables, the figures for life expectancy in these tables are meaningful and comparable to other like measures. This question arises because we have no information on the later survival history of the businesses which reached aged 10 and no information on the life span of businesses. Unlike humans, businesses do not have a natural limit to their lives. In this case, however, since the numbers of survivors to age 10 have been reduced to only one-quarter of their original size (equivalent to age 85 for the U.S. population currently!), the expectancy figures at age zero for 1992 and 1987 may be considered roughly comparable with one another and with other expectancy figures based on similarly constructed tables covering a similar number of ages. Test calculations would probably show that the life expectation figures at birth would differ little if different reasonable patterns of mortality over age 10 were assumed in the present cases.

Comparison of Dissolution Patterns and Life Expectancies

Many studies, in addition to those of King/Wicker and Nucci previously cited, show that, after an initial increase in the first year, dissolution rates fall steadily with advancing age, at least within the first decade. The age *pattern* of the rate of business closings is the same for many types of businesses, including those distinguished by broad industry sectors, specific lines of business,

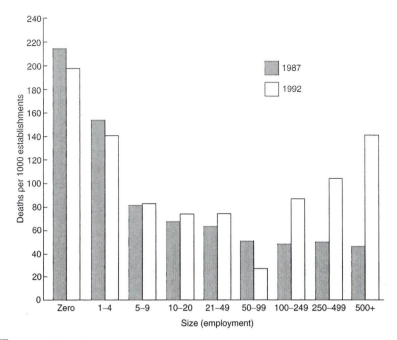

FIGURE 14.2 Death rates of private nonagricultural establishments with payroll, according to size of establishment: 1987 and 1992. *Source*: Alfred R. Nucci, "Comparison of 1987 and 1992 establishment life table survival distribution," presented at the Annual Meetings, Southern Demographic Association, Annapolis, MD, October 29–31, 1998.

employment-size classes, and regions.[14] The studies also show that the pattern is similar over time, even between phases of the business cycle.

Levels of dissolution rates, if not age patterns, vary greatly from one type of business to another, however. Closings are more likely in some industries than in others. For example, they are more common in mining, construction, and retail trade than in manufacturing, wholesale trade, and services. The rate of closings declines as establishment size (e.g., in terms of number of employees) increases, but then stops falling after about 20 employees (in 1992) and 100 employees (in 1987), with a pronounced upturn in the rate in the 1992 data as the number of employees increases (Figure 14.2). In some studies the rate of closings for large establishments starts out with low infant mortality and declines very little with age thereafter. Other evidence that small firms are more likely to die young is given by data on age at death by firm size. The median age of dissolution of U.S. establishments with payroll in 1987 rose steadily as employment-size of establishments rose until 100 to 249 employees, and then tended to level off for the largest establishments:

1987 employment	Median age	1987 employment	Median age
None	0.13	50–59	8.87
1–4	4.41	100–249	9.59
5–9	5.22	250–499	9.15
10–20	7.67	500 or more	9.26
21–49	8.20		

Source: Alfred R. Nucci, "The demography of business closings," *Small Business Economics* **12**(1): 25–39, February 1999, Table 1, p. 31.

In general, the rate of closings is greater in industries characterized by young, small, and autonomous establishments as compared with those characterized by older, larger, and affiliated establishments. Closings are greater in some growing parts of the country, but new business formations are greater as well since the same economic environment favors the formation of large numbers of new businesses.[15]

The similarities and differences in dissolution rates of businesses translate into similarities and differences in survival patterns and levels, and in life expectancies. For example, affiliated establishments are more likely to survive to higher ages than autonomous establishments. Among major industry groups, wholesale businesses, manufacturing, and services have the highest numbers of survivors and mining, construction, and retail trade the lowest. Establishments with no employees have the lowest survival rates and those with 50 to 99 employees have the highest survival rates among establishments with fewer than 100 employees.

In general, life expectancies for businesses increase with age monotonically and vary from one type of business to another in the same rank order as the survival numbers. Accordingly, life expectancy is greater for large establishments than for small establishments and for manufacturing and wholesale trade than for mining and construction.

Fertility

Once we have calculated the crude birthrate of established businesses, it is of interest to try to extend the analysis of the role of fertility in the dynamics of business populations. Although illustrative calculations or paradigms are not presented for calculation here, a few avenues of exploration are suggested. To calculate **age-specific birthrates**, we seek the following types of information: the number of new firms established, additional units of existing firms established at new locations, and firms started by merger, acquisition, spinoff, or breakup of parent companies during a year; the ages of the parent companies at the time of the birth; and the ages of all businesses of the same type at the middle of the year. Newly formed businesses present a special problem since they are parentless and yet they are likely to make up a substantial share of the starting events. One resolution of the problem of their parenthood is to include these businesses in the numerator and denominator of the zero age group.

The sum of age-specific rates, designated the **total fertility rate**, represents the total number of businesses that will be newly started or started by expansion, merger, acquisition, spinoff, or breakup during the lifetime of a hypothetical cohort of, say, 1000 businesses, according to the current age-specific birthrates of businesses, assuming that none of the businesses close. The cohort is a synthetic cohort inasmuch as its fertility experience is described in terms of the birthrates of a single calendar year. Since businesses can have births at any age in their lifetimes, the total fertility rate for businesses becomes a sum of birthrates over a multitude of ages, not just a limited few as in the case of the human total fertility rate. However, it is unlikely that the ages of older businesses can be readily ascertained and there may be a wide terminal age group. For example, if matching of lists of establishments is employed to identify age for this purpose, it would have to be applied over several decades with considerable risk of error. Appropriate lists may not be available and it may not be possible to construct them. Alternatively, an extensive historical analysis, such as was conducted by Hannan *et al.* (1997)[16] for the automobile industry, can be undertaken.

We can try to extend the analysis further by calculating the **net fertility rate**, or the total number of businesses that will be founded during the lifetime of a hypothetical cohort of 1000 businesses, allowing for any closings of new businesses (before they have attained the age of their parent business). This measure answers the question, are businesses replacing themselves in overall numbers during a "generation"? This measure may have an uncertain interpretation for cohorts of businesses because, without a defined reproduction period, the concept of a generation cannot easily be applied. Net fertility rates may drop to very low values since the number of openings and closings may approximate one another for any particular synthetic cohort (i.e., one described by the events of a single calendar year).[17]

An analysis of marriages and divorces of businesses would build on the research on the fertility analysis of businesses, exploiting principally the records relating to mergers, acquisitions, breakups, and spinoffs. The methods of demographic analysis of marriages and divorces of businesses and the required data, as for fertility analysis of businesses, have hardly been developed.

Projections of Sets of Businesses

There is a considerable literature relating to business forecasting, but it mainly concerns the "business outlook," production, productivity, interest rates, employment, prices, expenditures, and earnings. It is not particularly concerned with projections of the number and characteristics of businesses of specified types. In principle, a variety of methods can be employed to project the number and basic "demographic" characteristics (e.g., age, race/sex ownership, size, and major industry) of the businesses in the country or a region or of selected categories of businesses. These methods parallel those described in an earlier chapter as the methods useful for preparing projections of state or regional populations. They are broadly classified as mathematical and statistical analysis, economic analysis, and demographic analysis, and they may be combined in various ways. Various mathematical curves, time series methods, and regression models are applicable if data for a series of dates at short intervals can be compiled. Methods employing economic analysis may involve projections of the output of major industry groups in terms of dollar sales or units sold and the productivity of the industry group, or projections of the size of the industry group in terms of the number of employees or outlets. Methods of projection of sets of businesses employing demographic analysis, as for populations, would involve the projection of birth (formation) rates and death (dissolution) rates, and cohort-component calculations supported by life tables.

In one form or another the demographic and economic methods involve projecting past trends in the numbers and characteristics of the set of businesses in prior years. The procedures for projecting these parameters are often mathematical or statistical, such as applying a polynomial, exponential, or other mathematical curve, applying moving-averages or other smoothing models,[18] or applying regression analysis in one of its many variations. It should be apparent that the central problem now facing business forecasters is the development of the required historical series of comparable data, including detailed data on the demographic characteristics of the series. In addition to the general issues with which population forecasters have to deal, business forecasters face the special task of measuring seasonal and cyclical fluctuations in addition to secular trends.

Most business forecasting has been carried out by business economists, who have, as expected, employed the methods of economic analysis. They have yet to apply their techniques to organizational forecasting. Demographic methods have received little or no application in business forecasting; this development awaits the efforts of interested demographers.

NONPROFIT ORGANIZATIONS

The extension of demographic concepts and methods from business organizations to private nonprofit organizations is not a big leap since the concepts, issues, and measures are similar. Few demographic studies in this area are available, partly because much of the work done may be prepared as fugitive internal material and may not be published. Historians, political scientists, and sociologists have written numerous disquisitions regarding the history and characteristics of political movements and parties, activist organizations, voluntarist and fraternal organizations, and religious organizations, but little of this material has been subjected to quantitative demographic analysis.[19]

As with business organizations, demographic analysis of nonprofit organizations involves describing the demographic and socioeconomic characteristics of the organizations as a set, measuring growth trends, analyzing survival and other demographic and socieconomic patterns, and preparing projections of numbers and characteristics. The following discussion is largely limited to schools and colleges, with a short note on religious organizations. Similar considerations apply to the analysis of trade, professional, philanthropic, and fraternal organizations.

Schools and Colleges

The U.S. Office of Education, the education departments of the states, local school districts, the National Catholic Educational Association, and other educational associations have been engaged, to a limited degree, in the demographic analysis of the data on schools and school districts. This research is designed mainly to aid in planning school construction, estimating the requirements for teachers, and delineating school districts. Information on the distribution of schools and school districts in terms of age, race, socioeconomic status, and size are useful in developing policy and programs for educational administration. Specifically, items such as the age of school buildings,[20] the rates of new construction and of abandonment of schools, the race and socioeconomic status of the students, teachers, and the residents of the surrounding neighborhood and school district, and the size of the schools in terms of numbers of students, teachers, and classrooms are all pertinent to making decisions regarding school construction, hiring and deployment of teachers and administrators, and delineating school districts. They also may be viewed as part of the working materials of a field of educational demography.

Table 14.9 gives a simplistic illustration of such data and analysis. The table presents data on the size distribution of U.S. public schools and average enrollment for school year 1995–1996. A substantial share of elementary schools have only a few hundred pupils. Over two-fifths of the schools have fewer than 400 pupils and nearly three-quarters have fewer than 600 pupils. Mean enrollment is 476 pupils per school. There are many fewer secondary schools, and they tend to be more concentrated in the smallest and largest size intervals. One quarter of secondary schools have enrollments of fewer than 200, and one-quarter have enrollments of more than 1000. On average, they are more densely populated than the elementary schools, with a mean enrollment of 683 students. The population density of Catholic schools is far lower than for the public schools at both the elementary and secondary levels. The mean enrollment in Catholic schools was 286 and 508 for the two school levels, respectively, in fall 1995.[21]

TABLE 14.9 Percentage Distribution of Public Elementary and Secondary Schools by Size of School: 1995–1996

Size of school (no. of students)	Total[a]	Elementary[b]	Secondary[c]
Total			
Number of schools	87,125	61,165	20,997
Percentage of schools	100.0	100.0	100.0
Under 200	18.4	14.7	24.0
200 to 399	24.7	28.0	16.4
400 to 599	25.2	29.8	13.9
600 to 799	15.0	16.5	11.8
800 to 999	7.2	6.8	9.0
1000 to 1499	6.3	3.9	13.7
1500 and over	3.2	0.5	11.4
Mean enrollment[d]	513	476	683
Median enrollment[e]	451	446	537

[a] Includes 2796 combined schools (i.e., schools with both elementary and secondary grades) and 2167 other schools (i.e., special education, alternative, and other schools not classified by grade span).

[b] Includes schools beginning with grade 6 or below and with no grade higher than grade 8.

[c] Includes schools with no grade lower than grade 7.

[d] Mean enrollment for "combined" schools is 401 and for "other" schools it is 45.

[e] Median enrollment for "combined" schools is 248 and for "other" schools it is under 100.

Source: U.S. National Center for Education Statistics, *Digest of Education Statistics, 1995–1996*. See also U.S. Bureau of the Census, *Statistical Abstract of the United States, 1998*, Table 270.

Public schools have been becoming more densely populated. In 1985, mean enrollment per school was 476; in 1995–1996 it was 513. These data appear to suggest an increase in classroom size, one of the factors frequently cited as contributing to the decline in the quality of U.S. public education. In fact, however, pupil-teacher ratios at both the elementary and secondary levels were lower in the late 1990s than in the 1960s, 1970s, and early 1980s and have been nearly stationary at a relatively low level since 1985. The number of classrooms and teacher per school must have grown during this period.

Since 1985 the average number of students per school district has been rising as the number of school districts fell and the number of students enrolled rose:

Year	School districts[a]	Enrollment[b]	Enrollment per district
1998	14,822	45,924	3,098
1990	15,552	40,527	2,606
1985	15,812	39,354	2,489
1975	16,624	45,135	2,715

[a] For school year ending in year shown.
[b] Fall enrollment of previous year. In thousands.
Source: U.S. Bureau of the Census, *Statistical Abstract of the United States, 1999*, Table 274, and *1988*, Table 206. Basic data from National Education Association, Washington, DC, Estimates of School Statistics Database.

The average enrollment per school district was 24% greater in 1998 than in 1985. Before 1985, total enrollment and average enrollment were substantially higher because the baby-boom cohorts were passing through these grades. By 1998 the increased number of children of the baby-boom cohorts were populating the schools.

As with business units, so with colleges and universities, there are special problems of defining the population unit to be analyzed and of marking the occurrence of birth and death of the institution. The unit of analysis may be the collection of colleges and schools called a university in all its locations, the collection of units at one location under a common administration, or an individual college. Some universities have geographically dispersed campuses, while others have a single campus. In organizational research of universities, as of business organizations, the unit of analysis depends on the purposes of the specific study. For some studies, it may be best to define the unit of analysis as the entire complex of facilities, wherever located, under a single university administration; in others, the preferred unit of analysis may be the separate campus; and in still others, it may be the individual school or college.

Colleges and universities are frequently being established as new entities and closed as independent entities, but births have been far more frequent than deaths. Occasionally a university or college simply moves to a new location. Sometimes two colleges merge or a university divests itself of a unit. After a merger, the added unit may or may not maintain its separate identity and a spunoff unit may or may not continue as a separate operation. More often, universities establish a branch at another site in pursuance of an expansion plan. We may describe colleges as "marrying" when they merge, "divorcing" when coordinate units separate, and "becoming parents" when they spin off a college as an independent unit or expand with new branches. The concepts of parenthood, marriage, divorce, and widowhood are more difficult to apply to colleges than those of birth, death, and migration, as was the case for businesses. We should recognize the possibilities of analyzing the historical dynamics of colleges and universities in terms of growth rates, birthrates, death rates, marriage rates, and divorce rates, as was suggested for businesses. To the author's knowledge, no one has conducted a quantitative study in these terms. The task is to develop consistent operational definitions of the unit of analysis and of the concepts of change, compile a historical database with the number and characteristics of the organizations and their changes, and test-apply the measures of change.[22]

Colleges and universities can be classified in terms of various demographic and socioeconomic characteristics (e.g., age, sex, race/ethnicity, religious affiliation, socioeconomic status, and size), either on the basis of the characteristics of a majority of their students or on the basis of the characteristics of the institutions per se (e.g., their history, sponsorship, scholastic orientation, principal support, size of endowment). The classification on the basis of the characteristics of students resembles the internal demography of organizational units as discussed in Chapters 7 and 8 and the classification on the basis of the characteristics of the institution corresponds more closely to the demography of organizations as collectivities. We can draw on both these bases to describe the demographic characteristics of colleges as organizations.

As stated, to classify a college on the basis of its students' characteristics, we assign to the college the attributes of the majority of the students. There are colleges that can be characterized as women's colleges (e.g., Smith, Wellesley, Barnard), race-affiliated colleges (e.g., Spelman and Yavapai), age-selective colleges (e.g., Universities of the Third Age, 4-year undergraduate schools, community colleges), and colleges varying by socioeconomic status, as suggested by the mean income of students' families (e.g., Howard University, Stanford University).[23] Colleges may also differ with respect to the academic (i.e., educational) level of their students or curriculum (e.g., University of the District of Columbia, Harvard Unversity), and with respect to the religious affiliation of their students (e.g., Catholic University, Hebrew Union College, and Texas Christian University).

Historical, economic, and legal forces are changing the demographic face of our colleges and universities, as it is doing to our businesses. After 1954, when the Supreme Court outlawed the practice of public school segregation, in principle formerly black public schools and colleges could become racially mixed. For the most part, in spite of mandated school integration, little change has occurred among formerly black colleges, but some institutions have been gradually metamorphosed into their opposites, black colleges becoming predominantly white. This scenario is playing itself out, for example, at Bluefield State College in West Virginia. The college was founded in 1895 as a school for the children of black laborers but in 1997 it had a 93% white student body.[24] The admission of large numbers of whites at Bluefield State College appears to have been a strategy for survival in an area with only a small proportion of blacks. In fact, the 102 so-called black colleges are all admitting whites.

In addition to Bluefield, Western Virginia State College and Kentucky State University have a majority of white students.

The characterization of a college as black or white has important social and political implications. Bluefield State College still collects $1 million a year in federal funds targeted for black colleges. Black colleges produce a far larger proportion of all blacks who earn a college degree than attend such colleges. The shift to a majority of white students has had an effect on the admission requirements, the curriculum, and the goals of the schools. The change may be a harbinger of the forced retreat of the black college, consistent with other changes intended to diminish race-conscious social constructions in our society. As we saw, these changes are in part driven by recent legal decisions (Chapters 7 and 12). Advocates of the *status quo ante* interpret the change as an effort to destroy a distinctive heritage and diminish the importance of black-oriented studies in our society.

Institutions of higher learning may also be described by the characteristics of the institutions per se as opposed to the characteristics of the students. Geographic location in terms of regions or states or urban-rural is one such characteristic. Another is the age of the college—that is, the number of years since its founding. As a group, colleges have an age distribution and an average age, and these change over time. College branches on satellite campuses are typically much younger than the parent university on the main campus. Two-year colleges are typically much younger than 4-year colleges since most 2-year colleges came into existence as community colleges after World War II.

A college may also be described with reference to race, religion, or socioeconomic status on the basis of the institution's characteristics. Some of the illustrations given earlier are appropriate here also, but a few may be added. Morehouse College is black and Blackhawk Technical College is American Indian. As identified by sponsorship, Fordham University is Roman Catholic, Pacific Lutheran University and Pepperdine University are Protestant, and Brandeis University is Jewish. Differences in socioeconomic status, measured by endowment, are represented by Princeton University and Dartmouth College, on the one hand, and the University of Kentucky and University of Mississippi, on the other.

Colleges classified by nondemographic characteristics can be subjected to various types of demographic analysis. Such nondemographic characteristics include the type of program specialization (e.g., agriculture, art/music, business, health sciences), number of years in the academic program (2-year, 4-year, graduate, professional), and type of ownership (public, private). These special categories of colleges may be analyzed separately to understand their distinctive growth trends and their distinctive demographic characteristics. For example, the 1950s saw a large natural increase in 2-year public colleges, while the 1990s saw little change in their numbers.

Churches

Churches as organizational units offer the possibility of a variety of demographic investigations. We may be interested in comparing the demographic characteristics of different denominations of the same religion. For example, for the Protestant denominations, we may want to know how the age, sex, race, and family composition of congregations of Baptists, Methodists, Episcopalians, Lutherans, and other principal Protestant denominations differ among one another. We may want to explore the distribution of black congregations among the census tracts of a city. We may want to investigate the relation between the distribution of the physical structures maintained by a particular religious group (e.g., Roman Catholic churches, Jewish synagogues, or Shi-iah mosques) and the demographic and socioeconomic characteristics of the neighborhoods in which they are located.[25]

Because of the detailed records maintained by the Roman Catholic Church, there are many possibilities for demographic analysis of its organizational units. For example, with data on the number of parish churches in the country classified by the age of the church, and data on the number of parish churches sold, abandoned, or converted to other uses classified by the age of the church at the time of death, for a particular year, we could compute age-specific death rates for parish churches and hence construct a life table for them. On this basis, survival rates of parish churches over specified intervals of time at any given age and the average length of life of parish churchs at their founding and at other ages can be determined.

NATIONS AS QUASI-ORGANIZATIONAL UNITS

By analogy, we can expand the scope of organizational demography to include demographic studies of cities, states, and nations as collective units. We are accustomed to compare these geopolitical entities in terms of such summary demographic measures as population size, percentage urban, median age, infant mortality rate, life expectancy, and total fertility rate. We suggest the extension of the analysis to include the characteristics of the geopolitical entity per se, such as its age, relationship to other coordinate entities, and positions on various aspects of population policy (e.g., growth, immigration).

To narrow the discussion, let us consider only nations. Nations have life-history features that make them similar to organizations. Like organizations, a set of nations can be analyzed with respect to the changes in their numbers over time, the demographic factors accounting for these changes (i.e., births/formations, deaths/terminations, marriages/annexations or acquisitions), and their demographic characteristics, such as their ages. As Lazlett (1989) noted, however, the determination of these events and the assignment of an age to a country are uncertain and equivocal.[26] We can make much more certain determinations of the classification of nations, as for other geographic entities, with respect to the demographic characteristics of the populations within them than we can of the nation's characteristics per se. There is a gigantic difference, for example, between the age of a nation and the median age of its population. We are interested in classifying countries in both these ways, however.

Comparative analysis of countries as units of study on the basis of summary measures of their characteristics, while seemingly straightforward, does have its problems. Here is one such issue. Nations are often ranked with respect to some demographic measure such as the infant mortality rate, life expectancy at birth, or median age. All independent sovereign nation states may be included in the ranking. The issue is whether, in the determination of such ranking, all nations, including those that have uniquely different characteristics, should be included as units in the comparison with the other nations. Some "nations" are city-states (e.g., Hong Kong to July 1997, Singapore), diminutive principalities or kingdoms (e.g., Andorra, Liechtenstein, Monaco, San Marino, Bhutan), or nations with neglible populations (e.g., Netherlands Antilles, Western Samoa, Djibouti, Vanuatu). Consider the rank order of the nations with respect to the infant mortality rate according to the data compiled by the Population Reference Bureau for 1999.[27] The superior performers include several "odd" nations such as Andorra, Martinique, Netherlands Antilles, Hong Kong, Macao, San Marino, Singapore, and Luxembourg. If the exceptional areas are excluded from the ranking, many countries would have quite different ranks. The United States, for example, would move from 35th place to 27th place. The rankings would surely be more meaningful if the countries were classified and separated by type before being ranked with respect to analytic measures.

Determining the year of birth or death, or the age, of a nation can be "statistically" difficult. The constellation of countries underwent profound changes in the 20th century. Many were established and many were terminated. Many have been merged with or acquired by other countries, and many were spun off for independent existence. The pace of these changes was especially rapid just after World War II and in the early part of the 1990s.

Nations have frequently been created out of former nations. The consolidation of many city-states led to the formation of several independent sovereign nation-states in the late 19th century (e.g., Italy, Germany, Japan, China). Several countries were created following World War II, including some by consolidation (e.g., Israel, the Federal Republic of Yugoslavia, Czechoslovakia). Several countries were created by dismemberment of larger countries in the 1980s and 1990s (e.g., Slovenia, Bosnia, Federal Republic of Yugoslavia [i.e., Serbia and Montenegro], Slovakia, Ukraine, Russia, Moldova, Czech Republic), and several "new" countries were brought into being by the postwar decolonization of existing countries, mainly in Asia and Africa (e.g., India, Malaysia, Malawi, Kenya, Zambia, Malta).

The United States is an old country if we use a broad definition of nationhood—one that recognizes each change in dependency status, geographical composition, and international status. Alternatively, under a narrow concept of nationhood, the United States is young in comparison with many populous countries, not only Great Britain and France, but also China, Japan, and India. As implied, China, Japan, and India are young or old countries depending on the concept of nationhood invoked.

Given the many variations in the political status of nations, then, it is often difficult to state whether a given country is the same country under different circumstances. For example, England may be an old country (founded in the 14th or 15th century) but Great Britain, including Wales, Scotland, and Northern Ireland, is much younger. Are Great Britain's former colonies, such as India or Malaysia, old or new countries? We recognize the analogy to businesses that have changed ownership, products, and location, yet continue to trade under the same name as before the changes and report the earliest date of operation as the date of their founding.

It is tempting to apply such concepts as families, parenthood, and child status to countries, in addition to those of age, birth, and death. These concepts are sometimes used loosely in such expressions as the "mother country," "daughter countries," and "family of countries." They relate to a country and its colonies or its former colonies. The role of colonies is now largely historical since few colonies are left at the beginning of the new century. We still speak of the daughter nations of the British Commonwealth (e.g., Canada, Australia, New Zealand), the progeny of Spain and Portugal in Latin America (e.g., Argentina, Chile, Brazil), and the smaller joint brood of the United States and Spain in Latin America and Asia (e.g., Puerto Rico, Philippine Islands).

DETERMINANTS AND CONSEQUENCES OF ORGANIZATIONAL CHANGES

Much that is demographic with respect to organizations has been omitted or lightly touched on in this chapter. We can appreciate this point if we recall that the field of population studies is potentially very broad and encompasses the determinants and consequences of population changes as well as formal demography.

At first glance, the determinants and consequences of population changes would seem to bear little relation to the determinants and consequences of changes in organizations. Knowledge about the attitudes and practices with regard to childbearing, the socioeconomic differentials in the risks of sickness and death, and the basis for the variations in patterns of migration among the elderly is not very useful in understanding why and how organizations, such as businesses, professional associations, or philanthropic organizations, are created, thrive, struggle to exist, or disappear. The involvement of demography in organizational studies should not be limited to the application of demographic methods to organizational data, however. Demographers also have a substantive role to play in analyzing organizational changes. Demographic factors, particularly population growth, influence the formation and life course of organizations, and the existence of organizations in a community influences the course of population change. Two obvious illustrations are the effect of the growth of population on business expansion in a community and the effect of the demand by new businesses for new workers on migration and population growth. In many cases, however, concern by demographers with the determinants and consequences of changes in organizational structure and history would take them beyond their professional know-how into somewhat specialized areas of business economics, organizational sociology, management science, and public administration.

NOTES

1. U.S. Bureau of the Census, *Statistical Abstract of the United States, 1999*, Table 878.

2. For further information, see U.S. Bureau of the Census, "The Standard Statistical Establishment List Program," *Technical Paper* No. 44, U.S. Bureau of the Census, 1979; and Mitchell

L. Trager and Richard A. Moore (U.S. Bureau of the Census), "Development of a longitudinally linked establishment based register," March 1993 through April 1995, presented at the annual meeting of the American Statistical Association, Lake Buena Vista, FL, August 13–17, 1995.

3. Paul D. Reynolds, "Finding nascent entrepreneurs: The First stage in the firm life course," presented at the annual meeting of the Population Association of America, New York City, March 25, 1999; and "Participation in the entrepreneurial process and firm births: Estimates for the United States," pretest study results for the Panel Study of U.S. Business Start-Ups, a product of the Entrepreneurial Research Consortium, March 20, 1998.

4. See U.S. Bureau of the Census, *Survey of Minority-Owned Businesses, Summary 1992*, Series MB92-4. See also U.S. Bureau of the Census, *Statistical Abstract of the United States, 1998*. Tables 875 and 870.

5. See U.S. Bureau of the Census, *Survey of Minority-Owned Businesses, Summary 1992*, Series MB92-4. See also U.S. Bureau of the Census, *Statistical Abstract of the United States, 1998*, Tables 876 and 875.

6. In the Census Bureau's construction and use of the SSEL, the physical location, the affiliation status, major industry, and size, as they describe the business in the initial year, are assumed to apply throughout the year. For example, if a business is transferred to a new owner during the year but remains at the same location, this business remains the same business with the same identification number.

7. U.S. Bureau of the Census, *1992 Economic Censuses, Survey of Minority-Owned Business Enterprises, Summary*. See also U.S. Bureau of the Census, *Statistical Abstract of the United States, 1997*, Table 850.

8. Here are some illustrations. Starbucks Coffee, Valuejet Airlines, and Virgin Airways were started as totally new companies. Pan-American Airlines and Eastern Airlines terminated service. Novartis was formed from the merger of Ciba-Geigy and Sandoz, both giant pharmaceutical firms, in 1997; Gillette merged with Duracel in 1996; and Travelers Group, Inc., merged with Citicorp to become Citigroup. There are numerous examples of recent acquisitions. First Union Corp. acquired CoreStates Financial and WorldCom, Inc., acquired MCI Communications in 1998. Boeing acquired McDonnell Douglas and Bell Atlantic acquired NYNEX in 1997. The breakup of Bell Telephone Company into the "Baby Bells" in the 1970s illustrates a case of multiple births and the death of the parent. Lucent Technologies was spun off from AT&T Corporation in 1996, as was the NCR Corporation. Bally Entertainment Corporation spun off Bally Total Fitness Holding Corporation in 1995. May Department Stores spun off Payless ShoeSource and PepsiCo., Inc., divested itself of Tricon Global Restaurants. In a major industrial transformation, Westinghouse Corporation discontinued the manufacture of household appliances and became a radio and television broadcasting company.

9. For example, after Lucent Technologies was spun off from AT&T in 1996, it acquired Agile Networks in 1996 and Octel Communications, Livingston Enterprises, and Philips Electronics in 1997.

10. The frequency (e.g., quarterly) of the observations of the population of business units during a period (e.g., a year) affects the number of births and deaths of business units that are recorded during the period. The more frequent the observations, the greater the number of births and deaths that are recorded, and hence the greater the difference between the gross changes through births and deaths and the net changes during the period.

11. Jeanne C. King and Allan W. Wicker, "Demography for organizational populations: Methodological review and application," in *Advances in Entrepreneurship, Firm Emergence, and Growth*, pp. 83–143, Vol. 1, Greenwich, CT: JAI Press, 1993.

12. An observed death rate of businesses for a broad terminal band of ages is, implicitly, the average of the set of actual, even if unknown, death rates by age within this band of ages, weighted by the actual population of businesses at these ages. However, the life table generates its own implied group death rate if age-specific rates within the terminal group are used in constructing the table. The life table death rate for a broad terminal age group may then be quite different from the observed death rate for this group.

13. Alfred R. Nucci, "Preliminary evidence on establishment dissolution by age during expansions and contractions," presented at the Annual Meeting of the American Statistical Association, Anaheim, CA, August 10–14, 1997.

14. Alfred Nucci, "Business failure in the 1992 establishment universe: Source of population heterogeneity," unpublished paper presented at the Sixth International Applied Demography Conference, Bowling Green State University, Bowling Green, OH, September 19–21, 1996; Alfred R. Nucci, "The demography of business closings," *Small Business Economics* 12(1): 25–39, February 1999; Josef Bruderl and Rudolf Schussler, "Organizational mortality: The liabilities of newness and adolescence," *Administrative Sciences Quarterly* 35: 530–547, 1990; Jeanne C. King and Allan W. Wicker, "The population demography of organizations: An application to retail and service establishments," in F. Hoy (ed.), *Academy of Management Best Paper Proceedings 1988*, pp. 373–377, Mississippi, MS: Academy of Management, 1988; and Joel Popkin and Company, "Business survival rates by age cohort of business," report prepared for the U.S. Small Business Administration, Office of Advocacy, 1991.

15. Alfred R. Nucci, "Comparison of 1987 and 1992 establishment life table survival distributions," presented at the Annual Meeting of the Southern Demographic Association, October 29–31, 1998, Annapolis, MD, Center for Economic Studies, U.S. Bureau of the Census, unpublished paper, 1998.

16. Michael T. Hannan *et al.*, "Organizational mortality in European and American automobile industries, Part I: Revisiting the effects of size and age," *European Sociological Review* 14(3): 279–302, 1998.

17. King and Wicker (1993) also considered the interesting question of whether shifts in the birth and death rates of businesses in their study or other studies parallel the shifts described by demographic transition theory. The theory has been used as a framework for explaining in social, economic, and psychological terms the great transition in population trends in Western Europe in the 18th and 19th centuries. This theory identified a first stage of population development with high fertility and high mortality, a second stage with declining mortality and rapidly increasing natural increase, and a third stage with declining fertility, low mortality, and low natural increase. Are there circumstances where the death rate of a set of businesses drops sharply after a period of high birthrates, high death rates, and low rates of natural increase? Then, after a period of high growth, the birthrate and the rate of natural increase fall sharply until birthrates and death rates are both low and natural increase is low. Could the theory apply to a major industrial group or a specific line of business, if not to a broad geographic area? This is merely speculative, and the theory may not apply to business organizations at all. See Jeanne C. King and Allan W. Wicker, "The population demography of organizations: An application to retail and service establishments," in F. Hoy (ed.), *Academy of Management Best Paper Proceedings 1988*, pp. 373–377, Mississippi, MS: Academy of Management, 1988.

18. See, for example, the discussion of ramp filters in Foster Morrison and Nancy L. Morrison, "A phase plane model of the business cycle," in U.S. National Center for Education Statistics, *The Eighth Federal Forecasters Conference, 1996, and The Seventh Federal Forecasters Conference, 1994, Combined Papers and Proceedings*, 1997, pp. 93–112.

19. See, for example, B. Edwards and S. Marullo, "Organizational mortality in a declining social movement: The demise of peace movement organizations and the end of the Cold War era," *American Sociological Review* 60: 908–927, 1995; and D. C. Minkoff, "The organization of survival: Women's and racial-ethnic voluntarist and activist organizations," *Social Forces* 71: 887–908, 1993.

20. School buildings are to be interpreted here, not simply as physical structures, but as organizations of students, teachers, and administrators meeting and interacting at a common place.

21. Calculated from data in U.S. Bureau of the Census, *Statistical Abstract of the United States, 1998*, Table 288. Basic data compiled by the National Catholic Educational Association.

22. The histories of different individual colleges and universities offer some illustrations of the types of demographic changes they have experienced. The University of Pennsylvania was established as a single college in Philadelphia in 1740 and has remained in continuous existence since then on essentially the same campus, expanding to encompass numerous colleges and institutes. Pennsylvania State University, established in 1855 in University Park, now occupies several campuses with 4-year colleges, the latest college having been set up in Harrisburg in 1966. Radcliffe College was chartered by the Commonwealth of Massachusetts in 1894 and, after a series of collaborative steps with Harvard University, formally merged with Harvard University in 1999. Montgomery College is a group of three 2-year colleges established in Montgomery County, Maryland, in 1946, 1965, and 1975 on separate campuses. A striking example of a college that

experienced several demographic events in a short lifetime is offered by the history of the Friends World College. This liberal arts college was established in Huntington, New York, in the early 1960s and closed its doors in the early 1990s. For a brief period the parent college sponsored five smaller satellite colleges in five countries and a program on a ocean-going vessel.

23. The students at Spelman College are largely black and Yavapai College is a tribal college. Universities of the Third Age enroll elderly students. An example is the Institute for Learning in Retirement, which is affiliated with American University in Washington, DC. Students at undergraduate colleges are mainly 18 to 21 years old, the students at community colleges are somewhat older, being a mixture of recent high-school graduates and young working adults, and students at "adult education" schools tend to be young working adults. For example, the median age of students at University College, University of Maryland, is above 25 years, the median age of students at Montgomery (Community) College, Montgomery County, Maryland, is 23.0 years, and the median age of students in the undergraduate schools of the University of Maryland is under 21 years.

24. The Washington Post, "A college fades to white: Historically black roots engulfed at Bluefield State," by Michael A. Fletcher, *The Washington Post*, December 8, 1997, pp. A1, A12–13.

25. From this point of view, the structures represent organizations of congregants and religious leaders who meet and interact with one another at a common place.

26. Lazlitt makes some interesting comments on measuring the age of a country. See Peter Laslett, *A Fresh Map of Life: The Emergence of the Third Age*, London: Weidenfeld and Nicolson, 1989, Chapter 3.

27. Population Reference Bureau, *1999 World Population Data Sheet*, Washington, DC: Population Reference Bureau.

SUGGESTED READINGS

Bruderl, Josef, Preisendofer, Peter, and Ziegler, Rolf. (1992). "Survival chances of newly founded business organizations." *American Sociological Review* 57: 227–242.

Carroll, Glenn R. (1997). "Models of long-term organizational evolution: Theory, models, and evidence from industrial demography." *Industrial and Corporate Change* 6: 119–143.

Carroll, Glenn R., and Hannan, Michael T. (2000). *The Demography of Corporations and Industries*. Princeton, NJ: Princeton University Press.

Churchill, Betsey C. (1955, December). "Age and life expectancy of business firms." *Survey of Current Business*: 15–19, 24.

Edwards, B., and Marullo, S. (1995). Organizational mortality in a declining social movement: The demise of peace movement organizations and the end of the Cold War era." *American Sociological Review* 60: 908–927.

Freeman, J. M., Carroll, G. R., and Hannan, M. T. (1983). "The liability of newness: Age dependence in organizational death rates." *American Sociological Review* 48: 692–710.

Joel Popkin and Company. (1991). "Business survival rates by age cohort of business." Report prepared for the U.S. Small Business Administration, Office of Advocacy.

King, Jeanne C., and Wicker, Allan W. (1993). "Demography for organizational populations: Methodological review and application." In *Advances in Entrepreneurship, Firm Emergence, and Growth*, pp. 83–143, Vol. 1. Greenwich, CT: JAI Press.

Hannan, Michael T., Carroll, Glenn R., Dobrev, Stanislav D., and Han, Joon. (1998). "Organizational mortality in European and American automobile industries. Part I: Revisiting the effects of age and size." *European Sociological Review* 14(3): 279–302.

Hannan, Michael T., Carroll, Glenn R., Dobrev, Stanislav D., Han, Joon, and Torres, J. C. (1998). "Organizational mortality in European and American automobile industries. Part II: Coupled clocks." *European Sociological Review* 14(3): 303–313.

Hannan, Michael T., and Freeman, John H. (1989). *Organizational Ecology*. Cambridge, MA: Harvard University Press.

McGuckin, Robert, and Nucci, Alfred. (1991, November 14–15). "Survival patterns for small business: Who survives?" U.S. Internal Revenue Service, *1991 Internal Revenue Service Research Conference*. Washington, DC.

Minkoff, D. C. (1993). "The organization of survival: Women's and racial-ethnic voluntarist and activist organizations." *Social Forces* 71: 887–908.

Nucci, Alfred R. (1999, February). "The demography of business closings." *Small Business Economics* 12(1): 25–39.

Nucci, Alfred R. (1998, October 29–31). "Comparison of 1987 and 1992 establishment life table survival distribution." Paper presented at the Annual Meetings, Southern Demographic Association, Annapolis, MD, U.S. Census Bureau, unpublished paper.

Nucci, Alfred R. (1997, August 10–14). "Preliminary evidence on establishment dissolution by age during expansions and contractions." Presented at the annual meeting of the American Statistical Association, Anaheim, CA, U.S. Census Bureau, unpublished paper.

Phillips, B. D., and Kirchhoff, B. A. (1989). "Formation, growth, and survival: Small firm dynamics in the U.S. economy." *Small Business Economics* 1: 65–74.

Reynolds, Paul D. (1998, October 30–31). "Business start-ups: The beginning of the firm life course." Paper presented at the annual meeting of the Southern Demographic Association, Annapolis, MD.

U.S. Small Business Administration, Office of Advocacy. (1998). *Annual Report on Small Business and Competition, 1997.*

U.S. Small Business Administration, Office of Advocacy. (1998). *Women in Business.*

U.S. Small Business Administration, Office of Advocacy. (1999). *Minorities in Business.*

EPILOGUE

APPENDIX A: PROFESSIONAL ASSOCIATIONS
APPENDIX B: PUBLICATIONS OF INTEREST TO
APPLIED DEMOGRAPHERS

This final note is intended to highlight a few selected items on applied demography scattered through the book and to call attention to a few additional items not previously mentioned. This epilogue is not intended to summarize the book.

It should be apparent to the reader that applied demography has no well-defined boundaries and that its interests and scope overlap with those of its parent discipline, general demography, and a whole host of other disciplines. This is as expected for a scientific field today, but it is especially to be expected for a field that "reaches out" for areas of application.

Applied demography was described at the outset as a tool for making informed decisions in the conduct of public and private programs. This is widely accepted as the principal role of applied demography. I am inclined to believe, however, that decision making defines the role of the field too narrowly. It may fit demography as applied in business and even private nonprofit organizations. However, it hardly fits the work of numerous demographers in the federal government who are employed in the primary statistical agencies that have no administrative or regulatory functions, such as the Census Bureau, the National Center for Health Statistics, and the Bureau of Labor Statistics. The demographers who prepare population estimates and projections for local governments, states, the federal government, and the United Nations usually have only a remote relation to any decision-making activity and may simply be developing and providing basic data for other demographers and other social scientists engaged in research, with no immediate program applications intended. Many applied demographers work with no sense of the direct use of their efforts in decision making. I prefer to say that the work of applied demographers has the distinctive quality of being potentially practical and is available to others for whatever practical uses they choose.

As we saw, applied demographers may be found everywhere—in government, business, academia, or private practice. The largest group today is probably in government and the smallest is in private practice. Private practice may be the fastest growing group and is certainly the most interesting. Private practitioners may serve as expert witnesses or take on government or private contracts. The range of subjects on which applied demographers have testified or prepared affidavits as expert witnesses suggests the range of subjects concerning the field. Here is an illustrative list: the method of taking the census, the issues in the adjustment of the census for undercount, the costs of rearing a child in child-support cases or in cases of "wrongful birth" (i.e, births not averted by sterilization), income lost through "wrongful death" in casualty cases, methods of preparing population estimates and their accuracy in connection with the distribution state funds to local areas, the delineation of new congressional districts and their conformity with voting rights legislation, practices in hiring workers and their adherence to equal employment legislation, adequacy of local population estimates for determinations of certificates of need when licensing is sought for new businesses, and the selection of students for magnet schools according to affirmation action guidelines. We are seeing the emergence of the field of forensic demography.

A reading of this book should have brought home the need, in the practice of applied demography, for a sound knowledge of basic census and other demographic concepts, the basic sources of demographic data, and their limitations. Among these sources the products of the Census Bureau are at the top of the list because they underlie and support many of the other data that the applied demographer may have to work with. Moreover, the dictum that all data have limitations and suffer from errors of one sort or another is well to keep in mind. We need to recognize at once that, in general, the data essentially reflect reality and yet in many comparisons the unpleasant facts of undercounting, overcounting, misreporting, nonreporting, and large variances confuse the interpretation of the differences. This is in part why reputable demographers line up on opposite sides in court cases as expert witnesses.

Applied demography deals with the development of data for planning. This usually means the need to prepare forecasts of population and other demographic variables. The reader should have developed a sense of the uncertainty that must be attached to any forecasts, especially forecasts that extend far into the future, relate to small geographic areas, and involve future births or the oldest ages. The level of uncertainty should decrease as the future "approaches" the present, data sources are improved, and knowledge of social-economic-demographic relationships increases, but a degree of uncertainty will forever characterize any type of projection. Evaluative techniques for measuring this uncertainty are being developed and refined, and the reader will find it profitable to keep informed of, and even participate in, these developments. The measures of uncertainty are themselves uncertain, however.

I hope I have made the reader recognize the need for a sound knowledge of the basic techniques of demography and statistics as used in applied demography. I am referring to such methods as those described or suggested in Chapter 1 and elsewhere in this book—component estimation analysis, use of life tables in survival and socioeconomic analysis, cohort analysis, standardization of proportions and rates, methods of making population estimates and projections, forms of interpolation, calculation and interpretation of averages, comparison of demographic distributions, and regression analysis. He or she needs these tools to be a successful practitioner. Application of these techniques has progressed more slowly than it might have because this fact has not been recognized. Many of the techniques of demographic analysis that could usefully be employed in the analysis of business and government issues are not employed because their value is unrecognized or the analyst is unfamiliar with them.

Applied demography has a country-specific quality because of the variations from country to country in geographic structure, demographic and social history, laws, and sources of data. In the United States, some issues are so pervasive that they receive considerable attention from applied demographers. An example is the matter of race. It impinges on many aspects of public and private administration. American demographic data are developed in race categories, and many applications involve interpretation and use of race categories. This situation may not apply to other countries where other matters may require major attention in their data. I am hopeful that works on applied demography will be prepared dealing with the special situation in other countries. In time, this effort will permit the emergence of a more general text in the field.

I have at once stressed both the need to take account of demographic facts and factors in the interpretation and solution of issues and the need to avoid a stance of demographic determinism. The title of a recent publication of the National Academy on an Aging Society, *Demography Is Not Destiny*,[1] calls the issue sharply to our attention in its exploration of the facts and issues relating to the historical and prospective state of the elderly population. Demographic, economic, political, geographic, cultural, aesthetic, and other factors need to be considered in exploring most social problems. We saw how economic factors may play a larger role than demographic factors in the outcome of the impending Social Security crunch and how cultural factors may play a role in matters of international business. On the other hand, economic determinism and cultural determinism are extreme positions as well. Clearly, as demographers, we should be concerned in particular when demographic factors are neglected and a stance of economic determinism is taken with respect to issues in our society.

The reader may have observed how much of the interface of applied demography with other disciplines has the quality of flux. It is not simply a matter of technical improvements; the law or "the culture" may be changing. With historical change and developments, the situation is always in process, and what prevailed yesterday may have changed by today. This is especially true with regard to statistical administration, law, and public policy. Note, for example, how the methods of taking the census have evolved, how the laws pertaining to legislative redistricting have been reinterpreted, and how the role of demographic factors as compared with nondemographic factors in a number of public policy matters shifts as time passes. Since the situation in the applied area is in flux, it has to be evaluated on a continuining basis. For example, use of administrative records and file matching is *in*, and the conventional census is on its way *out*. Delineation of congressional districts solely on the basis of race is *out*, and delineation on multiple criteria is *in*. The dissemination of statistical data largely by printed reports is *out*, and computer and Internet dissemination is *in*.

I have tried to suggest that the scope of applied demography has been steadily expanding. It knows no obvious bounds. Applied demographers have become interested in the description and analysis of social institutions, social groups, social problems, and social processes of all kinds, provided they can find some association with demographic variables. Consider our social institutions. Applied demographers are playing an increasingly important role in connection with the analysis of programs relating to the family, education, health, recreation, government, business, and religion, including such specialized areas as work and retirement, income security, crime and punishment, and civil rights. New subspecialties of formal demography and applied demography, such as family and institutional demography, business demography, political demgraphy, educational demography, and health demography, have appeared. Interest has extended even to the physical and built environment, including the interrelationships with climate, environmental quality, and housing. One field that has been neglected is recreational demography or the demography of leisure, while one that has been progressing rapidly is health demography. Specialized works have emerged to cover some of the subfields.[2]

Applied demographers have been engaged in developing demographic profiles and analyses of all kinds of groups. The possibilities are endless. Consider an occupational group, such as librarians, clinical social workers, croupiers, or the armed forces; a sports group, such as professional soccer players or Olympic gold-medal winners; a group involved in various leisure or arts activities, such as pet owners, opera-goers, or gamblers; or the great groups of unpaid workers and nonworkers, such as homemakers, informal caregivers, volunteer workers, unpaid farm workers, and retired persons. The group studied may have just undergone a special experience, such as persons who have had open-heart surgery, bought a house, or been discharged from a mental institution in the previous year. Whoever they are, they have a demographic profile that can be described and analyzed, and the results of these analyses are of interest to a class of businesses, government agencies, charitable groups, or other organizations. The applied demographer is well equipped to carry out these studies in an insightful and informative way.

The wide interests of applied demographers is reflected further in their willingness to move beyond the study of human populations to the application of the demographic perspective and methods to nonhuman populations. The populations to be analyzed may be manufactured products, groups of organizations, or other living things.

Since applied demography draws from and interfaces with a wide range of disciplines, applied demographers come in all stripes in addition to their identity as applied demographers. They may be economists, sociologists, historians, political scientists, geographers, statisticians, gerontologists, and urban planners, even social workers, lawyers, and computer scientists. The extensive contacts that applied demographers have with practitioners in other disciplines is suggested by the list of professional associations to which applied demographers may belong (Appendix A) and the list of professional journals and other publications that may carry articles on applied demography (Appendix B).

APPENDIX A: PROFESSIONAL ASSOCIATIONS

Population Association of America
Southern Demographic Association
American Statistical Association
American Public Health Association
Gerontological Society of America
Association of Public Data Users
American Marketing Association
American Economic Association
American Political Science Association
Association for Applied Sociology
American Sociological Association
International Union for the Scientific Study of Population
International Institute of Forecasters
Association of American Geographers
American Planning Association

APPENDIX B: PUBLICATIONS OF INTEREST TO APPLIED DEMOGRAPHERS

There is no journal of applied demography. *Population Research and Policy Review* comes nearest to filling this role. Articles of interest to applied demographers are scattered in many different publications. The following publications are among those that may carry such articles.

Journals

Demography
Review of Public Data Use
Journal of the American Planning Association
Journal of Marketing Research
Journal of Regional Science
American Statistician
Journal of the American Statistical Association
Population Research and Policy Review
Population Studies (Br.)
Population (Fr.)
Population Index
Population and Development Review
Genus (It.)
Journal of Official Statistics
Canadian Studies in Population
International Migration Review
Population Bulletin (Population Reference Bureau)

International Journal of Forecasting
Journal of the American Public Health Association
Journal of Marriage and the Family
American Sociological Review
Journal of Health and Behavior
Journal of Gerontology: Social Sciences
Gerontologist
Evaluation Review
American Economic Review
American Political Science Review
Land Economics
Annals of the American Association of Geographers
Monthly Labor Review
Social Security Bulletin
Health Care Financing Review

Other Publications

Applied Demography, newsletter of the State and Local Demography Group and the Business Demography Group, Population Association of America

Occasional papers of the Rand Corporation, Santa Monica, California

Proceedings of the International Conference on Applied Demography, Bowling Green State University, Bowling Green, Ohio

American Demographics, a proprietary magazine, Stamford, Connecticut

Population Today, Population Reference Bureau, Washington, D.C.

Reports of various U.S. government agencies, particularly the Bureau of the Census, the Bureau of Labor Statistics, the National Center for Health Statistics, the National Center for Education Statistics, the Immigration and Naturalization Service, the Social Security Administration, and the General Accounting Office

Daily newspapers, such as *New York Times, Washington Post, Los Angeles Times, Wall Street Journal*, and *USA Today*

NOTES

1. Robert B. Friedland and Laura Summer, *Demography Is Not Destiny*, National Academy on an Aging Society, Gerontological Society of America, 2000.

2. For example, Louis G. Pol, and Richard K. Thomas, *Demography for Business Decision Making*, Westport, CT: Greenwood Press, 1997; Louis G. Pol and Richard K. Thomas, *The Demography of Health and Health Care*, 2nd ed., Norwell, MA: Kluwer Academic Publishers, 2000; and Dowell Myers (ed.), *Housing Demography: Linking Demographic Structure and Housing Markets*, Madison, WI: University of Wisconsin Press, 1991.

Legal Cases Cited

INDEX

Employment discrimination, *see* Discrimination, employment

Employment, by size of firms/establishments, 629–630

Employment expectancies, 354–356

Employment projections, national, 513, state, 521–522

Employment prospects/promotions effect of mortality, 340–341 effect of population growth, 340–341

Endogenous diseases, 592

Endogenous variables, 54, 70

End point, 202, 203

England, 654, 655

English language instruction, 306 as official language, 327*n*.24 percent of adults lacking knowledge, 300 proficiency, 307, 314, 316, 320, 326*n*.17 varieties of, 251

Enrollment, *see* School enrollment

Enumeration, 88, 538, 559

Environmental impact, 251

Enumeration district, 185*t*

Environmental equity, 251–252

Environmental Research Systems Institute, 204, 212

Epidemics, evolution of, 254

Equal Employment Opportunity Commission, *see* U.S. Equal Employment Opportunity Commission

Equal Employment Opportunity Special File, 113

Equal Pay Act of 1963, 372, 378, 381, 593

Equal proportions, method of, 542–544

Equal protection of the law, 323, 376, 378, 382, 439, 551

Equal representation, 546, 547, 548, 553, 562

Equal Rights Amendment, 372, 378

Equal worth, *see* Comparable worth

Equality, 377–378

Equilibrium households, 59, 83*n*.16 labor force, 513

Equity, 377–378

Ergodicity, 336

Erroneous inclusions, 147

Errors in single ages, 179*n*.11

Error of closure, 7, 402–403

Errors due to sampling, 170–178

Eskimos, *see* Alaska natives

Establishment data, 331

Establishments defined, 623 with payroll, 629 by size, 629–630

Estimates, *see specific types*

Ethnographic analysis limitations, 158 results, 159 uses, 157

Europe, 80, 279, 280

Evaluation Census; *see also* Coverage error, Response error population estimates design, 423, 425 measures, 423–425 other parameters, 425–427 results, 427, 428, 432 population projections national, 456–459 subnational, design, 470–471; measures, 471–474; results, 474–479

Evenness, residential, 283*n*.26

Event-exposure method, 344, 345; *see also* Life Tables

Executive Order 11246, 382

Exemptions, 412, 416, 505

Exit surveys, 227

Exogenous variable, 53, 70

Expectation of life, *see* Life expectancy

Expert witness, 2, 254, 389, 438, 662

Exponential function distribution, 284*n*.47 growth, 16 negative (decay), 244–245, 282n.23 reverse, 245–246, 282n.24 smoothing, 516

Exposure, residential, 283*n*.26

Extended cities, 196

External client population, 290–291, 292

Fair Housing Act of 1968 (Title VIII, Civil Rights Act of 1968), 249

Family defined, 225 types, 225–226

Family demography, 66, 664

Feature segment, 202

Federal Aid-Highway programs, 572

Federal fund allocations, *see* Fund allocations

Federal Privacy Act, 131

Federal-State Cooperative Program in Population Estimates, 428, 577

Federal-State Cooperative Program in Population Projections, 577

Federal statistical agencies, as source of demographic data, 89

Female-headed households, 225, 606

FERRET, 114

Fertility, *see also* Birth fluctuations, Birthrates, Pregnancy, teenage nonmarital, 38 state variations, 38, 71*t*–72*t* teenage, 38 total rate, 38, 461 trends, 37

Fetal deaths, *see* Fetal losses

Fetal losses, 302, 303, 304, 305 Certificate of fetal death, 116, 119*f* rate, 303, 304 source/limitations of data, 303 synthetic estimate, 303–304

Fictitious enumerations, 147, 160

Filipino, 110

Finland, 139*n*.4, 404

Firms defined, 625 employer (with paid employees), 626 by mean number of establishments, 625 minority-owned, by size, 631, 632 women-owned by major industry group, 632

Flagging, 200

Flexible diskettes, 112

Flex time, 64

Flow measures, 11, 12*f*, 307

Food stamp recipients, 130